DISCARD

lonely planet

England

D0201510

**Newcastle &
Northeast England**
p601

**The Lake District
& Cumbria**
p564

Yorkshire
p475

**Manchester, Liverpool
& Northwest England**
p529

**Birmingham,
the Midlands &
the Marches**
p389

**Cambridge &
East Anglia**
p349

**Oxford, Cotswolds
& Around**
p175

London
p54

**Bath &
Southwest
England**
p218

**Canterbury &
Southeast England**
p140

Belinda Dixon, Oliver Berry, Fionn Davenport, Marc Di Duca, Damian
Harper, Catherine Le Nevez, Isabella Noble, Neil Wilson

Contents

PLAN YOUR TRIP

Welcome to England 6
England Map 8
England's Top 20 10
Need to Know 20
First Time England..... 22
What's New 24
If You Like..............25
Month by Month....... 29
Itineraries 34
The Great Outdoors.... 39
Travel with Children.... 46
Regions at a Glance.... 49

PORTOBELLO ROAD
MARKET, LONDON P134

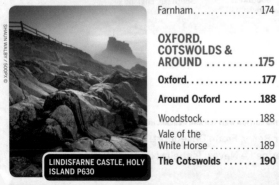

LINDISFARNE CASTLE, HOLY
ISLAND P630

ON THE ROAD

LONDON 54

CANTERBURY &
SOUTHEAST
ENGLAND 140
Kent 141
Canterbury 141
Whitstable............. 149
Margate 150
Broadstairs 151
Ramsgate.............. 152
Sandwich.............. 153
Dover 155
The White Cliffs
of Dover 157
East Sussex...........158
Rye 158
Hastings............... 161
Eastbourne 162
South Downs
National Park 163
Lewes 164
Brighton & Hove........ 165
West Sussex 171
Arundel 171
Chichester............. 172
Surrey................174
Farnham............... 174

OXFORD,
COTSWOLDS &
AROUND 175
Oxford................177
Around Oxford 188
Woodstock............. 188
Vale of the
White Horse 189
The Cotswolds 190

Cirencester 190
Bibury................. 191
Burford................ 193
Minster Lovell 196
Northleach............. 196
The Slaughters 197
Stow-on-the-Wold 197
Chipping Norton........ 198
Moreton-in-Marsh 199
Chipping Campden 200
Broadway.............. 201
Winchcombe........... 202
Painswick............. 203
Uley.................. 204
Western
Gloucestershire 205
Cheltenham........... 205
Forest of Dean 207
Buckinghamshire,
Bedfordshire &
Hertfordshire 210
Woburn................ 210
Waddesdon 210
St Albans 212
The Thames Valley 213
Windsor & Eton......... 213
Bray 217
Henley-on-Thames...... 217

BATH &
SOUTHWEST
ENGLAND 218
Hampshire........... 222
Winchester 222
Portsmouth............ 226
New Forest............ 229
Isle of Wight 233
Cowes & Around........ 235

Contents

Ryde & Around 235

Ventnor & Around 236

Steephill Cove. 237

West Wight 238

Dorset. 238

Bournemouth 238

Poole. 240

Corfe Castle 242

Lulworth Cove
& Around 243

Dorchester
& Around 244

Cerne Abbas &
the Cerne Giant 246

Weymouth 247

Isle of Portland. 248

Chesil Beach. 249

Lyme Regis 250

Sherborne 251

Wiltshire. 252

Salisbury 253

Stonehenge. 256

Stourhead 258

Longleat. 259

Lacock 259

Avebury & Around 260

**Exmoor
National Park 262**

Dulverton. 263

Exford. 265

Dunster 265

Porlock & Around. 266

Lynton & Lynmouth 267

Devon 268

Exeter. 268

Torquay & Around 274

Brixham 276

Dartmouth & Around. . . .276

Totnes & Around. 278

Plymouth & Around. 280

Dartmoor
National Park 284

Croyde & Braunton 291

Ilfracombe
& Around 292

Clovelly. 293

Bristol. 293

Bath 303

Somerset 312

Wells & Around 313

Glastonbury. 315

Cornwall. 318

Bude. 319

Boscastle. 321

Tintagel 321

Port Isaac 322

Padstow & Rock 323

Newquay 325

Perranporth
to Porthtowan. 327

St Ives 328

Zennor & St Just 332

Sennen &
Land's End. 333

Mousehole. 333

Penzance 334

The Lizard 336

Falmouth
& Around 337

Truro. 340

Fowey 342

Looe 343

Bodmin Moor 344

Isles of Scilly. 345

St Mary's 345

Tresco. 346

Bryher 347

St Martin's. 347

St Agnes 348

**CAMBRIDGE &
EAST ANGLIA 349**

Cambridgeshire 352

Cambridge. 353

Grantchester. 365

Ely. 365

Essex. 367

Colchester. 367

Dedham Vale. 368

Saffron Walden. 369

Southend-on-Sea
& Around 370

Suffolk 371

Long Melford. 371

Lavenham 372

Bury St Edmunds. 373

Orford. 375

Aldeburgh 376

Southwold 377

Norfolk 378

Norwich 378

Cromer. 382

Cley-next-the-Sea 383

Blakeney 384

Wells-next-the-Sea. 385

Holkham 386

Burnham Deepdale 386

King's Lynn
& Around 387

**BIRMINGHAM,
THE MIDLANDS &
THE MARCHES 389**

Birmingham. 392

ON THE ROAD

Warwickshire **402**

Coventry 402

Warwick 403

Kenilworth 405

Stratford-upon-Avon 406

Rugby 411

Staffordshire **412**

Lichfield 412

Worcestershire **414**

Worcester 414

Great Malvern 416

Herefordshire **417**

Hereford 418

Ross-on-Wye 420

Ledbury 420

Shropshire **421**

Shrewsbury 421

Ironbridge Gorge 424

Much Wenlock
& Around 428

Bridgnorth
& Around 429

Church Stretton
& Around 430

Bishop's Castle 431

Ludlow 432

Nottinghamshire **436**

Nottingham
& Around 436

Southwell 442

Newark-on-Trent 442

Lincolnshire **443**

Lincoln 443

Stamford 448

Boston 449

Northamptonshire **450**

Stoke Bruerne 450

TATE BRITAIN'S SPIRAL STAIRCASE P79

PHILLIP BIRD LRPS CPAGB /SHUTTERSTOCK ©

Leicestershire **451**

Leicester 451

Rutland **456**

Rutland Water 456

Derbyshire **457**

Derby 457

Ashbourne 460

Matlock Bath 460

Chesterfield
& Around 462

Peak District **463**

Buxton 465

Castleton
& Around 468

Derwent Reservoirs 471

Edale 471

Eyam 472

Bakewell & Around 472

YORKSHIRE **475**

North Yorkshire **479**

York 480

Castle Howard 490

Harrogate 491

Scarborough 494

**North York Moors
National Park** **498**

Helmsley & Around 499

Pickering 501

Whitby 502

Robin Hood's Bay 506

**Yorkshire Dales
National Park** **506**

Skipton 506

Grassington 508

Malham 509

Ribblesdale &
the Three Peaks 510

Hawes 511

Richmond 512

West Yorkshire **514**

Leeds 514

Bradford 519

Hebden Bridge 520

Haworth 522

South Yorkshire **523**

Sheffield 523

**East Riding
of Yorkshire** **525**

Hull 525

Beverley 527

Contents

MANCHESTER, LIVERPOOL & NORTHWEST ENGLAND 529

Manchester 532

Chester.............. 543

Liverpool 547

Lancashire........... 556

Blackpool.............556
Lancaster.............557
Clitheroe 559
Forest of Bowland 559

Isle of Man........... 560

Douglas 561
Around Douglas 562
Castletown
& Around 562
Peel..................563

THE LAKE DISTRICT & CUMBRIA......... 564

The Lake District 568

Windermere & Around...568
Troutbeck 574
Ambleside 574
Grasmere............. 577
Hawkshead 579
Coniston 581
Elterwater &
Great Langdale........583
Eskdale...............586
Wasdale..............586
Cockermouth 587
Keswick 588
Borrowdale 591
Buttermere 592
Ullswater & Around 592

Kendal 595

Cumbrian Coast 596

Northern &
Eastern Cumbria 597
Carlisle...............598
Penrith...............600

NEWCASTLE & NORTHEAST ENGLAND 601

Newcastle-upon-Tyne ...605
Tynemouth 613
Durham 614
Barnard Castle 616
Hadrian's Wall......... 617
Northumberland
National Park 624
Northumberland
Coast 626

UNDERSTAND

England
Today 634

History 636

Food & Drink 648

Architecture 655

The English
Landscape........... 660

Arts................. 665

Sporting England 672

SURVIVAL GUIDE

Directory A–Z 676

Transport 684

Index................ 691

Map Legend......... 702

SPECIAL FEATURES

Royal London.......... 62

Tower of London
3D Illustration..........76

Victoria & Albert
Museum
3D Illustration........ 84

British Museum
3D Illustration........ 92

The River Thames
3D Illustration........ 98

Hampton
Court Palace
3D Illustration........ 104

Flavours of England... 434

England's
Great Outdoors....... 584

Hadrian's Wall
3D Illustration........ 620

Welcome to England

This green land, this sceptred isle, this crucible of empire and pioneer of parliamentary democracy, is the most eccentric, extraordinary and downright intriguing place on Earth.

Variety Packed

From the Roman remains of Hadrian's Wall to London's incomparable theatre scene, England is full of astounding variety. In the cities, the streets buzz day and night, filled with tempting shops and restaurants, and some of the finest museums in the world. After dark, cutting-edge clubs, top-class performing arts and formidable live music provide a string of nights to remember. Next day, you're deep in the English countryside or enjoying a classic seaside resort. There really is something for everyone, whether you're eight or 80, going solo, or travelling with your friends, your kids or your grandma.

Time Travel

A journey through England is a journey through history. But not history that's dull and dusty – history you can feel and re-live. You can lay your hands on the ancient megaliths of a 5000-year-old stone circle, or walk the battlements of a medieval fortress – just as they were patrolled by chain-mail-clad defenders many centuries ago. Visit the sites of the legend of King Arthur, the sonnets of Shakespeare and the palaces of monarchs – past and present. Then fast forward to the future and admire 21st-century architecture in Manchester, or explore the space-age domes of Cornwall's Eden Project.

English Spoken Here

While England has developed a culture and tradition that may appear complex, much of it will be familiar – on the surface at least – to many visitors, thanks to the vast catalogue of British pop music, films and TV programs that have been exported around the world. The same applies when it comes to communication – this is, after all, the home turf of the English language. For many visitors this means there's no need to carry a phrasebook, although you might get a little confused by local accents in places such as Devon or Liverpool.

Easy Does It

Travel here is a breeze. Granted, it may not be totally effortless, but it's easy compared with many parts of the world. And although the locals may grumble (in fact, it's a national pastime), public transport is very good, and a train ride through the English landscape can be a highlight in itself. But whichever way you get around, in this compact country you're never far from the next town, the next pub, the next restaurant, the next national park or the next impressive castle on your hit list of highlights. The choice is endless.

Why I Love England

By Neil Wilson, Writer

England's most appealing feature is the aura of deep-rooted history that emanates from almost every corner of the land. There's a sense that its towns and villages, castles and cathedrals have grown organically over many centuries, to create calming and comfortable landscapes that the mind settles into like a favourite armchair. It's a place that encourages leisurely contemplation, whether gazing at dreaming spires from a thousand-year-old bridge, taking in the view at the top of a not-too-tiring hill or – best of all – ensconced in the corner of a thatch-roofed, stone-floored country pub with a well-earned pint in hand.

For more about our writers, see p704

Above: Clifford's Tower (p485), York

England

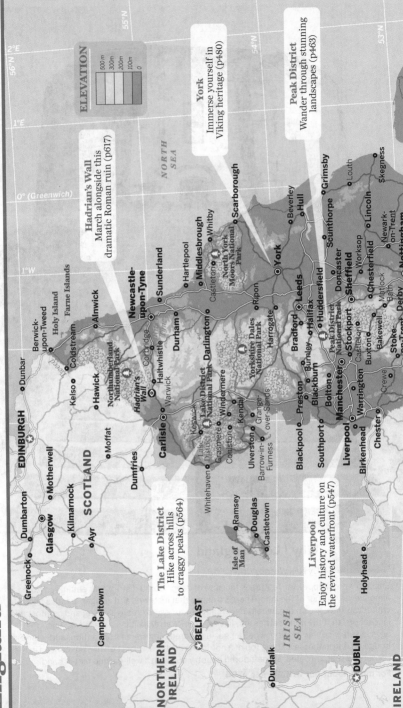

ELEVATION
- 500m
- 300m
- 200m
- 100m
- 0

Hadrian's Wall
March alongside this dramatic Roman ruin (p617)

York
Immerse yourself in Viking heritage (p480)

Peak District
Wander through stunning landscapes (p463)

The Lake District
Hike across hills to craggy peaks (p564)

Liverpool
Enjoy history and culture on the revived waterfront (p547)

0 100 km
0 50 miles

2°E
1°E
0° (Greenwich)
1°W

56°N
55°N
54°N
53°N

NORTH SEA
IRISH SEA

SCOTLAND
NORTHERN IRELAND
IRELAND

Campbeltown
Greenock
Dumbarton
Glasgow
Kilmarnock
Ayr
Motherwell
EDINBURGH
Dunbar
Berwick-upon-Tweed
Holy Island
Farne Islands
Coldstream
Kelso
Hawick
Moffat
Dumfries

Alnwick
Northumberland National Park
Hadrian's Wall
Warwick
Haltwhistle
Corbridge
Carlisle
Newcastle-upon-Tyne
Sunderland
Hartlepool
Durham
Darlington
Middlesbrough
Whitby
Scarborough
North York Moors National Park
Castleton
Ripon
Harrogate
York
Beverley
Hull

Keswick
Lake District National Park
Grasmere
Coniston
Windermere
Kendal
Ulverston
Grange-over-Sands
Barrow-in-Furness
Whitehaven

Yorkshire Dales National Park

BELFAST
DUBLIN

Isle of Man
Ramsey
Douglas
Castletown

Holyhead

Blackpool
Preston
Blackburn
Burnley
Bradford
Leeds
Halifax
Huddersfield
Southport
Bolton
Manchester
Warrington
Stockport
Liverpool
Birkenhead
Chester
Crewe

Doncaster
Worksop
Sheffield
Chesterfield
Peak District National Park
Castleton
Buxton
Bakewell
Matlock
Stoke-on-Trent
Derby
Burton-on-Trent
Nottingham
Newark-on-Trent
Lincoln
Louth
Skegness
Grimsby
Scunthorpe

Belfast
Dundalk

N

Cambridge
Attempt to punt on the picturesque 'Backs' (p353)

Canterbury
Be awed by its historic place of worship (p141)

Seven Sisters
Stroll across England's iconic white cliffs (p163)

London
Don't miss its world-class theatre scene (p54)

Stonehenge
Go mystic at England's famous prehistoric site (p256)

Eden Project
Marvel at Cornwall's three gigantic greenhouses (p338)

Bath
Admire beautiful Georgian architecture (p303)

The Cotswolds
Enjoy classic chocolate-box English countryside (p190)

Oxford
Wonder at archaic colleges and traditions (p177)

Stratford-upon-Avon
See a Shakespeare play at the Bard's birthplace (p406)

England's
Top 20

1

Stonehenge

1 Mysterious and compelling, Stonehenge (p256) is England's most iconic ancient site. People have been drawn to this myth-laden ring of boulders for more than 5000 years, and we still don't know quite why it was built. Most visitors gaze at the 50-tonne stones from behind the perimeter fence, but with enough planning you can arrange an early-morning or evening tour and gain access to the inner ring itself. In the slanting sunlight, away from the crowds, it's an ethereal place. This is an experience that stays with you.

Oxford

2 A visit to Oxford (p177) is as close as most of us will get to the brilliant minds and august institutions that have made this city famous across the globe. But you'll catch a glimpse of this rarefied world in the cobbled lanes and ancient quads where cycling students and dusty academics roam. The beautiful college buildings, archaic traditions and stunning architecture have changed little over the centuries, coexisiting with a lively, modern, working city. Below: The Radcliffe Camera (p179)

JUSTIN BLACK / SHUTTERSTOCK ©

CHRISTIAN OFFENBERG / SHUTTERSTOCK ©

JOE DANIEL PRICE / GETTY IMAGES / FLICKR RF ©

The Lake District

3 William Wordsworth and his Romantic friends were the first to champion the charms of the Lake District (p568) and it's not hard to see what stirred them. The dramatic landscape of whale-backed hills, deep valleys, misty mountain lakes and high peaks (including England's highest summit) makes this craggy corner of the country the spiritual home of English hiking. Strap on the boots, stock up on mint cake and drink in the views: inspiration is sure to follow. Top left: Keswick (p588), on the shore of Derwentwater

York

4 With its Roman and Viking heritage, ancient city walls and maze of cobbled streets, York (p480) is a living showcase for the highlights of English history. Join one of the city's many walking tours and plunge into the network of snickelways (narrow alleys), each one the focus of a ghost story or historical character. Explore the intricacies of York Minster, the biggest medieval cathedral in all of northern Europe, or admire the exhibits from more recent times at the National Railway Museum, the world's largest collection of historic locomotives. Below left: York Minster (p480)

Bath

5 In a nation packed with pretty cities, Bath (p303) still stands out as the belle of the ball. Founded by the Romans, who established the spa resort of Aquae Sulis to take advantage of the area's hot springs, Bath hit its stride in the 18th century when the rich industrialist Ralph Allen and architects John Wood the Elder and John Wood the Younger oversaw the city's reinvention as a model of Georgian architecture. Awash with golden stone townhouses, sweeping crescents and Palladian mansions, Bath demands your undivided attention. Above: Roman Baths (p303)

MARBURY / SHUTTERSTOCK ©

STOCKER1970 / SHUTTERSTOCK ©

DAVID HUGHES / SHUTTERSTOCK ©

Liverpool Museums

6 After a decade of development, the reborn waterfront is once again the heart of Liverpool. The focal point is Albert Dock (p550), a World Heritage Site of iconic and protected buildings, including a batch of top museums: the Merseyside Maritime Museum and International Slavery Museum ensure the good and bad sides of Liverpool's history are not forgotten, while the Tate Liverpool and the Beatles Story museum (pictured above left, p550) celebrate popular culture and the city's most famous musical sons (still).

Hadrian's Wall

7 Hadrian's Wall (p617) is one of the country's most revealing and dramatic Roman ruins, its 2000-year-old procession of abandoned forts, garrisons, towers and milecastles marching across the wild and lonely landscape of northern England. This wall was about defence and control, but this edge-of-empire barrier also symbolised the boundary of civilised order – to the north lay the unruly land of the marauding Celts, while to the south was the Roman world of orderly tax-paying, underfloor heating and bathrooms.

The Cotswolds

8 The most wonderful thing about the Cotswolds (p190) is that no matter where you go or how lost you get, you'll still end up in an impossibly quaint village of rose-clad cottages and honey-coloured stone. There'll be a charming village green, a pub with sloping floors and fine ales, and a view of the lush green hills. It's easy to leave the crowds behind and find your very own slice of medieval England here – and some of the best boutique hotels in the country. Above bottom right: Broadway (p201)

Stratford-upon-Avon

9 The pretty town of Stratford-upon-Avon (p406) is where William Shakespeare, the world's most famous playwright, was born and later shuffled off this mortal coil. Today, its tight knot of Tudor streets form a living map of Shakespeare's life. Huge crowds of thespians and theatre lovers come to take in a play at the famous theatre. Visit the five historic houses owned by Shakespeare and his relatives, and the school room where he was educated, then take a respectful detour to the old stone church where the Bard was laid to rest.

Cambridge

10 One of England's two great historic university cities, Cambridge (p352) highlights include a tour of at least one of the ancient colleges, and time spent marvelling at the intricate vaulting of King's College Chapel. But no trip to Cambridge is complete without an attempt to take a punt (flat-bottomed boat) along the river by the picturesque 'Backs' – the leafy, green lawns behind the city's finest colleges. Polish off the day with a pint in one of the many historic pubs. You'll soon wonder how you could have studied anywhere else.

Peak District

11 Curiously, you won't find many peaks in the Peak District (p463). But you will find blissful miles of tumbling moorland, plunging valleys, eroded gritstone crags, lush farmland and ancient villages. This beautiful landscape attracts a veritable army of outdoor enthusiasts – cyclists, hikers, cavers and rock climbers – on summer weekends, while those seeking relaxation can admire the rural market and famous puddings of Bakewell, the Victorian pavilions of spa-town Buxton, and the architectural drama of Chatsworth House (pictured).

Tower of London

12 Begun in the 11th century by William the Conqueror, the Tower of London (p71) is Europe's best-preserved medieval fortress and one of Britain's famous attractions. At almost 1000 years old (more if you count the Roman foundations) it's an enduring landmark of the capital, and over the centuries this sturdy fortress has served the nation as a palace, prison, arsenal and mint. Today it's home to the spectacular crown jewels, the legendary 'Beefeaters' with their distinctive red uniforms, and ravens that are attributed with mythical powers.

JASON BATTERHAM / SHUTTERSTOCK ©

DONSIMON / SHUTTERSTOCK ©

Afternoon Tea

13 Among England's many and varied traditions, afternoon tea is one of the most enticing, and certainly one of the tastiest. Centre of the ritual is the iconic beverage itself – brewed in a pot, ideally silver-plated, and poured carefully into fine bone-china cups and saucers. Depending where you are in the country, this hot drink is served with scones and cream, fruitcake or feather-light cucumber sandwiches. Fancy city hotels and traditional tearooms, such as Bettys (p492) in Harrogate, are among the best places to sample this epicurean delight.

London's Theatre Scene

14 However you budget your time and money in London, make sure you take in a show (p128). For big names, head for the West End (London's equivalent of Broadway), where famous spots include the National Theatre, Old Vic, Shaftesbury and Theatre Royal at Drury Lane. For new and experimental works, try the Donmar Warehouse and Royal Court. Either way, you'll see that London's theatre scene easily lives up to its reputation as one of the finest in the world – whatever New Yorkers say. Above top right: National Theatre (p128)

Canterbury Cathedral

15 Few other English cathedrals come close to Canterbury Cathedral (p144), the very fulcrum of the Anglican Church and a place of worship for over 15 centuries. Its intricate tower dominates the city skyline, while at its heart lies a 12th-century crime scene, where Archbishop Thomas Becket was put to the sword after disagreements with the king – an event that launched a million pilgrimages and still pulls in the crowds today. A lone candle mourns the gruesome deed, the pink sandstone before it smoothed by 800 years' worth of devout kneeling.

MAT ROBINSON / 500PX ©

NAIPUNG / SHUTTERSTOCK ©

JUSTIN FOULKES / LONELY PLANET ©

Walking in England

16 Call it hiking or rambling – but most often simply walking – England is the perfect place to explore on two feet, thanks to its compact nature and protected network of 'rights of way'. You can stroll the narrow streets and hidden alleyways of the nation's famous historic towns, then head for the national parks and open countryside where a gentle walk alongside meandering southern rivers or a serious trek over the Peak District hills can be an excellent way to get to know England and the English a little better. Above left: Winnats Pass, Peak District (p463)

Football

17 Much of the world may call it 'soccer' but to the English the name of the national sport is definitely 'football'. And despite what fans may say in Italy or Brazil, the English Premier League has some of the finest football teams in the world, with many of the world's best players. The most famous club on the planet is still Manchester United, while other big names include rival Manchester City, Arsenal, Liverpool and Chelsea. Tickets for the biggest matches are like gold dust, but most stadiums are open to visitors outside match days. Above top right: Old Trafford (p539), home to Manchester United

Seven Sisters Chalk Cliffs

18 Dover's iconic white cliffs grab the most attention, but the colossal chalky walls of the Seven Sisters (p163) are a much more spectacular affair. This 4-mile roller coaster of sheer white rock rollicks along the Sussex shore overlooking the waters of the English Channel, an impressive southern border to the South Downs National Park and most dramatic at the towering headland of Beachy Head. Hikes through the grassy clifftop fields provide wide sea views, breathtaking in every sense.

The Eden Project

19 Looking like a cross between a lunar landing station and a James Bond villain's lair, the gigantic hemispherical greenhouses of the Eden Project (p338) have become a symbol of Cornwall's renaissance. Dreamt up by ex-record producer Tim Smit, and built in an abandoned clay pit near St Austell, Eden's glass-domed 'biomes' re-create major world climate systems in microcosm, from the lush jungles of the Amazon rainforest to the olive trees, citrus groves and colourful flowers of the Mediterranean, South Africa and California.

England's Pubs

20 Despite the growth of stylish clubs and designer bars, the traditional neighbourhood or village pub – Ye Olde Trip to Jerusalem (pictured; p440) is the country's oldest – is still the centre of social life in England, and a visit can be one of the best ways to get under the skin of the nation. A drink or two may be necessary as well, and ideally that means traditional beer. To outsiders it may be 'warm and flat', but give it a chance and you'll soon learn to savour the complex flavours of the country's many regional varieties.

Need to Know

For more information, see Survival Guide (p675)

Currency
Pound sterling (£)

Language
English

Visas
Generally not needed for stays of up to six months. Not a member of the Schengen Zone.

Money
ATMs widely available; credit cards widely accepted.

Mobile Phones
The UK uses the GSM 900/1800 network, which covers the rest of Europe, Australia and New Zealand, but isn't compatible with the North American GSM 1900. Most modern mobiles can function on both networks, but check before you leave home.

Time
Greenwich Mean Time (UTC/GMT)

When to Go

Carlisle
GO May–Sep

York
GO May–Sep

Liverpool
GO May–Sep

Norwich
GO May–Sep

London
GO Any time

Exeter
GO Apr–Sep

High Season
(Jun–Aug)

➡ Weather at its best. Accommodation rates high, particularly in August (school holidays).

➡ Roads busy, especially in seaside areas, national parks and popular cities such as Oxford, Bath and York.

Shoulder
(Easter–May, mid-Sep–Oct)

➡ Crowds reduce. Prices drop.

➡ Weather often good: March to May sun mixes with sudden rain; September and October can feature balmy 'Indian summers'.

Low Season
(Dec–Feb)

➡ Wet and cold is the norm. Snow can fall, especially up north.

➡ Opening hours reduced October to Easter; some places shut for the winter. Big-city sights (especially London's) operate all year.

Useful Websites

BBC (www.bbc.co.uk) News and entertainment.

Enjoy England (www.visit england.com) Official tourism website.

Lonely Planet (www.lonely planet.com/england) Destination information, hotel bookings, traveller forum and more.

National Traveline (www. traveline.info) Great portal site for all public transport around England.

British Arts Festivals (www. artsfestivals.co.uk) Lists festivals – art, literature, dance, folk and more.

Important Numbers

England (and UK) country code	44
International access code	00
Emergency (police, fire, ambulance, mountain rescue or coastguard)	112 or 999

Exchange Rates

Australia	A$1	£0.58
Canada	C$1	£0.58
Eurozone	€1	£0.85
Japan	Y100	£0.75
New Zealand	NZ$1	£0.55
USA	US$1	£0.75

For current exchange rates, see www.xe.com.

Daily Costs

Budget: Less than £55

➡ Dorm beds: £15–30

➡ Cheap meals in cafes and pubs: £7–11

➡ Long-distance coach: £15–40 (200 miles)

Midrange: £55–120

➡ Double room in midrange hotel or B&B: £65–130 (London £100–200)

➡ Main course in midrange restaurant: £10–20

➡ Long-distance train: £20–80 (200 miles)

Top End: More than £120

➡ Four-star hotel room: from £130 (London from £200)

➡ Three-course meal in a good restaurant: around £40

➡ Car rental per day: from £35

Opening Hours

Opening hours may vary throughout the year, especially in rural areas where many places have shorter hours, or close completely, from October or November to March or April.

Banks 9.30am to 4pm or 5pm Monday to Friday; some open 9.30am to 1pm Saturday.

Pubs & Bars 11am to 11pm Monday to Thursday, 11am to 1am Friday and Saturday, 12.30pm to 11pm Sunday.

Shops 9am to 5.30pm or 6pm Monday to Saturday, and often 11am to 5pm Sunday.

Restaurants Lunch is noon to 3pm, dinner 6pm to 9pm or 10pm (later in cities).

Arriving in England

Heathrow Airport Trains, London Underground (tube) and buses to central London from just after 5am to before midnight (night buses run later) £5.70 to £21.50; taxi £45 to £85.

Gatwick Airport Trains to central London from 4.30am to 1.35am £10 to £20; hourly buses to central London around the clock from £5; taxi £100.

St Pancras International Train Station In Central London (for Eurostar train arrivals from Europe) and connected by many underground lines to other parts of the city.

Getting Around

Transport in England can be expensive compared to Continental Europe; bus and rail services are sparse in the more remote parts of the country. For timetables, check out www. traveline.info.

Car Useful for travelling at your own pace, or for visiting regions with minimal public transport. Cars can be hired in every town or city.

Train Relatively expensive, with extensive coverage and frequent departures throughout most of the country.

Bus Cheaper and slower than trains, but useful for more remote regions that aren't serviced by rail.

For much more on **getting around**, see p685

First Time England

For more information, see Survival Guide (p675)

Checklist

➡ Check the validity of your passport.

➡ Check any visa or entry requirements.

➡ Make any necessary bookings (sights, accommodation, travel).

➡ Check the airline baggage restrictions.

➡ Put all restricted items (eg hair gel, pocketknife) in your check-in baggage.

➡ Inform your credit/debit card company.

➡ Organise travel insurance.

➡ Check mobile (cell) phone compatibility.

➡ Check rental-car requirements.

What to Pack

➡ Electrical plug adaptor (UK-specific)

➡ Umbrella – the rumours about the weather are true

➡ Waterproof jacket – because sometimes the umbrella is not enough

➡ Comfortable walking shoes – England's towns and countryside are best explored on foot

➡ Taste for warm beer

Top Tips for Your Trip

➡ At major London airports, tickets for express trains into central London are usually available in the baggage arrivals hall; this saves queuing or dealing with machines on the station platform.

➡ The best way to get local currency is usually from an ATM, but this term is rarely used in England – 'cash machine' is more common.

➡ If staying more than a few days in London, get an Oyster card, the travel card the locals use.

➡ Pickpockets and hustlers lurk in the more crowded tourist areas, especially in London. No need to be paranoid, but do be on your guard.

➡ Britain's electrical plugs are unlike those in the rest of Europe, so bring (or buy) a UK-specific plug adaptor.

What to Wear

A rain jacket is essential, and a small backpack to carry it in when the sun comes out. In summer, you'll need sunscreen and an umbrella – possibly on the same day.

For sightseeing, comfortable shoes can make or break a trip. If you plan to enjoy Britain's great outdoors, suitable hiking gear is required in higher/wilder areas, but not for casual strolls in the countryside.

Some bars and restaurants have dress codes banning jeans, T-shirts and trainers (sneakers or runners).

Sleeping

Booking your accommodation in advance is recommended, especially in summer, at weekends and on islands (where options are often limited). Book at least two months ahead for July and August.

➡ **B&Bs** These small, family-run houses generally provide good value. More luxurious versions are more like a boutique hotel.

➡ **Hotels** English hotels range from half a dozen rooms above a pub to restored country houses and castles, with a commensurate range of rates.

➡ **Hostels** There's a good choice of both institutional and independent hostels, many housed in rustic and/or historic buildings.

Money

ATMs (which are usually called 'cash machines' in England) are common in cities and even small towns. Watch out for tampering though; one ruse by scammers is to attach a card-reader or minicamera to the slot.

Cash withdrawals from ATMs are often free, but some may be subject to a small charge. If you're not from the UK, your home bank will probably charge you for withdrawing money overseas – check before you leave.

Bargaining

A bit of mild haggling is acceptable at flea markets and antique shops, but everywhere else you're expected to pay the advertised price.

Tipping

➡ **Restaurants** Around 10% in restaurants and tearooms with table service, 15% at smarter restaurants. Tips may be added to your bill as a 'service charge'. Not compulsory.

➡ **Pubs & Bars** Not expected if you order drinks (or food) and pay at the bar; usually 10% if you order at the table and your meal is brought to you.

➡ **Taxis** Usually 10%, or rounded up to the nearest pound, especially in London.

A sign for the London Underground

Etiquette

➡ **Manners** The English have a reputation for being polite, and good manners are considered important in most situations. When asking directions, 'Excuse me, can you tell me the way to...' is better than 'Hey, where's...'

➡ **Queues** In England, queuing ('standing in line') is sacrosanct, whether to board a bus, buy tickets at a kiosk or enter the gates of an attraction. Any attempt to 'jump the queue' will result in an outburst of tut-tutting and hard stares – which is about as angry as most locals get in public.

➡ **Escalators** If you take an escalator (especially at London tube stations) or a moving walkway (eg at an airport) be sure to stand on the right, so folks can pass on the left.

Eating

It's wise to book ahead for midrange restaurants, especially at weekends. Top-end restaurants should be booked at least a couple of weeks in advance.

➡ **Restaurants** England's restaurants range from cheap-and-cheerful to Michelin-starred, and cover every cuisine you can imagine.

➡ **Cafes** Open during daytime (rarely after 6pm), cafes are good for a casual breakfast or lunch, or simply a cup of coffee.

➡ **Pubs** Most of England's pubs serve reasonably priced meals, and many can compete with restaurants on quality.

What's New

Charcuterie

Having successfully irritated the French by producing world-class sparkling wines and farmhouse cheeses, the English are getting further up Gallic noses by turning their hand to artisanal charcuterie. Some producers create their own versions of Italian and French classics; others try to create products that are more English. Check out **Cannon & Cannon** (www.cannonandcannon.com), or head to places such as the Reliance, a Leeds bar that serves its own home-cured Yorkshire charcuterie. (p517)

The Night Tube

It's only taken 153 years since its opening day, but London's Underground railway finally began operating around the clock (on Friday and Saturday nights) in August 2016. (p139)

Shakespeare's School Room

The Stratford school room where the world's most famous playwright was taught the three Rs from 1571 to 1578 was opened to the public in 2016. (p407)

Lakes Distillery

Watch out, Scotland! The first English whisky distillery for more than a century has opened in Keswick; its first single malt will be available from 2018. (p589)

i360 Tower

Sprouting from the ashes of Brighton's historic West Pier (destroyed by fire in 2003), this futuristic 162m-tall tower with a circular, glass viewing pod is Brighton's answer to the London Eye. (p167)

Magna Carta

The 800th anniversary of the signing of the Magna Carta in 2015 saw a £22 million restoration of Lincoln Castle create a subterranean vault to house one of only four original copies of this iconic document. (p444)

York City Art Gallery

Yorkshire's reputation as the epicentre of UK sculpture was further enhanced with the opening in 2015 of the revamped York art gallery's Centre of Ceramic Arts. (p485)

National Parks Get Bigger

The Lake District and Yorkshire Dales National Parks were both extended in 2016, by 3% and 24% respectively. The latter, controversially, now includes Leck Fell, the highest point in Lancashire (Yorkshire's traditional rival). (p564 & p506)

Sky Garden

20 Fenchurch St, one of London's recent landmark skyscrapers (nicknamed the Walkie Talkie), now has free access to its spectacular 155m-high rooftop garden and viewing gallery. (p123)

For more recommendations and reviews, see lonelyplanet.com/England

If You Like...

Royal England

Queen Elizabeth II celebrated her Diamond Jubilee in 2012 after 60 years on the throne. With a monarch at the top for a virtually unbroken 1500-year stretch, it's no surprise that many reminders of England's royal heritage dot the country today.

Buckingham Palace The Queen's official London residence, best known for its royal-waving balcony and the Changing of the Guard. (p61)

Westminster Abbey Where English monarchs are crowned and married – most recently William and Kate. (p58)

Tower of London A castle and royal palace for centuries, now holding the Crown Jewels; 900 years of history in one iconic building. (p71)

Sandringham The monarch's country residence, with a royal memorabilia museum. (p387)

Royal Pavilion Opulent and fantastical palace built for King George IV. (p165)

Althorp House Ancestral home and burial place of Diana, Princess of Wales. (p451)

Osborne House Royal retreat on the Isle of Wight, built for Queen Victoria. (p235)

Castles

Windsor Castle Largest and oldest occupied fortress in the world, and the Queen's weekend retreat. (p213)

Warwick Castle One of the finest castles in England; this well-preserved castle is both impressive and romantic. (p403)

Tintagel Castle Atmospheric clifftop ruin, and the legendary birthplace of King Arthur. (p322)

Bamburgh Castle Spectacularly positioned and largely rebuilt fortress on the Northumberland coast. (p628)

Richmond Castle Among England's oldest castles, with fantastic views from the medieval keep. (p512)

Skipton Castle Little known, but probably the best-preserved medieval castle in the country. (p507)

Cathedrals

St Paul's Cathedral Symbol of London for centuries, and still an essential part of the city's skyline. (p73)

York Minster One of the largest medieval cathedrals in all of Europe, especially renowned for its windows. (p480)

Canterbury Cathedral Mothership of the Anglican Church, still attracting pilgrims and visitors in their thousands. (p144)

Salisbury Cathedral Truly majestic cathedral and an English icon, topped by the tallest spire in England. (p253)

Ely Cathedral Visible for miles across the flatlands of eastern England, and locally dubbed the 'Ship of the Fens'. (p366)

Liverpool Cathedral The largest Anglican cathedral in the world. (p549)

Museums

British Museum England's largest and most visited museum is also one of the oldest and finest in the world. (p90)

National Railway Museum The epicentre of the nation's obsession with steam engines and railway history. (p481)

Natural History Museum A surefire hit with kids of all ages, with dinosaur skeletons, earthquake simulators and interactive exhibits. (p82)

Museum of Liverpool The city's multilayered past is celebrated at this interactive exploration of cultural and historical milestones. (p551)

Ashmolean Museum England's oldest museum, established in 1683, crammed with Egyptian mummies, rare porcelain and priceless musical instruments. (p183)

Mary Rose Museum Superb modern facility built around the remains of King Henry VIII's 16th-century flagship. (p226)

Historic Houses

Blenheim Palace Monumental baroque fantasy, Winston Churchill's birthplace and one of England's greatest stately homes. (p189)

Castle Howard Another impressive baroque edifice, best known as the setting for TV's *Brideshead Revisited*. (p490)

Audley End One of England's grandest country houses set amid glorious 'Capability' Brown landscaped gardens. (p369)

Chatsworth House Quintessential stately home and gardens; a treasure trove of heirlooms and works of art. (p473)

Longleat The first of England's stately homes to be opened to the public, complemented by a safari park on the grounds. (p259)

Wilton House Packed with exquisite art and period furniture; gives a glimpse into the rarefied existence of British aristocracy. (p255)

Quaint Villages

Clovelly A picture-postcard fishing village with cute cottages tumbling down a steep cobbled hill to the harbour. (p293)

Lavenham A collection of exquisitely preserved medieval buildings in East Anglia virtu-

Top: Barbara Hepworth sculpture in the grounds of the Tate Modern (p78)
Bottom: Blenheim Palace (p189)

ally untouched since the 15th century. (p372)

Painswick Hilltop Painswick is an absolute gem, unassuming and gloriously noncommercial. (p203)

Goathland One of Yorkshire's most attractive villages, complete with village green and traditional steam railway station. (p507)

Hawkshead This maze of cobbled lanes and whitewashed cottages is the Lake District's most handsome village. (p579)

Moors & Mountains

North York Moors National Park Wild and windswept, with whale-back hills stretching all the way to the sea, topped by England's largest expanse of heather. (p498)

The Lake District A feast of mountains, valleys, views and – of course – lakes; the hilltops that inspired William Wordsworth. (p568)

Yorkshire Dales National Park With scenic valleys, high hills and deep caves, the Dales are designed for hiking, biking and caving. (p506)

Dartmoor Exhilarating wilderness, hidden valleys and southern England's highest hills. (p284)

Peak District OK, so it's the most visited national park in Europe, but all those outdoor enthusiasts can't be wrong. (p463)

Shopping

Portobello Road Market One of the best-known street markets,

surrounded by quirky boutiques and gift stores. (p134)

Victoria Quarter In Leeds; lovely arcades of wrought iron-work and stained glass, home to several top fashion boutiques. (p518)

North Laine The perfect place in Brighton to pick up vegan shoes, Elvis outfits and circus monocycles. (p170)

Ludlow Foodie heaven, where almost everything is organic, artisan, sustainable or locally sourced. (p432)

Art Galleries

Tate Britain The best-known gallery in London, full to the brim with the finest works. (p79)

Tate Modern London's other Tate focuses on modern art in all its wonderful permutations. (p78)

BALTIC – Centre for Contemporary Art The 'Tate of the North' features work by some of contemporary art's biggest show-stoppers. (p607)

Hepworth Wakefield An award-winning gallery of contemporary sculpture, anchored by a world-class collection of works by local lass Barbara Hepworth. (p520)

Barber Institute of Fine Arts With works by Rubens, Turner and Picasso this provincial gallery is no lightweight. (p396)

Turner Contemporary The south coast's newest art space occupies a purpose-built structure next to the sea. (p150)

Yorkshire Sculpture Park England's biggest outdoor sculpture collection, dominated by the works of Henry Moore and Barbara Hepworth. (p520)

Festivals

Notting Hill Carnival London's Caribbean community shows the city how to party. (p106)

Glastonbury More than 40 years on and still going strong, Britain's biggest and best-loved music festival. (p315)

Brighton Festival You know a festival's matured when it grows a fringe; this gathering of all things arts is now firmly placed on the calendar. (p167)

Latitude An eclectic mix of music, literature, dance, drama and comedy, with a stunning location in Southwold. (p377)

Grassington Festival A village in the scenic Yorkshire Dales hosts this amazing two-week cultural extravaganza. (p509)

Reading Festival Venerable rock gathering that traces its roots back to the 1960s. (p216)

Leeds Festival Northern companion to the long-established Reading Festival. (p516)

Coastal Beauty

Holkham Bay Pristine 3-mile beach; the vast expanse of sand gives a real sense of isolation. (p386)

Jurassic Coast Towering rock stacks, sea-carved arches and fossils aplenty, plus some of the best beaches in the country. (p246)

Beachy Head & Seven Sisters Where the South Downs plunge into the sea, these mammoth chalk cliffs provide a dramatic finale. (p163)

Robin Hood's Bay Picturesque fishing village nestled in a nook amid impressive sea-cliff scenery. (p506)

ANDREW MONTGOMERY / LONELY PLANET ©

North York Moors National Park (p498)

Land's End The cliffs and coves are some of the most dramatic in the country (if you can ignore the theme park). (p333)

Seaside Towns

Scarborough The original British seaside resort, where it all began back in the 17th century. (p494)

Southwold A genteel seaside town with lovely sandy beach, charming pier and rows of colourful beach huts. (p377)

Bournemouth Seven miles of sandy beach, 3000 deckchairs, 1800 beach huts and a pair of Edwardian cliff lifts. (p238)

Brighton Away from the ubercool scene, there are still plenty of naughty postcards and kiss-me-quick hats in 'London-by-the-Sea'. (p165)

Eastbourne Once known as the nation's retirement home; new attractions and lively ambience now attract a considerably younger crowd. (p162)

Month by Month

January

After the festivities of Christmas and New Year's Eve, the first few weeks of the year can feel a bit of an anticlimax – never helped by the often bad weather.

✯ The London Parade

A ray of light in the gloom, the New Year's Day Parade in London (to use its official title) is one of the biggest events of its kind in the world, featuring marching bands, street performers, classic cars, floats and displays, winding their way through the streets. See www.londonparade.co.uk.

✯ Chinese New Year

Late January or early February sees London's Chinatown snap, crackle and pop with fireworks, a colourful street parade, lion dances and dim sum aplenty.

February

February is midwinter in England. The country may be scenic under snow and sunshine, but more likely grey and gloomy. Festivals and events to brighten the mood are still thin on the ground.

☆ Six Nations Rugby Championship

Highlight of the rugby calendar (www.rbs6nations.com) runs from late January to March, with the England team playing its home matches at London's Twickenham stadium.

✯ Jorvik Viking Festival

In chilly mid-February, the ancient Viking capital of York becomes home once again to invaders and horned helmets galore, with the intriguing addition of longship races. (p485)

March

Spring starts to show itself, with daffodil blooms brightening up the month.

Some people cling to the winter mood, but hotels and inns offer special weekend rates to tempt them out from under their duvets.

☆ University Boat Race

An annual race in late March down the River Thames in London between the rowing teams from Cambridge and Oxford Universities – an institution (since 1856) that still enthrals the country. (p103)

April

The weather is looking up, with warmer and drier days bringing out the spring blossoms. Sights and attractions that closed for the low season open up around the middle of the month or at Easter.

☆ Grand National

Half the country has a flutter on the highlight of the three-day horse race meeting at Aintree: a steeplechase with a testing course and high jumps. First Saturday in April. (p552)

🏃 London Marathon

In early April, super-fit athletes cover 26 miles, 385 yards in just over two hours. Others dress up in daft costumes and take considerably longer. (p103)

May

With sunny spring days, the calendar fills with more events. Two public holidays (the first and last Mondays of May) mean road traffic is very busy over the adjoining long weekends.

☆ FA Cup Final

The highlight of the football season for more than a century. All winter, teams from all of England's football divisions have been battling it out in a knockout tournament, culminating in this heady spectacle at Wembley Stadium – the home of English football. Held in early May.

🍴 Cotswold Food & Farming Festival

A celebration of local food and farming at the Cotswold Farm Park near Cheltenham, with stalls, displays, activities and demonstrating chefs. Main festival in May; others later in the year. See www.thecotswoldfoodandfarmingfestival.com.

🎵 Chelsea Flower Show

The Royal Horticultural Society flower show in late May is the highlight of the gardener's year. Top garden designers take gold, silver and bronze medals (and TV accolades), while the punters take the plants in the last-day giveaway. (p103)

☆ Glyndebourne

From late May till the end of August, this open-air festival of world-class opera enlivens the pastoral surroundings of Glyndebourne House in East Sussex.

🏃 Keswick Mountain Festival

A long weekend in late May in the heart of the Lake District is dedicated to celebrating all things outdoor-related, from outdoor activities and celebrity speakers to live music and sporting events.

June

Now it's almost summer. You can tell because June sees the music-festival season kick off properly, while sporting events – from rowing to racing – fill the calendar.

🎵 Salisbury Festival

A prestigious, eclectic event running from late May to early June, encompassing classical, world and pop music plus theatre, literature and art.

☆ Derby Week

Horse racing, people-watching and clothes-spotting are on the agenda at this weeklong race meeting in Epsom, Surrey, in early June. See www.epsomderby.co.uk.

☆ Isle of Wight Festival

Originally held from 1968 to 1970 during the high point of hippie counterculture, this musical extravaganza was resurrected in 2002. Today it attracts top bands, especially from the indie and rock fraternities. Held in mid-June; see www.isleofwightfestival.com. (p237)

👁 Trooping the Colour

Military bands and bearskinned grenadiers march down London's Whitehall in this mid-June martial pageant to mark the monarch's birthday. (p103)

☆ Royal Ascot

It's hard to tell which matters more – the fashion or the fillies – at this highlight of the horse-racing year, held in mid-June at Berkshire's Royal Ascot racetrack. Expect top hats, designer frocks and plenty of frantic betting. (p212)

☆ Wimbledon Lawn Tennis Championships

Correctly titled the All England Club Championship, and the best-known grass-court tennis tournament in the world, Wimbledon attracts all the big names. Held in late June. (p106)

🎵 Glastonbury Festival

England's favourite pop and rock fest held (nearly) every year on a dairy farm in Somerset in late June. Invariably muddy and still a rite of passage for every self-respecting British music fan. (p315)

☆ Royal Regatta

In late June or early July, boats of every description take to the water for an

IVAN VANG / SHUTTERSTOCK ©

upper-crust river regatta at Henley-on-Thames. (p217)

✨ Broadstairs Dickens Festival

Charles Dickens is one of England's best-known writers, celebrated at this literary festival in the town where he spent his summers and based many of his novels. (p152)

✨ Aldeburgh Festival

Founded by composer Benjamin Britten in 1948, this exploration of of classical music is East Anglia's biggest festival, taking in new, reinterpreted and rediscovered pieces, and extending into the visual arts.

✨ Pride

The big event on the gay-and-lesbian calendar, a technicolour street parade through London's West End, culminating in a concert in Trafalgar Sq. Late June or early July. (p106)

July

This is it: summer, with weekly festivals and country shows. Schools break up at the end of the month, so there's a holiday tingle in the air, dulled only by busy Friday-evening roads.

✨ Great Yorkshire Show

The charming town of Harrogate plays host to one of England's largest county shows. Expect Yorkshire grit, Yorkshire tykes, Yorkshire puddings, Yorkshire beef... See www.greatyorkshireshow.co.uk. (p492)

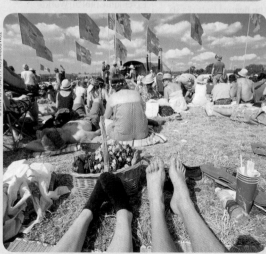

TOM ROBINSON / LONELY PLANET ©

Top: A Notting Hill Carnival (p106) participant
Bottom: Glastonbury Festival (p315)

✱✱ Latitude Festival

Popular and eclectic festival held near the lovely Suffolk seaside town of Southwold, with top names from the alternative-music scene complemented by theatre, cabaret and literary events. Held in mid-July. (p377)

☆ Cowes Week

The country's biggest yachting spectacular hits the choppy seas around the Isle of Wight in late July. (p235)

✱✱ Womad

In late July, roots and world music take centre stage at this former Reading-based festival, now in a country park near Malmesbury in the south Cotswolds. See www.womad.org.

✱✱ Truck

Held in late July, this indie music festival in Steventon, Oxfordshire, has a loyal following and is known for its eclectic acts. See www.thisistruck.com.

August

Schools and colleges are closed, parliament is in recess, the sun is shining (hopefully), most people go on holiday for a week or two (some of them abroad), and England is in a holiday mood.

✱✱ Notting Hill Carnival

A multicultural, Caribbean-style street carnival in late August in London's district of Notting Hill. Steel drums, dancers and outrageous costumes. (p106)

✱✱ Reading Festival

England's second-oldest music festival. Originally a rock fest, it veers a bit more towards pop these days, but it's still a good bet for big-name bands. Happens in late August. (p216)

✱✱ Leeds Festival

Leeds' major music festival, and the northern sister of the festival in Reading. The two festivals are the same late-August weekend, with the same lineup. If they play Reading on the Friday they'll play Leeds on Saturday, and vice versa. (p516)

✱✱ Manchester Pride

One of England's biggest celebrations of gay, bisexual and transgender life. Happens in late August; see www.manchesterpride.com. (p541)

☆ International Beatleweek

In the last week of August, the world's biggest tribute to the Beatles features six days of music, exhibitions, tours and memorabilia sales in Liverpool. (p552)

September

The first week of September feels more like August, but then the schools open up again, motorway traffic returns to normal and the summer party's over for another year. Good weather is still a chance.

☆ International Birdman Competition

In the first weekend in September, competitors dressed as batmen, fairies and flying machines compete in an outlandish celebration of self-powered flight at West Sussex' Bognor Regis. The furthest flight takes home a £30,000 prize. So far no one's got near the hallowed 100m goal. See www.birdman.org.uk.

✱✱ Bestival

Quirky music festival in early September, with a different fancy-dress theme every year. Held at Robin Hill Country Park on the Isle of Wight. (p237)

☆ World Gurning Championships

Gurning is face-pulling, and this has to be one of the weirdest events of the year. Elastic-faced contestants come to Egremont in Cumbria in mid-September every year, contorting their features in a bid to pull the most grotesque expressions. See www.facebook.com/EgremontCrabFairWorldGurningChampionships.

🏃 Great North Run

Britain's biggest marathon is in London, but the Great North Run in Tyneside in September is the biggest half-marathon in the world, with the greatest number of runners of any race over this distance. (p608)

October

October means autumn. Leaves turn golden-brown and, unless there's an 'Indian Summer', the weather starts to get cold. Sights and attractions start to shut down for the low season, and accommodation rates drop.

☆ Horse of the Year Show

The country's major indoor horse show, with dressage, show-jumping and other equine activities. Held in early October at the NEC arena near Birmingham. See www.hoys.co.uk.

✕ Falmouth Oyster Festival

The westcountry port of Falmouth hosts this event to mark the start of the traditional oyster-catching ('dredging') season, and to celebrate local food from the sea and farmland of Cornwall. (p340)

🎊 Cheltenham Literature Festival

Established in 1949, the world's longest-running book-focused festival showcases the biggest names in literature over 10 days in autumn, (p207)

November

Winter's here, and November is dull. The weather's often cold and damp, summer is a distant memory and Christmas seems far away: suitably sombre for Remembrance Day, while Guy Fawkes Night sparks up some fun.

☆ Guy Fawkes Night

Also called Bonfire Night and Fireworks Night, 5 November sees fireworks filling the country's skies in commemoration of a failed attempt to blow up parliament in 1605. Effigies of Guy Fawkes, the leader of the Gunpowder Plot, often burn on bonfires. See www.bonfirenight.net.

◉ Remembrance Day

On 11 November, red poppies are worn and wreaths are laid in towns and cities around the country. The day commemorates military personnel killed and injured in the line of duty, from the world wars to modern conflicts. See www.poppy.org.uk.

December

Schools break up around mid-December, but most shops and businesses keep going until Christmas Eve. Many towns and cities hold Christmas markets, ideal places for picking up Christmas presents.

🎊 Victorian Festival of Christmas

Portsmouth's historic dockyard, home to HMS *Victory* and the Mary Rose Museum, gets a Dickensian makeover for this celebration of Victorian Christmas traditions including street entertainment, carol singing and a Christmas market. First weekend in December or last weekend in November. See www.christmasfestival.co.uk.

🎊 New Year Celebrations

On 31 December, fireworks and street parties happen in town squares across the country, lighting up the nation to welcome in the New Year.

Itineraries

 8 DAYS England Express

Just over a week is long enough to tick off many of England's highlights. This tour takes in a dozen of the nation's top sights, from London to the Lakes.

Start with a full day in the nation's capital, **London**, simply walking the streets to admire the world-famous sights: Buckingham Palace, Tower Bridge, Trafalgar Square and more. Then head west for one or both of the grand cathedral cities of **Winchester** and **Salisbury**. Next stop: ancient history – the iconic megaliths of **Stonehenge**.

A short hop northwest leads to the beautiful city of **Bath**, for Roman history and fabulous Georgian architecture. Then cruise across the classic English countryside of the **Cotswolds** to reach that ancient seat of learning, **Oxford**. Not far away is **Stratford-upon-Avon**, for everything Shakespeare.

Next, strike out north for the **Lake District**, one of the country's most scenic areas, then across to **York** for Viking remains and the stunning Minster. End your trip with a visit to **Cambridge**, England's other great university city. Then a final day back in **London**, immersed in galleries, museums, luxury shops, street markets, West End shows or East End cafes – or whatever takes your fancy.

The Full Monty

4 WEEKS

With a month to spare, you can enjoy a trip taking in all the very best that England offers, without the pressure of a crowded schedule. This circuit covers all the bases.

Kick off in **London,** and spend a couple of days seeing the big-ticket attractions, but make the time for exploratory saunters as well – along the south bank of the River Thames, or through the markets of the East End. Next, go down to the sea at the buzzy coastal resort of **Brighton;** then west, via **Portsmouth** for the historic dockyard, to reach the picturesque **New Forest.** Head inland to the grand cathedral cities of **Winchester** and **Salisbury,** and on to England's best-known ancient site, **Stonehenge,** and nearby **Avebury Stone Circle** – bigger than Stonehenge but a more intimate experience.

Onwards into deepest Wessex, via Thomas Hardy's hometown, **Dorchester,** to reach the wild expanse of **Dartmoor National Park.** Then it's time for another historic city, **Wells,** with its beautiful cathedral, en route to the Georgian masterpiece of **Bath** and the southwest's big little city, **Bristol.** Next comes the classic English countryside of the **Cotswolds,** with a pause at delightful Stow-on-the-Wold, and maybe Broadway or Chipping Campden, before reaching **Oxford,** England's oldest seat of learning. Not far away is Shakespeare Central at **Stratford-upon-Avon** – take in a play by the Bard himself. Continue north via the heather-clad moors and limestone dales of the **Peak District** to reach England's second city, **Manchester,** and cultural crossroads **Liverpool.**

Then it's back to the wilds again with a short hop to the scenic wonders of the **Lake District.** From the sturdy border-town of **Carlisle,** follow the ancient Roman landmark of **Hadrian's Wall** all the way to revitalised city **Newcastle-upon-Tyne.** Then it's into the home stretch, south via **Durham** and its world-class cathedral, and then **York** for its Viking remains and stunning minster, to reach **Cambridge,** England's other great university city. From here it's a hop back to **London,** to use up the last few days of your grand tour, taking in highlights such as Trafalgar Square, the National Gallery, Tate Modern and the Tower of London, all polished off with a stroll across Westminster Bridge as Big Ben chimes the hour.

The Wild Side

2 WEEKS

This is a tour through the best of England's natural landscape, the inspiration for generations of poets, writers and composers. So put on your hiking boots, or have a camera at the ready, as we take a northeast–southwest meander through some of the country's finest national parks and stretches of open countryside.

Start at the spectacular Roman remains of **Hadrian's Wall**, one of England's finest reminders of the classical era, where you can explore the ancient forts and stride beside the ramparts centurion-style. Then continue into Cumbria for the high peaks of the **Lake District National Park**, once the spiritual home of Wordsworth and the Romantic poets, now a mecca for outdoor enthusiasts, with hikes and strolls for all abilities, plus cosy inns and traditional country hotels.

Travelling east from the Lakes carries you across the Pennines – the chain of hills known as the backbone of England – to reach the green hills and valleys of the **Yorkshire Dales National Park**. Nearby are the moors around **Haworth** – inspiration for Emily Brontë's *Wuthering Heights*.

Travel south through the hills and dales of the **Peak District National Park** – stopping off to explore the great park around Chatsworth if time allows – then through central England, via Elgar's beloved **Malvern Hills**, to reach the classic English countryside of the **Cotswolds**. Then continue southwards again to enjoy the epic emptiness of **Salisbury Plain**, home to **Stonehenge** and other archaeological intrigues. Nearby is **Avebury**, England's other great stone circle. A few miles more and you're on Dorset's spectacular, fossil-ridden **Jurassic Coast**.

Then head into England's toe, the Westcountry Peninsula, jutting deep into the Atlantic. Take in the farmland of Devon and the heathery hills and sandy coves of **Exmoor National Park**, then it's on to the granite tors of **Dartmoor National Park**, which offer some of the country's most bleakly beautiful views. Next stop: **Cornwall**, for pretty ports, gorse-clad cliffs and sparkling bays. Then finish this bucolic excursion at **Land's End**, where the English mainland finally plunges headlong into the restless ocean.

SCOTLAND
Newcastle-upon-Tyne
Angel of the North
NORTHERN
IRELAND
Isle of
Man
Leeds
Pennines — National Coal
Mining Museum
Liverpool
Manchester
IRISH
SEA
NORTH SEA
IRELAND
ENGLAND
Birmingham
WALES
Warwick
Stratford-upon-Avon
The
Cotswolds
Oxford
Cirencester
LONDON
Bristol
Windsor
Bath
Leeds Castle
Canterbury
BELGIUM
Salisbury
Winchester
English
Channel
FRANCE

Legend:
Heart of England
Urban Adventure

2 WEEKS Heart of England

This journey through the country's heartland takes in the best of 'Olde England', concentrating on castles, cathedrals and picturesque medieval towns and villages.

Start in **London**, with its biggest landmarks: Westminster Abbey, the Tower of London, St Paul's Cathedral and Buckingham Palace. Out of the centre, the gorgeous gardens at Kew, Eton College and **Windsor Castle** are also must-see sights.

Beyond the capital lies old England proper, especially around the market towns of Kent, where **Canterbury Cathedral** and **Leeds Castle** are top sights.

Then head into Hampshire, where **Winchester**, the ancient capital, boasts another fine cathedral. Jostling for prominence is nearby **Salisbury**, whose famous cathedral spire dominates the landscape.

Out west, **Bath** is crammed with Georgian architecture, while the **Cotswolds** conceal a host of pretty towns, such as Northleach, Wantage and **Cirencester**. On to picturesque **Oxford** and **Stratford-upon-Avon**, the home of Shakespeare, leaving enough time to top up on English history at **Warwick Castle**.

8 DAYS Urban Adventure

Outside of London, England's provincial cities provide a vibrant counterpoint to the country's tranquil coast and countryside.

Start in **Bristol**, a thriving regional capital famed for its engineering heritage and lively cultural scene. Then to **Birmingham**, once forlorn and now a byword for successful urban renewal.

Continue north to **Manchester**, famous for its music and football team, where architectural highlights include the stunning Imperial War Museum North. Nearby **Liverpool** is reinventing itself as a cultural capital, with the redevelopment most apparent at the historic Albert Dock.

Cross the Pennines to reach **Leeds**, the 'Knightsbridge of the North', where rundown factories and abandoned warehouses are now apartments and ritzy boutiques. But don't forget the past: go underground at the **National Coal Mining Museum**.

Further north is **Newcastle-upon-Tyne** and neighbouring Gateshead, where heavy industries have given way to art and architecture. Conclude your urban tour with a visit to England's best-known public art, the iconic **Angel of the North**.

2 WEEKS Edge of England

If you like the outdoors, and prefer flocks of birds to crowds of people, try this backwater route along England's eastern fringe.

Start in **Colchester**, with its magnificent castle, then visit sleepy Suffolk, where quaint villages and market towns such as Sudbury and Lavenham dot the landscape. Along the coast you'll discover wildlife reserves, shingle beaches, fishing ports such as **Aldeburgh,** and the delightfully retro seaside resort of **Southwold**.

Things get even quieter in Norfolk, especially around the misty lakes and rivers of the **Norfolk Broads**. For beach strolls or country pubs head for the coastal villages near **Wells-next-the-Sea**.

North of Norfolk lies the eerie landscape of the **Fens**, now a haven for otters and bird life. Then it's north again into Yorkshire to the heather-clad **North York Moors**, where hills roll all the way to the coast to drop dramatically into the North Sea.

Round things off with a stroll between the castles of Bamburgh and Dunstanburgh on the wild **Northumberland Coast**, finishing your tour at the historic island priory of **Lindisfarne**.

2 WEEKS Southwestern Wander

The southwest of England takes a bit of effort to reach but repays in full with a rich green landscape dotted with hills and moors, surrounded by glittering seas.

Start in **Bristol**, the capital of the West Country, then saunter down through Somerset to **Glastonbury**, famous for its annual music festival. South leads to Dorset, where highlights include picturesque **Shaftesbury**.

West leads to heathery **Exmoor National Park**, then it's onwards into Devon, where there's a choice of coasts, as well as **Dartmoor National Park**, the highest and wildest hills in southern England.

Cross into Cornwall to explore the space-age biodomes of the **Eden Project**. Nearby, but in another era entirely, is Tintagel Castle, the legendary birthplace of King Arthur. You can hang ten in surf-flavoured party town **Newquay**, or browse the galleries at **St Ives.**

Land's End is the natural finish to this wild west meander, where the English mainland comes to a full stop. Sink a drink in the First & Last Inn at nearby Sennen, and promise to return some day…

A rock climber at a crag in Great Langdale (p583).

Plan Your Trip

The Great Outdoors

What's the best way to slow down, meet the locals and get off the beaten track as you travel around England? Simple: go for a walk or get on a bike. Getting involved in the great outdoors is much more rewarding than staring at it through a car window or a camera lens.

Best Outdoors

Best Long-Distance Walks
Coast to Coast, Hadrian's Wall, Cotswold Way, South West Coast Path

Best Areas for Short Walks
Lake District, Yorkshire Dales, Cotswolds, Dartmoor

Best for Coast Walks
Northumberland, Devon & Cornwall, Norfolk & Suffolk, Dorset

Best Time to Go
Summer (June to August) The best time for walking: weather usually warm and hopefully dry; plenty of daylight too.

Late spring (May) and early autumn (September) The seasons either side of summer can be great for walking: fewer crowds; days often mild and sunny.

Best Maps for Walking
Ordnance Survey (UK's national mapping agency) Explorer series 1:25,000 scale.

Harvey Maps (specially designed for walkers) Superwalker series 1:25,000 scale.

Walking

Walking is the most popular outdoor activity in England – for locals and visitors alike – first, because it opens up some beautiful corners of the country, and secondly, because it can be done virtually on a whim. In fact, compared to hiking and trekking in some other parts of the world, it doesn't take much planning at all.

England's Footpaths

England is covered in a vast network of footpaths, many of which are centuries old, dating from the time when walking was the only way to get from farm to village, from village to town, from town to coast, or valley to valley. Any walk you do today will follow these historic paths. Even England's longest walks simply link up these networks of many shorter paths. You'll also sometimes walk along 'bridleways' originally for horse transport, and old unsurfaced roads called 'byways'.

Rights of Way

Nearly all footpaths in England are 'rights of way' – public paths and tracks across private property. Even though most land in England is privately owned, from tiny cultivated areas to vast mountain ranges, a right of way across the land cannot be overruled by the owner.

If you come from Australia, America or a country where a lot of land is jealously guarded with padlocked gates and barbed-wire fences, this can be a major revelation.

So if there is a right of way, you can follow it through fields, woods, pastures, paddocks, even farmhouse yards, as long as you keep to the correct route and do no damage.

In some mountain and moorland areas, it gets even better: walkers can move beyond the rights of way, and explore at will. Known as 'freedom to roam', where permitted it's clearly advertised with markers on gates and signposts.

Experience Required?

When deciding which area of England to visit for walking, a lot may depend on your own experience. Generally speaking, the lower and more cultivated the landscape, the easier the walking, with clear paths and signposts – ideal for beginners.

As the landscape gets higher, conditions tend to get more serious. In mountain and moorland areas, if the route is popular there will be a path (although sometimes this is faint), but not many signposts. This option is suitable if you already have a bit of walking/hiking experience.

In the more remote areas, if the route is rarely trodden, there may be no visible path at all, and absolutely no signposts, so you'll need to know what you're doing – and take a detailed map and compass for navigation.

England's Best Walking Areas

Although you can walk pretty much anywhere in England, some areas are better than others. Some are suitable for short walks of a couple of hours, others for longer all-day outings.

Lake District

If anywhere is the heart and soul of walking in England, it's the Lake District – a wonderful area of soaring peaks, endless views, deep valleys and, of course, beautiful lakes. Protected by the Lake District National Park (and often abbreviated to simply 'The Lakes', but never the 'Lakes District'), it is loved by walkers, partly because of the landscape, and partly because of the history; thanks to poet Wordsworth and his Romantic chums, this is where walking for enjoyment really began.

Southwest Coast

West Country gems Cornwall and Devon enjoy the best of the English climate and some of the finest scenery in the country, especially on the coast. But the rugged landscape means tough days on the trail. Thanks to those beautiful rivers flowing down steep valleys to the sea, you're forever going up or down. The coastline in neighbouring Dorset – known as the Jurassic Coast thanks to the proliferation of fossils – is less arduous and another great area for seaside walks.

Peak District

Despite the name, the Peak District has very few soaring summits. But there are plenty of hills, valleys and moors, making it a favoured walking area in northern England. Protected as a national park, the landscape falls into two zones: the south is mainly farmland, cut by limestone valleys; in the north are high peaty moors with rocky outcrops, and a more austere character.

Yorkshire Dales

With rolling hills, wild moors, limestone outcrops and green valleys cut by scenic streams, the Yorkshire Dales National Park is one of the most popular walking areas in England. Paths are a little gentler and conditions a little less serious than in the Lake District, with the happy addition of some delightful villages nestling in the dales – many with pubs and tearooms providing refreshments for walkers.

Cotswolds

One of the most popular areas for walkers in southern England, the Cotswold Hills offer classic English countryside, where paths meander through neat fields, past pretty villages with cottages of honey-coloured stone. The eastern side of the Cotswolds tends to be a gentler landscape, while the paths undulate more on the western side, especially along the Cotswold Escarpment – although the views are better here.

Dartmoor

In England's southwest, Dartmoor National Park boasts the highest hills for miles around, and a great sense of space on the uplands, where much of the landscape is devoid of trees and surprisingly wild. Meanwhile, below the hills, delightful valleys cut into the edges of the moor, perfect for picnics and riverside strolls in summer.

North Downs & South Downs

Between London and the south coast (and within easy reach of both), the North and South Downs are two parallel ranges of broad chalky hills. On the map, the North Downs appear hemmed-in by motorways

---

WALKING WEBSITES

Before you set off, take a look at the comprehensive website of the **Ramblers** (www.ramblers.org.uk), the country's leading organisation for walkers. Also great for specifics on some longer routes is www.national trail.co.uk.

BE PREPARED

While enjoying your walking in England, it's always worth remembering the fickle nature of English weather. The countryside can appear gentle and welcoming, and often is, but sometimes conditions can turn nasty – especially on the higher ground. At any time of year, if you're walking on the hills or open moors, it's vital to be well equipped. You should carry warm and waterproof clothing (even in summer), a map and compass (that you know how to use), some water, food and high-energy fuel such as chocolate. If you're really going off the beaten track, leave details of your route with someone.

JUSTIN FOULKES / LONELY PLANET ©

Walking the Hadian's Wall Path (p618)

and conurbations, and while this area can never be described as wilderness, the walking here is often unexpectedly tranquil. The South Downs are higher, and not so cramped by urban expansion, with more options for walks, and a landscape protected by England's newest national park.

Exmoor

Just to the north of Dartmoor, and sometimes overshadowed by its larger neighbour, southwest England's other national park is Exmoor. Heather-covered hills cut by deep valleys make it a perfect walking area, edged with the added bonus of a spectacular coastline of cliffs and beaches.

Northumberland

On northern England's frontier, keen walkers love the starkly beautiful moors of Northumberland National Park. For a change of scene, the high cliffs and vast empty beaches on the nearby Northumberland coast are less daunting but just as dramatic – perfect for wild seaside strolls.

Best Long-Distance Walks

Some long-distance routes traverse the country from west to east, while many more follow the coastline or traverse national parks and other scenic areas.

South West Coast Path

➡ 630 miles; 8-10 weeks; www. southwestcoastpath.com

A roller-coaster romp around England's southwest peninsula, past beaches, bays, shipwrecks, seaside resorts, fishing villages and clifftop castles. Given its length, most walkers do it in sections: the two-week stretch between Padstow and Falmouth around Land's End is most popular.

Pennine Way

➡ 256 miles; 14-21 days; www.nationaltrail. co.uk/pennineway

The granddaddy of them all, an epic trek along the mountainous spine of northern England, via some of the highest, wildest countryside in the country. Even in the summer, the elements can be dire, and many walkers find it an endurance test – but not one without rewards.

through time, passing prehistoric hill forts, Roman reminders and fine stately homes.

South Downs Way

➡ 100 miles; 7-9 days; www.nationaltrail.co.uk/southdowns

A sweeping hike through southeast England, along an ancient chalky highway from Winchester to the sea, mostly following a line of rolling hills, meaning big skies and wonderful views, plus picture-perfect villages and prehistoric sites.

Dales Way

➡ 85 miles; 6 days; www.dalesway.org.uk

A non-strenuous walk through the delightful Yorkshire Dales, via some of the most scenic valleys in northern England, to end at Windermere in the Lake District.

Cycling & Mountain Biking

A bike is the perfect mode of transport for exploring back-road England. Once you escape the busy main highways, a vast network of quiet country lanes winds through fields and peaceful villages, ideal for cycle touring. You can cruise through gently rolling landscapes, taking it easy and stopping for cream teas, or you can thrash all day through hilly areas, revelling in steep ascents and swooping downhill sections. You can cycle from place to place, camping or staying in B&Bs (many of which are cyclist-friendly), or you can base yourself in one area for a few days and go out on rides in different directions. All you need is a map and a sense of adventure.

Mountain bikers can go further into the wilds on the tracks and bridleways that criss-cross Britain's hills and high moors, or head for the many dedicated mountain-bike trail centres where specially built single-track trails wind through the forests. Options at these centres vary from delightful dirt roads ideal for families to gnarly rock gardens and precipitous drop-offs for hard-core riders, all classified from green to black in ski-resort style.

www.sustrans.org.uk Details of Britain's national network of cycling trails.

www.forestry.gov.uk/england-cycling Guide to forest cycling trails in England.

Signpost on the Pennine Way (p479)

Coast to Coast Walk

➡ 190 miles; 12-14 days; www.wainwright.org.uk/coasttocoast.html

Also known as Wainwright's Coast to Coast (after the man who devised it), this is not a national trail, but it is England's number-one long-distance route for locals and visitors alike – through three national parks via a spectacular mix of valleys, plains, mountains, dales and moors.

Hadrian's Wall Path

➡ 84 miles; 7-8 days; www.nationaltrail.co.uk/hadrianswall

A footpath following the world-famous Roman structure across northern England, via forts, castles, ramparts and battlements, and giving the Coast to Coast a run for its money in the popularity stakes.

Cotswold Way

➡ 102 miles; 7-10 days; www.nationaltrail.co.uk/cotswold

A picturesque and dramatic route, delivering England at its most enchanting, from villages in intimate valleys to escarpment ridges with bird's-eye views. It's also a trail

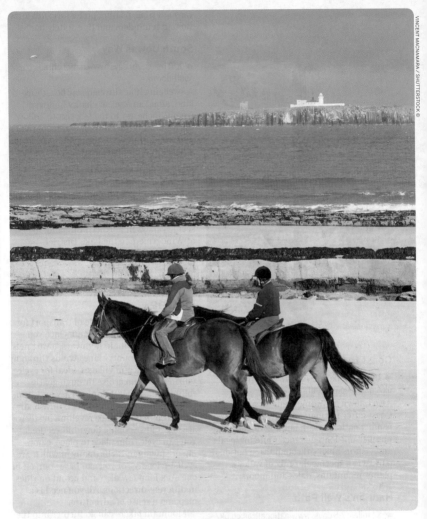

VINCENT MACNAMARA / SHUTTERSTOCK ©

JENNYT / SHUTTERSTOCK ©

Top: Horseriding on the beachfront at Seahouses

Bottom: Kitesurfing on the Devon coast

Surfing & Windsurfing

England may not seem an obvious destination for surfing, but conditions are surprisingly good and the large tidal range often means a completely different set of breaks at low and high tides. If you've come from the other side of the world, you'll be delighted to learn that summer water temperatures in southern England are roughly equivalent to winter temperatures in southern Australia (ie you'll still need a wetsuit). At the main spots, it's easy enough to hire boards and wetsuits.

Top of the list are the Atlantic-facing coasts of Cornwall and Devon (Newquay is surf-central, with all the trappings from Kombi vans to bleached hair), and there are smaller surf scenes elsewhere, notably Norfolk and Yorkshire in eastern England.

Windsurfing is hugely popular all around the coast. Top areas include Norfolk, Suffolk, Devon and Cornwall, and the Isle of Wight.

http://ukwindsurfing.com Good source of info on windsurfing.

http://surfinggb.com Listings of approved surf schools, courses, competitions and so on.

Canoeing & Kayaking

Southwest England's coast, with its sheltered inlets and indented shoreline, is ideal for sea kayaking, while inland lakes and canals across the country are great for Canadian canoeing. Although tame by comparison with alpine torrents, the turbulent spate rivers of the Lake District, Northumberland and Devon offer challenging whitewater kayaking.

Equipment rental and instruction are readily available in major centres such as Cornwall, Devon and the Lake District.

www.gocanoeing.org.uk Lists approved canoeing centres in England.

Sailing & Boating

The south coast of England, with its superb scenery and challenging winds and tides, is one of Europe's most popular yachting areas, while the English canals offer a classic narrow-boating experience. Beginners can take a Royal Yachting Association training course in yachting or dinghy sailing at many sailing schools around the coast. Narrow-boaters only need a quick introductory lesson at the start of their trip.

www.rya.org.uk The Royal Yachting Association's website.

www.canalholidays.com For more info on narrow boats and lessons.

Horse Riding & Pony Trekking

If you want to explore the hills and moors but walking or cycling is too much of a sweat, seeing the wilder parts of England from horseback is highly recommended. In rural areas and national parks such as Dartmoor and Northumberland, riding centres cater to all levels of proficiency, with ponies for kids and beginners, and horses for the more experienced.

British Horse Society (www.bhs.org.uk) Lists approved riding centres offering day rides or longer holidays on horseback.

Rock Climbing

England has a long history of rock climbing and mountaineering, with many of the classic routes having been pioneered in the 19th century. The main rock-climbing areas include the Lake District, the Peak District and Yorkshire, plus the sea cliffs of Devon and Cornwall, but there are also hundreds of smaller crags situated all over the country.

Comprehensive climbing guidebooks are published by the **Fell & Rock Climbing Club** (www.frcc.co.uk) and the **Climbers Club** (www.climbers-club.co.uk).

www.ukclimbing.com The UK Climbing website is crammed with useful information.

Plan Your Trip
Travel with Children

England is ideal for travelling with children because of its compact size, packing a lot of attractions into a small area. So when the kids in the back of the car say, 'Are we there yet?' your answer can often be 'Yes, we are'.

Best Regions for Kids

London
Children's attractions galore – some put a strain on parental purse strings, but many others are free.

Southwest England
Some of the best beaches in England, and fairly reliable holiday weather – though crowded in summer.

Peak District
Former railways that are now traffic-free cycle routes make the Peak District perfect for family outings by bike.

Oxford & the Cotswolds
Oxford has kid-friendly museums plus Harry Potter connections; the Cotswold countryside is ideal for little-leg strolls.

Shropshire
The historic England–Wales borderland has many castles to explore, plus excellent museums for inquisitive minds.

Lake District & Cumbria
This is Outdoor Activity Central: zip wires and mountain bikes for teenagers; boat rides and Beatrix Potter for the youngsters.

England for Kids

Many places of interest cater for kids as much as adults. At the country's historic castles, for example, mum and dad can admire the medieval architecture, while the kids will have great fun striding around the battlements or watching falconry demonstrations. In the same way, many national parks and holiday resorts organise specific activities and events for children. Everything ramps up in the school holidays.

Bargain Hunting

Most visitor attractions offer family tickets – usually two adults plus two children – for less than the sum of the individual entrance charges. Most offer cheaper rates for solo parents and kids too. Be sure to ask, as these are not always clearly displayed.

On the Road

If you're going by public transport, trains are great for families: intercity services have plenty of room for luggage and extra stuff like 'buggies' (prams), and the kids can move about a bit if they get bored. In contrast, they need to stay in their seats on long-distance coaches.

If you're hiring a car, most (but not all) rental firms can provide child seats – you'll need to check this in advance. Most will not actually fit the child seats; you must do that yourself, for insurance reasons.

Dining, not Whining

When it comes to refuelling, most cafes and teashops are child-friendly. Restaurants are mixed: some offer highchairs and kiddy portions; others firmly say, 'No children after 6pm'.

In some pubs, those under 18 are not allowed, but most pubs in tourist areas serve food, making them 'family-friendly'. If in doubt, simply ask the bar staff.

And finally, a word on another kind of refuelling: England is still slightly buttoned up about breastfeeding. Older folks may tut-tut a bit if you give junior a top-up in public, but if done modestly it's usually considered OK.

Children's Highlights

Best Hands-on Action

'Please Do Not Touch'? No chance! Here are some places where grubby fingers and enquiring minds are positively welcomed.

Science Museum, London (p82) Seven floors of educational exhibits at the mother of all science museums.

Discovery Museum, Newcastle (p605) Tyneside's rich history on display; highlights include a buzzers-and-bells science maze.

National Railway Museum, York (p481) Clambering into the driver's cab on a steam locomotive, exploring a Royal Mail train, taking part in engineering demonstrations...it's all here.

Action Stations!, Portsmouth (p227) Toys with a military spin; your chance to fly a helicopter, control an aircraft carrier, or up-periscope in a submarine.

Enginuity, Ironbridge (p427) Endless interactive displays at the birthplace of the Industrial Revolution.

Best Fresh-Air Fun

If the kids tire of England's castles and museums, you're never far from a place for outdoor activities to blow away the cobwebs.

Conkers, Leicestershire (p458) Play indoors, outdoors or among the trees in the heart of the National Forest.

Puzzlewood, Forest of Dean (p208) A wonderful woodland playground with maze-like paths, weird rock formations and eerie passageways to offer a real sense of discovery.

Whinlatter Forest Park, Cumbria (p589) Highlights include a 'Go Ape' adventure park, excellent mountain-bike trails, plus live video feeds from squirrel-cams.

Bewilderwood, Norfolk (p384) Zip wires, jungle bridges, tree houses, marsh walks, boat trips, mazes and all sorts of old-fashioned outdoor adventure.

North York Moors, Yorkshire (p478) Easy, scenic bike trails at Sutton Bank, hard-core mountain biking at Dalby Forest.

Lyme Regis & the Jurassic Coast, Dorset (p250) Guided tours show you how to find your very own prehistoric fossil.

Tissington Trail, Derbyshire (p463) Cycling this former railway is fun and almost effortless. You can hire kids' bikes, tandems and trailers. Don't forget to hoot in the tunnels!

Best Rainy-Day Distractions

On those inevitable gloomy days, head for the indoor attractions, including the nation's great collection of museums. Alternatively, try outdoor stuff like coasteering in Cornwall or canyoning (check conditions) in the Lake District – always fun, wet or dry.

Cadbury World, Birmingham (p396) Your dentist may cry, but kids love the story of chocolate. And yes, there are free samples.

Eden Project, Cornwall (p338) It may be raining outside, but inside these gigantic semispherical greenhouses, it's forever tropical forest or Mediterranean climate.

Cheddar Gorge Caves, Wessex (p314) Finally nail the difference between stalactites and stalagmites in the West Country's deep caverns.

Underground Passages, Exeter (p270) Explore medieval catacombs – the only system of its kind open to the public in England.

National Media Museum, Bradford (p519) Attractions include a TV studio where you can film yourself, a gallery of 1980s video games (yes, you can play them) and an IMAX cinema.

Best Stealth Learning

Secretly exercise their minds while the little darlings think they are 'just' having fun.

At-Bristol Science Centre, Bristol (p297) One of the best interactive science museums in England, covering space, technology and the human brain.

Jorvik Viking Centre, York (p483) An excellent smells-and-all Viking settlement reconstruction.

Natural History Museum, London (p82) Animals everywhere! Highlights include the life-size blue whale and the animatronics dinosaurs.

Thinktank, Birmingham (p393) Every display comes with a button or a lever at this edu-taining science museum.

National Space Centre, Leicester (p453) Space-suits, zero-gravity toilets and mini-astronaut training – all guaranteed to fire-up little minds.

Planning

When to Go

The best time for families to visit England is pretty much the best time for everyone else – any time from April/May till the end of September. It's worth avoiding August – the heart of school summer holidays – when prices go up and the roads are busy, especially near the coast.

Places to Stay

Some hotels welcome kids (with their parents!) and provide cots, toys and babysitting services, while others maintain an adult atmosphere. Many B&Bs offer 'family suites' – two adjoining bedrooms with one bathroom – and an increasing number of hostels (YHA and independent) have family rooms with four or six beds, some even with private bathroom attached. If you want to stay in one place for a while, renting a holiday cottage is ideal. Camping is very popular with English families, and there are lots of fantastic campsites, but you'll usually need all your own equipment.

Nappy Changing

On the sticky topic of dealing with nappies (diapers), most museums and other attractions in England have good baby-changing facilities. Elsewhere, some city-centre public toilets have baby-changing areas, although these can be a bit grimy; your best bet for clean facilities is an upmarket department store. On the road, baby-changing facilities are usually OK at motorway service stations or out-of-town supermarkets.

Regions at a Glance

From the multicultural melting pot of London to the lonely spiritual outpost of Lindisfarne, England's regions offer a kaleidoscope of classic experiences. Southern England is where you'll find the archetypal English countryside of lush meadows, thatched cottages and games of cricket on the village green. The southwestern counties of Devon and Cornwall are wilder in nature, known for their surf beaches and seafood restaurants. Lovers of moor and mountain will be spoilt for choice in the Lake District and Peak District, while those who prefer gritty industrial heritage and lively nightlife will enjoy the northern cities of Manchester, Liverpool and Newcastle. And bang in the middle is Yorkshire, with everything from the gorgeous city of York to the rolling hills of the Yorkshire Dales.

London

History
Entertainment
Culture

Historic Streets

London's ancient streets contain many of Britain's most famous and history-steeped landmarks. The echoes of the footfalls of monarchs, poets, whores and saints can still be detected in places such as the Tower of London, Westminster Abbey and St Paul's Cathedral, as well as the pubs and coaching inns that once served Dickens, Shelley, Keats and Byron.

Entertainment

From West End theatres to East End clubs, from Camden's rock venues to Covent Garden's opera house, from tennis at Wimbledon to cricket at Lord's or football at Wembley, London's world-famous venues and arenas offer a perpetual clamour of entertainment.

Museums

While the British Museum is the big crowd-puller, the capital has museums and galleries of every shape and size – and many of the very best are free.

p54

Canterbury & Southeast England

Cathedral
History
Food & Drink

Canterbury Cathedral

A major reason to visit southeast England, Canterbury Cathedral is one of the finest in Europe, and one of the most holy places in Christendom. Write your own Canterbury tale as you explore its atmospheric chapels, cloisters and crypts.

Invasion Heritage

The southeast has always been a gateway for arrivals from the Continent, some more welcome than others. Castles and fortresses, the 1066 battlefield and Dover's secret wartime tunnels all tell the region's story of invasion and defence.

Hops & Grapes

Kent is deservedly known as the Garden of England, long celebrated for its hops, which are still used to flavour traditional English beers. Sussex isn't far behind, with England's finest sparkling wine giving the French stuff a run for its euro.

p140

Oxford, Cotswolds & Around

Architecture
Stately Homes
Villages

Oxford Colleges

Oxford's architecture will never leave you indifferent, whether you gaze across the 'dreaming spires' from the top of Carfax Tower, or explore the medieval streets on foot, or simply admire the fantastic gargoyles on college facades.

Blenheim Palace

Favoured by the rich and powerful for centuries, this region is scattered with some of the finest country houses in England. Top of the pile is the baroque masterpiece of Blenheim Palace, birthplace of Sir Winston Churchill.

Cotswold Villages

Littered with picturesque 'chocolate box' scenes of honey-coloured stone cottages, thatched roofs, neat greens and cobbled lanes, the villages of the Cotswolds provide a charming snapshot of rural England.

p175

Bath & Southwest England

Coastline
History
Activities

Cornish Beaches

England's southwest peninsula juts determinedly into the Atlantic, fringed by an almost endless chain of sandy beaches, from the picturesque scenery of Kynance Cove to the rolling surf of Newquay.

Roman Remains

The handsome Georgian city of Bath – the whole town is a Unesco World Heritage Site – is home to one of the best preserved Roman bath complexes in the world.

Hiking & Surfing

If you like to take it nice and easy, come to walk the moors or tootle along cycle trails. If you prefer life fast and furious, come to surf the best waves in England or learn to dive or kitesurf.

p218

Cambridge & East Anglia

Architecture
Coastline
Waterways

Historic Churches

From the magnificent cathedrals of Ely, Norwich and Peterborough to Cambridge's King's College Chapel, Trinity's Great Court and the New Court at St John's, East Anglia's architectural splendour is second to none.

Seaside Resorts

With wide sandy beaches, great seafood, delightful old pubs, globally important bird reserves, historic villages still proud of their nautical heritage, and classic seaside resorts including Southwold and Cromer, the coastline of East Anglia is rich and varied.

The Broads

The Norfolk and Suffolk Broads are a tranquil haven of lakes and meandering rivers, and an ideal spot for boating, birdwatching, canoeing, cycling or walking, or just getting back to nature at a leisurely pace.

p349

Birmingham, the Midlands & the Marches

Activities
Stately Homes
Food & Drink

Hiking & Biking

The Peak District National Park, Cannock Chase, the Shropshire Hills, the Roaches, the Malvern Hills, Offa's Dyke Path, the Tissington Trail and the Pennine Cycleway all make this region great for hiking and biking.

Chatsworth

Grand houses including Haddon Hall, Burghley House and especially Chatsworth – the magnificent home of the Duke and Duchess of Devonshire – promise sprawling landscaped gardens adorned with classical sculptures, grand interiors full of priceless heirlooms and walls dripping with oil paintings.

Curry Capital

Foodies take note: Birmingham is the curry capital of the country (and, increasingly, a magnet for Michelin-starred chefs), while the tiny town of Ludlow is an epicentre of gastronomic exploration.

p389

Yorkshire

Activities
Food & Drink
History

Hiking & Biking

With rolling hills, scenic valleys, high moors and a cliff-lined coast, all protected by two of England's best-loved national parks, Yorkshire is a natural adventure playground for hiking, biking, surfing and rock climbing.

Roast Beef & Real Ale

Rich farmland and lush pasture means Yorkshire beef and lamb are much sought-after, while the famous Theakston's and Black Sheep breweries of Masham turn out excellent real ales, best sampled in one of Yorkshire's equally excellent traditional pubs.

Ancient Abbeys

From York's Roman and Viking heritage and the ancient abbeys of Rievaulx, Fountains and Whitby to the industrial archaeology of Leeds, Bradford and Sheffield, Yorkshire allows you to explore several of Britain's most important historical narratives.

p475

Manchester, Liverpool & Northwest England

History
Sport
Seaside Resorts

Museums

The northwest's collection of heritage sites, from the wonderful People's History Museum in Manchester to the International Slavery Museum in Liverpool, is testament to the region's rich history and its ability to keep it alive.

Football

Two cities, Liverpool and Manchester, give the world four famous clubs, including the two most successful in English history. The National Football Museum in Manchester is just another reason for football fans to visit this region.

Blackpool

The epitome of the classic English seaside resort just keeps on going, thanks to the rides of the Pleasure Beach amusement park, where adrenalin junkies can always find a fix.

p529

The Lake District & Cumbria

Scenery
Activities
Literature

Lakes & Mountains

The Lake District National Park is the most mountainous part of England, home to Scafell Pike (England's highest summit) and countless scenic lakes. Some are big and famous – Windermere, Coniston, Ullswater – while others are small, hidden and little known.

Walking

If anywhere is the heart and soul of walking in England, it's the Lake District. Casual strollers find gentle routes through foothills and valleys, while serious hikers hit the high fells and mountains – many heading to the top of Scafell Pike.

William Wordsworth

The beauty of the Lake District famously moved William Wordsworth to write his ode to 'a host of golden daffodils', and visiting Wordsworth landmarks such as Dove Cottage and Hawkshead Grammar School is one of the region's big draws.

p564

Newcastle & Northeast England

History
Landscapes
Castles

Hadrian's Wall

One of the world's premier Roman sites, this potent symbol of imperial power strides for over 70 miles across the neck of England, from Tyneside to the Solway Firth. You can travel its length, stopping off at forts along the way.

Northumberland National Park

If it's widescreen vistas you're after, the broad moors, stone villages and expansive views of England's most northerly national park never fail to please. As well as landscapes there are starscapes to be enjoyed, in the heart of England's biggest dark-sky park.

Alnwick Castle

Northumberland is dotted with some of Britain's finest castles, including the coastal fortresses of Bamburgh and Dunstanburgh, but Alnwick – setting for the Harry Potter movies – is the most famous.

p601

On the Road

Newcastle &
Northeast England
p601

The Lake District
& Cumbria
p564

Yorkshire
p475

Manchester, Liverpool
& Northwest England
p529

Birmingham,
the Midlands &
the Marches
p389

Cambridge &
East Anglia
p349

Oxford, Cotswolds
& Around
p175

London
p54

Bath &
Southwest
England
p218

Canterbury &
Southeast England
p140

London

POP 8.7 MILLION / ⏱ 020 / AREA 1 569 SQ KM

Includes ➡

History 55
Sights 58
Tours 102
Activities 103
Festivals & Events 103
Sleeping 106
Eating 112
Drinking & Nightlife 122
Entertainment 128
Shopping 132

Best Places to Eat

➡ Gymkhana (p113)

➡ Dinner by Heston Blumenthal (p116)

➡ Brasserie Zédel (p113)

➡ Gordon Ramsay (p116)

➡ Ledbury (p117)

Best Places to Sleep

➡ Zetter Hotel & Townhouse (p112)

➡ Citizen M (p108)

➡ Clink78 (p111)

➡ Beaumont (p107)

➡ Hoxton Hotel (p108)

Why Go?

Everyone comes to London with preconceptions shaped by a multitude of books, movies, TV shows and songs. Whatever yours are, prepare to have them exploded by this endlessly fascinating, amorphous city. You could spend a lifetime exploring it and still find that the slippery thing's gone and changed on you. One thing though is constant: that great serpent of a river enfolding the city in its sinuous loops, linking London both to the green heart of England and the world. From Roman times people from around the globe have come to London, put down roots and complained about the weather. This is one of the world's most multicultural cities – any given street yields a rich harvest of languages, and those narrow streets are also steeped in fascinating history, magnificent art, imposing architecture and popular culture. When you add an endless reserve of cool to this mix, it's hard not to conclude that London is one of the world's great cities, if not the greatest.

When to Go

London is a place that you can visit any time of the year. That said, different months and seasons boast different charms.

➡ Spring in the city sees daffodils in bloom and blossom in the trees.

➡ In June, the parks are filled with people, there's Trooping the Colour, summer arts festivals, Field Day in Victoria Park, other music events, gay pride and Wimbledon.

➡ Although the days are getting shorter, autumn in London is alive with festivals celebrating literature, the arts and culture.

➡ London in December is all about Christmas lights on Oxford and Regent Sts, and perhaps a whisper of snow.

History

London first came into being as a Celtic village near a ford across the River Thames, but the city only really took off after the Roman conquest in AD 43. The invaders enclosed their 'Londinium' in walls that still find refrain in the shape of the City (with a capital 'C') of London today.

By the end of the 3rd century AD, Londinium was home to some 30,000 people. Internal strife and relentless barbarian attacks wore the Romans down, however, and they abandoned Britain in the 5th century, reducing the settlement to a sparsely populated backwater.

The Saxons moved in next, their 'Lundenwic' prospering and becoming a large, well-organised town. As the city grew in importance, it caught the eye of Danish Vikings,who launched numerous invasions. In 1016 the Saxons, finally beaten down, were forced to accept the Danish leader Knut (Canute) as King of England, after which London replaced Winchester as capital. In 1042, the throne reverted to the Saxon Edward the Confessor, who built Westminster Abbey.

The Norman Conquest of 1066 saw William the Conqueror march into London, where he was crowned king. He built the White Tower (the core of the Tower of London), negotiated taxes with the merchants, and affirmed the city's right to self-government. From then until the late 15th century, London politics were largely taken up by a three-way power struggle between the monarchy, the Church and city guilds. An uneasy political compromise was reached between the factions, and the city expanded rapidly in the 16th century under the House of Tudor.

In a rerun of the disease that wiped out half of London's population between 1348 and1350, the Great Plague struck in 1665, and by the time the winter cold arrested the epidemic,100,000 Londoners had perished. The cataclysm was followed by further devastation when the Great Fire of 1666 sent the city skywards. One upshot of the conflagration was a blank canvas for master architect Sir Christopher Wren to build his magnificent churches.

Despite these setbacks, London continued to grow, and by 1700 it was Europe's largest city, with 600,000 people. An influx of foreign workers brought expansion to the east and south, while those who could afford it headed to the more salubrious environs of the north and west. Georgian London saw a surge in artistic creativity, with the likes of Dr Johnson, Handel, Gainsborough and Reynolds enriching the city's culture, while architects fashioned an elegant new metropolis.

In 1837, 18-year-old Victoria began her epic reign, as London became the fulcrum of the British Empire. The Industrial Revolution saw the building of new docks and railways (including the first underground line in 1863), while the Great Exhibition of 1851 showcased London to the world. During the Victorian era, the city's population mushroomed from just over two million to 6.6 million.

Although London suffered a relatively minor bruising during WWI, it was devastated by the Luftwaffe in WWII, when huge swaths of the centre and East End were flattened and 32,000 people were killed. Ugly housing and low-cost developments followed, and pollutants – both residential and industrial – rose steadily into the air. On 6 December 1952, the Great Smog (a lethal combination of fog, smoke and pollution) descended, killing some 4000 people.

Prosperity gradually returned to the city, and creative energy bottled up in the postwar years was suddenly unleashed. In the 'Swinging Sixties', London became the capital of cool in fashion and music – a party followed morosely by the austere 1970s. Since then the city has surfed up and down the waves of global fortunes, hanging on to its position as the world's leading financial centre.

In 2000, the modern metropolis won its first mayor of London, an elected role covering the City and all 32 urban boroughs. Bicycle-riding Boris Johnson, a Tory (Conservative) with a shock of blond hair and an affable persona, was elected in 2008, and retained his post in the 2012 mayoral election.

Triggered by the shooting of a man by police in Tottenham in August 2011, numerous London boroughs were rocked by riots characterised by looting and arson. Analysts still debate the causes of the disorder, ascribing any number of factors from single-parent families to gang culture, unemployment and criminal opportunism.

Both the Olympics and the Queen's Diamond Jubilee concocted a splendid display of pageantry for London in 2012. New overground train lines opened, a cable car was flung across the Thames and a once rundown and polluted area of East London was regenerated for the Olympic Park. The games themselves were a universally applauded success, kicked off by a stupendous Opening Ceremony orchestrated by Danny Boyle.

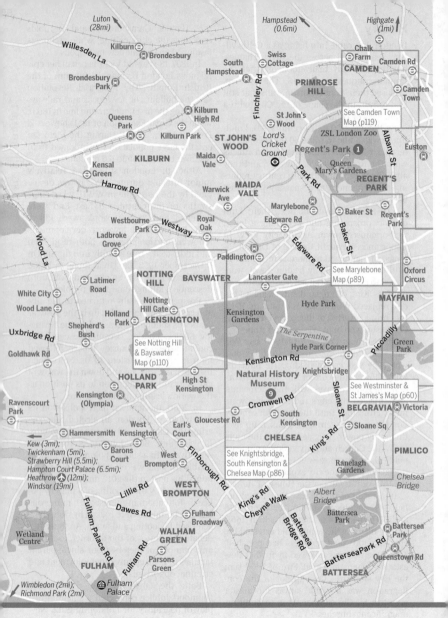

London Highlights

1 Regent's Park (p88)
Watching the world pass by in one of London's loveliest parks.

2 British Museum (p90)
Sifting through the booty of an empire at this fine museum.

3 Tower of London (p71)
Exploring the famous castle where several royals met their deaths by guillotine.

4 Westminster Abbey (p58)

Enjoying the awe-inspiring architecture at this holy spot.

5 Lamb & Flag (p122)
Raising a glass while overlooking the Thames from here or another riverside pub.

6 **Shoreditch bar hop**
Meeting locals on a cruise
around trendy Shoreditch (p121).

7 **St Paul's Cathedral** (p73)
Reaching for the heavens at the
top of the dome.

8 **Tate Modern** (p78)
Embarking on a tour of
modern and contemporary art.

9 **Natural History
Museum** (p82) Revelling in

the astounding displays and
gardens set in 5.7 hectares.

10 **Shakespeare's Globe**
(p128) Getting your drama fix
at a Shakespearean outdoor
theatre.

◉ Sights

The city's main geographical feature is the murky Thames, which snakes around, but roughly divides the city into north and south. The old City of London is the capital's financial district, covering roughly a square mile bordered by the river and the many gates of the ancient (long-gone) city walls: Newgate, Moorgate etc. The areas east of the City are collectively known as the East End. The West End, on the City's other flank, is effectively the centre of London gravity. It actually falls within the City of Westminster, one of London's 32 boroughs and long the centre of government and royalty.

Surrounding these central areas are dozens of former villages (Camden Town, Islington, Clapham etc), each with its own High St, long ago swallowed by London's sprawl.

When the sun shines, make like a Londoner and head to the parks.

◉ Westminster & St James's

Purposefully positioned outside the old City (London's fiercely independent burghers preferred to keep the monarch and parliament at arm's length), Westminster has been the centre of the nation's political power for nearly a millennium. The area's many landmarks combine to form an awesome display of authority, pomp and gravitas. St James's is an aristocratic enclave of palaces, famous hotels, historic shops and elegant edifices, with some 150 historically noteworthy buildings in its 36 hectares.

★Westminster Abbey   CHURCH
(Map p60; ☑020-7222 5152; www.westminster-abbey.org; 20 Dean's Yard, SW1; adult/child £20/9, verger tours £5, cloister & gardens free; ◉9.30am-4.30pm Mon, Tue, Thu & Fri, to 7pm Wed, to 2.30pm Sat; ◉Westminster) A splendid mixture of architectural styles, Westminster Abbey is considered the finest example of Early English Gothic (1190–1300). It's not merely a beautiful place of worship – the Abbey also serves up the country's history cold on slabs of stone. For centuries, the country's greatest have been interred here, including 17 monarchs from Henry III (died 1272) to George II (1760). Never a cathedral (the seat of a bishop), Westminster Abbey is what is called a 'royal peculiar', administered by the Crown.

Every monarch since William the Conqueror has been crowned here, with the exception of a couple of unlucky Eds who were either murdered (Edward V) or abdicated (Edward VIII) before the magic moment.

At the heart of the Abbey is the beautifully tiled sanctuary (or sacrarium), a stage for coronations, royal weddings and funerals. George Gilbert Scott designed the ornate high altar in 1873. In front of the altar is the Cosmati marble pavement dating to 1268. It has intricate designs of small pieces of marble inlaid into plain marble, which predicts the end of the world in AD 19,693! At the entrance to the lovely Chapel of St John the Baptist is a sublime alabaster Virgin and Child bathed in candlelight.

The most sacred spot in the Abbey, the shrine of St Edward the Confessor, lies behind the high altar; access is generally restricted to protect the 13th-century flooring. St Edward was the founder of the Abbey and the original building was consecrated a few weeks before his death. His tomb was slightly altered after the original was destroyed during the Reformation but still contains Edward's remains – the only complete saint's body in Britain. Ninety-minute verger-led tours of the Abbey include a visit to the shrine.

The Quire, a sublime structure of gold, blue and red Victorian Gothic by Edward Blore, dates back to the mid-19th century. It sits where the original choir for the monks' worship would have been but bears no resemblance to the original. Nowadays, the Quire is still used for singing, but its regular occupants are the Westminster Choir – 22 boys and 12 'lay vicars' (men) who sing the daily services.

Henry III began work on the new building in 1245 but didn't complete it; the Gothic nave was finished under Richard II in 1388. Henry VII's magnificent Perpendicular Gothic-style Lady Chapel was consecrated in 1519 after 16 years of construction. The vestibule of the Lady Chapel is the usual place for the rather ordinary-looking Coronation Chair, upon which every monarch since the early 14th century has been crowned (apart from joint-monarch Mary II, who had her own chair fashioned for her coronation, which is now in the Westminster Abbey Museum (Map p60; ◉10.30am-4pm).

Apart from the royal graves, keep an eye out for the many famous commoners interred here, especially in Poets' Corner, where you'll find the resting places of Chaucer, Dickens, Hardy, Tennyson, Dr Johnson and Kipling, as well as memorials to the other greats (Shakespeare, Jane Austen, Brontë

LONDON IN ...

Two Days

Start in **Trafalgar Sq** and see at least the outside of all the big-ticket sights – **London Eye**, **Houses of Parliament**, **Westminster Abbey**, **St James's Park and Palace**, **Buckingham Palace**, **Green Park**, **Hyde Park** and **Kensington Gardens** – and then motor around the **Tate Modern** until you get booted out. In the evening, explore **Soho**. On day two, race around the **British Museum**, then head to the **City**. Start with our **walking tour** and finish in the **Tower of London**. In the evening, head to **Clerkenwell** for international eats, then **Hoxton** and **Shoreditch** for hip bars.

Four Days

Take the two-day itinerary but stretch it to a comfortable pace, spending extra time in the Tate Modern, British Museum and Tower of London. Stop at the **National Gallery** while you're in Trafalgar Sq and explore inside Westminster Abbey and **St Paul's Cathedral**. On your extra evenings, check out **Camden** and **Islington** or enjoy a no-expenses-spared dinner in **Kensington** or **Knightsbridge**.

One Week

As above, but add a day each for **Greenwich**, **Kew Gardens** and **Hampton Court Palace**

---

etc). Nearby you'll find the graves of Handel and Sir Isaac Newton.

The octagonal **Chapter House** dates from the 1250s and was where the monks would meet for daily prayer before Henry VIII's suppression of the monasteries some three centuries later. To the right of the entrance to Chapter House is what is claimed to be the oldest door in Britain – it's been there for 950 years. Used as a treasury and 'Royal Wardrobe', the crypt-like **Pyx Chamber** dates from about 1070. Next door in the vaulted undercroft, the museum exhibits the death masks of generations of royalty, wax effigies representing Charles II and William III (who is on a stool to make him as tall as his wife, Mary II), armour and stained glass. Highlights are the graffiti-inscribed Mary Chair (used for the coronation of Mary II) and the Westminster Retable, England's oldest altarpiece, from the 13th century.

Parts of the Abbey complex are free to visitors. This includes the **Cloister** and the 900-year-old **College Garden** (Map p60; ⏰10am-6pm Tue-Thu Apr-Sep, to 4pm Oct-Mar). Adjacent to the abbey is **St Margaret's Church**, the House of Commons' place of worship since 1614, where windows commemorate churchgoers Caxton and Milton, and Sir Walter Raleigh is buried by the altar.

In the works are the **Queen's Diamond Jubilee Galleries**, a new museum and gallery space located in the medieval triforium, and due to open in 2018.

★**Houses of Parliament** HISTORIC BUILDING
(Map p60; www.parliament.uk; Parliament Sq, SW1; ⊖Westminster) FREE A visit here is a journey to the heart of UK democracy. Officially called the Palace of Westminster, the Houses of Parliament's oldest part is 11th-century **Westminster Hall**, one of only a few sections that survived a catastrophic fire in 1834. Its roof, added between 1394 and 1401, is the earliest-known example of a hammer-beam roof. The rest is mostly a neo-Gothic confection built by Charles Barry and Augustus Pugin (1840–58).

The palace's most famous feature is its clock tower, Elizabeth Tower, aka **Big Ben** (Map p60; ⊖Westminster).

Ben is actually the 13.5-ton bell, named after Benjamin Hall, who was Commissioner of Works when the tower was completed in 1858.

At the business end, parliament is split into two houses. The green-hued **House of Commons** (Map p60; www.parliament.uk/business/commons; ⏰2.30-10pm Mon & Tue, 11.30am-7.30pm Wed, 10.30am-6.30pm Thu, 9.30am-3pm Fri) is the lower house, where the 650 elected Members of Parliament sit. Traditionally the home of hereditary blue bloods, the scarlet-decorated **House of Lords** (Map p60; www.parliament.uk/business/lords; Parliament Sq, SW1; ⏰2.30-10pm Mon & Tue, 3-10pm Wed, 11am-7.30pm Thu, 10am-close of session Fri; ⊖Westminster), with 763 members, now has peers appointed through various means. Both houses debate and vote on legislation, which is then presented to the Queen for her Royal

Westminster & St James's

0 ————— 500 m
0 ————— 0.25 miles

River Thames

Victoria Embankment

Whitehall Pl

Richmond Tce

Whitehall 7

Horse Guards Parade

Treasury

HorseGuards Rd

Foreign & Commonwealth Office

Churchill War Rooms 5

King Charles St

Great George St

13

Westminster 2
Bridge St

Big Ben

24
23
25

10 2
12
11

St Margaret St

18
19

Abingdon St

Millbank

Victoria Tower Gardens

Tate Britain (500m)

Parliament Sq

Westminster Abbey 6

21

8

Great College St

Tufton St

Old Queen St

Great Smith St   Marsham St

St James's Park

Broadway

Tothill St

Great Peter St

Monck St

Medway St

Old Pye St

St James's Park Lake

Birdcage Walk

Petty France

Caxton St

Victoria St

Howick Pl

ST JAMES'S

The Mall

St James's Park

Marlborough Rd

Pall Mall

17

Buckingham Gate

Castle La

Cardinal Walk

Victoria St

Ashley Pl

22

Caton Grd

King St

St James's St

16

Queen's Walk

Green Park

Queen Victoria Monument

Spur Rd

Palace St

Bressenden Pl

Victoria St

Victoria

Green Park 9

Buckingham Palace 3

Changing of the Guard 4

14

15
Lower Grosvenor

Buckingham Palace Rd

Eaton La

26

Hobart Pl

BELGRAVIA

Eaton Sq

Piccadilly

Constitution Hill

Buckingham Palace Gardens

Grosvenor Pl

Upper Belgrave St

Belgrave Pl

Belgrave Pl

Curzon St
Market Mews
Shepherd St

Hertford St

Brick St

Old Park La

Hamilton Pl

27

Duke of Wellington Pl

Apsley House 1

Hyde Park Corner

20

Grosvenor Cres

Halkin St

Chapel St

Chester St

Wilton St

Belgrave Sq

Eaton Pl

Lyall Mews

Hyde Park

Serpentine Rd

Rotten Row

Park La

Westminster & St James's

◉ Top Sights
1 Apsley House..A2
2 Big Ben...G3
3 Buckingham Palace...............................C2
4 Changing of the Guard.........................C3
5 Churchill War Rooms............................F2
6 Westminster Abbey...............................F3

◉ Sights
7 Banqueting House.................................G1
8 College Garden......................................F3
9 Green Park...C1
10 House of Commons...............................G3
11 House of Lords......................................G3
12 Houses of Parliament..........................G3
13 No 10 Downing Street...........................F2
14 Queen's Gallery....................................C3
15 Royal Mews...C3
16 Spencer House.......................................D1

17 St James's Park....................................E2
18 St Stephen's Entrance.........................G3
19 Supreme Court......................................F3
20 Wellington Arch....................................B2
21 Westminster Abbey Museum...............F3
22 Westminster Cathedral........................D4

✚ Activities, Courses & Tours
23 City Cruises...G2
   Houses of Parliament Tours.........(see 12)
24 Thames River Boats.............................G2
25 Westminster Passenger Services
   Association...G2

⊜ Sleeping
26 Goring..C4

⊜ Drinking & Nightlife
27 Galvin at Windows................................B1

Assent (in practice, this is a formality; the last time Royal Assent was denied was in 1708). At the annual State Opening of Parliament, which takes place in May, the Queen takes her throne in the House of Lords, having arrived in the gold-trimmed Irish State Coach from Buckingham Palace (her crown travels alone in Queen Alexandra's State Coach). It's well worth lining the route for a gawk at the crown jewels sparkling in the sun.

On Saturdays year-round and on most weekdays during parliamentary recesses including Easter, summer and Christmas, visitors can join a 90-minute **guided tour** (Map p60; ☑ 020-7219 4114; www.parliament.uk/visiting/visiting-and-tours; adult/child £25.50/11) of both chambers, Westminster Hall and other historic buildings conducted by qualified Blue Badge Tourist Guides in seven languages. Afternoon tea in the Terrace Pavilion overlooking the River Thames is a popular add-on to the tours. Tour schedules change with every recess and are occasionally subject to variation or cancellation due to the State Opening of Parliament and other parliamentary business, so check ahead and book. UK residents can approach their MPs to arrange a free tour and to climb the Elizabeth Tower.

The public entrance to the Houses of Parliament is **St Stephen's Entrance** (Map p60; www.parliament.uk; Parliament Sq, SW1; ⊜ Westminster), housed within St Stephen's Tower.

★ **Buckingham Palace** PALACE
(Map p60; ☑ 020-7766 7300; www.royalcollection.org.uk; Buckingham Palace Rd, SW1; adult/child/child under 5 £21.50/12.30/free; ⊙ 9.30am-7.30pm late Jul–Aug, to 6.30pm Sep; ⊜ St James's Park, Victoria or Green Park) Built in 1703 for the Duke of Buckingham, Buckingham Palace replaced St James's Palace as the monarch's official London residence in 1837. When she's not delivering her trademark wave to far-flung parts of the Commonwealth, Queen Elizabeth II divides her time between here, Windsor and, in summer, Balmoral. If she's at home, the yellow, red and blue standard is flying. Some 19 lavishly furnished **State Rooms** are open to visitors when Her Royal Highness takes her holidays from late July to September.

Hung with artworks by the likes of Rembrandt, Van Dyck, Canaletto, Poussin and Vermeer, the State Rooms are open for two-hour tours that include the **Throne Room**, with his-and-hers pink chairs initialed 'ER' and 'P'. Access is by timed tickets with admission every 15 minutes (audio guide included).

From 2016, admission included access to *Fashioning a Reign: 90 Years of Style from The Queen's Wardrobe*, an exhibition affording a glimpse at royal couture during the Queen's reign.

Admission also includes access to part of the garden at Buckingham Palace as you exit, although you will have to join the three-hour State Rooms and Garden Highlights Tour (adult/child £27.50/16.40) to see the wisteria-clad Summer House and other famous features, and get an idea of the garden's full 16-hectare size.

Your ticket to Buckingham Palace is good for a return trip if bought direct from the palace ticket office (ask to have it stamped). You can even make your ticket purchase a

1. Tower of London 2. Windsor Castle 3. Hampton Court Palace
4. Buckingham Palace

Royal London

Along with Stonehenge and Big Ben, the current monarch, Queen Elizabeth II, is one of the most potent symbols of England. Pretty much anything connected to the country's royal heritage is a guaranteed attraction – especially the capital's fine collection of palaces and castles.

The Tower of London (p71)

The Tower of London has a 1000-year-old history and foundations that date back to Roman times. Over the centuries it's been a royal residence, treasury, mint, prison and arsenal. Today it's home to the spectacular Crown Jewels, as well as red-coated Beefeaters and ravens attributed with mythical power.

Windsor Castle (p213)

Although not actually in London, Windsor Castle is near enough to visit on a day-trip. This is the wlargest and oldest occupied fortress in the world, an astounding edifice of defensive walls, towers and battlements, used for state occasions and as the Queen's weekend retreat.

Buckingham Palace (p61)

Buckingham Palace has been the monarch's London residence since 1837, and the current Queen divides her time between here, Windsor Castle and Balmoral in Scotland. If she's at home, the 'royal standard' flag flies on the roof. If she's out, you can take a tour to see inside. Either way, don't miss the famous Changing of the Guard.

Hampton Court Palace (p101)

Hampton Court Palace is England's largest and grandest Tudor structure, used by King Henry VIII as a riverside hideaway. After admiring the grand interior, you can relax in the extensive gardens, but don't get lost in the 300-year-old maze.

LONDON: TOP TIPS

➡ London is huge – work by neighbourhood to avoid wasting time (and money) on transport.

➡ An Oyster Card is a cheaper and convenient way to use public transport, but you can also pay by credit or debit card provided it has a contactless function indicated by a symbol of four wavy lines.

➡ Walk – it's cheaper than transport and the best way to discover central London.

➡ For West End performances at bargain prices, opt for standby tickets (which you buy on the day at the venue) or last-minute ticket-booth tickets on Leicester Sq.

➡ To treat yourself to fine dining without breaking the bank, opt for lunch rather than dinner, or try for pre- or post-theatre dinner deals.

donation and gain free access for a whole year (ask at the ticket office).

At 11.30am daily from April to July (on alternate days, weather permitting, for the rest of the year), the old guard (Foot Guards of the Household Regiment) comes off duty to be replaced by the new guard on the forecourt of Buckingham Palace, an event known as the **Changing of the Guard**. Highly popular, the show lasts about 40 minutes (brace for crowds).

Originally designed by John Nash as a conservatory, the **Queen's Gallery** (Map p60; Southern wing, Buckingham Palace, Buckingham Gate, SW1; adult/child £10.30/5.30, with Royal Mews £17.70/9.70; ⊙10am-5.30pm; ⊜St James's Park, Victoria or Green Park) showcases some of the palace's treasures on a rotating basis, through temporary exhibitions. Entrance to the gallery is through Buckingham Gate.

Indulge your Cinderella fantasies while inspecting the exquisite state coaches in the **Royal Mews** (Map p60; www.royal collection.org.uk; Buckingham Palace Rd, SW1; adult/child £9.30/5.50, with Queen's Gallery £17.70/9.70; ⊙10am-5pm daily Apr-Oct, to 4pm Mon-Sat Nov-March; ⊜Victoria), a working stable looking after the royals' immaculately groomed horses and the opulent vehicles they use for getting from A to B. Highlights include the magnificent Gold State Coach of 1762 and the 1911 Glass Coach.

A Royal Day Out (adult/child £35.60/20) is a combined ticket including the State Rooms, Queen's Gallery and Royal Mews.

Supreme Court
LANDMARK

(Map p60; ☎020-7960 1500, 020-7960 1900; www.supremecourt.uk; Parliament Sq, SW1; ⊙9.30am-4.30pm Mon-Fri; ⊜Westminster) **FREE** The Supreme Court, the highest court in the UK, was the Appellate Committee of the House of Lords until 2009. It is now housed in the neo-Gothic Middlesex Guildhall (1913) on Parliament Sq. There's a permanent exhibition looking at the work and history of the UK's highest court as well as the building's history on the lower-ground floor. The self-guided tour booklet is £1; tours are also available on Fridays (£5; 11am, 2pm and 3pm).

St James's Park
PARK

(Map p60; www.royalparks.org.uk; The Mall, SW1; deckchairs per hr/day £1.50/7; ⊙5am-midnight, deckchairs daylight hours Mar-Oct; ⊜St James's Park or Green Park) At just 23 hectares, St James's is one of the smallest but best groomed of London's royal parks. It has brilliant views of the London Eye, Westminster, St James's Palace, Carlton Tce and the Horse Guards Parade; the photo-perfect sight of Buckingham Palace from the footbridge spanning the central lake is the best you'll find.

The lake brims with ducks, geese, swans and general fowl, and the rocks on its southern side serve as a rest stop for a half-dozen pelicans (fed at 2.30pm daily).

Green Park
PARK

(Map p60; www.royalparks.org.uk; ⊙24hr; ⊜Green Park) Less manicured than adjoining St James's, 19-hectare Green Park has huge oaks and hilly meadows, and it's never as crowded as its neighbour. It was once a duelling ground and, like Hyde Park, served as a vegetable garden during WWII.

Westminster Cathedral
CHURCH

(Map p60; www.westminstercathedral.org.uk; Victoria St, SW1; tower adult/child/family £6/3/12; ⊙7am-7pm church, 9.30am-5pm Mon-Fri, to 6pm Sat & Sun Bell Tower & exhibition; ⊜Victoria) With its distinctive candy-striped red-brick and white-stone tower features, John Francis Bentley's 19th-century cathedral, the mother church of Roman Catholicism in England and Wales, is a splendid example of neo-

Byzantine architecture. Although construction started here in 1896 and worshippers began attending services seven years later, the church ran out of money and the gaunt interior remains largely unfinished, although some radiant mosaics dazzle from the gloom.

Banqueting House
PALACE

(Map p60; ☎ 020-3166 6000; www.hrp.org.uk/banquetinghouse; Whitehall, SW1; adult/child £6.60/free; ⊙ 10am-5pm; ⊜ Westminster) After the Holbein Gate was demolished in 1759, this is the sole surviving part of the Tudor Whitehall Palace (1532) that once stretched most of the way down Whitehall before going skywards in a 1698 conflagration. Designed by Inigo Jones in 1622 and controversially refaced in Portland stone in the 19th century, Banqueting House was England's first purely Renaissance building and resembled no other structure in the country at the time. The English apparently loathed it for over a century.

No 10 Downing Street
HISTORIC BUILDING

(Map p60; www.number10.gov.uk; 10 Downing St, SW1; ⊜ Westminster) The official office of British leaders since 1732, when George II presented No 10 to Robert Walpole, this has also been the prime minister's London residence since refurbishment in 1902. For such a famous address, No 10 is a small-looking Georgian building on a plain-looking street, hardly warranting comparison with the White House, for example. Yet it is actually three houses joined into one and boasts roughly 100 rooms plus a 2000-sq-metre garden with a lovely L-shaped lawn.

★ Churchill War Rooms
MUSEUM

(Map p60; www.iwm.org.uk; Clive Steps, King Charles St, SW1; adult/child £17.25/8.60; ⊙ 9.30am-6pm, last entry 5pm; ⊜ Westminster) Winston Churchill coordinated the Allied resistance against Nazi Germany on a Bakelite telephone from this underground military HQ during WWII. The Cabinet War Rooms remain much as they were when the lights were flicked off in 1945, capturing the drama and dogged spirit of the time, while the multimedia Churchill Museum affords intriguing insights into the resolute, cigar-smoking wartime leader.

Spencer House
HISTORIC BUILDING

(Map p60; ☎ 020-7514 1958; www.spencerhouse.co.uk; 27 St James's Pl, SW1; adult/child £13/11; ⊙ 10am-4.45pm Sun Feb-Jul & Sep-Dec; ⊜ Green Park) Just outside Green Park is Spencer House, completed in the Palladian style in 1766 for the first Earl Spencer, an ancestor of Princess Diana. The Spencers moved out in 1927 and their grand family home was used as an office, until Lord Rothschild stepped in and returned it to its former glory in 1987 with an £18 million restoration.

★ Apsley House
HISTORIC BUILDING

(Map p60; www.english-heritage.org.uk/visit/places/apsley-house; 149 Piccadilly, Hyde Park Corner, W1; adult/child £8.80/5.20, with Wellington Arch £10.50/6.30; ⊙ 11am-5pm Wed-Sun Apr-Oct, 10am-5pm Sat & Sun Nov-Mar; ⊜ Hyde Park Corner) This stunning house, containing exhibits about the Duke of Wellington, victor of Waterloo against Napoleon Bonaparte, was once the first building to appear when entering London from the west and was therefore known as 'No 1 London'. Wellington memorabilia, including the duke's death mask, fills the basement gallery, while an astonishing collection of china and silver, and paintings by Velasquez, Rubens, Van Dyck, Brueghel, Murillo and Goya awaits in the 1st-floor Waterloo Gallery.

Wellington Arch
MUSEUM

(Map p60; www.english-heritage.org.uk/visit/places/wellington-arch; Hyde Park Corner, W1; adult/child £4.70/2.80, with Apsley House £10.50/6.30; ⊙ 10am-6pm Apr-Sep, to 4pm Nov-Mar; ⊜ Hyde Park Corner) Dominating the green space throttled by the Hyde Park Corner roundabout, this imposing neoclassical 1826 arch originally faced the Hyde Park Screen, but was shunted here in 1882 for road widening. Once a police station, it is now a gallery with temporary exhibitions and a permanent display about the history of the arch. The open-air balconies (accessible by lift) afford unforgettable views of Hyde Park, Buckingham Palace and the Mall.

⊙ West End

A strident mix of culture and consumerism, but more a concept than a fixed geographical area, the West End is synonymous with roof-raising musicals, bright lights, outstanding restaurants and bag-laden shoppers. It casts its net around Piccadilly Circus and Trafalgar Sq to the south, Regent St to the west, Oxford St to the north, Covent Garden to the east and the Strand to the southeast.

Named after the elaborate collars (picadils) that were the sartorial staple of a local 17th-century tailor, Piccadilly became the fashionable haunt of the well-heeled (and collared), and still boasts establishment icons such as the Ritz hotel and the Fortnum &

West End

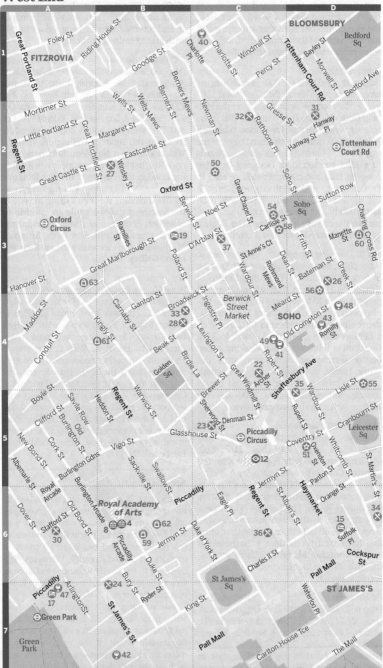

BLOOMSBURY

Bedford Sq

Bedford Ave

FITZROVIA

Foley St

Riding House St

Great Portland St

Goodge St

Charlotte Pl

Charlotte St

Windmill St

Percy St

Bayley St

Morwell St

Tottenham Court Rd

Mortimer St

Wells St

Wells Mews

Berners Mews

Berners St

Newman St

Gresse St

32

31

Hanway Pl

Little Portland St

Margaret St

Great Titchfield St

Eastcastle St

Rathbone Pl

Hanway St

Tottenham Court Rd

Regent St

Great Castle St

Winsley St

27

50

Soho St

Sutton Row

Oxford St

Soho Sq

Oxford Circus

Ramillies St

Berwick St

Noel St

Great Chapel St

54

Carlisle St

58

Manette St

Charing Cross Rd

60

19

D'Arblay St

37

St Anne's Ct

Frith St

Bateman St

Great Marlborough St

Poland St

Wardour St

Richmond Mews

Dean St

Greek St

26

56

Hanover St

63

Ganton St

Broadwick St

Theatre Pl

Berwick Street Market

Meard St

SOHO

Old Compton St

48

43

Romilly St

Maddox St

Carnaby St

33

28

Lexington St

49

41

Conduit St

Kingly St

61

Beak St

Birdie La

Brewer St

Great Windmill St

22

Archer

Rupert St

35

Shaftesbury Ave

Lisle St

55

Golden Sq

Warwick St

Sherwood St

Denman St

Rupert St

Wardour St

Cranbourn St

Leicester Sq

Boyle St

Clifford St

Savile Row

Old Burlington St

Heddon St

23

Glasshouse St

Piccadilly Circus

Coventry St

Ovenden St

Whitcomb St

51

St Martin's St

New Bond St

Cork St

Burlington Gdns

Vigo St

Sackville St

Swallow St

12

Jermyn St

St Alban's St

Panton St

Haymarket

Orange St

34

Albemarle St

Royal Arcade

Old Bond St

Royal Academy of Arts

8

4

62

Piccadilly

Eagle Pl

Regent St

36

15

Suffolk Pl

Dover St

Stafford St

30

Burlington Arcade

Piccadilly Arcade

59

Jermyn St

Duke of York St

Charles II St

Pall Mall

Cockspur St

Piccadilly

47

17

Arlington St

24

Bury St

Duke St

Ryder St

King St

St James's Sq

ST JAMES'S

Green Park

Green Park

St James's St

Pall Mall

Carlton House Tce

Waterloo Pl

The Mall

42

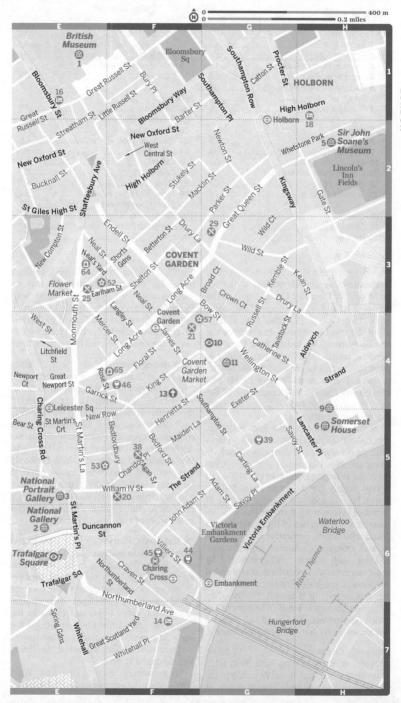

0 400 m
0 0.2 miles

British Museum 1

Bloomsbury Sq

Southampton Row

Procter St

HOLBORN

16

Bloomsbury St

Great Russell St

Little Russell St

Bury Pl

Bloomsbury Way

Southampton Pl

Barter St

High Holborn

Holborn 18

Great Russell St

Streatham St

New Oxford St

West Central St

Newton St

Whetstone Park

Sir John Soane's Museum 5

New Oxford St

Bucknall St

Shaftesbury Ave

High Holborn

Stukely St

Macklin St

Parker St

Great Queen St

Kingsway

Gate St

Lincoln's Inn Fields

St Giles High St

New Compton St

Endell St

Neal St

Shorts Gdns

Betterton St

Drury La

29

Wild St

Wild Ct

Kemble St

Kean St

COVENT GARDEN

Neal's Yard 64

52

Flower Market

25

Earlham St

Shelton St

Neal St

Long Acre

Broad Ct

Crown Ct

Crown Ct

Russell St

Drury La

Tavistock St

Aldwych

West St

Langley St

Mercer St

Covent Garden 57

Bow St

21

10

Catherine St

Strand

Litchfield St

Long Acre

Floral St

James St

Covent Garden Market

11

Wellington St

Exeter St

Newport Ct

Rose St 65

46

Garrick St

King St

13

Henrietta St

Southampton St

Great Newport St

Charing Cross Rd

Leicester Sq

St Martin's Crt

New Row

Bedfordbury

Maiden La

39

9

6 **Somerset House**

Lancaster Pl

Savoy St

Bear St

St Martin's La

Chandos Pl

Agar St

38

53

Carting La

The Strand

Adam St

Savoy Pl

Victoria Embankment

National Portrait Gallery 3

William IV St

20

John Adam St

National Gallery 2

St Martin's Pl

Duncannon St

Victoria Embankment Gardens

Waterloo Bridge

Trafalgar Square 7

Villiers St

45

44

Trafalgar Sq

Northumberland St

Craven St

Charing Cross

Embankment

River Thames

Spring Gdns

Whitehall

Northumberland Ave

Great Scotland Yard

14

Hungerford Bridge

Whitehall Pl

West End

◎ Top Sights
1 British Museum	E1
2 National Gallery	E6
3 National Portrait Gallery	E5
4 Royal Academy of Arts	B6
5 Sir John Soane's Museum	H2
6 Somerset House	H5
7 Trafalgar Square	E6

◎ Sights
8 Burlington Arcade	B6
9 Courtauld Gallery	H4
10 Covent Garden Piazza	G4
11 London Transport Museum	G4
12 Piccadilly Circus	C5
13 St Paul's Church	F4

⊜ Sleeping
14 Corinthia	F7
15 Haymarket Hotel	D6
16 Morgan Hotel	E1
17 Ritz	A7
18 Rosewood	H1
19 YHA London Oxford Street	B3

⊗ Eating
20 Barrafina	F5
21 Battersea Pie Station	F4
22 Bocca di Lupo	C4
23 Brasserie Zédel	C5
24 Cafe Murano	B7
25 Canela	E3
26 Ceviche	D3
27 Ethos	B2
28 Fernandez & Wells	B4
29 Great Queen Street	G3
30 Gymkhana	A6
31 Hakkasan Hanway Place	D2
32 Lima	C2

Mason department store. It meets Regent St, Shaftesbury Ave and Haymarket at the neon-lit swirl of Piccadilly Circus, home to the ever-popular and ever-misnamed Eros statue.

Mayfair, west of Piccadilly Circus, hogs all of the most expensive streets from the Monopoly board, including Park Lane and Bond St, which should give you an idea of what to expect: lots of pricey shops, Michelin-starred restaurants, society hotels and gentlemen's clubs. The elegant bow of Regent St and frantic Oxford St are the city's main shopping strips.

At the heart of the West End lies Soho, a boho grid of narrow streets and squares hiding gay bars, strip clubs, cafes and advertising agencies. Carnaby St was the epicentre of the swinging London of the 1960s, but is now largely given over to chain fashion stores. Lisle St and, in particular, Gerrard St (north of Leicester Sq) form the heart of Chinatown, a convergence of reasonably priced Asian restaurants, decorative Chinese arches and aromatic Cantonese supermarkets. Heaving with tourists and dominated by huge cinemas (with occasional star-studded premieres), neighbouring Leicester Sq (lester) has undergone a facelift. Described by Benjamin Disraeli in the 19th century as Europe's finest street, the Strand still boasts a few classy hotels, but its lustre has dimmed.

Piccadilly Circus SQUARE

(Map p66; ⊜ Piccadilly Circus) John Nash originally designed Regent St and Piccadilly in the 1820s to be the two most elegant streets in town but, curbed by city planners, couldn't realise his dream to the full. He may be disappointed, but suitably astonished, with Piccadilly Circus today: a traffic maelstrom, deluged with visitors and flanked by flashing advertisement panels. 'It's like Piccadilly Circus', as the saying goes, but it's certainly fun.

⭐**Trafalgar Square** SQUARE

(Map p66; ⊜ Charing Cross) In many ways Trafalgar Square is the centre of London, where rallies and marches take place, tens of thousands of revellers usher in the New Year and locals congregate for anything from communal open-air cinema and Christmas celebrations to various political protests. It is dominated by the 52m-high **Nelson's Column** and ringed by many splendid buildings, including the National Gallery and St Martin-in-the-Fields. The Nazis once planned to shift Nelson's Column to Berlin in the wake of a successful invasion.

⭐**National Gallery** GALLERY

(Map p66; www.nationalgallery.org.uk; Trafalgar Sq, WC2; ⊙10am-6pm Sat-Thu, to 9pm Fri; ⊜ Charing Cross) **FREE** With some 2300 European paintings on display, this is one of the world's great art collections, with seminal works from every important epoch in the history of art – from the mid-13th to the early 20th century, including masterpieces by Leonardo da Vinci, Michelangelo, Titian, Van Gogh and Renoir.

Many visitors flock to the East Wing (1700–1900), where works by 18th-century

33	Mildreds	B4
34	National Dining Rooms	D6
35	Palomar	D5
36	Shoryu	C6
37	The Breakfast Club	C3
38	Wahaca	F5

⊜ Drinking & Nightlife

39	American Bar	G5
40	Draft House	C1
41	Duke of Wellington	C4
42	Dukes Bar	B7
43	French House	D4
44	Gordon's Wine Bar	F6
45	Heaven	F6
46	Lamb & Flag	F4
47	Rivoli Bar	A7
48	She Soho	D4
49	Village	C4

☺ Entertainment

50	100 Club	C2
51	Comedy Store	D5
52	Donmar Warehouse	E3
53	London Coliseum	E5
54	Pizza Express Jazz Club	C3
55	Prince Charles	D4
56	Ronnie Scott's	D3
57	Royal Opera House	F4
58	Soho Theatre	C3

☖ Shopping

59	Fortnum & Mason	B6
60	Foyles	D3
61	Hamleys	B4
62	Hatchards	B6
63	Liberty	A3
64	Monmouth Coffee Company	E3
65	Stanford's	F4

British artists such as Gainsborough, Constable and Turner, and seminal Impressionist and post-Impressionist masterpieces by Van Gogh, Renoir and Monet await.

★**National Portrait Gallery** GALLERY
(Map p66; www.npg.org.uk; St Martin's Pl, WC2; ⊙10am-6pm Sat-Wed, to 9pm Thu & Fri; ⊜; ⊜Charing Cross or Leicester Sq) FREE What makes the National Portrait Gallery so compelling is its familiarity; in many cases you'll have heard of the subject (royals, scientists, politicians, celebrities) or the artist (Andy Warhol, Annie Leibovitz, Lucian Freud). Highlights include the famous 'Chandos portrait' of William Shakespeare, the first artwork the gallery acquired (in 1856) and believed to be the only likeness made during the playwright's lifetime, and a touching sketch of novelist Jane Austen by her sister.

★**Royal Academy of Arts** GALLERY
(Map p66; www.royalacademy.org.uk; Burlington House, Piccadilly, W1; adult/child £10/6, prices vary for exhibitions; ⊙10am-6pm Sat-Thu, to 10pm Fri; ⊜Green Park) Britain's oldest society devoted to fine arts was founded in 1768, moving to Burlington House exactly a century later. The collection contains drawings, paintings, architectural designs, photographs and sculptures by past and present Academicians such as Joshua Reynolds, John Constable, Thomas Gainsborough, JMW Turner, David Hockney and Norman Foster.

Covent Garden Piazza SQUARE
(Map p66; ⊜Covent Garden) London's first planned square is now mostly the preserve of visitors, who flock here to shop among the quaint old arcades, browse through eclectic market stalls and shops, cast coins at street performers pretending to be statues and traipse through the fun London Transport Museum (p69). On the square's west side rises handsome **St Paul's Church** (Map p66; www.actorschurch.org; Bedford St, WC2; ⊙8.30am-5pm Mon-Fri, varies Sat, 9am-1pm Sun; ⊜Covent Garden), built in 1633.

London Transport Museum MUSEUM
(Map p66; www.ltmuseum.co.uk; Covent Garden Piazza, WC2; adult/child £17/free; ⊙10am-6pm Sat-Thu, 11am-6pm Fri; ⊜Covent Garden) This entertaining and informative museum looks at how London developed as a result of better transport and contains everything from horse-drawn omnibuses, early taxis, underground trains you can drive yourself, a forward look at Crossrail (a high-frequency rail service linking Reading with east London, southeast London and Essex, due to open in 2018), plus everything in between. Check out the museum shop for imaginative souvenirs, including historical tube posters and 'Mind the Gap' socks.

★**Sir John Soane's Museum** MUSEUM
(Map p66; www.soane.org; 13 Lincoln's Inn Fields, WC2; ⊙10am-5pm Tue-Sat, plus 6-9pm 1st Tue of month; ⊜Holborn) FREE This museum is one of the most atmospheric and fascinating

🏃 City Walk
A Taste of the City

START ST BARTHOLOMEW-THE-GREAT
END 30 ST MARY AXE (THE GHERKIN)
LENGTH 1.5 MILES; THREE HOURS

The City of London has as much history in its square mile as the rest of London put together; this walk picks out just a few of its highlights.

Start by exploring the wonderful 12th-century ❶ **St Bartholomew-the-Great** (p75), whose atmospheric interior has been used frequently as a film set. Head through the Tudor gatehouse and turn right towards the colourful Victorian arches of ❷ **Smithfield Market** (p75), London's last surviving meat market.

Take a right down Long Lane and another at Aldersgate St. Follow the roundabout to the right and nip up the stairs (or take the lift) to the ❸ **Museum of London** (p74). Explore the museum's excellent galleries or head to the right to the ruins of the ❹ **Roman city walls** and behind them the distinctive towers of the ❺ **Barbican** (p130).

Turn right at Wood St to find the remaining ❻ **tower of St Alban** (1698), all that's left of

a Wren-designed church destroyed in WWII bombing in 1940. Turn left into Love Lane and right into Aldermanbury – the impressive 15th-century ❼ **Guildhall** (p74) is on your left. Crossing its courtyard – note the black outline of the Roman amphitheatre – continue east onto Gresham St, taking a right into Prince's St and emerging onto the busy Bank intersection lined with neoclassical temples to commerce. Behind the Duke of Wellington statue is a metal pyramid detailing the many significant buildings here.

From the ❽ **Royal Exchange** (p75), follow Cornhill and take a right down Gracechurch St. Turn left into wonderful ❾ **Leadenhall Market** (p134), roughly where the Roman forum once stood. As you leave the market's far end, ❿ **Lloyd's of London** (p75) displays its innards for all to see. Once you turn left onto Lime St, ⓫ **30 St Mary Axe** (p75), or 'the Gherkin', looms before you. Built nearly 900 years after St Bartholomew-the-Great, it's tangible testimony to the city's ability to constantly reinvent itself.

in London. The building was the beautiful, bewitching home of architect Sir John Soane (1753–1837), which he left brimming with his vast architectural and archaeological collection, as well as intriguing personal effects and curiosities. The museum represents his exquisite and eccentric tastes, persuasions and proclivities.

★ **Somerset House** HISTORIC BUILDING
(Map p66; www.somersethouse.org.uk; The Strand, WC2; ⊘ galleries 10am-6pm, Safra Courtyard 7.30am-11pm; ⊜ Charing Cross, Embankment or Temple) Designed by William Chambers in 1775 for royal societies, Somerset House now contains two fabulous galleries. Near the Strand entrance, the **Courtauld Gallery** (Map p66; www.courtauld.ac.uk; Somerset House, The Strand, WC2; adult/child Tue-Sun £7/ free, temporary exhibitions an additional £1.50; ⊘10am-6pm; ⊜ Charing Cross, Embankment or Temple) displays a wealth of 14th- to 20th-century art, including masterpieces by Rubens, Botticelli, Cézanne, Degas, Renoir, Seurat, Manet, Monet, Leger and others. Downstairs, the Embankment Galleries are devoted to temporary (mostly photographic) exhibitions; prices and hours vary.

Burlington Arcade HISTORIC BUILDING
(Map p66; www.burlington-arcade.co.uk; 51 Piccadilly, W1; ⊘ 9am-7.30pm Mon-Sat, 11am-6pm Sun; ⊜ Green Park) Flanking Burlington House, home to the Royal Academy of Arts, is this delightful arcade, built in 1819. Today it is a shopping precinct for the wealthy, and is most famous for the Burlington Berties, uniformed guards who patrol the area keeping an eye out for such offences as running, chewing gum, whistling, opening umbrellas or anything else that could lower the tone (that the arcade once served as a brothel is kept quiet).

◉ **The City**

With beguiling churches, hidden gardens and atmospheric lanes stuffed between iconic corporate towers and office blocks, you could spend weeks exploring the City of London, which, for most of its history, *was* London. Its boundaries have changed little since the Romans first founded their gated community here two millennia ago.

It's only in the last 250 years that the City has gone from being the very essence of London and its main population centre to just its central business district. But what a business district it is – the 'square mile' remains at the very heart of world capitalism.

Currently fewer than 10,000 people actually live here, although some 300,000 descend on it each weekday, to generate almost three-quarters of Britain's GDP before squeezing back onto the tube. On Sundays the City (capital 'C') becomes a virtual ghost town; it's nice and quiet, but come with a full stomach – most shops, eateries and pubs are closed.

★ **Tower of London** CASTLE
(Map p72; ☑ 0844 482 7777; www.hrp.org.uk/toweroflondon; Tower Hill, EC3; adult/child £25/12, audio guide £4/3; ⊘ 9am-5.30pm Tue-Sat, 10am-5.30pm Sun & Mon Mar-Oct, 9am-4.30pm Tue-Sat, 10am-4.30pm Sun & Mon Nov-Feb; ⊜ Tower Hill) The unmissable Tower of London (actually a castle of 22 towers) offers a window into a gruesome and compelling history. This was where two kings and three queens met their deaths and countless others were imprisoned. Come here to see the colourful Yeoman Warders (or Beefeaters), the spectacular Crown Jewels, the soothsaying ravens and armour fit for a *very* large king.

In the 1070s, William the Conqueror started work on the White Tower to replace the castle he'd previously had built here. By 1285, two walls with towers and a moat were built around it and the defences have barely been altered since. A former royal residence, treasury, mint and armoury, it became most famous as a prison when Henry VIII moved to Whitehall Palace in 1529 and started meting out his preferred brand of punishment.

The most striking building is the central **White Tower**, with its solid Norman architecture and four turrets. Today, on the entrance floor it houses a collection from the **Royal Armouries**, including Henry VIII's commodious suit of armour. On the 1st floor is **St John's Chapel**, dating from 1080 and therefore the oldest church in London. To the north stands Waterloo Barracks, which now contains the spectacular **Crown Jewels**, including the platinum crown of the late Queen Mother, set with the 106-carat **Koh-i-Noor (Mountain of Light) diamond**, and the Imperial State Crown, worn by the Queen at the State Opening of Parliament. Slow-moving travelators shunt wide-eyed visitors past the collection. On the far side of the White Tower is the **Bloody Tower**, where the 12-year-old Edward V and his little brother Richard were held 'for their own safety' and later murdered, perhaps by their uncle, the future Richard III. Sir Walter Raleigh

The City

CLERKENWELL

Gray's Inn Gardens
Gray's Inn Rd
Portpool La
Leather Lane Market
Cross St
Farringdon
Hatton Garden
Leather La
Greville St
Cowcross St
Charterhouse St
Farringdon
Barbican
Long La
Beech St
Aldersgate St
St Bartholomew-the-Great
Little Britain
14
West Smithfield
Snow Hill
Hosier La
Giltspur St
2 Museum of London
Chancery La
High Holborn
HOLBORN
Holborn
Furnival St
Fetter La
New Fetter La
Holborn Viaduct
Newgate St
Angel St
Gresham St
Noble St
Wood St
Foster La
Gutter La
Lincoln's Inn Fields
Chancery La
Bream's Bldgs
Farringdon St
Old Bailey St
St Paul's
Lincoln's Inn Fields
Serle St
Carey St
Fetter La
Fleet St
Shoe La
St Bride St
Ludgate Hill
St Paul's Cathedral 4
St Paul's Churchyard 21
22
Fleet St
Bouverie St
New Bridge St
City Thameslink
Carter La
18
Strand
Essex St
Milford La
Temple Ave
Carmelite St
Tudor St
Puddle Dock
Queen Victoria St
Castle Baynard St
Surrey St
Arundel St
Temple
Victoria Embankment
Blackfriars
White Lion Hill
Blackfriars Bridge
Millennium Bridge
Bankside Pier
The Queen's Walk
Tate Modern
New Globe Walk
Waterloo Rd
Upper Ground
Stamford St
Rennie St
Hopton St
Holland St
Sumner St
SOUTHWARK
Southwark St
Zoar St
Southwark Bridge Rd

23
Greville St

did a 13-year stretch here too under James I, when he wrote his *History of the World*.

In front of the Chapel Royal of St Peter ad Vincula stood Henry VIII's scaffold, where nobles such as Anne Boleyn and Catherine Howard (Henry's second and fifth wives) were beheaded. Look out for the latest in the Tower's long line of famous ravens, which legend says could cause the White Tower to collapse should they leave (their wing feathers are clipped in case they get any ideas).

To get your bearings, take the entertaining (and free) guided tour with any of the Beefeaters. Hour-long tours leave every 30 minutes from the bridge near the main entrance; the last tour is an hour before closing.

The red-brick New Armouries Cafe in the southeastern corner of the inner courtyard offers hot meals and sandwiches. Book online for cheaper rates for the Tower.

★ Tower Bridge   BRIDGE
(Map p72; ⊖ Tower Hill) London was a thriving port in 1894 when elegant Tower Bridge was built. Designed to be raised to allow ships to pass, electricity has now taken over from the original steam and hydraulic engines. A lift leads up from the northern tower to the

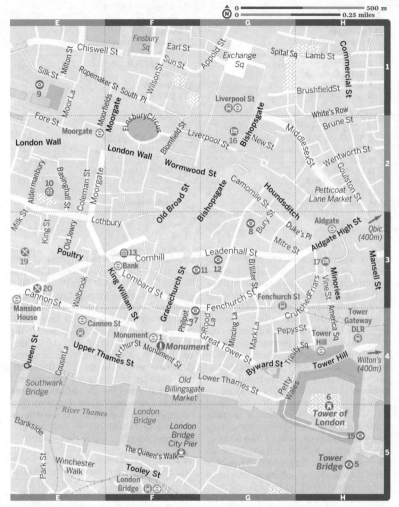

Tower Bridge Exhibition (Map p72; ☎020-7403 3761; www.towerbridge.org.uk; Tower Bridge, SE1; adult/child £9/3.90, incl Monument £11/5; ⏰10am-6pm Apr-Sep, 9.30am-5.30pm Oct-Mar, last admission 30min before closing; ⊖Tower Hill), where the story of its building is recounted within the upper walkway. You then walk down to the fascinating Victorian Engine Rooms, which powered the bridge lifts.

★ **St Paul's Cathedral**   CATHEDRAL
(Map p72; ☎020-7246 8350; www.stpauls.co.uk; St Paul's Churchyard, EC4; adult/child £18/8; ⏰8.30am-4.30pm Mon-Sat; ⊖St Paul's) Tower-

ing over Ludgate Hill, in a superb position that's been a place of Christian worship for over 1400 years, St Paul's Cathedral is one of London's most majestic and iconic buildings. For Londoners, the vast dome, which still manages to dominate the skyline, is a symbol of resilience and pride, standing tall for more than 300 years. Viewing Sir Christopher Wren's masterpiece from the inside and climbing to the top for sweeping views of the capital is an exhilarating experience.

The cathedral was designed by Wren after the Great Fire and built between 1675 and 1710; it opened the following year. The site is

The City

◉ Top Sights
1 Monument F4
2 Museum of London D2
3 St Bartholomew-the-Great C1
4 St Paul's Cathedral D3
5 Tower Bridge H5
6 Tower of London H5

◉ Sights
7 20 Fenchurch St F4
8 30 St Mary Axe G3
9 Barbican E1
10 Guildhall E2
11 Leadenhall Market F3
12 Lloyd's of London G3
13 Royal Exchange F3
14 Smithfield Market C1
15 Tower Bridge Exhibition H5

◉ Sleeping
16 Andaz Liverpool Street G2
17 Hotel Indigo Tower Hill H3
18 London St Paul's YHA C3

❌ Eating
19 Café Below E3
    Restaurant at St Paul's .... (see 4)
20 Sweeting's E3

◉ Drinking & Nightlife
21 Madison D3
    Sky Pod .... (see 7)
22 Ye Olde Cheshire Cheese B3
23 Ye Olde Mitre B2

◉ Entertainment
    Barbican .... (see 9)

ancient hallowed ground, with four other cathedrals preceding Wren's English baroque masterpiece here, the first dating from 604.

The dome, the world's second-largest cathedral dome and weighing in at 65,000 tons, is famed for sidestepping Luftwaffe incendiary bombs in the 'Second Great Fire of London' of December 1940, becoming an icon of London resilience during the Blitz. Outside the cathedral, to the north, a monument to the people of London is a simple and elegant memorial to the 32,000 Londoners killed.

Inside, some 30m above the main paved area, is the first of three domes (actually a dome inside a cone inside a dome) supported by eight huge columns. The walkway around its base, 257 steps up a staircase on the western side of the southern transept, is called the Whispering Gallery, because if you talk close to the wall, your words will carry to the opposite side, 32m away. A further 119 steps brings you to the Stone Gallery, 152 iron steps above which is the Golden Gallery at the very top, rewarded with unforgettable views of London. As part of its 300th anniversary celebrations in 2011, St Paul's underwent a £40-million renovation project that gave the church a deep clean. It's not looked this good since they cut the blue ribbon opening the cathedral in 1711.

The crypt has memorials to up to 300 heroes and military demigods, including Wellington and Nelson, whose body lies directly below the dome. But the most poignant memorial is to Wren himself. On a simple slab bearing his name, part of a Latin inscription translates as: 'If you seek his memorial, look around you'. Also here is the **Crypt Café** and the excellent Restaurant at St Paul's (p115).

Free multimedia tours lasting 1½ hours are available. Free 1½-hour guided tours leave the tour desk four times a day (typically at 10am, 11am, 1pm and 2pm); head to the desk just past the entrance to check times and book a place. Around twice a month, 60-minute tours (£8) also visit the astonishing Library, the Geometric Staircase and Great Model, and include impressive views down the nave from above the Great West Doors; check the website for dates and hours and book well ahead. Filming and photography is not permitted within the cathedral.

★ **Museum of London**   MUSEUM
(Map p72; www.museumoflondon.org.uk; 150 London Wall, EC2; ⊙10am-6pm; ⊖Barbican) FREE
One of the capital's best museums, this is a fascinating walk through the various incarnations of the city from Roman Londinium and Anglo-Saxon Ludenwic to 21st-century metropolis contained in two-dozen galleries. There are a lot of interactive displays with an emphasis on experience rather than learning.

Guildhall   HISTORIC BUILDING
(Map p72; ☑020-7332 1313; www.guildhall.cityoflondon.gov.uk; Gresham St, EC2; ⊖Bank) FREE
Bang in the centre of the Square Mile, Guildhall has been the City's seat of government for more than 800 years. The present building dates from the early 15th century, making it the only existing secular stone structure to have survived the Great Fire of 1666,

although it was severely damaged both then and during the Blitz of 1940.

★ **Monument** TOWER
(Map p72; www.themonument.info; Junction of Fish Street Hill & Monument St, EC3; adult/child £4/2, incl Tower Bridge Exhibition £10.50/4.70; ⊙ 9.30am-6pm Apr-Sep, to 5.30pm Oct-Mar; ⊜ Monument) Sir Christopher Wren's 1677 column, known simply as the Monument, is a memorial to the Great Fire of London of 1666, whose impact on London's history cannot be overstated. An immense Doric column made of Portland stone, the Monument is 4.5m wide and 60.6m tall – the exact distance it stands from the bakery in Pudding Lane where the fire is thought to have started.

Inns of Court HISTORIC BUILDINGS
All London barristers work from within one of the four atmospheric Inns of Court, positioned between the walls of the old City and Westminster. It would take a lifetime working here to grasp all the intricacies of their arcane protocols, originating in the 13th-century. It's best just to soak up the dreamy ambience of the alleys and open spaces and thank your lucky stars you're not one of the bewigged barristers scurrying about.

★ **St Bartholomew-the-Great** CHURCH
(Map p72; ✆ 020-7600 0440; www.greatstbarts.com; West Smithfield, EC1; adult/concession £5/4.50; ⊙ 8.30am-5pm Mon-Fri, 10.30am-4pm Sat, 8.30am-8pm Sun; ⊜ Farringdon or Barbican) Dating back to 1123 and adjoining one of London's oldest hospitals, St Bartholomew-the-Great is one of London's most ancient churches. The authentic Norman arches and profound sense of history lend this holy space an ancient calm, while approaching from nearby Smithfield Market through the restored 13th-century half-timbered archway is like walking back in time. The church was originally part of the monastery of Augustinian Canons, but became the parish church of Smithfield in 1539 when King Henry VIII dissolved the monasteries.

Smithfield Market MARKET
(Map p72; www.smithfieldmarket.com; West Smithfield, EC1; ⊙ 2-10am Mon-Fri; ⊜ Farringdon) Smithfield is central London's last surviving meat market. Its name derives from 'smooth field', where animals could graze, although its history is far from pastoral as this was once a place where public executions were held. Visit the market by 7am at the latest to see it in full swing. The Museum of London (p74) is

due to move into Smithfield Market by 2021 in a relocation costing £70 million.

Royal Exchange HISTORIC BUILDING
(Map p72; www.theroyalexchange.co.uk; Royal Exchange, EC3; ⊙ shops 10am-6pm, restaurants 8am-11pm Mon-Fri; ⊜ Bank) The Royal Exchange was founded by Thomas Gresham in 1564, and this imposing, colonnaded building at the juncture of Threadneedle St and Cornhill is the third building on the site – the first was officially opened by Elizabeth I in 1570. It ceased functioning as a financial institution in the 1980s and now houses posh shops, cafes and restaurants.

Lloyd's of London NOTABLE BUILDING
(Map p72; www.lloyds.com/lloyds/about-us/the-lloyds-building; 1 Lime St, EC3; ⊜ Aldgate or Monument) While the world's leading insurance brokers are inside underwriting everything from astronauts' lives to Mariah Carey's legs and Tom Jones' chest hair, people outside still stop to gawp at the stainless-steel external ducting, vents and staircases of this 1986 postmodern building designed by Richard Rogers, one of the architects of Paris' Pompidou Centre.

30 St Mary Axe NOTABLE BUILDING
(Gherkin; Map p72; www.30stmaryaxe.info; 30 St Mary Axe, EC3; ⊜ Aldgate) Nicknamed 'the Gherkin' for its unusual shape, 30 St Mary Axe is arguably the City's most distinctive skyscraper, dominating the skyline despite actually being slightly smaller than the neighbouring NatWest Tower. Built in 2003 by award-winning Norman Foster, the Gherkin's futuristic exterior has become an emblem of modern London – as recognisable as Big Ben and the London Eye.

◉ South Bank

Londoners once crossed the river to the area controlled by the licentious Bishops of Southwark for all manner of bawdy frolicking frowned upon in the City. It's a much more seemly and temperate area these days, but the frisson of theatre and entertainment survives. While South Bank only technically refers to the area of river bank between Westminster and Blackfriars Bridges (parts of which are actually on the east bank due to the way the river bends), we've used it as a convenient catch-all for those parts of Southwark and Lambeth that sit closest to the river.

Tower of London

TACKLING THE TOWER

Although it's usually less busy in the late afternoon, don't leave your assault on the Tower until too late in the day. You could easily spend hours here and not see it all. Start by getting your bearings on one of the Yeoman Warder (Beefeater) tours; they are included in the cost of admission, entertaining and the easiest way to access the **Chapel Royal of St Peter ad Vincula ❶**, which is where they finish up.

When you leave the chapel, the **Scaffold Site ❷** is directly in front. The building immediately to your left is Waterloo Barracks, where the **Crown Jewels ❸** are housed. These are the absolute highlight of a Tower visit, so keep an eye on the entrance and pick a time to visit when it looks relatively quiet. Once inside, take things at your own pace. Slow-moving travelators shunt you past the dozen or so crowns that are the treasury's centrepieces, but feel free to double-back for a second or even third pass.

Allow plenty of time for the **White Tower ❹**, the core of the whole complex, starting with the exhibition of royal armour. As you continue onto the 1st floor, keep an eye out for **St John's Chapel ❺**.

The famous **ravens ❻** can be seen in the courtyard south of the White Tower. Head next through the towers that formed the **Medieval Palace ❼**, then take the **East Wall Walk ❽** to get a feel for the castle's mighty battlements. Spend the rest of your time poking around the many other fascinating nooks and crannies of the Tower complex.

BEAT THE QUEUES

» **Buy** tickets online, avoid weekends and aim to be at the Tower first thing in the morning, when queues are shortest.

» **Become a member** An annual Historic Royal Palaces membership allows you to jump the queues and visit the Tower (and four other London palaces) as often as you like.

Chapel Royal of St Peter ad Vincula
This chapel serves as the resting place for the royals and other members of the aristocracy who were executed on the small green out front. Several other historical figures are buried here too, including Thomas More.

Scaffold Site
Seven people, including three queens (Anne Boleyn, Catherine Howard and Jane Grey), lost their heads here during Tudor times, saving the monarch the embarrassment of public executions on Tower Hill. The site features a rather odd 'pillow' sculpture by Brian Catling.

Dry Moat

Beauchamp Tower

Main Entrance

Middle Tower

Byward Tower

Bell Tower

White Tower
Much of the White Tower is taken up with an exhibition on 500 years of royal armour. Look for the virtually cuboid suit made to match Henry VIII's bloated 49-year-old body, complete with an oversized armoured codpiece to protect, ahem, the crown jewels.

St John's Chapel
Kept as plain and unadorned as it would have been in Norman times, the White Tower's 1st-floor chapel is the oldest surviving church from 1080.

Crown Jewels
When they're not being worn for ceremonies of state, Her Majesty's bling is kept here. Among the 23,578 gems, look out for the 530-carat 1st Star of Africa diamond at the top of the Sovereign's Sceptre with cross, the largest part of what was then the largest diamond ever found.

TOM HANLEY / ALAMY ©

Bowyer Tower

Martin Tower

Queen's House

Constable Tower

Bloody Tower

Broad Arrow Tower

New Armouries

Traitors' Gate & St Thomas's Tower

Wakefield & St Thomas's Towers

Salt Tower

River Thames

Medieval Palace
This part of the Tower complex was begun around 1220 and was home to England's medieval monarchs. Look for the recreations of the bedchamber of Edward I (1272–1307) in St Thomas's Tower and the throne room of his father, Henry III (1216–72) in the Wakefield Tower.

CRISTIAN SANTINON / SHUTTERSTOCK ©

Ravens
This stretch of green is where the Tower's half-dozen ravens are kept, fed on raw meat and blood-soaked biscuits. According to legend, if the ravens depart the fortress, the Tower will fall.

East Wall Walk
Follow the inner ramparts, starting from the 13th-century Salt Tower, passing through the Broad Arrow and Constable Towers, and ending at the Martin Tower, where the Crown Jewels were stored till the mid-19th century.

⭐ **Tate Modern**   MUSEUM
(Map p80; www.tate.org.uk; Queen's Walk, SE1; ⏲10am-6pm Sun-Thu, to 10pm Fri & Sat; 🛜🚻; 🚇Blackfriars, Southwark or London Bridge) **FREE**
One of London's most amazing attractions, this outstanding modern- and contemporary-art gallery is housed in the creatively revamped **Bankside Power Station** south of the Millennium Bridge. A spellbinding synthesis of modern art and capacious industrial brick design, Tate Modern has been extraordinarily successful in bringing challenging work to the masses, both through its free permanent collection and fee-paying, big-name temporary exhibitions. A stunning new extension opened in 2016, increasing the available exhibition space by 60%.

The 4.2 million bricks of the 200m-long Tate Modern is an imposing sight, designed by Swiss architects Herzog and de Meuron, who scooped the prestigious Pritzker Prize for their transformation of the empty power station. Leaving the building's central 99m-high chimney, adding a two-storey glass box onto the roof and employing the cavernous Turbine Hall as a dramatic entrance space were three huge achievements. Herzog and de Meuron also designed the new 11-storey Tate extension.

As a supreme collection of modern art, the contents of the museum are, however, the main draw. At their disposal, the curators have paintings by Georges Braque, Henri Matisse, Piet Mondrian, Andy Warhol, Mark Rothko and Jackson Pollock as well as pieces by Joseph Beuys, Damien Hirst, Claes Oldenburg and Auguste Rodin.

Tate Modern's permanent collection is arranged by both theme and chronology on levels 2, 3 and 4. More than 60,000 works are on constant rotation, so if there's a particular work you would like to see, check the website to see if (and where) it's hanging.

The location is also supreme, as the ever-popular balconies on level 3 with their magnificent views of St Paul's will attest. The **Millennium Bridge** (Map p80; 🚇St Paul's or Blackfriars) elegantly conveys views direct from the Tate Modern to St Paul's Cathedral in the City on the far bank of the river.

Free guided highlights tours depart at 11am, noon, 2pm and 3pm daily. Audio guides (in five languages) are available for £4 – they contain information about 50 artworks across the gallery and offer suggested tours for adults or children.

To visit the sister-museum Tate Britain, hop on the Tate Boat (Map p80; www.tate.org.uk/visit/tate-boat; 1-way adult/child £7.50/3.75) from Bankside Pier.

⭐ **Shakespeare's Globe**   HISTORIC BUILDING
(Map p80; www.shakespearesglobe.com; 21 New Globe Walk, SE1; adult/child £14/8; ⏲9am-5pm; 🚻; 🚇Blackfriars, Southwark or London Bridge)
Unlike other venues for Shakespearean plays, the new Globe was designed to resemble the original as closely as possible, which means having the arena open to the fickle London skies, leaving the 700 'groundlings' to stand in London's spectacular downpours. Visits to the Globe include tours of the theatre (half-hourly, generally in the morning from 9.30am, with afternoon tours on Monday too) as well as access to the exhibition space, which has fascinating exhibits about Shakespeare and theatre in the 17th century.

⭐ **London Eye**   VIEWPOINT
(Map p80; ☎0871 781 3000; www.londoneye.com; adult/child £21.20/16.10; ⏲10am-8pm, to 9.30pm in summer; 🚇Waterloo) Standing 135m high in a fairly flat city, the London Eye affords views 25 miles in every direction, weather permitting. Interactive tablets provide great information (in six languages) about landmarks as they appear in the skyline. Each rotation – or 'flight' – takes a gracefully slow 30 minutes. At peak times (July, August and school holidays) it may seem like you'll spend more time in the queue than in the capsule. For £27.95, showcase your fast-track swagger.

⭐ **Imperial War Museum**   MUSEUM
(Map p80; www.iwm.org.uk; Lambeth Rd, SE1; ⏲10am-6pm; 🚇Lambeth North) **FREE** Fronted by a pair of intimidating 15in naval guns, this riveting museum is housed in what was the Bethlehem Royal Hospital, a psychiatric hospital also known as Bedlam. Although the museum's focus is on military action involving British or Commonwealth troops largely during the 20th century, it rolls out the carpet to war in the wider sense. Highlights include the state-of-the-art **First World War Galleries** and **Witnesses to War** in the forecourt and atrium above.

Shard   NOTABLE BUILDING
(Map p80; www.theviewfromtheshard.com; 32 London Bridge St, SE1; adult/child £30.95/24.95; ⏲10am-10pm; 🚇London Bridge) Puncturing the skies above London, the dramatic splinter-like form of the Shard has rapidly become

TATE BRITAIN

Splendidly reopened a few years back with a stunning new art-deco-inspired staircase and a rehung collection, the older and more venerable of the two Tate siblings **Tate Britain** (www. tate.org.uk; Millbank, SW1; ⊘10am-6pm, to 10pm 1st Fri of month; ⊜Pimlico) celebrates paintings from 1500 to the present, with works from Blake, Hogarth, Gainsborough, Barbara Hepworth, Whistler, Constable and Turner, as well as vibrant modern and contemporary pieces from Lucian Freud, Francis Bacon and Henry Moore. Join a free 45-minute **thematic tour** (⊘11am) and 15-minute **Art in Focus talks** (Millbank, SW1; ⊘1.15pm Tue, Thu & Sat).

The stars of the show at Tate Britain are, undoubtedly, the light infused visions of JMW Turner in the Clore Gallery. After he died in 1851, his estate was settled by a decree declaring that whatever had been found in his studio – 300 oil paintings and about 30,000 sketches and drawings – would be bequeathed to the nation. The collection at the Tate Britain constitutes a grand and sweeping display of his work, including classics such as *The Scarlet Sunset* and *Norham Castle, Sunrise*.

There are also seminal works from Constable, Gainsborough and Reynolds, as well as the pre-Raphaelites, including William Holman Hunt's *The Awakening Conscience*, John William Waterhouse's *The Lady of Shalott*, *Ophelia* by John Everett Millais and Edward Burne-Jones's *The Golden Stairs*. Look out also for Francis Bacon's *Three Studies for Figures at the Base of a Crucifixion*. Tate Britain hosts the prestigious and often controversial Turner Prize for Contemporary Art from October to early December every year.

The Tate Britain also has a program of ticketed exhibitions which changes every few months; consult the website for details of the latest exhibition. The ticket office closes at 5.15pm.

an icon of London. The viewing platforms on floors 68, 69 and 72 are open to the public and the views are, as you'd expect from a 244m vantage point, sweeping, but they come at a hefty price – book online at least a day in advance to save £5.

Old Operating Theatre Museum & Herb Garret

MUSEUM

(Map p80; www.thegarret.org.uk; 9a St Thomas St, SE1; adult/child £6.50/3.50; ⊘10.30am-5pm; ⊜London Bridge) This unique museum, 32 steps up a spiral stairway in the tower of **St Thomas Church** (1703), is the unlikely home of Britain's oldest operating theatre. Rediscovered in 1956, the garret was used by the apothecary of St Thomas's Hospital to store medicinal herbs. The museum looks back at the horror of 19th-century medicine – all pre-ether, pre-chloroform and pre-antiseptic.

★Southwark Cathedral

CHURCH

(Map p80; ☑020-7367 6700; www.cathedral.southwark.anglican.org; Montague Cl, SE1; ⊘8am-6pm Mon-Fri, 9am-6pm Sat & Sun; ⊜London Bridge) The earliest surviving parts of this relatively small cathedral are the retrochoir at the eastern end, which contains four chapels and was part of the 13th-century Priory of St Mary Overie, some ancient arcading by the southwest door and an arch that dates to the original Norman church. But most of the ca-

thedral is Victorian. Inside are monuments galore, including a Shakespeare memorial. Catch evensong at 5.30pm on Tuesdays, Thursdays and Fridays, 4pm on Saturdays and 3pm on Sundays.

Design Museum

MUSEUM

(☑020-7940 8790; www.designmuseum.org; 224-238 Kensington High St, W8; ⊘10am-5.45pm; ⊜High St Kensington) Dedicated to popularising the importance of good design in everyday life, the Design Museum has a revolving program of special exhibitions. Past shows have ranged from Manolo Blahnik shoes to Formula One racing cars. The annual 'Design of the Year' exhibition showcases the best and latest design innovations – as the museum's tagline has it, 'Someday, the other museums will be showing this stuff'.

HMS Belfast

SHIP

(Map p80; www.iwm.org.uk/visits/hms-belfast; Queen's Walk, SE1; adult/child £14.50/7.25; ⊘10am-6pm Mar-Oct, to 5pm Nov-Feb; ⊜London Bridge) HMS *Belfast* is a magnet for naval-gazing kids of all ages. This large, light cruiser – launched in 1938 – served in WWII, helping to sink the German battleship *Scharnhorst*, shelling the Normandy coast on D Day and later participating in the Korean War. Its 6in guns could bombard a target 14 land miles distant. Displays offer a great insight into

South Bank

0   500 m
0   0.25 miles

River Thames

Victoria Embankment
Lower Thames St
Old Billingsgate Market
London Bridge
Waterloo Bridge
Golden Jubilee Bridge
Hungerford Bridge
Jubilee Gardens
Waterloo Rd
Belvedere Rd
Upper Ground
Tenison Way
Stamford St
York Rd
Addington St
Westminster Bridge Rd
Carlisle La
Lambeth Palace Rd
Archbishop's Park
Lambeth La
Lower Marsh
Baylis Rd
Coin St
Cornwall Rd
Upper Ground
Rennie St
Paris Garden
Hatfields St
Duchy St
Meymott St
Roupell St
Theed St
Wootton St
Waterloo East
The Cut
Nrtford St
Mitre Rd
Surrey Row
Lancaster St
Webber St
Great Suffolk St
Glasshill St
Copperfield St
Union St
Great Guildford St
Sumner St
Holland St
Hopton St
Blackfriars Rd
Southwark St
Southwark Bridge Rd
Redcross Way
Ayres St
Lant St
Borough High St
Newcomen St
Crosby Row
Snowsfields
St Thomas St
Tooley St
The Queen's Walk
Battle Br La
Crucifix La
Tanner St
Bermondsey St
Abbey St
Grange Rd
Tower Bridge Rd
Bermondsey Market
Rothsay St
Law St
Long La
Weston St
Kipling St
Guy St
Great Dover St
Trinity St
Swan St
Harper Rd
Tabard St
Newington Causeway
Borough Rd
Garden Row
London Rd
St George's Rd
Westminster Bridge Rd
Lambeth Rd
Kennington Rd
Cosser St
Pearman St
Coral St
Morley St
Waterloo Rd
Elephant & Castle
William Curtis Park

BERMONDSEY
BOROUGH
SOUTHWARK
SOUTH BANK
LAMBETH

Little Bird Gin (350m);
Maltby Street Market (150m)

Imperial War Museum
Shakespeare's Globe
Tate Modern
Tate Boat
New Globe Walk
Millennium Bridge
Blackfriars Bridge
London Eye
London Dungeon
Borough Market
Southwark Cathedral
London Bridge App
Railway
London Bridge
Park St
Stoney St
Bankside
Southwark Bridge
London Bridge
Bermondsey Market

Oval (1mi);
RVT (1mi)

1   Borough Market
2   Imperial War Museum
3   London Dungeon
4   London Eye
5   New Globe
6   Southwark Cathedral
7   Tate Modern
9
10
11 Shakespeare's Globe
12
13
14
15
16
17
18
19
21
22
23
24
25
26
27
20

South Bank

◎ Top Sights
1 Borough Market.................................E2
2 Imperial War Museum.......................C4
3 London Dungeon...............................A3
4 London Eye.......................................A2
5 Shakespeare's Globe.........................D1
6 Southwark Cathedral.........................E1
7 Tate Modern.....................................D1

◎ Sights
8 Hayward Gallery................................A2
9 HMS Belfast.....................................G1
10 London Sea Life Aquarium................A3
11 Millennium Bridge............................D1
12 National Theatre...............................B1
13 Old Operating Theatre Museum &
   Herb Garret...................................F2
14 Shard..F2
15 White Cube Bermondsey....................G3

◎ Activities, Courses & Tours
16 London Bicycle Tour..........................B1
17 London Duck Tours............................A3

◎ Sleeping
18 Citizen M...D2
   Shangri-La Hotel at the Shard......(see 14)
19 St Christopher's Inn..........................E2
20 St Christopher's Village.....................E2

◎ Eating
21 Arabica Bar & Kitchen.......................E2
22 M Manze...G4
   Skylon..(see 26)

◎ Drinking & Nightlife
23 Ministry of Sound..............................D4
   Oblix...(see 14)
   Skylon..(see 26)

◎ Entertainment
24 BFI Southbank...................................B1
   National Theatre..........................(see 12)
25 Old Vic...B3
26 Royal Festival Hall.............................A2
   Shakespeare's Globe......................(see 5)
27 Southbank Centre...............................A2

what life on board was like, in peace times and during military engagements.

★ **London Dungeon**   HISTORIC BUILDING
(Map p80; www.thedungeons.com/london; County Hall, Westminster Bridge Rd, SE1; adult/child £28.95/24.45; ⊙10am-5pm, to 6pm Sat & Sun; ⊖Waterloo or Westminster) Older kids tend to love the London Dungeon, as the terrifying queues during school holidays and weekends testify. It's all spooky music, ghostly boat rides, macabre hangman's drop-rides, fake blood and actors dressed up as torturers and gory criminals (including Jack the Ripper and Sweeney Todd) with interactive scares galore.

London Sea Life Aquarium   AQUARIUM
(Map p80; www.visitsealife.com; County Hall, Westminster Bridge Rd, SE1; adult/child £24.50/18.10; ⊙10am-7pm Mon-Fri, 9am-7pm Sat & Sun; ⊖Waterloo or Westminster) Displays look somewhat dated, but there are a couple of stand-out sights, including the shark tunnel, ray lagoon, the Gentoo penguin enclosures (penguins jump and dive at mesmerising speed) and Frozen Planet, with its flickering northern lights. Feeds and talks are scheduled throughout the day so your chances of catching one during your visit are high.

White Cube Bermondsey   GALLERY
(Map p80; www.whitecube.com; 144-152 Bermondsey St, SE1; ⊙10am-6pm Tue-Sat, noon-6pm

Sun; ⊖London Bridge) **FREE** The newest and largest of the White Cube galleries – the brainchild of Jay Jopling, dealer to the stars of the Brit Art movement who made his reputation in the 1990s by exhibiting then-unknown artists such as Damien Hirst and Antony Gormley – this gallery impresses with its large exhibition spaces, which lend themselves to monumental pieces or expansive installations using several mediums.

Hayward Gallery   GALLERY
(Map p80; www.southbankcentre.co.uk; Belvedere Rd, SE1; ⊙noon-6pm Mon, 11am-7pm Tue-Wed, Sat & Sun, to 8pm Thu & Fri; 📷; ⊖Waterloo) Part of the Southbank Centre, the Hayward hosts a changing roster of contemporary art (video, installations, photography, collage, painting etc) in a 1960s Brutalist building. The gallery was closed for works at the time of research; check the website for details.

★ **Borough Market**   MARKET
(Map p80; www.boroughmarket.org.uk; 8 Southwark St, SE1; ⊙10am-5pm Wed & Thu, 10am-6pm Fri, 8am-5pm Sat; ⊖London Bridge) Located here in some form or another since the 13th century (and possibly since 1014), 'London's Larder' has enjoyed an astonishing renaissance in the past 15 years. Always overflowing with food lovers, inveterate gastronomes, wide-eyed visitors and Londoners in search of inspiration for their dinner

party, this fantastic market has become firmly established as a sight in its own right. The market specialises in high-end fresh products; there are also plenty of takeaway stalls and an unreasonable number of cake stalls!

⊙ Chelsea & Kensington

Known as the royal borough, Chelsea and Kensington lays claim to the highest income earners in the UK. Kensington High St has a lively mix of chains and boutiques, while even the charity shops along King's Rd resemble fashion outlets. Some of London's most beautiful and fascinating museums, clustered together in South Kensington, are must-sees come rain or shine.

★Victoria & Albert Museum   MUSEUM
(V&A; Map p86; www.vam.ac.uk; Cromwell Rd, SW7; ⊙10am-5.45pm Sat-Thu, to 10pm Fri; ⊜South Kensington) FREE The Museum of Manufactures, as the V&A was known when it opened in 1852, was part of Prince Albert's legacy to the nation in the aftermath of the successful Great Exhibition of 1851. It houses the world's largest collection of decorative arts, from Asian ceramics to Middle Eastern rugs, Chinese paintings, Western furniture, fashion from all ages and modern-day domestic appliances. The temporary exhibitions are another highlight, covering anything from David Bowie retrospectives to designer Alexander McQueen, special materials and trends.

There are more than 100 galleries in the museum, so pick carefully or join a free one-hour guided tour; there are several a day (they meet close to the information desk in the main hall) on a variety of themes including introductory tours, medieval and Renaissance tours and theatre and performance tours.

★Natural History Museum   MUSEUM
(Map p86; www.nhm.ac.uk; Cromwell Rd, SW7; ⊙10am-5.50pm; 🐾; ⊜South Kensington) FREE This colossal and magnificent-looking building is infused with the irrepressible Victorian spirit of collecting, cataloguing and interpreting the natural world. The Dinosaurs Gallery (Blue Zone) is a must for children, who gawp at the animatronic T-Rex, fossils and excellent displays. Adults for their part will love the intriguing Treasures exhibition in the Cadogan Gallery (Green Zone), which houses a host of unrelated objects each telling its own unique story, from a chunk of moon rock to a dodo skeleton.

Also in the Green Zone, the Mineral Gallery is a breathtaking display of architectural perspective leading to the Vault, where you'll find the Aurora Collection of almost 300 coloured diamonds. In the Orange Zone, the vast Darwin Centre focuses on taxonomy, showcasing 28 million insects and six million plants in a giant cocoon; glass windows allow you to watch scientists at work.

At the centre of the museum is Hintze Hall, which resembles a cathedral nave – quite fitting for a time when the natural sciences were challenging the biblical tenets of Christian orthodoxy. The hall is dominated by the over-arching cast of a Diplodocus skeleton (nicknamed Dippy), which is due to be replaced by the real skeleton of a diving blue whale (*Balaenoptera musculus*), hung from the ceiling, in 2017.

A slice of English countryside in SW7, the beautiful Wildlife Garden next to the West Lawn encompasses a range of British lowland habitats, including a meadow with farm gates and a bee tree where a colony of honey bees fills the air.

In 2018, the eastern grounds are also due to be redesigned to feature a geological and palaeontological walk, with a bronze sculpture of Dippy as well as ferns and cycads.

The entire museum and its gardens cover a huge 5.7 hectares and contains 80 million specimens from across the natural world. More than five million visitors come each year, so queues can sometimes get long, especially during the school holidays.

★Science Museum   MUSEUM
(Map p86; www.sciencemuseum.org.uk; Exhibition Rd, SW7; ⊙10am-6pm; 🐾; ⊜South Kensington) FREE With seven floors of interactive and educational exhibits, this scientifically spellbinding museum will mesmerise adults and children alike, covering everything from early technology to space travel. A perennial favourite is Exploring Space, a gallery featuring genuine rockets and satellites and a full-size replica of the 'Eagle', the lander that took Neil Armstrong and Buzz Aldrin to the moon in 1969. The Making the Modern World Gallery next door is a visual feast of locomotives, planes, cars and other revolutionary inventions.

The fantastic Information Age Gallery on level 2 showcases how information and communication technologies – from the telegraph to smartphones – have transformed our lives since the 19th century. Standout displays include wireless sent by a sinking

Titanic, the first BBC radio broadcast and a Soviet BESM 1965 super-computer. Also on level 2 is Media Space, a gallery dedicated to excellent photographic exhibitions from the National Photography Collection (adult/child £8/free).

The 3rd-floor Flight Gallery (free tours 1pm most days) is a favourite place for children, with its gliders, hot-air balloons and aircraft, including the Gipsy Moth, which Amy Johnson flew to Australia in 1930. This floor also features a Red Arrows 3D flight simulation theatre (adult/children £6/5) and Fly 360-degree flight-simulator capsules (£12 per capsule). Launchpad, on the same floor, is stuffed with (free) hands-on gadgets exploring physic and the properties of liquids.

Glimpses of Medical History on level 4 isn't as high-tech as the rest of the museum but is highly evocative with models and life-size reconstructions showing how medicine – from childbirth to dentistry – was practised through the ages.

If you've kids under the age of five, pop down to the basement and the Garden, where there's a fun-filled play zone, including a water-play area, besieged by tots in orange waterproof smocks.

★ Hyde Park
PARK

(Map p86; www.royalparks.org.uk/parks/hyde-park; ⊙ 5am-midnight; ⊜ Marble Arch, Hyde Park Corner or Queensway) At 145 hectares, Hyde Park is central London's largest open space, expropriated from the Church in 1536 by Henry VIII and turned into a hunting ground and later a venue for duels, executions and horse racing. The 1851 Great Exhibition was held here, and during WWII the park became an enormous potato field. These days, there's boating on the Serpentine, summer concerts (Bruce Springsteen, Florence + The Machine, Patti Smith), film nights and other warm-weather events.

★ Kensington Palace
PALACE

(Map p110; www.hrp.org.uk/kensingtonpalace; Kensington Gardens, W8; adult/child £16.30/free; ⊙ 10am-6pm Mar-Oct, to 5pm Nov-Feb; ⊜ High St Kensington) Built in 1605, the palace became the favourite royal residence under William and Mary of Orange in 1689, and remained so until George III became king and relocated to Buckingham Palace. Today, it is still a royal residence, with the likes of the Duke and Duchess of Cambridge (Prince William and his wife Catherine) and Prince Harry living there. A large part of the palace is open to the public, however, including the King's and Queen's State Apartments.

Kensington Gardens
PARK

(Map p110; www.royalparks.org.uk/parks/kensington-gardens; ⊙ 6am-dusk; ⊜ Queensway or Lancaster Gate) Kensington Gardens is a gorgeous collection of manicured lawns, tree-shaded avenues and basins immediately west of Hyde Park. The picturesque 107-hectare expanse is technically part of Kensington Palace, located in the far west of the gardens. The large Round Pond is enjoyable to amble around and also worth a look are the lovely fountains in the Italian Gardens (Map p86; Kensington Gardens; ⊜ Lancaster Gate), believed to be a gift from Albert to Queen Victoria.

Albert Memorial
MONUMENT

(Map p86; ☑ tours 020-8969 0104; Kensington Gardens; tours adult/concession £8/7; ⊙ tours 2pm & 3pm 1st Sun of month Mar-Dec; ⊜ Knightsbridge or Gloucester Rd) This splendid Victorian confection on the southern edge of Kensington Gardens is as ostentatious as its subject. Purportedly humble, Queen Victoria's German husband Albert (1819–61) explicitly insisted he did not want a monument. Ignoring the good prince's wishes, the Lord Mayor instructed George Gilbert Scott to build the 53m-high, gaudy Gothic memorial – the 4.25m-tall gilded statue of the prince, surrounded by 187 figures representing the continents (Asia, Europe, Africa and America), the arts, industry and science, went up in 1876.

Saatchi Gallery
GALLERY

(Map p86; www.saatchigallery.com; Duke of York's HQ, King's Rd, SW3; ⊙ 10am-6pm; ⊜ Sloane Sq) **FREE** This enticing gallery hosts temporary exhibitions of experimental and thought-provoking work across a variety of media. The white and sanded bare-floorboard galleries are magnificently presented, but save some wonder for Gallery 15, where Richard Wilson's *20:50* is on permanent display. Mesmerising, impassive and ineffable, it's a riveting tour de force. A cool shop chips in on the 1st floor.

Royal Hospital Chelsea
HISTORIC BUILDINGS

(Map p86; www.chelsea-pensioners.co.uk; Royal Hospital Rd, SW3; ⊙ grounds 10am-4.30pm Mon-Sat, Great Hall shuts daily noon to 2pm, museum 10am-4pm Mon-Fri; ⊜ Sloane Sq) **FREE** Designed by Christopher Wren, this superb structure was built in 1692 to provide shelter for ex-servicemen. Since the reign of Charles

Victoria & Albert Museum

HALF-DAY HIGHLIGHTS TOUR

The art- and design-packed V&A is vast: we have devised an easy-to-follow tour of the museum highlights to help cover some signature pieces while also allowing you to appreciate some of the grandeur of the museum architecture.

Enter the V&A by the Grand Entrance off Cromwell Rd and immediately turn left to explore the Islamic Middle East Gallery and to discover the sumptuous silk-and-wool **Ardabil Carpet** ❶. Among the pieces from South Asia in the adjacent gallery is the terrifying automated **Tipu's Tiger** ❷. Continue to the outstanding **Fashion Gallery** ❸ with its displays of clothing styles through the ages. The magnificent gallery opposite houses the **Raphael Cartoons** ❹, large paintings by Raphael used to weave tapestries for the Vatican. Take the stairs to Level 2 and the Britain 1500–1760 Gallery; turn left in the

Raphael Cartoons
These seven drawings by Raphael, depicting the acts of St Peter and St Paul, were the full-scale preparatory works for seven tapestries that were woven for the Sistine Chapel in the Vatican.

Fashion Gallery
With clothing from the 18th century to the present day, this circular and chronologically arranged gallery showcases evening wear, undergarments and iconic fashion milestones, such as 1960s dresses designed by Mary Quant.

The Great Bed of Ware
Created during the reign of Queen Elizabeth I, its headboard and bedposts are etched with ancient graffiti; the 16th-century oak Great Bed of Ware is famously name-dropped in Shakespeare's *Twelfth Night*.

Britain 1500-1760 Gallery

Stairs to Level 2

Stairs from Level 1

Stairs to Level 3

Main Entrance

Gift Shop

John Madejski Garden

T.T Tsui China collection

Japan Gallery

Cast Courts

LEVEL 1

LEVEL 2

The Ardabil Carpet
One of the world's most beautiful carpets, the Ardabil was completed in 1540, one of a pair commissioned by Shah Tahmasp, ruler of Iran. The piece is most astonishing for the artistry of the detailing and the subtlety of design.

Tipu's Tiger
This disquieting 18th-century wood-and-metal mechanical automaton depicts a European being savaged by a tiger. When a handle is turned, an organ hidden within the feline mimics the cries of the dying man, whose arm also rises.

gallery to find the **Great Bed of Ware** ⑤, beyond which rests the exquisitely crafted artistry of **Henry VIII's Writing Box** ⑥. Head up the stairs into the Metalware Gallery on Level 3 for the **Hereford Screen** ⑦. Continue through the Ironwork and Sculpture Galleries and through the Leighton Corridor to the glittering **Jewellery Gallery** ⑧. Exit through the Stained Glass gallery, at the end of which you'll find stairs back down to level 1.

TOP TIPS

» **More Info** Museum attendants are always at hand along the route.

» **Photography** Allowed in most galleries, except the Jewellery Gallery, the Raphael Cartoons and in exhibitions.

» **Evening Exploration** Avoid daytime crowds: visit the V&A till 10pm on Friday.

MARTIN HESKO / SHUTTERSTOCK ©

Henry VIII's Writing Box
This exquisitely ornate walnut and oak 16th-century writing box has been added to over the centuries, but the original decorative motifs are superb, including Henry's coat of arms, flanked by Venus (holding Cupid) and Mars.

Jewellery Gallery
The beautifully illuminated Jewellery Gallery has a stunning collection of items from ancient Greece to the modern day, including a dazzling gold Celtic breastplate, art-nouveau jewellery and animals fashioned by Fabergé.

Stairs to Other Levels

20th Century Gallery

Stairs from Level 2

⑦

National Art Library

Ironwork Gallery

⑧

Leighton Corridor

Sculpture Gallery

Photographers Gallery

LEVEL 3

LEVEL 4

The Hereford Screen
Designed by Sir George Gilbert Scott, this awe-inspiring choir screen is a labour of love, originally fashioned for Hereford Cathedral. An almighty conception of wood, iron, copper, brass and hardstone, there were few parts of the V&A that could support its great mass.

Knightsbridge, South Kensington & Chelsea

0 500 m
0 0.25 miles

Leinster Tce
Porchester Tce
Bayswater Rd
Lancaster Gate
Paddington (300m)
Lancaster Gate
Bayswater Rd
Buck Hill Walk
North Ride

Budge's Walk
Kensington Gardens
The Long Water
Lancaster Walk
W Carriage Dr

Round Pond
The Flower Walk
Palace Gate
Kensington Rd
Kensington Rd
Prince Consort Rd
Exhibition Rd
Kensington Gore
Kensington Rd
Knightsbridge
KNIGHTSBRIDGE
Rutland Gate
Montpelier St
Ennismore Gdns

Hyde Park
Hyde Park
The Serpentine
Serpentine Rd
Rotten Row
South Carriage Dr

Park La
Park La
Park La
Park La
Marble Arch (150m)
Woods Mews
Culross St
Upper Grosvenor St
Aldford St
South St
Deanery St
MAYFAIR
Mount Row
Grosvenor Sq
Adam's Row
Mount St
Farm St
Hill St
Hay's Mews
Charles St
Hill St
Curzon Sq
Curzon St
Curzon St
Shepherd St
Hertford St
Brick St
Piccadilly
Green Park
Buckingham Palace Gardens
Grosvenor Pl
Chapel St
Chester St
Halkin St
Belgrave Sq
Motcomb St
Hyde Park Corner
Knightsbridge
Kinnerton St
Lowndes St
South Carriage Dr
Sloane St
Knightsbridge
Basil St
Brompton Rd
Raphael St

1
5
7
12
16
20
21
22
23
25
26

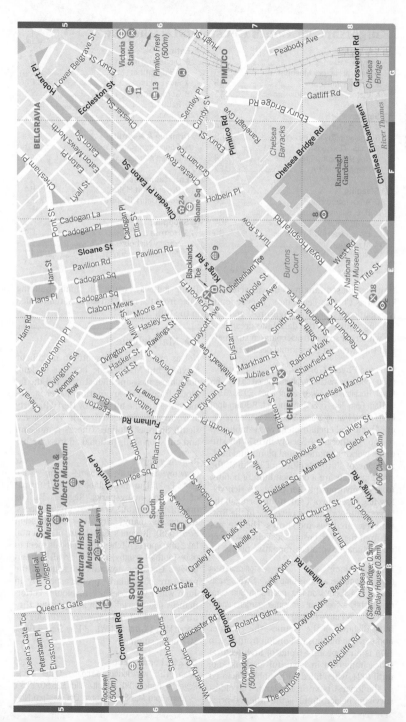

LONDON

BELGRAVIA

PIMLICO

SOUTH KENSINGTON

CHELSEA

Victoria Station

Pimlico Fresh (500m)

Peabody Ave

Grosvenor Rd

Chelsea Bridge

River Thames

Gatliff Rd

Ebury Bridge Rd

Chelsea Barracks

Ranelagh Gardens

Chelsea Embankment

Hobart Pl

Lower Belgrave St

Ebury St

Eccleston St

Chester Sq

Eaton Mews North

Eaton Sq

Eaton Pl

Chesham Pl

Lyall St

Pont St

Cadogan La

Cadogan Pl

Cadogan Pl

Ellis St

Cadogan Pl

Clivedon Pl

Eaton Sq

Sloane Sq

Holbein Pl

Sloane St

Pavilion Rd

Pavilion Rd

Cadogan Sq

Hans St

Hans Pl

Cadogan Sq

Clabon Mews

Hans Rd

Hans St

Beauchamp Pl

Ovington Sq

Yeoman's Row

Cheval Pl

Egerton Gdns

Walton St

Donne Pl

South Tce

Pelham St

Thurloe Pl

Thurloe Sq

Thurloe St

South Kensington

Onslow Sq

Onslow Sq

South Pde

Cranley Pl

Foulis Tce

Neville St

Queen's Gate

Cromwell Rd

Gloucester Rd

Stanhope Gdns

Wetherby Gdns

Queen's Gate

Queen's Gate Tce

Petersham Pl

Elvaston Pl

Imperial College Rd

Science Museum 3

Victoria & Albert Museum 4

Natural History Museum 2

East Lawn

10

15

14

Gloucester Rd

Old Brompton Rd

Cranley Gdns

Roland Gdns

Drayton Gdns

Gilston Rd

Redcliffe Rd

Fulham Rd

King's Rd

Mallord St

Beaufort St

Elm Pk Rd

Old Church St

Manresa Rd

Chelsea Sq

Dovehouse St

Oakley St

Glebe Pl

Cale St

Britten St

Jubilee Pl

Markham St

Radnor Walk

Shawfield St

Flood St

Chelsea Manor St

Elystan Pl

Lucan Pl

Ixworth Pl

Sloane Ave

Denyer St

Rawlings St

Hasker St

First St

Ovington St

Milner St

Hasley St

Moore St

Draycott Ave

Whitehead's Gve

Draycott Pl

Blacklands Tce

Cheltenham Tce

Walpole St

Royal Ave

Smith St

St Leonard's Tce

Redburn St

Christchurch St

Tedworth Sq

Flood St

Smith Tce

Burtons Court

Royal Hospital Rd

Turk's Row

Tite St

West Rd

National Army Museum

Chelsea Bridge Rd

Pimlico Rd

Ranelagh Gve

Ebury Sq

Cundy St

Graham Tce

Chester Row

Graham Tce

Semley Pl

Hugh St

Hugh St

11

13

24

6

27

19

18

9

8

King's Rd

King's Rd

606 Club (0.8m)

Chelsea FC (Stamford Bridge; 0.5m); Barclay House (0.8m)

Troubadour (500m)

The Boltons

Rockwell (500m)

Knightsbridge, South Kensington & Chelsea

◎ Top Sights
1 Hyde Park D2
2 Natural History Museum B5
3 Science Museum B5
4 Victoria & Albert Museum C5

◎ Sights
5 Albert Memorial B4
6 Chelsea Physic Garden E8
7 Italian Gardens B1
8 Royal Hospital Chelsea F8
9 Saatchi Gallery E7

◎ Sleeping
10 Ampersand Hotel B6
11 B+B Belgravia G6
12 Levin Hotel E4
13 Lime Tree Hotel G6
14 Meininger B5
15 Number Sixteen B6

◎ Eating
16 Dinner by Heston
   Blumenthal E4
17 Five Fields E7
18 Gordon Ramsay E8
19 Rabbit D7
20 Zuma D4

◎ Drinking & Nightlife
21 Connaught Bar G1
22 Queen's Arms A4

◎ Entertainment
23 Royal Albert Hall B4
24 Royal Court Theatre F6

◎ Shopping
25 Harrods D4
26 Harvey Nichols E4
27 John Sandoe Books E7

II, it has housed hundreds of war veterans, known as Chelsea Pensioners. They're fondly regarded as national treasures, and cut striking figures in the dark-blue greatcoats (in winter) or scarlet frock coats (in summer) that they wear on ceremonial occasions.

Chelsea Physic Garden GARDENS
(Map p86; www.chelseaphysicgarden.co.uk; 66 Royal Hospital Rd, SW3; adult/child £9.50/6.95; ⏰11am-6pm Tue-Fri & Sun Apr-Oct, 9.30am-4pm Mon-Fri Nov-Mar; ⊜Sloane Sq) This walled pocket of botanical enchantment was established by the Apothecaries' Society in 1673 for students working on medicinal plants and healing. One of Europe's oldest of its kind, the small grounds are a compendium of botany, from carnivorous pitcher plants to rich yellow flag irises, a cork oak from Portugal, the largest outdoor fruiting olive tree in the British Isles, rare trees and shrubs. The site, not far from the river, ensures a slightly warmer microclimate to protect nonnative plants.

Fulham Palace HISTORIC BUILDING
(www.fulhampalace.org; Bishop's Ave, SW6; ⏰palace 12.30-4.30pm Mon-Thu, noon-5pm Sun summer, slightly earlier hours in winter, gardens dawn-dusk daily; ⊜Putney Bridge) FREE Within stumbling distance of the Thames, this summer home of the bishops of London from 704 to 1975 is an appealing blend of architectural styles immersed in beautiful gardens and, until 1924, when filled with rubble, enclosed by the longest moat in England. The oldest surviving palace chunk is the little red-brick Tudor gateway, while the main building dates from the mid-17th century, remodelled in the 19th century.

◎ Marylebone

Not as exclusive as its southern neighbour Mayfair, hip Marylebone has one of London's most pleasant high streets and the famous, if rather disappointing, Baker St, immortalised in the hit song by Gerry Rafferty and strongly associated with Victoria-era sleuth Sherlock Holmes (there's a museum and gift shop at his fictional address, 221b).

Regent's Park PARK
(www.royalparks.org.uk; ⏰5am-9.30pm; ⊜Regent's Park) The most elaborate and formal of London's many parks, Regent's Park is one of the capital's loveliest green spaces. Among its many attractions are London Zoo (p88), Regent's Canal, an ornamental lake and sports pitches where locals meet to play football, rugby and volleyball. **Queen Mary's Gardens**, towards the south of the park, are particularly pretty, especially in June when the roses are in bloom. Performances take place here in an **open-air theatre** (📞0844 826 4242; www.openairtheatre.org; Queen Mary's Gardens, NW1; ⏰May-Sep; ⊜Baker St) during summer.

★ ZSL London Zoo ZOO
(Map p119; www.londonzoo.co.uk; Outer Circle, Regent's Park, NW1; adult/child £25.50/18.50; ⏰10am-6pm Mar-Sep, to 5pm Oct, to 4pm Nov-

Marylebone

Feb; 📮 274) Established in 1828, these 15-hectare zoological gardens are among the oldest in the world. The emphasis nowadays is firmly placed on conservation, education and breeding. Highlights include Penguin Beach, Gorilla Kingdom, Tiger Territory, the walk-through In with the Lemurs, In with the Spiders and Meet the Monkeys. Land of the Lions is a new enclosure to house its Asiatic lions. Feeding sessions and talks take place throughout the day – join in with a spot of afternoon tea (adults/children £19.75/10).

Regent's Canal   CANAL
(Map p119) To escape the crowded streets and enjoy a picturesque, waterside angle on North London, take to the canals that once played such a vital role in the transport of goods across the capital. The towpath of the Regent's Canal also makes an excellent shortcut across North London, either on foot or by bike. In full, the ribbon of water runs 9 miles from Little Venice (where it connects with the Grand Union Canal) to the Thames at Limehouse.

Marylebone

⊙ Top Sights
1 Madame Tussauds A1
2 Wallace Collection B3

⊜ Sleeping
3 Beaumont B5

⊗ Eating
4 Chiltern Firehouse B3
5 Foyer at Claridge's C5
6 La Fromagerie B2
7 Locanda Locatelli A4
8 Monocle Cafe B3

⊙ Drinking & Nightlife
American Bar .... (see 3)
9 Artesian D3
10 Purl B3

⊜ Shopping
11 Cadenhead's Whisky &
     Tasting Shop B3
12 Daunt Books B2
13 Selfridges B5

★ **Madame Tussauds**　　　　　MUSEUM
(Map p89; ☑ 0870 400 3000; www.madame-
tussauds.com/london; Marylebone Rd, NW1; adult/
child £35/29.50; ⊙ 8.30am-6pm Mon-Thu, 9am-
6pm Fri-Sun; ⊜ Baker St) It may be kitschy and
pricey (book online for much cheaper rates),
but Madame Tussauds makes for a fun-filled
day. There are photo ops with your dream
celebrity (Daniel Craig, Miley Cyrus, Audrey
Hepburn, the Beckhams), the Bollywood
gathering (studs Hrithik Roshan and Sal-
man Khan) and the Royal Appointment (the
Queen, Harry, William and Kate).

⊙ Bloomsbury & St Pancras

With the University of London and British
Museum within its genteel environs, it's little wonder that Bloomsbury has attracted a
lot of very clever, bookish people over the
years. Between the world wars, these pleasant streets were colonised by a group of
artists and intellectuals known collectively
as the Bloomsbury Group, which included
novelists Virginia Woolf and EM Forster and
the economist John Maynard Keynes. Russell Sq, its very heart, was laid out in 1800
and is one of London's largest and loveliest.

★ **British Museum**　　　　　MUSEUM
(Map p66; ☑ 020-7323 8299; www.britishmuseum.
org; Great Russell St, WC1; ⊙ 10am-5.30pm Sat-Thu,

to 8.30pm Fri; ⊜ Russell Sq or Tottenham Court Rd)
FREE The country's largest museum and one
of the oldest and finest in the world, this famous museum boasts vast Egyptian, Etrus-
can, Greek, Roman, European and Middle
Eastern galleries, among others. It is frequently London's most-visited attraction, drawing
more than six million visitors annually.

Don't miss the **Rosetta Stone**, the key to
deciphering Egyptian hieroglyphics, discovered in 1799; the controversial **Parthenon
Sculptures**, taken from the Parthenon in
Athens by Lord Elgin (the British ambassa-
dor to the Ottoman Empire); and the large
collection of **Egyptian mummies**. Other
must-sees include the Anglo-Saxon **Sutton
Hoo burial relics** and the **Winged Bulls
from Khorsabad**.

Begun in 1753 with a 'cabinet of curiosities' sold to the nation by royal physician
Sir Hans Sloane, the collection mushroomed
over the ensuing years partly through acquisitions, bequests and plundering the empire.
The grand Enlightenment Gallery was the
first section of the redesigned museum to be
built in the 1820s.

The **Great Court**, restored and augment-
ed by Norman Foster in 2000, has a spectacular glass-and-steel roof, making it one of the
most impressive architectural spaces in the
capital. In the centre is the **Reading Room**,
with its stunning blue-and-gold domed ceiling made of papier mâché, where Karl Marx
researched and wrote *Das Kapital*.

The British Museum's extension, the £135
million World Conservation and Exhibitions
Centre in its northwestern corner, opened
in 2014, in the same year as the Sainsbury
Exhibitions Gallery, which hosts high-profile
exhibitions.

The museum is huge, so make a few
focused visits if you have time, and consider taking one of the free tours. There are 15
free 30- to 40-minute **eye-opener tours** of
individual galleries per day. The museum
also has free daily gallery talks, a **highlights
tour** (adult/child £12/free, 11.30am and 2pm
Friday, Saturday and Sunday), free 45-min-
ute **lunchtime gallery talks** (1.15pm Tuesday to Friday) and free 20-minute **spotlight
tours** on Friday evenings. Audio guides (£5)
can be found at the audio-guide desk in the
Great Court.

★ **British Library**　　　　　LIBRARY
(Map p94; www.bl.uk; 96 Euston Rd, NW1; ⊙ galleries 9.30am-6pm Mon & Fri, 9.30am-5pm Sat,
9.30am-8pm Tue-Thu, 11am-5pm Sun; ☏; ⊜ King's

FREE LONDON

Natural History Museum (p82) Every British child visits this building at least once, and so should you.

Tate Modern (p78) Hosts art designed to perplex and enthral.

Victoria & Albert Museum (p82) It's not overstating it to say that this is the world's greatest art-and-design museum.

National Gallery (p68) One of the world's great art collections, with some 2300 European paintings on display.

Hyde Park (p83) Millions of people come to sunbathe, boat, swim and picnic around the Serpentine, or to hear soapbox oratory at Speaker's Corner.

Science Museum (p82) Seven floors of interactive and educational exhibits.

Wallace Collection (Map p89; www.wallacecollection.org; Hertford House, Manchester Sq, W1; ⏰10am-5pm; ⊖Bond St) An enthralling glimpse into 18th-century aristocratic life.

Grant Museum of Zoology (Map p94; www.ucl.ac.uk/museums/zoology; Rockefeller Building, University College London, 21 University St, WC1; ⏰1-5pm Mon-Sat; ⊖Euston Sq) Collects 68,000 specimens from around the animal kingdom.

Highgate Cemetery (p100) London's most famous graveyard is also a de facto nature reserve.

Tate Britain (p79) Displays paintings from 1500 to the present; the works of JMW Turner are a particular highlight.

Regent's Park (p88) One of the city's most pleasant green spaces.

Wellcome Collection (p91) Celebrates the intersection of art, science and medicine.

Hampstead Heath (p100) Woodlands and meadows sprawled across 320 hectares.

Cross St Pancras) FREE Consisting of low-slung red-brick terraces and fronted by a large plaza featuring an oversized statue of Sir Isaac Newton, Colin St John Wilson's British Library building is a love-it-or-hate-it affair (Prince Charles likened it to a secret-police academy). Completed in 1997, it's home to some of the greatest treasures of the written word, including the *Codex Sinaiticus* (the first complete text of the New Testament), Leonardo da Vinci's notebooks and a copy of the Magna Carta (1215).

★**Wellcome Collection**　　MUSEUM
(Map p94; www.wellcomecollection.org; 183 Euston Rd, NW1; ⏰10am-6pm Tue, Wed & Fri-Sun, to 10pm Thu; ⊖Euston Sq) FREE Focusing on the interface of art, science and medicine, this clever and resourceful museum is fascinating. There are interactive displays where you can scan your face and watch it stretched into the statistical average, wacky modern sculptures inspired by various medical conditions, and downright creepy things, such as an actual cross-section of a body and enlargements of parasites (fleas, body lice, scabies) to terrifying proportions.

Charles Dickens Museum　　MUSEUM
(Map p94; www.dickensmuseum.com; 48 Doughty St, WC1; adult/child £9/4; ⏰10am-5pm, last admission 4pm; 📷; ⊖Chancery Lane or Russell Sq) A £3.5-million renovation made this museum, located in a handsome four-storey house that was the great Victorian novelist's sole surviving residence in London, bigger and better than ever. A period kitchen in the basement and a nursery in the attic were added, and newly acquired 49 Doughty St increased the exhibition space substantially.

⊙ Hoxton, Shoreditch & Spitalfields

These revitalised and hip areas northeast of the City have enough sightseeing allure to keep daytime travellers occupied, but things really get going in the evening, when the late-night pubs, clubs and restaurants come into their own. Vibrant Hoxton and Shoreditch form the centre of gravity for nightlife, while Sunday is optimum for strolling leisurely through Spitalfields after a Saturday night out. Over the centuries, waves of immigrants have left their mark here, and it's

The British Museum

A HALF-DAY TOUR

The British Museum, with almost eight million items in its permanent collection, is so vast and comprehensive that it can be daunting for the first-time visitor. To avoid a frustrating trip – and getting lost on the way to the Egyptian mummies – set out on this half-day exploration, which takes in some of the museum's most important sights. If you want to see and learn more, join a tour or grab an audioguide (£5).

A good starting point is the **Rosetta Stone ❶**, the key that cracked the code to ancient Egypt's writing system. Nearby treasures from Assyria – an ancient civilisation centred in Mesopotamia between the Tigris and Euphrates Rivers – including the colossal **Khorsabad Winged Bulls ❷**, give way to the **Parthenon Sculptures ❸**, highpoints of classical Greek art that continue to influence us today. Be sure to see both the sculptures and the monumental frieze celebrating the birth of

Winged Bulls from Khorsabad
This awesome pair of alabaster winged bulls with human heads once guarded the entrance to the palace of Assyrian King Sargon II at Khorsabad in Mesopotamia, a cradle of civilisation in present-day Iraq.

Parthenon Sculptures
The Parthenon, a white marble temple dedicated to Athena, was part of a fortified citadel on the Acropolis in Athens. There are dozens of sculptures and friezes with models and interactive displays explaining how they all once fitted together.

GROUND FLOOR

Rosetta Stone
Written in hieroglyphic, demotic (cursive ancient Egyptian script used for everyday use) and Greek, the 762kg stone contains a decree exempting priests from tax on the first anniversary of young Ptolemy V's coronation.

Bust of Ramesses the Great
The most impressive sculpture in the Egyptian galleries, this 7.5-tonne bust portrays Ramesses II, scourge of the Israelites in the Book of Exodus, as great benefactor.

Athena. En route to the West Stairs is a huge bust of **Pharaoh Ramesses II** ④, just a hint of the large collection of **Egyptian mummies** ⑤ upstairs. (The earliest, affectionately called Ginger because of wispy reddish hair, was preserved simply by hot sand.) The Romans introduce visitors to the early Britain galleries via the rich **Mildenhall Treasure** ⑥. The Anglo-Saxon **Sutton Hoo Ship Burial** ⑦ and the medieval **Lewis Chessmen** ⑧ follow.

EATING OPTIONS

» **Court Cafes** At the northern end of the Great Court; takeaway counters with salads and sandwiches; communal tables

» **Gallery Cafe** Slightly out of the way near Room 12; quieter; offers hot dishes

» **Court Restaurant** Upstairs overlooking the former Reading Room; sit-down meals

Lewis Chessmen
The much-loved 78 chess pieces portray faceless pawns, worried-looking queens, bishops with their mitres turned sideways and rooks as 'warders', gnawing away at their shields.

FEARGUS COONEY / GETTY IMAGES ©

Egyptian Mummies
Among the rich collection of mummies and funerary objects is 'Ginger', who was buried at the site of Gebelein, in Upper Egypt, more than 5000 years ago, and Katebet, a one-time chantress (ritual performer) at the Amun temple in Karnak.

Greece & Rome

Stairs

Medieval Europe

Court Restaurant

Ancient Egypt ⑤

⑧

⑦ ⑥

Ancient Middle East

UPPER FLOOR

Sutton Hoo Ship Burial
This unique grave of an important (but unidentified) Anglo-Saxon royal has yielded drinking horns, gold buckles and a stunning helmet with face mask.

Mildenhall Treasure
Roman gods such as Neptune and Bacchus share space with early Christian symbols like the *chi-rho* (short for 'Christ') on the find's three dozen silver bowls, plates and spoons.

North Central London

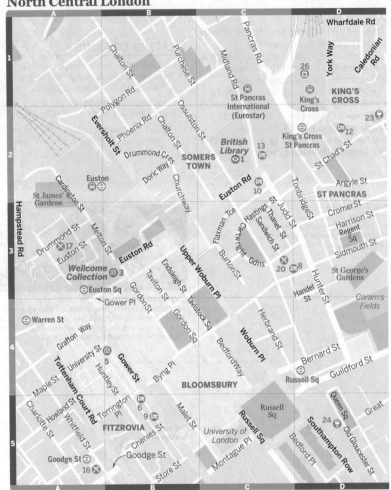

a great place to come for diverse cuisine and vibrant nightlife.

⭐ **Dennis Severs' House** MUSEUM
(Map p120; ☎020-7247 4013; www.dennissevers house.co.uk; 18 Folgate St, E1; day/night £10/15; ⌚noon-2pm & 5-9pm Mon, 5-9pm Wed & Fri, noon-4pm Sun; ⊖Shoreditch High St) This extraordinary Georgian House is set up as if its occupants – a family of Huguenot silk weavers – had just walked out the door. There are half-drunk cups of tea and partially consumed food, lit candles and, in perhaps unnecessary attention to detail, a full chamber pot by the

bed. More than a museum, it's an opportunity to meditate on the minutiae of everyday Georgian life through silent exploration.

⭐ **Geffrye Museum** MUSEUM
(Map p120; www.geffrye-museum.org.uk; 136 Kingsland Rd, E2; ⌚10am-5pm Tue-Sun; ⊖Hoxton) **FREE** If you like nosing around other people's homes, you'll love this museum, entirely devoted to middle-class domestic interiors. Built in 1714 as a home for poor pensioners, these beautiful ivy-clad brick almshouses have been converted into a series of living rooms, dating from 1630 to the

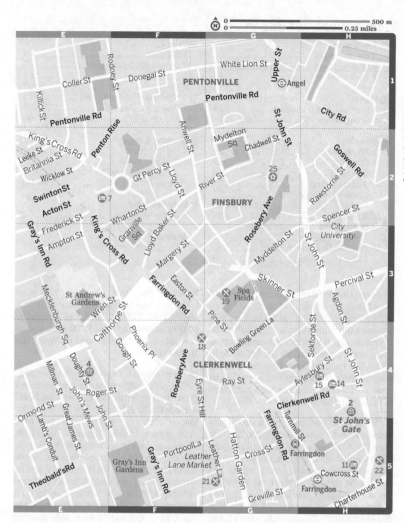

present day. The rear garden is also organised by era, mirroring the museum's exploration of domesticity through the centuries. There's also a very impressive walled herb garden, featuring 170 different plants.

★ St John's Gate   HISTORIC BUILDING

(Map p94; www.museumstjohn.org.uk; St John's Lane, EC1M; tour suggested donation £5; ☉10am-5pm Mon-Sat year-round, 10am-5pm Sun July-Aug, tours 11am & 2.30pm Tue, Fri & Sat; ⊖Farringdon) **FREE** This remarkable Tudor gate dates to 1504. During the 12th century, the Knights Hospitaller (a Christian and military order

with a focus on providing care to the sick) established a priory here. Inside is a small museum that covers the history of the order (including rare examples of the knights' armour), as well as its 19th-century revival in Britain as the secular Order of St John and the foundation of St John Ambulance.

◉ The East End & Docklands

A huge area, the East End and Docklands are not rich in sights, but a dramatic new focus has emerged in the Olympic Park, while new Overground lines make transport

North Central London

◎ Top Sights

1 British Library	C2
2 St John's Gate	H4
3 Wellcome Collection	B3

◎ Sights

4 Charles Dickens Museum	E4
5 Grant Museum of Zoology	B4

◎ Sleeping

6 Arosfa Hotel	B5
7 Clink78	E2
8 Generator	D3
9 Jesmond Hotel	B5
10 London St Pancras YHA	C2
11 Rookery	H5
12 Rough Luxe	D2
13 St Pancras Renaissance London Hotel	C2
14 Zetter Hotel & Townhouse	H4
15 Zetter Townhouse	H4

◎ Eating

16 Dabbous	A5
17 Diwana Bhel Poori House	A3
18 Little Bay	F4
19 Morito	G3
20 North Sea Fish Restaurant	C3
21 Prufrock Coffee	G5
22 St John	H5

◎ Drinking & Nightlife

23 Big Chill House	D2
24 Queen's Larder	D5
Zetter Townhouse Cocktail Lounge	(see 14)

◎ Entertainment

25 Sadler's Wells	G2

◎ Shopping

26 Harry Potter Shop at Platform 9¾	D1

a breeze. The Docklands' Canary Wharf and Isle of Dogs are an island of tower blocks, rivalling those of the City itself. London's port was once the world's greatest, the hub of the enormous global trade of the British Empire. Since being pummelled by the Luftwaffe in WWII, its fortunes have been topsy-turvy, but massive development of Canary Wharf replaced its crusty seadogs with battalions of dark-suited office workers.

★ Museum of London Docklands   MUSEUM
(www.museumoflondon.org.uk/docklands; West India Quay, E14; ◎10am-6pm; ⓢDLR West India Quay) FREE Housed in an 1802 warehouse, this educational museum combines artefacts and multimedia displays to chart the history of the city through its river and docks. The best strategy is to begin on the 3rd floor, where displays cover the Roman settlement of Londinium, and work your way down through the ages. Perhaps the most illuminating and certainly the most disturbing gallery is London, Sugar and Slavery, which examines the capital's role in the transatlantic slave trade.

★ Queen Elizabeth Olympic Park   PARK
(www.queenelizabetholympicpark.co.uk; E20; ⓢStratford) The glittering centrepiece of London's 2012 Olympic Games, this vast 227-hectare expanse includes the main Olympic venues as well as playgrounds, walking and cycling trails, gardens and a diverse mix of wetland, woodland, meadow and other wildlife habitats as an environmentally fertile

legacy for the future. The main focal point is the **stadium** (www.london-stadium.com; tours adult/child £19/11), with a Games capacity of 80,000, scaled back to 54,000 seats for its new role as the home ground for West Ham United FC.

★ ArcelorMittal Orbit   TOWER
(☏0333 800 8099; www.arcelormittalorbit.com; Queen Elizabeth Olympic Park, E20; adult/child £12/7, with slide £15/10; ◎10am-6pm Apr-Sep, to 5pm Oct-Mar; ⓢStratford) Love it or loathe it, Turner Prize–winner Anish Kapoor's 115m-high, twisted-steel sculpture towers strikingly over the southern end of Olympic Park. In essence it's an artwork, but at the 80m mark it also offers a stunning panorama from its mirrored viewing platform, which is accessed by a lift from the base of the sculpture (the tallest in the UK). A dramatic tunnel slide running down the tower is the world's highest and longest, coiling 178m down to ground level.

House Mill   HISTORIC BUILDING
(www.housemill.org.uk; Three Mill Lane, E3; adult/child £3/free; ◎11am-4pm Sun May-Oct, 1st Sun only Mar, Apr & Dec; ⓢBromley-by-Bow) One of two remaining mills from a trio that once stood on this small island in the River Lea, House Mill (1776) operated as a sluice tidal mill, grinding grain for a nearby distillery until 1941. Tours, which run according to demand and last about 45 minutes, take visitors to all four floors of the mill and offer a fascinating look at traditional East End industry.

★Viktor Wynd Museum of
Curiosities, Fine Art &
Natural History   MUSEUM
(www.thelasttuesdaysociety.org; 11 Mare St, E8;
admission £5; ⊙11am-10pm Wed-Sun; ⊜Bethnal
Green) Museum? Art project? Cocktail bar?
This is not a venue that's easily classifiable.
Inspired by Victorian-era cabinets of curiosities (*wunderkabinnet*), Wynd's wilfully
eccentric collection includes stuffed birds,
pickled genitals, two-headed lambs, shrunk-
en heads, a key to the Garden of Eden, dodo
bones, celebrity excrement, ancient Chinese
dildos and toys from McDonald's Happy
Meals. A self-confessed 'incoherent vision of
the world displayed through wonder', make
of it what you will. Or stop by for a cocktail
(£8) at the tiny bar.

⊙ Greenwich

Greenwich (*gren*-itch) straddles the hemispheres and the ages, retaining its own
sense of identity based on historic associations with the sea and science and an extraordinary cluster of buildings that have
earned 'Maritime Greenwich' a Unesco
World Heritage listing.

★Old Royal
Naval College   HISTORIC BUILDING
(www.ornc.org; 2 Cutty Sark Gardens, SE10;
⊙grounds 8am-6pm, to 11pm in summer; ⏏DLR
Cutty Sark) FREE Designed by Christopher
Wren, the Old Royal Naval College is a magnificent example of monumental classical
architecture. Parts are now used by the
University of Greenwich and Trinity College
of Music, but you can still visit the **chapel**
and the extraordinary **Painted Hall**, which
took artist Sir James Thornhill 19 years to
complete. Hour-long, yeomen-led tours (£6)
leave at noon daily, taking in areas not otherwise open to the public. Free 45-minute
tours take place at least four times daily.

★National Maritime Museum   MUSEUM
(www.rmg.co.uk/national-maritime-museum; Romney Rd, SE10; ⊙10am-5pm; ⏏DLR Cutty Sark)
FREE Narrating the long, briny and eventful
history of seafaring Britain, this excellent
museum's exhibits are arranged thematical-
ly, with highlights including *Miss Britain III*
(the first boat to top 100mph on open water)
from 1933, the 19m-long golden state barge
built in 1732 for Frederick, Prince of Wales,
the huge ship's propeller and the colourful
figureheads installed on the ground floor.
Families will love these, as well as the ship
simulator and the 'All Hands' children's gallery on the 2nd floor.

★Royal Observatory   HISTORIC BUILDING
(www.rmg.co.uk;   Greenwich Park, Blackheath
Ave, SE10; adult/child £9.50/5, with Cutty Sark
£18.50/8.50; ⊙10am-5pm Sep-Jun, to 6pm Jul &
Aug; ⏏DLR Cutty Sark, ⏏DLR Greenwich, ⏏Green-
wich) Rising south of Queen's House, idyllic
Greenwich Park (www.royalparks.org.uk; King
George St, SE10; ⊙6am-6pm winter, to 8pm spring
& autumn, to 9pm summer; ⏏DLR Cutty Sark,
⏏Greenwich or Maze Hill) climbs up the hill, affording stunning views of London from the
Royal Observatory, which Charles II had built
in 1675 to help solve the riddle of longitude.
To the north is lovely **Flamsteed House** and
the **Meridian Courtyard**, where you can
stand with your feet straddling the western
and eastern hemispheres; admission is by
ticket. The southern half contains the highly
informative and free **Weller Astronomy Galleries** and the **Peter Harrison Planetarium**
(⏃020-8312 6608; www.rmg.co.uk/whats-on/plan
etarium-shows; adult/child £7.50/5.50).

Queen's House   HISTORIC BUILDING
(www.rmg.co.uk/queens-house; Romney Rd, SE10;
⊙10am-5pm; ⏏DLR Cutty Sark) FREE The first
Palladian building by architect Inigo Jones after he returned from Italy is as enticing for its
form as for its art collection. The Great Hall
is a lovely cube shape with an elaborately

EMIRATES AIR LINE CABLE CAR

Capable of ferrying 2400 people per hour across the Thames in either direction, the cable
car run by **Emirates Air Line** (www.emiratesairline.co.uk; 27 Western Gateway, E16; one-way
adult/child £4.50/2.30, with Oyster Card or Travelcard £3.40/1.70; ⊙7am-9pm Mon-Fri, 8am-9pm
Sat, 9am-9pm Sun, closes 8pm Oct-Mar; ⏏DLR Royal Victoria, ⊜North Greenwich) makes quick
work of the journey from the Greenwich Peninsula to the Royal Docks. Although it's mostly patronised by tourists for the views over the river – and the views are ace – it's also
listed on the London Underground map as part of the transport network. Oyster Card and
Travelcard holders nab discounts for journeys, which are bike-friendly, too.

The River Thames

A FLOATING TOUR

London's history has always been determined by the Thames. The city was founded as a Roman port nearly 2000 years ago and over the centuries since then many of the capital's landmarks have lined the river's banks. A boat trip is a great way to experience the attractions.

There are piers dotted along both banks at regular intervals where you can hop on and hop off the regular services to visit places of interest. The best place to board is Westminster Pier, from where boats head downstream, taking you from the City of Westminster, the seat of government, to the original City of London, now the financial district and dominated by a growing band of skyscrapers. Across the river, the once shabby and neglected South Bank now bristles with as many top attractions as its northern counterpart, including the slender Shard.

In our illustration we've concentrated on the top highlights you'll enjoy from a waterborne

KIEVVICTOR / SHUTTERSTOCK ©

St Paul's Cathedral
Though there's been a church here since AD 604, the current building rose from the ashes of the 1666 Great Fire and is architect Christopher Wren's masterpiece. Famous for surviving the Blitz intact and for the wedding of Charles and Diana, it's looking as good as new after a major clean-up for its 300th anniversary in 2011.

Blackfriars

Somerset House
This grand neoclassical palace was once one of many aristocratic houses lining the Thames. The huge arches at river level gave direct access to the Thames until the Embankment was built in the 1860s.

Temple

Blackfriars Pier
Blackfriars Bridge

Charing Cross

Savoy Pier   Waterloo Bridge

Victoria Embankment Gardens

National Theatre

OXO Tower

Embankment

Queen Elizabeth Hall
Southbank Centre

London Eye
Built in 2000 and originally temporary, the Eye instantly became a much-loved landmark. The 30-minute spin takes you 135m above the city from where the views are unsurprisingly amazing.

Waterloo Millennium Pier

Westminster Pier

Houses of Parliament
Rebuilt in neo-Gothic style after the old Palace of Westminster burned down in 1834, the most famous part of the British parliament is the clocktower. Generally known as Big Ben, it's named after Benjamin Hall who oversaw its construction.

Westminster
Westminster Bridge

VERDOONIE / BUDGET TRAVEL ©

vessel. These are, from west to east, the **Houses of Parliament** ❶, the **London Eye** ❷, **Somerset House** ❸, **St Paul's Cathedral** ❹, **Tate Modern** ❺, **Shakespeare's Globe** ❻, the **Tower of London** ❼ and **Tower Bridge** ❽.

Apart from covering this central section of the river, boats can also be taken upstream as far as Kew Gardens and Hampton Court Palace, and downstream to Greenwich and the Thames Barrier.

BOAT HOPPING

Thames Clippers hop-on/hop-off services are aimed at commuters but are equally useful for visitors, operating every 15 minutes on a loop from piers at Embankment, Waterloo, Blackfriars, Bankside, London Bridge and the Tower. Other services also go from Westminster. Oyster cardholders get a discount off the boat ticket price.

30 St Mary Axe (Gherkin)

Leadenhall Building (Cheese Grater)

20 Fenchurch St (Walkie Talkie)

Cannon St

Monument

Millennium Bridge

Southwark Bridge

Bankside Pier

London Bridge

Southwark Cathedral

London Bridge Pier

London Bridge

HMS Belfast

Tower Pier

Shard

City Hall

Tower of London
It's not the tallest building in London anymore, but with the Crown Jewels and execution site, the 900-year-old Tower still overshadows the city's other attractions. From the river you can clearly see Traitors' Gate through which enemies of the crown entered the prison.

Tate Modern
Directly across the river from St Paul's, this museum of modern art is the world's most visited. Built as a power station in the late 1940s, its industrial architecture is as popular as its artworks, while a splendid new extension was completed in 2016.

Shakespeare's Globe
The reconstructed Globe stands on the river a few hundred metres from where the original stood (and burnt down in 1613 during a performance). The life's work of American actor Sam Wanamaker, the theatre runs a hugely popular season from April to October each year.

Tower Bridge
It might look as old as its namesake neighbour but one of the world's most iconic bridges was only completed in 1894. Not to be confused with London Bridge upstream, this one's famous raising bascules allowed tall ships to dock at the old wharves to the west and are still lifted up to 1000 times a year.

tiled floor. Climb the beautiful helix-shaped Tulip Stairs up to the 1st floor, where there's a rich collection of paintings and portraits with a sea or seafaring theme from the National Maritime Museum's collection.

★**Cutty Sark** MUSEUM

(☏020-8312 6608; www.rmg.co.uk/cuttysark; King William Walk, SE10; adult/child £13.50/7, with Royal Observatory £18.50/8.50; ◷10am-5pm Sep-Jun, to 6pm Jul & Aug; ☒DLR Cutty Sark) This Greenwich landmark, the last of the great clipper ships to sail between China and England in the 19th century, saw £25 million of extensive renovations largely precipitated by a disastrous fire in 2007. The exhibition in the ship's hold tells its story as a tea clipper at the end of the 19th century.

◉ Hampstead & Highgate

These quaint and well-heeled villages, perched on hills north of London, are home to a litany of A- and B-list celebrities.

★**Hampstead Heath** PARK

(☒Hampstead Heath) Sprawling Hampstead Heath, with its rolling woodlands and meadows, feels a million miles away – despite being approximately 4 miles – from the City of London. Covering 320 hectares, most of it woods, hills and meadows, it's home to about 180 bird species, 23 species of butterflies, grass snakes, bats and a rich array of flora.

★**Kenwood** HISTORIC BUILDING

(EH; www.english-heritage.org.uk; Hampstead Lane, NW3; ◷10am-5pm; ☒210) **FREE** This magnificent neoclassical mansion stands at the northern end of Hampstead Heath (p100) in a glorious sweep of landscaped gardens leading down to a picturesque lake. The 17th-century house was substantially remodelled in the 1760s and rescued from developers by Edward Cecil Guinness, 1st Earl of Iveagh, who donated it and the wonderful collection of art it contains to the nation in 1927. Among its treasures are paintings by such greats as Rembrandt (one of his many self-portraits), Constable, Gainsborough and Vermeer.

★**Highgate Cemetery** CEMETERY

(www.highgatecemetery.org; Swain's Lane, N6; East Cemetery adult/child £4/free; ◷10am-5pm Mon-Fri, 11am-5pm Sat & Sun; ☒Archway) A Gothic wonderland of shrouded urns, obelisks, broken columns, sleeping angels, Egyptian-style tombs and overgrown graves, Highgate is a Victorian Valhalla spread over 20 wonderfully wild and atmospheric hectares. On

---

TRIPS ON THE THAMES

London Waterbus Company (☏020-7482 2550; www.londonwaterbus.co.uk; 58 Camden Lock Pl, NW1; adult/child one-way £8.50/7, return £12.50/10.50; ◷hourly 10am-5pm Apr-Sep; ☒Warwick Ave or Camden Town) This enclosed barge runs enjoyable 50-minute trips on Regent's Canal between Little Venice and Camden Lock, passing by Regent's Park and stopping at London Zoo. There are fewer departures outside high season – check the website for schedules. One-way tickets (adult/child £25/18), including entry to London Zoo, are also available for passengers to disembark within the zoo grounds.

Thames River Boats (Map p60; ☏020-7930 2062; www.wpsa.co.uk; Westminster Pier, Victoria Embankment, SW1; Kew adult/child one-way £13/6.50, return £20/10, Hampton Court one-way £17/8.50, return £25/12.50; ◷10am-4pm Apr-Oct) These boats go upriver from Westminster Pier to the Royal Botanic Gardens at Kew (1½ hours, four per day) and on to Hampton Court Palace (another 1½ hours, 11am sailing only), a distance of 22 miles. It's possible to get off the boats at Richmond, but it depends on the tides; check before you sail.

London Duck Tours (Map p80; ☏020-7928 3132; www.londonducktours.co.uk; County Hall, SE1; adult/child from £26/18; ☒Waterloo) Amphibious craft based on D-Day landing vehicles depart from behind the **London Eye** (p78) near the County Hall and cruise the streets of central London before making a dramatic descent into the Thames at Vauxhall. There's a variety of tours, from the classic sightseeing tour to a James Bond tour and a D Day Duck tour, as well as private tours.

City Cruises (Map p60; ☏020-7740 0400; www.citycruises.com; single/return from £12.50/16.50, day pass £16.65) Ferry service departing every 30 minutes between Westminster, the London Eye, Bankside, Tower and Greenwich piers, with circular cruises (£11.70) going from Tower and Bankside.

the eastern side, you can pay your respects to the graves of Karl Marx and Mary Ann Evans (better known as novelist George Eliot). The real highlight, however, is the overgrown **West Cemetery**, which can only be visited on a **guided tour** (adult/child £12/6; ⊙1.45pm Mon-Fri, every 30min 11am-3pm Sat & Sun Nov-Mar, to 4pm Apr-Oct); bookings are essential for weekday tours.

⊙ Outside Central London

★**Kew Gardens**   GARDENS
(www.kew.org; Kew Rd; adult/child £15/3.50; ⊙10am-6.30pm Apr-Aug, closes earlier Sep-Mar; ⊵Kew Pier, ⊠Kew Bridge, ⊜Kew Gardens) In 1759 botanists began rummaging around the world for specimens to plant in the 3-hectare Royal Botanic Gardens at Kew. They never stopped collecting, and the gardens, which have bloomed to 120 hectares, provide the most comprehensive botanical collection on earth (including the world's largest collection of orchids). A Unesco World Heritage Site, the gardens can easily devour a day's exploration; for those pressed for time, the **Kew Explorer** (adult/child £5/2) hop-on/hop-off road train takes in the main sights.

Don't worry if you don't know your golden slipper orchid from your fengoky or your quiver tree from your alang-alang; a visit to Kew is a journey of discovery for everyone. Highlights include the enormous early **Victorian Palm House**, a hothouse of metal and curved sheets of glass; the impressive **Princess of Wales Conservatory**; the red-brick, 1631 **Kew Palace** (www.hrp.org. uk/kewpalace; with admission to Kew Gardens; ⊙10.30am-5.30pm Apr-Sep), formerly King George III's country retreat; the celebrated **Chinese Pagoda** designed by William Chambers in 1762 (closed for restoration until 2018); the **Temperate House**, the world's largest ornamental glasshouse (closed for restoration until 2018); and the very enjoyable **Rhizotron & Xstrata Treetop Walkway**, where you can survey the tree canopy from 18m up in the air. A lattice fashioned from thousands of pieces of aluminium illuminated with hundreds of LED lights, the 17m-high **Hive** mimics activity within a real beehive (it's on show till late 2017). Check the website for a full list of activities at Kew from free one-hour walking tours (daily), photography walks, theatre performances, outside cinema as well as a host of seasonal events and things to do.

WORTH A TRIP

ABBEY ROAD STUDIOS

Beatles aficionados can't possibly visit London without making a pilgrimage to the famous **Abbey Road Studios** (www.abbeyroad.com; 3 Abbey Rd, NW8; ⊜St John's Wood) in St John's Wood. The recording studios themselves are off-limits, so you'll have to content yourself with examining the decades of fans' graffiti on the fence outside. Stopstart local traffic is long accustomed to groups of tourists lining up on the zebra crossing to re-enact the cover of the fab four's 1969 masterpiece *Abbey Road*. In 2010 the crossing was rewarded with Grade II heritage status.

Kew Gardens are easily reached by tube, but you might prefer to take a cruise on a riverboat from the **Westminster Passenger Services Association** (Map p60; ⌨020-7930 2062; www.wpsa.co.uk; return to Hampton Court adult/child £25/12.50; ⊜Westminster), which runs several daily boats from April to October, departing from Westminster Pier.

★**Hampton Court Palace**   PALACE
(www.hrp.org.uk/hamptoncourtpalace; adult/child/family £19/9.50/47; ⊙10am-6pm Apr-Oct, to 4.30pm Nov-Mar; ⊵Hampton Court Palace, ⊠Hampton Court) Built by Cardinal Thomas Wolsey in 1514 but coaxed from him by Henry VIII just before Wolsey (as chancellor) fell from favour, Hampton Court Palace is England's largest and grandest Tudor structure. It was already one of Europe's most sophisticated palaces when, in the 17th century, Christopher Wren designed an extension. The result is a beautiful blend of Tudor and 'restrained baroque' architecture. You could easily spend a day exploring the palace and its 24 hectares of riverside gardens, including a 300-year-old **maze** (adult/child/family £4.40/2.80/13.20; ⊙10am-5.15pm Apr-Oct, to 3.45pm Nov-Mar).

Take a themed tour led by costumed historians or, if you're in a rush, visit the highlights: **Henry VIII's State Apartments**, including the **Great Hall** with its spectacular hammer-beamed roof; the **Tudor Kitchens**, staffed by 'servants'; the **Wolsey Closet**; the **Chapel Royal**; **William III's & Mary II's Apartments**, the **King's Staircase** and the **Chocolate Kitchens**; Mantegna's **The Triumphs of Caesar**; the restored and recently opened **Cumberland Art Gallery** off Clock

Court; and the magnificent gardens, including the **Kitchen Garden** – and don't miss getting lost in the maze. The **Magic Garden** is a new interactive garden attraction for children and families. Also keep an eye out for the **Real Tennis Court**, dating from the 1620s. Do not overlook exploring the palace's magnificent riverside **gardens**; on a sunny day it reveals London at its very finest and most beautiful. Check the schedule for spectacular shows and **events**, including Tudor jousting, falconry displays, ghost hunts (for children), garden adventures, family trails and more. In summer, fun 15- to 20-minute shire-horse-drawn **charabanc tours** (adult/child £6/3) depart from the East Front Garden between 11am and 5pm.

Ask one of the red-tunic-garbed warders for anecdotes and information. The excellent **audio guides** can be picked up just off Base Court and then dropped off in the bin as you exit the palace to the gardens.

Hampton Court is 13 miles southwest of central London and is easily reached by train from Waterloo. Alternatively, the riverboats that head from Westminster to Kew continue here (adult/child £17/8.50, three hours).

See p100 for more information.

Richmond Park   PARK
(⊙7am-dusk; @Richmond) At almost 1000 hectares (the largest urban parkland in Europe), this park offers everything from formal gardens and ancient oaks to unsurpassed views of central London 12 miles away. It's easy to flee the several roads slicing up the rambling wilderness, making the park perfect for a quiet walk or a picnic with the kids, even in summer when Richmond's riverside heaves. Coming from Richmond, it's easiest to enter via Richmond Gate or from Petersham Rd.

Strawberry Hill   HISTORIC BUILDING
(www.strawberryhillhouse.org.uk; 268 Waldegrave Rd, TW1; adult/child £12/free; ⊙house 1.40-5.30pm Mon-Wed, noon-5.30pm Sat & Sun Mar-Oct, garden 10am-6pm daily; @Strawberry Hill, @Richmond Station, then bus R68) With its snow-white walls and Gothic turrets, this fantastical and totally restored 18th-century creation in Twickenham is the work of art historian, author and politician Horace Walpole. Studded with elaborate stained glass, the building reaches its astonishing apogee in the gallery, with its magnificent papier-mâché ceiling. For the full magic, join a twilight tour (£20). Last admission to the house is 4pm.

Wimbledon Lawn Tennis Museum   MUSEUM
(☑020-8946 6131; www.wimbledon.com/museum; Gate 4, Church Rd, SW19; adult/child £13/8, museum & tour £24/15; ⊙10am-5.30pm, last admission 5pm; @Wimbledon, then bus 93, @Wimbledon) This ace museum details the history of tennis – from its French precursor *jeu de paume* (which employed the open hand) to the supersonic serves of today's champions. It's a state-of-the-art presentation, with plenty of video clips and a projection of John McEnroe in the dressing room at Wimbledon, but the highlight is the chance to see Centre Court from the **360-degree viewing box**. During the championships in June/July, only those with tickets to the tournament can access the museum.

 Tours

From erudite to eccentric, tours on offer to see the sights are legion in London. Bus tours, although not particularly cool, are good for those who are short on time. Those with special interests – Jewish London, bird watching, pop music – might consider hiring their own guide.

Original Tour   BUS
(www.theoriginaltour.com; adult/child £30/15; ⊙8.30am-8.30pm) A 24-hour hop-on, hop-off bus service with a river cruise thrown in, as well as three themed walks: Changing of the Guard, Rock 'n' Roll and Jack the Ripper. Buses every five to 20 minutes; you can buy tickets on the bus or online. There's also a 48-hour ticket available (adult/child £40/19), with an extended river cruise.

Big Bus Tours   BUS
(www.bigbustours.com; adult/child £26/12.50; ⊙every 20min 8.30am-6pm Apr-Sep, to 5pm Oct & Mar, to 4.30pm Nov-Feb) Informative commentaries in 12 languages. The ticket includes a free river cruise with City Cruises and three thematic walking tours (Royal London, film locations, mysteries). Good online booking discounts available.

London Mystery Walks   WALKING
(☑07957 388280; www.tourguides.org.uk; adult/child/family £10/9/20) Tour Jack the Ripper's old haunts at 7pm on Monday, Wednesday, Friday and Sunday. London chocolate tours too (£39) on Sunday at 12.30pm. You must book in advance.

London Beatles Walks   WALKING
(☑07958 706329; www.beatlesinlondon.com; adult/child £10/free) Public and private tours

following in the footsteps of the fab four. Most tours are just over two hours.

London Bicycle Tour CYCLING
(Map p80; ☑020-7928 6838; www.londonbicycle.com; 1 Gabriel's Wharf, 56 Upper Ground, SE1; tour incl bike from £23.95, bike hire per day £20; ☻Southwark, Waterloo or Blackfriars) Three-hour tours begin in the South Bank and take in London's highlights on both sides of the river; a night ride is also available. You can also hire traditional or speciality bikes, such as tandems and folding bikes, by the hour or day.

 Activities

London Aquatics Centre SWIMMING
(www.londonaquaticscentre.org; Queen Elizabeth Olympic Park, E20; adult/child £4.95/2.50; ☺6am-10.30pm; ☻Stratford) The sweeping lines and wave-like movement of Zaha Hadid's award-winning Aquatics Centre make it the architectural highlight of Olympic Park (p96). Bathed in natural light, the 50m competition pool beneath the huge undulating roof (which sits on just three supports) is an extraordinary place to swim. There's also a second 50m pool, a diving area, gym, creche and cafe.

Lee Valley VeloPark CYCLING
(☑0300 0030 610; www.visitleevalley.org.uk/velopark; Abercrombie Rd, E20; 1hr taster adult/child £40/30, pay & ride weekend/weekday £5/4, bike & helmet hire from £8; ☺9am-10pm; ☻Hackney Wick) An architectural highlight of Olympic Park (p96), the cutting-edge velodrome is open to the public – either to wander through and watch the pros tear around the steep-sloped circuit, or to have a go yourself. Both the velodrome and the attached BMX park offer taster sessions. Mountain bikers and road cyclists can attack the tracks on a pay-and-ride basis.

Up at the O2 ADVENTURE SPORTS
(www.theo2.co.uk/upattheo2; O2, Greenwich Peninsula, SE10; weekdays/weekends from £28/35; ☺hours vary; ☻North Greenwich) London isn't exactly your thrill-seeking destination, but this ascent of the O2 dome is not for the faint-hearted. Equipped with climbing suit and harness, you'll scale the famous white dome to reach a viewing platform perched 52m above the Thames with sweeping views of Canary Wharf, the river, Greenwich and beyond. Hours vary depending on the season (sunset climbs also available).

✈ Festivals & Events

Chinese New Year CULTURAL
(☺late Jan or early Feb) Chinese New Year sees Chinatown snap, crackle and pop with fireworks, a colourful street parade and eating aplenty.

University Boat Race ROWING
(www.theboatrace.org; ☺late Mar) A posh-boy grudge match held annually since 1829 between the rowing crews of Oxford and Cambridge universities.

Virgin Money London Marathon MARATHON
(www.virginmoneylondonmarathon.com; ☺late Apr) Up to half a million spectators watch the whippet-thin champions and bizarrely clad amateurs take to the streets.

Chelsea Flower Show HORTICULTURE
(www.rhs.org.uk/chelsea; Royal Hospital Chelsea; admission from £23; ☺May) Arguably the world's most renowned horticultural show attracts green fingers from near and far.

Trooping the Colour PARADE
(☺Jun) Celebrating the Queen's official birthday, this ceremonial procession of troops, marching along the Mall for their monarch's inspection, is a pageantry overload.

Field Day MUSIC
(www.fielddayfestivals.com; Victoria Park, Grove Rd, E3; ☺Jun; ☻Hackney Wick) The annual Field Day music festival has been running in **Victoria Park** (www.towerhamlets.gov.uk/victoria park; Grove Rd, E3; ☺7am-dusk; ☻Hackney Wick) since 2007, with performances in recent years from PJ Harvey, Air and James Blake.

Royal Academy Summer Exhibition ART
(www.royalacademy.org.uk; adult/child £9.50/5; ☺mid-Jun–mid-Aug) This is an annual showcase of works submitted by artists from all over Britain, mercifully distilled to 1200 or so pieces.

OUTDOOR CITY SWIMMING

Built in the 1930s but abandoned by the '80s, the **London Fields Lido** (☑020-7254 9038; www.better.org.uk/leisure/london-fields-lido; London Fields Westside, E8; adult/child £4.80/2.85; ☺6.30am-9pm; ☻Hackney Central) heated 50m Olympic-size outdoor pool gets packed with swimmers and sunbathers during summer.

Hampton Court Palace

A DAY AT THE PALACE

With so much to explore and seemingly infinite gardens, it can be tricky knowing where to begin. It helps to understand how the palace has grown over the centuries and how successive royal occupants embellished Hampton Court to suit their purposes and to reflect the style of the time.

As soon as he had his royal hands upon the palace from Cardinal Thomas Wolsey, Henry VIII began expanding the **Tudor architecture ①**, adding the **Great Hall ②**, the exquisite **Chapel Royal ③**, the opulent Great Watching Chamber and the gigantic **kitchens ④**. By 1540 it had become one of the grandest and most sophisticated palaces in Europe. James I kept things ticking over, while Charles I added a new tennis court and did some serious art-collecting, including pieces that can be seen in the recently opened **Cumberland Art Gallery ⑤**.

VISITBRITAIN / GETTY IMAGES ©

⑦ The Maze
Around 150m north of the main bulding
Created from hornbeam and yew and planted in around 1700, the maze covers a third of an acre within the famous palace gardens. A must-see conclusion to Hampton Court, the maze takes the average visitor about 20 minutes to reach the centre.

Tudor Architecture
Dating to 1515, the heart of the palace serves as one of the finest examples of Tudor architecture in the nation. Cardinal Thomas Wolsey was responsible for transforming what was originally a grand medieval manor house into a stunning Tudor palace.

KIEVVICTOR / SHUTTERSTOCK ©

Tudor Kitchens
These vast kitchens were the engine room of the palace. With a staff of 200 people, there were six spit-rack-equipped fireplaces, with roast meat always on the menu (to the tune of 8200 sheep and 1240 oxen per year).

Information Centre

Main Entrance

① Base Court

Anne Boleyn's Gateway

↑ North Direction

OPEN FOR INSPECTION

The palace was opened to the public by Queen Victoria in 1838.

After the Civil War, puritanical Oliver Cromwell warmed to his own regal proclivities, spending weekends in the comfort of the former Queen's bedroom and selling off Charles I's art collection. In the late 17th century, William and Mary employed Sir Christopher Wren for baroque extensions, chiefly the William III Apartments, reached by the **King's Staircase** ⑥. William III also commissioned the world-famous **maze** ⑦.

The Great Hall
This grand dining hall is the defining room of the palace, displaying what is considered England's finest hammer-beam roof, 16th-century Flemish tapestries telling the story of Abraham, and some exquisite stained-glass windows.

Chapel Royal
The blue-and-gold vaulted ceiling was originally intended for Christ Church, Oxford, but was installed here instead; the 18th-century oak reredos was carved by Grinling Gibbons. Books on display include a 1611 1st edition of the King James Bible, printed by Robert Barker.

Chapel Court Garden

Clock Court

② ⑤ ③

Fountain Court

⑥

The King's Staircase
One of five rooms at the palace painted by Antonio Verrio and a suitably bombastic prelude to the King's Apartments, the overblown King's Staircase adulates William III by elevating him above a cohort of Roman emperors.

Cumberland Art Gallery
The former Cumberland Suite, designed by William Kent, has been restored to accommodate a choice selection of some of the finest works from the Royal Collection.

er

s, I revel in all our
- Big Ben, Tower
hames, the London
former government
that made some of the greatest museums and art galleries in the world free to one and all. The choice of restaurants, bars and clubs is legion, and what's not to love about a city with more lush parkland than any other world capital? But the one thing that sets my adopted city apart from any other is its amazing tolerance. 'As long as you don't scare the horses, mate, you'll be all right here,' I was told when I arrived here more than 20 years ago. Guess what...it still hasn't happened.

Meltdown Festival MUSIC
(www.southbankcentre.co.uk; ⊘late Jun) The Southbank Centre hands over the curatorial reigns to a legend of contemporary music (Morrissey, Patti Smith or David Byrne) to pull together a full program of concerts, talks and films.

Wimbledon Lawn Tennis Championships SPORTS
(www.wimbledon.com; ⊘late Jun; ⊜Wimbledon) The world's most splendid tennis event takes place in late June.

Wireless MUSIC
(www.wirelessfestival.co.uk; Finsbury Park, N4; ⊘Jul) This popular rock and pop festival is held over three days in July every year.

Pride GAY & LESBIAN
(www.prideinlondon.org; ⊘late Jun or early Jul) The big event on the gay and lesbian calendar, a technicolour street parade heads through the West End, culminating in a concert in Trafalgar Sq.

Lovebox MUSIC
(www.loveboxfestival.com; Victoria Park, E9; ⊘mid-Jul) London's contribution to the summer music-festival circuit, held in Victoria Park.

Notting Hill Carnival CARNIVAL
(www.thenottinghillcarnival.com; ⊘Aug) Every year, for three days during the last weekend of August, Notting Hill echoes to the calypso, ska, reggae and soca sounds of the

Notting Hill Carnival. Launched in 1964 by the local Afro-Caribbean community, keen to celebrate its culture and traditions, it has grown to become Europe's largest street festival (up to one million people) and a highlight of London's calendar.

Sleeping

Hanging your hat (and anything else you care to remove) in London can be painfully expensive, and you'll almost always need to book your room well in advance. Decent, central hostels are easy enough to find and also offer reasonably priced double rooms. Bed and breakfasts are a dependable and inexpensive, if rather simple, option. Hotels range from cheap, no-frills chains through boutique choices to luxury five-star historic hotels.

West End

Like in Monopoly, land on a Mayfair hotel and you may have to sell your house, or at least remortgage. This is the heart of the action, and a couple of hostels cater for would be Soho hipsters of more modest means.

YHA London Oxford Street HOSTEL £
(Map p66; ☑020-7734 1618; www.yha.org.uk; 14 Noel St, W1; dm/tw from £18/46; @♠; ⊜Oxford Circus) The most central of London's eight YHA hostels is also one of the most intimate with just 104 beds, and excellent shared facilities, including the fuchsia kitchen and the bright, funky lounge. Dormitories have three and four beds and there are doubles and twins. The in-house shop sells coffee and beer. Wi-fi (common areas) is free. Free daily walking tours too.

Morgan Hotel B&B ££
(Map p66; ☑020-7636 3735; www.morganhotel. co.uk; 24 Bloomsbury St, WC1; s/d/tr incl breakfast £120/145/165, ste from £175; ❋@♠; ⊜Tottenham Court Rd) In a delightful row of 18th-century Georgian houses, the family-owned 17-room Morgan offers friendliness, fine service, breakfast fit for a king, and excellent value for central London. Room decor may be somewhat dated, but cleanliness is a strong point. Larger suites (single/double/triple £175/205/250, no air-con) are worth the extra outlay. There's no lift, and the top floor is a clamber for some.

Jesmond Hotel B&B ££
(Map p94; ☑020-7636 3199; www.jesmondhotel. org.uk; 63 Gower St, WC1; s/d/tr/q incl breakfast from £70/90/120/150; @♠; ⊜Goodge St) The

rooms – cheapest with shared bathroom – at this popular, 15-room family-run Georgian hotel in Bloomsbury are basic but clean and cheerful, there's a small, pretty garden and the price tag is very attractive indeed. There's also laundry service, free wi-fi and good breakfasts for kicking off your London day. Location is highly central.

★ Beaumont HOTEL £££
(Map p89; ☑020-7499 1001; www.thebeaumont. com; Brown Hart Gardens, W1; d/studio/ste incl breakfast from £395/625/900; ❄ ☎; ⊜ Bond St) A stylish, handsome and luxurious hotel, the 73-room Beaumont is all deco opulence. Fronted by an arresting chunk of deco-inspired stainless steel and fumed oak sculpture from Antony Gormley called *Room* (part of a £1130-per-night suite), the striking white building dates from 1926. Rooms and suites are swish and elegant, with a 1920s modernist aesthetic. Room prices include local drop-offs in the hotel's vintage Daimler.

★ Corinthia HOTEL £££
(Map p66; ☑020-7930 8181; www.corinthia. com; Whitehall Place, SW1; d/ste/penthouse £425/1380/3000; ❄ ☎ ✄; ⊜ Embankment) With hotels from Malta to St Petersburg, the Corinthia group's crown jewel is this grand Victorian property in Whitehall. It's as smart as can be, but never overbearing and stuffy. A stay here is a delight, from perfect rooms to flawless service, tempting afternoon tea and a location that ensconces you at the very heart, but just beyond the bustle of London.

★ Haymarket Hotel HOTEL £££
(Map p66; ☑020-7470 4000; www.haymarket hotel.com; 1 Suffolk Pl, off Haymarket, SW1; r/ste from £336/504; ❄ ☎ ✄; ⊜ Piccadilly Circus) With the trademark colours and lines of hoteliers and designers Tim and Kit Kemp, the Haymarket is beautiful, with hand-painted Gournay wallpaper, signature fuchsia and green designs in the 50 guest rooms, a sensational 18m pool with mood lighting, an exquisite library lounge with honesty bar, and original artwork throughout. Just love the dog silhouettes on the chairs and bar stools.

★ Rosewood HOTEL £££
(Map p66; ☑020-7781 8888; www.rosewood hotels.com/en/london; 252 High Holborn, WC1; d from £380-750, ste £1140-9000; ❄ @ ☎; ⊜ Holborn) An £85-million refurb transformed the grand Pearl Assurance building (dating from 1914) into the stunning Rosewood ho-

tel, where an artful marriage of period and modern styles can be found in its 262 rooms and 44 suites. British heritage is carefully woven throughout the bar, restaurant, deli, lobby and even the housekeepers' uniforms.

★ Ritz LUXURY HOTEL £££
(Map p66; ☑020-7493 8181; www.theritzlondon. com; 150 Piccadilly, W1; r/ste from £380/770; ❄ @ ☎; ⊜ Green Park) What can you say about a hotel that has lent its name to the English lexicon? This 136-room caravanserai has a spectacular position overlooking Green Park and is supposedly the Royal Family's home away from home (it does have a royal warrant from the Prince of Wales and is very close to the palace). All rooms have period interiors and antique furniture.

🛏 The City

It bristles with bankers during the week, but you can often net considerable bargains in the City come weekends.

London St Paul's YHA HOSTEL £
(Map p72; ☑020-7236 4965; www.yha.org.uk/ hostel/london-st-pauls; 36 Carter Lane, EC4; dm £17-30, d £65-79; @ ☎; ⊜ St Paul's) This 213-bed hostel is housed in the former boarding school for choir boys from St Paul's Cathedral, almost next door. Dorms have between three and 11 beds, and twins and doubles are available. There's a great lounge, licensed cafeteria (breakfast £5.25, dinner from £7 to £10) but no kitchen – and lots and lots of stairs (and no lift). Seven-night maximum stay.

Hotel Indigo Tower Hill BOUTIQUE HOTEL ££
(Map p72; ☑020-7265 1014; www.ihg.com; 142 Minories, EC3; r weekend/weekday from £100/260; ❄ ☎; ⊜ Aldgate) This branch of the US InterContinental group's boutique-hotel chain offers 46 differently styled rooms, all with four-poster beds and iPod docking stations. Larger-than-life drawings and photos of the neighbourhood won't let you forget where you are.

Andaz Liverpool Street HOTEL ££
(Map p72; ☑020-7961 1234; www.london.liver poolstreet.andaz.hyatt.com; 40 Liverpool St, EC2; r weekday/weekend from £180/365; ❄ ☎; ⊜ Liverpool St) This is the London flagship for Hyatt's sophisticated Andaz chain. There's no reception, just black-clad staff who check you in on iPads. The 267 rooms are cool and spacious, with interesting furnishings and lighting scheme. On top of this there are

HOXTON HOTEL

In the heart of hip Shoreditch, the sleek **Hoxton Hotel** (Map p120; ☑ 020-7550 1000; www.hoxtonhotels.com; 81 Great Eastern St, EC2; r from £49; ✳ @ 🛜; ⊖ Old St) takes the easyJet approach to selling its rooms – book long enough ahead and you might pay just £49. The 210 renovated rooms are small but stylish, with flat-screen TVs, a desk, fridge with complimentary bottled water and milk, and breakfast (orange juice, granola, yoghurt, banana) in a bag delivered to your door.

king-size beds), state-of-the-art technology (everything in the room from mood lighting to the TV is controlled through a tablet computer) and superb decor.

Shangri-La Hotel at the Shard HOTEL **£££** (Map p80; ☑ 020-7234 8000; www.shangri-la. com/london/shangrila; 31 St Thomas St, SE1; d/ ste from £420/750; ✳ @ 🛜 ☲; ℝ London Bridge, ⊖ London Bridge) The UK's first five-star hotel south of the Thames has breathtaking views from the highest hotel (above ground level) in Western Europe, occupying levels 34 to 52 of the Shard. From the 35th-floor sky lobby to the rooms, the Shangri-La concocts a stylish blend of Chinese aesthetics, Asian hospitality and sharp modernity.

five restaurants, two bars, a health club and a subterranean Masonic temple discovered during the hotel's refit in the '90s.

🛏 South Bank

Immediately on the south side of the Thames is a fab perch for reaching the central sights, while gauging the personality of South London.

St Christopher's Village HOSTEL **£** (Map p80; ☑ 020-7939 9710; www.st-christophers. co.uk; 163 Borough High St, SE1; dm/r from £15.90/43; @ 🛜; ⊖ London Bridge) This 194-bed party-zone hostel has new bathrooms, fresh paint, pod beds with privacy curtains, reading lights, power sockets (British and European) and USB ports, and refurbished common areas. Its two bars, Belushi's and Dugout, are perennially popular. Dorms have four to 22 beds (female-only dorms available); breakfast and linen are included.

The hotel has another branch 100m up the road: **St Christopher's Inn** (Map p80; ☑ 020-7407 2392; www.st-christophers.co.uk; 121 Borough High St, SE1; dm/r from £13.90/50; @ 🛜; ⊖ London Bridge), which sits above a traditional pub. The dorms are smaller and look a little tired, but it's altogether quieter than at the Village.

★**Citizen M** BOUTIQUE HOTEL **££** (Map p80; ☑ 020-3519 1680; www.citizenm.com/ london-bankside; 20 Lavington St, SE1; r £109-249; ✳ @ 🛜; ⊖ Southwark) If Citizen M had a motto, it would be 'less fuss, more comfort'. The hotel has done away with things it considers superfluous (room service, reception, bags of space) and instead gone all out on mattresses and bedding (heavenly super-

🛏 Pimlico & Belgravia

Lime Tree Hotel BOUTIQUE HOTEL **££** (Map p86; ☑ 020-7730 8191; www.limetreehotel. co.uk; 135-137 Ebury St, SW1; s £120-160, d & tw £180-210, tr £230 incl breakfast; @ 🛜; ⊖ Victoria) Family-run for 30 years, this beautiful 25-bedroom Georgian town-house hotel is all comfort, British designs and understated elegance. Rooms are individually decorated, many with open fireplaces and sash windows, but some are smaller than others, so enquire. There is a lovely back garden for late-afternoon rays (picnics encouraged on summer evenings). Rates include a hearty full-English breakfast. No lift.

B+B Belgravia B&B **££** (Map p86; ☑ 020-7259 8570; www.bb-belgravia. com; 64-66 Ebury St, SW1; d £79-209, studio £130-279; @ 🛜; ⊖ Victoria) This spiffing six-floor Georgian B&B, remodelled with contemporary flair, boasts crisp common areas and a chic lounge. The 17 rooms (some with shower, others with bath, half facing the street, half facing the garden) aren't enormous but there's a further batch of studio rooms with compact kitchens at No 82 Ebury St. A pleasant courtyard garden is out back. No lift.

★**Goring** HOTEL **£££** (Map p60; ☑ 020-7396 9000; www.thegoring.com; Beeston Pl; r/ste from £395/825; ✳ 🛜; ⊖ Victoria) Kate Middleton spent her last night as a commoner in the Royal Suite (£8400 per night) before joining the Royal Family, propelling the Goring into an international media glare. Glistening with chandeliers, dotted with trademark fluffy sheep and overseen by highly professional staff, this family-owned hotel is a supremely grand, albeit highly relaxed, slice of England and Englishness, with a sumptuous garden.

🛏 Knightsbridge

Named after a bridge over the River Westbourne, Knightsbridge is where you'll find some of London's best-known department stores and some top hotels.

Levin Hotel   HOTEL £££

(Map p86; 🕿 020-7589 6286; www.thelevinhotel. co.uk; 28 Basil St, SW3; r from £374, ste from £619 incl breakfast; ❋ @ 🛜; ⊖ Knightsbridge) The luxury 12-room Levin is a bijou boutique gem. Attention to detail (US, EU, UK and Asian sockets in every room, Nespresso coffee machines, fine Egyptian linen, underfloor heating in bathrooms, iPads on request), exquisite design and highly hospitable service create a delightful stay. The gorgeous continental buffet breakfast is complimentary. Room rates start at £274 in low season.

🛏 Chelsea & Kensington

Well-turned-out Chelsea and Kensington offer easy access to the museums, natty shopping choices and some of London's best-looking streets.

Meininger   HOSTEL £

(Map p86; 🕿 020-3318 1407; www.meininger-hostels.com; Baden Powell House, 65-67 Queen's Gate, SW7; dm £16-50, s/tw from £60/70; ❋ @ 🛜; ⊖ Gloucester Rd or South Kensington) Housed in the late-1950s Baden Powell House opposite the Natural History Museum, this 48-room German-run 'city hostel and hotel' has spick-and-span rooms – most are dorms of between four and 12 beds, with pod-like showers. There is also a handful of private rooms. There's good security and nice communal facilities, including a bar and a big roof terrace, plus a fantastic location.

★ Number Sixteen   HOTEL £££

(Map p86; 🕿 020-7589 5232; www.firmdalehotels. com/hotels/london/number-sixteen; 16 Sumner Pl, SW7; s from £192, d £240-396; ❋ @ 🛜 ☷; ⊖ South Kensington) With uplifting splashes of colour, choice art and a sophisticated-but-fun design ethos, Number Sixteen is simply ravishing. There are 41 individually designed rooms, a cosy drawing room and a fully stocked library. And wait till you see the idyllic, long back garden set around a fountain, or sit down for breakfast in the light-filled conservatory. Great amenities for families.

Ampersand Hotel   BOUTIQUE HOTEL £££

(Map p86; 🕿 020-7589 5895; www.ampersand hotel.com; 10 Harrington Rd, SW7; s £170-192, d £216-360; ❋ @ 🛜; ⊖ South Kensington) It feels light, fresh and bubbly in the Ampersand, where smiling staff wear denims and waistcoats rather than impersonal dark suits. The common rooms are colourful and airy, and the stylish rooms are decorated with wallpaper designs celebrating the nearby arts and sciences of South Kensington's museums.

🛏 Earl's Court & Fulham

West London's Earl's Court is lively, cosmopolitan and so popular with travelling Antipodeans it's nicknamed Kangaroo Valley. There are no real sights, but it has inexpensive digs, an infectious holiday atmosphere and it's a short hop to the action. Further west and abutting the Thames, Fulham is the home of its famous riverside palace.

★ Barclay House   B&B ££

(🕿 077 6742 0943; www.barclayhouselondon.com; 21 Barclay Rd, SW6; s £110, d £135-168; @ 🛜; ⊖ Fulham Broadway) The three dapper, thoroughly modern and comfy bedrooms in this shipshape Victorian house are a dream, from the Phillipe Starck shower rooms, walnut furniture, new double-glazed sash windows and underfloor heating to the small, thoughtful details (fumble-free coat hangers, drawers packed with sewing kits and maps). The cordial, music-loving owners – bursting with tips and handy London knowledge – concoct an inclusive, homely atmosphere.

Rockwell   BOUTIQUE HOTEL ££

(🕿 020-7244 2000; www.therockwell.com; 181-183 Cromwell Rd, SW5; s £120-125, d £145-180, ste from £200; ❋ @ 🛜; ⊖ Earl's Court) With an understated-cool design ethos and some lovely floor tiling, things are muted, dapper and more than a tad minimalist at the 'budget boutique' 40-room Rockwell. Spruce and stylish, all rooms have showers, the mezzanine suites are peaches and the three rooms looking on to the walled garden (LG1, 2 and 3) are particularly fine.

🛏 Notting Hill, Bayswater & Paddington

Don't be fooled by Julia Roberts' and Hugh Grant's shenanigans, Notting Hill and the areas immediately north of Hyde Park are as shabby as they are chic, but they're still cool.

Notting Hill & Bayswater

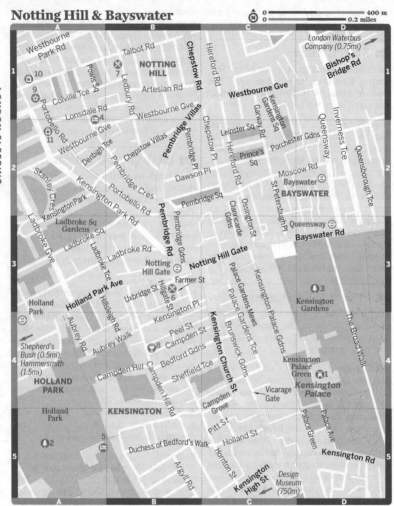

There are some gorgeous gated squares surrounded by Georgian town houses, but the area is better exemplified by the Portobello Road Market and the Notting Hill Carnival. Scruffy Paddington has lots of cheap hotels, with a major strip of unremarkable ones along Sussex Gardens that may be worth checking if you're short on options.

Safestay Holland Park
HOSTEL **£**

(Map p110; 📞 020-3326 8471; www.safestay.co.uk; Holland Walk, W8; dm £18, tw from £58, s from £66; 🛜; 🚇 High St Kensington or Holland Park) This new place replaced the long-serving

YHA hostel running here since 1958. With a bright and bold colour design, the hostel has four- to eight-bunk dorm rooms, twin-bunk and single-bunk rooms, free wi-fi in the lobby and a fabulous location in the Jacobean east wing of Holland House in **Holland Park** (Map p110; Ilchester Pl; ⏰ 7.30am–dusk; 🚇 High St Kensington or Holland Park).

★ Main House
HOTEL **££**

(Map p110; 📞 020-7221 9691; www.themainhouse. co.uk; 6 Colville Rd, W11; ste £120-150; 🛜; 🚇 Ladbroke Grove, Notting Hill Gate or Westbourne Park) The four adorable suites at this peach of

Notting Hill & Bayswater

◎ **Top Sights**
1 Kensington Palace...............................D4

◎ **Sights**
2 Holland Park...A5
3 Kensington Gardens............................D3

🛏 **Sleeping**
4 Main House..A1
5 Safestay Holland Park.........................A5

🍽 **Eating**
6 Geales..B3
7 Ledbury...B1

🍷 **Drinking & Nightlife**
8 Windsor Castle.....................................B4

🎭 **Entertainment**
9 Electric Cinema....................................A1

🛍 **Shopping**
10 Ceramica Blue.....................................A1
11 Portobello Road Market.....................A2

a Victorian midterrace house on Colville Rd make this a superb choice. Bright and spacious, with vast bathrooms, rooms are excellent value and include endless tea and coffee. Cream of the crop is the uppermost suite, occupying the entire top floor. There's no sign, but look for the huge letters 'SIX'. Minimum three-night stay.

🛏 Bloomsbury & St Pancras

One step from the West End and crammed with Georgian town-house conversions, these are more affordable neighbourhoods. A stretch of lower-priced hotels runs along Gower St and on the pretty Cartwright Gardens crescent. While hardly a salubrious location, St Pancras is handy with some excellent budget options.

⭐ **Clink78**   HOSTEL **£**
(Map p94; ☎020-7183 9400; www.clinkhostels. com/london/clink78; 78 King's Cross Rd, WC1; dm/r from £16/65 incl breakfast; @🗗; ⊖King's Cross/St Pancras) This fantastic 630-bed hostel is housed in a 19th-century magistrates' courthouse where Dickens once worked as a scribe and members of the Clash stood trial in 1978. Rooms feature pod beds (including overhead storage space) in four- to 16-bed dormitories. There's a top kitchen with a huge dining area and the busy Clash bar in the basement.

Parts of the hostel, includin[g] verted to bedrooms and a pai[r] elled court rooms used as a [...] internet room, are heritage-list[ed ...] all-female dorms too. You'll fi[nd ...] and change machine convenie[... th]e lobby. Free breakfast included: toast and spreads, cereal, juice, tea and coffee (7am to 10.30am).

Generator   HOSTEL **£**
(Map p94; ☎020-73887666; www.generatorhostels. com/london; 37 Tavistock Pl, WC1; dm/r from £18/68; @🗗; ⊖Russell Sq) With its industrial lines and funky decor, the huge Generator (more than 870 beds) is one of central London's grooviest budget spots. The bar, complete with pool tables, stays open until 2am and there are frequent themed parties. Dorm rooms have between six and 12 beds; backing it up are twins, triples and quad rooms.

London St Pancras YHA   HOSTEL **£**
(Map p94; ☎020-7388 9998; www.yha.org.uk; 79-81 Euston Rd, NW1; dm/r from £16/60; @🗗; ⊖King's Cross/St Pancras) This hostel with 186 beds spread over eight floors has modern, clean dorms sleeping four to six (nearly all with private facilities) and some private rooms. There's a good bar and cafe, although there are no self-catering facilities. Check out time is 10am.

Arosfa Hotel   B&B **££**
(Map p94; ☎020-7636 2115; www.arosfalondon. com; 83 Gower St, WC1; incl breakfast s/tw/tr/f from £82/135/145/178, d £139-175; 🗗; ⊖Goodge St) The Philippe Starck furniture and modern look in the lounge is more lavish than the decor in the hotel's 16 rooms, with cabin-like bathrooms in many of them. About half have been refurbished; they are small but remain good value. There are a couple of family rooms; room 4 looks on to a small but charming garden. Prices rise on Saturdays.

Rough Luxe   BOUTIQUE HOTEL **£££**
(Map p94; ☎020-7837 5338; www.roughluxe.co.uk; 1 Birkenhead St, WC1; r £209-239; ❋🗗; ⊖King's Cross/St Pancras) Half-rough, half-luxury is the strapline of this nine-room hotel, and the distressed interior is true to its word. Scraps of old newspaper adorn the walls, along with original artwork, while the vintage 1970s TVs are for show only. Some rooms are admittedly small but service, location and the delightful patio garden at the back more than make up for it.

**ras Renaissance
.on Hotel** LUXURY HOTEL £££

.ap p94; ☑ 020-7841 3540; www.stpancrasrenais-sance.co.uk; Euston Rd, NW1; d from £230; ✳ 🛜 🏊; ◉ King's Cross/St Pancras) Housed in the former Midland Grand Hotel (1873), a Gothic, red-brick Victorian marvel designed by Sir George Gilbert Scott, the St Pancras Renaissance counts 245 rooms but only 38 of them are are in the original building; the rest are in an extension at the back and rather bland.

🛏 Clerkenwell & Farringdon

★ Zetter Hotel & Townhouse
BOUTIQUE HOTEL £££

(Map p94; ☑ 020-7324 4444; www.thezetter.com; 86-88 Clerkenwell Rd, EC1; d from £222, studio £300-438; ✳ 🛜; ◉ Farringdon) 🏄 The Zetter comprises two quite different properties. The original Zetter Hotel is a temple of cool with an overlay of kitsch on Clerkenwell's main thoroughfare. Built using sustainable materials on the site of a derelict office, its 59 rooms are small but perfectly formed. The **Zetter Townhouse** (Map p94; 49-50 St John's Sq; r £222-294, ste £438-480), on a pretty square behind, has just 13 rooms in a lovely Georgian pile.

At the main Zetter, the rooftop studios are the real treat, with terraces commanding superb views across the city. The rooms in the Zetter Townhouse are uniquely decorated in period style but with witty touches such as headboards made from reclaimed fairground carousels. The fantastic cocktail bar is a destination in itself.

Rookery HERITAGE HOTEL £££

(Map p94; ☑ 020-7336 0931; www.rookery hotel.com; 12 Peter's Lane, Cowcross St, EC1; s/d £222/294, ste £474-660; ✳ 🛜; ◉ Farringdon) This charming warren of 33 rooms has been built within a row of 18th-century Georgian houses and fitted out with period furniture (including a museum-piece collection of Victorian baths, showers and toilets), original wood panelling shipped over from Ireland and artwork selected personally by the owner. Highlights: the small courtyard garden and the two-storey Rook's Nest penthouse suite.

🛏 East End & Docklands

★ Qbic
DESIGN HOTEL ££

(☑ 020-3021 3300; www.london.qbichotels.com; 42 Adler St, E1; d £70-250; ✳ 🛜; ◉ Aldgate East) The 171 rooms of this snappy hotel south of Brick Lane are based around a 'cubi', with

each bed and bathroom part of a square-box design. There's a very modern feel throughout, with white tiling, neon signs, and vibrant art and textiles. Rooms are sound-insulated, mattresses excellent and rainforest showers powerful. A great continental buffet breakfast is available for £9.95.

40 Winks BOUTIQUE HOTEL ££

(☑ 020-7790 0259; www.40winks.org; 109 Mile End Rd, E1; s/d £120/195 incl breakfast; 🛜; ◉ Stepney Green) Short on space but not on style, this two-room boutique guesthouse, housed in an early-18th-century town house in Stepney Green, oozes quirky charm. Owned by a successful designer, the hotel has been used as a location for a number of fashion shoots and the rooms (the single is quite compact) are uniquely decorated with an expert's eye. Book far ahead.

🍴 Eating

Dining out in London has become so fashionable that you can hardly open a menu without banging into some celebrity chef or other. The range and quality of eating options has increased exponentially over the last few decades. Waves of immigrant flavours have deeply infused London cuisine and the expectations of modern-day Londoners are demanding. In this section we have sieved out choicer restaurants and cafes noted for their location, value for money, unique character, ambience and, of course, good food. Vegetarians needn't fret: London has a host of dedicated meat-free joints, while most others have veggie offerings.

🍴 West End

Mayfair, Soho and Covent Garden are the gastronomic heart of London, with a blinding choice of restaurants and cuisines at budgets to suit booze hounds, theatregoers or determined grazers.

★ Shoryu
NOODLES £

(Map p66; www.shoryuramen.com; 9 Regent St, SW1; mains £9-15; ⊙ 11.15am-midnight Mon-Sat, to 10.30pm Sun; ◉ Piccadilly Circus) Compact, well-mannered noodle-parlour Shoryu draws in reams of noodle diners to feast at its wooden counters and small tables. It's busy, friendly and efficient, with helpful and informative staff. Fantastic *tonkotsu* pork-broth ramen is the name of the game here, sprinkled with *nori* (dried, pressed seaweed), spring onion, *nitamago* (soft-boiled eggs) and sesame seeds. No bookings.

Ceviche
SOUTH AMERICAN £

(Map p66; www.cevicheuk.com; 17 Frith St, W1; mains £6-13.50; ⊘ noon-11.30pm Mon-Sat, to 10.15pm Sun; 🛜; ⊖ Leicester Sq) This colourfully decorated *bodega* serves some of the most authentic Peruvian food in town. Start with *cancha* (large crunchy corn kernels) and move on to one of the signature dishes of ceviche (fish or shellfish marinated in lime juice with chillies, onion and coriander). Salads made with quinoa and palm hearts are excellent.

The Breakfast Club
BREAKFAST £

(Map p66; 🖅 020-7434 2571; www.thebreakfastclubcafes.com; 33 D'Arblay St; mains £5-12.50; ⊘ 8am-10pm Mon-Sat, to 7pm Sun; 🛜; ⊖ Oxford Circus) This fun and friendly original branch of The Breakfast Club has been successfully frying up for more than a decade and has spawned seven other branches in town. Full or half Monty or All American brekkies are the natural inclination, but chorizo hash browns, pancakes and delights of the El Butty also await (once you reach the front of the queue).

Wahaca
MEXICAN $

(Map p66; www.wahaca.com; 66 Chandos Pl, WC2; mains £7-10.50; ⊘ noon-11pm Mon-Sat, to 10.30pm Sun; 🛜; ⊖ Covent Garden) 🍴 This delightful but frequently busy carbon-neutral cantina, part of an ever-expanding and ever-popular chain, styles itself as a 'Mexican-market eating' experience. Choose to share a selection of street snacks (tacos, tostadas, *quesadillas*) or aim for a more traditional main such as chargrilled chicken breast marinated in Yucatecan spices and pineapple juice. Wash it down with one of a dozen tequilas.

Fernandez & Wells
CAFE £

(Map p66; www.fernandezandwells.com; 73 Beak St, W1; dishes £4.50-6; ⊘ 7.30am-6pm Mon-Fri, 9am-6pm Sat & Sun; ⊖ Piccadilly Circus) A wonderful taste of Spain in Soho, Fernandez serves simple lunches of *jamón* (ham) and cured meats and cheese platters. Grilled chorizo sandwiches are perfect for quick lunchtime bites. The place is usually busy, with a relaxed atmosphere. Excellent coffee.

Mildreds
VEGETARIAN £

(Map p66; www.mildreds.co.uk; 45 Lexington St, W1; mains £8.0-12; ⊘ noon-11pm Mon-Sat; 🛜🍴; ⊖ Oxford Circus or Piccadilly Circus) Central London's most inventive vegetarian restaurant,

Mildred's heaves at lunchtime so don't be shy about sharing a table in the skylit dining room. Expect the likes of Sri Lankan sweet-potato and cashew-nut curry, pumpkin and ricotta ravioli, Middle Eastern mezze, wonderfully exotic (and filling) salads and delicious stir-fries. There are also vegan and gluten-free options.

Monocle Cafe
CAFE £

(Map p89; http://cafe.monocle.com; 18 Chiltern St, W1; mains from £5.50; ⊘ 7am-7pm Mon-Wed, 7am-8pm Thu & Fri, 8am-8pm Sat, 8am-7pm Sun; 🛜; ⊖ Baker St) A small and cool ground-floor and basement hideout for the Marylebone hipster set, Monocle Cafe (from the eponymous magazine) is a delightful addition to buzzing Chiltern St. It offers eclectic flavours from Swedish pastries to Japanese and Scandinavian breakfasts, Bircher muesli with strawberries or shrimp *katsu* (breaded shrimp) sandwiches.

★ Gymkhana
INDIAN ££

(Map p66; 🖅 020-3011 5900; www.gymkhanalondon.com; 42 Albemarle St, W1; mains £8-38, 2/3-course lunch £25/30; ⊘ noon-2.30pm & 5.30-10.30pm Mon-Sat; 🛜; ⊖ Green Park) The rather sombre setting is all British Raj: ceiling fans, oak ceiling, period cricket photos and hunting trophies, but the menu is lively, bright and inspiring. For lovers of variety, the seven-course tasting menu (£70; vegetarian menu available £65) or vault menu (£75; vegetarian menu £70) is the way to go, or aim for the seafood menu instead (seven courses £80).

★ Brasserie Zédel
FRENCH ££

(Map p66; 🖅 020-7734 4888; www.brasseriezedel.com; 20 Sherwood St, W1; mains £8.75-30; ⊘ 11.30am-midnight Mon-Sat, to 11pm Sun; 🛜; ⊖ Piccadilly Circus) This brasserie in the renovated art-deco ballroom of a former hotel is the Frenchest eatery west of Calais. Favourites include *choucroute Alsacienne* (sauerkraut with sausages and charcuterie, £14) or a straight-up *steak haché, sauce au poivre et frites* (chopped steak with pepper sauce; £9.75). Set menus (£9.75/12.75 for two/three courses) and *plats du jour* (£14.25) offer excellent value, in a terrific setting.

There's a vegetarian menu available, too. Also here, the **Bar Américain** is a classic deco spot for a pre-dinner libation.

★ Barrafina
SPANISH ££

(Map p66; www.barrafina.co.uk; 10 Adelaide St, WC2; tapas £6-14.50; ⊘ noon-3pm & 5-11pm Mon-Sat, 1-3.30pm & 5.30-10pm Sun; ⊖ Embankment or

Leicester Sq) With no reservations, you may need to get in line for an hour or so at this restaurant that does a brisk service in some of the best tapas in town. Divine mouthfuls are served on each plate, from the stuffed courgette flower to the suckling pig and crab on toast, so diners dig their heels in, prepared to wait.

★ Palomar   JEWISH ££

(Map p66; ☑ 020-7439 8777; 34 Rupert St, W1; mains £6.50-19; ⊙ noon-2.30pm & 5.30-11pm Mon-Sat, noon-3.30pm & 6-9pm Sun; ☜; ⊖ Piccadilly Circus) The buzzing vibe at this good-looking celebration of modern-day Jerusalem cuisine (in all its inflections) is infectious, but we could enjoy the dishes cooked up here in a deserted warehouse and still come back for more. The Jerusalem-style polenta and Josperised aubergine are fantastic, but portions are smallish, so sharing is the way to go. Reservations essential.

★ Cafe Murano   ITALIAN ££

(Map p66; ☑ 020-3371 5559; www.cafemurano.co.uk; 33 St James's St, SW1; mains £9-24, 2/3-course set meal £19/23; ⊙ noon-3pm & 5.30-11pm Mon-Sat; ⊖ Green Park) The setting may seem somewhat demure at this superb and busy restaurant, but with such a sublime North Italian menu on offer, it sees no need to be flash and of-the-moment. You get what you come for, and the beef carpaccio, crab linguine and lamb ragu are as close to culinary perfection as you can get. Reserve.

Battersea Pie Station   BRITISH £

(Map p66; www.batterseapiestation.co.uk; Lower Ground Floor, 28 The Market, Covent Garden, WC2; mains from £7.50; ⊙ 11am-7pm Sun-Thu, to 8pm Fri-Sat; ⊖ Covent Garden) Just what Covent Garden needs, this small, white-tiled cafe has a terrific choice of pies (baby or big) to satisfy all levels of hunger, from careful nibblers to voracious teens. Meat is all free-range, flavours are classic and rich (lamb and mint, fish, steak and ale, chicken and mushroom, butternut squash and goat's cheese), each coming with a dollop of mash.

Great Queen Street   BRITISH ££

(Map p66; ☑ 020-7242 0622; www.greatqueenstreetrestaurant.co.uk; 32 Great Queen St, WC2; mains £16.80-18; ⊙ noon-2.30pm & 5.30-10.30pm Mon-Sat, 1-3.30pm Sun; ⊖ Holborn) The menu at one of Covent Garden's best places to eat is seasonal (and changes daily), with an emphasis on quality, hearty dishes and fine ingredients – there are always delicious stews, roasts and

simple fish dishes. The atmosphere is lively, with a small **cellar bar** (⊙ 5-12pm Tues-Sat) for cocktails and drinks. Booking is essential (do it online).

National Dining Rooms   BRITISH ££

(Map p66; ☑ 020-7747 2525; www.peytonandbyrne.co.uk; 1st fl, Sainsbury Wing, National Gallery, Trafalgar Sq, WC2; mains £14.50-21.50; ⊙ 10am-5.30pm Sat-Thu, to 8.30pm Fri; ☜; ⊖ Charing Cross) Right at the very heart of town, chef Oliver Peyton's restaurant at the National Gallery (p68) is a superb choice, its menu featuring an extensive and wonderful selection of British cheeses for a light lunch. For something more filling, go for the monthly changing County Menu, honouring regional specialities from across the British Isles. Set lunch is £19.50 for two courses.

Ethos   VEGETARIAN ££

(Map p66; 48 Eastcastle St, W1; lunch/dinner £2.60/2.85 per 100g; ⊙ 8am-10pm Mon-Fri, 11.30am-10pm Sat, 10am-4pm Sun; ☜ ☑; ⊖ Oxford Circus) 🌢 Busy, self-service Ethos sells creative, meat-free food chosen from the buffet and then priced by weight. Doors open for breakfast (smashed avocado on toast, gluten-free porridge with almond milk etc), moving through lunch and dinner (guacamole, chickpea and coconut curry, Japanese-miso aubergine etc) via afternoon tea (£20 per person) and brunch on Sundays.

Bocca di Lupo   ITALIAN ££

(Map p66; ☑ 020-7734 2223; www.boccadilupo.com; 12 Archer St, W1; mains £8-23; ⊙ 12.30-3pm & 5.30-11pm Mon-Sat, 12.15-3.15pm & 5.15-9.30pm Sun; ⊖ Piccadilly Circus) Bocca radiates elegant sophistication from its dark Soho backstreet setting. The menu has dishes from across Italy (with pointers of what region they're from), and every main course can be ordered as a large or small portion, rounded off with a good selection of Italian wines and terrific desserts. It's often full, so make sure to book.

Canela   PORTUGUESE ££

(Map p66; www.canelacafe.com; 33 Earlham St, WC2; mains £11-13; ⊙ 8am-10.30pm Mon-Thu, to 11pm Fri & Sat, to 9pm Sun; ☜; ⊖ Covent Garden) This small cafe in Seven Dials at the heart of Covent Garden serves tasty Portuguese and Brazilian dishes. Try the classic dish of the day, opt for the Portuguese national dish *feijoada,* a bean stew with smoked meat, or stop by early for a rustic brekkie. There's a good selection of vegetarian dishes, as well as a strong Portuguese wine list.

★ **Foyer at Claridge's** BRITISH £££
(Map p89; www.claridges.co.uk; 49-53 Brook St, W1; afternoon tea £58, with champagne £68; ⊗ tea served 2.45-5.30pm; 🕾; ⊖ Bond St) Extend that pinkie finger to partake in afternoon tea within the classic art-deco-style foyer of this landmark hotel where the gentle clink of fine porcelain and champagne glasses could be a defining memory of your trip to London. The setting is gorgeous and dress is elegant, smart casual (ripped jeans and baseball caps won't get served).

Chiltern Firehouse MODERN EUROPEAN £££
(Map p89; 🖉 020-7073 7676; www.chilternfire-house.com; 1 Chiltern St, W1; mains £24-42; ⊗ 7-10.30am Mon-Fri, 9-10.30am Sat & Sun, noon-2.30pm Mon-Wed, noon-3pm Thu & Fri, 11am-3pm Sat & Sun, 5.30-10.30pm Mon-Wed, 6-10.30pm Thu-Sun; 🕾; ⊖ Baker St or Bond St) When they can secure a table, diners come to this splendidly dapper Marylebone Fire Station to celeb-spot and bask in its glorious setting as much as to dine. Chef Nuno Mendes has worked some considerable culinary flair into his menu, but the hype and overarching trendiness guarantee an outlay almost as high as the red-brick chimneys aloft.

✖ The City

You'll be sorely dismayed if you've got an empty belly on a Sunday morning in the City. Even during the busy weekdays, the chain eateries are often your best option.

Café Below CAFE £
(Map p72; 🖉 020-7329 0789; www.cafebelow.co.uk; St Mary-le-Bow, Cheapside, EC2; mains £8-15.50; ⊗ 7.30am-2.30pm Mon-Fri, to 9.30pm Wed-Fri; 🖉; ⊖ Mansion House or St Paul's) This very atmospheric cafe-restaurant, in the crypt of one of London's most famous churches, offers excellent value and a tasty range of international fare, with as many vegetarian choices as meat choices. Summer sees tables outside in the shady courtyard. Occasional set dinners are available, but check the website or phone in for details.

★ **Restaurant at St Paul's** MODERN BRITISH ££
(Map p72; 🖉 020-7248 2469; www.harbourand jones.com/restaurant/restaurant-at-st-pauls; Crypt, St Paul's Cathedral, EC4; mains from £14, brunch menu £25; ⊗ breakfast 9-11am Thu & Fri, lunch noon-2.15pm, tea 3-4.15pm Mon-Sat; 🕾; ⊖ St Paul's) The quality of the dishes at this restaurant in the crypt of St Paul's (p73) lives up to the grandeur above. The menu offers two- or three-course lunches, including dishes such as pork-belly confit and goat's-cheese ravioli with spiced tomato.

Sweeting's SEAFOOD £££
(Map p72; 🖉 020-7248 3062; www.sweetingsres taurant.co.uk; 39 Queen Victoria St, EC4; mains £15-45; ⊗ 11.30am-3pm Mon-Fri; ⊖ Mansion House) 🖋 A City institution, Sweeting's dates to 1889. It hasn't changed much, with its small sit-down dining area, mosaic floor and narrow counters, behind which stand waiters in white aprons. Dishes include sustainably sourced fish of all kinds (grilled, fried or poached), potted shrimps, eels and Sweeting's famous fish pie (£16). Round it all off with a plate of spotted dick.

✖ South Bank

Popular restaurants feast on iconic riverside views, but cast your net wider and gems crop up everywhere. For a feed with a local feel, head to Borough Market (p81) or Bermondsey St.

M Manze BRITISH £
(Map p80; www.manze.co.uk; 87 Tower Bridge Rd, SE1; mains from £2.95; ⊗ 11am-2pm Mon, 10.30am-2pm Tue-Thu, 10am-2.30pm Fri, 10am-3pm Sat; ⊖ Borough) Dating to 1902, M Manze started off as an ice-cream seller before moving on to selling its legendary staples: pies (minced beef). It's a classic operation, from the ageing tile work to the traditional working-man's menu: pie and mash (£4), pie and liquor (£2.95), and you can take your eels jellied or stewed (£4.65).

★ **Skylon** MODERN EUROPEAN ££
(Map p80; 🖉 020-7654 7800; www.skylon-restaurant.co.uk; 3rd fl, Royal Festival Hall, Southbank Centre, Belvedere Rd, SE1; grill 3-course menu £25, restaurant 3-course menu £32; ⊗ grill noon-11pm Mon-Sat, to 10.30pm Sun, restaurant noon-2.30pm & 5.30-10.30pm Mon-Sat & noon-4pm Sun; 🕾; ⊖ Waterloo) This excellent restaurant inside the Royal Festival Hall (p130) is divided into grill and fine-dining sections by a large **bar** (⊗ noon-1am Mon-Sat, to 10.30pm Sun). The decor is cutting-edge 1950s: muted colours and period chairs (trendy then, trendier now) while floor-to-ceiling windows bathe you in magnificent views of the Thames and the City. The six-course restaurant tasting menu is £59. Booking is advised.

★ **Arabica Bar**
& Kitchen MIDDLE EASTERN £££
(Map p80; ☑ 020-3011 5151; www.arabicabarand
kitchen.com; 3 Rochester Walk, Borough Market,
SE1; dishes £6-14; ⊙ 11am-11pm Mon-Wed, 8.30am-
11pm Thu, 8.30am-11.30pm Fri & Sat, 11am-4pm
Sun; ☑; ⊜ London Bridge) Pan Middle-Eastern
cuisine is a well-rehearsed classic these days,
but Arabica Bar & Kitchen has managed to
bring something fresh to its table: the decor
is contemporary and bright, the food delicate and light, with an emphasis on sharing
(two to three small dishes per person). The
downside of this tapas approach is that the
bill adds up quickly.

✕ Belgravia

★ **Pimlico Fresh** CAFE £
(86 Wilton Rd, SW1; mains from £4.50; ⊙ 7.30am-
7.30pm Mon-Fri, 9am-6pm Sat & Sun; ⊜ Victoria)
This friendly two-room cafe will see you
right whether you need breakfast (French
toast, bowls of porridge laced with honey
or maple syrup), lunch (homemade quiches
and soups, 'things' on toast) or just a good
old latte and cake.

✕ Knightsbridge

★ **Dinner by**
Heston Blumenthal MODERN BRITISH £££
(Map p86; ☑ 020-7201 3833; www.dinnerbyheston.
com; Mandarin Oriental Hyde Park, 66 Knightsbridge, SW1; 3-course set lunch £40, mains £28-42;
⊙ noon-2pm & 6-10.15pm; ☎; ⊜ Knightsbridge)
Sumptuously presented Dinner is a gastronomic tour de force, taking diners on a journey through British culinary history (with
inventive modern inflections). Dishes carry
historical dates to convey context, while the
restaurant interior is a design triumph, from
the glass-walled kitchen and its overhead
clock mechanism to the large windows looking onto the park. Book ahead.

Also at hand is a 16th-century Tudor-style
private room that seats 12 guests, dining
from an extravagant Sapele and Rosewood
oval table. Set lunches are available Monday
to Friday.

Zuma JAPANESE £££
(Map p86; ☑ 020-7584 1010; www.zumarestaurant.
com; 5 Raphael St, SW7; mains £15-75; ⊙ noon-
3pm Mon-Fri, noon-3.30pm Sat & Sun, 6-11pm Mon-
Sat, 6-10.30pm Sun; ☎; ⊜ Knightsbridge) Zuma
oozes style – a modern-day take on the traditional Japanese *izakaya* ('a place to stay and

drink sake'), where drinking and eating har-
monise. The *robata* (chargrilled) dishes are
the stars of the show; wash them down with
one of 40 types of sake on offer. Booking is
advised, although there are walk-in spaces
at the *robata* and sushi counters.

✕ Chelsea & Kensington

These highbrow neighbourhoods harbour
some of London's very best (and priciest)
restaurants.

★ **Rabbit** MODERN BRITISH ££
(Map p86; ☑ 020-3750 0172; www.rabbit-restau
rant.com; 172 King's Rd, SW3; mains £6-24, set
lunch £13.50; ⊙ noon-midnight Tue-Sat, 6-11pm
Mon, noon-6pm Sun; ☑; ⊜ Sloane Sq) Three
brothers grew up on a farm. One became a
farmer, another a butcher, while the third
worked in hospitality. So they pooled their
skills and came up with Rabbit, a breath of
fresh air in upmarket Chelsea. The restaurant rocks the agri-chic (yes) look and the
creative, seasonal modern British cuisine is
fabulous.

★ **Five Fields** MODERN BRITISH £££
(Map p86; ☑ 020-7838 1082; www.fivefieldsre
staurant.com; 8-9 Blacklands Tce, SW3; 3-course
set meal £60; ⊙ 6.30-10pm Tue-Sat; ☎; ⊜ Sloane
Sq) The inventive British cuisine, consum-
mate service and enticingly light and inviting decor of Five Fields are hard to resist,
at this triumphant Chelsea restaurant, but
you'll need to plan early and book way up
front. It's only open five nights a week.

★ **Gordon Ramsay** FRENCH £££
(Map p86; ☑ 020-7352 4441; www.gordonramsay.
com; 68 Royal Hospital Rd, SW3; 3-course lunch/
dinner £65/110; ⊙ noon-2.30pm & 6.30-11pm Mon-
Fri; ⊜ Sloane Sq) One of Britain's finest restaurants and London's longest-running with
three Michelin stars, this is hallowed turf for
those who worship at the altar of the stove.
It's true that it's a treat right from the taster
to the truffles, but you won't get much time
to savour it all. The blowout tasting Menu
Prestige (£145) is seven courses of perfection.

Bookings are made in specific sittings and
you dare not linger; book as late as you can
to avoid that rushed feeling.

✕ Notting Hill, Shepherd's Bush
& Hammersmith

Notting Hill teems with good places to eat,
from cheap takeaways to atmospheric pubs

and restaurants worthy of the fine-dining tag. Shepherd's Bush and Hammersmith to the west pitch in with some fine contenders.

★ Potli
INDIAN **£**

(www.potli.co.uk; 319-321 King St, W6; weekday 1-/2-course set lunch £7.95/10.95, mains £7.50-15; ⊙ noon-2.30pm Mon-Sat, 6-10.15pm Mon-Thu, 5.30-10.30pm Fri-Sat, noon-10pm Sun; 🤖; ⊜ Stamford Brook or Ravenscourt Park) With its scattered pieces from Mumbai's Thieves Market, Indian-market-kitchen/bazaar cuisine, home-made pickles and spice mixes, plus an accent on genuine flavour, tantalising Potli deftly captures the aromas of its culinary home. Downstairs there's an open kitchen and service is friendly, but it's the alluring menu – where flavours are teased into a rich and authentic India culinary experience – that's the real crowd-pleaser.

★ Geales
SEAFOOD **££**

(Map p110; 📞 020-7727 7528; www.geales.com; 2 Farmer St, W8; 2-course express lunch £9.75, mains £9-39.50; ⊙ noon-3pm & 6-10.30pm Tue-Fri, noon-10.30pm Sat, noon-4pm Sun; ⊜ Notting Hill Gate) Frying since 1939 – a bad year for the restaurant trade – Geales has endured with its quiet location on the corner of Farmer St in Hillgate Village. The succulent fish in crispy batter is a fine catch from a menu that also runs to other British faves such as pork belly with apple sauce and crackling, and beef and bacon pie.

★ Ledbury
FRENCH **£££**

(Map p110; 📞 020-7792 9090; www.theledbury. com; 127 Ledbury Rd, W11; 4-course set lunch £85, 4-course dinner £95; ⊙ noon-2pm Wed-Sun & 6.30-9.45pm daily; 🤖; ⊜ Westbourne Park or Notting Hill Gate) Two Michelin stars and swooningly elegant, Brett Graham's artful French restaurant attracts well-heeled diners in jeans with designer jackets. Dishes – such as hand-dived scallops, ceviche, seaweed and herb oil with frozen English wasabi or Herdwick lamb with salt-baked turnips, celery cream and wild garlic – are triumphant. London gastronomes have the Ledbury on speed-dial, so reservations well in advance are crucial.

✘ Marylebone

You won't go too far wrong planting yourself on a table anywhere along Marylebone's charming High St.

La Fromagerie
CAFE **££**

(Map p89; www.lafromagerie.co.uk; 2-6 Moxon St, W1; mains £8.50-18; ⊙ 8am-7.30pm Mon-Fri, 9am-7pm Sat, 10am-6pm Sun; 🤖; ⊜ Baker St) 🍴 This deli-cafe has bowls of delectable salads, antipasto, peppers and beans scattered about the long communal table. Huge slabs of bread invite you to tuck in, and all the while the heavenly waft from the cheese room beckons. Cheese boards come in small and large (£9.25 and £16) and breakfast is always a good choice.

Locanda Locatelli
ITALIAN **££**

(Map p89; 📞 020-7935 9088; www.locandalocatelli.com; 8 Seymour St, W1; mains from £13.50; ⊙ noon-3pm daily, 6-11pm Mon-Thu, to 11.30pm Fri & Sat, to 10.15pm Sun; 🤖; ⊜ Marble Arch) This dark but quietly glamorous restaurant in an otherwise unremarkable Marble Arch hotel remains one of London's hottest tables, and you're likely to see some famous faces being greeted by celebrity chef Giorgio Locatelli. The restaurant is renowned for its pasta dishes, and the mains include six fish and five meat dishes. Booking is essential.

✘ Bloomsbury & St Pancras

Diwana Bhel Poori House
INDIAN **£**

(Map p94; 📞 020-7387 5556; www.diwanabph.com; 121-123 Drummond St, NW1; mains £5.10-8.95; ⊙ noon-11.30pm Mon-Sat, to 10.30pm Sun; 📷; ⊜ Euston) One of the best Indian vegetarian restaurants in London, Diwana specialises in Bombay-style *bhel poori* (a tangy, soft and crunchy 'party mix' dish) and *dosas* (filled crispy pancakes made from rice flour). Solo diners should consider a *thali* (a complete meal consisting of lots of small dishes). The all-you-can-eat lunchtime buffet (£7) is legendary while daily specials are £6.60.

North Sea Fish Restaurant
FISH & CHIPS **££**

(Map p94; www.northseafishrestaurant.co.uk; 7-8 Leigh St, WC1; mains £9.95-23; ⊙ noon-10.30pm Mon-Sat, 2.30-9.30pm Sun; ⊜ Russell Sq) The North Sea sets out to cook fresh fish and potatoes – a simple ambition in which it succeeds admirably. Look forward to jumbo-sized plaice or halibut fillets, deep-fried or grilled, and a huge serving of chips. There's takeaway next door if you can't face the rather austere dining room.

✘ Fitzrovia

Tucked away behind busy Tottenham Court Rd, Fitzrovia's Charlotte and Goodge Sts form one of central London's most vibrant eating precincts.

CAMDEN MARKET

Although (or perhaps because) it stopped being cutting-edge several thousand cheap leather jackets ago, **Camden Market** (Map p119; www. camdenmarket.com; Camden High St, NW1; ⊙10am-6pm; ⊖Camden Town) gets a whopping 10 million visitors each year and is one of London's most popular attractions. What started out as a collection of attractive craft stalls by Camden Lock on the Regent's Canal now extends most of the way from Camden Town tube station to Chalk Farm tube station.

Dabbous MODERN EUROPEAN **££**
(Map p94; ☑020-7323 1544; www.dabbous. co.uk; 39 Whitfield St, W1; set lunch 3/4 courses £28/35, set dinner 4 courses £59; ⊙noon-3pm & 5.30-11.30pm Tue-Sat; 🛜; ⊖Goodge St) This award-winning eatery is the creation of Ollie Dabbous, everyone's favourite new chef, so book ahead for dinner or come for lunch. The combination of flavours is inspired – king crab in warm garlic buttermilk, pork with mango, rhubarb with lavender – and at first seems at odds with the industrial, hard-edged decor. But it all works exceedingly well. Reservations essential.

Lima SOUTH AMERICAN **£££**
(Map p66; ☑020-3002 2640; www.limalondon. com; 31 Rathbone Pl, W1; mains £22-29; ⊙noon-2.30pm Tue-Sun, 5.30-10.45pm Mon-Sat, 5-9pm Sun; 🛜; ⊖Tottenham Court Rd) Sublimely zestful and piquant Peruvian flavours percolate at the heart of this fantastic and unassuming Fitzrovia restaurant. The stunningly presented cuisine has pulled a Michelin star, while helpful staff take pride in their work.

Hakkasan Hanway Place CHINESE **£££**
(Map p66; ☑020-7927 7000; www.hakkasan.com; 8 Hanway Pl, W1; mains £13.80-100; ⊙noon-3pm Mon-Fri, to 4pm Sat & Sun, 5.30-11pm Sun-Wed, to 12.15am Thu-Sat; 🛜; ⊖Tottenham Court Rd) This basement Michelin-starred restaurant – hidden down a back alleyway – successfully combines celebrity status, stunning design, persuasive cocktails and sophisticated Chinese food. The low, nightclub-style lighting makes it a good spot for dating or a night out with friends (the bar serves seriously creative cocktails). Book far in advance or come for lunch (three courses £38, also available from 6pm to 7pm).

✗ Camden Town

Camden is great for cheap eats, while neighbouring Chalk Farm and Primrose Hill are salted with gastropubs and upmarket restaurants.

★**Hook Camden Town** FISH & CHIPS **£**
(Map p119; www.hookrestaurants.com; 65 Parkway Rd, NW1; mains £8-12; ⊙noon-3pm & 5-10pm Mon-Thu, noon-10.30pm Fri & Sat, noon-9pm Sun; ⊖Camden Town) 🌿 Working entirely with sustainable small fisheries and local suppliers, Hook also makes all its sauces on-site and wraps its fish in recycled materials, supplying London diners with some extraordinarily fine-tasting morsels. Totally fresh, the fish arrives in panko breadcrumbs or tempura batter, with seaweed salted chips. Craft beers and fine wines are also to hand.

Mango Room CARIBBEAN **££**
(Map p119; ☑020-7482 5065; www.mangoroom. co.uk; 10-12 Kentish Town Rd, NW1; mains £12.50-17; ⊙noon-11pm; ⊖Camden Town) With its modern, bright decor and excellent service, Mango Room promises a sophisticated Caribbean experience, with food to match: seafood soup, grilled goat's cheese with pesto and mixed-leaf salad, salt fish with ackee (a yellow-skinned Jamaican fruit that has an uncanny resemblance to scrambled eggs), and curried goat with hot pepper and spices, all presented with origami intricacy. Booking recommended.

✗ Islington

Allow at least an evening to explore Islington's Upper St, along with the lanes leading off it.

★**Ottolenghi** BAKERY, MEDITERRANEAN **££**
(☑020-7288 1454; www.ottolenghi.co.uk; 287 Upper St, N1; breakfast £5.50-10.50, lunch mains from £12.90, dinner mains from £11; ⊙8am-10.30pm Mon-Sat, 9am-7pm Sun; 🖋; ⊖Highbury & Islington) Mountains of meringues tempt you through the door of this deli-restaurant, where a sumptuous array of baked goods and fresh salads greets you. Meals are as light and bright as the brilliantly white interior design, with a strong influence from the eastern Mediterranean.

Trullo ITALIAN **££**
(☑020-7226 2733; www.trullorestaurant.com; 300-302 St Paul's Rd, N1; mains £15-21; ⊙12.30-2.45pm & 6-10.15pm Mon-Sat, 12.30-3pm Sun; ⊖Highbury & Islington) Trullo's homemade pasta is delicious, but the main attraction here is the

Camden Town

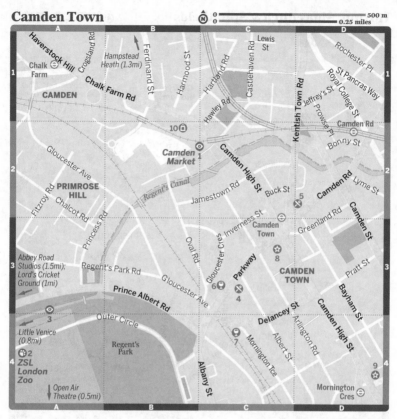

charcoal grill, which churns out the likes of succulent Italian-style pork chops, steaks and fish. The service is excellent, too, although dinner time can get packed.

Le Mercury FRENCH **££**
(☏ 020-7354 4088; www.lemercury.co.uk; 140a Upper St, N1; mains £10.95; ☺ noon-1am Mon-Sat, to 11pm Sun; ☺ Highbury & Islington or Angel) An excellent and wildly popular budget French eatery, Le Mercury seems to have all you need in its winning formula: romantic atmosphere with candlelit, petite tables and plants everywhere, combined with superb French food at unbeatable prices. Londoners have long known about this place, so reservations are advised.

✖ Clerkenwell & Farringdon

Clerkenwell's hidden gems are well worth digging for. Pedestrianised Exmouth Market is a good place to start.

Camden Town

◉ **Top Sights**
1 Camden Market B2
2 ZSL London Zoo A4

◉ **Sights**
3 Regent's Canal A3

✖ **Eating**
4 Hook Camden Town C3
5 Mango Room D2

◉ **Drinking & Nightlife**
6 Dublin Castle C3
7 Edinboro Castle C4

✪ **Entertainment**
8 Jazz Cafe C3
9 KOKO D4

⊜ **Shopping**
10 Stables Market B2

Hoxton, Shoreditch & Spitalfields

0 200 m
0 0.1 miles

Vortex Jazz Club (1.2mi)

Broadway Market (0.75mi);
Viktor Wynd Museum of Curiosities,
Fine Art & Natural History (0.75mi);
London Fields (1mi);
London Fields Lido (1.2mi)

Geffrye Museum

HOXTON

SHOREDITCH

Corner Room (0.75mi)

Carpenter's Arms (250m)

SPITALFIELDS

Dennis Severs' House

★ **Prufrock Coffee**   CAFE £
(Map p94; www.prufrockcoffee.com; 23-25 Leather Lane, EC1N; mains £4-7; ⊙8am-6pm Mon-Fri, 10am-5pm Sat & Sun; 🛜✐; 🚇Farringdon) Not content with being one of the kings of London's coffee-bean scene (it offers barista training and workshops in 'latte art'), Prufrock also dishes up delicious breakfasts, lunches and cuppa-friendly pastries and snacks. Judging by the number of laptops, plenty of customers treat it as their office.

Hoxton, Shoreditch & Spitalfields

⊚ **Top Sights**
1 Dennis Severs' House C5
2 Geffrye Museum C1

🛏 **Sleeping**
3 Hoxton Hotel B4

🍴 **Eating**
4 Brawn D2
5 Brick Lane Beigel Bake D4
6 Poppies D5
7 Sông Quê C2

🍸 **Drinking & Nightlife**
8 Book Club.. B4

9 BrewDog D4
10 Cargo... C3
11 Happiness Forgets B3
12 Sager + Wilde....................................... D1
13 Ten Bells D6
14 Worship St Whistling Shop A5
15 XOYO... A3

🎭 **Entertainment**
16 Comedy Cafe Theatre.......................... B3

🛍 **Shopping**
17 Old Spitalfields Market C5
18 Rough Trade East D5
19 Sunday UpMarket D5

★**St John**   BRITISH ££

(Map p94; ☎020-7251 0848; www.stjohnrestaurant.com; 26 St John St, EC1M; mains £18-21.50; ⊙noon-3pm & 6-11pm Mon-Fri, 6-11pm Sat, 12.30-4pm Sun; ⊕Farringdon) Whitewashed brick walls, high ceilings and simple wooden furniture keep diners free to concentrate on St John's famous nose-to-tail dishes. Serves are big, hearty and a celebration of England's culinary past. Don't miss the signature roast bone marrow and parsley salad (£8.90).

★**Morito**   TAPAS ££

(Map p94; ☎020-7278 7007; www.morito.co.uk; 32 Exmouth Market, EC1R; tapas £4.50-9.50; ⊙noon-4pm daily, 5-11pm Mon-Sat; 🎤; ⊕Farringdon) This diminutive eatery is a wonderfully authentic take on a Spanish tapas bar, with excellent eats. Seats are at the bar, along the window, or on one of the small tables inside or out. It's relaxed, convivial and often completely crammed; reservations are taken for lunch, but dinner is first come, first served, with couples generally going to the bar.

Little Bay   EUROPEAN ££

(Map p94; ☎020-7278 1234; www.littlebayfarringdon.co.uk; 171 Farringdon Rd, EC1R; mains from £7; ⊙noon-midnight Mon-Sat, to 11pm Sun; ⊕Farringdon) We're talking crushed-velvet ceiling, handmade twisted lamps that improve around the room (as the artist got better) and elaborately painted bar and tables where nymphs frolic. Totally bonkers, but fun. Food is hearty, and good value, with two-course set meals a bargain £10 before 6pm.

✗ Hoxton, Shoreditch & Spitalfields

From the hit-and-miss Bangladeshi restaurants of Brick Lane to the Vietnamese strip on Kingsland Rd, and the Jewish, Spanish, French, Italian and Greek eateries in between, the East End's cuisine is as multicultural as its residents.

Sông Quê   VIETNAMESE £

(Map p120; www.songque.co.uk; 134 Kingsland Rd, E2; mains £7.40-9.50; ⊙noon-3pm & 5.30-11pm Mon-Fri, noon-11pm Sat, noon-10.30pm Sun; ⊕Hoxton) With the kind of demand for seats that most London restaurants can only dream of, this no-frills, hospital-green Vietnamese joint often has a line of people waiting. Feeding the denizens of London for almost 15 years, service can be abrupt, but the food is spot-on, with two dozen types of fantastic *pho* (noodle soup) to choose from.

Brick Lane Beigel Bake   BAKERY £

(Map p120; 159 Brick Lane, E2; bagels £1-4.20; ⊙24hr; ⊕Shoreditch High St) This relic of the Jewish East End still makes a brisk trade serving dirt-cheap homemade bagels (filled with salmon, cream cheese and/or salt beef) to hungry shoppers and late-night boozers.

Poppies   FISH & CHIPS ££

(Map p120; www.poppiesfishandchips.co.uk; 6-8 Hanbury St, E1; mains £5.90-18; ⊙11am-11pm Mon-Thu, to 11.30pm Fri & Sat, to 10.30pm Sun; 🎤; ⊕Shoreditch High St) This glorious re-creation of a 1950s East End chippy comes complete with waitresses in pinnies and hairnets, and Blitz memorabilia. As well as the usual fishy suspects, it does those old-time London staples – jellied eels and mushy peas – plus kid-pleasing, sweet-tooth desserts (sticky toffee pudding or apple pie with ice cream) and a wine list.

✖ The East End

★ Corner Room   MODERN BRITISH ££

(✆ 020-7871 0460; www.townhallhotel.com/cornerroom; Patriot Sq, E2; mains £10-14, 2/3-course lunch £19/23; ⏱ 7.30-10am Mon-Fri, 7.30-10.30am Sat & Sun, noon-3pm Mon-Thu, noon-4pm Fri-Sun, 6-10pm Mon-Wed & Sun, 6-10.30pm Thu-Sat; ⊖ Bethnal Green) Someone put this baby in the corner, but we're certainly not complaining. Tucked away on the 1st floor of the Town Hall Hotel, this relaxed restaurant serves expertly crafted dishes with complex yet delicate flavours, highlighting the best of British seasonal produce. The six-course tasting menu is £45.

★ Brawn   BRITISH, FRENCH ££

(Map p120; ✆ 020-7729 5692; www.brawn.co; 49 Columbia Rd, E2; mains £11.50-28; ⏱ noon-3pm Tue-Sat, 6-10.30pm Mon-Sat, noon-4pm Sun; ⊖ Hoxton) There's a Parisian bistro feel to this relaxed corner restaurant, yet the menu walks a fine line between British and French traditions. Hence oxtail and veal kidney pie sits alongside plaice Grenobloise, and souffles are filled with Westcombe cheddar. Try its legendary spicy Scotch-egg starter – a Brit classic delivered with French finesse. The three-course Sunday lunch is £28.

Drinking & Nightlife

You need only glance at William Hogarth's Gin Lane prints from 1751 to realise that Londoners and alcohol have more than a passing acquaintance. The metropolis offers a huge variety of venues to wet your whistle in – from neighbourhood pubs to all-night clubs, and everything in between.

🍷 West End

Lamb & Flag   PUB

(Map p66; www.lambandflagcoventgarden.co.uk; 33 Rose St, WC2; ⏱ 11am-11pm Mon-Sat, noon-10.30pm Sun; 🐾; ⊖ Covent Garden) Pocket-sized Lamb & Flag is brimful of charm and history, squeezed into an alley (where poet John Dryden was mugged in December 1679) on the site of a pub that dates to at least 1772. Rain or shine, you'll have to elbow your way to the bar through the merry crowd drinking outside. Inside are brass fittings and creaky wooden floors.

★ Dukes Bar   COCKTAIL BAR

(Map p66; ✆ 020-7491 4840; www.dukeshotel.com; 35 St James's Pl, SW1; ⏱ 2-11pm Mon-Sat, 4-10.30pm Sun; 🐾; ⊖ Green Park) Sip to-die-for martinis like royalty in a gentleman's-club-like ambience at this tidily tucked-away classic bar where white-jacketed masters mix up some awesomely good preparations. Ian Fleming used to drink here, perhaps perfecting his 'shaken, not stirred' Bond maxim. Smokers can ease into the secluded Cognac and Cigar Garden to light up (but cigars must be purchased here).

★ American Bar   BAR

(Map p89; www.thebeaumont.com; The Beaumont, Brown Hart Gardens, W1; ⏱ 11.30am-midnight Mon-Sat, to 11pm Sun; 🐾; ⊖ Bond St) Sip a bourbon or a classic cocktail in the classic 1930s art-deco striped-walnut ambience of this stylish bar at the hallmark Beaumont hotel (p107). It's central, period and like a gentleman's club, but far from stuffy. Only a few years old, the American Bar feels like its been pouring drinks since the days of the Eton Crop and the Jazz Age.

★ American Bar   COCKTAIL BAR

(Map p66; www.fairmont.com/savoy-london/dining/americanbar; The Strand, WC2; ⏱ 11.30am-midnight Mon-Sat, noon-midnight Sun; ⊖ Covent Garden) Home of the Hanky Panky, White Lady and other classic infusions invented here, the seriously dishy and elegant American Bar is an icon of London, with soft cream and blue deco lines and live piano. Cocktails start at £16.50 and peak at a stupefying £5000 (The Original Sazerac, containing Sazerac de Forge from 1857).

Galvin at Windows   BAR

(Map p60; www.galvinatwindows.com; London Hilton on Park Lane, 28th fl, 22 Park Lane, W1; ⏱ 11am-1am Mon-Wed, 11am-2am Thu-Fri, 3pm-2am Sat, 11am-11pm Sun; 🐾; ⊖ Hyde Park Corner) On the 28th floor of the London Hilton on Park Lane, this swish bar gazes on to awesome views, especially come dusk. Cocktail prices reach similar heights (£12 to £40) but the leather seats are inviting and the marble bar is gorgeous. The one-Michelin-star restaurant (same views) offers a giveaway lunch menu (two/three courses £28/33; Monday to Friday).

Connaught Bar   COCKTAIL BAR

(Map p86; www.the-connaught.co.uk; Connaught Hotel, Carlos Pl, W1; ⏱ 4pm-1am Mon-Sat, to midnight Sun; ⊖ Bond St) Drinkers who know their stuff single out the Martini trolley for particular praise, but almost everything at this sumptuous bar at the exclusive and very British Connaught Hotel gets the nod: lavish deco-inspired lines, excruciating attention to detail, faultless service, and some of the best drinks in town. Cocktails, classic and those given a thoroughly contemporary twist, start at £17.

Rivoli Bar
COCKTAIL BAR

(Map p66; www.theritzlondon.com/rivoli-bar; Ritz, 150 Piccadilly, W1; ☺11.30am-11.30pm Mon-Sat, noon-10.30pm Sun; ☎; ⊖Green Park) You may not quite need a diamond as big as the Ritz to drink at this art-deco marvel, but it always helps. All camphor wood, illuminated glass, golden ceiling domes and stunning cocktails, the bar is a lavish art-deco gem. Unlike in some other parts of the Ritz, dress code at the Rivoli is smart casual.

Gordon's Wine Bar
BAR

(Map p66; www.gordonswinebar.com; 47 Villiers St, WC2; ☺11am-11pm Mon-Sat, noon-10pm Sun; ⊖Embankment) Cavernous, dark, candlelit, atmospheric and founded in 1890, Gordon's is a victim of its own success – it's relentlessly busy and unless you arrive before the office crowd does (around 6pm), forget about landing a table. The French and New World wines are heady and reasonably priced. You can nibble on bread, cheese and olives and there's outside garden seating in summer.

French House
BAR

(Map p66; www.frenchhousesoho.com; 49 Dean St, W1; ☺noon-11pm Mon-Sat, to 10.30pm Sun; ⊖Leicester Sq) French House is Soho's legendary boho boozer with a history to match: this was the meeting place of the Free French Forces during WWII, and De Gaulle is said to have drunk here often, while Dylan Thomas, Peter O'Toole and Francis Bacon all ended up on the wooden floor at least once.

🍸 The City

⭐ Sky Pod
BAR

(Map p72; ☑0333-772 0020; http://skygarden.london/sky-pod-bar; 20 Fenchurch St, EC3; ☺7am-1am Mon, 7am-2am Tue-Fri, 8am-2am Sat, 9am-midnight Sun; ⊖Monument) One of the best places in the City to get high is the Sky Pod in the Sky Garden on level 35 of the so-called Walkie Talkie. The views are nothing short of phenomenal – especially from the open-air South Terrace – the gardens are lush and it's the only place where this obstructive and clumsy-looking building won't be in your face.

Madison
COCKTAIL BAR

(Map p72; ☑020-3693 5160; www.madisonlondon.net; Rooftop Terrace, One New Change, EC4; ☺11am-midnight Mon-Wed, to 1am Thu-Sat, to 9pm Sun; ⊖St Paul's) Perched atop One New Change with a drop-dead view of St Paul's and beyond, Madison offers one of the largest public open-air roof terraces you'll ever encounter. There's a full restaurant and bar on one side and a cocktail bar with outdoor seating on the other. We come for the latter. Drinkers must be over 21; dress code is smart casual.

Ye Olde Cheshire Cheese
PUB

(Map p72; ☑020-7353 6170; Wine Office Court, 145 Fleet St, EC4; ☺11.30am-11pm Mon-Fri, noon-11pm Sat; ⊖Chancery Lane) The entrance to this historic pub is via a narrow alley off Fleet St. Over its long history, locals have included Dr Johnson, Thackeray and Dickens. Despite (or possibly because of) this, the Cheshire can feel a bit like a museum. Nevertheless it's one of London's most famous and historic pubs and well worth popping in for a pint.

🍸 South Bank

⭐ Little Bird Gin
COCKTAIL BAR

(www.littlebirdgin.com; Maltby St, SE1; ☺10am-4pm Sat, from 11am Sun; ⊖London Bridge) The South London–based distillery opens a pop-up bar in a workshop on **Maltby Street Market** (www.maltby.st; Maltby St, SE1; ☺9am-4pm Sat, 11am-4pm Sun; ⊖London Bridge) to ply merry punters with devilishly good cocktails (£5 to £7), served in jam jars or apothecary's glass bottles.

⭐ Oblix
BAR

(Map p80; www.oblixrestaurant.com; 32nd fl, Shard, 31 St Thomas St, SE1; ☺noon-11pm; ⊖London Bridge) On the 32nd floor of the Shard (p78), Oblix offers mesmerising vistas of London. You can come for anything from a coffee (£3.50) to a cocktail (from £10) and enjoy virtually the same views as the official viewing galleries of the Shard (but at a reduced cost and with the added bonus of a drink). Live music every night from 7pm.

Ministry of Sound
CLUB

(Map p80; www.ministryofsound.com; 103 Gaunt St, SE1; entry £10-22; ☺10pm-6.30am Fri, 11am-7am Sat; ⊖Elephant & Castle) This legendary club-cum-enormous-global-brand (four bars, three dance floors) lost some 'edge' in the early noughties but, after pumping in top DJs, firmly rejoined the top club ranks. Friday is the Gallery trance night, while

GAY & LESBIAN LONDON

The West End, particularly Soho, is the visible centre of gay and lesbian London, with venues clustered around Old Compton St and its surrounds. However, Soho doesn't hold a monopoly on gay life. Generally, London is a safe place for lesbians and gays. It's rare to encounter any problem with sharing rooms or holding hands in the inner city, although it would pay to keep your wits about you at night and be conscious of your surroundings.

Some venues to get you started include the following:

Village (Map p66; www.village-soho.co.uk; 81 Wardour St, W1; ⊙ 5pm-1am Mon-Tue, to 2am Wed-Sat, to 11.30pm Sun; ⊖ Piccadilly Circus) The Village is always up for a party, whatever the night of the week. There are karaoke nights, 'discolicious' nights, go-go-dancer nights – take your pick. And if you can't wait until the clubs open to strut your stuff, there is a dance floor downstairs, complete with pole, of course. Open till 3am on the last weekend of the month.

She Soho (Map p66; ☑ 020-7287 5041; www.she-soho.com; 23a Old Compton St, W1D; ⊙ 4-11.30pm Mon-Thu, to 12.30am Fri & Sat, to 10.30pm Sun; ⊖ Leicester Sq) Soho lost a lesbian bar (Candy Bar) but gained another with this intimate and dimly lit basement place with DJs at weekends, comedy, cabaret, live music and party nights. Open till 3am on the last Friday and Saturday of the month.

Heaven (Map p66; www.heavennightclub-london.com; Villiers St, WC2; ⊙ 11pm-5am Mon, Thu & Fri, 10pm-5am Sat; ⊖ Embankment or Charing Cross) This 37-year-old, perennially popular gay club under the arches beneath Charing Cross station is host to excellent live gigs and club nights. Monday's Popcorn (mixed dance party, all-welcome door policy) offers one of the best weeknight's clubbing in the capital. The celebrated G-A-Y takes place here on Thursday (G-A-Y Porn Idol), Friday (G-A-Y Camp Attack) and Saturday (plain ol' G-A-Y).

Duke of Wellington (Map p66; 77 Wardour St, W1; ⊙ noon-midnight Mon-Fri, 11am-midnight Sat, noon-11.30pm Sun; ⊖ Leicester Sq) This seasoned pub off Old Compton St is often busy but has few pretensions, attracting a more beardy, fun-loving gay crowd, many of whom gather outside in warmer months.

RVT (Royal Vauxhall Tavern; www.rvt.org.uk; 372 Kennington Lane, SE11; entry £4-8; ⊙ 7pm-midnight Mon-Thu, 9pm-3am Fri, 9pm-2am Sat, 3pm-midnight Sun; ⊖ Vauxhall) Rough around the edges to say the least, the Royal Vauxhall Tavern is the perfect antidote to the gleaming new wave of uppity gay venues now crowding Vauxhall's gay village. Saturday's Duckie, tagged 'London's Authentic Honky Tonk', is the club's signature queer performance night, while Sunday Social is cabaret and dance, till midnight.

Two Brewers (www.the2brewers.com; 114 Clapham High St, SW4; admission after 10pm £3-6; ⊙ 4pm-2am Sun-Thu, to 4am Fri & Sat; ⊖ Clapham Common) Clapham exudes an inner suburban feel, the High St in particular, but the long-standing Two Brewers endures as one of the best London gay bars outside the gay villages of Soho, Shoreditch and Vauxhall. Here there's a friendly, laid-back, local crowd who come for a quiet drink during the week and some madcap cabaret and dancing at weekends.

Saturday sessions offer the crème de la crème of house, electro and techno DJs.

🍺 Chelsea & Kensington

Queen's Arms   PUB
(Map p86; www.thequeensarmskensington.co.uk; 30 Queen's Gate Mews, SW7; ⊙ noon-11pm Mon-Sat, to 10.30pm Sun; ⊖ Gloucester Rd) Just around the corner from the Royal Albert Hall, this godsend of a blue-grey painted pub in an adorable cobbled mews setting off bustling Queen's Gate beckons with a cosy interior and a right royal selection of ales – including selections from small, local cask brewers – and ciders on tap.

The fine pub menu can sew up din-dins, with burger-and-a-beer offers on Mondays for a tenner.

🍺 Bloomsbury & St Pancras

Big Chill House   PUB
(Map p94; www.wearebigchill.com; 257-259 Pentonville Rd, N1; ⊙ 11am-midnight Sun-Wed, to 1am Thu, to 3am Fri & Sat; ☎; ⊖ King's Cross St Pan-

cras) Come the weekend, the only remotely chilled-out space in this large, buzzy Victorian pub is its first-rate and generously proportioned rooftop terrace. It's run by the people behind the Big Chill record label, so it can be counted on for a varied roster of live music and DJs. The sound system is fantastic and entry is free most nights.

Queen's Larder
PUB

(Map p94; www.queenslarder.co.uk; 1 Queen Sq, WC1; ⊘ 11.30am-11pm Mon-Sat, noon-10.30pm Sun; ☻ Russell Sq) In a lovely square southeast of Russell Sq is this pub, so called because Queen Charlotte, wife of 'Mad' King George III, rented part of the pub's cellar to store special foods for her husband while he was being treated nearby. It's a tiny but wonderfully cosy pub; there are benches outside for fair-weather fans and a dining room upstairs.

69 Colebrooke Row
COCKTAIL BAR

(www.69colebrookerow.com; 69 Colebrooke Row, N1; ⊘ 5pm-midnight Sun-Thu, to 2am Fri & Sat; ☻ Angel) Also known as 'the bar with no name', this tiny establishment may be nothing much to look at, but it has a stellar reputation for its cocktails (£10.50). The seasonal drinks menu is steeped in ambitious flavours and blends, with classic drinks for more conservative palates. Hard to find a seat at the best of times, so make sure you book ahead.

Draft House
BAR

(Map p66; www.drafthouse.co.uk; 43 Goodge St, W1; ⊘ noon-11pm Mon-Thu, to midnight Fri & Sat; ☏; ☻ Goodge St) Although you can line your tummy with good nosh, Draft House is largely about the beer choice it crams into its pea-sized premises. This is a public house for ale aficionados, where you can happily corner a Flying Dog Gonzo Imperial Porter or a head-spinning Samichlaus 14%.

Notting Hill, Bayswater & Paddington

★ Troubadour
BAR

(www.troubadour.co.uk; 263-267 Old Brompton Rd, SW5; ⊘ 8.30am-midnight; ☏; ☻ Earl's Court) On a compatible spiritual plane to Paris' Shakespeare and Company Bookshop, this eccentric, time-warped and convivial boho bar-cafe has been serenading drinkers since the 1950s. (Deep breath) Adele, Paolo Nutini, Joni Mitchell and (deeper breath) Jimi Hendrix and Bob Dylan have performed here, and there's still live music (folk, blues) and a large, pleasant garden open in summer.

Windsor Castle
PUB

(Map p110; www.thewindsorcastlekensington.co.uk; 114 Campden Hill Rd, W11; ⊘ noon-11pm Mon-Sat, to 10.30pm Sun; ☏; ☻ Notting Hill Gate) A classic tavern on the brow of Campden Hill Rd, this place has history, nooks and charm on tap. It's worth the search for its historic compartmentalised interior, roaring fire (in winter), delightful beer garden (in summer) and affable regulars (most always). According to legend, the bones of Thomas Paine (author of *Rights of Man*) are in the cellar.

Dove
PUB

(☏ 020-8748 9474; www.dovehammersmith.co.uk; 19 Upper Mall, W6; ⊘ 11am-11pm Mon-Sat, noon-10.30pm Sun; ☏; ☻ Hammersmith or Ravenscourt Park) Severely inundated by the epic floodwaters of 1928, this gem of a 17th-century Fuller's pub revels in historic charm and superb Thames views. Scottish poet James Thompson was reputedly inspired to write the lyrics to 'Rule Britannia' here in the 18th century. It was Graham Greene's local, Hemingway and Dylan Thomas drank here, too, and William Morris lived nearby.

Marylebone

Purl
COCKTAIL BAR

(Map p89; ☏ 020-7935 0835; www.purl-london.com; 50-54 Blandford St, W1; ⊘ 5-11.30pm Mon-Thu, to midnight Fri & Sat; ☻ Baker St or Bond St) Purl is a fabulous underground drinking den. Decked out in vintage furniture, it serves original and intriguingly named cocktails (What's Your Poison? or Mr Hyde's No 2) and a punch of the day. It's all subdued lighting and hushed-tone conversations, which only adds to the mysterious air. Booking recommended.

Artesian
BAR

(Map p89; ☏ 020-7636 1000; www.artesian-bar.co.uk; Langham Hotel, 1c Portland Pl, W1; ⊘ 11am-2am Mon-Sat, to midnight Sun; ☏; ☻ Oxford Circus) For a dose of colonial glamour with a touch of Oriental elegance, the sumptuous bar at the Langham hits the mark, though it's often packed. With the largest collection in town, rum is the speciality here and award-winning cocktails (£17) are concocted from the 60 varieties on offer.

Camden Town

★ Dublin Castle
PUB

(Map p119; www.thedublincastle.com; 94 Parkway, NW1; ⊘ 1pm-2am; ☻ Camden Town) There's live punk or alternative bands most nights in this comfortingly grungy pub's back room (cover charges are usually between £4.50 and £7). DJs take over after the bands on Friday, Saturday and Sunday nights.

★ **Edinboro Castle**   PUB
(Map p119; www.edinborocastlepub.co.uk; 57 Mornington Tce, NW1; ⊘noon-11.30pm Mon-Fri, 10am-11.30pm Sat, noon-10.30pm Sun; ☏; ☻Camden Town) Large and relaxed Edinboro enjoys a refined atmosphere, gorgeous furniture perfect for slumping, a fine bar and a full menu. The highlight, however, is the huge beer garden, complete with warm-weather BBQs and foosball table and adorned with coloured lights on long summer evenings.

Clerkenwell & Farringdon

★ **Zetter Townhouse Cocktail Lounge**   COCKTAIL BAR
(Map p94; ☏020-7324 4545; www.thezettertownhouse.com; 49-50 St John's Sq, EC1V; ⊘7.30am-12.45am; ☻Farringdon) Tucked away behind an unassuming door on St John's Sq, this ground-floor bar is quirkily decorated with plush armchairs, stuffed animal heads and a legion of lamps. The cocktail list takes its theme from the area's distilling history – recipes of yesteryear and homemade tinctures and cordials are used to create interesting and unusual tipples. House cocktails are all £10.50.

★ **Ye Olde Mitre**   PUB
(Map p72; www.yeoldemitreholborn.co.uk; 1 Ely Ct, EC1N; ⊘11am-11pm Mon-Fri; ☏; ☻Farringdon) A delightfully cosy historic pub with an extensive beer selection, tucked away in a backstreet off Hatton Garden, Ye Olde Mitre was built in 1546 for the servants of Ely Palace. There's no music, so the rooms only echo with amiable chit-chat. Queen Elizabeth I danced around the cherry tree by the bar, they say. Closed Saturday and Sunday.

Hoxton, Shoreditch & Spitalfields

★ **XOYO**   CLUB
(Map p120; www.xoyo.co.uk; 32-37 Cowper St, EC2A; ⊘hours vary; ☻Old St) This fantastic Shoreditch warehouse club throws together a pulsingly popular mix of gigs, club nights and art events. Always buzzing, the varied line-up – expect indie bands, hip hop, elec-

tro, dubstep and much in between – attracts a mix of clubbers, from skinny-jeaned hipsters to more mature hedonists (but no suits).

★ **Worship St Whistling Shop**   COCKTAIL BAR
(Map p120; ☏020-7247 0015; www.whistlingshop.com; 63 Worship St, EC2A; ⊘5pm-midnight Mon & Tue, to 1am Wed & Thu, to 2am Fri & Sat; ☻Old St) While the name is Victorian slang for a place selling illicit booze, this subterranean drinking den's master mixologists explore the experimental outer limits of cocktail chemistry and aromatic science, as well as concocting the classics. Many ingredients are made with the rotary evaporators in the on-site lab. Cocktail masterclasses also run.

Happiness Forgets   COCKTAIL BAR
(Map p120; www.happinessforgets.com; 8-9 Hoxton Sq, N1; ⊘5-11pm; ☏; ☻Old St) This low-lit, basement bar with good-value cocktails is relaxed and intimate, overseen by considerate and professional staff. You won't want to leave: look for the signs for Ruby cafe and take the stairs heading down. It's worth reserving.

BrewDog   BAR
(Map p120; www.brewdog.com; 51-55 Bethnal Green Rd, E1; ⊘noon-midnight; ☏; ☻Shoreditch High St) BrewDog is an ale aficionado's paradise, with 18 different brews on tap, hundreds by the bottle and Dirty Burgers to soak it all up with. Its own crowd-funded ecobrewery sits up in Scotland, near Aberdeen, but it stocks plenty of other microbrewery beers, too.

Book Club   BAR
(Map p120; ☏020-7684 8618; www.wearetbc.com; 100-106 Leonard St, EC2A; ⊘8am-midnight Mon-Wed, to 2am Thu & Fri, 10am-2am Sat, 10am-midnight Sun; ☏; ☻Old St) A creative vibe animates this fantastic one-time Victorian warehouse, which hosts DJs and oddball events (life drawing, workshops, twerking lessons, the Crap Film Club) to complement the drinking and enthusiastic ping-pong and pool playing. Food is served throughout the day and there's a scruffy basement bar below.

Sager + Wilde   WINE BAR
(Map p120; www.sagerandwilde.com; 193 Hackney Rd, E2; ⊘5pm-midnight Mon-Fri, 2pm-midnight Sat & Sun; ☏; ☻Hoxton) A handsome addition to the East End drinking scene, this quietly stylish wine bar offers a modish bar-

bites menu, an eye-catching glass-brick bar counter and excellent wines by the bottle and glass. There are a few outdoor tables for street-side supping.

Ten Bells

PUB

(Map p120; www.tenbells.com; 84 Commercial St, E1; ⊘ noon-midnight Sun-Wed, to 1am Thu-Sat; ☎; ⊜ Shoreditch High St) With its large windows and beautiful tiles, this landmark Victorian pub is perfectly positioned for a pint after a wander around Spitalfields Market. The most famous Jack the Ripper pub, it was patronised by his last victim before her grisly end – and possibly by the serial killer himself. Gin menu and homemade pork scratchings offered.

Cargo

BAR, CLUB

(Map p120; www.cargo-london.com; 83 Rivington St, EC2A; ⊘ noon-1am Sun-Thu, to 3am Fri & Sat; ⊜ Shoreditch High St) Cargo is one of London's most eclectic clubs. Under its brick railway arches you'll find a dance floor, bar and outside terrace adorned with two original Banksy images. The music policy (hip hop, pop, R&B, club classics) is varied, with plenty of up-and-coming bands also in the line-up. Food is available throughout the day.

The East End

★ Prospect of Whitby

PUB

(57 Wapping Wall, E1; ⊘ noon-11pm; ☎; ⊜ Wapping) Once known as the Devil's Tavern, the Whitby is said to date from 1520, making it the oldest riverside pub in London. Famous patrons have included Charles Dickens and Samuel Pepys. It's firmly on the tourist trail, but there's a smallish terrace overlooking the Thames, a restaurant upstairs, open fires in winter and a pewter-topped bar.

★ Carpenter's Arms

PUB

(www.carpentersarmsfreehouse.com; 73 Cheshire St, E2; ⊘ 4-11.30pm Mon-Wed, noon-11.30pm Thu & Sun, noon-12.30pm Fri & Sat; ☎; ⊜ Shoreditch High St) Once owned by infamous gangsters the Kray brothers (who bought it for their old ma to run), this chic yet cosy pub has been beautifully restored and its many wooden surfaces positively gleam. A back room and small yard provide a little more space for the convivial drinkers. There's a huge range of draught and bottled beers and ciders.

Greenwich

★ Cutty Sark Tavern

PUB

(www.cuttysarktavern.co.uk; 4-6 Ballast Quay, SE10; ⊘ 11am-11pm Mon-Sat, noon-10.30pm Sun; ⊠ DLR Cutty Sark) Housed in a delightful bow-windowed, wood-beamed Georgian building directly on the Thames, the Cutty Sark is one of the few independent pubs left in Greenwich. Half a dozen cask-conditioned ales on tap line the bar, there's an inviting riverside seating area opposite and an upstairs dining room looking out on to glorious views. It's a 10-minute walk from the DLR station.

Trafalgar Tavern

PUB

(☑ 020-8858 2909; www.trafalgartavern.co.uk; 6 Park Row, SE10; ⊘ noon-11pm Mon-Thu, noon-midnight Fri, 10am-midnight Sat, 10am-11pm Sun; ⊠ DLR Cutty Sark) This elegant tavern with big windows overlooking the Thames is steeped in history. Dickens apparently knocked back a few here – and used it as the setting for the wedding breakfast scene in *Our Mutual Friend* – and prime ministers Gladstone and Disraeli used to dine on the pub's celebrated whitebait.

Hampstead & Highgate

★ Holly Bush

PUB

(www.hollybushhampstead.co.uk; 22 Holly Mount, NW3; ⊘ noon-11pm Mon-Sat, to 10.30pm Sun; ☎ ♿; ⊜ Hampstead) This beautiful Grade II–listed Georgian pub opens to an antique interior, with a secluded hilltop location, open fires in winter and a knack for making you stay longer than you planned. Set above Heath St, it's reached via the Holly Bush Steps.

Outside Central London

★ White Cross

PUB

(www.thewhitecrossrichmond.com; Water Lane, TW9; ⊘ 10am-11pm Mon-Sat, to 10.30pm; ☎; ⊜ Richmond) The riverside location and fine food and ales make this bay-windowed pub on the site of a former friary a winner. There are entrances for low and high tides, but when the river is at its highest, Cholmondeley Walk running along the Thames floods and the pub is out of bounds to those not willing to wade. Wellies are provided.

★ City Barge

PUB

(www.metropolitanpubcompany.com/our-pubs/the-city-barge; 27 Strand on the Green, W4; ⊘ noon-

11pm Mon-Thu, noon-midnight Fri, 10am-midnight Sat, 10am-10.30pm Sun; 🛜; ⊜Gunnersbury) In a line of small riverside cottages facing wooded Oliver's Island (where Cromwell is alleged to have taken refuge), this excellent pub looks straight onto the muddy Thames. Once known as the Navigators Arms, there has been a pub here since the Middle Ages (1484, to be exact), although the Luftwaffe gave it a dramatic facelift (as has a recent, attractive refurb).

☆ Entertainment

From West End luvvies to East End geezers, Londoners have always loved a spectacle. With bear-baiting and public executions long on the no-no list, they've fallen back on what London does well: some of the world's best theatre and live-music choices. For a comprehensive list of what to do on any given night, check out *Time Out*, the *Evening Standard* and *Metro*.

☆ Theatre

From West End luvvies to East End geezers, Londoners have always loved a spectacle. With bear-baiting and public executions long on the no-no list, they've fallen back on what London does well: some of the world's best theatre and live-music choices. The term 'West End' – as with Broadway – generally refers to the big-money productions such as musicals, but also includes other heavyweights. Off West End – including venues such as the Almeida and Donmar Warehouse – is where you'll generally find the most original works.

★ Shakespeare's Globe   THEATRE
(Map p80; ☑020-7401 9919; www.shakespeares globe.com; 21 New Globe Walk, SE1; seats £10-43, standing £5; ⊜Blackfriars or London Bridge) If you love Shakespeare and the theatre, the Globe will knock your theatrical socks off. This authentic Shakespearean theatre is a wooden 'O' without a roof over the central stage area, and although there are covered wooden bench seats in tiers around the stage, many people (there's room for 700) do as 17th-century 'groundlings' did, standing in front of the stage.

Because the building is quite open to the elements, you may have to wrap up. Groundlings note: umbrellas are not allowed, but cheap raincoats are on sale. A warning: two pillars holding up the stage canopy (the so-called Heavens) obscure much of the view in section D; you'd almost do better to stand. Unexpected aircraft noise features in some plays.

The theatre season runs from late April to mid-October and includes works by Shakespeare and his contemporaries such as Christopher Marlowe.

If you don't like the idea of standing in the rain or sitting in the cold, opt for an indoor candlelit play in the Sam Wanamaker Playhouse, a Jacobean theatre similar to the one Shakespeare would have used in winter. The programming also includes opera.

★ Wilton's   THEATRE
(☑020-7702 2789; www.wiltons.org.uk; 1 Graces Alley, E1; tour £6; ⊙tours 6pm most Mon, bar 5-11pm Mon-Sat; ⊜Tower Hill) A gloriously atmospheric example of one of London's Victorian public-house music halls, Wilton's hosts a variety of shows, from comedy and classical music to theatre and opera. One-hour guided tours offer an insight into its fascinating history. The Mahogany Bar is a great way to get a taste of the place if you're not attending a performance.

National Theatre   THEATRE
(Map p80; ☑020-7452 3000; www.nationaltheatre. org.uk; South Bank, SE1; ⊙9.30am-11pm Mon-Sat, noon-6pm Sun; ⊜Waterloo) England's flagship theatre (its full name is the Royal National Theatre) showcases a mix of classic and contemporary plays performed by excellent casts in three theatres (Olivier, Lyttelton and Dorfman). Outstanding artistic director Nicholas Hytner oversaw a golden decade at the theatre, with landmark productions such as *War Horse*. His replacement, Rufus Norris, started in April 2015.

Travelex tickets costing just £15 are available to certain performances during the peak period; same-day tickets also cost £15. Under-18s pay half price. Likened by Prince Charles to a nuclear power station, the theatre's purpose-designed architecture is considered an icon of the Brutalist school.

Almeida   THEATRE
(☑020-7359 4404; www.almeida.co.uk; Almeida St, N1; £10-38; ⊜Highbury or Islington) Housed in a Grade II–listed Victorian building, this plush 325-seat theatre can be relied on for imaginative programming.

Donmar Warehouse   THEATRE
(Map p66; ☑0844 871 7624; www.donmarware house.com; 41 Earlham St, WC2; ⊜Covent Garden) The cosy Donmar Warehouse is London's

FOOTBALL IN LONDON

As the capital of a football-mad nation, expect half of London to be watching the beautiful game during the cooler months.

Wembley Stadium (☑ 0800 169 9933; www.wembleystadium.com; tours adult/child £19/11; ⊕ Wembley Park) The city's landmark national stadium where England traditionally plays its international matches and where the FA Cup final is contested. Tours visit the England changing rooms, the players' tunnel, the Royal Box and you can get your hands on (a replica of) the FA Cup.

Chelsea (☑ 0871 984 1955; www.chelseafc.com; Stamford Bridge, Fulham Rd, SW6; stadium tours & museum adult/child £20/13; ⊘ museum 9am-5pm, 10am-4pm Sun; ⊕ Fulham Broadway) Tours of Stamford Bridge, Chelsea FC's football ground and access to the museum.

West Ham United (www.whufc.com; Boleyn Ground, Green St, Upton Park, E13; tours adult/child £19/11; ⊕ Upton Park) From the start of the new season in 2016, the Olympics Stadium became West Ham United's new ground. See the website for details of tours.

Tottenham Hotspur (www.tottenhamhotspur.com; White Hart Lane, 748 High Rd, N17; tour adult/child £20/9; ⊠ White Hart Lane) The 90-minute to two-hour tour takes Spurs supporters to all key areas of White Hart Lane, including the players' dressing room.

'thinking person's theatre'. Current artistic director Josie Rourke has staged some intriguing and successful productions, including the well-received comedy *My Night with Reg*.

Royal Court Theatre　　　　THEATRE
(Map p86; ☑ 020-7565 5000; www.royalcourt theatre.com; Sloane Sq, SW1; tickets £12-38; ⊕ Sloane Sq) Equally renowned for staging innovative new plays and old classics, the Royal Court is among London's most progressive theatres and has continued to foster major writing talent across the UK. There are two auditoriums: the main Jerwood Theatre Downstairs, and the much smaller studio Jerwood Theatre Upstairs. Tickets for Monday performances are £10.

Old Vic　　　　THEATRE
(Map p80; ☑ 0844 871 7628; www.oldvictheatre. com; The Cut, SE1; ⊕ Waterloo) American actor Kevin Spacey took the theatrical helm of this stalwart of the London theatre scene in 2003, giving it a new lease of life. He was succeeded in April 2015 by Matthew Warchus (who directed *Matilda the Musical* and the film *Pride*). In 2016, Warchus was directing the musical *Groundhog Day*, which was set to start at the Old Vic.

☆ Live Music

It goes without saying that London is a crucible of musical talent, with young bands gigging around venues citywide.

★ Jazz Cafe　　　　LIVE MUSIC
(Map p119; ☑ 020-7485 6834; www.thejazzcafelon don.com; 5 Parkway, NW1; ⊕ Camden Town) The name would have you think jazz is the main staple, but it's only a small slice of what's on offer. The intimate club-like space also serves up funk, hip hop, R&B, soul and rare groove, with big-name acts regularly dropping in. Saturday club night is soul night.

★ Pizza Express Jazz Club　　　　JAZZ
(Map p66; ☑ 020-7439 4962; www.pizzaexpress live.com; 10 Dean St, W1; admission £10-35; ⊘ live music 7-10.30pm Mon-Thu, 7-11pm Fri & Sat, midday-3.30pm & 6.30-10pm Sun; ⊕ Tottenham Court Rd) Pizza Express has been one of the best jazz venues in London since opening in 1969. It may be a strange arrangement, in a basement beneath the main chain restaurant, but it's highly popular. Lots of big names perform here and promising artists such as Norah Jones, Jamie Cullum and the late Amy Winehouse played here in their early days.

★ 606 Club　　　　BLUES, JAZZ
(☑ 020-7352 5953; www.606club.co.uk; 90 Lots Rd, SW10; ⊘ 7-11.15pm Sun-Thu, 8pm-12.30am Fri & Sat; ⊠ Imperial Wharf) Named after its old address on King's Rd, which cast a spell over jazz lovers London-wide back in the '80s, this fantastic, tucked-away basement jazz club and restaurant gives centre stage to contemporary British-based jazz musicians nightly. The club can only serve alcohol to

people who are dining and it is highly advisable to book to get a table.

★ Vortex Jazz Club   JAZZ
(📞 020-7254 4097; www.vortexjazz.co.uk; 11 Gillet Sq, N16; ⊙ 8pm-midnight; 🚇 Dalston Kingsland) With a fantastically varied menu of jazz, the Vortex hosts an outstanding line-up of musicians, singers and songwriters from the UK, US, Europe, Africa and beyond. It's a small venue so make sure you book if there's an act you particularly fancy.

★ O2 Academy Brixton   LIVE MUSIC
(www.o2academybrixton.co.uk; 211 Stockwell Rd, SW9; ⊙ doors open 7pm most nights; 🚇 Brixton) It's hard to have a bad night at the Brixton Academy, even if you leave with your soles sticky with beer, as this cavernous former-5000-capacity art-deco theatre always thrums with bonhomie. There's a properly raked floor for good views, as well as plenty of bars and an excellent mixed bill of established and emerging talent. Most shows are 14-plus.

★ KOKO   LIVE MUSIC
(Map p119; 📞 020-7388 3222; www.koko.uk.com; 1a Camden High St, NW1; ⊙ 7-11pm Sun-Thu, 6.30pm-4am Fri, from midnight Sat; 🚇 Mornington Cres) Once the legendary Camden Palace, where Charlie Chaplin, the Goons and the Sex Pistols performed, KOKO is maintaining its reputation as one of London's better gig venues. The theatre has a dance floor and decadent balconies and attracts an indie crowd with Club NME on Friday. There are live bands most nights and it has a great roof terrace.

O2 Arena   LIVE MUSIC
(www.theo2.co.uk; Peninsula Sq, SE10; 🚇 North Greenwich) One of the city's major concert venues, hosting all the biggies – the Rolling Stones, Paul Simon and Sting, One Direction, Ed Sheeran and many others – inside the 20,000-capacity arena. It's also a popular venue for sporting events. The smaller Indigo at the O2 seats 2350.

Ronnie Scott's   JAZZ
(Map p66; 📞 020-7439 0747; www.ronniescotts. co.uk; 47 Frith St, W1; ⊙ 7pm-3am Mon-Sat, to midnight Sun; 🚇 Leicester Sq or Tottenham Court Rd) Ronnie Scott originally opened his jazz club on Gerrard St in 1959 under a Chinese gambling den. It moved here six years later and became widely known as Britain's best jazz club. Gigs are at 8.15pm (8pm Sunday) with a second sitting at 11.15pm Friday and Saturday (check though), followed by the more informal Late, Late Show until 3am.

100 Club   LIVE MUSIC
(Map p66; 📞 020-7636 0933; www.the100club. co.uk; 100 Oxford St, W1; admission £8-20; ⊙ check website for gig times; 🚇 Oxford Circus or Tottenham Court Rd) This legendary London venue has always concentrated on jazz, but also features swing and rock. It's showcased Chris Barber, BB King and the Stones, and was at the centre of the punk revolution and the '90s indie scene. It hosts dancing swing gigs and local jazz musicians, the occasional big name, where-are-they-now bands and top-league tributes.

☆ Classical Music

With a raft of world-class symphony orchestras, a batch of opera companies, various smaller ensembles, brilliant venues, reasonable prices and high standards of performance, London is a classical capital. Keep an eye out for the free (or nearly so) lunchtime concerts held in many of the city's churches.

Royal Albert Hall   CONCERT VENUE
(Map p86; 📞 0845 401 5034; www.royalalberthall. com; Kensington Gore, SW7; 🚇 South Kensington) This splendid Victorian concert hall hosts classical-music, rock and other performances, but is famously the venue for the BBC-sponsored Proms. Booking is possible, but from mid-July to mid-September Proms punters queue for £5 standing (or 'promenading') tickets that go on sale one hour before curtain-up. Otherwise, the box office and prepaid-ticket collection counter are through door 12 (south side of the hall).

Royal Festival Hall   CONCERT VENUE
(Map p80; 📞 0844 875 0073; www.southbankcentre. co.uk; Southbank Centre, Belvedere Rd, SE1; admission £6-60; 🚇; 🚇 Waterloo) The hall's amphitheatre seats 3000 and is one of the best places for catching world- and classical-music artists. The sound is fantastic, the programming impeccable and there are frequent free gigs in the wonderfully expansive foyer.

Barbican   PERFORMING ARTS
(Map p72; 📞 box office 020-7638 8891; www.barbican.org.uk; Silk St, EC2; ⊙ box office 10am-8pm Mon-Sat, from 11am Sun; 🚇 Barbican) Home to the wonderful London Symphony Orchestra

and its associate orchestra, the lesser-known BBC Symphony Orchestra, the arts centre also hosts scores of other leading musicians, focusing in particular on jazz, folk, world and soul artists. Dance is another strong point here, while film covers recent releases as well as film festivals and seasons.

☆ Opera & Dance

Royal Opera House OPERA
(Map p66; ☑ 020-7304 4000; www.roh.org.uk; Bow St, WC2; tickets £7-250; ⊖ Covent Garden) The £210-million redevelopment for the millennium gave classic opera a fantastic setting in London, and coming here for a night is a sumptuous – if pricey – affair. Although the program has been fluffed up by modern influences, the main attractions are still the opera and classical ballet – all are wonderful productions and feature world-class performers.

Midweek matinees are usually cheaper than evening performances and restricted-view seats cost as little as £7. There are same-day tickets (one per customer available to the first 67 people in the queue) from 10am for £8 to £44 and student standby tickets for £10. Half-price standby tickets four hours before the performance are only occasionally available. Free lunchtime recitals are held on Mondays, when possible, in the Crush Room or Paul Hamlyn Hall, depending on the program.

Sadler's Wells DANCE
(Map p94; ☑ 020-7863 8000, 0844 412 4319; www.sadlerswells.com; Rosebery Ave, EC1R; ⊖ Angel) A glittering modern venue that was, in fact, first established in 1683, Sadler's Wells is the most eclectic modern-dance and ballet venue in town, with experimental dance shows of all genres and from all corners of the globe. The Lilian Baylis Studio stages smaller productions.

London Coliseum OPERA
(Map p66; ☑ 020-7845 9300; www.eno.org; St Martin's Lane, WC2; ⊖ Leicester Sq) The London Coliseum is home to the English National Opera (ENO), celebrated for making opera modern and more relevant, as all productions are sung in English. The building, built in 1904 and lovingly restored 100 years later, is very impressive. The English National Ballet also does regular performances at the Coliseum. Tickets range from £12 to £99.

☆ Comedy

Comedy Store COMEDY
(Map p66; ☑ 0844 871 7699; www.thecomedystore.co.uk; 1a Oxendon St, SW1; admission £8-23.50; ⊖ Piccadilly Circus) One of the first (and still one of the best) comedy clubs in London. Wednesday and Sunday night's Comedy Store Players is the most famous improvisation outfit in town, with the wonderful Josie Lawrence; on Thursdays, Fridays and Saturdays' Best in Stand Up features the best on London's comedy circuit.

Comedy Cafe Theatre COMEDY
(Map p120; ☑ 020-7739 5706; www.comedycafetheatre.co.uk; 68 Rivington St, EC2A; admission free-£12; ⊖ Shoreditch High St) This purpose-built comedy venue offers comedy and dinner, with two-hour shows starting at 8pm most Friday and Saturday nights. The free New Act Night on Wednesdays is a good option for some wincing entertainment. The attached **Bedroom Bar** (www.bedroom-bar.co.uk) has live music most nights.

Soho Theatre COMEDY
(Map p66; ☑ 020-7478 0100; www.sohotheatre.com; 21 Dean St, W1; admission £10-25; ⊖ Tottenham Court Rd) The Soho Theatre has developed a superb reputation for showcasing new comedy-writing talent and comedians. It's also hosted some top-notch stand-up or sketch-based comedians including Alexei Sayle and Doctor Brown, plus cabaret.

☆ Cinemas

Glitzy premieres usually take place in one of the mega multiplexes in Leicester Sq.

Electric Cinema CINEMA
(Map p110; ☑ 020-7908 9696; www.electriccinema.co.uk; 191 Portobello Rd, W11; tickets £8-22.50; ⊖ Ladbroke Grove) Having notched up its first centenary a few years back, the Electric is one of the UK's oldest cinemas, updated. Avail yourself of the luxurious leather armchairs, sofas, footstools and tables for food and drink in the auditorium, or select one of the six front-row double beds! Tickets are cheapest on Mondays.

Prince Charles CINEMA
(Map p66; www.princecharlescinema.com; 7 Leicester Pl, WC2; tickets £8-16; ⊖ Leicester Sq) Leicester Sq cinema-ticket prices are brutal, so wait until the first-runs have moved to the Prince Charles, central London's cheapest

HARRY POTTER SHOP

With Pottermania refusing to die down and Diagon Alley impossible to find, if your junior witches and wizards are seeking a wand of their own, take the family directly to King's Cross Station to **Harry Potter Shop at Platform 9¾** (Map p94; www.harrypotterplatform934. com; King's Cross Station, N1; ⏰8am-10pm Mon-Sat, 9am-9pm Sun; King's Cross St Pancras). This little wood-panelled store also stocks jumpers sporting the colours of Hogwarts' four houses (Gryffindor having pride of place) and assorted merchandise, including, of course, the books.

cinema, where nonmembers pay only £8 to £10 for new releases. Also on the cards are minifestivals, Q&As with film directors, classics, sleepover movie marathons and exuberant sing-along screenings of *Frozen, The Sound of Music* and *Rocky Horror Picture Show*.

BFI Southbank   CINEMA
(Map p80; ☑020-7928 3232; www.bfi.org.uk; Belvedere Rd, SE1; tickets £8-12; ⏰11am-11pm; Waterloo) Tucked almost out of sight under the arches of Waterloo Bridge is the British Film Institute, containing four cinemas that screen thousands of films each year (mostly art house), a gallery devoted to the moving image and the mediatheque, where you watch film and TV highlights from the BFI National Archive.

☆ Rugby

World Rugby Museum   MUSEUM
(☑020-8892 8877; www.rfu.com; adult/child £8/6, with tour £20/12; ⏰10am-5pm Tue-Sat, 11am-5pm Sun) In the east stand of Twickenham Stadium, this museum exhibits the world's largest and most comprehensive collection of rugby memorabilia.Tours are an extra feature.

☆ Cricket & Tennis

Wimbledon Championships   SPECTATOR SPORT
(☑020-8944 1066; www.wimbledon.com/championships/tickets) For a few weeks each June and July, the sporting world's attention is fixed on the quiet southern suburb of Wimbledon, as it has been since 1877. Most show-court tickets for the Wimbledon Champi-

onships are allocated through public ballot, applications for which usually begin in early August of the preceding year and close at the end of December.

Entry into the ballot does not mean entrants will get a ticket. A quantity of show-court, outer-court, ground tickets and late-entry tickets are also available if you queue on the day of play, but if you want a show-court ticket it is recommended you camp the night before in the queue. See www.wimbledon.com for details.

Lord's   STADIUM
(☑tour info 020-7616 8595; www.lords.org; St John's Wood Rd, NW8; tours adult/child £20/12; ⏰tours hourly 10am-3pm; St John's Wood) The 'home of cricket' is a must for any devotee of this particularly English game. Book early for the Test matches here, but cricket buffs should also take the absorbing and anecdote-filled 100-minute tour of the ground and facilities. Tours take in the famous Long Room, where members watch the games surrounded by portraits of cricket's great and good, and a museum featuring evocative memorabilia that will appeal to fans old and new.

Oval   SPECTATOR SPORT
(☑0844 375 1845; www.kiaoval.com; Kennington, SE11; international match £20-350, county £20-35; Oval) Home to the Surrey County Cricket Club, the Oval is London's second cricketing venue after Lord's. As well as Surrey matches, it also regularly hosts international test matches. Getting tickets for county games is relatively straightforward, but it's much harder for international fixtures. The season runs from April to September.

🛍 Shopping

From charity-shop finds to designer bags, there are thousands of ways to spend your hard-earned cash in London. Many of the big-name shopping attractions, such as Harrods, Hamleys, Camden Market and Old Spitalfields Market, have become must-sees in their own right. Chances are that with so many temptations, you'll give your wallet a full workout.

🛍 West End

Oxford St is the place for high-street fashion, while Regent St cranks it up a notch. Bond St has designers galore, Savile Row is all about bespoke tailoring and Jermyn St is the place for smart clobber (particularly shirts).

★ Fortnum & Mason   DEPARTMENT STORE

(Map p66; www.fortnumandmason.com; 181 Picca-dilly, W1; ⊙10am-9pm Mon-Sat, 11.30am-6pm Sun; ⊖Piccadilly Circus) With its classic *eau de nil* colour scheme, London's oldest grocery store (established 1707), refuses to yield to modern times. Its staff still clad in old-fashioned tailcoats, its glamorous food hall supplied with hampers, cut marmalade, speciality teas and so forth, Fortnum and Mason is *the* quintessential London shopping experience.

Hatchards   BOOKS

(Map p66; www.hatchards.co.uk; 187 Piccadilly, W1; ⊙9.30am-8pm Mon-Sat, noon-6.30pm Sun; ⊖Green Park or Piccadilly Circus) London's oldest bookshop dates to 1797. Holding three royal warrants (hence the portrait of the Queen), it's a stupendous independent bookstore, with a solid supply of signed editions and bursting at its smart seams with very browsable stock. There's a strong selection of first editions on the ground floor as well as regular literary events.

Selfridges   DEPARTMENT STORE

(Map p89; www.selfridges.com; 400 Oxford St, W1; ⊙9.30am-10pm Mon-Sat, 11.30am-6pm Sun; ⊖Bond St) Selfridges loves innovation – it's famed for its inventive window displays by international artists, gala shows and, above all, its amazing range of products. It's the trendiest of London's one-stop shops, with labels such as Boudicca, Luella Bartley, Emma Cook, Chloé and Missoni; an unparalleled food hall; and Europe's largest cosmetics department.

Liberty   DEPARTMENT STORE

(Map p66; www.liberty.co.uk; Great Marlborough St, W1; ⊙10am-8pm Mon-Sat, noon-6pm Sun; ⊖Oxford Circus) An irresistible blend of contemporary styles in an old-fashioned mock-Tudor atmosphere, Liberty has a huge cosmetics department and an accessories floor, along with a breathtaking lingerie section, all at very inflated prices. A classic London souvenir is a Liberty fabric print, especially in the form of a scarf.

Stanford's   BOOKS, MAPS

(Map p66; www.stanfords.co.uk; 12-14 Long Acre, WC2; ⊙9am-8pm Mon-Sat, 11.30am-6pm Sun; ⊖Leicester Sq or Covent Garden) Trading from this address for more than 100 years, this granddaddy of travel bookshops and seasoned seller of maps, guides and literature is a destination in its own right. Ernest Shackleton and David Livingstone and, more recently, Michael Palin and Brad Pitt have all popped in here.

Hamleys   TOYS

(Map p66; www.hamleys.com; 188-196 Regent St, W1; ⊙10am-9pm Mon-Fri, 9.30am-9pm Sat, noon-6pm Sun; ⊖Oxford Circus) Claiming to be the world's oldest (and some say, the largest) toy store, Hamleys moved to its address on Regent St in 1881. From the ground floor – where staff glide UFOs and foam boomerangs through the air with practised nonchalance – to Lego World and a cafe on the 5th floor, it's a layer cake of playthings.

Foyles   BOOKS

(Map p66; www.foyles.co.uk; 107 Charing Cross Rd, WC2; ⊙9.30am-9pm Mon-Sat, 11.30am-6pm Sun; ⊖Tottenham Court Rd) With four miles of shelving, you can bet on finding even the most obscure of titles in London's most legendary bookshop. Once synonymous with chaos, Foyles long ago got its act together and in 2014 moved just down the road into the spacious former home of Central St Martins. Thoroughly redesigned, its stunning new home is a joy to explore.

Cadenhead's Whisky & Tasting Shop   DRINK

(Map p89; www.whiskytastingroom.com; 26 Chiltern St, W1; ⊖Baker St) Scotland's oldest independent bottler of pure, nonblended whisky from local distilleries, this excellent shop is a joy for anyone with a passion for *uisge* (the gaelic word for 'water'). All bottled whiskies derive from individually selected casks, without any filtrations, additions or colouring, guaranteeing purity. Regular whisky tastings are held downstairs (maximum 12 people).

Monmouth Coffee Company   FOOD & DRINKS

(Map p66; www.monmouthcoffee.co.uk; 27 Monmouth St, WC2; pastry & cakes from £2.50; ⊙8am-6.30pm Mon-Sat; ⊖Tottenham Court Rd or Leicester Sq) Essentially a shop selling beans from just about every coffee-growing country, Monmouth, here since 1978, has a few wooden alcoves at the back where you can squeeze in and savour blends from around the world as well as cakes from local patisseries.

🏠 Knightsbridge, Kensington & Chelsea

Knightsbridge draws the hordes with quintessentially English department stores.

LOCAL KNOWLEDGE

LONDON'S MARKETS

Perhaps the biggest draw for visitors are the capital's famed markets. A treasure trove of small designers, unique jewellery pieces, original framed photographs and posters, colourful vintage pieces and bric-a-brac, they are the antidote to impersonal, carbon-copy shopping centres.

The most popular markets are Camden, Old Spitalfields and Portobello Road, which operate most days, but there are dozens of others, such as Brick Lane's excellent Sunday Upmarket, which only pop up on the weekend. Camden and Old Spitalfields are both mainly covered, but even the outdoor markets are busy, rain or shine.

Portobello Road Market (Map p110; www.portobellomarket.org; Portobello Rd, W10; ⊙8am-6.30pm Mon-Wed, Fri & Sat, to 1pm Thu; ⊝Notting Hill Gate or Ladbroke Grove) Lovely on a warm summer's day, Portobello Road Market is an iconic London attraction with an eclectic mix of street food, fruit and veg, antiques, curios, collectables, vibrant fashion and trinkets. Although the shops along Portobello Rd open daily and the fruit and veg stalls (from Elgin Cres to Talbot Rd) only close on Sunday, the busiest day by far is Saturday, when antique dealers set up shop (from Chepstow Villas to Elgin Cres).

Sunday UpMarket (Map p120; www.sundayupmarket.co.uk; Old Truman Brewery, 91 Brick Lane, E1; ⊙10am-5pm Sun; ⊝Shoreditch High St) The best of all the Sunday markets, this workaday covered car park fills up with young designers selling their wares, quirky crafts and a drool-inducing array of food stalls.

Stables Market (Map p119; Chalk Farm Rd, NW1; ⊙10am-6pm; ⊝Chalk Farm) Connected to the Lock Market, the Stables is the best part of the Camden Market complex, with antiques, Asian artefacts, rugs, retro furniture and clothing.

Camden Passage Market (www.camdenpassageislington.co.uk; Camden Passage, N1; ⊙8am-6pm Wed & Sat, 11am-6pm Sun-Tue, Thu & Fri; ⊝Angel) Not to be confused with Camden Market, Camden Passage is a pretty cobbled lane in Islington lined with antique stores, vintage-clothing boutiques and cafes. Scattered along the lane are four separate market areas devoted to antique curios and whatnots. The main market days are Wednesday and Sunday. Stallholders know their stuff, so bargains are rare.

Old Spitalfields Market (Map p120; www.oldspitalfieldsmarket.com; Commercial St, E1; ⊙10am-5pm Mon-Fri, 11am-5pm Sat, 10am-5pm Sun; ⊝Shoreditch High St) Traders have been hawking their wares here since 1638 and it's still one of London's best markets. Today's covered market was built in the late 19th century, with the more modern development added in 2006. Sundays are the biggest and best days, but Thursdays are good for antiques and Fridays for independent fashion. There are plenty of food stalls, too.

Broadway Market (www.broadwaymarket.co.uk; Broadway Market, E8; ⊙9am-5pm Sat; ⊠394) There's been a market down this pretty street since the late 19th century. The focus these days is artisan food, arty knick-knacks, books, records and vintage clothing. Stock up on edible treats then head to London Fields (Richmond Rd, E8; ⊝Hackney Central) for a picnic.

Leadenhall Market (Map p72; www.cityoflondon.gov.uk/things-to-do/leadenhall-market; Whittington Ave, EC3; ⊙10am-6pm Mon-Fri; ⊝Bank or Monument) A visit to this covered mall off Gracechurch St is a step back in time. There's been a market on this site since the Roman era, but the architecture that survives is all cobblestones and late-19th-century Victorian ironwork. Leadenhall Market appears as Diagon Alley in *Harry Potter and the Philosopher's Stone* and an optician's shop was used for the entrance to the Leaky Cauldron wizarding pub in *Harry Potter and the Goblet of Fire*.

Greenwich Market (www.greenwichmarketlondon.com; College Approach, SE10; ⊙10am-5.30pm; ⊠DLR Cutty Sark) One of the smallest of London's ubiquitous markets, but Greenwich Market holds its own in quality. On Tuesdays, Wednesdays, Fridays and weekends, stallholders tend to be small, independent artists, offering original prints, wholesome beauty products, funky jewellery and accessories, cool fashion pieces and so on. On Tuesdays, Thursdays and Fridays, you'll find vintage, antiques and collectables. Loads of street food too.

★ **John Sandoe Books** BOOKS
(Map p86; www.johnsandoe.com; 10 Blacklands Tce, SW3; ⊙9.30am-6.30pm Mon-Sat, 11am-5pm Sun; ⊜Sloane Sq) The perfect antidote to impersonal book superstores, this atmospheric three-storey bookshop in 18th-century premises is a treasure trove of literary gems and hidden surprises. It's been in business for almost 60 years and loyal customers swear by it, while knowledgeable booksellers spill forth with well-read pointers and helpful advice.

Harrods DEPARTMENT STORE
(Map p86; www.harrods.com; 87-135 Brompton Rd, SW1; ⊙10am-9pm Mon-Sat, 11.30am-6pm Sun; ⊜Knightsbridge) Garish and stylish in equal measures, perennially crowded Harrods is an obligatory stop for visitors, from the cash-strapped to the big spenders. The stock is astonishing, as are many of the price tags. High on kitsch, the 'Egyptian Elevator' resembles something out of an Indiana Jones epic, while the memorial fountain to Dodi and Di (lower ground floor) merely adds surrealism.

Harvey Nichols DEPARTMENT STORE
(Map p86; www.harveynichols.com; 109-125 Knightsbridge, SW1; ⊙10am-8pm Mon-Sat, 11.30am-6pm Sun; ⊜Knightsbridge) At London's temple of high fashion, you'll find Chloé and Balenciaga bags, the city's best denim range, a massive make-up hall with exclusive lines and great jewellery. The food hall and in-house restaurant, **Fifth Floor**, are, you guessed it, on the 5th floor. From 11.30am to midday, it's browsing time only.

🏠 Notting Hill, Bayswater & Paddington

Ceramica Blue HOMEWARES
(Map p110; www.ceramicablue.co.uk; 10 Blenheim Cres, W11; ⊙10am-6.30pm Mon-Sat, noon-5pm Sun; ⊜Ladbroke Grove) A lovely spot for colourful, eclectic and handsome crockery, imported from more than a dozen countries. There are Japanese eggshell-glaze teacups, serving plates with tribal South African designs, candelabra from Italy, gorgeous table cloths from Provence, Turkish hand-decorated glass and much more.

🏠 Marylebone

Daunt Books BOOKS
(Map p89; www.dauntbooks.co.uk; 83 Marylebone High St, W1; ⊙9am-7.30pm Mon-Sat, 11am-6pm Sun; ⊜Baker St) An original Edwardian bookshop, with oak panels and gorgeous skylights, Daunt is one of London's loveliest travel bookshops. It has two floors and stocks general fiction and nonfiction titles as well.

🏠 Hoxton, Shoreditch & Spitalfields

★ **Rough Trade East** MUSIC
(Map p120; www.roughtrade.com; Old Truman Brewery, 91 Brick Lane, E1; ⊙9am-9pm Mon-Thu, 9am-8pm Fri, 10am-8pm Sat, 11am-7pm Sun; ⊜Shoreditch High St) No longer directly associated with the legendary record label (home to The Smiths, The Libertines and The Strokes, among many others), but this huge record store is still the best place to come for music of an indie, soul, electronica and alternative bent. Apart from the impressive selection of CDs and vinyl, it also dispenses coffee and stages promotional gigs.

🏠 The East End & Docklands

Westfield Stratford City MALL
(http://uk.westfield.com; Westfield Ave, E20; ⊙10am-9pm Mon-Fri, 9am-9pm Sat, noon-6pm Sun; ⊜Stratford) Right by Queen Elizabeth Olympic Park (p96), this is Britain's third-largest mall – a behemoth containing more than 250 shops, 70 places to eat and drink, a 17-screen Vue cinema, a bowling alley, a 24-hour casino and a Premier Inn hotel. In its first week of trading in 2011, it raked in £20 million from shoppers.

ℹ Information

DANGERS & ANNOYANCES
London is a fairly safe city for its size, so exercising common sense should keep you secure.

If you're getting a cab after a night's clubbing, make sure you go for a black taxi or a licensed minicab firm. Many of the touts operating outside clubs and bars are unlicensed and can therefore be unsafe.

Pickpocketing does happen in London, so keep an eye on your handbag and wallet, especially in bars and nightclubs, and in crowded areas such as the Underground.

EMERGENCY
Police/Fire/Ambulance (📞999)
Rape & Sexual Abuse Support Centre (📞0808 802 9999; www.rasasc.org.uk; ⊙noon-2.30pm & 7-9.30pm)

Samaritans (toll-free 116 123; www.samaritans.org) For anyone in emotional distress.

INTERNET ACCESS

Virtually every hotel in London now provides wi-fi free of charge (only a couple of budget places have it as an add-on).

A huge number of cafes, and an increasing number of restaurants, offer free wi-fi to customers, including chains such as Starbucks, Costa and Pret a Manger.

MEDICAL SERVICES

St Thomas' Hospital (020-7188 7188; www.guysandstthomas.nhs.uk; Westminster Bridge Rd, SE1; ⊖ Waterloo or Westminster) Large hospital across the Thames from Westminster.

University College London Hospital (0845 155 5000, 020-3456 7890; www.uclh.nhs.uk; 235 Euston Rd, NW1; ⊖ Warren St or Euston) One of central London's busiest hospitals.

TOURIST INFORMATION

Visit London (www.visitlondon.com) can fill you in on everything from attractions and events to tours and accommodation.

City of London Information Centre (Map p72; www.visitthecity.co.uk; St Paul's Churchyard, EC4; ⊗ 9.30am-5.30pm Mon-Sat, 10am-4pm Sun; ⊛; ⊖ St Paul's) Multilingual tourist information, fast-track tickets to City attractions and guided walks (adult/child £7/6).

Greenwich Tourist Office (0870 608 2000; www.visitgreenwich.org.uk; Pepys House, 2 Cutty Sark Gardens, SE10; ⊗ 10am-5pm; ℝ DLR Cutty Sark) Has a wealth of information about Greenwich and the surrounding areas. Free daily guided walks leave at 12.15pm and 2.15pm.

ⓘ PLAN YOUR TRIP

Three months before Book weekend performances of top shows; make dinner reservations for renowned restaurants with celebrity chefs; snap up tickets for must-see temporary exhibitions; book accommodation at boutique properties.

One month before Check listings on entertainment sites such as **Time Out** (www.timeout.com/london) for fringe theatre, live music and festivals, and book tickets.

A few days before Check the weather with the **Met Office** (www.met office.gov.uk) .

ⓘ Getting There & Away
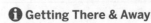

AIR

There are a number of London Airports. For more information, see p684.

BUS

Victoria Coach Station (Map p86; 164 Buckingham Palace Rd, SW1; ⊖ Victoria) Long-distance and international buses arrive and depart fromVictoria coach station, close to the Victoria tube and rail stations.

TRAIN

Main national rail routes are served by a variety of private train-operating companies. Tickets are not cheap, but trains between cities are usually quite punctual. Check **National Rail** (www.nationalrail.co.uk) for timetables and fares.

Eurostar (www.eurostar.com) is the high-speed passenger rail service that links St Pancras International Station with Gare du Nord in Paris (or Bruxelles Midi in Brussels), with between 14 and 16 daily departures. Fares vary enormously, from £69 for the cheapest return to upwards of £300 for a fully flexible return at busy periods.

ⓘ Getting Around

TO/FROM THE AIRPORTS
Gatwick

Gatwick Express (www.gatwickexpress.com; 1-way/return adult £19.90/34.90, 1-way/return child £9.95/17.45) This dedicated train service links the station near the South Terminal with Victoria station in central London every 15 minutes. From the airport, there are services between 4.35am and 12.50am. From Victoria, they leave between 3.30am and at 12.32am. The journey takes 30 minutes.

National Rail (www.nationalrail.co.uk) has regular train services to/from London Bridge (30 minutes, every 15 to 30 minutes), London King's Cross (55 minutes, every 15 to 30 minutes) and London Victoria (30 minutes, every 10 to 15 minutes). Fares vary depending on the time of travel and the train company, but allow £10 to £20 for a single.

National Express (www.nationalexpress.com) coaches (one-way from £6, 80 minutes to two hours) run throughout the day from Gatwick to Victoria Coach station. Services leave hourly around the clock.

EasyBus (www.easybus.co.uk) runs 19-seater minibuses to Gatwick every 15 to 20 minutes on two routes: one from Earl's Court/West Brompton and from Waterloo (one-way from £5.95). The service runs round the clock. Journey time averages 75 minutes.

Heathrow

Heathrow Express (www.heathrowexpress. com; 1-way/return £22/36) This high-speed train whisks passengers from Heathrow Central station (serving Terminals 2 and 3) and Terminal 5 to Paddington in 15 minutes. Terminal 4 passengers should take the free interterminal shuttle train to Heathrow Central and board there. Trains run every 15 minutes from just after 5am in both directions to between 11.25pm (from Paddington) and 11.40pm (from the airport). Three Underground stations on the Piccadilly line serve Heathrow: one for Terminals 2 and 3, another for Terminal 4, and the terminus for Terminal 5. The Underground, commonly referred to as 'the tube' (one-way £5.10, from central London one hour, every three to nine minutes) is the cheapest way of getting to Heathrow. Leaving from the airport, it runs from just after 5am to 11.45pm, and heading to the airport it runs from 5.45am to 12.30am (and all night Friday and Saturday, with reduced frequency). Buy tickets at the station.

National Express (www.nationalexpress.com) coaches (one-way from £6, 35 to 90 minutes, every 30 minutes to one hour) link the Heathrow Central bus station with Victoria coach station. The first bus leaves the Heathrow Central bus station (at Terminals 2 and 3) at 4.40am, with the last departure just before 11pm. The first bus leaves Victoria at 3am, the last just before midnight.

At night, the **N9 bus** (£1.50, 1¼ hours, every 20 minutes) connects Heathrow with central London, terminating at Aldwych.

London City

The **Docklands Light Railway** (DLR; www.tfl. gov.uk/dlr) stops at the London City Airport station (one-way £2.80 to £3.30). The journey to Bank takes just over 20 minutes, and trains go every eight to 10 minutes from just after 5.30am to 12.15am Monday to Saturday, and 7am to 11.15pm Sunday.

Luton

National Rail (www.nationalrail.co.uk) services (one-way from £10, 35 to 50 minutes, every six to 30 minutes, from 7am to 10pm) run from London Bridge and London King's Cross stations to Luton Airport Parkway station, from where an airport shuttle bus (one-way £1.60) will take you to the airport in 10 minutes.

Stansted

Stansted Express (☑ 0845 8500150; www. stanstedexpress.com; one-way/return £19/32) This rail service (45 minutes, every 15 to 30 minutes) links the airport and Liverpool St station. From the airport the first train leaves at 5.30am, the last about 12.30pm. Trains depart Liverpool St station from 3.40am to 11.25pm.

ⓘ INTERNET RESOURCES

Lonely Planet (www.lonelyplanet.com/london) Bookings, traveller forum and more.

Londonist (www.londonist.com) A website about London and everything that happens in it.

Transport for London (www.tfl.gov.uk) Essential tool for staying mobile in the capital.

BBC London (www.bbc.co.uk/news/england/london) The latest news about London.

National Express (www.nationalexpress.com) coaches run around the clock, offering well over 100 services per day. The A6 runs to Victoria coach station (one-way from £12, 85 minutes to more than two hours, every 20 minutes) via North London. The A9 runs to Liverpool St station (one-way from £10, 60 to 80 minutes, every 30 minutes).

EasyBus (www.easybus.co.uk) runs services to Baker St and Old St tube stations every 15 minutes. The journey (one-way from £4.95) takes one hour from Old St, 1¼ hour from Baker St.

Terravision (www.terravision.eu) coaches link Stansted to both Liverpool St train station (bus A51, one-way/return from £8/14, 55 minutes) and Victoria coach station (bus A50, one-way/return from £9/15, 75 minutes) every 20 to 40 minutes between 6am and 1am.

BICYCLE

Like Paris and other European cities, London has its own cycle-hire scheme called **Santander Cycles** (☑ 0343 222 6666; www.tfl.gov.uk/modes/cycling/santander-cycles), also variously referred to as 'Barclays Bikes' after their former sponsor, or 'Boris bikes' after the city's mayor, Boris Johnson (2008–16), who launched the initiative. The bikes have proved as popular with visitors as with Londoners.

The idea is simple: pick up a bike from one of the 700 docking stations dotted around the capital. Cycle. Drop it off at another docking station.

The access fee is £2 for 24 hours. All you need is a credit or debit card. The first 30 minutes are free. It's then £2 for any additional period of 30 minutes.

You can take as many bikes as you like during your access period (24 hours), leaving five minutes between each trip.

The pricing structure is designed to encourage short journeys rather than longer rentals; for those, go to a hire company. You'll also find that although easy to ride, the bikes only have three

OYSTER CARD

The Oyster Card is a smart card on which you can store credit towards 'prepay' fares, as well as Travelcards valid for periods from a day to a year. Oyster Cards are valid across the entire public transport network in London. All you need to do when entering a station is touch your card on a reader (which has a yellow circle with the image of an Oyster Card on it) and then touch again on your way out. The system will then deduct the appropriate amount of credit from your card, as necessary. For bus journeys, you only need to touch once upon boarding.

The benefit lies in the fact that fares for Oyster Card users are lower than standard ones. If you are making many journeys during the day, you will never pay more than the appropriate Travelcard (peak or off-peak) once the daily 'price cap' has been reached.

Oyster Cards can be bought (£5 refundable deposit required) and topped up at any Underground station, travel information centre or shop displaying the Oyster logo.

To get your deposit back along with any remaining credit, simply return your Oyster Card at a ticket booth.

Contactless cards (which do not require chip and pin or a signature) can now be used directly on Oyster Card readers and are subject to the same Oyster fares. The advantage is that you don't have to bother with buying, topping up and then returning an Oyster Card, but foreign visitors should bear in mind the cost of card transactions.

gears and are quite heavy. You must be 18 to buy access and at least 14 to ride a bike.

CAR

London has a congestion charge in place to reduce the flow of traffic into its centre. For full details, log on to www.tfl.gov.uk/roadusers/congestioncharging.

The congestion-charge zone encompasses Euston Rd and Pentonville Rd to the north, Park Lane to the west, Tower Bridge to the east and Elephant and Castle and Vauxhall Bridge Rd to the south. As you enter the zone, you will see a large white 'C' in a red circle.

If you enter the zone between 7am and 6pm Monday to Friday (excluding public holidays), you must pay the £11.50 charge (payable in advance or on the day) or £14 on the first charging day after travel to avoid receiving a fine (£130, or £65 if paid within 14 days).

You can pay online, at newsagents, petrol stations or any shop displaying the 'C' sign.

PUBLIC TRANSPORT
Boat

There are a number of companies operating along the River Thames. Only **Thames Clippers** (www. thamesclippers.com) really offers commuter services, however. It's fast, pleasant and you're almost always guaranteed a seat and a view.

Thames Clipper boats run regular services between Embankment, Waterloo (London Eye), Blackfriars, Bankside (Shakespeare's Globe), London Bridge, Tower Bridge, Canary Wharf, Greenwich, North Greenwich and Woolwich piers (adult/child £7.50/3.75), from 6.55am to around midnight (from 9.29am weekends).

Thames Clipper River Roamer tickets (adult/child £17.35/8.65) give freedom to hop on and hop off boats on most routes all day.

You can get a discount of one-third off the standard fare and off the price of River Roamer tickets if you're a pay-as-you-go Oyster Card holder or Travelcard holder (paper ticket or on Oyster Card). Children under five go free on most boats.

Bus

London's ubiquitous red double-decker buses afford great views of the city, but be aware that the going can be slow, thanks to traffic jams and dozens of commuters getting on and off at every stop.

There are excellent bus maps at every stop detailing all routes and destinations served from that particular area (generally a few bus stops within a two- to three-minute walk, shown on a local map).

Bus services normally operate from 5am to 11.30pm.

➡ More than 50 night-bus routes (prefixed with the letter 'N') run from around 11.30pm to 5am.

➡ There are also another 60 bus routes operating 24 hours; the frequency decreases between 11pm and 5am.

➡ Oxford Circus, Tottenham Court Rd and Trafalgar Sq are the main hubs for night routes.

➡ Night buses can be infrequent and stop only on request, so remember to ring for your stop.

➡ Don't forget the Night Tube which runs along five lines for 24 hours on Fridays and Saturdays, and can either be used as an alternative or in concert with night buses.

Underground, DLR & Overground

The London Underground ('the tube'; 11 colour-coded lines) is part of an integrated-transport system that also includes the Docklands Light Railway (DLR; www.tfl.gov.uk/dlr; a driverless overhead train operating in the eastern part of the city) and Overground network (mostly outside of Zone 1 and sometimes underground). Despite the never-ending upgrades and 'engineering works' requiring weekend closures, it is overall the quickest and easiest way of getting around the city, if not the cheapest.

The first trains operate from around 5.30am Monday to Saturday and 6.45am Sunday. The last trains leave around 12.30am Monday to Saturday and 11.30pm Sunday.

Additionally, selected lines (the Victoria and Jubilee lines, plus most of the Piccadilly, Central and Northern lines) run all night on Fridays and Saturdays to get revellers home, with trains every 10 minutes or so.

During weekend closures, schedules, maps and alternative route suggestions are posted in every station, and staff are at hand to help redirect you.

Some stations, most famously Leicester Sq and Covent Garden, are much closer in reality than they appear on the map.

MINICABS

➤ Minicabs, which are licensed, are cheaper (usually) competitors of black cabs.

➤ Unlike black cabs, minicabs cannot legally be hailed on the street; they must be hired by phone or directly from one of the minicab offices (every high street has at least one and most clubs work with a minicab firm to send revellers home safely).

➤ Don't accept unsolicited offers from individuals claiming to be minicab drivers – they are just guys with cars.

➤ Minicabs don't have meters; there's usually a fare set by the dispatcher. Make sure you ask before setting off.

➤ Your hotel or host will be able to recommend a reputable minicab company in the neighbourhood; every Londoner has the number of at least one company. Or phone a large 24-hour operator such as **Addison Lee** (☑020-7387 8888; www.addisonlee.com).

➤ Apps such as **Uber** (www.uber.com) or **Kabbee** (www.kabbee.com) allow you to book a minicab in double-quick time.

TAXI

The black cab is as much a feature of the London cityscape as the red double-decker bus. Licensed black-cab drivers have the 'Knowledge', acquired after rigorous training and a series of exams. They are supposed to know 25,000 streets within a six-mile radius of Charing Cross/Trafalgar Sq and the 100 most-visited spots of the moment, including clubs and restaurants.

➤ Cabs are available for hire when the yellow sign above the windscreen is lit; just stick your arm out to signal one.

➤ Fares are metered, with the flagfall charge of £2.60 (covering the first 248m during a weekday), rising by increments of 20p for each subsequent 124m.

➤ Fares are more expensive in the evenings and overnight.

➤ You can tip taxi drivers up to 10%, but most Londoners simply round up to the nearest pound.

➤ Apps such as Hailo (www.hailocab.com) use your smartphone's GPS to locate the nearest black cab. You only pay the metered fare.

Canterbury & Southeast England

Includes ➡

Canterbury 141
Margate 150
Broadstairs 151
Ramsgate. 152
Sandwich. 153
Dover 155
Rye 158
Hastings. 161
Lewes 164
Brighton & Hove. 165
Arundel 171
Chichester 172
Farnham. 174

Best Places to Eat

➡ Deeson's (p147)
➡ Allotment (p157)
➡ Iydea (p169)
➡ Terre à Terre (p169)
➡ Town House (p172)

Best Places to Sleep

➡ Bleak House (p152)
➡ Jeake's House (p160)
➡ Wallett's Court (p156)
➡ Reading Rooms (p151)
➡ Hotel Una (p169)

Why Go?

Rolling chalk hills, venerable Victorian resorts, fields of hops and grapes sweetening in the sun: welcome to England's southeast, four soothing counties' worth of country houses, fairy-tale castles and the country's finest food and drink. That fruit-ripening sun shines brightest and longest on the coast, warming a string of seaside towns wedged between formidable chalk cliffs. There's something for everyone here, from the medieval quaintness of Sandwich to the bohemian spirit of hedonistic Brighton and the more genteel grandeur of Eastbourne.

The southeast is also pock-marked with reminders of darker days. The region's position as the front line against Continental invaders has left a wealth of turbulent history, including the 1066 battlefield, Dover Castle's secret war tunnels and scattered Roman ruins.

England's spiritual heart is Canterbury; its cathedral and ancient Unesco-listed attractions are essential viewing for any 21st-century pilgrim.

When to Go

➡ May is a good time to get creative in Brighton at Great Britain's second-largest arts festival.

➡ During June, don your top hat and breeches to revel in frilly Victoriana at the Dickens festival in Broadstairs.

➡ Any time between May and October is ideal for a hike along the South Downs Way, which runs the length of England's newest national park.

➡ In summer, head to Thanet's glorious beaches for some proper seaside fun.

🏃 Activities

The southeast of England may be Britain's most densely populated corner, but there are still plenty of off-the-beaten-track walking and cycling routes to enjoy.

Cycling

Finding quiet roads for cycle touring takes a little extra perseverance in the southeast of England, but the effort is richly rewarded. Long-distance routes that form part of the **National Cycle Network** (NCN; www.sustrans.org.uk) include the **Downs & Weald Cycle Route** (110 miles; NCN Routes 2, 20 and 21) from London to Brighton and on to Hastings, and the **Garden of England Cycle Route** (165 miles; NCN Routes 1 & 2) from London to Dover and then Hastings.

You'll also find less demanding routes on the NCN website. Meanwhile, there are plenty of uppers and downers to challenge mountain bikers on walking trails, such as the **South Downs Way National Trail** (100 miles), which takes between two and four days to complete.

Walking

Two long-distance trails meander steadily westward through the region, and there are plenty of shorter ambles to match your schedule, stamina and scenery wish-list.

South Downs Way National Trail (www.nationaltrail.co.uk/south-downs-way) This 100-mile National Trail through England's newest national park is a beautiful roller-coaster walk along prehistoric drove roads between Winchester and Eastbourne.

North Downs Way National Trail (www.nationaltrail.co.uk/north-downs-way) This 153-mile walk begins near Farnham in Surrey, but one of its most beautiful sections runs from near Ashford to Dover; a loop takes in Canterbury near its end.

1066 Country Walk Heads from Pevensey Castle to Rye (32 miles) and serves as a continuation of the South Downs Way.

ℹ Information

Kent Attractions (www.kentattractions.co.uk)

Tourism South East (www.visitsoutheastengland.com) The official website for south and southeast England.

Visit Kent (www.visitkent.co.uk)

Visit Surrey (www.visitsurrey.com)

Visit Sussex (www.visitsussex.org)

ℹ Getting There & Around

The southeast is easily explored by train or bus, and many attractions can be visited as a day trip from London. Contact the **National Traveline** (www.travelinesoutheast.org.uk) for comprehensive information about public transport in the region.

BUS

Explorer tickets (adult/child £7.20/5.10) provide unlimited day-long travel on most buses throughout the region. Buy them on the first bus you board.

TRAIN

Secure 33% discounts on most rail fares in the southeast by purchasing a **Network Railcard** (per year £30). Three adults can travel with you for the same discounted fare, and you save 60% on fares for children under 15.

KENT

Kent isn't described as the garden of England for nothing. Within its sea-lined borders you'll find a fragrant landscape of gentle hills, fertile farmland, cultivated country estates and fruit-laden orchards. It could also be described as the beer garden of England as it produces the world-renowned Kent hops and some of the country's finest ales and wines from its numerous vineyards. At its heart is spellbinding Canterbury, crowned by its enthralling cathedral. You'll also find beautiful coastal stretches dotted with beach towns and villages, from old-school Broadstairs to gentrified Whitstable and the aesthetically challenged port town of Dover.

Canterbury

POP 55,240

Canterbury tops the charts for English cathedral cities and is one of southern England's top attractions. Many consider the World Heritage–listed cathedral that dominates its centre to be one of Europe's finest, and the town's narrow medieval alleyways, riverside gardens and ancient city walls are a joy to explore. But Canterbury isn't just a showpiece for the past – it's a bustling, busy place with an energetic student population and a wide choice of contemporary bars, restaurants, venues and independent shops. Book ahead for the best hotels and eateries: pilgrims may no longer flock here in their thousands, but tourists certainly do.

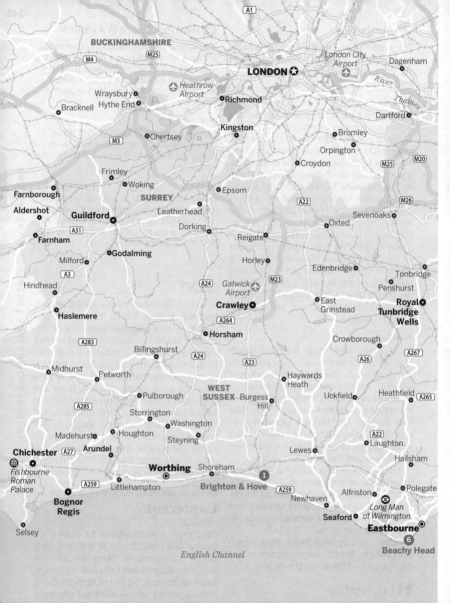

Canterbury & the Southeast Highlights

1 Brighton & Hove
(p165) Shopping, tanning and partying in the hedonist capital of the southeast.

2 Canterbury (p141)
Making a pilgrimage to one

of England's most important religious sites.

3 Dover Castle (p155)
Exploring the atmospheric WWII tunnels beneath this sprawling castle.

4 Rye (p158) Wandering the cobbled lanes of one of England's prettiest towns.

5 Leeds Castle (p148)
Kicking back at this moated marvel.

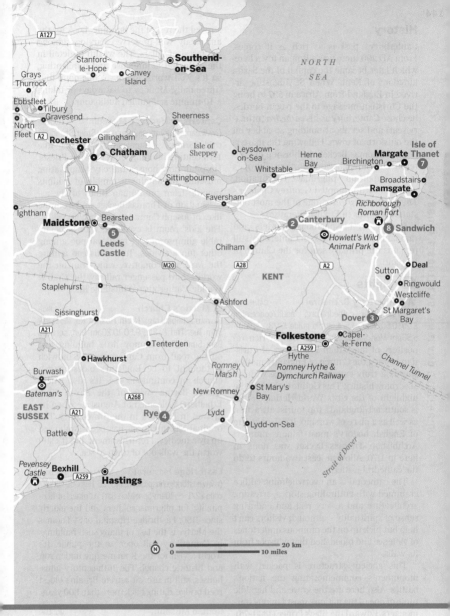

6 **Beachy Head** (p163)
Scrambling up this spectacular headland in snow-white chalk.

7 **Isle of Thanet** (p151)

Shaking out your beach towel for some seaside fun.

8 **Sandwich** (p153) Getting hopelessly lost in crooked medieval streets.

History

Canterbury's past is as rich as it comes. From AD 200 there was a Roman town here, which later became the capital of the Saxon kingdom of Kent. When St Augustine arrived in England from Africa in 597 to bring the Christian message to the pagan hordes, he chose Canterbury as his *cathedra* (primary seat) and set about building an abbey on the outskirts of town. Following the martyrdom of Thomas Becket, Archbishop of Canterbury, the town became northern Europe's most important pilgrimage destination, which in turn prompted Geoffrey Chaucer's *The Canterbury Tales,* one of the most outstanding works in English literature.

Despite its blasphemous murders and rampant tourism, the city of Canterbury still remains the primary seat for the Church of England.

⊙ Sights

★**Canterbury Cathedral**　　CATHEDRAL
(www.canterbury-cathedral.org; adult/concession £12/10.50, tours £5/4, audio guide £4/3; ⊘9am-5.30pm Mon-Sat, 12.30-2.30pm Sun) A rich repository of more than 1400 years of Christian history, the Church of England's mother ship is a truly extraordinary place with an absorbing history. This Gothic cathedral, the highlight of the city's World Heritage Sites, is southeast England's top tourist attraction as well as a place of worship. It's also the site of English history's most famous murder: Archbishop Thomas Becket was done in here in 1170. Allow at least two hours to do the cathedral justice.

The cathedral is an overwhelming edifice crammed with enthralling stories, arresting architecture and a very real and enduring sense of spirituality – although visitors can't help but pick up on the ominous undertones of violence and bloodshed that whisper from its walls.

This ancient structure is packed with monuments commemorating the nation's battles. Also here are the grave and heraldic tunic of one of the nation's most famous warmongers, Edward the Black Prince (1330–76). The spot in the northwest transept where Becket met his grisly end has drawn pilgrims for more than 800 years and is marked by a flickering candle and a striking modern altar.

The doorway to the crypt is beside the altar. This cavernous space is the cathedral's highlight, the only survivor from the cathedral's last devastating fire in 1174, which destroyed the rest of the building. Look for the amazingly well-preserved carvings among the forest of pillars. The wealth of detail in the cathedral is immense and unrelenting, so it's well worth joining a one-hour tour (three daily, Monday to Saturday) or taking a 40-minute self-guided audio tour.

Canterbury Heritage Museum　　MUSEUM
(www.canterbury-museums.co.uk; Stour St; adult/child £8/free; ⊘11am-5pm daily) This fine 14th-century building, once the Poor Priests' Hospital, now houses the city's captivating museum. It contains a jumble of exhibits ranging from pre-Roman times to the assassination of Thomas Becket, and from the likes of Joseph Conrad to locally born celebs. The kids' room is excellent, with a memorable glimpse of real medieval poo among other fun activities. Train fans can admire the *Invicta* locomotive, which ran on the world's third passenger railway, the 'Crab & Winkle' Canterbury–Whitstable line.

St Martin's Church　　CHURCH
(www.martinpaul.org; North Holmes Rd; ⊘11am-3pm Tue, Thu & Sat, 9.50-10.20am Sun, services 9am Sun) This stumpy little building just off the road from Canterbury to Sandwich is thought to be England's oldest parish church in continuous use. It's also where Queen Bertha (wife of the Saxon King Ethelbert) welcomed St Augustine when he arrived in England in the 6th century. The original Saxon church has been swallowed up by a medieval refurbishment, but it's still worth the walk out of town to see.

Eastbridge Hospital　　HISTORIC BUILDING
(www.eastbridgehospital.org.uk; 25 High St; adult/child £2/1; ⊘10am-5pm Mon-Sat) A 'place of hospitality' for pilgrims, soldiers and the elderly since 1180, Eastbridge Hospital of St Thomas the Martyr is the last of many such buildings in Canterbury still open to the public. It's worth a visit for the Romanesque undercroft and historic chapel. The 16th-century almshouses, still in use, sit astride Britain's oldest road bridge, dating back more than 800 years.

Roman Museum　　MUSEUM
(www.canterburymuseums.co.uk; Butchery Lane; adult/child £8/free; ⊘10am-5pm) This fascinating subterranean archaeological site gives an insight into Canterbury's everyday life almost two millennia ago. Visitors can stroll a reconstructed Roman marketplace and rooms, including a kitchen, as well as view Roman mosaic floors. Everything you see

Canterbury

Canterbury

◎ Top Sights
1 Canterbury Cathedral C2

◎ Sights
2 Beaney House of Art &
    Knowledge B2
3 Canterbury Heritage Museum B3
4 Eastbridge Hospital B2
5 Greyfriars Chapel B3
6 Roman Museum C3
7 West Gate Towers B2

◈ Activities, Courses & Tours
8 Canterbury Guided Tours C2
9 Canterbury Historic River
    Tours B2
10 Canterbury River Navigation
    Company B2

▣ Sleeping
11 ABode Canterbury B2
12 Castle House A4
13 Cathedral Gate Hotel C2

14 House of Agnes A1

✕ Eating
15 Boho B2
16 Deeson's C2
17 Goods Shed B1
18 Refectory Kitchen B1
19 Tiny Tim's Tearoom B3

◆ Drinking & Nightlife
20 Alberry's Wine Bar B3
21 Foundry Brewpub B3
22 Micro Roastery B3
23 Parrot C1
24 Steinbeck & Shaw C3

◆ Entertainment
25 New Marlowe Theatre B2

◆ Shopping
26 Chaucer Bookshop B3
27 Revivals B2

THE MARTYRDOM OF THOMAS BECKET

Not one to shy away from cronyism, in 1162 King Henry II appointed his good mate Thomas Becket to the highest clerical office in the land, figuring it would be easier to force the increasingly vocal religious lobby to fall into line if he was pals with the archbishop. Unfortunately for Henry, he underestimated how seriously Thomas would take the job, and the archbishop soon began to disagree with almost everything the king said or did. By 1170, Henry had become exasperated with his former favourite and suggested to four of his knights that Thomas was too much to bear. Becket was murdered on 29 December. Becket's martyrdom – and canonisation in double-quick time (1173) – catapulted Canterbury Cathedral to the top of the league of northern European pilgrimage sites. Mindful of the growing criticism of his role in Becket's murder, Henry arrived in Canterbury in 1174 for a dramatic *mea culpa* and, after allowing himself to be whipped and scolded, was granted absolution.

here was only discovered after WWII bombs did a bit of impromptu excavation.

West Gate Towers
MUSEUM

(www.onepoundlane.co.uk; St Peter's St; adult/concession £4/3; ⏲11am-4pm) The city's only remaining medieval gateway (1380) has been Canterbury's most controversial sight in recent years, opening and closing more than a parson's Bible. But in 2015 it was taken over by a private company who have reopened the museum inside, which focuses on the building's use as a prison. The views from the top are pretty good, but if you don't go inside, you can always entertain yourself watching buses, wing mirrors folded back, as they squeeze through the medieval archway.

Greyfriars Chapel
CHURCH

(⏲2-4pm Mon-Sat Easter-Sep) You'll find Greyfriars Chapel in serene riverside gardens behind Eastbridge Hospital. The first monastery built in England by Franciscan monks in 1267, its grounds are a tranquil city-centre spot to unfurl the picnic blanket.

Beaney House of Art & Knowledge
MUSEUM

(18 High St; ⏲9am-5pm Mon-Wed, Fri & Sat, 9am-7pm Thu, 10am-5pm Sun) **FREE** This mock-Tudor edifice is the grandest on the main shopping thoroughfare, if not the most authentic. Formerly called the Royal Museum & Art Gallery, it has housed Canterbury's main library, a museum and an art gallery since 1899 – it's current name is in honour of the 19th-century benefactor who funded the original building. In addition to the city's main library and the tourist office, the mixed bag of museum exhibitions is worth half an hour between the main sights.

🕽 Tours

Canterbury Historic River Tours
BOATING

(📞07790-534744; www.canterburyrivertours.co.uk; Kings Bridge; adult/child £9/5; ⏲10am-5pm Mar-Oct) Knowledgeable guides double up as energetic oarsmen on these fascinating, multi-award-winning River Stour mini cruises, which depart from behind the Old Weaver's House.

Canterbury River Navigation Company
BOATING

(📞07816-760869; www.crnc.co.uk; Westgate Gardens; adult/child from £10/6; ⏲Apr-Oct) Weather permitting, this company offers relaxing punt trips on the pretty River Stour.

Canterbury Guided Tours
WALKING

(📞01227-459779; www.canterburyguidedtours.com; adult/child/concession £7.50/5.50/7; ⏲11am Feb-Oct, plus 2pm Jul-Sep) Guided walking tours leave from opposite the Canturbury Cathedral entrance. Tickets can be purchased from the tourist office.

⚒ Festivals & Events

Canterbury Festival
PERFORMING ARTS

(📞box office 01227-787787; www.canterburyfestival.co.uk; ⏲mid-Oct–early Nov) Myriad musicians, comedians, theatre groups and other artists from around the world come to party during this festival, which runs for almost three weeks.

🛏 Sleeping

Kipp's Independent Hostel
HOSTEL £

(📞01227-786121; www.kipps-hostel.com; 40 Nunnery Fields; dm £16.50-24.50, s £25-35, d £50-70; @ 🛜) Occupying a red-brick town house in a quietish residential area less than a mile from the city centre, these superb backpacker digs enjoy a homey atmosphere, clean (though cramped) dorms and rave reviews.

House of Agnes
HOTEL ££

(☎01227-472185; www.houseofagnes.co.uk; 71 St Dunstan's St; r from £89-125; @🛜) This rather wonky 13th-century beamed inn, mentioned in Dickens' *David Copperfield*, has eight themed rooms bearing names such as 'Marrakesh' (Moorish), 'Venice' (carnival masks), 'Boston' (light and airy) and 'Canterbury' (antiques and heavy fabrics). If you prefer your room to have straight lines and right angles, there are eight less exciting, but no less comfortable, 'stable' rooms in the garden annexe.

Cathedral Gate Hotel
HOTEL ££

(☎01227-464381; www.cathgate.co.uk; 36 Burgate; s/d £50/112, without bathroom £50/81.50; 🛜) Predating the spectacular cathedral gate it adjoins, this quaint 15th-century hotel is a medieval warren of steep staircases and narrow passageways leading to 27 pleasingly old-fashioned rooms with angled floors, low doors and cockeyed walls. Some have cathedral views, while others overlook pretty Buttermarket. There's no lift.

Arthouse B&B
B&B ££

(☎07976-725457; www.arthousebandb.com; 24 London Rd; r from £65; P🛜) A night at Canterbury's most laid-back digs, housed in a 19th-century fire station, is a bit like sleeping over at a really cool art student's pad. The theme is funky and eclectic, with furniture by local designers and artwork by the instantly likeable artist owners, who have a house-studio out back.

Castle House
B&B ££

(☎01227-761897; www.castlehouse hotel.co.uk; 28 Castle St; r from £90; P🛜) This historic guesthouse sits opposite the ruins of Canterbury's Norman castle, and incorporates part of the old city walls. The spacious, tasteful, high-ceilinged Georgian-style rooms have pretty views and bags of space and there's a secluded garden out back.

★ABode Canterbury
HOTEL £££

(☎01227-766266; www.abodecanterbury.co.uk; 30-33 High St; r from £98; 🛜) The 72 rooms at this supercentral hotel, the only boutique hotel in town, are graded from 'comfortable' to 'fabulous', and for the most part live up to their names. They come with features such as handmade beds, chesterfield sofas, tweed cushions and beautiful modern bathrooms. There's a splendid champagne bar, restaurant and tavern, too.

Eating

★Tiny Tim's Tearoom
CAFE £

(www.tinytimstearoom.com; 34 St Margaret's St; mains £6-10.50; ⊙9.30am-5pm Tue-Sat, 10.30am-4pm Sun) It's no mean feat to be declared 'Kent Tearoom of the Year', but this swish 1930s cafe was awarded the accolade in 2015. It offers hungry shoppers big breakfasts bursting with Kentish ingredients, and tiers of cakes, crumpets, cucumber sandwiches and scones plastered in clotted cream. On busy shopping days you are guaranteed to queue for a table.

Refectory Kitchen
BRITISH £

(☎01227-638766; www.refectorykitchen.com; 16 St Dunstan's St; mains around £8; ⊙8am-5pm Mon-Wed, 8am-4pm & 6-9.30pm Thu & Fri, 9am-4pm & 6-9.30pm Sat, 9am-3pm Sun) This tiny, wood-beamed cafe serves all-day breakfasts and a short menu of light lunch and dinner mains containing Kentish ingredients as far as possible. The welcome is friendly, the atmosphere welcoming, but things get very busy at mealtimes.

Boho
INTERNATIONAL £

(43 St Peter's St; snacks £4-14; ⊙9am-6pm Mon-Thu, to 10pm Fri & Sat, 10am-5pm Sun) This hip eatery in a prime spot on the main drag is extraordinarily popular and you'll be lucky to get a table on busy shopping days. Cool tunes lilt through the chic retro dining space while chilled diners chow down on humongous burgers, full-monty breakfasts and imaginative, owner-cooked international mains. Boho doesn't do bookings, so be prepared to queue.

★Deeson's
BRITISH ££

(☎01227-767854; www.deesonsrestaurant. co.uk; 25-26 Sun St; mains £15-24; ⊙noon-3pm & 5-10pm) Put the words 'local', 'seasonal' and 'tasty' together and you have this superb British eatery. Local fruit and veg; award-winning wines, beers and ciders; fish from Kent's coastal waters; and the odd ingredient from the proprietor's own allotment are all served in a straightforward, contemporary setting just a Kentish apple's throw from the Canterbury Cathedral gates.

Goods Shed
MARKET ££

(☎01227-459153; www.thegoodsshed.co.uk; Station Rd West; mains £17-20; ⊙market 9am-7pm Tue-Sat, 10am-4pm Sun, restaurant 8am-9.30pm Tue-Sat, 9am-3pm Sun) Farmers market, food hall and fabulous restaurant rolled into one, this converted warehouse by the Canterbury West train station is a hit with everyone

WORTH A TRIP

LEEDS CASTLE

The immense moated pile **Leeds Castle** (www.leeds-castle.com; adult/child £24.50/16.50; ⏰10am-6pm Apr-Sep, to 5pm Oct-Mar), just east of Maidstone is, for many, the world's most romantic castle, and it's certainly one of the most visited in Britain. The formidable, hefty structure balancing on two islands is known as something of a 'ladies castle'. This stems from the fact that in its more than 1000 years of history, it has been home to a who's who of medieval queens, most famously Henry VIII's first wife, Catherine of Aragon.

The castle was transformed from fortress to lavish palace over the centuries, and its last owner, the high-society hostess Lady Baillie, used it as a princely family home and party pad to entertain the likes of Errol Flynn, Douglas Fairbanks and John F Kennedy.

The castle's vast estate offers enough attractions of its own to justify a day trip: peaceful walks, a duckery, aviary and falconry demonstrations. You'll also find possibly the world's sole dog-collar museum, plenty of kids' attractions and a hedge maze, overseen by a grassy bank from where fellow travellers can shout encouragement or misdirections.

Since Lady Baillie's death in 1974, a private trust has managed the property. This means that some parts of the castle are periodically closed for private events.

Trains run from London Victoria to Bearsted, where you catch a special shuttle coach to the castle.

from self-caterers to sit-down gourmets. The chunky wooden tables sit slightly above the market hubbub but in full view of its appetite-whetting stalls. Daily specials exploit the freshest farm goodies the Garden of England has to offer.

 Drinking & Nightlife

Steinbeck & Shaw CLUB
(www.steinbeckandshaw.co.uk; 41 St George's Pl; ⏰6pm-2am Mon-Thu, to 3am Fri & Sat) Canterbury's newest nightclub has a super-cool, 21st-century interior with urban and retro elements. The weekly program is a mixed bag of rock and house and is as popular with students as with tourists and Kentish trendoids.

Foundry Brewpub BREWERY
(www.thefoundrycanterbury.co.uk; White Horse Lane; ⏰noon-midnight Mon-Thu, noon-late Fri & Sat, noon-11pm Sun) Canterbury's brewpub pumps out award-winning craft beers in the industrial setting of a former foundry. It also stocks a wide range of local and national ales and ciders and serves light snacks and meals.

Micro Roastery COFFEE
(www.microroastery.co.uk; 4 St Margaret's St; ⏰8am-6pm Mon-Fri, 9am-6pm Sat, 10am-5pm Sun; 📶) Owned by an Anglo-Peruvian couple, this new cafe imports, roasts, grinds and sells its unsurpassed beans and blends. There's local art on the walls; the furniture is upholstered in coffee-bean sacks; and a La Marzocco espresso machine pumps out strong brews.

Parrot PUB
(www.theparrotonline.com; 1-9 Church Lane; ⏰noon-10pm Mon-Sat, to 9.30pm Sun) Built in 1370 on Roman foundations, Canterbury's oldest boozer has a snug, beam-rich pub downstairs and a much-lauded dining room upstairs under yet more ageing oak. Many a local microbrewed ale is pulled in both venues.

Alberry's Wine Bar CLUB
(www.alberrys.co.uk; 38 St Margaret's St; ⏰11am-3am) An after-hours music bar that puts on everything from smooth live jazz to DJ-led drum and bass to commercial pop. It's a two-level place where you can relax over a cocktail upstairs before heading down to the basement bar.

 Entertainment

New Marlowe Theatre THEATRE
(📞01227-787787; www.marlowetheatre.com; The Friars) Canterbury's main theatre attracts popular, fast-selling productions on national tour. Check out that bizarre auditorium, with its dark faux veneers contrasting sharply with the lifejacket-orange seating. The Studio in the same complex is a more intimate performance venue.

🛍 **Shopping**

Chaucer Bookshop BOOKS
(6-7 Beer Cart Lane; ⏰10am-5pm Mon-Sat, 11am-4pm Sun) Antiquarian and used books plus interesting prints and drawings.

Revivals   CLOTHING
(42 St Peter's St; ⏱10am-5pm Mon-Sat, to 4pm Sun)
The city's best vintage-clothing emporium.

ℹ Information

Post Office (19 St George's St; ⏱9am-5.30pm
Mon-Sat, 10.30am-2.30pm Sun) On the 1st
floor of WH Smiths.

Tourist Office (☏01227-862162; www.canter-
bury.co.uk; 18 High St; ⏱9am-5pm Mon-Wed,
Fri & Sat, to 7pm Thu, 10am-5pm Sun) Located
in the Beaney House of Art & Knowledge. Staff
can help book accommodation, excursions and
theatre tickets.

ℹ Getting There & Away

BUS

The city's **bus station** (St George's Lane) is just
within the city walls. Canterbury connections:

Dover (National Express; £5.80, 40 minutes,
hourly)

London Victoria (National Express; £15.50,
two hours, hourly)

Margate (£5.30, 50 minutes, four hourly)

Ramsgate (£5.30 45 minutes, hourly)

Sandwich (£3.70, 40 minutes, three hourly)

Whitstable (£4.70, 30 minutes, every 10
minutes)

TRAIN

There are two train stations, Canterbury East
for London Victoria and Canterbury West for
London's Charing Cross/St Pancras stations.
Canterbury connections:

Dover Priory (£8.20, 25 minutes, half-hourly)
Runs from Canterbury East train station.

London St Pancras (£34.80, one hour, hourly)
High-speed service.

London Victoria/Charing Cross (£29.30, 1¾
hours, two hourly)

ℹ Getting Around

Canterbury's centre is mostly set up for pedestrians. Car parks are dotted along and just inside
the walls, but to avoid heavy traffic, day trippers
may prefer to use one of three Park & Ride sites,
which cost £3 per day and connect to the centre
by bus every eight minutes (7am to 7.30pm Monday to Saturday, 10am to 6pm Sun).

Whitstable

POP 30,195

Perhaps it's the oysters, harvested since Roman times? Maybe it's the weatherboard
houses and shingle beach? Or perhaps it's
the pleasingly old-fashioned main street with
petite galleries, been-there-forever outfitters

and emporia of vintage clothing? Most likely
it's for all of these reasons that Whitstable has
become a bit of a weekend mecca for metropolitan types looking for refuge from the city
hassle. It's also a simple day trip from Canterbury, to which it is linked by regular local bus.

◉ Sights

Whitstable Museum & Gallery   MUSEUM
(www.canterburymuseums.co.uk; 5 Oxford St; adult/
concession £3/2; ⏱11am-4.30pm) This modest
museum has glass cases examining Whitstable's oyster industry, the Crab & Winkle Railway which once ran from Canterbury, and
the local fishing fleet, as well as a corner dedicated to actor Peter Cushing, star of several
Hammer Horror films and the town's most
famous resident, who died in 1994.

✦ Festivals & Events

Whitstable Oyster Festival   FOOD & DRINK
(www.whitstableoysterfestival.co.uk; ⏱late Jul)
For a week in late July, the town hosts a seafood, arts and music extravaganza offering
a packed schedule of events, from history
walks, crab catching and oyster-eating competitions to a beer festival and traditional
'blessing of the waters'.

🛏 Sleeping

Hotel Continental   HOTEL ££
(☏01227-280280; www.hotelcontinental.co.uk; 29
Beach Walk; r from £75; 🅰) The rooms at this
elegant seaside art-deco building have undergone a complete refit and are now bright
and breezy quarters with light-painted wood
cladding, brilliant white beds and sparkling
bathrooms. There's a decent restaurant and
bar on the premises.

Whitstable Bay   B&B ££
(☏01227-779362; www.whitstablebay.com; 74
Joy Lane; s/d from £65/70; 🅿🅰) This much-
lauded B&B is a short stroll southwest of
High St and offers three very well-appointed and stylishly decorated doubles in a quiet residential area. Continental breakfast is
free, but a full English is £6.50 extra.

✕ Eating

Samphire   MODERN BRITISH ££
(☏01227-770075; www.samphirewhitstable.co.uk;
4 High St; mains £10-19; ⏱10am-10pm) The shabby-chic jumble of tables and chairs, big-print
wallpaper and blackboard menus create the
perfect stage for meticulously crafted mains
containing East Kent's most flavour-packed

ingredients. An interesting side dish is its namesake samphire, an asparagus-like plant that grows on sea-sprayed rocks and cliffs, often found on menus in these parts.

 Sportsman Pub BRITISH £££
(www.thesportsmanseasalter.co.uk; Faversham Rd; mains around £20; ⊘ restaurant noon-2pm & 7-9pm Tue-Sat, 12.30-2.45pm Sun, bar noon-3pm & 6-11pm Tue-Sat, noon-10pm Sun) The anonymous and oddly named village of Seasalter, 4 miles east of Whitstable, would hardly receive a trickle of visitors wereit not for the deceivingly ramshackle Sportsman Pub, East Kent's only eatery adorned with a Michelin star. Local ingredients from sea, marsh and woods are crafted by Whitstable-born chef Stephen Harris into taste-packed Kentish creations that have food critics drooling.

Wheeler's Oyster Bar SEAFOOD £££
(☏ 01227-273311; www.wheelersoysterbar.com; 8 High St; mains £18.50-22.50; ⊘10.30am-9pm Mon, Tue & Thu, 10.15am-9.30pm Fri, 10am-10pm Sat, 11.30am-9pm Sun) Squeeze onto a stool by the bar or into the four-table Victorian dining room of this baby-blue and pink restaurant, choose from the seasonal menu and enjoy the best seafood in Whitstable. This place knows its stuff, as it's been serving oysters since 1856. Bookings are highly recommended unless you're travelling solo. Cash only.

🍸 Drinking & Nightlife

Old Neptune PUB
(www.neppy.co.uk; Marine Tce; ⊘noon-10.30pm) A ramshackle pub about as far onto the beach as it's possible to get (it's been washed away several times by high tides) with cosy winter window seats and wonky floorboards. Summer sees drinkers tumble out onto the shingle and there's regular live music.

❶ Getting There & Away

BUS

Whitstable has connections to Canterbury (£4.70, 30 minutes, every 10 minutes) and London Victoria (£15.50, 2¼ hours, three daily).

TRAIN

Whitstable has the following connections:
London St Pancras (£28, one hour 20 minutes, hourly)
London Victoria (£22, one hour 20 minutes, hourly)
Margate (£7.20, 20 minutes, twice hourly)
Ramsgate (£9.30, 36 minutes, twice hourly)

Margate
POP 49,700

A popular resort for more than two centuries, Margate's late-20th-century slump was long and bleak as British holidaymakers ditched Victorian frump for the carefree *costas* of Spain. But this grand old seaside, with fine-sand beaches and artistic associations, has bounced off the bottom. Major cultural regeneration projects – including the spectacular Turner Contemporary art gallery – are slowly reversing the town's fortunes, and on busy days even the odd non-English speaker can be overheard in the newly minted cafes and rejuvenated old town.

◎ Sights

 Turner Contemporary GALLERY
(www.turnercontemporary.org; Rendezvous; ⊘10am-6pm Tue-Sun) [FREE] This blockbuster contemporary art gallery, bolted together on the site of the seafront guesthouse where master painter JMW Turner used to stay, is one of East Kent's top attractions. Within the strikingly featureless shell the only thing distracting the eye, apart from the artwork on display, is the sea view from the floor-to-ceiling windows. These allow you to appreciate the very thing Turner loved so much about Margate – the sea, sky and refracted light of the north Kent coast.

The gallery is attracting top-notch contemporary installations by high-calibre artists such as Tracey Emin (who grew up in Margate) and Alex Katz. When you're finished with the art, culinary creations await in the cafe and the gift shop is excellent.

Shell Grotto GROTTO, CAVE
(www.shellgrotto.co.uk; Grotto Hill; adult/child £3.50/1.50; ⊘10am-5pm Apr-Oct, 11am-4pm Sat & Sun Nov-Mar) Margate's unique attraction is a mysterious subterranean grotto, discovered in 1835. It's a claustrophobic collection of rooms and passageways embedded with 4.6 million shells arranged in symbol-rich mosaics. It has inspired feverish speculation over the years; some think it a 2000-year-old pagan temple, others an elaborate 19th-century hoax. Either way, it's an exquisite place worth seeing.

Dreamland AMUSEMENT PARK
(www.dreamland.co.uk; Marine Terrace; adult/child £18/15; ⊘11am-9pm May-Oct) Given the kiss of life using lottery and council funds, Margate's famous amusement park is slowly coming back to life after a decade of lying

derelict. The main attraction here is the so-called Scenic Railway, a 1920s heritage-listed wooden roller coaster that was rebuilt after an arson attack in 2008. But there are plenty of other period rides and attractions to keep adults and kiddies thrilled, some shipped in from other defunct, 20th-century amusement parks across the country.

🛏 Sleeping & Eating

★ Reading Rooms
B&B £££

(📞 01843-225166; www.thereadingroomsmargate. co.uk; 31 Hawley Sq; r £180; 🛜) Occupying an unmarked 18th-century Georgian town house on a tranquil square just five minutes' walk from the sea, this luxury boutique B&B is as stylish as they come. Generously cut rooms with waxed wooden floors and beautiful French antique reproduction furniture contrast with the 21st-century bathrooms fragrant with Ren cosmetics. Breakfast is served in your room. Bookings essential; no children or pets.

Sands Hotel
BOUTIQUE HOTEL £££

(📞 01843-228228; www.sandshotelmargate.co.uk; 16 Marine Dr; r £120-200; ✱🛜) This beautifully styled boutique hotel sits right on the Margate seafront. It features an understated sand-hued theme throughout, the southeast's best bathrooms, and a restaurant with spectacular bay views, which around half of the rooms also share. The entrance is hidden under the arches on the seafront next to the hotel's very own summertime ice-cream parlour.

★ Mad Hatter
CAFE £

(www.facebook.com/TheMadHatterMargate; 9 Lombard St; snacks & light meals £3.50-11; ⊙11am-5.30pm Sat, other days occasionally Jul & Aug) This unmissable, completely cuckoo eatery run by a top-hatted proprietor packs two rooms of a 1690s house with regalia and knick-knackery from down the ages. Christmas decorations stay up all year and the toilets are original Victorian porcelain. The yummy cakes and snacks are all homemade. Just a shame it isn't open more often.

Great British Pizza Company
PIZZA £

(www.greatbritishpizza.com; 14 Marine Dr; pizzas £4-9.50; ⊙noon-9pm Tue-Sat, to 3pm Sun; 🛜) A world away from your normal 'British pizza', the delicious cheese-topped wheels at this cool hang-out are made using the best local and Italian ingredients. Right on the seafront, this popular spot has a funkily eclectic but simple dining space, heart-pumping coffees and gelato containing nothing that it shouldn't.

ISLE OF THANET

You won't need a wetsuit or a ferry to reach the Isle of Thanet and its towns of Margate, Ramsgate and Broadstairs: the 2-mile-wide Wantsum Channel, which divides the island from the mainland, silted up in the 16th century, transforming the East Kent landscape forever. In its island days, Thanet was the springboard for several epoch-making episodes in English history. It was here that the Romans kicked off their invasion in the 1st century AD and where St Augustine landed in AD 597 to launch his conversion of the pagans. If global warming forecasts are right, Thanet could once again be an island by the end of the century.

ℹ Information

Tourist Office (📞 01843-577577; www.visit-thanet.co.uk; Droit House, Stone Pier; ⊙10am-5pm daily Easter-Oct, 10am-5pm Tue-Sat Nov-Easter) Next to the Turner Contemporary art gallery, the tourist office serves all of the Isle of Thanet. It hands out *The Isle*, a glossy magazine crammed with Thanet listings.

ℹ Getting There & Away

BUS

Departure and arrival points for local buses are Queen St and adjacent Cecil St.

Broadstairs (Thanet Loop Bus; £1.90, up to every 10 minutes)

Canterbury (£5.20, 50 minutes, three hourly)

London Victoria (National Express; £14.50, three hours, seven daily)

Ramsgate (Thanet Loop Bus; £2.30, up to every 10 minutes)

TRAIN

The train station is just a few steps from the beach. There are twice-hourly services to London Victoria (£35.50, one hour 50 minutes) and a high-speed service to London St Pancras (£41.40, 1½ hours) every hour.

Broadstairs

POP 25,000

While its bigger, brasher neighbours seek to revive and regenerate themselves, quaint little Broadstairs quietly gets on with what it's done best for the past 150 years – wowing visitors with its tight sickle of reddish sand (Viking Bay) and sun-warmed lapping sea.

Charles Dickens certainly thought it a pretty spot, spending most summers here between 1837 and 1859. The resort now plays the Victorian nostalgia card at every opportunity and names every second business after the works of its most famous holidaymaker.

◉ Sights

Dickens House Museum MUSEUM
(www.dickensfellowship.org; 2 Victoria Pde; adult/child £3.75/2.10; ⊙1-4.30pm Easter–mid-Jun & mid-Sep–Oct, 10am-4.30pm mid-Jun–mid-Sep, 1-4.30pm Sat & Sun Nov) This quaint museum is Broadstairs' top attraction and the former home of Mary Pearson Strong – Dickens' inspiration for the character of Betsey Trotwood in *David Copperfield*. Diverse Dickensiana on display includes letters from the author.

✷ Festivals & Events

Dickens Festival CULTURAL
(www.broadstairsdickensfestival.co.uk; ⊙late Jun) Broadstairs' biggest bash, this annual, weeklong festival held in mid-June culminates in a banquet and ball in Victorian fancy dress.

⌷ Sleeping & Eating

Copperfields Guest House B&B ££
(☎01843-601247; www.copperfieldsbb.co.uk; 11 Queen's Rd; s/d £65/85; 🐾) 🌿 This vegetarian B&B offers three homely rooms with en suite, and a warm welcome from the owners and pet Yorkie. It also caters for vegans, and all products in the bathrooms are cruelty-free.

★ Bleak House HISTORIC HOTEL £££
(☎01843-865338; www.bleakhousebroadstairs. co.uk; Fort Rd; r £155-250, apt £300; 🐾) This former Napoleonic-era fortress overlooking the beach was converted into an opulent Victorian residence just in time for one Charles Dickens to rent it for 22 summers (1837–59). From the lounge bar to the Copperfield suite with its Viking Bay views and five-star bathroom, the whole caboodle oozes unique period character. Building tours run from 10am to 6pm.

★ Wyatt & Jones BRITISH ££
(www.wyattandjones.co.uk; 23-27 Harbour St; mains £6-19; ⊙9-11am, noon-3pm & 6.30-9pm Wed & Thu, to 10pm Fri & Sat, 9am-5pm Sun) Broadstairs' best offering is this contemporary British restaurant just a few steps off the beach. Savour unashamedly local dishes such as Whitstable oysters, local bream, mussels and chips, or a day-launching breakfast in the uncluttered interior of gun-metal blue and scratched timber floors. Then admire your expanding waistline in the retro mirror wall.

Tartar Frigate BRITISH ££
(www.tartarfrigate.co.uk; 42 Harbour St; mains £16.50-24.50; ⊙11am-11pm) Dating back to the 18th century, this seafront pub is a great place to be in summer when tourists and locals alike spill out onto the beach. The seafood restaurant upstairs serves up excellent fare and there are great views of the bay. The pub also puts on regular live folk music.

ⓘ Getting There & Away

BUS
Broadstairs connections include the following:
Canterbury (£5.20, 1½ hours, twice hourly)
London Victoria (National Express, £14.50, 3¼ hours, seven daily)
Margate (Thanet Loop Bus; £1.90, 21 minutes, up to every 10 minutes)
Ramsgate (Thanet Loop Bus; £1.50, 14 minutes, up to every 10 minutes)

TRAIN
Broadstairs is connected to London Victoria (£22.50, two hours, hourly) and by high-speed service to London St Pancras (£39.30, one hour 20 minutes, twice hourly).

Ramsgate

POP 39,600
The most varied of Thanet's towns, Ramsgate has a friendlier feel than rival Margate and is more vibrant than its quaint little neighbour Broadstairs. A forest of masts whistles serenely in the breeze below the handsomely curved walls of Britain's only royal harbour, and the seafront is surrounded by bars and cosmopolitan street cafes. Just one celebrity chef away from being described as 'up and coming', Ramsgate retains a shabbily undiscovered charm, its sweeping, environmentally sanctioned Blue Flag beaches and some spectacular Victorian architecture making it well worth the visit.

◉ Sights

Spitfire Memorial Museum MUSEUM
(www.spitfiremuseum.org.uk; Manston Rd; ⊙10am-5pm Apr-Oct, to 4pm Nov-Mar) FREE Around 4 miles northwest of Ramsgate's town centre at Manston Airport, this purpose-built museum stores two WWII planes: one a Spitfire, the other a Hurricane. Both look factory-fresh but are surprisingly delicate so, sadly, there's

no clambering on board. Gathered around the planes are myriad flight-associated exhibits, many relating to Manston's role as an airfield during the Battle of Britain. Take bus 38 or 11 from King St and ask the driver to drop you off as near as possible.

Ramsgate Maritime Museum MUSEUM
(www.ramsgatemaritimemuseum.org; The Clock House, Royal Harbour; adult/child £2/1; ☉10am-5pm Tue-Sun Easter-Sep) Interesting but erratically opening museum displaying loot from the more than 600 ships that have been wrecked on the notorious Goodwin Sands off this stretch of coast.

🛏️ Sleeping & Eating

Royal Harbour Hotel HOTEL ££
(☑ 01843-591514; www.royalharbourhotel.co.uk; Nelson Crescent 10/11; s/d from £79/100) Occupying two regency town houses on a glorious seafront crescent, this boutique hotel feels enveloped in warmth and quirkiness – an eclectic collection of books, magazines, games and artwork line the hotel. Rooms range from tiny nautical-esque 'cabins' to country-house style, four-poster doubles, most with postcard views over the forest of masts below and all are perfectly appointed with bags of character.

Glendevon Guesthouse B&B ££
(☑ 01843-570909; www.glendevonguesthouse. co.uk; 8 Truro Rd; s/d from £52.50/70; P🐾) 🍃 Run by energetic and very knowledgeable hosts, this comfy guesthouse takes the whole ecofriendly thing very seriously, with guest recycling facilities, eco-showers and even energy-saving hairdryers. The hallways of this grand Victorian house, a block back from the Ramsgate seafront, are decorated with work by local artists. All rooms have kitchenettes, and breakfast is a convivial affair taken around a communal table.

Vinyl Head Cafe CAFE £
(2-3 Addington Street; snacks £1-5; ☉9am-3pm Tue-Sun) Located off the beaten track on a quiet road running up from the western end of the harbour, this groovy community cafe offers great coffee and homemade cakes, locals to chat with and retro sounds on vinyl.

Bon Appetit FRENCH ££
(www.bonappetitramsgate.co.uk; 4 Westcliff Arcade; mains £7-21; ☉noon-2.30pm & 7pm-late Tue-Sat) The best eatery on Westcliff, this first-rate bistro serves up French-inspired dishes in a simple dining room or with alfresco harbour views. Ingredients on the menu are of the seasonal and locally sourced ilk, with finely crafted mains including delights such as pan-fried Kentish pheasant and Dover sole.

ℹ️ Information

Tourist Office (☑ 01843-598750; www.ramsgatetown.org; Customs House, Harbour Pde; ☉10am-4pm Mon-Sun) A small, staffed visitor centre with out-of-hours brochure stands.

ℹ️ Getting There & Away

BUS
Ramsgate has the following bus connections:
Broadstairs (Thanet Loop Bus; £1.50, up to every 10 minutes)
London Victoria (National Express; £14.50, three hours, six daily)
Margate (Thanet Loop Bus; £2.30, up to every 10 minutes)
Sandwich (£3, 25 minutes, hourly)

TRAIN
Ramsgate has train services to London Victoria (£22.50, two hours, twice hourly) and a high-speed service to London St Pancras (£39.70, 1¼ hours, twice hourly).

Sandwich

POP 5000
As close as you'll get to a living museum, Sandwich was once England's fourth city (after London, Norwich and Ipswich). It's a fact hard to grasp as you wander its drowsy medieval lanes, ancient churches, Dutch gables, crooked peg-tiled roofs and overhanging timber-framed houses. Once a port to rival London, Sandwich began its decline when the entrance to the harbour silted up in the 16th century, and this once-vital gateway to and from the Continent spent the next 400 years retreating into quaint rural obscurity. Preservation is big here, with huge local interest in period authenticity. The tiny 100-seat cinema is preserved as an art-deco museum piece and the 1920s garage deals more in classic cars than modern vehicles. Within the town's historical core, unlisted buildings are the exception.

⊙ Sights

Sandwich's web of medieval and Elizabethan streets is perfect for ambling through and getting pleasantly lost (as many do). Strand Street in particular has one of the country's highest concentrations of half-timbered buildings. Ornate brickwork on some houses betrays the strong influence of 350 Protestant Flemish refugees (referred to as 'the Strangers'), who settled in the town in the 16th century at the invitation of Elizabeth I.

Sandwich Quay
WATERFRONT

Several attractions line the River Stour. First up is a cute little flint-chequered Barbican tollgate built by Henry VIII, which controls traffic flow over the river's only road bridge. Nearby rises Fishergate, built in 1384 and once the main entrance to the town, through which goods from the Continent and beyond once passed. On fair-weather days, hop aboard the **Sandwich River Bus** (☑ 07958 376183; www.sandwichrb.uk; adult/child 30min trip £7/5, 1hr £12/8; ⊙ every 30-60min 11am-6pm Thu-Sun Apr-Sep) beside the toll bridge for seal-spotting trips along the River Stour and in Pegwell Bay, or for an interesting way to reach the **Richborough Roman Fort** (Richborough Rd; h 10am-6pm Apr-Sep, to 5pm Wed-Sun Oct, to 4pm Sat & Sun Nov-Mar; adult/child £5.80/3.40).

Salutation Gardens
GARDENS

(www.the-salutation.com; The Salutation, Knightrider St; admission £7; ⊙ 10am-5pm) Just along from Fishergate, this set of exquisite gardens was laid out behind a 1912 mansion by leading early-20th-century garden designers Jekyll and Lutyens. In the mid-noughties the exquisite site was brought back to life by Dom and Steph Parker, nationally known as minor celebrities from British TV's *Gogglebox* show. The gardens suffered major flooding in 2013 but have largely recovered. There's a superb tearoom in the grounds and you can stay with Dom and Steph in their multi-million-pound mansion.

St Peter's
CHURCH

(King St; ⊙ 10am-5pm) The oldest church in Sandwich is now no longer used for worship. It's a real mixture of styles and years: its tower collapsed in dramatic fashion in 1661 and it was rebuilt with a bulbous cupola by the Flemish 'Strangers'. At the time of research, work was underway to make this accessible to visitors for unsurpassed views of Sandwich.

Guildhall Museum
MUSEUM

(www.guildhalltowncouncil.gov.uk; Guildhall; adult/child £1/50p; ⊙ 10.30am-12.30pm & 2-4pm Tue, Wed, Fri & Sat, 2-4pm Thu & Sun Apr-Nov) Sandwich's small but thorough museum is a good place to start exploring the town. Exhibitions examine the town's rich past as a

Cinque Port, its role in various wars, and the gruesome punishments meted out to felons, fornicators and phoney fishers.

🛏 Sleeping & Eating

★ Bell Hotel
HOTEL ££

(☑ 01304-613388; www.bellhotelsandwich.co.uk; Sandwich Quay; s/d from £100/105; 🖝) Today the haunt of celebrity golfers, the Bell Hotel has been sitting on the town's quay since Tudor times, though much of the remaining building is from the 19th century. A splendid sweeping staircase leads to luxurious rooms, some with pretty quay views. The Old Dining Room restaurant is one of East Kent's poshest nosh spots.

No Name Shop
DELI, BISTRO ££

(www.nonameshop.co.uk; No Name St; snacks £1.90-6.25, meals £6.95-13.50; ⊙ 8am-5pm Mon-Sat, 9am-4pm Sun) This far-from-anonymous French-owned deli (downstairs) and bistro (upstairs) near the bus stop is a pleasantly aromatic spot for a quick sandwich in Sandwich or an 'oozylicious' *croque monsieur*, as well as more sophisticated dishes, followed by a relaxing glass of something Gallic. Very popular among locals, some of whom seem to regularly prefer it over their own kitchens.

King's Arms
BRITISH ££

(☑ 01304-617330; www.kingsarms-sandwich. co.uk; cnr Church & Strand Sts; light meals £4-11, mains £11-17; ⊙ noon-3pm & 6-10pm; 🖝) This cosy 15th-century inn opposite St Mary's church serves quality English food and very popular Sunday lunches in a beamed dining room heated by large fireplaces. There are six B&B rooms upstairs.

ℹ Information

Tourist Office (☑ 01304-613565; www. open-sandwich.co.uk; Guildhall, Cattle Market; ⊙ 10am-4pm Mon-Sat Apr-Oct) Located in the historic Guildhall.

ℹ Getting There & Away

BUS

Buses go to Ramsgate (£3, 22 minutes, hourly), Dover (£7.90, 45 minutes, hourly) and Canterbury (£5.20, 40 minutes, three hourly).

TRAIN

Trains run from Dover Priory train station (£6.90, 22 minutes, hourly), Ramsgate (£5, 12 minutes, hourly) and London St Pancras (£30.20, two hours, hourly).

Dover

POP 37,400

Down-in-the-dumps Dover has certainly seen better days. Its derelict postwar architecture and shabby town centre is a sad introduction to England for travellers arriving on cross-Channel ferries and cruise ships, most of whom pass through quickly. Lucky, then, that the town has a couple of stellar attractions to redeem it. The port's vital strategic position so close to mainland Europe gave rise to a sprawling hilltop castle, which has some 2000 years of history to its credit. The spectacular white cliffs, as much a symbol of English wartime resilience as Winston Churchill or the Battle of Britain, rear in chalky magnificence to the east and west.

◉ Sights

★ **Dover Castle**   CASTLE
(EH; adult/child £18.30/11; ⊙ 10am-6pm Apr-Jul & Sep, 9.30am-6pm Aug, to 5pm Oct, 10am-4pm Sat & Sun Nov-Mar; P) Occupying top spot, literally and figuratively, in Dover's townscape, this most impressive of castles was built to bolster the country's weakest point at the shortest sea crossing to mainland Europe. The highlights here are the unmissable **secret wartime tunnels** (Dover Castle; adult/child £18.30/11; ⊙ 10am-6pm Apr-Jul & Sep, 9.30am-6pm Aug, to 5pm Oct, 10am-4pm Sat & Sun Nov-Mar) and the **Great Tower**, but the huge area it sprawls across has a lot of other bits, so allow at least three hours for your visit, more if you stand to admire the views across the Channel to France.

The site has been in use for as many as 2000 years. On the vast grounds are the remains of a **Roman lighthouse**, which dates from AD 50 and may be the oldest standing building in Britain. Beside it lies the restored Saxon **Church of St Mary** in Castro.

The robust 12th-century Great Tower, with walls up to 7m thick, is a medieval warren filled with interactive exhibits and light-and-sound shows that take visitors back to the times of Henry II.

However the biggest draw of all is the network of secret wartime tunnels. The claustrophobic chalk-hewn passageways were first excavated during the Napoleonic Wars and then expanded to house a command post and hospital in WWII. The highly enjoyable 50-minute guided tour (every 20 minutes, included in the ticket price) tells the story of one of Britain's most famous wartime operations, code-named Dynamo, which was directed from here in 1940 and saw hundreds of thousands of men evacuated from the beaches at Dunkirk. The story is told in a very effective way, with video projected sharply onto the tunnel walls and sounds rumbling through the rock. At one point, the entire passageway is consumed in flames and at others visitors are plunged into complete darkness.

Roman Painted House   RUINS
(www.theromanpaintedhouse.co.uk; New St; adult/child £3/2; ⊙ 10am-5pm Tue-Sun Jun-Sep; P) A crumbling 1960s bunker is the unlikely setting for some of the most extensive, if stunted, Roman wall paintings north of the Alps. Several scenes depict Bacchus (Roman god

---

A SWIG OF KENT & SUSSEX

With booze cruises over to Calais almost a thing of the past, many Kent and Sussex drinkers are rediscovering their counties' superb home-grown beverages. Both counties produce some of the most delicious ales in the country and the southeast's wines are even outgunning some traditional Continental vintners.

Kent's **Shepherd Neame Brewery** (☎ 01795-542016; www.shepherdneame.co.uk; 10 Court St, Faversham; tours £11.50) is Britain's oldest and cooks up aromatic ales brewed from Kent-grown premium hops. Sussex's reply is **Harveys Brewery** (p164), which perfumes Lewes town centre with a hop-laden scent. Book in advance for tours of either brewery.

Mention 'English wine' not too long ago and you'd likely hear a snort of derision. Not any more. Thanks to warmer temperatures and determined winemakers, English wine, particularly of the sparkling variety, is developing a fan base all of its own.

Award-winning vineyards can be found in both Sussex and Kent, whose chalky soils are likened to France's Champagne region. Many vineyards now offer tours and wine tastings. Some of the most popular are **Biddenden Vineyards** (☎ 01580-291726; www.biddendenvineyards.com; tours free; ⊙ tours 10am Wed & Sat), 1.2 miles from Wealden, and **Chapel Down Vinery** (☎ 01580-766111; www.englishwinesgroup.com; Tenterden; tours £10; ⊙ tours daily Apr-Nov), located 2.5 miles south of Tenterden on the B2082.

Dover

Dover

◎ **Top Sights**

1 Dover Castle C1

◎ **Sights**

2 Roman Painted House B2
3 Secret Wartime Tunnels D1

🛏 **Sleeping**

4 Dover Marina Hotel B3
5 East Lee Guest House B1

✴ **Eating**

6 Allotment A1
7 La Salle Verte B2

of wine and revelry), which makes perfect sense as this large villa was built around AD 200 as a *mansio* (hotel) for travellers needing a little lubrication to unwind.

🛏 Sleeping

Dover Marina Hotel HOTEL ££
(☑ 01304-203633; www.dovermarinahotel.co.uk; Waterloo Cres; r £97-164; 🛜) Just a few steps from Dover's beach, this seafront hotel crams 81 rooms of varying dimensions into a gently curving 1870s edifice. The undulating corridors show the building's age,

but there's nothing wonky about the rooms with their trendy ethnic fabrics, big-print wallpaper and contemporary artwork. Half the rooms have unrivalled sea views and 10 boast much-sought-after balconies.

East Lee Guest House B&B ££
(☑ 01304-210176; www.eastlee.co.uk; 108 Maison Dieu Rd; d £65-80; 🅿🛜) This lovely terracotta-shingled town house impresses with its grand, elegantly decorated communal areas, scrupulously maintained rooms, energetic hosts and excellent, varied breakfasts.

★ **Wallett's Court** HOTEL £££
(☑ 01304-852424; www.wallettscourt.com; Westcliffe, St Margaret's-at-Cliffe; d from £135; 🅿🛜🏊) With its soothing spa, first-rate restaurant and perky service, this is one relaxing country house retreat. Digs at this country house set in rolling farmland range from spacious Jacobean guest rooms to beamed converted barns to a canvas wigwam (for a night of 'glamping'). Heading towards Deal, turn right off the A258 after almost 2 miles for Westcliffe.

✕ Eating

La Salle Verte CAFE £
(14-15 Cannon St; snacks £2-6; ⊙9am-5pm Mon-Sat) A much-loved coffee or lunch halt with fascinating black-and-white images of old

Dover lining the walls, an intimate cellar and friendly staff. Fills up at lunch, even on winter Wednesdays.

★ **Allotment** BRITISH ££
(www.theallotmentdover.com; 9 High St; mains £8.50-16; ⊙8.30am-10pm Tue-Sat) Dover's best dining spot plates up local fish and meat from around Canterbury, seasoned with herbs from the tranquil garden out back, for breakfast, lunch and dinner. Cleanse your palette with a Kentish wine in a relaxed, understated setting as you admire the view of the Maison Dieu (13th-century pilgrims' hospital) directly opposite through the exquisite stained-glass frontage.

ℹ Information

Tourist Office (☑01304-201066; www.whitecliffscountry.org.uk; Market Sq; ⊙9.30am-5pm Mon-Sat year-round, 10am-3pm Sun Apr-Sep) Located in the Dover Museum.

ℹ Getting There & Away

BOAT

Ferries depart for France from the Eastern Docks below the castle. Fares vary according to season and advance purchase. Services seem to be in a constant state of flux with companies rising and falling as often as the Channel's swell.

DFDS (☑0871-5747235; www.dfdsseaways.co.uk) Services to Dunkirk (two hours, every two hours) and Calais (1½ hours, at least hourly).

P&O Ferries (☑0871-6642020; www.poferries.com) Runs to Calais (1½ hours, every 40 to 60 minutes).

BUS

Dover has bus connections to the following:
Canterbury (£5.10, 40 minutes, four hourly)
London Victoria (coach 007; £15.50, 2½ to 3½ hours, 12 daily)
Sandwich (£5.70, 50 minutes, hourly)

TRAIN

Dover is connected by train to Ramsgate (£9.60, 35 minutes, hourly) via Sandwich and by high-speed service to London St Pancras (£40, one hour, hourly).

ℹ Getting Around

It's quite a long walk between the Eastern Docks and the train station, especially with luggage. The special bus was discontinued a couple of years ago so you'll have to take a **taxi** (☑01304-201915; www.dovertaxis.com). It's also quite an uphill slog to the castle.

The White Cliffs of Dover

Immortalised in song, film and literature, the iconic white cliffs of Dover are embedded in the national consciousness, and are a big 'Welcome Home' sign to generations of travellers and soldiers. The cliffs rise to 100m high and extend on either side of Dover, but the best bit is the 6-mile stretch that starts about 2 miles east of town, properly known as the Langdon Cliffs. A trail runs along the cliffs as far as St Margaret's Bay, a popular spot among locals.

◉ Sights & Activities

South Foreland Lighthouse HISTORIC BUILDING
(NT; adult/child £6/3; ⊙guided tours 11am-5.30pm Fri-Mon mid-Mar–Oct) From the Langdon Cliffs tourist office, follow the stony path east along the clifftops for a bracing 2-mile walk to the stout Victorian South Foreland Lighthouse. This was the first lighthouse to be powered by electricity and is the site of the first international radio transmissions, in 1898.

St Margaret's Bay VILLAGE
A mile further along the clifftop trail from the South Foreland Lighthouse, you will reach the delightful village of St Margaret's Bay, a gap in the chalk with a sun-trapping shingle beach. This is the closest point to France and many a cross-Channel swimmer has stepped into the briny here.

Dover Sea Safari BOATING
(☑01304-212880; www.doverseasafari.co.uk; Dover Sea Sports Centre, Esplanade; adult/child £35/20; ⊙year-round) This company offers exciting, fast-moving rigid inflatable tours of the White Cliffs plus seal-spotting trips to Pegwell Bay.

Dover White Cliffs Tours BOATING
(☑07971-301379; www.doverwhiteclifftours.com; adult/child £10/5; ⊙daily Jul & Aug, Sat & Sun Apr-Jun, Sep & Oct) This company runs 40-minute sightseeing trips at least three times daily from Dover's Western Docks.

✕ Eating

Coastguard Pub PUB FOOD ££
(www.thecoastguard.co.uk; St Margaret's Bay; mains £10-16; ⊙10am-11pm Mon-Sat, to 10pm Sun; P 🖥) This welcoming seafront pub at St Margaret's Bay is the closest tavern to France in England. Recently refurbished, the bar and dining room are a cosy spot on winter evenings, heated by a real fire. In

summer, retreat to the terrace with lovely beach and Channel views. The British pub-food menu features superb fish and chips.

ℹ Getting There & Away

At the end of the trail along the cliffs at St Margaret's Bay, bus 15 shuttles back to Dover or onto Deal every hour.

EAST SUSSEX

Home to rolling countryside, medieval villages and gorgeous coastline, this inspiring corner of England is besieged by weekending Londoners whenever the sun pops out. And it's not hard to see why as you explore the cobbled medieval streets of Rye; wander around historic Battle, where William the Conqueror first engaged the Saxons in 1066; and peer over the edge of the breathtaking Seven Sisters chalk cliffs and Beachy Head near the genteel seaside town of Eastbourne. Brighton, a highlight of any visit, offers some kicking nightlife, offbeat shopping and British seaside fun. Off the beaten track, you can stretch your legs on the South Downs Way, which traverses England's newest national park, the South Downs National Park.

Rye

POP 4770

Possibly the south of England's quaintest town, Rye is a little nugget of the past, a medieval settlement that looks like someone hit the pause button on time. Even the most hard-boiled cynic can't fail to be softened by Rye's cobbled lanes, mysterious passageways and crooked half-timbered Tudor buildings. Tales of resident smugglers, ghosts, writers and artists abound.

Rye was once one of the Cinque Ports, occupying a high promontory above the sea. Today the town rises 2 miles from the briny; sheep graze where the Channel's strong tides once swelled.

◉ Sights

Mermaid Street   AREA

Most start their exploration of Rye on famous Mermaid St, a short walk from the Rye Heritage Centre. It bristles with 15th-century timber-framed houses with quirky house names such as 'The House with Two Front Doors' and 'The House Opposite'.

Driving Tour
Dover to Rye

START DOVER EASTERN DOCKS
END RYE
LENGTH 35.5 MILES; AT LEAST FOUR HOURS (WITHOUT DUNGENESS PENINSULA DETOUR)

If you've just rolled off a cross-Channel ferry or have a day away from a cruise ship docked in Dover, instead of heading north to London, why not take this fascinating route along the white cliffs and across the flat marshes of the Kent–Sussex border to discover some of the southeast's hidden corners. Buses 100, 101 and 102 follow this route between Dover, Lydd and Hastings.

Starting at the exit to Dover's frantic ❶ **Eastern Docks**, where all cross-Channel ferries tie up, take the A20 along the seafront. After a few minutes, this dual carriageway begins to climb onto the famous white cliffs west of Dover. Your first stop is just outside town – take the turning for ❷ **Samphire Hoe** nature park, a ledge of parkland created between the white cliffs and the sea using 5 million cu metres of chalk excavated during the construction of the Channel tunnel. It's a fine spot for a picnic as you watch the 30 local species of butterfly flutter by.

Back on the A20, it's a mere 1¾ miles to the exit for the village of Capel-Le-Ferne (on the B2011). Well signposted at the end of the village is the ❸ **Battle of Britain Memorial**, a striking monument to the airmen who took part in the decisive struggle with the Luftwaffe in the skies above Kent and Sussex. An airman seated at the centre of a huge Spitfire propeller looks out serenely across the Channel and there's a new multimedia visitors centre and museum experience to enjoy. Returning to the B2011, a few gear changes will have you on the outskirts of ❹ **Folkestone**. Take a left at the first roundabout then the sixth right onto Dover Rd. This will take you into the centre of this formerly grand old resort, once a favourite stomping ground of royal *bon viveur* King Edward VII and a forgotten piece of England's seaside past. Take a stroll through the seafront Leas Coastal Park with its subtropical flora, then halt for fish and chips at the old fish market before ambling up through the Creative Quarter,

Folkestone's old town now occupied by artists studios and craft shops.

Heading out of Folkestone to the west on the A259 Sandgate Rd, you pass through Sandgate with its antique shops and shingle beach. From there it's another 2.5 miles to fascinating little **⑤ Hythe**. You could spend a full day in this original Cinque Port. Not only is it the eastern terminus of the fascinating narrow-gauge Romney, Hythe and Dymchurch Railway (RH&D Railway), but the Royal Military Canal also flows through the town and there's a quaint high street and beach to explore.

Heading ever west, a series of not-so-attractive shingle resorts such as Dymchurch and St Mary's are strung along the A259, cowering below their huge dykes, which keep the high tides from turning this stretch of the coast into sea bottom. You've now left the white cliffs behind and are entering the **⑥ Romney Marsh**, a flat, sparsely populated landscape of reed beds and sheep-dotted fields. There's a visitor centre (www. kentwildlifetrust.org.uk) between St Mary's Bay and New Romney (on the A259) for those with time.

Having negotiated New Romney, another of the original five Cinque Ports, just outside the town take the turning to the left onto the B2075, which leads to **⑦ Lydd**, a quaint former corporate member of the Cinque Ports. From here, detour along the lonely Dungeness Rd, which heads across the flats of the eerie **⑧ Dungeness Peninsula**, a low shingle spit dominated by a brooding nuclear power station. As well as boasting the southeast's largest seabird colony, it's also the western terminus of the RH&D Railway.

Back in Lydd, stick with the B2075 heading west for 6 miles until you reach Camber. Thought the entire south coast had just shingle beaches? Well, the main attraction here is **⑨ Camber Sands**, a wide expanse of golden grains and dunes, ideal for picnicking and strolling.

The B2075 winds through shingly, scrubby wetlands until it rejoins the A259 at the hamlet of East Guldeford, where you should turn left towards Rye. Along the roads around here you will see the main source of revenue from the Romney Marsh – thousands of sheep grazing on the verdant flats. The A259 barrels across the marshes, eventually depositing you in **⑨ Rye** (p158), one of the southeast's quaintest towns.

BATTLE VILLAGE & ABBEY

'If there'd been no battle, there'd be no Battle,' goes the saying in this unassuming village, which grew up around the hillside where invading French duke William of Normandy, aka William the Conqueror, scored a decisive victory over local king Harold in 1066. The epicentre of 1066 country, visitors flock here to see the spot where Harold got it in the eye, with the biggest crowd turning up mid-October to witness the annual re-enactment on the original battlefield.

The **Battle Abbey** (EH; adult/child £10.10/6; ⊙10am-6pm Apr-Sep, to 4pm Sat & Sun Oct-Mar) is where the pivotal battle in the last successful invasion of England in 1066 raged: an event that had an unparalleled impact on the country's subsequent social structure, language and, well, pretty much everything. Four years after, the Normans began constructing an abbey on the battlefield, a penance ordered by the pope for the loss of life incurred here. Only the foundations of the original church remain; the altar's position is supposedly the spot King Harold famously took an arrow in his eye.

Bus 304/305 goes hourly to Hastings (£2.70, 28 minutes). There are train connections to Hastings (£4.20, 15 minutes, twice hourly) and London Charing Cross (£22.30, one hour and 20 minutes, twice hourly).

Ypres Tower   MUSEUM

(www.ryemuseum.co.uk; Church Sq; adult/child £4/free; ⊙10.30am-5pm Apr-Oct, to 3.30pm Nov-Mar) Just off Church Sq stands the sandcastle-esque Ypres Tower (pronounced 'wipers'). You can scramble through the 13th-century building to learn about its long history as a fort, prison, mortuary and museum (the last two at overlapping times), and an annexe contains one of the last surviving Victorian women's prisons in the country. From here, there are widescreen views of Rye Bay, Dungeness nuclear power station and even France on very clear days.

Church of St Mary the Virgin   CHURCH

(Church Sq; tower adult/child £3.50/1; ⊙9am-5.30pm Apr-Sep, to 4.30pm Nov-Mar) Rye's church is a hotchpotch of medieval and later styles. Its turret clock is the oldest in England (1561) still working with its original pendulum, which swings above your head as you enter. Climb the tower for pretty views of the town and surroundings, then inspect the small exhibition of interesting old objects found in and around Rye.

🛏 Sleeping

★ Jeake's House   HOTEL ££

(☎01797-222828; www.jeakeshouse.com; Mermaid St; s/d from £75/95; P🅟🛜) Situated on ancient Mermaid St, this 17th-century town house once belonged to US poet Conrad Aitken. The 11 rooms are named after writers who stayed here. The decor was probably slightly less bold then, minus the beeswaxed antiques and lavish drapery. Take a pew in the snug book-lined bar and, continuing the theme, enjoy breakfast in an 18th-century former Quaker chapel.

Windmill Guesthouse   B&B ££

(☎01797-224027; www.ryewindmill.co.uk; Mill Lane; d from £80; P🛜) This white windmill, sails still intact, houses perhaps Rye's oddest digs. The shape of the building means room sizes vary, as do standards. The two-storey much sought-after 'Windmill Suite' is located almost at the top, enjoying 360-degree views. Breakfast is served in the former granary and the octagonal guest lounge occupies the mill's base. Book ahead.

George in Rye   HOTEL £££

(☎01797-222114; www.thegeorgeinrye.com; 98 High St; d from £135; @🛜) This old coaching inn has managed to reinvent itself as a contemporary boutique hotel while staying true to its roots. Downstairs, an old-fashioned wood-panelled lounge is warmed by roaring log fires, while the guest rooms in the main building, created by the set designer from the film *Pride & Prejudice,* are chic and understated.

Mermaid Inn   HOTEL £££

(☎01797-223065; www.mermaidinn.com; Mermaid St; s/d from £90/150; P) Few inns can claim to be as atmospheric as this ancient hostelry, dating from 1420. Each of the 31 rooms is different, but all are thick with dark beams and lit by leaded windows, and some are graced by secret passageways that now act as fire escapes. It also has one of Rye's best restaurants.

Eating

Simon the Pieman CAFE **£**
(3 Lion St; snacks £2.50-9; ◷ 9.30am-4.45pm Mon-Fri, to 5.30pm Sat, 12.30-5.30pm Sun) Many local cream-tea cognoscenti assert this traditional tearoom, Rye's oldest, does the best scone-cream-jam combo this side of Romney Marsh. Further foes of tooth and waistline tempt from the shop's window.

Haydens CAFE **£**
(www.haydensinrye.co.uk; 108 High St; snacks/meals £4.50-9; ◷10am-5pm) Long-time believers in organic and fair-trade produce, Haydens dishes up delicious omelettes, ploughman's lunches, salads and bagels in a light, breezy cafe. There's a wonderful elevated terrace at the back with great views over town and country. Also runs an excellent seven-room ecofriendly guesthouse upstairs.

Landgate Bistro BRITISH **££**
(www.landgatebistro.co.uk; 5-6 Landgate; mains £14-20; ◷noon-3.30pm Sat & Sun, 7-11pm Wed-Sat) Escape the medieval excesses of Rye's central eateries to this fresh-feeling bistro, slightly off the tourist trail near the impressive 14th-century Landgate. The focus here is on competently crafted dishes using local lamb and fish. The dining space is understated with tables gathered around an ancient fireplace.

ⓘ Information

Rye Heritage Centre (☏ 01797-226696; www.ryeheritage.co.uk; Strand Quay; ◷10am-5pm Apr-Oct, shorter hours Nov-Mar) See a town-model audiovisual history (£3.50) and, upstairs, a freaky collection of still-functional penny-in-the-slot novelty machines. Also runs themed walking tours of the town; see the website for details.

ⓘ Getting There & Away

There are twice-hourly buses to Dover (bus 100; £6.40, two hours) and Hastings (bus 100/101; £5.60, 40 minutes).

Change in Ashford for services to London St Pancras (£31.70, 1½ hours, hourly).

Hastings

POP 90,300

Forever associated with the Norman invasion of 1066 (even though the crucial events took place 6 miles away), Hastings thrived as one of the Cinque Ports and, in its Victorian heyday, was one of the country's most fashionable resorts. After a period of steady decline, the town is enjoying a mini-renaissance, and these days is an intriguing mix of tacky resort, fishing port and arty New Age hang-out.

◉ Sights

Stade AREA
(Rock-A-Nore Rd) The seafront area known as the Stade (below East Hill) is home to distinctive black clapboard structures known as Net Shops. These were built to store fishing gear back in the 17th century, but some now house fishmongers who sell off the catch of Europe's largest beach-launched fishing fleet, usually hauled up on the shingle behind. All these fishy goings-on keep the Stade very much a working place, with the combined pong of diesel and guts scenting the air.

Hastings Museum & Art Gallery MUSEUM
(www.hmag.org.uk; Johns Place, Bohemia Rd; ◷10am-5pm Tue-Sat, noon-5pm Sun Apr-Sep, shorter hours Oct-Mar) `FREE` A short walk west of the train station, this marvellous little museum is housed in a red-brick mansion. Highlights inside include the intricately Moorish Durbar Hall and a section on John Logie Baird, who invented television while recuperating from an illness in Hastings between February 1923 and November 1924.

Jerwood Gallery GALLERY
(www.jerwoodgallery.org; Rock-A-Nore Rd; adult/child £9/3.50; ◷11am-5pm Tue-Sun) Large, purpose-built exhibition venue at the end of the Stade used for temporary shows of contemporary British art as well as themed installations from the Jerwood collection. The building has a great cafe with sunny Channel views.

Hastings Castle RUINS
(www.discoverhastings.co.uk; Castle Hill Rd; adult/child £7/5; ◷10am-4pm Easter-Sep) This fortress was built by William the Conquerer, and an exhibition in the grounds tells the story of the castle and the Battle of Hastings in 1066.

🛏 Sleeping & Eating

Swan House B&B **££**
(☏ 01424-430014; www.swanhousehastings.co.uk; 1 Hill St; s/d from £90/120; @ 🛜) Inside its 15th-century timbered shell, this place blends contemporary and vintage chic to perfection. The four rooms feature organic toiletries, fresh flowers, hand-painted walls

and huge beds. The guest lounge, where pale sofas, painted floorboards and striking modern sculpture rub shoulders with beams and a huge stone fireplace, is a stunner.

The Laindons   B&B **££**
(01424-437710; www.thelaindons.com; 23 High St; s/d from £105/120;) Occupying a Georgian grade II–listed former coaching inn, this cosy B&B is just five minutes' amble from the seafront at the quieter end of High St. The five beautifully appointed rooms flood with sea-refracted light from the huge Georgian windows, illuminating the blend of breezy contemporary design and antique furnishings. Owner-cooked breakfasts are taken around a communal table.

Dragon Bar   INTERNATIONAL **££**
(www.dragon-bar.uk; 71 George St; mains £10-17.50, weekday lunch menu £7; noon-11pm;) The younger end of the alternative old-town crowd is attracted to this atmospheric, hip bar-restaurant hang-out. It's full of dark walls, mismatched furniture and beaten leather sofas, and the eclectic menu features everything from Madras curry to Winchelsea lamb and pizzas.

Drinking & Nightlife

Hanushka Coffee House   CAFE
(28 George St; 9.30am-6pm) Hastings' best caffeine stop resembles a very well-stocked secondhand bookshop with every inch of wall space packed with browsable titles. The low-lit and tightly packed space in between provokes inter-table interaction, or you can seek sanctuary on the sofas and perches in the window.

Information

Tourist Office (01424-451111; www.visit-1066country.com; Aquila House, Breeds Pl; 9am-5pm Mon-Fri, 9.30am-5.30pm Sat, 10.30am-4pm Sun Apr-Sep, slightly shorter hours Oct-Mar)

Getting There & Away

BUS

Hastings has the following bus connections:
Eastbourne (bus 98/99; £4.60, 75 minutes, four hourly)
London Victoria (National Express; £14.40, three hours, daily)
Rye (buses 100/101; £5.60, 40 minutes, twice hourly)

TRAIN

Hastings has connections with Brighton (£13.30, one hour to 80 minutes, three hourly), via Eastbourne, and London Victoria (£17.80, two hours, hourly).

Getting Around

Hastings has two delightful old Victorian funiculars, the East Hill Cliff and West Hill Cliff Railways, useful if you need to get up onto the cliffs and don't fancy the walk. The **East Hill Cliff Railway** (Rock-A-Nore Rd; adult/child return £2.50/1.50; 10am-5.30pm Apr-Sep, 11am-4pm Sat & Sun Oct-Mar) funicular ascends from the Stade to Hastings Country Park, while the **West Hill Cliff Railway** (George St; adult/child return £2.50/1.50; 10am-5.30pm Mar-Sep, 11am-4pm Oct-Mar) funicular saves visitors' legs when climbing up to Hastings Castle. Otherwise the town can be easily tackled on foot.

Eastbourne

POP 99,400

Despite its official title as 'Britain's sunniest town', Eastbourne has been slow to throw off its unattractive image as death's waiting room by the chilly Channel, all snoozing octogenarians in deckchairs and fusty guesthouses populated by vitamin D–deprived bank-holidaying Scots. But while much of this is still to be found here, in the last decade or so an influx of students and the arrival of the southeast's largest Polish community have given the town a sprightlier feel.

Eastbourne's 3.5-mile sweeping, palm-tree-lined seafront is one of the UK's grandest. Add to this a fresh modern art gallery and the recently created South Downs National Park that nudges its western suburbs and Eastbourne certainly makes an enjoyable day trip from London or Brighton. It's also the start and end point for a hike along the 100-mile South Downs Way.

Sights

Towner Art Gallery   GALLERY
(01323-434670; www.townereastbourne.org.uk; Devonshire Park, College Rd; 10am-5pm Tue-Sun) **FREE** One of the southeast's most exciting exhibition spaces, this purpose-built structure has temporary shows of contemporary work on the ground and 2nd floors, while the 1st floor is given over to rotating themed shows created from the gallery's 5000-piece collection. Building tours include a peek inside the climate-controlled art store; see the website for times.

Eastbourne Pier LANDMARK

(⊙24hr) Mercifully saved by some clever firefighting when a huge blaze broke out in the amusement arcade at the land end of the structure on 30 July 2014, it took just over a year for this ramshackle piece of rusty Victoriana jutting into the Channel to come back from the dead. The amusement arcade wasn't rebuilt, a pleasant open decking space replacing the slot machines. This is part of a long-overdue clean-up of the town's most lovable sight.

🖝 Tours

Sussex Voyages BOATING

(☑ 01293-888780; www.sussexvoyages.co.uk; Lower Quayside, The Waterfront, Sovereign Harbour Marina; adult/child £25/14) Hour-long Beachy Head and Seven Sisters boat tours leaving from Sovereign Harbour (take hourly bus 51) on rigid-hulled inflatables. Reservations essential.

🛏 Sleeping & Eating

Albert & Victoria B&B ££

(☑ 01323-730948; www.albertandvictoria.com; 19 St Aubyns Rd; s/d from £35/70; 🖵) Book ahead to stay at this delightful Victorian terraced house, whose fragrant rooms, canopied beds, crystal chandeliers and secluded walled garden for summer breakfasts are mere paces from the seafront promenade. The four rooms are named after four of Queen Victoria's offspring.

Big Sleep HOTEL ££

(☑ 01323-722676; www.thebigsleephotel.com; King Edward's Pde; s/d from £44/59; 🖵) Hip, fresh and friendly, this seafront hotel has 50 gob-smacking rooms with big-print wallpaper, retro furnishings, and curtains that resemble sheep that might have been grazing on Beachy Head just a few hours prior. A trendy bar, big basement games room and Channel views make this Eastbourne's coolest kip.

Lamb Inn PUB FOOD ££

(www.thelambeastbourne.co.uk; 36 High St; mains £10-17; ⊙11am-11pm Sun-Thu, to midnight Fri & Sat) This ancient Eastbourne institution located less than a mile northwest of the train station in the under-visited Old Town has been plonking Sussex ales on the bar for eight centuries, and now also serves gourmet British pub grub. A holidaying Charles Dickens also left a few smudged napkins

here when he stayed across the road. Buses 1, 1A and 12 stop nearby.

Belgian Cafe BELGIAN ££

(www.thebelgiancafe.co.uk; 11-23 Grand Pde; mains £10-18.50; ⊙11am-11pm) If you didn't know that Belgian beer can taste of fruit; the national dish is mussels and chips; and Tintin hails from its capital, Brussels, you will once you've experienced this popular cafe near the pier. Fifty types of mussel dishes and the same number of Belgian ales are available.

ℹ Information

Tourist Office (☑ 01323-415 415; www.visit eastbourne.com; Cornfield Rd; ⊙9am-5.30pm Mon-Fri, to 5pm Sat, 10am-1pm Sun May-Sep, closed Sun & shorter hours Oct-Apr)

ℹ Getting There & Away

There are buses to Brighton (bus 12; £4, 75 minutes, up to every 10 minutes) and Hastings (bus 98/99; £4.50, one hour and 10 minutes, three hourly). Twice-hourly trains service Brighton (£10.60, 30 to 40 minutes) and London Victoria (£17.80, 1½ hours).

South Downs National Park

The South Downs National Park, more than 600 sq miles of rolling chalk downs, stretches west from Eastbourne for about 100 miles. The South Downs Way extends its entire length.

⊙ Sights

Beachy Head LANDMARK

(www.beachyhead.org.uk) The famous cliffs of Beachy Head are the highest point of the chalky rock faces that slice across the rugged coastline at the southern end of the South Downs. It's off the B2103, from the A259 between Eastbourne and Newhaven. From here the stunning Seven Sisters Cliffs undulate their way west. A clifftop path (a branch of the South Downs Way) rides the waves of chalk as far as picturesque Cuckmere Haven.

Pevensey Castle RUINS

(EH; Castle Rd, Pevensey; adult/child £5.80/3.40; ⊙10am-6pm Apr-Sep) The ruins of William the Conqueror's first stronghold sit 5 miles east of Eastbourne, just off the A259. Regular train services between London Victoria and Hastings via Eastbourne stop at

Westham, half a mile from Pevensey. Picturesquely dissolving into its own moat, the castle marks the point where William the Conqueror landed in 1066, just two weeks before the Battle of Hastings.

Sleeping

★ Belle Tout Lighthouse
B&B £££

(☑ 01323 423-185; www.belletout.co.uk; South Downs Way, Beachy Head, Eastbourne; d from £165) Perched precariously close to the edge of the white cliffs, this decommissioned lighthouse is a truly wonderful place to stay. The building has had an incredible past, almost destroyed in WWII, used by the BBC to film *The Life and Loves of a She-Devil* and famously moved back from the cliff edge in 1999 before becoming a quirky guesthouse.

Lewes

POP 17,300

Strung out along an undulating High St flanked by elegant Georgian buildings, a part-ruined castle and a traditional brewery, Lewes (pronounced 'Lewis') is a charmingly affluent hillside town with a turbulent past and fiery traditions. Off the main drag, however, there's a more intimate atmosphere as you descend into twisting narrow streets called twittens – the remainder of the town's original medieval street plan.

One of Lewes' claims to fame is that it straddles the 0 degrees line of longitude. An inconspicuous plaque on Western Rd marks the meridian, though modern measuring methods have actually placed the line around 100m to the east.

Sights & Activities

Lewes Castle &
Barbican House Museum
CASTLE

(www.sussexpast.co.uk; 169 High St; adult/child £7.40/4; ⊙ 10am-5.30pm Tue-Sat, 11am-5.30pm Sun & Mon; P) Now little more than a set of ruins, this castle was built shortly after the 1066 Norman invasion. It never saw warfare, but there were riotous celebrations following the navy's victory over the Spanish Armada in 1588, when happy citizens blew great chunks out of the castle's walls. They left enough standing for it to remain an impressive sight though, and its windy keep, visible for miles around, affords panoramic views across the town and beyond.

The attached Barbican House Museum has a good collection of Lewesiana, but the star attraction is the incredibly accurate town model, glued together by an army of volunteers in the mid-1980s and showing how the town looked a century earlier. Viewing is accompanied by a 12-minute film relating the homo-Sussexicus' historical advancement from cavemen to Victorians.

Harveys Brewery
TOURS

(☑ 01273-480217; www.harveys.org.uk; Bridge Wharf; per person £3; ⊙ three evenings a week Jun, Jul & Sep-Nov) Sussex's Harveys Brewery perfumes Lewes town centre with a hop-laden scent. Book several months in advance for tours.

Festivals & Events

★ Lewes Bonfire Celebrations
FIREWORKS

(www.lewesbonfirecelebrations.com; ⊙ 5 Nov) Lewes holds what it claims is the biggest Bonfire Night bash in the world with tens of thousands of people descending on the town to watch a carnival, fireworks display and effigies of villains of the day going up in flames.

Sleeping & Eating

Castle Banks Cottage
B&B ££

(☑ 01273-476291; www.castlebankscottage.co.uk; 4 Castle Banks; s/d £42.50/85; 🖥) Tucked away in a quiet lane near the castle, this tiny guesthouse has just two rooms. The easygoing travel-writer proprietor is a mine of information about the area's local history. Breakfast is served in the secluded garden in summer.

Shelleys
HOTEL £££

(☑ 01273-472361; www.the-shelleys.co.uk; 135-136 High St; r from £130; 🖥) Full of old-fashioned charm, this 16th-century manor house was once home to the earl of Dorset and was owned by the Shelley family (of Percy Bysshe fame). It has cosy, country rooms and an above standard restaurant overlooking a lovely walled garden.

Bill's
CAFE £

(www.bills-website.co.uk; 56 Cliffe High St; mains & snacks £3.50-12; ⊙ 8am-11pm) Part grocers, part delicatessen, part rustic-styled cafe, this insanely popular place envelopes customers in its colours and smells then dishes up melt-in-the-mouth tartlets, gourmet pizzas, salads, desserts and other artisanal snacks. Get here early at meal times, and even in-between times, as it's normally chock-a-block.

Real Eating Company BRITISH ££
(18 Cliffe High St; mains £10-19; ⊘8.30am-9pm Mon-Sat, 10am-5pm Sun) This large, airy cafe-brasserie stretches back to a lovely outside terrace and serves kick-starting breakfasts, gourmet fish and chips, and substantial British meat-and-two-veg combos, all made with Sussex ingredients as much as possible.

🛍 Shopping

Fifteenth Century Bookshop BOOKS
(www.oldenyoungbooks.co.uk; 99 High St; ⊘10am-5.30pm Mon-Sat) Rummage through antiquarian treasures and new editions at the fabulous, half-timbered bookshop housed in a former candle factory.

ℹ Information

Tourist Office (☑01273-483448; www.lewes. gov.uk; 187 High Street; ⊘9.30am-4.30pm Mon-Fri, to 4pm Sat, 10am-2pm Sun Apr-Sep, closed Sunday & shorter hours Sat Oct-Mar)

ℹ Getting There & Away

Lewes' only useful bus connection goes to Brighton (£3.50, 30 minutes, four hourly).

Lewes has the following rail connections:
Brighton (£4.30, 15 minutes, four hourly)
Eastbourne (£7.70, 20 minutes, three hourly)
London Victoria (£17.80, one hour to 1½ hours, four hourly)

Brighton & Hove

POP 275,800

Raves on the beach, Graham Greene novels, mods and rockers in bank-holiday fisticuffs, naughty weekends for Mr and Mrs Smith, the UK's biggest gay scene and the Channel's best clubbing – this coastal city evokes many images for the British. But one thing is certain: with its bohemian, hedonistic vibe, Brighton is where England's seaside experience goes from cold to cool.

Brighton is without doubt Britain's most colourful and outrageous city. Here burlesque meets contemporary design; grotty hostels share thin walls with kinky boutique hotels; microbrewed ales share bar space with 'sex on the beach'; and stags watch drag. The city returned the UK's first Green Party MP, Valentine's Day is celebrated with unusual gusto, and according to the 2001 census, it has the UK's highest Jedi population.

The highlight for the sightseeing visitor is the Royal Pavilion, a 19th-century party palace built by the Prince Regent, who kicked off Brighton's love of the outlandish.

GLYNDEBOURNE THEATRE

In 1934, science teacher John Christie and his opera-singer wife Audrey Mildmay decided to build a 1200-seat opera house in the middle of nowhere. It seemed a magnificent folly at the time, but now **Glyndebourne** (☑01273-812321; www.glyndebourne.com; Glyndebourne) is one of England's best venues for the lyric arts, from late May to the end of August. Tickets can be like gold dust, so book well ahead. Glyndebourne is 4 miles east of Lewes off the B2192.

◎ Sights

★**Royal Pavilion** PALACE
(☑03000-290901; http://brightonmuseums.org. uk/royalpavilion; Royal Pavilion Gardens; adult/child £12.30/6.90; ⊘9.30am-5.45pm Apr-Sep, 10am-5.15pm Oct-Mar) The city's must-see attraction is the Royal Pavilion, the glittering party pad and palace of Prince George, later Prince Regent and then King George IV. It's one of the most opulent buildings in England, and certainly the finest example of early-19th-century chinoiserie anywhere in Europe. It's an apt symbol of Brighton's reputation for decadence. An unimpressed Queen Victoria called the Royal Pavilion 'a strange, odd Chinese place', but for visitors to Brighton it's an unmissable chunk of Sussex history.

The entire palace is an eye-popping spectacle, but some interiors stand out even amid the riot of decoration. The dragon-themed banqueting hall must be the most incredible in all of England. More dragons and snakes writhe in the music room, with its ceiling of 26,000 gold scales, and the then-state-of-the-art kitchen must have wowed Georgians with its automatic spits and hot tables. Prince Albert carted away all of the furniture, some of which has been loaned back by the present queen.

Brighton Museum & Art Gallery MUSEUM, GALLERY
(www.brighton-hove-museums.org.uk; Royal Pavilion Gardens; adult/child £5.20/3; ⊘10am-5pm Tue-Sun) Set in the Royal Pavilion's renovated stable block, this museum and art gallery has a glittering collection of 20th-century art and design, including a crimson

Brighton & Hove

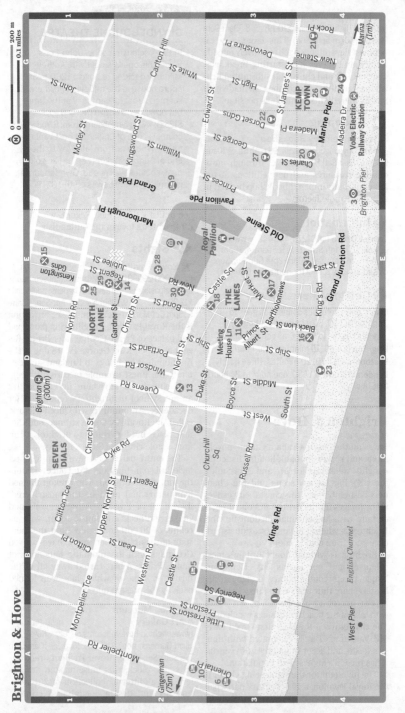

SEVEN DIALS

NORTH LAINE

THE LANES

KEMP TOWN

English Channel

West Pier

Brighton Pier

Marina (1mi)

Rock Pl

New Steine

Marine Pde

Madeira Dr

Volks Electric Railway Station

Grand Junction Rd

King's Rd

King's Rd

Churchill Sq

Regency Sq

Royal Pavilion

Grand Pde

Pavilion Pde

Marlborough Pl

Old Steine

St James's St

Devonshire Pl

High St

White St

Carlton Hill

John St

Morley St

Kingswood St

William St

Edward St

George St

Charles St

Dorset Gdns

Princes St

Kensington Gdns

Regent St

Jubilee St

New Rd

Bond St

North St

Castle Sq

Market St

East St

Black Lion St

Ship St

Ship St

Middle St

South St

West St

Boyce St

Duke St

North St

Portland St

Windsor Rd

Queens Rd

Gardner St

Church St

North Rd

Dyke Rd

Church St

Regent Hill

Upper North St

Dean St

Western Rd

Castle St

Castle St

Little Preston St

Preston St

Oriental Pl

Clifton Pl

Clifton Tce

Montpelier Tce

Montpelier Rd

Russell Rd

Meeting House Ln

Prince Albert St

Bartholomews

Jew St

Brighton (300m)

Brighton (R)

Gingerman (75m)

0   200 m
0   0.1 miles

1 2 3 4

A B C D E F G

Salvador Dalí sofa modelled on Mae West's lips. There's also an enthralling gallery of world art, an impressive collection of Egyptian artefacts, and an 'Images of Brighton' multimedia exhibit containing a series of oral histories and a model of the defunct West Pier.

i360 Tower

TOWER

(☑ 03337-720 360; www.britishairwaysi360.com; Lower King's Rd; adult/child £15/7.50; ⊙ 10am-7.30pm Sun-Thu, to 9.30pm Fri & Sat) Brighton's newest attraction opened in 2016, at the point the now defunct West Pier used to make landfall. The world's most slender tower is a brutal, 162m-tall column of reinforced steel and concrete rising rudely in space-age spectacle from the seafront, a huge, impaled, glass doughnut taking 'passengers' 138m above the city for some gob-smacking vistas of the Sussex coast. The idea is that profits from the i360, a 21st-century 'vertical pier', will one day be used to rebuild the West Pier.

Brighton Pier

LANDMARK

(www.brightonpier.co.uk; Madeira Dr) This grand century-old pier is the place to experience Brighton's tackier side. There are plenty of stomach-churning fairground rides and dingy amusement arcades to keep you entertained, and candy floss and Brighton rock to chomp on while you're doing so. Just west are the sad remains of the **West Pier** (www.westpier.co.uk), a skeletal iron hulk that attracts flocks of starlings at sunset.

✰ Festivals & Events

Brighton Festival

PERFORMING ARTS

(☑ 01273-709709; www.brightonfestival.org; ⊙ May) After Edinburgh, this is the UK's biggest arts festival. It draws star performers from around the globe for three weeks by the sea.

Brighton Pride

LGBT

(www.brighton-pride.org; ⊙ early Aug) One of the UK's biggest gay bashes, with a rainbow-hued parade and concerts in Preston Park.

🛏 Sleeping

Kipps Brighton

HOSTEL £

(☑ 01273-604182; www.kipps-brighton.com; 76 Grand Pde; dm £14-35, d £42-90; @ 🛜) The owners of Canterbury's award-winning hostel have created equally commendable budget digs here in Brighton. There's a real cafe vibe around reception, and facilities include a communal kitchen. Free movie, pizza and pub nights successfully separate guests from their wi-fi-enabled devices.

Baggies Backpackers

HOSTEL £

(☑ 01273-733740; www.baggiesbackpackers.com; 33 Oriental Pl; dm/d £16/40; 🛜) With a warm, familial atmosphere, worn-in charm, attentive service and clean, snug dorms, this long-established hostel is a Brighton institution.There's a cosy basement music and chill-out room, and a TV lounge piled high with video cassettes that have somehow survived the digital revolution. The hostel has sister establishments in Bath and Bournemouth.

Brighton & Hove

◎ Top Sights
1 Royal Pavilion E3

◎ Sights
2 Brighton Museum & Art Gallery E2
3 Brighton Pier F4
4 i360 Tower B3

🛏 Sleeping
5 Artist Residence B2
6 Baggies Backpackers A3
7 Hotel Pelirocco B3
8 Hotel Una B3
9 Kipps Brighton F2
10 Neo Hotel A2

🍴 Eating
11 Choccywoccydoodah D3
12 English's of Brighton E3
13 Foodilic D2
14 Infinity Foods Kitchen E2

15 Iydea E1
16 JB's American Diner D4
17 Plateau E3
18 Riddle & Finns E3
19 Terre à Terre E4

🍸 Drinking & Nightlife
20 A Bar F4
21 Brighton Rocks G4
22 Bulldog F3
23 Coalition D4
24 Concorde 2 .... G4
25 Dorset E1
26 Legends Club G4
   Patterns .... (see 20)
27 Queen's Arms F3

🎭 Entertainment
28 Brighton Dome E2
29 Komedia Theatre E1
30 Theatre Royal E2

★ **No 27 Brighton** B&B ££

(☑ 01273-694951; www.brighton-bed-and-breakfast.co.uk; 27 Upper Rock Gardens; s £61.50-72.50, d £84-110) Brighton's top B&B has five sumptuous rooms, perfectly done out with antique flourish. All the fabrics, furniture and decoration has been painstakingly selected to fit an understated theme, the overarching topic being people related to King George IV. Some rooms have sea views, but the superb decor may have you looking around more than out. Breakfast (£7.50) is served on crisp linen and fine English china.

Hotel Pelirocco HOTEL ££

(☑ 01273-327055; www.hotelpelirocco.co.uk; 10 Regency Sq; s £65-125, d £95-125; ☎) One of Brighton's sexiest and nuttiest places to stay, the Pelirocco has become the ultimate venue for a flirty rock-and-roll weekend. Flamboyant rooms, some designed by artists, include the 'Dollywould' room paying homage to Dolly Parton, the 'Modrophenia' room on a Mod and pop art theme, and the 'Pretty Vacant' double, a shrine to the Sex Pistols.

The room everyone wants, or wishes they could have, is the 'Kraken's lair' suite with 3m circular bed, mirrored ceiling and pole-dancing area.

Snooze HOTEL ££

(☑ 01273-605797; www.snoozebrighton.com; 25 St George's Tce; s/d from £75/95; ☎) The retro styling at this eccentric Kemptown pad features everything from vintage posters and bright '60s and '70s wallpaper to Bollywood film posters, floral sinks and mad clashes of colour. It's more than just a gimmick – the rooms are comfortable and spotless, and there are great meat-free breakfasts. You'll find it just off St James' St, about 500m east of New Steine.

Blanch House BOUTIQUE HOTEL ££

(☑ 01273-603504; www.blanchhouse.co.uk; 17 Atlingworth St; r from £109; @☎) Themed rooms are the name of the game at this boutique hotel, but there's nothing tacky about them – swish art-deco styling rules in the Legacia Room, while the Snowstorm is a frosty vision in white and tinkling ice. The magnificently stylish fine-dining restaurant is all white leather banquettes and space-age swivel chairs and there's a fine cocktail bar. From New Steine, walk for 150m east along St James' St then turn right into Atlingworth St.

Neo Hotel BOUTIQUE HOTEL ££

(☑ 01273-711104; www.neohotel.com; 19 Oriental Pl; r £90-200; ☎) You won't be surprised to learn the owner of this gorgeous hotel is an interior stylist. The nine rooms could have dropped straight from the pages of a design magazine, each finished in rich colours and tactile fabrics, with bold floral and Asian motifs, and black-tiled bathrooms. Wonderful breakfasts include homemade smoothies and pancakes.

★ **Hotel Una** BOUTIQUE HOTEL £££

(☑ 01273-820464; www.hotel-una.co.uk; 55-56 Regency Sq; s £55-75, d £115-200, all incl breakfast; ✴☎) All of the 19 generous rooms here wow guests with their bold-patterned fabrics, supersized leather sofas, in-room free-standing baths and vegan, veggie or carnivorous breakfast in bed. Some, such as the two-level suite with its own mini-cinema, and the under-pavement chambers with their own spa and Jacuzzi, are truly show-stopping and not as expensive as you might expect.

All this plus a cool cocktail bar and lots of time-warp period features make the Una our numero uno.

★ **Artist Residence** BOUTIQUE HOTEL £££

(☑ 01273-324 302; www.artistresidencebrighton.co.uk; 33 Regency Sq; d £129-260; ☎) Eclectic doesn't quite describe the rooms at this wonderful 23-room town-house hotel, set amid the splendour of Regency Sq. As befits the name, every bedroom is a work of funky art with bold wall murals, bespoke and vintage furniture, rough wood cladding and in-room roll-top baths. The Set Restaurant downstairs already has a glowing reputation. Book direct and breakfast is free.

✗ Eating

★ **Iydea** VEGETARIAN £

(www.iydea.co.uk; 17 Kensington Gardens; mains £6-8; ⊙ 9.30am-5.30pm; ☎✎) Even by Brighton's lofty standards, the food at this multi-award-winning vegetarian cafe is a treat. The daily-changing choices of curries, lasagnes, felafel, enchiladas and quiches are full of flavour and can be washed down with a selection of vegan wines, organic ales and homemade lemonades. If you're on the hop, you can get any dish to takeaway in environmentally-friendly packaging.

Choccywoccydoodah CAFE £

(www.choccywoccydoodah.com; 3 Meeting House Lane; cakes & snacks £2-5; ⊙ 10am-6pm Mon-Sat, 11am-5pm Sun) Even if you're not hungry or thirsty, this incredible chocolate emporium, painted blood red inside and out, is a must-see. The downstairs is packed with outrageous Belgian chocolate creations, fake rococo mirrors, sprays of artificial flowers and tassled lampshades. Head upstairs to the small cafe where every single item on sale contains chocolate. Madly popular so be prepared to queue.

Foodilic   BUFFET **£**
(www.foodilic.com; 60 North St; takeaway box £5, buffet £7; ☺8am-9.30pm Mon-Sat, to 6pm Sun) It's as good for breakfast (£4.50) as for a late dinner, but it's the eat-till-you-burst buffet of scrumptious healthy fare that packs out this funky place all day long. Slightly a victim of its own success, it could do with bigger premises – you'll queue at lunchtime and inside things get cramped.

Infinity Foods Kitchen   VEGETARIAN **£**
(www.infinityfoodskitchen.co.uk; 50 Gardner St; mains £3.50-8; ☺9am-5pm Mon-Sat, 10am-4pm Sun; 🐾🍴) The sister establishment of Infinity Foods wholefoods shop (health-food co-operative and Brighton institution) serves a wide variety of vegetarian and organic food, with many vegan and wheat- or gluten-free options including tofu burgers, mezze platters and veggie sausage sandwiches. There's seating upstairs with views of the passing hipster mob.

★**Terre à Terre**   VEGETARIAN **££**
(☎01273-729051; www.terreaterre.co.uk; 71 East St; mains £15; ☺noon-10.30pm Mon-Fri, 10am-11pm Sat, 10am-10pm Sun; 🍴) Even staunch meat eaters will rave about this legendary vegetarian restaurant. A sublime dining experience, from the vibrant modern space to the entertaining menus and inventive dishes stuffed with excitingly zingy ingredients. There's also plenty for vegans. Desserts are on the steep side.

Gingerman   MODERN EUROPEAN **££**
(☎01273-326688; www.gingermanrestaurants.com; 21a Norfolk Sq; 2-/3-course menu £17/20; ☺12.30-2pm & 7-10pm Tue-Sun) Hastings seafood, Sussex beef, Romney Marsh lamb, local sparkling wines and countless other seasonal, local and British treats go into the adroitly flash-fried and slow-cooked dishes served at this snug 32-cover eatery. Reservations are advised. Norfolk Sq is a short walk west along Western Rd from the Churchill Square shopping centre.

Riddle & Finns   SEAFOOD **££**
(www.riddleandfinns.co.uk; 12 Meeting House Lane; mains £14-36; ☺noon-late Sun-Fri, 11.30am-11pm Sat) Regarded as the town's most refined

seafood spot, R&F is light on gimmicky interiors (think white butcher's shop tiles, marble tables and candles) but heavy on taste. With the kitchen open to the street outside, chefs put on a public cooking class with every dish as they prepare your smoked haddock in champagne sauce or wild sea bass.

English's of Brighton   SEAFOOD **££**
(☎01273-327980; www.englishs.co.uk; 29-31 East St; mains £15-30; ☺noon-10pm) A 70-year-old institution and celebrity haunt, this local seafood paradise dishes up everything from Essex oysters to locally caught lobster and Dover sole. It's converted from fishers' cottages, with shades of the elegant Edwardian era inside and alfresco dining on the pedestrian square outside.

Plateau   INTERNATIONAL **££**
(☎01273-733085; www.plateaubrighton.co.uk; 1 Bartholomews; tapas £6-16, mains around £30; ☺noon-4pm & 6-10pm) This relative newcomer to the Brighton feeding scene serves up superb tapas such as Sussex chorizo, roast bone marrow and mozzarella with peas, mint and lemon as well as pricey mains. The shabby-retro interior includes scuffed floorboards and stained glass that belonged to a previous incarnation of the building. At night the place morphs into a wine and cocktail bar.

JB's American Diner   FAST FOOD **££**
(http://jbsdiner.co.uk; 31 King's Rd; burgers £7-10, mains £6.50-15; ☺10am-10pm Mon-Sat, 9am-10pm Sun) The waft of hot dogs as you push open the door, the shiny red-leather booths, the stars and stripes draped across the wall, the 1950s soundtrack twanging in the background and the colossal portions of burgers, fries and milkshakes – in short, this is a hefty slab of authentic Americana teleported to the Brighton seafront.

🍷 Drinking & Nightlife

Concorde 2   CLUB
(www.concorde2.co.uk; Madeira Dr) Brighton's best-known and best-loved club is a disarmingly unpretentious den, where DJ Fatboy Slim pioneered the Big Beat Boutique and still occasionally graces the decks. Each month there's a huge variety of club nights, live bands and concerts by international names.

Coalition   BAR
(www.coalitionbrighton.com; 171-181 Kings Rd Arches; ☺10am-5am Mon-Fri, to 7am Sat) On a sum-

GAY & LESBIAN BRIGHTON

Brighton has the most vibrant gay community in the country outside London and Kemptown (aka Camptown). On and off St James's St is where it's all at. The old Brunswick Town area of Hove is a quieter alternative to the traditionally cruisy (and sometimes seedy) scene in Kemptown. For up-to-date information on the gay scene in Brighton, check out www.gay.brighton.co.uk and www.realbrighton.com, or pick up the free monthly magazine *Gscene* (www.gscene.com) from gay venues.

Legends Club (www.legendsbrighton.com; 31-34 Marine Pde; ⊗ bar 11am-5am, club 10pm-5am Wed & Fri-Sun) Located beneath the Legends Hotel this is arguably the best gay bar and club in town.

A Bar (www.amsterdam.uk.com; 11-12 Marine Pde; ⊗ noon-2am; 🛜) Extremely hip bar and sauna in the Amsterdam hotel; its sun terrace is a particular hit.

Brighton Rocks (www.brightonrocksbar.co.uk; 6 Rock Pl; ⊗ 4-11pm Mon-Thu, to 1am Sat, noon-11pm Sun; 🛜) Incongruously located in an alley of garages and used-car lots, this cocktail bar is firmly established on the Kemptown gay scene, but welcomes all-comers with Sussex Martinis, well-executed plates of food and theme parties.

Queen's Arms (www.queensarmsbrighton.com; 7 George St; ⊗ 3pm-late) And they ain't talking Victoria or Elizabeth! Plenty of camp cabaret and karaoke at this pub.

Bulldog (www.bulldogbrighton.com; 31 St James's St; ⊗ 11am-late) Longest-running gay bar in Brighton; mostly frequented by men.

mer's day, there's nowhere finer to sit and watch the world go by than at this popular beach bar, diner and club. All sorts of events happen here, from comedy to live music and club nights.

Black Dove PUB
(www.blackdovebrighton.com; 74 St James's St; ⊗ 4pm-late) Eclectic hangout with shabby-chic furnishings, huge antique ceiling fans, a bar stocked with unusual tipples and a quirky basement snug. Live acoustic music and local DJs provide the soundtrack for evening quaffing that spills out onto the pavements when the mercury is high.

Patterns CLUB
(www.patternsbrighton.com; 10 Marine Pde; ⊗ Wed-Sat, hours vary) Some of the city's top club nights are held at this ear-numbing venue. The music is top priority here, attracting a young, up-for-it crowd.

Dorset PUB
(www.thedorset.co.uk; 28 North Rd; ⊗ 9am-late; 🛜) In fine weather this laid-back Brighton institution throws open its doors and windows, and tables spill out onto the pavement. You'll be just as welcome for a morning coffee as for an evening pint here, and should you not leave between the two, there's a decent gastropub menu.

⭐ Entertainment

Brighton Dome THEATRE
(🖉 01273-709709; www.brightondome.org; Church St) Once the stables for King George IV's horses, this art-deco complex houses three theatre venues within the Royal Pavilion estate. ABBA famously won the 1974 Eurovision Song Contest here.

Theatre Royal THEATRE
(🖉 0844 871 7650; New Rd) Built by decree of the Prince of Wales in 1806, this grand venue hosts musicals, plays and operas.

Komedia Theatre COMEDY
(🖉 0845 293 8480; www.komedia.co.uk; 44-47 Gardner St) A stylish comedy, theatre and cabaret venue attracting the best stand-up acts from the English-speaking world.

🔒 Shopping

In the market for a pair of vegan shoes, a gauche portrait of a Lego man or a letter opener in the shape of something naughty? Whatever item you yearn for, old or new, you'll probably find it in Brighton. The tightly packed **Lanes** is the most popular shopping district, its every twist and turn jam-packed with jewellers and gift shops, coffee shops and boutiques selling everything from antique firearms to hard-to-find vinyls.

There's another, less-claustrophobic shopping district in **North Laine**, a series of partially pedestrian thoroughfares north of the Lanes, including Bond, Gardner, Kensington and Sydney Sts, lined with retro-cool boutiques and bohemian cafes. Mainstream chains gather within the Churchill Square shopping centre and along Western Rd.

❶ Information

Incredibly, Brighton closed its busy tourist office in 2013, replacing it with 15 information points across the city, mostly racks of brochures in hotels, shops and museums. Contact **Visit Brighton** (☑ 01273-290337; www.visitbrighton.com) for information.

Jubilee Library (Jubilee St; ◷10am-7pm Mon, Tue & Thu, to 5pm Wed, Fri & Sat, 11am-5pm Sun) Bring ID to sign up for free internet sessions.

Post Office (2-3 Churchill Sq; ◷9am-5.30pm Mon-Sat, 11am-3pm Sun) Located within WH Smiths.

❶ Getting There & Away

BUS

Standard bus connections:
Arundel (bus 700; two hours, twice hourly)
Chichester (bus 700; three hours, twice hourly)
Eastbourne (bus 12; 70 minutes, up to every 10 minutes)
London Victoria (National Express; from £10, 2½ hours, hourly)

TRAIN

London-bound services pass through Gatwick Airport (£9.80, 25 to 40 minutes, up to five hourly).
Chichester (£13, 50 minutes, half-hourly)
Eastbourne (£10.60, 30 to 40 minutes, half-hourly)
Hastings (£13.30, one hour 20 minutes, half-hourly)
London St Pancras (£17.20, 1¼ hours, half-hourly)
London Victoria (£17.80, one hour, three-hourly)
Portsmouth (£15.30, 1½ hours, hourly)

❶ Getting Around

Day bus tickets (£5) are available from the drivers of all Brighton and Hove buses. Alternatively, a £3.60 PlusBus ticket on top of your rail fare gives unlimited bus travel for the day.

The city operates a pricey pay-and-display parking scheme. In the town centre, it costs between £1 and £3.60 per hour for a maximum stay of two hours. Alternatively, there's a Park & Ride 2.5 miles northwest of the centre at Withdean, from where bus 27 zips into town.

Cab companies include **Brighton Streamline Taxis** (☑ 01273-202020) and **City Cabs** (☑ 01273-205205), and there's a taxi rank at the junction of East and Market Sts.

WEST SUSSEX

West Sussex offers a welcome respite from fast-paced adventures. The serene hills and valleys of the South Downs ripple across the county, fringed by sheltered coastline. Beautiful Arundel and cultured Chichester make good bases from which to explore the county's winding country lanes and remarkable Roman ruins.

Arundel

POP 3500

Arguably the prettiest town in West Sussex, Arundel is clustered around a vast fairy-tale castle, and its hillside streets overflow with antique emporiums, teashops and a host of eateries. While much of the town appears medieval – the whimsical castle has been home to the Dukes of Norfolk for centuries – most of it dates back to Victorian times.

◉ Sights

Arundel Castle   CASTLE
(www.arundelcastle.org; adult/child £18/9; ◷10am-5pm Tue-Sun Easter-Oct) Arundel Castle was first built in the 11th century but all that's left of the early structure are the modest remains of the keep. It was ransacked during the English Civil War, and most of what you see today is the result of reconstruction by the eighth, 11th and 15th dukes of Norfolk between 1718 and 1900. The current duke still lives in part of the castle, whose highlights include the atmospheric keep, the massive Great Hall and the library.

Arundel Cathedral   CATHEDRAL
(www.arundelcathedral.org; London Rd; ◷9am-6pm Apr-Oct, to dusk Nov-Mar) FREE Arundel's ostentatious 19th-century Catholic cathedral is the other dominating feature of the town's impressive skyline. Commissioned by the 15th duke of Norfolk in 1868, the impressive structure was designed by Joseph Aloysius Hansom (inventor of the Hansom cab) in the French Gothic style, but shows much

Victorian economy and restraint. Although small for a cathedral – it holds just 500 worshippers – Hansom's clever layout makes the building seem a lot bigger.

Sleeping & Eating

Arundel House
B&B ££

(☎ 01903-882136; www.arundelhouseonline.com; 11 High St; d/ste from £90/125; 🛜) The contemporary chambers at this lovely 'restaurant with rooms' may be slightly low-ceilinged, but they're clean-cut and very comfortable, with showers big enough for two. The restaurant downstairs serves some of the best food in Arundel, which, happily, extends to breakfast.

Arden Guest House
B&B ££

(☎ 01903-884184; www.ardenguesthouse.net; 4 Queens Lane; d £99, without bathroom £89; P 🛜) For the classic British B&B experience, head to this seven-room guesthouse just over the river from the historical centre. Rooms are kept fresh and tick all the boxes; the hosts are amiable; and the breakfasts are cooked. No pets or children under 14 and only 10% off if you're travelling solo.

Bay Tree
MODERN EUROPEAN ££

(www.thebaytreearundel.com; 21 Tarrant St; mains £11-18; ⊙11.30am-3pm & 6.30pm-late Mon-Fri, 10.30am-4.30pm & 6.30pm-late Sat & Sun) The ideal lunch stop after a spot of antique hunting on Tarrant St, the Bay Tree serves up expertly prepared dishes in a pleasingly simple setting with just varnished oak tables and the odd objet d'art to distract you from your food. Pastas, panini, risottos and dishes large and small inhabit the menu, as does a highly recommended full English breakfast.

★ Town House
BRITISH £££

(☎ 01903-883847; www.thetownhouse.co.uk; 65 High St; set lunch/dinner from £17.50/25.50; ⊙noon-2.30pm & 7-9.30pm Tue-Sat) The only thing that rivals the 16th-century Florentine gilded-walnut ceiling in this compact and very elegant eatery is the sparkling atmosphere and acclaimed British cuisine with a European twist. Book ahead. Town House also has well-appointed rooms to let.

❶ Getting There & Away

Bus 700 runs to Brighton (two hours, twice hourly).

Arundel has the following train connections:

Brighton (£10.70, 1¼ hours, twice hourly) Change at Ford or Barnham.

Chichester (£4.60, 25 minutes, twice hourly) Change at Ford or Barnham.

London Victoria (£17.80, 1½ hours, twice hourly)

Chichester

POP 28,700

A lively Georgian market town still almost encircled by its medieval town walls, the administrative capital of West Sussex keeps watch over the plains between the South Downs and the sea. Visitors flock to Chichester's splendid cathedral, streets of handsome 18th-century town houses and its famous theatre, and of course to its pedestrianised shopping streets packed with big-name and independent shops. A Roman port garrison in its early days, the town is also a launch pad to other fascinating Roman remains, as well as to Arundel and the coast.

◉ Sights

Chichester Cathedral
CATHEDRAL

(www.chichestercathedral.org.uk; West St; ⊙7.15am-7pm, free tours 11.15am & 2.30pm Mon-Sat) This understated cathedral was begun in 1075 and largely rebuilt in the 13th century. The free-standing church tower went up in the 15th century; the spire dates from the 19th century, when its predecessor famously toppled over. Inside, three storeys of beautiful arches sweep upwards and Romanesque carvings are dotted around. Interesting features to track down include a smudgy stained-glass window added by artist Marc Chagall in 1978 and a glassed-over section of Roman mosaic flooring.

On the left as you enter there's a small exhibition on the history of the building, and little further on the treasury displays heaps of church plates and an interesting collection of 13th-century oak chests. The peaceful cloisters are home to an excellent cafe, all the profits from which go to the upkeep of the cathedral.

Pallant House Gallery
GALLERY

(www.pallant.org.uk; 9 North Pallant; adult/child £9/free; ⊙10am-5pm Tue, Wed, Fri & Sat, to 8pm Thu, 11am-5pm Sun) A Queen Anne mansion built by a local wine merchant, handsome Pallant House and a 21st-century wing host this superb gallery. The focus is on mostly British, 20th-century art. Show-stoppers Patrick Caulfield, Lucian Freud, Graham Sutherland, Frank Auerbach and Henry Moore are interspersed with international names such as Emil Filla, Le Corbusier and RB Kitaj. Most of these older works are in the mansion, while the newer wing is packed with pop art and temporary shows of modern and contemporary work.

Novium Museum MUSEUM
(www.thenovium.org; Tower St; ⊙10am-5pm Mon-Sat, to 4pm Sun Apr-Oct, 10am-5pm Mon-Sat Nov-Mar) FREE Chichester's purpose-built museum provides a home for the eclectic collections of the erstwhile District Museum, as well as some artefacts from Fishbourne Palace and a huge mosaic from Chilgrove Roman villa. The highlight is the set of Roman *thermae* (baths) discovered in the 1970s, around which this six-million-pound wedge of architecture was designed.

🛏 Sleeping & Eating

Trents B&B **££**
(✆ 01243-773714; www.trentschichester.co.uk; 50 South St; d from £75; 🛜) Just about the only place to sleep in the thick of the city centre action, the five snazzy rooms above this trendy bar-cum-restaurant are understandably popular.

Ship Hotel BOUTIQUE HOTEL **£££**
(✆ 01243-778000; www.theshiphotel.net; North St; s/d from £103/145; 🛜) The grand central staircase in this former Georgian town house climbs to 36 fairly spacious rooms of commanding period chic. It's the most enticing option in town and it also boasts a snazzily styled restaurant. Book well ahead.

Duke & Rye AMERICAN **£**
(14 West St; mains £4-11; ⊙11am-11pm Mon-Sat, noon-8pm Sun; 🛜) Occupying a large deconsecrated church opposite Chichester Cathedral, this temple of food and ale allows you to refuel and kick back in an incongruously ecclesiastical setting, recently updated to include shabby-chic areas of funky wallpaper, frilly standard lamps and Persian carpets. The US diner-style menu of burgers and sundaes is sure to bust your belt and invoke a holy thirst.

Amelie & Friends INTERNATIONAL **££**
(✆ 01243-771444; www.amelieandfriends.com; 31 North St; mains £12.50-18; ⊙noon-2.30pm & 5.30-9pm Mon-Fri, noon-3pm & 5-9pm Sat, noon-2.30pm Sun) This award-winning, vaguely Gallic-feeling restaurant serves up finely crafted seasonal dishes with a slight bias towards seafood in a stylishly simple dining room and a peaceful garden out back.

WORTH A TRIP

ROMAN FISHBOURNE PALACE

Fishbourne Palace (www.sussexpast.co.uk; Roman Way; adult/child £8.90/4.70; ⊙10am-5pm Mar-Oct, reduced hours & days rest of the year) is the largest-known Roman residence in Britain. The palace lies 1.5 miles west of Chichester, just off the A259 (take bus 700 from outside Chichester Cathedral). Happened upon by labourers in the 1960s, it's thought that this once-luxurious mansion was built around AD 75 for a romanised local king. Housed in a modern pavilion are its foundations, hypocaust and painstakingly re-laid mosaics.

The centrepiece is a spectacular floor depicting Cupid riding a dolphin, flanked by sea horses and panthers. There's also a fascinating little museum and replanted Roman gardens.

Service is the best in the city and the menu is a mix of the familiar (gourmet fish and chips, banoffee pie) and less oft encountered (chicory-stuffed crêpes, Bermuda Seafood Chowder).

☆ Entertainment

Chichester Festival Theatre THEATRE
(✆ 01243-781312; www.cft.org.uk; Oakland's Park) Built in 1962, this somewhat Soviet-looking playhouse has a long and distinguished history. Sir Laurence Olivier was the theatre's first director, and Ingrid Bergman, Sir John Gielgud and Sir Anthony Hopkins have all played here. Today it hosts a mix of entertainment from musicals to opera, stand-up comedy to Shakespeare.

ℹ Information

Tourist Office (✆ 01243-775888; www.visitchichester.org; Novium Museum, Tower St; ⊙10am-5pm Mon-Sat, to 4pm Sun) Located in the Novium Museum.

ℹ Getting There & Away

BUS
Chichester has bus connections to the following:
Brighton (bus 700; £4.80, three hours, up to three hourly)
London Victoria (National Express; £16, three hours 40 minutes, eight daily) Change at Gatwick Airport.

Portsmouth (bus 700, £4.50, one hour 10 minutes, up to three hourly)

TRAIN
Chichester has train connections to the following:
Arundel (£4.60, 20 minutes, twice hourly)
Change at Ford or Barnham.
Brighton (£13, 50 minutes, twice hourly)
London Victoria (£17.50, 1½ hours, half-hourly)
Portsmouth (£7.60, 30 to 40 minutes, twice hourly)

SURREY

Surrey is popular with affluent London commuters who've had kids, moved out of the city and bought a country pad. For the most part, though, it's made up of uninspiring towns and dull, sprawling suburbs. Further away from the roaring motorways and packed rush-hour trains, the county reveals some inspiring landscapes made famous by authors Sir Arthur Conan Doyle, Sir Walter Scott and Jane Austen.

Farnham

POP 39,500

Nudging the border with Hampshire and joined at the hip with the garrison settlement of Aldershot, affluent Farnham is Surrey's prettiest town and its most worthwhile destination. Blessed with lively shopping streets of Georgian symmetry, a 12th-century castle and some soothing river walks, this easygoing market town makes for an undemanding day trip from London, just an hour away.

⊙ Sights

Museum of Farnham   MUSEUM
(www.farnhammaltings.com; 38 West St; ⊙10am-5pm Tue-Sat) FREE This engaging little museum is located in the splendid Willmer House, a Georgian mansion built in 1718 for the wealthy hop merchant and maltster John Thorne. Themed rooms trace Farnham's history from flint-tool days to Bakelite nostalgia. A corner is dedicated to William Cobbett, the town's most famous son, a 19th-century reformer, radical member of parliament, writer and journalist who established Hansard (the official record of what is said in parliament).

Cobbett's bust takes pride of place in the peaceful garden out the back, where you'll also find a timber gallery housing temporary exhibitions.

Farnham Castle   CASTLE
(EH; ☑01252-721194; www.farnhamcastle.com; Castle St; palace adult/child £3.50/2.50, keep free; ⊙palace 2-4pm Wed, keep 9am-5pm Mon-Fri, 10am-4pm Sat & Sun, closed Jan) Farnham Castle was constructed in 1138 by Henry de Blois, the grandson of William the Conqueror. There's not much left of the castle keep today except the beautiful old ramparts. Even if the keep is closed, it's worth walking around the outside for the picturesque views.

Open only one afternoon a week, the residential palace was built in the 13th century as a stopover for the bishops of Winchester on London journeys. From 1926 to the 1950s, it was used by the bishops of Guildford.

🛌 Sleeping & Eating

Bush Hotel   HOTEL ££
(☑01252-234800; www.mercure-uk.com; The Borough; r from £89; P❋⊛) Farnham's top address is this finely appointed 17th-century inn right in the heart of the action. Rolling renovations keep things fresh, and there's a snug beamed bar and highly recommended restaurant that spills into the pretty courtyard.

Brasserie Blanc   FRENCH ££
(www.brasserieblanc.com; 5 Castle St; mains £13.50-20; ⊙8am-10pm Mon-Thu, to 10.30pm Fri & Sat, 8.30am-9pm Sun) For a bit of Gallic class, head to this understated eatery near Farnham Castle, one of French chef Raymond Blanc's 18 UK restaurants. The simply laid tables, low-watt art-deco lighting and art-covered walls create a modestly stylish atmosphere, and there's a walled garden out the back. The menu is a mostly seasonal list of finely crafted dishes cooked using choice ingredients shipped in from France.

❶ Getting There & Away

There is a daily bus to London Victoria (National Express; £9.90, 1½ hours) and half-hourly services to Hindland (30 minutes to one hour).

There are twice-hourly train services to both London Waterloo (£15.70, one hour) and Winchester (£19.90, 60 to 80 minutes); you will need to change at Woking for the latter.

Oxford, Cotswolds & Around

Includes ➜

Oxford 177
Woodstock 188
Cirencester 190
Burford 193
Northleach 196
Stow-on-the-Wold . . .197
Moreton-in-Marsh . . .199
Chipping Campden . 200
Broadway 201
Winchcombe 202
Cheltenham 205
Forest of Dean 207
Windsor & Eton 213

Best Places to Eat

➜ Hind's Head (p217)

➜ Edamamé (p185)

➜ Le Champignon Sauvage (p207)

➜ Waterside Inn (p217)

➜ Wheatsheaf (p197)

Best Places to Sleep

➜ Star Cottage (p193)

➜ Barnsley House (p192)

➜ Glove House (p189)

➜ Bradley (p205)

Why Go?

Sprinkled with gorgeous little villages, this part of the country is as close to the old-world English idyll as you'll get. It's a haven of rolling green-cloaked hills, rose-clad cottages, graceful stone churches and thatched roofs. Add to this alluring mix the legendary university city of Oxford, with its majestic architecture, historic air and lively student scene, and it's obvious why the region is a magnet for visitors.

Although the roads and most popular villages are busy in summer, it's easy to get off the tourist trail. The golden-hued Cotswolds work their finest magic when you find your very own romantic hideaway. Buckinghamshire, Bedforshire and Hertfordshire conceal splendid country houses, while Windsor delights with regal character. In the far west, the Forest of Dean beckons with outdoor-adventure appeal.

Much of the area is an easy day trip from London, but Oxford and the Cotswolds deserve at least several leisurely days.

When to Go

➜ Welcome the dawn with Oxford's Magdalen College Choir, which sings hymns from atop the college tower, on May Morning (1 May).

➜ In July, sip champagne and watch the rowers whizz by at Henley Royal Regatta.

➜ Walking in the Cotswolds is ideal from April to June and in September, when the weather is (mostly) in your favour, without the July and August crowds.

➜ In early October, Cheltenham kicks into bookish action for its famous 10-day Literature Festival.

➜ Gather among glamorous crowds in June for the country's greatest annual racing meet, Royal Ascot.

Oxford, Cotswolds & Around Highlights

① **Oxford** (p177) Following in the footsteps of JRR Tolkien, CS Lewis and Oscar Wilde as you explore magical colleges.

② **The Cotswolds** (p190) Wandering between perfect gold-tinged Cotswolds villages, such as Chipping Campden.

③ **Windsor** (p213) Catching a glimpse of regal life at the Queen's weekend hideaway.

④ **Blenheim Palace** (p189) Lording it up at one of Britain's greatest stately homes in Woodstock.

⑤ **Stowe** (p210) Getting lost in a serene world of spectacular 18th-century landscaped gardens.

⑥ **Gloucester Cathedral** (p208) Strolling the elegant cloisters of this exquisite Perpendicular Gothic creation.

⑦ **Painswick** (p203) Exploring a beautiful and unspoilt town in the Cotswolds.

⑧ **Making of Harry Potter** (p211) Unleashing your inner wizard at this studio tour.

Activities

Cycling

Gentle gradients and wonderfully scenic panoramas make the Cotswolds ideal for cycling, with only the steep western escarpment offering a challenge to the legs. Plenty of quiet country lanes and byways criss-cross the region. You can also follow the signposted Thames Valley Cycle Way (NCN Routes 4 and 5) between Oxford and Windsor (and on to London).

Mountain bikers can use a variety of bridleways in the Cotswolds and Chilterns. In the west of the region, the Forest of Dean has many dirt-track options and some dedicated mountain-bike trails.

Walking

The Cotswolds offer endless opportunities for day hikes as well as something for the more ambitious.

Cotswold Way (www.nationaltrail.co.uk/cotswold-way) The 102-mile path between Bath and Chipping Campden takes about a week to walk; it's easily accessed from many points en route if you'd like to hike a smaller section.

Thames Path (www.nationaltrail.co.uk/thamespath) This 184-mile path follows the river downstream from its source near Cirencester to London.

Gloucestershire Way This 100-mile path links Chepstow to Tewkesbury via Stow-on-the-Wold.

Oxfordshire Way (www.oxfordshire.gov.uk/countryside) In Oxfordshire, this 65-mile signposted trail tracks from Bourton-on-the-Water to Henley-on-Thames.

Wychwood Way (www.oxfordshire.gov.uk/countryside) The 37-mile loop from Woodstock runs through an ancient royal forest.

Ridgeway (www.nationaltrail.co.uk/ridgeway) This picturesque 87-mile walk meanders along the chalky grassland of the Wiltshire Downs near Avebury, down into the Thames Valley and then along the spine of the Chilterns to Ivinghoe Beacon near Aylesbury in Buckinghamshire.

❶ Getting There & Around

A car will give you the most freedom, especially for exploring the small villages of the Cotswolds. Oxford, Moreton-in-Marsh, Stroud, Cheltenham, Gloucester, Bletchley, Hatfield, St Albans, Henley-on-Thames and Windsor are plugged into the train network; all have services to London, in most cases direct. Other direct trains go as far afield as Birmingham, Manchester and Newcastle (from Oxford), and Cardiff, Edinburgh and Exeter (from Cheltenham).

Local buses link larger towns to each other and to their surrounding villages. Services are run by various operators. For timetables, use the journey planner tool on **Traveline** (www.traveline.info).

OXFORD

POP 159,994

One of the world's most famous university cities, Oxford is a beautiful, privileged place. It is steeped in history and studded with august buildings, yet maintains the feel of a young city, thanks to its large student population. The elegant honey-toned buildings of the university's colleges, scattered throughout the city, wrap around tranquil courtyards along narrow cobbled lanes, and, inside their grounds, a studious calm reigns. The city's famed spires twirl into the sky above.

Oxford is a wonderful place to wander: the oldest colleges date back to the 13th century, and little has changed inside the hallowed walls since. But along with the rich history, tradition and energetic academic life, there is a busy, lively world beyond the college walls, and the city's non-university majority far outnumber the academic elite. Just as in Cambridge, the existence of 'town' beside 'gown' makes Oxford more than simply a bookish place of learning.

History

Strategically placed at the confluence of the Rivers Cherwell and Thames (called the Isis here, from the Latin *Tamesis*), Oxford was a key Saxon town, heavily fortified by Alfred the Great during the war against the Danes. It continued to grow under the Normans, who founded its castle in 1071.

By the 11th century, the Augustinian abbey in Oxford had begun training clerics, and when Anglo-Norman clerical scholars were expelled from the Sorbonne in 1167, the abbey began to attract students in droves. The first three colleges – University, Balliol and Merton – were founded in the mid-13th century. Alongside Oxford's growing prosperity grew the enmity between local townspeople and new students ('town and gown'), culminating in the St Scholastica's Day Massacre in 1355, which started as an argument over beer but resulted in 90 deaths.

Thereafter, the king ordered that the university be broken up into colleges, each of which developed its own traditions.

The university, largely a religious entity at the time, was rocked in the 16th century by the Reformation; the public trials and burning at the stake of Protestant heretics under Mary I; and by the subsequent hanging, drawing and quartering of Catholics under her successor Elizabeth I. As the Royalist headquarters, Oxford backed the losing side during the Civil War, but flourished after the restoration of the monarchy, with some of its most notable buildings constructed in the late 17th and early 18th centuries.

The arrival of the canal system in 1790 had a profound effect on Oxford. By creating a link with the Midlands' industrial centres, work and trade suddenly expanded beyond the academic core. This was further strengthened by the construction of the railways.

The city's real industrial boom came, however, when William Morris began producing cars here in 1913. With the success of his Bullnose Morris and Morris Minor, his Cowley factory went on to become one of the largest motor plants in the world. Although works have been scaled down since, Minis still run off BMW's Cowley production line today.

◉ Sights

University of Oxford

For those wondering where exactly to find the University of Oxford, the usual answer is: everywhere. Much of Oxford's centre is taken up by graceful university buildings and elegant colleges, each one individual in its appearance and academic specialities. The most visited strip, flanked by colleges and the Bodleian Library, is Catte St.

The first colleges (Balliol, Merton and University) were built in the 13th century, with at least three more being added in each of the following three centuries. Newer colleges, such as Keble, were added in the 19th and 20th centuries to accommodate an ever-expanding student population. Tradition dies hard at Oxford, however: it wasn't until 1877 that lecturers were allowed to marry, and female students were only finally admitted in 1878. It took another 42 years before women were granted degrees. To date, 26 British prime ministers have been educated at the University of Oxford.

Today, there are 38 colleges catering to 22,600 students. Not all are open to the public. For those that are, visiting hours change with term and exam schedules, and there's usually an admission fee. Check www.ox.ac.uk for full visiting details.

★ Pitt Rivers Museum   MUSEUM

(☑ 01865-270927; www.prm.ox.ac.uk; South Parks Rd; ⊙ noon-4.30pm Mon, 10am-4.30pm Tue-Sun) FREE Hidden away through a door at the back of the Oxford University Museum of Natural History (p178), this wonderfully creepy anthropological museum houses a treasure trove of half a million objects from around the world – more than enough to satisfy any armchair adventurer. One of the reasons it's so brilliant is the fact there are no computers, interactive displays or shiny modern gimmicks. Dim lighting lends an air of mystery to glass cases stuffed with the prized booty of Victorian explorers.

Trinity College   COLLEGE

(☑ 01865-279900; www.trinity.ox.ac.uk; Broad St; adult/child £2/1; ⊙ 10am-12.15pm & 1.30-4pm Mon-Fri, 1.30-4pm Sat & Sun) Founded in 1555, this small college is worth a visit to see the lovely 17th-century garden quad, designed by Christopher Wren. Its exquisitely carved chapel is one of the city's most beautiful and a masterpiece of English baroque. Famous students have included Cardinal Newman, William Pitt the Elder and two other British prime ministers.

Exeter College   COLLEGE

(☑ 01865-279600; www.exeter.ox.ac.uk; Turl St; ⊙ 2-5pm) FREE Founded in 1314, Exeter is known for its elaborate 17th-century dining hall and ornate Victorian Gothic chapel housing The Adoration of the Magi, a William Morris tapestry (Morris was an undergraduate here), and a psychedelic bombast of gold mosaic and stained glass. The college inspired the fictional Jordan College in the His Dark Materials trilogy by Philip Pullman, who also studied at Exeter.

Sheldonian Theatre   THEATRE

(☑ 01865-277299; www.admin.ox.ac.uk/sheldonian; Broad St; adult/child £3.50/2.50, tours £8/6; ⊙ 10am-4pm daily Mar-Nov, to 3pm Mon-Sat Dec-Feb) Begun in 1663, this monumental building was the first major work of Christopher Wren, then a professor of astronomy. Inspired by the classical Theatre of Marcellus in Rome, it has a rectangular front end, a semicircular back and railings decorated with classical busts. The ceiling in the main hall is blanketed by a fine 17th-century painting of the triumph of truth over ignorance; the ceiling's remarkable length was made possible by ingenious braces made of shorter timbers.

New College
COLLEGE

(📞01865-279500; www.new.ox.ac.uk; Holywell St; adult/child £4/3; ⏲11am-5pm Easter-Oct, 2-4pm Nov-Feb) Established in 1379, New College was the first in Oxford for undergraduates and is a fine example of the glorious Perpendicular Gothic style. The chapel is full of treasures, including superb medieval stained glass (much of it original) and Sir Jacob Epstein's disturbing statue of Lazarus. The 15th-century cloisters and 19th-century evergreen oak featured in *Harry Potter and the Goblet of Fire*. During term time, visitors can attend the beautiful Evensong, a choral church service held nightly at 6.15pm.

Bridge of Sighs
BRIDGE

(Hertford Bridge; New College Lane) As you stroll along New College Lane, look up at the steeped Bridge of Sighs linking the two halves of Hertford College. Completed in 1914, it's sometimes erroneously referred to as a copy of the famous bridge in Venice, but it bears a much closer resemblance to that city's Rialto Bridge.

★ Bodleian Library
LIBRARY

(📞01865-287400; www.bodleian.ox.ac.uk/bodley; Catte St; tours £6-14; ⏲9am-5pm Mon-Sat, 11am-5pm Sun) Oxford's Bodleian Library is one of the oldest public libraries in the world and quite possibly the most impressive one you'll ever see. Visitors are welcome to wander around the central quad and the foyer exhibition space. For £1 you can visit the Divinity School, but the rest of the complex is only accessible on guided tours. Check timings online or at the information desk. Advance tickets are only available for extended tours; others must be purchased on the day.

Radcliffe Camera
LIBRARY

(www.bodleian.ox.ac.uk; Radcliffe Sq) The sandy-gold Radcliffe Camera is the quintessential Oxford landmark and undoubtedly one of the city's most photographed buildings. This beautiful circular, columned library and reading room, filled with natural light and focused on the humanities, was built between 1737 and 1749 in grand Palladian style, and has Britain's third-largest dome. The only way to see the interior is to join an extended 1½-hour tour (£14) of the Bodleian Library (p179).

University Church of St Mary the Virgin
CHURCH

(📞01865-279111; www.university-church.ox.ac.uk; High St; ⏲9.30am-5pm Mon-Sat, 11.30am-5pm Sun Sep-Jun, 9am-6pm daily Jul & Aug) **FREE** With a tower dating from 1280 and a Perpendicular Gothic nave, this relatively unadorned church is most famous as the site of the 1556 trial of three Anglican bishops during the reign of Mary I. All three were later burned at the stake for heresy on Broad St. Inside, there's a memorial to the victims of the Reformation – both Protestant and Catholic.

All Souls College
COLLEGE

(📞01865-279379; www.asc.ox.ac.uk; High St; ⏲2-4pm Mon-Fri, closed Aug) **FREE** One of the wealthiest and most peaceful Oxford colleges, All Souls was founded in 1438 as a centre of prayer and learning. It's one of several graduate colleges, though it doesn't accept just any old Oxford graduate. Each year, the university's top finalists sit a fellowship exam, with an average of only two achieving the grade. It's said to be the hardest entrance exam in the world, and fellowship of the college is one of the country's highest academic honours.

St Edmund Hall
COLLEGE

(📞01865-279000; www.seh.ox.ac.uk; Queen's Lane; ⏲10am-4pm) **FREE** St Edmund Hall ('Teddy Hall' to residents) was founded sometime before 1317 and is the sole survivor of the original medieval halls, the teaching institutions that preceded colleges in Oxford. It's best known for its small late-17th-century chapel, later decorated by William Morris and Edward Burne-Jones. Mohawk chief Oronhyatekha studied here in 1862 (and eloped with the principal's daughter).

Magdalen College
COLLEGE

(📞01865-276000; www.magd.ox.ac.uk; High St; adult/child £5/4, 45min tours £6; ⏲1-6pm Oct-Jun, noon-7pm Jul-Sep, tours 6pm daily Jul-Sep) Set amid 40 hectares of private lawns, woodlands, river walks and deer park, Magdalen (*mawd*-lin), founded in 1458, is one of the wealthiest and most beautiful of Oxford's colleges. It has a reputation as an artistic college. Some of its notable students have included writers Julian Barnes, Alan Hollinghurst, CS Lewis, John Betjeman, Seamus Heaney and Oscar Wilde, not to mention Edward VIII, TE Lawrence 'of Arabia', Dudley Moore and Cardinal Thomas Wolsey.

Beyond the elegant Victorian gateway, you'll find the medieval chapel (with its

Oxford

glorious 15th-century tower). From here, move on to the remarkable, now-restored 15th-century cloisters, some of Oxford's finest and with strange animals perched on the buttresses. The fantastic gargoyles and grotesques along the frontage here are thought to have inspired CS Lewis' stone statues in *The Chronicles of Narnia*. Behind the cloisters, lovely Addison's Walk leads through the grounds and along the banks of the River Cherwell for just under a mile. In the mid-1870s, you might have encountered Oscar Wilde taking his pet lobster for a stroll.

The college also has a fine choir that sings Hymnus Eucharisticus at 6am on May Day (1 May) from the top of the 44m bell tower.

Botanic Garden GARDENS
(☎01865-286690; www.botanic-garden.ox.ac.uk; High St; adult/child £5/free; ⊙9am-6pm May-Aug, to 5pm Mar, Apr, Sep & Oct, to 4pm Nov-Feb) Sweeping along the banks of the River Cherwell, Oxford's peaceful botanic garden was founded in 1621 for the study of medicinal plants; it's the oldest of its kind in England and remains a department of the university. Inside, you'll find a lily house, a rock garden

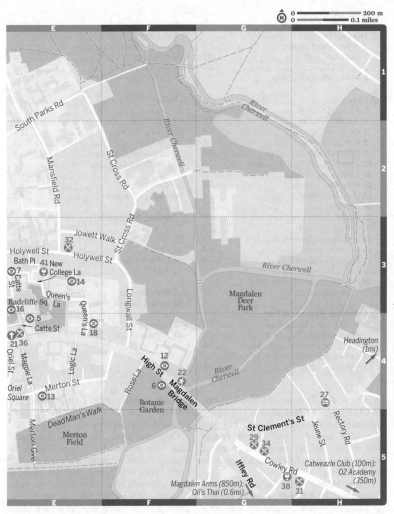

and the bench that Lyra and her extra-universal lover Will vow to visit once a year in Phillip Pullman's *His Dark Materials*.

Merton College
COLLEGE

(☏ 01865-276310; www.merton.ox.ac.uk; Merton St; adult/child £3/free; ⊙ 2-5pm Mon-Fri, 10am-5pm Sat & Sun) Founded in 1264, Merton is the oldest of Oxford's colleges and the first to adopt collegiate planning, bringing scholars and tutors together into a formal community and providing a planned residence for them. Its distinguishing architectural features include large gargoyles, whose expres-

sions suggest that they're about to throw up, and the charming 14th-century **Mob Quad** – the first of the college quads.

Just off the quad is a 13th-century **chapel** and the **Old Library** (admission on guided tour only), the oldest medieval library in use (look for the chained books). It is said that Tolkien, a Merton English professor, spent many hours here writing *The Lord of the Rings* and that the trees in the Fellows' Garden inspired the ents of Middle Earth. Other literary giants associated with Merton include TS Eliot and Louis MacNeice;

Oxford

◉ Top Sights
1 Ashmolean Museum C3
2 Bodleian Library D3
3 Christ Church D5
4 Pitt Rivers Museum D1

◎ Sights
5 All Souls College E4
6 Botanic Garden F4
7 Bridge of Sighs E3
8 Carfax Tower D4
9 Christ Church Cathedral D5
10 Christ Church Picture Gallery D5
11 Exeter College D3
12 Magdalen College F4
13 Merton College E4
14 New College E3
15 Oxford Castle Unlocked B4
16 Radcliffe Camera E3
17 Sheldonian Theatre D3
18 St Edmund Hall E4
19 St Mary's Passage D4
20 Trinity College D3
21 University Church of St Mary
     the Virgin E4

◉ Activities, Courses & Tours
Bill Spectre's Ghost Trails .... (see 15)
Blackwell's Walking Tours .... (see 43)
22 Magdalen Bridge Boathouse F4
23 Oxford Official Guided
     Walking Tours D3

◉ Sleeping
24 Central Backpackers B4
25 Malmaison C4
26 Old Parsonage Hotel C1
27 Oxford Coach & Horses H4

◉ Eating
28 Branca B1
29 Café Coco G5
30 Chiang Mai Kitchen D4
31 Door 74 .... H5
32 Edamamé E3
33 Handle Bar Cafe & Kitchen C3
34 Kazbar G5
35 Turl St Kitchen D3
36 Vaults & Garden E4

◉ Drinking & Nightlife
37 Bear Inn D4
38 Café Tarifa G5
39 Eagle & Child C2
40 Lamb & Flag C2
41 Turf Tavern E3

◉ Entertainment
42 Oxford Playhouse C3

◉ Shopping
43 Blackwell's D3

Thomas Bodley, founder of Oxford's Bodleian Library, was a fellow here.

From July to September, you can join 40-minute guided tours of the college grounds (£5). Also in summer, keep an eye out for posters advertising candlelit concerts in the chapel.

Behind Merton College is the ominously named **Dead Man's Walk**, so called because the medieval Jewish community, who were not allowed to bury their dead within the city, would take bodies along this route to the Jewish cemetery (now the Botanic Garden).

★ **Christ Church**   COLLEGE
(☑ 01865-276492; www.chch.ox.ac.uk; St Aldate's; adult/child £8/7; ☺ 10am-4.15pm Mon-Sat, 2-4.15pm Sun) The largest of all of Oxford's colleges, with 650 students, and the one with the grandest quad, Christ Church is also its most popular. Its magnificent buildings, illustrious history and latter-day fame as a location for the *Harry Potter* films have tourists visiting in droves. The college was founded in 1524 by Cardinal Thomas Wolsey,

who suppressed the 9th-century monastery existing on the site to acquire the funds for his lavish building project.

Over the years, numerous luminaries have been educated at Christ Church, including Albert Einstein, philosopher John Locke, poet WH Auden, Charles Dodgson (Lewis Carroll; who immortalised the then-dean's daughter in his *Alice in Wonderland* tales), and no fewer than 13 British prime ministers. The main entrance is below the imposing 17th-century **Tom Tower**, the upper part of which was designed by former student Sir Christopher Wren. Great Tom, the 6-tonne tower bell, still chimes 101 times each evening at 9.05pm (Oxford is five minutes west of Greenwich) to sound the curfew imposed on the original 100 students – plus the one added in 1663.

Visitors must head further south down St Aldate's to the visitors' entrance (where there may be queues). From here, you go up to the **Great Hall**, the college's spectacular dining room, with its hammer-beam roof and imposing portraits of past scholars. It was replicated in film studios as the Hogwarts dining hall for the *Harry Potter* films. The hall often closes between noon and 2pm.

Coming down the grand fan-vaulted staircase (where Professor McGonagall welcomed Harry in *Harry Potter and the Philosopher's Stone*), you'll enter **Tom Quad**, Oxford's largest and arguably most impressive quadrangle, with a statue of Mercury in its pond.

From the quad, you access 12th-century **Christ Church Cathedral** (☑ 01865-276150; www.chch.ox.ac.uk/cathedral; St Aldate's; admission free; ☉ 10am-4.15pm Mon-Sat, 2-4.15pm Sun). It was originally the abbey church and then the college chapel, but was declared a cathedral by Henry VIII when he broke from the Catholic Church, suppressed more monasteries and convents, and gave the college its current name in 1546. It was formerly known as Cardinal's College.

Inside, brawny Norman columns are topped by elegant vaulting, and beautiful stained-glass windows illuminate the walls. Keep an eye out for the 13th-century reliquary of St Frideswide, Oxford's patron saint, whose Anglo-Saxon shrine was a focus of pilgrimage prior to the college being built. Other notable features include the stained-glass depiction of the murder of Thomas Becket, dating from 1320, above the side altar on the right. As this is a working Anglican cathedral, there's no charge to visit it for private prayer or to attend a service – talk to the porters at the main gate. Evensong is held at 6pm most days.

Finally, you'll pass through the 15th-century **cloister**, a relic of the ancient Priory of St Frideswide.

To the south of the college is **Christ Church Meadow**, a leafy expanse bordered by the Rivers Cherwell and Isis, ideal for leisurely walking.

Christ Church Picture Gallery   GALLERY
(☑ 01865-276172; www.chch.ox.ac.uk/gallery; Oriel Sq; adult/child £4/2; ☉ 10.30am-4.15pm Mon-Sat, 2-4.15pm Sun, closed Tue Oct-Jun) Christ Church's impressive stash of precious masterpieces dates from 1300 to 1750, and has a particular focus on the Italian Renaissance. Paintings by such greats as Tintoretto, Veronese and van Dyck take pride of place, and there's an exalted collection of drawings by Michelangelo, Leonardo da Vinci, Rubens and Raphael. Admission is half-price with a valid Christ Church ticket. Free guided tours at 2.30pm on Monday.

Other Sights

★ Ashmolean Museum   MUSEUM
(☑ 01865-278000; www.ashmolean.org; Beaumont St; ☉ 10am-5pm Tue-Sun) **FREE** Britain's oldest public museum, second in repute only to London's British Museum, was established in 1683 when Elias Ashmole presented the university with the collection of curiosities amassed by the well-travelled John Tradescant, gardener to Charles I. Today its four floors feature interactive displays, a giant atrium, glass walls revealing galleries on different levels and a beautifully sited rooftop restaurant.

Collections, displayed in bright, spacious, attractive galleries within one of Britain's best examples of neoclassical architecture, span the world.

Historical treasures include Egyptian mummies, Islamic art, Indian textiles, ancient documents, rare porcelain, tapestries, silverware, priceless musical instruments, extensive displays of European art and, famously, the Anglo-Saxon Alfred Jewel.

Carfax Tower   TOWER
(Queen St; adult/child £2.50/1.50; ☉ 10am-5pm) This central landmark, towering over what has been a crossroads for 1000 years, is the sole reminder of Oxford's medieval St Martin's Church and affords good views over the city centre.

St Mary's Passage   STREET
With a doorway sporting a lion's head knocker, flanked by two golden fawns, this tiny alley is often said to have inspired CS Lewis' magical world in *The Chronicles of Narnia*. While this may or may not be true, it's nonetheless a pretty little corner, tucked between High St and the much-photographed Radcliffe Camera.

🏃 Activities

A quintessential Oxford experience, punting is all about sitting back in a flat-bottomed boat and sipping Pimms (the typical English summer drink) as you watch the city's glorious architecture float by. This, of course, requires someone else to do the hard work – punting is far more difficult than it appears. If you decide to give it a go alone, a deposit for the punt is usually charged. Most punts hold five people including the punter. Punt rental typically costs £16 to £24 per hour.

Magdalen Bridge Boathouse   BOATING
(☑ 01865-202643; www.oxfordpunting.co.uk; High St; chauffeured 4-person punt per 30min £30,

WORTH A TRIP

TOLKIEN'S RESTING PLACE

Lord of the Rings author JRR Tolkien is buried with his wife Edith at **Wolvercote Cemetery** (Banbury Rd, Wolvercote; admission free; ⊙7am-8pm Mon-Fri, 8am-8pm Sat & Sun Apr-Sep, to 5pm Oct-Mar), 2 miles north of Oxford city centre. The names Beren and Lúthien are carved on their gravestone, a reference to the love between a mortal man and an elf maiden who gave up her immortality to be with him.

punt rental per hour £24; ⊙9.30am-dusk Feb-Nov) Right beside Magdalen Bridge, this is the most central location to hire a punt, chauffeured or otherwise. From here, you can head downstream around the Botanic Garden and Christ Church Meadow or upstream around Magdalen Deer Park. You can also hire row boats and pedaloes.

Cherwell Boat House   BOATING
(☑01865-515978; www.cherwellboathouse.co.uk; 50 Bardwell Rd; punt rental per hour £16-18; ⊙10am-dusk mid-Mar–mid-Oct) Head a mile north of central Oxford (along Banbury Rd then right onto Bardwell Rd) for a countryside punt on the River Cherwell, where the most popular destination is the busy Victoria Arms pub. Row boats and canoes are also available.

☞ Tours

Bill Spectre's Ghost Trails   WALKING
(☑07941 041811; www.ghosttrail.org; Oxford Castle Unlocked; adult/child £8/6; ⊙6.30pm Fri & Sat) For a highly entertaining, theatrical and informative look at Oxford's dark underbelly, join Victorian undertaker Bill Spectre on a 1¾-hour tour of the city's most haunted sites. It departs from **Oxford Castle Unlocked** (www.oxfordcastleunlocked.co.uk; 44-46 Oxford Castle); no bookings needed. Audience participation likely.

**Oxford Official Guided
Walking Tours**   WALKING
(☑01865-686441; www.experienceoxfordshire. org/official-tours; 15-16 Broad St; adult/child from £12/7.50) Tours of Oxford city and colleges (10.45am and 1pm year-round, plus 11am and 2pm at busy times), along with a bewildering array of themed tours, from *Inspector Morse, Alice in Wonderland* and *Harry Potter* to medieval Oxford, William Morris

and stained-glass itineraries. Check online for details or book at the tourist office (p188).

Blackwell's Walking Tours   WALKING
(☑01865-333602; www.blackwells.co.uk/oxford; 48-53 Broad St; tours £9; ⊙mid-Apr–Oct) From spring to autumn, Oxford's most renowned bookshop runs a variety of literary-themed walking tours. Choices include the Inklings Walking Tour, which leads you to favourite haunts of JRR Tolkien, CS Lewis and other Inklings-group members.

⌂ Sleeping

Book ahead between May and September and on weekends. If you're stuck, you'll find plenty of B&Bs along Iffley, Abingdon, Banbury and Headington Rds. There's a cluster of budget accommodation near the train station.

Central Backpackers   HOSTEL £
(☑01865-242288; www.centralbackpackers.co.uk; 13 Park End St; dm £20-25; 🛜) A welcoming budget option between the train station and town centre, above a bar. This small hostel has basic, bright and cheerful dorms, with lockers, for four to 12 people, a rooftop terrace and a small TV lounge. There's a six-bed women-only dorm.

★**Oxford Coach & Horses**   B&B ££
(☑01865-200017; www.oxfordcoachandhorses. co.uk; 62 St Clement's St; s/d/tr £125/135/165; 🅿🛜♿) Once an 18th-century coaching inn, this fabulous English-Mexican-owned boutique B&B hides behind a fresh powder-blue exterior, just a few metres from the Cowley Rd action. The eight light-filled rooms are cosy, spacious and individually styled in soothing pastels with the odd splash of purple, turquoise or exposed wood. The converted ground floor houses an airy, attractive breakfast room.

Burlington House   B&B ££
(☑01865-513513; www.burlington-hotel-oxford. co.uk; 374 Banbury Rd, Summertown; s/d from £70/96; 🅿🛜) Twelve elegantly contemporary rooms with patterned wallpaper, immaculate bathrooms, dashes of colour and luxury touches are available at this beautifully refreshed Victorian merchant's house. Personal service is as sensational as the delicious breakfast, complete with organic eggs, fresh orange juice and homemade bread, yoghurt and granola. It's 2 miles north of central Oxford, with good public transport links.

Remont
B&B **££**

(📞 01865-311020; www.remont-oxford.co.uk; 367 Banbury Rd, Summertown; r £127-147; 🅿 @ 🛜) All modern style, subtle lighting and colourful furnishings, this 25-room guesthouse has a range of rooms decked out in cool neutrals with silky bedspreads, abstract art, vibrant bedheads, writing desks and plasma-screen TVs. There's a sunny garden and roomy breakfast hall out the back, plus good public transport into the centre (it's 2.5 miles north).

University Rooms
Oxford
UNIVERSITY ACCOMMODATION **££**

(www.universityrooms.com; s £37-70, d £75-110, q 138-195; 🛜) During university holidays (Christmas, Easter and summer), you can sleep inside Oxford's hallowed colleges and breakfast in a grand hall by staying in student rooms. Most are functional singles with basic furnishings and shared bathrooms, though there are also a few en suites, twins and small flats available. Some rooms have views over college quads.

Oxford Townhouse
BOUTIQUE HOTEL **£££**

(📞 01865-722500; www.theoxfordtownhouse. co.uk; 90 Abingdon Rd; s £120, d £145-175, all incl breakfast; 🅿🛜) Just two months old at research time, this gorgeously restyled duo of Victorian town houses combines subtly chic rooms, good breakfasts and a warm welcome, half a mile south of the centre. Rooms are comfy, grey-toned and minimalist-modern in style, with white-and-navy stripy blankets, varnished-wood desks and blue flourishes, though mostly quite small (considering prices). Colourful paintings of Oxford adorn the walls.

Malmaison
HISTORIC HOTEL **£££**

(📞 01865-689944; www.malmaison.com; Oxford Castle, 3 New Rd; d/ste from £190/325; 🅿🛜) This converted former Victorian prison is one place you might just wish to be locked up in. Attached to Oxford's castle, it's now a sophisticated, thoroughly contemporary hotel with plush interiors, sultry lighting and polished service. Each of the 95 slick rooms has a giant bed and is made from three cells.

Old Parsonage Hotel
BOUTIQUE HOTEL **£££**

(📞 01865-310210; www.oldparsonage-hotel.co.uk; 1-3 Banbury Rd; r from £229; 🅿🛜) Tucked into a 17th-century stone house cloaked in wisteria, this 35-room boutique property achieves the perfect blend of period charm and modern luxury. Oscar Wilde once made it his home. The atmospheric interior has an impressive contemporary art collection, artfully mismatched furniture and tastefully styled rooms in reds, purples and greys, with handmade beds and marble bathrooms.

✕ Eating

★ Edamamé
JAPANESE **£**

(📞 01865-246916; www.edamame.co.uk; 15 Holywell St; mains £6-9.50; ⏱ 11.30am-2.30pm Wed, 11.30am-2.30pm & 5-8.30pm Thu-Sat, noon-3.30pm Sun; 🍴) The queue out the door speaks volumes about the food quality at this tiny, deliciously authentic place. All light wood, dainty trays and friendly bustle, this is Oxford's top spot for gracefully simple, flavour-packed Japanese cuisine. Dishes include fragrant chicken-miso ramen, tofu stir-fry and, on Thursday night, sushi. No bookings; arrive early and be prepared to wait. Cash only at lunch.

★ Vaults & Garden
CAFE **£**

(📞 01865-279112; www.thevaultsandgarden.com; University Church of St Mary the Virgin, Radcliffe Sq; mains £7-10; ⏱ 8.30am-6pm; 🛜🍴) Hidden away in the vaulted 14th-century Old Congregation House of the University Church, this buzzy local favourite serves a wholesome seasonal selection of soups, salads, pastas, curries, sandwiches and cakes, including plenty of vegetarian and gluten-free options. It's one of Oxford's most beautiful lunch venues, with additional tables in a pretty garden overlooking Radcliffe Sq.

Handle Bar Cafe & Kitchen
CAFE **£**

(Bike Zone, 28-32 St Michael's Street; dishes £5-7; ⏱ 8am-10pm Mon-Sat, 10am-7pm Sun; 🛜🍴) Hot on Oxford's simmering coffee-culture scene, this bubbly bike-themed cafe gets packed with students, professionals and a few lucky tourists. They're here for luscious, health-focused bites, such as spiced avocado-and-feta toast, kale-wrapped halloumi and fresh-fruit smoothie 'pots', plus tasty cakes, teas and coffees. A raised penny-farthing serves as centrepiece and bikes dangle from the ceiling.

Oli's Thai
THAI **£**

(📞 01865-790223; www.olisthai.com; 38 Magdalen Rd; mains £6-12; ⏱ noon-3pm Tue, noon-2pm & 5-10pm Wed-Sat) With a sunny front terrace and a tiny interior, family-run Oli's is well off the tourist track but absolutely worth seeking out. A Thai chef lends authenticity to the short but delicate, dynamic menu. It's a mile southeast of Magdalen Bridge, along Iffley Rd then Magdalen Rd. Tables get booked up months in advance, so reserve well ahead.

Fishes
PUB FOOD ££

(☑ 01865-249796; www.fishesoxford.co.uk; North Hinksey Village; mains £13-20; ⊙ 9.30am-11pm Mon-Thu, to midnight Fri & Sat, to 10.30pm Sun; ℗) In a delightful country setting, 1.5 miles west of central Oxford, this buzzy gastropub draws a regular local crowd with its excellent menu of classy modern-British offerings like crunchy ricotta-filled pastry, dry-aged steaks, enormous deli boards and chalkboard specials. Dine in the bright, cosy-smart interior or grab a deck chair or picnic rug in the chilled-out garden. Bookings recommended.

Turl St Kitchen
MODERN BRITISH ££

(☑ 01865-264171; www.turlstreetkitchen.co.uk; 16-17 Turl St; mains £11-19; ⊙ 8-10am, noon-2.30pm & 6.30-10pm; ☑) ✐ A twice-daily-changing menu transforms meals into exquisite surprises at this lively, super-central multi-level cafe-restaurant. Fresh, organic, sustainable and locally sourced produce is thrown into creative contemporary combinations, perhaps starring veggie tajines, roast beef, hake-and-chorizo skewers or fennel-infused salads. Proceeds support a local charity. The interior is a rustic-chic mix of blue-tiled floors, faded-wood tables and fairy lights. Good cakes and coffee.

Kazbar
TAPAS ££

(☑ 01865-202920; www.kazbar.co.uk; 25-27 Cowley Rd; tapas £3.50-6; ⊙ 5pm-midnight Mon-Fri, noon-12.30am Sat, noon-11pm Sun; ☑) Both sultry and stylish, this energetic Moroccan-inspired bar-restaurant has hanging lanterns, draped fabrics, low lighting, warm colours and a fun, fresh vibe. It's usually filled with a fashionable crowd sipping cocktails and tucking into superb Spanish and North African tapas, perhaps hummus dips, chilli-prawns or cheese platters.

Chiang Mai Kitchen
THAI ££

(☑ 01865-202233; www.chiangmaikitchen.co.uk; 130a High St; mains £7-15; ⊙ noon-10.30pm Mon-Sat, noon-10pm Sun; ☑) Real-deal Thai cuisine in a little heart-of-Oxford alley, complete with tear-jerkingly hot *sôm·dam* (spicy papaya salad), a range of curries, plenty of seafood, rice and noodle favourites, and standout classics such as stir-fried chicken with cashew nuts. There's an excellent vegetarian menu.

Café Coco
MEDITERRANEAN ££

(☑ 01865-200232; www.cafecoco.co.uk; 23 Cowley Rd; breakfast £4.50-9, mains £7-12; ⊙ 10am-10pm Mon-Thu, to midnight Fri, 9am-midnight Sat, 9am-10pm Sun; ☑) This Cowley Rd institution is a hugely popular brunching destination, decorated with classic posters, warm yellow walls, chunky mirrors and a plaster-cast clown in an ice bath. The global menu ranges from cooked and 'healthy' breakfasts to pizzas, salads, burgers, pastas, mezze platters, Mediterranean mains and zingy fresh juices. Or just swing by for cocktails (happy hour 5pm to 7.30pm).

Door 74
MODERN BRITISH ££

(☑ 01865-203374; www.door74.co.uk; 74 Cowley Rd; mains £10-14; ⊙ 11am-2.30pm & 5-9.30pm Tue-Sat, 11am-2.30pm Sun; ☑) This cosy little place woos fans with its rich mix of British and Mediterranean flavours, friendly service and intimate setting. The menu is limited and tables are tightly packed, but the cooking is consistently good (pastas, risottos, burgers) and weekend brunches (full English, French toast, salmon with scrambled eggs etc) are supremely filling. Book ahead.

Branca
ITALIAN ££

(☑ 01865-556111; www.branca.co.uk; 110-111 Walton St, Jericho; mains £8-17; ⊙ 10am-10pm) Big, bright and bustling, glitzy Jericho favourite Branca serves cool cocktails and savoury focaccia to complement elegant, well-prepped pizzas, pastas, risottos, and Italian meat and seafood grills. It fills up fast and also runs the deli next door. There's a decent-value, two-course lunch deal (£14) from Monday to Saturday.

🍷 Drinking & Nightlife

Bear Inn
PUB

(☑ 01865-728164; www.bearoxford.co.uk; 6 Alfred St; ⊙ 11am-11pm Sun-Thu, to midnight Fri & Sat) Arguably Oxford's oldest pub (there's been a pub on this site since 1242), the atmospherically creaky Bear requires all but the most vertically challenged to duck their heads when passing through doorways. A curious tie collection covers the walls and ceilings, and there are usually a couple of worthy guest ales and artisan beers.

Eagle & Child
PUB

(☑ 01865-302925; www.nicholsonspubs.co.uk/theeagleandchildoxford; 49 St Giles; ⊙ noon-11pm) Affectionately known as the 'Bird & Baby', this quirky pub dates from 1650 and was once a favourite haunt of authors JRR Tolkien and CS Lewis and a few other Inklings. Its narrow wood-panelled rooms and selection of real ales, craft beers and gins still attract a mellow crowd.

Turf Tavern
PUB

(☎ 01865-243235; www.turftavern-oxford.co.uk; 4-5 Bath Pl; ⊙11am-11pm) Squeezed down a narrow alleyway, this tiny medieval pub (from at least 1381) is one of Oxford's best loved. It's where US president Bill Clinton famously 'did not inhale'; other patrons have included Oscar Wilde, Stephen Hawking and Margaret Thatcher. Home to 11 real ales, it's always crammed with students, professionals and the odd tourist. Plenty of outdoor seating.

Café Tarifa
BAR

(☎ 01865-256091; www.cafe-tarifa.co.uk; 56-60 Cowley Rd; ⊙5pm-midnight Mon-Fri, to 1am Sat, to 11pm Sun) Themed around a Spanish kitesurfing town, this low-key lounge spot is big on neo-Moorish style, with cushioned booths, low-slung tables, tile-patterned sinks and cushy beanbags. There's a wide selection of cocktails, plus movie nights and live music.

Lamb & Flag
PUB

(cnr St Giles & Lamb & Flag Passage; ⊙noon-11pm Mon-Sat, to 10.30pm Sun) Born as a 17th-century tavern, this relaxed wood-walled hideaway is still a good bet for a sturdy pint or glass of wine. It's said that Thomas Hardy wrote part of his novel *Jude the Obscure* within its walls, while authors CS Lewis and JRR Tolkien were once regulars. Pint purchases help fund PhD scholarships at St John's College (which manages the pub).

☆ Entertainment

If you're a fan of classical music you'll be spoilt for choice in Oxford, which has a host of excellent venues and regular concerts throughout the year. There's also a lively theatre scene. See www.dailyinfo.co.uk or www.musicatoxford.com for listings.

★ Creation Theatre
THEATRE

(☎ 01865-766266; www.creationtheatre.co.uk) Performing in a variety of nontraditional venues, including city parks, Blackwell's bookshop, Oxford Castle and various colleges, this ambitious theatre company produces highly original, mostly Shakespearean shows featuring plenty of magic, quirk and special effects.

Oxford Playhouse
THEATRE

(☎ 01865-305305; www.oxfordplayhouse.com; Beaumont St) The city's main stage for quality drama also hosts an impressive selection of touring music, dance and theatre performances. The Burton Taylor Studio often features quirky student productions and other innovative pieces.

Catweazle Club
LIVE MUSIC

(www.catweazleclub.com; East Oxford Social Club, 44 Princes St; admission £6; ⊙8pm Thu) Legendary open-mic night, featuring musicians, poets, writers and all sorts of bohemian performers.

O2 Academy
LIVE MUSIC

(☎ 01865-813500; www.academymusicgroup.com/o2academyoxford; 190 Cowley Rd) Oxford's busiest club and live-music venue hosts everything from big-name DJs and international touring artists to indie bands and hard rock.

🛍 Shopping

★ Blackwell's
BOOKS

(☎ 01865-792792; www.blackwell.co.uk; 48-51 Broad St; ⊙9am-6.30pm Mon-Sat, 11am-5pm Sun) The most famous bookshop in the most studenty of cities, Blackwell's is a book-lover's dream with its vast range of literature, academic treatises and guilty pleasures. Make sure you visit the Norrington Room in the basement – an immense inverted step pyramid lined with 3 miles of shelves, constructed in 1966. From April to October, Blackwell's runs literary-themed walking tours (p184).

ℹ Information

John Radcliffe Hospital (☎ 01865-741166; www.ouh.nhs.uk; Headley Way, Headington; ⊙24hr) Located 2.5 miles east of Oxford city centre.

WORTH A TRIP

LE MANOIR AUX QUAT'SAISONS

As Oxford itself has no Michelin-starred restaurants, local food lovers make the 10-mile pilgrimage east to the impressive stone manor house **Le Manoir aux Quat'Saisons** (☎ 01844-278881; www.belmond.com/le-manoir-aux-quat-saisons-oxfordshire; Church Rd, Great Milton; 5-course lunch/dinner £82/138; ⊙7.30-10am, 11.45am-2.15pm & 6.45-9.30pm; ✦). Chef Raymond Blanc has been working his magic here for over 30 years, presenting imaginative, complex and exquisitely presented dishes. Book well ahead and dress smartly.

Post Office (102 St Aldate's; ◷ 9am-5.30pm Mon-Sat)

Tourist Office (◪ 01865-686430; www.experienceoxfordshire.com; 15-16 Broad St; ◷ 9.30am-5pm Mon-Sat, 10am-3.30pm Sun) Covers the whole of Oxfordshire, stocks printed Oxford walking guides, and books official walking tours.

ⓘ Getting There & Away

BUS

Oxford's **bus station** (Gloucester Green) is in the centre, near the corner of Worcester and George Sts. The main bus companies are **Oxford Bus Company** (◪ 01865-785400; www.oxford-bus.co.uk), **Stagecoach** (◪ 01865-772250; www.stagecoachbus.com) and **Swanbrook** (◪ 01452-712386; www.swanbrook.co.uk).

Destinations include the following:

Burford (route 853; £3.80, 45 minutes)

Cambridge (X5; £13, 3¾ hours)

Chipping Norton (S3; £4.60, one hour)

Cheltenham (route 853; £8, 1½ hours)

London Victoria (Oxford Tube/X90; £15, 1¾ hours)

Woodstock (S3; £3.70, 30 minutes)

National Express (◪ 0871-7818181; www.nationalexpress.com) coach destinations service the following:

Bath (£7, two hours)

Birmingham (£13.50, two hours)

Bristol (£7, three hours)

London Victoria (£16, two hours)

Oxford Bus Company runs 'The Airline' service to/from Heathrow (£23, 1½ hours) and Gatwick (£28, two hours) airports.

CAR

Driving and parking in central Oxford is a nightmare. There are five Park & Ride car parks on major routes leading into town. Parking costs £2 to £4 per day; buses run to/from the centre every 15 to 30 minutes (return £2.80, 12 to 25 minutes).

TRAIN

Oxford's main train station (Botley Rd) is conveniently placed on the western side of the city centre. Destinations include the following:

Birmingham (£18, 1¼ hours)

London Paddington (£25, 1¼ hours)

Manchester (£50, three hours)

Moreton-in-Marsh (£9.90, 35 minutes)

Newcastle (£111, 4½ hours)

Winchester (£17, 1¼ hours)

Oxford Parkway station (Banbury Rd), 4 miles north of the centre, has trains to London Marylebone (£25, one hour). It's convenient if you're staying in Summertown and has bus links to central Oxford.

ⓘ Getting Around

BICYCLE

Cycling is a popular way to get around Oxford. **Cyclo Analysts** (◪ 01865-424444; www.cycloanalysts.com; 150 Cowley Rd; per day/week from £10/36; ◷ 9am-6pm Mon-Sat) and **Summertown Cycles** (◪ 01865-316885; www.summertowncycles.co.uk; 200-202 Banbury Rd, Summertown; per day/week £18/35; ◷ 9am-5.30pm Mon-Sat, 10am-4pm Sun) sell, repair and rent out bikes, including hybrids.

BUS

Oxford Bus Company (p188) and **Stagecoach** (p188) serve an extensive local network with regular buses on major routes. A short journey costs £2.10 (return £3.50); consider a day pass (£4). Tickets are purchased on the bus (cash only).

TAXI

There are taxi ranks at the train station and bus station, as well as on St Giles and at Carfax. Alternatively, contact **001 Taxis** (◪ 01865-240000; www.001taxis.com; New Inn Yard, 108 St Aldate's) or **Oxford Minicab Service** (◪ 01865-987749; www.oxfordminicab.co.uk; 25 Croft Rd).

AROUND OXFORD

Rustic charm is in abundant supply in the villages and towns surrounding Oxford. They make excellent day-trip options or stop-off destinations if you're heading west into the Cotswolds. To the northwest, Witney has a pretty town centre, but the major highlight is Woodstock's magnificent Blenheim Palace (p189), birthplace of Sir Winston Churchill. Southwest of Oxford, the Vale of the White Horse offers some intriguing prehistoric attractions.

Woodstock

POP 2521

Old pubs, antique stores and fine stone houses dominate the well-heeled centre of beautiful Woodstock, 8 miles northwest of Oxford, which has long been linked to royal history. But what really draws the crowds here is Blenheim Palace, the extravagant baroque pile that was the birthplace of Sir Winston Churchill.

⊙ Sights

★ Blenheim Palace
PALACE

(☎ 01993-810530; www.blenheimpalace.com; Woodstock; adult/child £24.90/13.90, park & gardens only £14.90/6.90; ⊙ palace 10.30am-5.30pm, park & gardens 9am-6pm; P) One of Britain's greatest stately homes, Blenheim Palace is a monumental baroque fantasy designed by Sir John Vanbrugh and Nicholas Hawksmoor, and built between 1705 and 1722. The land and funds to build the house were granted to John Churchill, Duke of Marlborough, by a grateful Queen Anne, after his victory over the French at the 1704 Battle of Blenheim. Sir Winston Churchill was born here in 1874. Now a Unesco World Heritage Site, Blenheim (*blen*-num) is home to the 12th duke.

Inside, beyond majestic oak doors, the house is stuffed with statues, tapestries, ostentatious furniture, priceless china and giant oil paintings in elaborate gilt frames. Visits start in the Great Hall, a soaring space topped by a 20m-high ceiling adorned with images of the first duke. To the right upon entering is the Churchill Exhibition, dedicated to the life, work, paintings and writings of Winston Churchill. The British prime minister was a descendant of the Dukes of Marlborough, as was Princess Diana, and is buried nearby in Bladon graveyard.

From here, you can wander through the various grand state rooms independently or join one of the free 45-minute guided tours, which depart every 30 minutes throughout the day (except Sunday, when there are guides in all rooms). Highlights include the famous Blenheim Tapestries, a set of 10 large wall hangings commemorating the first duke's triumphs; the State Dining Room, with its painted walls and *trompe l'oeil* ceilings; and the magnificent Long Library, overlooked by an elaborate 1738 statue of Queen Anne.

Afterwards, head upstairs to the 'Untold Story', where a ghostly chambermaid leads you through a series of tableaux recreating important scenes from the palace's history. From February to September, you can also join additional tours (adult/child £6/5) of the Duke's private apartments, the palace's bedrooms or the household staff areas.

If the crowds in the house become too oppressive, escape into the vast, lavish gardens and parklands, parts of which were landscaped by the great Lancelot 'Capability' Brown. A minitrain (50p) takes visitors to the Pleasure Gardens, which feature a yew maze, adventure playground, lavender

WORTH A TRIP

KELMSCOTT MANOR

Tucked away in the countryside 20 miles west of Oxford Kelmscott Manor (☎ 01367-252486; www.sal.org.uk/kelmscott-manor; Kelmscott; adult/child £9.50/5; ⊙ 11am-5pm Wed & Sat Apr-Oct) is a gorgeous garden-fringed Tudor pile that was once the summer home of 19th-century poet and artist William Morris, founder of the Arts and Crafts movement. The interior is true to his philosophy that one should not own anything that is neither beautiful nor useful, and the house contains many of Morris' personal effects, as well as fabrics and furniture designed by him and his associates.

garden and butterfly house. For quieter and longer strolls, there are glorious walks of up to 4.5 miles, leading past lakes to an arboretum, rose garden, cascade and temple, and Vanbrugh's Grand Bridge.

Tickets can be purchased on arrival or online up to 24 hours in advance.

🛏 Sleeping & Eating

★ Glove House
B&B £££

(☎ 01993-813475; www.theglovehouse.co.uk; 24 Oxford St; s £155-165, d £170-180, ste £200-220; �) Luxuriously renovated but proudly displaying evidence of its venerable age, this elegant 400-year-old town house conceals three sumptuous rooms with the added bonus of a glorious rear garden. The Charlbury suite has a free-standing copper bath-tub in its wonderful lounge-equipped bathroom.

La Galleria
ITALIAN ££

(☎ 01993-813381; www.lagalleriawoodstock.com; 2 Market Pl; mains £11-23; ⊙ noon-2pm & 7-10pm Tue-Sun; 🖉) Big windows bathe the simple interior of this much-loved Italian restaurant in light. It's an old-fashioned kind of place, with heavy swag curtains, pink tablecloths and flowers on every table. Primarily Sardinian, the menu ranges from silky pastas and light salads to smartly cooked veal and fish. There's a decent-value three-course lunch menu (£14.95) Tuesday to Saturday.

Vale of the White Horse

Lying around 20 miles southwest of Oxford, this verdant valley is notable for the historic market town of Wantage, birthplace of

Alfred the Great (AD 849–899). But it's most interesting attractions are far older. Clustered together 8 miles west of Wantage on White Horse Hill, you'll find the Uffington White Horse (Britain's most ancient chalk figure), 700 BC Uffington Castle and Wayland's Smithy (a neolithic long barrow).

◉ Sights

Uffington White Horse   LANDMARK
(NT; www.nationaltrust.org.uk; White Horse Hill; ☺dawn-dusk) [FREE] Just below Oxfordshire's highest point, this highly stylised horse image is the oldest chalk figure in Britain, dating from the Bronze Age. It was created around 3000 years ago by cutting trenches out of the hill and filling them with blocks of chalk; local inhabitants have maintained the figure for centuries. Perhaps it was planned for the gods: it's best seen from the air above. It's a half-mile walk east through fields from the hillside car park, signposted off the B4507.

Dragon Hill   LANDMARK
(NT; www.nationaltrust.org.uk; White Horse Hill; ☺dawn-dusk) [FREE] A 10m-high, flat-topped mound, Dragon Hill was believed by locals to be the site where St George slew the dragon, although it's possibly an Iron Age ritual site. It sits just below the Uffington White Horse (p190), signposted off the B4507.

THE COTSWOLDS

Rolling gracefully across six counties, the Cotswolds are a delightful tangle of gloriously golden villages, thatch-roofed cottages, evocative churches, rickety almshouses and ancient mansions of honey-coloured stone. If you've ever lusted after exposed beams, cream teas or cuisine crammed full of local produce, look no further.

The booming medieval wool trade brought wealth to the Cotswolds, leaving behind a proliferation of exquisite buildings. In 1966, the region was declared an Area of Outstanding Natural Beauty (AONB). At 790 sq miles, it's England's second-largest protected area after the Lake District. Though it extends from north of Chipping Campden to south of Bath, the bulk of it lies in Gloucestershire. More than 83% is farmland but, even so, around 139,000 people live within the AONB itself.

These gentle yet dramatic hills are perfect for walking, cycling and horse riding, crisscrossed by a network of long-distance tracks, most notably the 102-mile Cotswold Way.

Cirencester

POP 16,325

Charming Cirencester (siren-sester) is the most significant town in the southern Cotswolds, just 15 miles south of Cheltenham. Refreshingly unpretentious, it's nonetheless an elegant and affluent town. It's difficult to believe that under the Romans (who called the town Corinium), Cirencester was second only to London in terms of size and importance (though little of this period remains). The medieval wool trade brought more success, with wealthy merchants funding the building of a superb church.

Today, Cirencester's lively Monday and Friday markets and warren-like antique shops remain as important as the upmarket boutiques and fashionable delis that line its narrow streets. Beautiful Victorian architecture flanks the busy Market Sq (the heart of the town) and the surrounding streets showcase a harmonious medley of buildings from various eras.

◉ Sights

★**Corinium Museum**   MUSEUM
(☑01285-655611; www.coriniummuseum.org; Park St; adult/child £5.20/2.50; ☺10am-5pm Mon-Sat, 2-5pm Sun Apr-Oct, to 4pm Nov-Mar; ☷) Most of this wonderful modern, well-presented museum is, of course, dedicated to Cirencester's Roman past, with reconstructed rooms, videos and interactive displays that bring the era to life. Among an array of highlights, you'll see a beautiful set of floor mosaics (including a 4th-century mosaic showing mythical musician Orpheus charming animals) and the 2nd-century 'Jupiter column', a carved capital depicting Bacchus and his drunken mates. There's also an excellent Anglo-Saxon section, plus exhibits on medieval Cirencester and the town's prosperous wool trade.

St John the Baptist's Church   CHURCH
(☑01285-659317; www.cirenparish.co.uk; Market Sq; ☺10am-4pm) Commenced in 1100, the cathedral-like St John's is one of England's largest parish churches. It boasts an outstanding Perpendicular Gothic tower with flying buttresses (c 1400) and a majestic three-storey south porch, which was built as an office by late-15th-century abbots but subsequently became the medieval town hall. Soaring arches, magnificent fan vaulting and a Tudor nave adorn the light-filled

interior, where, in a wall safe, you'll find the **Boleyn Cup**, made for Anne Boleyn in 1535.

🛏 Sleeping

★ No 12
B&B ££

(☑ 01285-640232; www.no12cirencester.co.uk; 12 Park St; d/ste £130/150; P 🐾) A welcoming Georgian town house right in the centre of Cirencester, No 12 offers four gloriously unfussy, very private rooms kitted out with a tasteful mix of antiques and modern furnishings. Romantic room 1 has an in-room bath, the suite overlooks the lovely garden, and there are piles of feather pillows, extra-long beds, splashes of red and slick modern bathrooms throughout.

Kings Head
LUXURY HOTEL £££

(☑ 01285-700900; www.kingsheadhotel.co.uk; 24 Market Pl; d/ste from £125/300; 🐾🛗🌐) At this plush spot opposite Cirencester's church, a glam refurb means super-polished service and slick boudoirs behind a 19th-century facade. Original exposed beams, red-brick walls and wood panelling pop up between Nespresso machines and Apple TVs. Standard rooms are wonderfully contemporary and comfy; suite 103 is a stunner with an in-room copper bath. Enjoy the tucked-away spa, cosy bar and smart **restaurant** (☑ 01285-700900; www.kingsheadhotel.co.uk; 24 Market Pl; mains £11-17; ⏱ 7.30am-10am, noon-2.30pm & 6.30-9.30pm Mon-Sat, 7.30-10.30am, noon-4pm & 6-9pm Sun).

🍴 Eating

Jack's
CAFE £

(☑ 01285-640888; wwww.facebook.com/jackscoffeecirencester; 44 Black Jack St; dishes £4-8; ⏱ 9am-5pm Mon-Sat, 11am-5pm Sun) Raid the stunning display of home-baked cakes, brownies, scones and flapjacks and snuggle into a cosy corner at this lively, locally popular cafe, right next to Cirencester's museum. There's also good coffee, along with tasty soups, salads, sandwiches and other light lunches.

Made by Bob
MODERN BRITISH ££

(☑ 01285-641818; www.foodmadebybob.com; Corn Hall, 26 Market Pl; mains £10-20; ⏱ 7.30-10am & noon-5.30pm Mon-Thu, 7.30-10am, noon-5pm & 7-9pm Fri, 8-10am & noon-5.30pm Sat) Part deli, part fashionable brasserie, Bob's is a huge hit for its casual atmosphere and sophisticated, inventive modern British fare featuring locally sourced products and cooked in an enormous open-plan kitchen. The break-

fast selection is excellent (granola, smashed avocado, full English), while lunch bites include salads, soups, pastas, risottos and charcuterie platters. No bookings taken.

Jesse's Bistro
MODERN BRITISH £££

(☑ 01285-641497; www.jessesbistro.co.uk; The Stableyard, 14 Black Jack St; mains £14.50-24; ⏱ 11.45am-2.45pm Mon, 11.45am-2.45pm & 6.45-9.30pm Tue-Sat, 11.45am-5pm Sun) Hidden away in a cobbled stable yard, Jesse's is a wonderful little place, filled with flagstone floors, wood-beamed ceilings and mosaic tables. Delectable dishes come fresh from the semi-open-plan kitchen and feature local, seasonal produce, such as Cornish fish and Cotswolds meat from the adjacent butcher.

ℹ Information

Tourist Office (☑ 01285-654180; www.cotswolds.com; Corinium Museum, Park St; ⏱ 10am-5pm Mon-Sat, 2-5pm Sun Apr-Oct, to 4pm Nov-Mar) Stocks a leaflet detailing a self-guided walk around the town (50p).

ℹ Getting There & Away

Trains run between London Paddington (£25, 1¾ hours) and Kemble, 4.5 miles south of Cirencester.

Stagecoach, Pulhams and Cotswold Green serve Cirencester. Most buses stop outside the Corn Hall on Market Pl. Buses run to/from the following:

Cheltenham (route 51; £3.60, 40 minutes)

Gloucester (route 852; £2.60, 1¼ hours)

Northleach (route 855; £2.70, 20 minutes)

Stroud (route 54/54A; £3.50, 40 minutes)

Tetbury (route 881; £2.50, 30 minutes)

National Express (www.nationalexpress.com) coach destinations:

Birmingham (£15, 2½ hours)

Leeds (£53, 6¾ hours)

London Victoria (£13, 2½ hours)

Newcastle-upon-Tyne (£60, 11 hours)

Nottingham (£28, 5¼ hours)

Bibury

POP 627

Once described by William Morris as England's most beautiful village, Bibury is the Cotswolds at its most picturesque (and popular), with a cluster of perfect riverside cottages and a tangle of narrow streets flanked by attractive stone buildings. It's 8 miles northeast of Cirencester.

The Cotswolds

⊙ Sights

★ Arlington Row   STREET

This perfectly rustic sweep of cottages (originally a 14th-century wool store, converted in the 17th century) is Bibury's most famous attraction and overlooks Rack Isle, a riverside wildlife refuge once used as a cloth-drying and cattle-grazing area. It has served as a backdrop for many films (most notably *Stardust*) and is thought to be a contender for Britain's most photographed street.

Church of St Mary the Virgin   CHURCH

(Church Rd; ⊗10am-dusk) Bibury's Saxon-built church has been much altered since its original construction, but many 8th-century features are still visible among the 12th-, 13th- and 15th-century additions. It's just off the B4425 as you enter the village from the northeast.

🛏 Sleeping

New Inn   PUB ££

(☎01285-750651; www.new-inn.co.uk; Main St, Coln St Aldwyns; r incl breakfast £79-169; P🕏🛜🐾) The popular jasmine-clad New Inn offers quirky contemporary comfort in 16th-century surroundings, both in the main pub building and a neighbouring cottage. The 15 bedrooms are spacious and atmospheric, with bold colours, fluffy throws, smart furnishings, the odd free-standing bath-tub and a few wood beams. It's 2 miles southeast of Bibury.

★ Barnsley House   LUXURY HOTEL £££

(☎01285-740000; www.barnsleyhouse.com; B4425, Barnsley; r incl breakfast from £249; P🕏🞥) For pure Cotswolds indulgence and romance, this 1697 country house and its famously beautiful garden take some beating. Each of the 18 rooms is individually styled, and while some have lavish oriental touch-

WARWICKSHIRE

Banbury

M40

Chipping Norton • Great Tew

A44

Woodstock

Wychwood

Swinbrook

Witney A40

Minster Lovell

Windrush

Thames (Isis)

Oxford

Thames (Isis)

OXFORDSHIRE

Thames Path

A34

Faringdon

Uffington

Ardington

Vale of the White Horse

Wantage

es or in-room baths overlooking private gardens, most are elegantly understated in their decor. Facilities include a soothing spa, heated pool, private cinema, restaurant and pub. Service is superb.

ⓘ Getting There & Away

Pulhams bus 855 heads to/from Cirencester (£2.20, 15 minutes), Barnsley (£1.50, 10 minutes) and Northleach (£2.20, 20 minutes); there is no Sunday service.

Burford

POP 1410

Slithering down a steep hill to a medieval crossing point on the River Windrush, the remarkable village of Burford, 20 miles west of Oxford, is little changed since its glory days at the height of the wool trade. It's a particularly picturesque place with

a striking mix of stone cottages, fine gold-tinged Cotswold town houses and the odd Elizabethan or Georgian treasure. Throw in a wonderfully well-preserved, centuries-old church and an array of delightful hotels and restaurants, and Burford makes an attractive stop. Antique shops, chintzy tearooms and specialist boutiques peddle nostalgia to the many visitors who make it here in summer, but, despite the crowds, it's easy to get off the main drag and wander along quiet side streets seemingly lost in time.

◉ Sights

St John the Baptist's Church CHURCH (www.burfordchurch.org; Church Lane; ⊙9am-5pm) Commenced in 1175 and added to over the years, Burford's sturdy stone church has managed to survive reformers and Round-heads (supporters of parliament against the king in the English Civil War) with its fan-vaulted ceiling, Norman west doorway, 15th-century spire and several grand tombs intact. The finest of these is the macabre 1625 Tanfield tomb, with colourful effigies of a noble couple in all their finery on top and as skeletons below.

Cotswold Wildlife Park ZOO (☎01993-823006; www.cotswoldwildlifepark. co.uk; Bradwell Grove; adult/child £15/10; ⊙10am-6pm Apr-Oct, to 5pm Nov-Mar, last admission 1½hr before closing; P🚻) 🐾 Younger visitors in particular will enjoy this hugely popular 64-hectare wildlife centre, 3 miles south of Burford. Among its vast 250-specie menagerie, there are penguins, zebras, lions, reindeer, otters, endangered white rhinos and much more. A miniature train takes the excitement up a notch.

🛏 Sleeping & Eating

★**Star Cottage** B&B ££ (☎01993-822032; www.burfordbedandbreakfast. co.uk; Meadow Lane, Fulbrook; r £110-125, apt £115-140; 🛜🚻) A mile northeast of Burford, this wonderful old Cotswold cottage has two brilliantly comfortable and character-filled en-ˋsuite rooms done up in tastefully creative blues, whites and greys, with gorgeous quilted curtains. The smaller room has a grand canopied bed; the bigger one includes a beautiful bathroom; and the back barn hosts an independent four-person apartment. Home-cooked, locally sourced breakfasts are fantastic.

OXFORD, COTSWOLDS & AROUND BURFORD

Swan Inn
PUB ££

(☎ 01993-823339; www.theswanswinbrook.co.uk; Swinbrook; s £90-100, d £125-150, ste £195, all incl breakfast; ⓟ 🛜 🐾) All soft pastels, country comfort and dashes of colour, The Swan sits right by the River Windrush in tiny Swinbrook, 3 miles east of Burford. The six cosy, elegant stable-building rooms overlook orchards, including a plush top-floor suite with sloping ceilings (perfect for families). The newer riverside cottage has five delightful rooms in slightly more contemporary style. There's an excellent **restaurant** (☎ 01993-823339; mains £15-20; ⏱ noon-2pm & 7-9pm; ⓟ).

Bull
HOTEL ££

(☎ 01993-822220; www.bullatburford.co.uk; 105 High St; s £70-120, d £75-180, all incl breakfast; ⓟ 🛜) Stay at this refurbished 15th-century coaching inn and you'll be following in the footsteps of guests as illustrious as Charles II and Horatio Nelson. Plusher rooms feature four-poster beds, floral fabrics and antique furniture, but all rooms have old-world charm. The **restaurant** (mains £12-18; ⏱ noon-2.30pm & 6.30-9pm) delivers beautifully executed dishes that make the most of local ingredients.

Angel
PUB FOOD ££

(☎ 01993-822714; www.theangelatburford.co.uk; 14 Witney St; mains £14-17; ⏱ noon-10pm; 🛜 🍴 🐾) Set in a stylishly revamped 16th-century coaching inn, this buzzy pub turns out a tasty modern British menu with a choice between refined flavour-packed mains and 'pub classics'. Enjoy roaring fires and cosy cushioned booths in winter, or eat alfresco in the lovely walled garden in warmer weather. There are three homey rooms upstairs (£110 to £130, including breakfast).

❶ Information

Tourist Office (☎ 01993-823558; www.oxfordshirecotswolds.org; 33a High St; ⏱ 9.30am-5pm Mon-Sat, 10am-4pm Sun) Advises on local walks.

❶ Getting There & Away

Stagecoach and Swanbrook buses run to/from Burford. Most buses stop on High or Sheep St. Bus destinations include the following:

Cheltenham (route 853; £4.20, 45 minutes)

Gloucester (route 853; £5.50, 1¼ hours)

Oxford (route 853; £3.80, 45 minutes)

Minster Lovell (route 233/853; £1.80, 10 to 20 minutes)

Witney (route 233/853; £3.20, 19 minutes)

Woodstock (route 233; £4, one hour)

Driving Tour
Classic Cotswolds

START BURFORD
END WINCHCOMBE
LENGTH 54 MILES; ONE TO THREE DAYS

Given its large network of winding country lanes linking ancient market towns, time-warped villages and majestic stately homes, it's impossible to cover all the Cotswolds' highlights in one day. This tour spans three counties and ticks off some of the most picturesque parts of the range's northern half. While it can be driven in a day, if you fancy stopping off along the way, it's better stretched into two or three.

Begin in Oxfordshire at the gorgeous hillside market town of ❶ **Burford**, then head 10 miles west on the A40 into Gloucestershire, following signs to classic Cotswolds town ❷ **Northleach**. The Cotswolds Discovery Centre (p197) here has excellent displays covering all you need to know about the history, geography, flora and fauna of the Cotswolds Area of Outstanding Natural Beauty (AONB).

From Northleach, spin 7 miles northeast on the A429 to signposted ❸ **Lower Slaughter**, a serene riverside village lined with houses made of that typical golden Cotswolds stone. If time allows, take the 1-mile walk northwest to ❹ **Upper Slaughter**, less visited than its sibling but no less attractive, thanks to its idyllic setting between a small ford and the hills. If you've booked ahead, stop for lunch at Michelin-starred Lords of the Manor (p197), housed in an exquisite Jacobean mansion.

Continue 3 miles north on the A429 to ❺ **Stow-on-the-Wold**, the highest of the Cotswold villages at 244m and a market town since the 12th century. Peruse the market square, then take the A429 north. After 4.5 miles you'll reach busy ❻ **Moreton-in-Marsh**, known for its weekly Tuesday market and excellent local food shops.

Next, zip 3 miles west on the A44 to tiny ❼ **Bourton-on-the-Hill**, filled with attractive 17th- and 18th-century cottages. It's famous for two things: the gibbeting cage in which the bodies of dead highwaymen were hung in the 19th century, and horse training – there are several stud farms in the vicinity of the village. Horse & Groom (p199) here is a good alternative spot to pause for lunch.

Head 3 miles west on the A44, then turn right (northeast) onto the B4081 to **⑧ Chipping Campden**, one of the Cotswold's most bucolic towns. After admiring 15th-century **St James' Church** (p200) and the honey-toned buildings along High St backtrack to the A44. Drive a mile northwest, crossing into the Worcestershire corner of the Cotswolds, and turn off at signposted **⑨ Broadway Tower** (www.broadwaytower.co.uk), an 18th-century Gothic folly perched spectacularly atop the escarpment.

Leaving Broadway Tower, continue 1 mile south and turn right (southwest) at the crossing. You'll soon see signs to pretty little **⑩ Snowshill**, a mile further on and one-time film set for *Bridget Jones's Diary*. If you're visiting in June or July, you'll swing by spectacularly purple fields of flowering lavender. From Snowshill, whizz 2.5 miles north to **⑪ Broadway**. After cruising along broad High St, hop on the B4632 southwest towards Cheltenham.

After 3 miles, take the left (east) turn-off to **⑫ Stanton**, a tiny stunner of a village. Its houses are crafted out of gold-tinged Cotswolds stone, with not a shop or quaint

tearoom in sight. The buildings most likely to catch your eye are Jacobean **Stanton Court** and **St Michael & All Angels' Church**, with its fine Perpendicular tower and beguiling medieval interior.

You'll undoubtedly see walkers passing through Stanton, heading along the Cotswold Way to **⑬ Stanway**, a mile south; follow the narrow road that runs parallel to the trail. There is little more to idyllic Stanway than a few thatched-roofed cottages, a church and Stanway House (www.stanwayfountain.co.uk), a magnificent Jacobean mansion hidden behind a triple-gabled gatehouse. Its beautiful baroque water gardens feature Britain's tallest fountain. The manor has been the private home of the Earls of Wemyss for 500 years and has a delightful, lived-in charm.

Traverse Stanway, turn right (west) onto the B4077 and then left (southwest) back onto the B4632. After 3.5 miles, you'll reach **⑭ Winchcombe**, an ancient Anglo-Saxon town and walkers' favourite with good sleeping and eating options, including 5 North St (p203). You'll probably want to stay overnight to explore wonderful Sudeley Castle (p202) in the morning. Otherwise, continue 8 miles southwest on the B4632 to Cheltenham.

LOCAL KNOWLEDGE

COTSWOLDS FOOD & FARMERS MARKETS

When the locally sourced, seasonal food movement took off, the Cotswolds were already there. Organic, ethically produced produce has long been a staple in its villages, where restaurants thrill with wonderfully fresh local ingredients. In delis and independent food shops all over the Cotswolds, visiting food-lovers will make tempting discoveries.

Edible goodies to look out for include cheese from **Simon Weaver Organic** (www.simonweaver.net), from a farm near Upper Slaughter; organic beef from **LoveMyCow** (www.lovemycow.com) in Bourton-on-the-Water; smoked fish and meats from **Upton Smokery** (www.uptonsmokery.co.uk) in Burford; and fantastic ice cream from **Chedworth's Cotswold Ice Cream Company** (www.cotswold-icecream.co.uk).

Farmers markets take place monthly or fortnightly in many Cotswolds villages and towns, with a multitude of local producers selling their seasonal delights to the public. **Cotswolds.org** (www.cotswolds.org) publishes an online schedule, though it's best to check locally. The best market is held every Saturday morning in **Stroud** (◷Sat).

Minster Lovell

POP 1236

Set on a gentle slope leading down to the meandering River Windrush, Minster Lovell is a gorgeous village with a cluster of thatch-roofed stone cottages nestled beside an ancient pub and riverside mill. One of William Morris' favourite spots, the peaceful flower-filled village has changed little since medieval times. It's 18 miles west of Oxford and divided into two halves: Old Minster, recorded in the Domesday Book (1086), and the rather newer (less charming) Minster Lovell, across the river and up the hill.

◉ Sights

Minster Lovell Hall   HISTORIC BUILDING
(EH; www.english-heritage.org.uk; Old Minster; ◷24hr) **FREE** Old Minster's main sight is Minster Lovell Hall, the 15th-century riverside manor house that was originally home to Viscount Francis Lovell. Abandoned in 1747, the manor is now in ruins. You can pass through the vaulted porch to peek past blackened walls into the roofless great hall, the interior courtyard and the crumbling tower, while the wind whistles eerily through the gaping windows. To get here, walk through the church gardens at the eastern end of Old Minster.

🛏 Sleeping & Eating

Old Swan & Minster Mill   LUXURY HOTEL £££
(☎01993-774441; www.oldswanandminstermill.com; Old Minster; r/ste incl breakfast from £125/295; P🛜🏊♿🐾🚭) 🍴 This luxurious, mostly hydro-powered complex has 14 charming period-style rooms in a 600-year-old pub and 39 sleek, contemporary-design pads in a converted 19th-century mill, opposite. Minster Mill offers a spa, tennis courts, fire pits and an idyllic riverside setting. The Old Swan serves excellent gastropub food (mains £12 to £20, open 12.30 to 3pm and 6.30 to 9pm), including light pastas, daily fish, dinner game and lunchtime sandwiches.

ℹ Getting There & Away

Stagecoach and/or Swanbrook buses serve the following:
Burford (route 233/853; £1.70, 10 to 20 minutes)
Cheltenham (route 853; £5.10, 50 minutes)
Gloucester (route 853; £6.20, 1¼ hours)
Oxford (route S2/853; £4, one hour)
Witney (route 233/S2/853; £2.70, seven to 30 minutes)

Northleach

POP 1923

Little visited and underappreciated, Northleach has been a small market town since 1227 and comprises late-medieval cottages, imposing merchants' stores and half-timbered Tudor houses. A wonderful mix of architectural styles clusters around Market Sq and the narrow laneways leading off it. Northleach is 14 miles southeast of Cheltenham.

◉ Sights

Chedworth Roman Villa   ARCHAEOLOGICAL SITE
(NT; ☎01242-890256; www.nationaltrust.org.uk; Yanworth; adult/child £9/4.50; ◷10am-5pm Mar-Oct, to 4pm Feb & Nov; P) Rediscovered by a gamekeeper in 1864, Chedworth's extensive ruins represent one of the largest, most lux-

urious Roman villas in England. Though the earliest section dates to around AD 175, it's thought to have been at its most magnificent around AD 362, with two sets of bathhouses, a water shrine and a formal dining room with underfloor heating. The stars are the exquisite, well-preserved mosaics. Free guided 45-minute tours offer a good introduction. It's 4.5 miles west of Northleach, signposted from the A429.

Church of St Peter & St Paul CHURCH
(www.northleach.org; Church Walk; ⊙9am-5pm) The grandeur and complexity of this masterpiece of the Cotswold Perpendicular style is testimony to its wool-era wealth. Although the chancel and 30m tower date to the 14th century, the building was extensively reworked during the 15th-century wool boom. A modern highlight is the 1964 stained-glass window behind the altar (depicting Christ in Glory), while earlier treasures include an unusual 14th-century font.

**Cotswolds
Discovery Centre** INTERPRETATION CENTRE
(Escape to the Cotswolds; www.cotswoldsaonb. org.uk; A429; ⊙9.30am-4.30pm; P 🏠) FREE Housed in Northleach's Old Prison, this is the official visitors centre for the Cotswolds Area of Outstanding Natural Beauty (AONB), with displays outlining the area's history, ecology, traditions and attractions. There's also a cosy cafe and a collection of agricultural wagons in the rear courtyard.

🛏 Sleeping & Eating

★**Wheatsheaf** BOUTIQUE HOTEL £££
(☑01451-860244; www.cotswoldswheatsheaf.com; West End; r incl breakfast £123-255; P 🏠 🔌 🐾) The 14 different rooms at this former coaching inn blend atmospheric period touches, such as free-standing bath-tubs, with modern comforts that include power showers, organic toiletries and country-chic decor. Downstairs, there's an outrageously popular **restaurant** (mains £14-27; ⊙8-10am, noon-3pm & 6-9pm Mon-Thu & Sun, to 10pm Fri & Sat; P 🏠 🔌) dishing up delightful seasonal British dishes with a contemporary twist.

❶ Getting There & Away

Swanbrook or Pulhams buses head to/from the following destinations:
Burford (route 853; £2.20, 15 minutes)
Cheltenham (route 801/853; £2.70, 30 minutes)
Cirencester (route 855; £2.70; 20 minutes)

Gloucester (route 853; £3.30, one hour)
Moreton-in-Marsh (route 801; £2.20, 45 minutes)
Oxford (route 853; £6.60, one hour)

The Slaughters
POP 400
The picture-postcard villages of Upper and Lower Slaughter, 3.5 miles southwest of Stow-on-the-Wold, manage to maintain their unhurried medieval charm despite receiving a multitude of visitors. The village names have nothing to do with abattoirs; they are derived from the Old English 'sloughtre', meaning slough or muddy place. Today the River Eye is contained within limestone banks and meanders peacefully through the two villages past classic gold-tinged Cotswolds houses and the 17th-century Slaughters Manor House (now an upmarket hotel).

🛏 Sleeping & Eating

Lords of the Manor MODERN BRITISH £££
(☑01451-820243; www.lordsofthemanor.com; Upper Slaughter; 3-course dinner £72.50; ⊙noon-1.30pm Sat & Sun, 6.45-9pm daily; P) Set inside a dazzling countryside manor, this romantic Michelin-starred restaurant concocts imaginative, beautifully presented dishes with French touches and plenty of quality local produce. It also serves popular afternoon teas and has 26 plush, comfy **rooms** (r incl breakfast £150-465; P 🏠 🐾). Book ahead.

❶ Getting There & Away

Buses are not permitted through the Slaughters, so a car is your best option (unless you're hiking).

Stow-on-the-Wold
POP 2042
The highest town in the Cotswolds (244m), 4.5 miles south of Moreton-in-Marsh, Stow is anchored by a large market square surrounded by handsome buildings and steep-walled alleyways, originally used to funnel sheep into the fair. It's still an important market town and has long held a strategic place in Cotswold history, standing on the Roman Fosse Way (now the A429 here) and at the junction of six roads. Today it's famous for its twice-yearly Stow Horse Fair, and at other times, it attracts plenty of visitors with its scenic hilltop market-town appeal.

WORTH A TRIP

DAYLESFORD ORGANIC

A country-chic temple to the Cotswolds' organic movement, **Daylesford Organic** (☑01608-731700; www.daylesford. com; Daylesford; ⊙8am-5pm Mon-Wed, 8am-8pm Thu-Sat, 10am-4pm Sun) is a sprawling, award-winning agricultural operation that grew from turning a family farm sustainable over 35 years ago. The gleaming food hall is crammed with Daylesford-brand produce. The excellent (though pricey) cafe-restaurant dishes up daily-changing menus of organic-fuelled treats (£7 to £17). There's also a luxury spa, plus an upmarket boutique. It's 4 miles east of Stow-on-the-Wold.

◉ Sights

Cotswold Farm Park ZOO
(☑01451-850307; www.cotswoldfarmpark.co.uk; Guiting Power; adult/child £10.50/9.50; ⊙10.30am-5pm mid-Feb–Oct, to 4.30pm Nov–mid-Dec; ⓟ⊞) 🖉 Owned by TV presenter Adam Henson, Cotswold Farm Park is designed to introduce little ones to the world of farm animals while also preserving rare breeds, such as Exmoor ponies and Cotswold Lion sheep. There are milking demonstrations, lamb-feeding sessions, an adventure playground, a 2-mile wildlife walk and pedal tractors to ride on. It's 6 miles west of Stow-on-the-Wold, signposted from the B4077 and B4068.

🛏 Sleeping & Eating

King's Head Inn PUB ££
(☑01608-658365; www.thekingsheadinn.net; The Green, Bledington; s £75-100, d £100-130, all incl breakfast; ⓟ🛜) Overlooking a peaceful green 4.5 miles southeast of Stow, this stylishly revamped 15th-century cider house blends old and new to perfection, with 12 subtly luxurious, individually styled rooms and a good **restaurant** (mains £12-18; ⊙noon-2pm & 6.30-9pm Mon-Sat, noon-3pm & 6.30-9pm Sun; ⓟ🖉) 🖉. Cosy rooms in the original building burst with old-world character (exposed beams, check-print rugs). The six quieter, contemporary-design courtyard rooms are more sumptuous, featuring power showers and Nespresso machines.

Old Stocks Inn BOUTIQUE HOTEL £££
(☑01451-830666; www.oldstocksinn.com; Market Sq; r £139-279; 🛜⊞☀) Right on Stow's

square, this 17th-century inn is looking fantastically fresh after a bold, contemporary makeover that beautifully mixes period charm (exposed beams, slender staircases) with modern comforts (capsule-coffee kits, retro phones). Decor features bright whites, hot turquoises and patterned pillows. The most affordable rooms are snug attic-style affairs with sloping ceilings, while more lavish 'Great' rooms have claw-foot baths.

❶ Getting There & Away

Pulhams buses serve the following destinations, Monday to Saturday:
Cheltenham (route 801; £3, 1¼ hours)
Moreton-in-Marsh (route 801; £1.70, 10 minutes)
Northleach (route 801; £2.10, 30 minutes)

Chipping Norton
POP 6300

Often overlooked, the hilly, pretty town of Chipping Norton ('Chippy') has plenty of quiet side streets to wander, a fine wool-era church and none of the classic Cotswolds crowds. Handsome Georgian buildings, old coaching inns and the pillared 19th-century town hall cluster around the market square, while on Church St you'll find a row of beautiful honey-tinged almshouses built in the 17th century.

◉ Sights

St Mary's Church CHURCH
(☑01608-646202; www.stmaryscnorton.com; Church St; ⊙10am-dusk) Chipping Norton's secluded church is a classic example of the Cotswold wool churches, with a magnificent Perpendicular nave and clerestory, several alabaster tombs and fluted, diamond-shaped pillars. While it was mostly built in 1448, two of the arches in the chancel date to around 1200. In the hexagonal porch, carved 15th-century ceiling bosses include a sheep overpowering a wolf and the possibly pagan but common visitor to British churches, the Green Man.

🍴 Eating

Wild Thyme MODERN BRITISH ££
(☑01608-645060; www.wildthymerestaurant. co.uk; 10 New St; mains £18-20, 2-/3-course set menu from £20/25; ⊙7-9pm Tue & Wed, noon-2pm & 7-9pm Thu, noon-2pm & 6.30-9.30pm Fri & Sat) A little 'restaurant with rooms', Wild Thyme thrills palates with top-notch creative dishes

packed with flavour, such as asparagus and goat's cheese risotto or steamed brill with shellfish ravioli. The desserts – from apple crumble to chocolate sharing platters – are nothing short of sublime. Hidden upstairs are three brilliantly cosy pastel-painted **rooms** (s £65-75, d £75-85; 🛜).

🛍 Shopping

⭐ **Jaffé & Neale Bookshop Cafe** BOOKS
(📞 01608-641033; www.jaffeandneale.co.uk; 1 Middle Row; ⏰ 9.30am-5.30pm Mon-Sat, 11am-5pm Sun; 🛜) This brilliant independent bookshop serves delicious cakes and coffees to tables squeezed between the bookshelves or in the cosy upstairs reading lounge with sofas.

ℹ Getting There & Away

Stagecoach and/or Pulhams buses head to/from the following destinations:
Oxford (route S3; £4.60, one hour)
Stratford-upon-Avon (route 50; £5.85, 50 minutes)
Witney (route X9; £3.90, 40 minutes)
Woodstock (route S3; £4, 20 minutes)

Moreton-in-Marsh

POP 3493

Home to some beautiful 17th- and 18th-century buildings but plagued by the heavy traffic that clogs up its broad High St (A429; built on top of the Roman Fosse Way), Moreton-in-Marsh is a major transport hub known for its excellent food shops stocking local Cotswold produce. On Tuesday, the town bursts into life for its weekly market. It's 4.5 miles north of Stow-on-the-Wold.

◎ Sights

⭐ **Cotswold Falconry Centre** AVIARY
(📞 01386-701043; www.cotswold-falconry.co.uk; Batsford Park; adult/child £10/5; ⏰ 10.30am-5pm mid-Feb–mid-Nov; 🅿) Home to over 150 birds of prey (owl, vulture, eagle and, of course, falcon), this exciting spot offers displays of the ancient practice of falconry at 11.30am, 1.30pm and 3pm daily (plus 4.30pm April to October). The birds fly at their best on windy days. Various hands-on experiences (from £40) include a one-hour 'Flying Start' during which visitors get to fly hawks.

Batsford Arboretum PARK
(📞 01386-701441; www.batsarb.co.uk; Batsford Park; adult/child £7.20/3.15; ⏰ 9am-5pm Mon-Sat, 10am-5pm Sun; 🅿🐾) 🖉 Created by Ber-

COTSWOLDS DISTILLERY

Launched in 2014, the ambitious, ecofriendly gin and whisky distillery-**Cotswolds Distillery** (📞 01608-238533; www.cotswoldsdistillery.com; Phillip's Field, Whichford Road, Stourton; tours without/with tasting £6/10; ⏰ tours 11am & 2pm, shop 9am-5pm Mon-Sat, 11am-4pm Sun) sits tucked into the northern Cotswolds, 7 miles north of Chipping Norton. You can tour the facilities and learn all about how its delicious Cotswolds-flavoured liquors are produced, before wrapping up with a tasting session. Book ahead.

tie Mitford (Lord Redesdale) in 1880, these exotic 22-hectare woodlands feature around 1600 species of labelled trees, bamboos and shrubs from Nepal, China, Japan and North America. Many of these are rare or endangared, or were planted pre-WWI. Highlights include vast American redwoods, flowering Japanese cherries (at their best in spring), an enormous davidia and the strangely churchlike 'cathedral' lime.

🛌 Sleeping & Eating

White Hart Royal Hotel HOTEL ££
(📞 01608-650731; www.whitehartroyal.co.uk; High St; s/d incl breakfast from £75/95; 🅿🛜) 'Royal' relates to the fact that Charles I once stayed here during the Civil War, and while he probably didn't use the iPod docks, flat-screen TVs and en-suite rooms, he certainly walked down the atmospheric half-timbered corridors. Standard rooms aren't particularly characterful, though they're comfy and well equipped. The downstairs restaurant (mains £12 to £20, open from 6pm to 9pm Monday to Saturday, noon to 2pm and 6pm to 9pm Sunday) has plenty of charm.

⭐ **Horse & Groom** PUB FOOD ££
(📞 01386-700413; www.horseandgroom.info; Bourton-on-the-Hill; mains £12.50-21.50; ⏰ noon-2pm daily, 7-9pm Mon-Sat; 🅿🛜) 🖉 The bubbly, laid-back Horse & Groom, 2 miles west of Moreton-in-Marsh, excels at upmarket country cooking showcasing local lamb, beef and vegetables, alongside flavour-filled fish dishes, all colourfully chalked up on a board in the bar. It's a firm favourite with well-heeled horsey types. It also has five swish rooms upstairs (single £80, double £120 to £170).

❶ Getting There & Away

BUS
From Monday to Saturday, Pulhams, Stagecoach and/or Johnsons Excelbus buses head to/from the following:

Broadway (route 21/22; £3.20, 30 minutes)
Cheltenham (route 801; £3.30, 1½ hours)
Chipping Campden (route 21/22; £3.20, 50 minutes)
Cirencester (route 855; £2.70, one hour)
Northleach (route 855; £2.20, 40 minutes)
Stow-on-the-Wold (route 801; £1.70, 10 minutes)
Stratford-upon-Avon (route 21/22/23/50; £5.85, one hour)

TRAIN
The train station is towards the northern end of town, just off High St. Trains head to/from the following:

Hereford (£18, 1¾ hours)
Ledbury (£17, 1½ hours)
London Paddington (£35, 1½ hours)
Oxford (£9.90, 35 minutes)
Worcester (£12.40, 40 minutes)

Chipping Campden
POP 2037

An absolute gem in an area full of pretty towns, Chipping Campden is a glorious reminder of Cotswolds life in medieval times. The graceful curving main street is flanked by a perfectly picturesque array of stone cottages, fine terraced houses, ancient inns and historic homes, most made of that beautiful honey-coloured Cotswolds stone. There are particularly striking thatch-roofed cottages along Westington, at the southwestern end of town. Despite its obvious allure, Chipping Campden remains relatively unspoiled by visiting crowds. It is, however, popular with walkers rambling along the Cotswold Way, which tracks 102 miles northeast from Bath to Chipping Campden.

While the village's name derives from the Old English 'ceapen', meaning 'market', 'Chippy's' visible prosperity derives from its past as a successful wool town.

◎ Sights

St James' Church   CHURCH
(☎01386-841927; www.stjameschurchcampden. co.uk; Church St; admission by donation; ◎10am-4.30pm Mon-Sat, noon-4pm Sun Apr-Oct, 11am-3pm Mon-Sat, 2-4pm Sun Nov-Mar) Built in the late 15th century in Perpendicular Gothic style, on wool-trade riches, imposing St James' has a splendid tower and some graceful 17th-century monuments. Inside, you can see one of the earliest priest vestments on record, dating back to 1400. On Church St, just outside, stands a remarkable row of almshouses constructed in 1612.

Grevel House   HISTORIC BUILDING
(High St; ◎closed to the public) One of the grandest residences on High St, 14th-century Grevel House was once home to highly successful wool merchant William Grevel and is Chipping Campden's oldest building. Admire the splendid Perpendicular Gothic–style gabled window and sundial from the street.

Hidcote   GARDENS
(NT; www.nationaltrust.org.uk; Hidcote Bartrim; adult/child £10.90/5.45; ◎10am-6pm, to 5pm Oct, shorter hours Nov, Dec & mid-Feb–Mar, closed Jan; P) About 4 miles northeast of Chipping Campden, Hidcote is one of the finest examples of Arts and Crafts landscaping in Britain, with a series of outdoor 'rooms' filled with flowers and rare plants from across the globe. It owes its unique beauty to 20th-century avid garden designer Lawrence Johnston.

🛏 Sleeping & Eating

Eight Bells Inn   PUB ££
(☎01386-840371; www.eightbellsinn.co.uk; Church St; s £60-95, d £95-140, all incl breakfast; 🤶) This refurbished 14th-century inn is a particularly friendly and atmospheric place to stay, featuring six bright, modern rooms with iron bedsteads, soothing neutral decor, flowery wallpaper and warm accents. Room 7, with its chunky old-world beams, is especially striking. The cosy **pub** (mains £13-16; ◎noon-2pm & 6.30-9pm Mon-Thu, noon-2.30pm & 6.30-9.30pm Fri & Sat, 12.15-9pm Sun; 👪🍴) downstairs serves good modern British country cooking.

Chef's Dozen   MODERN BRITISH ££
(☎01386-840598; www.thechefsdozen.co.uk; High St; 3-/4-course set menu £28/45; ◎6.30-9pm Tue-Thu, noon-1.30pm & 6.30-9pm Fri & Sat) 🌱 Superb organic, field-to-fork cooking powered by local produce and delivered by changing seasonal menus is the draw at this fresh, friendly culinary star. Settle into the tastefully understated cream-coloured dining room for skilfully concocted, beautifully creative dishes, such as wild-rabbit ravioli or

risotto filled with Cotswolds cheeses. Outside, tables dot a sweet, discreet courtyard.

ⓘ Information

Tourist Office (☑ 01386-841206; www.campdenonline.org; Old Police Station, High St; ☺ 9.30am-5pm daily mid-Mar–mid-Nov, 9.30am-1pm Mon-Thu, to 4pm Fri-Sun mid-Nov–mid-Mar) Pick up a town guide (£1.50) for a self-guided walk around Chipping Campden's most significant buildings. Guided tours are run by the Cotswold Voluntary Wardens from May to September (suggested donation £3).

ⓘ Getting There & Away

From Monday to Saturday, Johnsons Excelbus services head to/from Moreton-in-Marsh (route 21/22; £3.20, 50 minutes), Broadway (route 21/22/24; £2.70, 20 minutes) and Stratford-up-on-Avon (route 21/22/24; £4.20, 50 minutes).

Marchants bus 606S (Sunday only) runs to/from Broadway (£4.50, 20 minutes), Cheltenham (£8, one hour), Stratford-upon-Avon (£4.50, 25 minutes) and Winchcombe (£8, 35 minutes). Marchants bus 606 runs to the same destinations Monday to Saturday.

Broadway

POP 2540

A quintessentially English village with a smattering of antique shops, tearooms and art galleries, Broadway has inspired writers, artists and composers in times past with its graceful, golden-hued cottages set at the foot of a steep escarpment. Unsurprisingly, it's one of the more popular Cotswolds spots, just 5 miles west of Chipping Campden.

If the village of Snowshill, 2.5 miles south, looks familiar, that's because it featured in hit film *Bridget Jones's Diary*. A local house was used as Bridget's parents' home.

◉ Sights

Ashmolean Museum Broadway MUSEUM
(☑ 01386-859047; www.ashmoleanbroadway.org; Tudor House, 65 High St; adult/child £5/2; ☺ 10am-5pm Tue-Sun) Partnered with Oxford's famous Ashmolean Museum, this grand converted 17th-century coaching inn has fascinating displays of local crafts, antiques and historical detail spanning from the 17th-century to the present day. Collections include Winchcombe pottery, vintage furniture, elaborate tapestries and paintings by 18th-century artists Joshua Reynolds and Thomas Gainsborough.

Snowshill Manor & Garden HOUSE
(NT; www.nationaltrust.org.uk; Snowshill; adult/child £10.40/5.40; ☺ noon-5pm mid-Mar–Oct) About 3 miles south of Broadway lies this wonderful Cotswold mansion, once home to marvellously eccentric poet and architect Charles Paget Wade (1883–1956). The house contains Wade's extraordinary collection of crafts and design, taking in everything from musical instruments to Southeast Asian masks and Japanese samurai armour. The impressive gardens were designed as an extension of the house, with pools, terraces and wonderful views.

🛏 Sleeping & Eating

Russell's HOTEL ££
(☑ 01386-853555; www.russellsofbroadway.co.uk; The Green, 20 High St; r incl breakfast from £120; ☺ restaurant noon-2.15pm & 6-9.15pm Mon-Sat, noon-2.30pm Sun; ℗ 🕸 🐾) Sleek and stylish Russell's has seven spacious, individually designed rooms, some with exposed beams, four-poster beds and armchairs, and all with modern luxuries such as contemporary bathrooms and fresh white styling. It's known for its beautifully executed modern-British fare (mains £16 to £26), including Sunday roasts.

Foxhill Manor DESIGN HOTEL £££
(☑ 01386-852711; www.foxhillmanor.com; Farmcombe Estate; r incl breakfast from £375; ℗ 🕸 🐾) Occupying a 1904 mansion on 160 hectares of hillside estate, 2.5 miles northeast of Broadway, ultra-luxurious Foxhill is all Cotswolds chic with stripped-back Scandi-influenced style. From dazzlingly bold decor (leopard-print cushions, a hot-pink bathroom, twin window-facing baths) to period stucco-work, the eight sleek all-different suites sparkle with character. The in-house chef cooks according to personal requests.

Mount Inn PUB FOOD ££
(☑ 01386-584316; www.themountinn.co.uk; Stanton; mains £13-22; ☺ noon-1pm & 6-9pm; ℗) Perched above pretty honey-washed Stanton, 3 miles southwest of Broadway, the Mount Inn is one of the Cotswolds' most idyllically positioned pubs. The food's fantastic too: hearty country fare carefully prepared with contemporary flair. Menus range over breaded local St Eadburgha cheese, beer-battered haddock, gammon steaks, mushroom-halloumi burgers and daily-changing seasonal specials. Outdoor benches revel in those glorious hilltop views.

ℹ Information

Tourist Office (☑ 01386-852937; www.
visit-broadway.co.uk; Russell Sq; ⊙10am-5pm
Mon-Sat, 11am-3pm Sun Apr-Oct, 10am-4pm
Mon-Sat Nov-Mar) Sells maps of local walks.

ℹ Getting There & Away

Marchants and Johnsons Excelbus buses head
to the following destinations:

Cheltenham (route 606/606S; £3.10, 35
minutes)

Chipping Campden (route 21/22/24/606S;
£2.70 to £4.50, 20 minutes)

Moreton-in-Marsh (route 21/22; £3.20, 30
minutes)

Stratford-upon-Avon (route 21/22/24/606S;
£4.20, one hour)

Winchcombe (route 606/606S; £2.80, 30
minutes)

Winchcombe

POP 4538

Winchcombe, 8 miles northeast of Cheltenham, is very much a working, living town,
where butchers, bakers and independent
shops line the main streets. It was capital of
the Anglo-Saxon kingdom of Mercia and one
of the major towns in the Cotswolds until the
Middle Ages, as well as an important tobacco
producer. Today, the remnants of this illustrious past can still be seen in Winchcombe's
dramatic stone and half-timbered buildings.
Keep an eye out for the picturesque cottages
on Vineyard St and Dents Tce.

Winchcombe is particularly popular with
and ideally situated for walkers.

◉ Sights

Sudeley Castle   CASTLE
(☑ 01242-604244; www.sudeleycastle.co.uk; adult/
child £14.50/5.50; ⊙10am-5pm mid-Mar–Oct;
℗ 🚻) Winchcombe's main attraction, this
magnificent castle has welcomed many a
monarch over its thousand-year history, including Richard III, Henry VIII and Charles
I. It's most famous as the home and final resting place of Catherine Parr (Henry VIII's wid-
ow), who lived here with her fourth husband,
Thomas Seymour. You'll find **Catherine's
tomb** in the castle's Perpendicular Gothic St
Mary's Church, making this the only private
house in England where a queen is buried.
There are also 10 splendid gardens here.

Henry VIII and Anne Boleyn visited Sudeley together in 1535. Princess Elizabeth (before becoming Elizabeth I) was part of the
household until Seymour's inappropriate
displays of affection towards her prompted
Catherine to banish her from the premises. Lady Jane Grey (the ill-fated 'Nine Days
Queen') was also sent here to live with the
Seymours, and was the chief mourner at
Catherine's funeral (1548).

The house is still a family home and some
of the interior may be off-limits to visitors,
but you can get a good sense of its grand
proportions while visiting the exhibitions of
costumes, memorabilia and paintings, and
the gorgeous surrounding grounds. The gardens include spectacular avenues of sculpted
yews, an intricate knot garden (inspired by
the pattern of one of Elizabeth I's gowns) and
aviaries containing magnificently coloured
pheasants. The rose-filled **Queen's Garden**,
based on its original Tudor parterre, gets its
name from having been strolled in by four
English queens (Anne Boleyn, Catherine
Parr, Lady Jane Grey and Elizabeth I).

Hailes Abbey   RUINS
(EH; www.english-heritage.org.uk; Hailes; adult/
child £5/3; ⊙10am-6pm Jul & Aug, to 5pm East-
er-Jun, Sep & Oct; ℗) Three miles northeast
of Winchcombe lie the meagre ruins of this
13th-century Cistercian abbey, once one of
England's main pilgrimage centres, due to
a long-running medieval scam. The abbey
was said to possess a vial of Christ's blood,
which turned out to be merely coloured water; before the deception came to light, thousands of pilgrims contributed to the abbey's
wealth. Free audio guides lead you around.

Belas Knap Long Barrow   ARCHAEOLOGICAL SITE
(EH; www.english-heritage.org.uk; near Charlton Abbots; ⊙dawn-dusk) FREE Dating from around
3000 BC, Belas Knap is one of the country's
best-preserved neolithic burial chambers,
with a 'false' portal leading to nowhere. The
remains of 31 people were found when its four
chambers were excavated. At 290m, views
across Sudeley Castle and the surrounding
countryside are breathtaking. The barrow can
be accessed from Winchcombe by a 2½-mile
hike south along the Cotswold Way. Alternatively, park on Corndean Lane and take a
steep half-mile walk up across fields.

🛏 Sleeping & Eating

Wesley House   B&B ££
(☑ 01242-602366; www.wesleyhouse.co.uk; High
St; s £70-95, d £85-110; ⊙restaurant noon-2pm &
7-9pm Tue-Sat, noon-2pm Sun; 🛜🐾) Methodist
founder John Wesley once stayed in this

wonderful 15th-century half-timbered town house with five pleasantly styled rooms and a warm welcome. 'Mumble Meadow', splashed with reds, overlooks the street, while 'Almsbury' has its own terrace gazing out across the countryside. Downstairs is split between a relaxed bar and grill, and a more formal restaurant serving fabulous modern-British cuisine (mains £16 to £24).

⭐ **5 North St**   MODERN EUROPEAN **£££**
(☑ 01242-604566; www.5northstreetrestaurant. co.uk; 5 North St; 2-/3-course lunch £26/30, 3- to 7-course dinner £47-70; ☉ 7-9pm Tue, noon-1.30pm & 7-9pm Wed-Sat, noon-1.30pm Sun; ☑) This long-standing Michelin-starred restaurant is a treat from start to finish, from its splendid 400-year-old timbered exterior to the elegant, inventive creations you eventually find on your plate. Marcus Ashenford's cooking is rooted in traditional seasonal ingredients, but the odd playful experiment (such as duck-egg pasta or malt ice cream) adds that extra magic. Vegetarians will enjoy their own dedicated menu.

ℹ Information

Tourist Office (☑ 01242-602925; www.winchcombe.co.uk; Town Hall, High St; ☉10am-4pm daily Apr-Oct, to 3pm Sat & Sun Nov-Mar) Has maps of local walks and runs free guided town tours at 11am and 2.30pm on Sunday, Easter to October.

ℹ Getting There & Away

The **Gloucestershire Warwickshire Railway** (GWR; ☑ 01242-621405; www.gwsr.com; day pass adult/child £16/7; ☉ Mar-Dec; 🚻) runs between Winchcombe and Cheltenham (£12, 25 minutes).

Marchants buses travel to/from Broadway (route 606/606S; £2.80, 30 minutes) and Cheltenham (route 606/606S/W1/W2; £2.50, 20 to 45 minutes).

Painswick

POP 1762

One of the most beautiful and unspoilt towns in the Cotswolds, hilltop Painswick sits 10 miles southwest of Cheltenham, but it sees only a trickle of visitors. You can wander the narrow winding streets and admire the picture-perfect cottages, handsome stone town houses and medieval inns at your own leisure. Keep an eye out for Bisley St, the original main drag, which was superseded by the now ancient-looking New St in medieval times.

WORTH A TRIP

PRINCE CHARLES' HIGHGROVE

The private residence of Prince Charles and the Duchess of Cornwall, **Highgrove** (☑ 0303 123 7310; www.highgrovegardens.com; Doughton; tours £25; ☉ Apr–mid-Oct) is famous for its exquisite, sustainable, organic gardens, which include rows of shape-clipped yews and a 'carpet garden' modelled on an oriental rug. Two-hour garden tours run on select days. Tickets (prebooked) sell out far in advance, though last-minute tickets are sometimes available through **Highgrove Shop** (www.highgroveshop. com; 10 Long St; ☉ 9.30am-5pm Mon-Sat, 10.30am-4pm Sun). Highgrove is a mile southwest of Tetbury.

The bucolic little village of Slad, 2 miles south of Painswick in the Slad Valley, was once the much-loved home of writer Laurie Lee, who immortalised its beauty in *Cider with Rosie*.

◉ Sights

Painswick Rococo Garden   GARDENS
(☑ 01452-813204; www.rococogarden.org.uk; off B4073; adult/child £7/3.30; ☉10.30am-5pm mid-Jan–Oct; 🅿🚻) Just north of Painswick, this stunner is the only garden of its type in England, designed by Benjamin Hyett in the 1740s as a vast 'outdoor room' and now restored to its former glory. Winding paths soften the otherwise strict geometrical precision, leading visitors around the central vegetable garden, plunge pool and pond to the many Gothic follies dotted across the grounds. Among these is the eccentric Red House, with Latin quotes from the Song of Solomon etched into its stained-glass windows.

St Mary's Church   CHURCH
(www.stmaryspainswick.org.uk; New St; ☉ 9.30am-dusk) Painswick centres on this fine 14th-century, Perpendicular Gothic wool church, surrounded by 18th-century tabletop tombs and clipped yew trees that resemble giant lollipops. Legend has it that only 99 trees could ever grow here, as the devil would shrivel the 100th tree. They planted it anyway, to celebrate the millennium and – lo and behold! – one of the trees toppled several years later. In the street, at the foot of the churchyard, stands a rare set of iron stocks.

📷 Sleeping & Eating

Troy House
B&B ££

(☑ 01452-812339; www.troyguesthouse.co.uk; Gloucester St; s/d £75/85; 🛜) This great little B&B sleeps guests in four sweet, spacious rooms, two of which occupy their own separate rear cottage accessed from a pretty courtyard. They're prettily decked out with soothing cream decor, comfy beds and baskets of toiletries, and freshly cooked breakfasts are excellent.

⭐ The Painswick
LUXURY HOTEL £££

(☑ 01452-813688; www.thepainswick.co.uk; Kemps Lane; r/ste from £119/344; ⊙ restaurant noon-2.30pm & 7-9.30pm; 🅿🛜♿) Relaunched in 2016 after a seriously chic makeover, The Painswick blends 18th-century architecture with boldly contemporary decor, a laid-back feel and 16 individually decorated, pastel-painted rooms. All come with luxury comforts, including Nespresso machines; some have claw-foot bath-tubs, others four-poster beds or tile-floored bathrooms. There are massage/treatment rooms, plus a futuristic bar, colour-popping lounge and good modern restaurant (mains £15 to £24).

Woolpack
PUB FOOD ££

(☑ 01452-813429; www.thewoolpackslad.com; Slad; mains £11-16; ⊙ noon-midnight; 🍴) A wonderfully authentic old-world village pub with a lively local buzz, the Woolpack was a favourite watering hole of Slad-based writer Laurie Lee, whose portrait and books adorn the walls. It's perfect for a pint, stocking excellent locally brewed beers including Uley Bitter. The tempting daily-changing seasonal menu delivers classic gammon or fish and chips alongside pastas, burgers, curries and pizzas (Monday). Slad is 2 miles south of Painswick.

ℹ Information

Tourist Office (☑ 01452-812278; www.painswicktouristinfo.co.uk; Gravedigger's Hut, St Mary's Church, New St; ⊙ 10am-4pm Mon & Wed-Fri, to 1pm Tue & Sat Mar-Oct) In the church grounds.

ℹ Getting There & Away

Stagecoach bus 61 heads to/from Cheltenham (£3.40, 32 minutes) and Stroud (£2, 15 minutes).

Uley

POP 998

This lovely little hamlet, with its quaint village green and jumble of pretty houses, sits below the overgrown remains of the largest Iron Age hill fort in England, Uley Bury. There are some fascinating sights nearby, including two prehistoric long barrows. Uley is 7.5 miles southwest of Stroud.

⊙ Sights

Uley Bury
ARCHAEOLOGICAL SITE

(⊙ 24hr) FREE England's largest Iron Age hill fort dates from about 300 BC and sprawls across 13 (overgrown) hectares above Uley. You can follow the 1.1-mile perimeter track around its ramparts, which afford fabulous views over Uley and the Severn Vale. If you're driving, an unsignposted 100m track leads to a corner of the bury from a small car park, 1 mile north of Uley on the B4066. For walkers, a steep path climbs up to the bury from Uley's village church.

From the car park, you can also follow part of the Cotswold Way a short distance north to Uley Long Barrow, a 3500 BC burial mound.

Woodchester Mansion
HOUSE

(☑ 01453-861541; www.woodchestermansion.org.uk; Woodchester Park, Nympsfield; adult/child £7.50/free; ⊙ 11am-5pm Tue-Sat late Mar-Oct) Untouched since the mid-1870s, grand, graceful Woodchester Mansion was abandoned before it was finished. Doors open to nowhere, fireplaces are stuck halfway up walls, and corridors end at ledges with views of the ground

WORTH A TRIP

SLIMBRIDGE WETLAND CENTRE

A pioneer in wetlands conservation, the 325-hectare reserve **Slimbridge Wetland Centre** (WWT; ☑ 01453-891900; www.wwt.org.uk/slimbridge; Bowditch, Slimbridge; adult/child £11.90/6.55; ⊙ 9.30am-5.30pm Apr-Oct, to 5pm Nov-Mar; 🅿) has provided a haven for thousands of migratory and resident birds since 1946. The observation tower affords spectacular 360-degree views for spotting some of the 200-plus feathered species, which range from visiting swallows, peregrine falcons, white-fronted geese and Bewick's swans to hot-pink resident flamingos. Migratory birds visit in winter, while spring brings plenty of chicks. There's an array of activities, including self-led canoeing (£5). The reserve is 5 miles northeast of Berkeley, off the A38.

below. The house also features some impressive gruesome gargoyles and is home to one of England's most important colonies of horseshoe bats and several resident ghosts. Marked trails lead through the surrounding parkland. It's 3 miles north of Uley, off the B4066.

ℹ Getting There & Away

Stagecoach bus 35 heads to/from Stroud (£2.80, 35 minutes), though you're better off with your own car.

WESTERN GLOUCESTERSHIRE

West of the Cotswolds, Gloucestershire's greatest asset is the elegant Regency town of Cheltenham, home to tree-lined terraces, upmarket boutiques and a tempting collection of hotels and restaurants. The county capital, Gloucester, is well worth a visit for its magnificent Perpendicular Gothic cathedral. Just southwest lies Berkeley, with its historic Norman castle. Further west, the Forest of Dean is a leafy backwater perfect for walking, cycling, kayaking and other adventure activities.

Cheltenham

POP 115,700

Cheltenham, on the western edge of the Cotswolds, is the region's major town, and retains an air of gracious refinement left over from its heyday as a spa resort in the 18th century. At the time, it rivalled Bath as the place for sick rich people to go, and today it still has many graceful Regency buildings and manicured squares. These days, however, it's best known for its racecourse and mid-March horse races.

Cheltenham's excellent hotel and restaurant offerings make it a much more appealing base to the region than the county town of Gloucester (12 miles west), but it's unlikely to be the highlight of your trip.

Central Cheltenham extends around the grand tree-lined Promenade, at the southern end of which lies the fashionable Montpellier area.

◉ Sights

Montpellier   AREA

As well as its handsome architecture, Montpellier hosts a lively collection of bars, restaurants, hotels and independent shops

BERKELEY CASTLE

The fine red-stone **Berkeley Castle** (☑ 01453-810303; www.berkeley-castle. com; adult/child £11/6; ⊙ 11am-5pm Sun-Wed Apr-Oct; P ⛟) has been the home of the Berkeleys for nearly 900 years, and little has changed since it was built as a sturdy Norman fortress. Edward II was imprisoned and then allegedly murdered here in 1327 on the order of his wife and her lover. Visits include the 12th-century keep, the King's Gallery (with cell and dungeon) and the spectacular medieval Great Hall (lined with tapestries). Free 45-minute guided tours run every 30 minutes.

and boutiques. Along **Montpellier Walk**, 32 caryatids (draped female figures based on those of Athens' Acropolis) act as structural supports between the 1840s shops, each balancing an elaborately carved cornice on her head. Directly opposite are the pretty Montpellier Gardens, established in 1809.

The Wilson   MUSEUM, GALLERY
(☑ 01242-237431; www.thewilson.org.uk; Clarence St; ⊙ 9.30am-5.15pm) **FREE** Cheltenham's excellent museum depicts local life through the ages and has wonderful displays on William Morris and the Arts and Crafts movement, including a painted pine table designed by Morris. It also contains exhibits on British ceramics, fine art and jewellery, and the Roman era. A section on Captain Scott's ill-fated expedition to Antarctica highlights the important role of local lad Edward Wilson, for whom the museum is named.

🛏 Sleeping

★ Bradley   B&B **££**
(☑ 01242-519077; www.thebradleyhotel.co.uk; 19 Royal Pde, Bayshill Rd; s/d from £94/99; P ⛟) This brilliantly preserved Regency house in Montpellier has lost none of its original flair in its transition into a fabulous, wonderfully comfortable B&B. Each of the six rooms has its own individual style, combining antique furniture, vintage trinkets and original artwork with modern amenities.

Wyastone Townhouse   B&B **££**
(☑ 01242-245549; www.wyastonehotel.co.uk; Parabola Rd; s/d from £75/125; P ⛟) A keen young couple heads up this lovely white

Cheltenham

Cheltenham

◉ Sights
1 Montpellier	A4
2 The Wilson	B2

⌂ Sleeping
3 Bradley	A4
4 No 131	B4
5 Wyastone Townhouse	A4

⊗ Eating
6 L'Artisan	B2
7 Le Champignon Sauvage	B5

◉ Drinking & Nightlife
8 John Gordons	A4

Victorian house in Montpellier. Rooms in the main house are grander than those surrounding the pretty back courtyard, but all 16 are comfortable and well equipped. Decor is bright and fresh, with paintings by local artists. There are plenty of tips on Cheltenham and the Cotswolds, plus wonderful homemade breakfasts. Excellent value.

No 131   BOUTIQUE HOTEL **£££**
(☎ 01242-822939; www.no131.com; 131 The Promenade; r incl breakfast £145-335; ☜) Housed in a stunning Georgian building, No 131 is an exquisite luxury addition to Cheltenham's hotel

scene. The 11 supremely comfortable, country-chic rooms combine original artwork, antique touches (such as 19th-century claw-foot baths) and contemporary comforts (Nespresso machines, iPod docks). Some have in-room baths, others step-down walk-in showers. Scented candles dot the corridors, the bar buzzes and there's a luxe, laid-back vibe.

✕ Eating & Drinking

L'Artisan FRENCH ££
(☑ 01242-571257; www.lartisan-restaurant.com; 30 Clarence St; mains £12-20; ☺ noon-2pm & 6-9pm Tue-Sat; ☑) Decked with ornate mirrors, red-striped velvet chairs and mini-chandeliers, yellow-walled L'Artisan delights with its bubbly atmosphere and smartly prepared, thoroughly French food. Meals begin with homemade breads and spreads, followed by fluffy risotto, stuffed chicken breast, a choice of omelettes or a 'fish-duo' dish. Service from the efficient staff is superb.

★ Le Champignon Sauvage FRENCH £££
(☑ 01242-573449; www.lechampignonsauvage.co.uk; 24-28 Suffolk Rd; 2-/3-/4-course menu £50/63/73; ☺ 12.30-1.30pm & 7.30-8.45pm Tue-Sat) For nearly 30 years, this two-Michelin-starred Cheltenham institution has been delighting visitors and locals alike with chef David Everitt-Matthias' finely executed dishes and imaginative flavour combinations. We're not alone in thinking it's Gloucestershire's best restaurant. The set lunch and dinner menus are good value.

John Gordons WINE BAR
(☑ 01242-245985; www.johngordons.co.uk; 11 Montpellier Arcade; ☺ 10.30am-10pm Mon-Wed, to 11pm Thu, to 1am Fri & Sat, noon-9pm Sun) This elegantly low-key wine-and-spirits bar delivers a wonderful globetrotting selection of whiskies, gins, wines, beers and ciders, accompanied by local cheese boards, charcuterie platters and other light bites (£3 to £14). Perfect for sampling enormous glass goblets of highly popular Cotswolds-distilled gin (with tonic, of course).

✦ Festivals

Cheltenham Literature Festival LITERATURE
(www.cheltenhamfestivals.com; ☺ early Oct) One of the world's oldest book-focused festivals kicks off over 10 days in autumn, hosting an astounding array of talks, workshops, interviews and debates by 600 top writers, actors, scholars and other literary figures.

ℹ Information

Tourist Office (☑ 01242-237431; www.visitcheltenham.com; The Wilson, Clarence St; ☺ 9.30am-5.15pm) Inside the town museum.

ℹ Transport

BUS

Stagecoach, Pulhams, Marchants and Swanbrook operate local buses from Cheltenham. Most buses depart from the **bus station** (Royal Well Rd); some use stops along the Promenade. Bus destinations include the following:

Broadway (route 606/606S; £3.10, 35 minutes)
Cirencester (route 51; £3.60, 40 minutes)
Gloucester (route 10/94/97/98/99; £3.20, 45 minutes)
Oxford (route 853; £8, 1½ hours)
Stow-on-the-Wold (route 801; £3, 1¼ hours)
Stratford-upon-Avon (route 606S, Sunday only; £8, 1½ hours)
Stroud (route 61; £3.60, 45 minutes)
Winchcombe (route 606/606S; £2.50, 20 minutes)

National Express coach destinations:
Birmingham (£12, 1½ hours)
Bristol (£9, 1½ hours)
Leeds (£42, 5½ hours)
London Victoria (£7, three hours)
Newcastle-upon-Tyne (£56, eight hours)
Nottingham (£25, four hours)

TRAIN

Cheltenham Spa train station is a mile west of the centre. Buses (£2) run to/from the station every 10 minutes. Services include the following:
Bath (£14.30, 1½ hours)
Bristol (£9, 40 minutes)
Cardiff (£18, 1½ hours)
Edinburgh (£130, six hours)
Exeter (£23, 1¾ hours)
Gloucester (£4.60, 10 minutes)
London Paddington (£33, 2¼ hours)

Forest of Dean

The Forest of Dean is the oldest oak forest in England and a wonderfully scenic place for outdoor adventure activities. The 42-sq-mile woodland, designated England's first National Forest Park in 1938, was formerly a royal hunting ground and a centre of iron and coal mining. Its mysterious depths supposedly inspired the forests of JRR Tolkien's Middle Earth books, and key scenes in *Harry Potter & the Deathly Hallows* were filmed here.

GLOUCESTER CATHEDRAL

The spectacular **Gloucester Cathedral** (☑ 01452-528095; www.gloucestercathedral.org. uk; 12 College Green; admission free, tower tours adult/child £7/1; ☉ 7.30am-6pm) is among the first and finest examples of the English Perpendicular Gothic style. A Norman church was built here by a group of Benedictine monks in the 12th century, on the site of a Saxon abbey, and further elements (including the present-day tower) were added in the 15th century. When Edward II died in 1327 under suspicious circumstances at nearby Berkeley Castle, the church became his burial place.

Inside, the best of Norman Romanesque and Gothic design are skilfully combined with sturdy columns, creating a sense of gracious solidity. From the 14th-century wooden choir stalls, you'll get a good view of the imposing 22m-high **Great East Window**, the largest in Europe when it was installed in the 1350s. Beneath the window in the northern ambulatory is **Edward II's tomb**, a magnificently elaborate work in alabaster that turned the place into a important pilgrimage spot for 70 years after his death. Right behind the altar is the late-15th-century **Lady Chapel**, a glorious patchwork of carved stone and stained glass.

One of the cathedral's most resplendent treasures is the exquisite **Great Cloister**, which featured in the first, second and sixth *Harry Potter* films. Completed in 1367, it contains the earliest example of fan vaulting in England and is matched in beauty only by Henry VII's chapel at Westminster Abbey. When the sun shines through, stained-glass windows tinge the cloister pink.

The Forest of Dean also gives its name to one of Gloucestershire's districts, which includes the towns of Newent and Coleford, north and west (respectively) of the forest itself. To the northwest, the forest spills over into Herefordshire. The River Wye skirts its west edge, offering glorious views to canoeists paddling out from the village of Symonds Yat.

A good place to begin exploring the forest proper is the **Dean Heritage Centre** (☑ 01594-822170; www.deanheritagecentre.com; Camp Mill, Soudley; adult/child £7.20/5.40; ☉ 10am-5pm Apr-Oct, to 4pm Nov-Mar; ℗ ♿), just outside Soudley, within the forest's eastern fringe.

◉ Sights

★ International Centre for Birds of Prey
AVIARY
(☑ 01531-820286; www.icbp.org; Boulsdon House, Newent; adult/child £10.90/7; ☉ 10.30am-4.30pm Feb-Nov; ℗) Watch raptors swoop and dive at this large, long-standing countryside complex, 2 miles southwest of Newent (follow the signs). There are three flyings per day (11.30am, 2pm and 4.15pm), along with aviaries housing 70 species of owls, falcons, kestrels, eagles, buzzards, hawks, kites and other birds of prey from all over the world. For the hands-on feel, choose from a range of 'experience days', such as Hunting or Owls (from £70).

Clearwell Caves
CAVE
(☑ 01594-832535; www.clearwellcaves.com; Clearwell; adult/child £6.50/4.50; ☉ 10am-5pm mid-Feb-Dec; ℗ ♿) Descend into the damp subterranean world of a 4500-year-old iron and ochre mine, comprising a warren of dimly lit passageways, caverns and pools, and home to several species of bats. 'Deep Level Caving' sessions (adult/child £25/18) take you even further in. From November, the caves are transformed into a hugely popular Christmas grotto. They're signposted off the B4228, a mile south of Coleford.

Puzzlewood
FOREST, FARM
(☑ 01594-833187; www.puzzlewood.net; Perrygrove Rd, Coleford; adult/child £6.50/5; ☉ 10am-5pm Apr-Sep, to 3.30pm Wed, Sat & Sun Mar, Nov & Dec; ℗ ♿) A pre-Roman open-cast ore mine, overgrown with eerie moss-covered trees, Puzzlewood is a 6-hectare woodland web of paths, weird rock formations, tangled vines, rickety bridges, 200 uneven steps and dark passageways seemingly designed to leave you disorientated. Parts of hit TV shows *Doctor Who* and *Merlin*, as well as *Star Wars: The Force Awakens*, were shot here. There's a mile of pathways to explore and kids will love the farm animals. Find it a mile south of Coleford on the B4228.

WORTH A TRIP

SYMONDS YAT VILLAGE & ROCK

Symonds Yat Right on the northwest edge of the Forest of Dean, squeezed between the River Wye and the towering limestone outcrop Symonds Yat Rock, Symonds Yat is a tiny, endearing tangle of pubs, guesthouses and campsites, with great walks and a couple of canoeing centres. It's split into two halves by the river, which are connected by an ancient hand-hauled ferry (adult/child/bicycle £1.20/60p/60p; dawn to dusk).

Symonds Yat Rock (Symonds Yat East; admission free; ⊗24hr; P) Soaring 504m high above Symonds Yat East, this limestone outcrop has outstanding wraparound views of the River Wye and the surrounding countryside. It's a favourite spot for birdwatchers; you may be lucky enough to spot the resident pair of peregrine falcons whooshing by the drop-off. You can walk up from Symonds Yat East. A kiosk atop the rock sells drinks and snacks, and peaceful walking trails continue east through the forest.

Wyedean Canoe & Adventure Centre (☑01600-890238; www.wyedean.co.uk; Symonds Yat East; half-day hire from £23) Hires out canoes and kayaks, and organises white-water trips, archery, high ropes, abseiling, caving, rock climbing and stand-up paddle-boarding (SUP). Opening hours depend on the conditions.

🏃 Activities

Way2Go Adventures ADVENTURE SPORTS
(☑01594-800908; www.way2goadventures.co.uk; 20 Forest Rd, Milkwall) Offers a range of canoeing, kayaking, raft-building, stand-up paddle-boarding (SUP) and Nordic-walking expeditions. Opening hours depend on the conditions. Milkwall is 1 mile southeast of Coleford.

🛏 Sleeping

Wye Valley YHA HOSTEL £
(☑0845 371 9666; www.yha.org.uk; Welsh Bicknor; dm £15-25, d £30, summer bell tents from £49; ⊗Mar-Oct; P🛜🚗) This austere former Victorian rectory overlooks the countryside from lovely riverside grounds, 2 miles southeast of Goodrich. It offers neat shared-bathroom doubles and dorms for four to 10 people, plus breakfast, dinner, riverside barbecues and walking tips. It's well signposted, but drivers should expect a long, steep, difficult access road; follow signs near Goodrich Castle and fork right where the road splits.

Garth Cottage B&B ££
(☑01600-890364; www.garthcottage-symondsyat.com; Symonds Yat East; s/d £50/85; ⊗mid-Mar–Oct; P🛜) Garth Cottage is an exceedingly friendly and efficiently run family-owned B&B, right by the River Wye, next to the ferry crossing. Comfy, chintzy, spotlessly maintained rooms have floral fabrics, tea and coffee kits and gorgeous river views. Home-cooked breakfasts are excellent. Discounted rates available for longer stays.

⭐**Tudor Farmhouse** BOUTIQUE HOTEL £££
(☑01594-833046; www.tudorfarmhousehotel.co.uk; High St, Clearwell; d £100-200, ste £200-230, all incl breakfast; P🛜🚗) Sleep in a chic, contemporary world of whites, creams and spiralling Tudor-era staircases, inside a beautifully updated farmhouse. A range of stylish rooms, most with exposed beams, check-print blankets and Nespresso machines, rambles across the main house. The spacious 'Roost' suite, with its claw-foot bath, is particularly romantic. More rooms sit in adjacent buildings. There's also an exceptional modern British **restaurant** (mains £13-25, 2-/3-course set lunch £22/25; ⊗8am-10pm, noon-5pm & 6.30-9pm; P🛜).

⭐**Saracens Head Inn** MODERN BRITISH ££
(☑01600-890435; www.saracensheadinn.co.uk; Symonds Yat East; mains £11-18; ⊗noon-2.30pm & 6.30-9pm; P🛜🚗🚗) Creatively prepared modern British dishes crammed with local ingredients tick all boxes at this welcoming riverside gastropub, right beside the ferry crossing. Menus range from garlic-grilled chicken, brioche burgers and veggie risottos to baked Camembert platters, featuring plenty of seasonal specials. Delicious desserts might include sensational smashed cheesecake. Dine in the warm pub-restaurant or at river-view benches outside. Bookings recommended.

BUCKINGHAMSHIRE, BEDFORDSHIRE & HERTFORDSHIRE

Now on the edge of London's commuter belt, these three green-clad counties once served as rural boltholes for the city's rich and titled, especially when the stench and grime of the industrial age was at its peak. The sweeping valleys and forested hills are still scattered with majestic stately homes and splendid gardens, many of which are open to the public.

The 324-sq-mile **Chilterns Area of Outstanding Natural Beauty** (AONB; www.visitchilterns.co.uk) extends southwest from Hitchin (Hertfordshire), through Bedfordshire and Buckinghamshire, to Oxfordshire.

Woburn

POP 933

Blissfully set within the Bedfordshire countryside, 6 miles southeast of Milton Keynes, this peaceful village has existed since the 10th century. Despite hosting a couple of big attractions, the county's only Michelin-starred restaurant and a busy main road, it's still charmingly sleepy.

OFF THE BEATEN TRACK

STOWE GARDENS

Covering 160 hectares, the glorious **Stowe Gardens** (NT; ☑01280-817156; www.nationaltrust.org.uk; New Inn Farm; adult/child £11.20/5.60; ☺10am-6pm Mar-Oct, to 4pm Nov-Feb; P) were shaped in the 18th century by Britain's greatest landscape gardeners. Among them was master landscape architect Lancelot 'Capability' Brown, who kickstarted his career at Stowe. The gardens are best known for their many temples and follies, commissioned by the super-wealthy Richard Temple (1st Viscount Cobham), whose family motto was *Templa Quam Dilecta* (How Delightful are Your Temples). Paths meander past lakes, bridges, temples, fountains and cascades, and through Capability Brown's Grecian Valley.

◉ Sights

Woburn Abbey   HOUSE
(☑01525-290333; www.woburnabbey.co.uk; Park St; adult/child £16/7.25; ☺house 11am-5pm mid-Mar–Oct, gardens 10am-5pm mid-Mar–Oct; P) Originally a Cistercian abbey but dissolved by Henry VIII and awarded to the Earl of Bedford (the current Duke of Bedford still calls it home), Woburn Abbey is a wonderful country pile set within a 1200-hectare deer park. The opulent house displays paintings by Gainsborough, Reynolds and van Dyck, and an impressive 21 views of Venice by Canaletto. Highlights include Queen Victoria's bedroom, beautiful wall hangings and cabinets in the Chinese Room, plus the mysterious story of the Flying Duchess.

Woburn Safari Park   ZOO
(www.woburnsafari.co.uk; Woburn Park; adult/child £23/16; ☺10am-5pm mid-Feb–Oct) Sprawling across 150 hectares, this is the country's largest drive-through animal reserve. Rhinos, tigers, lions, zebras, bison, monkeys, elephants, giraffes, wolves and wallabies roam the grounds, while in the 'foot safari' area, you can see sea lions, penguins, meerkats and lemurs.

✗ Eating

★ **Paris House**   MODERN BRITISH £££
(☑01525-290692; www.parishouse.co.uk; Woburn Park, London Rd; lunch £43, dinner £91-109; ☺noon-1.30pm & 7-8.30pm Wed & Thu, to 9pm Fri & Sat, noon-2pm Sun) On the Woburn Estate, Paris House is a handsome black-and-white structure that the 9th duke of Bedford took a shine to on a visit to the French capital and had shipped back here. During WWII, the Queen often stayed here. Now it's Bedfordshire's top and only Michelin-starred restaurant, serving exquisite, six- to 10-course set tasting menus of beautifully presented contemporary cuisine.

❶ Information

The Woburn Passport ticket (adult/child £29.99/18.99), valid April to November, can be used on two separate days within any 12-month period and gives access to both Woburn Abbey and Woburn Safari Park.

Waddesdon

POP 1797

Straddling the A41, 5 miles northwest of Aylesbury, sleepy little Waddesdon is well worth a visit for its splendid 19th-century manor.

WARNER BROS STUDIO TOUR: THE MAKING OF HARRY POTTER

Whether you're a fair-weather fan or a full-on Potterhead, the magical **Warner Bros Studio Tour: The Making of Harry Potter** (☑ 0345 084 0900; www.wbstudiotour.co.uk; Studio Tour Dr, Leavesden, WD25; adult/child £35/27; ⊘ 10am-8pm, hours vary; ℗; ⊠ Watford Junction, then shuttle bus) is well worth the admittedly hefty admission price. You'll need to book your visit for an allocated time slot, arrive 20 minutes beforehand and allow two to three hours to do the complex full justice. It starts with a short film before you're ushered through giant doors into the actual set of Hogwarts' Great Hall – just the first of many 'wow' moments.

From here, you're free to explore the rest of the complex at your own pace, including a large hangar featuring all the most familiar interior sets (Dumbledore's office, the Gryffindor common room, Hagrid's hut), another starring Platform 9¾ and the Hogwarts Express, and an outdoor section with the exterior of Privet Dr, the purple triple-decker Knight Bus, Sirius Black's motorbike and a shop selling snacks and butterbeer (sickly sweet). Along the way, video screens burst into life to discuss elements of the production.

Other highlights include the animatronic workshop (say 'Hi' to the Hippogriff) and a stroll down Diagon Alley. All your favourite *Harry Potter* creatures are on display, from an enormous Aragog to Dobby the House-Elf. But the most magical treat is saved for last – a shimmering, gasp-inducing 1:24 scale model of Hogwarts, used for the exterior shots.

Then comes the biggest challenge for true fans and parents: a quite extraordinary gift shop stocked with all your wizardry accessories, including uniforms for each of the Hogwarts houses and replicas of the individually designed wands used by pretty much any character you can think of.

If you're driving, there's a large free car park, plus extensive directions on the website. Otherwise, catch a train to Watford Junction from London Euston (£9.80, 20 minutes), then take the shuttle bus (return £2.50, 10 minutes).

◉ Sights

Waddesdon Manor   HOUSE

(NT; ☑ 01296-653226; www.waddesdon.org.uk; off A41; adult/child £18/9, gardens only £9/4.50; ⊘ house noon-4pm Wed-Fri, 11am-4pm Sat & Sun, gardens 10am-5pm Wed-Sun late Mar-Dec; ℗) A remarkable French Renaissance chateau-style fairy-tale palace, Waddesdon Manor was completed in 1889 for the Baron Ferdinand de Rothschild so that he could showcase his collection of French decorative arts and throw glamorous parties. Taking in its ostentatious gold-stone magnificence, it's easy to imagine the greats of Victorian society living it up in the palatial rooms. Admission to the house is by guided tours (book ahead); guests are free to wander the exquisite gardens.

Very little indoors space is left unadorned; only the Bachelors' Wing stands out as being noticeably more restrained. On display is an outstanding collection of Dutch Old Masters paintings, English portraits (by the likes of Reynolds and Gainsborough), Sèvres porcelain and ornate furniture, and the extensive wine cellars.

The beautiful gardens boast a superb formal parterre, adorned with colour-bursting flowers and a Pluto and Proserpine fountain, as well as contemporary sculptures, a rose garden and a rococo-revival aviary filled with rare, exotic birds.

From April to October, the manor operates a free daily shuttle bus to/from Aylesbury (check times online).

🛏 Sleeping & Eating

Five Arrows Hotel   HOTEL £££

(☑ 01296-651727; www.thefivearrows.co.uk; High St; s/d incl breakfast from £85/210; ℗ 🛜) Five Arrows is an elaborate half-timbered inn that was originally built to house the artisans working on nearby Waddesdon Manor. The 16 rooms have been stylishly renovated, and guests are entitled to free access to the manor gardens. The bright, elegant **restaurant** (mains £17-23; ⊘ noon-2.15 & 6.30-9.15pm; ℗) serves excellent refined modern British fare in a plush setting.

❶ Getting There & Away

Waddesdon is on the A41, 5 miles northwest of Aylesbury, which has two train stations with regular links to London Marylebone (£16, one hour). **Red Rose Travel** (www.redrosetravel.com)

ROYAL ASCOT

Join the glitterati in your finest outfit for **Royal Ascot** (☑ 0844 346 3000; www. ascot.co.uk; Ascot; Windsor Enclosure per day from £34, Queen Anne Enclosure per day from £75; ⊙ mid-Jun), the biggest racing meet of the year, going strong since 1711. The royal family, A-list celebrities and other rich and famous gather here to show off their Jimmy Choos and place the odd bet. It's essential to book tickets well in advance for this five-day festival.

You can soak up the atmosphere from the Windsor Enclosure or head for the Queen Anne Enclosure to rub shoulders with the ladies in fancy hats.

buses 16 and 17 run between Waddesdon and Aylesbury (£3, 15 minutes) Monday to Saturday.

St Albans

POP 82,146

Under the name Verulamium, St Albans was the third-biggest city in Roman Britain. Its current name derives from Alban, a Christian Roman soldier who was martyred here in about AD 250, becoming the first English martyr. These days, it's a bustling and prosperous market town bordering London's northwestern fringes, with a host of crooked Tudor buildings, elegant Georgian town houses and a fantastic multi-era cathedral.

◉ Sights

★ **St Albans Cathedral**   CATHEDRAL
(☑ 01727-890200; www.stalbanscathedral.org; off High St & Holywell Hill; admission free; ⊙ 8.30am-5.45pm, free tours 11.30am & 2.30pm Mon-Fri, 11.30am & 2pm Sat, 2.30pm Sun) Built by King Offa of Mercia in 793 around the tomb of St Alban, who was martyred here in approximately AD 250, this massive cathedral is a magnificent melange of Norman Romanesque and Gothic architecture. The longest medieval nave in the country gives way to ornate ceilings, semi-lost 13th-century wall paintings, rounded Norman arches built with reused brick from Roman Verulamium and, of course, the shrine of St Alban, hidden behind a stone reredos.

Verulamium Museum   MUSEUM
(☑ 01727-751810; www.stalbansmuseums.org. uk; St Michael's St; adult/child £5/2.50; ⊙ 10am-5.30pm Mon-Sat, 2-5.30pm Sun) This fantastic multimedia exposé of everyday life in Roman Verulamium includes household objects, farming utensils, legionnaires' armour, statuary, jewellery, glassware, coins, potttery and grave goods. The big highlight, however, is the Mosaic Room, where five superb mosaic floors, uncovered between 1930 and 1955, are laid out, including a beautiful shell-shaped mosaic dating to around AD 130. The adjacent Verulamium Park contains the remains of a basilica, bathhouse, mosaic and parts of the city wall.

🛏 Sleeping & Eating

St Michael's Manor Hotel   HOTEL £££
(☑ 01727-864444; www.stmichaelsmanor.com; Fishpool St; d incl breakfast £145-200; 🅿 🛜) In a lovely lakeside position, this 500-year-old manor offers 30 opulent, individually styled rooms hidden down hushed carpeted corridors. The eight contemporary-design 'luxury garden' rooms are sumptuously sleek, with deep purples, rich reds, patterned wallpaper and, for 'Mulberry', a four-poster bed and mirrored bathroom door. Rooms in the manor itself are less sparkly, but win fans with comfortably updated historical charm.

Lussmanns Fish & Grill   MODERN BRITISH ££
(☑ 01727-851941; www.lussmans.com; Waxhouse Gate, off High St; mains £13-20; ⊙ noon-9.30pm Sun-Thu, to 10.30pm Fri & Sat; 🍴) 🌱 A bright, modern restaurant just steps from the cathedral, Lussmanns serves a changing, season-focused, ethically sourced menu of creative British dishes with Mediterranean touches and mostly local ingredients, such as pomegranate-infused salad or chicken with pancetta. There's a good-value set lunch with a glass of wine (two/three courses £12.50/17.95).

ⓘ Information

Tourist Office (☑ 01727-864511; www.enjoys-talbans.com; Alban Arena, off St Peter's St; ⊙ 10am-4.30pm Mon-Sat)

ⓘ Getting There & Away

Regular trains run between St Albans City, a mile east of the centre, and London King's Cross/St Pancras (£11.60, 20 minutes) and London Blackfriars (£11.60, 30 minutes).

THE THAMES VALLEY

This prosperous part of the world, spreading west from London, acts as a country getaway for some of England's most influential figures. Within easy reach of the capital and yet entirely different in character, its pastoral landscape features handsome villages, historic houses and some of the top attractions in the country. Windsor Castle draws crowds to Windsor and Eton in search of royal pomp, while Henley-on-Thames is famous for its July rowing regatta. Meanwhile, the little village of Bray stakes its claim as the country's gastronomic capital with a string of Michelin-starred restaurants.

Windsor & Eton

POP 31,225

Dominated by the massive bulk of Windsor Castle, the twin Thames-side towns of Windsor and Eton have a rather surreal atmosphere, with the morning pomp and ceremony of the changing of the guards in Windsor, and the sight of schoolboys dressed in formal tailcoats wandering the streets of tiny Eton.

Windsor town centre is full of expensive boutiques, grand cafes and buzzing restaurants. Eton, immediately north across the river, is far quieter, its one-street centre flanked by antique shops and art galleries. Both are easily accessible as a day trip from London.

⊙ Sights

★ **Windsor Castle**   CASTLE, PALACE
(☏0303 123 7304; www.royalcollection.org.uk; Castle Hill; adult/child £20/11.70; ⊙9.30am-5.15pm Mar-Oct, 9.45am-4.15pm Nov-Feb; 👣; ☒702 from London Victoria, ☒London Waterloo to Windsor & Eton Riverside, ☒London Paddington to Windsor & Eton Central via Slough) The world's largest and oldest continuously occupied fortress, Windsor Castle is a majestic vision of battlements and towers. It's used for state occasions and is one of the Queen's principal residences; if she's at home, the Royal Standard flies from the Round Tower. Join a free guided tour (every half-hour) of the wards or take a handheld multimedia tour of the lavish State Apartments and beautiful chapels. Some sections may be off-limits if in use. Book tickets online to avoid queues.

William the Conqueror first established a royal residence in Windsor in 1080. Since then successive monarchs have rebuilt, remodelled and refurbished the castle complex to create the massive, sumptuous palace that stands here today. Henry II replaced the original wooden stockade in 1170 with a stone round tower and built the outer walls to the north, east and south; Elizabeth I carried out major palace-wide renovations; Charles II gave the State Apartments a glorious baroque makeover; George IV swept in with his team of artisans; and Queen Victoria refurbished an ornate chapel in memory of her beloved Albert.

➡ **Queen Mary's Dolls' House**
Your first stop is likely to be the incredible dolls' house designed by Sir Edwin Lutyens for Queen Mary between 1921 and 1924, on a scale of 1:12. The attention to detail is spellbinding: there's running water, electricity and lighting, tiny Crown Jewels, vintage wine in the cellar and mini-books by literary greats in the library. You may have to queue.

➡ **State Apartments**
The Grand Staircase, flanked by armour, weapons and a statue of Queen Victoria, sets the tone for a collection of absolutely spectacular rooms, dripping in gilt and screaming 'royal' from every painted surface and sparkling chandelier. Highlights include St George's Hall, used for state banquets of up to 162 people; its soaring ceilings are covered in the painted shields of the Knights of the Garter. For more intimate gatherings (just 60 people), the Queen entertains in the Waterloo Chamber, commemorating the 1815 victory over Napoleon, with portraits of

---

WORTH A TRIP

BLETCHLEY PARK

Once England's best-kept secret **Bletchley Park** (☏01908-640404; www.bletchleypark.org.uk; Bletchley; adult/child £17.25/10.25; ⊙9.30am-5pm; ℗) was the scene of an enormous code-breaking operation during WWII, dramatised in the 2014 film *The Imitation Game*. At its peak, almost 8500 people worked here in total secrecy, intercepting up to 20,000 enemy messages a day, then decrypting, translating and interpreting the correspondence. Inside Block B, you can see the Bombe machine itself, crucial to the breaking of the code; volunteers will happily explain its inner workings.

Windsor & Eton

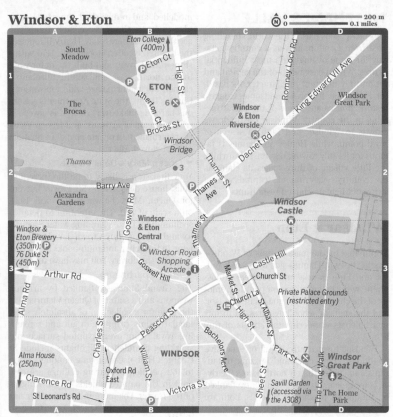

Windsor & Eton

◎ Top Sights
1 Windsor Castle C3
2 Windsor Great Park D4

◆ Activities, Courses & Tours
3 French Brothers B2
4 Royal Windsor Town Walks B3

◉ Sleeping
5 Macdonald Windsor Hotel C3

⊗ Eating
6 Gilbey's..B1
7 Two Brewers D4

statesmen including the Duke of Wellington and George IV.

The State Apartments house some exquisite pieces of art, among them works by Rubens, Canaletto and Anthony van Dyck.

➡ **St George's Chapel**

This elegant chapel, commissioned for the Order of the Garter by Edward IV in 1475, is one of England's finest examples of Perpendicular Gothic architecture. The nave and beautiful fan-vaulted roof were completed under Henry VII, but the final nail was driven under Henry VIII in 1528.

Along with Westminster Abbey, it serves as a royal mausoleum, housing the remains of 10 monarchs, including Henry VIII, Jane Seymour, Charles I and the present queen's father (King George VI), mother (Queen Elizabeth) and sister (Princess Margaret).

St George's Chapel closes on Sunday, but time your visit well and you can attend a morning service or Evensong at 5.15pm.

➡ **Albert Memorial Chapel**

Built in 1240 and dedicated to St Edward the Confessor, the small Albert Memorial Chapel was the place of worship for the Order of the Garter until St George's Chapel snatched away that honour. After the death of Prince Albert at Windsor Castle in 1861, Queen Victoria ordered its elaborate redecoration as a tribute to her husband and consort. A major feature of the restoration is the magnificent vaulted roof, whose gold mosaic pieces were crafted in Venice.

There's a monument to the prince, although he's actually buried with Queen Victoria in the Royal Mausoleum at Frogmore House in Windsor Great Park. Their youngest son, Prince Leopold (Duke of Albany), is, however, buried in the Albert Memorial Chapel.

⇒ **Changing of the Guard**

A fabulous spectacle, with triumphant tunes from a military band and plenty of foot stamping from smartly attired lads in red uniforms and bear-skin caps, the changing of the guard draws crowds to Windsor Castle each day. It takes place at 11am Monday to Saturday from April to July, and on alternate days from August to March.

★ **Windsor Great Park**   PARK
(📞 01753-860222;   www.windsorgreatpark.co.uk; Windsor; ☉ dawn-dusk) **FREE** Stretching from Windsor Castle almost all the way southwest to Ascot, Windsor Great Park covers just under 8 sq miles and features a lake, walking tracks, a bridleway, gardens and a deer park with 500 free-roaming red deer. Its popular Long Walk is a 2.7-mile jaunt south from King George IV Gate, south of the castle, to the 1831 Copper Horse statue of George III on Snow Hill, the park's highest point. From Windsor, public access is via Park St.

Eton College   NOTABLE BUILDING
(📞 01753-370100; www.etoncollege.com; High St, Eton; ☉ closed to the public) Eton College is the largest and most famous public (meaning private and fee-paying) boys' school in England, and arguably the most enduring symbol of England's class system. High-profile alumni include 19 British prime ministers, countless princes, kings and maharajas, famous explorers, authors, actors and economists – among them Princes William and Harry, George Orwell, Ian Fleming, John Maynard Keynes, Bear Grylls and Eddie Redmayne.

Eton was founded by Henry VI in 1440 with a view towards educating 70 highly qualified boys awarded a scholarship from a fund endowed by the king. Every year since then, 70 King's Scholars have been chosen based on the results of a highly competitive exam; these pupils are housed in separate quarters from the 1300 or so other students. All pupils are boarders and must wear formal tailcoats, waistcoats and white collars to lessons (though the top hats went out in 1948).

At the time of writing, no public visits or tours of Eton College were available. Small-group tours may begin in early 2017; check the website.

Runnymede   HISTORIC SITE
(NT; www.nationaltrust.org.uk; Windsor Rd, Old Windsor; parking per hr £1.50; ☉ site dawn-dusk, car park 8.30am-7pm Apr-Sep, to 5pm Oct, Nov, Feb & Mar, to 4pm Dec & Jan; **P**) **FREE** In June 1215, King John met his barons in this field, 3 miles southeast of Windsor; over the following days they hammered out an agreement on a basic charter of rights guaranteeing the liberties of the king's subjects and restricting the monarch's absolute power. The document they signed was the Magna Carta, the world's first constitution. Today, the field remains much as it was, yet adorned with several modern-day memorials and two 1929 lodges, designed by Edwin Lutyens.

The Magna Carta formed the basis for statutes and charters throughout the world's democracies. Both the national and state constitutions of the USA, drawn up more than 500 years later, paraphrase it. To recognise its importance, the American Bar Association erected the **Memorial to Magna Carta** here in 1957 in the style of a Greek temple, across the field from the car park. A short uphill path nearby leads to the 1965 **President John F Kennedy Memorial**, which sits between trees on an acre of land gifted to the US. In the middle of the main field stands **The Jurors**, a 12-bronze-chair memorial honouring the Magna Carta's 800th anniversary (2015).

After stomping through the muddy field to these three memorials, it's possible to continue uphill on a 1.5-mile loop track to the moving **Commonwealth Airforces Memorial**, where the names of 20,000 WWII airmen without graves from the UK, Canada, New Zealand, Australia, India and South Africa are inscribed.

Bus 71 from Windsor (£4.20, 10 minutes) stops half a mile northwest of Runnymede, on Windsor Rd (A308).

READING FESTIVAL

Each August Bank Holiday weekend, up to 87,000 revellers descend on the industrial town of Reading for one of the country's biggest rock-music events. The **Reading Festival** (📞020-70093001; www.readingfestival.com; Reading; tickets day/weekend £66.50/213; ⏱ Aug). is a three-day extravaganza featuring a top line of rock, indie, punk, metal and alternative artists. Set up camp for the weekend or just book a day ticket.

👉 Tours

French Brothers   BOATING
(📞01753-851900;   www.frenchbrothers.co.uk; Windsor Promenade, Barry Ave, Windsor; ⏱10am-5pm mid-Feb–Oct) Offers a variety of boat trips along the Thames to/from Runnymede (return adult/child £14.40/9.60) and around Windsor (adult/child from £7.40/4.95).

Royal Windsor Town Walks   WALKING
(📞01753-743900; www.windsor.gov.uk; Tourist Office, Old Booking Hall, Windsor Royal Shopping Arcade, Thames St; adult/child £7.50/6.50; ⏱11.45am Sat & 2.30pm Sun Easter-Aug) Detailed one-hour tours depart from the tourist office (p216); you can also book online.

🛏 Sleeping

Alma House   B&B ££
(📞01753-862983; www.almahouse.co.uk; 56 Alma Rd, Windsor; s/d from £65/75; 🛜🚲) Within this pretty Victorian town house, half a mile southwest of the castle, the four smartly revamped rooms feature comfy beds, plenty of light and tasteful cream or purple decor. Two rooms accommodate families, as does the equally homey annexe room out the back. Breakfast is a minimal self-service continental spread.

Macdonald Windsor Hotel   HOTEL £££
(📞0344 879 9101; www.macdonaldhotels.co.uk/Windsor; 23 High St, Windsor; r from £158; P🛜🐾) Looking small and quaint from the road but magically transforming into 120 elegant rooms beyond its revolving door, the floral-scented Windsor is the slickest choice in town. Dark browns, creams, reds and purples add a plush, rich feel to the resolutely modern decor and facilities (such as capsule-coffee kits), and service hits that perfect

friendly and professional note. Some rooms have castle glimpses.

🍴 Eating & Drinking

Two Brewers   PUB FOOD ££
(📞01753-855426; www.twobrewerswindsor.co.uk; 34 Park St, Windsor; mains £12.50-17; ⏱11.30am-11pm Mon-Thu, 11.30am-11.30pm Fri & Sat, noon-10.30pm Sun) Pack into this atmospheric 18th-century inn perched on the edge of Windsor Great Park for tasty, well-prepped pub meals that are a cut above the usual pub grub. Menus range from soups, salads and tapas to steaks, fishcakes and cheese boards. Outdoor sunny benches front the flower-covered exterior; inside, think low-beamed ceilings, dim lighting and a roaring winter fire.

Gilbey's   MODERN BRITISH £££
(📞01753-854921; www.gilbeygroup.com; 82-83 High St, Eton; mains £17-23, 2-/3-course menu £22.50/28.50; ⏱6-10pm Mon, noon-3pm & 6-10pm Tue-Sun) Small but perfectly formed, this bistro-restaurant in the heart of Eton is one of the area's best. Terracotta tiling, deep-green decor and a sunny courtyard garden and conservatory give Gilbey's the feel of a European cafe, complemented by an extensive wine list and a superb modern-British menu of soups, steaks, pies, artisan cheeses and Sunday lunches.

Windsor & Eton Brewery   BREWERY
(📞01753-854075; www.webrew.co.uk; 1 Vansittart Estate, Windsor; ⏱8am-6pm Mon-Fri, 10am-3pm Sat) Call into this boutique brewery, just west of Windsor's centre, to sample and stock up on hoppy delights such as the award-winning Knight of the Garter pale ale, Eton Rifles or the royal-wedding special, the Windsor Knot. It's worth enquiring about the occasional two-hour tours, which take you behind the scenes.

ℹ Information

Tourist Office (📞01753-743900; www.windsor.gov.uk; Old Booking Hall, Windsor Royal Shopping Arcade, Thames St; ⏱10am-5pm Apr-Sep, to 4pm Oct-Mar) Pick up a heritage walk map (£2.20).

ℹ Getting There & Away

BUS

From Windsor, Courtney buses head to/from Bray (route 16/16A; £3.30, 30 minutes). First buses connect Windsor and Eton with Heathrow terminal 5 (route 60/61/71/77; £5, 30 to 50 minutes). Green Line (www.greenline.co.uk) coaches head to/from London Victoria (£6, two hours).

TRAIN

Trains from Windsor & Eton Riverside (Dachet Rd) go directly to London Waterloo (£10, one hour). Trains from Windsor & Eton Central (Thames St), changing at Slough for London Paddington (£10, 28 to 46 minutes), are quicker.

Bray

POP 8425 (PARISH)

It's strange to think that this tiny village of flint, brick and half-timbered cottages strung along the Thames, 4.5 miles northwest of Windsor, could be Britain's gastronomic capital. Yet Bray is home to one of only three restaurants in the UK to be rated three-star (the highest possible honour) in 2016 by foodie bible, the Michelin guide. On top of that, two of the local pubs also sport a Michelin star, while Heston Blumenthal's much-garlanded Fat Duck (p217) restaurant reopened in Bray in late 2015.

There's little more to do here than to dine fabulously.

✖ Eating

★ **Waterside Inn**   FRENCH £££
(✆01628-620691; www.waterside-inn.co.uk; Ferry Rd; mains £53-59, 2-/3-course lunch £49.50/62; ☺noon-2pm & 7-10pm Wed-Sun, closed end Dec–end Jan) From the moment the uniformed valet opens your car door, until the last tray of petit fours is served, you know this three-Michelin-starred restaurant is something special. For more than 40 years, chef Alain Roux has been working his magic, constructing exceptional dishes for a small army of staff to serve, in a room looking out on the Thames. It also has rooms (from £260).

★ **Hind's Head**   GASTROPUB £££
(✆01628-626151; www.hindsheadbray.com; High St; mains £18-30; ☺noon-2.30pm & 6.15-9.15pm Mon-Sat, noon-3.30pm Sun; P) Oozing atmosphere, this 15th-century pub offers the chance to experience Heston Blumenthal's highly creative cuisine in a relatively affordable, informal setting. The food's less zany than his signature cooking style, but there are still plenty of whimsical touches. Try the chicken, ham and leek pie with wholegrain mustard cream or the onion-wrapped bread-and-cheese royale with Marmite emulsion.

Fat Duck   MODERN BRITISH £££
(✆01628-580333; www.thefatduck.co.uk; High St; degustation menu per person £255; ☺noon-2pm & 7-9pm Tue-Sat) Arguably the most famous restaurant in the country, the Fat Duck – whizz-bang chef Heston Blumenthal's signature eatery – is exceedingly difficult to get into at the best of times. Following a 2015 sojourn in Melbourne, Australia, it's now back with a hungrily awaited, eye-poppingly priced journey-themed menu for those lucky enough to score a reservation (available three months in advance).

Henley-on-Thames

POP 11,494

The attractive commuter town of Henley, 15 miles northwest of Windsor, is synonymous with the world-famous Henley Royal Regatta rowing tournament. At other times of year, it remains a pretty riverside town that's a delight to stroll around, particularly along the Thames, and has a couple of minor attractions.

◉ Sights

River & Rowing Museum   MUSEUM
(✆01491-415600; www.rrm.co.uk; Mill Meadows; adult/child £11/9; ☺10am-5pm; P) For the lowdown on Henley's rowing tradition, visit this excellent, modern museum, half a mile south of the train station. The airy 1st-floor galleries tell the story of rowing as an Olympic sport, alongside striking boat displays that include the early-19th-century Royal Oak, Britain's oldest racing boat. Downstairs, a sweet 3D exhibition pays homage to Kenneth Grahame's *The Wind in the Willows*, whose river is thought to have been inspired by this area's section of the Thames.

✩ Festivals & Events

Henley Royal Regatta   SPORTS
(www.hrr.co.uk; tickets £27-30; ☺Jul) This world-renowned, five-day rowing tournament sees Henley burst into action. Although rowers of the highest calibre compete, it has grown into a major social fixture for the upwardly mobile and the main event can be overshadowed by their champagne-fuelled antics. Still, picnicking in the public enclosure and watching the rowers' boats whizz by makes for a good, sunny day out.

Bath & Southwest England

Includes ➡

Hampshire......... 222
Isle of Wight 233
Dorset............. 238
Exmoor
National Park 262
Devon............. 268
Bristol............. 293
Bath 303
Somerset..........312
Cornwall...........318
Isles of Scilly....... 345

Best Places to Eat

➡ Paul Ainsworth at No 6 (p324)

➡ Riverford Field Kitchen (p279)

➡ Menu Gordon Jones (p311)

➡ Boathouse (p237)

Best Places to Sleep

➡ Vintage Vacations (p236)

➡ Scarlet (p326)

➡ Queensberry Hotel (p308)

➡ Hotel du Vin Exeter (p271)

Why Go?

England's southwest is simply spectacular. Here the past is ever present – prepare for close encounters with iconic stone circles, Iron Age hill forts and Roman baths. Blockbuster stately homes border romantic castles; serene cathedrals frame sumptuous Georgian cityscapes. The landscape immerses you in the myths of kings Arthur and Alfred the Great, and the writings of Thomas Hardy, Jane Austen and Daphne du Maurier.

But the southwest also has an eye to the future. Here you can tour alternative eco-towns, pioneering restaurants and cool surfer hang-outs, and sleep in campsites peppered with chic yurts and retro campervans. Then there are three wildlife-rich national parks, fossil-studded shores, England's best surf spots and a coastline flecked with exquisite bays, towering rock formations and tranquil sweeps of sandy beach. It all gives you a bit of a dilemma – with England's West Country you won't know what to do first.

When to Go

➡ Cliffs, hillsides and formal gardens burst into fragrance and blooms in April and May, when seasonal attractions also reopen and boat trips start.

➡ Music festival fever takes hold in June at ultracool Glastonbury, and on the funky Isle of Wight.

➡ The peak holiday season and the best weather (in theory) is in July and August.

➡ The end of school summer holidays in September brings cheaper sleep spots, quieter beaches and warmer seas. The Isle of Wight goes all groovy at bohemian Bestival.

➡ Bigger waves draw surfers to Cornwall and north Devon in October; meanwhile Exmoor's deer rut sees huge stags battle for supremacy, and the winter storm-watching season begins.

Activities

Cycling

Cycling the southwest is a superb, if strenuous, way to experience England's great outdoors. The region's National Cycle Network (NCN) routes include the **West Country Way** (NCN Route 3), a 240-mile jaunt from Bristol to Padstow via Glastonbury, Taunton and Barnstaple, and the 103-mile **Devon Coast to Coast Cycle Route** between Ilfracombe and Plymouth.

The 160-mile, circular **Wiltshire Cycleway** skirts the county's borders. In Hampshire, the New Forest's hundreds of miles of cycle paths snake through a wildlife-rich environment, while the Isle of Wight boasts 62 miles of bike-friendly routes and its very own cycling festival (p233).

Off-road mountain-biking highlights include the North Wessex Downs, Exmoor National Park and Dartmoor National Park. Many cycle trails trace the routes of old railway lines, including Devon's 11-mile **Granite Way** between Okehampton and Lydford, and Cornwall's popular 18-mile **Camel Trail** linking Padstow with Bodmin Moor.

For more information contact **Sustrans** (www.sustrans.org.uk) and local tourist offices.

Walking

Often called the 630-mile adventure, the **South West Coast Path** is Britain's longest national walking trail, stretching from Minehead in Somerset via Land's End to Poole in Dorset. You can pick it up along the coast for short and spectacular day hikes or tackle longer stretches. The **South West Coast Path Association** (www.southwestcoastpath.org.uk) has a detailed website and publishes an annual guide.

For wilderness hikes, the national parks of **Dartmoor** and **Exmoor** are hard to beat. Dartmoor is bigger and more remote; Exmoor's ace in the pack is a cracking 34 miles of precipitous coast. The region's third national park, the **New Forest**, is an altogether gentler affair, offering hundreds of miles of heritage trails.

Other hiking highlights are Exmoor's 51-mile **Coleridge Way** (www.coleridgeway.co.uk), the Isle of Wight and Bodmin Moor, while Wiltshire's 87-mile **Ridgeway National Trail** (www.nationaltrail.co.uk/ridgeway) starts near Avebury and winds through chalk downland and the wooded Chiltern hills.

Surfing & Boating

North Cornwall, and to a lesser extent north Devon, serves up the best surf in England. Party town Newquay is the epicentre; other top spots are Bude in Cornwall and Croyde in Devon. Region-wide surf conditions can be found at www.magicseaweed.com.

For sailing, highlights includes Britain's 2012 Olympic sailing venues at Weymouth and Portland, and the yachting havens of the Isle of Wight, Falmouth, Dartmouth and Poole.

Other Activities

The southwest is prime territory for kitesurfing, windsurfing, diving, sea kayaking, white-water kayaking and wakeboarding. The sport of stand-up paddleboarding (SUP) continues to grow in popularity, especially in calm water spots.

Plenty of firms also offer caving, coasteering, mountainboarding, climbing and kitebuggying. Check out www.visitsouthwest.co.uk for links to the region's counties and activity operators.

ⓘ Getting Around

BUS

The region's bus network is fairly comprehensive, but becomes patchy away from main towns. **National Express** (www.nationalexpress.com) often provides the quickest bus link between cities and larger towns. **PlusBus** (www.plusbus.info) adds local bus travel to your train ticket (from £2 per day). Participating cities include Bath, Bournemouth, Bristol, Exeter, Plymouth, Salisbury, Truro and Weymouth. Buy tickets at train stations.

First (www.firstgroup.com) One of the region's largest bus companies, operating in Bath, Bristol, Cornwall, Dorset, Portsmouth and Somerset. It offers subregional tickets, such as the Freedom Travelpass, covering Bath, Bristol and northeast Somerset (one day/week £13.50/59).

More (www.wdbus.co.uk) Useful service across Wiltshire and Dorset and into the New Forest. Does day tickets (adult/child £8.50/5.50) and seven-day network tickets (£25) for south-coast routes.

Stagecoach (www.stagecoachbus.com) A key provider in Cornwall, Devon, Hampshire and Somerset. Offers a range of one-day tickets (adult/child from £4/3) and weekly Megarider fares from £8 (no child fare).

CAR

The main car-hire firms have offices at the region's airports and main-line train stations; rates reflect those elsewhere in the UK.

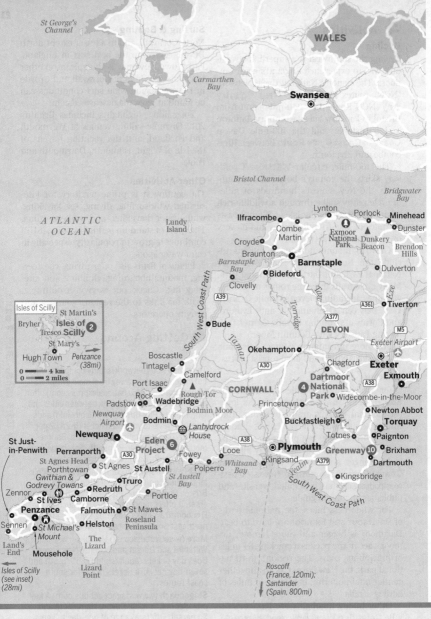

Bath & Southwest England Highlights

1 Stonehenge (p256)
Taking a magical dawn walk inside the massive sarsen ring.

2 Isles of Scilly (p345)
Ferry-hopping around the UK's most idyllic archipelago.

3 Royal Crescent (p306)
Strolling England's most glorious Georgian street.

4 Dartmoor National Park (p284) Striding the park's remote, high hills.

5 Portsmouth (p226)
Staring at the vast, ancient timbers of Henry VIII's warship.

6 Eden Project (p338)
Marvelling at space-age biomes.

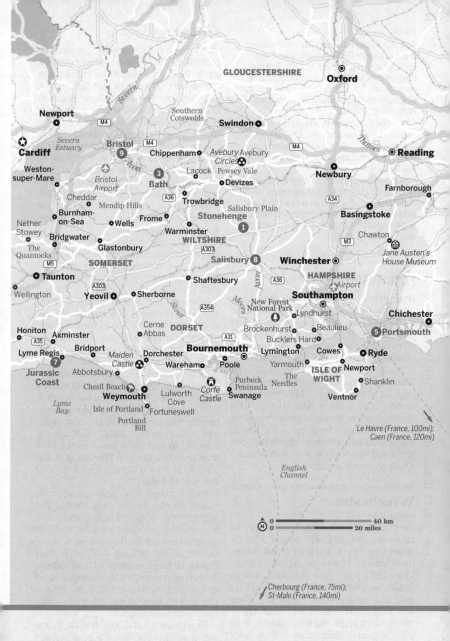

GLOUCESTERSHIRE

Oxford

Newport

Southern
Cotswolds

Swindon

Severn
Estuary

Bristol

Reading

Chippenham

Avebury Avebury
Circles

M4

Cardiff

Weston-
super-Mare

Bristol
Airport

Bath

Lacock

Pewsey Vale

Devizes

Newbury

Cheddar

Mendip Hills

Trowbridge

Farnborough

Nether
Stowey

Burnham-
on-Sea

Wells

Frome

Salisbury Plain

Stonehenge

Basingstoke

Chawton

The
Quantocks

Bridgwater

Warminster

WILTSHIRE

Jane Austen's
House Museum

Taunton

Glastonbury

SOMERSET

Salisbury

Winchester

Wellington

Shaftesbury

HAMPSHIRE
Airport

Yeovil

Sherborne

New Forest
National Park

Southampton

Lyndhurst

Chichester

Honiton

Axminster

DORSET

Cerne
Abbas

Brockenhurst

Beaulieu

Portsmouth

Lyme Regis

Bridport

Maiden
Castle

Dorchester

Bucklers Hard

Cowes

Ryde

**Jurassic
Coast**

Abbotsbury

Wareham

Bournemouth

Poole

Lymington

Yarmouth

Newport

Chesil Beach

Weymouth

Lulworth
Cove

Corfe
Castle

Swanage

ISLE OF
WIGHT

Shanklin

Isle of Portland

Fortuneswell

Purbeck
Peninsula

The
Needles

Ventnor

Lyme
Bay

Portland
Bill

Le Havre (France, 100mi);
Caen (France, 120mi)

English
Channel

0   40 km
0   20 miles

Cherbourg (France, 75mi);
St-Malo (France, 140mi)

7 Jurassic Coast (p250)
Foraging for 200-million-year-old fossils on Dorset's shore.

8 Salisbury (p253)
Savouring the city's soaring, serene cathedral.

9 SS Great Britain (p295)
Stepping on the deck of Brunel's groundbreaking steamship in Bristol.

10 Greenway (p277)
Discovering the locations

behind the murder plots at Agatha Christie's enchanting home.

TRAIN

Bristol is a main train hub with links including those to London Paddington, Scotland and Birmingham, plus services to Bath, Swindon, Chippenham, Weymouth, Southampton and Portsmouth. Trains from London Waterloo travel to Bournemouth, Salisbury, Southampton, Portsmouth and Weymouth.

Stops on the London Paddington–Penzance service include Exeter, Plymouth, Liskeard, St Austell and Truro. Spur lines run to Barnstaple, Paignton, Gunnislake, Looe, Falmouth, St Ives and Newquay.

The Freedom of the South West Rover pass (adult/child £112/56) allows eight days' unlimited travel over 15 days in an area west of, and including, Salisbury, Bath, Bristol, Portsmouth and Weymouth. A three-in-seven-day pass is also available (£81/41).

HAMPSHIRE

Hampshire's history is regal and rich. Kings Alfred the Great, Knut and William the Conqueror all based their reigns in its ancient cathedral city of Winchester, whose jumble of historic buildings sits in the centre of undulating chalk downs. The county's coast is awash with heritage too – in rejuvenated Portsmouth you can clamber aboard the pride of Nelson's navy, HMS *Victory*, and wonder at the *Mary Rose* (Henry VIII's flagship), before wandering wharfs buzzing with restaurants, shops and bars. Hampshire's southwestern corner claims the open heath and woods of the New Forest (p229), which is covered separately.

Winchester

POP 116,600

Calm, collegiate Winchester is a mellow must-see. The past still echoes strongly around the flint-flecked walls of this ancient cathedral city. It was the capital of Saxon kings and a power base of bishops, and its statues and sights evoke two of England's mightiest myth-makers: Alfred the Great and King Arthur (he of the round table). Winchester's architecture is exquisite, from the handsome Elizabethan and Regency buildings in the narrow streets to the wondrous cathedral at its core, while its river valley location means there are charming waterside trails to explore.

 Sights

★ **Winchester Cathedral** CATHEDRAL

(☑ 01962-857225; www.winchester-cathedral. org.uk; The Close; adult/child incl cathedral body & crypt tours £8/free; ⊘ 9.30am-5pm Mon-Sat, 12.30-3pm Sun) One of southern England's most awe-inspiring buildings, 11th-century Winchester Cathedral boasts a fine Gothic facade, one of the longest medieval naves in Europe (164m), and a fascinating jumble of features from all eras. Other highlights include the intricately carved medieval choir stalls, which sport everything from mythical beasts to a mischievous green man, Jane Austen's grave (near the entrance, in the northern aisle) and one of the UK's finest illuminated manuscripts.

As the biggest, brightest and best surviving 12th-century English Bible, the dazzling, four-volume **Winchester Bible** has vivid illuminated pages. It was commissioned in 1160, possibly by the grandson of William the Conqueror. At time of writing, the Bible was being re-bound (with one volume still on display). It's then due to form the centrepiece of a new exhibition inside the cathedral that charts the story of how it was made. Check online for the latest.

Today's cathedral sits beside foundations that mark Winchester's original 7th-century minster church. The cathedral was begun in 1070 and completed in 1093, and was subsequently entrusted with the bones of its patron saint, St Swithin (Bishop of Winchester from 852 to 862). He is best known for the proverb stating that if it rains on St Swithin's Day (15 July), it will rain for a further 40 days and 40 nights.

Soggy ground and poor construction spelled disaster for the early church. The original tower collapsed in 1107 and major restructuring continued until the mid-15th century. Look out for the monument at the far end of the building to diver William Walker; he saved the cathedral from collapse by delving repeatedly into its waterlogged underbelly from 1906 to 1912 to bolster rotting wooden foundations with vast quantities of concrete and brick.

Choral **evensong** (5.30pm Mon-Sat, 3.30pm Sun) is atmospheric; other Sunday services take place at 8am, 9.45am and 11am.

The highly informative, one-hour **Cathedral Body Tours** (10am-3pm Mon-Sat) and atmospheric **Crypt Tours** (10.30am, 12.30pm & 2.30pm Mon-Sat) are included in the admission price for Winchester

Winchester

N 0 ———— 500 m
0 ———— 0.25 miles

Winchester

◎ **Top Sights**
1 Winchester Cathedral C2
2 Winchester College C3
3 Wolvesey Castle C3

◎ **Sights**
4 City Museum B2
5 Round Table & Great Hall A2
6 Royal Green Jackets Museum A2

◉ **Activities, Courses & Tours**
7 Guided Walks C2

◉ **Sleeping**
8 5 Clifton Terrace A2
9 Magdalen House D2
10 No 5 .... D2

11 St John's Croft D2
12 Wykeham Arms B3

◉ **Eating**
13 Black Rat D3
14 Chesil Rectory D2
15 Old Vine B2
16 River Cottage Canteen C2

◉ **Drinking & Nightlife**
17 Black Boy D3

◉ **Entertainment**
18 Railway Inn A1

◉ **Shopping**
19 Deanery Porch C3

Cathedral. **Tower and Roof Tours** (2.15pm Monday, Wednesday, Friday and Saturday, plus 11.30am Saturday, May to September) cost £6 and take you on to the roof for views as far as the Isle of Wight. These tours are popular – book well in advance.

On the Crypt Tour look out for Sound II, an enigmatic life-size depiction of a contemplative man by Anthony Gormley. The Tower and Roof Tour will see you clambering 213 steps up narrow stairwells, navigating an interior gallery high above the nave and visiting the bell chamber.

The cathedral's **tree-fringed lawns** make for tranquil spots to take time out, especially on the quieter south side beyond the cloisters; the permanent secondhand book stall in the **Deanery Porch** (The Close; ⊘10am-4pm Sat & Sun) provides great bargain hunting.

★**Winchester College**   HISTORIC BUILDING
(☑01962-621209; www.winchestercollege.org; College St; adult/child £7/free; ⊘tours 10.15am,

11.30am, 2.15pm, 3.30pm Mon, Wed, Fri-Sun) Winchester College delivers a rare chance to nosey around a prestigious English private school. It was set up by William Wykeham, Bishop of Winchester, in 1393, 14 years after he founded Oxford's New College. Hour-long guided tours take in the 14th-century Gothic chapel, complete with wooden vaulted roof, the dining room (called College Hall), and a vast 17th-century open classroom (called School) where exams are still held. A revealing insight into how the other half learns.

★ **Wolvesey Castle**   CASTLE
(EH; ☑ 0370-333 1181; www.english-heritage.org. uk; College St; ⊗ 10am-5pm Apr-Oct) FREE The fantastical, crumbling remains of early-12th-century Wolvesey Castle huddle in the protective embrace of the city's walls. Completed by Henry de Blois, it served as the Bishop of Winchester's residence throughout the medieval era, with Queen Mary I and Philip II of Spain celebrating their wedding feast here in 1554. According to legend, its name comes from a Saxon king's demand for an annual payment of 300 wolves' heads. Today, the bishop lives in the (private) **Wolvesey Palace**, next door.

City Museum   MUSEUM
(www.hampshireculturaltrust.org.uk; The Square; ⊗ 10am-4pm Mon-Sat, noon-4pm Sun, closed Mon Nov-Mar) FREE A people-centred canter through Winchester's past with jewellery, mosaics, sculpture, coins and tobacco tins charting a narrative from the Iron Age, via the Romans and Anglo-Saxons, to the present day.

Round Table & Great Hall   HISTORIC BUILDING
(☑ 01962-846476; www.hants.gov.uk/greathall; Castle Ave; suggested donation £3; ⊗ 10am-5pm) FREE Winchester's cavernous Great Hall is the only part of the 11th-century Winchester Castle that Oliver Cromwell spared from destruction. Crowning the wall like a giant-sized dartboard of green and cream spokes is what centuries of mythology have dubbed King Arthur's Round Table. It's actually a 700-year-old copy, but is fascinating nonetheless. It's thought to have been constructed in the late 13th century and then painted in the reign of Henry VIII (King Arthur's image is unsurprisingly reminiscent of Henry's youthful face).

Royal Green Jackets Museum   MUSEUM
(The Rifles; ☑ 01962-877826; www.winchestermilitarymuseums.co.uk; Peninsula Barracks, Romsey Rd; adult/child £4/free; ⊗ 10am-5pm Tue-Sat year-round, plus Mon & Sun Jul-Sep) The pick of Winchester's cluster of army museums, with its mini rifle-shooting range, a room of 6000 medals and an impressive blow-by-blow diorama of Napoleon's downfall, the Battle of Waterloo.

Hospital of St Cross   HISTORIC BUILDING
(☑ 01962-851375; www.stcrosshospital.co.uk; St Cross Rd; adult/child £4.50/2.50; ⊗ 9.30am-5pm Mon-Sat, 1-5pm Sun Apr-Oct, 10.30am-3.30pm Mon-Sat Nov-Mar) Welcome to the oldest charitable institution in the country, founded in 1132 by the grandson of William the Conqueror, Henry de Blois. As well as healing the sick and housing the needy, the hospital was built to care for pilgrims and crusaders en route to the Holy Land. Today, it's roamed by elderly black- and red-gowned brothers, who hand out the Wayfarer's Dole; a crust of bread and horn of ale (now a swig of beer) from the Porter's Gate.

🏃 **Activities**

Winchester's tempting walks include the 1-mile **Keats' Walk** through the water meadows to the Hospital of St Cross. Its beauty is said to have prompted the poet to pen the ode *To Autumn*; pick up the trail near Wolvesey Castle. Alternatively, head down Wharf Hill, through the water meadows to St Catherine's Hill (1 mile), or take the tranquil **Riverside Walk** from Wolvesey Castle along the River Itchen's banks to High St.

👉 **Tours**

Guided Walks   WALKING
(☑ 01962-840500; www.winchestertouristguides. com; adult/child £5/free; ⊗ Mon-Sat Apr-Oct, weekly Nov-Mar) These 90-minute walks include City Highlights and Upper and Lower Winchester. In peak season, up to four leave daily from the tourist office (p226).

🛏 **Sleeping**

★ **St John's Croft**   B&B ££
(☑ 01962-859976; www.st-johns-croft.co.uk; St John's St; s/d/f £55/90/120; 🅿 🛜) You may well fall in love with this oh-so-casually stylish, rambling Queen Anne town house, where rattan carpets are teamed with bulging bookcases, and Indian art with shabby-chic antiques. The rooms are vast, the garden is tranquil and breakfast is served beside the Aga in the country-house kitchen.

5 Clifton Terrace   B&B ££
(☑ 01962-890053; cliftonterrace@hotmail.co.uk; 5 Clifton Tce; s £75-85, d £80-90, f from £110; 🛜)

There's a captivating air of easygoing elegance about this tall Georgian town house. Family heirlooms sit beside candy-striped rugs and peppermint-green, claw-foot baths – it's great value too.

Magdalen House
B&B ££

(☎01962-869634; www.magdalen-house.co.uk; 5 Magdalen Hill; s/d/f £60/70/112; P⊛) Pastel-themed bedrooms are arranged over three floors in this peaceful, modern hillside house. The family room opens out directly on to a sunny terrace – the doubles trump that though, with views over rooftops to Winchester Cathedral.

No 5
B&B ££

(☎01962-863838; www.no5bridgestreet.co.uk; 5 Bridge St; d £121-146; ⊛) Subtle tweedy-meets-tartan motifs are used to good effect here, with soft, checked throws bookending beds draped in gentle grey. Spacious bathrooms, feature fireplaces and a downstairs bistro add to the appeal. Choosing not to have breakfast knocks £22 off the price of a double room.

★ Wykeham Arms
INN £££

(☎01962-853834; www.wykehamarmswinchester. co.uk; 75 Kingsgate St; s/d/ste £85/150/200; P⊛) At 250-odd years old, the Wykeham bursts with history – it used to be a brothel and also put Nelson up for a night (some say the events coincided). Creaking stairs lead to plush bedrooms that manage to be both deeply established but also on-trend; brass bedsteads meet jazzy throws, oak dressers sport stylish lights. Simply smashing.

The eccentric bar is a bit of a mustn't-miss experience. Tankards and school canes hang from the ceiling; worn school desks lend pint-supping an illicit air and sizzling sausages (75p each) are served nightly at 6pm.

There's also a wide-ranging food menu, from juicy burgers and fish 'n' chips to satisfying creations adorned with cheffy flourishes.

✕ Eating

River Cottage Canteen
BRITISH ££

(☎01962-457747; www.rivercottage.net; Abbey Mill, Abbey Mill Gardens; mains £9-17; ⊛noon-3pm & 6-9.15pm Tue-Sat; ⊿) The setting is pretty idyllic – beside a rushing river in an imaginatively converted Georgian mill. And the food is memorable too: plump for vegetable or meat sharing platters, sole with seaweed butter, or a spicy white bean and leek soup.

Chesil Rectory
BRITISH ££

(☎01962-851555; www.chesilrectory.co.uk; 1 Chesil St; mains £14-21; ⊛noon-2.20pm & 6-9.30pm) It's almost as if they created a checklist for a great date: hushed tones, flickering candles, dark beams. They get the food right too, from lighter offerings such as white onion risotto, to sticky, glossy beef ribs, and pork made fragrant by apple and vanilla.

Old Vine
PUB FOOD ££

(☎01962-854616; www.oldvinewinchester.com; 8 Great Minster St; mains £10-20; ⊛noon-2.30pm & 6.30-9pm) Ask for table with a view of Winchester's captivating Cathedral Green, soak up the mellow, old-inn atmosphere, then choose between comfort food (beef, mushroom and ale pie) and fancier fare: perhaps a melting lamb shank braised in red wine.

★ Black Rat
MODERN BRITISH £££

(☎01962-844465; www.theblackrat.co.uk; 88 Chesil St; mains £20-24, 2/3 course lunch £26/29; ⊛7-9.15pm daily, noon-2.15pm Sat & Sun) The aromas are irresistible, the food frankly fabulous, the cooking highly technical and the ingredients dare to surprise – expect lamb neck to be joined by beer-and-onion purée, black pudding by scallops, and charred octopus by chorizo. That'll be why the Black Rat deserves its Michelin star.

▽ Drinking & Nightlife

Black Boy
PUB

(www.theblackboypub.com; 1 Wharf Hill; ⊛noon-11pm Mon-Thu, to midnight Fri & Sat, to 10.30pm Sun) Two open fires, a battered foosball table, a random array of dented antiques, a clutch of draught ciders and five real ales make this a legendary local. Any time after noon, check to see if they still have any Black Boy Bangers (£2.50) – a sausage in a crispy roll – the fried onions and mustard are optional.

Railway Inn
LIVE MUSIC

(www.railwayinn.pub; 3 St Paul's Hill; ⊛5pm-midnight Sun-Thu, to 2am Fri, to 1am Sat) Easily the area's best live-music and DJ space, the two-venue Railway's offer of local and touring bands showcases everything from rock and blues to folk and jazz.

ⓘ Information

Discovery Centre (www3.hants.gov.uk/wdc; Jewry St; ⊛9am-6.45pm Mon-Fri, to 4.45pm Sat, 11am-2.45pm Sun; ⊛) Free internet access.

Tourist Office (☑ 01962-840500; www. visitwinchester.co.uk; High St; ☺10am-5pm Mon-Sat, plus 11am-4pm Sun May-Sep)

❶ Getting There & Away

Winchester is 65 miles west of London. Direct National Express **buses** shuttle to London Victoria every two hours (£14, 1¾ hours). Trains leave half-hourly to hourly for London Waterloo (£32, 1¼ hours) and hourly for Portsmouth (£11, 1¼ hours). There are also fast links to the Midlands.

❶ Getting Around

Bikes can be hired from the tourist office, per half-/full day £7/10 (a £50 deposit is needed).

Park & Ride car parks (per day £3) are signed off junctions 10 and 11 of the M3. There are taxi ranks on the High St, and outside the train station and tourist office, or call **Wintax** (☑ 01962-878727; www.wintaxcars.com).

BATH & SOUTHWEST ENGLAND PORTSMOUTH

Portsmouth

POP 205,100

The world-class collection of maritime heritage at Portsmouth more than demands a day trip. Here you can roam around three stunning historic ships, a submarine and an impressive cluster of museums. Nauticalia done, the city's Point district tempts with cobbled streets and ancient pubs, the Spinnaker Tower delivers jaw-dropping views, and the port makes a prime launch pad for the Isle of Wight.

◉ Sights

★**Portsmouth
Historic Dockyard**   HISTORIC SHIPS
(☑ 02392-839766; www.historicdockyard.co.uk; Victory Gate; All Attractions ticket adult/child £33/23; ☺10am-5.30pm Apr-Oct, to 5pm Nov-Mar) Portsmouth's blockbuster draw sees you gazing at the evocative hulk of Henry VIII's flagship, the Mary Rose (p226), and jumping aboard HMS Victory (p226) – the warship Nelson captained at the Battle of Trafalgar. Then there's the Victorian HMS Warrior, the WWII-era submarine HMS Alliance (p228) and a wealth of imaginative, maritime-themed museums, along with waterborne harbour tours. Visiting more than one exhibit makes the All Attractions ticket (rather than single attraction tickets) the best value. There's a 20% discount for buying online.

Harbour tours (p228) are also included in the All Attractions ticket. Last admission to the dockyard is one hour before closing.

★**Mary Rose Museum**   MUSEUM
(www.maryrose.org; Portsmouth Historic Dockyard; adult/child £18/13; ☺10am-5.30pm Apr-Oct, to 5pm Nov-Mar) The raising of the 16th-century warship the *Mary Rose* in 1982 was an extraordinary feat of marine archaeology. The £35-million, boat-shaped museum that's been built around her gives uninterrupted views of the preserved timbers of her massive hull. The ship can also be seen from tiered galleries that reconstruct life on each deck, using some of the 19,000 artefacts that were raised with her. Items on display range from the military, including scores of cannons and hundreds of longbows, to the touchingly prosaic: water jugs, hair combs, leather shoes and even the skeleton of Hatch, the ship's dog.

This 700-tonne floating fortress was Henry VIII's favourite vessel, but she sank suddenly off Portsmouth while fighting the French in 1545. Of a crew of 400, it's thought 360 died.

★**HMS Victory**   HISTORIC SHIP
(www.hms-victory.com; Portsmouth Historic Dockyard; adult/child £18/13; ☺10am-5.30pm Apr-Oct, to 5pm Nov-Mar) As resplendent as she is venerable, HMS *Victory* was Lord Nelson's flagship at the Battle of Trafalgar (1805) and the site of his famous dying words 'Kiss me, Hardy', after victory over the French had been secured. This remarkable ship is topped by a forest of ropes and masts, and weighted by a swollen belly filled with cannons and paraphernalia for an 850-strong crew. Clambering through the low-beamed decks and crew's quarters is an evocative experience.

In the summer, tours are self-guided. But between November and March, hugely popular 50-minute guided tours are held. Arrive early to bag a place – you can't book in advance.

★**HMS Warrior**   HISTORIC SHIP
(www.hmswarrior.org; Portsmouth Historic Dockyard; adult/child £18/13; ☺10am-5.30pm Apr-Oct, to 5pm Nov-Mar) Anywhere else, the magnificent warship HMS *Warrior* would grab centre stage. This stately dame was at the cutting edge of technology when she was built in 1860, riding the transition from wood to iron and sail to steam. The gleaming upper deck, vast gun deck and dimly lit cable lockers conjure up vivid pictures of life in the Victorian navy.

Portsmouth

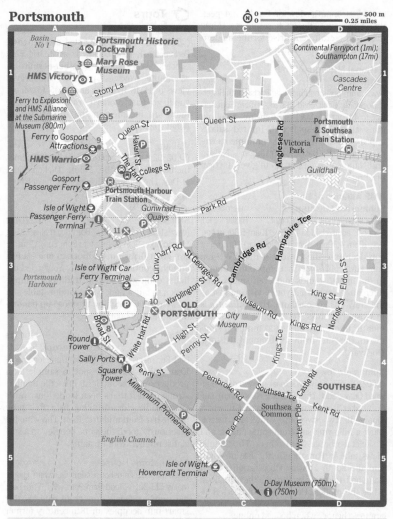

Portsmouth

◎ Top Sights
1 HMS Victory	A1
2 HMS Warrior	A2
3 Mary Rose Museum	A1
4 Portsmouth Historic Dockyard	A1

◎ Sights
5 Action Stations!	B1
6 National Museum of the Royal Navy	A1

7 Spinnaker Tower	A3
8 The Point	B4

✦ Activities, Courses & Tours
9 Harbour Tours	A2

✕ Eating
10 A Bar	B3
11 Old Customs House	B3
12 Still & West	A3

Action Stations!   MUSEUM
(www.actionstations.org; Portsmouth Historic Dockyard; adult/child £18/13; ☺10am-5.30pm Apr-Oct,

to 5pm Nov-Mar) Stroll into Action Stations!, a warehouse full of child-friendly interactive gadgets, to command a warship, gaze at an astronaut's view of Earth, and peek up a periscope. The whole set-up is a thinly disguised recruitment drive for the modern navy, but it's fun nonetheless.

National Museum of the Royal Navy
MUSEUM

(www.nmrn-portsmouth.org.uk; Portsmouth Historic Dockyard; adult/child £13/8; ☻10am-5pm Apr-Oct, to 4.15pm Nov-Mar) Cannon-fire, recoiling guns and blood-spattered, injured sailors appear in this museum's multimedia re-creation of the Battle of Trafalgar – Nelson and Napoleon even pop up to give a tactical briefing.

HMS Alliance at the Submarine Museum
HISTORIC SHIP

(www.submarine-museum.co.uk; Haslar Rd, Gosport; adult/child £14/10; ☻10am-5.30pm Apr-Oct, 10am-4.30pm Wed-Sun Nov-Mar) Taking a trip deep into the bowels of the WWII-era sub HMS *Alliance* is compelling, thanks to the lights, sounds and even smells used to create a sense that you're visiting just as the crew has gone ashore. HMS *Alliance* is in Gosport, across the harbour from Portsmouth; free water buses (30 minutes) shuttle to the site from Portsmouth Historic Dockyard.

Spinnaker Tower
TOWER

(☎02392-857520; www.spinnakertower.co.uk; Gunwharf Quays; adult/child £10/8; ☻10am-6pm) The Spinnaker Tower soars 170m above Gunwharf Quays, its two sweeping white arcs resembling a billowing sail from some angles, and a skeletal ribcage from others. The 23-mile views take in Portsmouth, the Isle of Wight and the South Downs. Observation Deck 1 has a hair-raising view through the glass floor, while the roofless Crow's Nest on Deck 3 allows you to feel the wind on your face. Tickets are 15% cheaper when booked online.

The Point
HISTORIC SITE

The Point's characterful cobbled streets are dotted with higgledy-piggledy houses and salty sea-dog pubs, their terraces prime places to watch streams of ferries and naval ships. Here you can climb Henry V's **Round Tower** and stroll along the fort's walls to the 15th-century **Square Tower**. Underneath, cavernous vaults frame **Sally Ports**: openings in the defences that used to give captains access to the sea, and now lead naval worshippers on to a tiny shingle beach.

Tours

Harbour Tours
BOATING

(☎02392-839766; www.historicdockyard.co.uk; Portsmouth Historic Dockyard; adult/child £7/5; ☻hours vary) These weather-permitting, 45-minute voyages provide salt-sprayed views of HMS *Warrior* and HMS *Victory* – you'll go past modern warships too. The tours are included in the All Attractions ticket (p226).

Walking Tours
WALKING

(☎02392-826722; adult/child £3/free) Themes include Nelson, the Point, Dickens and D-Day. The tourist office has details of times.

✗ Eating

Still & West
PUB FOOD £

(www.stillandwest.co.uk; 2 Bath Sq; mains £10-17; ☻food noon-9pm Mon-Sat, to 8pm Sun) Genius: two great British institutions in one – a fish and chip outlet inside a pub. Your fried delights come wrapped in traditional chippy paper, so buy a pint, bag a window table and tuck in while watching the close-up panorama of passing boats.

A Bar
BISTRO ££

(☎02392-811585; www.abarbistro.co.uk; 58 White Hart Rd; mains £13-22; ☻11am-11pm, food noon-10pm; 🐾) A laid-back spot to sample local produce and soak up local life – the menu is strong on fish that's been landed just yards away, while cider-drinking fisherfolk prop up the bar from midafternoon. The wine list is seriously good; the same people run a specialist retailer from upstairs.

Old Customs House
PUB FOOD ££

(www.theoldcustomshouse.com; Gunwharf Quays; mains £13-20; ☻food 9am-9pm; 🐾) The best of Gunwharf Quays' numerous eateries, this smart pub occupies an 18th-century former Royal Marine hospital. Now better-than-average bar food (think confit rabbit leg, goats cheese and quinoa salad, and sea trout with pickled samphire) is served up alongside its raspberry-red walls and gilt-framed mirrors.

ℹ Information

Portsea Library (www.johnpoundscentre.co.uk; John Pounds Centre, 23 Queen St; ☻10.30am-4.30pm Mon-Fri) Free internet access.

Tourist Office (☎02392-826722; www.visitportsmouth.co.uk; Clarence Esplanade;

⊘10am-5.30pm Apr-Sep, to 5pm Oct-Mar) In the D-Day Museum in Southsea.

ⓘ Getting There & Away

Portsmouth is 100 miles southwest of London.

BOAT

Car and **passenger** ferries and **hovercraft** link Portsmouth to the **Isle of Wight** (p233).

Several routes run from Portsmouth to France. Prices vary wildly depending on times and dates of travel – an example one-way fare is £130 for a car and two adults on the Portsmouth–Cherbourg route. Book in advance, be prepared to travel off-peak and look out for special deals.

Brittany Ferries (www.brittanyferries.co.uk) Runs regular services from Portsmouth to St Malo (10¾ hours), Caen (seven hours), Cherbourg (three hours) and Le Havre (eight hours) in France, and twice weekly services to Santander (24 hours) and Bilbao (24 hours) in Spain.

Condor Ferries (www.condorferries.co.uk) Runs a weekly car-and-passenger service from Portsmouth to Cherbourg (6½ hours) between June and September.

BUS

From Monday to Saturday, there are hourly, direct National Express buses from London Victoria (£14, two hours). Bus 700 runs to Chichester (£4.50, one hour).

TRAIN

Direct trains run hourly from London Victoria (£33, two hours) and half-hourly from London Waterloo (£33, 2½ hours). For the Historic Dockyard, get off at the final stop, Portsmouth Harbour.

Other departures:

Brighton £16, two hours, hourly

Chichester £8, 40 minutes, two per hour

Southampton £10, one hour, three trains per hour

Winchester £11, 1¼ hours, hourly

ⓘ Getting Around

Bus 1 runs every 20 minutes between Portsmouth Harbour bus station and South Parade Pier in Southsea, via Old Portsmouth. An all-day ticket is £4.20.

Every 15 minutes the **Gosport Passenger Ferry** (www.gosportferry.co.uk; The Hard; adult/child/bicycle return £3.30/2.10/1.20; ⊘5.30am-midnight) shuttles from **Portsmouth Harbour** train station to Gosport.

Taxi ranks are near the Portsmouth Harbour bus and train stations. Or call **Aquacars** (☏02392-654321; www.aquacars.co.uk; ⊘24hr).

New Forest

With typical, accidental, English irony the New Forest is anything but new – it was first proclaimed a royal hunting preserve in 1079. It's also not much of a forest, being mostly heathland ('forest' is from the Old French for 'hunting ground'). Designated a national park in 2005, the forest's combined charms make it a joy to explore. Wild ponies mooch around pretty scrubland, deer flicker in the distance and rare birds flit among the foliage. Genteel villages dot the landscape, connected by a web of walking and cycling trails.

🏃 Activities

New Forest Activities   ADVENTURE SPORTS
(☏01590-612377; www.newforestactivities.co.uk; High St, Beaulieu) Runs sessions in canoeing (adult/child per two hours £32/17), kayaking (per two hours £32) and archery (adult/child per 1½ hours £22/17).

Walking

The forest is prime hiking territory. Ordnance Survey (OS) produces a detailed, 1:25,000 Explorer map (New Forest; No 22, £9); Crimson's *New Forest Short Walks* (£8) features 20 day hikes of 2 to 6 miles.

Lyndhurst tourist office (p230) stocks maps and guides; they're also available from its website.

Ranger Walks   WALKING
(☏0300 068 0400; www.forestry.gov.uk/newforest-events; from £5.50) Day walks including those themed around photography, ponies and the unique way the New Forest is managed.

Cycling

➜ The New Forest makes for superb cycling country, with 100 miles of routes linking the main villages and the key railway station at Brockenhurst.

➜ *The New Forest By Bike* map (£3.50) features 22 routes ranging from 8 to 32 miles. The *New Forest Cycling Guide* (£4) features six day-cycle routes of between 4 and 22 miles on a 1:25,000 OS map.

➜ Maps and guides can be bought from Lyndhurst tourist office (p230) or via its website.

➜ To rent bikes, you'll need to pay a deposit (usually £20) and provide identification.

BATH & SOUTHWEST ENGLAND NEW FOREST

ℹ CAMPING IN THE NEW FOREST

The New Forest is a haven for campers. The **Forestry Commission** (www.campingintheforest.co.uk) runs 10 relatively rural sites. Lyndhurst's **tourist office** (p230) has a leaflet (50p) detailing other designated areas; see also www.thenewforest.co.uk.

AA Bike Hire   CYCLING
(☑ 02380-283349; www.aabikehirenewforest.co.uk; Fern Glen, Gosport Lane, Lyndhurst; adult/child per day £10/5) Based in Lyndhurst's main car park.

Cyclexperience   CYCLING
(New Forest Cycle Hire; ☑ 01590-624808; www.newforestcyclehire.co.uk; 2 Brookley Rd, Brockenhurst; adult/child per day £17.50/9) Based at Brockenhurst train station.

Country Lanes   CYCLING
(☑ 01590-622627; www.countrylanes.co.uk; train station, Brockenhurst; adult/child per day £18/9) Based in a vintage railway carriage.

Forest Leisure Cycling   CYCLING
(☑ 01425-403584; www.forestleisurecycling.co.uk; The Cross, Burley; adult/child per day £17/9) Has easy links on to nine cycle routes.

Horse Riding
A number of stables welcome beginners.

Arniss Equestrian Centre   HORSE RIDING
(☑ 01425-654114; www.arnissequestrian.co.uk; Godshill, Fordingbridge; per hr £27) Caters for all skill levels.

Burley Manor   HORSE RIDING
(☑ 01425-403489; www.burleymanorridingstables.com; Ringwood Rd, Burley; per 1/2 hr £33/60) Also does pub rides.

Burley Villa   HORSE RIDING
(Western Riding; ☑ 01425-610278; www.burleyvilla.co.uk; near New Milton; per hr from £35) Runs rides using traditional English and also Western saddle styles (per 90 minutes £48).

ℹ Information

Tourist Office (☑ 02380-282269; www.thenewforest.co.uk; main car park, Lyndhurst; ⊙10am-5pm Easter-Oct, to 4pm Nov-Easter) The national park's main tourist office, set in the New Forest Centre, has a wealth of information including walking and cycling maps, and camping guides.

ℹ Getting There & Around

BUS
➡ National Express buses stop at Lyndhurst, Lymington and Ringwood.

➡ Regular local services run between the park's main towns, Bournemouth (£8.50) and Southampton (£7.40).

➡ The **New Forest Tour** (www.thenewforesttour.info; adult per 1/2/5 days £15/20/30, child £8/10/15; ⊙ hourly 10am-6pm mid-Jun–mid-Sep) has three connecting routes of hop-on/hop-off buses, passing through Lyndhurst's main car park, Brockenhurst train station, Lymington, Beaulieu and Exbury.

TRAIN
➡ Two trains an hour run to Brockenhurst from London Waterloo (£18, two hours) via Winchester (£12, 30 minutes) and on to Bournemouth (£8, 20 minutes).

➡ Local trains also shuttle twice an hour between Brockenhurst and Lymington (£4, 10 minutes).

Lyndhurst, Brockenhurst & Around

The quaint country villages of Lyndhurst and Brockenhurst are separated by just 4 miles. Their picturesque accommodation options and superb eateries ensure they're atmospheric bases from which to explore the New Forest.

◎ Sights

New Forest Museum   MUSEUM
(www.newforestcentre.org.uk; main car park, Lyndhurst; ⊙10am-5pm Apr-Oct, to 4pm Nov-Mar) **FREE** Features a local labourer's cottage (complete with socks drying beside the fire), potato dibbles and a cider press. The mini-film makes for an accessible introduction to the park – listen too for recordings of the autumn pony sales, which take place after the annual drifts (round-ups).

Beaulieu   HISTORIC BUILDING
(☑ 01590-612345; www.beaulieu.co.uk; adult/child £24/12; ⊙10am-6pm Apr-Sep, to 5pm Oct-Mar) Petrolheads, historians and ghost-hunters gravitate to Beaulieu (*bew*-lee) – a vintage car museum, stately home and tourist complex centred on a 13th-century Cistercian monastery. Motor-maniacs will be in raptures at Lord Montague's **National Motor Museum**. Tickets are valid for a year; it's up to £5 cheaper to buy in advance, online. Beaulieu is served by the New Forest Tour (p230).

The abbey at the heart of modern-day Beaulieu was a key one. After Henry VIII's monastic land-grab of 1536, it fell to the ancestors of the current proprietors, the Montague family. Today the motor museum presents a splendid collection that spans early classics, F1 cars and jet-powered land-speed record-breakers including *Bluebird*, which broke the 403mph (649km/h) limit in 1964. Celebrity wheels include those driven by James Bond and Mr Bean.

Beaulieu's grand but homely **palace** began life as a 14th-century Gothic abbey gate-house, and received a 19th-century Scottish baronial makeover from Baron Montague in the 1860s. Listen out for eerie Gregorian chanting – the abbey is supposedly one of England's most haunted buildings.

🛏 Sleeping

Daisybank Cottage
B&B ££

(☏ 01590-622086; www.bedandbreakfast-newforest.co.uk; Sway Rd, Brockenhurst; s £90, d £110-130; P 🛜) The five gorgeous themed suites here are mini pamper palaces. Expect aromatic smellies in gleaming bathrooms, stylish luxurious furnishings and lots of little extras: breakfasts laden with New Forest goodies, handmade chocolates, smartphone docks, DAB radios and range-baked cakes on arrival.

Little Hayes
B&B ££

(☏ 02380-283816; www.littlehayesguesthouse.co.uk; 43 Romsey Rd, Lyndhurst; s £70-80, d £100-110) Pine mini-four-poster beds, smart bathrooms and bright colour schemes, ranging from raspberry to aquamarine, lift this friendly B&B above the crowd. Bedroom 5, with its slanting ceiling and roomy bathroom, is particularly appealing.

★ The Pig
BOUTIQUE HOTEL £££

(☏ 0345 225 9494; www.thepighotel.co.uk; Beaulieu Rd, Brockenhurst; r £175-265; P 🛜) One of the New Forest's classiest hotels remains an utter delight: log baskets, croquet mallets and ranks of guest gumboots give things a country-house air; espresso machines and minilarders lend bedrooms a luxury touch. In fact, all this effortless elegance makes it feel like you've just dropped by a friend's (very stylish) rural retreat.

🍴 Eating

★ The Pig
MODERN BRITISH ££

(☏ 0345 225 9494; www.thepighotel.co.uk; Beaulieu Rd, Brockenhurst; mains £10-17; ⊘ noon-2.30pm & 6.30-9.30pm; 🛜) Add this to your must-eat-here list. The Pig's creative chefs devise menus by the 'micro-season'; they change hourly depending on what's been found when foraging or in the hotel's kitchen garden. This results in imaginative combos, which might feature pungent wild garlic, punchy, house-smoked ham or a creamy risotto of just-picked mushrooms.

Oak Inn
PUB FOOD ££

(☏ 02380-282350; www.oakinnlyndhurst.co.uk; Pinkney Lane, Bank; mains £12-24; ⊘ noon-2.30pm & 6-9pm Mon-Fri, noon-9pm Sat & Sun) The essence of old England has been poured into this convivial, flower-framed inn. Horse brasses and dried hops hang over diners tucking into charcuterie platters, succulent pan-seared New Forest venison, roasted Hampshire pheasant and Lymington crab.

ℹ️ Getting There & Away

Bus 6 shuttles between Lyndhurst, Brockenhurst and Lymington (£3.70, hourly Monday to Saturday, five on Sunday); so does the **New Forest Tour** (p230).

Trains run twice an hour between Brockenhurst and Lymington (£4, 10 minutes).

Buckler's Hard

For such a tiny place, this picturesque huddle of 18th-century cottages, near the mouth of the River Beaulieu, has a big history. It started in 1722, when a duke of Montague built a port to finance a Caribbean expedition. His dream faltered, but when war with France came, this embryonic village and sheltered gravel waterfront became a secret boatyard where several of Nelson's triumphant Battle of Trafalgar warships were built. In the 20th century it played its part in the preparations for the D-Day landings.

◉ Sights

Buckler's Hard Story
MUSEUM

(☏ 01590-616203; www.bucklershard.co.uk; adult/child £6.50/4.50; ⊘ 10am-5pm Apr-Sep, to 4pm Oct-Mar) The hamlet's fascinating Maritime Museum and heritage centre chart the inlet's shipbuilding history and role in WWII, and feature immaculately preserved 18th-century labourers' cottages.

🛏 Sleeping & Eating

Master Builder's House Hotel
HOTEL ££

(☏ 01590-616253; www.hillbrookehotels.co.uk; d £105-170; ⊘ food noon-3pm & 7-9pm; P) In this beautifully restored 18th-century hotel, 25 stately but stylish rooms feature soft lighting, burnished trunks and plush fabrics.

The atmospheric river-view **restaurant** (mains £12-23) delivers classy, classic dishes, while the wood-panelled **Yachtsman's Bar** serves quality pub grub (mains £7-16).

Lymington

POP 15,400

Yachting haven, New Forest base and jumping-off point to the Isle of Wight – the appealing Georgian harbour town of Lymington has several strings to its tourism bow. This former smuggler's port offers nautical shops, prime eating and sleeping spots and, in Quay St, an utterly quaint cobbled lane.

◉ Sights & Activities

St Barbe Museum   MUSEUM
(☑ 01590-676969; www.stbarbe-museum.org.uk; New St; adult/child £5.45/2.70; ☺ 10am-4pm Mon-Sat) Explores tales of boatbuilders, sailors, smugglers, salt-makers and farmers through a mix of models, hands-on displays and artefacts. The museum was closed at the time of writing for a £2-million revamp but due to reopen soon.

Puffin Cruises   BOATING
(☑ 07850-947618; www.puffincruiseslymington. com; Town Quay) The best trip is an exhilarating, three-hour sunset surge across the Solent to the Isle of Wight (adult/child £20/9, 6pm Monday, Wednesday, Friday and Saturday, May to October), where the Needles lighthouse and towering chalk stacks loom from the water.

🛏 Sleeping

Auplands   B&B ££
(☑ 01590-675944; www.auplands.com; 22 Southampton Rd; s £55-65, d £75-85; 🅿 🛜) Your genial hosts have been running this B&B for more than 30 years, and it shows in their supremely efficient systems and easy charm. Snug rooms feature pine, bottled water and big plants, while the eateries of Lymington are only a 10-minute stroll away.

★ Mill at Gordleton   BOUTIQUE HOTEL £££
(☑ 01590-682219; www.themillatgordleton.co.uk; Silver St, Hordle; d £195-175, ste £175-295; 🅿 🛜) Step inside here and know, instantly, you're going to be looked after, beautifully. Wicker, velvet and gingham dot exquisite rooms (each one comes with a sweet soft toy duck), while the garden is a magical mix of rushing water, fairy lights and modern sculpture. The Mill is 4 miles west of Lymington.

Stanwell House   BOUTIQUE HOTEL £££
(☑ 01590-677123; www.stanwellhouse.com; 14 High St; d £145-205, ste £256; @ 🛜) There are boutique tweaks everywhere at Stanwell. Swish Georgian rooms manage to be both period and modern: the four-poster ones feature dark woods and zingy colours, while the high-tech suites are simply irresistible – two even have their own roof terrace for sunny days and moonlit nights.

🍴 Eating

Fish & Chips   FISH & CHIPS £
(130 High St; mains £8; ☺ noon-2.30pm & 4.30-8.30pm Mon-Fri, noon-9pm Sat, noon-7.30pm Sun) They're often queuing out the door at this classic British chippy, which boasts great fish, laminate tables and pickled eggs. Eat in or take away.

Ship Inn   PUB FOOD ££
(☑ 01590-676903; www.theshiplymington.co.uk; The Quay; mains £9-17; ☺ food noon-10pm; 🍴) A pub for all seasons: knock back summertime drinks on the waterside terrace; in winter, a toasty log burner gets you warm. Hearty food ranges from sticky, marinated chicken to homemade beetroot and truffle ravioli; drinks totter from tangy real ales to vintage champagne.

★ Elderflower   MODERN BRITISH £££
(☑ 01590-676908; www.elderflowerrestaurant. co.uk; 5 Quay St; mains £19-24; ☺ noon-2.30pm & 6.30-9.30pm Tue-Sat, noon-2.30pm Sun) An Anglo-French feel infuses Elderflower – from the truffle-scented braised New Forest venison, to the apple and vanilla soufflé, which comes with custard laced with Calvados. Or opt for the tapas-style *petites assiettes* (£2 to £10); perhaps pine-smoked mussels, wild mushroom *bordaliase* or beef rib that's been slow-cooked for 72 hours.

ⓘ Information

Library (☑ 0300 555 1387; North Close; ☺ 9am-5pm Mon, Wed, Thu & Sat, to 7pm Tue & Fri; 🛜) Free internet access.

ⓘ Getting There & Away

Lymington has two train stations: Lymington Town and Lymington Pier. Isle of Wight ferries connect with Lymington Pier. Trains run to

Southampton (£11, 40 minutes), with a change at Brockenhurst, twice an hour.

Wightlink Ferries (☏ 0333 999 7333; www.wightlink.co.uk) has car and passenger ferries that run hourly to Yarmouth on the Isle of Wight (30 minutes). An adult/child foot-passenger day-return costs £14.60/7.30. Car fares start at around £60 for a short-break return.

ISLE OF WIGHT

On the Isle of Wight these days there's something groovy in the air. For decades this slab of rock anchored off Portsmouth has been a magnet for family holidays, and it still has seaside kitsch by the bucket and spade. But now the proms and amusement arcades are framed by pockets of pure funkiness. A brace of music festivals draws partygoers, just-caught seafood is served in kooky fishers' cafes, and cool camping rules – here sites are dotted with ecoyurts and vintage campervans. Yet still the isle's principal appeal remains: a mild climate, myriad outdoorsy activities and a 25-mile shore lined with beaches, dramatic white cliffs and tranquil sand dunes.

🏃 Activities

Cycling
With 200 miles of cycle routes, the Isle of Wight makes pedal pushers smile. The island's official visitor website (www.visitisleofwight.co.uk) lists suggested trips (complete with maps), ranging from family-friendly tootles along former railway routes to the 50-mile, cliff-climbing **Chalk Ridge Extreme**. A **Cycling Festival** (☏ 01983-821000; www.sunseaandcycling.com) is held every September.

Bike rentals start at around £13/45 per day/week. Many firms deliver and collect on orders over £30.

Tavcycles   CYCLING
(☏ 01983-812989; www.tavcycles.co.uk; 140 High St, Ryde) Offers rates ranging from half-day (£7) and 24 hours (£15) to one week (£45).

Top Gear   CYCLING
(☏ 01983-299056; www.top-gearhire.com; 1 Terminus Rd, Cowes; adult per day/week £15/70, child per day/week £13/70) Delivers bikes island-wide.

Wight Cycle Hire   CYCLING
(☏ 01983-761800; www.wightcyclehire.co.uk; Station Rd, Yarmouth; adult day/week £16/70, child

day/week £10/40) Also rents electric bikes (per day £35) and tandems (per day £32).

Walking
This is one of the best spots in southern England for rambling, with 500 miles of well-marked walking paths, including 67 miles of coastal routes. The island's two-week **walking festival** (www.isleofwightwalkingfestival.co.uk; ☺May) is billed as the UK's largest.

Water Sports
Water sports are serious business on the Isle of Wight. Cowes is the sailing centre, surfers and wind- and kitesurfers flock to the southwest, especially around Compton Bay, while powerboats run trips out to the Needles rocks.

Isle of Wight Adventure
Activities   ADVENTURE SPORTS
(☏ 01983-755838; www.isleofwightadventureactivities.co.uk; Freshwater) Runs activities ranging from surfing, stand-up paddleboarding and kayaking (per two hours adult/child £40/25) to archery (per hour £12).

ℹ Information

The Isle of Wight's main **tourist office** (☏ 01983-813813; www.visitisleofwight.co.uk; High St, Newport; ☺10.30am-3.30pm Mon-Fri, to 2.30pm Sat) is in Newport; small-scale information points include those at the main ferry ports.

ℹ Getting There & Away

Hovertravel (☏ 01983-717700; www.hovertravel.co.uk; day-return adult/child £19/9.60) Shuttles foot passengers between Southsea (a Portsmouth suburb) and Ryde, half-hourly to hourly.

Red Funnel (☏ 02380-019192; www.redfunnel.co.uk) Runs car-and-passenger ferries between Southampton and East Cowes (same-day return adult/child £16.80/8.40, from £45 with car, 60 minutes, hourly) and high-speed passenger ferries between Southampton and West

> ℹ **CAR FERRY COSTS**
>
> The cost of car ferries to the Isle of Wight can vary enormously. Save by booking ahead, asking about special offers and travelling off-peak (midweek and later in the day). Long stays are cheaper and some deals include admission to island attractions. Booking online can mean paying £20 less.

Isle of Wight

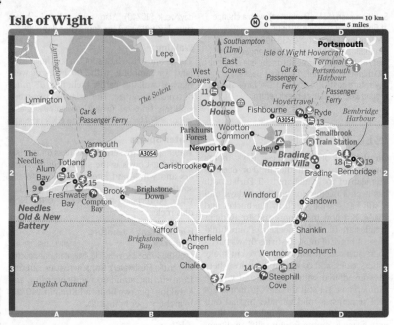

Isle of Wight

◎ Top Sights
1 Brading Roman Villa	D2
2 Needles Old & New Battery	A2
3 Osborne House	C1

◎ Sights
4 Carisbrooke Castle	C2
5 St Catherine's Lighthouse	C3
St Catherine's Oratory	(see 5)
6 St Helens Duver	D2

✪ Activities, Courses & Tours
7 Blackgang Chine	C3
8 Isle of Wight Adventure Activities	A2
9 Needles Pleasure Cruises	A2
Tavcycles	(see 13)
Top Gear	(see 11)
10 Wight Cycle Hire	A2

🛏 Sleeping
11 Fountain	C1
Hambrough	(see 12)
12 Harbour View	C3
13 Kasbah	D1
14 Lighthouse	C3
onefiftycowes	(see 11)
15 Really Green	A2
16 Totland Bay YHA	A2
17 Vintage Vacations	C2
18 Xoron Floatel	D2

✕ Eating
Ale & Oyster	(see 12)
Black Sheep	(see 13)
Boathouse	(see 14)
Crab Shed	(see 14)
Floating Cafe & Shop	(see 18)
19 Pilot Boat	D2
Spyglass Inn	(see 12)

Cowes (same-day return adult/child £24/12, 25 minutes, one to two per hour).

Wightlink Ferries (📞 0333 999 7333; www.wightlink.co.uk) Operates passenger ferries every half-hour from Portsmouth to Ryde (day-return adult/child £18.40/9.20, 22 minutes). It also runs hourly car-and-passenger ferries from Portsmouth to Fishbourne (45 minutes) and from Lymington to Yarmouth (30 minutes). For both, an adult/child foot passen-

ger day-return costs £14.60/7.30. Car fares start at around £60 for a short-break return.

🛈 Getting Around

BUS

Southern Vectis (www.islandbuses.info) runs buses between the eastern towns roughly every 30 minutes. Regular services to the remoter southwest, especially between Blackgang Chine and Brook, are less frequent, but between April and September, the **Island Coaster** (www.islandbuses.info; per day adult/child £10/5, per 2 days adult/child £15/7.30) makes four return circuits a day along the southern shore from Ryde around to Yarmouth, in the west.

Rover Tickets cover all Southern Vectis routes: one day (adult/child £10/5) or two days (adult/child £15/7.30).

CAR

1st Call (☑ 01983-400055; www.1stcallcar-sales.com; 15 College Close, Sandown; per day/week from £30/150) Collects and delivers island-wide.

TRAIN

Island Line trains (www.southwesttrains.co.uk) run twice hourly from Ryde to Shanklin (same-day return £4.40, 25 minutes), via Smallbrook Junction, Brading and Sandown.

Cowes & Around

Pack your yachting cap – the hilly Georgian harbour town of Cowes is famous for Cowes Week in early August; first held in 1826, it's one of the biggest and longest-running sailing regattas in the world. Fibreglass playthings and vintage sailing boats line Cowes' waterfronts, which are lopped into East and West Cowes by the picturesque River Medina. The island's capital, Newport, is 5 miles south.

◉ Sights

★ Osborne House HISTORIC BUILDING
(EH; ☑ 01983-200022; www.english-heritage.org.uk; York Ave, East Cowes; adult/child £15/9; ⊘ 10am-6pm Apr-Sep, to 5pm Oct; P) Lemon-frosted and Italianate, Osborne House is pure Victorian pomp. Built in the 1840s at the behest of Queen Victoria, the monarch grieved here for many years after her husband's death. Extravagant rooms include the opulent Royal Apartments and Durbar Room; other highlights are horse and carriage rides, the Swiss Cottage – where the royal ankle-biters would play – and the stroll down Rhododendron Walk to Her Majesty's private beach.

Carisbrooke Castle CASTLE
(EH; ☑ 01983-522107; www.english-heritage.org.uk; Castle Hill, Newport; adult/child £9/5; ⊘ 10am-6pm Apr-Sep, to 5pm Oct, to 4pm Sat & Sun Nov-Mar; P) Charles I was imprisoned here before his execution in 1649. Today you can clamber the sturdy ramparts and play bowls on the very green the doomed monarch used.

⭐ Festivals & Events

Cowes Week SPORTS
(www.aamcowesweek.co.uk; ⊘ Aug) One of the biggest and longest-running sailing regattas in the world.

🛏 Sleeping

★ onefiftycowes B&B ££
(☑ 07795 296399; www.onefiftycowes.co.uk; 150 Park Rd, West Cowes; s £60-75, d £85-90; P 🛜) All the trappings of a luxury hotel, all the individuality of a B&B – at onefiftycowes, wicker chairs sit beside stand-alone sinks; feature fireplaces are stacked with sea-smoothed pebbles. The best room is Solent, where a pair of binoculars is waiting to help you gaze at the partial sea views.

Fountain HOTEL ££
(☑ 0845 608 6040; www.fountaininn-cowes.co.uk; High St, West Cowes; s £60-100, d £75-110; 🛜) Georgian-repro style rules at this appealing harbourside inn, where mock-flock wallpaper and old, wooden furniture define comfy rooms; number 21 has slanting ceilings and prime views of the bustling quay. The snug bar and sunny terrace are good places to sample pints and pub-grub classics (mains £9; open 11am to 10pm).

Ryde & Around

The nippiest foot-passenger ferries between Wight and Portsmouth alight in **Ryde**, a workaday but appealing Victorian town rich in the trappings of the British seaside. Next come the cutesy village of **Brading**, with its fine Roman villa, and photogenic **Bembridge Harbour**, which is fringed by sandy beaches.

Further south lie the twin resort towns of **Sandown** and **Shanklin**, boasting promenades and hordes of families wielding buckets and spades.

◉ Sights

★ Brading Roman Villa RUINS
(☑ 01983-406223; www.bradingromanvilla.org.uk; Morton Old Rd, Brading; adult/child £9.50/4.75; ⊘ 10am-5pm) The exquisitely preserved mosaics here (including a famous cockerel-headed man) make this one of the finest Romano-British sites in the UK. Wooden walkways lead over rubble walls and brightly painted tiles, allowing you to gaze right down on to the ruins below.

St Helens Duver　　　　NATURE RESERVE
(NT; www.nationaltrust.org.uk; ⊘24hr; **P**) At this idyllic sand-and-shingle spit bordering the mouth of the River Yar, trails snake past swathes of sea pink, marram grass and rare clovers. It's signed from the village of St Helens, near Bembridge Harbour.

Isle of Wight
Steam Railway　　　　HERITAGE RAILWAY
(☑01983-882204; www.iwsteamrailway.co.uk; return adult/child £12/6, 1st class £17/11; ⊘mid-Apr–Sep) Regularly chugs the one-hour journey from Smallbrook Junction to Wootton Common.

🛏 Sleeping

★**Vintage Vacations**　　　CAMPGROUND **£**
(☑07802 758113; www.vintagevacations.co.uk; Ashey, near Ryde; 4-person caravans per week £475-710; ⊘Apr-Oct; **P**) The bevy of 1960s Airstream trailers on this farm are vintage chic personified. The gleaming aluminium shells shelter lovingly selected furnishings ranging from cheerful patchwork blankets to vivid tea cosies. Alternatively, opt for a beach-shack retreat, a 1930s scout hut, or the Mission: a late-Victorian tin chapel.

Xoron Floatel　　　　B&B **££**
(☑01983-874596; www.xoronfloatel.co.uk; Bembridge Harbour; d £70; **P**) A truly unique spot to drop off – this former WWII gunboat is now a cheery, bunting-draped houseboat. Tiny, comfy cabins come complete with pocket-sized bathrooms, while the harbour views from the flower-framed sun deck are simply superb.

Kasbah　　　　　　B&B **££**
(☑01983-810088; www.kasbahiw.com; 76 Union St, Ryde; d £70; 🛜) Kasbah brings a burst of North Africa to the streets of East Wight. Chunky wooden furniture and vibrant furnishings give bedrooms a Moroccan feel; some also have water views. The downstairs bar is lively – if you're not a night owl, avoid weekends or ask for a room on the top floor.

🍴 Eating

Pilot Boat　　　　　PUB FOOD **£**
(☑01983-872077; www.thepilotboatinn.com; Station Rd, Bembridge; mains £9; ⊘noon-2pm & 6-8pm; **P**🛜) It's a good sign when customers can just sit down and play the pub's piano and guitars – a convivial atmosphere that's enhanced by a log-burner, ships' flags and quality homemade grub (think local crab

salad and big bowls of chilli). Meanwhile, the spick-and-span bedrooms (doubles £90) are attractively nautically themed.

Black Sheep　　　　　　CAFE **£**
(☑01983-811006; www.theblacksheepbar.co.uk; 53 Union St, Ryde; mains £8-10; ⊘noon-3pm Mon-Thu, to 8pm Fri & Sat) Chilled tunes on the music system, piles of newspapers and a palm-dotted terrace draw the locals to this laid-back Ryde venue – as do the regular live music sessions and a menu that spans homemade burgers, steaming bowls of mussels, and honey, fig and black pudding focaccia.

Floating Cafe & Shop　　　SEAFOOD **££**
(☑01983-874758; www.thebestdressedcrabintown. co.uk; Fisherman's Wharf, Bembridge Harbour; mains £6-22; ⊘10am-4pm daily Easter-Dec, 10am-4pm Sat & Sun Jan-Easter) Welcome to an idyllic spot to munch your lunch. At this bijou cafe tacked on to a pontoon, the day's crab and lobster harvest is turned into supremely tasty sandwiches, salads and soups. Best eaten at one of the tables perched beside the water as local fishing boats unload their catch. It's deservedly popular – book. From mid-July to late August the cafe is open until 8.30pm.

Ventnor & Around

The Victorian town of Ventnor slaloms so steeply down the island's southern coast that it feels more like the south of France. The shops in the town's winding streets are worth browsing and the seafront is well worth a stroll.

⊙ Sights & Activities

St Catherine's Lighthouse　　　LIGHTHOUSE
(☑01983-730435; www.trinityhouse.co.uk; near Niton; adult/child £4/3; ⊘1-4.30pm Jul & Aug, hours vary Apr-Jun & Sep) A crenellated 19th-century navigational aid that marks the island's southernmost point. Tours climb the 90-odd steps up to the lantern room, revealing sweeping sea views.

St Catherine's Oratory　　　LIGHTHOUSE
(near Niton) **FREE** Known locally as the Pepperpot, this 10.5m, octagonal, 14th-century tower constitutes England's only surviving medieval lighthouse.

Blackgang Chine　　　AMUSEMENT PARK
(☑01983-730330; www.blackgangchine.com; Blackgang; admission £91.50; ⊘10am-5pm Apr-Jul, to 6pm Aug, to 4pm Sep-Mar) A kid-friendly

ISLE OF WIGHT MUSIC FESTIVALS

The isle's festival tradition kicked off in 1968, when an estimated 200,000 hippies came to see the Doors, the Who, Joni Mitchell and rock icon Jimi Hendrix' last performance. A generation on, its gatherings are still some of England's top musical events.

Isle of Wight Festival (www.isleofwightfestival.com; ☉ mid-Jun) Held in mid-June, past headline acts include Stereophonics, Muse, the Red Hot Chili Peppers, the Kings of Leon and the Rolling Stones.

Bestival (www.bestival.net; ☉ Sep) Held in early September, Bestival delights in an eclectic, alternative feel, drawing the Super Furry Animals, Scissor Sisters, Candi Staton and more.

attraction themed around dinosaurs, pirates and dragons, which features water gardens, animated shows and a hedge maze.

🛏 Sleeping & Eating

Harbour View   B&B ££
(St Augustine Villa; ☑ 01983-852285; www.harbour-viewhotel.co.uk; The Esplanade, Ventnor; s £80-96, d £89-105; ℗ 🛜) Country-house collectables dot this Italianate Victorian villa, where wing-backed chairs sit in stately bedrooms and rich red fabrics frame sea views. And what views! Watch the sun set from your sofa or the waves roll from your four-poster bed.

Hambrough   B&B £££
(☑ 01983-856333; www.thehambrough.com; Hambrough Rd, Ventnor; d £120-230; ℗ 🛜) It's the little touches that make a big difference at this boutique B&B. Subtle, sleek furnishings, espresso machines (which even froth the milk) and Isle of Wight smoked salmon for breakfast. Two bedrooms have balconies directly overlooking the sea – in some top-floor rooms you can even watch the waves from your bath-tub.

Spyglass Inn   PUB FOOD ££
(☑ 01983-855338; The Esplanade, Ventnor; mains £10-25; ☉ noon-9.30pm) When a beachfront pub is this bedecked with pirate paraphernalia, ships' lanterns and lifebelts, you tend to be wary of the meals. No need. The seafood platters and salads here are superb, especially the grilled, garlic-butter-laced lobster – book these, they tend to sell out.

Ale & Oyster   BISTRO ££
(☑ 01983-857025; www.thealeandoyster.co.uk; The Esplanade, Ventnor; mains £9-20; ☉ noon-2pm & 6-9pm Wed-Sun) Modern takes on Isle of Wight produce include wild mushroom and smoked garlic risotto, crab mornay, and hazelnut-dusted pan-seared scallops. Best enjoyed on the terrace set right beside Ventnor's esplanade.

Steephill Cove

Steephill Cove's tiny, sandy beach is fringed by buildings that range from stone cottages to rickety-looking shacks. Beach finds festoon porches dotted with driftwood furniture and draped with fishing nets; a tiny clapboard lighthouse presides over the scene. It's all studiedly nautical, but still very nice.

🛏 Sleeping & Eating

★ Lighthouse   APARTMENT £
(☑ 07903-689984; www.steephill-cove.co.uk; Steephill Cove; 6 people per week £990-1950) This is the sea-view sleep spot of your dreams. A white, two-storey, clapboard lighthouse where the style is pure New England beach chic and the setting is right beside the shore. Lie in bed watching the waves, take a few steps to the beach to swim in the sea, stroll out to dine on your private deck. Heavenly.

The same people run a boathouse (sleeping six people, per week £950 to £1490) and the romantic, two-person Crow's Nest (£390 to £600) nearby.

Crab Shed   CAFE £
(Steephill Cove; snacks £5; ☉ noon-3pm Apr-Sep) Lobster pots and fishing boats line the slipway outside a shack that's a riot of sea-smoothed spas, cork floats and faded buoys. Irresistible treats include meaty crab salads, mackerel ciabatta and crumbly crab pasties.

★ Boathouse   SEAFOOD £££
(☑ 01983-852747; www.steephill-cove.co.uk; Steephill Cove; mains £19-41; ☉ noon-3pm Thu-Tue late May–early Sep) Arrive early enough, and you'll see Steephill Cove's fishers (Jimmy and Mark) landing your lunch – the sanded wooden tables here are just steps from the sea. It makes a spellbinding spot to sip chilled wine, sample succulent lobster and revel in Wight's new-found driftwood chic. Booking essential.

ⓘ Getting There & Away

Steephill Cove is 1 mile west of Ventnor and is off-limits to cars. Walk from the nearby Botanical Gardens (parking £5), or hike from the hillside car park 200m west of Ventnor Esplanade, then follow the (sometimes steep) coast path until you arrive.

West Wight

Rural and remote, Wight's westerly corner is where the island really comes into its own. Sheer white cliffs rear from a surging sea as the stunning coastline peels west to Alum Bay and the most famous chunks of chalk in the region: the **Needles**. These jagged rocks rise, shardlike, out of the sea, like the backbone of a prehistoric sea monster. West Wight is also home to arguably the isle's best beach: sandy, windswept **Compton Bay**.

◉ Sights & Activities

★ Needles Old & New Battery   FORT

(NT; ☎ 01983-754772; www.nationaltrust.org.uk; The Needles; adult/child £6.30/3.10; ⊙ 11am-4pm mid-Mar–Oct) The Victorian fort complex at Wight's western tip is home to two gun emplacements where engrossing displays reveal how the site was established in 1862, served in two world wars and then became a secret Cold War rocket-testing base. Walk to the battery along the cliffs from Alum Bay (1 mile) or hop on the **tourist bus** (www.islandbuses.info; per 24hr adult/child £10/5; ⊙ 10am-5pm mid-Mar–Sep) that runs twice hourly between battery and bay.

Needles Pleasure Cruises   BOATING

(☎ 01983-761587; www.needlespleasurecruises.co.uk; Alum Bay; adult/child £5.50/3.50; ⊙ 10.30am-4.30pm Easter-Oct) Twenty-minute voyages run half-hourly from Alum Bay beach to the towering Needles chalk stacks, providing cracking views of those soaring white cliffs.

🛏 Sleeping

★ Really Green   CAMPGROUND £

(☎ 07802 678591; www.thereallygreenholidaycompany.com; Blackbridge Rd, Freshwater Bay; yurt per week £375-705; ⊙ Easter-Oct; 🅿) 🡒 Roughing it has never been so smooth. The two- to five-person, fully furnished yurts on this tree-shaded site feature four-poster beds, futons, wood-burning stoves and time-worn antiques. It's set amid secluded fields with river views. A local farm shop–deli is just a few minutes' walk away.

Totland Bay YHA   HOSTEL £

(☎ 0845 371 9348; www.yha.org.uk; Hirst Hill, Totland Bay; dm/d £18/25; 🅿 🛜) Creaking, cheerfully run Victorian house with a maximum of eight beds per room and staff happy to share local info.

DORSET

Holiday hot spot Dorset offers a checklist of charms. Its shoreline is one of Britain's best and boasts the Jurassic Coast – a World Heritage Site flecked with sea-carved bays, crumbly cliffs and beaches loaded with fossilised souvenirs. Swimming, kayaking and hiking here are memorable indeed. Inland, Thomas Hardy's lyrical landscape serves up vast Iron Age hill forts, rude chalk figures, fairy-tale castles and must-see stately homes. Then there are resorts alive with party animals, golden beaches flanked by millionaires' mansions, and sailing waters that have hosted Olympic events. Time then to add Dorset to your holiday list.

ⓘ Information

Visit Dorset (www.visit-dorset.com) The county's official tourism website.

ⓘ Getting There & Around

TRAIN

One train route runs from Bristol through Bath and Dorchester West to Weymouth (£20, three hours, at least six daily).

Another hourly service connects London Waterloo with Weymouth (£20, three hours), via Southampton, Bournemouth, Poole and Dorchester South.

BUS

First (www.firstgroup.com) runs bus routes linking the main towns.
More (www.morebus.co.uk) is the key bus operator in Bournemouth, Poole and surrounding rural areas.

Bournemouth

POP 183,491

If one thing has shaped Bournemouth, it's the beach. This glorious, 7-mile strip of soft sand first drew holidaymakers in the Victorian days. Today the resort attracts both elderly coach parties and youthful stag parties – on Saturday nights fancy-dress is everywhere; angels in L-plates meet men in mankinis. But

Bournemouth is more than just a full-on party town. It also boasts some hip hideaways, great restaurants, tempting water sports, and in Boscombe, 2 miles east of the centre, a suburb with a cool urban-surfer vibe.

◉ Sights & Activities

Bournemouth Beach
BEACH

Bournemouth's sandy shoreline regularly clocks up seaside awards. It stretches from Southbourne in the far east to Alum Chine in the west – an immense promenade backed by some 3000 deckchairs, ornamental gardens, kids' playgrounds and cafes. The resort also has two piers. Around **Bournemouth Pier** you can hire brightly painted **beach huts** (☏01202-451781; www.bournemouthbeachhuts.co.uk; per day/week £40/158), deckchairs (per day £3), windbreaks (£5.50) and parasols (£6). **Boscombe Pier** is a focus for water sports.

Russell-Cotes
MUSEUM

(☏01202-451858; www.russellcotes.com; Russell-Cotes Rd; adult/child £6/4; ◎10am-5pm Tue-Sun) Ostentation oozes from almost every inch of this arresting structure – a mash-up of Italianate villa and Scottish baronial pile. It was built at the end of the 1800s for Merton and Annie Russell-Cotes as somewhere to showcase the remarkable range of souvenirs gathered on their world travels.

Alum Chine
GARDENS

(Mountbatten Rd; ◎24hr) Bournemouth's 1920s heyday is beautifully evoked at a subtropical enclave containing plants from the Canary Islands, New Zealand, Mexico and the Himalayas; their bright-red bracts, silver thistles and purple flowers are set against a glittering sea. It's 1.5 miles west of Bournemouth Pier.

Sorted Watersports
WATER SPORTS

(☏01202-300668; www.sortedsurfschool.co.uk; Overstrand Bldg, Undercliff Dr) From its base on Boscombe promenade, Sorted runs lessons in surfing and stand-up paddleboarding (per two hours £30). It also hires out wetsuits (two/eight hours £10/30), surfboards (two/eight hours £10/30), stand-up paddleboards (one/two hours £15/25), and kayaks (one/two hours £15/25).

🛏 Sleeping

Bournemouth Backpackers
HOSTEL £

(☏01202-299491; www.bournemouthbackpackers.co.uk; 3 Frances Rd; dm/d £15/34; P🛜) Three-to six-bed dorms in a suburban house dotted with travellers' totems – one wall is lined with chocolate-bar wrappers from around the world. It's for non-UK citizens only, and reservations are only accepted via the booking form on the website.

★ B&B by the Beach
B&B ££

(☏01202-433632; www.bedandbreakfastbythebeach.co.uk; 7 Burtley Rd, Southbourne; d £110; P🛜) Prepare for a winning combo: charming owners and delightful rooms. Themes and colours encompass yachting, deep aquamarine and ruby red. Relaxation comes courtesy of the flower-framed terrace, posh chocs and homemade cake – best sampled with the complimentary glass of wine.

★ Urban Beach
BOUTIQUE HOTEL ££

(☏01202-301509; www.urbanbeach.co.uk; 23 Argyll Rd; s £72, d £99-180; P@🛜) Still slumber spot of choice for Bournemouth's hip visitors, Urban Beach revels in a 'no-worries' air that sees free loans of wellingtons, umbrellas and DVDs. Bold black, dark grey and vivid lime define stylish bedrooms, while the decked terrace is full of fashionistas tucking into fare from the upscale bistro (open noon to 10pm).

Mory House
B&B ££

(☏01202-433553; www.moryhouse.co.uk; 31 Grand Ave, Southbourne; s £55-70, d £75-97, f from £117; P🛜) In this serene, pristine B&B, stained glass and an elegant stairwell hint at the house's Edwardian age. Contemporary bedrooms are styled in muted colours; the pick is number 3, where a pint-sized balcony is an ideal spot to nibble one of the cookies or sweets you'll find scattered around. There's also a family room (sleeps four).

Amarillo
B&B ££

(☏01202-553884; www.amarillohotel.co.uk; 52 Frances Rd; s £35-45, d £70-90; P🛜) Amarillo's smart, stylish bedrooms are great value; expect jazzy wallpaper, snazzy throws and subtle lighting.

🍴 Eating

★ Urban Reef
BISTRO ££

(☏01202-443960; www.urbanreef.com; Undercliff Dr, Boscombe; mains £8-22; ◎9am-10pm, winter times vary; 🛜) On sunny weekends a cool crowd queues out the door at funky Urban Reef. No wonder: a waterfront deck and balcony, punchy coffee, top-notch snacks and quality, sustainable restaurant fare. On stormy days snuggle down beside the log burner and listen to the sound of sea.

Reef Encounter
BISTRO **££**

(www.reef-encounter.com; 42 Sea Rd, Boscombe; mains £7-15; ⏲11am-10pm Mon-Fri, 9am-10pm Sat & Sun, shorter hours winter; 🛜) Big squishy sofas, a mellow soundtrack and a sea-view terrace give this chilled-out eatery a surf bar vibe. Imaginative takes on brunch include smoked salmon, egg and avocado, or opt for tasty burgers, ribs and wings – perhaps while sipping a cool beer, watching the waves.

West Beach
SEAFOOD **££**

(☎01202-587785; www.west-beach.co.uk; Pier Approach; mains £15-35; ⏲noon-3pm & 6-10pm) The seafood and setting are hard to beat – bag a chair on the decking beside the sand, watch the waves lap Bournemouth Pier and tuck into perfectly cooked, perfectly fresh fish; perhaps grey mullet with chorizo and saffron oil, or a shellfish platter piled high with oysters, langoustines, cockles and clams.

Drinking & Nightlife

Sixty Million Postcards
PUB

(www.sixtymillionpostcards.com; 19 Exeter Rd; ⏲noon-midnight Sun-Thu, to 2am Fri & Sat) An oasis of hipster grunginess amid pound-a-pint Bournemouth, Sixty Million draws a decidedly beatnik crowd. Worn wooden floors and fringed lampshades frame events encompassing retro DJ sets, live bands, discos, movie and comedy nights, Sunday pub quizzes and jazz 'n' jumble sales.

Old Firestation
CLUB

(www.oldfirestation.co.uk; 36 Holdenhurst Rd; ⏲Thu-Sat 10pm-3am) Mixes touring gigs, club nights and student parties; music takes in indie, punk, rock 'n' roll and old skool.

ℹ️ Information

Rio Internet Cafe (☎01202-312021; 130 Commercial Rd; per hr £1.80; ⏲10am-7pm Mon-Fri, to 5pm Sat & Sun)

Tourist Office (☎01202-451734; www.bournemouth.co.uk; Pier Approach; ⏲10am-5pm Apr-Oct, to 4pm Nov-Mar) Set right beside Bournemouth Pier.

ℹ️ Getting There & Around

BUS

Direct National Express routes include the following:

Bristol £20, four hours, daily Monday to Saturday

London £15, 2½ hours, hourly

Oxford £18, 3½ hours, three daily

Southampton £8, 50 minutes, hourly

Useful local buses:

Poole bus M1/M2; £2.30, 25 minutes, every 15 minutes

Salisbury bus X3; £8.50, 1¼ hours, at least hourly

A Morebus Zone A Dayrider (adult/child £4.10/3.60) gives a day's unlimited travel in much of Poole, Bournemouth and neighbouring Christchurch.

TRAIN

Destinations include the following:

Dorchester South £12, 45 minutes, hourly

London Waterloo £24, 2¾ hours, hourly

Poole £4.10, 12 minutes, half-hourly

Weymouth £14.60, one hour, hourly

Poole

POP 147,645

In the quaint old port of Poole there's a whiff of money in the air: the town borders Sandbanks, a gorgeous beach backed by some of the world's most expensive chunks of real estate. Big bucks aside, Poole also boasts excellent eateries and is the springboard for a raft of water sports and some irresistible boat trips.

👁️ Sights

Brownsea Island
ISLAND

(NT; ☎01202-707744; www.nationaltrust.org.uk; adult/child £6.30/3.15; ⏲10am-5pm late Mar–Oct) On this small, wooded island in the middle of Poole Harbour, trails weave through heath and woods, past peacocks, red squirrels, red deer and a wealth of bird life – the water-framed views on to the Isle of Purbeck are stunning. Free guided walks focus on the wartime island, smugglers and pirates. Boats, run by **Brownsea Island Ferries** (☎01929-462383; www.brownseaislandferries.com; ⏲10am-5pm late Mar-Oct), leave from Poole Quay (adult/child return £10.75/6.75) and Sandbanks (adult/child return £6.50/5) at least hourly.

Waterfront Museum
MUSEUM

(☎01202-262600; www.boroughofpoole.com/museums; 4 High St; ⏲10am-5pm Mon-Sat, noon-5pm Sun) **FREE** The building alone is worth seeing – a beautifully restored 15th-century warehouse. The star exhibit is a 2300-year-old **Iron Age logboat** dredged up from Poole Harbour. At 10m long and 14 tonnes, it's the largest to be found in southern Britain and probably carried 18 people.

Sandbanks
BEACH

A 2-mile, wafer-thin peninsula of land that curls around the expanse of Poole Harbour, Sandbanks is studded with some of the most expensive houses in the world. But the white-sand beaches that border them are free, have some of the best UK water-quality standards and are home to a host of water-sports operators.

🛏 Sleeping

Old Townhouse
B&B ££

(☑ 01202-670950; www.theoldtownhouse.co.uk; 7 High St; s/d £65/95; 🐾) A delightful air of old England settles cosily over this quayside B&B. It's largely down to the gleaming wood, big burnished brass taps and furnishings that aren't afraid to echo heritage styles. A central setting and tiny patio add to the appeal.

Quayside
B&B ££

(☑ 01202-683733; www.poolequayside.co.uk; 9 High St; s/d/f £45/75/85; 🐾) Snug rooms in pine and bright, blocky prints in the heart of the old harbour.

Merchant House
B&B £££

(☑ 01202-661470; www.themerchanthouse.org.uk; 10 Strand St; s £110, d £140-160) Tucked just one street back from the water's edge, tall, red-brick Merchant House is boutiquery at its best. Hefty wood sculptures, wicker rocking chairs and crisp linen ensure it's stylish; the odd teddy bear keeps it cheery too.

🍴 Eating

Storm
SEAFOOD ££

(☑ 01202-674970; www.stormfish.co.uk; 16 High St; mains £16-20; ⊙6-10pm Mon-Sat) How rare is this: the dish you're eating could well have been caught by the chef? At chilled-out Storm, fisher Pete also rattles the pots 'n' pans, delighting in dishing up intense Goan fish curry, local pollack with Welsh rarebit crust, and spicy Dorset clams.

Poole Arms
PUB FOOD ££

(www.poolearms.co.uk; Poole Quay; mains £9-16; ⊙noon-9pm Sun-Thu, to 9.30pm Fri & Sat) The grub at this ancient pub is strong on locally landed seafood – try the homemade fish pie, local crab or pan-fried herring roe. Order some New Forest beer, then settle down in the snug, wood-lined bar with the locals, or on the terrace overlooking the quay.

★ Guildhall Tavern
FRENCH £££

(☑ 01202-671717; www.guildhalltavern.co.uk; 15 Market St; mains £18-20; ⊙noon-4pm & 6pm-midnight Tue-Sat) Poole's top table consistently delights as it combines local ingredients with lashings of French flair. Predictably, fish features strongly – the vanilla-infused confit salmon is superb; succulent skate wing comes *à la Provençale* – but *boeuf bourguignon* and rosemary-scented Dorset lamb also make carnivores smile. Book.

ℹ Information

Tourist Office (☑ 01202-262600; www.pooletourism.com; 4 High St; ⊙10am-5pm Sep-Jun, to 6pm Jul & Aug) Now set inside the Waterfront Museum.

ℹ Getting There & Around

BOAT

Brittany Ferries (☑ 0330 159 7000; www.brittany-ferries.com) sails between Poole and Cherbourg in France (4½ hours, one daily). Summer return prices start at around £85 for foot passengers and £310 for a car and two adults.

Sandbanks Ferry (☑ 01929-450203; www.sandbanksferry.co.uk; per pedestrian/car £1/4.10; ⊙7am-11pm) makes the four-minute trip from Sandbanks to Studland every 20 minutes. It's a shortcut from Poole to Swanage, Wareham and the Isle of Purbeck, but the summer queues can be a pain.

WATER SPORTS – POOLE HARBOUR

Poole Harbour's sheltered coasts may inspire you to get on the water. Operators cluster near the Sandbanks peninsula.

Poole Harbour Watersports (☑ 01202-700503; www.pooleharbour.co.uk; 284 Sandbanks Rd) Does lessons in stand-up paddleboarding (SUP; per 1½ hours £20), windsurfing (per three hours £45) and kitesurfing (per day £99), plus memorable kayak and SUP tours (per three hours £30 to £40).

Watersports Academy (☑ 01202-708283; www.thewatersportsacademy.com; 15 Banks Rd) Offers kitesurfing lessons (per day £100), windsurfer sessions (per two hours/days £25/110), sailing courses (per two hours/days £65/165) and wakeboarding and water-skiing lessons (per hour £60).

KINGSTON LACY

Dorset's must-see stately home **Kingston Lacy** (NT; ☏ 01202-883402; www.nationaltrust.org.uk; Wimborne Minster; adult/child £13.50/6.70; ⊘ house 11am-5pm Mar-Oct, to 4pm Nov-Dec, grounds 10am-6pm Mar-Oct, to 4pm Nov-Feb; P) looks every inch the setting for a period drama. It overflows with rich decor, most famously in the Spanish Room, which is smothered with gold and gilt. Other highlights are the hieroglyphics in the Egyptian Room and the elegant marble staircase and loggia. Artworks include the overwhelming ceiling fresco *The Separation of Night and Day,* by Guido Reni, and paintings by Rubens, Titian and Van Dyck. Kingston Lacy is 2.5 miles west of Wimborne.

BUS

Bournemouth bus M1/M2; £2.30, 25 minutes, every 15 minutes

London Victoria National Express; £25, 3½ hours, every two hours

Sandbanks bus 52; £3.50, 25 minutes, hourly Monday to Saturday

A Morebus Zone A Dayrider (adult/child £4.10/3.60) gives a day's unlimited travel in much of Poole and Bournemouth.

TAXI

Dial-a-Cab (☏ 01202-666822; www.pooletaxis.co.uk)

TRAIN

Bournemouth £4.10, 12 minutes, half-hourly

Dorchester South £10.20, 30 minutes, at least hourly

London Waterloo £17, 2¼ hours, half-hourly

Weymouth £14, 45 minutes, hourly

Corfe Castle

The massive, shattered ruins of Corfe Castle loom so dramatically from the landscape it's like blundering into a film set. The defensive fragments tower over an equally photogenic village, which bears the castle's name and makes for a romantic spot for a meal or an overnight stay.

⊙ Sights

★ **Corfe Castle**   CASTLE
(NT; ☏ 01929-481294; www.nationaltrust.org.uk; The Square; adult/child £8.50/4.25; ⊘ 10am-6pm Apr-Sep, to 4pm Oct-Mar) The startling, fractured battlements of one of Dorset's most famous landmarks were once home to Sir John Bankes, Charles I's right-hand man. The Civil War saw the castle besieged by Cromwellian forces; in 1646 the plucky Lady Bankes directed a six-week defence and the castle fell only after being betrayed from within. The Roundheads then gunpowdered Corfe Castle

apart; turrets and soaring walls still sheer off at precarious angles – the splayed-out gatehouse looks like it's just been blown up.

Swanage Steam Railway   HERITAGE RAILWAY
(☏ 01929-425800; www.swanagerailway.co.uk; adult/child return £12.50/7.60; ⊘ daily Apr-Oct, Sat & Sun Nov-Mar) Vintage steam trains puff at least hourly between Swanage and Norden (25 minutes), stopping at Corfe Castle.

🛏 Sleeping & Eating

Ammonite   B&B **£**
(☏ 01929-480188; www.ammonite-corfecastle.co.uk; 88 West St; s £55, d £65-85; P ☞) The pleasing bedrooms at this tranquil edge-of-village B&B feature pastels and pine, while the Aga-cooked breakfast includes local eggs, homemade jams and crusty bread from Corfe Castle's bakery.

Olivers   B&B **££**
(☏ 01929-477111; www.oliverscorfecastle.com; 5 West St; s/d/f £80/95/105) Tucked away in the heart of the old village in a charismatic street, Olivers combines honey-coloured beams with country-cottage chic: repro-heritage armchairs, mock-flock wallpaper and chunky wood furniture. Stylish, restful, great-value rooms.

Castle Inn   PUB FOOD **££**
(☏ 01929-480208; www.castleinncorfe.co.uk; 63 East St; mains £12-20; ⊘ noon-3pm & 6-9pm Mon-Sat, noon-9pm Sun; ☞) The locals' choice. Prepare to dine, beside flagstone floors and ancient beams festooned with fairy lights, on tasty pub classics, plus some specials-board surprises: perhaps sea bass given a kick by smoked paprika, or a gutsy chickpea stew.

ℹ Getting There & Away

Bus 40 shuttles hourly between Poole, Wareham, Corfe Castle and Swanage. The 15-minute trip to Wareham costs £4.40.

Lulworth Cove & Around

POP 740

In this stretch of southeast Dorset the coast steals the show. For millions of years the elements have been creating an intricate shoreline of curved bays, caves, stacks and weirdly wonderful rock formations – most notably the massive natural arch at Durdle Door.

The charismatic hamlet of Lulworth Cove is a pleasing jumble of thatched cottages and fishing gear, which winds down to a perfect crescent of white cliffs.

⊙ Sights & Activities

Lulworth Cove Heritage
Centre INTERPRETATION CENTRE
(☑ 01929-400587; www.lulworth.com; main car park, Lulworth Cove; ⊘ 10am-5pm) Excellent displays outline how geology and erosion have combined to shape the area's remarkable shoreline. Staff can advise about walks too.

Stair Hole Bay BAY
(Lulworth Cove) Stair Hole Bay sits just a few hundred yards west of Lulworth Cove. This diminutive semicircle is almost enclosed by cliffs that feature tiny rock arches – a route in that's popular with kayakers. On the landward side is the delightfully named Lulworth Crumple, where layers of rock form dramatically zigzagging folds.

★ Durdle Door LANDMARK
The poster child of Dorset's Jurassic Coast, this immense, sea-fringed, 150-million-year-old Portland stone arch was created by a combination of massive earth movements and erosion. Today it's framed by shimmering bays; bring a swimsuit and head down the hundreds of steps for an unforgettable dip. You can park at the top of the cliffs (two hours £3, four hours £4), but it's best to hike the coast path from Lulworth Cove (1 mile).

Lulworth Castle CASTLE
(EH; ☑ 01929-400352; www.lulworth.com; East Lulworth; adult/child £5/3; ⊘ 10.30am-5pm Sun-Fri Apr-Dec) A confection in creamy, dreamy white, this baronial pile looks more like a French chateau than a traditional English castle. Built in 1608 as a hunting lodge, it's survived extravagant owners, extensive remodelling and a disastrous fire in 1929. It has been extensively restored – check out the reconstructed kitchen and cellars, then climb the tower for sweeping coastal views. It costs £3 to park.

★ Jurassic Coast
Activities ADVENTURE SPORTS
(☑ 01305-835301; www.jurassiccoastactivities.co.uk; Lulworth Cove; per person £60; ⊘ up to 3 tours daily) This unmissable, three-hour paddle offers jaw-dropping views of Dorset's heavily eroded coast. Starting at Lulworth Cove, you glide through Stair Hole's caves and stacks, across Man O'War Bay, then under the stone arch at Durdle Door, stopping for swims and picnics along the way.

🛏 Sleeping

Lulworth YHA HOSTEL £
(☑ 0845 371 9331; www.yha.org.uk; School Lane, West Lulworth; dm £13-23, d £40; ℗) Hills stretch out alongside, and sheep bleat outside this cosy, chalet-style, edge-of-village hostel.

Durdle Door Holiday Park CAMPGROUND £
(☑ 01929-400200; www.lulworth.com; sites £26-43; ⊘ Mar-Oct; ℗) Attractive, spacious site, just minutes from the creamy cliffs, and 1.5 miles west of the hamlet of Lulworth Cove.

★ Lulworth Cove INN ££
(☑ 01929-400333; www.lulworth-coveinn.co.uk; Main Rd, Lulworth Cove; d £110-150; ℗ 🛜) What do you get for a £1.4-million refurbishment? A veritable vision of driftwood chic – whitewashed floorboards, aquamarine panels, painted wicker chairs and roll-top baths. Add cracking sea views, a mini roof terrace

---

LAWRENCE OF ARABIA

The tiny cottage Clouds Hill (NT; ☑ 01929-405616; www.nationaltrust.org.uk; near Bovington; adult/child £6/3; ⊘ 11am-5pm Mar-Oct; ℗) that was home to TE Lawrence (1888–1935), provides a compelling insight into a complex man. The British soldier became legendary after working with Arab tribes against Turkish forces in WWI. Look out for Lawrence's evocative desert-campaign photos, his French crusader castle sketches and the desk where he abridged Seven Pillars of Wisdom.

The four idiosyncratic rooms include a surprisingly comfortable cork-lined bathroom, an aluminium foil–lined bunk room and a heavily beamed music room. The house is much as Lawrence left it – he died at the age of 46 after a motorbike accident on a nearby road.

and top-quality gastropub grub (mains £9 to £15; food served from noon to 9pm) and you have an irresistible inn.

Bishops INN £££

(☑ 01929-400552; www.bishopslulworth.co.uk; Main Rd, Lulworth Cove; d £160-180; ❄ ✿) An idyllic setting, pared-down designs, top-notch linen and pamper-yourself toiletries combine to make this a memorable place to stay – especially if you opt for a room with Lulworth Cove views. Or just lounge beside the pool, which also overlooks that circle of bay. Tasty food (mains £15 to £20; served from noon to 2.30pm and 7pm to 9pm) spans lobster, risotto and *moules*.

✗ Eating & Drinking

Cove Fish SEAFOOD £

(☑ 01929-400807; Lulworth Cove; fish from £3, crab £3-4; ⊙ 10am-4pm Tue-Sun Easter-Sep, plus some winter weekends) The seafood piled high in this shed by the path to the beach has been caught by ninth- and 10th-generation fishermen Joe and Levi. Bag some fish for the barbecue, or settle at the wobbly table and tuck into Lulworth Cove crab (£3 to £4) or lobster – a meal that's travelled food yards not miles.

★ Castle PUB

(www.thecastleinn-lulworthcove.co.uk; West Lulworth; ⊙ noon-10pm; ☎) A head-spinning array of 40-plus ciders make this thatched pub a magnet for fans of the golden elixir. From quaffable Bumble Berry (4%) to epic Old Rosie (7.3%), this 'permanent cider festival' thoughtfully offers sampler trays (three different thirds of a pint) to help you get through a few.

❶ Getting There & Away

Bus 104 links Lulworth with Wareham (£5, 35 minutes, two daily, Monday to Saturday).

Dorchester & Around

POP 19,143

With Dorchester, you get two towns in one: a real-life, bustling county town and Thomas Hardy's fictional Casterbridge. The Victorian writer was born nearby and his literary locations can still be found among Dorchester's white- and red-brick Georgian terraces. Here you can also visit Hardy's former homes and see his original manuscripts. Add cracking archaeological sites and attractive places to eat and sleep and you have an appealing base for a night or two.

◉ Sights

★ Dorset County Museum MUSEUM

(☑ 01305-262735; www.dorsetcountymuseum.org; High West St; adult/child £5.35/3.50; ⊙ 10am-5pm Mon-Sat Apr-Oct, to 4pm Nov-Mar) The Thomas Hardy collection here is the world's largest, offering extraordinary insights into his creative process. You can see from text in Hardy's cramped handwriting where he's crossed out one word and substituted another. There's also an atmospheric reconstruction of his study at Max Gate and a letter in which Siegfried Sassoon requests permission to dedicate his first book of poems to Hardy.

Jurassic Coast fossil exhibits include a huge ichthyosaur and 1.8m plesiosaur fore paddle. Bronze and Iron Age finds from Maiden Castle include a treasure trove of coins and neck rings, while Roman artefacts include 70 gold coins, nail cleaners and (toe-curlingly) ear-picks.

Roman Town House HISTORIC BUILDING

(www.romantownhouse.co.uk; Northern Hay; ⊙ 24hr) FREE The knee-high flint walls and beautifully preserved mosaics here powerfully conjure up the Roman occupation of Dorchester (then Durnovaria). Peek into the summer dining room to see the underfloor heating system (hypocaust), where charcoal-warmed air circulated around pillars to produce a toasty 18°C (64°F).

Maiden Castle ARCHAEOLOGICAL SITE

(EH; www.english-heritage.org.uk; ⊙ dawn-dusk; ℗) FREE Occupying a massive slab of horizon on the southern fringes of Dorchester, Maiden Castle is the largest and most complex Iron Age hill fort in Britain. The first defences were built on the site around 500 BC – in its heyday it was densely populated with clusters of roundhouses and a network of roads. The Romans besieged and captured Maiden Castle in AD 43 – an ancient Briton skeleton with a Roman crossbow bolt in the spine was found at the fort.

⬛ Sleeping

★ Beggars Knap B&B ££

(☑ 01305-268191; www.beggarsknap.co.uk; 2 Weymouth Ave; s £60-80, d £80-100, f from £115; ℗ ☎) Despite the name, this altogether fabulous, vaguely decadent guesthouse is far from impoverished. Opulent rooms drip with chandeliers and gold brocades; beds draped in fine cottons range from French sleigh

THOMAS HARDY'S DORCHESTER

Thomas Hardy fans can hunt down the *Mayor of Casterbridge* locations hidden among modern Dorchester. They include **Lucetta's House** (Trinity St), a grand Georgian affair with ornate doorposts in Trinity St, while in parallel South St, a red-brick, mid-18th-century building (now a bank) is named as the inspiration for the **house of the mayor** (South St) himself. The **tourist office** (p245) sells book location guides.

Max Gate (NT; ☑ 01305-262538; www.nationaltrust.org.uk; Alington Ave; adult/child £6/3; ⊙ 11am-5pm Wed-Sun mid-Mar–Oct; ℗) Novelist Thomas Hardy was a trained architect and designed this attractive house, where he lived from 1885 until his death in 1928. *Tess of the D'Urbervilles* and *Jude the Obscure* were both written here, and the house contains several pieces of original furniture. It's a mile east of Dorchester, on the A352.

Hardy's Cottage (NT; ☑ 01305-262366; www.nationaltrust.org.uk; Higher Bockhampton; adult/child £6/3; ⊙ 11am-5pm Wed-Sun mid-Mar–Oct; ℗) This picturesque cob-and-thatch house is the birthplace of writer Thomas Hardy. It features evocative, sparsely furnished rooms and a lush garden. It's in Higher Bockhampton, 3 miles northeast of Dorchester.

to four-poster. You could pay much, much more and get something half as nice.

Westwood B&B ££
(☑ 01305-268018; www.westwoodhouse.co.uk; 29 High West St; s/d/f £75/95/130; ☏) A skilled designer has been at work in this 18th-century town house, producing a contemporary-meets-Georgian style: muted greens, brass lamps, subtle checks and minisofas. The modern bathrooms glint, while tiny fridges harbour fresh milk for your tea.

Yalbury Cottage HOTEL ££
(☑ 01305-262382; www.yalburycottage.com; Lower Bockhampton; s/d £85/120; ℗ ☏) It's almost your archetypal English cottage: framed by flowers and crowned by moss-studded thatch. Inside fresh, simple, gently rustic bedrooms overlook the garden or fields. The restaurant (two/three courses £33/38) serves up top-notch takes on British classics in convivial, clublike rooms; it's open 6.30pm to 8.30pm daily and noon to 2pm Sunday; bookings required.

It's in Lower Bockhampton, 3 miles east of Dorchester.

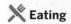 Eating

★ No 6 FRENCH ££
(☑ 01305-267679; www.no6-restaurant.co.uk; 6 North Sq; mains £20; ⊙ noon-2pm & 6.30-9pm Tue-Fri, 6-10pm Sat) The local goodies here are dished up with more than a soupçon of French finesse. Expect oven-roasted duck with a Normandy cider sauce; net-fresh, simply cooked fish, and a corker of a West Country–themed cheese board, showcasing caved-aged Cheddar, Somerset Brie and smoked Dorset Red.

Trinity SEAFOOD ££
(☑ 01305-757428; Trinity St; mains from £11-20; ⊙ noon-3pm & 7-10pm Wed-Sat) Trinity's open-plan kitchen-dining room means mouthwatering aromas waft around you. A menu that spans continents means those aromas might involve anything from smoked haddock chowder and hake linguine to jerk fish. It's no frills but great fun and the seafood is super fresh. Cash only.

Sienna MODERN BRITISH ££
(☑ 01305-250022; www.siennadorchester.co.uk; 36 High West St; mains £16-19; ⊙ noon-2pm & 7-9pm Tue-Sat) The menu at Sienna is peppered with rarities; expect to find barbecue broccoli, jerk carrot or squid ink arranged on your plate. The puddings are imaginative too – perhaps try the chocolate mousse with hints of prune, orange and earl grey.

☆ Entertainment

Plaza Cinema CINEMA
(☑ 01305-262488; www.plazadorchester.com; Trinity St) A four-screen art-deco gem, resplendent in red, black and gold, where the glamorous setting upstages the movies.

ℹ Information

Tourist Office (☑ 01305-267992; www.visit-dorset.com; Antelope Walk; ⊙ 9am-5pm Mon-Sat Apr-Oct, to 4pm Nov-Mar)

ℹ Getting There & Away

BUS

London Victoria National Express; £23, four hours, one daily

BATH & SOUTHWEST ENGLAND DORCHESTER & AROUND

JURASSIC COAST

The kind of massive, hands-on geology lesson you wish you had had at school, the Jurassic Coast is England's first natural World Heritage Site, putting it on a par with the Great Barrier Reef and the Grand Canyon. This striking shoreline stretches from Exmouth in East Devon to Swanage in Dorset, encompassing 185 million years of the Earth's history in just 95 miles. It means you can walk, in just a few hours, many millions of years in geological time.

It began when layers of rocks formed, their varying compositions determined by different climates: desertlike conditions gave way to higher then lower sea levels. Massive earth movements then tilted all the rock layers, forcing most of the oldest formations to the west, and the youngest to the east. Next, erosion exposed the different strata.

The differences are very tangible. Devon's rusty-red Triassic rocks are 200–250 million years old. Lyme Regis' fossil-rich, dark-clay Jurassic cliffs are 190 million years old. Pockets of much younger, creamy-coloured Cretaceous rocks (a mere 65–140 million years old) pop up, notably around Lulworth Cove, where erosion has sculpted a stunning display of bays, stacks and rock arches.

The coast's website (www.jurassiccoast.com) is a great information source; also look out locally for the highly readable *Official Guide to the Jurassic Coast* (£4.95), or buy it at www.jurassiccoasttrust.org.

Lyme Regis Bus X51; £4.60, 1¼ hours, hourly Monday to Saturday

Sherborne Bus 216 via Cerne Abbas; £4.50, one hour, four to six daily Monday to Saturday

Weymouth Bus 10; £1.80, 30 minutes, half-hourly

TRAIN

Dorchester has two train stations.

Trains leave Dorchester West for Bath and Bristol (£20, three hours, at least six daily).

Services from Dorchester South, running at least hourly, include the following:

Bournemouth £12, 45 minutes

London Waterloo £32, 2¾ hours

Southampton £25, 1½ hours

Weymouth £5, 10 minutes

Cerne Abbas & the Cerne Giant

If you had to describe an archetypal sleepy Dorset village, you'd come up with something a lot like Cerne Abbas: houses run the gamut of English architectural styles, roses climb countless doorways and half-timbered houses frame a honey-coloured, 12th-century church. But this village also packs one heck of a surprise: the Cerne Giant; a vast chalk figure of a naked man.

⊙ Sights

★**Cerne Giant**   LANDMARK

(⊙24hr; P) FREE Rarely do you find such a nudge-nudge, wink-wink tourist attraction.

Nude, full frontal and notoriously well endowed, this hillside chalk figure is revealed in all his glory. And he's in a stage of excitement that wouldn't be allowed in most magazines. The giant is around 60m high and 51m wide and his age remains a mystery; some claim he's Roman but the first historical reference comes in 1694, when three shillings were set aside for his repair. These days a car park provides grandstand views.

The Victorians found it all deeply embarrassing and allowed grass to grow over his most outstanding feature. Today the hill is grazed by sheep and cattle, though only the sheep are allowed to do their nibbling over the giant – the cows would do too much damage to his lines.

🛏 Sleeping & Eating

★**New Inn**   INN ££

(📞01300-341274; www.thenewinncerneabbas.co.uk; 14 Long St; d £95-140, ste £170; P🛜) Only in England could the New Inn actually be more than 400 years old. Rooms are crammed with heritage character; expect dark panelling, vast gilt mirrors and beams in the bathrooms. Or opt for the modern annex where painted wood and blue-and-white furnishings rule. The suites (especially Cerne) are gorgeous, boasting stand-alone baths in the bedrooms.

Abbots   B&B ££

(📞01300-341349; www.abbotsbedandbreakfast.co.uk; 7 Long St; s/f £60/130, d £75-85; 🛜) The top-floor rooms here are big on atmosphere and small on head space, with duck-orregret-it lintels for those over 6ft. It's charming throughout though, with rooms decked-out in light grey, lemon and blue. The cakes in the cafe (open 10am to 4pm) are real diet busters.

❶ Getting There & Away

Dorchester is 8 miles south. Bus X11 (four to six daily Monday to Saturday) goes to Dorchester (£2.60, 30 minutes) and Sherborne (£3, 30 minutes).

Weymouth

POP 52,168

At just over 225 years old, Weymouth is a grand dame of a resort with a couple of tricks up her faded sleeve. Candy-striped kiosks and deckchairs line a golden, 3-mile beach; chuck in cockles and chippies and prepare to promenade down seaside memory lane. But Weymouth is about more than just that sandy shore; the town boasts a bustling harbour, some superb seafood restaurants and easy access to the water sports centres of the neighbouring Isle of Portland.

◎ Sights & Activities

Weymouth Beach   BEACH
The nostalgia-inducing offerings along Weymouth's fine sandy shore could see you marvelling at highly skilled sand sculptors, renting a deckchair or pedalo, descending a helter-skelter, trampoline-bouncing, watching Punch and Judy shows, or riding a donkey.

Nothe Fort   FORT
(☑ 01305-766626; www.nothefort.org.uk; Barrack Rd; adult/child £8/1; ◷ 10.30am-5.30pm Apr-Sep) Weymouth's photogenic 19th-century defences are studded with cannons, searchlights and 30cm coastal guns. Exhibits detail Dorset's Roman invasion, a Victorian soldier's drill and Weymouth in WWII.

Sea Life   AQUARIUM
(☑ 0871 423 2110; www.sealifeweymouth.com; Lodmoor Country Park; £23; ◷ 10am-5pm Apr-Oct, to 4pm Nov-Mar; ℗) Highlights include sharks, penguins and seahorses. Tickets fall to £16.50 if bought in advance.

Coastline Cruises   BOATING
(☑ 01305-785000; www.coastlinecruises.co.uk; Brewers Quay; adult/child return £10/6; ◷ 10.30am daily Apr-Oct) This wind-blown 90-minute jaunt passes Weymouth's historic fortifications and crosses Portland Harbour's vast 2012 Olympic sailing waters before sailing into Portland Harbour. Boats leave from Weymouth Harbour's west side.

🛏 Sleeping

★ Roundhouse   B&B **££**
(☑ 01305-761010; www.roundhouse-weymouth.com; 1 The Esplanade; d £85-145; ⍾) The decor here is as gently eccentric as the owner – vivid interiors combine sky blue, purple and shocking pink with fluffy cushions and snazzy modern art. But the best bit is the views; you can see both the beach out front and the harbour behind from all bedrooms.

B+B   B&B **££**
(☑ 01305-761190; www.bb-weymouth.com; 68 The Esplanade; s £60-80, d £70-100; ℗ ⍾) As far a cry from chintz and pine as you can imagine, this style-conscious B&B opts for minimalist rooms (some have sea views) and a host of freebies – mineral water, biscuits and espressos that are best enjoyed in the hip 1st-floor lounge overlooking the bay.

Old Harbour View   B&B **££**
(☑ 01305-774633; www.oldharbourviewweymouth.co.uk; 12 Trinity Rd; s/d £70/98; ℗ ⍾) In this pristine Georgian terrace, you get boating themes in the fresh, white bedrooms, and boats right outside the front door. One room overlooks the busy quay, the other faces the back.

✖ Eating

★ Marlboro   FISH & CHIPS **£**
(www.marlbororestaurant.co.uk; 46 St Thomas St; mains from £7.50; ◷ noon-9.45pm) A sustainable slant and a 40-year history help lift this traditional chippy, just yards from Weymouth's quay, above its rivals – mackerel features among the long list of super-fresh fish. Take it away and duck the seagulls or get munching in the bay-windowed, licensed cafe (open till 8pm).

Dining Room Steakhouse   MODERN BRITISH **££**
(☑ 01305-783008; www.thediningroomweymouth.co.uk; 67 St Mary St; mains £10-25; ◷ 6-9pm Wed-Sat) Despite the name, it's not all steaks here; you could also plump for grilled lobster, marinated lamb or slow-braised barbecue ribs. But it's the sirloin, fillet, rib-eye and T-bone most folks comes for. That or a Tomahawk – a whopping 46oz slab of meat that feeds two to three.

Dorset Burger Co   BURGERS **££**
(DBC; ☑ 01305-780888; www.thedorsetburgercompany.co.uk; 6 King St; burgers £9-13; ◷ 6-8pm

WATER SPORTS – PORTLAND HARBOUR

At 890-hectare Portland Harbour, just south of Weymouth, you can glide in 2012 Olympic sailing waters. Local waters also offer superb diving, with a huge variety of depths, seascapes and wrecks. In addition to local operators, Weymouth's **Old Harbour Dive Centre** (☑ 01305-760888; www.oldharbourdivecentre.co.uk; 11 Nothe Pde) runs a range of PADI courses (90 minutes/four days £45/430), hires equipment and charters RIBs.

OTC (☑ 07817 717904; http://uk.otc-windsurf.com; Osprey Quay, Portland Harbour) Offers lessons in stand-up paddleboarding (SUP; one/two hours £25/40) and windsurfing (£45/95/185 per two hours/one day/two days). It also rents out SUP boards (per hour £10) and windsurfing boards and sails (per hour £15).

Andrew Simpson Sailing Centre (☑ 01305-457400; www.andrewsimpsonsailing.org; Osprey Quay, Portland Harbour) Runs RYA lessons (adult/child per two days £175/199).

Dive Beyond (☑ 01305-861441; www.divebeyond.co.uk; Castletown, Portland) Runs a five-day PADI open-water course (£475), rents equipment (full kit per day £45) and runs RIB trips to dive sites (from £15).

Mon-Fri, noon-8.30pm Sat & Sun) Hand-patted, juicy, chargrilled burgers, made mostly from Dorset produce.

No 4 SEAFOOD ££
(☑ 01305-780010; www.no4.restaurant; 4 Trinity Rd; mains £13-20; ☺ noon-2pm Tue-Sun, 6.30-9pm Tue-Sat) Fittingly, given the many fishing boats moored right outside, at driftwood-dotted No 4 the seafood is as fresh as it comes. Feast on a simply grilled catch of the day that's dotted with capers or laced with lemon butter. Or plump for some flavour-packed fish soup.

ℹ Information

Tourist Office (☑ 01305-561983; www.visit-dorset.com; 7 Coburg Place, St Thomas St; ☺ 10am-5pm Mon-Sat year-round, plus 10am-4pm Sun Apr-Oct)

ℹ Getting There & Away

BUS

The Jurassic Coaster bus X53 (four daily to hourly, no service winter Sundays) travels from Weymouth to Wareham (50 minutes), Poole (1½ hours), Abbotsbury (35 minutes), Lyme Regis (1¾ hours), Axminster (two hours) and Exeter (three hours). A Day Rider ticket costs adult/child £10/5; shorter fares are available.

Dorchester Bus 10; £1.80, 30 minutes, half-hourly

Fortuneswell, Isle of Portland Bus 1; £1.80, 20 minutes, four per hour

London National Express; £23, 4¼ hours, one direct daily

Portland Bill, Isle of Portland Bus 501; £1.80, 45 minutes, five daily June to September only

TRAIN

At least hourly services include the following:

Bournemouth £15, one hour

Dorchester South £5, 10 minutes

London Waterloo £25, three hours

Services every two hours:

Bath £26, two hours

Bristol £18, 2¾ hours

Isle of Portland

The 'Isle' of Portland is a hard, high comma of rock fused to the rest of Dorset by the ridge of Chesil Beach. On its 150m central plateau, a quarrying past still holds sway, evidenced by huge craters and large slabs of limestone. Portland offers jaw-dropping views down on to 18-mile Chesil Beach and the neighbouring Fleet – Britain's biggest tidal lagoon.

Proud, and at times bleak and rough around the edges, Portland is decidedly different from the rest of Dorset, and is all the more compelling because of it. The Isle's industrial heritage, water-sport facilities, rich bird life and starkly beautiful cliffs make it worth at least a day trip.

◎ Sights

★ **Tout Quarry** OUTDOORS
(near Fortuneswell; ☺ 24hr; ℗) FREE Portland's white limestone has been quarried for centuries and has been used in some of the world's finest buildings, such as the British Museum and St Paul's Cathedral. Tout Quarry's disused workings now house 53 sculptures that have been carved into the rock in situ, resulting in a fascinating combination

of the raw material, the detritus of the quarrying process and the beauty of chiselled works.

Portland Castle
CASTLE

(EH; ☑01305-820539; www.english-heritage.org.uk; Liberty Rd, Chiswell; adult/child £5.30/3.10; ⊙10am-6pm Apr-Sep, to 5pm Oct) A particularly fine product of Henry VIII's castle-building spree, with expansive views over Portland harbour.

Portland Lighthouse
LIGHTHOUSE

(☑01305-821050; www.trinityhouse.co.uk; Portland Bill; adult/child £7/5; ⊙10am-5pm Jun-Sep; ℗) For a real sense of Portland's remote nature, head to its southern tip, Portland Billt, to climb the 41m-high, candy-striped lighthouse. It offers breathtaking views of rugged cliffs and the Race, a surging vortex of conflicting tides. The interactive displays in the former lighthousekeepers' cottages include Into the Dark; a re-creation of sailing into stormy seas.

The lighthouse is also open some weekends outside the main season – call for the latest times.

🛏 Sleeping & Eating

Portland YHA
HOSTEL £

(☑0845-3719339; www.yha.org.uk; Castle Rd, Castletown; dm £19, q £39-60; ℗ 🗟) Comfy, rambling Edwardian house with sea views from most dorms.

⭐ Queen Anne House
B&B ££

(☑01305-820028; www.queenannehouse.co.uk; 2 Fortuneswell; s £55-60, d £80-95; 🗟) It's impossible to know which room to pick: White, with skylight, beams and a hobbit-esque door; Lotus, with its grand furniture; ornate Oyster with its half-tester bed; or the suite with a French bath and miniconservatory. It doesn't matter though – they're all great value and gorgeous.

⭐ Crab House Cafe
SEAFOOD ££

(☑01305-788867; www.crabhousecafe.co.uk; Portland Rd, Wyke Regis; mains £11-22; ⊙noon-2pm & 6-8.30pm Wed-Sat, noon-3.30pm Sun) This is where the locals make for on hot summer days, to sit beside the Fleet Lagoon amid beach-shack-chic tucking into fresh-as-it-gets seafood. Fish is enlivened by chilli, curry, lemon and herbs; crab comes spicy Chinese-style or whole for you to crack; and the oysters come with either pesto and Parmesan or bacon and cream.

Cove House
PUB FOOD ££

(☑01305-820895; www.thecovehouseinn.co.uk; Chiswell Seafront; mains £10-18; ⊙noon-2.30pm & 6-9pm Mon-Fri, noon-9pm Sat & Sun) Extraordinary Chesil Beach views, memorable sunsets and great grub (try the Lyme Bay scallops) in a history-rich fishers' inn.

❶ Getting There & Away

Bus 1 runs from Weymouth to Fortuneswell (£1.80, 20 minutes, four per hour).

Between June and September only bus 501 goes from Weymouth to Portland Bill (£1.80, 45 minutes, five daily).

Chesil Beach

One of the most breathtaking beaches in Britain, Chesil is 18 miles long, 15m high and moving inland at the rate of 5m a century. This mind-boggling, 100-million-tonne pebble ridge is the baby of the Jurassic Coast. A mere 6000 years old, its stones range from pea-sized in the west to hand-sized in the east.

◉ Sights & Activities

Chesil Beach Centre
INTERPRETATION CENTRE

(Fine Foundation; ☑01305-206191; www.dorsetwildlifetrust.org.uk; Ferrybridge; ⊙10am-5pm Easter-Sep, to 4pm Oct-Easter) FREE This centre, at the start of the bridge to Portland, is a great gateway to the beach. The pebble ridge is at its highest here – 15m compared to 7m at Abbotsbury. From the car park an energy-sapping hike up sliding pebbles leads to the constant surge and rattle of waves on stones and dazzling views of the sea, with the thin pebble line and the expanse of the Fleet Lagoon behind.

⭐ Abbotsbury Swannery
WILDLIFE RESERVE

(☑01305-871130; www.abbotsbury-tourism.co.uk; New Barn Rd, Abbotsbury; adult/child £12/9; ⊙10am-5pm late Mar–Oct) Every May some 600 free-flying swans choose to nest at this swannery, which shelters in the Fleet Lagoon, protected by the ridge of Chesil Beach. Wandering the network of trails that winds between the swans' nests is an awe-inspiring experience that's punctuated by occasional territorial displays (think snuffling coughs and stand-up flapping), ensuring that even the liveliest children are stilled.

The swannery is at the picturesque village of Abbotsbury, 10 miles from Weymouth off the B3157.

Lyme Regis

POP 3637

Fantastically fossiliferous Lyme Regis packs a heavyweight historical punch. Rock-hard relics of the past pop out repeatedly from the surrounding cliffs – exposed by the landslides of a retreating shoreline. Lyme is now a pivot point of the Unesco-listed Jurassic Coast: fossil fever is definitely in the air and everyone, from proper palaeontologists to those out for a bit of fun, can engage in a spot of coastal rummaging. Add sandy beaches and some delightful places to sleep and eat, and you get a charming base for explorations.

◎ Sights

Lyme Regis Museum   MUSEUM
(✆ 01297-443370; www.lymeregismuseum.co.uk; Bridge St; adult/child £4/free; ◉ 10am-5pm Easter-Oct, 11am-4pm Wed-Sun Nov-Easter) In 1814 local teenager Mary Anning found the first full ichthyosaur skeleton near Lyme Regis, propelling the town on to the world stage. A famous fossilist in her day, Miss Anning did much to pioneer the science of modern-day palaeontology. This museum, on the site of her former home, tells her story and exhibits spectacular fossils and prehistoric finds.

Cobb   LANDMARK
First built in the 13th century, Lyme's iconic, curling sea defences have been strengthened and extended over the years, and so don't present the elegant line they once did, but it's still hard to resist wandering their length to the tip.

Dinosaurland   MUSEUM
(✆ 01297-443541; www.dinosaurland.co.uk; Coombe St; adult/child £5/4; ◉ 10am-5pm mid-Feb–mid-Oct) This joyful, mini, indoor Jurassic Park overflows with fossilised remains; look out for belemnites, a plesiosaurus and an impressive locally found ichthyosaur. Lifelike dinosaur models will thrill youngsters – the rock-hard tyrannosaur eggs and 73kg dinosaur dung will have them in raptures.

Town Mill   HISTORIC BUILDING
(✆ 01297-444042; www.townmill.org.uk; Mill Lane; requested donation £2.50; ◉ 11am-2pm Mon-Fri, to 4pm Sat & Sun Apr-Oct) FREE An atmospheric, creaking, grinding, 14th-century working watermill. Cafes, art galleries, a jewellery workshop and microbrewery sit alongside. Winter hours vary; call to check.

🏃 Activities

Undercliff   WALKING
This wildly undulating, 304-hectare nature reserve just west of Lyme was formed by massive landslides. They've left a challenging hiking landscape of slipped cliffs, fissures and ridges, where paths snake between dense vegetation, exposed tree roots and tangles of brambles. The Undercliff starts a mile west of central Lyme Regis; follow footpath signs from Holmbush Car Park.

🛌 Sleeping

Sanctuary   B&B £
(✆ 01297-445815; www.lyme-regis.demon.co.uk; 65 Broad St; s/d £45/56) A B&B for bibliophiles: the charming, chintzy, volume-filled bedrooms here sit inside a four-floor, 18-room bookshop. Ancient tomes that just beg to be perused are everywhere – they can delay you en route to (the excellent) breakfast, but handily there's a wonderfully relaxed vibe. And yes – that price *is* right.

FOSSIL HUNTING

Fossil fever is catching. Lyme Regis sits in one of the most unstable sections of Britain's coast, and regular landslips mean nuggets of prehistory keep tumbling from the cliffs.

Joining a guided walk aids explorations. Three miles east of Lyme, the **Charmouth Heritage Coast Centre** (✆ 01297-560772; www.charmouth.org; Lower Sea Lane, Charmouth; ◉ 10.30am-4.30pm daily Easter-Oct, Thu-Sun Nov-Easter) FREE runs one to seven trips a week (adult/child £7.50/3). Or, in Lyme itself, **Lyme Regis Museum** (p250) holds three to seven walks a week (adult/child £11/6); local expert **Brandon Lennon** (✆ 07854 377519; www.lymeregisfossilwalks.com; adult/child £8/6; ◉ Sat-Mon) also leads expeditions. All walks are popular, so book early.

For the best chances of a find, visit within two hours of low water. If you do hunt by yourself, official advice is to check tide times and collect on a falling tide, observe warning signs, keep away from cliffs, only pick up from the beach and always leave some behind for others. Oh, and tell the experts if you find a stunner.

Coombe House   B&B ££
(📞01297-443849; www.coombe-house.co.uk; 41
Coombe St; d £64-72, 5-person apt per week £360-
630; 🅿) The airy, easygoing, stylish bedrooms in this fabulous-value guesthouse are
full of bay windows, wicker and white wood.
Breakfast is delivered to your room on a trolley, complete with homemade bread and a
toaster – perfect for a lazy lie-in in Lyme.

★ **Hix Townhouse**   B&B £££
(📞01297-442499; www.hixtownhouse.co.uk; 1
Pound St; d £120-150, ste £165; 📶) With its
witty designer decor, luxury flourishes and
in-town location, this 18th-century terrace
is hard to resist. Each room playfully conjures a leisure theme (think gardening, fishing, reading etc); the pick is Sailing with its
mock portholes, artfully arranged ropes,
mini roof terrace and gorgeous sea views.

✖ Eating

★ **Alexandra**   BRITISH £
(📞01297-442010; www.hotelalexandra.co.uk;
Pound St; afternoon tea £7.50-29; ⏰3-5.30pm;
🅿📶) It's like the setting for an Agatha
Christie, minus the murder. Wicker chairs
dot manicured lawns, glittering Lyme Bay
sweeps out behind. The perfect spot for a
proper English afternoon tea, complete with
scones, jam and dainty sandwiches.

Harbour Inn   PUB FOOD ££
(📞01297-442299; www.harbourinnlymeregis.
co.uk; Marine Pde; mains £9-25; ⏰noon-2.30pm
& 6-9pm) A flower-framed, beachside veran-
dah, smart but snug interior and some of the
best bistro–pub grub in town – the bouillabaisse is suitably intense.

Millside   MODERN BRITISH ££
(📞01297-445999; www.themillside.co.uk; 1 Mill
Lane; mains £13-18; ⏰noon-2.30pm Tue-Sun, 6.30-
9pm Tue-Sat) West Country foodstuffs pack
the menu in this stylish eatery, from juicy
burgers topped with Cheddar from Cheddar,
to fish freshly caught on the local day boats.
Millside's compact terrace makes a tempting
spot for lunch on a sunny day.

★ **Hix Oyster & Fish House**   SEAFOOD £££
(📞01297-446910; www.hixoysterandfishhouse.
co.uk; Cobb Rd; mains £13-23; ⏰noon-10pm) Expect sweeping views of the Cobb and dazzling food at this super-stylish, open-plan
cabin. Lyme Bay shellfish soup comes with
Cornish pastis liqueur; Newlyn hake head
comes with Poole cockles. Perhaps start by

WORTH A TRIP

FORDE ABBEY
....

Built in the 12th century as a Cistercian
monastery, **Forde Abbey** (📞01460-
220231; www.fordeabbey.co.uk; Chard; house
adult/child £12.50/free, gardens £10/free;
⏰ house noon-5pm Tue-Fri & Sun May-Oct,
gardens 10am-5.30pm daily year-round) has
been a private home since 1649. The
building boasts magnificent plasterwork
ceilings and fine tapestries but the gardens steal the show: 12 hectares of lawns,
ponds, shrubberies and flower beds with
hundreds of rare and beautiful species.
Forde Abbey is 10 miles north of Lyme
Regis; public transport is a nonstarter.

---

slurping oysters: Brownsea Island or Portland molluscs come at £2.75 a pop.

ℹ Information

Tourist Office (📞01297-442138; www.visit-
dorset.com; Church St; ⏰10am-5pm Mon-Sat
Apr-Oct, to 3pm Nov-Mar)

ℹ Getting There & Away

Bus X51 (£4.60, 1¼ hours, hourly Monday to
Saturday) shuttles to Dorchester.

Bus X53 (four daily to hourly, no service winter
Sundays) goes west to Exeter (£7.20) and east to
Weymouth (£7.40) via Chesil Beach.

Sherborne
POP 9581

Sherborne gleams with a mellow, oran-
gey-yellow stone - it's been used to build a
cluster of 15th-century buildings and the
impressive abbey church at their core. This
serene town exudes wealth.

◉ Sights

Sherborne Abbey   CHURCH
(📞01935-812452; www.sherborneabbey.com;
Abbey Cl; suggested donation £4; ⏰8am-6pm
Apr-Sep, to 4pm Oct-Mar) At the height of its
influence, the magnificent Abbey Church of
St Mary the Virgin was the central cathedral
of 26 succeeding Saxon bishops. Established
early in the 8th century, it became a Benedictine abbey in 998 and functioned as a
cathedral until 1075. The church has mesmerising fan vaulting that's the oldest in the
country, a central tower supported by Saxon
Norman piers and an 1180 Norman porch.

Sherborne Old Castle
CASTLE

(EH; ☑ 01935-812730; www.english-heritage.org.uk; Castleton; adult/child £4/2.40; ☺ 10am-5pm Apr-Jun, Sep & Oct, to 6pm Jul & Aug) These days the epitome of a picturesque ruin, Sherborne's Old Castle was built by Roger, Bishop of Salisbury, in 1120 – Elizabeth I gave it to her one-time favourite Sir Walter Raleigh in the late 16th century. It became a Royalist stronghold during the English Civil War, but Cromwell reduced it to rubble after a 16-day siege in 1645, leaving just the fractured southwest gatehouse, great tower and north range.

Sherborne New Castle
CASTLE

(☑ 01935-812072; www.sherbornecastle.com; New Rd; house & gardens adult/child £11/free, gardens only £6/free; ☺ 11am-5pm Tue-Thu, Sat & Sun Apr-Oct) Sir Walter Raleigh began building the impressive Sherborne New Castle in 1594, but only got as far as the central block before being imprisoned by James I. James promptly sold the castle to Sir John Digby who added the splendid wings you see today. In 1753 the grounds received a mega-makeover at the hands of landscape-gardener extraordinaire Capability Brown who added a massive lake and the 12-hectare waterside gardens.

☞ Tours

Walking Tours
WALKING

(www.sherbornewalks.co.uk; tours £5; ☺ 10.30am Tue & Thu Jul-Sep) Ninety-minute trips exploring the photogenic old town, leaving from the tourist office.

🛏 Sleeping & Eating

★Cumberland House
B&B ££

(☑ 01935-817554; www.bandbdorset.co.uk; Green Hill; d £75-80; P 🛜) Artistry oozes from these history-rich rooms – bright scatter rugs sit on flagstone floors; lemon and oatmeal walls undulate between wonderfully wonky beams. Gourmet breakfasts include freshly squeezed orange juice; arrive around 4pm and expect an offer of tea, taken in the garden or beside the fire.

Stoneleigh Barn
B&B ££

(☑ 01935-389288; www.stoneleighbarn.co.uk; North Wootton; s £60-75, d £80-95, f from £160; P 🛜) Warm, weathered stone and extensive gardens ensure this 18th-century barn delights on the outside. Inside, exposed trusses frame spacious rooms that are decorated in line with the colours of their namesake flowers; choose from orchid, lilac or rose. Stoneleigh is 3 miles southeast of Sherborne.

George
PUB FOOD ££

(www.thegeorgesherborne.co.uk; 4 Higher Cheap St; mains £9-13; ☺ noon-2.30pm & 6-9pm; 🛜) It's five centuries since Sherborne's oldest, cosiest inn pulled its first pint; today it signals its age with wooden settles polished smooth by countless behinds. The food is enduring pub grub fare: robust steaks, ham and egg, homemade puds and a 'roast of the day'.

★Green
MODERN BRITISH £££

(☑ 01935-813821; www.greenrestaurant.co.uk; 3 The Green; mains £20-25; ☺ noon-2.30pm & 6.30-9.30pm Tue-Sat) In this affable, elegant eatery, the furniture is more chic than shabby and the food is pure West Country élan. Dorset goodies might include steamed Lyme Bay brill made fragrant with wild garlic, or saddle of local rabbit studded with wild mushrooms. For a great-value feed, plump for the cracking *menu du jour* (three courses £20).

❶ Information

Tourist Office (☑ 01935-815341; www.visit-dorset.com; Digby Rd; ☺ 9.30am-4pm Mon-Sat Apr-Nov, to 3pm Dec-Mar)

❶ Getting There & Away

BUS

Dorchester (Bus X1; £4.50, one hour, four to six daily Monday to Saturday) Via Cerne Abbas (30 minutes)

Yeovil Bus 57/58; £4.50, 15 minutes, 10 daily Monday to Saturday

TRAIN

Hourly services:

Exeter £18, 1¼ hours

London Waterloo £20, 2½ hours

Salisbury £14, 45 minutes

Wiltshire

Wiltshire is rich in the reminders of ritual and packed with not-to-be-missed sights. Its verdant landscape is littered with more mysterious stone circles, processional avenues and ancient barrows than anywhere else in Britain. It's a place that teases and tantalises the imagination – here you'll experience the prehistoric majesty of Stonehenge and the atmospheric stone ring at Avebury. Add the serene 800-year-old cathedral at Salisbury, the supremely stately homes at Stourhead and Longleat and the impossibly pretty village of Lacock, and you have a county crammed full of English charm waiting to be explored.

ℹ️ Information

There's a large tourist office in **Salisbury** (p256). **Visit Wiltshire** (www.visitwiltshire.co.uk) also has tourist information.

ℹ️ Getting There & Around

BUS

Wiltshire's bus coverage can be patchy, especially in the northwest.

First (www.firstgroup.com) Serves west Wiltshire.

Salisbury Reds (www.salisburyreds.co.uk) Covers Salisbury and many rural areas; offers one-day Rover Tickets (£8.50) and seven-day passes (Salisbury area £13.50, network-wide £24).

Stagecoach (www.stagecoachbus.com) Provides services around Swindon and Salisbury.

TRAIN

Rail lines run from London Waterloo to Salisbury (£25, 1½ hours, half-hourly), and beyond to Exeter and Plymouth, branching off north to Bradford-on-Avon, Bath and Bristol.

Salisbury

POP 40,300

Centred on a majestic cathedral that's topped by the tallest spire in England, Salisbury makes an appealing Wiltshire base. It's been an important provincial city for more than a thousand years, and its streets form an architectural timeline ranging from medieval walls and half-timbered Tudor town houses to Georgian mansions and Victorian villas. Salisbury is also a lively, modern town, boasting plenty of bars and restaurants, plus a concentrated cluster of excellent museums.

👁 Sights

⭐**Salisbury Cathedral**   CATHEDRAL
(📞01722-555120;   www.salisburycathedral.org.uk; Cathedral Close; requested donation adult/child £7.50/free; ☺9am-5pm Mon-Sat, noon-4pm Sun) England is endowed with countless stunning churches, but few can hold a candle to the grandeur and sheer spectacle of 13th-century Salisbury Cathedral. This early English Gothic–style structure has an elaborate exterior decorated with pointed arches and flying buttresses, and a sombre, austere interior designed to keep its congregation suitably pious. Its statuary and tombs are outstanding; don't miss the daily tower tours and the cathedral's original, 13th-century copy of the **Magna Carta** (www.salisburycathedral.org.uk; Cathedral Close; ☺9.30am-4.30pm Mon-Sat, noon-3.45pm Sun).

The cathedral was built between 1220 and 1258. Beyond its highly decorative **West Front**, a small passageway leads into the 70m-long **nave**, lined with handsome pillars of Purbeck stone. In the north aisle look out for a fascinating **medieval clock** dating from 1386, probably the oldest working timepiece in the world. At the eastern end of the ambulatory the glorious **Prisoners of Conscience** stained-glass window (1980) hovers above the ornate **tomb** of Edward Seymour (1539–1621) and Lady Catherine Grey. Other monuments and tombs line the sides of the nave, including that of William Longespée, son of Henry II and half-brother of King John. When the tomb was excavated a well-preserved rat was found inside Longespée's skull.

Salisbury's 123m crowning glory, its **spire**, was added in the mid-14th century, and is the tallest in Britain. It represented an enormous technical challenge for its medieval builders; it weighs around 6500 tons and required an elaborate system of cross-bracing, scissor arches and supporting buttresses to keep it upright. Look closely and you'll see the additional weight has buckled the four central piers of the nave.

Sir Christopher Wren surveyed the cathedral in 1668 and calculated that the spire was leaning by 75cm. A brass plate in the floor of the nave is used to measure any shift, but no further lean was recorded in 1951 or 1970. Despite this, reinforcement of the notoriously 'wonky spire' continues to this day.

The cathedral really comes into its own during **evensong**, which takes place at 5.30pm Monday to Saturday and 4.30pm on Sunday, during term time only.

The best way to experience the cathedral is on a 90-minute tower tour (there are one to five daily), which sees you climbing 332 vertigo-inducing steps to the base of the spire for jaw-dropping views across the city and the surrounding countryside. They only take 12 people on each tour; booking is essential. Adults £12.50, children £8.

Cathedral Close   HISTORIC SITE
Salisbury's medieval cathedral close, a hushed enclave surrounded by beautiful houses, has an other-worldly feel. Many of the buildings date from the 13th century, although the area was heavily restored during an 18th-century clean-up by James Wyatt. The close is encircled by a sturdy outer wall,

Salisbury

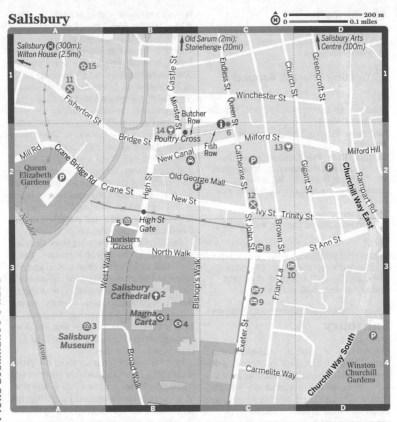

Salisbury ⓟ (300m);
Wilton House (2.5mi)

Old Sarum (2mi);
Stonehenge (10mi)

Salisbury Arts
Centre (100m)

Salisbury

◉ Top Sights
1 Magna Carta	B4
2 Salisbury Cathedral	B3
3 Salisbury Museum	A4

◉ Sights
4 Cathedral Close	B4
5 Mompesson House	B3

✦ Activities, Courses & Tours
6 Salisbury Guides	C2

🛏 Sleeping
7 Cathedral View	C3

8 Chapter House	C3
9 Spire House	C3
10 St Ann's House	C3

⊗ Eating
11 Anokaa	A1
12 Cloisters	C2

● Drinking & Nightlife
13 Chapel	C2
14 Haunch of Venison	B2

✪ Entertainment
15 Salisbury Playhouse	A1

constructed in 1333; the stout gates leading
into the complex are still locked every night.

★ Salisbury Museum   MUSEUM
(☎ 01722-332151; www.salisburymuseum.org.uk;
65 Cathedral Close; adult/child £8/4; ⏱ 10am-
5pm Mon-Sat year-round, plus noon-5pm Sun Jun-

Sep) The hugely important archaeological
finds here include the Stonehenge Archer,
the bones of a man found in the ditch surrounding the stone circle – one of the arrows
found alongside probably killed him. With
gold coins dating from 100 BC and a Bronze

Age gold necklace, it's a powerful introduction to Wiltshire's prehistory.

Mompesson House
HISTORIC BUILDING

(NT; ☑ 01722-335659; www.nationaltrust.org.uk; Cathedral Close; adult/child £6.30/3; ⊙ 11am-5pm Sat-Wed mid-Mar–Oct) Magnificent plasterwork ceilings, exceptional period furnishings and a sweeping carved staircase grace this fine Queen Anne (1701) building. All that made it the perfect location for the 1995 film *Sense and Sensibility*.

Old Sarum
ARCHAEOLOGICAL SITE

(EH; ☑ 01722-335398; www.english-heritage.org.uk; Castle Rd; adult/child £4.50/2.70; ⊙ 10am-6pm Apr-Sep, to 5pm Oct, to 4pm Nov-Mar; P) The huge ramparts of Old Sarum sit on a grass-covered hill 2 miles north of Salisbury. You can wander the grassy ramparts, see the original cathedral's stone foundations, and look across the Wiltshire countryside to the spire of the present Salisbury Cathedral. Medieval tournaments, open-air jousts and mock battles are held on selected days. Bus X5 runs twice an hour from Salisbury to Old Sarum (£2.30, hourly on Sundays). It's also a stop on the Stonehenge Tour bus (p256).

★ Wilton House
HISTORIC BUILDING

(☑ 01722-746714; www.wiltonhouse.com; Wilton; house & grounds adult/child £15/8; ⊙ 11.30am-5pm Sun-Thu May-Aug; P) Stately Wilton House provides an insight into the rarefied world of the British aristocracy. One of Britain's finest stately homes, it's been the house of the earls of Pembroke since 1542, and has been expanded, improved and embellished by successive generations. Highlights are the **Single** and **Double Cube Rooms**, designed by the pioneering 17th-century architect Inigo Jones.

Wilton House is 2.5 miles west of Salisbury; bus R3 runs from Salisbury (£2.70, 10 minutes, one to three hourly Monday to Saturday).

⌖ Tours

Salisbury Guides
WALKING

(☑ 07873-212941; www.salisburycityguides.co.uk; adult/child £6/3; ⊙ 11am daily Apr-Oct, 11am Sat & Sun Nov-Mar) These 90-minute trips leave from the tourist office.

🛏 Sleeping

★ Chapter House
INN ££

(☑ 01722-412028; www.thechapterhouseuk.com; 9 St Johns St; r £100-140) In this 800-year-old

boutique beauty, wood panels and wildly wonky stairs sit beside duck-your-head beams. The cheaper bedrooms are swish but the posher ones are stunning, starring slipper baths and the odd heraldic crest. The pick is room 6, where King Charles is reputed to have stayed. Lucky him.

St Ann's House
B&B ££

(☑ 01722-335657; www.stannshouse.co.uk; 32 St Ann St; s £64, d £89-110; 🛜) The aromas wafting from breakfast may well spur you from your room: powerful coffee; cinnamon-and-lemon banana bread; chilli and beef sausages; poached eggs and Parma ham. Utter elegance reigns upstairs where well-chosen antiques, warm colours and Turkish linen ensure a supremely comfortable stay.

Cathedral View
B&B ££

(☑ 01722-502254; www.cathedral-viewbandb.co.uk; 83 Exeter St; s £75-85, d £80-100; P 🛜) Admirable attention to detail defines this Georgian town house, where miniature flower displays and home-baked biscuits sit in quietly elegant rooms. Breakfasts include prime Wiltshire sausages and the B&B's own bread and jam, while homemade lemon drizzle cake will be waiting for your afternoon tea.

Spire House
B&B ££

(☑ 01722-339213; www.salisbury-bedandbreakfast.com; 84 Exeter St; s/d/f £60/75/90; P 🛜) In this B&B of beautifully kept, sweet rooms, the easygoing vibe extends to breakfast (add £5): chalk up your choice on a blackboard the night before. Options include slow-cooked blueberry-studded porridge, croissants and pastries, and local bacon and eggs.

✗ Eating & Drinking

Anokaa
INDIAN ££

(☑ 01722-414142; www.anokaa.com; 60 Fisherton St; mains £12-18; ⊙ noon-2pm & 5.30-11pm; ✗) The pink-neon and multicoloured bubble displays signal what's in store here: a supremely modern version of Indian cuisine. The spice and flavour combos make the ingredients sing; the meat-free menu makes vegetarians gleeful, and the lunchtime buffet (£9) makes everyone smile.

Cloisters
PUB FOOD ££

(www.cloisterspubsalisbury.co.uk; 83 Catherine St; mains £9-19; ⊙ noon-9pm) The building dates from 1350, it's been a pub since the 1600s and, today, improbably warped beams reinforce an age-old vibe. It's a convivial spot for beefy burgers and homemade pies, or classier evening fare such as pesto-dusted salmon fillet, and lamb steaks with redcurrant sauce.

Haunch of Venison   PUB
(www.haunchpub.co.uk; 1 Minster St; ⊙ 11am-11pm Mon-Sat, to 6pm Sun) Featuring wood-panelled snugs, spiral staircases and crooked ceilings, this 14th-century drinking den is packed with atmosphere – and ghosts. One is a cheating whist player whose hand was severed in a game – look out for his mummified bones on display inside.

Chapel   CLUB
(www.chapelnightclub.co.uk; 34 Milford St; ⊙ 9.30pm-3am Thu-Sat) Buzzing three-room club with adjoining bar where the DJ sets range from funk to '90s hip hop and chart 'n' cheese.

☆ Entertainment

Salisbury Playhouse   THEATRE
(☎ 01722-320333; www.salisburyplayhouse.com; Malthouse Lane) A producing theatre that also hosts top touring shows and musicals.

Salisbury Arts Centre   ARTS CENTRE
(☎ 01722-321744; www.salisburyartscentre.co.uk; Bedwin St) An innovative venue showcasing cutting-edge theatre, indie films, dance and live gigs.

❶ Information

Library (www.wiltshire.gov.uk; Market Walk; internet per 30min £1; ⊙ 10am-7pm Mon, Tue, Fri, 9am-5pm Wed, Thu & Sat; 🛜)
Tourist Office (☎ 01722-342860; www.visitsalisbury.co.uk; Fish Row; ⊙ 9am-5pm Mon-Fri, 10am-4pm Sat, 10am-2pm Sun)

❶ Getting There & Away

BUS
Direct National Express services:
Bath £11, 1¼ hours, one daily
Bristol £11, 2¼ hours, one daily

> ### ❶ TICKETS FOR STONEHENGE
>
> Stonehenge operates by timed tickets, meaning if you want to guarantee your entry you have to book in advance – even English Heritage and National Trust members entitled to free admission.
> If you're planning a peak-season visit, it's best to secure your ticket well in advance.

London (£17, three hours, three daily) Via Heathrow.
Local services include the following:
Devizes Bus 2; £5.50, one hour, hourly Monday to Saturday
Shaftesbury Bus 29; £4.80, 1¼ hours, five daily Monday to Saturday
Tour buses leave to **Stonehenge** (☎ 01202-338420; www.thestonehengetour.info; adult/child £27/17) regularly.

TRAIN
Half-hourly connections include the following:
Bath £10, one hour
Bradford-on-Avon £13, 40 minutes
Bristol £15, 1¼ hours
London Waterloo £25, 1½ hours
Southampton £10, 30 minutes
Hourly connections:
Exeter £20, two hours
Portsmouth £20, 1¼ hours

Stonehenge

Welcome to Britain's most iconic archaeological site. This compelling ring of monolithic stones has been attracting a steady stream of pilgrims, poets and philosophers for the last 5000 years and is still a mystical, ethereal place – a haunting echo from Britain's forgotten past, and a reminder of those who once walked the ceremonial avenues across Salisbury Plain.

◎ Sights

★ Stonehenge   ARCHAEOLOGICAL SITE
(EH; ☎ 0370 333 1181; www.english-heritage.org.uk; adult/child same-day tickets £18/11, advance booking £15.50/9.30; ⊙ 9am-8pm Jun-Aug, 9.30am-7pm Apr, May & Sep, 9.30am-5pm Oct-Mar; ℗) An ultra-modern makeover at ancient Stonehenge has brought an impressive visitor centre and the closure of an intrusive road (now restored to grassland). The result is a far stronger sense of historical context; dignity and mystery returned to an archaeological gem.

A pathway frames the ring of massive stones. Although you can't walk in the circle, unless on a recommended Stone Circle Access Visit (p258), you can get close-up views. Admission is through timed tickets – secure a place well in advance.

Stonehenge is one of Britain's great archaeological mysteries: despite countless theories about the site's purpose, ranging from a sacrificial centre to a celestial timepiece, in truth, no one knows for sure what

Stonehenge

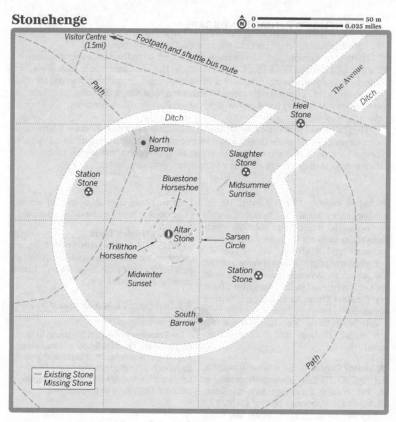

N

0 ————— 50 m
0 ————— 0.025 miles

Visitor Centre (1.5mi)

Footpath and shuttle bus route

Path

The Avenue

Ditch

Heel Stone

Ditch

North Barrow

Slaughter Stone

Station Stone

Bluestone Horseshoe

Midsummer Sunrise

Altar Stone

Sarsen Circle

Trilithon Horseshoe

Station Stone

Midwinter Sunset

South Barrow

Path

Existing Stone
Missing Stone

drove prehistoric Britons to expend so much time and effort on its construction.

The first phase of building started around 3000 BC, when the outer circular bank and ditch were erected. A thousand years later, an inner circle of granite stones, known as bluestones, was added. It's thought that these mammoth 4-tonne blocks were hauled from the Preseli Mountains in South Wales, some 250 miles away – an almost inexplicable feat for Stone Age builders equipped with only the simplest of tools. Although no one is entirely sure how the builders transported the stones so far, it's thought they probably used a system of ropes, sledges and rollers fashioned from tree trunks – Salisbury Plain was still covered by forest during Stonehenge's construction.

Around 1500 BC, Stonehenge's main stones were dragged to the site, erected in a circle and crowned by massive lintels to make the trilithons (two vertical stones topped by a horizontal one). The sarsen (sandstone) stones were cut from an extremely hard rock found on the Marlborough Downs, 20 miles from the site. It's estimated dragging one of these 50-tonne stones across the countryside would require about 600 people.

Also around this time, the bluestones from 500 years earlier were rearranged as an inner **bluestone horseshoe** with an **altar stone** at the centre. Outside this the **trilithon horseshoe** of five massive sets of stones was erected. Three of these are intact; the other two have just a single upright. Then came the major **sarsen circle** of 30 massive vertical stones, of which 17 uprights and six lintels remain.

Much further out, another circle was delineated by the 58 Aubrey Holes, named after John Aubrey, who discovered them in the 1600s. Just inside this circle are the **South** and **North Barrows**, each originally topped by a stone. Like many stone circles in Britain

STONEHENGE'S RITUAL LANDSCAPE

Stonehenge actually forms part of a huge complex of ancient monuments.

North of Stonehenge and running roughly east–west is the **Cursus**, an elongated em-banked oval; the smaller **Lesser Cursus** is nearby. Theories abound as to what these sites were used for, ranging from ancient sporting arenas to processional avenues for the dead. Two clusters of burial mounds, the **Old** and **New Kings Barrows**, sit beside the ceremonial pathway **the Avenue**, which originally linked Stonehenge with the River Avon, 2 miles away.

The **National Trust** (www.nationaltrust.org.uk) website has a downloadable 3.5-mile circular walk (A King's View) that traces tracks across the chalk downland from Stone-henge, past the Cursus and Kings Barrows and along a section of the Avenue itself. The Stonehenge **visitor centre** also has leaflets detailing walking routes.

(including Avebury, 22 miles away), the in-ner horseshoes are aligned to coincide with sunrise at the midsummer solstice, which some claim supports the theory that the site was some kind of astronomical calendar.

Prehistoric pilgrims would have entered the site via the **Avenue**, whose entrance to the circle is marked by the **Slaughter Stone** and the **Heel Stone**, located slightly further out on one side.

Admission to the Stonehenge site is free for English Heritage and National Trust members.

★ **Visitor Centre**   INTERPRETATION CENTRE
(EH; ☑ 0370 333 1181; www.english-heritage.org.uk; incl access to Stonehenge, same-day tickets adult/child £18/11, advance booking £15.50/9.30; ⊙ 9am-8pm Jun-Aug, 9.30am-7pm Apr, May & Sep, 9.30am-5pm Oct-Mar) Stonehenge's swish new visitor centre sees you standing in the mid-dle of an atmospheric 360-degree projection of the stone circle through the ages and sea-sons – complete with midsummer sunrise and swirling star-scape. Engaging audiovis-ual displays detail the transportation of the stones and the building stages, while 300 finds from the wider site include flint chip-pings, bone pins and arrowheads, there's also a striking re-creation of the face of a Neolith-ic man whose body was found nearby.

☞ Tours

★ **Stone Circle Access Visits**   WALKING
(☑ 0370 333 0605; www.english-heritage.org.uk; adult/child £32/19) Circle-access visits are an unforgettable experience. Visitors normally have to stay outside the stone circle itself, but on these self-guided walks, you get to wander around the core of the site, getting up-close views of the iconic bluestones and trilithons.

Each visit only takes 26 people; to secure a place book at least two months in advance.

Salisbury Guided Tours   HISTORY
(☑ 07775 674816; www.salisburyguidedtours.com; per person from £80) Runs a wide range of ex-pert-led trips to Stonehenge, the wider ritual landscape and Salisbury.

❶ Getting There & Away

No regular buses go to the site.

The **Stonehenge Tour** (p256) leaves Salis-bury's railway station half-hourly from June to August, and hourly between September and May. The ticket includes admission to Stone-henge and the Iron Age hill fort at **Old Sarum** (p255); it stops there on the return leg.

Stourhead

★ **Stourhead**   HISTORIC BUILDING
(NT; ☑ 01747-841152; www.nationaltrust.org.uk; Mere; adult/child £14.10/7.10; ⊙ 11am-4.30pm mid-Feb–late Oct, to 3.30pm late Oct–late Dec; ⓟ) Overflowing with vistas, temples and follies, Stourhead is landscape gardening at its fin-est. The Palladian house has some fine Chip-pendale furniture and paintings by Claude and Gaspard Poussin, but it's a sideshow to the magnificent 18th-century gardens (open 9am to 5pm, November to March, to 6pm April to October), which spread out across the valley. Stourhead is off the B3092, 8 miles south of Frome.

A picturesque 2-mile garden circuit takes you past the most ornate follies, around the lake and to the Temple of Apollo; a 3.5-mile side trip can be made from near the Pan-theon to **King Alfred's Tower** (NT; ☑ 01747-841152; www.nationaltrust.org.uk; near Mere; adult/child £4/2; ⊙ noon-4pm Sat & Sun Mar-Oct), a 50m-high folly with wonderful views.

Longleat

★**Longleat** ZOO
(☑ 01985-844400;www.longleat.co.uk;all-inclusive ticket adult/child £34/24, house & grounds £18.50/13.50; ⊘10am-5pm Feb–mid-Oct, to 7pm late Jul & Aug; P) Half ancestral mansion, half wildlife park, Longleat was transformed into Britain's first safari park in 1966, turning Capability Brown's landscaped grounds into an amazing drive-through zoo populated by a menagerie of animals more at home in the African wilderness than the fields of Wiltshire. Longleat also has a throng of attractions, including a historic house, narrow-gauge railway, Doctor Who exhibit, Postman Pat village, pets' corner and butterfly garden.

Longleat was the first English stately home to open its doors to the public. That decision was prompted by finance: heavy taxes and mounting post-WWII bills meant the house had to earn its keep.

The house itself contains fine tapestries, furniture and decorated ceilings, as well as seven libraries containing around 40,000 tomes. The highlight, though, is an extraordinary series of paintings and psychedelic murals by the present-day marquess, who was an art student in the '60s and upholds the long-standing tradition of eccentricity among the English aristocracy – check out his website (www.lordbath.co.uk).

Longleat is just off the A362, 3 miles from Frome. It's open until 6pm on many summer weekends.

Lacock

POP 1159
With its geranium-covered cottages and higgledy-piggledy rooftops, pockets of the medieval village of Lacock seem to have been preserved in mid-19th-century aspic. The village has been in the hands of the National Trust since 1944, and in many places is remarkably free of modern development – there are no telephone poles or electric street lights and the main car park on the outskirts keeps it largely traffic-free. Unsurprisingly, it's a popular location for costume dramas and feature films – the village and its abbey pop up in the Harry Potter films, *Downton Abbey*, *The Other Boleyn Girl* and BBC adaptations of *Wolf Hall*, *Moll Flanders* and *Pride and Prejudice*.

◉ Sights

Lacock Abbey ABBEY
(NT; ☑ 01249-730459; www.nationaltrust.org.uk; Hither Way; adult/child £12/6; ⊘10.30am-5.30pm Mar-Oct, 11am-4pm Nov-Feb) Lacock Abbey is a window into a medieval world. Founded as an Augustinian nunnery in the 13th century, its deeply atmospheric rooms and stunning Gothic entrance hall are lined with bizarre terracotta figures; spot the scapegoat with a lump of sugar on its nose. Some of the original structure is evident in the cloisters and there are traces of medieval wall paintings too.

Fox Talbot Museum MUSEUM
(NT; ☑ 01249-730459; www.nationaltrust.org.uk; Hither Way; incl Lacock Abbey adult/child £12/6; ⊘10.30am-5.30pm Mar-Oct, 11am-4pm Nov-Feb) William Henry Fox Talbot (1800–77) pioneered the photographic negative. A prolific inventor, he began developing the system in 1834 while working at Lacock Abbey. The museum details his groundbreaking work and displays a superb collection of his images.

🛏 Sleeping & Eating

★**Sign of the Angel** INN ££
(☑ 01249-730230; www.signoftheangel.co.uk; 6 Church St; r £120-140; P 🛜) Every inch of this gorgeous, 15th-century restaurant-with-rooms is rich in heritage pizzazz. Burnished beams, slanting floors and open fires meet duck-down duvets, upcycled furniture and neutral tones, delivering a fresh provincial rustic feel. Treats include luxury toiletries, chef-baked cookies and a free glass of prosecco (if you book one of the swisher rooms).

Red Lion INN ££
(☑ 01249-730456; www.redlionlacock.co.uk; 1 High St; d £120; P 🛜) In atmospheric Lacock, where better to sleep than a Georgian coaching inn that oozes ambience. Step on flagstone floors past open fires, up a grand staircase to sweet rooms where padded cushions line mullioned windows with picture-postcard views of ancient streets. The food's notable too (mains £13, served noon to 8pm).

King John's Hunting Lodge CAFE £
(☑ 01249-730313; www.kingjohnslodge.2day.ws; 21 Church St; snacks from £5; ⊘10.30am-4pm Wed-Sun Feb–mid-Dec; P) Afternoon tea is a must at Lacock's oldest building, where a cosy, beam-lined room and a peaceful garden set the scene for dainty china, light lunches and tasty cakes.

George Inn
PUB FOOD **££**

(www.georgeinnlacock.co.uk; 4 West St; mains £10-16; ⊙food noon-2.30pm & 6-9pm Mon-Sat, 6-8pm Sun) Sample well-executed, classic pub grub and some of the six local ales at this 14th-century, horse brass–hung pub.

Avebury & Around

POP 530

While the tour buses head straight for Stonehenge, prehistoric purists make for the massive stone circle at Avebury. Though it lacks the dramatic trilithons of its sister site across Salisbury Plain, Avebury is just as rewarding to visit. It's bigger and older, and a large section of the village is actually inside the stones – footpaths wind around them, allowing you to really soak up the extraordinary atmosphere. Avebury also boasts an encircling landscape that's rich in prehistoric sites and a manor house where restored rooms span five completely different eras.

◉ Sights

★ **Avebury Stone Circle**   ARCHAEOLOGICAL SITE

(NT; ☑01672-539250; www.nationaltrust.org.uk; ⊙24hr; ℗) **FREE** With a diameter of 348m, Avebury is the largest stone circle in the world. It's also one of the oldest, dating from 2500 to 2200 BC. Today, more than 30 stones are in place; pillars show where missing stones would have been. Wandering between them emphasises the site's sheer scale, evidenced also by the massive bank and ditch that line the circle; the quieter northwest sector is particularly atmospheric. National Trust-run guided walks (£3) are held on most days.

Avebury henge originally consisted of an outer circle of 98 standing stones of up to 6m in length, many weighing 20 tonnes. The stones were surrounded by another circle delineated by a 5m-high earth bank and a ditch up to 9m deep. Inside were smaller stone circles to the north (27 stones) and south (29 stones).

In the Middle Ages, when Britain's pagan past was an embarrassment to the Church, many of the stones were buried, removed or broken up. In 1934 wealthy businessman and archaeologist Alexander Keiller supervised the re-erection of the stones; he later bought the site for posterity using funds from his family's marmalade fortune.

Modern roads into Avebury neatly dissect the circle into four sectors. Starting at High St, near the Henge Shop (p262), and walking round the circle in an anticlockwise direction, you'll encounter 11 standing stones in the southwest sector. They include the **Barber Surgeon Stone**, named after the skeleton of a man found under it – the equipment buried with him suggests he was a barber-cum-surgeon.

The southeast sector starts with huge **portal stones** marking the entry to the circle from **West Kennet Ave**. The **southern inner circle** stood in this sector and within this ring was the obelisk and a group of stones known as the Z Feature. Just outside this smaller circle, only the base of the Ring Stone survives.

In the **northern inner circle** in the northeast sector, three sarsens remain of what would have been a rectangular **cove**. The northwest sector has the most complete collection of standing stones, including the massive 65-tonne **Swindon Stone**, one of the few never to have been toppled.

★ **Avebury Manor**   HISTORIC BUILDING

(NT; ☑01672-539250; www.nationaltrust.org.uk; adult/child £6.75/3.35; ⊙11am-5pm Apr-Oct, to 4pm mid-Feb–Mar, 11am-4pm Thu-Sun Nov & Dec) The mother of all makeovers at this 16th-century manor house used original techniques and materials to recreate interiors spanning five periods. Being hands-on is encouraged here, so now you can sit on beds, play billiards and listen to the gramophone in rooms that range from Tudor, through Georgian to the 1930s. Visits are by timed ticket only; arrive early to bag a slot.

Silbury Hill
ARCHAEOLOGICAL SITE

(EH; www.english-heritage.org.uk; ℗) **FREE** Rising abruptly from the fields just south of Avebury, 40m-high Silbury Hill is the largest artificial earthwork in Europe, comparable in height and volume to the Egyptian pyramids. It was built in stages from around 2500 BC, but the precise reason for its construction remains unclear. Direct access to the hill isn't allowed, but you can view it from a lay-by on the A4.

West Kennet Long Barrow   ARCHAEOLOGICAL SITE

(EH; ☑0370 333 1181; www.english-heritage.org.uk; ⊙dawn-dusk) **FREE** England's finest burial mound dates from around 3500 BC. Its entrance is guarded by huge sarsens and its roof is made out of gigantic overlapping capstones. About 50 skeletons were found when it was excavated; finds are on display at the Wiltshire Heritage Museum in Devizes. The

Avebury

barrow is a half-mile walk across fields from the parking lay-by.

A footpath also leads from Avebury Stone Circle to West Kennet (2 miles), passing the vast earthwork of Silbury Hill en route.

🛏 Sleeping & Eating

⭐ **Manor Farm**   B&B **££**

(☑ 01672-539294; www.manorfarmavebury.com; High St; s £70-80, d £90-100; **P**🛜) A rare chance to sleep in style inside a stone circle – this red-brick farmhouse snuggles just inside Avebury henge. The elegant, comfy rooms blend old woods with bright furnishings, while the windows provide spine-tingling views of those 4000-year-old standing stones.

Avebury Lodge   B&B **£££**

(☑ 01672-539023; www.aveburylodge.co.uk; High St; s/d £140/175; **P**🛜) It's as if gentlemanly archaeologists are still in situ: antiquarian

Avebury

◎ Top Sights
1 Avebury Manor	A2
2 Avebury Stone Circle	B2

◎ Sights
3 Barber Surgeon Stone	C4
4 Obelisk	C3
5 Ring Stone	D3
6 Swindon Stone	B1
7 Z Feature	C3

🛏 Sleeping
8 Avebury Lodge	B3
9 Manor Farm	B3

🍴 Eating
10 Circle	B2

🍷 Drinking & Nightlife
11 Red Lion	C2

🛍 Shopping
12 Henge Shop	B3

prints of stone circles smother the walls, pelmets and chandeliers are dotted around. And whenever you glance from a window, a bit of Avebury henge appears. It's lovely, but you might consider it overpriced – it's the location that pushes the room rates up here.

Red Lion
PUB

(www.oldenglishinns.co.uk; High St; ⊘11am-11pm) Having a pint here means downing a drink at the only pub in the world inside a stone circle. Food (mains £8 to £16) is served noon to 9pm (to 8pm on Sunday). It's firmly traditional stuff – think pork belly and sausage 'n' mash.

🛍 Shopping

Henge Shop
GIFTS & SOUVENIRS

(☑01672-539229; www.hengeshop.com; High St; ⊘9.30am-5pm) Stocks as many souvenirs and stone circle–related books, maps, jewellery and gifts as you could wish for.

ℹ Getting There & Away

Bus 49 runs hourly to Swindon (£2.80, 30 minutes) and Devizes (£2.80, 10 minutes).

EXMOOR NATIONAL PARK

Exmoor is more than a little addictive. Even when you get home, your mind could well return to its broad, russet views. In the middle sits the higher moor, an empty, expansive, other-worldly landscape of tawny grasses and huge skies. Here picturesque Exford makes an ideal village base. In the north, sheer, rock-strewn river valleys cut into the plateau and coal-black cliffs lurch towards the sea. Amid these towering headlands, charismatic Porlock and the twin villages of Lynton and Lynmouth are atmospheric places to stay. Relaxed Dulverton delivers a country-town vibe, while appealing Dunster boasts cobbled streets and a russet-red castle. And everywhere on Exmoor, life is attuned to the rhythm of the seasons; it's a glimpse into another world. Visit – but you're likely to be planning to return before you leave.

🏃 Activities

Exmoor Adventures
OUTDOORS

(☑07976-208279; www.exmooradventures.co.uk) Runs kayaking, canoeing, mountain-biking, coasteering and rock-climbing sessions.

Cycling

Despite the formidable hills, cycling is hugely popular on Exmoor. Several sections of the **National Cycle Network** (NCN; www.sustrans.org.uk) cross the park, including the West Country Way (NCN route 3) from Bristol to Padstow, and Devon Coast to Coast (NCN route 27), between Ilfracombe and Plymouth, via Dartmoor and Exmoor.

Exmoor is also one of the county's most exhilarating off-road cycling destinations, with a wealth of bridleways and permitted tracks. The ENPA has produced a colour-coded, off-road cycle map (£10); buy it at tourist offices.

Exmoor Adventures (p262) runs a five-hour mountain-biking skills course (£50) and also hires bikes (per day £25).

Pompys
CYCLING

(☑01643-704077; www.pompyscycles.co.uk; Mart Rd, Minehead; per day £18; ⊘9am-5pm Mon-Sat) Bike sales and hire.

Pony Trekking & Horse Riding

Exmoor is prime riding country, with stables offering pony and horse treks from around £40 to £45 for a two-hour ride.

Brendan Manor Stables
HORSE RIDING

(☑01598-741246; www.ridingonexmoor.co.uk; Brendon Manor) Runs a full range of horse-riding trips, from one to three hours, that head on to the open moor and down into the valleys. Prices start at £30. Lynton-based.

Burrowhayes Farm
HORSE RIDING

(☑01643-862463; www.burrowhayes.co.uk; West Luccombe; per 1/2 hr £22/42) Based near Porlock, Burrowhayes runs a wide range of treks that go into the Horner Valley and on to the moor. Plus special half-hour pony rides for children (£12).

Outovercott Stables
HORSE RIDING

(☑01598-753341; www.outovercott.co.uk; near Lynton; per hr £30) Outovercott's treks on to Exmoor's exposed moorland range from one-hour trips for novices to excursions for more experienced riders, which take in views of the Valley of Rocks and the coastline.

Walking

The open moors and a profusion of marked bridleways make Exmoor an excellent area for hiking. The best-known routes are the **Somerset & North Devon Coast Path**, which is part of the **South West Coast Path** (www.southwestcoastpath.org.uk), and the Exmoor section of the **Two Moors Way**,

Exmoor National Park

which starts in Lynmouth and travels south to Dartmoor and beyond.

Another superb route is the **Coleridge Way** (www.coleridgeway.co.uk), which winds for 51 miles through Exmoor, the Brendon Hills and the Quantocks. Part of the 180-mile **Tarka Trail** cuts through the park; join it at Combe Martin, hike along the cliffs to Lynton/Lynmouth, then head across the moor towards Barnstaple.

Organised walks run by the ENPA are held throughout the year and include deer safaris, nightjar walks and dark-sky strolls.

ⓘ Information

Active Exmoor www.activeexmoor.com
Snowdrop Valley www.wheddoncross.org.uk/snowdropvalley.htm
Visit Exmoor www.visit-exmoor.co.uk
What's On Exmoor www.whatsonexmoor.com

There are three Exmoor National Park Authority tourist offices, in **Dulverton** (☑ 01398-323841; www.exmoor-nationalpark.gov.uk; 7-9 Fore St; ☺10am-5pm Apr-Oct, limited winter hours), **Dunster** (☑ 01643-821835; www.exmoor-nationalpark.gov.uk; The Steep; ☺10am-5pm Apr-Oct, limited winter hours) and **Lynmouth** (p268).

ⓘ Getting Around

The **MoorRover** (☑ 01643-709701) is an on-demand minibus that can take you anywhere on Exmoor. Prices range from £10 to £30, depending on distances involved. It'll also carry bikes and provide a luggage transfer service. Book at least a day ahead.

Exmoor's bus routes are listed at the **ExploreMoor** (www.exploremoor.co.uk) website. Be aware: some services are seasonal, and the more remote ones are particularly prone to change. Services include the following:

28 (at least hourly) Shuttles from Taunton to the resort of Minehead (1¼ hours).

300 (two services a day from Monday to Saturday in July and August only) Heads along the coast from Minehead to Lynmouth, via Porlock.

309/310 (13 services daily, Monday to Saturday) Runs from Barnstaple via Parracombe to Lynton or Lynmouth, year-round.

467 (one daily, Monday to Friday) Runs from Minehead to Dulverton (one hour), via Dunster and Wheddon Cross.

Dulverton

POP 1500

The southern gateway to Exmoor National Park, Dulverton sits at the base of the Barle Valley near the confluence of two key rivers: the Exe and Barle. A traditional country town, it's home to a collection of gun sellers, fishing-tackle stores and gift shops, and makes an attractive edge-of-moor base.

⊙ Sights

★**Tarr Steps**   LANDMARK
(☺24hr) **FREE** Exmoor's most famous landmark is an ancient stone clapper bridge shaded by gnarled old trees. Its huge slabs are propped up on stone columns embedded in the River Barle. Local folklore aside (which declares it was used by the devil for sunbathing), it first pops into the historical record in the 1600s, and has had to be rebuilt after 21st-century floods. The steps are signed off the B3223 Dulverton-to-Simonsbath road, 5 miles northwest of Dulverton.

WILDLIFE-WATCHING

Exmoor supports one of England's largest wild red deer populations, best experienced in autumn when the annual 'rutting' season sees stags bellowing, charging at each other and clashing horns in an attempt to impress prospective mates. Despite their numbers, these skittish creatures are notoriously difficult to spot without some local knowledge.

The **Exmoor National Park Authority** (ENPA; www.exmoor-nationalpark.gov.uk) runs regular wildlife-themed guided walks (free), which include evening deer-spotting hikes. Or head out on an organised jeep safari to combine scenic sightseeing with a couple of hours of off-road wildlife-watching.

Barle Valley Safaris (☏ 01643-841326; www.exmoorwildlifesafaris.co.uk; adult/child £35/25) Runs half-day 4WD wildlife-watching safaris on to the moor. Trips leave from Dulverton and Dunster, with pickups from Exford and Wheddon Cross.

Discovery Safaris (☏ 01643-863444; www.discoverysafaris.com; per person £25) These twice-daily jeep safaris set off from Porlock and head up on to open moorland searching for wildlife, especially Exmoor's famous red deer.

Exmoor Safari (☏ 01643-831229; www.exmoorsafari.co.uk; Exford; adult/child £35/16) Long-running wildlife-watching operator that uses 4WD vehicles and local knowledge to search out red deer. Also does special photography-themed trips.

🛏 Sleeping

★ Streamcombe Farm
B&B ££

(☏ 01398-323775; www.streamcombefarm.co.uk; Streamcombe Lane, near Dulverton; s £65-75, d £80-100; ℗) In this enchanting, 18th-century farmhouse, stylish, rustic-chic bedrooms feature chimney breasts and reclaimed joists, and the only sounds are the sheep, deer and pheasants outside. There's woodland camping (per person £9) and a two-person shepherd's hut (£85) too.

Town Mills
B&B ££

(☏ 01398-323124; www.townmillsdulverton.co.uk; High St; s/d £85/95; ℗ 🛜) The top choice if you want to stay in Dulverton itself is a thoroughly contemporary riverside mill with creamy carpets, magnolia walls and bursts of floral art.

Tarr Farm
HOTEL £££

(☏ 01643-851507; www.tarrfarm.co.uk; Tarr Steps; s/d £90/150; ℗ 🛜) This is the place to really lose yourself: a charming farmhouse nested among the woods near Tarr Steps, 7 miles from Dulverton. The nine rooms are spacious and luxurious, with spoil-yourself extras such as organic bath goodies and homemade biscuits.

🍴 Eating

Exclusive Cake Co
BAKERY £

(www.exclusivecakecompany.co.uk; 19 High St; snacks from £3; ⊙ 9am-4pm Mon-Fri, to 2pm Sat) Real rarities stack the shelves here: Exmoor ale, cheese and wholegrain-mustard bread; Somerset cider cake; venison and port pie. Note the typically Exmoor warning: 'Game pies may contain lead shot'.

★ Woods
BISTRO ££

(☏ 01398-324007; www.woodsdulverton.co.uk; 4 Bank Sq; mains £15-20; ⊙ noon-2pm & 7-9.30pm) With its deer antlers, hunting prints and big wood-burning stove, Woods is Exmoor to its core. No surprise then to find menus full of full-bodied flavours: expect venison confit, belly pork with black pudding, and wild mushrooms with truffle and white wine.

The bar menu (£10 to £12, served between 6pm and 9.30pm) is simpler stuff – think steak, omelette Arnold Bennett and lamb rogan josh.

Tarr Farm Inn
RESTAURANT ££

(☏ 01643-851507; www.tarrfarm.co.uk; Tarr Steps; snacks from £5, dinner mains £13-27; ⊙ 11am-2.30pm & 6.30-9.30pm) All comers are welcome here: walkers and families come for cream teas (served from 11am to 5pm) and hearty lunches, while after-dark diners sample more formal country fare. It's all deservedly a hit with the waxed-jacket-wearing regulars.

The inn is set beside the Tarr Steps stone bridge; it's signed off the B3223 Dulverton–Simonsbath road, 5 miles northwest of Dulverton.

Exford

Tucked into the banks of the River Exe at the heart of Exmoor, Exford is a delightful medley of cottages and slate-roofed houses clustered around a village green.

🛏 Sleeping

Exford YHA   HOSTEL £
(📞01643-831229; www.yha.org.uk; Exe Mead, Exford; dm/d £20/50; 🅿) An imaginative revamp has given the lounge and kitchen of this hikers' favourite a glamorous edge. A cracking cooked breakfast (£8) is served in the White Horse inn, opposite, while the hostel's woodland setting, beside the babbling River Exe (campsites per adult £10), is divine.

Exmoor White Horse   INN £££
(📞01643-831229; www.exmoor-whitehorse.co.uk; Exford; d £180-205; 🅿🛜) Step through the door here to find everything you want from an Exmoor coaching inn: a friendly bar with a real fire, a local-produce packed restaurant (mains £14 to £22) and smoothly comfy rooms. On summer afternoons, the riverside beer terrace is a firm favourite with the locals – an idyllic spot to watch the horse riders trot by.

Dunster

POP 850

Centred on a scarlet-walled castle and a medieval yarn market, Dunster is one of Exmoor's oldest villages, a tempting tangle of cobbled streets, bubbling brooks and packhorse bridges.

◉ Sights

★ Dunster Castle   CASTLE
(NT;   📞01643-821314; www.nationaltrust.org.uk; Castle Hill; adult/child £10.30/5.15; ⊙11am-5pm Mar-Oct; 🅿) Rosy-hued Dunster Castle crowns a densely wooded hill. Built by the Luttrell family, who once owned much of northern Exmoor, the oldest sections are 13th century, although the turrets and exterior walls are 19th-century additions. Look out for Tudor furnishings, 17th-century plasterwork and a ridiculously grand staircase. Leave time to explore the colourful terraced gardens, with their riverside walks and views across Exmoor's shores.

Watermill   HISTORIC BUILDING
(NT;   📞01643-821759; www.nationaltrust.org.uk; Mill Lane; ⊙10am-5pm Mar-Oct) Most of the original cogs, wheels and grinding stones still rotate away in this working 18th-century mill; there's a picturesque riverside tearoom alongside.

Admission to the mill is included in tickets to Dunster Castle.

🛏 Sleeping & Eating

Spears Cross   B&B ££
(📞01643-821439; www.spearscross.co.uk;   1 West St; d £97-107; 🅿🛜) 'We simply like to make breakfasts more fun', says the owner of this 15th-century B&B. That explains tummy-tempting options such as scrambled egg with watercress, tomatoes and Cheddar, and muffins topped with asparagus and poached egg. The just-as-delicious decor sees age-old beams frame wood panels, floral furnishings and raspberry-red walls.

Mill Stream Cottage   B&B ££
(📞01643-821966;   www.millstreamcottagedunster.co.uk; 2 Mill Lane; s £60, d £74-84) In the 1600s this was Dunster's workhouse; now it's a sweet-as-pie guesthouse with country cottage–style rooms. There are homemade cakes on arrival and home-baked biscuits on the tea tray, plus an oh-so-comfy guest lounge where you can snooze in front of the wood burner.

Luttrell Arms   INN £££
(📞01643-821555; www.luttrellarms.co.uk; High St; r £140-195; 🅿🛜) You almost need a ladder to climb up to the high four-poster bed in the feature room at this exquisite old coaching inn. In medieval times, this was the guesthouse of the Abbots of Cleeve. Even the more standard rooms are gorgeous; expect a plethora of brass plates, beams and a plaster fireplace or two.

Reeve's   BRITISH ££
(📞01643-821414;   www.reevesrestaurantdunster.co.uk; 20 High St; mains £18; ⊙7-9pm Tue-Sat, noon-2pm Sun) The eponymous chef at seriously stylish Reeve's is an award winner. No wonder: the complex creations here truly showcase Exmoor produce. Perhaps opt for slow-roast pig's cheek with veal and cider jus, or tender lamb roasted with rosemary and garlic.

ℹ Getting There & Away

Bus 467 (one daily, Monday to Friday) runs north to Minehead and south to Dulverton (one hour), via Wheddon Cross.

The 22-mile **West Somerset Railway** (📞01643-704996; www.west-somerset-railway.

co.uk; 24hr rover tickets adult/child £19/9.50) stops at Dunster during the summer, with four to seven trains daily from May to October.

Porlock & Around

The coastal village of Porlock is one of the prettiest on the Exmoor coast; the huddle of thatched cottages lining its main street is framed on one side by the sea, and on the other by houses clinging to the steeply sloping hills behind. Winding lanes lead to the charismatic breakwater of Porlock Weir, 2 miles to the west, with its arching pebble beach and striking coastal views.

◉ Sights

Porlock Weir   HARBOUR

(☉24hr; P) FREE Porlock Weir's stout granite quay curves around a shingly beach, which is backed by pubs, fishers' storehouses and a scattering of seasonal shops. The weir has been around for almost a thousand years (it's named in the Domesday Book as 'Portloc') and makes a glorious place for a pub lunch and a stroll, with stirring views across the Vale of Porlock and easy access to the coast path.

Holnicote Estate   HISTORIC BUILDINGS

(NT; ☑ 01643-862452; www.nationaltrust.org.uk; near Porlock; ☉24hr; P) FREE The 50-sq-km Holnicote Estate sweeps southeast out of Porlock, taking in a string of impossibly pretty villages. Picturesque **Bossington** leads to charming **Allerford**, with its 15th-century packhorse bridge. The biggest, **Selworthy**, offers eye-catching Exmoor views, a cafe, a shop, and cob-and-thatch cottages clustering around the village green.

🛏 Sleeping & Eating

★ **Millers at the Anchor**   BOUTIQUE HOTEL ££

(☑ 01643-862753; www.millersuk.com/anchor; Porlock Weir; s £85-105, d £85-155; P🐾) Stuffed with antiques, overflowing with piled-up books, and scattered with exotic rugs, Millers delivers an enjoyably overwhelming dose of English eccentricity. Gilt-framed mirrors jostle with marble busts, vast beds and captivating views of Porlock Weir. But the chess set in the lounge and the quirky home cinema may tempt you from your room.

Sea View   B&B ££

(☑ 01643-863456; www.seaviewporlock.co.uk; High Bank, Porlock; d £65-70; 🐾) If somewhere is this cheap it really shouldn't be this nice. But Sea View actually is. Tiny rooms are pleasantly packed with painted furniture, trinkets and oil paintings plus thoughtful extras – blister plasters and muscle soak for hikers tackling Porlock's precipitous hills.

Ship Inn   PUB FOOD ££

(Top Ship; ☑ 01643-862507; www.shipinnporlock. co.uk; High St, Porlock; mains £8-16; ☉noon-2.30pm & 6-8.30pm; P) Poet Coleridge and pal Robert Southey both downed pints in this 13th-century thatched Porlock inn – you can even sit in a snug still dubbed 'Southey's Corner'. Substantial pub food – mainly steaks, roasts and stews – is served in the bar.

Culbone   BRITISH ££

(☑ 01643-862259; www.theculbone.com; near Porlock; mains £9-25; ☉noon-2.30pm & 6-9pm Mon-Sat, noon-3pm Sun; P🐾) This smart restaurant-with-rooms is a carnivore's delight. Plump for the 28-day aged Devon Red steaks and choose from three different cuts, and sauces including horseradish and rosemary, garlic and shallot, or creamy Devon Blue cheese.

Cafe Porlock Weir   BRITISH ££

(☑ 01643-863300; www.thecafeporlockweir.co.uk; Porlock Weir; mains £10-20; ☉noon-8pm Wed-Sun) The food here regularly notches up awards; shore views and an assured, country-house ambience add to the appeal. Ingredients from moor and shore pack the menu, making a window table an atmospheric spot to tuck into crab risotto, nutty butter-doused skate or chargrilled rib-eye steak.

ℹ Information

Porlock Tourist Office (☑ 01643-863150; www.porlock.co.uk; West End, Porlock; ☉10am-5pm Mon-Sat Easter-Oct, to 12.30pm Tue-Sat Nov-Easter)

ℹ Getting There & Away

Bus 300 (two services a day from Monday to Saturday in July and August only) heads from Porlock east along the coast to Minehead, and west to Lynmouth.

Drivers can choose from two picturesque routes into Porlock village. The New Road Toll Road sweeps through pine forests and round U-bends, while Porlock Hill (A39) is a brake-burning 1:4 descent. Another toll road, the Porlock Scenic (Worthy) Toll Road, provides an alternative, bouncing, route up out of Porlock Weir.

Lynton & Lynmouth

Tucked in amid precipitous cliffs and steep, tree-lined slopes, these twin coastal towns are a landscape painter's dream. Bustling Lynmouth sits beside the shore, a busy harbour lined with pubs and souvenir shops. On the clifftop, Lynton feels much more genteel and well-to-do. A cliffside railway links the two: it's powered by the rushing West Lyn river, which feeds numerous cascades and waterfalls nearby.

◎ Sights

★ Cliff Railway
HERITAGE RAILWAY

(☎01598-753486; www.cliffrailwaylynton.co.uk; adult single/return £2.70/3.70, child £1.60/2.20; ⊙10am-5pm Feb-May, Sep & Oct, to 7pm Jun-Aug) This extraordinary piece of Victorian engineering sees two cars, linked by a steel cable, descend and ascend the sloping cliff face according to the weight of water in the cars' tanks. All burnished wood and polished brass, it's been running since 1890 and makes for an unmissable ride.

Flood Memorial Hall
INTERPRETATION CENTRE

(The Esplanade, Lynmouth; ⊙9am-5pm Easter-Oct) FREE On 16 August 1952 a huge wave of water swept through Lynmouth after torrential rain. The devastation was immense: 34 people lost their lives; four bridges and countless houses were washed away. This exhibition features photos of the destroyed buildings and the personal testimonies of those involved.

🏃 Activities

Popular hiking trails among Lynton and Lynmouth's spectacular scenery include ones to the lighthouse at **Foreland Point**; to **Watersmeet**, 2 miles east of Lynmouth (reached via the gorgeous East Lyn river glade); and along the scenic **Glen Lyn Gorge**.

Valley of the Rocks
WALKING

The dramatic geology in this valley was described by poet Robert Southey as 'rock reeling upon rock, stone piled upon stone, a huge terrifying reeling mass'. Look out for the formations dubbed the Devil's Cheesewring and Ragged Jack – and also the feral goats that wander the tracks. Its a mile's walk west of Lynton along a cracking coast path.

🛏 Sleeping

★ Rock House
B&B ££

(☎01598-753508; www.rock-house.co.uk; Manor Green, Lynmouth; s £45-88, d £110-125) The setting is simply superb: right on Lynmouth's pocket-sized harbour, steep hills sloping up on three sides. Contemporary rooms sport leather headboards, lilac scatter cushions and mini-armchairs. All have extraordinary views; the best is number 4, where the window is right next to the beach.

Bath Hotel
HOTEL ££

(☎01598-752238; www.bathhotellynmouth.co.uk; The Esplanade, Lynmouth; d £78-130; P 🖤) A pair of third-generation hoteliers are breathing fresh life into the Bath Hotel, a feature of the town since Victorian days. To a stylish new cocktail bar add rooms teaming lime fabrics with dark leather and cracking harbour and headland views.

North Walk House
B&B ££

(☎01598-753372; www.northwalkhouse.co.uk; North Walk, Lynton; d £66-71; P 🖤) Stripped wooden floors, stripy bedspreads and colourful rugs give North Walk House a gently funky feel. The views over the sea and rugged cliffs are fantastic, while the all-organic breakfasts feature Exmoor bacon and sausages, and Aga-baked eggs.

Rising Sun
INN £££

(☎01598-753223; www.risingsunlynmouth.co.uk; Harbourside, Lynmouth; d £160-190) At the Rising Sun a 14th-century smugglers' haunt has been transformed into a romantic hideaway with a sleek designer feel. Elegant flourishes are everywhere, from the anglepoise lamps and local art to the soft, tasteful throws. Ask for a sea-view room to watch the tide rise and fall in the harbour just outside.

STARGAZING ON EXMOOR

Exmoor holds the distinction of being named Europe's first International Dark Sky Reserve. The ENPA runs free night-time stargazing strolls; eerie hilltop hikes where the inky blackness is punctuated by mesmerising constellations. The authority's (free) *Dark Sky Discovery* leaflets feature star charts and maps. For optimum views, central, higher Exmoor is best; try the hills around Dunkery Beacon.

Eating

Charlie Friday's   CAFE £
(www.charliefridays.co.uk; Church Hill, Lynton; snacks from £4; ⊙10am-5pm Tue-Sun Feb-Nov) A funky, friendly hang-out serving melting pastries, thick sarnies and fair-trade, two-shot espresso that really packs a punch.

Bath Bar   PUB FOOD ££
(☑01598-752238; www.bathhotellynmouth.co.uk; The Esplanade, Lynmouth; mains £14; ⊙noon-9pm, winter hours vary) The Bath brings a burst of shipwreck chic to Lynmouth, thanks to a copper bar top, curved ship's decking and a figurehead who isn't entirely clothed. Best surveyed while tucking into a stacked-high Bath Burger, complete with Exmoor ale and black treacle–braised brisket, onion jam and blue-cheese mousse.

Rising Sun   MODERN BRITISH ££
(☑01598-753223; www.risingsunlynmouth.co.uk; Harbourside, Lynmouth; mains £14-26; ⊙noon-2.30pm & 6-9pm) At the harbourside Rising Sun, head chef Matthew Terrett delights in showcasing not only Exmoor meat and vegetables, but also the fresh seafood landed along this rugged shore. Seasonal treats might include succulent lobster, fresh sea bass and local mussels, all served up with confidence and more than a dash of élan.

ⓘ Information

Lynmouth Tourist Office (☑01598-752509; www.exmoor-nationalpark.gov.uk; The Esplanade, Lynmouth; ⊙10am-5pm) An Exmoor National Park Authority Tourist Office.

Lynton Tourist Office (☑01598-752225; www. lynton-lynmouth-tourism.co.uk; Lynton Town Hall, Lee Rd; ⊙10am-5pm Mon-Sat, to 2pm Sun)

DEVON

Devon offers freedom. Its rippling, beach-fringed landscape is studded with historic homes, vibrant cities and wild, wild moors. So here you can ditch schedules and to-do lists and hike a rugged coast path, take a scenic boat trip, or get lost in hedge-lined lanes that aren't even on your map.

Discover collegiate Exeter, touristy Torquay, yachting-haven Dartmouth and alternative Totnes. Or escape to wilderness Dartmoor and the remote, surf-dashed north coast. Sample wine made from the vines beside you and food that's fresh from field, furrow or sea. Go surfing, cycling, kayaking, horse riding, sea swimming and bare-foot beachcombing.

ⓘ Information

Visit Devon (www.visitdevon.co.uk) The first port of call for all things Devonian.

ⓘ Getting Around

BUS

Most bus services between larger towns and villages are now run by Stagecoach, with a number of smaller coach companies offering infrequent services to other areas. Dartmoor is poorly served by buses, so you'll need a car or bike to explore here.

There are several bus passes available: the **Devon Day Ticket** (adult/child/family £8.50/5.70/17) covers all companies, while the **Stagecoach Explorer** (adult/child/family £7.70/5.10/15.40) and **Megarider Gold** (1/4 weeks £27/97) tickets only cover Stagecoach buses.

Traveline South West (www.travelinesw.com) is a great online tool for travel planning, while the Devon interactive bus map (https://new. devon.gov.uk/travel) provides a useful visual map of bus routes.

TRAIN

Devon's main line skirts southern Dartmoor, running from Exeter to Plymouth and on to Cornwall. Branch lines include the 39-mile Exeter–Barnstaple Tarka Line; the 15-mile Plymouth–Gunnislake Tamar Valley Line and the scenic Exeter–Torquay Paignton line. There are also several lovely steam railways.

The **Freedom of Devon & Cornwall Rover** (3 days adult/child £46.45/23.30, 8 days £71.20/35.60) ticket is good value if you're doing a lot of travel by train, offering three days travel out of seven days, or eight days of travel out of 15 days.

Exeter

POP 117,800

Well heeled and comfortable, Exeter exudes evidence of its centuries-old role as the spiritual and administrative heart of Devon. The city's Gothic cathedral presides over pockets of cobbled streets; medieval and Georgian buildings, and fragments of the Roman city stretch out all around. A snazzy new shopping centre brings bursts of the modern, thousands of university students ensure a buzzing nightlife, and the vibrant quayside acts as a launch pad for cycling or kayaking trips. Throw in some stylish places

Exeter

Exeter

◎ Top Sights
1 Exeter Cathedral	C3
2 RAMM	C2
3 Underground Passages	D2

◎ Sights
4 St Nicholas Priory	B3

⊕ Activities, Courses & Tours
Exeter Cathedral Guided Tours	(see 1)
Exeter Cathedral Roof Tours	(see 1)
5 Redcoat Tours	C3
6 Saddles & Paddles	C4

▣ Sleeping
7 ABode Exeter	C3
8 Globe Backpackers	C4
9 Hotel du Vin Exeter	D4

10 Raffles	D1
11 St Olaves	B3
12 Townhouse	A1

⊗ Eating
13 @Angela's	B4
14 Herbies	B3
15 Jasmine Thai	B3
16 Ruby	C2
17 Rusty Bike	C1

⊜ Drinking & Nightlife
18 Old Firehouse	D2
19 Timepiece	C2

⊕ Entertainment
20 Bike Shed	B3
21 Exeter Phoenix	C2
22 Exeter Picturehouse	B4

to stay and eat and you have a relaxed but lively base for explorations.

History

Exeter's past can be read in its buildings. The Romans marched in around AD 55 – their 17-hectare fortress included a 2-mile defensive wall, crumbling sections of which remain, especially in Rougemont and Northernhay Gardens. Saxon and Norman times saw growth: a castle went up in 1068, the cathedral 40 years later. The Tudor wool boom brought Exeter an export trade, riches and half-timbered houses; prosperity continued into the Georgian era when hundreds of merchants built genteel homes. The Blitz of WWII brought devastation. In 1942 in just one night, 156 people died and 12 hectares of the city were flattened. In the 21st century, the £220-million Princesshay Shopping Centre added shimmering glass and steel lines to the architectural mix.

◎ Sights

★**Exeter Cathedral**   CATHEDRAL
(Cathedral Church of St Peter; ☑ 01392- 285983; www.exeter-cathedral.org.uk; The Close; adult/child £7.50/free; ☉ 9.30am-5pm Mon-Sat, 11.30am-3.30pm Sun) Magnificent in warm, honey-coloured stone, Exeter's cathedral is one of Devon's most impressive ecclesiastical sights. Dating largely from the 12th and 13th centuries, the **west front** is framed by extraordinary medieval statuary, while inside the ceiling soars upwards to the longest span of unbroken Gothic vaulting in the world, dotted with ornate ceiling bosses in gilt and vibrant colours. Look out for the scale Lego model that's being built beside the main entrance; for £1 you can add a brick.

The site has been a religious one since at least the 5th century, but the Normans started the current building in 1114; the towers of today's cathedral date from that period. In 1270 a 90-year remodelling process began, introducing a mix of Early English and Decorated Gothic styles.

Above the **Great West Front** scores of weather-worn figures line a once brightly painted screen that now forms England's largest collection of 14th-century sculpture. Inside, the exquisitely symmetrical ceiling soars up and along, towards the north transept and the 15th-century **Exeter Clock**: in keeping with medieval astronomy it shows the earth as a golden ball at the centre of the universe with the sun, a fleur-de-lys,

travelling round. Still ticking and whirring, it chimes on the hour.

The huge oak canopy over the **Bishop's Throne** was carved in 1312, while the 1350 **minstrels' gallery** is decorated with 12 angels playing musical instruments. Cathedral staff will point out the famous sculpture of the lady with two left feet and the tiny **St James Chapel**, built to repair the one destroyed in the Blitz. Look out for its unusual carvings: a cat, a mouse and, oddly, a rugby player.

There are free informative **guided tours** of the cathedral every day, or you can self-guide with one of the free audio guides. But to get the most dramatic perspective you really need to head up into the tower and drink in the views. **Roof tours** (☑ 01392-285983; www.exeter-cathedral.org.uk; incl Exeter Cathedral admission adult/child £12.50/5; ☉ 2pm Tue, 10.30am Sat Apr-Sep) run only on Tuesdays and Fridays (you can book in advance online). There's a minimum age of eight.

Choral **evensong** services are held at 5.30pm Monday to Friday, and 4pm Saturday and Sunday.

★**RAMM**   MUSEUM
(Royal Albert Memorial Museum & Art Gallery; ☑ 01392-265858; www.rammuseum.org.uk; Queen St; ☉ 10am-5pm Tue-Sun; ☎) FREE The imposing, red-brick exterior looks every inch the Victorian museum, but a £24-million revamp has brought the exhibits bang up to date. Interactive displays focus on Exeter's heritage from prehistory to the present, as well as global exploration and the concept of collecting. Look out for Exeter's Roman-era artefacts, local Tudor carvings and the striking ethnographic displays, which include African masks, samurai armour and the mummy of Shep en-Mut.

★**Underground Passages**   UNDERGROUND
(☑ 01392-665887; www.exeter.gov.uk/passages; Paris St; adult/child £6/4; ☉ 9.30am-5.30pm Mon-Sat, 10am-4pm Sun Jun-Sep, 10.30am-4.30pm Tue-Fri, 9.30am-5.30pm Sat, 11am-4.30pm Sun Oct-May) Prepare to crouch down, don a hard hat and possibly get spooked in what is the only publicly accessible system of its kind in England. These medieval vaulted passages were built to house pipes bringing fresh water to the city. Guides lead you on a scramble through the network telling tales of ghosts, escape routes and cholera. The last tour is an hour before closing; they're popular – book ahead.

Bill Douglas Cinema Museum MUSEUM

(☎01392-724321; www.bdcmuseum.org.uk; Old Library, Prince of Wales Rd; ⏰10am-5pm; P) **FREE** This eccentric museum is a must for cinephiles, containing a vast hoard of film-themed memorabilia amassed by Scottish filmmaker Bill Douglas, best known for his semi-autobiographical trilogy about his childhood. Douglas was also an avid collector, amassing more than 50,000 cinematic collectibles, encompassing magic lanterns, peep shows, original cels from Disney films, Charlie Chaplin bottle stoppers, James Bond board games, vintage film posters, *Star Wars* toys and more. It's on the Exeter University campus, a mile northwest of the city centre.

St Nicholas Priory HISTORIC BUILDING

(☎01392-265858; www.exeter.gov.uk/priory; The Mint) Originally part of a medieval Benedictine monastery, and later a lavish Elizabethan manor house, this 900-year-old building is currently closed for renovations – check the website for updates.

Powderham Castle HISTORIC BUILDING

(☎01626-890243; www.powderham.co.uk; adult/child £11.50/9.50; ⏰11am-4.30pm Sun-Fri Apr-Jun, Sep & Oct, to 5.30pm Jul & Aug; P) The historic, and current, home of the Earl of Devon, Powderham is a stately but still friendly place that was built in 1391 and remodelled in the Victorian era. A visit takes in a fine wood-panelled Great Hall, parkland with 650 deer and glimpses of life 'below stairs' in the kitchen. Powderham is on the River Exe near Kenton, 8 miles south of Exeter.

🏃 Activities

Saddles & Paddles OUTDOORS

(☎01392-424241; www.sadpad.com; Exeter Quay; ⏰9am-6pm) Rents out bikes (adult per hour/day £6/15), kayaks (£10/35) and Canadian canoes (£15/50); the tourist office stocks maps.

👉 Tours

★Redcoat Tours WALKING

(☎01392-265203; www.exeter.gov.uk/visiting; ⏰3-6pm daily Apr-Oct, 2 daily Nov-Mar) **FREE** For an informed and entertaining introduction to Exeter's history, tag along on one of these 1½-hour tours. Themes range from murder and trade to the Tudors and religion – there are even torchlight prowls through the catacombs and evening ghost walks. Tours leave from Cathedral Yard or the Quay; there's no need to book.

LOCAL KNOWLEDGE

CATHEDRAL ROOF TOURS

For a sensational view of **Exeter Cathedral** (p270), book one of these high-rise guided **walks** (p270). Climb 251 steps up spiral staircases, head out onto the sweeping roof, then gaze down on the city from the edge of the North Tower. They're popular so book two weeks ahead.

🛏 Sleeping

Globe Backpackers HOSTEL £

(☎01392-215521; www.exeterbackpackers.co.uk; 71 Holloway St; dm/d £17.50/45; ⏰reception 8.30am-noon & 3.30-11pm; P🛜) Rightly a firm favourite among budget travellers, this spotlessly clean, relaxed, rambling former town house boasts three doubles, roomy dorms and six shared wet-room showers. There's a pleasant lounge, a rather undersized kitchen, free wi-fi and lockers for storage.

Townhouse B&B ££

(☎01392-494 994; www.townhouseexeter.co.uk; 54 St David's Hill; s £52-72, d £80-100; P🛜) One of the better B&B options in Exeter – built from red brick, clad in ivy, and with nine smart rooms with wood floors, grey-and-crimson colour schemes and plenty of original features, such as fireplaces and sash windows.

St Olaves HOTEL ££

(☎01392-217736; www.olaves.co.uk; Mary Arches St; s £75-90, d £90-109; P🛜) Whitewashed and Georgian, this smart house was built for a wealthy merchant and later served as a vicarage. These days it's a stylish if rather staid hotel, with 15 spacious rooms featuring brass bedsteads and plush furnishings; some overlook the garden. The central staircase is seriously grand.

Raffles B&B ££

(☎01392-270200; www.raffles-exeter.co.uk; 11 Blackall Rd; s £48-55, d/f from £78/88; P🛜) The antique dealer owner has peppered each room of this late-Victorian town house with heritage features – look out for Bakelite radios, wooden plant stands and polished trunks. Largely organic breakfasts and a walled garden add to the appeal.

★Hotel du Vin Exeter BOUTIQUE HOTEL £££

(☎01392-790120; www.hotelduvin.com/locations/exeter; Magdalen St; d £119-169, ste £189; @🛜🏊) This impressive red-brick edifice (once

Exeter's eye hospital) has recently been acquired by the plush Hotel du Vin chain. Quietly stylish, the rooms incorporate aspects of the building's Victorian architecture (bay windows, cornicing, wood floors) into their palette of muted colours, offbeat wallpapers and Scandi-style sofas. Elsewhere, there's a stylish octagon-shaped restaurant, an excellent bar and design touches aplenty.

ABode Exeter   HOTEL £££
(☑01392-319955; www.abodehotels.co.uk/exeter; Cathedral Yard; r £100-350; ☎) Of all the city's hotels, this one surely boasts the best location – it's smack bang on the cathedral green, and you'll be able to see the towers from your window if you bag one of the top-drawer 'Fabulous' rooms. The building is Georgian, but the style is contemporary: off-kilter floors and stained glass meet muted colours and minimalist furnishings.

✗ Eating

★ Rusty Bike   MODERN BRITISH ££
(☑01392-214440; www.rustybike-exeter.co.uk; 67 Howell Rd; mains £13-20; ☺5-10pm Mon-Sat, noon-10.30pm Sun) It's in the city, but Rusty's soul is rooted deep in the countryside. It's all about farm-to-plate dining here (or 'welly to belly', as they put it), with as much as possible coming from local suppliers – game from local estates, wild veg foraged by hand, Aberdeen Angus beef reared at nearby farms.

Jasmine Thai   BISTRO ££
(☑01392-689988; www.jasmine-thai.co.uk; 153 Fore St; mains £11-19; ☺noon-2.30pm Mon-Sat, 6-10pm daily) A spicy new addition to Exeter, this Thai restaurant has proved very popular. You can play safe with the classics – red, green, Penang or jungle curries – or go for something special, like whole sea bass with Thai herbs or 'weeping tiger' steak. Thai-style decor – Buddhas, pagodas and the like – complete the Far Eastern feel.

Ruby   BURGERS ££
(☑01392-436168; www.rubyburgers.com; 74 Queen St; mains £6-11; ☺10am-10pm) Exeter's boutique burger joint, beloved by hipsters, students and local diners of all ages. It's all studiously trendy: retro in style, fast and furious in service, with a menu that takes in classic burgers plus sliders, panko-crusted chicken fillets and 'falloumi' burgers for veggies. Extra marks for the puns on the specials board – fancy a 'Mother Ducka' or 'Notorious P.I.G', anyone?

Herbies   VEGETARIAN ££
(☑01392-258473; 15 North St; mains £7-12; ☺11am-2.30pm Mon-Sat, 6.30-9.30pm Tue-Sat; ☒) Cosy and gently groovy, Herbies has been cheerfully feeding Exeter's veggies and vegans for more than 20 years. Tuck into delicious Tuscan mushrooms, Moroccan tagine, or butter bean, thyme and squash risotto.

@Angela's   MODERN BRITISH £££
(☑01392-499038; www.angelasrestaurant.co.uk; 38 New Bridge St; mains £19.50-28.50; ☺6-9.30pm Mon-Sat) A slightly old-fashioned fine-dining restaurant, big on rich, filling dishes such as rosemary-garlic lamb loin and roast monkfish in a creamy sauce. The feel is rather formal, with starched white tablecloths and napkins shaped like shells – lovely, if you like that sort of thing.

🍷 Drinking & Nightlife

★ Old Firehouse   PUB
(☑01392-277279; www.oldfirehouseexeter.co.uk; 50 New North Rd; ☺noon-2am Mon-Wed, to 3am Thu-Sat, to 1am Sun) Step into the snug, candlelit interior of this Exeter institution and feel instantly at home. Here, dried hops hang from rafters above flagstone floors and walls of exposed stone. The range of draught ciders and cask ales is truly impressive, while the pizzas, served after 9pm, have kept countless students fed.

Timepiece   CLUB
(www.timepiecenightclub.co.uk; Little Castle St; ☺9.30pm-1.30am Mon-Wed, 10pm-2am Fri & Sat) A student's late-night favourite, with nights devoted to indie, electro, house and cheesy club classics.

☆ Entertainment

Bike Shed   THEATRE
(☑01392-434169; www.bikeshedtheatre.co.uk; 162 Fore St; ☺noon-midnight Mon-Thu, to 2am Fri & Sat, 5-11pm Sun) Emerging writers are profiled in the Bike Shed's rough 'n' ready subterranean, brick-lined performance space. Its vintage cocktail bar makes a hip setting for live music and DJ sets on Friday and Saturday nights.

Exeter Phoenix   ARTS CENTRE
(☑01392-667080; www.exeterphoenix.org.uk; Bradninch Pl, Gandy St; ☺10am-11pm Mon-Sat,; ☎) Exeter's art and soul, the Phoenix is a buzzing blend of indie cinema, performance space, galleries and a cool cafe-bar (snacks to 9pm).

RIVER COTTAGE CANTEEN

Known for his media campaigns on sustainability and organic food, TV chef Hugh Fearnley-Whittingstall has broadcast most of his TV shows from his home base at **River Cottage HQ** (☏01297-630300; www.rivercottage.net; Trinity Hill Rd, Axminster; 2-course lunch £55, 4-course dinner £70-90), near Axminster, 30 miles from Exeter. Though the house suffered a serious fire in 2012, it's since been rebuilt and is very much back in business. If you fancy seeing where the magic happens, you can book in for a sumptuous four-course meal, made with produce from Hugh's own garden, or attend one of the regular cooking courses. A cheaper option is to dine at his **canteen** (☏01297-631715; www.rivercottage.net; Trinity Sq, Axminster; mains £8-16; ☺9am-5pm daily, 6.30-9pm Tue-Sat; ✔) in Axminster village nearby.

Exeter Picturehouse   CINEMA
(☏0871 902 5730; www.picturehouses.co.uk; 51 Bartholomew St West) An intimate, independent cinema, screening mainstream and arthouse movies.

ℹ Information

Custom House Visitor Centre (☏01392-271611; customhouse@exeter.gov.uk; 46 The Quay; ☺10am-5pm daily Apr-Oct, 11am-4pm Nov-Mar) is a small tourist office near the quay.

Exeter Library (Castle St; per 30min £3; ☺9am-6pm Mon, Tue, Thu & Fri, 10am-5pm Wed, 9am-4pm Sat; 🛜) has internet access and free wi-fi.

Exeter Tourist Office (☏01392-665700; www.heartofdevon.com; Dix's Field; ☺9am-5pm Mon-Sat Apr-Sep, 9.30am-4pm Mon-Sat Oct-Mar) is efficient and well run, with plenty of info on Exeter and the rest of Devon.

Police Station (☏08452-777444; Heavitree Rd; ☺24hr)

Royal Devon & Exeter Hospital (Barrack Rd) caters for accident and emergency.

ℹ Getting There & Away

AIR

Exeter International Airport (www.exeter-airport.co.uk) is 6 miles east of the city. Flights connect with several UK cities, including Manchester, Newcastle, Edinburgh and Glasgow, as well as to the Isles of Scilly and the Channel Islands. Flights also travel to European cities, including Paris, Amsterdam and Dublin.

Bus 56 runs from Exeter St David's train station and Exeter bus station to Exeter International Airport (£3, 30 minutes, hourly 7am to 6pm).

BUS

Services include the following:

Lyme Regis (£7.70, six daily Monday to Friday, five on Saturday and Sunday) Bus X52 runs via Beer; four services continue to Bridport.

Plymouth bus X38; £9.70, 1¼ hours, every other hour Monday to Saturday, two on Sunday

Totnes bus X64; £9.70, 50 minutes, eight daily Monday to Friday, seven on Saturday, three on Sunday

Transmoor Link/Bus 82 runs on summer Saturdays and Sundays only (mid-May to mid-September), making one trip each way from Exeter to Tavistock (£5.80) via Moretonhampstead, Postbridge, Princetown and Yelverton.

TRAIN

Main-line trains stopping at St David's train station include the following:

Bristol £27.50, 1¼ hours, half-hourly

London Paddington £47.50, 2½ hours, half-hourly

Paignton £6.60, 50 minutes, half-hourly

Penzance £20.40, three hours, half-hourly to hourly

Plymouth £9.10, one hour, half-hourly

Torquay £6.60, 45 minutes, half-hourly to hourly

Totnes £11, 35 minutes, half-hourly

Some branch-line services also go through Central train station.

ℹ Getting Around

BICYCLE

Saddles & Paddles (p271) rents out bikes.

BUS

Bus H (two to four per hour) links St David's train station with Central train station and the High St, passing near the bus station.

CAR

Most of the major car-hire firms have desks at the airport, and a few have concessions at the train station too.

There are plenty of car parks in the city centre, but there can be heavy traffic during rush hour and on weekends. Park & Ride buses (adult/child return £2.50/1.60) operate every 20 minutes, running from Sowton (near M5, junction 30) and Matford (near M5, junction 31) Monday to Saturday, and from Honiton Rd (near M5, junction 29) daily.

TAXI

There are taxi ranks at St David's train station and on High and Sidwell Sts.

Capital Taxis (☑ 01392-434343)
Club Cars (☑ 01392-213030)
Gemini (☑ 01392-666666)

Torquay & Around

POP 114, 266

It may face the English Channel, rather than the Med, but the coast around Torquay has long been dubbed the English Riviera; famous for palm trees, piers and russet-red cliffs. At first glance, Torquay itself is the quintessential English seaside resort in flux, beloved by both the coach-tour crowd and stag- and hen-party animals. But a mild microclimate and an azure circle of bay have also drawn a smarter set and Torquay now competes with foodie-hub Dartmouth for fine eateries. The area also boasts unique attractions that range from an immense aviary to a surreal model village. Add an Agatha Christie connection, fishing boats and steam trains, and it all adds up to some grand days out beside the sea.

Torquay's neighbouring resort, Paignton, and its Victorian pier, sits 3 miles south. The fishing port of Brixham is 5 miles further south again.

◉ Sights & Activities

Torquay boasts no fewer than 20 beaches and an impressive 22 miles of coast. Holidaymakers flock to the central (but tidal) **Torre Abbey Sands**; locals head for the sand-and-shingle beaches beside the 73m red-clay cliffs around **Babbacombe**.

Train buffs won't want to miss a trip from Paignton aboard the Dartmouth Steam Railway (p277).

Living Coasts   ZOO
(☑ 0844-474 3366; www.livingcoasts.org.uk; Beacon Quay; adult/child £12.20/9.15; ☺10am-5pm) An enormous open-plan aviary bringing you up close to free-roaming penguins, punk-rocker-style tufted puffins and irresistibly cute otters. Booking online saves money and queues.

Babbacombe Model Village   EXHIBITION
(☑ 01803-315315; www.model-village.co.uk; Hampton Ave; adult/child £10.95/8.95; ☺10am-4pm,

until 9pm some summer evenings) Prepare for a fabulously eccentric, 1.6-hectare world in miniature, complete with small-scale Stonehenge, football stadium, beach, castle (under attack from a fire-breathing dragon) and thatched village where firefighters are tackling a blaze. Visit in the evening for illuminations; think pocket-sized Piccadilly Circus, complete with flashing signs. The height of kitsch, but improbably good fun.

Babbacombe Cliff Railway   RAIL
(☑ 01803-328750; www.babbacombecliffrailway. co.uk; adult/child return £2.20/1.50; ☺9.30am-4.55pm Feb-Oct) At Babbacombe, a glorious 1920s funicular railway sees you climbing into a tiny wooden carriage and rattling up and down rails set into the cliff.

Paignton Zoo   ZOO
(☑ 0844-474 2222; www.paigntonzoo.org.uk; Totnes Rd, Paignton; adult/child £16.95/12.75; ☺10am-5pm; ☐) A conservation charity runs this innovative, 32-hectare zoo, where spacious enclosures recreate habitats as varied as savannah, wetland, tropical forest and desert. High spots include the orangutan island, a vast glass-walled lion enclosure and a lemur wood, where you walk over a plank suspension bridge as the primates leap around in the surrounding trees. Then there's the steamy crocodile swamp with pathways winding over and beside Nile, Cuban and saltwater crocs, some up to 6m long.

🛏 Sleeping

Torquay Backpackers   HOSTEL £
(☑ 01803-299924; www.torquaybackpackers. co.uk; 119 Abbey Rd; dm/d £17/38; @🤶) Photos of grinning past guests plaster noticeboards; flags of all nations drape the walls at this budget stalwart. There are luxuries too: a DVD den and a decked, alfresco pool-table terrace, but dorms can be a bit noisy as it's popular with stag and hen dos. There's a £1 surcharge for Friday and Saturday stays.

Hillcroft   B&B ££
(☑ 01803-297247; www.thehillcroft.co.uk; 9 St Lukes Rd; r £79, d £105-120; ☐@🤶) One of the better B&B options in Torquay town, with rooms styled after Morocco, Bali, Lombok and Tuscany. The pick of the rooms are the spacious suites: Provençal, with ormolu bed and sitting room, or India with Indian art and four-poster bed.

AGATHA CHRISTIE

Torquay is the birthplace of the 'Queen of Crime', Agatha Christie (1890–1976), author of 75 novels and 33 plays, and creator of Hercule Poirot, the moustachioed, immodest Belgian detective, and Miss Marple, the surprisingly perceptive busybody spinster. Born Agatha Miller, she grew up, courted and honeymooned in Torquay, and also worked as a hospital dispenser here during WWI, thus acquiring her famous knowledge of poisons.

The tourist office stocks the free Agatha Christie Mile leaflet, which guides you around significant local sites, while **Torquay Museum** (☏ 01803-293975; www.torquaymuseum. org; 529 Babbacombe Rd; adult/child £6.45/3.95; ⊙10am-4pm) has a collection of photos, handwritten notes and displays devoted to her famous detectives. The highlight, though, is **Greenway** (p277), her summer home near Dartmouth. The **Greenway Ferry** (p278) sails there from Torquay's Princess Pier – it's best to book. Boats also go from Dartmouth and Totnes; a steam train runs from Paignton.

★**Cary Arms** BOUTIQUE HOTEL **£££**
(☏ 01803-327110; www.caryarms.co.uk; Babbacombe Beach; d £195-295, ste £375-450; P 🔊 🐾) In a dreamy spot beside Babbacombe's sands, this heritage hotel has more than a hint of a New England beach retreat. Bright, light-filled rooms with candy-stripe throws and white furniture shimmer with style, and the best have sea-view balconies. There's a divine spa, too.

Orestone HOTEL **£££**
(☏ 01803-328098; www.orestonemanor.com; Rock House Lane; r £150-275, ste £350; P 🔊) A refined hideaway, in a wooded valley 3 miles north of Torquay. With its gabled facade and plush public areas, there's a dash of period elegance here, and the rooms vary widely in terms of space and comfort: classic doubles are a bit small and floral, so it's worth spending for extra style and roominess. The terrace is gorgeous, overlooking subtropical gardens to the sea.

✕ Eating

★**The Elephant** MODERN BRITISH **££**
(☏ 01803-200044; www.elephantrestaurant.co.uk; 3 Beacon Tce; 2-course lunch menu £14.50, mains £15.50-24; ⊙noon-2pm & 6.30-9pm Tue-Sat) This fine-dining beauty remains Torquay's premier foodie destination, although it's slimmed down operations by combining two restaurants into one. It's run by chef Simon Hulstone, who still has a taste for seasonal food and elaborate presentation, but these days it's a more relaxed affair. Expect quality bistro dishes like scallop ceviche and sticky-braised pig's cheeks, made with top Devonian ingredients.

Number 7 SEAFOOD **££**
(☏ 01803-295055; www.no7-fish.com; 7 Beacon Tce; mains £13.75; ⊙noon-1.45pm Wed-Sat year-round, 7-9pm daily Jul-Sep, Tue-Sat Oct-Jun) No-fuss fish is the order of the day at this small family-run bistro. The decor's a bit dated, but the food is as fresh as ever: crab, lobster, scallops and cod steaks, laced with garlic butter or dusted with Moroccan spices.

Rockfish SEAFOOD **££**
(☏ 01803-212175; 20 Victoria Pde; mains £11.95-18.95; ⊙noon-9.30pm) Mitch Tonks' rapidly expanding mini-chain of seafood restaurants has opened a new branch on the Torquay seafront, and its taste for relaxed catch-of-the-day dining has unsurprisingly proved popular. Whitewashed wood and nautical knick-knacks give it a shipshape ambience, and the food takes in everything from classic fish and chips to a take on Italian *fritto misto* (mixed fried fish).

ℹ Information

Post Office (7-13 Union St)
Torquay Tourist Office (☏ 01803-211211; www.theenglishriviera.co.uk; Vaughan Pde; ⊙9.30am-2pm Mon-Sat) Torquay's main tourist office covers Torquay, Paignton and Brixham.

ℹ Getting There & Away

BUS
Brixham (Bus 12; £4.10, 50 minutes, half-hourly) Via Paignton.
Dartmouth (£4.50, 1¼ hours, hourly Mon-Sat) Stagecoach Gold.
Totnes (£3.50, 45 minutes, half-hourly Mon-Sat, seven on Sunday) Stagecoach Gold.

FERRY

Regular **ferries** (p279) shuttle between Torquay and Brixham (one way/return £2/3).

TRAIN

Trains run from Exeter via Torquay (£6, 45 minutes, half-hourly to hourly) to Paignton (£6, 52 minutes).

Brixham

POP 17,457

An appealing, pastel-painted tumbling of fishermen's cottages leads down to Brixham's horseshoe harbour where arcades and gift shops coexist with winding streets, brightly coloured boats and one of England's busiest fishing ports. Although picturesque, Brixham is far from a neatly packaged resort, and its brand of gritty charm offers an insight into work-a-day life along Devon's coast.

◉ Sights

Golden Hind   HISTORIC SHIP

(☎01803-856223; www.goldenhind.co.uk; The Quay; adult/child £7/5; ◉10.30am-4pm Mar-Oct) Devon explorer Sir Francis Drake carried out a treasure-seeking circumnavigation of the globe aboard the *Golden Hind,* in the late 1500s. This full-sized replica sees you crossing the gangplank, clambering below decks, peering into the captain's cabin and prowling around the poop deck.

Brixham Heritage Museum   MUSEUM

(☎01803-856267; www.torbaymuseums.com; Bolton Cross; adult/child £2/free; ◉10am-4pm Tue-Fri, 10am-1pm Sat) An eclectic collection of exhibits explores the town's salty history, majoring on sailboats, smuggling, shipbuilding and sea rescues. There are reconstructions of a fisherman's cottage and police cell, but it's the sepia-tinted photos of the town's past that steal the imagination.

☞ Tours

★Fish Market   FOOD & DRINK

(☎07973 297620; bfmt2014@gmail.com; The Quay; tours incl breakfast £12.50) Life in Brixham revolves around the fish market, and it's possible to book a guided tour during summer months. You'll see ice-lined fish trays, white-coated buyers and a bustling auction, then have breakfast at the Fishermen's Mission – but you'll need to be an early riser, as the action kicks off at 6am. Bookings essential.

✗ Eating & Drinking

David Walker & Son   SEAFOOD £

(www.davidwalkerandson.com; Unit B, Fish Market; ◉9am-3pm Mon-Fri, 8am-3pm Sat) Fish doesn't get any fresher than at Mr Walker's fish stall, where all the catches of the day are piled high on beds of ice. Crab, lobster, skate, hake and sea bass – there's no telling which little fishy you'll find for your dishy.

Beamers   SEAFOOD ££

(☎01803-854777; www.beamersrestaurant.co.uk; 19 The Quay; mains £16.95-29.95; ◉6.30-9pm Wed-Mon; ☑) A superior seafood choice, where all the fish is sourced on a daily basis straight from the quayside market. Samphire, saffron and Pernod spring some menu surprises; bagging a window table secures an absorbing harbour view.

Maritime   PUB

(www.themaritime.co.uk; 79 King St; ◉7-11pm) Eccentric old boozer smothered in thousands of key rings, stone jugs and chamber pots, presided over by a chatty parrot called Mr Tibbs.

ℹ Getting There & Away

Regular **ferries** (p279) shuttle between Brixham and Torquay (one way/return £2/3).

Kingswear (bus 22; £3.20, 15 minutes, half-hourly to hourly) **Ferry** (p278) connections continue to Dartmouth.

Torquay (bus 12; £4.10, 50 minutes, half-hourly) Via Paignton.

Dartmouth & Around

POP 10,716

Home to the nation's most prestigious naval college, the riverside town of Dartmouth is surely one of Devon's prettiest, awash with pastel-coloured, punch-drunk 17th- and 18th-century buildings leaning at crazy angles, and a picturesque harbour stacked with yachts and clanking boat masts. It's distinctly chic these days, but it's still a working port, and the triple draw of regular riverboat cruises, the art-deco house of Coleton Fishacre and Agatha Christie's former home at Greenway make Dartmouth all but irresistible.

Dartmouth is on the west side of the Dart estuary. It's linked to the village of Kingswear on the east bank by fleets of car and foot ferries, providing a key transport link to Torquay.

Sights

★ Greenway
HISTORIC BUILDING

(NT; ☎ 01803-842382; www.nationaltrust.org.uk; Greenway Rd, Galmpton; adult/child £10.30/5.10; ⏱ 10.30am-5pm) High on Devon's must-see list, the captivating summer home of crime writer Agatha Christie sits beside the placid River Dart. Part-guided tours allow you to wander between rooms where the furnishings and knick-knacks are much as she left them. The bewitching waterside gardens include features that pop up in her mysteries, so you get to spot locations made notorious by fictional murders. Car parking needs to be prebooked; the best way to arrive is by Greenway Ferry (p278) or on foot.

Christie owned Greenway between 1938 and 1959, and the house feels frozen in time: check out the piles of hats in the lobby, the books in her library, the clothes in her wardrobe, and listen to her speak (via a replica radio) in the drawing room. In the gardens, woods are speckled with splashes of magnolias, daffodils and hydrangeas frame the water, while the planting creates intimate, secret spaces – the boathouse and views over the river are sublime. In Christie's book *Dead Man's Folly*, Greenway doubles as Nasse House, with the boathouse making an appearance as a murder scene.

The Greenway Ferry runs to the house year-round, or you can take the Dartmouth Steam Railway from Paignton to Greenway Halt and walk half a mile through the woods. The last way to arrive is to hike along the picturesque **Dart Valley Trail** from Kingswear (4 miles).

★ Coleton Fishacre
HISTORIC BUILDING

(NT; ☎ 01803-842382; www.nationaltrust.org.uk; Brownstone Rd, near Kingswear; adult/child £10.30/5.10; ⏱ 10.30am-5pm; P) For an evocative glimpse of Jazz Age glamour, drop by the former home of the D'Oyly Carte family of theatre impresarios. Built in the 1920s, its faultless art-deco embellishments include original Lalique tulip uplighters, comic bathroom tiles and a stunning saloon – complete with tinkling piano. The croquet terrace leads to deeply shelved subtropical gardens and vistas of the sea. Hike the 4 miles along the cliffs from Kingswear, or drive.

Dartmouth Castle
CASTLE

(EH; ☎ 01803-833588; www.english-heritage.org.uk/visit/places/dartmouth-castle; adult/child £6.10/3.70; ⏱ 10am-6pm Apr-Sep, to 5pm Oct, to 4pm Sat & Sun Nov-Mar) Encounter mazy passages, atmospheric guardrooms and great views from the battlements. Get there via the tiny, open-top Castle Ferry (p278).

★ Dartmouth Steam Railway
RAIL

(☎ 01803-555872; www.dartmouthrailriver.co.uk; Torbay Rd, Paignton; adult/child/family return £16/9.50/43.25; ⏱ 4-9 trains daily Mar-Nov) Chugging from seaside Paignton to the beautiful banks of the River Dart, these vintage trains roll back the years to the age of steam. The 7-mile, 30-minute journey puffs past Goodrington Sands stopping at Greenway Halt (near Agatha Christie's former home), then the village of Kingswear, where ferries shuttle across to picturesque Dartmouth.

There are various other trips available, involving coastal cruises and excursions on a paddle steamer; see the website for the full round-up.

Sleeping

★ Bayard's Cove
B&B ££

(☎ 01803-839278; www.bayardscoveinn.co.uk; 27 Lower St; d £125-155, f £185; ⏱) Crammed with character and bursting with beams, Bayard's Cove sees you sleeping amid whitewashed stone walls and huge church candles. The lavish family suites feature grand double beds and kids' cabins, complete with bunk beds and tiny TVs; there are even estuary glimpses from the rooms.

Alf Resco
B&B ££

(☎ 01803-835880; www.cafealfresco.co.uk; Lower St; d from £70-90, apt £100) Ahoy, me hearties – not content with providing some of the town's yummiest food, Alf's also offers a couple of cosy rooms, bunk beds in the 'Crew's Quarters' and a 'Captain's Cabin', squeezed in under the rafters with all the atmosphere of a ship's cabin (lanterns, panelled walls, watery views and all).

Just B
GUESTHOUSE ££

(☎ 01803-834311; www.justbdartmouth.com; reception 17 Fosse St; r £75-110) The nine chi-chi options here range from bedrooms with bathrooms to mini-apartments, all featuring snazzy furnishings, crisp cottons and comfy beds. They're scattered over three central properties, and the 'just B' policy (no '&B' means no breakfast) keeps prices down.

Eating

★ Alf Resco
CAFE £

(☎ 01803-835880; www.cafealfresco.co.uk; Lower St; mains from £6; ⏱ 7am-2pm; ⏱) An eclectic crowd hangs out at Alf's – you'll be eating among hipsters, families, tourists and river-boat crews. The same menu spans breakfast through to lunch; expect piled-high fry-ups, irresistible pastries and eye-opening espressos. The gorgeous B&B rooms (p277) are pure shabby chic.

Rockfish
FISH & CHIPS ££

(☑ 01803-832800; www.rockfishdevon.co.uk; 8 South Embankment; mains £10-18; ☺ noon-9.30pm) The Dartmouth outpost of Mitch Tonks' four-strong bistro chain. Seafood is the speciality, and the weathered boarding and maritime decor fit right in along Dartmouth's streets. The fish and chips are delicious.

★ Seahorse
SEAFOOD £££

(☑ 01803-835147; www.seahorserestaurant.co.uk; 5 South Embankment; mains £19-28; ☺ noon-3pm Tue-Sun, 6-10pm Tue-Sat) What Rick Stein is to Cornwall, Mitch Tonks is to Devon – a seafood supremo, with a clutch of restaurants across the county. The Seahorse is the Tonks original, and still the best: a classic fish restaurant where the just-landed produce is roasted over open charcoals. Leather banquettes, wood floors and a wine wall give it a French bistro feel.

ℹ Information

Tourist Office (☑ 01803-834224; www.discoverdartmouth.com; Mayor's Ave; ☺ 10am-4pm Mon, Tue & Thu-Sat)

ℹ Getting There & Away

BUS

Plymouth (£7.20, 2½ hours, hourly Monday to Saturday) Stagecoach bus 3. Two buses run as far as Kingsbridge on Sunday.

Totnes (£3.70, 50 minutes, hourly Monday to Saturday) Stagecoach bus X64 continues to Exeter.

FERRY

Several ferries run from Dartmouth's quay:

Castle Ferry (www.dartmouthcastleferry. co.uk; adult/child return £5/3; ☺ 10am-4.45pm Apr-Oct) Runs to Dartmouth Castle.

Dartmouth–Kingswear Higher Ferry (☑ 07866 531687; www.dartmouthhigherferry. com; car/pedestrian one way £5.60/60p; ☺ 6.30am-10.45pm) Carries cars and pedestrians across the estuary every six minutes, and enables you to avoid the town's narrow streets.

Dartmouth–Kingswear Lower Ferry (www. southhams.gov.uk/DartmouthLowerFerry; car/ pedestrian £4.50/1.50; ☺ 7.10am-10.55pm) The town's oldest ferry service, in business since the 1300s. It's a float boat that's pulled by a tug moored alongside.

Greenway Ferry (☑ 01803-882811; www. greenwayferry.co.uk; adult/child return £8.50/6.50) Boats to Greenway and Dittisham, plus scenic river cruises.

TRAIN

The **Dartmouth Steam Railway** (p277) links Kingswear and Paignton.

Totnes & Around

POP 8041

Totnes has such a reputation for being alternative that local jokers wrote 'twinned with Narnia' under the town sign. For decades famous as Devon's hippie haven, ecoconscious Totnes also became Britain's first 'transition town' in 2005, when it began trying to wean itself off a dependence on oil. Sustainability aside, Totnes boasts a tempting vineyard, a gracious Norman castle and a mass of fine Tudor buildings, and is the springboard for a range of adrenaline sports.

◎ Sights & Activities

★ Sharpham Wine & Cheese
WINERY

(☑ 01803-732203; www.sharpham.com; ☺ 10am-6pm May-Sep, 10am-5pm Mar & Apr, 10am-3pm Oct-Dec, booking required for some tours; ℙ) This is one of Devon's most prestigious vineyards, particularly known for its crisp, sparkling whites. You can explore the steep vine-covered hills on your own (£8.95), and then head for the shop for a taste or a sit-down meal in the excellent **Anchorstone Café** (☑ 01803-732178; www.anchorstoneatsharphamvineyard.co.uk; Sharpham Vineyard; mains £7-15; ☺ 10am-4.30pm, lunch served noon-2.30pm Apr-Sep; ✔). Longer tours including tutored tastings are available by reservation.

The vineyard is 3 miles south of Totnes, off the A381.

Totnes Castle
CASTLE

(EH; ☑ 01803-864406; www.english-heritage.org.uk; Castle St; adult/child £4/2.40; ☺ 10am-6pm Apr-Sep, to 5pm Oct, to 4pm Sat & Sun Nov-Mar) The outer keep of Totnes' Norman motte-and-bailey fortress crowns a hill at the top of town, providing engrossing views over higgledy-piggledy rooftops and the river valley. Look out for the medieval toilet, too (but maybe don't use it).

Dartington Estate
HISTORIC SITE

(☑ 01803-847000; www.dartington.org; ☺ gardens dawn-dusk, visitor centre 9am-5pm) Henry VIII gave this pastoral 324-hectare estate to two of his wives (Catherines Howard and Parr). For many years it was home to the town's art college; now the 14th-century manor house hosts events, including the renowned classical music and literature festivals. There's also a great art-house cinema, a decent pub and you can even stay here if you like – but the gorgeous grounds are definitely worth a wander even if not. It's about 2 miles northwest of Totnes.

★ **Dynamic Adventures**   ADVENTURE SPORTS
(☑ 01803-862725; www.dynamicadventurescic.co.uk; The Shops at Dartington, Dartington) The superb activities on offer here include canoeing and kayaking (per half-/full day £35/70) and sea kayaking (from £75), as well as rock climbing and archery (both per hour £15). It also rents bikes (half-/full day £12/16).

It's based 2 miles northwest of Totnes.

Totnes Kayaks   KAYAKING
(☑ 07799 403788; www.totneskayaks.co.uk; The Quay, Stoke Gabriel; 1/3/6hr £20/25/40) On these self-guided paddles beside unspoilt hills, it's best to go with the tide (owner Tom will advise); so either upriver past Sharpham Vineyard, or downriver to the charming village of Dittisham. You set off from sleepy Stoke Gabriel, 5 miles southeast of Totnes.

🛏 Sleeping & Eating

★ **Dartington Hall**   B&B ££
(☑ 01803-847147; www.dartington.org; Dartington, near Totnes; s/d from £59/99; 🅿 🛜) The wings of this idyllic, ancient manor house have been carefully converted into rooms that range from heritage themed to deluxe modern. Ask for one overlooking the grassy, cobble-fringed courtyard and settle back for a truly tranquil night's sleep. The estate is about 1.5 miles from Totnes.

Willow   VEGETARIAN £
(☑ 01803-862605; 87 High St; mains £5-10; ⊙ 11am-8pm Sun-Tue, 11am-9pm or 10pm Wed-Sat; 🥄) 🍴 Totnes' alternative crowd makes a beeline for this long-standing veggie and wholefood cafe, as homely as an old tie-dyed T-shirt. Quiches, hotpots, salads, moussaka, gluten-free cakes – you'll find them all here. There's a weekly curry night.

★ **Riverford Field Kitchen**   MODERN BRITISH ££
(☑ 01803-762074; www.riverford.co.uk; Wash Barn; 3-course lunch/dinner £23.50/27; ⊙ noon-2.30pm daily, 6-10pm most evenings; 🥄) 🍴 This ecofriendly, organic, plough-to-plate farm is where everyone wants to eat when they come to Totnes (booking essential). It began as a food-box scheme, and has now branched out with a delightful barn bistro, where diners sit communally at long wooden tables and hand round dishes of the day. Rustic flavours rule: delicious salads, roast meats, imaginative veggie options.

Rumour   PUB FOOD ££
(☑ 01803-864682; www.rumourtotnes.com; 30 High St, Totnes; mains £9-18; ⊙ noon-3pm Mon-Sat, 6-9pm daily) 🍴 Rumour is a local institution – a narrow, cosy pub-restaurant with low lighting, funky local art and newspapers to read. It's legendary for its pizzas (£9), but there's lots more choice too – risottos, steaks, stews and fish of the day.

ℹ Information

Tourist Office (☑ 01803-863168; www.totnesinformation.co.uk; Coronation Rd; ⊙ 10am-4pm Mon-Sat Apr-Oct, 10am-4pm Mon-Fri, 10am-1pm Sat Nov-Mar) Small but well-stocked tourist office with lots of good links to local accommodation and activity providers.

ℹ Getting There & Around

BOAT

Boats shuttle downriver to Dartmouth with the **Dartmouth Steam Railway and Riverboat Company** (☑ 01803-555872; www.dartmouthrailriver.co.uk).

BUS

Totnes has a good bus service, although some buses and coaches run a rather Byzantine timetable. Useful options:

Exeter (£9.70, every two hours Monday to Saturday, three on Sunday) Stagecoach Bus X64; continues to Dartmouth in the opposite direction.

Plymouth (£3.40, one hour, half-hourly Monday to Friday, hourly at weekends) Stagecoach Gold.

Torquay (£3.70, 45 minutes, half-hourly Monday to Friday, hourly at weekends) Stagecoach Gold.

TRAIN

Trains go at least hourly to Exeter (£11, 35 minutes) and Plymouth (£8, 30 minutes).

The quaint **South Devon Steam Railway** (www.southdevonrailway.co.uk; adult/child return £14/8.40; ⊙ 3-9 trains daily Apr-Oct) chuffs to Buckfastleigh, on the edge of Dartmoor.

Plymouth & Around

POP 258,000

For decades, some have dismissed Plymouth as sprawling and ugly, pointing to architectural eyesores and sometimes palpable poverty. But the arrival of high-profile chefs Hugh Fearnley-Whittingstall and Mitch Tonks, and ongoing waterfront regeneration begs a rethink. Yes, the city, an important Royal Naval port, suffered WWII bomb damage, and today it is still sometimes more gritty than pretty, but Plymouth is also packed with possibilities: swim in an art-deco lido; tour a gin distillery; learn to kayak; roam an aquarium; take a boat trip across the bay; then see a top-class theatre show and party till dawn. And the ace in the pack? Plymouth Hoe – a cafe-dotted, wide grassy headland offering captivating views of a boat-studded bay.

History

Plymouth's history is dominated by the sea. The first recorded cargo left in 1211 and by the late 16th century it was the port of choice for explorers and adventurers. It's waved off Sir Francis Drake, Sir Walter Raleigh, the fleet that defeated the Spanish Armada, the pilgrims who founded America, Charles Darwin, Captain Cook and countless boats carrying emigrants to Australia and New Zealand.

During WWII Plymouth suffered horrendously at the hands of the Luftwaffe – more than 1000 civilians died in the Blitz, which reduced the city centre to rubble. The 21st century has brought regeneration to waterfront areas, a £200-million Drake Circus shopping centre and a growing university, bringing a burst of new buildings and 30,000 students to the heart of town.

◎ Sights

★ Plymouth Hoe   LANDMARK

Francis Drake supposedly spied the Spanish fleet from this grassy headland overlooking Plymouth Sound (the city's wide bay); the bowling green on which he finished his game was probably where his **statue** now stands. The wide villa-backed promenade features scores of war memorials, including the immense **Plymouth Naval Memorial**, which commemorates Commonwealth WWI and WWII sailors who have no grave but the sea.

Smeaton's Tower   LIGHTHOUSE

(☑ 01752-304774; www.plymouth.gov.uk/museumsmeatonstower; The Hoe; adult/child £3/1.50; ◎10am-5pm Tue-Sun) The red-and-white stripes of Smeaton's Tower rise from the middle of the Plymouth Hoe headland. The whole 21m structure used to stand on the Eddystone Reef, 14 miles offshore, and was transferred here, brick by brick, in the 1880s. For an insight into past lighthouse keepers' lives, head up 93 stone steps and through the circular rooms to emerge onto an open-air platform with stunning views of the city, Dartmoor and the sea.

★ Barbican   AREA

(www.plymouthbarbican.com) For a glimpse of what Plymouth might have looked like before the bombers of the Luftwaffe had their way, head down to this historic harbour area, where the part-cobbled streets are lined with Tudor and Jacobean buildings, and old dockside warehouses have been turned into bars, restaurants and art galleries. It's also famous as the point from which the Pilgrim Fathers set sail for the New World in 1620: the **Mayflower Steps** mark the spot.

The original passenger list can be seen on the side of **Island House** nearby. The steps also commemorate Captain James Cook's 1768 voyage of discovery and the first emigrant ships to Australia and New Zealand.

These days the Barbican is one of the city's liveliest, funkiest areas – not to mention one of its prettiest. Drink it all in, me hearties.

★ Plymouth Gin Distillery   DISTILLERY

(☑ 01752-665292; www.plymouthdistillery.com; 60 Southside St; tours £7; ◎ 6 tours daily) This heavily beamed distillery has been concocting gin since 1793, making it the oldest producer of the spirit in the world. The Royal Navy ferried it round the world in countless officers' messes and the brand was specified in the first recorded recipe for a dry martini in the 1930s. Tours thread past the stills and take in a tutored tasting before retiring to the beautiful, Grade II-listed cocktail bar for a complimentary G&T. You can book places online.

Plymouth Fish Market   MARKET

(☑ 01752-204738; www.plymouthfisheries.co.uk; Sutton Harbour) Around 60,000 tonnes of fish pass through this fish market on Sutton Harbour, making it the second biggest by volume in England after Billingsgate. It's an amazing sight when it's in full flow, and it's possible to arrange a guided tour with the harbour-

Plymouth

Plymouth

◎ Top Sights
1	Barbican	D3
2	Plymouth Gin Distillery	C3
3	Plymouth Hoe	B4

◎ Sights
4	Drake Statue	B3
5	Island House	D3
6	Mayflower Steps	D3
7	National Marine Aquarium	D3
8	Plymouth Fish Market	D3
9	Plymouth Naval Memorial	B3
10	Smeaton's Tower	B4

◎ Activities, Courses & Tours
11	Plymouth Boat Trips	D3
12	Tinside Lido	B4

◎ Sleeping
13	Acorns & Lawns	B3
14	Imperial	B3
15	Sea Breezes	A4

◎ Eating
16	Catch 22	C3
17	Rockfish	D3
18	Supha's Street Emporium	D2

◎ Drinking & Nightlife
19	Dolphin	D3
20	Live Lounge	C2

◎ Entertainment
21	Annabel's	C2
22	Plymouth Arts Centre	C2
23	Theatre Royal	B2

master (p.bromley@sutton-harbour.co.uk). There are also regular Fish In Sutton Harbour (FISH) guided tours with a local fisherman; check its Facebook page for the latest.

National Marine Aquarium   AQUARIUM
(☎0844 893 7938; www.national-aquarium.co.uk; Rope Walk; adult/child £14.95/10.95; ⊕10am-5pm, to 6pm Apr-Sep) The sharks here swim in coral

LOCAL KNOWLEDGE

ROYAL WILLIAM YARD

This cluster of 1830s waterfront warehouses once supplied stores for countless Royal Navy vessels. Today it's home to sleek apartments, a couple of art galleries, a relaxed pub, a chic wine bar and a string of eateries; the best are **River Cottage Canteen** (p283) and the **Royal William Bakery** (p283).

The yard is 2 miles west of the city centre; bus 34 (£1.20, eight minutes, half-hourly) runs there; better still, catch the **ferry** (☑ 07979 152008; www.royalwilliamyardharbour.co.uk/ferry.php; adult/child £3/2; ☺ 10am-5pm May-Sep to 6pm Jul & Aug) from the Barbican Pontoon.

seas that teem with moray eels and vividly coloured fish – there's even a loggerhead turtle called Snorkel who was rescued from a Cornish beach. Walk-through glass arches ensure huge rays glide over your head, while the gigantic Atlantic reef tank reveals just what's lurking a few miles offshore. Key events include Shark Shows at 11am and 3pm, plus chances to meet octopuses at 1.30pm and 4pm.

There's a slight discount for buying tickets online.

🏊 Activities

★ Tinside Lido   SWIMMING
(☑ 01752-261915; www.everyoneactive.com; Hoe Rd; adult/child/family £4/3/11.60; ☺ noon-6pm daily Mon-Fri Oct-May, 10am-6pm Jun-Sep, evening swim 6-7.30pm Wed) This glorious outdoor swimming pool is one of Plymouth's great surprises. Nestled beneath the Hoe with views over Plymouth Sound, it's a gem of the Jazz Age: built in 1935 with a blend of sleek white curves and chequerboard blue tiles, it's like something straight out of an F Scott Fitzgerald novel (only in Plymouth).

Mount Batten Centre   WATER SPORTS
(☑ 01752-404567; www.mount-batten-centre.com; 70 Lawrence Rd) A great way to explore Plymouth from a different angle is to get onto the water. This water sports and activity centre is out on the Mount Batten peninsula, linked to the Barbican by a passenger ferry (www.mountbattenferry.com; adult/child return £3/2). Two-hour taster sessions in a sit-on-top kayak cost £18.50, or you can try out sailing or stand-up paddleboarding for £19.95.

Plymouth Boat Trips   BOAT TOUR
(☑ 01752-253153; www.plymouthboattrips.co.uk; Barbican Pontoon; ☺ 4 daily Apr–mid-Oct) This boat-trip company runs various scenic expeditions from the Barbican quayside, including regular one-hour excursions around Plymouth's Dockyards and naval base (adult/child £8.50/5), plus a longer 4½-hour trip up the Tamar Valley to the Cornish village of Calstock (£17.50/12).

🛌 Sleeping

★ St Elizabeth's House   BOUTIQUE HOTEL ££
(☑ 01752-344840; www.stelizabeths.co.uk; Longbrook St, Plympton St Maurice; d £119-129; P 🛜) Prepare to be pampered. In this 17th-century manor house turned boutique bolthole, free-standing slipper baths, oak furniture and Egyptian cotton grace the rooms; the suites feature palatial bathrooms and private terraces. The only drawback is its out-of-town location: it's in the suburb-cum-village of Plympton St Maurice, 5 miles east of Plymouth.

Imperial   HOTEL ££
(☑ 01752-227311; www.imperialplymouth.co.uk; Lockyer St; s £80, d £90-110, f £140; P 🛜) Probably the pick of the options in the B&B-heavy area around the Hoe: an 1840s town house that once belonged to an admiral, now thoroughly updated. There are still a few heritage features around, but it all feels quite modern: think beige carpets, wooden furniture and the odd bit of Orla Kiely wallpaper. There's a 12-space car park.

Acorns & Lawns   B&B ££
(☑ 01752-229474; www.acornsandlawnsguesthouse.com; 171 Citadel Rd; d £60-75; 🛜) A small, modern B&B set back a little from the Hoe, with views to grassy lawns from the front-facing rooms. It concentrates on getting the basics right: there's a touch of Ikea-chic to the rooms, with minimal clutter and fresh, modern decor, and a pleasant lounge-breakfast room with varnished laminate floors and colourful art. On-street parking costs £2 per day.

Sea Breezes   B&B ££
(☑ 01752-667205; www.plymouth-bedandbreakfast.co.uk; 28 Grand Pde; s/d/f £55/85/105; P) 'Luxury to rival the finest 5* hotels' trumpets the blurb – well let's not get carried away, but this six-roomer is still a good option, with tasteful rooms in whites and sea blues, complete with plush cushions, cast-iron bedsteads, old-fashioned alarm clocks and

other thoughtful touches. Sea views abound, and owner Anne Anderson is a fine hostess.

Premier Inn Sutton Harbour HOTEL ££

(✐ 0871 527 8882; www.premierinn.com; 28 Sutton Rd; r £69-99; ✳ 🕾 👪) Yes, yes, it's part of a national chain, and it might be corporate and functional, but it's still an eminently practical sleep. The decor is inoffensive bordering on bland – cream walls, MDF furniture, plain bathrooms – but you're in a prime spot here overlooking Sutton Harbour. It won't be your most memorable night's sleep, but practicality trumps posh sometimes.

✗ Eating

★ Supha's Street Emporium ASIAN £

(✐ 01752-228513; www.suphas.co.uk; Unit 1, East Quay House; dishes £6.95-14.95; ☺ noon-9pm Tue & Sun, noon-10pm Wed-Sat; 🍴) An exotic new addition to the up-and-coming area around Sutton Harbour, this joint specialises in spicy, flavourful Thai-style street food: classic massaman curry, steamed sea bass, larb and papaya salads, and much more. There's a choice of ways to dine: small street plates, platters to share, mix-and-match curries. All are authentic and delicious, and there are plenty of veggie options, too.

Royal William Bakery CAFE, BAKERY £

(www.royalwilliambakery.com; Royal William Yard; mains £3-6; ☺ 8.30am-4.30pm; 🍴) Piles of huge, just-cooked loaves, tureens full of soup, crumbly pastries and irresistible cakes – this is a bakery like few others. The serve-yourself style is so laid-back you don't get a bill – just tell them what you've eaten and they'll tot it up at the end. The Royal William Yard is 2 miles west of the city centre, on bus route 34.

★ Rock Salt MODERN BRITISH ££

(✐ 01752-225522; www.rocksaltcafe.co.uk; 31 Stonehouse St; mains lunch £12.95-14.95, dinner £14.95-19.95; ☺ noon-3pm & 5-9.30pm; 🕾) Local boy Dave Jenkins has worked wonders at his little brasserie, which has deservedly built up a loyal local following and scooped foodie awards, too. It suits all times of day: tuck into fluffy eggs royale for breakfast, enjoy a light butternut squash risotto for lunch, and savour slow-braised ox cheek for dinner. A local diner par excellence.

Catch 22 SEAFOOD

(✐ 07557 476530; @Catch22; Quay Rd; mains £10-14; ☺ noon-8pm) This fishy pop-up has taken the harbour by storm since it opened.

Run by Mark Tam and Sam Johnson, it began as a hole-in-the-wall, serving simple, no-nonsense seafood such as fresh mussels, tempura squid and garlic king prawns. It's proved a huge hit, so they've teamed up with neighbours at the Live Lounge to offer seating, evening barbecues and feast nights.

River Cottage Canteen MODERN BRITISH ££

(✐ 01752-252702; www.rivercottage.net; Royal William Yard; mains £10-18; ☺ 10am-11pm Mon-Sat, to 4pm Sun; 🍴) Hugh Fearnley-Whittingstall's gaff focuses firmly on local, sustainable, seasonal, organic goodies. Expect meats to be roasted beside an open fire, fish to be simply grilled and familiar veg to be given a revelatory makeover. It's in the Royal William Yard, 2 miles west of the city centre; catch bus 34.

Rockfish SEAFOOD ££

(✐ 01752-255974; www.therockfish.co.uk; 3 Rope Walk; mains £9.95-14.95; ☺ noon-9.30pm) In renowned southwest chef Mitch Tonks' cheery bistro (handily set right beside the fish market), perfectly cooked cod comes with as many chips as you can eat; roasted scallops, steamed prawns and sweet Devon crab feature on the imaginative menu, too.

🍷 Drinking & Nightlife

Like any Royal Navy city, Plymouth has a more-than-lively nightlife. Union St is clubland, Mutley Plain and North Hill have a studenty vibe, while the Barbican has more restaurants amid the bars. All three areas can get rowdy, especially at weekends.

Dolphin PUB

(✐ 01752-660876; 14 The Barbican; ☺ 10am-11pm) This gloriously unreconstructed Barbican boozer is all scuffed tables, padded bench seats and an authentic, no-nonsense atmosphere. Feeling peckish? Get a fish-and-chip takeaway from two doors down, then settle down with your pint.

Live Lounge BAR

(✐ 07714 001991; 11 The Parade; ☺ 10am-4am) One of many bars and clubs dotted around the Barbican, this night spot is worth a look for its vaulted interior and decent cocktails.

Vignoble WINE BAR

(www.levignoble.co.uk; Royal William Yard; ☺ noon-11.30pm) A bijou hang-out where you can sample taster-sized glasses of your chosen vintages. It's at the Royal William Yard, 2 miles west of the city centre.

☆ Entertainment

★ Annabel's CABARET
(www.annabelscabaret.co.uk; 88 Vauxhall St;
⊙9pm-2am Thu, 8.30pm-3am Fri & Sat) Saucy
showmanship comes to the Barbican at Annabel's, a late-night cabaret club where you
never quite know what the night's entertainment might be – be it burlesque or blues,
comedy or country. It's great fun, and the
lounge-bar vibe is spot on.

Plymouth Arts Centre CINEMA
(☑01752-206114; www.plymouthartscentre.org;
38 Looe St; ⊙10am-8.30pm Tue-Sat, from 4pm
Sun) Combines a cracking independent cinema, modern-art exhibitions, and a licensed,
vegetarian-friendly bistro (closed Sunday).

Theatre Royal THEATRE
(TRP; ☑01752-267222; www.theatreroyal.com;
Royal Pde) Plymouth's main theatre stages
large-scale touring and home-grown productions; its studio space, the Drum, is renowned for featuring new writing.

❶ Information

Plymouth Library (Drake Circus; per 30min
£2; ⊙9am-6pm Mon-Fri, to 5pm Sat; 🛜)
Internet access and free wi-fi.
Police Station (Charles Cross; ⊙24hr)
Tourist Office (☑01752-306330; www.visit-
plymouth.co.uk; 3 The Barbican; ⊙9am-5pm
Mon-Sat, 10am-4pm Sun Apr-Oct, 10am-4pm
Mon-Sat Nov-Mar) Local literature aplenty, plus
advance tickets for many attractions.

❶ Getting There & Away

BUS

National Express services include the following:
Bristol £16 to £21, three hours, four to six daily
Exeter £5, one to 1½ hours, four daily
London £27.80, five to six hours, six daily
Penzance £6.20, 3¼ hours, five daily
Local services:
Exeter Bus X38; £9.70, 1¼ hours, twice hourly
Monday to Saturday, three on Sunday
Totnes Stagecoach Gold; £3.40, one hour, half-
hourly Monday to Friday, hourly at weekends

TRAIN

Services include the following:
Bristol £18.50 to £27.90, two hours, two or
three hourly
Exeter £8.60, one hour, half-hourly
London Paddington £54, 3¼ hours, half-hourly
Penzance £10, two hours, half-hourly
Totnes £8, 30 minutes, half-hourly to hourly

Dartmoor National Park

Dartmoor is Devon's wild heart. Covering
368 sq miles, this vast national park feels
like it's tumbled straight out of a Tolkien
tome, with its honey-coloured heaths, moss-
smothered boulders, tinkling streams and
eerie granite hills (known locally as tors).

On sunny days, Dartmoor is idyllic: ponies wander at will and sheep graze beside
the road, making for a cinematic location
used to memorable effect in Steven Spiel-
berg's WWI epic *War Horse.* But Dartmoor
is also the setting for Sir Arthur Conan
Doyle's *The Hound of the Baskervilles,* and
in sleeting rain and swirling mists you'll understand why; the moor morphs into a bleak
wilderness where tales of a phantom hound
can seem very real indeed.

It's a haven for outdoor activities, including hiking, cycling, riding, climbing and
white-water kayaking, and there are plenty
of rustic pubs and country-house hotels to
hunker down in when the fog rolls in.

🏃 Activities

Dartmoor is a fantastic place to get out and
active, whether that means an afternoon
hike or a horseback hack. For a broad-based
overview, multi-activity providers such as
CRS Adventures (☑01364-653444; www.crs-
adventures.co.uk; Holne Park, Ashburton) and Adventure Okehampton (p286) offer a range of
ways to get your pulse racing.

Walking

Some 730 miles of public footpaths snake
across Dartmoor's open heaths and rocky
tors. The Pathfinder *Dartmoor Walks* (£12)
guide has 28 hikes of up to 9 miles, while
its *Dartmoor Short Walks* (£8) focuses on
family-friendly treks.

The 18-mile **Templer Way** is a two- to
three-day stretch from Haytor to Teign-
mouth, while the **West Devon Way** forms a
36-mile trek linking Okehampton and Plymouth. The 95-mile **Dartmoor Way** circles
from Buckfastleigh in the south, through
Moretonhampstead, northwest to Okehampton and south through Lydford to Tavistock. The 117-mile **Two Moors Way** runs
from Wembury on the south Devon coast,
across Dartmoor and Exmoor to Lynmouth,
on the north coast.

Be prepared for Dartmoor's notoriously
fickle weather and carry a map and compass –
many trails are not way-marked. The Ord-

Dartmoor National Park

nance Survey (OS) Explorer 1:25,000 map No 28, *Dartmoor* (£8), is the most comprehensive and shows park boundaries and Ministry of Defence firing-range areas.

★**Moorland Guides**   HIKING
(www.moorlandguides.co.uk; adult £5-10, child free) Wide range of walks, from one-hour rambles to strenuous all-day hikes, on themes spanning heritage, geology, wildlife, myths and navigation.

DNPA Guided Walks   HIKING
(www.dartmoor.gov.uk/visiting; adult/child £5/free) Led by national park rangers, these organised hikes cover a variety of aspects of the moor (geology, natural history and so on), and cater for various fitness levels. They range from one to six hours.

Cycling

Routes include the 11-mile **Granite Way**, which runs, now entirely off-road, along a former railway line between Okehampton and Lydford. The 13-mile **Princetown & Burrator Mountain Bike Route** is a challenging moorland circuit along tracks and bridleways taking in Princetown, Sheepstor village and Burrator Reservoir. Tourist offices also sell the *Dartmoor Cycling Map* (£13).

Devon Cycle Hire   CYCLING
(☑ 01837-861141; www.devoncyclehire.co.uk; Sourton Down, near Okehampton; per day adult/child £16/12; ⊙9am-5pm Thu-Tue Apr-Sep) On the Granite Way. It will deliver bikes for a small charge.

Princetown Cycle Hire   CYCLING
(☑ 01822-890238; www.princetowncyclehire.co.uk; Fox Tor Cafe, Two Bridges Rd, Princetown; per day adult/child £18.50/10; ⊙9am-5pm) Based at the Fox Tor Cafe, this is handy for the Princetown & Burrator Mountain Bike Route.

ⓘ WARNING

The military uses three adjoining areas of Dartmoor as training ranges where live ammunition is used. Tourist offices can outline their locations; they're also marked on Ordnance Survey (OS) maps. You're advised to check if the route you're planning falls within a range; if it does, find out if firing is taking place when you want to walk via the **Firing Information Service** (☑ 0800 458 4868; www.mod.uk/access). During the day, red flags fly at the edges of in-use ranges, while red flares burn at night. Even when there's no firing, beware of unidentified metal objects lying in the grass. Don't touch anything you find: note its position and report it to the **Commandant** (☑ 01837-650010).

Horse Riding

A number of local stables across the moor cater to all abilities.

Babeny Farm   HORSE RIDING
(☑ 01364-631296;   www.babenystables.co.uk;
Poundsgate, near Ashburton; 1/2hr hack £25/50)
A family-run farm that offers hacks, riding lessons and a rather British 'ride to the pub'.

Cholwell   HORSE RIDING
(☑ 01822-810526;   www.cholwellridingstables.
co.uk; near Mary Tavy; 1/2hr £22/40) A family-run stables that caters for novices and experts. It's near an old silver mine on the edge of the moor near the village of Mary Tavy, about halfway between Okehampton and Tavistock.

Shilstone Rocks   HORSE RIDING
(☑ 01364-621281;   www.dartmoorstables.com;
Widecombe-in-the-Moor; per 1/2hr £40/55) This experienced riding centre offers one- and two-hour hacks from its base near Widecombe (advance bookings are required). It also breeds Dartmoor ponies.

White-Water Sports

The raging River Dart makes Dartmoor a top spot for thrill seekers. Experienced kayakers can get permits from the Dartmoor National Park Authority. For white-water kayaking, go for Dynamic Adventures (p279), near Totnes. Rivers are only open from October to mid-March.

Climbing

Adventure Okehampton   OUTDOORS
(☑ 01837-53916;   www.adventureokehampton.
com; Klondyke Rd, Okehampton; per day from £60; ⊙ school holidays only) Runs wall- and rock-climbing sessions, plus activities including archery, abseiling and wild camping.

ⓘ Information

Dartmoor National Park Authority (DNPA; www.dartmoor.gov.uk) The official national park site.
DNPA Haytor (☑ 01364-661520; ⊙ 10am-5pm Apr-Sep, to 4pm Mar & Oct, 10.30am-3.30pm Thu-Sun Nov-Feb)
DNPA Postbridge (☑ 01822-880272; ⊙ 10am-5pm Apr-Sep, to 4pm Mar & Oct, 10.30am-3.30pm Thu-Sun Nov-Feb)
Higher Moorland Tourist Office (DNPA; ☑ 01822-890414; www.dartmoor.gov.uk; Princetown; ⊙ 10am-5pm Apr-Sep, to 4pm Mar & Oct, 10.30am-3.30pm Thu-Sun Nov-Feb)
Visit Dartmoor (www.visitdartmoor.co.uk)

ⓘ Getting There & Around

Theoretically it's possible to get around Dartmoor by bus, but services can be frustratingly infrequent, and are very seasonal.

Tourist offices stock bus timetables; see also https://new.devon.gov.uk/travel.
Bus 98 (one daily Monday to Saturday) This is the only regular bus into the centre of the moor. It runs from Tavistock to Princetown, Two Bridges and Postbridge, then circles back to Yelverton. A couple of afternoon buses repeat the run as far as Princetown and back.
Bus 23 (first Saturday every month) Travels from Tavistock to Exeter via Princetown, Postbridge, Two Bridges and Moretonhampstead, but it only runs once a month.
Bus 6A (hourly Monday to Saturday, three Sunday) Skirts the northern edge of the moor en route from Bude to Exeter, stopping in Okehampton.
Bus 178 (two daily Monday to Saturday) Travels from Newton Abbot to Okehampton, via Bovey Tracey, Chagford and Morteonhampstead.
Haytor Hoppa Runs on Saturdays between June and September only, providing four buses between Newton Abbot, Bovey Tracey, Haytor and Widecombe-in-the-Moor (daily fare £5).

Princetown

POP 1767

Set in the heart of the remote, higher moor, Princetown is dominated by the grey, foreboding bulk of Dartmoor Prison and on bad weather days the town can have a bleak feel.

But it's also a useful insight into the harsh realities of moorland life and makes an atmospheric base for some excellent walks.

◉ Sights

Higher Moorland Tourist Office
INTERPRETATION CENTRE

(DNPA; ☑ 01822-890414; Tavistock Road, Princetown; ☉ 10am-5pm daily Apr-Sep, to 4pm Mar & Oct, 10.30am-3.30pm Thu-Sun Nov-Feb) Heritage displays include those on tin workings, gunpowder factories and legends, and there's a stunning time-lapse video. The office used to be the Duchy Hotel; one former guest was Sir Arthur Conan Doyle, who went on to write *The Hound of the Baskervilles*. Dartmoor lore recounts local man Henry Baskerville took the novelist on a carriage tour, and the brooding landscape he encountered, coupled with legends of huge phantom dogs, inspired the thriller.

Dartmoor Prison Museum
MUSEUM

(☑ 01822-322130; www.dartmoor-prison.co.uk; Princetown; adult/child £3.50/2.50; ☉ 9.30am-4.30pm Mon-Thu & Sat, 9.30am-4pm Fri & Sun; ℗) In the early 1800s Princetown's jail was home to French and American prisoners of war, becoming a convict jail in 1850. Just up from the looming gates, this museum provides a chilling glimpse of life inside. Look out for straitjackets, manacles, escape stories and the makeshift knives made by modern prisoners. You can also book a guided walk (adult/child £6.50/5.50) that skirts the prison perimeter and heads into otherwise out-of-bounds French and American cemeteries.

The prison itself is still in use: it's currently home to around 640 inmates.

🛏️ Sleeping & Eating

Prince of Wales
PUB, HOSTEL £

(☑ 01822-890219; www.theprinceofwalesprincetown.co.uk; Tavistock Rd; dm/s/d £10/45/65; ℗) Roaring fires, low ceilings, a friendly landlord – the Prince is the place where everyone pops in for a pint of home-brewed Jail Ale and a plate of something hot and filling. But there's another reason to stop in. There are simple B&B rooms, and a bargain bunkhouse out the back, with unexpected luxuries including central heating and a drying room.

Tor Royal Farm
B&B ££

(☑ 01822-890189; www.torroyal.co.uk; Tor Royal Lane, near Princetown; s £60, d £80-100; ℗🛜) An easygoing, country cottage–styled farmhouse packed with lived-in charm. The rooms are rather old-fashioned – cream-and-white furniture, puffy bedspreads, easy chairs – but they're very cosy, and the sumptuous afternoon tea (£14) is reason to stay here alone, with Victoria sponges, cupcakes and fancies galore.

Two Bridges
HOTEL £££

(☑ 01822-892300; www.twobridges.co.uk; Two Bridges; r £120-230; ℗🛜) Perhaps the definitive historic moorland hotel: polished wood panels, huge inglenook fireplaces, and a guest list that includes Wallis Simpson, Winston Churchill and Vivien Leigh. The Premier and Historic rooms look positively museum worthy, with massive wooden four-poster beds and antique furniture aplenty; cheaper rooms are heavy on the florals. It's 1.5 miles northeast of Princetown.

Fox Tor Cafe
CAFE £

(☑ 01822-890238; www.foxtorcafe.com; Two Bridges Rd; mains £3-12; ☉ 9am-5pm Mon-Fri, 7.30am-5pm Sat, 7.30am-5pm Sun) Known as FTC to locals, this friendly little cafe is a favourite for hearty breakfasts, doorstep sandwiches and massive chunks of cake, but it does more filling fare too, such as spicy chillis and mushroom stroganoff. There's a basic bunkhouse (dorm £11) out the back where hikers and bikers stay.

Postbridge & Around
POP 170

The quaint hamlet of Postbridge owes its popularity, and its name, to its medieval stone slab or clapper bridge; a 13th-century structure with four, 3m-long slabs propped up on sturdy columns of stacked stones. Walking over takes you across the rushing East Dart River; a picturesque spot to whip off your boots and plunge your feet into water that's quite possibly never felt so cold.

🛏️ Sleeping & Eating

Brimpts Farm
B&B £

(☑ 0845 034 5968; www.brimptsfarm.co.uk; sites per person £5, s/d/f £42.50/65/97.50; ℗) A beauty of a Dartmoor farm, as traditional as afternoon tea, and all the better for it. There's a choice of sleeps: quaint, frilly B&B rooms, two camping fields or five timber-and-aluminium camping pods, all with bewitching moorland views. It does lovely grub, too: hearty breakfasts, packed lunches and cracking cream teas. It's off the B3357, Two Bridges–Dartmeet road.

> ## ⓘ DRIVING ON DARTMOOR
>
> Dartmoor's roads are exciting to drive, but large stretches have unfenced grazing so you'll come across Dartmoor ponies, sheep and even cows in the middle of the road. Many sections have a 40mph speed limit. Car parks on the moor can be little more than lay-bys; their surface can be rough to very rough.

Dartmoor YHA

HOSTEL £

(Bellever; ☑ 0845 371 9622; www.yha.org.uk; dm £19-23, q £59-89; ℗) A characterful former farm on the edge of a conifer plantation, with a huge kitchen, lots of rustic stone walls and cosy dorms. It also rents out bikes. It's a mile south of Postbridge.

Runnage Farm Camping Barns

HUT £

(☑ 01822-880222; www.runnagecampingbarns. co.uk; dm £10; ℗) A couple of old barns on this handsome farm have been turned into bunkhouses, with basic raised beds, simple cooking facilities, and toilets and showers in a separate building. They can be centrally heated for £13 a night. There's another barn reserved for groups. It's 1.5 miles east of Postbridge: take the 'Widecombe' turning off the B3212 Moretonhampstead road.

★ Warren House Inn

PUB FOOD £

(www.warrenhouseinn.co.uk; mains £8.75-12.75; ⊙ kitchen noon-8.30pm, shorter hours winter) Marooned amid miles of moorland, this Dartmoor institution exudes a hospitality only found in pubs in the middle of nowhere. A fire that's been burning (apparently) since 1845 warms stone floors, trestle tables and hikers munching robust food; the Warreners' Pie (local rabbit) is legendary. It's on the B3212, some 2 miles northeast of Postbridge. The bar's open 11am to 11pm.

Widecombe-in-the-Moor

POP 566

With its honey-grey buildings and imposing church tower, this is archetypal Dartmoor, down to the ponies grazing on the village green. The village is commemorated in the traditional English folk song of Widecombe Fair, a traditional country pageant that takes place on the second Tuesday of September.

◉ Sights

St Pancras Church

CHURCH

St Pancras' immense 40m tower has seen it dubbed the Cathedral of the Moor. Inside search out the boards telling the fire-and-brimstone tale of the violent storm of 1638 – it knocked a pinnacle from the roof, killing several parishioners. As ever on Dartmoor, the devil was blamed, said to be in search of souls.

🛏 Sleeping & Eating

Manor Cottage

B&B £

(☑ 01364-621218; www.manorcottagedartmoor. co.uk; d £50-65; ℗ 🛜) Roses climb around the doorway of this quaint, ancient, village-centre cottage. The best billet is a bedroom-bathroom suite at the top of its own spiral staircase. Breakfasts feature berry compote, local sausages and eggs freshly laid by the hens clucking around outside.

★ Rugglestone Inn

PUB FOOD ££

(☑ 01364-621327; www.rugglestoneinn.co.uk; mains £11; ⊙ meals served noon-2pm & 6.30-9pm) Just one pint at this wisteria-clad pub is enough to make you want to drop everything and move to Dartmoor. It's a classic wood-beamed, low-ceilinged, old-fashioned village boozer, full of local characters and packed with history. There are lots of real ales on tap, and the menu features pies, lasagne, quiches and potted crab.

ⓘ Getting There & Away

Widecombe's bus service is woeful – bus 672 stops once a week (Wednesday) en route to Buckfastleigh and Newton Abbot. On summer Saturdays Widecombe is served by the Haytor Hoppa (p286).

Chagford & Moretonhampstead

With its wonky thatches and cream- and white-fronted buildings, Chagford clusters on the edge of Dartmoor around a picturesque square. But this apparently timeless moorland scene is also now home to some supremely stylish places to eat and sleep.

The bustling market town of Moretonhampstead sits 5 miles east.

◉ Sights

★ Castle Drogo

HISTORIC BUILDING

(NT; ☑ 01647-433306; www.nationaltrust.org.uk; near Drewsteignton; adult/child £9/4.45; ⊙ 11am-5pm mid-Mar–Oct; ℗) Three miles northeast

Driving Tour
A Dartmoor Road Trip

START TAVISTOCK
END CHAGFORD
LENGTH 20 MILES; ONE DAY

Driving on Dartmoor is like being inside a feature film: compelling 360-degree views are screened all around. This scenic, west-to-east transmoor traverse sweeps up and through this wilderness, taking in a bleak prison, prehistoric remains, a rustic pub and a unique castle.

Start by strolling among the fine 19th-century architecture of **1 Tavistock**, perhaps dropping by its Pannier Market to rummage for antiques. Next take the B3357 towards Princetown. It climbs steeply (expect ears to pop), crosses a cattle grid (a sign you're on the moor 'proper') and crests a hill to reveal swaths of honey-coloured tors. Soon you're at **2 Merrivale**. Park up on the right, just after the Dartmoor Inn, and stroll over the rise (due south) to discover a snaking stone row; a tiny stone circle and a standing stone are just 100m further on.

Back in the car, after a short climb, turn right towards Princetown, glimpsing the brooding bulk of Dartmoor Prison (you can't stop here; there's a better vantage point later). Call in at the **3 Dartmoor Prison Museum** (p287) to explore the jail's grim story. Cut through rugged **4 Princetown**, before picking up the B3212 towards Two Bridges; the **5 lay-by** immediately after you leave Princetown provides prime Dartmoor Prison views. As you follow signs for Moretonhampstead, an expansive landscape unfurls. At **6 Postbridge**, park and stroll over the 700-year-old bridge, then dangle hot feet in the cold River Dart. A few miles further on, the **7 Warren House Inn** (p288) makes an atmospheric spot for lunch. Around **8 Lettaford** take one of the signed, plunging lanes to **9 Chagford** to visit its quaint, thatch-dotted square. Scour some of its wonderfully old-fashioned shops, then head to **10 Castle Drogo** (p288) to explore a unique 1920s stately home. Finish the day back at Chagford at **11 22 Mill Street** (p290); a truly classy spot to eat and sleep.

of Chagford, this outlandish architectural flight of fancy was designed by Sir Edwin Lutyens for self-made food-millionaire Julius Drewe, and built between 1911 and 1931, it was intended to be a modern-day medieval castle with all the comforts of a country house. Unfortunately, Drewe's grand vision came at a price: the castle has been steadily falling to bits ever since, and it's currently the focus of a massive five-year restoration project. Parts of the house remain open during renovations.

🛏️ Sleeping & Eating

Sparrowhawk   HOSTEL £
(📞 01647-440318; www.sparrowhawkbackpackers.co.uk; 45 Ford St, Moretonhampstead; dm/d £17/38) 🚲 At this long-standing backpackers' favourite, primary colours meet beams and exposed stone in light dorms overlooking a central courtyard that's ringed by rickety outbuildings.

⭐Gidleigh Park   HOTEL £££
(📞 01647-432367; www.gidleigh.com; Gidleigh; r £315-1050; 🅿️📶) Without doubt Devon's grandest, fanciest, priciest hotel. At the end of a long private drive, the mock-Tudor house is an unashamedly opulent pamper pad: vast suites with wet-room showers, luxurious lounges with crackling fires, and a stellar restaurant (lunch/dinner menu from £30/118) overseen by multiple-Michelin-starred Michael Wignall. It's 2 miles west of Chagford.

Horse   GASTROPUB ££
(📞 01647-440242; www.thehorsedartmoor.co.uk; 7 George St, Moretonhampstead; mains £5-19; ⏱️food served 12.30-2.30pm Tue-Sat, 6.30-10pm daily) You've got to love a place that bills itself as a 'pub and nosebag'. Despite the village location, this is a hip gastropub that wouldn't feel out of place in the big city: it serves simple, well-done food including mussels, antipasti, chargrilled rib-eye and lots of pizzas.

Sandy Park   INN ££
(📞 01647-433267; www.sandyparkinn.co.uk; Sandy Park, Chagford; mains £8-12; ⏱️4-11pm Tue, noon-11pm Wed-Sat; 🅿️) This thatched pub is a good bet for no-nonsense, back-to-basics nosh that won't break the bank – battered haddock, beef lasagne and korma curry.

22 Mill Street   RESTAURANT £££
(📞 01647-432244; www.22millst.com; 22 Mill St, Chagford; 2-/3-course lunch menu £19/24, 2-/3-course dinner menu £36/42; ⏱️noon-2.30pm & 7-9pm Wed-Sat) You might not be expecting a fine-dining bistro of this calibre in quaint Chagford, but prepare to be pleasantly surprised: the food is first-rate, making maximum use of Moorland produce in its rich, French-tinged dishes. It's a smart space, with polished wood tables and light filtering through slatted blinds. There are also two upstairs rooms (from £169).

Okehampton & Lydford

Okehampton huddles on the edge of an uninhabited tract of bracken-covered slopes and granite tors – the mind-expanding landscape known as the higher moor. The town has a staging-post feel, and its traditional shops and pubs are good places to prepare for a foray into the wilderness.

Nine miles southwest of Okehampton, the little village of Lydford is best known for the dramatic gorge that cuts through the landscape nearby en route to a beautiful waterfall. Once a strategic stronghold, its medieval castle has long since tumbled into ruins.

👁️ Sights

⭐Lydford Gorge   WATERFALL
(NT; 📞 01822-820320; www.nationaltrust.org.uk; Lydford; adult/child £7.40/3.70; ⏱️10am-5pm mid-Mar–Oct) This plunging gorge is the deepest in the southwest, and can be reached via a 1.5-mile rugged riverside hike past a series of bubbling whirlpools (including the fearsome Devil's Cauldron) to the thundering, 30m-high White Lady waterfall.

Okehampton Castle   CASTLE
(EH; 📞 01837-52844; www.english-heritage.org.uk; Castle Lodge, Okehampton; adult/child £5/3; ⏱️10am-5pm Apr-Oct, to 6pm Jul & Aug) The town's castle dates back to Norman times, strategically sited on top of a rocky escarpment. Once Devon's largest castle, it's now a picturesque ruin; little remains of the interior, but several of the stout exterior walls still stand.

Finch Foundry   HISTORIC SITE
(NT; 📞 01837-840046; www.nationaltrust.org.uk; Sticklepath; adult/child £5.60/2.80; ⏱️11am-5pm mid-Mar–Oct; 🅿️) A century ago, this dramatic building would have thundered to the sound of clanging hammers and grinding metal. It was one of the busiest tool factories in the southwest, turning out hundreds of chisels, knives, shears and scythes a day. Though it's not quite the industrial powerhouse of yesteryear, it's still a working forge, powered by three working watermills. You can drive

or cycle there, or follow a 4-mile (3½-hour) walk east along the Tarka Trail from Okehampton.

🛏 Sleeping & Eating

Okehampton Bracken Tor YHA   HOSTEL £
(☎0844 293 0555; www.yha.org.uk/hostel/okehampton-bracken-tor; Saxongate; dm £24; ⊙reception 8-10am & 4-8pm; 🅿 @ 🛜) Budget-conscious outdoors types love this one: a 100-year-old country house, set in 1.6-hectare grounds on the fringe of the higher moor – it also offers climbing, canoeing and bike hire. It's a mile south of Okehampton; be aware, there's another YHA hostel in Okehampton itself.

★ Dartmoor Inn   INN ££
(☎01822-820221; www.dartmoorinn.com; Moorside, Lydford; d £115; 🅿) It might look venerable, but don't be fooled: behind the whitewashed exterior, this coaching inn is a thoroughly modern affair, light, bright and bang up to date. Most people stop in for the superb food, such as confit duck leg and butterflied lamb rump (mains £11.95 to £19.95), but it's worth spending the night: rooms sparkle with Roberts radios, sleigh beds and posh linens.

Castle   INN ££
(☎01822-820241; www.castleinnlydford.com; Lydford; d £70-95; 🅿 🛜) With nearly five centuries of pint-pulling behind it (parts of the building date from the 16th century), this village inn has views of Lydford's castle to match its beamed, olde-worlde interior. The grub is hardly haute cuisine – steaks, beef-and-ale pies, beer-battered fish – but it's enough to stave off hunger after a long hike along the gorge. Chintzy rooms are also available.

ℹ Information

Tourist Office (☎01837-53020; www.everythingokehampton.co.uk; Museum Courtyard, 3 West St, Okehampton; ⊙10am-5pm Mon-Sat Apr-Oct, to 4pm Mon, Fri & Sat Nov-Mar)

Croyde & Braunton

POP 8131
While surfers in Cornwall head for Newquay, bros and bro-ettes in Devon make a beeline for Croyde. Devon's north coast receives essentially the same swell as Cornwall's, but the scene is a lot less brash than around Newquay: here, the thatched cottages and pubs of the old village sit happily alongside the surf shops and wetsuit-hire firms. It's a fun, friendly mix, and ideal for some seaside fun.

The more run-of-the-mill market town of Braunton is 4 miles inland.

◉ Sights & Activities

The water's hard to resist in Croyde. **Ralph's** (☎01271-890147; Hobbs Hill, Croyde; surfboard & wetsuit per 4/24hr £12/18, bodyboard & wetsuit £10/15; ⊙9am-dusk mid-Mar–Dec) is among those hiring equipment. Lessons are provided by **Surf South West** (☎01271-890400; www.surfsouthwest.com; Croyde Burrows, Croyde; per half-/full day £34/64; ⊙Mar-Nov) and **Surfing Croyde Bay** (☎01271-891200; www.surfing-croydebay.co.uk; 8 Hobbs Hill, Croyde; per half-/full day £35/70).

★ Museum of British Surfing   MUSEUM
(☎01271-815155; www.museumofbritishsurfing.org.uk; Caen St, Braunton; adult/child £2/free; ⊙11am-3pm Wed-Mon Easter-Dec) Few museums are this cool. Vibrant surfboards and vintage wetsuits line the walls, sepia images catch your eye. The stories are compelling: 18th-century British sailors riding Hawaiian waves; England's 1920s home-grown surf pioneers – here heritage meets hanging ten.

Braunton Burrows   WILDLIFE RESERVE
(www.brauntonburrows.org; ⊙24hr) FREE The vast network of dunes here is the UK's largest. Paths wind past sandy hummocks, salt marshes, purple thyme, yellow hawkweed and pyramidal orchids. The burrows were also the main training area for American troops before D-Day. Mock landing craft are still hidden in the tufted dunes near the car park at its southern tip.

🛏 Sleeping & Eating

★ Baggy   HOSTEL, B&B £
(www.baggys.co.uk; Baggy Point; dm/d from £35/110; 🛜) It doesn't get much sleeker than this surf lodge–cum-cafe set right on the coast path beside Croyde Bay. The dorms are supersmart, the sea-view doubles positively boutiquey, and breakfast (served till 11am) can be eaten on decking watching the waves.

Ocean Pitch   CAMPGROUND £
(☎07581 024348; www.oceanpitch.co.uk; Moor Lane, Croyde; sites per 2 adults £26-30; ⊙mid-Jun–Sep; 🅿 🛜) A surfers' favourite, set at the northern end of Croyde Bay with brilliant views of the breakers. If you don't feel like pitching, you can rent a pre-erected bell tent

(£85 per night, two-night minimum) or even a classic VW camper (£99 per night, two-night minimum).

Thatch
INN **££**

(☑01271-890349; www.thethatchcroyde.com; 14 Hobbs Hill, Croyde; d £60-110, f £130) A legendary venue among surfers, this cavernous, thatched pub's trendy bedrooms feature subtle creams, stripes and checks; the owners offer extra rooms above another pub and in the cottage opposite. The pick, though, are at their nearby (quieter) Priory, where elegant beams frame exposed stone. Decent pub grub, too (mains £9.95 to £14.95).

Devonia Cottage
B&B **££**

(☑01271-891434; www.devoniacottage.com; 32 St Marys Rd, Braunton; d £95-105; ☎) Far and away the best B&B in Braunton, this bewitching place is run by a husband-and-wife team who've previously run a chalet in the Alps, so they know how to look after guests. The two rooms feel up to date but still have country touches such as hefty beams and pine doors – we liked Mavericks for its Velux skylights and cosy spot under the eaves.

ℹ Information

Tourist Office (☑01271-816688; www.visit-braunton.co.uk; Caen St, Braunton; ⊙10am-3pm Mon-Fri, to 1pm Sat) Inside Braunton's museum.

Ilfracombe & Around

POP 11,509

If there's anywhere that sums up the faded grandeur of the British seaside, it's surely Ilfracombe. Framed by precipitous cliffs, elegant town houses, crazy golf greens and a promenade strung with twinkling lights, it's a place that sometimes seems pickled in a bygone age. But look beneath the surface and you'll find there's another side to Ilfracombe – it's a favourite hang-out for the artist Damien Hirst, who's donated a controversial statue to the seafront, and is now home to some intriguing eateries. St-Tropez it may not be, but Ilfracombe deserves a look.

⊙ Sights & Activities

★**Verity**
LANDMARK

(The Pier) **FREE** Pregnant, naked and holding aloft a huge spear, *Verity*, towers above Ilfracombe's harbour mouth. On the seaward side her skin is peeled back, revealing sinew, fat and foetus.

Critics say she detracts from the scenery, the artist says she's an allegory for truth and justice. Either way, she's drawing the crowds.

Ilfracombe Aquarium
AQUARIUM

(☑01271-864533; www.ilfracombeaquarium.co.uk; The Pier; adult/child £4.50/3.50; ⊙10am-4.30pm, to 5.45pm late Jul & Aug) Recreates aquatic environments from Exmoor to the Atlantic, via estuary, rock pool and harbour.

★**Tunnelsbeaches**
SWIMMING

(☑01271-879882; www.tunnelsbeaches.co.uk; Granville Rd; adult/child £2.50/1.95; ⊙10am-5pm Apr-Jun, Sep & Oct, to 7pm Jul & Aug) It was a remarkable feat – in 1823 hundreds of Welsh miners hacked, by hand, the four tunnels here out of solid rock. They lead to a strip of beach where you can still plunge into the sea from Victorian tidal bathing pools.

🛏 Sleeping & Eating

Ocean Backpackers
HOSTEL **£**

(☑01271-867835; www.oceanbackpackers.co.uk; 29 St James Pl; dm £16-19, d £42-48, f £68-75; **P**@☎) Brightly painted en-suite dorms, a convivial kitchen and free coffee lend this long-established indie hostel a laid-back vibe; the giant world map in the lounge has kick-started countless travellers' tales. The doubles and family rooms are great value.

★**Norbury House**
B&B **££**

(☑01271-863888; www.norburyhouse.co.uk; Torrs Park; d £85-110, f £120-145; **P**☎) Each of the rooms in this gorgeous guesthouse is done up in a different style: choose from pop art, art deco or contemporary chic. Fabulous soft furnishings, a light-filled sitting room (complete with baby grand piano), charming hosts and cracking sea-and-town views seal the deal.

Olive Branch & Room
BISTRO **££**

(☑01271-879005; www.olivebranchguesthouse. co.uk; 56 Fore St; mains £21-23; ⊙6.30-9pm Tue-Sat; ☎) Up-and-coming chef Thomas Carr (a protégé of Nathan Outlaw) has recently taken over the reigns of this smart bistro-B&B, so you can expect top-class seafood and other refined dishes served in an intimate Georgian town-house setting. The upstairs rooms are lovely too (doubles £85 to £105), spacious and stylish, with grandstand bay views.

The Quay
EUROPEAN **££**

(☑01271-868090; www.11thequay.co.uk; 11 The Quay; mains £15-25; ⊙10am-10pm) Ilfracombe's hippest harbourside hang-out by far is owned by artist Damien Hirst (he of the cut-in-half cows and pickled sharks). His creations line the walls, so you get to tuck into lobster macaroni or Exmoor Angus steaks while studying models of his statue *Verity* and, with delicious irony, fish in formaldehyde.

ℹ Information

Tourist Office (📞 01271-863001; www.visitilfracombe.co.uk; The Seafront; ⊙ 9.30am-4.30pm Mon-Fri, from 10.30am Sat & Sun) Inside the Landmark Theatre.

ℹ Getting There & Away

Services include the following:

Bus 21/21A (half-hourly Monday to Saturday, hourly Sunday) Runs to Barnstaple (£2.40, 40 minutes) via Braunton (£1.80).

Bus 300 Heads to Lynton and Lynmouth (£3.80, 45 minutes) twice on Saturday and once on Sunday.

Clovelly

POP 440

Clovelly is the quintessential, picture-postcard Devon village. Its cottages cascade down cliffs to meet a curving crab claw of a harbour that is lined with lobster pots and set against a deep-blue sea. A clutch of impossibly picturesque inns and B&Bs makes it even harder to leave.

◉ Sights & Activities

Clovelly Historic Village HISTORIC SITE (www.clovelly.co.uk; adult/child £7/4.40; ⊙ 9am-6.30pm Jun-Sep, 9.30am-5pm Apr, May & Oct, 10am-4pm Nov-Mar; 🅿) Clovelly is privately owned, and admission is charged at the hilltop visitor centre. The village's cobbled streets are so steep that cars can't cope, so supplies are still brought in by sledge; you'll see these big bread baskets on runners leaning outside homes. Charles Kingsley, author of the children's classic *The Water Babies,* spent much of his early life in Clovelly – don't miss his former **house**, or the highly atmospheric **fisherman's cottage** and the village's twin **chapels**.

🛌 Sleeping & Eating

Donkey Shoe Cottage B&B £ (📞 01237-431601; www.donkeyshoecottage.co.uk; 21 High St; s/d £30/60) A country-style B&B plumb on Clovelly's crazily steep hill, with wooden floors, raspberry-red walls and sea views – the best is from room 3, under the eaves.

★**Berridon Farm** CAMPGROUND ££ (📞 01409-241552; www.berridonfarm.co.uk; near Bradworthy; 3 nights £400-680, 7 nights £500-1060; ⊙ Easter–mid-Oct; 🅿) At Berridon, camping goes seriously comfy. Here five- or six-person, insulated safari-style tents sport a leather sofa and wood-burner oven, plus proper beds and a flushing toilet. If it's wet, head for the shabby-chic sitting-eating-playing space in a converted barn. It's all tucked away 11 miles south of Clovelly.

Red Lion INN £££ (📞 01237-431237; www.stayatclovelly.co.uk/redlion; d £156-190) The best of the village's brace of inns, in a super waterside position with quaint, low-ceilinged rooms offering a choice of aspects: big, blue sea views, or an equally sweet outlook across the harbour front. It's plush and rather old-fashioned, and there's a choice of settings for dinner: the atmospheric bar for pub grub, or a smarter dining room for formal food.

ℹ Information

Clovelly Visitor Centre (📞 01237-431781; www.clovelly.co.uk; ⊙ 9am-6.30pm Jun-Sep, 9.30am-5pm Apr, May & Oct, 10am-4pm Nov-Mar) The visitor centre and ticket office is at the entrance to the village.

ℹ Getting There & Away

Bus 319 (five daily Monday to Saturday) runs between Clovelly, Hartland Village, Bideford (£2.20, 40 minutes) and Barnstaple (£3, one hour). This bus goes to Bude (£3.80, one daily Monday to Saturday) in the opposite direction.

BRISTOL

POP 442,500

If ever there was a British city on the rise, it's Bristol. Once a centre for heavy industry, over the last few decades the southwest's largest city has reinvented itself as a hub of culture and creativity. From Clifton's iconic suspension bridge to Brunel's groundbreaking steamship, the SS *Great Britain,* it's a city that's awash with historical interest. But Bristol is also known for its offbeat, alternative character, and you'll find a wealth of art collectives, community-run cafes and music venues dotted around – not to mention murals left behind by the city's most notorious son, the mischievous street artist Banksy.

Throw in the revamped harbourside, the landmark new M Shed history museum and

Bristol

a fast-growing foodie reputation, and it's little wonder that Bristol was recently named Britain's most liveable city. Gert lush, as they might say round these parts.

History

The city began as a Saxon village and developed into the medieval river port of Brigstow, an important trading centre for cloth and wine.

In 1497 'local hero' John Cabot (actually a Genoese sailor called Giovanni Caboto) sailed from Bristol to discover Newfoundland in 1497. The city subsequently become one of Britain's major ports, growing rich on the 'Triangular Trade', in which African slaves were shipped across the Atlantic to New World colonies, where they were bartered for luxury goods such as sugar, rum, tobacco and cotton that fetched a healthy profit back home. Much of Bristol's 18th-century splendour – including Clifton's terraces and the Old Vic theatre – were partly financed on profits from the trade.

After being usurped by rival ports in London and Liverpool, Bristol repositioned itself as an industrial and shipbuilding centre, and in 1840 became the western terminus

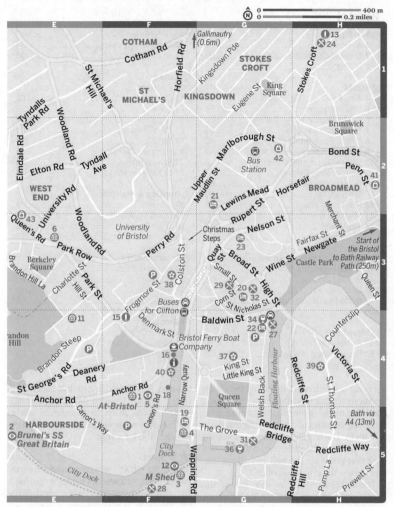

for the newly built Great Western Railway line from London.

In the early 20th century, local engineers pioneered the development of a ground-breaking aeroplane design known as the Bristol Boxkite, and the city became a hub for aeronautics; many parts for Concorde were made in nearby Filton. Unfortunately, Bristol's industrial importance made it a target for German bombing during WWII, and much of the city centre and harbourside was reduced to rubble.

In 2006, the city celebrated the bicentenary of the birth of Isambard Kingdom Brunel, the pioneering Victorian engineer responsible for (among many other things) the Great Western Railway, the Clifton Suspension Bridge and SS *Great Britain*.

⊙ Sights

★ **Brunel's SS Great Britain**   HISTORIC SITE
(📞0117-926 0680; www.ssgreatbritain.org; Great Western Dock, Gas Ferry Rd; adult/child £14/8; ⊙10am-5.30pm Apr-Oct, to 4.30pm Nov-Mar) Bristol's pride and joy is the mighty, innovative steamship, the SS *Great Britain,* designed by engineering genius Isambard Kingdom Brunel in 1843. The ship's interior has been

Bristol

◎ **Top Sights**
1 At-Bristol F4
2 Brunel's SS Great Britain E5
3 M Shed F5

◎ **Sights**
4 Arnolfini F5
5 Bristol Aquarium F4
6 Bristol Museum & Art Gallery E3
7 Bristol Zoo Gardens B1
8 Clifton Observatory A3
9 Clifton Suspension Bridge A3
10 Clifton Suspension Bridge
   Information Centre A3
11 Georgian House E4
   Giant's Cave .... (see 8)
12 Matthew F5
13 Mild Mild West H1
14 The Downs A3
15 Well Hung Lover F4

◎ **Activities, Courses & Tours**
16 Bristol Highlights Walk F4
17 Bristol Lido D2
18 Bristol Packet F4
   Cycle The City .... (see 16)
   Lanes .... (see 23)

◎ **Sleeping**
19 Bristol YHA F5
20 Brooks Guest House G3

21 Hotel du Vin G2
22 Mercure Brigstow G4
23 Rock n' Bowl G3

◎ **Eating**
24 Canteen H1
25 Cowshed D1
26 Fishers B3
27 Glassboat G4
28 Olive Shed F5
29 Ox G3
30 Primrose Café C3
31 Riverstation G5
32 St Nicholas Market G3

◎ **Drinking & Nightlife**
33 Albion C3
34 BrewDog Bristol G4
35 Grain Barge D5
36 Thekla G5

◎ **Entertainment**
37 Bristol Old Vic G4
38 Colston Hall F3
39 Fleece H4
40 Watershed F4

◎ **Shopping**
41 Cabot Circus H2
42 Loot G2
43 Rise Music E3

impeccably refurbished, including the galley, the surgeon's quarters, the dining saloon and a working model of the original steam engine (weighing 340 tons and measuring three storeys high). The highlight is the 'glass sea' on which the ship sits, enclosing an airtight dry dock that preserves the hull and allows visitors to view the screw propeller.

The SS *Great Britain* was one of the largest and most technologically advanced steamships ever built, measuring 98m from stern to tip. The ship has had a chequered history. Between 1843 and 1886, she served her intended duty as a passenger liner, completing the transatlantic crossing between Bristol and New York in just 14 days. Unfortunately, enormous running costs and mounting debts led her towards an ignominious fate: she was eventually sold off and subsequently served as a troop vessel, quarantine ship, emigration transport and coal hulk, before finally being scuttled near Port Stanley in the Falklands in 1937.

Happily, that wasn't the end. The ship was towed back to Bristol in 1970, and has since undergone an impressive 30-year res-

toration. It's resulted in a multisensory experience: prepare to stroll the deck, peep into luxury cabins, listen to passengers' stories and catch a whiff of life on board. Tickets remain valid for a year.

★ **M Shed**   MUSEUM
(☏ 0117-352 6600; www.bristolmuseums.org.uk; Princes Wharf; ◷ 10am-5pm Tue-Fri, to 6pm Sat & Sun) **FREE** Set amid the iconic cranes of Bristol's dockside, this impressive museum is a treasure trove of memorabilia. The exhibits are divided into three sections (People, Place and Life), and provide a panoramic overview of Bristol's history – from slaves' possessions and vintage buses to Wallace and Gromit figurines and a set of decks once used by Massive Attack.

Banksy's unsettling *Grim Reaper* stencil was right on the waterline of the party boat *Thekla*, but it was removed amid much controversy and now sits on the 1st floor.

It's all highly interactive and child-friendly. In summer, look out for special weekend activities including the chance to ride on the dock cranes, watch the old Pyronaut fireboat in action or catch a lift aboard one of the world's oldest steam tugs (see the website for times). The museum also runs guided tours exploring the harbour's history.

Matthew
HISTORIC SITE

(☑ 0117-927 6868; www.matthew.co.uk; Princes Wharf; ◷10am-4pm Tue-Sun Mar-Oct, Sat & Sun Nov-Feb) **FREE** The most striking thing about this replica of the vessel in which John Cabot made his landmark voyage from Bristol to Newfoundland in 1497 is its size. At 24m it seems far too small, but it would have carried a crew of around 18. Step aboard to climb below into their quarters, walk the deck and gaze up at the rigging.

Arnolfini
GALLERY

(☑ 0117-917 2300; www.arnolfini.org.uk; 16 Narrow Quay; ◷10am-6pm Tue-Sun) **FREE** The city's avant-garde art gallery occupies a hulking warehouse by the river, and remains the top venue in town for modern art, as well as occasional exhibitions of dance, film and photography.

Bristol Aquarium
AQUARIUM

(☑ 0117-929 8929; www.bristolaquarium.co.uk; Harbourside; adult/child £14.50/10; ◷10am-5pm) The underwater habitats you'll encounter here include a Bay of Rays, a Coral Sea, a Shark Tank and an Amazon River Zone. The underwater viewing tunnel adds extra appeal. There's a £2 discount per ticket for buying online.

★ At-Bristol
MUSEUM

(☑ 0845 345 1235; www.at-bristol.org.uk; Anchor Rd; adult/child £14.60/9.40; ◷10am-5pm Mon-Fri, to 6pm Sat & Sun) Bristol's interactive science museum has zones featuring space, technology, sport, the sea and the human brain. In the Curiosity Zone you get to walk through a tornado, spin on a human gyroscope and strum the strings of a virtual harp. There's also a 3D planetarium with evening stargazing shows. It's fun, interactive, and should keep you and the kids entertained for hours.

Georgian House
HISTORIC BUILDING

(www.bristolmuseums.org.uk; 7 Great George St; ◷11am-4pm Sat-Tue Apr-Oct) **FREE** Once the home of the wealthy West India merchant John Pinney, this 18th-century house provides an evocative insight into aristocratic life in Bristol during the Georgian era. It's decorated in period style, typified by the huge kitchen (complete with cast-iron roasting spit), book-lined library and grand drawing rooms, as well as Pinney's cold-water plunge-pool in the basement.

Bristol Museum & Art Gallery
MUSEUM

(☑ 0117-922 3571; www.bristolmuseums.org.uk; Queen's Rd; ◷10am-5pm Mon-Fri, to 6pm Sat & Sun) **FREE** You're in for a few surprises at this classic old Edwardian museum. Look out for the *Paint-Pot Angel* by world-famous street artist Banksy in the entrance hall; a funerary statue with an upturned pink paint pot on her head, she's designed to challenge our expectations of museum exhibits and the value of art. It's also a reminder of the artist's hugely popular 2009 exhibition here. Just above sits the Bristol Boxkite, a prototype propeller-powered biplane, which dangles from the ceiling.

Clifton Suspension Bridge
BRIDGE

(www.cliftonbridge.org.uk) Clifton's most famous (and photographed) landmark is the 76m-high Clifton Suspension Bridge, which spans the Avon Gorge. It was designed by master engineer Isambard Kingdom Brunel with construction beginning in 1836, although Brunel died before its completion in 1864. It's free to walk or cycle across; car drivers pay a £1 toll.

There's an **information centre** (www.cliftonbridge.org.uk; ◷10am-5pm) near the tower on the Leigh Woods side. Free bridge tours take place at 3pm on Saturday and Sunday from Easter to October.

The Downs
PARK

(🖽🕿) The grassy parks of Clifton Down and Durdham Down (often referred to as just the Downs) fan out from the Clifton Suspension Bridge (p297) and make a fine spot for a picnic. Nearby, the **Clifton Observatory** (☑ 0117-974 1242; www.cliftonobservatory.com; Litfield Rd, Clifton Down; adult/child £2.50/1.50; ◷10am-5pm Feb-Oct, to 4pm Nov-Jan) houses a **camera obscura** and a tunnel leading down to the **Giant's Cave,** a natural cavern that emerges halfway down the cliff with dizzying views across the Avon Gorge.

Bristol Zoo Gardens
ZOO

(☑ 0117-974 7399; www.bristolzoo.org.uk; Cecil Rd; adult/child £17/11; ◷9am-5.30pm; 🅿) Highlights at the city's award-winning zoo include a family of eight western lowland gorillas (bossed by silverback Jock) and the Seal and Penguin Coast, where African penguins, eider ducks and South American fur seals lounge around. There's also a reptile and bug zone, a butterfly forest, a lion enclosure, a monkey jungle and the **Zooropia** (adult/child £8/7) treetop adventure park. Online tickets are 15% cheaper. To get here from the city centre, catch bus 8/9.

Activities

Lanes
BOWLING
(☑0117-325 1979; www.thelanesbristol.co.uk; Nelson St; games £4-6; ⊙noon-11pm Sun-Thu, to 2am Fri & Sat) The five vintage Brunswick lanes at this boutique bowling alley are all gleaming metal and polished wood. You'll also find a craft-beer bar and huge, crispy New York–style pizzas.

Bristol Packet
BOATING
(☑0117-926 8157; www.bristolpacket.co.uk; Wapping Wharf, Gas Ferry Rd) This boat company cruises around the harbour area (adult/child £6/4, six sailings daily April to October, and on winter weekends). There are also weekly cruises to the spectacular Avon Gorge from April to September (adult/child £17/13) and a Sunday afternoon trip to Beese's Tea Gardens (£13/8, runs April to September). Cruises to Bath (£28.50/21) run once a month from May to September.

Cycle the City
CYCLING
(☑07873-387167; www.cyclethecity.org; 1 Harbourside; tours £15) These 1½-hour bike tours of Bristol's expansive harbourside are an ideal way to take in the city's main waterfront sights. The fee includes bike, helmet and an expert guide. The same firm also rents out bikes (per day £16). They don't have a shop, so bike hire and tours need to be prebooked. The bike collection point, and starting point for the tours, is No 1 Harbourside.

Bristol Highlights Walk
WALKING
(www.bristolwalks.co.uk; adult/child £6/3; ⊙11am Sat Mar-Nov) Tours the old town, city centre and harbourside, leaving from the tour-

BANKSY – STREET ARTIST

If there's one Bristolian nearly everyone has heard of, it's **Banksy** (www.banksy.co.uk) – the guerrilla street artist whose distinctive stencilled style and provocative artworks have earned him worldwide notoriety.

Though his true identity is a secret, it's believed Banksy was born in 1974 in Yate, 12 miles from Bristol, and honed his artistic skills in a local graffiti outfit. His works take a wry view of 21st-century culture – especially capitalism, consumerism and the cult of celebrity. Among his best-known pieces are the production of spoof banknotes (featuring Princess Diana's head instead of the Queen's), a series of murals on Israel's West Bank barrier (depicting people digging holes under and climbing ladders over the wall) and a painting of a caveman pushing a shopping trolley at the British Museum (which the museum promptly claimed for its permanent collection). His documentary *Exit Through the Gift Shop*, about an LA street artist, was nominated for an Oscar in 2011.

Long despised by the authorities, Banksy has become an unlikely tourist magnet. Though many of his works are short-lived, a good few still survive around the city. The **Well Hung Lover** (Frogmore St) depicts an angry husband, a two-timing wife, and a naked man dangling from a window. The startling **Paint-Pot Angel** (think pink paint meets funerary monument) resides in the foyer of the **Bristol Museum & Art Gallery** (p297) and is a reminder of the artist's hugely popular 2009 exhibition there. **Mild Mild West** (80 Stokes Croft) features a Molotov cocktail–wielding teddy bear facing three riot police and is thought to be a wry comment on Bristol's edgy-yet-comfy vibe. A stencil of the **Grim Reaper** rowing a boat, which used to sit right on the waterline of the party boat the *Thekla*, is now on the 1st floor of the city's **M Shed Museum** (p296). There are other artworks further out from the city centre; the **tourist office** (p302) sells an excellent Banksy info sheet (50p) and can advise on locations.

Banksy hit the headlines once more in 2014 when one of his murals unexpectedly appeared on a wooden panel outside the Broad Plain Boys' Club. Known as **Mobile Lovers**, the mural depicted a young couple who appear to be embracing but are actually staring into their phones. Predictably enough, a furore over ownership ensued, but the artist made it clear that he had painted the mural as a gift to the boys' club (which he's thought to have attended as a young man). After a few months on display at the Bristol City Museum, the work was sold for £400,000 to a private collector in August 2014, with all the proceeds going to fund the boys' club's ongoing projects. Good on ya, Banksy.

ist office (p302) – there's no need to book. Themed tours exploring Clifton, medieval Bristol and the history of Bristol's slave and wine trades run on request.

Festivals & Events

Bristol Shakespeare Festival THEATRE
(www.bristolshakespeare.org.uk; ⊘ Jul) One of Britain's biggest outdoor festivals devoted to the Bard runs throughout July.

Encounters FILM
(www.encounters-festival.org.uk; ⊘ Sep) Bristol's largest film fest.

Sleeping

Bristol YHA HOSTEL £
(☎ 0845 371 9726; www.yha.org.uk; 14 Narrow Quay; dm £13-22, d £30-70; @ 🖤) Few hostels can boast a position as good as this one, beside the river in a red-brick warehouse. Facilities include kitchens, a cycle store, a games room and the excellent Grainshed coffee lounge. As ever, the dorms are fairly functional, while the doubles can be expensive.

Rock n' Bowl HOSTEL £
(☎ 0117-325 1980; www.thelanesbristol.co.uk/hostel; 22 Nelson St; dm £13-18, d £45; 🖤) A cheery, well-run backpackers' favourite set in a rambling 1930s building, with street art covering the walls, a table-tennis table in the huge chill-out room, and free breakfast.

Brooks Guest House B&B ££
(☎ 0117-930 0066; www.brooksguesthousebristol. com; Exchange Ave; d £90-130, trailers £100-105; 🖤) Improbable as it seems, three vintage Airstream trailers sit on the AstroTurf of the bijou roof garden at this central Bristol B&B. They're predictably tiny but still feature seating areas and pocket-sized bathrooms. In the guesthouse, bedrooms are compact but pleasing, with olive colour schemes and tartan throws.

Greenhouse B&B ££
(☎ 0117-902 9166; www.thegreenhousebristol. co.uk; 61 Greenbank Rd; s/d £85/115; P 🖤) 🌿 No bells and whistles here – just a lovely, friendly, quiet B&B in Southville, a few minutes' stride to the river and the centre. Cream rooms, white sheets and an excellent organic breakfast make it well worth considering. The free parking is a real bonus.

Mercure Brigstow HOTEL ££
(☎ 0117-929 1030; www.mercure.com; Welsh Back; d £90-200; 🖤) A harbourside location and attractive modern design make the Mercure a good, central option. All rooms boast 'floating' beds, curved panel walls and tiny TVs set into bathroom tiles (gimmicky, yes, but fun). The cheaper rooms face the back, the pricier ones look out over the water; some have balconies and pod coffee machines.

★ Number 38 B&B £££
(☎ 01179-466 905; www.number38clifton.com; 38 Upper Belgrave Rd, Clifton; s/ste £115/180, d £130-165; P 🖤) Perched on the edge of the Downs, this upmarket B&B is *the* choice for style-conscious travellers. The rooms are huge and contemporary – sombre greys and smooth blues dictate the palette, luxury is provided by waffle bathrobes and designer bath goodies, and city views unfold from the roof terrace. The two suites have gleaming, old-fashioned metal baths.

Hotel du Vin HOTEL £££
(☎ 0117-403 2979; www.hotelduvin.com; Narrow Lewins Mead; d £145-170, ste £194-260; P 🖤) This luxury British hotel brand is a fave with well-heeled city-breakers. Their Bristol outpost occupies an old sugar warehouse, and mixes industrial chic and sleek minimalism: exposed brick and iron pillars meet futon beds and claw-foot baths. The rooms are named after vintage champagnes; the best are the split-level mezzanine suites.

The stylish bistro is great, too.

Eating

Canteen CAFE £
(☎ 0117-923 2017; www.canteenbristol.co.uk; 80 Stokes Croft; mains £4-10; ⊙ 10am-midnight Mon-Thu, to 1am Fri & Sat, to 11pm Sun; 🖤) 🌿 Occupying the ground floor of an old office block, this community-run cafe sums up Bristol's alternative character: it's all about slow food, local suppliers and fair prices, whether you pop in for a bacon butty, veggie chilli or sit-down supper. It's not signed on the outside – look out for the hipsters on the terrace and the lettering: Hamilton House.

St Nicholas Market MARKET £
(www.stnicholasmarketbristol.co.uk; Corn St; ⊙ 9.30am-5pm Mon-Sat) The city's lively street market has a bevy of food stalls selling everything from mezze platters to pulled-pork rolls from barbecue specialists **Grillstock**. Lines can be long at lunchtime, but it's worth the wait. Look out too for the Wednesday **farmers markets**.

Olive Shed

BISTRO £

(☎ 0117-929 1960; www.theoliveshed.com; Princes Wharf; mains £4-8; ☉ 11am-10pm Tue-Sat, to 4pm Sun) With tables right beside Bristol's Floating Harbour, this rustic eatery is a top spot for a waterfront lunch. It serves tapas and twists on Mediterranean food; think cured and torched mackerel, mushrooms made pungent by smoked garlic, and smoked chicken made spicy by harissa.

★ Riverstation

BRITISH ££

(☎ 0117-914 4434; www.riverstation.co.uk; The Grove; lunch 2/3 courses £14/17, dinner mains £15-18; ☉ noon-2.30pm & 6-10.30pm) Riverstation is one of Bristol's original dining-out destinations, and still leads the pack. The waterside location is hard to beat, with a view over the Floating Harbour, but it's the food that keeps the punters coming back: classic in style with a strong European flavour, from French fish soup to steak *à la béarnaise*.

Fishers

SEAFOOD ££

(☎ 0117-974 7044; www.fishers-restaurant.com; 35 Princess Victoria St; mains £14-25; ☉ noon-3pm & 5.30-10pm daily, closed Mon lunch) Bristol's top choice for fish dishes rustles up everything from pan-fried sea bass with chorizo to succulent grilled whole lobster. The hot shellfish platter (£46 for two people) is made for sharing. The simple setting, with its whitewashed walls, ships' lanterns and nautical knick-knacks, adds to the maritime vibe.

Cowshed

BRITISH ££

(☎ 0117-973 3550; www.thecowshedbristol.com; 46 Whiteladies Rd; 2/3-course lunch £11/13, dinner mains £14-26; ☉ noon-2.45pm & 6-10pm Mon-Sat, noon-4pm & 6.30-9.15pm Sun) Country food with a modern twist is served at the Cowshed. The focus is on quality, locally sourced meat – aged beef, wild rabbit, pork belly, plus the *pièce de résistance,* 'steak on stone',

served sizzling on a hot lava rock. The three-course lunch is excellent value.

Primrose Café

BISTRO ££

(☎ 0117-946 6577; www.primrosecafe.co.uk; 1 Boyce's Ave; lunch mains £7-9, dinner mains £14-20; ☉ 9am-5pm & 6-10pm Tue-Sat, 9.30am-3pm Sun, 9am-5pm Mon) A Clifton classic, as perfect for morning coffee as for a proper sit-down dinner. With its pavement tables and wooden interior, it feels like a Bristolian version of a Parisian street cafe. It's particularly choice for breakfast: the eggs Benedict and Belgian waffles are legendary.

Ox

BRITISH ££

(☎ 0117-922 1001; www.theoxbristol.com; The Basement, 43 Corn St; mains £13-29; ☉ noon-2.30pm Mon-Fri, 5-10.30pm Mon-Sat, noon-4pm Sun) Gorgeous, highly polished wood, glinting brass, low lighting and cool jazz ensure this sleek eatery resembles a posh Pullman dining car that's somehow been bestowed with some Pre-Raphaelite murals. The food is aimed firmly at the carnivores; expect charcuterie platters, gourmet burgers and five choices of steak cut.

It's very easy to miss – look for the marble stairs winding down beneath the Wetherspoon pub.

Soukitchen

MIDDLE EASTERN ££

(☎ 0117-966 6880; www.soukitchen.co.uk; 277 North St; mains £8-14; ☉ noon-2.30pm Wed-Sun, 5.30-9pm Tue-Sun) Middle Eastern market food is the stock-in-trade at this friendly diner in Southville, with characteristic dishes such as borek (filo pies stuffed with meat or vegetables), mix-and-match mezze platters and flame-grilled kebabs. Honest food with heart.

Glassboat

FRENCH ££

(☎ 0117-332 3971; www.glassboat.co.uk; Welsh Back; lunch 2/3 courses £10/12, dinner mains £17-21; ☉ 8-11.30am, noon-3pm & 5.30-10pm daily,

BATH & SOUTHWEST ENGLAND BRISTOL

WORTH A TRIP

TYNTESFIELD HOUSE

Formerly the aristocratic home of the Gibbs family, **Tyntesfield** (NT; ☎ 01275-461900; www.nationaltrust.org.uk; Wraxall; adult/child £14/7, gardens only £9/4.50; ☉ house 10am-6pm Mar-Oct, 11am-3pm Nov-Feb, gardens 10am-5pm year-round) is one of the National Trust's most important acquisitions of recent years. A fairy-tale mansion bristling with pinnacles and turrets, brimful of sweeping staircases and cavernous, antique-filled rooms, the house gives an insight into the lavish lives once enjoyed by England's aristocratic families. Entry is via timed ticket and includes a guided tour. The house is 7 miles southwest of Bristol, off the B3128.

BRISTOL LIDO

Bath isn't the only southwestern city with its own outdoor hot tub. It's a little-known fact that Bristol sits on its own system of geothermal springs, which bubble up through the rocks beneath the Avon Gorge. During the 19th century, these naturally heated waters turned the area around Hotwells into a popular spa resort, where Georgian bathers flocked to try the curative waters (which were believed to alleviate a variety of conditions including consumption, asthma, dropsy and venereal diseases). The area even had its own funicular railway between Hotwells and Clifton, which served as a bomb shelter during WWII.

Though Bristol's days as a spa town may be over, you can still experience a flavour of its hot-water heyday thanks to the wonderful **Bristol Lido** (☑ 0117-933 9530; www. lidobristol.com; Oakfield Pl; nonmembers £20; ☺ nonmembers 1-4pm Mon-Fri). Originally opened as the Clifton Lido in 1849, the baths fell into disrepair and were closed in 1990, but have been carefully restored over the last few years. They're now a real local secret, with a beautiful 24m outdoor swimming pool that's kept at a constant temperature of around 24°C. Spa treatments and massage sessions are also available, and there's even an excellent bistro.

The only drawback for nonlocals is that priority is given to members. On weekends and busy days, the lido is closed for day visitors, so phone ahead to make sure there's space.

closed Sun evening) This converted river barge is great for a romantic dinner, with candle-lit tables and harbour views through a glass extension. The stylish food revolves around French and Italian flavours.

🍷 Drinking & Nightlife

BrewDog Bristol PUB
(www.brewdog.com; 58 Baldwin St; ☺ noon-midnight Sun-Wed, to 1am Thu-Sat) The Bristol outlet of Britain's punk brewery draws both the just-finished work crowd and those who want to linger – the cluster of tables out front prove popular on warm nights. Expect to find ales such as Libertine Black, Vagabond Pale and Hardcore on tap.

Thekla CLUB
(www.theklabristol.co.uk; The Grove, East Mud Dock; ☺ Thu-Sat 9.30pm-3am or 4am) Bristol's club-boat has nights for all moods: electro-punk, indie, disco and new wave, plus regular live gigs during the week. Check the website for the latest.

Albion PUB
(www.thealbionclifton.co.uk; Boyce's Ave; ☺ 9am-midnight Mon-Sat, to 11pm Sun) The well-heeled drinkers of Clifton make a beeline for this smart pub for a postwork pint. It also dishes up top-notch food, the likes of which range from classy bar-menu classics to trea-cle-marinated pork chops (mains £9 to £14).

Grain Barge PUB
(www.grainbarge.com; Mardyke Wharf, Hotwell Rd; ☺ noon-11pm Sun-Thu, to 11.30pm Fri & Sat) This

lovingly converted 1930s cargo vessel used to transport barley and wheat. Fittingly it's now used by the Bristol Beer Factory to showcase its craft ales. There's live music on Thursday nights (from 8pm).

☆ Entertainment

Watershed CINEMA
(www.watershed.co.uk; 1 Canon's Rd) Bristol's digital-media centre hosts regular art-house programs and film-related events, including the Encounters Festival (p299) in September.

Bristol Old Vic THEATRE
(☑ 0117-987 7877; www.bristololdvic.org.uk; 103 The Cut) Bristol's much-respected, stately theatre (one of England's oldest) hosts big touring productions in its ornate audito-rium, plus more experimental work in its smaller studio.

Fleece LIVE MUSIC
(www.thefleece.co.uk; 12 St Thomas St) A gig-pub favoured by indie artists.

Colston Hall LIVE MUSIC
(☑ 0844 887 1500; www.colstonhall.org; Colston St) Bristol's historic concert hall now has a new gleaming five-floor annex. It tends to attract the best bands and big-name comedy acts.

🛍 Shopping

Bristol is good for shopping, but you'll need to get out of the centre if you want to avoid the high-street chains, which cluster around **Cabot Circus** (www.cabotcircus.com; Glass

House; ⊘10am-8pm Mon-Sat, 11am-5pm Sun) and **Broadmead**.

Stokes Croft and Gloucester Rd are the best areas for independent shops, especially vintage clothing, crafts and secondhand music. Clifton is more upmarket, with high-end designer, homeware and antiques shops.

Rise Music   MUSIC
(☑0117-929 7511; www.rise-music.co.uk; 70 Queen's Rd; ⊘10am-7pm Mon-Sat, noon-6pm Sun) Bristol's top independent record shop has racks of CDs and vinyl, regular events and a coffee bar downstairs.

Loot   CLOTHING
(☑0117-922 0633; www.gimmetheloot.co.uk; 9 Haymarket Walk; ⊘10am-5.30pm Mon-Sat, 11am-5pm Sun) The city's largest vintage clothing shop is lodged, incongruously, at the base of the Premier Inn.

ⓘ Information

Bristol Royal Infirmary (www.uhbristol.nhs.uk; Marlborough St; ⊘24hr)
Bristol Tourist Office (☑0906 711 2191; www.visitbristol.co.uk; E-Shed, 1 Canons Rd; ⊘10am-4pm Mon-Sat, 11am-4pm Sun) Calling the phone number costs the premium rate of 50p per minute.

ⓘ Getting There & Away

AIR

Bristol International Airport (☑0871-3344344; www.bristolairport.co.uk) Bristol's airport is 8 miles southwest of the city. Destinations in the UK and Ireland include Aberdeen, Edinburgh, Cork, Glasgow and Newcastle (mainly handled by easyJet). Direct flights to cities in mainland Europe include those to Barcelona, Berlin, Milan and Paris. On-the-day parking at the airport is expensive; booking online in advance is much cheaper.
Bristol Airport Flyer (http://flyer.bristolairport.co.uk; ⊘24hr) Runs shuttle buses (one way/return £7/11, 30 minutes, every 10 minutes at peak times) from the bus station and Temple Meads.
Checker Cars (☑01446-711747; www.checkercars.com) Bristol Airport's official taxi service. Prices start from around £27 from the city centre.

BUS

National Express coaches go to Birmingham (£22, two hours, six to eight daily), London (£21, 2½ hours, hourly), Cardiff (£10, 1¼ hours, every two hours) and Exeter (£15, two hours, five daily).

Useful local buses include:
Bath (£5.50, 50 minutes, four per hour Monday to Saturday, half-hourly on Sunday) Bus 38/39/X39.
Wells (£5.50, one hour, half-hourly to hourly) Bus 376, which then goes on to Glastonbury (£5.50, 1¼ hours).

TRAIN

Bristol is an important rail hub, with regular services to London Paddington provided by the **Great Western Railway** (www.gwr.com) and services to northern England and Scotland mainly covered by **CrossCountry** (www.crosscountrytrains.co.uk). Book ahead for the best deals.

DESTINATION	COST (£)	TIME (HR)	FREQUENCY
Birmingham	26	1½	hourly
Edinburgh	80	6½	hourly
Exeter	14	1	half-hourly
Glasgow	85	6½	hourly
London	32	1¾	half-hourly
Penzance	35	5½	hourly
Truro	40	4	hourly

ⓘ Getting Around

Traveline South West (www.travelinesw.com) provides comprehensive details of both travel around the region, and in and around Bristol city.

BICYCLE

Bristol Bike Project (☑0117-942 1794; www.thebristolbikeproject.org; City Rd; per day Mon-Fri £12, per weekend £25; ⊘9am-6pm Mon-Fri, 10.30am-5.30pm Sat) A community-run bike shop and rental outlet in Stokes Croft.
Roll for the Soul (☑07856-544471; www.rollforthesoul.org; 2 Quay St; ⊘8am-6pm Mon & Tue, to 9pm Wed-Fri, 10am-9pm Sat) Not-for-profit bike cafe and bike workshop – great for meeting like-minded cycling buddies.

BOAT

Bristol Ferry Boat Company (☑0117-927 3416; www.bristolferry.com) Ferry services feature two, hourly routes: Hotwells runs west, with stops including Millennium Sq and the SS *Great Britain*. Temple Meads runs east, with stops including Welsh Back, Castle Park (for Cabot Circus) and Temple Meads (for the train station). Boats leave from the dock near the tourist office. Fares depend on distance travelled; an all-day pass is adult/child £6.50/5.50.

BUS

Bus journeys in Bristol's city centre cost £1 for up to three stops; longer trips cost £1.50. A Day-Rider pass (£4.50) provides unlimited travel.

Bus 8/9 To Clifton (10 minutes), Whiteladies Rd and Bristol Zoo Gardens every 15 minutes from St Augustine's Pde. Add 10 minutes from Temple Meads.

Bus 73/X73 Runs every 20 minutes from Bristol Parkway Station to the centre (£3.50, 30 minutes).

CAR & MOTORCYCLE

Heavy traffic and pricey parking make driving in Bristol a headache. **Park & Ride Buses** (☑ 0117-9020 157; www.ctplusbristol.org; peak/off-peak return £4/3; ☺ 6am-9.30pm Mon-Fri, 7am-8pm Sat) run every 20 minutes from Portway, Bath Rd and Long Ashton. Note that overnight parking is not permitted at the Park & Ride car parks.

TAXI

You can usually find a cab at the taxi rank on **St Augustine's Pde** (St Augustine's Pde), and there are plenty of dial-a-fares: try **Streamline Taxis** (☑ 0117-926 4001; www.bristolstreamlinetaxis. com) or **1st Call Taxi** (☑ 0117-955 5111; www. 1stcalltaxis.net). If you're taking a nonmetered cab, agree on the fare in advance.

BATH

POP 88,900

Britain's littered with beautiful cities, but precious few compare to Bath. Home to some of the nation's grandest Georgian architecture – not to mention one of the world's best-preserved Roman bathhouses – this slinky, sophisticated, snooty city, founded on top of natural hot springs, has been a tourist draw for nigh on 2000 years.

Bath's heyday really began during the 18th century, when local entrepreneur Ralph Allen and his team of father-and-son architects, John Wood the Elder and Younger, turned this sleepy backwater into the toast of Georgian society, and constructed fabulous landmarks such as the Circus and Royal Crescent.

History

Legend has it King Bladud, a Trojan refugee and father of King Lear, founded Bath some 2800 years ago when his pigs were cured of leprosy by a dip in the muddy swamps. The Romans established the town of Aquae Sulis in AD 44 and built the extensive baths complex and a temple to the goddess Sulis-Minerva.

Long after the Romans decamped, the Anglo-Saxons arrived, and in 944 a monastery was founded on the site of the present abbey. Throughout the Middle Ages, Bath was an ecclesiastical centre and a wool-trading town, but it wasn't until the early 18th century that Ralph Allen and the celebrated dandy Richard 'Beau' Nash made Bath the centre of fashionable society. Allen developed the quarries at Coombe Down, constructed Prior Park and employed the two John Woods (father and son) to create Bath's signature buildings.

During WWII, Bath was hit by the Luftwaffe during the so-called Baedeker raids, which targeted historic cities in an effort to sap British morale. Several houses on the Royal Crescent and the Circus were badly damaged, and the city's Assembly Rooms were gutted by fire, although all have since been restored.

In 1987, Bath became the only city in Britain to be declared a Unesco World Heritage Site in its entirety, leading to many subsequent wrangles over construction and development, most recently concerning the design of the redeveloped Thermae Bath Spa and SouthGate shopping centre.

☉ Sights

★ **Roman Baths**　　　HISTORIC BUILDING
(☑ 01225-477785; www.romanbaths.co.uk; Abbey Churchyard; adult/child £15/9.50; ☺ 9am-9pm Jul & Aug, to 5pm Sep-Jun) In typically ostentatious style, the Romans constructed a complex of bathhouses above Bath's three natural hot springs, which emerge at a steady 46°C (115°F). Situated alongside a temple dedicated to the healing goddess Sulis-Minerva, the baths now form one of the best-preserved ancient Roman spas in the world, and are encircled by 18th- and 19th-century buildings. Bath's premier attraction can get very busy. To dodge the worst crowds, avoid weekends, July and August.

The heart of the complex is the **Great Bath**, a lead-lined pool filled with steaming, geothermally heated water from the so-called 'Sacred Spring' to a depth of 1.6m. Though now open-air, the bath would

---

ⓘ MUSEUM DISCOUNTS

Saver tickets covering the Roman Baths and the Fashion Museum cost adult/child/family £21/11/53. There's also a joint ticket covering No 1 Royal Crescent and the Museum of Bath Architecture for £13/5/28.

Bath

originally have been covered by a 45m-high, barrel-vaulted roof.

More bathing pools and changing rooms are situated to the east and west, with excavated sections revealing the **hypocaust system** that heated the bathing rooms. Af-

ter luxuriating in the baths, Romans would have reinvigorated themselves with a dip in the circular **cold-water pool**, which now has life-size films of bathers projected on to the walls.

Bath

◉ **Top Sights**
1 Bath Abbey D4
2 Roman Baths D4
3 Royal Crescent A1

◉ **Sights**
4 Bath Assembly Rooms C2
  Fashion Museum .... (see 4)
5 Georgian Garden B2
6 Herschel Museum of
    Astronomy B3
7 Jane Austen Centre C3
8 Museum of Bath Architecture C2
9 No 1 Royal Crescent B2
10 Pump Room C4
11 The Circus B2

◆ **Activities, Courses & Tours**
12 Bath Abbey Tower Tours D4
13 Bath City Boat Trips D3
14 Bizarre Bath Comedy Walk D4
15 Mayor's Guide Tours C4
16 Pulteney Cruisers D3
17 Thermae Bath Spa C4

◉ **Sleeping**
18 Bath Backpackers D4
19 Grays Bath A6
20 Halcyon Apartments C2
21 Henry D4
22 Hill House Bath C1
23 Queensberry Hotel C2

24 Three Abbey Green D4

✖ **Eating**
25 Acorn D4
26 Adventure Cafe Bar C2
27 Bertinet Bakery C3
28 Café Retro D4
29 Chequers B1
30 Circus B2
31 Green Park Station B4
32 Hudson Steakhouse D1
33 Marlborough Tavern A1
  Pump Room Restaurant .... (see 10)
  Sally Lunn's .... (see 25)
34 Sotto Sotto D4
35 Tasting Room C3
36 Thoughtful Bread Company C3

◉ **Drinking & Nightlife**
37 Bell Inn D1
38 Colonna & Smalls B3
39 Moles C2
40 Same Same But Different C2
41 Star Inn C1

✪ **Entertainment**
42 Komedia C4
43 Little Theatre Cinema C4
44 Theatre Royal C4

◉ **Shopping**
45 SouthGate D5

The **King's Bath** was added sometime during the 12th century around the site of the original Sacred Spring. Every day, 1.5 million litres of hot water still pour into the pool. Beneath the Pump Room are the remains of the **Temple of Sulis-Minerva**.

There is also a fascinating **museum** displaying artefacts discovered on the site. Look out for the famous gilded bronze head of Minerva and a striking carved Gorgon's Head, as well as some of the 12,000-odd Roman coins thrown into the spring as votive offerings to the goddess.

The complex of buildings around the baths were built in stages during the 18th and 19th centuries. The two John Woods designed the buildings around the Sacred Spring, while the famous **Pump Room** (www.romanbaths.co.uk; Stall St; ⊙10am-5pm) **FREE** was built by their contemporaries, Thomas Baldwin and John Palmer, in neoclassical style, complete with soaring Ionic and Corinthian columns. The building now houses a restaurant (p310) which serves a magnificent afternoon tea (£22, or £31 with champagne). You can also sample the spring waters, which were believed in Victorian times to have curative properties. If you're lucky, you might even have music provided by the Pump Room's string trio.

Admission to the Roman Baths includes an audio guide, featuring a commentary in eight languages. One of the English guides is read by bestselling author Bill Bryson. Free hourly guided tours start at the Great Bath. Saver tickets covering the Roman Baths and the Fashion Museum cost adult/child/family £21/11/53.

★**Bath Abbey**   CHURCH
(www.bathabbey.org; Abbey Churchyard; requested donation adult/student £2.50/1.50; ⊙9.30am-5.30pm Mon, 9am-5.30pm Tue-Fri, 9am-6pm Sat, 1-2.30pm & 4.30-5.30pm Sun) Looming above the city centre, Bath's huge abbey church was built between 1499 and 1616, making it the last great medieval church raised in England. Its most striking feature is the west facade, where angels climb up and down

PRIOR PARK ESTATE

Partly designed by the landscape architect Capability Brown, the grounds of **Prior Park** (NT; ☎01225-833977; www.nationaltrust.org.uk; Ralph Allen Dr; adult/child £6.50/3.40; ⏰10am-5.30pm Feb-Oct daily, to 4pm Sat & Sun Nov-Jan), an 18th-century estate on Bath's southern fringe, feature cascading lakes and a graceful **Palladian bridge**. It's one of only four such structures in the world (look out for the period graffiti, some of which dates back to the 1800s).

The park is a mile south of Bath's centre. Bus 1 (every 45 minutes) stops nearby, as does Bath City Sightseeing's 'City Skyline' **tour** (p307).

stone ladders, commemorating a dream of the founder, Bishop Oliver King.

Tower tours (www.bathabbey.org; adult/child £6/3; ⏰10am-5pm Apr-Aug, 11am-3pm Sep-Mar, no tours Sun) leave on the hour from Monday to Friday, and every half-hour on Saturday.

Jane Austen Centre   MUSEUM
(☎01225-443000; www.janeausten.co.uk; 40 Gay St; adult/child £11/5.50; ⏰9.45am-5.30pm Apr-Oct, 10am-4pm Nov-Mar) Bath is known to many as a location in Jane Austen's novels, including *Persuasion* and *Northanger Abbey*. Although Austen lived in Bath for only five years, from 1801 to 1806, she remained a regular visitor and a keen student of the city's social scene. Here, guides in Regency costumes regale you with Austen-esque tales as you tour memorabilia relating to the writer's life in Bath.

Herschel Museum of Astronomy   MUSEUM
(☎01225-446865; www.herschelmuseum.org.uk; 19 New King St; adult/child £6.50/3; ⏰1-5pm Mon-Fri, 11am-5pm Sat & Sun Mar-Sep) In 1781 astronomer William Herschel discovered Uranus from the garden of his home, now converted into a museum. The house is little changed since the 18th century; an astrolabe in the garden marks the position of Herschel's telescope.

★**Royal Crescent**   ARCHITECTURE
(Royal Cres) Bath is famous for its glorious Georgian architecture, and it doesn't get any grander than this semicircular terrace of majestic town houses overlooking the green sweep of Royal Victoria Park. Designed by John Wood the Younger (1728–82) and built between 1767 and 1775, the houses appear perfectly symmetrical from the outside, but the owners were allowed to tweak the interiors, so no two houses are quite the same. **No 1 Royal Crescent** offers you an intriguing insight into life inside.

A walk east along Brock St from the Royal Crescent leads to **the Circus** (The Circus), a ring of 33 houses divided into three semicircular terraces. Plaques on the houses commemorate famous residents such as Thomas Gainsborough, Clive of India and David Livingstone. The terrace was designed by John Wood the Elder, but he died in 1754, and the terrace was completed by his son in 1768.

To the south along Gravel Walk is the **Georgian Garden** (off Royal Ave; ⏰9am-5pm) **FREE**, restored to resemble a typical 18th-century town-house garden.

Bath Assembly Rooms   HISTORIC BUILDING
(NT; www.nationaltrust.org.uk; 19 Bennett St; ⏰10.30am-5pm Mar-Oct, to 4pm Nov-Feb) **FREE** When they opened in 1771, the city's glorious Assembly Rooms were where fashionable Bath socialites gathered to waltz, play cards and listen to the latest chamber music. Rooms open to the public include the card room, tearoom and ballroom – all lit by their original 18th-century chandeliers.

Fashion Museum   MUSEUM
(☎01225-477789; www.fashionmuseum.co.uk; Assembly Rooms, 19 Bennett St; adult/child £8.75/6.75; ⏰10.30am-5pm Mar-Oct, to 4pm Nov-Feb) The collections on display in the basement of the Assembly Rooms include costumes from the 17th to late 20th centuries. Some exhibits change annually; check the website for the latest.

Museum of Bath Architecture   MUSEUM
(☎01225-333895; www.museumofbatharchitecture.org.uk; The Vineyards, The Paragon; adult/child £5.50/2.50; ⏰2-5pm Tue-Fri, 10.30am-5pm Sat & Sun mid-Feb–Nov) The stories behind the building of Bath's most striking structures are explored here, using antique tools, displays on Georgian construction methods and a 1:500 scale model of the city.

A joint ticket covering the Museum of Bath Architecture and No 1 Royal Crescent costs adult/child/family £13/5/28.

Holburne Museum
GALLERY

(☑ 01225-388569; www.holburne.org; Great Pulteney St; ☺ 10am-5pm Mon-Sat, 11am-5pm Sun) FREE Sir William Holburne, the 18th-century aristocrat and art fanatic, amassed a huge collection, which now forms the core of the Holburne Museum, in a lavish mansion at the end of Great Pulteney St. The museum houses a roll call of works by artists including Turner, Stubbs, William Hoare and Thomas Gainsborough, as well as 18th-century majolica and porcelain.

American Museum in Britain
MUSEUM

(☑ 01225-460503; www.americanmuseum.org; Claverton Manor; adult/child £11/6.50; ☺ noon-5pm Tue-Sun late Mar-Oct, to 4.30pm late Nov–mid-Dec) Britain's largest collection of American folk art, including First Nations textiles, patchwork quilts and historic maps, is housed in a fine mansion a couple of miles from the city centre. Several rooms have been decorated to resemble a 17th-century Puritan house, an 18th-century tavern and a New Orleans boudoir c 1860. A free shuttle bus (11.40am to 5pm) leaves from Terrace Walk, beside Parade Gardens.

🏃 Activities

Various cruise operators offer boat trips up and down the River Avon from the Pulteney Bridge area, including **Pulteney Cruisers** (☑ 01225-863600; www.bathboating.com; Pulteney Bridge; adult/child £9/4; ☺ mid-Mar–Nov) and **Bath City Boat Trips** (☑ 07974 560197; www.bathcityboattrips.com; Pulteney Sluice Gate; adult/child £10/8). There's not much difference between the tours; most last around an hour. Between mid-March and November there are at least five sailings a day.

⭐ Thermae Bath Spa
SPA

(☑ 01225-331234; www.thermaebathspa.com; Hot Bath St; Mon-Fri £34, Sat & Sun £37; ☺ 9am-9.30pm, last entry 7pm) Taking a dip in the Roman Baths might be off-limits, but you can still sample the city's curative waters at this fantastic modern spa complex, housed in a shell of local stone and plate glass. The showpiece is the open-air rooftop pool, where you can bathe in naturally heated, mineral-rich waters with a backdrop of Bath's cityscape – a mustn't-miss experience, best enjoyed at dusk.

Tickets includes steam rooms, waterfall showers and a choice of two swimming pools.

Bath Boating Station
BOATING

(☑ 01225-312900; www.bathboating.co.uk; Forester Rd; 1st hr adult/child £7/3.50, additional hrs £4/2; ☺ 10am-6pm Easter-Sep) You can pilot your own vessel down the Avon from this Victorian-era boathouse, which rents out traditional skiffs, rowing boats and Canadian canoes. It's in the suburb of Bathwick, a 20-minute walk northeast from the city centre.

☞ Tours

⭐ Bizarre Bath Comedy Walk
WALKING

(☑ 01225-335124; www.bizarrebath.co.uk; adult/student £8/5; ☺ 8pm Mar-Oct) Fabulously daft city tour mixing street theatre and live performance. Leaves nightly from outside the Huntsman Inn on North Pde Passage. Most of the walk is wheelchair-accessible.

Mayor's Guide Tours
WALKING

(☑ 01225-477411; www.bathguides.org.uk; ☺ 10.30am & 2pm Sun-Fri, 10.30am Sat) FREE Excellent historical tours provided free by the Mayor's Corp of Honorary Guides; tours cover about 2 miles and are wheelchair-accessible. They leave from within the Abbey Churchyard, outside the Pump Room. There are extra tours at 7pm on Tuesdays and Thursdays May to September.

Bath City Sightseeing
BUS

(Bath Bus Company; ☑ 01225-444102; www.bathbuscompany.com; adult/child £14.50/9; ☺ 10am-5pm, reduced services Jan-Mar) Two hop-on/hop-off city tours on open-topped buses, with commentary in seven languages. Tickets last 24 hours, or two consecutive days.

🎊 Festivals & Events

Bath has a busy program of festivals. All bookings are handled by **Bath Festivals** (☑ 01225-462231; www.bathfestivals.org.uk).

Bath Literature Festival
LITERATURE

(www.bathlitfest.org.uk; ☺ Feb & Mar) Major book festival in late February or early March.

Bath International Music Festival
MUSIC

(www.bathmusicfest.org.uk; ☺ May) Mainly classical and opera, plus smaller gigs of jazz, folk and world. Events run mid- to late May.

Bath Fringe Festival　　THEATRE

(www.bathfringe.co.uk; ☉May-Jun) Major theatre festival around mid-May to early June.

🛏 Sleeping

Bath has a wide range of hotels and B&Bs, and gets extremely busy in the height of summer when prices peak. Be aware, they also rise by anything from £10 to £50 a room at weekends year-round. Few hotels have on-site parking, although some offer discounted rates at municipal car parks.

Bath Backpackers　　HOSTEL £

(☑01225-446787; www.hostels.co.uk/bath; 13 Pierrepont St; dm £12-17) The showers are scarce, and it's a bit grimy and battered, but this hostel is still beloved by budget travellers for bargain rates, a prime location, a friendly vibe and a 24-hour 'dungeon' (in truth a sound-proofed basement where you don't have to 'keep the noise down').

Bath YHA　　HOSTEL £

(☑0845 371 9303; www.yha.org.uk; Bathwick Hill; dm £13-22, d from £39; ☉reception 7am-11pm; P@☎) Split across an Italianate mansion and a modern annex, this impressive hostel is a steep climb (or a short hop on bus U1 or U18) from the city. The listed building means the rooms are huge, and some have period features such as cornicing and bay windows.

★ Three Abbey Green　　B&B ££

(☑01225-428558; www.threeabbeygreen.com; 3 Abbey Green; d £90-200, apt £160; ☎) Rarely in Bath do you get somewhere as central as this Georgian town house with such spacious rooms. Elegant, 18th-century-style furnishings are teamed with swish wet-room bathrooms, and the opulent Lord Nelson suite features a vast four-poster bed. There's also a two-person, self-catering apartment nearby (two-night minimum stay).

Henry　　B&B ££

(☑01225-424052; www.thehenry.com; 6 Henry St; s £80-95, d £100-145, f from £175; ☎) This tall town house has one of the best positions in Bath, literally steps from the centre. The seven rooms and a self-catering apartment are jazzed up by modern floral motifs, striped cushions and mints on the pillows. The family room and free cot may also suit.

Appletree　　B&B ££

(☑01225-337642; www.appletreebath.com; 7 Pulteney Gardens; s £80-150, d £90-160; P☎)

Owner, Ling, ran a city-centre hotel for 15 years, and those skills shine throughout this classy B&B. Bedrooms are named after the eponymous fruit. The best is Royal Gala, which features a sleigh bed and sofa, but even the cheaper rooms are bright and fresh and dotted with Asian art.

★ Queensberry Hotel　　HOTEL £££

(☑01225-447928; www.thequeensberry.co.uk; 4 Russell St; r £125-185, ste £225-275; ☎) Award-winning, quirky Queensberry is Bath's best boutique spoil. Four Georgian town houses have been combined into one seamlessly stylish whole, where heritage roots meet snazzy designs; expect everything from gingham checks and country creams to bright upholstery, original fireplaces and free-standing tubs. Rates exclude breakfast; parking is £7. The hotel's Olive Tree Restaurant is excellent, too.

Grays Bath　　B&B £££

(☑01225-403020; www.graysbath.co.uk; Upper Oldfield Park; d £90-205; ☎) Boutique treat Grays is a beautiful blend of modern, pared-down design and family treasures, many picked up from the owners' travels. All the rooms are individual: choose from floral, polka dot or maritime stripes. Perhaps the pick is the six-sided, curling room 12 in the attic, with partial city views.

The owners also run a smaller but equally smart B&B on the east side of town, **Brindleys** (☑01225-310444; www.brindleysbath.co.uk; 14 Pulteney Gardens; d £135-200; P☎).

Halcyon Apartments　　RENTAL HOUSE £££

(☑01225-585100; www.thehalcyon.com/apartments; 15a George St; apt £150-300; ☎) The spacious, two- to four-people apartments set in this Georgian building blend heritage features (sash windows and high ceilings) with modern fixtures and furnishings. Quite the stylish pied-à-terre.

Hill House Bath　　B&B £££

(☑01225-920520; www.hillhousebath.co.uk; 25 Belvedere; r £150-170; P☎) When you walk through the door here it almost feels like you're staying with friends. The decor showcases the owners' quirky tastes – dog-print cushions, retro pictures and objets d'art abound. Breakfasts are packed with local ingredients and include homemade marmalade and jam.

🏃 Walking Tour
Bath

START BATH ABBEY
FINISH ROYAL CRESCENT
LENGTH 1.5 MILES; TWO HOURS

Start this architectural amble at **1 Bath Abbey** (p305), the city's iconic ecclesiastical edifice, built on the site of an 8th-century chapel. From the abbey square, head south along Stall St for a view of the 19th-century **2 Pump Room** (p305). Turn left onto York St, and follow it east to **3 Parade Gardens**, a Victorian park framed by the River Avon.

From here, the Grand Parade leads north; look out for the building on the corner, **4 The Empire**, built as a luxurious hotel in 1901. At the northern end of the Grand Parade is **5 Pulteney Bridge**, designed by Robert Adams in 1773, one of only a handful in the world to be lined with shops. West of the bridge, **6 Upper Borough Walls** marks the northern extent of medieval Bath; if you look closely, you might spot some sections of the medieval wall that remain.

At Sawclose, you'll see the elaborate facade of Bath's **7 Theatre Royal** (p311),

which has been staging productions since 1805. From here, follow Barton St on to **8 Queen Square**, the oldest of Bath's Georgian squares, built as a showpiece development between 1728 and 1736 to demonstrate the talents of its architect, John Wood the Elder.

Head north on to Gay St, and right on to George St. Next to the Porter pub, an alley leads north, emerging next to the **9 Assembly Rooms** (p306), the heart of Georgian Bath's social life. Continue to Bennett St and turn left until you reach **10 the Circus** (p306), designed to echo the Colosseum in Rome. The three-tiered pillars exhibit the key styles of classical architecture (Doric, Ionic and Corinthian) and the facades are supposedly studded with masonic symbols.

From here, Brock St leads west to Bath's Georgian glory, the **11 Royal Crescent** (p306). Constructed by John Wood the Younger in 1774, the terrace is now Grade I listed, making it as architecturally significant as Buckingham Palace. The elegant Royal Crescent Hotel is at number 16.

✗ Eating

Many bakeries and cafes serve the city's famous 'Bath Bun', somewhere between a brioche and a bread, and not to be confused with the London Bath Bun, which is small and sweet.

There's a Saturday morning farmers market at **Green Park Station** (Green Park; ⊙8am-1pm Sat), where you can pick up local cheeses, meats and ciders, plus bread from the **Thoughtful Bread Company** (www.thethoughtfulbreadcompany.com; 19 Barton St; ⊙9am-4pm Tue-Sun).

Bertinet Bakery BAKERY £
(www.bertinet.com/bertinetbakery; 1 New Bond St Pl; baked goods £2.50-5; ⊙8am-5pm Mon-Fri, 8.30am-5.30pm Sat) The flavourful fillings and light pastry of the pasties at baker Richard Bertinet's take-out shop could change your view of that foodstuff for good. You'll also be tempted by rich quiches, cheese-studded croissants, French-inspired cakes and irresistible pistachio swirls.

Café Retro CAFE £
(☎01225-339347; www.caferetro.co.uk; 18 York St; mains £5-11; ⊙9am-5pm Mon-Sun) A poke in the eye for the corporate coffee chains. The paint job's scruffy, the crockery's ancient and none of the furniture matches, but that's all part of the charm: this is a cafe from the old school, and there are few places better for burgers, butties or cake. Takeaways (in biodegradable containers) are available from Retro-to-Go next door.

Adventure Cafe Bar CAFE £
(www.adventurecafebar.co.uk; 5 Princes Bldgs, George St; mains £5-10; ⊙8.30am-3am Mon-Fri, 9am-3am Sat & Sun) This cool cafe-bar, just a slipper's throw from the Assembly Rooms, offers something to everyone at most times of the day: morning cappuccino, lunchtime ciabatta and late-night beer and cocktails. There's great outdoor seating in the back.

Sally Lunn's CAFE £
(☎01225-461634; www.sallylunns.co.uk; 4 North Pde Passage; mains £6-17; ⊙10am-9.30pm Sun-Thu, to 10pm Fri & Sat) Eating a bun at Sally Lunn's is just one of those things you have to do in Bath. It's all about proper English tea here, brewed in bone-china teapots, with finger sandwiches and dainty cakes served by waitresses in frilly aprons.

★ Circus MODERN BRITISH ££
(☎01225-466020; www.thecircuscafeandrestaurant.co.uk; 34 Brock St; mains lunch £10-15, dinner £19; ⊙10am-midnight Mon-Sat) Chef Ali Golden has turned this bistro into one of Bath's destination addresses. Her taste is for British dishes with a continental twist, à la Elizabeth David: rabbit, Wiltshire lamb and West Country fish are all infused with herby flavours and rich sauces. It occupies an elegant town house near the Circus. Reservations recommended.

Acorn VEGETARIAN ££
(☎01225-446059; www.acornvegetariankitchen.co.uk; 2 North Pde Passage; lunch mains £12, dinner 2/3 courses £27/33; ⊙noon-3pm & 5.30-9.30pm; ☑) Proudly proclaiming 'plants taste better', Bath's premier vegetarian restaurant tempts you inside with aromas reflecting its imaginative, global-themed cuisine. The wine flights (two/three courses £12/18) matched to the set dinner menus are good value; or opt for a pear Bellini (£7) to get the liquid refreshments under way.

Pump Room Restaurant CAFE ££
(☎01225-444477; www.romanbaths.co.uk; Stall St; snacks £6-8, dishes £8-12; ⊙10am-5pm) Elegance is everywhere in this tall, Georgian room, from the string trio and Corinthian columns to the oil paintings and glinting chandeliers. It sets the scene perfectly for morning coffee, classic lunches and the dainty sandwiches and cakes of their famous afternoon tea (£22 to £40 per person).

Chequers GASTROPUB ££
(☎01225-360017; www.thechequersbar.com; 50 Rivers St; mains £10-25; ⊙bar noon-11pm daily, food 6-9pm daily, noon-2.30pm Sat & Sun) A discerning crowd inhabits Chequers, a pub that's been in business since 1776, but which has a menu that's bang up to date thanks to head chef Tony Casey. Forget bar-food staples, here it's hake with octopus and wild rice.

Sotto Sotto ITALIAN ££
(☎01225-330236; www.sottosotto.co.uk; 10 North Pde; mains £10-20; ⊙noon-2pm & 5-10pm) The setting is superb – an artfully lit vaulted brick chamber – and the food matches it for style. Authentic Italian dishes are likely to include Parma ham–wrapped sea bass sautéed in white wine, and a spicy seafood and Tuscan bean pasta. A top tip: don't forgo the garlicky sautéed spinach side.

Tasting Room
TAPAS **££**

(✐01225-483070; www.tastingroom.co.uk; 6 Green St; mains £6-13; ◷10.30am-11pm Wed-Sat, to 4.30pm Mon & Tue) High-class vintages, tapas and piled-high platters of meats and cheese are the *modi operandi* of this slinky cafe-bar, located above Bath's premier wine merchant.

Marlborough Tavern
GASTROPUB **££**

(✐01225-423731; www.marlborough-tavern.com; 35 Marlborough Bldgs; mains £13-25; ◷bar noon-11pm, food noon-2pm & 6-9.30pm) The queen of Bath's gastropubs has food that's closer to that of a fine-dining restaurant – think duo of venison and pork tenderloin rather than bog-standard meat-and-two-veg. Chunky wooden tables and racks of wine behind the bar give it an exclusive, classy feel.

★ Menu Gordon Jones
MODERN BRITISH **£££**

(✐01225-480871; www.menugordonjones.co.uk; 2 Wellsway; 5-course lunch £40, 6-course dinner £55; ◷12.30-2pm & 7-9pm Tue-Sat) If you enjoy dining with an element of surprise, then Gordon Jones' restaurant will be right up your culinary boulevard. Menus are dreamt up daily and showcase the chef's taste for experimental ingredients (eel, haggis and smoked milk foam) and madcap presentation (test tubes, edible cups, slate plates). It's superb value given the skill on show. Reservations essential.

Hudson Steakhouse
STEAK **£££**

(✐01225-332323; www.hudsonsteakhouse.co.uk; 14 London St; mains £22-34; ◷5-10.30pm) Steak, steak and more steak is this acclaimed eatery's raison d'être. Tuck into top-quality cuts from porterhouse to prime fillet, all sourced from a Staffordshire farmers' co-op.

Their early-evening special of a steak and a glass of wine (£15) is a bargain.

🍷 Drinking & Nightlife

★ Colonna & Smalls
CAFE

(www.colonnaandsmalls.co.uk; 6 Chapel Row; ◷8.30am-5.30pm Mon-Sat, 10am-4pm Sun; 🛜) If you're keen on caffeinated beans, this is a cafe not to miss. A mission to explore coffee ensures that there are three guest espresso varieties and smiley staff happy to share their expertise. They'll even tell you that black filter coffee – yes, filter coffee – is actually the best way to judge high-grade beans.

★ Star Inn
PUB

(www.abbeyales.co.uk; 23 The Vineyards, off the Paragon; ◷noon-2.30pm & 5.30-11pm Mon-Fri, noon-11pm Sat, noon-10.30pm Sun) Not many pubs are registered relics, but the Star is – it still has many of its 19th-century bar fittings. It's the brewery tap for Bath-based Abbey Ales; some ales are served in traditional jugs, and you can even ask for a pinch of snuff in the 'smaller bar'.

Bell Inn
PUB

(www.thebellinnbath.co.uk; 103 Walcot St; ◷11.30am-11pm Mon-Sat, noon-10.30pm Sun) To join Bath's bohemian muso crowd, head to this welcoming, laid-back locals' favourite. You'll find a real fire, swathes of draped hops and a bar billiards table (£1 a go). Plus live music (Monday and Wednesday at 9pm, Sunday at 1pm) that ranges from acoustic, country and folk to echoes of the blues.

Same Same But Different
BAR

(www.same-same.co.uk; 7a Prince's Bldgs, Bartlett St; ◷8am-11pm Tue-Fri, 9am-11pm Sat, 10am-5pm Sun) Boho hang-out for the town's trendies, tucked down an alley off George St. Savour wine by the glass, snack on tapas or sip a cappuccino with the Sunday papers.

Moles
CLUB

(www.moles.co.uk; 14 George St) Bath's main music venue keeps the crowds happy with a musical diet of indie, electro pop, club classics and cheese.

☆ Entertainment

Komedia
COMEDY

(✐0845 293 8480; www.komedia.co.uk; 22-23 Westgate St) Renowned comedy venue featuring touring shows and the sell-out Krater Saturday Comedy Club. Also live music and films.

Little Theatre Cinema
CINEMA

(www.picturehouses.com; St Michael's Pl) Bath's excellent art-house cinema screens fringe films and foreign-language flicks.

Theatre Royal
THEATRE

(✐01225-448844; www.theatreroyal.org.uk; Sawclose) Bath's historic theatre dates back 200 years. Major touring productions go in the main auditorium and smaller shows appear in the Ustinov Studio.

🛍 Shopping

Bath's main shopping centre is **SouthGate** (www.southgatebath.com), where you'll find all the major chain stores.

Smaller shops tend to be a little north of the centre. Milsom St is good for upmarket fashion, while Walcot St is lined by quirky independent food shops, design stores and vintage-clothing retailers.

❶ Information

Bath Tourist Office (☎ 0844 847 5256; www. visitbath.co.uk; Abbey Chambers, Abbey Churchyard; ☺ 9.30am-5.30pm Mon-Sat, 10am-4pm Sun) Calls are charged at the premium rate of 50p per minute.

Royal United Hospital (☎ 01225-428331; www.ruh.nhs.uk; Combe Park)

❶ Getting There & Away

BUS

Bath's **bus and coach station** (Dorchester St) is near the train station.

National Express coaches run direct to London (£33, 3½ hours, eight to 10 daily). Two-hourly services also run to London Heathrow (£27, three hours). Services to many other destinations change at Bristol.

Local buses include the following:

Bristol bus 38/39/X39; £5.50, 50 minutes, four per hour Monday to Saturday, half-hourly on Sunday

Wells bus 173; £5.50, one hour 15 minutes, two per hour Monday to Saturday, hourly Sunday)

TRAIN

Bath Spa station is at the south end of Manvers St. Many services connect through Bristol, including those to the southwest and north of England.

Direct services include:

Bristol £7.30, 15 minutes, three per hour
Cardiff Central £20, one hour, hourly
London Paddington £38, 1½ hours, half-hourly
Salisbury £18, one hour, hourly

❶ Getting Around

BICYCLE

Bath is hilly, but the canal paths along the Kennet and Avon Canal and the 13-mile **Bristol & Bath Railway Path** (www.bristolbathrailway-path.org.uk) are great to explore by bike.

Bath Bike Hire (☎ 01225-447276; www. bath-narrowboats.co.uk; Sydney Wharf; per day £15; ☺ 9am-5pm, shorter hours in winter) Ten-minute walk from the centre. Handy for the canal and railway paths.

Take Charge Bikes (☎ 01225-789568; www. takechargebikes.co.uk; 1 Victoria Bldgs, Lower Bristol Rd; per day £17; ☺ 9am-5.30pm Mon-Fri, to 4.30pm Sat) Rents electric bikes.

BUS

Bus U18 runs from the bus station, High St and Great Pulteney St up Bathwick Hill past the YHA to the university every 20 minutes (£1.20).

Bus 4 runs to Bathampton (£1.50, 30 minutes, one to two per hour).

CAR & MOTORCYCLE

Bath has serious traffic problems, especially at rush hour. **Park & Ride services** (☎ 0871-2002233; return Mon-Fri £3.30, Sat & Sun £2.60; ☺ 6.15am-8.30pm Mon-Sat, 9.30am-6pm Sun) operate from Lansdown to the north, Newbridge to the west and Odd Down to the south. It takes about 10 minutes to the centre; buses leave every 10 to 15 minutes.

There's a good, central car park underneath the SouthGate shopping centre (two/eight hours £3.50/14, after 6pm £2 to £5).

SOMERSET

With its pastoral landscape of hedgerows, fields and hummocked hills, sleepy Somerset is the very picture of the rural English countryside, and makes the perfect escape from the bustle of Bath and the hustle of Bristol. Things certainly move at a drowsier pace around these parts – it's a place to wander, ponder and drink in the sights at your own pace.

The cathedral city of Wells is an atmospheric base for exploring the limestone caves and gorges around Cheddar, while the hippie haven of Glastonbury is handy for venturing on to the wetlands of the Somerset Levels and the high hills of the Quantocks.

❶ Information

➡ The Taunton **tourist office** (☎ 01823-340470; www.visitsomerset.co.uk/taunton; Fore St; ☺ 9.30am-4.30pm Mon-Sat) is the best source of information about Somerset as a whole.

➡ www.visitsouthsomerset.co.uk is another useful source of information.

❶ Getting There & Around

➡ The M5 heads south past Bristol to Bridgwater and Taunton, while the A39 leads west across the Quantocks to Exmoor.

➡ Key train services link Bath, Bristol, Bridgwater, Taunton and Weston-super-Mare.

➡ **First** (www.firstgroup.com) is a key local bus operator. For timetables and general information, contact **Traveline South West** (www. travelinesw.com).

Wells & Around

POP 11,340

In Wells, small is beautiful. This is England's smallest city, and only qualifies for the title thanks to a magnificent medieval cathedral, which sits beside the grand Bishop's Palace – the official residence of the Bishop of Bath and Wells since the 12th century.

Medieval buildings and cobbled streets radiate out from the cathedral green to a marketplace that has been the bustling heart of Wells for some nine centuries (Wednesday and Saturday are market days). Film buffs might also recognise it from the hit British comedy *Hot Fuzz* – the film's final shoot-out was filmed here.

◎ Sights

★ Wells Cathedral   CATHEDRAL

(Cathedral Church of St Andrew; www.wellscathedral.org.uk; Cathedral Green; requested donation adult/child £6/3; ⊘7am-7pm Apr-Sep, to 6pm Oct-Mar) Wells' gargantuan Gothic cathedral sits plumb in the centre of the city, surrounded by one of the largest cathedral closes anywhere in England. It was built in stages between 1180 and 1508, and consequently showcases several Gothic styles. Among its notable features are the **West Front**, decorated with more than 300 carved figures, and the famous **scissor arches** – an ingenious architectural solution to counter the subsidence of the central tower.

In the north transept is a **mechanical clock** dating from 1392 – the second-oldest in England after the one at Salisbury Cathedral – which shows the position of the planets and the phases of the moon.

Other highlights include the elegant **Lady Chapel** (1326), the fan-vaulted **Chapter House** (1306) and the celebrated **chained library**, which contains books and manuscripts dating back to 1472. Outside, the covered cloister known as the **Chain Bridge** enabled clerics to reach the cathedral without getting their robes wet.

Free guided tours run regularly from Monday to Saturday. You'll need a photography permit (£3) to take pictures.

Cathedral Close   HISTORIC SITE

Wells Cathedral forms the centrepiece of a cluster of ecclesiastical buildings dating back to the Middle Ages. Facing the west front, on the left are the 15th-century **Old Deanery** and the **Wells Museum** (www.wells-museum.org.uk; 8 Cathedral Green; adult/child £3/1; ⊘10am-5pm Mon-Sat Easter-Oct, to 4pm Nov-Easter).

Further north, **Vicars' Close** is a stunning 14th-century cobbled street, with a chapel at the end; members of the cathedral choir still live here. It is thought to be the oldest complete medieval street in Europe.

Bishop's Palace   HISTORIC BUILDING

(www.bishopspalacewells.co.uk; Market Place; adult/child £7/3; ⊘10am-6pm Apr-Oct, to 4pm Nov-Mar) Built for the bishop in the 13th century, this moat-ringed palace is purportedly the oldest inhabited building in England. Inside, the palace's state rooms and ruined great hall are worth a look, but it's the shady gardens that are the real draw. The natural springs after which Wells is named bubble up in the palace's grounds.

Wookey Hole   CAVE

(www.wookey.co.uk; adult/child £18.50/14; ⊘10am-5pm Apr-Oct, to 4pm Nov-Mar) The River Axe has gouged out this network of deep limestone caverns, which are famous for striking stalagmites and stalactites, one of which is the legendary Witch of Wookey Hole, who was turned to stone by a local priest. Admission to the caves is by guided tour; up on top you'll find beyond-kitsch tourist attractions ranging from a penny arcade to a mirror maze. Wookey Hole is 3 miles northwest of Wells; look out for brown signs on the A371.

⌇ Sleeping

Stoberry House   B&B ££

(☏01749-672906; www.stoberryhouse.co.uk; Stoberry Park; s £85, d £95-155; ℗⑉) It's hard to know which is more beautiful: the lush, 2.5-hectare garden, or the house that overflows with rich fabrics, plush cushions and boutique flourishes. Expect pod coffee machines, luxury teas, books to browse and the use of a well-stocked pantry. It's all tucked away in a private estate.

Ancient Gate House Hotel   HOTEL ££

(☏01749-672029; www.ancientgatehouse.co.uk; 20 Sadler Street,; s £90-95, d £110-125; ⑉) This old hostelry is partly built right into the cathedral's west gate. Rooms are decorated in regal reds and duck-egg blues; the best have four-poster beds and knockout cathedral views through latticed windows. They're £15 extra, and worth it.

CHEDDAR GORGE

Cheddar Gorge (www.cheddargorge.co.uk; Cheddar Gorge; Explorer Ticket adult/child £20/14; ⊘10.30am-5.30pm) Carved out by glacial meltwater during the last ice age, these limestone cliffs form England's deepest natural canyon, in places towering 138m above the twisting B3135. Beneath the cliffs, the gorge is riddled with miles of subterranean caves. Cox's Cave and Gough's Cave are the easiest to reach, decorated with impressive displays of stalactites and stalagmites. Admission covers parking in the gorge and entry to the caves. Cheddar Gorge is about 20 miles northwest of Wells on the A371.

X-Treme (☑01934-742343; www.cheddargorge.co.uk/x-treme; 1½-hr trips adult/child £22/20) The Cheddar Gorge's main outdoors company offers guided caving trips lasting around 1½ hours. Crawling, climbing ladders and squeezing through small spaces inevitably means you'll get wet and dirty. But that photo featuring mud-caked dungarees, helmet and head torch is worth it. X-Treme runs rock-climbing sessions too (adult/child £22/20).

Cheddar Gorge Cheese Company (☑01934-742810; www.cheddargorgecheeseco.co.uk; The Cliffs, Cheddar; adult/child £2/free; ⊘10am-5pm Easter-Oct, winter hours vary) Along with its caves, Cheddar is also famous as the home of the nation's favourite cheese, produced here since the 12th century (Henry II considered it 'the best cheese in Britain', and the king's accounts from 1170 record that he purchased around 4644kg of the stuff). At this cheesemaker you can watch the whole creamy, gooey transformation process from a viewing gallery, then buy some tangy, whiffy souvenirs at the shop.

Beryl
B&B ££

(☑01749-678738; www.beryl-wells.co.uk; Hawkers Lane; s £75-95, d £110-160; P🐾🛜🏊) This grand gabled mansion offers a taste of English eccentricity. Every inch of the house is crammed with antique atmosphere, and the rooms boast grandfather clocks, chaises longues and four-posters galore. It's about a mile from Wells.

★ Babington House
LUXURY HOTEL £££

(☑01373-812266; www.babingtonhouse.co.uk; near Frome; r £270-410; P🐾🛜🏊) It's eye-poppingly pricey, but this lauded design hotel is one of Britain's most luxurious. It's a mash-up of *Homes & Gardens* and *Wallpaper:* heritage beds, antique dressers and period fireplaces meet minimalist furniture, sanded wood floors and retro lamps. There's a cool library, 45-seat private cinema and spa in the old cowshed. It's 14 miles east of Wells.

✖ Eating

Strangers with Coffee
CAFE £

(☑07728 047233; 31 St Cuthbert St; cakes £2-5; ⊘7.30am-4pm Tue-Sat) 'Life is too short to drink bad coffee' says the sign – something they've taken to heart here as they work caffeinated magic with some of the best beans in town. There's a tempting selection of cakes to match.

★ Goodfellows Cafe & Seafood Restaurant
CAFE ££

(☑01749-673866; www.goodfellowswells.co.uk; 5 Sadler St; mains £11-24; ⊘11am-3pm daily, 6-9.30pm Wed-Sat) There's a choice of eating options in Goodfellows' three vibrant rooms: the continental cafe menu offers cakes, pastries and light lunches (opt to pay either £10 or £19 for two courses and a drink). Or book for an evening fine-dining experience; £29 gets you three classy courses, while the five-course seafood tasting menu (£49) is an absolute treat.

Square Edge
BISTRO ££

(☑01749-671166; www.square-edgecafe.co.uk; 2 Town Halls Bldgs; mains £8-18; ⊘9am-5pm Mon-Wed, to 8.30pm Thu-Sat, 10am-3pm Sun) There's an easygoing charm to Square Edge, a retro eatery where 1950s movie posters frame old jukeboxes and vintage radios. Treats range from garlicky portobello mushrooms on soda bread toast, to steak with Stilton sauce. Hard-to-resist puddings might include blueberry Bakewell slice or a supremely sticky Eton mess.

ℹ Information

Tourist Office (☑01749-671770; www.wells-somerset.com; 8 Cathedral Green; ⊘10am-5pm Mon-Sat Easter-Oct, to 4pm Nov-Easter)

ⓘ Getting There & Away

The bus station is south of Cuthbert St, on Princes Rd. Useful services include the following:

Bath bus 173; £5.50, 1¼ hours, half-hourly Monday to Saturday, hourly Sunday

Bristol bus 376; £5.50, one hour, half-hourly

Cheddar Bus 26 (£4.50, 25 minutes, hourly Monday to Saturday) continues to Weston-super-Mare (£5.50, 1¼ hours).

Glastonbury bus 37/375/376; £3.50, 15 minutes, several times an hour

Glastonbury

POP 8900

Ley lines converge, white witches convene and every shop is filled with the aroma of smouldering joss sticks in good old Glastonbury, the southwest's undisputed capital of alternative culture. Now famous for its annual musical mudfest, held on Michael Eavis' farm in nearby Pilton, Glastonbury has a much more ancient past: the town's iconic tor was an important pagan site, and is rumoured by some to be the mythical Isle of Avalon, King Arthur's last resting place. It's also allegedly one of the world's great spiritual nodes, marking the meeting point of many mystical lines of power – so if you feel the need to get your chakras realigned, this is definitely the place. Whatever the truth of the various legends swirling round Glastonbury, one thing's for certain – watching the sunrise from the top of the tor is an experience you won't forget in a hurry.

◉ Sights

★ **Glastonbury Tor**   LANDMARK
(NT; www.nationaltrust.org.uk) **FREE** Topped by the ruined, medieval **Chapel of St Michael**, the iconic hump of Glastonbury Tor is visible for miles around, and provides Somerset with one of its most unmistakable landmarks. It takes half an hour to walk up from the start of the trail on Well House Lane; the steepest sections are stepped. Between April and Septembe,r a regular Tor Bus (adult/child £3/1.50) shuttles from St Dunstan's car park near Glastonbury Abbey to the trailhead on Well House Lane; alternatively, it's a 20-minute walk.

The tor is the focal point for a wealth of local lore. According to Celtic legend, the tor is the home of Arawn or Gwyn ap Nudd, king of the underworld and lord of the faeries. A more famous legend identifies the tor as the mythic Isle of Avalon, where King Arthur was taken after being mortally wounded in battle, and where Britain's 'once and

---

GLASTONBURY FESTIVAL

To many people, Glastonbury is synonymous with the **Glastonbury Festival of Contemporary Performing Arts** (www.glastonburyfestivals.co.uk; tickets from £228; ☉ Jun or Jul), a majestic (and frequently mud-soaked) extravaganza of music, theatre, dance, cabaret, carnival, spirituality and general all-round weirdness that's been held on and off on farmland in Pilton, just outside Glastonbury, for the last 40-plus years (bar the occasional off-year to let the farm recover).

The first event was held in 1970, when young dairy farmer Michael Eavis decided to stage his own British version of Woodstock on his land at Worthy Farm. Eavis borrowed £15,000 and invited some bands to play on a couple of makeshift stages in a field. Entry was £1, which included a pint of milk from Eavis' dairy herd; among the performers was Marc Bolan of T-Rex, who arrived in typically flamboyant style in his own velvet-covered Buick.

Forty-something years later, the festival has become the world's longest-running pop-music festival, attracting crowds of more than 120,000. It's even had a feature-length film made about it, directed by Julien Temple. Eavis' daughter Emily has since taken over the day-to-day running of the festival, and her decision to give headline slots to artists such as Dolly Parton, Jay-Z and U2 has led many people to grumble that Glastonbury's gone mainstream – but with acts such as the Rolling Stones and the Arctic Monkeys still lining up to play, Glastonbury's status as the UK's premier outdoor party looks safe for years to come.

More importantly, even the local councillors seem to have come around; after years of wrangling, in 2014 the festival was granted an unprecedented 10-year licence, a sign that the powers-that-be have recognised the festival's status as a national treasure. Tickets usually go on sale in the autumn, and always sell out within a matter of minutes, so you need to get in lightning-quick if you want to go.

Glastonbury

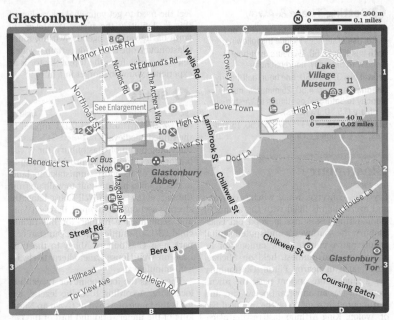

Glastonbury

◎ Top Sights
1 Glastonbury Abbey	B2
2 Glastonbury Tor	D3
3 Lake Village Museum	D1

◎ Sights
4 Chalice Well & Gardens	D3

🛏 Sleeping
5 Covenstead	B2
6 Crown Glastonbury Backpackers	C1
7 Glastonbury Townhouse	A3
8 Glastonbury White House	B1
9 Magdalene House	B2

✕ Eating
10 Hundred Monkeys Cafe	B2
11 Rainbow's End	D1
12 Who'd a Thought It Inn	A2

future king' sleeps until his country calls again. Others believe that the tor marks an ancient mystical node where invisible lines of energy, known as ley lines, converge.

It's easy to see why the tor has inspired so many myths. It's a strange presence in an otherwise pan-flat landscape, and in ancient times (when the area around Glastonbury was covered by water for much of the year),

the tor would indeed have appeared as an island, wreathed in mists and cut off by rivers, marshes and bogs.

Chalice Well & Gardens   GARDENS

(📞01458-835528; www.chalicewell.org.uk; Chalkwell St; adult/child £4.20/2.10; ⊙10am-6pm Apr-Oct, to 4.30pm Nov-Mar) Shaded by yew trees and criss-crossed by quiet paths, the Chalice Well & Gardens have been sites of pilgrimage since the days of the Celts. The iron-red waters from the 800-year-old well are rumoured to have healing properties, good for everything from eczema to smelly feet; some legends also identify the well as the hiding place of the Holy Grail.

★ Glastonbury Abbey   RUINS

(📞01458-832267; www.glastonburyabbey.com; Magdalene St; adult/child £7.60/4.70; ⊙9am-8pm Jun-Aug, to 6pm Mar-May, Sep & Oct, to 4pm Nov-Feb) The scattered ruins of Glastonbury Abbey give little hint that this was once one of England's great seats of ecclesiastical power. It was torn down following Henry VIII's dissolution of the monasteries in 1539, and the last abbot, Richard Whiting, was hung, drawn and quartered on the tor. Today's striking ruins include some of the nave walls, the remains of **St Mary's chapel**, and the crossing arches, which may have been scissor-shaped like those in Wells Cathedral.

The grounds also contain a **museum**, **cider orchard** and **herb garden**. According to legend, the abbey's famous holy thorn tree sprang from the staff of Joseph of Arimathea, Jesus' great-uncle, who supposedly visited the abbey following Christ's death. It blooms at Christmas and Easter.

The abbey even has an Arthurian connection. In the 12th century, monks supposedly uncovered a tomb in the abbey grounds inscribed *Hic iacet sepultus inclitus rex arturius in insula avalonia,* or 'Here lies buried the renowned King Arthur in the Isle of Avalon'. Inside the tomb were two entwined skeletons, purportedly those of Arthur and his wife Guinevere. The bones were reburied beneath the altar in 1278, but were lost following the abbey's destruction.

★**Lake Village Museum**　　MUSEUM
(The Tribunal, 9 High St; adult/child £3.50/2; ⊙10am-3pm Mon-Sat) The Lake Village Museum displays finds from a prehistoric bog village discovered in nearby Godney. The houses were clustered in about six groups and built from reeds, hazel and willow. It's thought they were occupied by summer traders who lived the rest of the year around Glastonbury Tor.

🛏 **Sleeping**

Crown Glastonbury Backpackers　HOSTEL £
(☑01458-833353; 4 Market Pl; dm £25, d £35-50; @🛜) Well worn, grungy and set above a proper boozers bar, this friendly, erstwhile backpackers' favourite still draws in the travellers thanks to the big kitchen, comfy lounge, heart-off-the-action location and cheap beds.

Covenstead　　B&B ££
(☑01458-830278; www.covenstead.co.uk; Magdalene St; s £60, d £70-90; P🛜) It's as if they've distilled the wacky essence of Glastonbury and poured it all over this weirdly wonderful B&B. The downstairs is a riot of oddities: mock skeletons, witches hats, upcycled antlers and draped python skins. Bedroom themes range from fairy via green man and Gothic to Halloween honeymoon. A tad crazy, yes, but also delightfully done.

Magdalene House　　B&B ££
(☑01458-830202; www.magdalenehouseglastonbury.co.uk; Magdalene St; s £70-95, d £90-105, f £130-140; P🛜) Artfully decorated Magdalene used to be a school run by Glastonbury's nuns, and one room still overlooks the abbey grounds. Each of the tall, light rooms is an array of olive, oatmeal and other soft tones, while tasteful knick-knacks give it all a homely feel.

Glastonbury Townhouse　　B&B ££
(☑01458-831040; www.glastonburytownhouse.co.uk; Street Rd; r £75-120; P🛜) Nothing too outlandish about this place – just a solid, red-brick, Edwardian town house, with a clutch of quiet rooms, lots of painted furniture and a contemporary vibe. Breakfast, served overlooking the garden, can be vegetarian, vegan, or dairy- or gluten-free.

Glastonbury White House　　B&B ££
(☑01458-830886; www.theglastonburywhitehouse.com; 21 Manor House Rd; s/d £60/80; P🛜) There's a serene feel to this two-room guesthouse with its subtle, natural tones, clawfoot baths, cast-iron fireplaces and polished wooden floors. Organic elements feature strongly, from handmade cotton fabrics and fair-trade soap to optional vegetarian breakfasts (£10 extra each) served till 10.30am. Checkout is also delightfully relaxed: noon.

🍴 **Eating**

Rainbow's End　　VEGETARIAN £
(☑01458-833896; www.rainbowsendcafe.com; 17b High St; mains £5-9; ⊙10am-4pm; 🌿) This psychedelic cafe sums up the Glastonbury spirit, with its all-veggie food, potted plants and mix-and-match furniture. Tuck into homity pie or a hot quiche, followed by scrumptious homemade cake. There's a small patio out back.

WORTH A TRIP

LORD POULETT ARMS

Hinton St George's deliciously olde-worlde village pub **Lord Poulett Arms** (☑01460-73149; www.lordpoulettarms.com; Hinton St George; mains £14-20; ⊙noon-2pm & 6-9pm; P) has been named Somerset Dining Pub of the Year numerous times. No wonder: the hearty food is fantastic and the building oozes country atmosphere, with beams, roaring fires and stacks of ale barrels behind the bar. Hard to fault.

It even has quirky rooms (singles £60 to £65, doubles £85 to £95) upstairs. It's roughly 15 miles from Yeovil and Taunton.

SOMERSET LEVELS

Flat as a pancake, sub-sea-level and criss-crossed with canals (known locally as rhynes), the Somerset Levels are one of England's largest native wetlands. Covering almost 250 sq miles between the Quantock and Mendip Hills, they're brilliant for bird-spotters – particularly in October and November, when huge flocks of starlings (properly known as murmurations) descend on the area. Nature reserves have been established at Ham Wall, Shapwick Heath, Sedgemoor and Westhay.

The flat landscape of the Levels also makes it ideal for cycling. Several trails pass through the village of Langport, including the long-distance River Parrett Trail.

Bocabar   BRITISH ££
(☑ 01458-440558; http://glastonbury.bocabar. co.uk; Morland Rd; lunch £5-10, dinner £13.50-19.95; ⊙9.30am-11pm Tue-Thu, to 1am Fri & Sat, 10am-5pm Sun & Mon) There's been quite a transformation at this cavernous red-brick building: from old sheepskin factory to hip hang-out. It's now home to live bands and events several times a week, and features a pan-global menu that takes in Thai curries, classic steaks, gourmet burgers and adventurous crêpes. The industrial-chic vibe adds appeal.

It's about 1.5 miles southwest of the town centre along Morland Rd.

Hundred
Monkeys Cafe   BISTRO ££
(www.hundredmonkeyscafe.com; 52 High St; mains £8-15; ⊙8am-6pm Sun-Wed, to 10pm Thu, to 9pm Fri & Sat; ☑) A buzzy bistro featuring pine furniture, handwritten blackboards and a fair-trade, seasonal ethos that infuses the mezze platters, pasta dishes, curries and risottos – with plenty of gluten-free and vegan options. The tea selection is enormous and the wines are biodynamic; best enjoyed on Thursday, acoustic music night.

Who'd a Thought It Inn   PUB FOOD ££
(www.whodathoughtit.co.uk; 17 Northload St; mains £11-21; ⊙noon-9pm) In this pleasantly peculiar locals' pub, antique bottles and vintage advertising signs sit beside swathes of dried hops and an old red telephone box, while an upside-down bike dangles from the ceiling. The food is solid pub fare – think sausages, pies and steaks – but there are usually specials chalked above the bar.

ⓘ Information

Glastonbury Tourist Office (☑ 01458-832954; www.glastonburytic.co.uk; The Tribunal, 9 High St; ⊙10am-3.30pm Mon-Fri, to 4.30pm Sat)

ⓘ Getting There & Away

There is no train station in Glastonbury.
   Useful bus routes include:
Taunton bus 29; £5.50, 1½ hours, four daily Monday to Saturday
Wells bus 37/375/376; £3.50, 15 minutes, several times an hour

CORNWALL

You can't get further west than the ancient Celtic kingdom of Cornwall (or Kernow, as it's known to Cornish speakers). Blessed with the southwest's wildest coastline and most breathtakingly beautiful beaches, this proudly independent peninsula has always marched to its own tune.

While the staple industries of old – mining, fishing and farming – have all but disappeared, Cornwall has since reinvented itself as one of the nation's creative corners. Whether it's exploring the space-age domes of the Eden Project, sampling the culinary creations of a celebrity chef or basking on a deserted beach, you're guaranteed to feel the itch of inspiration. Time to let a little Kernow into your soul.

Since 2006, Cornwall's historic mining areas have formed part of the UK's newest Unesco World Heritage Site, the Cornwall & West Devon Mining Landscape (www. cornish-mining.org.uk).

ⓘ Getting There & Away

It's pretty easy to get to Cornwall these days, although its far westerly location means travel times from most locations in the UK are long.

The county's main airport is located just outside Newquay, with links to London Gatwick and other major cities.

The main train line from London Paddington runs through the centre of the county before terminating at Penzance.

The major road into Cornwall, the A30, is prone to traffic jams in summer. The A38 from

Plymouth over the Tamar Bridge into Cornwall is an alternative, but it's a more circuitous route.

Five miles from Newquay, Cornwall's main airport **Newquay Cornwall Airport** (01637-860600; www.newquaycornwallairport.com) currently offers direct daily flights to Manchester and London Gatwick with **Flybe** (www.flybe.com) and the Isles of Scilly with **IoS Skybus** (p345).

First Kernow bus 56 (26 minutes, hourly Monday to Saturday, five on Sunday) runs from Newquay's bus station to Padstow. A taxi will cost £15 to £25 from the town centre.

Various seasonal destinations around the UK and Europe are also offered during the summer.

Getting Around

Bus, train and ferry timetables can be found on the **Traveline South West** (0871 200 2233; www.travelinesw.com) website.

The useful **Great Scenic Railways** (www.greatscenicrailways.com) website features online booking and timetables for Cornwall's regional railways.

BUS

Cornwall's main bus provider is **First Kernow** (customer service 0845 600 1420, timetables 0871 200 2233; www.firstgroup.com/cornwall), which operates the majority of services between major towns. The county's other big bus company, Western Greyhound, went into administration in 2015, and although some of its routes are now operated by smaller coach companies, many were axed, leaving some rural communities stranded without a regular bus service.

TRAIN

Cornwall's main railway line follows the coast as far as Penzance, with branch lines to Gunnislake, Looe, Falmouth, St Ives and Newquay.

Most trains are provided by **Great Western Railway** (0345 7000 125; www.gwr.com), although **Crosscountry Trains** (0844 811 0124; www.crosscountrytrains.co.uk) also run through major stations.

TRANSPORT PASSES

Several passes cover public transport in Cornwall.

Ride Cornwall Ranger (adult/child/family £10/7.50/20) is the best all-round value covering bus and train travel across Cornwall.

There are also Day Ranger tickets for all of Cornwall's branch railway lines, as well as 'Two Together' and 'Groupsave' tickets for two and four adults travelling together.

Freedom of Devon & Cornwall Rover (3-day adult/child £46.45/23.20, 8-day adult/child £71.20/35.60) provides three days' train travel in seven, or eight days' travel in 14. Valid after 9am and anytime weekends.

Bude
POP 9242

Just a scant few miles across the Devon border, Bude is a breezy seaside town with a bevy of impressive beaches, as well as a lovely seawater lido built in the 1930s. The town itself isn't much to look at, but the stunning coastline on its doorstep makes it worthy of a stop.

Sights & Activities

Bude's beaches are definitely its main asset. Closest is **Summerleaze**, a bucket-and-spade affair with lots of space at low tide, and the beautiful **Bude Sea Pool** (www.budeseapool.net) FREE. North across Summerleaze Down is **Crooklets**, offering golden sand and rock pools at low tide.

To reach Bude's other beaches requires either a car or a hike along the coast path. Three miles south of town is **Widemouth Bay** (*wid*-mouth), a broad, sandy beach good for both families and surfers. Two miles further is the shingly beach of **Millook**, followed by the dramatic cliffs around **Crackington Haven**.

Three miles north of town are the National Trust–owned **Northcott Mouth** and **Sandymouth**.

A mile further on is pebbly **Duckpool**, often quiet even in summer.

Bude Castle MUSEUM
(www.thecastlebude.org.uk; The Castle; 10am-5pm Easter-Oct, 10am-4pm Nov-Easter;) FREE Housed in a peculiar folly behind

WORTH A TRIP

MONTACUTE HOUSE

Built in the 1590s for Sir Edward Phelips, a speaker of the House of Commons, **Montacute House** (NT; 01935-823289; www.nationaltrust.org.uk; Montacute; adult/child £11.40/5.70; house 11am-4.30pm Mar-Oct, noon-3pm Sat & Sun Nov-Feb, gardens 10am-5pm daily Mar-Oct, 11am-4pm Wed-Sat Nov-Feb) contains some of the finest 16th- and 17th-century interiors in the country. It's plasterwork, chimney pieces and tapestries are renowned, but the highlight is the **Long Gallery** – the longest such hall in England, it's rich in Elizabethan portraits.

Montacute is 5 miles west of Yeovil on the A3088.

CAMEL VALLEY VINEYARD

Cornwall might not seem like an obvious place for wine-making, but local entrepreneur Bob Lindo has been producing award-winning vintages at his **Camel Valley Vineyard** (☑ 01208-77959; www.camelvalley.com; ☺ shop 10am-5pm Mon-Sat, tours 2.30pm Mon-Fri & 5pm Wed) since 1989. The range includes award-winning whites and rosés, and a bubbly that's Champagne in all but name. Aficionados say the wines have a fresh, light quality that comes from the mild climate and pure sea air. Vineyard tours run regularly and you can taste and buy the goods in the on-site shop.

Summerleaze beach, Bude Castle was built by local inventor Sir Goldsworthy Gurney, whose creations included theatrical limelight and steam carriages. The building now houses a small **heritage centre**, which roves through Bude's maritime, geological and social history. There's also a cafe on the top floor.

Raven Surf School
SURFING
(☑ 07860-465499; www.ravensurf.co.uk; per lesson £35) A reliable school run by Mike Raven, a former surfing champion. It also offers surf life-saving and instructor courses, as well as accommodation in 'surf pods' (ecofriendly wooden cabins) and a campsite nearby.

Big Blue Surf School
SURFING
(☑ 01288-331764; www.bigbluesurfschool.co.uk; per lesson £30) A recommended school that offers lessons mainly to beginner and intermediate surfers. Special lessons for disabled surfers and a 'women's club' on Tuesday evenings and Saturday mornings are some of its main attractions.

🛏 Sleeping & Eating

Bangor's Organic
B&B ££
(☑ 01288-361297; www.bangorsorganic.co.uk; Poundstock; d £100; ⊞) 🍴 This ecofriendly B&B sits near Poundstock, 7 miles from Bude. The house is elegantly Victorian and the two rooms are fairly frilly, but the draw is the rural setting; it's set among 2 hectares, and you'll find fresh-picked veg and just-laid eggs on the breakfast table. Gill and Neil are your friendly hosts, and also run an excellent farm shop.

Elements Hotel
HOTEL ££
(☑ 01288-275066; www.elements-life.co.uk; Marine Dr; s £60, d £79-120; ⊞ ⎙) Smart clifftop hotel with 11 rooms in whites and creams, big coastal views from the outdoor deck, a gym and Finholme sauna, and surf packages courtesy of nearby Raven Surf School. The downstairs bar does decent food, too.

Beach at Bude
HOTEL £££
(☑ 01288-389800; www.thebeachatbude.co.uk; Summerleaze Cres; r £135-237.50; ⊞ ⎙ ⎙) For a proper hotel stay, complete with all the pampering, this is definitely the choice in Bude. The main sell is the fine position behind Summerleaze beach, but the rooms are attractive too: spacious and smart, with neutral tones, pine headboards and Lloyd Loom chairs, conjuring the feel of a New England beach cabin.

The Bank
TAPAS £
(☑ 01288-352070; www.thebankatbude.co.uk; Pethericks Mill; tapas £4.25-8.95; ☺ 3-10pm Tue-Sat) It's a little way from the town centre, but this relaxed joint is a popular weekend haunt for locals, serving authentic Spanish tapas in a sweet setting inside a former mill. It also serves paella and more substantial fish and shellfish dishes. Follow the road south from the tourist office towards the A39 and look out for signs.

Life's a Beach
CAFE ££
(☑ 01288-355222; www.lifesabeach.info; Summerleaze; mains lunch £8-12, dinner £16.50-22.50; ☺ 10.30am-3pm & 7-10pm Mon-Sat year-round, 10.30am-3pm Sun) This beachside bistro overlooking Summerleaze has a split personality: by day it's a beach cafe serving coffees, panini and ice creams; by night it's a smart seafood restaurant. It's the most popular place to eat in town, so book ahead.

ℹ Information

Bude Tourist Office (☑ 01288-354240; www.visitbude.info; The Crescent; ☺ 10am-5pm Mon-Sat, plus 10am-4pm Sun summer) Beside the main car park near Bude Castle.

ℹ Getting There & Away

First Kernow bus 95/96 (six daily Monday to Saturday, four on Sunday) stops in Bude en route from Camelford (one hour 10 minutes) via Tintagel (50 minutes), Boscastle (40 minutes) and the beaches south of Bude.

Most buses also connect onwards to Wadebridge via Port Isaac, Polzeath, Rock and nearby beaches.

Boscastle

POP 641

Nestled in the crook of a steep coombe (valley) at the confluence of three rivers, Boscastle's seagoing heritage stretches back to Elizabethan times. With its quaint cottages, flower-clad cliffs, tinkling streams and sturdy quay, it's almost impossibly photogenic.

But the peaceful setting belies some turbulent history: in 2004 Boscastle was devastated by one of Britain's largest-ever flash floods, which carried away cars, bridges and buildings. The village has since been rebuilt, but look closely and you'll still spot reminders of the floods dotted around.

◉ Sights

Museum of Witchcraft   MUSEUM
(☑ 01840-250111; www.museumofwitchcraftand-magic.co.uk; The Harbour; adult/child £5/4; ⊙ 10.30am-6pm Mon-Sat, 11.30am-6pm Sun Mar-Nov) This oddball museum claims to house the world's largest collection of witchy memorabilia, from haunted skulls to hags' bridles and voodoo dolls. It's half-tacky, half-spooky, and some of the more 'controversial' exhibits might perturb kids of a sensitive disposition (or adults, for that matter).

⏹ Sleeping & Eating

Boscastle YHA   HOSTEL £
(☑ 0845 371 9006; boscastle@yha.org.uk; Palace Stables, The Harbour; dm £19-25; ⊙ Apr-Nov) Boscastle's shoebox-sized hostel was all but washed away by the floods, but it's been completely renovated. It's in one of the village's oldest buildings beside the harbour, but be prepared for small dorms, especially considering the price.

Orchard Lodge   B&B ££
(☑ 01840-250418; www.orchardlodgeboscastle. co.uk; Gunpool Lane; d £95-110; [P][🖥]) Uphill from the harbour, Geoff and Shirley Barratt have turned their whitewashed house into a charming B&B bolthole, with each room boasting its own mix-and-match furnishings and fabrics, and hallways plastered with Thomas Hardy quotes. There's a two-night minimum stay in summer, and rates get cheaper the longer you stay.

Boscastle House   B&B ££
(☑ 01840-250654; www.boscastlehouse.co.uk; Tintagel Rd; s/d from £60/110; [P][🖥]) The fanciest of Boscastle's B&Bs, in a Victorian house overlooking the valley, with five classy rooms with a bright, contemporary feel, mixing neutral colours with bold print wallpapers. Charlotte has bay-window views, Nine Windows has his-and-hers sinks and a free-standing bath, and Trelawney has ample space and its own sofa.

Boscastle Farm Shop   CAFE £
(☑ 01840-250827; www.boscastlefarmshop.co.uk; cakes & teas £3-5; ⊙ 10am-5pm; [P]) Half a mile from the harbour on the B3263, this excellent farm shop sells its own produce, including ruby-red beef and possibly the best sausages on the north coast. In the cafe, tall windows look onto fields and coast – the perfect setting for a cream tea.

Waterloo Restaurant   BRITISH £££
(☑ 01840-250202; www.wellingtonhotelboscastle. com; The Harbour; 2-/3-course menu £30/37.50; ⊙ dinner 6.30-9.30pm Tue-Sat) This turreted coaching inn dates back to the 16th century (previous guests include King Edward VII and Guy Gibson of Dambusters fame). It's an old-fashioned place – flock carpets, burnished furniture, upholstered chairs – and the restaurant continues the trad theme. It's now run by Kit Davis, who previously ran his own restaurant in Bude.

ⓘ Information

Boscastle Tourist Office (☑ 01840-250010; www.visitboscastleandtintagel.com; The Harbour; ⊙ 10am-5pm Mar-Oct, 10.30am-4pm Nov-Feb) Not far from the quay, and with some useful leaflets on local history and walks.

ⓘ Getting There & Away

The coastal 95/96 bus (six daily Monday to Saturday, four on Sunday) stops in Tintagel as it trundles from Camelford to Bude.

Tintagel

POP 1822

The spectre of King Arthur looms large over Tintagel and its clifftop castle. Though the present-day ruins mostly date from the 13th century, archaeological digs have revealed the foundations of a much earlier fortress, fuelling speculation that Arthur may indeed have been born at the castle as locals like to claim.

The village itself isn't terribly exciting, but if you're looking for a cheesy King Arthur souvenir, you'll find them in ample supply.

◉ Sights

★ Tintagel Castle
CASTLE

(EH; ☑01840-770328; adult/child £7.90/4.70; ◷10am-6pm Apr-Sep, to 5pm Oct, to 4pm Nov-Mar) Famous as the supposed birthplace of King Arthur, Tintagel's stunning clifftop castle has been occupied since Roman times and once served as a residence for Cornwall's Celtic kings, but the present castle is largely the work of Richard, Earl of Cornwall, who built a castle here during the 1230s. Though the Arthurian links may be tenuous, it's certainly a fine spot for a fortress: clinging to black granite cliffs, surrounded by booming surf and wheeling gulls, it's the classic fairytale castle.

Though much of the structure has crumbled away, it's still possible to make out several walls and much of the original layout. Part of the castle stands on a rocky outcrop cut off from the mainland, and is accessed via a wooden bridge and a very steep staircase (vertigo sufferers beware).

Trails lead along the headland to the atmospheric medieval chapel of St Glebe's, and down on the beach below the castle, the rocky mouth of Merlin's Cave is exposed at low tide – local legend claims it's where the wizard once wove his spells.

It's a steep walk down to the castle from the village car parks; in summer, Land Rover taxis shuttle up and down throughout the day.

Old Post Office
HISTORIC BUILDING

(NT; ☑01840-770024; Fore St; adult/child £4/2; ◷10.30am-5.30pm mid-Mar–Sep, 11am-4pm Oct) One of the National Trust's oldest properties, this is one of the best-preserved examples of a traditional 16th-century Cornish longhouse, topped by pepper-pot chimneys and riddled with tiny rooms. As its name suggests, it was used as a post office during the 19th century.

ℹ Getting There & Away

First Kernow bus 95/96 (six daily Monday to Saturday, four on Sunday) stops in Tintagel en route from Camelford (15 minutes) to Bude (50 minutes).

Port Isaac

POP 721

A few miles southwest of Tintagel is the classic Cornish fishing harbour of Port Isaac, a cluster of cobbled alleyways, slender opes (lanes) and cobwalled cottages collected around a medieval harbour and slipway.

Though still a working harbour, Port Isaac is best known as a filming location: the Brit film *Saving Grace* and the TV series *Doc Martin* have both used the village as a ready-made backdrop. A short walk west leads to the neighbouring harbour of Port Gaverne, while a couple of miles west is Port Quin, now owned by the National Trust.

Cornwall's chef *du jour*, Nathan Outlaw, has made the village his culinary centre of operations.

🛏 Sleeping & Eating

Old School Hotel
HOTEL ££

(☑01208-880721; www.theoldschoolhotel.co.uk; Fore St; d £115-165; 🅿🛜) A small hotel that was originally Port Isaac's schoolhouse (*Doc Martin* fans might recognise it as the village school in the TV show). Appropriately, rooms are named after school subjects: top of the class are Latin, with its sleigh bed and cupboard bathroom; Biology, with its sofa and church-style windows; and split-level Mathematics, with shared terrace and bunk-beds for the kids.

Outlaw's Fish Kitchen
SEAFOOD £

(☑01208-881183; www.outlaws.co.uk/fishkitchen; 1 Middle St; mains £6-10; ◷noon-3pm & 6-9pm Tue-Sun Jun-Sep, Mon-Sat Oct-May) Nathan Outlaw's newest venture is this tiny fish restaurant, which specialises in small seafood tasting plates made to share. The exact menu is dictated by whatever's brought in on the day by Port Isaac's fishermen, and the restaurant is tiny, so bookings are essential.

Fresh from the Sea
SEAFOOD ££

(☑01208-880849; www.freshfromthesea.co.uk; 18 New Rd; sandwiches £5.50-9.50, mains £10.50-20) Local man Callum Greehalgh takes out his boat daily in search of crab and lobster, then brings it back to sell at his dinky Port Isaac shop. Seafood doesn't get any fresher – a crab salad with glass of wine costs £12.50, and a whole lobster is £20. Depending on the season, oysters from nearby Porthilly cost £1.50 each.

★ **Restaurant Nathan Outlaw** SEAFOOD £££
(☑ 01208-862737; www.nathan-outlaw.com; 6 New Rd; tasting menu £119; ⊙ 7-9pm Wed-Sat, plus noon-2pm Fri & Sat) Port Isaac's prestige has skyrocketed since Cornwall's top chef, Nathan Outlaw, moved his main operation here from Rock. This is the place to experience Outlaw's passion for Cornish fish and seafood. His style is surprisingly classic, relying on top-notch ingredients rather than cheffy tricks. As you'd expect from a twice Michelin-starred restaurant, it's expensive, but very much a tell-your-friends experience.

ⓘ Getting There & Away

First Kernow bus 95/96 stops in Port Isaac at least four times daily en route between Camelford and Bude.

Padstow & Rock

POP 3162

If anywhere symbolises Cornwall's changing character, it's Padstow. This once-sleepy fishing port has been transformed into one of the county's most cosmopolitan corners thanks to celebrity chef Rick Stein, whose property portfolio encompasses several restaurants, shops and hotels, as well as a seafood school and fish-and-chip bar.

The 'Stein Effect' has certainly changed the place: Padstow feels more Kensington chic than Cornish quaint these days, with fancy restaurants and boutiques sitting alongside the old pubs and pasty shops. Whether the town's managed to hold on to its soul in the process is debatable, but it's still hard not to be charmed by the setting.

Across the Camel Estuary from Padstow is Rock, a once-quiet village that's been reinvented as an über-exclusive holiday destination. Nearby lies the long sweep of Daymer Bay, and between the two resorts is the treacherous sandbank known as the Doom Bar.

⊙ Sights & Activities

Padstow is surrounded by fine beaches, including the so-called Seven Bays: Trevone, Harlyn, Mother Ivey's, Booby's, Constantine, Treyarnon and Porthcothan.

National Lobster Hatchery NATURE DISPLAY
(☑ 01841-533877; www.nationallobsterhatchery.co.uk; South Quay; adult/child £3.75/1.75; ⊙ 10am-7.30pm Jul & Aug, to 4pm or 5pm Sep-Jun) 🌫 In an effort to combat falling lobster stocks, this harbourside hatchery rears baby lobsters in tanks before returning them to the wild. Displays detail the crustaceans' life cycle, and there are viewing tanks where you can watch the residents in action. You can also book 30-minute 'Meet the Expert' tours (adult/child £12/6), which allow you a glimpse into work behind the scenes.

Prideaux Place HISTORIC BUILDING
(☑ 01841-532411; www.prideauxplace.co.uk; Prideaux Pl; house & grounds adult £8.50, grounds only £3; ⊙ house 1.30-4pm Sun-Thu, grounds & tearoom 12.30-5.30pm Apr-Oct) Much favoured by directors of costume dramas, the stately Grade I-listed manor was built by the Prideaux-Brune family, purportedly descendants of William the Conqueror. Guided tours last around an hour and take in state rooms, staircases and Prideaux-Brune heirlooms, as well as the house's extensive collection of teddy bears.

Camel Trail CYCLING
(www.cornwall.gov.uk/cameltrail) The old Padstow-Bodmin railway was closed in the 1950s, and has now been turned into Cornwall's most popular bike trail. The main section starts in Padstow and runs east through Wadebridge (5.75 miles), but the trail runs on all the way to Poley Bridge on Bodmin Moor (18.3 miles).

Bikes can be hired from **Padstow Cycle Hire** (☑ 01841-533533; www.padstowcyclehire.com; South Quay; per day adult/child £15/7; ⊙ 9am-5pm, to 9pm summer) or **Trail Bike Hire** (☑ 01841-532594; www.trailbikehire.co.uk; Unit 6, South Quay; adult £14, child £5-8; ⊙ 9am-6pm) at the Padstow end, or from **Bridge Bike Hire** (☑ 01208-813050; www.bridgebikehire.co.uk; adult £12-14, child £6-9; ⊙ 10am-5pm) at the Wadebridge end.

Pumps and helmets are usually included, but tandems and kids' trailers cost extra.

Most people do the route from Padstow and back, so it's often quieter (and much easier to find parking) if you start from the Wadebridge side.

Padstow Boat Trips BOATING
(www.padstowboattrips.com; South Quay) Between Easter and October, the **Jubilee Queen** (☑ 07836-798457; www.padstowboattrips.co.uk; South Quay; adult/child £12/7) runs scenic trips along the coastline, while **Padstow Sealife Safaris** (☑ 01841-521613; www.padstowsealifesafaris.co.uk; 2hr cruise adult/child £39/25) visits local seal and seabird colonies.

For something racier, 15-minute **speedboat trips** (£7) zip past the treacherous sandbank of Doom Bar and the beaches of Daymer Bay, Polzeath, Hawkers Cove and Tregirls.

The main Padstow Boat Trips website keeps listings of all the local operators.

🛏 Sleeping

Treyarnon Bay YHA
HOSTEL £

(☑ 0845 371 9664; treyarnon@yha.org.uk; Treyarnon Bay; dm £22-25; ⊙ reception 8-10am & 2-10pm; P 🛜) A super 1930s-built beach hostel on the bluffs above Treyarnon Bay. Rooms are big and there's a good cafe, plus barbecues in summer – and the sunsets are spectacular. It's 4.5 miles east of Padstow: there's parking on-site, but the nearest bus stop is at Constantine, about a 20-minute walk away.

Althea Library
B&B ££

(☑ 01841-532579; www.altheahouse-padstow.co.uk; 64 Church St, Padstow; d £90-120; P 🛜) If you want to be in Padstow proper, this charming ivy-clad house is hard to better. There are two stylish self-catering suites: Rafters is accessed via a private staircase, while Driftwood has a pine four-poster bed. It's luxurious – both suites have sofas, Nespresso coffee machines, baths and small studio kitchens. There's also a nearby cottage for longer stays.

Woodlands
B&B ££

(☑ 01841-532426; www.woodlands-padstow.co.uk; Treator; d £118-138; P 🛜) A mile or so from Padstow's harbourside on the A389, offering green fields and distant flashes of sea, this is a great B&B base for Padstow, run by larger-than-life Hugo Woolley, who masterminds the legendary breakfasts and also sells his own boutique brand of granolas and mueslis. Rooms are a bit heavy on the creams and frills, but cosy nonetheless.

St Enodoc Hotel
HOTEL £££

(☑ 01208-863394; www.enodoc-hotel.co.uk; Rock Rd; r £195-495; P 🛜) Supremely sophisticated this place most certainly is, but cheap it certainly isn't (hardly a surprise in uberchic Rock). Rooms are elegant, with muted tones offset by bright scatter cushions, cappuccino-coloured carpets, distressed dressers and artwork by Penzance painter Jessica Cooper. There's a very smart spa, too.

🍴 Eating

Chough Bakery
BAKERY £

(☑ 01841-533361; www.thechoughbakery.co.uk; 1-3 The Strand, Padstow; pasties £3-5) Padstow's finest pasties, bar none – they've scooped top honours in the World Pasty Championships several times.

Cornish Arms
GASTROPUB ££

(☑ 01841-520288; www.rickstein.com/the-cornish-arms.html; St Merryn; mains £7-18; ⊙ 11.30am-11pm) This country pub near the village of St Merryn is now owned by the Stein empire, and offers updated pub classics such as scampi-and-chips and pint-of-prawns, with a characteristically creative spin. The Sunday roast is phenomenally popular, so arrive early. It's a 3-mile drive from Padstow.

Rojano's in the Square
ITALIAN ££

(☑ 01841-532796; www.rojanos.co.uk; 9 Mill Sq, Padstow; pizzas & pastas £8.50-17) Now under the stewardship of Paul Ainsworth, this excellent little Italian bistro turns out fantastic wood-fired pizzas, spicy pastas and antipasti.

Rick Stein's Cafe
EUROPEAN ££

(☑ 01841-532700; Middle St, Padstow; mains £10.95-19.95; ⊙ 8am-9.30pm) Stein's backstreet bistro takes its inspiration from the chef's globetrotting travels, with dishes ranging all the way from the Far East to the Mediterranean: classic mussels with saffron, or Thai-spiced seafood broth. The vibe is relaxed, but you'll still need to book.

★ Paul Ainsworth at No 6
BRITISH £££

(☑ 01841-532093; www.paul-ainsworth.co.uk/number6; 6 Middle St, Padstow; 2-/3-course lunch £19/26, dinner mains £28-40; ⊙ noon-2.30pm & 6-10pm Tue-Sat) Rick Stein might be the household name, but Paul Ainsworth is touted by those in the know as Padstow's top chef. His food combines surprising flavours and impeccable presentation with a refreshingly unpretentious approach, and the town-house setting along one of Padstow's backstreets makes a relaxed, unfussy place to dine. Now Michelin-starred, this is Padstow's prime table.

TV fans might recognise his signature dessert, 'A Fairground Tale', from BBC2's *Great British Menu*.

Seafood Restaurant
SEAFOOD £££

(☑ 01841-532700; www.rickstein.com; Riverside, Padstow; 3-course lunch £40, mains £19.50-65.50; ⊙ noon-2pm & 6.30-10pm) Rick Stein's flagship seafooderie needs no introduction – it's one of Britain's foremost fish addresses, with an expensive menu offering treats such as fresh Padstow lobster and sumptuous *fruits de mer*. The setting is lovely, with a light-filled dining room and a conservatory overlooking the harbour. You'll generally need to book months in advance, although last-minute lunch tables sometimes crop up.

ℹ Information

Padstow Tourist Information Centre
(📞 01841-533449; www.padstowlive.com; North Quay; ⊙10am-5pm Mon-Sat, 10am-4pm Apr-Sep, 10am-4pm Mon-Sat Oct-Mar) In a red-brick building on the quayside.

ℹ Getting There & Away

There are a couple of car parks beside the harbour in Padstow, but they fill up quickly, so it's usually a better idea to park at one of the large car parks at the top of town and walk down.

The only useful bus is First Kernow bus 56 (hourly Monday to Saturday, five on Sunday, one hour 25 minutes) which runs along the coast via Harlyn Bay, Constantine Bay, Porthcothan, Mawgan Porth, Newquay Cornwall Airport, Porth Beach and Newquay.

Newquay

POP 19,423

If Padstow is Cornwall's Cannes, then Newquay is its Costa del Sol. Perched on the cliffs above a cluster of white-sand beaches, and packed with enough pubs, bars and dodgy clubs to give Ibiza a run for its money, it's become the summer venue of choice for beer boys, beach bums and surf addicts alike, all of whom descend on the town in their droves in summer. Newquay is also the capital of Cornish surfing, and if you're looking to learn how to brave the waves, this is the place to do it.

⊙ Sights

Newquay has a truly stunning location among some of North Cornwall's finest beaches. The best known is **Fistral**, England's most famous surfing beach. It's nestled on the west side of Towan Head, a 10-minute walk from the town centre.

To the east of Towan Head are Newquay's other main beaches. Just below town are **Towan**, **Great Western** and **Tolcarne**, followed by nearby **Lusty Glaze**. All offer good swimming and lifeguard supervision throughout summer.

You'll need transport to reach Newquay's other beaches. North of Lusty Glaze is **Porth**, a long, narrow beach that's popular with families, followed a couple of miles further by the massive curve of **Watergate Bay**, home to Jamie Oliver's much-vaunted restaurant, Fifteen Cornwall. Two miles north brings you to **Mawgan Porth**, a horseshoe-shaped bay that often stays quieter than its neighbours.

BEDRUTHAN STEPS

Roughly halfway between Newquay and Padstow loom the stately rock stacks **Bedruthan Steps** (Carnewas; NT; www.nationaltrust.org.uk/carnewas-and-bedruthan-steps) . These mighty granite pillars have been carved out by the relentless action of thousands of years of wind and waves, and now provide a stirring spot for a stroll. The area is owned by the National Trust, who also runs the car park and cafe. There's no admission fee, but if you're not a NT member you will have to pay for parking.

You'll find even more beaches to the southwest of Newquay, including the large, sandy, family-friendly beaches of **Crantock** (about 3 miles from town) and **Holywell Bay** (6 miles from town).

Blue Reef Aquarium   AQUARIUM
(📞 01637-878134; www.bluereefaquarium.co.uk/newquay; Towan Promenade; adult/child/family £10.50/8.25/35.50; ⊙10am-6pm; 🚻) Small aquarium on Towan beach, with touch pools and various deep-sea denizens, including reef sharks, loggerhead turtles and a giant Pacific octopus. There's a discount for online bookings.

Newquay Zoo   ZOO
(📞 01637-873342; www.newquayzoo.org.uk; Trenance Gardens; adult/child/family £13.60/10.20/42.60; ⊙10am-5pm; 🚻) Newquay's miniature zoo isn't a world-beater, but its population of penguins, lemurs, parrots and snakes will keep the kids happy. The Tropical House and Toad Hall are particularly good fun, and key events include penguin feeding at noon and lion feeding at 2.30pm.

Trerice   HISTORIC BUILDING
(NT; 📞 01637-875404; www.nationaltrust.org.uk/trerice; adult/child £7.65/3.80; ⊙house 11am-5pm, gardens 10.30am-5pm) Built in 1751, this National Trust–owned Elizabethan manor is most famous for the elaborate barrel-roofed ceiling of the Great Chamber, and some fantastic original 16th-century stained glass among the 576 panes that make up the great window. It's 3.3 miles southeast of Newquay.

🏃 Activities

Newquay's brimming with surf schools, but the quality is variable. Choose one that offers small-group sessions, and ideally has a no-stag-party policy. Ask about teachers' accreditation and experience, and whether they travel to beaches other than Fistral – good schools follow the best waves.

English Surfing Federation
Surf School
SURFING

(☑01637-879571; www.englishsurfschool.com; lessons from £35) One of the most experienced and efficient large schools, linked with Rip Curl and staffed by fully English Surfing Federation–approved instructors (including the British team coach). It also offers coasteering and bodyboarding.

Kingsurf Surf School
SURFING

(☑01637-860091; www.kingsurf.co.uk; lessons from £30) A good option if you prefer to avoid the Fistral hustle, this school at Mawgan Porth has five young instructors and gets a tick for personal attention and small class sizes.

Extreme Academy
ADVENTURE SPORTS

(☑01637-860840; www.extremeacademy.co.uk; Watergate Bay) Owned by the Watergate Bay Hotel, this is a large and efficient operation that offers the full gamut of water sports: surfing, of course, as well as more unusual options such as stand-up paddleboarding and handplaning (which involves catching a wave with a miniature surfboard attached to your wrist).

EboAdventure
OUTDOORS

(☑0800 781 6861; www.eboadventure.co.uk) Surfing's not the only sport in Newquay – you could also try kitebuggying, kayaking, stand-up paddleboarding and coasteering (a mix of rock climbing, scrambling and wild swimming). This multi-activity centre is based at the Penhale Training Camp, at the northern end of Holywell Bay.

🛏 Sleeping

Newquay Townhouse
B&B £

(☑01637-620009; www.newquaytownhouse.co.uk; 6 Tower Rd; d £50-70; ℗🖥) A decent B&B near Newquay's town centre, with bright rooms livened up with stripy cushions and wicker furniture.

★ Scarlet
HOTEL £££

(☑01637-861600; www.scarlethotel.co.uk; Mawgan Porth; r from £240; ℗🖥☲) For out-and-out luxury, Cornwall's fabulously chic, adults-only ecohotel takes the crown. In a regal location above Mawgan Porth, 5 miles from Newquay, it screams designer style, from the huge sea-view rooms with their funky furniture and minimalist decor to the luxurious spa, complete with meditation lounge, outdoor hot tubs and wild swimming pool. The restaurant's a beauty, too.

Watergate Bay Hotel
HOTEL £££

(☑01637-860543; www.watergatebay.co.uk; Watergate Bay; d £265-410, ste £365-490; ℗🖥) Originally built for Victorian tourists arriving on the (long-disappeared) railway line from Newquay, this old hotel has had a totally 21st-century transformation: its rooms shine in slinky pinks, candy stripes and sea blues, the style is sleek and minimal, and there's a choice of restaurants. It's big on activities, too, provided by the attached Extreme Academy.

🍴 Eating

Zacry's
MODERN BRITISH ££

(☑01637-861231; www.watergatebay.co.uk/food-and-drink/zacrys; Watergate Bay; 2-/3-course menu £29.50/36.50; ☉6.30-9.30pm) The newest offering at the Watergate Bay Hotel is a faintly American affair: a smart bistro with wooden booths arranged in a gentle curve, overlooking a semi-open-plan kitchen. Head chef Neil Haydock has a taste for Stateside flavours, so expect things like chargrilled sirloin and seafood succotash on the menu. The food is great, but kids aren't encouraged.

Boathouse
BISTRO ££

(☑01637-874062; www.the-boathouse-newquay.co.uk; South Quay Hill; mains £12.35-18.40, seafood platters £42-64; ☉10am-11pm) The pick of the places to eat in downtown Newquay, hidden away from the hustle at the bottom of the hill beside the fishing quay. Appropriately enough, it's a seafood specialist, taking its catch straight from the day boats – lemon sole, pollock, crawfish, spider crab and lobster, plus sumptuous *fruits de mer* platters. A lovely surprise.

Beach Hut
BISTRO ££

(☑01637-860877; Watergate Bay; mains £10-18; ☉9am-9pm) Lodged beneath Jamie Oliver's Fifteen Cornwall, this beachside bistro is a great bet for simple surf 'n' turf: sticky pork ribs, 'extreme' burgers and a different fish every day.

Lewinnick Lodge
BISTRO ££

(☑01637-878117; www.lewinnicklodge.co.uk; Pentire Head, Newquay; mains £12.50-20; ☉8am-10pm) For lunch with a view, this smart cafe-bistro is the choice. It's perched right on the cliffs of Pentire Head, giving a knock-out perspective on the coastline around Newquay. The style is modern, all bleached wood and plate glass, and the food is decent too: gourmet burgers, mussels and Thai-style salads are on the menu. Rooms (from £170) are extremely pleasant.

Fifteen Cornwall ITALIAN £££
(☑ 01637-861000; www.fifteencornwall.com; Watergate Bay; 2-/3-course lunch menu £26/32, 5-course dinner menu £65; ⊘ 8.30am-10am, noon-2.30pm & 6.15-9.15pm) Owned by celeb chef Jamie Oliver, this restaurant on Watergate Bay serves Jamie's trademark Italian food while simultaneously training young apprentices. The vibe is relaxed (white walls, street-art murals, retro furniture) and the beach view is stunning through the floor-to-ceiling windows, but the prices are on the high side.

🍷 Drinking & Nightlife

Newquay's drinking spots aren't sophisticated: cheesy clubs and brash bars abound, and the town centre gets notoriously rowdy on Friday and Saturday nights, especially in summer.

Chy BAR
(http://chybarandkitchen-newquay.co.uk; 12 Beach Rd; ⊘9am-11pm) Chrome, wood and leather dominate this cafe-bar overlooking Towan beach. The action continues till late at the Koola nightclub downstairs.

Central PUB
(11 Central Sq; ⊘11am-midnight Sun-Thu, to 1am Fri & Sat) As its name suggests, this pre-club pub is in the heart of town, and is usually packed at weekends.

ℹ Information

Newquay Tourist Office (☑ 01637-854020; www.visitnewquay.org; Marcus Hill; ⊘9.15am-5.30pm Mon-Fri, 10am-4pm Sat & Sun) Small but well-stocked office, which can help you arrange everything from accommodation to surf lessons.

ℹ Getting There & Away

AIR

Five miles from town, **Newquay Cornwall Airport** (p319) currently offers direct daily flights to Manchester and London Gatwick with **Flybe** (www.flybe.com) and the Isles of Scilly with **Isles of Scilly Skybus** (p345). Various seasonal destinations around the UK and Europe are also offered during summer.

BUS

Newquay's bus station is on Manor Rd. Useful destinations:

Newquay Cornwall Airport Bus 56; 26 minutes, hourly Monday to Saturday, five on Sunday

Padstow Bus 56; 26 minutes, hourly Monday to Saturday, five on Sunday

St Agnes (bus 87; 50 minutes, hourly) Also stops at Crantock, Holywell Bay and Perranporth before continuing to Truro.

Truro (bus 90/92/93; 70 minutes, half-hourly Monday to Saturday) The fastest bus to Truro; the various routes travel via different villages but all terminate in Truro.

Wadebridge Bus 95; 50 minutes, five daily Monday to Saturday

TRAIN

Newquay is on the branch line between Newquay and Par (Atlantic Coast Line; £4.70, 45 minutes), from where you can hop aboard the main London–Penzance line.

Perranporth to Porthtowan

Southwest of Newquay, Cornwall's craggy northern coastline dips and curves through a stunning panorama of wild, sea-smacked cliffs and golden bays, including the family-friendly beach of Perranporth, the old mining town of St Agnes and the surfy hangout of Porthtowan.

◎ Sights & Acitivities

Perranporth Beach BEACH
(🅿) Perranporth's huge, flat, sandy beach is popular with bucket-and-spading families and surfers alike. It's over a mile long, backed by dunes and rocky cliffs, and usually has space even on the busiest days, and it's home to the Watering Hole (p328).

★ Chapel Porth COVE
(🅿) Two miles from St Agnes is one of Cornwall's most beautiful coves, Chapel Porth, a wild, rocky beach framed by steep, gorse-covered cliffs, owned by the National Trust. Above the cove is the ruined engine stack of **Wheal Coates**, which still boasts its chimney and winding house, from where the coast path winds all the way to the blustery outcrop of **St Agnes Head**.

Blue Hills Tin Streams EXHIBITION
(☑ 01872-553341; www.bluehillstin.com; adult/child £6.50/3; ⊘10am-2pm Tue-Sat mid-Apr–mid-Oct) A

mile east of St Agnes (signed to Wheal Kitty) is the rocky valley of Trevellas, home to one of Cornwall's last tin manufacturers where you can watch the whole tinning process, from mining and smelting through to casting and finishing. Handmade jewellery is sold in the shop.

Eating & Drinking

Chapel Porth Cafe
CAFE £

(Chapel Porth; sandwiches & cakes £2-4; ⏱10am-5pm) The Chapel Porth Cafe is a local institution, serving hot chocolate, cheesy baguettes and the house speciality: hedgehog ice cream (vanilla ice cream topped with clotted cream and hazelnuts).

Blue Bar
BISTRO ££

(☏01209-890329; www.blue-bar.co.uk; Porthtowan; mains £8-16; ⏱10am-11pm) For a seaside sundowner or a lunchtime snack by the sand, this Porthtowan cafe is tough to beat (unfortunately everyone knows about it, so arrive early).

Bolingey Inn
PUB FOOD ££

(☏01872-571626; Penwartha Rd, Bolingey; mains £10-16; ⏱noon-11pm) The ivy-covered Bolingey Inn is the best pub around Perranporth for food, and has a valley location about 2 miles drive inland.

Watering Hole
BAR

(www.the-wateringhole.co.uk; Perranporth Beach; ⏱10am-11pm) One of Cornwall's oldest beach bars, the Watering Hole was nearly washed away during heavy storms in 2014. It's a nice spot for a sundowner, and has regular bands.

❶ Getting There & Away

First Kernow buses:

Bus 57 (two daily) To Perranporth and St Agnes in one direction, to Porthtowan, Gwithian and St Ives in the other direction.

Bus 87 (hourly Monday to Saturday, slightly fewer on Sunday) Stops in St Agnes on its way from Newquay via Crantock, Holywell and Perranporth to Truro.

St Ives

POP 9870

Even if you've seen St Ives many times before, it's still hard not to be dazzled as you gaze across its improbably pretty jumble of slate roofs, church towers and turquoise bays. Once a busy pilchard harbour, St Ives

later became the centre of Cornwall's arts scene in the 1920s and '30s, and the town is still an artistic centre, with numerous galleries and craft shops lining its winding cobbled streets, as well as the southwestern outpost of the renowned Tate Museum.

Unfortunately, change has come at a price – St Ives is packed throughout summer, and prices here are substantially higher than other parts of Cornwall. To see it at its best, avoid school holidays an July and August.

◉ Sights & Activities

The largest town beaches are Porthmeor and Porthminster, both of which have sand and space aplenty. Between them juts the grassy promontory known as the Island, topped by the tiny pre-14th-century Chapel of St Nicholas. On the peninsula's east side is the little cove of Porthgwidden, often a good place to escape the crowds.

★ Tate St Ives
GALLERY

(☏01736-796226; www.tate.org.uk/stives; Porthmeor Beach) Hovering like a concrete curl above Porthmeor Beach, St Ives' celebrated art museum has been closed for a huge renovation project, which will include the addition of an entire new wing. Work was scheduled for completion in spring 2017 – check the website for the latest news.

Barbara Hepworth Museum
MUSEUM

(☏01736-796226; Barnoon Hill; adult/child £6.60/5.50; ⏱10am-5pm Mar-Oct, to 4pm Nov-Feb) Barbara Hepworth (1903–75) was one of the leading abstract sculptors of the 20th century and a key figure in the St Ives art scene. Her studio on Barnoon Hill has remained almost untouched since her death and the adjoining garden contains several of her most notable sculptures, many of which were inspired by the elemental forces she discovered in her adopted Cornish home: rock, sea, sand, wind, sky. Free private tours are also available to provide extra context.

St Ives Boats
BOATING

(☏0777 300 8000; www.stivesboats.co.uk; adult/child £10/8) From the harbour front, several operators including St Ives Boats offer fishing trips and scenic cruises, including to the grey seal colony on Seal Island. If you're really lucky, you might even spot a porpoise or a basking shark in summer.

Leach Pottery
GALLERY

(☏01736-796398; www.leachpottery.com; Higher Stennack; adult/child £4.50/free; ⏱10am-5pm

West Cornwall

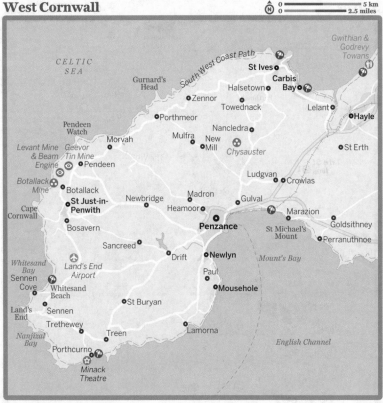

CELTIC SEA

Gwithian & Godrevy Towans

Gurnard's Head

South West Coast Path

St Ives

Carbis Bay

Halsetown

Lelant

Hayle

Zennor

Towednack

Porthmeor

Nancledra

St Erth

Pendeen Watch

Morvah

Mulfra

New Mill

Chysauster

Levant Mine & Beam Engine

Geevor Tin Mine

Pendeen

Ludgvan

Crowlas

Botallack Mine

Botallack

Newbridge

Madron

Gulval

St Just-in-Penwith

Heamoor

Marazion

Goldsithney

Cape Cornwall

Bosavern

Penzance

St Michael's Mount

Perranuthnoe

Sancreed

Drift

Newlyn

Mount's Bay

Whitesand Bay

Land's End Airport

Paul

Sennen Cove

Whitesand Beach

Mousehole

Land's End

Sennen

St Buryan

Trethewey

Treen

Lamorna

English Channel

Nanjizal Bay

Porthcurno

Minack Theatre

Mon-Sat, 11am-4pm Sun) While other St Ives artists broke new ground in sculpture and abstract art, the potter Bernard Leach was hard at work reinventing British ceramics in his studio in Higher Stennack. Drawing inspiration from Japanese and oriental sculpture, and using a unique hand-built 'climbing' kiln based on ones he had seen in Japan, Leach's pottery created a unique fusion of Western and Eastern ideas.

🛏 Sleeping

Primrose Valley Hotel   HOTEL **££**
(📞 01736-794939;   www.primroseonline.co.uk;
Primrose Valley; r £135-180; 🅿🛜) Reopened after comprehensive refurbishment, this chic hotel has one massive selling point – it's a minute's walk from Porthminster's sands. But there are plenty more pluses too – such as its light, attractive rooms in taupes, greys, checks and sea blues, and quirky design touches including wicker lamps, Scan-

di-style dressers and model ships. It feels very modern and impeccably designed throughout.

11 Sea View Terrace   B&B **££**
(📞 01736-798440; www.11stives.co.uk; 11 Sea View Tce; d £120-140; 🅿🛜) Occupying one of the classic Edwardian villas lining the upper part of St Ives, this three-suite B&B is a chic place to stay. The two front 'suites' have lovely town and sea views, while the rear one overlooks a garden patio; for more space, there's a smart holiday flat (£350 to £975 per week).

Treliska   B&B **££**
(📞 01736-797678; www.treliska.com; 3 Bedford Rd; d £70-90; 🛜) This B&B is a bargain in pricey St Ives, especially given the location, just steps from the town centre. The trade-off is the room size: most are on the small side (ask for room 5 if it's space you're after).

St Ives

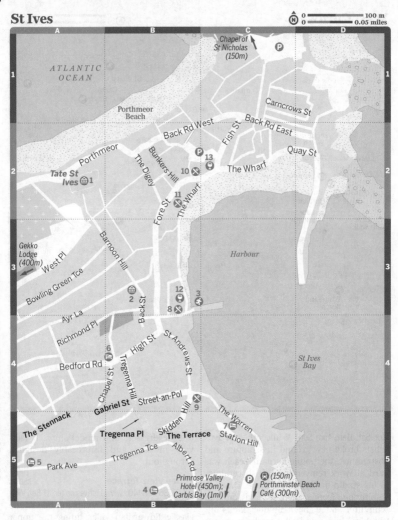

ATLANTIC OCEAN

Porthmeor Beach

St Ives Bay

Harbour

St Ives

◎ Top Sights
1 Tate St Ives A2

◎ Sights
2 Barbara Hepworth Museum B3

◉ Activities, Courses & Tours
3 St Ives Boats B3

◉ Sleeping
4 11 Sea View Terrace.............................. B5
5 Little Leaf Guest House........................ A5

6 Treliska.. B4
7 Trevose Harbour House C5

⊗ Eating
8 Alba B3
9 Blas Burgerworks.................................... B4
10 Moomaid of Zennor............................... B2
11 Porthminster Kitchen B2

⊙ Drinking & Nightlife
12 Hub B3
13 Sloop Inn... C2

Little Leaf Guest House
B&B ££

(☑ 01736-795427; www.littleleafguesthouse.co.uk; Park Ave; r £85-125; 🐾) A reliable, ecofriendly B&B in the upper part of town, which offers excellent rates, especially in the low season. It's on a terrace overlooking the town's rooftops. Rooms are sweet and simple, finished in creamy colours and pine furniture. Ask for rooms 2 or 5 if you're after a sea view. Parking is the only problem.

Trevose Harbour House
B&B £££

(☑ 01736-793267; www.trevosehouse.co.uk; 22 The Warren; d £185-275; 🐾) A stylish six-room town house on the winding Warren, restored with a sea-themed combo of fresh whites and stripy blues. It's been beautifully finished – Neal's Yard bathstuffs, iPod docks and retro design pieces in the rooms, plus a book-lined lounge and minimalist courtyard patio. It's boutique through and through.

Boskerris
HOTEL £££

(☑ 01736-795295; www.boskerrishotel.co.uk; Boskerris Rd, Carbis Bay; d £170-280; P🐾) Just along the coast from St Ives in the suburb of Carbis Bay, this upmarket mini-hotel offers plenty of reasons to stay: smart rooms in cool monotones, an elegantly uncluttered design aesthetic, lovely bathrooms with freestanding bath-tubs and swish ceramic sinks, and a cracking patio overlooking the bay. It's great value in the low season.

Blue Hayes
HOTEL £££

(☑ 01736-797129; www.bluehayes.co.uk; Trelyon Ave; r £150-270; P🐾) Riviera luxury in a St Ives hotel, with manicured grounds, a balustraded breakfast terrace and five suite-sized rooms. The Trelyon Suite even has its own private roof terrace.

✗ Eating

Moomaid of Zennor
ICE CREAM £

(www.moomaidofzennor.com; Wharf; from £2; ⊙9am-5pm) This ice-cream maker is a local legend, and makes all of its 30 flavours on the home farm just outside Zennor, using only its own milk and Rodda's clotted cream. Exotic concoctions include fig and mascarpone and pear cider sorbet.

★ Porthminster Beach Café
BISTRO ££

(☑ 01736-795352; www.porthminstercafe.co.uk; Porthminster Beach; mains £15-22; ⊙9am-10pm) This is no ordinary beach cafe: it's a full-blown bistro with a gorgeous sun-trap terrace and a superb Mediterranean-influenced menu, specialising in seafood. Tuck into rich bouillabaisse, seafood curry or Provençal fish soup, and settle back to enjoy the breezy beach vistas. It's published its own cookbook, too, if you fancy taking the recipes home.

Porthminster Kitchen
BISTRO ££

(☑ 01736-799874; www.porthminster.kitchen; Wharf; mains lunch £7.50-15, dinner £11-17; ⊙9am-10pm) Run by the same team as Porthminster Beach Café, this is a welcome new addition to the harbourside in St Ives. It showcases fresh, zingy, fusion food, from tuna sashimi and sea trout with Asian mushrooms to Malay veggie curry – there's an emphasis on minimising gluten and dairy too. The quayview dining room is lovely.

Blas Burgerworks
CAFE ££

(☑ 01736-797272; The Warren; burgers £10-12.50; ⊙noon-9.30pm Jul & Aug, 5.30-9.30pm rest of year) 🍴 St Ives' boutique burger joint, with an ecofriendly manifesto and an imaginative menu. Go for a 6oz Classic Blasburger, or branch out with a guacamole and corn salsa–topped Rancheros, or a Smokey with beetroot, aged cheddar and homemade piccalilli (plenty of veggie options, too). The owners also run the excellent Halsetown Inn, just outside St Ives.

Halsetown Inn
PUB FOOD ££

(☑ 01736-795583; www.halsetowninn.co.uk; Halsetown; mains £13-22.50; ⊙noon-2pm & 6-9pm) Prime pub grub a mile from St Ives in tiny Halsetown. It's still the village boozer – local ales, first-name bar staff, cosy crannies to hunker down in – but the food is a notch above the norm thanks to the owners, who also run Blas Burgerworks. Expect posh mains such as chicken pithivier and cider-baked ham, plus a cracking Sunday roast.

Alba
MODERN BRITISH £££

(☑ 01736-797222; www.thealbarestaurant.com; Old Lifeboat House; 2-/3-course dinner menu £21.95/25.95, mains £16-28.95; ⊙noon-2pm & 6-10pm) Other restaurants have come and gone in St Ives, but this harbourside bistro next to the old lifeboat station continues to excel. It's in a converted boathouse, with a split-level layout: diner-style downstairs, more formal upstairs (book well ahead for the prime window tables). First-class fish and seafood are the mainstays. The set dinner menu is only available from 5.30pm to 7pm.

Drinking & Entertainment

Sloop Inn
INN

(☎01736-796584; www.sloop-inn.co.uk; Wharf; ☺11am-11pm) This beam-ceilinged boozer is as comfy as an old pair of slippers, with a few tables on the harbour and lots of local ales.

Hub
BAR

(www.hub-stives.co.uk; Wharf; ☺9am-11pm) The open-plan Hub is the heart of St Ives' (limited) nightlife: coffee and burgers by day, cocktails after dark.

Getting There & Away

BUS

Bus 17/17A/17B (£5, 30 minutes, half-hourly Monday to Saturday, hourly Sunday) The quickest route to Penzance, via Lelant and Marazion.

Bus 16/16A (£5, hourly Monday to Saturday) An alternative route to Penzance; bus 16A travels via Zennor and the Gurnard's Head pub, while bus 16 goes via Halsetown, Ludgvan and Gulval.

TRAIN

The branch train line from St Ives is worth taking just for the coastal views.

Trains shuttle between St Ives train station and St Erth (£3, 14 minutes, half-hourly), where you can catch connections along the Penzance–London Paddington main line.

Zennor & St Just

The twisting B3306 from St Ives is a roller coaster of a road, winding through a stark landscape of ancient drystone walls, barren moorland, tiny villages and rocky bluffs. The landscape here feels wild and ancient, a world away from some of Cornwall's more gentrified corners.

Sights

Church of St Senara
CHURCH

(Zennor) This little church in the hamlet of Zennor dates from at least 1150. Inside, a famous carved chair depicts the legendary Mermaid of Zennor, who is said to have fallen in love with the singing voice of local Matthew Trewhella. Locals say you can still sometimes hear them singing down at nearby Pendour Cove – and even if you don't, the views along the coast path are reward enough.

★ Geevor Tin Mine
MINE

(☎01736-788662; www.geevor.com; adult/child £12.95/7.50; ☺9am-5pm Sun-Fri Mar-Oct, to 4pm

Nov-Feb) Just north of St Just near Pendeen, this historic mine closed in 1990 and now provides a powerful insight into the dark, dingy and dangerous conditions in which Cornwall's miners worked. Above ground, you can view the dressing floors and the original machinery used to sort the minerals and ores, before taking a guided tour into some of the underground shafts. Claustrophobes need not apply.

Botallack Mine
RUINS

Clinging to the cliffs near Levant, this dramatic engine house has abandoned mine shafts extending right out beneath the raging Atlantic waves. It's a treacherous climb down, so it's best viewed from a distance from nearby **Botallack Head**.

Levant Mine & Beam Engine
HISTORIC SITE

(www.nationaltrust.org.uk/main/w-levantmineand-beamengine; adult/child £7.20/3.60; ☺10.30am-5pm Sun-Fri) At this clifftop site, one of the world's only working beam engines is still in thunderous action. Built in 1840, these great engines were the powerhouses behind the Cornish mining boom, powering mineral trains and pumping water from the shafts. Lovingly restored by a team of enthusiasts, it's a sight to behold when it's in full steam.

Cape Cornwall
LANDMARK

Jutting out from the cliffs near St Just is Cornwall's only 'official' cape, a craggy finger of land topped by an abandoned minestack. Below the cape is the rocky beach of **Priest's Cove**, while nearby are the ruins of **St Helen's Oratory**, supposedly one of the first Christian chapels built in West Cornwall.

Sleeping & Eating

Zennor Chapel Guesthouse
B&B

(☎01736-798307; www.zennorchapelguesthouse. com; r from £80; P) As its name hints, this attractive B&B (previously a hostel) occupies a former church on the edge of the village. There are five rooms, most of which still boast original ecclesiastical features, including beautiful arched windows. There's a range of sleeping configurations – doubles, twins and family with bunkbeds. There's also a cafe and gift shop downstairs.

★ Gurnard's Head
BRITISH ££

(☎01736-796928; www.gurnardshead.co.uk; near Zennor; mains £12-19.95, r £115-180; P🔊🐾) On the wonderful coast road between Zennor and St Just, you can't miss the Gurnard's – its name is emblazoned on the roof. Run by

MINACK THEATRE & PORTHCURNO

In terms of theatrical settings, the **Minack** (☑ 01736-810181; www.minack.com; tickets from £10) takes top billing. Carved into the crags overlooking Porthcurno and the azure-blue Atlantic, this amazing clifftop amphitheatre was the lifelong passion of theatre-lover Rowena Cade, who dreamt up the idea in the 1930s. It's now a hugely popular place for alfresco theatre, with plays staged from mid-May to mid-September.

Just up the valley from the Minack Theatre, the redeveloped **Porthcurno Telegraph Museum** (☑ 01736-810966; www.telegraphmuseum.org; adult/child £8.50/5; ☉ 10am-5pm) recounts the area's role as Britain's first hub for transatlantic telecommunications – until 1970, sub-sea cables carried messages here from all over the world. There's an intriguing museum containing a communications kit – vintage radios, transistor valves and so on – and you can explore a network of underground tunnels built here during WWII.

the Inkin brothers (who also own Mousehole's Old Coastguard Hotel) this is the quintessential Cornish country pub, with wooden furniture, book-lined shelves and sepia prints conjuring a cosy, lived-in feel. It's renowned for its food.

Sennen & Land's End

Beyond St Ives, the coastline gets wilder and emptier as you near Cornwall's tip at Land's End, the westernmost point of mainland England, where the coal-black cliffs plunge into the pounding surf, and the views stretch all the way to the Isles of Scilly on a clear day.

Unfortunately, the decision to build the **Legendary Land's End** (☑ 0871 720 0044; www.landsend-landmark.co.uk; day ticket adult/child £12/9; ☉ 9am-5pm Mar-Oct; 🚸) theme park on the headland in the 1980s hasn't done much to enhance the view. Take our advice: just pay for the car park, skip the tacky multimedia shows and opt for an exhilarating clifftop stroll instead. Look for the historic **Longships Lighthouse**, on a reef 1.25 miles out to sea.

From Land's End, follow the coast path west to the secluded cove of **Nanjizal Bay**, or east to the old harbour of Sennen, which overlooks the glorious beach of **Whitesand Bay**, the area's most impressive stretch of sand.

Mousehole

POP 697

With a tight tangle of cottages and alleyways gathered behind the granite breakwater, Mousehole (mowzle) looks like something from a children's storybook (a fact not unno-

ticed by author Antonia Barber, who set her much-loved fairy tale *The Mousehole Cat* here). In centuries past, this was Cornwall's busiest pilchard port, but the fish dried up at the turn of the century, and the village now survives mostly on tourist traffic.

Packed in summer and deserted in winter, it's ripe for a wander, with a maze of slips, net-lofts and courtyards. It's also well known for its Christmas lights, and as the home of 'stargazey pie', a pilchard pie in which the fish heads are left poking through the pie's crust.

🛏 Sleeping & Eating

Old Coastguard Hotel HOTEL £££
(☑ 01736-731222; www.oldcoastguardhotel.co.uk; The Parade; d £187.50-277.50; 🅿 🛜 🐾) Now run by the owners of the Gurnard's Head, this coastal beauty has a much more relaxed atmosphere than it used to be. Rooms are still classic – restrained colour schemes, stately beds – and the best ones obviously have a sea view. Seafood takes prominence in the smart sea-view restaurant (mains £13.50 to £18.50), and there's a cliff garden for soaking up the rays.

★ **2 Fore St** FRENCH ££
(☑ 01736-731164; www.2forestreet.co.uk; Fore St; mains £11-20; ☉ noon-2pm & 7-9pm) Culinary sophistication on the Mousehole seafront. It's young but has already gained plenty of admirers, including *Harden's* and the *Good Food Guide*. Inside, stripped wood, cool colours and harbour views; outside, a sweet garden shaded by palms and canvas umbrellas. The menu wears its French influences on its sleeve, as you might expect from a head chef who trained under Raymond Blanc.

Penzance

POP 21,168

Overlooking the majestic sweep of Mount's Bay, the old harbour of Penzance has a salty, sea-blown charm that feels altogether more authentic than many of Cornwall's polished-up ports. Its streets and shopping arcades still feel real and a touch ramshackle, and there's nowhere better for a windy-day walk than the town's seafront Victorian promenade. Along the way look out for the elegant sight of Jubilee Pool, the town's lovely outdoor lido, recently restored.

The nearby harbour of Newlyn is still home to Cornwall's largest fishing fleet, and the harbour is filled with bobbing boats of every shape and description.

Sights & Activities

Penlee House Gallery & Museum GALLERY
(www.penleehouse.org.uk; Morrab Rd; adult/child £4.50/3; ⊙10am-5pm Mon-Sat Easter-Sep, 10.30am-4.30pm Oct-Easter) Penzance's historic art gallery displays paintings by artists of the Newlyn School (including Stanhope Forbes and Lamorna Birch) and hosts regular exhibitions. The nearby Penlee Gardens are well worth a stroll.

Tremenheere Sculpture Garden GARDENS
(☑01736-448089; www.tremenheere.co.uk; adult/child £8/4.50; ⊙10am-4pm Mon-Thu, 10am-5pm Fri-Sun; ⊞) This inventive garden opened just outside Penzance in 2012. The landscaped gardens sit in a sheltered valley awash with artworks and installations: look out for a 'sky-view' chamber by James Turrell, a 'black mound' of tree stumps by David Nash and a 'Camera Obscura' by Billy Wynter, offering a unique panorama of the gardens and Mount's Bay.

There's also a super cafe, Tremenheere Kitchen (lunches £8 to £14), and there are family events such as den-building and art workshops during school holidays.

★ Jubilee Pool SWIMMING
(www.jubileepool.co.uk; Western Promendade Rd; adult/child £4.75/3.80; ⊙10.30am-6pm Wed-Mon, to 8pm Tue late-May-early-Sep) After being thoroughly battered during recent winter storms, Penzance's glorious seawater lido has reopened and regained its place as the town's pride and joy. Built in 1935, it's a bold statement of art-deco styling, sleek, sharp and whitewashed – the perfect backdrop for sea bathing in style. There's discounted entry after 3.30pm (adult/child £3.10/2.50).

Sleeping

Penzance YHA HOSTEL £
(☑0845 371 9653; penzance@yha.org.uk; Castle Horneck, Alverton; dm £19-25; P ⊞) Penzance's YHA is inside an 18th-century house on the edge of town. It's a rambling place, with a cafe, laundry and four- to 10-bed dorms. It's a 15-minute walk from the harbour front.

★ Venton Vean B&B ££
(☑01736-351294; www.ventonvean.co.uk; Trewithen Rd; r £86-97; ⊞) The picture of a modern B&B, finished in stylish greys and blues, with stripped wood floors, bay windows and a keen eye for design. Rooms 1 and 2 are the most spacious; the former overlooks Penlee Memorial Park. The sumptuous breakfast choice includes pancakes, smoked Newlyn fish, avocado on sourdough toast, and a Mexican-style feast of tortillas and refried beans.

★ Artist Residence Penzance B&B ££
(☑01736-365664; www.arthotelcornwall.co.uk; 20 Chapel St; d £115-145, 2-bed apt from £255; ⊞) Hands down the most entertaining place to stay in Penzance, this B&B on Chapel St is like sleeping inside an art gallery. All rooms are designed by a local artist, and all are bright, colourful and brimming with imagination (we particularly liked the Attic Lofts). There are apartments for longer stays, and food is available in the Cornish Barn.

Chapel House Penzance B&B ££
(☑01736-362024; www.chapelhousepz.co.uk; Chapel St; r from £150; ⊞) In one of Chapel St's most historic buildings – a sea-captain's house that was for many years an arts centre – this beautiful B&B has become a favourite of travel supplements, and it's not hard to see why. The six rooms ooze design credentials: retro furniture, waterfall baths, oak beds, sleek bathrooms, all carefully blended with the house's Georgian architecture.

Eating

★ Shore MODERN BRITISH ££
(☑01736-362444; www.theshorerestaurant.uk; 13/14 Alverton St; 2-/3-course lunch £18/24, dinner mains £17.50-20; ⊙noon-2pm & 6.30-9pm Tue-Sat) Penzance's hottest new table (and one of the hottest in Cornwall, come to think of it) is this barn-storming bistro overseen by chef Bruce

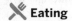

BATH & SOUTHWEST ENGLAND PENZANCE

Penzance

Rennie, a veteran of many a Michelin-starred kitchen. It's all about seafood here, sourced from the Newlyn day boats and served with a strong French-Italian influence.

★ **Ben's Cornish Kitchen**   BRITISH ££
(☎ 01736-719200; www.benscornishkitchen.com; Marazion; 2-/3-course dinner £24/29; ⊙noon-1.30pm & 7-8.30pm Tue-Sat; ✐) Blink and you'll miss Ben Prior's unassuming restaurant as you zip along Marazion's main street, but diners travel from far and wide to taste his classical cooking, which majors in meaty Cornish flavours with a French influence. It's won national awards from Waitrose, *The Good Food Guide* and the Trencherman's guide, and tables are getting scarce – book well ahead.

★ **Tolcarne Inn**   PUB FOOD ££
(☎ 01736-363074; www.tolcarneinn.co.uk; Tolcarne Pl, Newlyn; mains £15-22; ⊙noon-2.15pm & 7-9pm Tue-Sat, noon-2.15pm Sun) This old Newlyn inn is run by talented local chef Ben Tunnicliffe, who's fast turned it into the area's primo gastropub. The ethos is refreshingly honest – top-quality fish, seafood and locally sourced meat, served with minimal fuss. Bookings advisable, especially for Sunday lunch.

Penzance

◎ Sights
1 Penlee House Gallery & Museum B2

✪ Activities, Courses & Tours
2 Jubilee Pool D3

⊨ Sleeping
3 Artist Residence Penzance C2
4 Chapel House Penzance.....................C2
5 Venton Vean A3

✸ Eating
6 Bakehouse C2
7 Shore B2

⊜ Drinking & Nightlife
8 Admiral Benbow................................C2
9 Zero Lounge C2

Bakehouse   MEDITERRANEAN ££
(☎ 01736-331331; www.bakehouserestaurant.co.uk; Chapel St; mains £10.95-19.95; ⊙6-10pm Mon-Sat) Down an alley off Chapel St, this no-nonsense bistro serves unpretentious food such as fish served with Med-style marinades, and steaks with spicy rubs.

Drinking & Nightlife

Admiral Benbow PUB

(☑ 01736-363448; 46 Chapel St; ⊙ 11am-11pm)
On historic Chapel St, the salty old Benbow
looks like it's dropped from the pages of
Treasure Island, with nautical decor mostly
reclaimed from shipwrecks: anchors, lanterns, figureheads and all.

Zero Lounge BAR

(Chapel St; ⊙ 11am-11pm) More urban chic
than olde worlde, this open-plan bar also
has the town's best beer garden – a hidden
patio with sofas and wicker chairs to lounge
on. DJs play at weekends.

ⓘ Getting There & Away

BUS

Local destinations include the following:

Helston (bus 2/2A; £5, hourly Monday to Saturday, two hourly Sunday) Travels via Marazion
and connects onwards to Falmouth.

St Ives buses 17/17A/17B; £5, 30 minutes, half-
hourly Monday to Saturday, hourly Sunday

TRAIN

Penzance is the last stop on the line from London Paddington.

Truro £6.60, 30 minutes

St Ives £4.20, 50 minutes) Change at St Erth.

Exeter £20.40, three hours

London Paddington £62.60, 5½ hours

The Lizard

Once notorious as a smugglers' haven and
an ill-famed graveyard for ships, the rugged
Lizard Peninsula offers Cornwall's wildest
coastal panoramas. Wind-lashed in winter,
in summer its heaths and cliffs blaze with
wild flowers, and its beaches and coves are
perfect for a bracing swim.

The main town is **Helston**, famous for
its annual street party, **Flora Day**, held on
8 May. Pretty villages are dotted along the
peninsula's coastline: the old harbour of
Coverack, the beaches of **Mullion** and the
idyllic thatched-cottage cove of **Cadgwith**
are well worth a visit.

Towards Lizard Point lie the dramatic
satellite dishes of **Goonhilly Downs** and the
beautiful National Trust beach of **Kynance
Cove**, which has to be one of Cornwall's
most photogenic beaches.

Along the peninsula's northern edge runs
Helford River, lined with creeks and inlets
that famously inspired Daphne du Maurier's

smuggling yarn, *Frenchman's Creek.* Several local companies offer kayaking tours.

◉ Sights & Activities

★**Kynance Cove** BEACH

A mile north of Lizard Point, this National
Trust–owned inlet is a showstopper, studded with offshore islands rising out of sear-
ingly blue seas. The cliffs around the cove
are rich in serpentine, a red-green rock popular with Victorian trinket-makers. Drinks
and snacks are available at the ecofriendly
cafe (www.kynancecovecafe.co.uk; mains £5-14;
⊙ 9am-5.30pm).

Lizard Lighthouse Heritage Centre MUSEUM

(☑ 01326-290202; www.lizardlighthouse.co.uk;
adult/child £3/2; ⊙ 11am-5pm Sun-Thu Mar-Oct)
Rising above Lizard Point, the whitewashed
lighthouse was built in 1751 and has protected shipping from the treacherous rocks ever
since. Although it's now automated like all
the UK's lighthouses, you can still visit the
heritage centre to learn more about its mechanics and the many ships that have come
to grief nearby. You can also take informative guided tours (adult/child £7.50/4.50)
into the tower to see the lamp room and
foghorn.

Cornish Seal Sanctuary WILDLIFE RESERVE

(☑ 01326-221361; www.visitsealife.com/gweek;
adult/child £14.95/12.50; ⊙ 10am-5pm; ⊞)
Towards the northwest of the Lizard Peninsula, this sanctuary cares for sick and or-
phaned seals washed up along the Cornish
coastline before returning them to the wild.
There are also resident populations of otters,
penguins and Californian sea lions.

Aberfal Outdoor Pursuits KAYAKING

(☑ 07968 770756; www.aberfaloutdoorpursuits.
co.uk; half-/full day £35/50) Half- and full-day
guided kayaking trips along the Helford on
sit-on-top kayaks.

🛏 Sleeping & Eating

Lizard YHA HOSTEL £

(☑ 0845 371 9550; www.yha.org.uk; Lizard Point;
dm £19-25; ⊙ Apr-Oct) Once a Victorian hotel
next to the lighthouse, now a YHA hostel,
this has to rank pretty high in the 'UK's best
budget beds' list. It's in a spectacular situation, overlooking miles of wild cliffs and
coast, and it's typically well run: a range of
dorms, a self-catering kitchen, a spacious
lounge, but no cafe.

ST MICHAEL'S MOUNT

Looming in the middle of Mount's Bay and connected to the mainland via a cobbled causeway, the abbey-crowned island **St Michael's Mount** (NT; ☑01736-710507; www.stmichaelsmount.co.uk; house & gardens adult/child £12.50/6; ☺house 10.30am-5.30pm Sun-Fri Jul-Sep, 10.30am-5pm Mar-Jun & Oct) is an unforgettable sight – and one of Cornwall's most iconic images. Initially a Benedictine monastery, and later the seat of the St Aubyn family, it's a must-visit. You can catch the ferry (adult/child £2/1) from nearby Marazion at high tide, but it's worth arriving at low tide so you can walk across the causeway, as pilgrims did centuries ago.

There's been a monastery here since at least the 5th century, but the present abbey was mostly built by Benedictine monks during the 12th century. Highlights include the rococo drawing room, the armoury, the 14th-century church and the amazing clifftop gardens.

Recent excavations including a Bronze Age axe head, dagger and metal clasp have proved the island has been inhabited since ancient times.

Though it's still owned by the St Aubyn family, the abbey is run by the National Trust. The hourly 17B bus shuttles between Marazion and Penzance (£2).

★ Kota

INTERNATIONAL ££

(☑01326-562407; www.kotarestaurant.co.uk; 2-/3-course menu £20/25, mains £13.95-21.95; ☺6-9pm Tue-Sat) Half-Maori, half Chinese-Malay, chef Jude Kereama takes his culinary inspiration from his globetrotting travels, and his menu is spiced with exotic flavours, from Szechuan to Thai and Malaysian. His main restaurant is in a converted mill in Porthleven, 3 miles south of Helston. He also has another cafe-bistro, Kota Kai, along the quay.

Kota Kai Bar & Kitchen

CAFE ££

(☑01326-574411; www.kotakai.co.uk; mains £7.95-18.95; ☺noon-2pm & 5.30-9.30pm Mon, Tue & Thu-Sat, noon-2.30pm Sun; 🛜) On the 1st floor of a waterfront building overlooking Porthleven's harbour, this zingy cafe is run by chef Jude Kereama, and showcases his taste for spicy, exotic dishes: laksa curry, tom yum soup, five-spiced squid. The views over the quay are super.

Halzephron Inn

PUB FOOD ££

(☑01326-240406; www.halzephron-inn.co.uk; mains £10.25-21.95; ☺11am-11pm) On the cliffs above the cove of Gunwalloe, 5 miles south of Helston, this is a historic Cornish local, whitewashed and slate-topped, with brassy trinkets above the bar, stout beams and a menu of beer-battered fish, grilled gammon steak, duck breast and the like. It's cosy and stone-walled, with lots of nooks and crannies, and a small patio outside.

Falmouth & Around

POP 20,775

Few seaside towns in Cornwall boast such an arresting location as Falmouth, overlooking the broad Fal River as it empties into the English Channel. Backed by green hills and blue water, Falmouth is criss-crossed by cobbled lanes, salty old pubs and trendy cafes. It makes an ideal base for exploring Cornwall's south coast, and has a wealth of bars and bistros, a trio of beaches and the nation's foremost maritime museum.

Though it's now mainly supported by students at Falmouth University in nearby Penryn, the town made its fortune during the 18th and 19th centuries thanks to lucrative maritime trade – the deep water offshore is the third-deepest natural harbour in the world, and the town grew rich when tea clippers, trading vessels and mail packets stopped here to unload their cargoes. Falmouth is still an important centre for ship repairs – you can look over the dockyard cranes as you head to Pendennis Point.

⊙ Sights & Activities

Falmouth's bucket-and-spade beaches aren't quite up to north coast standards, but they're nice enough for paddling and sun lounging. All the beaches have car parks, but they fill up quickly in summer. The 367 bus (hourly Monday to Friday, four times on Saturday) runs from the Moor bus station to Gyllyngvase and Swanpool.

National Maritime Museum MUSEUM
(☎01326-313388; www.nmmc.co.uk; Discovery Quay; adult/child £12.50/5; ☺10am-5pm) Falmouth's most high-profile museum is located on the much revamped area around Discovery Quay. It's the sister outpost of the National Maritime Museum in Greenwich, London, and focuses on Falmouth's history as a seafaring port, supplemented by regular nautically themed exhibitions. The centrepiece is the impressive **Flotilla Gallery**, where an array of small boats is suspended from the ceiling on steel wires.

Pendennis Castle CASTLE
(EH; ☎01326-316594; www.english-heritage.org.uk; adult/child £7.90/4.70; ☺10am-6pm daily Mar-Sep, 10am-5pm Oct, 10am-4pm Sat & Sun Nov-Feb) Designed to work in tandem with its sister castle in St Mawes across the estuary, this Tudor castle sits proudly on Pendennis Point, and was built as part of Henry VIII's massive castle-building program to reinforce England's coastline. You can wander around several of the castle floors and the Tudor gun deck, as well as the governor's bedroom, a WWI guardhouse and the WWII-era Half-Moon Battery. Listen out for the Noonday Gun blasting out at midday.

Fal River Boat Trips BOATING
Falmouth's main pier is the departure point for boat trips along the Fal River and ferries to Flushing and St Mawes. There are several operators, all offering similar routes: Enterprise Boats (p341) is the best known, and runs regular trips to Truro and St Mawes via Trelissick Gardens.

CORNWALL'S GREAT GARDENS

Eden Project (☎01726-811911; www.edenproject.com; adult/child/family £25/15/69, joint ticket with Lost Gardens of Heligan £34.65/18/93.50; ☺9.30am-6pm, last admission 4.30pm) Lodged at the bottom of a disused clay pit, the giant biomes of the Eden Project – the largest greenhouses in the world – have become Cornwall's most celebrated landmark and an essential visit. Looking like a Bond villain's lair, Eden's bubble-shaped biomes maintain miniature ecosystems that enable all kinds of weird and wonderful plants to flourish – from stinking rafflesia flowers and banana trees in the rainforest biome to cacti and soaring palms in the Mediterranean biome.

Lost Gardens of Heligan (☎01726-845100; www.heligan.com; adult/child £13.50/6; ☺10am-6pm Mar-Oct, to 5pm Nov-Feb) This is Cornwall's real-life secret garden. Formerly the family estate of the Tremaynes, Heligan's magnificent 19th-century gardens fell into disrepair following WWI, and have since been restored to their former splendour by the brains behind the Eden Project, Tim Smit, and a huge army of gardeners, horticulturalists and volunteers.

Trebah Garden (☎01326-252200; www.trebahgarden.co.uk; adult/child £9/3; ☺10.30am-5.30pm, last entry 4.30pm) Trebah Garden was planted in 1840 by Charles Fox, younger brother of Alfred, who established nearby Glendurgan Garden. It's less formal, with gigantic rhododendrons, gunnera and jungle ferns lining the sides of a steep ravine leading down to the quay and shingle beach. There's a pleasant cafe and souvenir shop beside the ticket office. Admission to the gardens is half-price from November to February.

Glendurgan Garden (NT; ☎01326-250906; www.nationaltrust.org.uk/glendurgan-garden; adult/child £8.10/4.05; ☺10.30am-5.30pm Tue-Sun) Glendurgan was established by Alfred Fox in the 1820s to show off the many weird and wonderful plants being brought back from the far corners of the empire, from Himalayan rhododendrons to Canadian maples and New Zealand tree ferns. Tumbling down a stunning subtropical valley, the garden offers breathtaking views of the Helford, as well as a lovely ornamental maze and a secluded beach near Durgan village. The gardens are now owned by the National Trust.

Potager Garden (☎01326-341258; www.potagergarden.org; suggested donation £3; ☺10am-5pm Thu-Sun) It's a considerable drive from Falmouth but this gorgeous kitchen garden near Constantine is well worth the detour. Rescued from dilapidation by its current owners, it's been renovated by volunteers into a delightful working garden modelled on the French 'potager'. Highlights include the 30m greenhouse and super cafe, and there are outdoor games to play and hammocks to lounge around on. The garden also hosts craft workshops from time to time. Check the website for directions.

🛏 Sleeping

Falmouth Lodge Backpackers
HOSTEL **£**

(✆ 01326-319996; www.falmouthbackpackers.
co.uk; 9 Gyllyngvase Tce; dm/s £19/28, d per person from £28) In a mock-Tudor house at the top of town, this friendly hostel makes a fun budget stay. Rooms are small but clean and cosy, there's an Aga in the kitchen and a DVD lounge, and owner Judi often holds impromptu barbecues for guests.

Highcliffe Contemporary B&B
B&B **££**

(✆ 01326-314466; www.highcliffefalmouth.com; 22 Melvill Rd; s £68, d £99-150; 🛜) Vintage furniture and upcycled design pieces give each of the rooms here its own individual feel. The pick of the bunch is the light-filled Attic Penthouse, with skylight windows overlooking Falmouth Bay. Room service breakfasts are served in picnic baskets, or you can tuck into pancakes and Hog's pudding in the dining room.

Bosanneth
B&B **££**

(✆ 01326-314649; www.bosanneth.co.uk; Gyllyngvase Hill; d from £90; 🛜) There's a mix-and-match decorative vibe running through this eight-room B&B. Some of the rooms feel vintage, with old mirrors, reclaimed furniture and classic colours, while others go for a more up-to-date look. The 'oasis' garden is a particular delight.

Greenbank
HOTEL **£££**

(✆ 01326-312440; www.greenbank-hotel.co.uk; Harbourside; r £129-259; 🅿🛜) The queen of Falmouth's hotels, with a knockout position overlooking the boat-filled estuary towards Flushing. It feels rather like the setting for an Agatha Christie novel – nautical knickknacks and ships in cabinets dot the public areas, and tall windows look out onto the water. The rooms are more modern, decorated in inoffensive beiges and creams. Sea views command premium prices.

🍴 Eating

Good Vibes Café
CAFE **£**

(✆ 01326-211870; 28 Killigrew St; sandwiches and salads £5.95-7.45; ⏱8.30am-5.30pm Mon-Sat) Look no further for lunch than this lovely, contemporary cafe on the Moor, which does a brisk trade from breakfast through to teatime. It's popular for its copious breakfasts, creative sandwiches (which range from pulled spiced chicken to peanut-and-mackerel bagel), crunchy salads and irresistible cakes. There's free cucumber water on tap, plus smoothies and juices galore.

★ Oliver's
BISTRO **££**

(✆ 01326-218138; www.oliversfalmouth.com; 33 High St; mains £16.50-23.50; ⏱noon-2pm & 7-9pm Tue-Sat) Run by chef Ken Oliver, this little bistro is the place everyone wants to dine in Falmouth, but the tiny dining room means you'll have to book well ahead. White walls and pine tables provide a stripped-back match for Ken's imaginative, Mediterranean-inspired food. Local foragers provide many ingredients.

★ Wildebeest
VEGAN **££**

(✆ 01326-210602; 13 Arwenack St; mains £8.25-10.25; ⏱10am-4pm & 5.30-11pm Mon & Wed-Sat) Veggies rejoice: this superb bistro serves up some of the most delicious food of any of Falmouth's restaurants, all 100% vegan. From fiery Malaysian laksa to raw pad Thai, every dish here sparkles with exotic flavours – and the icecream (made with coconut oil and cashew nuts) has to be tasted to be believed. The only drawback? It's tiny.

★ Wheelhouse
SEAFOOD **££**

(✆ 01326-318050; Upton Slip; mains £8-15; ⏱6-10pm Wed-Sat) Hidden down a narrow alley off Church St, this backstreet shellfish bar is all about the hands-on dining experience: crab, scallops, mussels and lobsters are served in their shells, complete with cracking tools. There are two sittings, but both are always packed out – you will need to book well ahead, ideally a week or two in advance.

Star & Garter
GASTROPUB **££**

(✆ 01326-316663; http://starandgarter.square space.com; 52 High St; mains £15-20; ⏱noon-3pm & 6-9pm) At the top of the old High Street among antique shops and health-food stores, this ancient old boozer has been slaking the town's thirst for several centuries. Its most recent reincarnation is as a gourmet gastropub focusing on nose-to-tail dining, so the menu is meat-heavy (think ox tongue and chargrilled pork leg). Ask for one of the harbour-view tables.

Courtyard Deli
DELI, CAFE **££**

(✆ 01326 319526; www.courtyarddeli.co.uk; 2 Bells Court; mains £8-12; ⏱8.30am-5.30pm Mon-Sat, 10.30am-4pm Sun) Small is beautiful, as this cosy deli-diner ably demonstrates. Charcuterie, tarts, salads and quiches fill the counter cabinets, and there are regular evening dinner sessions. It's up an easy-to-miss alley, next to Beerwolf Books.

Drinking & Nightlife

★Beerwolf Books PUB
(☎01326-618474; www.beerwolfbooks.com; 3 Bells Court; ⊙noon-midnight) Quite possibly the greatest idea ever, anytime, anywhere: a pub and bookshop rolled into one, meaning you can browse for reading material before settling down for a pint of real ale.

Hand Bar BAR
(☎01326-319888; 3 Old Brewery Yard; ⊙noon-1am) Pete Walker's craft-beer bar showcases his knowledge, gained while running Leeds' North Bar: esoteric choices such as New York's Brooklyn Brewery and Bodmin's Harbour Brewing Co are among the regulars on tap – although esoterica equals expensiveness. It's fittingly situated in a former brewery, with a few courtyard tables outside, but space is limited inside.

The Front PUB
(☎01326-212168; Custom House Quay; ⊙11am-11.30pm) The beer-buffs' choice: a cosy spit-and-sawdust pub, with scuffed wood floors and a copious choice of real ales served straight from wooden casks. The entrance is down a small hill off Arwenack St.

Boathouse PUB
(☎01326-315425; Trevethan Hill) Lively split-level pub offering great views across the river to Flushing, and decent food.

✵ Festivals

Falmouth Oyster Festival FOOD & DRINK
(www.falmouthoysterfestival.co.uk; ⊙Oct) Feast on fresh oysters, mussels and other crustaceans during this October festival, which also hosts cookery classes and culinary demos.

ℹ Information

Fal River Information Centre (☎01326-741194; www.falriver.co.uk; 11 Market Strand, Prince of Wales Pier; ⊙9.30am-5.30pm Mon-Sat, 10am-4pm Sun)

ℹ Getting There & Away

Falmouth is at the end of the branch train line from Truro (£4.20, 24 minutes), where you can catch connections with the mainline service from Penzance to stations including Plymouth, Exeter and London Paddington.

Falmouth's **Moor Bus Station** (The Moor) is central. **First Kernow** (www.firstgroup.com/cornwall) has the following bus routes:

U1 (£5, half-hourly Monday to Saturday, hourly Sunday) To Truro via Penryn.

FERRYBOAT INN

The lovely riverside pub **Ferryboat Inn** (☎01326-250625; www.thewrightbrothers.co.uk/ferryboat-inn.html; Helford Passage; mains £8-20; ⊙11am-11pm) is now owned by the Wright Brothers, Britain's premier oyster entrepreneurs, who also run the oyster farm at nearby Porth Navas. Outside, there are wooden picnic tables with dreamy views over the Helford River; inside, it's all wood, slate and open plan. It's great for food – oysters, shellfish and the Sunday roast are strong points. Bus 35 passes hourly from Falmouth.

U2 (£5, hourly) To Redruth via Penryn.
2 (every two hours Monday to Saturday) To Penzance via Helston.
35/35A (£5, hourly Monday to Saturday) Stops at Glendurgan and Trebah Gardens en route to Helston.

Truro

POP 17,431

Centred on its three-spired 19th-century cathedral, Truro is Cornwall's capital city. Once a busy river port and one of Cornwall's five Stannary towns (where tin was assayed and stamped for export), these days it's a busy commercial city, with a lively centre dominated by the usual coffee shops and chain stores.

Remnants of the city's elegant Georgian past can be seen on **Lemon St** and **Walsingham Place**.

◎ Sights & Activities

Truro Cathedral CHURCH
(www.trurocathedral.org.uk; High Cross; suggested donation £5; ⊙7.30am-6pm Mon-Sat, 9am-7pm Sun) Built on the site of a 16th-century parish church in soaring Gothic Revival style, Truro Cathedral was completed in 1910, making it the first cathedral built in England since St Paul's. Inside, the vast nave contains some fine Victorian stained glass and the impressive Father Willis Organ.

Royal Cornwall Museum MUSEUM
(☎01872-272205; www.royalcornwallmuseum.org.uk; River St; ⊙10am-5pm Mon-Sat) FREE Collections at the county's main museum encompass everything from geological specimens

to Celtic torques and a ceremonial carriage. Upstairs there's an Egyptian section and a little gallery with some surprising finds: a Turner here, a van Dyck there, and several works by the Newlyn artist Stanhope Forbes.

★**Enterprise Boats**   BOATING
(📞 01326-374241; www.falriver.co.uk; return adult/child £15/7.50) Two miles downriver from Truro's city centre, past the green expanse of Boscawen Park, is the riverside hamlet of Malpas, from where ferries chug out along the River Fal all the way to Falmouth. It's a wonderfully scenic trip that putters past wooded riverbanks and hidden inlets; some boats also stop at Trelissick en route. Free double-deckers run from the Truro harbour-master's office to the pontoon at Malpas, although depending on the tides you can often ride the boat right back to Truro.

🛏 **Sleeping**

Mannings Hotel   HOTEL **££**
(📞 01872-270345; www.manningshotels.co.uk; Lemon St; r £105-115, apt £135; 🅿🛜) The best place to stay in the city centre. The part-Georgian building has been tastefully modernised, with bright colours and functional furniture, even if the general vibe feels a tad corporate. There are 'aparthotels' for longer stays, and the private car park is useful.

Merchant House Hotel   HOTEL **££**
(📞 01872-272450; www.merchant-house.co.uk; 49 Falmouth Rd; s/d/f £79/99/119; 🅿) This Victorian house is handy for town, and refurbishment has brightened up the rooms. Some have skylights, others overlook the garden. It's popular with business travellers and organised coach tours, however, so it's worth reserving well ahead.

✕ **Eating & Drinking**

★**Falmouth Bay Seafood Café**   SEAFOOD **££**
(📞 01872-278884; www.falmouthbayseafoodcafe. com; Castle Villa, 53 Castle St; mains £11.95-22.95; ⊙noon-3.30pm, 5.30-10pm Mon-Sat) Rightly touted as Truro's top restaurant, this smart seafooderie focuses on the fruits of the sea – tuck into fresh Fal oysters or Falmouth Bay scallops, then go for the seafood platter (£38). The pre-theatre menu is good value: £14.50/17.50 for two/three courses, served from 5.30pm to 7pm.

Sam's in the City   BISTRO **££**
(📞 01872-859819; www.samscornwall.co.uk; 1-2 New Bridge St; mains £11.95-21.95; ⊙9am-10pm) Fowey's long-standing restaurant has come to the city, in a former jeweller's on one of Truro's oldest streets. The menu is split between seafood classics, steaks, city salads and sharing platters – plus bouillabaisse and seafood feasts for the very hungry.

★**108 Coffee**   CAFE
(📞 07582 339636; www.108coffee.co.uk; 108c Kenwyn St; ⊙7am-6pm Mon-Fri, 8am-6pm Sat) Set up in 2011 by unapologetic coffee nuts Paul and Michelle, this is the premier place for a caffeine fix in Truro. The beans come courtesy of Cornwall's renowned coffee roasters Origin Coffee, and the flat whites and espressos are as good as any the county has to offer (you can even text your order ahead to save waiting).

Old Ale House   PUB
(📞 01872-271122; 7 Quay St; ⊙noon-11pm) A proper ale-drinker's pub, with sawdust on the floor, beer mats on the ceiling and a menu of guest ales. Ask at the bar for a handful of peanuts to snack on.

ℹ **Information**

Tourist Office (📞 01872-274555; www.visittruro.org.uk; Boscawen St; ⊙9am-5.30pm Mon-Fri, to 5pm Sat) In a small office beside the Hall for Cornwall's rear entrance.

ℹ **Getting There & Away**

BUS
Truro's bus station is beside Lemon Quay.
Bus U1 (£5, half-hourly Monday to Saturday, hourly Sunday) To Truro via Penryn.
Bus 14/14A (£5, 1½ hours, hourly Monday to Saturday) To St Ives.
Bus 18 (£5, half-hourly Monday to Saturday, hourly Sunday) To Penzance.

TRAIN
Truro is on the main London Paddington–Penzance line and the branch line to Falmouth.
Bristol £46.50, 3½ hours
Exeter £18.40, 2¼ hours
Falmouth £4.20, 30 minutes
London Paddington £62.60, 4½ hours
Penzance £6.60, 30 minutes

Fowey

POP 2273

In many ways, Fowey feels like Padstow's south-coast sister; a workaday port turned well-heeled holiday town, with a tumble of pastel-coloured houses, portside pubs and tiered terraces overlooking the wooded banks of the Fowey River. The town's wealth was founded on the export of china clay from the St Austell pits, but it's been an important port since Elizabethan times, and later became the adopted home of the thriller writer Daphne du Maurier, who used the nearby house at Menabilly Barton as the inspiration for *Rebecca*.

Today it's an attractive and increasingly upmarket town, handy for exploring Cornwall's southeastern corner.

◉ Sights & Activities

Readymoney Cove
BEACH

From the town centre, the Esplanade leads down to this little cove and the remains of the small Tudor fort of **St Catherine's Castle** FREE.

Polkerris Beach
BEACH

(www.polkerrisbeach.com) A couple of miles west of Fowey, this is the area's largest and busiest beach. Sailing lessons, windsurfing and stand-up paddleboarding are all available.

Hall Walk
HIKING

(www.nationaltrust.org.uk/fowey-estuary/trails/fowey-hall-walk) This 3.5-mile circular walk starts across the river from Fowey in Bodinnick, winding along the wooded shores of Pont Pill Creek before following the coastline to the harbour of Polruan, from where you can catch a ferry back to Fowey. You can download a route guide from the National Trust website.

Encounter Cornwall
KAYAKING

(☏ 07976 466123; www.encountercornwall.com; Golant; adult/child £25/15) Three-hour trips from Golant, just north of Fowey, with a choice of exploring creek or coastline. It also offers two-hour 'sundowner' expeditions and stand-up paddleboarding trips.

🛌 Sleeping

★ Coriander Cottages
B&B ££

(☏ 01726-834998; www.foweyaccommodation.co.uk; Penventinue Lane; r £100-135; P 🛜) 🌿
A delightfully rural cottage complex on the outskirts of Fowey, with ecofriendly accommodation in a choice of open-plan, self-catering barns, all with quiet country views. The stone barns have been beautifully modernised, and use a combination of solar panels, ground-source heating and rainwater harvesting to reduce environmental impact. A lovely retreat.

Cormorant Hotel
HOTEL ££

(☏ 01726-833426; www.cormoranthotel.co.uk; Golant; d £135-235) Up the creek in Golant (about 5 miles by road), this small hotel has a superb riverside location, and many of its rooms have water-view balconies. They're split into three comfort levels: go for a Superior with view for the premium price-comfort ratio.

Old Quay House
HOTEL £££

(☏ 01726-833302; www.theoldquayhouse.com; 28 Fore St; d £160-340; 🛜) The epitome of Fowey's upmarket trend, this exclusive quayside hotel is all natural fabrics, rattan chairs and tasteful tones, and the rooms are a mix of estuary-view suites and attic penthouses. Very Kensington, not very Cornish.

WORTH A TRIP

POLPERRO

Even in a county where picturesque fishing harbours seem to fill every cove, it's hard not to fall for Polperro – a warren of cottages, boat stores and alleyways, all set around a stout granite harbour. Unsurprisingly, this was once a smugglers' hideout, and it's still a place with a salty, sea-dog atmosphere, despite the inevitable summer crowds. The coast path between Polperro and Looe is particularly scenic, especially around **Talland Bay**.

The main car park is 750m uphill from the village, from where it's a 15-minute stroll down to the quayside. Apart from simply wandering and soaking up the scenery, it's worth popping into the ramshackle **Heritage Museum** (☏ 01503-272423; The Warren; adult/child £2/0.50; ⊙10am-4.30pm or 5pm Mar-Oct), which explores the town's maritime history.

✗ Eating & Drinking

Lifebuoy Cafe CAFE **£**
(☑07715 075869; www.thelifebuoycafe.co.uk; 8 Lostwithiel St; mains £5-10; ⊗8am-5pm) Everyone's favourite brekkie stop in Fowey, this friendly cafe is a riot of character, from the brightly coloured furniture and polka-dot bunting to the vintage Action Men on the shelves. Wolf down a Fat Buoy brekkie or a classic fish-finger butty, washed down with a mug of good old English tea.

Dwelling House CAFE **£**
(☑01726-833662; 6 Fore St; tea £3-6; ⊗10am-6.30pm May-Sep, to 5.30pm Wed-Sun Oct-Apr) Top spot for tea (20-plus varieties) and dainty cakes (decorated with sprinkles and icing swirls, and served on a proper cake stand).

Sam's BISTRO **££**
(☑01726-832273; http://samscornwall.co.uk/fowey; 20 Fore St; mains £7.95-15.95; ⊗noon-9pm) Sam's has been a stalwart in Fowey for years. Booth seats, day-glo menus and a lively local vibe keep the feel laid-back, and the menu of burgers, fish, salads and steaks proves perenially popular. No bookings.

King of Prussia PUB
(www.kingofprussia.co.uk; Town Quay; ⊗11am-11pm) Fowey has lots of pubs, but you might as well go for the one with the best harbour view, named after notorious 'free trader' (otherwise known as smuggler) John Carter.

❶ Information

Fowey Tourist Information Centre (☑01726-833616; www.fowey.co.uk; 5 South St; ⊗9.30am-5pm Mon-Sat, 10am-4pm Sun) Lots of information on Fowey and southeast Cornwall.

❶ Getting There & Away

Bus services are limited: the only really useful service is bus 24 (hourly Monday to Saturday, six on Sunday), which runs to St Austell, Heligan and Mevagissey. It also stops at Par train station, where you can catch trains on the main London–Penzance line.

Polruan Ferry (www.ctomsandson.co.uk/polruan-ferry; adult/child/bicycle £1.80/0.80/1; ⊗last ferry 11pm May-Sep, 7pm Oct-Apr) Passenger ferry to Polruan. In winter and on summer evenings, it runs from Town Quay; during the day, it runs from Whitehouse Slipway on the Esplanade.

Bodinnick Ferry (www.ctomsandson.co.uk/bodinnick-ferry; car & 2 passengers/pedestrian/bicycle £4.60/1.80/free; ⊗last ferry 8.45pm Apr-Oct, 7pm Nov-Mar) Car ferry crossing the river to Bodinnick.

Looe
POP 5280

Tucked into the long curve of coast between the Fowey River and Plymouth Sound, Looe is half historic fishing port, half bucket-and-spade resort. Split into East and West Looe and linked by a historic arched bridge, it's a pleasant base for exploring Cornwall's southeastern reaches, and has some lovely beaches nearby.

◎ Sights

Looe Island ISLAND
A mile offshore from Hannafore Point is the densely wooded Looe Island (officially known as St George's Island), a 9-hectare nature reserve and a haven for marine wildlife. Between May and September, trips are offered by the **Islander** (☑07814 139223; return adult/child £7/5, plus landing fee £3/1) from the quayside near the lifeboat station, but they're dependent on the weather and tides.

Wild Futures Monkey Sanctuary WILDLIFE RESERVE
(☑01503-262532; www.monkeysanctuary.org; St Martins; adult/child £8.50/5; ⊗11am-4.30pm Sat-Thu; ▣) Half a mile west of town, this wildlife centre is guaranteed to raise some 'aaahhhhs' over its woolly and capuchin monkeys, many of which were rescued from captivity.

🛏 Sleeping

Penvith Barns B&B **££**
(☑01503-240772; www.penvithbarns.co.uk; St-Martin-by-Looe; r £75-80; ▣🛜🐾) Escape the Looe crowds at this rural barn conversion in the nearby hamlet of St-Martin-by-Looe, run by friendly owners Graham and Jules. Rooms range from small to spacious: the Piggery is tiny and tucked under the eaves, while the Dairy has enough space for a spare bed and sofa. A bit of a bargain.

Commonwood Manor B&B **£££**
(☑01503-262929; www.commonwoodmanor.com; St Martins Rd; d £75-95; ▣🛜🏊) In a prime position on the hillside of East Looe, this elegant manor house is a cut above the bargain-basement B&Bs you'll find around the rest of Looe. Rooms are a touch frilly and pastel heavy, but if you can bag one of the bay-window bedrooms you'll be rewarded with the best sea views in town.

ⓘ Information

Looe Tourist Office (☎ 01503-262072; www. visit-southeastcornwall.co.uk; Guildhall, Fore St; ⊙ 10am-5pm Easter-Oct)

ⓘ Getting There & Away

Plymouth Citybus provides the only buses to Looe. Bus 71A/72 (hourly Monday to Saturday, five on Sunday) runs from Plymouth via Looe and Polperro.

Bodmin Moor

It can't quite boast the wild majesty of Dartmoor, but Bodmin Moor has a bleak beauty all of its own. Pockmarked with heaths and granite hills, including **Rough Tor** (row-tor; 400m) and Cornwall's highest point, **Brown Willy** (419m), it's a desolate place that works on the imagination; for years there have been reported sightings of the Beast of Bodmin, a large, black catlike creature, although no one's ever managed to snap a decent picture.

Apart from the hills, the moor's main landmark is **Jamaica Inn**, made famous by Daphne du Maurier's novel of the same name – although it's disappointingly been modernised since the author's day.

◉ Sights & Activities

Golitha Falls WATERFALL
Around 1.25 miles west of St Cleer, these crashing waterfalls are one of the most renowned beauty spots on the moor. Around

---

WORTH A TRIP

COTEHELE HOUSE

At the head of the Tamar Valley sits the Tudor manor of **Cotehele** (NT; ☎ 01579-351346; St Dominick; adult/child £10/5, grounds only £6.50/3.25; ⊙ house 11am-4pm, gardens dawn-dusk daily), one of the Edgcumbe dynasty's modest country retreats. The cavernous great hall is the centrepiece, and the house has an unparalleled collection of Tudor tapestries, armour and furniture.

Outside, the gardens sweep down past the 18th-century Prospect Folly to Cotehele Quay, where there's a discovery centre exploring the history of the Tamar Valley and a vintage sailing barge, the **Shamrock**.

---

the falls are the remains of the ancient oak woodland that once covered much of the moor. There is a car park half a mile's walk from the reserve near Draynes Bridge.

Carnglaze Caverns CAVE
(☎ 01579-320251; www.carnglaze.com; adult/child £6/4; ⊙ 10am-5pm) Slate was once extensively mined on the moor, leaving behind a network of deep caverns such as these ones outside St Neot. Several of the caves are open to the public and can be visited on an underground tour.

Bodmin & Wenford Railway RAIL
(☎ 01208-73555; www.bodminandwenfordrailway. co.uk; rover pass adult/child £13/6; ⊙ 3-5 daily trains May-Sep, fewer at other times) Run by enthusiasts, this steam railway – the only 'standard gauge' line of its type left in Cornwall – chuffs and clatters for 6.5 miles between Bodmin and Boscarne Junction. Many trains are still decked out in their original 1950s livery. At the Boscarne end, the line links up with the Camel Trail (p323); bikes can be taken on the trains if there's space.

Look out for special trips in summer, including Pullman-style dining trains with a silver-service supper, plus murder mystery and pub quiz trains.

✕ Eating

★ St Tudy Inn MODERN BRITISH ££
(☎ 01208-850656; www.sttudyinn.com; St Tudy; mains £14-25; ⊙ meals served noon-2.30pm & 6.30-9pm Mon-Sat, noon-2.30pm Sun) Run by the locally lauded chef Emily Scott, whose previous restaurant in Port Isaac received rave reviews, this village pub has fast become one of east Cornwall's top dining destinations. The old pub has been stripped down and sleekened, and Scott's trademark light, fresh, imaginative food takes centre stage. It's a gastropub of the first order – bookings essential.

★ Woods Cafe CAFE ££
(☎ 01208-78111; www.woodscafecornwall.co.uk; Cardinham Woods; mains £6-12; ⊙ 10.30am-4.30pm) In an old woodsman's cottage lost among the trees of Cardinham, this cracking cafe has become a dining destination in its own right – it's locally famous for its homebaked cakes, cockle-warming soups and sausage sarnies.

ISLES OF SCILLY

While only 28 miles west of the mainland, in many ways the Isles of Scilly feel like a different world. Life on this archipelago of around 140 tiny islands seems hardly to have changed in decades: there are no traffic jams, no supermarkets, no multinational hotels, and the only noise pollution comes from breaking waves and cawing gulls. That's not to say that Scilly is behind the times – you'll find a mobile signal and broadband on the main islands – but life ticks along at its own island pace. Renowned for glorious beaches, there are few places better to escape the outside world.

Only five islands are inhabited: St Mary's is the largest, followed by Tresco, while only a few hardy souls remain on Bryher, St Martin's and St Agnes. Regular ferry boats run between all five islands.

Unsurprisingly, summer is by far the busiest time. Many businesses shut down completely in winter.

ℹ️ Information

Isles of Scilly Tourist Information Centre
(☑ 01720-424031; www.visitislesofscilly.com; Porthcressa Beach, St Mary's; ⊙ 9am-5.30pm Mon-Sat, 9am-2pm Sun Mar-Oct, 10am-2pm Mon-Fri Nov-Feb)
Scilly Online (www.scillyonline.co.uk)
Simply Scilly (www.simplyscilly.co.uk)

ℹ️ Getting There & Away

Bookings for flights and ferries are handled by the **Isles of Scilly Travel Centre** (☑ 0845 710 5555; www.islesofscilly-travel.co.uk; Quay St; ⊙ 8am-6.30pm Mon-Sat) in Penzance. There's also a small enquiries office in High Town on St Mary's.

Bad weather and fog often play havoc with the islands' travel schedules, so it's worth checking on the latest status before you set out – the Ios Travel Twitter account is very useful (@IoSTravel).
Isles of Scilly Skybus (☑ 01736-334220; www.islesofscilly-travel.co.uk) Since the closure of the helicopter service in 2013, planes provide the only air link to the islands. There are several flights daily from Land's End Airport, near Zennor, and Newquay Airport. Adult fares start at £70 one way. Summer flights also run from Exeter, Bristol and Southampton.
Scillonian III (☑ 0845 710 5555; www.islesof scilly-travel.co.uk; ⊙ Apr-Oct) Scilly's ferry plies the notoriously choppy waters between Penzance and St Mary's (one-way adult

£49.50). There's at least one daily crossing in summer, but there are no ferries in winter. Seasickness is a distinct possibility: be prepared

ℹ️ Getting Around

Inter-island ferries between St Mary's and the other islands are provided by the **St Mary's Boatmen's Association** (p346). If you're staying at one of the hotels on Tresco, there's also a separate transfer service.

The only bus and taxi services are on St Mary's. All flights are met by **Paulgers Transport** (☑ 01720-423701; adult/child return £7.50/3.50), who will run you to wherever you're staying, or straight to the quayside if you're travelling to other islands.

St Mary's

POP 2200

St Mary's is the largest and busiest island in Scilly, and the main point of arrival for flights and ferries. About a mile west of the airport is the main settlement of **Hugh Town**, home to most of the island's hotels, shops and guesthouses, as well as the main harbour.

Most people never get much further than **Porthcressa**, Hugh Town's narrow sandy beach, but there are plenty of other coves that can be reached on foot or by bike, including **Porth Hellick**, **Watermill Cove** and the remote **Pelistry Bay**.

◉ Sights

Isles of Scilly Museum MUSEUM
(Church St, Hugh Town; adult/child £3.50/1; ⊙ 10am-4.30pm Mon-Fri, 10am-noon Sat Easter-Sep, 10am-noon Mon-Sat Oct-Easter) The small Isles of Scilly Museum explores the islands' history, with an eclectic mix of archaeological finds and shipwreck artefacts. Among the collection are Neolithic remains such as tools and jewellery, clay pipes left behind by generations of sailors, a couple of sailing boats and a small exhibition on Ted Heath, the English prime minister who loved Scilly so much he was buried here.

☞ Tours

Scilly Walks WALKING
(☑ 01720-423326; www.scillywalks.co.uk; adult/child £6/3) Three-hour archaeological and historical tours, plus guided walking trips to other islands, conducted by local historian and archaeologist Katherine Sawyer.

Island Wildlife Tours WALKING

(☏ 01720-422212; www.islandwildlifetours.co.uk; half-/full day £6/12) Regular birdwatching and wildlife walks with local character and resident twitcher Will Wagstaff, the undisputed authority on Scilly's natural history. Most tours start at 9.45am or 10am on St Mary's, but there are regular tours on other islands too; you need to add on the cost of the boat transfer.

Island Sea Safaris BOATING

(☏ 01720-422732; www.islandseasafaris.co.uk) Trips to see local seabird and seal colonies (adult/child £33/25), plus one-hour 'island taster' tours (£24 per person). Also rents wetsuits and snorkelling gear.

🛏 Sleeping

Garrison Campsite CAMPGROUND £

(☏ 01720-422670; tedmoulson@aol.com; Tower Cottage, Garrison; sites £9.20-11.45; 🛜) Three and a half hectares of sea-view camping above Hugh Town, with electrical hook-ups, wi-fi and a laundry-cum-shower block. It'll even pitch a tent for you.

Mincarlo B&B

(☏ 01720-422513; www.mincarlo.info; s £42-50, d £85-112; 🛜🚗) You couldn't ask for a better location on St Mary's than this little guesthouse: it's in a prime spot with views all the way to Hugh Town from the western end of Town Beach. Rooms are plain and cosy (the attic's a bargain), there's a lounge with local books to browse, breakfast is great, and owners Nick and Bryony are full of local info.

Isles of Scilly
Country Guesthouse B&B ££

(☏ 01720-422440; www.scillyguesthouse.co.uk; High Lanes; d £94-114; 🛜) Run by Bavarian expat Sabine Schraudolph, this guesthouse is one of the comfiest on St Mary's. The large rooms are chintz-free and look out across St Mary's fields, and Sabine serves Bavarian goodies such as *apfelstrudel* in her conservatory-cum-coffee house.

Star Castle Hotel HOTEL £££

(☏ 01720-422317; www.star-castle.co.uk; The Garrison; r incl dinner £127-324; 🛜🚗🚗) Shaped like an eight-pointed star, this former fort on Garrison Point is one of Scilly's star hotels, with heritage-style castle rooms and more modern garden suites. It's stuffy and expensive, but the views are the best on the

island, and at least prices include dinner. It gets a lot cheaper outside the peak months between May and September.

🍴 Eating

Juliet's Garden Restaurant RESTAURANT ££

(☏ 01720-422228; www.julietsgardenrestaurant. co.uk; lunch mains £7-12, dinner mains £14-24.95; ⏰ noon-4pm & 6-9pm) St Mary's long-standing bistro, in business for three decades, is still the best place to eat. It's in a converted barn 15 minutes' walk from town: expect gourmet salads and sandwiches by day, plus classier plates of pan-roasted bream, slow-roast lamb and whole lobster after dark, served by candlelight. The garden is glorious on a sunny day.

Dibble & Grub CAFE ££

(☏ 01720-423719; www.dibbleandgrub.com; lunch £6-12, dinner £10-16; ⏰ 10am-10pm Apr-Sep) Smart beachside cafe beside Porthcressa, housed in the island's old fire station. The menu dabbles in tapas and Mediterranean-style classics.

ℹ Getting Around

The airport bus (£3) departs from Hugh Town 40 minutes before each flight, while the **Island Rover** (☏ 01720-422131; www.islandrover.co.uk; tickets £8) offers a twice-daily sightseeing trip in a vintage bus in summer.

For taxis on St Mary's, try **Island Taxis** (☏ 01720-422126), **Scilly Cabs** (☏ 01720-422901) or **St Mary's Taxis** (☏ 01720-422142) or airport taxi **Paulgers Transport** (p345).

St Mary's Boatmen's Association (☏ 01720-423999; www.scillyboating.co.uk) provides regular ferry services from St Mary's to Scilly's other islands. Returns to/from one island cost adult/child £9.50/4.50, or you can take a 'circular' return via another island for £15/7.50.

Tresco

POP 175

A short boat hop across the channel from St Mary's brings you to Tresco, the second-largest island, once owned by the monks of Tavistock Abbey and now leased by locals from the Duchy of Cornwall. It's a proper old-fashioned island getaway – for decades there was just one pub and one hotel on the island. The main attraction here is the island's fabulous subtropical garden, but it's a lovely place just to wander.

◉ Sights

★ **Tresco Abbey Garden**　　GARDENS
(✆01720-424105; www.tresco.co.uk/stay/abbey-garden; adult/child £15/free; ⏰10am-4pm) One of Scilly's great attractions is this subtropical estate, laid out in 1834 on the site of a 12th-century Benedictine priory by the horticultural visionary Augustus Smith. The gardens are now home to more than 20,000 exotic species, from towering palms to desert cacti and crimson flame trees, all nurtured by the temperate gusts of the Gulf Stream. Admission also covers the **Valhalla collection**, made up of figureheads and nameplates salvaged from the many ships that have foundered off Tresco's shores.

⌂ Sleeping & Eating

New Inn　　PUB, HOTEL £££
(✆01720-422849; contactus@tresco.co.uk; r £120-320) Compared with Tresco's two wallet-shreddingly expensive hotels, the New Inn is a comparative bargain. The rooms are soothingly finished in buttery yellows and pale blues, although inevitably you'll have to fork out for a view. The inn itself serves good food (mains £10 to £18), mainly standards such as pollock and chips, steaks and the like.

Bryher

Only around 70 people live on Bryher, Scilly's smallest and wildest inhabited island. Covered by rough bracken and heather, and fringed by white sand, this slender chunk of rock takes a fearsome battering from the Atlantic – Hell Bay hasn't earned its name for nothing. But on a bright sunny day, it's an island idyll par excellence, ideal for exploring on foot. Several small sandy beaches can be reached along the coast path, including the impressive sweep of **Rushy Bay**. For the best views, hike up to the top of **Watch Hill**, from where you can drink in a panorama right across Scilly.

⌂ Sleeping & Eating

Bryher Campsite　　CAMPGROUND £
(✆01720-422886; www.bryhercampsite.co.uk; sites £10.25; ❄) Bare-bones camping, in a secluded spot surround by drystone walls and just steps from the sea. Hot showers and tractor transport are included in the nightly rates.

Hell Bay Hotel　　HOTEL £££
(✆01720-422947; www.hellbay.co.uk; d £205-350) Pretty much the poshest place to stay in Scilly – a true island getaway blending New England–style furnishings with sunny golds, sea blues and pale wood beams. It has the feel of a luxurious beach villa, with lovingly tended gardens and an excellent restaurant (three-course menu £45). Garden-view suites are the cheapest.

Fraggle Rock　　CAFE ££
(✆01720-422222; www.bryher.co; mains £8-15; ⏰9am-9pm; 🖥) This relaxed cafe also doubles as Bryher's pub. The menu's mainly quiches, salads and burgers, ideally served in the front garden, where chickens scratch around and there are views out to Hangman's Rock. It's a lively evening hang-out in season. There are a few timber-clad cabins (£620 to £1090 per week) if you feel like staying.

Bryher Shop　　DELI
(✆01720-423601; www.bryhershop.co.uk; ⏰9am-5.30pm Mon-Sat, 10am-1pm Sun) Pick up all your essential supplies at the island's charming general store.

St Martin's

POP 136

The northernmost of the main islands, little St Martin's is rightly renowned for its beaches. Worth hunting out are **Lawrence's Bay** on the south coast, which becomes a broad sweep of sand at low tide; the secluded cove of Perpitch in the southeast; and **Great Bay** on the north, arguably Scilly's finest beach.

◉ Sights & Activities

St Martin's Vineyard　　WINERY
(✆01720-423418; www.stmartinsvineyard.co.uk; ⏰tours 10.45am-4pm Tue-Thu) The UK's smallest and most southwesterly vineyard produces its own range of white wines. Tours are conducted by owners Val and Graham Thomas.

Scilly Diving　　DIVING
(✆01720-422848; www.scillydiving.com) Situated in Higher Town, this dive outfit offers diving courses and single dives.

⌂ Sleeping

Accommodation is limited apart from one super-expensive hotel, **St Martin's on the Isle** (✆01720-422090; www.stmartinshotel.co.uk; d £300-560), and a handful of B&Bs.

St Martin's Campsite
CAMPGROUND £

(☑ 01720-422888; www.stmartinscampsite.co.uk; sites £10-11.50; ☺ Mar-Oct) The second-largest campsite in Scilly at the western end of Lawrence's Bay, with 50 pitches spread across three fields. There are coin-operated washing machines and showers, and eggs and veg are available for your morning fry-up.

Polreath
B&B ££

(☑ 01720-422046; www.polreath.com; Higher Town; d £110-120) This friendly granite cottage has small rooms and a sunny conservatory serving cream teas, homemade lemonade and evening meals. Weekly stays required May to September.

✖ Eating & Drinking

Little Arthur Farm
CAFE £

(☑ 01720-422457; www.littlearthur.co.uk; ☺ 10.30am-4pm daily) ❂ A little slice of the good life on St Martin's, this small-scale farm has diversified in all kinds of imaginative directions. There's a cafe-bistro, it grows its own produce and even makes shoes – and there's an ecocabin to stay in too (£380 per week).

Adam's Fish & Chips
SEAFOOD £

(☑ 01720-422457; takeaway fish & chips £8; ☺ 6-8.30pm Tue-Thu, noon-2.30pm Sat Jul & Aug, 6-8.30pm Tue & Thu Sep-Jun) The fish here is as fresh as it gets – whatever's caught on the day is what ends up in your batter. It's run by Adam and Emma, who live and work on Little Arthur Farm nearby.

Island Bakery
BAKERY £

(☑ 01720-42211; www.theislandbakery-stmartins.com; ☺ 9am-5pm Mon-Sat) This homespun bakery run by Barney and Ella McLachlan turns out fresh bread, pizzas and, of course, homemade pasties.

Seven Stones
PUB

(☑ 01720-423777; sevenstonesinn@gmail.com; mains £8-12; ☺ 10am-11pm) Gorgeous pub and the island's only boozer, so it's the heart of the action every night of the week. Decent grub, Cornish ales and super views of the other islands from the terrace.

St Agnes
POP 170

Scilly's southernmost island feels really remote, with a string of empty coves and a scattering of prehistoric sites. Visitors disembark at Porth Conger, near the old lighthouse, from where you wander along the coast path around the whole island.

At low tide, a narrow sand bar appears to the neighbouring island of **Gugh**, where many ancient burial sites and a few chamber tombs can be found. The **Troy Town Maze** is slightly more recent, thought to have been fashioned from stones around 200 years ago.

🛏 Sleeping & Eating

Troytown Farm
CAMPGROUND £

(☑ 01720-422360; www.troytown.co.uk; adult £9.50, tents £2-8) Once a flower farm, St Martin's minuscule campsite offers meadow camping with superb sea views, and also rents three self-catering cottages (from £550 per week). Transport by tractor from the quay costs £3.50.

Covean Cottage
COTTAGE ££

(☑ 01720-422620; http://st-agnes-scilly.org/covean.htm; d £88-104) Pretty much the only B&B on the island, this little stone-walled cottage has three pretty sea-view rooms. There's also a small cafe, which serves brekkies and light meals cooked up by the owner.

★ Turk's Head
PUB FOOD ££

(☑ 01720-422434; mains £8-14; ☺ 11am-11pm Mon-Sat, noon-10.30pm Sun) You can almost smell the history at Britain's most southerly alehouse. It's covered in maritime memorabilia – model ships in glass cabinets, vintage maps of the islands, black-and-white photos of seafarers – and there are few finer places to sup a pint. You might even be treated to a sea shanty if the local lads are in the mood.

Cambridge & East Anglia

Includes →

Cambridge	353
Ely	365
Colchester	367
Dedham Vale	368
Saffron Walden	369
Southend-on-Sea	370
Lavenham	372
Bury St Edmunds	373
Aldeburgh	376
Southwold	377
Norwich	378
King's Lynn	387

Best Places to Eat

→ Midsummer House (p363)

→ Roger Hickman's (p381)

→ Butley Orford Oysterage (p376)

→ Great House (p373)

→ Picnic Fayre (p383)

Best Places to Sleep

→ Varsity (p362)

→ Sutherland House (p377)

→ Swan (p373)

→ Dedham Hall (p368)

→ Cley Windmill (p383)

Why Go?

Unfurling gently eastwards to the sea, the vast flatlands of East Anglia are a rich web of lush farmland, melancholy Fens and sparkling rivers. The area is justly famous for its sweeping sandy beaches, big skies and the bucolic landscape that once inspired Constable and Gainsborough.

It's not all rural idyll though: rising out of the Fens is the world-famous university town of Cambridge, with its stunning classical architecture and earnest attitude, and to the east is the cosmopolitan city of Norwich. Around them, magnificent cathedral cities, pretty market towns and implausibly picturesque villages are testament to the enormous wealth amassed here during medieval times, when the wool and weaving industries flourished.

Meanwhile, the meandering coastline is peppered with pretty fishing villages and traditional bucket-and-spade resorts, while inland is the languid, hypnotic charm of the Norfolk Broads, an ideal location for serious relaxation.

When to Go

→ To best explore the Cambridge colleges, avoid Spring (early April to mid-June), when they close to visitors as students prepare for exams.

→ June and August show the Norfolk and Suffolk beaches and the Norfolk Broads at their best. But in school holidays (late July to August) it gets busy and accommodation prices rise.

→ World-class classical music comes to Suffolk in the Aldeburgh Festival in June. In July, Southwold's eclectic Latitude Festival offers alternative rock, comedy and theatre.

→ November's Ways With Words literature festival draws big-name authors to Southwold.

→ Exquisite music fills Cambridge's King's College Chapel in December, culminating in the Festival of Nine Lessons and Carols on Christmas Eve.

Cambridge & East Anglia Highlights

1 **Cambridge** (p353) Punting past historic colleges then enjoying the heavenly evensong at King's College Chapel.

2 **Lavenham** (p372) Soaking up the medieval architecture in this atmospheric market town.

3 **Norwich** (p378) Marvelling at the exquisite rib vaulting in the city's fine cathedral.

4 **Aldeburgh** (p376) Dining on sublime seafood and walking the prom in a laid-back resort.

5 **Sandringham** (p387) Nosying around the drawing room of the Queen's country estate.

6 **Norfolk Broads** (p385) Canoeing your way through unique tranquil waterways.

7 **Imperial War Museum** (p364) Discovering the history of the British and American air forces.

8 **Holkham Beach** (p386) Wandering barefoot along immense, pine-backed golden sands.

9 **Audley End** (p369) Delighting in one of Britain's grandest stately homes.

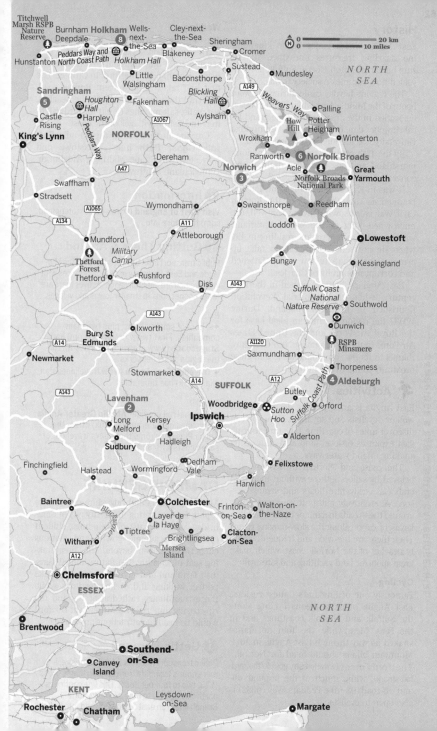

History

East Anglia was a major Saxon kingdom; the dazzling treasures unearthed in the ship burial at Sutton Hoo in Suffolk have revealed how complex a society it was.

The region's heyday came during the wool boom of the Middle Ages when Flemish weavers settled in the area; many of the grand local churches date from this time – Cambridge University was founded in this period, too.

By the 17th century, much of the region's marshland and bog had been drained and converted into arable land.

It was in East Anglia's emergent, Puritan bourgeoisie that the seeds of the English Civil War were sown. Oliver Cromwell, the uncrowned king of the parliamentarians, was a small-time merchant residing in Ely when he answered God's call to take up arms against what he saw as the fattened and corrupt monarchy of Charles I.

East Anglia's fortunes waned in the 18th century, when the Industrial Revolution flourished in northern England. During WWII the region became an ideal base for the Royal Air Force and the United States Air Force in the fight against Nazi Germany, thanks to its flat, open landscape and close proximity to mainland Europe.

Activities

East Anglia is an appealing destination for walkers, cyclists and kayakers. Here you can discover miles of coastline, take time touring vast expanses of level land and glide along snaking inland waterways.

The coast and Norfolk Broads are also beloved by sailors – those without their own craft can easily hire boats and arrange lessons. Alternatively putt-putt your way gently around the Broads in a motor boat or paddle a kayak or canoe along the slow-moving rivers. Then there are the wide and frequently empty beaches of the Norfolk coast, which make great spots for land yachting and kitesurfing.

Cycling

Famously one of England's flattest regions, East Anglia offers gorgeous cycling along the Suffolk and Norfolk coastlines and in the Fens. Meanwhile, the Tour de France snaked its way through East Anglia in 2014. Mountain bikers should head for Norfolk's **Thetford Forest** (www.forestry.gov.uk/thetford-forestpark), while much of the popular on- and off-road, 93-mile Peddars Way (p352) is also open to cyclists.

Walking

The **Peddars Way and Norfolk Coast Path** (www.nationaltrail.co.uk/peddarsway) is a seven-day, 93-mile national trail from Knettishall Heath, near Thetford, to Cromer. The first half takes in an ancient Roman road. The trail then meanders along the beaches, sea walls, salt marshes (great for birdwatching) and fishing villages of the coast.

Curving further south, the 50-mile **Suffolk Coast Path** links Felixstowe and Lowestoft, via Snape Maltings, Aldeburgh, Dunwich and Southwold.

ℹ Information

Visit East of England (www.visiteastofengland. com) has more info.

ℹ Getting There & Around

Public transport links between London, the Midlands and East Anglia are excellent. Services within the region are generally good; as ever there are fewer connections to smaller towns and villages.

BUS

➤ A host of smaller firms, plus two main companies, **First** (www.firstgroup.com) and **Stagecoach** (www.stagecoachbus.com), run the region's bus networks.

➤ **Traveline East Anglia** (www.travelineeastanglia.org.uk) has timetables.

TRAIN

➤ Regional rail provider **Abellio Greater Anglia** (www.abelliogreateranglia.co.uk) offers the Anglia Plus Pass (one/three days travel out of seven costs £18/36.)

CAMBRIDGESHIRE

Many visitors to Cambridgeshire never make it past the captivating university city of Cambridge, where august old buildings, student cyclists in academic gowns and glorious chapels await. But beyond this breathtaking seat of learning, the flat reclaimed Fens, lush farmland and myriad waterways make perfect walking and cycling territory, while the extraordinary cathedral at Ely and the rip-roaring Imperial War Museum at Duxford would be headline attractions anywhere else.

ℹ Getting Around

Public transport radiates from Cambridge, a mere hour's train ride from London King's Cross (£23, two to four per hour). This line continues north through Ely to King's Lynn in Norfolk. Branch lines run east to Norwich and into Suffolk.

Cambridge

POP 123,900

Abounding with exquisite architecture, exuding history and tradition and renowned for its quirky rituals, Cambridge is a university town extraordinaire. The tightly packed core of ancient colleges, the picturesque riverside 'Backs' (college gardens) and the leafy green meadows surrounding the city give it a more tranquil appeal than its historic rival Oxford.

Like 'the Other Place', as Oxford is known locally, the buildings here seem unchanged for centuries, and it's possible to wander the college buildings and experience them as countless prime ministers, poets, writers and scientists have done. Sheer academic achievement seems to permeate the very walls: cyclists loaded down with books negotiate cobbled passageways, students relax on manicured lawns and great minds debate life-changing research in historic pubs. First-time punters zigzag erratically across the river and those long past their student days wonder what it would have been like to study in such splendid surroundings.

History

Despite roots stretching back to the Iron Age, Cambridge was little more than a rural backwater until the 11th century, when an Augustinian order of monks set up shop here – the first of the religious institutions that eventually became the colleges. When the university town of Oxford exploded in a riot between town and gown in 1209, a group of scholars, fed up with the constant brawling between locals and students, upped and joined what was to become the University of Cambridge. Cambridge wasn't spared by the riots, and brawls between town and gown took place with disturbing regularity here as well.

The first Cambridge college, Peterhouse (never Peterhouse *College*), was founded in 1284, and in 1318 Pope John XXII's papal bull declared Cambridge to be an official university.

By the 14th century, royalty, nobility, churches, trade guilds and anyone rich enough could court prestige by founding their own colleges, though the system was shaken up during the Reformation with the dissolution of the monasteries. It was 500 years before female students were allowed into the hallowed grounds, though, and even then they were only allowed into the women-only colleges Girton and Newnham, founded in 1869 and 1871 respectively. By 1948, Cambridge minds had broadened sufficiently to allow women to actually graduate.

The honour roll of famous Cambridge students and affiliates reads like an international who's who of high achievers: 92 Nobel Prize winners (more than any other institution in the world), 13 British prime ministers, nine archbishops of Canterbury, an immense number of scientists, and a healthy host of poets and authors. This is the town where Newton refined his theory of gravity, Whipple invented the jet engine and Crick and Watson (relying heavily on the work of Rosalind Franklin, also a scientist at Cambridge) discovered DNA. William Wordsworth, Lord Byron, Vladimir Nabokov, Stephen Hawking and Stephen Fry all studied here too.

Today the university remains one of the best for research worldwide. Thanks to some of the earth-shaking discoveries made here, Cambridge is inextricably linked to the history of learning.

◉ Sights

Cambridge University comprises 31 colleges, though not all are open to the public.

★ **King's College Chapel**   CHURCH
(☑ 01223-331212; www.kings.cam.ac.uk/chapel; King's Pde; adult/child £9/6; ◷ 9.30am-3.15pm Mon-Sat & 1.15-2.30pm Sun term time, 9.30am-4.30pm daily, to 3.30pm Dec, Jan & university holidays) In a city crammed with showstopping buildings, this is the scene-stealer. Grandiose, 16th-century King's College Chapel is one of England's most extraordinary examples of Gothic architecture. Its inspirational, intricate 80m-long, fan-vaulted ceiling is the world's largest and soars upwards before exploding into a series of stone fireworks. This hugely atmospheric space is a fitting stage for the chapel's world-famous choir; hear it during the magnificent, free, **evensong** (term time only; 5.30pm Monday to Saturday, 10.30am and 3.30pm Sunday).

King's **steeples** have long been a magnet for student night climbers (p363) and today images of the chapel adorn thousands of postcards, tea towels and choral CDs. But it was begun in 1446 as an act of piety by Henry VI and was only finished by Henry VIII around 1516.

The lofty **stained-glass windows** that flank the chapel's sides ensure it's remarkably light. The glass is original, rare survivors of the excesses of the Civil War in this

Cambridge

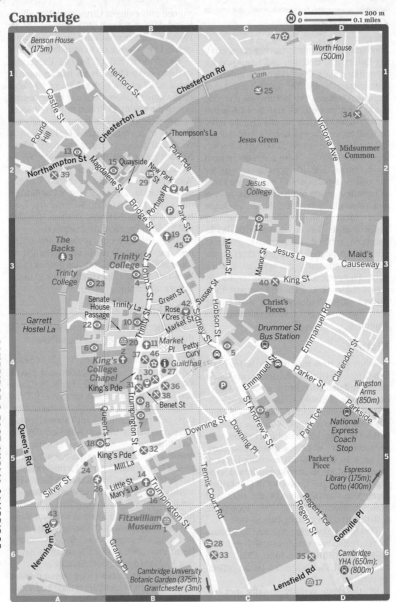

region. It's said that these windows were ordered to be spared by Cromwell himself, who knew of their beauty from his own studies in Cambridge.

The antechapel and the choir are divided by a superbly carved **wooden screen**, de-

signed and executed by Peter Stockton for Henry VIII. The screen bears his master's initials entwined with those of Anne Boleyn. Look closely and you may find an angry human face (possibly Stockton's) amid the elaborate jungle of mythical beasts and sym-

Cambridge

◉ Top Sights
1 Fitzwilliam Museum...............................B6
2 King's College Chapel..........................B4
3 The Backs..A3
4 Trinity College......................................B3

◉ Sights
5 Christ's College....................................C4
6 Clare College..A4
7 Corpus Christi College B5
8 Corpus Clock..B4
9 Emmanuel College...............................C5
10 Gonville & Caius College B4
11 Great St Mary's Church B4
12 Jesus College.......................................C3
13 Kettle's Yard..A2
14 Little St Mary's Church B5
15 Magdalene College..............................B2
   Pepys Library............................(see 15)
16 Peterhouse...B5
17 Polar Museum......................................D6
18 Queens' College...................................A5
19 Round Church.......................................B3
20 Senate House.......................................B4
21 St John's College..................................B3
22 Trinity Hall College A4
23 Wren Library..A3

◉ Activities, Courses & Tours
24 Cambridge Chauffeur Punts.................A5
   Granta Moorings.........................(see 43)

25 Jesus Green Pool C1
26 Scudamore's Punting A5
27 Walking Tours.......................................B4

◉ Sleeping
28 Hotel du Vin C6
29 Varsity..B2

◉ Eating
30 Aromi..B4
31 Chop House B4
32 Fitzbillies...B5
33 Hot Numbers..C6
34 Midsummer House D1
35 Oak Bistro D6
36 Pint Shop..B4
37 Rainbow B4
38 Smokeworks..B4
39 St John's Chop House A2
40 Urban Shed...C3

◉ Drinking & Nightlife
41 Eagle...B4
42 Fez..B3
43 Granta...A6
44 Maypole B2

◉ Entertainment
45 ADC...B3
46 Cambridge Arts Theatre.......................B4
47 Portland Arms C1

bolic flowers. Above is the magnificent bat-wing **organ**, originally constructed in 1686, though much altered since.

Beyond the thickly carved, dark-wood choir stalls, light suffuses the high **altar**, which is framed by Rubens' masterpiece *Adoration of the Magi* (1634) and the magnificent east window. To the left of the altar in the side chapels, an **exhibition** charts the construction stages and methods.

Note the chapel itself (but not the grounds) *is* open during the exam period (April to June).

Each Christmas Eve, King's College Chapel stages the **Festival of Nine Lessons & Carols**. It's broadcast globally by the BBC, and to around 300 American radio stations. You can also queue for a place – if you start early enough (often by around 9am), you could well get in.

Senate House HISTORIC BUILDING
(Senate House Passage) This beautiful classical structure (not open to the public), tucked in beside King's College, was designed in 1730 by James Gibbs. Graduations are held here in summer, when gowned and mortar-boarded students parade the streets. Look out for the degree class lists that are posted outside at the end of the academic year.

Great St Mary's Church CHURCH
(www.gsm.cam.ac.uk; Senate House Hill; ◷10am-4pm Mon-Sat, 1-4pm Sun) FREE The foundations of Cambridge's sublime university church date from 1010. It was burnt to the ground in the 1290s and rebuilt in 1351. The major expansion of 1478–1519 resulted in the late-Gothic Perpendicular style you see today. Striking features include the mid-Victorian stained-glass windows, seating galleries and two organs – unusual in a church. The **tower** (adult/child £3.90/2.50) was added in 1690; climb it for superb vistas of Cambridge's dreamy spires.

Gonville & Caius College COLLEGE
(www.cai.cam.ac.uk; Trinity St; ◷9am-2pm, closed late Apr–mid-Jun) FREE Known locally as Caius (pronounced 'keys'), Gonville and Caius boasts three fascinating **gates**: Virtue, Humility and Honour. They symbolise the progress of the good student, since the third

gate (the Porta Honoris, a fabulous domed and sundial-sided confection) leads to the Senate House (p355) and thus graduation. Former students include Francis Crick (of DNA-discoverers Crick and Watson) and Edward Wilson, of Scott's tragic Antarctic expedition. The megastar of astrophysics, Stephen Hawking, is currently a fellow here.

The college was actually founded twice, first by a priest called Gonville, in 1348, and then again in 1557 by Dr Caius (his given name was Keys – it was common for academics to use the Latin form of their names), a brilliant physician who supposedly spoiled his legacy by insisting in the statutes that the college admit no 'deaf, dumb, deformed, lame, chronic invalids, or Welshmen'.

Trinity Hall College   COLLEGE

(☎ 01223-332500; www.trinhall.cam.ac.uk; Trinity Lane; admission by donation; ☺ 9.15am-noon & 2pm-dusk, closed early Apr-Jun) Wedged cosily among the great and famous colleges (but unconnected to better-known Trinity), diminutive Trinity Hall was founded in 1350 as a refuge for lawyers and clerics escaping the ravages of the Black Death. The college's chapel is one of the most beautiful in Cambridge; you can visit for evensong during some terms; check with the college for details.

Graduates include writer JB Priestley, astrophysicist Stephen Hawking and actor Rachel Weisz. The college's 16th-century library (not normally open to the public) has original Jacobean reading desks and books chained to shelves.

★ Trinity College   COLLEGE

(www.trin.cam.ac.uk; Trinity St; adult/child £3/1; ☺ 10am-4.30pm, closed early Apr–mid-Jun) The largest of Cambridge's colleges, Trinity offers an extraordinary Tudor gateway, an air of supreme elegance and a sweeping Great Court – the largest of its kind in the world. It also boasts the renowned and suitably musty Wren Library (www.trin.cam.ac.uk; ☺ noon-2pm Mon-Fri, plus 10.30am-12.30pm Sat term time only) FREE, containing 55,000 books dated before 1820 and more than 2500 manuscripts. Works include those by Shakespeare, St Jerome, Newton and Swift – and AA Milne's original Winnie the Pooh; both Milne and his son, Christopher Robin, were graduates.

As you enter Trinity through the part-gilded gate, have a look at the statue of the college's founder, Henry VIII, that adorns it. His left hand holds a golden orb, while his right grips not the original sceptre but a table leg,

put there by student pranksters and never replaced. It's a wonderful introduction to one of Cambridge's most venerable colleges, and a reminder of who really rules the roost.

In the Great Court beyond, scholastic humour gives way to wonderment, thanks to its imposing architecture and sheer size. To the right of the entrance is a small tree, planted in the 1950s and reputed to be a descendant of the apple tree made famous by Trinity alumnus Sir Isaac Newton. Other alumni include Francis Bacon, Lord Byron, Tennyson, HRH Prince Charles (legend has it his bodyguard scored higher in exams than he did), at least nine prime ministers (British and international) and more than 30 Nobel Prize winners.

The college's vast hall has a dramatic hammer-beam roof and lantern; beyond lie the dignified cloisters of Nevile's Court. Henry VIII would have been proud to note, too, that his college would eventually come to throw the best party in town, the lavish May Ball (p361) in June, though you will need a fat purse, and a friend on the inside, to get an invitation.

St John's College   COLLEGE

(www.joh.cam.ac.uk; St John's St; adult/child £8/5; ☺ 10am-5pm Mar-Oct, to 3.30pm Nov-Feb, closed mid-Jun) Alma mater of six prime ministers, three saints and Douglas Adams (author of The Hitchhiker's Guide to the Galaxy), St John's is superbly photogenic. It's also the second-biggest college after Trinity. Founded in 1511 by Henry VII's mother, Margaret Beaufort, it sprawls along both riverbanks, joined by the Bridge of Sighs, a masterpiece of stone tracery and focus for student pranks. Going into St John's or taking a punting tour are the only ways to get a clear view of the structure.

Over the bridge is the 19th-century New Court, an extravagant neo-Gothic creation, and out to the left are impressive views of the Backs (p357). Parts of the college are much older and the chapel, though smaller than King's, is one of Cambridge's hidden gems.

Round Church   CHURCH

(www.christianheritage.org.uk; Bridge St; admission £2.50; ☺ 10am-5pm Mon-Fri, 1.30-5pm Sat, 1.30-4pm Sun) Cambridge's atmospheric Round Church is one of only four such structures in England. It was built by the mysterious Knights Templar in 1130 and shelters an unusual circular nave ringed by chunky Norman pillars – the carved stone faces that crown them bring the 12th century vividly to life.

Jesus College
COLLEGE

(www.jesus.cam.ac.uk; Jesus Lane; ⊙9am-5pm, closed early Apr–mid-Jun) **FREE** This tranquil 15th-century college was once a nunnery of St Radegund before the Bishop of Ely, John Alcock, expelled the nuns for 'improvidence, extravagance and incontinence'. Highlights include a Norman arched **gallery**, a 13th-century **chancel** and art-nouveau features by Pugin, Ford Madox Brown, William Morris (ceilings) and Burne-Jones (stained glass). Illustrious alumni include Thomas Cranmer, burnt in Oxford for his faith during the Reformation, and long-running BBC and PBS radio journalist and presenter Alistair Cooke.

Magdalene College
COLLEGE

(www.magd.cam.ac.uk; Magdalene St; ⊙8am-6pm, closed early Apr–mid-Jun) **FREE** Riverside Magdalene often catches people out – the college name is properly pronounced 'Maud-lyn'. This former Benedictine hostel's greatest asset is the **Pepys Library** (www.magd.cam.ac.uk; Magdalene St; ⊙2-4pm Mon-Fri year-round, 11.30am-12.30pm & 1.30-2.30pm Sat May-Aug, 2-4pm Mon-Sat Oct-Apr, closed Sep) **FREE** housing 3000 books bequeathed by the mid-17th-century diarist to his old college. This idiosyncratic collection of beautifully bound tomes is ordered by height. Treasures include vivid medieval manuscripts and the *Anthony Roll*, a 1540s depiction of the Royal Navy's ships.

Magdalene was the last college to let women study there; when they were finally admitted in 1988, some male students wore black armbands and flew the college flag at half mast.

Kettle's Yard
HOUSE

(www.kettlesyard.co.uk; Castle St) **FREE** Closed at time of writing but due to reopen in late 2017, Kettle's Yard offers a very personal glimpse into the incredible home of HS 'Jim' Ede, a former curator at the Tate Gallery in London. In his deceptively roomy cottage, all the furniture, ceramics and art – such as the collection of 20th-century works by Miró, Henry Moore and others – is arranged just so, allowing you a real sense of the man's intriguing personality.

★ The Backs
PARK

Behind the Cambridge colleges' grandiose facades and stately courts, a series of gardens and parks line up beside the river. Collectively known as the Backs, the tranquil green spaces and shimmering waters offer unparalleled views of the colleges and are often the most enduring image of Cambridge for visitors. The picture-postcard snapshots of student life and graceful bridges can be seen from the riverside pathways and pedestrian bridges – or the comfort of a chauffeur-driven punt.

For the best views of the fanciful **Bridge of Sighs** head into St John's College (p356). Built in 1831, it's best observed from the stylish bridge designed by Wren just to the south, also on St John's grounds. The oldest river crossing is at **Clare College** (www.clare.cam.ac.uk; Trinity Lane; £3.50; ⊙dawn-dusk, closed early Apr–mid-Jun), built in 1639 and ornamented with decorative balls. Its architect was paid a grand total of 15p for his design and, feeling aggrieved at such a measly fee, it's said he cut a chunk out of one of the balls adorning the balustrade so the bridge would never be complete.

Most curious of all is the flimsy-looking wooden construction (visible from Silver St) which joins the two halves of Queens' College. Known as the **Mathematical Bridge**, it was first built in 1749. Despite what unscrupulous guides may tell you, it wasn't the handiwork of Sir Isaac Newton (he died in 1727), originally built without nails, or taken apart by academics who then couldn't figure how to put it back together.

Queens' College
COLLEGE

(www.queens.cam.ac.uk; Queen's Lane; £3; ⊙10am-4pm, closed early Apr–mid-Jun) Gorgeous 15th-century Queens' College sits elegantly astride the river, connected by the unscientific-looking Mathematical Bridge. Highlights include: two enchanting medieval courtyards, **Old Court** and **Cloister Court**; the beautiful half-timbered **President's Lodge**; and the tower in which Dutch scholar and reformer Desiderius Erasmus lodged from 1510 to 1514.

Corpus Christi College
COLLEGE

(www.corpus.cam.ac.uk; King's Pde; £2.50; ⊙10.30am-4.30pm mid-Jun–Sep, 2-4pm Oct–early Apr) Corpus Christi was founded in 1352, a heritage reflected in its exquisite buildings and a monastic atmosphere that radiates from the medieval **Old Court**. Look out for the fascinating sundial and plaque to playwright and past student Christopher Marlowe (1564–93), who penned *Doctor Faustus* and *Tamburlaine*. New Court (a mere 200 years old) leads to the **Parker Library**, which holds the world's finest collection of Anglo-Saxon manuscripts (open Monday and Thursday afternoons to tourist office–run tours).

❶ VISITING THE COLLEGES

Colleges close to visitors over the two-week Christmas break, and while students are preparing for and sitting exams – between early April and mid-June. Be aware, too, that opening hours can vary from day to day, so if you have your heart set on visiting a particular college, contact it in advance to avoid disappointment.

Corpus Clock   LANDMARK

(Benet St) Made from 24-carat gold, the Corpus Clock displays the time through a series of concentric LED lights. A hideous-looking insect 'time-eater' crawls across the top. The clock is only accurate once every five minutes. At other times it slows or stops and then speeds up, which, according to its creator, JC Taylor, reflects life's irregularity.

Christ's College   COLLEGE

(www.christs.cam.ac.uk; St Andrew's St; ⊙ 9am-4pm, closed early May–mid-Jun) FREE Christ's College is a venerable institution at more than 500 years old. It's gleaming Great Gate is emblazoned with heraldic carvings of Tudor roses, a portcullis and spotted Beaufort yale (antelope-like creatures). Its founder, Lady Margaret Beaufort, hovers above like a guiding spirit. A stout oak door leads into First Court, one of Cambridge's more picturesque front courts and the only circular one. Hunt out the gardens dedicated to alumnus Charles Darwin; they feature species brought back from his famous Galapagos voyage.

Emmanuel College   COLLEGE

(www.emma.cam.ac.uk; St Andrew's St; ⊙ 9am-6pm, closed early Apr–mid-Jun) FREE The 16th-century Emmanuel College ('Emma' to students) is famous for its exquisite chapel designed by Sir Christopher Wren. Seek out the plaque commemorating John Harvard (who graduated with a BA in 1632), a scholar here who later settled in New England and left his money to a certain Cambridge College in Massachusetts – now Harvard University.

Little St Mary's Church   CHURCH

(www.lsm.org.uk; Trumpington St; ⊙ 9am-6pm) FREE The church's unwieldy original name was St Peter's-without-Trumpington-Gate, which gave St Peter's College itself its name. Inside is a memorial to student Godfrey Washington, great-uncle of George. His family coat of arms was the stars and stripes, the inspiration for the US flag. Henry Cavendish, the first person to measure the density of water, also studied here. He also calculated the planet's weight: about 6 billion trillion metric tons, by the way.

Peterhouse   COLLEGE

(www.pet.cam.ac.uk; Trumpington St; ⊙ 9am-5pm, closed early Apr–mid-Jun) FREE The oldest and smallest college, charming Peterhouse was founded in 1284. Much of the college was rebuilt or added to over the years, including the exceptional little chapel built in 1632, but the beautifully restored main hall is bona-fide 13th century.

★ Fitzwilliam Museum   MUSEUM

(www.fitzmuseum.cam.ac.uk; Trumpington St; donation requested; ⊙ 10am-5pm Tue-Sat, noon-5pm Sun) FREE Fondly dubbed 'the Fitz' by locals, this colossal neoclassical pile was one of the first public art museums in Britain, built to house the fabulous treasures that the seventh Viscount Fitzwilliam bequeathed to his old university. Expect Roman and Egyptian grave goods, artworks by many of the great masters and some quirkier collections: banknotes, literary autographs, watches and armour.

The building's unabashedly over-the-top appearance sets out to mirror its contents; this ostentatious jumble of styles mixes mosaic with marble, and Greek with Egyptian. The lower galleries are filled with priceless treasures spanning the ancient world; look out for a Roman funerary couch, an inscribed copper votive plaque from Yemen (c AD 100–200), a figurine of Egyptian cat goddess Bastet, splendid Egyptian sarcophagi and mummified animals, plus dazzling illuminated manuscripts. The upper galleries showcase works by Leonardo da Vinci, Titian, Rubens, the impressionists, Gainsborough and Constable, right through to Rembrandt and Picasso; standout works include the tender *Pietà* by Giovanni del Ponte and Salvator Rosa's dark and intensely personal *L'Umana Fragilita*.

The Fitz has a tragic footnote: although begun by George Basevi in 1837, he didn't live to see its completion. While working on Ely Cathedral he stepped back to admire his handiwork, slipped and fell to his death.

One-hour guided tours (£6) of the museum are held at 2.30pm Saturday.

City Walk
The Colleges and The Backs

START KING'S COLLEGE CHAPEL
END FITZBILLIES
LENGTH 3 MILES; FOUR HOURS

From divine **1** **King's** (p353), stroll north, diverting into **2** **Great St Mary's** (p355) and climbing the tower for fine Cambridge views. Next, dodge the cyclists and touting tour guides before ducking into atmospheric **3** **Gonville & Caius** (p355) to marvel at its ornate gates. **4** **Trinity's** (p356) elaborate entranceway towers up on the left; head through it into the college's Great Court; marvel at the architecture, then make for the absorbing **5** **Wren Library** (p356), with its extraordinary historic books. Next, pause to admire the gorgeous **6** **St John's** (p356) before dropping into the captivating, 12th-century **7** **Round Church** (p356). Cut right between the sweet terraces of narrow Portugal Pl – at the end, the **8** **Maypole** (p364) pub is a friendly place to eat or drink.

Next head diagonally across Jesus Green, to consider a dip in the bijou open-air **9** **pool** (p360). Then stroll southwest beside the river, passing locks and houseboats. Cross at the bridge beside **10** **Magdalene College** (p357), where the unique Pepys Library is well worth a detour.

Northampton St reminds you the 21st century does exist, then it's on to the path through the Backs, where the stately sweep of St John's College shelters amid the trees, Trinity sits next door. Next play zigzag with college paths and the river: nip up **11** **Garret Hostel Lane** for a closer view of punts, bridges and college facades. Then it's back to the path, before another detour left leads to the gates of **12** **Clare College** (p357), where the Fellow's Garden is a real must-see.

Back on the Backs, next comes the impressive west end of King's; the Palladian **13** **Fellows' Building** is just to the right. After curving beside **14** **Queens'** (p357), cut left. On Silver St's bridge spy the chunky **15** **Mathematical Bridge** (p357) on the left, and the fleets of punts on the right. Time to rest. Where better than **16** **Fitzbillies** (p362) for a Chelsea bun and a steaming cup of tea.

HOW TO PUNT

Punting looks pretty straightforward but, believe us, really – it's not. So here are some tips to stop you zigzagging wildly across the river, losing your pole and falling in.

➡ Standing at the back end of the punt, lift the pole out of the water at the side of the punt.

➡ Let the pole slide through your hands to touch the bottom of the river.

➡ Tilt the pole forward (that is, in the direction of travel of the punt) and push down to propel the punt forward.

➡ Twist the pole to free the end from the mud at the bottom of the river, and let it float up and trail behind the punt. You can then use it as a rudder to steer.

➡ If you haven't fallen in yet, raise the pole out of the water and into the vertical position to begin the cycle again.

➡ Hold on to the pole, particularly when passing under Clare Bridge, as students sometimes snatch them for a giggle.

Polar Museum　　　　　　　MUSEUM
(www.spri.cam.ac.uk/museum; Lensfield Rd; ⊙10am-4pm Tue-Sat) FREE Tales of hostile environments, dogged determination and, sometimes, life-claiming mistakes are evoked powerfully at this compelling museum. Its focus on polar exploration charts the feats of the likes of Roald Amundsen, Fridtjof Nansen and Captain Robert Falcon Scott. The affecting collections include paintings, photographs, clothing, equipment, maps, journals and last messages left for loved ones by Scott's polar crew.

Other exhibits include models of ships that ventured into sub-zero Arctic and Antarctic waters, innovative equipment such as the 'Nansen cooker' and interactive displays on ice and climate change. The section devoted to the people of the Arctic includes Inuit carvings and scrimshaw (etched bones), a Sami knife with a carved reindeer-horn sheath, a walrus tusk with walrus hunt scenes etched on it, and particularly fine examples of *tupilak* (carved caribou-horn figures with ancestor souls captured inside) from Greenland. The museum is run by the Scott Polar Institute, founded with part of the relief fund set up in the wake of the explorer's ill-fated South Pole expedition – these days it takes a lead role in climate-change research.

**Cambridge University
Botanic Garden**　　　　　　GARDENS
(www.botanic.cam.ac.uk; 1 Brookside; adult/child £5/free; ⊙10am-6pm Apr-Sep, to 5pm Feb, Mar & Oct, to 4pm Nov-Jan) Founded by Charles Darwin's mentor, Professor John Henslow, the beautiful Botanic Garden is home to 8000 plant species, a wonderful arboretum, glasshouses (containing both fierce carnivorous pitcher plants and the delicate slipper orchid), a winter garden and flamboyant herbaceous borders. The gardens are 1200m south of the city centre via Trumpington St.

 Activities

Swimming

Jesus Green Pool　　　　　　SWIMMING
(www.better.org.uk; Jesus Green; adult/child £4.50/2.40; ⊙7.30am-7.30pm Mon, Tue & Fri, noon-7.30pm Wed, Thu, Sat & Sun May-Sep) A slender, 100-yard, 1920s open-air swim spot; popular with poolside sunbathers too.

Punting

Gliding a self-propelled punt along the Backs is a blissful experience – once you've got the hang of it. It can also be a manic challenge to begin. If you wimp out, you can always opt for a relaxing chauffeured punt.

Punt hire costs around £20 to £28 per hour; 45-minute chauffeured trips of the Backs cost about £15 to £19 per person. One-way trips to Grantchester (1½ hours) start at around £18 per person.

Scudamore's Punting　　　　　BOATING
(☏01223-359750; www.scudamores.com; Granta Place; chauffeured punt per 45min per person £16-19, 6-person self-punt per hr £22-28; ⊙9am-dusk) Hires punts, rowing boats, kayaks and canoes. Offers up to £5 discount if you book online.

Cambridge Chauffeur Punts　　　BOATING
(www.punting-in-cambridge.co.uk; Silver St Bridge) Runs regular chauffeured punting tours (per hour adult/child £16/7) and also self-hire (six-person punt per hour £22).

Granta Moorings
BOATING

(www.puntingincambridge.com; Newnham Rd; chauffeured punt per 50min per person £15, 6-person self-punt per hr £24; ☺9.30am-dusk Mar-Oct) Handily sited punt-rental company if you're heading towards Grantchester. Runs reduced services in winter.

☞ Tours

★ Walking Tours
WALKING

(✆01223-791501; www.visitcambridge.org; Peas Hill) The tourist office runs **guided two-hour tours** (adult/child £19/9) taking in two of the most memorable colleges; they might include King's College Chapel, Queens', Pembroke or St John's. The price includes admission to the colleges. Tours leave from the tourist office. They're popular: book.

Year-round, tours run at 11am and 1pm Monday to Friday, at 11am, noon, 1pm and 2pm Saturday, and at 1pm Sunday. In July and August, there are extra daily tours at noon and 2pm.

Colourful, one-hour **Ghost Tours** (adult/child £7/5) take place on Friday and Saturday; start times vary from 6pm to 8pm. The Ghost Tours leave from the Guildhall.

♣ Festivals & Events

Cambridge has a jam-packed cultural schedule. For one-off events, check out the notices tied to railings all over the city centre, especially around St Mary's Church.

Bumps
SPORTS

(www.cucbc.org/bumps; ☺Feb & Jun) Traditional rowing races along the Cam (or the Granta, as the Cambridge stretch is called), in which college boat clubs compete to 'bump' the crew in front.

Beer Festival
BEER

(www.cambridgebeerfestival.com; ☺May) Hugely popular five-day beer and cider extravaganza on Jesus Green, featuring brews from all over the country as well as a great range of British cheeses.

May Balls
CULTURAL

(☺early Jun) The biggest student events of the year, the name of these formal balls don't match the month they're held in (June) because college authorities decided that May's traditional booze-fuelled revelry – just before the exams – wasn't such a great idea. Now they take place after the exams, but in a typically Cambridge quirk, they keep their old name.

Folk Festival
MUSIC

(www.cambridgefolkfestival.co.uk; ☺late Jul–early Aug) Acclaimed four-day music fest in Cherry Hinton Hall, 4 miles southeast of the city centre. It's hosted the likes of Van Morrison, Ladysmith Black Mambazo, Christy Moore, Imelda May, Paul Simon and KT Tunstall.

Cambridge Shakespeare Festival
THEATRE

(www.cambridgeshakespeare.com; ☺Jul & Aug) The bard's best-loved works performed in outdoor settings.

⌶ Sleeping

Cambridge YHA
HOSTEL £

(✆0845-371 9728; www.yha.org.uk; 97 Tenison Rd; dm £18-26, d £39-59; @⊚) Smart, friendly, recently renovated, deservedly popular hostel with compact dorms and good facilities. Handily, it's near the railway station.

University Rooms Cambridge
B&B ££

(www.universityrooms.com/en/city/cambridge/home; s/d from £46/80) For an authentic taste of university life, check into a student room in one of a range of colleges. Accommodation varies from functional singles (with shared bathroom) overlooking college courts to more modern, en-suite rooms in nearby annexes. Breakfast is often in hall (the students' dining room). Rooms are largely available during university holidays (June to August, Christmas, and March to April).

Worth House
B&B ££

(✆01223-316074; www.worth-house.co.uk; 152 Chesterton Rd; s £75-85, d £95-145; P⊚) The welcome is wonderfully warm, the great-value rooms utterly delightful. Soft grey and cream meets candy-stripe reds, fancy bathrooms boast claw-foot baths and tea trays are full of treats. There's also a three-person, self-catering apartment (per week £550) two doors down.

Benson House
B&B ££

(✆01223-311594; www.bensonhouse.co.uk; 24 Huntingdon Rd; s £75-115, d £110-115; P⊚) Lots of little things lift Benson a cut above – sleep among feather pillows and Egyptian cotton linen, sip tea from Royal Doulton bone china, then tuck into award-winning breakfasts featuring kippers, croissants and fresh fruit.

Tudor Cottage
B&B ££

(✆01223-565212; www.tudorcottageguesthouse.co.uk; 292 Histon Rd; s/d £50/80; P⊚) Sweet features help make this neat-as-a-pin guesthouse feel like a home from home, from bedrooms boasting gleaming bathrooms to the ranks of speciality teas, cereals, cakes and muffins at the breakfast table. It's just under 2 miles north of the city centre; bus 8 stops just outside.

Rosa's
B&B ££

(📞01223-512596; www.rosasbedandbreakfast. co.uk; 53 Roseford Rd; s £55-70; P 🛜) One for solo travellers: a friendly, family-run B&B where the two bright, snug, singles have accents of chocolate-brown and lime. It's 2 miles north of the city centre; there's free on-road parking outside and bus 8 runs nearby.

★ Varsity
BOUTIQUE HOTEL £££

(📞01223-306030; www.thevarsityhotel.co.uk; Thompson's Lane; d £190-350; @ 🛜) In the 44 individually styled rooms of riverside Varsity, wondrous furnishings and witty features (Union Jack footstools, mock-flock wallpaper) sit beside floor-to-ceiling glass windows, espresso machines and smartphone docks. The views out over the colleges from the roof terrace are, frankly, gorgeous.

★ Hotel du Vin
BOUTIQUE HOTEL £££

(📞01223-928991; www.hotelduvin.com; 15 Trumpington St; d £159-259, ste £250-425; @ 🛜) One of the country's swishest, coolest chains delivers again here. Achingly beautiful rooms sport roll-top baths, monsoon showers and custom-made beds, the cosy cellar bar is vaulted, the bistro (two/three courses £17/20) is chic, and the luxuriously appointed suites (expect rotating TVs, mini-cinemas and surround sound) are simply divine.

Felix
BOUTIQUE HOTEL £££

(📞01223-277977; www.hotelfelix.co.uk; Whitehouse Lane, Huntingdon Rd; s £205, d £220-285, ste £325-345; P @ 🛜) It's the bold modern art and imaginative design (fuchsia-pink chairs amid stately polished wood) that nudge Felix into the boutique sleep spots. That and the silk curtains, luxurious linens and stone-and-slate bathrooms. Felix is 1.5 miles north-west of the city. The Penthouse suite, up in the eaves, is an utterly romantic retreat.

✕ Eating

★ Urban Shed
SANDWICHES £

(www.theurbanshed.com; 62 King St; sandwiches from £4.25; ⊙8.30am-5pm Mon-Thu, 8.30am-4.30pm Fri, 9am-6pm Sat, 10am-4pm Sun) Somewhere between a retro goods shop and a sandwich bar, unorthodox Urban Shed has a personal service ethos so strong that regular customers have a locker for their own mug. Decor teams old aeroplane seats with cable-drum tables, their own-blend coffee is mellow and the sandwiches range is superb.

Hot Numbers
CAFE £

(www.hotnumberscoffee.co.uk; 4 Trumpington St; snacks from £5; ⊙7am-7pm Mon-Fri, 8am-6pm Sat & Sun; 🛜) Hipster hang-out with maple-smoked bacon for breakfast, single-origin bean coffee, craft beers, cool tunes and a laid-back vibe.

Espresso Library
CAFE £

(www.espressolibrary.co.uk; 210 East Rd; mains £5-9; ⊙7am-7pm Mon & Tue, to 9pm Wed & Thu, to 11pm Fri & Sat, 9am-6pm Sun; 🖋) A chilled soundtrack and a customer laptop on almost every table signal that this industrial-chic cafe is a student favourite. That'll be partly down to the wholesome food – think frittata with sweet potatoes and spinach, or juicy portobello mushrooms in brioche buns – and partly down to some cracking coffee.

Aromi
ITALIAN £

(www.aromi.co.uk; 1 Benet St; mains £4.50; ⊙9am-7pm Sun-Thu, to 8pm Fri & Sat; 🖋) Sometimes you should yield to temptation. So be drawn in by a window full of stunning Sicilian pizza and feast on light, crisp bases piled high with fresh spinach and Parma ham. Then succumb to the indecently thick hot chocolate; may as well make it a large.

Aromi also has another cafe a few doors down on Peas Hill.

Fitzbillies
CAFE £

(www.fitzbillies.com; 52 Trumpington St; mains £6-12; ⊙8am-6pm Mon-Fri, 9am-7pm Sat, 10am-6pm Sun) Cambridge's oldest bakery has a soft, doughy place in the hearts of generations of students, thanks to its ultrasticky Chelsea buns and other sweet treats. Pick up a bagful to take away or munch in comfort in the quaint cafe.

Rainbow
VEGETARIAN £

(www.rainbowcafe.co.uk; 9a King's Pde; mains £7-11; ⊙10am-10pm Tue-Sat, to 3pm Sun; 🖋) Quite a treat for non-meat-eaters: a cheery basement bistro, tucked away at the end of an alley off King's Parade. In this warren of cosy rooms, rickety tables set the scene for an eclectic range of veg that's been transformed into a variety of bakes, roasts, pastas and pies.

There are also tasty gluten-free options.

Pint Shop
MODERN BRITISH ££

(📞01223-352293; www.pintshop.co.uk; 10 Peas Hill; mains £12-21; ⊙noon-10pm) Popular Pint

PRANKSTERS, NIGHT CLIMBERS & CUBES

In a city with so much concentrated mental prowess, it is perhaps inevitable that the student community would excel at all kinds of mischief. The most impressive prank ever to take place in Cambridge – lifting an Austin Seven van on to the roof of the landmark Senate House (p355) in 1958 – involved a great deal of planning from four mechanical sciences students and spawned a number of copycat pranks, including suspending another Austin Seven from the ornate Bridge of Sighs (p356).

King's College has long been a target of night climbers – students who get their thrills by scaling the lofty heights of out-of-bounds buildings at night. The sport is taken very seriously – to the point where a Trinity College student, Geoffrey Winthrop Young, wrote the *Roof Climber's Guide to Trinity* in 1900. If you're in Cambridge after a particularly spectacular climber excursion, you may find some out-of-place objects atop the pinnacles of King's College Chapel (p353) – anything from a traffic cone to a Santa hat.

Finally, there's the Cubes (Cambridge University Breaking and Entering Society): its objective is to access places members shouldn't be and leave distinctive calling cards – the most famous being the wooden mallard in the rafters of Trinity's Great Hall.

Shop's vision is to embrace eating and drinking equally. So it's created both a busy bar specialising in craft beer (10 on keg and six on draft) and a stylish dining room serving classy versions of traditional grub (dry aged steaks, gin-cured sea trout, charcoal-grilled plaice). All in all, hard to resist.

Smokeworks   BARBECUE **££**
(www.smokeworks.co.uk; 2 Free School Lane; mains £9-17; ◷11.45am-10.30pm Mon-Thu, to 11pm Fri & Sat, to 9.30pm Sun; 🛜) This dark, industrial-themed dining spot draws discerning carnivores and local hipsters with its melt-in-your-mouth ribs, wings and wonderfully smoky pulled pork. The service is friendly and prompt and their salted caramel milkshakes come in a glass the size of your head.

Kingston Arms   PUB FOOD **££**
(www.kingston-arms.co.uk; 33 Kingston St; mains £5-16; ◷noon-2pm & 6-10pm Mon-Fri, noon-10pm Sat & Sun; 🛜) Great gastropub grub – from roasts to homemade risotto and recession-busting mains (held at £5) – keeps stomachs satisfied at the award-winning Kingston. More than 10 real ales, stacked board games and a students-meet-locals clientele deliver a contemporary Cambridge vibe.

It's 1 mile southeast of the centre.

Chop House   BRITISH **££**
(www.cambscuisine.com/cambridge-chop-house; 1 King's Pde; mains £15-22; ◷noon-10.30pm Mon-Sat, to 9.30pm Sun) The window seats here deliver some of the best views in town – on to King's College's hallowed walls. The food is pure English establishment too: hearty steaks and chops and chips, plus a scattering of fish dishes and suet puddings. It's also open from 10am to noon for coffee and cakes.

Sister restaurant **St John's Chop House** (www.cambscuisine.com/st-johns-chop-house; 21 Northampton St; mains £11-27; ◷noon-3pm & 6-10.30pm Mon-Fri, noon-11pm Sat, noon-9.30pm Sun) sits near the rear entrance to St John's College.

Oak Bistro   BISTRO **££**
(☑01223-323361; www.theoakbistro.co.uk; 6 Lensfield Rd; mains £14-24, set lunch 2/3 courses £14/17; ◷noon-2.30pm & 6-9.30pm Mon-Sat) Truffle oil, salsa verde and rosemary jus are the kind of flavour intensifiers you'll find at this friendly but classy neighbourhood eatery where locally sourced duck, lamb and beef come cooked just so. The set lunch remains a bargain.

★ **Midsummer House**   MODERN BRITISH **£££**
(☑01223-369299; www.midsummerhouse.co.uk; Midsummer Common; 5/8 courses £48/105; ◷noon-1.30pm Wed-Sat, 7-9.30pm Tue-Sat; ☑) At the region's top table, chef Daniel Clifford's double-Michelin-starred creations are distinguished by depth of flavour and immense technical skill. Sample transformations of coal-baked celeriac, Cornish crab, and roast pigeon with wild garlic before a pear, blueberry and white chocolate delight.

Wine flights start at £45. Unusually, there are vegetarian versions of both the set menus.

Cotto   INTERNATIONAL **£££**
(☑01223-302010; www.cottocambridge.co.uk; 183 East Rd; 3 courses £65-70; ◷6.30-9pm Wed-Sat; ☑) 🍽 An irresistible blend of artistry

WORTH A TRIP

IMPERIAL WAR MUSEUM

At Europe's biggest aviation museum, **Imperial War Museum** (www.iwm.org.uk; Duxford; adult/child £16.35/8.15; ⏱10am-6pm Easter-Oct, to 4pm Nov-Easter; Ⓟ 👪), some 200 lovingly preserved vintage aircraft are housed in several enormous hangars. The vast airfield showcases everything from dive bombers to biplanes, Spitfire and Concorde. The awe-inspiring **American Air Museum** hangar pays homage to US WWII servicemen, hosting the largest collection of American civil and military aircraft outside the USA.

Duxford is 9 miles south of Cambridge at Junction 10 of the M11. Buses only run to the museum on Sunday (bus 132; £3.90, 50 minutes).

and precision ensure chef Hans Schweitzer's creations look gorgeous and taste fabulous. Delights might include seafood velouté or the signature dish Cotto venison Wellington, followed perhaps by 'Hans-made chocolates' or coconut brûlée.

🍷 Drinking & Nightlife

★**Eagle** PUB
(www.eagle-cambridge.co.uk; Benet St; ⏱8am-11pm Mon-Sat, to 10.30pm Sun) Cambridge's most famous pub has loosened the tongues and pickled the grey cells of many an illustrious academic; among them Nobel Prize–winning scientists Crick and Watson, who discussed their research into DNA here (note the blue plaque by the door). Fifteenth-century, wood-panelled and rambling, its cosy rooms include one with WWII airmen's signatures on the ceiling. The food, served all day, is good too.

Fez CLUB
(www.cambridgefez.com; 15 Market Passage; ⏱10.30pm-3am Tue-Sat) Hip hop, dancehall, R&B, techno, funk, indie, house and garage; top-name DJs and club nights – you'll find it all at Cambridge's most popular club, the Moroccan-themed Fez.

Maypole PUB
(www.maypolefreehouse.co.uk; 20a Portugal Pl; ⏱11.30am-midnight Sun-Thu, to 1am Fri & Sat) A dozen pumps dispensing real ale, a roomy beer garden and a friendly, unreconstructed vibe make this red-brick pub popular with the locals. That and hearty, homemade Italian food and festivals championing regional and microbrewery beers.

Granta PUB
(www.granta-cambridge.co.uk; 14 Newnham Rd; ⏱11am-11pm) If the exterior of this picturesque waterside pub, overhanging a pretty mill pond, looks strangely familiar, it could be because it is the darling of many a TV di-

rector. No wonder: with its snug deck, riverside terrace and punts moored up alongside, it's a highly atmospheric spot to sup and watch the world drift by.

☆ Entertainment

ADC THEATRE
(☎01223-300085; www.adctheatre.com; Park St) This famous student-run theatre is home to the university's Footlights comedy troupe whose past members include Emma Thompson, Hugh Laurie and Stephen Fry.

Cambridge Arts Theatre THEATRE
(☎01223-503333; www.cambridgeartstheatre.com; 6 St Edward's Passage) Cambridge's biggest bona-fide theatre puts on everything from highbrow drama and dance, to panto and shows fresh from London's West End.

Junction PERFORMING ARTS
(☎01223-511511; www.junction.co.uk; Clifton Way) Theatre, dance, comedy, live bands and club nights at a contemporary performance venue near the railway station. It's 1.5 miles southeast of the city centre, down Regent St (later Hills Rd).

Portland Arms LIVE MUSIC
(www.theportlandarms.co.uk; 129 Chesterton Rd; ⏱noon-11.30pm Mon-Thu, to 12.30am Fri & Sat, to 11pm Sun) A popular student haunt, the 200-capacity Portland is the best spot in town to catch a gig and see the pick of up-and-coming bands. It has a wood-panelled saloon bar, a spacious terrace and monthly comedy nights too.

ℹ Information

Addenbrooke's (www.cuh.org.uk; Hills Rd; ⏱24hr emergency room) Four miles southeast of the centre.
Cantab Millenium Services (☎01223-322306; 95 Mill Rd; per hour £1.50; ⏱9.30am-6.30pm) Internet cafe.

Tourist Office (☑ 01223-791500; www.
visitcambridge.org; Peas Hill; ☺10am-5pm
Mon-Sat, 11am-3pm Sun Apr-Oct, 10am-5pm
Mon-Sat Nov-Mar)

❶ Getting There & Away

BUS

Buses run by **National Express** (☑ 0871 781
8181; www.nationalexpress.com; Parkside)
leave from Parkside. Direct services include the
following:

Gatwick £37, 3¾ hours, nine daily

Heathrow £25, 2¾ hours, hourly

London Victoria £5, 2½ hours, two-hourly

Oxford £12, 3½ hours, every 30 minutes

Stansted £10, 45 minutes, two-hourly

CAR

Cambridge's centre is largely pedestrianised.
The city's multistorey car parks charge between
£3 and £4.60 for two hours.

Five free Park & Ride car parks (parking per
day £1) circle the city on the major routes, with
buses (return tickets £2.70) shuttling into the
city centre every 10 to 15 minutes between
around 7am and 8pm Monday to Saturday, 9am
to 5.45pm Sunday.

TRAIN

The train station is 1.5 miles southeast of the
centre. Direct services:

Birmingham New Street £55, three hours,
hourly

Bury St Edmunds £10, 40 minutes, hourly

Ely £5,15 minutes, three per hour

King's Lynn £10, 50 minutes, hourly

London King's Cross £23, one hour, two to
four per hour

Stansted Airport £10, 35 minutes, hourly

❶ Getting Around

BICYCLE

Cambridge is incredibly bike-friendly, with two
wheels providing an ideal, and atmospheric, way
to get around town.

Recommended bicycle hire outfits:

City Cycle Hire (www.citycyclehire.com; 61
Newnham Rd; per half-day/day/week £7/10/25;
☺9am-5.30pm Mon-Fri, plus 9am-5pm Sat
Apr-Oct) A mile southwest of the city centre.

Rutland Cycling (☑ 01223-307655; www.
rutlandcycling.com; Corn Exchange St; per
4hr/day £7/10; ☺9am-6pm Mon-Fri, 10am-
5pm Sun) In the heart of town, underneath the
Grand Arcade shopping centre. There's another
branch on Station Rd at the train station.

BUS

➡ Bus routes run around town from the **main
bus station** (Drummer St).

➡ Many operate until around 11pm.

➡ C1, C3 and C7 stop at the train station.

➡ A Dayrider ticket (£4.10) provides 24 hours,
unlimited, citywide bus travel.

Grantchester

POP 540

Old thatched cottages with gardens covered in flowers, breezy meadows and classic
cream teas aren't the only reason to make
the pilgrimage along the Cam to the picture-postcard village of Grantchester. You'll
also be following in the footsteps of some of
the world's greatest minds on a 3-mile walk,
cycle or punt that has changed little since
Edwardian times.

✕ Eating

★**Orchard Tea Garden**   CAFE £
(☑ 01223-551125;   http://mlsb.org/orchard-
teagarden; Mill Way; lunch mains £4-10, cakes £3;
☺9.30am-7.30pm Jun-Aug, to 5.30pm Mar-May
& Sep-Nov, to 4.30pm Dec-Feb) After an idyllic
punt, walk or cycle to Grantchester from
Cambridge beside the Cam, flop into a deckchair under a leafy apple tree and wolf down
caloric cakes or light lunches at this quintessentially English spot. This was the favourite
haunt of the Bloomsbury Group who came to
camp, picnic, swim and discuss their work.

❶ Getting There & Away

➡ Grantchester is 3 miles from Cambridge; you
can punt, walk or cycle beside the Cam.

➡ Bus 18 runs from Cambridge to Grantchester
(£2.50, 15 minutes, hourly Monday to Saturday).

Ely

POP 20,256

A small but charming city dominated by a
jaw-dropping cathedral, Ely makes an excellent day trip from Cambridge. It takes
its name (*ee-lee*) from the eels that once
inhabited the surrounding undrained Fens.
From the Middle Ages onward, Ely was one
of the biggest opium-producing centres in
Britain, with high-class ladies holding 'poppy parties' and local mothers sedating their
children with 'poppy tea'. Today, beyond the
dizzying heights of the cathedral towers, Ely
is a cluster of medieval streets lined with

traditional tearooms and pretty Georgian houses; a quaint quayside adds extra appeal.

◎ Sights

★ Ely Cathedral
CATHEDRAL

(www.elycathedral.org; The Gallery; adult/child £8/ free, incl tower tour £15/free; ⊙ 7am-6.30pm) Ely Cathedral's stunning silhouette dominates the whole area; it's dubbed the 'Ship of the Fens' because it's so visible across the vast, flat sweeps of land. The early-12th-century nave dazzles with clean, uncluttered lines and a lofty sense of space. Look out for the entrancing ceiling, the masterly 14th-century Octagon, and towers that soar upwards in shimmering colours. Standard admission includes a ground-floor guided tour. The tower tours (three to five daily) deliver behind-the-scenes glimpses, 165 steps and remarkable views.

Ely has been a place of worship and pilgrimage since at least 673, when Etheldreda, daughter of the king of East Anglia, founded a nunnery here (shrugging off the fact that she had been twice married in her determination to become a nun). She was canonised shortly after her death. The nunnery was sacked by the Danes, rebuilt as a monastery, demolished and then resurrected as a church after the Norman Conquest. In 1109, Ely became a cathedral. Gothic arches were added later to support the weight of the mighty walls.

The vast 14th-century Lady Chapel is filled with eerily empty niches that once held statues of saints and martyrs. They were hacked out unceremoniously by iconoclasts during the English Civil War. But the delicate tracery remains, overseen by a rather controversial statue of *Holy Mary* by David Wynne, unveiled in 2000 to mixed reviews. The cathedral's beauty has made it a popular film location: you may recognise some of its fine details from scenes in *Elizabeth: The Golden Age* and *The Other Boleyn Girl*. For optimum atmosphere, visit during evensong (5.30pm Monday to Saturday, 4pm Sunday) or a choral service (10.30am Sunday).

Oliver Cromwell's House
MUSEUM

(www.olivercromwellshouse.co.uk; 29 St Mary's St; adult/child £4.90/3.40; ⊙ 10am-5pm Apr-Oct, 11am-4pm Nov-Mar) England's premier Puritan (p642) lived in this attractive, half-timbered house with his family from 1636 to 1647, when he was the local tithe collector. The interior has been restored to reflect the fixtures and fittings that would have been part of their daily lives – expect flickering candles, floppy hats and writing quills.

Ely Museum
MUSEUM

(www.elymuseum.org.uk; Market St; adult/child £4.50/1; ⊙ 10.30am-5pm Mon-Sat, 1-5pm Sun Apr-Oct, 10.30am-4pm Wed-Sat, 1-4pm Sun Nov-Mar) Housed in the Old Gaol House, this quirky little museum appropriately features gruesome prison tableaux inside prisoners' cells, plus displays on the Romans, the Anglo-Saxons, the Long Barrow burial ground at nearby Haddlington, and the formation of the Fens. You are also initiated into the mysteries of old Ely trades such as leatherwork and eel-catching.

🛏 Sleeping & Eating

★ Peacocks
B&B ££

(☎ 01353-661100; www.peacockstearoom.co.uk; 65 Waterside; d £125-150) Walk into the roomy suites here and feel instantly at home. In Cottage, floral Laura Ashley wallpaper graces a sweet sitting area and bedroom; in Brewery, the vintage books, gilt mirrors and burnished antiques are reminiscent of a grand gentlemen's club.

Riverside Inn
B&B ££

(☎ 01353-661677; www.riversideinn-ely.co.uk; 8 Annesdale; s £59-69, d £89-120; P 🛜) In this Georgian guesthouse on Ely's quay, rooms are enriched by dull golds, deep reds, brocade bedspreads, dark furniture and sparkling bathrooms. Just the place to gaze at the houseboats and rowers bobbing about on the River Great Ouse.

★ Peacocks
CAFE £

(www.peacockstearoom.co.uk; 65 Waterside; snacks from £7; ⊙ 10.30am-4.30pm Wed-Sun, plus Tue Jun-Sep) An award-winning cafe serving a vast selection of teas and cream teas, luscious homemade soups, salads, cakes and scones. Eat inside surrounded by fun knickknacks and bone china, or in the bijou garden framed by drooping wisteria.

Old Fire Engine House
BRITISH ££

(☎ 01353-662582; www.theoldfireenginehouse. co.uk; 25 St Mary's St; lunch 2/3 courses £17/22, mains £16; ⊙ noon-2pm & 7-9pm Mon-Sat, noon-2pm Sun) 🍴 Eating here is like sampling the dishes cooked up in a (decidedly classy) classic East Anglian farmhouse kitchen. Seasonal and local produce rule, so treats might include locally smoked eel or roast guinea fowl with wild mushrooms, rounded off with some custard-smothered, steamed treacle and ginger pudding.

ℹ️ Information

Tourist Office (☎ 01353-662062; www.visitely. org.uk; 29 St Mary's St; ⊙10am-5pm Apr-Oct, 11am-4pm Nov-Mar) Stocks leaflets on the picturesque Eel Trail (50p) and Fen Rivers Way (£2) circular walks.

ℹ️ Getting There & Away

You can walk to Ely from Cambridge, along the 17-mile, riverside Fen Rivers Way. Rail connections include the following:

Cambridge £3, 20 minutes, three per hour
King's Lynn £7, 30 minutes, every 30 minutes
Norwich £17, one hour, every 30 minutes

ESSEX

The county's inhabitants have been the butt of snobbery and some of England's cruellest jokes for years, thanks to pop-culture stereotypes. But beyond the fake tans and slots 'n' bumper car resorts, the county's still-idyllic medieval villages and rolling countryside provided inspiration for Constable, one of England's best-loved painters. Here, too, is the historic town of Colchester, while even Southend-on-Sea, the area's most popular resort, has a softer side in the traditional cockle-sellers and cobbled lanes of the sleepy suburb Old Leigh.

Colchester

POP 180,420

Dominated by its sturdy castle and extensive Roman walls, Colchester is Britain's oldest recorded city, dating from the 5th century BC. In AD 43 the Romans came, saw, conquered and constructed their northern capital Camulodunum. It was razed by Boudica just 17 years later. In the 11th century, the invading Normans built a mighty castle; today it's set amid narrow streets that are home to a striking new arts space and some half-timbered gems.

⊙ Sights

⭐**Colchester Castle**　　　　　　CASTLE
(www.cimuseums.org.uk; Castle Park; adult/child £7.60/4.75; ⊙10am-5pm Mon-Sat, 11am-5pm Sun) Built in 1076 on the foundations of the Roman Temple of Claudius, England's largest surviving Norman keep is bigger than that of the Tower of London. Over the centuries it's been a royal residence, a prison and home to a Witchfinder General. Now a £4-million restoration has brought 21st-century technology to its 11th-century walls. Look out for mobile phone apps and tablet hire, and a cracking *son et lumiere* recreating lost internal structures and bringing the building's history to life.

firstsite　　　　　　ARTS CENTRE
(www.firstsite.uk.net; Lewis Gardens; ⊙10am-5pm; ♿) **FREE** Colchester's shiny, curved, glass-and-copper arts centre brings the town bang up to date. It's as striking inside as out: installations flow seamlessly into one another amid a wealth of space and light. Temporary visual art displays are cunningly juxtaposed with historical works; the one permanent exhibition is the magnificent Berryfield Mosaic – a Roman artefact found on firstsite's location in 1923, and now under glass in the centre of the gallery space.

Hollytrees Museum　　　　　　MUSEUM
(www.cimuseums.org.uk; Castle Park; ⊙10am-5pm Mon-Sat) **FREE** It's like walking into a period drama: a Georgian town house dating from 1718, filled with toys and costumes, watches and clocks. Reminders of the domestic life of the wealthy owners and their servants are everywhere, with quirky exhibits that include a shipwright's baby carriage in the shape of a boat, a make-your-own Victorian silhouette feature and an intricate, envy-inducing doll's house.

🛏️ Sleeping & Eating

North Hill　　　　　　HOTEL **££**
(☎ 01206-574001; www.northhillhotel.com; 51 North Hill; s/d/ste £90/100/120; 🛜) Ask for a room in the characterful, cottage-style back building of this sleek sleep spot and you'll be rewarded with wonky beams, exposed red brick and plush modern furnishings. Stylish, more contemporary rooms sit in the former solicitor's chambers next door – it comes complete with ranks of law books on the shelves.

⭐**Company Shed**　　　　　　SEAFOOD **££**
(☎ 01206-382700; http://thecompanyshed.co; 129 Coast Rd, West Mersea; mains £5-16; ⊙9am-4pm Tue-Sat, 10am-4pm Sun) Bring your own bread and wine to this seaside shack to tuck into mussels, oysters, prawns, lobster, jellied eels, smoked fish or their signature seafood platter. It's all courtesy of the Howard

family, eighth-generation oyster-harvesters. The shed is on Mersea Island, 9 miles south of Colchester. Check the times of high water – it's not accessible on particularly high tides.

You can't book; arrive early (by 11.30am in the summer) to be sure of a meal.

Green Room
MODERN BRITISH **££**

(☑ 01206-574001; www.northhillhotel.com; 51 North Hill; mains £12-18; ⊙ noon-2.30pm & 6-9.30pm Mon-Sat, noon-8pm Sun) Local, seasonal comfort-food classics are given a contemporary twist at this smart, friendly restaurant, where dishes range from fish and chips or venison with wilted spinach to a gorgeously garlicky grilled lobster. Their working lunch (mains £6 to £8) is a snip.

ℹ Information

Tourist Office (☑ 01206-282920; www.visitcolchester.com; Castle Park; ⊙ 10am-5pm Mon-Sat) Inside the Hollytrees Museum.

ℹ Getting There & Away

➡ National Express buses run to London Victoria roughly every two hours (£10, 2½ hours).
➡ Trains shuttle to London Liverpool St (£15, one hour, every 15 minutes).

Dedham Vale

John Constable's romantic visions of country lanes, springtime fields and babbling creeks were inspired by and painted in this serene vale. The artist was born and bred in East Bergholt in 1776 and, although you may not see the rickety old cart pictured in his renowned painting *The Hay Wain,* the picturesque cottages, rolling countryside and languid charm remain.

Now known as Constable Country, Dedham Vale centres on the villages of Dedham, East Bergholt and Flatford. With leafy lanes, arresting pastoral views and graceful old churches, it's a glorious area to explore on foot or by bike.

◉ Sights

Flatford Mill
HISTORIC BUILDING

(Flatford, near East Bergholt; ℙ) Constable fans will recognise red-brick Flatford Mill immediately, as it appears in many of his canvases and remains as idyllic a setting today. It was once owned by the artist's family and is now used as an education centre, so although you can take in picture-perfect views from front and back, you can't go in.

Flatford
HISTORIC BUILDING

(Bridge Cottage, NT; ☑ 01206-298260; www.nationaltrust.org.uk; Bridge Cottage, near East Bergholt; parking £4; ⊙ 10.30am-5.30pm Apr-Oct, to 3.30pm Sat & Sun Nov-Mar; ℙ) **FREE** Set right beside Flatford Mill – a feature of several Constable paintings – thatched Bridge Cottage has an exhibition that provides a fine introduction to the artist's life and works. Daily guided tours (£3, noon and 2pm, April to October) take in views of Flatford Mill, Willy Lott's House (which features in *The Hay Wain*) and other sites that pop up in Constable's paintings. There are also self-guided routes.

⚲ Courses

Painting Courses
COURSE

(☑ 01206-323027; www.dedhamhall.co.uk; Brook St, Dedham; nonresidents per 3/7 days £325/380) For those inspired by Dedham Vale's bucolic landscapes, atmospheric Dedham Hall (p368) runs acclaimed painting courses in a converted, 14th-century barn. You can just visit each day for lessons, but it's more fun to stay, when the fee (double per three/seven nights from £450/740) includes dinner, bed and breakfast.

⬛ Sleeping & Eating

★ Dedham Hall
B&B **££**

(☑ 01206-323027; www.dedhamhall.co.uk; Brook St, Dedham; s/d £75/120; ℙ) An air of authentic old England infuses Dedham Hall, a delightfully relaxed 15th-century farmhouse where overstuffed armchairs sit beside ancient beams, candlesticks perch above red-brick fireplaces and plump pillows rest on cosy beds. Add a dappled garden dotted with chairs and it's really rather hard to leave.

Residents can also tuck into elegant, imaginative dinners (dinner and B&B for two costs £190).

Sun
INN **££**

(☑ 01206-323351; www.thesuninndedham.com; High St, Dedham; d £145; ℙ🛜) The centuries-old Sun is the epitome of heritage-chic: creaking floors and wonky walls surround upcycled mirrors, brass bedsteads and subtle colour schemes that team terracotta with a gentle yellow and olive with green. The pick of the rooms is church-view Elsa, where an immense bed is framed by armchairs and a bathroom is tucked in behind a wood-panelled door.

Milsoms
HOTEL ££

(📞 01206-322795; www.milsomhotels.com; Stratford Rd, Dedham; d £100-210; P 🛜) Sure-footed design gives the rooms here a real sense of fun: red-leather armchairs, anglepoise lamps and retro phones meet vast leaning mirrors and jazzy modern art. Their bicycle and canoe hire service opens up tranquil explorations of Dedham Vale.

Or drop by the hip, buzzy restaurant (open noon to 9.30pm, mains £9 to £28) for local steaks, mezze boards, duck tacos and lush ice cream.

Maison Talbooth
BOUTIQUE HOTEL £££

(📞 01206-322367; www.milsomhotels.com; Stratford Rd, Dedham; ste £150-450; P 🛜 🏊) In secluded grounds overlooking Constable's Dedham Vale, this fabulous retreat sees guests luxuriating in swish suites with goose-feather duvets and don't-want-to-get-up beds, and destressing in its hot tub, spa and heated outdoor pool, complete with pool house with a blazing log fire.

Sun
PUB FOOD ££

(www.thesuninndedham.com; High St, Dedham; mains £13-20; ⊘ noon-2.30pm & 6-9.30pm) Surprisingly, dishes infused with flavours of the Med appear on the scrubbed wooden tables of this old English inn. It's wood-panelled walls and beams provide a fine setting for risotto enriched with wild garlic, pasta stuffed with nettle and chard, and creamy vanilla-scented panna cotta.

ⓘ Getting There & Away

Flatford Mill is a lovely 2-mile walk from Manningtree train station.

Bus links from Colchester:

Dedham Buses 80, 81 and 102 (£2.40, 30 minutes, two to seven daily).

East Bergholt Buses 93 and 94 (£2.80, 40 minutes, hourly Monday to Saturday).

Saffron Walden
POP 15,210

The 12th-century market town of Saffron Walden is a delightful knot of half-timbered houses, narrow lanes, crooked roofs and ancient buildings. It gets its name from the purple saffron crocus (source of the world's most expensive spice), which was cultivated in the surrounding fields between the 15th and 18th centuries. If you can, time a visit to Tuesday or Saturday morning when markets stalls fill the centre of town.

⊙ Sights

Saffron Walden Museum
MUSEUM

(www.saffronwaldenmuseum.org; Museum St; adult/child £2.50/free; ⊘ 10am-4.30pm Tue-Sat, 2-4.30pm Sun) In the excellent museum, itself dating from 1835, you'll find an eclectic collection of artefacts covering everything from local history and 18th- and 19th-century costumes to geology, a partially interactive natural-history exhibit, Victorian toys and ancient Egyptian items. There's a sandpit for young archaeologists and a fascinating 'Worlds of Man' collection, ranging from West African carvings and weaponry to Inuit bone harpoons. The bramble-covered ruins of Walden Castle Keep, built about 1125, lie in the grounds.

St Mary the Virgin
CHURCH

(www.stmaryssaffronwalden.org; Church St; ⊘ 9am-5pm) FREE St Mary's oldest parts date back to 1250. A symbol of the town's saffron-inspired golden age, it is one of the largest churches in the county and features some impressive Gothic arches and local landowner Lord Audley's tomb.

Bridge End Gardens
GARDENS

(Bridge End; ⊘ gardens 24hr, maze & kitchen garden 9am-3pm Mon-Thu, to 1pm Fri, 10am-4pm Sat & Sun) FREE Careful restoration of these seven interlinked gardens has brought them back

CAMBRIDGE & EAST ANGLIA SAFFRON WALDEN

WORTH A TRIP

AUDLEY END HOUSE & GARDENS

Positively palatial in its scale, style and the all-too-apparent ambition of its creator, the first Earl of Suffolk, the fabulous early-Jacobean **Audley End House & Gardens** (EH; 📞 01799-522842; www.english-heritage.org.uk; off London Rd; adult/child £16.60/10; ⊘ house noon-5pm Apr-Sep, to 4pm Oct, gardens 10am-6pm Apr-Sep, to 5pm Oct) eventually did become a royal palace when it was bought by Charles II in 1668. Lavishly decorated rooms glitter with silverware, priceless furniture and paintings, making it one of England's grandest country homes. The fine landscaped park was designed by Lancelot 'Capability' Brown. Audley End House is 1 mile west of Saffron Walden off the B1383.

to their former Victorian glory. Try to visit when the maze and produce-packed kitchen garden are open too.

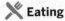 Eating

Eight Bells
PUB FOOD ££

(www.8bells-pub.co.uk; 18 Bridge St; mains £12-18; ⊙noon-9.30pm; 🍴) A warm mix of medieval character and contemporary style, this 16th-century gastropub serves up the likes of roast Suffolk lamb, lavender-cured duck and – fittingly – a vivid pea and courgette risotto, with saffron for extra spice.

Scrubbed wooden floors, half-timbered walls, abstract art, deep leather sofas and roaring fires make it an attractive place to sip on a pint, too.

Cafe Coucou
CAFE ££

(www.cafecoucou.co.uk; 17 George St; mains £8-11; ⊙9am-5pm Mon-Sat) Delicious homemade quiches, huge scones, chunky doorstep sandwiches and salads sell like hot cakes at this cheerful family-run cafe.

ℹ Information

Tourist Office (☑01799-524002; www.visitsaffronwalden.gov.uk; 1 Market Pl; ⊙9.30am-5pm Mon-Sat) Stocks a good leaflet (free) outlining a trail around the town's historic buildings.

ℹ Getting There & Away

Bus 7 runs between Saffron Walden and Cambridge (£4.40, 1¼ hours, seven daily Monday to Saturday).

The nearest train station is 2 miles west of Saffron Walden at Audley End. Bus 301 links Audley End train station with Saffron Walden (£1.90, 15 minutes, hourly Monday to Saturday). Train services from there include the following:

Cambridge £7, 15 minutes, every 20 minutes

London Liverpool St £10, one hour, twice hourly

Southend-on-Sea & Around

POP 177,900

Full of flashing lights and fairground rides, Southend is London's weekend playground, replete with gaudy amusements and packed-out nightclubs. But as well as all that, there's a glorious stretch of sandy beach, an absurdly long pier and, in the suburb of Old Leigh, echoes of a traditional fishing village.

Sights

Southend Pier
LANDMARK

(www.southend.gov.uk/pier; Western Esplanade; adult/child £2/1; ⊙8am-6pm Mon-Fri, to 8pm Sat & Sun Apr-Sep, 9am-5pm Wed-Sun Oct-Mar) Welcome to the world's longest pier – a staggering 1.341 miles long, to be precise – built in 1830 and a magnet for boat crashes, storms and fires, the last of which ravaged its tip in 2005. Today, a peaceful if windy stroll to the restored Pier Head reveals a cafe, sun deck, gift shop, exhibition space and active lifeboat station. Hopping on the **Pier Railway** (one-way adult/child £4/2.20) saves the long slog back.

Pier Museum
MUSEUM

(☑01702-611214; www.southendpiermuseum.co.uk; Western Esplanade; adult/child £1.50/50p; ⊙11am-5pm Sat, Sun, Tue & Wed May-Oct) Southend's seaside heyday springs to life in this charming museum, where a Victorian toast-rack tram from the pier sits beside a functioning signal box, sepia photos and period costumes. The best bits though are the still-working antique penny-slot machines.

Old Leigh
AREA

Cobbled streets, cockle sheds, art galleries and craft shops define atmospheric Old Leigh. It's a long stroll west along Southend's seafront, or a short hop on the local train.

🛏 Sleeping & Eating

Roslin Beach
HOTEL ££

(☑01702-586375; www.roslinhotel.com; Thorpe Esplanade; s £71-130, d £109-159, ste £154-245; ⊙food noon-3pm & 6-9.30pm Mon-Sat, noon-5pm & 7-9pm Sun; 🅿🛜🐾) Seafront Roslin is all New England beach-house chic: sculptural driftwood features, seashell-framed mirrors and sand drifting up the steps. De-knot in the sauna, soak in the spa then sample locally caught whitebait (mains £10 to £22) on the water-view terrace, framed by swaying palms.

Osborne Bros
SEAFOOD £

(www.osbornebros.co.uk; High St, Leigh-on-Sea; snacks/mains £2.50/8; ⊙8am-5pm) Part fish stall, part bare-bones cafe, Osbourne's is set right on Old Leigh's waterfront and serves up expansive Thames Estuary views. Best observed while tucking into crab, jellied eels or a seafood platter (cockles, mussels, prawns and crayfish; £8) and downing a pint from the pub next door.

They often stay open later in the summer and on fine weekends.

★ Simply Seafood
SEAFOOD £££

(☑ 01702-716645; www.simply-seafood.com; 1 The Cockle Sheds, Leigh-on-Sea; mains £18-35; ⊙ noon-3.30pm & 5-10pm Tue-Sat, noon-4.30pm Sun) Tucked under the flyover just west of Old Leigh, this bright little eatery lets locally sourced seafood shine. The oysters are from the River Chelmer, the crab is from Cromer and the fish is from the boats just outside. Scallops come perfectly seared and the *fruits de mer* platter is superb. Despite the name, there's a trio of steak options too.

ℹ Information

Tourist Office (☑ 01702-215620; www.visit-southend.co.uk; Southend Pier, Western Esplanade; ⊙ 8.30am-9pm Jun-Sep, 10am-6pm Wed-Sun Oct-May) At the entrance to the pier.

ℹ Getting There & Away

The easiest way to arrive is by train. The town's most useful train stations are Central (10 minutes' walk from the sea) and Victoria (15 minutes from the shore). Services include the following:

Leigh-on-Sea (from Central) £3, seven minutes, every 15 minutes.

London Fenchurch St (from Central) £12, 1¼ hours, three per hour.

London Liverpool St (from Victoria) £17, one hour, three per hour.

SUFFOLK

Suffolk is dotted with picturesque villages seemingly lost in time. The county made its money on the back of the medieval wool trade, and magnificent churches and lavish Tudor homes attest to the area's wealthy past. To the west are the picture-postcard villages of Lavenham and Long Melford. Further north, Bury St Edmunds ushers in historic buildings and a market-town vibe, while the appealing seaside resorts of Aldeburgh and Southwold overflow with genteel charm.

ℹ Getting Around

Ipswich is the county's main transport hub. **Traveline** (www.travelineeastanglia.org.uk) details bus routes.

Train connections from Ipswich include the following:

Bury St Edmunds £9, 30 minutes, one to two per hour

London Liverpool St £20, 1¼ hours, two per hour

Norwich £15, 40 minutes, two per hour

Long Melford
POP 2800

Two Elizabethan manors and some fine eateries make Long Melford deserving of a detour. Its expansive village green, antiques shops and string of independent stores provide other excellent reasons to meander on through.

◉ Sights

Kentwell Hall HISTORIC BUILDING

(☑ 01787-310207; www.kentwell.co.uk; adult/child £12.20/9.20; ⊙ hours vary; 🅿) Gorgeous, turreted Kentwell Hall may date from the 1500s and be full of Tudor grandeur, but it's still used as a private home, resulting in a wonderfully lived-in feel. Kentwell is framed by a rectangular moat, glorious gardens and an irresistible rare-breeds farm. Tudor re-enactment events see the whole estate bristle with bodices, codpieces and hose. Opening hours are erratic, it tends to be open 11am to 5pm during school summer holidays, plus other weekends; call to check.

Melford Hall HISTORIC BUILDING

(NT; www.nationaltrust.org.uk; Hall St; adult/child £7.50/3.75; ⊙ noon-5pm Wed-Sun Apr-Oct; 🅿) From outside, the romantic Elizabethan mansion of Melford Hall seems little changed since it entertained Queen Elizabeth I in 1578. Inside, there's a panelled banqueting hall, masses of Regency and Victorian finery, and a display on Beatrix Potter, a cousin of the Hyde Parkers, who owned the house from 1786 to 1960.

Holy Trinity CHURCH

(www.longmelfordchurch.com; Church Walk; ⊙ 10am-6pm Apr-Oct, to 4pm Nov-Mar) FREE Magnificent Holy Trinity is more cathedral-sized than church-sized, a spectacular example of a 15th-century wool church. The stained-glass windows and flint-and-stone flushwork are outstanding.

🛏 Sleeping & Eating

Black Lion HOTEL ££

(☑ 01787-312356; www.blacklionhotel.net; The Green; s/d/ste £100/125/175; 🅿🛜) There's more than a hint of the Scottish Highlands at the smashing Black Lion, thanks to tartan carpets, open fires and ancient-looking oil paintings. Flamboyant bedrooms, all swag curtains and feature beds, are named after classy wines – Yquem is, fittingly, floor-to-ceiling rich red.

GAINSBOROUGH'S HOUSE

Most visitors to Sudbury come to see Thomas Gainsborough's atmospheric birthplace **Gainsborough's House** (www.gainsborough.org; 46 Gainsborough St; adult/child £6.50/2; ⊙10am-5pm Mon-Sat, 11am-5pm Sun), now home to the world's largest collection of his work. The 16th-century house and gardens feature a Georgian facade built by the artist's father. Inside, look out for *Pitminster Boy* in the entrance hall; the exquisite *Portrait of Harriett; Viscountess Tracy*, celebrated for its delicate portrayal of drapery; and the landscapes that were his passion.

Bull   INN **££**
(📞01787-378494; www.oldenglishinns.co.uk; Hall St; s £60, d £80-120; 🅿🛜) Built, probably, for a wool merchant in 1450, this cavernous pub has been pulling pints since around 1580. The carved ceilings and heraldic crests in its bars attest to that grand age. Check into a front-facing bedroom for maximum atmosphere enhanced by aged beams and dark wood.

Decent pub grub (think slow-cooked lamb shank, and beef and ale pie) is served between noon and 9.30pm (mains £9 to £12).

⭐ **Scutcher's**   MODERN BRITISH **£££**
(📞01787-310200; www.scutchers.com; Westgate St; mains £19-29; ⊙noon-2pm & 7-9.30pm Thu-Sat) Beautiful reinventions of traditional ingredients ensure this unpretentious place is renowned throughout the Stour Valley. Local Gressingham duck is given an Asian twist; fish ragout comes with a vermouth sauce; the hot, grilled cheese is paired with quince. It's modern, classy and assured.

❶ Getting There & Away

Bus links include the following:
Bury St Edmunds £4.10, 50 minutes, hourly Monday to Saturday
Sudbury £1.50, 10 minutes, hourly Monday to Saturday

Lavenham
POP 1413

One of East Anglia's most beautiful and rewarding towns, the former wool-trade centre of Lavenham is home to a collection of exquisitely preserved medieval build-ings that lean and lurch to dramatic effect. Lavenham's 300 half-timbered, pargeted and thatched houses have been left virtually untouched since the 15th century; many are now superb places to eat and stay.

◉ Sights & Activities

Lavenham Guildhall   HISTORIC BUILDING
(NT; www.nationaltrust.org.uk; Market Pl; adult/child £6.20/3.10; ⊙11am-5pm daily Mar-Oct, to 4pm Sat & Sun Nov-Feb) Lavenham's most enchanting buildings are clustered along High St, Water St and around the unusually triangular Market Pl. They're dominated by this early-16th-century whitewashed guildhall – a superb example of a close-studded, timber-framed building. It is now a local-history museum with displays on the wool trade and medieval guilds; in its tranquil garden you can see dye plants that produced the typical medieval colours.

Little Hall   HISTORIC BUILDING
(www.littlehall.org.uk; Market Pl; adult/child £4/free; ⊙10am-1pm Mon, 1-4pm Tue-Sun Easter-Oct) Caramel-coloured, 14th-century Little Hall was once home to a successful wool merchant. Inside, the rooms of this medieval gem were restored to period splendour through the efforts of the Gayer-Anderson twins who made it their home in the 1920s and 1930s.

St Peter & St Paul   CHURCH
(www.lavenhamchurch.wordpress.com; Church St; ⊙8.30am-5.30pm) This late-Perpendicular structure seems to lift into the sky, with its beautifully proportioned windows, soaring flint tower and gargoyle waterspouts. Built between 1485 and 1530, it was one of Suffolk's last great wool churches, completed on the eve of the Reformation, and is now a lofty testament to Lavenham's past prosperity.

Guided Walks   WALKING
(📞01787-248207; adult/child £4.50/free; ⊙2.30pm Sat & 11am Sun Easter-Oct) Delve deep into the stories behind Lavenham's beautiful buildings on these guided strolls. They leave from the tourist office; there's no need to book.

🛏 Sleeping & Eating

Angel   HOTEL **££**
(📞01787-247388; www.cozypubs.co.uk; Market Pl; s £80-109, d £99-119; ⊙food noon-3pm & 6-10pm Mon-Fri, noon-10pm Sat, noon-8pm Sun; 🅿🛜) In Lavenham's oldest building, dark-green corridors lead to gorgeously renovated, large, bright, beam-scored rooms. The eclectic

decor in the bar (think theatrical spotlights and battered travelling trunks) echoes a menu that ranges confidently from English inn standards to superfood salads and hefty *a la carte* dishes (mains £12 to £24).

Brett Farm   B&B ££

(☑ 01787-248533; www.brettfarm.com; The Common; d £80) Totally tranquil Brett Farm is on the far fringe of Lavenham, a modern bungalow decked out in blue gingham and pine. But it's the setting that sells it – in its 11 hectares of fields and paddocks, alive with birdsong, tables and chairs sit in the shade beside a stream.

★ Swan   HOTEL £££

(☑ 01787-247477; www.theswanatlavenham.co.uk; High St; s/d/ste £100/140/315; P �) Marvellously medieval and utterly indulgent, the Swan might just spoil you in terms of other places to stay. Tasteful furnishings team oatmeal with olive and gentle reds, latticework of ancient wood climbs all around. The service is smooth, while the suites are simply stunning: expect soaring arched ceilings criss-crossed with beams.

The spa boasts a sauna, steam room and heated outdoor jacuzzi plunge-pool. Perhaps relax there before heading to the hotel's Airmen's Bar, so called because of the wall bearing the signatures of the US pilots based nearby during WWII.

Lavenham Priory   APARTMENT £££

(☑ 01787-247404; www.lavenhampriory.co.uk; Water St; 2-person apt per 2 nights/week £325/900; P �) A rare treat – sumptuously restored, two- to six-person, 13th-century cottages that steal your heart as soon as you walk in. The history-rich rooms feature crooked beams, carved oak staircases, wood-burning stoves and antique furniture. And a complimentary hamper full of local food.

★ Great House   MODERN BRITISH ££

(☑ 01787-247431; www.greathouse.co.uk; Market Pl; 3-course lunch/dinner £25/37; � noon-2.30pm Wed-Sun, 7-9.30pm Tue-Sat) Contrasting cultures combine so well here: traditional meets modern, East Anglian ingredients meet French cuisine. Which could see you eating roasted Norfolk (Gressingham) duck or braised Suffolk pork, then dispatching coffee and praline *millefeuille* or tangy morsels of French and Suffolk cheese.

They also do a great-value, two-course lunch (£20).

ℹ Information

Tourist Office (☑ 01787-248207; www.heartofsuffolk.co.uk; Lady St; � 10am-4.45pm Mar-Oct, 11am-3pm Sat & Sun Nov-Feb) Tucked in beside central Market Pl.

ℹ Getting There & Away

Bus 753 runs to Bury St Edmunds (£4, 30 minutes) hourly, Monday to Saturday.

Bury St Edmunds

POP 41,113

In Bury, the past is ever present. A centre of pilgrimage for centuries, its history-rich features include an atmospheric ruined abbey, handsome Georgian architecture and tranquil gardens. The chance to visit two breweries proves pretty tempting too.

◉ Sights

Abbey Gardens   RUINS

(Mustow St; � dawn-dusk) FREE Now a picturesque ruin in parkland behind the cathedral, Bury's once-mighty abbey still impresses despite the townspeople having made off with much of the stone after the dissolution of the monasteries. The walls are striking (especially on the west side), having crumbled and eroded into a series of fantastical shapes. Other highlights are the decorative Great Gate, the diminutive dovecote and the flower-filled gardens.

You enter the Abbey Gardens via one of two well-preserved old gates: the staunch mid-14th-century **Great Gate** is intricately decorated and ominously defensive, with battlements, a portcullis and arrow slits. The other entrance sits further up Angel Hill, where a gargoyle-studded early-12th-century **Norman Tower** looms.

Just beyond the Great Gate is a peaceful garden where the **Great Court** was once a hive of activity; further on a **dovecote** marks the only remains of the Abbot's Palace. Most impressive, however, are the remains of the western front, where the original abbey walls were burrowed into in the 18th century to make way for homes. The houses are still in use and look as if they've been carved out of the stone like caves. Nearby is **Samson Tower** and in front of it is a beautiful statue of St Edmund by Dame Elisabeth Frink (1976). The rest of the abbey spreads eastward like a ragged skeleton, with various lumps and pillars hinting at its immense size.

SUTTON HOO

Somehow missed by plundering grave robbers and left undisturbed for 1300 years, the hull of an enormous Anglo-Saxon ship was discovered at **Sutton Hoo** (NT; 01394-389700; www.nationaltrust.org.uk; Sutton Hoo, near Woodbridge; adult/child £8.20/4.10; 10.30am-5pm Easter-Oct, 10.30am-4pm Sat & Sun Nov-Easter; P) in 1939, buried under a mound of earth. The vessel was the final resting place of Raedwald, king of East Anglia until AD 625, and was stuffed with Saxon riches, reflecting a sophisticated culture that's conveyed beautifully in on-site displays.

The massive effort that went into Raedwald's burial gives some idea of just how important a man he was, while the elaborate nature of the treasures transformed perceptions of the era. Many of the original finds and a full-scale reconstruction of his ship and burial chamber can be seen in the visitor centre. The finest treasures, including the king's exquisitely crafted helmet, shields, gold ornaments and Byzantine silver, are displayed in London's British Museum, but replicas are on show here, along with an original prince's sword.

Paths encircle the 18 burial mounds (which look like bumps in the ground) that make up the 'royal cemetery'. You can only walk on to them as part of one-hour **guided tours** (adult/child £2.50/1.25), which provide a fascinating insight into the site. There's normally at least one tour a day; call to check for times. Sutton Hoo is 3 miles east of Woodbridge and 11 miles northeast of Ipswich off the B1083.

St Edmundsbury Cathedral   CATHEDRAL
(www.stedscathedral.co.uk; Angel Hill; requested donation adult/child £3/50p; 8.30am-6pm) The 45m-high tower of this cathedral was only completed in 2005 and is a vision in Lincolnshire limestone – its traditional Gothic-style construction conveys how many English cathedrals must have looked fresh from the stonemason's chisel. Most of the building is early 16th century, though the eastern end is post-1945. The overall effect is light and lofty, with a gorgeous hammer-beam roof and a striking sculpture of the crucified Christ by Dame Elisabeth Frink in the north transept. Free, 30-minute guided **tours** (11am Mon-Sat, May-Sep) provide an in-depth insight into the cathedral's heritage.

St Mary's Church   CHURCH
(www.wearechurch.net; Honey Hill; donation requested; 10am-4pm Mon-Sat, to 3pm Nov-Mar) St Mary's is one of the largest parish churches in England, and it contains the tomb of Mary Tudor – Henry VIII's sister and a one-time queen of France. Built around 1430, it's famous for its hammer-beam roof, which features a host of vampirelike angels swooping from the ceiling. A bell is still rung to mark curfew, as it was in the Middle Ages.

Greene King Brewery   BREWERY
(01284-714297; www.greeneking.co.uk; Westgate St; visitor centre free, tours £12; 10.30am-4.30pm Mon-Sat) They've been crafting some of England's favourite booze in this working brewery since 1799. Explore the town's 900-year-old brewing heritage in the visitor centre, then take a **tour** (2pm Mon-Fri, & 11am Wed-Sun, 12.30pm & 3.30pm Sat) that winds past the vats and pipes of the historic brewhouse, takes in sweeping town views from the roof, and heads to the Brewery Tap for tipples from the casks. The tours are popular – book.

Moyse's Hall   MUSEUM
(www.stedmundsbury.gov.uk/moyseshall; Cornhill; adult/child £4/2; 10am-5pm Mon-Sat, noon-4pm Sun) Set in an impressive 12th-century undercroft, Moyse's Hall's rarities include a locket containing some of Mary Tudor's hair and finds from Bury's ruined abbey. Displays chart the key episodes in the town's past, including the chilling Bury witch trials.

Theatre Royal   HISTORIC BUILDING
(NT; 01284-769505; www.theatreroyal.org; Westgate St) A real treat, Britain's only working Regency playhouse features ornate gilding, sweeps of boxes and a *trompe l'oeil* ceiling, all revealed on self-led (free) and guided (£6.50) front-of-house and backstage **tours**. These tend to be held between February and November; times vary – call to check.

🛏 Sleeping

★ **Chantry**   HOTEL **££**
(01284-767427; www.chantryhotel.com; 8 Sparhawk St; s/ste £75/145, d £115-130; P @) Pretty much everything feels right about the Chantry – a family-run town house that's

somewhere between a hotel and a B&B. Sash windows and cast-iron fireplaces signal its Georgian origins; French beds and walk-in showers add contemporary comfort; the convivial lounge and tiny bar help you feel at home.

Old Cannon B&B ££

(☎01284-768769; www.oldcannonbrewery.co.uk; 86 Cannon St; s/d £96/130) In these rooms run by a hip microbrewery, converted outhouses feature smart bedrooms with gentle checks and terracotta walls. Each room is named after one of their beers – you get a free bottle on arrival. If you like it, pop into the pub just next door.

Fox INN ££

(☎01284-705562; www.oldenglishinns.co.uk; 1 Eastgate St; d £119-150; P🖗) Slumber in these converted animal barns and be surrounded by carefully kept original features: bleached beams, weathered brick walls and even the livestock tethering rings. Painted wicker chairs and the odd chandelier add another layer of class. Cheap Sunday night deals mean prices can go as low as £85 for a double room.

Angel HOTEL ££

(☎01284-714000; www.theangel.co.uk; 3 Angel Hill; d £115-180, ste £330; P🖗) The more expensive rooms at this ivy-clad Georgian coaching inn are pretty special: expect luxury bathrooms, quirky mock-1700s furnishings (the odd bright-pink plastic chair) and suites with stand-alone copper baths. The cheaper rooms, although perfectly comfortable, have much less pizzazz.

🍴 Eating & Drinking

★**Pea Porridge** MODERN BRITISH ££

(☎01284-700200; www.peaporridge.co.uk; 29 Cannon St; mains £13-18; ☺noon-1.45pm Thu-Sat, 6.30-9pm Tue-Sat) Warmth, happy chatter and great aromas greet you at this intimate neighbourhood eatery. Imaginative dishes borrow from the cuisines of Italy and France – choose from salt cod, risotto, Normandy black sausage or Breckland muntjac loin – you're on to a winner any which way.

Their *menus du jour* (two/three courses £14.50/18.50) are a bargain.

Maison Bleue FRENCH £££

(☎01284-760623; www.maisonbleue.co.uk; 31 Churchgate St; mains £29-40; ☺noon-2pm & 7-9.30pm Tue-Sat) Settle into this elegant eatery for modern French cuisine that's su-

premely stylish and bursting with flavour. Creations might include roasted Norfolk black chicken, seared scallops, or caramelised Dingley Dell pork. The set menus (three-course lunch/dinner £25/37) are great value.

★**Old Cannon** PUB

(☎01284-768769; www.oldcannonbrewery.co.uk; 86 Cannon St; ☺11am-11pm) 🍺 In this microbrewery, gleaming mash tuns sit alongside the funky bar – try the Rusty Gun (ABV 4%) or the more feisty St Edmund's Head (5%). A fair bit of the ale goes into the food (served 8.30am to 9pm Monday to Saturday, to 3pm Sunday); perhaps sample some Gunner's Daughter sausages and bacon cured in stout.

Nutshell PUB

(www.thenutshellpub.co.uk; The Traverse; ☺11am-11pm Mon-Thu, to midnight Fri & Sat, noon-10.30pm Sun) Tiny benches, tiny tables, a ceiling smothered in international banknotes and a suspended pufferfish: it's amazing what they've squeezed into this thimble-sized, memorabilia-packed, timber-framed pub, recognised by the *Guinness Book of Records* as Britain's smallest.

If you're not squeamish, look out for the almost-mummified 400-year-old cat.

ℹ️ Information

Tourist Office (☎01284-764667; www. visit-burystedmunds.co.uk; The Apex Centre, Charter Sq; ☺10am-5pm Mon-Sat)

ℹ️ Getting There & Away

BUS

The main bus station is on St Andrew's St North.
Cambridge (£5, one hour, hourly Monday to Saturday) Stagecoach bus 11.
London Victoria (£12, 3½ hours, three daily) National Express.

TRAIN

The train station is a 10-minute walk north of the centre of town.
Cambridge £10, 40 minutes, hourly
Ely £10, 30 minutes, every two hours

Orford

POP 713

Secluded and seductive, the gorgeous village of Orford, 6 miles south of Snape Maltings, is well worth a detour. It's a laid-back spot dotted with pretty houses and dominated by a real rarity: curiously polygonal Orford Castle.

◉ Sights

Orford Castle   CASTLE
(EH; www.english-heritage.org.uk; Orford; adult/
child £6.90/4.10; ⊙10am-6pm Apr-Sep, to
5pm Oct, to 4pm Sat & Sun Nov-Mar; 🅿) This
12th-century structure has an innovative,
18-sided drum design with three square turrets. From the roof there are glorious views
of the nature reserve of Orford Ness.

Orford Ness   NATURE RESERVE
(NT; www.nationaltrust.org.uk; adult/child incl ferry
crossing £4/2; ⊙10am-5pm Tue-Sat Jul-Sep, 10am-
5pm Sat late Mar–Jun & Oct) Wind-whipped, remote Orford Ness is the largest vegetated
shingle spit in Europe and was once used as
a secret military testing ground; now it's a
nature reserve and is home to rare wading
birds, animals and plants. Ferries run from
Orford Quay: the last leaves at 2pm and returns from the reserve at 5pm. Spaces can be
limited – arrive early to reserve a seat.

✖ Eating

Pinney's   SEAFOOD £
(www.pinneysoforford.co.uk; The Quay; from £3.50;
⊙10am-4.30pm, to 4pm Sun) Sells own-smoked
seafood treats, including eel, prawns and
sardines, plus meats and just-caught fish.

★ Butley Orford Oysterage   SEAFOOD ££
(☎01394-450277;   www.pinneysoforford.co.uk;
Market Hill; mains £8-18; ⊙noon-2.15pm daily, plus
6.30-9pm daily Aug, Wed-Sat Apr-Jul, Sep & Oct, Fri
& Sat Nov-Mar) They catch and smoke much
of the superb seafood they serve here themselves; treats include Butley oysters and
garlic-laced griddled prawns. Expect metal
chairs, chalked-up menus, fabulous food
and bags of charm.

➊ Getting There & Away

Buses run to Melton (£2.20, 30 minutes, two
buses daily Monday to Saturday), with regular
connections from there to Aldeburgh and Ipswich.

Aldeburgh
POP 3225

The time-warped coastal town of Aldeburgh
(*orld*-bruh) is one of the region's most charming. Its picturesque streets and sweeping
shingle beach are lined with pastel-coloured
houses, independent shops, art galleries and
ramshackle fresh-fish kiosks. Its connections
with composer Benjamin Britten and two
festivals might also draw you to the town.

◉ Sights

Moot Hall   MUSEUM
(www.aldeburghmuseum.org.uk; Market Cross Pl;
adult/child £2/free; ⊙noon-5pm Jun-Aug, 2.30pm-
5pm Apr, May, Sep & Oct) Displays on fishing,
shipbuilding, coastal defences and Regen-
cy-era tourism set in an intricately carved,
timber-framed, 16th-century house.

Scallop   SCULPTURE
(near Thorpe Rd car park) Maggi Hambling's
sculpture commemorates Aldeburgh's links
with 20th-century composer Benjamin Britten, who spent much of his life in the town.
With 4m of inscribed, scallop shell–shaped
steel, its beachside setting has proved controversial locally. It's a short stroll north of
town along the seafront.

✦✦ Festivals & Events

Aldeburgh Festival   MUSIC
(www.aldeburgh.co.uk; ⊙Jun) Founded by local
composer Benjamin Britten in 1948, this
exploration of classical music is one of East
Anglia's biggest, taking in new, reinterpreted
and rediscovered pieces, and visual arts.

**Aldeburgh
Food & Drink Festival**   FOOD & DRINK
(www.aldeburghfoodanddrink.co.uk; ⊙late Sep) A
two-day celebration of Suffolk produce and
top-class cooking.

⌇ Sleeping & Eating

★ Ocean House   B&B ££
(☎01728-452094;   www.oceanhousealdeburgh.
co.uk; 25 Crag Path; s £50, d £100-120, apt per week
£1050) You are just seven paces (count them)
from the beach at Ocean House, and many
of the rustic-chic bedrooms directly overlook
the surging sea. The five-person self-catering
apartment comes with homely kitchen and
pint-sized balcony, while the top-floor double is a true delight: water views on three
sides and a sitting room with a baby grand.

Dunan House   B&B ££
(☎01728-452486; www.dunanhouse.co.uk; 41 Park
Rd; d £90-100, f £105-115; 🅿 🛜) Evidence of the
artist owners' efforts are everywhere: bright
abstracts, self-portraits and pottery galore.
Vivid walls alternate between red, orange
and lemon. Vintage books and battered travelling chests lie around, while the top-floor
family suite even has binoculars for zoomed-
in estuary views.

Fish & Chip Shop
FISH & CHIPS £

(www.aldeburghfishandchips.co.uk; 226 High St; mains £5-6; ☺noon-2pm Tue-Sun, 5-9pm Thu-Sat) Aldeburgh has a reputation for the finest fish and chips in the area; this is the best place to find out why.

★ Lighthouse
MODERN BRITISH ££

(☎01728-453377; www.lighthouserestaurant. co.uk; 77 High St; mains £11-19; ☺noon-2pm & 6.30-10pm; ✦) The new owner of this bright bistro was a waiter here for years and a sense of enthusiastic friendliness pervades the place. The food is special too; fish is a real strength, although meat-lovers might prefer guinea-fowl confit or a nice juicy steak. Be aware though, the local cod and seafood risotto is pretty hard to beat.

Regatta Restaurant
SEAFOOD ££

(☎01728-452011; www.regattaaldeburgh.com; 171 High St; mains from £10, 2/3 courses £15/18; ☺noon-2pm & 6-10pm) At Regatta, the fish is simple but good; from crispy salt and pepper squid, via their own-smoked salmon, to classic combinations such as halibut, samphire, new potatoes and salad.

❶ Information

Tourist Office (☎01728-453637; www. thesuffolkcoast.co.uk; 48 High St; ☺10am-3pm Mon-Sat, noon-4pm Sun)

❶ Getting There & Away

Bus 64/65 runs hourly Monday to Saturday to Ipswich (£7, 1½ hours), where you can make connections to the rest of the region.

Southwold

POP 1090

Southwold's reputation as a well-heeled holiday getaway has earned it the nickname 'Kensington-on-Sea', after the upmarket London borough, and its lovely sandy beach, pebble-walled cottages, cannon-dotted clifftop and rows of beachfront bathing huts are undeniably picturesque. It's all attracted many artists, including JMW Turner, Charles Rennie Mackintosh, Lucian Freud and Damien Hirst.

◉ Sights & Activities

Adnams
BREWERY

(☎01502-727225; www.adnams.co.uk; Adnams Pl; tours £12; ☺2-4 tours daily Mar-Sep) Spend an hour touring the high-tech kit inside this

Victorian brewery, indulge in a 30-minute tutored tasting, then select a free bottle of beer to take home. Book.

You can also now be shown around the Adnams gin distillery. Those under 18 can't go on the tours.

Seafront & Pier
AREA

(www.southwoldpier.co.uk; ☺pier 9am-5pm, to 8pm Fri-Sun) FREE Southwold's shore-front is its main attraction. Amble along the promenade, admire the squat 19th-century lighthouse then drop by the 190m pier, first built in 1899 and recently reconstructed. Its Under the Pier Show (☺10am-6pm, to 8pm Fri-Sun) sports a kooky collection of handmade amusement machines combining daft fun with political satire.

Coastal Voyager
BOATING

(☎07887 525082; www.coastalvoyager.co.uk; Blackshore, Southwold Harbour) Trips include a 30-minute high-speed blast around the bay (adult/child £26/13), a leisurely 3½-hour cruise up the Blyth Estuary (£30/15) and a three-hour voyage to Scroby Sands (£40/20) to see a seal colony and wind farm.

★☆ Festivals & Events

Latitude Festival
ART

(www.latitudefestival.co.uk; Henham Park; ☺Jul) An eclectic mix of music, literature, dance, drama and comedy set in a country estate.

Ways with Words
LITERATURE

(www.wayswithwords.co.uk; ☺Nov) Talks and readings by big-name authors in venues around town.

⌯ Sleeping & Eating

Home@21
B&B ££

(☎01502-722573; www.homeat21.co.uk; 21 North Pde; d £99-125; ☎) The sea-view bedrooms here are splendid: plenty of space, cosy furnishings and big windows overlooking Southwold's pier and shore. The back-facing rooms are less striking but still perfectly sweet.

The life-size plaster 'dancing girl' in the sunny guest lounge tends to prompt a smile.

★ Sutherland House
HOTEL £££

(☎01502-724544; www.sutherlandhouse.co.uk; 56 High St; d £90-199; P☎) Past guests at this former mayor's residence include a future James II and the Earl of Sandwich. They'd probably approve of the present appearance: pargeted ceilings, exposed beams and free-standing baths – it's top-quality, luxurious heritage-chic.

Supper time (mains £16 to £20; noon to 2pm and 7pm to 9pm, closed Monday) sees prime local ingredients transformed by flourishes such as bouillabaisse sauce, dill crackers and microherbs.

Swan HOTEL £££
(☑ 01502-722186; www.adnams.co.uk; Market Sq; s £115-125, d £185-255; P🛉🐾) It's a boon for beer lovers – an entire hotel owned by Southwold brewery giant Adnams. A £4-million refurbishment is bringing this venerable inn bang up to date. Expect vivid colours and contemporary bathrooms alongside plenty of 17th-century elegance. In the bar, staff are just itching to serve you a beer brewed right next door.

Coasters MODERN BRITISH ££
(☑ 01502-724734; www.coastersofsouthwold. co.uk; 12 Queen St; mains £10-22; ⏱noon-2.30pm & 6-9pm) Punchy flavours and rich ingredients are the mainstay of this intimate bistro, where a wide-ranging menu skips nimbly from whole crab and Stilton glazed beef to Dingley Dell Suffolk pork sausages with mustard mash.

❶ Information

Tourist Information (☑ 01502-523442; www. eastsuffolk.gov.uk/visitors; North Green; ⏱10am-1pm & 2-5pm Mon-Sat, 11am-4pm Sun) Southwold's tourist office has closed; this information point is inside the town library.

❶ Getting There & Away

Services are limited. Bus 146 runs to Norwich (£4, 1½ hours, hourly Monday to Saturday). For services south, including to Aldeburgh, catch bus 88A to Halesworth (£2.70, 30 minutes, hourly Monday to Saturday) and continue from there.

NORFOLK

Big skies, sweeping beaches, windswept marshes, meandering inland waterways and pretty flint houses combine to great effect in Norfolk. They say the locals have 'one foot on the land, and one in the sea' and you're never far from water here, whether it's beside the windmill-framed rivers of the tranquil Norfolk Broads or the wide, birdlife-rich sands of the shore. Inland, the bustling city of Norwich offers a fine castle and cathedral, a lively market and some truly excellent places to sleep and eat.

❶ Getting Around

Norwich is the transport hub. Train connections include those to London Liverpool St (£20, two hours, two per hour).

Traveline (www.travelineeastanglia.org.uk) details bus routes. One of the most useful is the frequent **Coasthopper Bus** (www.coast-hopper.co.uk), which hugs the shore on its route between Cromer and King's Lynn.

Norwich

POP 132,512

The affluent and easygoing city of Norwich (*norr*-ich) is a rich tapestry of meandering alleys liberally sprinkled with architectural jewels – spoils of the city's medieval wool boom. A magnificent cathedral and impressive Norman castle bookend the city centre; in between, crooked half-timbered buildings line quiet lanes. Thriving markets and a large student population enhance the city's relaxed vibe. Add quick access to the Broads and Norfolk's beaches, and you have an excellent base from which to explore.

◉ Sights

★**Norwich Cathedral** CATHEDRAL
(www.cathedral.org.uk; The Close; donations requested; ⏱7.30am-6pm) Norwich's most impressive landmark is a magnificent Anglican cathedral. Its barbed spire soars higher than any in England except Salisbury's, while the size of its cloisters is second to none. Highlights include the mesmerising ceiling and striking modern features of the **Hostry**, where high-tech displays explore the cathedral's past. The one-hour **guided tours** (donation requested, hourly Monday to Saturday, 11am to 3pm) are an engaging way to find out more.

Work started on the cathedral in 1096 and it remains one of the finest Anglo-Norman abbey churches in the country. The sheer size of its nave is striking, but its most renowned feature is the superb Gothic rib vaulting added in 1463. Among the spidery stonework are 1200 sculpted roof bosses depicting Bible stories. Together they represent one of the finest achievements of English medieval masonry.

Similar bosses can be seen in closer detail in the cathedral's remarkable, two-storey **cloisters**. Built between 1297 and 1430, they are unique in England and were originally built to house a community of about 100 monks.

Norwich

Norwich

◎ Top Sights
1	Museum of Norwich at the Bridewell	B3
2	Norwich Castle	B3
3	Norwich Cathedral	C2

◎ Sights
| 4 | Tombland & Elm Hill | C2 |

⊕ Activities, Courses & Tours
| | Ghost Walks | (see 14) |
| 5 | Guided Walks | B3 |

⊟ Sleeping
| 6 | 38 St Giles | A3 |

| 7 | Gothic House | B1 |
| 8 | St Giles House | A3 |

⊗ Eating
9	Bishops	B3
10	Grosvenor Fish Bar	A3
11	Library	B3
	Mustard	(see 1)
12	No 12	C4
13	Roger Hickman's	A3

◉ Drinking & Nightlife
| 14 | Adam & Eve | D1 |
| 15 | Birdcage | B3 |

Above the bronze font (which came from a nearby chocolate factory), look out for *Censing Angel* (2012) – a suspended celestial figure woven out of willow branches by sculptor Joy Whiddett, trailing the words 'peace', 'hope' and 'love'.

Outside the cathedral's eastern end is the grave of the WWI heroine Edith Cavell, a Norfolk-born nurse who was executed for helping hundreds of Allied soldiers escape from German-occupied Belgium. The handsome cathedral close also contains the old chapel of King Edward VI School (where naval hero Admiral Nelson was educated). Today's students make up the choir, which performs in services.

Tombland & Elm Hill
AREA

Leafy Tombland, near Norwich Cathedral, is where the market was originally located ('tomb' is an old Norse word for empty, hence space for a market). From there, follow Princes St to reach Elm Hill, Norwich's prettiest street, with its medieval cobblestones, crooked timber beams and doors, intriguing shops and tucked-away cafes.

★ Museum of Norwich at the Bridewell
MUSEUM

(www.museums.norfolk.gov.uk; Bridewell Alley; adult/child £5.50/4.40; ⊙10am-4.30pm Tue-Sat) Best be on your best behaviour: 14th-century Bridewell is a former house of correction, a 'prison for women, beggars and tramps'. Displays here explore Norwich's prominence as England's second city in the Middle Ages and its 19th-century industrial heritage. You can also play games in a 1950s parlour, listen to shoe workers' memories, and watch films in a pocket-sized cinema. Look out too for the eccentric, snake-proof boot.

★ Norwich Castle
MUSEUM

(www.museums.norfolk.gov.uk; Castle Hill; adult/child £8.80/7; ⊙10am-4.30pm Mon-Sat, 1pm-4.30pm Sun) Crowning a hilltop overlooking central Norwich, this massive, 12th-century castle is one of England's best-preserved examples of Anglo-Norman military architecture. Its superb **interactive museum** crams in lively exhibits on Boudica, the Iceni, the Anglo-Saxons and the Vikings. Perhaps the best bit though is the atmospheric keep itself with its graphic displays on grisly punishments meted out in its days as a medieval prison. Twice-daily **guided tours** (adult/child £3.50/2.80) run around the battlements and creepy dungeons.

Sainsbury Centre for Visual Arts
GALLERY

(www.scva.ac.uk; University of East Anglia; ⊙10am-6pm Tue-Fri, to 5pm Sat & Sun) FREE The region's most important centre for the arts is housed in the first major public building by renowned architect Norman Foster. Its eclectic collections include works by Picasso, Moore, Degas and Bacon, and are displayed beside curios from Africa, the Pacific and the Americas.

The gallery is in the University of East Anglia's grounds, 2 miles west of the city centre. To get there take bus 25, 22 or 26.

Tours

Ghost Walks
WALKING

(☑07831 189985; www.ghostwalksnorwich.co.uk; adult/child £7/5; ⊙2-3 per week mid-Apr–Dec) A lively immersion in Norwich's haunted history; the tours depart from the Adam & Eve pub (p382) on Bishopsgate at 7.30pm. There's no need to book.

Guided Walks
WALKING

(☑01603-213999; www.visitnorwich.co.uk; adult/child £5/1.50; ⊙11am or 2pm, 2-12 per week Easter-Oct) Art-nouveau Norwich, Georgian dandies and 1000 years of history are among the themes for these 1½-hour guided strolls. Run by the tourist office (p382), many leave from the Forum Centre, where the office is based; booking is advised.

🛏 Sleeping

Gothic House
B&B ££

(☑01603-631879; www.gothic-house-norwich.com; King's Head Yard, Magdalen St; s/d £65/95; 🅿🛜) Step through the door here and be whisked straight back to the Regency era. Original panelling, columns and cornices border the swirling stairs; fresh fruit and mini-decanters of sherry sit in elegant bedrooms that are studies in olive green, lemon yellow and duck-egg blue.

Wedgewood House
B&B ££

(☑01603-625730; www.wedgewoodhouse.co.uk; 42 St Stephens Road; d £80-90; 🅿🛜) The vibrant throws, contemporary prints, central location and parking all appeal at this homely B&B. But it's the breakfasts that really shine: home-baked bread, homemade yoghurt and no fewer than 10 jams and marmalades concocted by the owner – the rhubarb and ginger and the pink grapefruit and lemon are particularly zingy.

No 15
B&B ££

(☑01603-250283; www.number15bedandbreakfast.co.uk; 15 Grange Rd; s/d £55/75; 🛜) 🍽 The breakfasts at this vegetarian B&B are packed with treats: organic eggs, veggie sausages, artisan-baked walnut bread and grilled halloumi cheese. The furnishings are low allergy, but high on style – expect sanded wooden furniture, soft lights and bright fabrics. It's a mile west of the centre; bus 25 runs nearby.

★ 38 St Giles
B&B £££

(☑01603-662944; www.38stgiles.co.uk; 38 St Giles St; s/ste £95/245, d £130-160; 🅿🛜) At boutique 38 St Giles it seems everything gleams –

HAUNTED BLICKLING HALL

Largely remodelled in the 17th century for Sir Henry Hobart, James I's chief justice, **Blickling Hall** (NT; www.nationaltrust.org.uk; Blickling; adult/child £12.65/6.80; ☉house noon-5pm Wed-Mon Easter-Oct, grounds 11am-4pm Wed-Sun; P) began life in the 11th century as a manor house and bishop's palace. The grand Jacobean state rooms are stuffed with fine Georgian furniture, pictures and tapestries; the plaster ceiling in the Long Gallery is spectacular. The estate's vast parklands are criss-crossed with cycling and walking routes.

In 1437 the isolated house was claimed by the Boleyn family and passed through the generations to Thomas, father of Anne Boleyn. Anne was executed by her husband Henry VIII in 1533, who opted to have her beheaded. It's said that on the anniversary of her death a coach drives up to the house, drawn by headless horses, driven by headless coachmen and containing the queen with her head on her lap.

Blickling Hall is 15 miles north of Norwich off the A140.

from the highly polished floorboards to the aged cherry-red sofas. Mustard yellow and rich rugs add another layer of charm, while breakfast time brings local and organic meats and eggs, plus home-baked bread.

St Giles House
HOTEL £££
(☎01603-275180; www.stgileshousehotel.com; 41 St Giles St; d/ste £130/220; P ☎) There's more than a whiff of art nouveau about luxurious St Giles House; built in 1919, it teams a grand entrance hall with an ornate facade. Period flourishes echo on into bedrooms that are full of bold patterns and fluid curves – the spa, bistro and cocktail terrace are rather splendid too.

✗ Eating

Grosvenor Fish Bar
FISH & CHIPS £
(www.fshshop.com; 28 Lower Goat Lane; mains from £5; ☉11am-7.30pm Mon-Sat) At this groovy chippy-with-a-difference, chips come with fresh cod goujons, sea-bass wraps come with spicy mango salsa and a 'Big Mack' is crispy mackerel fillet tucked into a bread roll. Take away or chow down on the benches inside.

Mustard
CAFE £
(www.mustardcoffeebar.co.uk; 3 Bridewell Alley; snacks/mains £2/7; ☉8am-5pm Mon-Sat; ☎) You'll find a suitably bright-yellow colour scheme at this funky, student-friendly cafe set on the site of the original Colman's Mustard shop. Quality dishes delight in being homemade (think warm pitta stuffed full of halloumi and roasted peppers) and include rarities such as chorizo Scotch eggs. They even roast their own coffee beans.

Bishops
MODERN BRITISH ££
(☎01603-767321; www.bishopsrestaurant.co.uk; 8 St Andrew's Hill; lunch/dinner 2 courses £15/29; ☉noon-2.30pm & 6-9.45pm Tue-Sat) The unusual, the unexpected and Norfolk ingredients are the mainstays of menus at Bishops. Sample smoked eel with horseradish, pigeon Wellington or slow-braised Suffolk pork belly. Then satisfy your sweet tooth with a mocha fondant and salted-caramel ice cream.

Library
BRASSERIE ££
(☎01603-616606; www.thelibraryrestaurant.co.uk; 4a Guildhall Hill; mains £12-20; ☉noon-2.30pm & 6-10pm Mon-Sat, noon-4pm Sun) The chef here has a penchant for grilling over woodsmoke; those flavours infuse everything from chicken, lamb and beef to fennel seeds. It's a hit, as is the setting – with Victorian bookcases lining the walls of what was once a library, dining here has a clublike feel.

No 12
BISTRO ££
(www.number12norwich.org; 12 Farmers Ave; mains £7-15; ☉noon-3pm & 5-8.30pm Mon-Sat, noon-3pm Sun) Lounge music plays, heather-hued tartan covers the walls, beams sit above beige-leather bar stools: it sounds weird but it works. Food ranges from light lunch standards to truffle-infused risotto and beef *bourguignon*.

★ Roger Hickman's
MODERN BRITISH £££
(☎01603-633522; www.rogerhickmansrestaurant.com; 79 Upper St Giles St; dinner 2/3/7 courses £36/45/60; ☉noon-2.30pm & 7-10pm Tue-Sat) Understated elegance is everywhere here: pale floorboards, white linen and unobtrusive service. Dishes might include venison with figs, monkfish with octopus, or pork-cheek terrine –

flair, imagination and a simple dedication to quality run right through. The lunches (two/three courses £20/25) are a cracking deal.

Drinking & Nightlife

★ Birdcage
PUB

(www.thebirdcagenorwich.co.uk; 23 Pottergate; ⏰11am-midnight; 📶) Formica tables, chilled tunes, cupcakes and cocktails make this beatnik drinking den a one-of-a-kind delight. Drop by for a Bums Life Drawing session (yes, really) and classy nibbles; or ferry in fish and chips from the shop over the lane.

Adam & Eve
PUB

(Bishopsgate; ⏰11am-11pm Mon-Sat, noon-10.30pm Sun) Norwich's oldest-surviving pub has been slaking thirst since 1249, when the cathedral builders used to drop by. Tiny, with a sunken floor and part-panelled walls, it attracts a mixed band of regulars, choristers and ghost hunters, drawn by the fine malt whiskies and real ales.

ℹ️ Information

Tourist Office (☎01603-213999; www.visit-norwich.co.uk; Millennium Plain; ⏰9.30am-5.30pm Mon-Sat, plus 10.30am-3.30pm Sun mid-Jul–mid-Sep) Inside the Forum Centre.

ℹ️ Getting There & Away

AIR

Norwich International Airport (www.norwichinternational.com) is 4 miles north of town. Connections go to Amsterdam, Aberdeen, Edinburgh, Exeter and Manchester year-round; there are also summer flights to Spain and the Channel Islands.

BUS

The **bus station** (Queen's Rd) is 400m south of the castle. Follow Red Lion St into St Stephen's St and then turn left on to Surrey St. **National**

ℹ️ COASTHOPPER BUS

➡ The **Coasthopper Bus** (www.coasthopper.co.uk) runs from Cromer to King's Lynn; stops include Cley, Blakeney, Wells, Holkham and Burnham Deepdale.

➡ Services are frequent from April to September; less so the rest of the year.

➡ Single fares start at £1.40; passes are also available (one/three/seven days £9.50/20/33).

Express (www.nationalexpress.com) and **First** (www.firstgroup.com) are among the operators:

Cromer Bus X44; £3.60, one hour, hourly

King's Lynn Bus X1; £9, 1½ hours, hourly

London Victoria £10, three hours, every two hours

CAR

Norwich has free parking at six Park & Ride locations. Buses (£3.50) run to the city centre up to every 15 minutes from around 7am to 7pm, Monday to Saturday.

TRAIN

The train station is off Thorpe Rd, 600m east of the castle.

Cambridge £17, 1¼ hours, hourly

Ely £12, one hour, twice hourly

London Liverpool St £20, two hours, two per hour

Cromer

POP 7949

The once-fashionable Victorian resort of Cromer is a relaxed mix of old-school English seaside resort and appealing fishing port. Here, brightly painted houses line narrow lanes dotted with nonchain shops. Its main attractions remain sweet-tasting Cromer crab, the atmospheric pier and an appealing stretch of pebbly shore.

◉ Sights

Henry Blogg Museum
MUSEUM

(Lifeboat Museum; www.rnlicromer.org.uk; The Gangway; ⏰10am-5pm Tue-Sun Apr-Sep, to 4pm Oct-Mar) **FREE** Tap out a message in Morse and spell your name in semaphore flags – hands-on gizmos add to the appeal of this excellent museum, as do the well-told tales of brave sea rescues and the WWII lifeboat sitting proudly inside.

Felbrigg Hall
HISTORIC BUILDING

(NT; www.nationaltrust.org.uk; Felbrigg; adult/child £9.90/4.70; ⏰11am-5pm Sat-Wed Mar-Sep, to 4pm Oct; 🅿) An elegant Jacobean mansion boasting a fine Georgian interior and splendid facade, as well as gorgeous walled gardens and an orangery. It's 2 miles southwest of Cromer, off the B1436

🛏️ Sleeping & Eating

★ Red Lion
INN ££

(☎01263-514964; www.redlioncromer.co.uk; Brook St; s £63-95, d £115-140, ste £150-180; 🅿📶) Coloured floor tiles, wooden banisters and stained glass signal this seafront inn's 18th-century heritage; stylish, sea-themed rooms bring it right up to date. All bedrooms come with baths, cafetière coffee and fresh milk – the pick is the suite (room 7), where you can see the sea from both the balcony and the tub. The cosy, flint-walled, sea-view bar is the ideal spot to down a pint.

★ **Davies** SEAFOOD £
(7 Garden St; crab £3.50-6; ⊙ 8.30am-5pm Mon-Sat, 10am-4pm Sun Apr-Oct, 8.30am-4pm Tue-Sat Nov-Mar) Less a fish shop, more a local institution – at Davies the crab is caught by its own day boat (the *Richard William*) and is boiled, cracked and dressed on-site. Other treats include cockles, mussels and homemade pâté; the mackerel and horseradish one has quite a kick.

Rocket House CAFE £
(www.rockethousecafe.co.uk; The Gangway; mains £5-10; ⊙ 9am-4pm Mon-Fri, 10am-5pm Sat & Sun) Set right on the seafront, Rocket House delivers an airy interior and a balcony that almost overhangs the waves. Light dishes include ploughman's with Norfolk Dapple and Binham Blue cheese, locally smoked mackerel salad, and their renowned Cromer crab platter.

They're also open on summer Saturday evenings (6pm to 9.30pm from mid-May to September); it's best to book.

❶ Getting There & Away

Trains run to Norwich (£7, 45 minutes, hourly). The **Coasthopper Bus** (www.coasthopper. co.uk) shuttles west along the coast to King's Lynn, roughly every half-hour in summer.

Cley-next-the-Sea

POP 450

As the name suggests, the sleepy village of Cley (pronounced 'cly') huddles beside the shore. Here, a cluster of pretty cottages surrounds a photogenic windmill, and bird-rich marshes fan out all around.

◉ Sights

Cley Marshes NATURE RESERVE
(www.norfolkwildlifetrust.org.uk; near Cley-next-the-Sea; adult/child £5/free; ⊙ dawn-dusk; ▣) 🏊 One of England's premier birdwatching sites, Cley Marshes has more than 300 resident bird species, plentiful migrants and a network of walking trails and bird hides amid its golden reeds.

Even if you're not into birdwatching, don't miss the (free) cafe-cum-visitor centre where seats and telescopes line up beside vast picture windows with panoramic reserve views. This is birdwatching for softies; sip a latte while enjoying zoomed-in images of marsh harriers.

🛏 Sleeping & Eating

★ **Cley Windmill** B&B £££
(☎ 01263-740209; www.cleymill.co.uk; High St; d £160-200, apt per week £570; ▣) With the kind of wonky walls you'd expect from a circular, 18th-century agricultural building, Cley Windmill is packed with character. Rooms are named after their former functions (the crazy-shaped Barley Bin is gorgeous), and many look out directly over reed-filled salt marshes. A sweet, four-person self-catering cottage sits just next door.

George INN £££
(☎ 01263-740652; www.thegeorgehotelatcley. co.uk; High St; d £120-345) The George may be an age-old English inn, but the style is all contemporary north-Norfolk chic. Sure-footed design sees bare floorboards and feature fireplaces teamed with upcycled armchairs and quirky chests of drawers. Opt for a room overlooking the marshes for mesmerising views of wind-ruffled reeds.

★ **Picnic Fayre** DELI £
(www.picnic-fayre.co.uk; High St; ⊙ 9am-5pm Mon-Sat, 10am-4pm Sun) A deli to ditch the diet for, crammed full of imaginative versions of English picnic classics – pork pies with chorizo, sausages smothered with sweet chill sauce, and home-baked lavender bread. Plus gooey homemade fudge and Portuguese custard tarts. Yum.

Cley Smokehouse DELI £
(www.cleysmokehouse.com; High St; ⊙ 9.30am-4.30pm) Flavour-packed, home-smoked fish, shellfish and cured meats.

❶ Information

Visitor Centre (www.norfolkwildlifetrust. org.uk; Cley Marshes; ⊙ 10am-5pm Apr-Oct, to 4pm Nov-Mar) Here, seats and telescopes line up beside vast picture windows with panoramic views of the bird reserve. There's a cafe too.

EXPLORING THE NORFOLK BROADS

Why Should I Wish to Visit a Swamp?

These vast wetlands were formed when the rivers Wensum, Bure, Waveney and Yare flooded the big gaping holes inland, which had been dug by 12th-century crofters looking for peat. They comprise fragile ecosystems and, protected as a national park, are home to some of the UK's rarest plants and birds – the appeal to birdwatchers and naturalists is obvious. Apart from that, if you've ever envisioned yourself captaining your own boat and living afloat, there are 125 miles of lock-free waterways to explore. Or if paddling a canoe and losing yourself in the hypnotic lapping of water away from the rest of humanity appeals, there's plenty of scope for that, too.

What Is There to See and Do that Doesn't Involve Water?

Museum of the Broads (☑ 01692-581681; www.museumofthebroads.org.uk; The Staithe, Stalham; adult/child £5/2.50; ☺ 10am-4pm Easter-Oct) Five miles north of Potter Heigham off the A149, this museum features fine boats and colourful displays on the local marshmen, their traditional lifestyles, peat extraction and modern conservation. You can ride on a steam launch too.

Toad Hole Cottage (How Hill; ☺ 10.30am-5pm Mon-Sat Apr-Oct) FREE The life of Fen dwellers is revealed at this tiny cottage, which shows how an eel-catcher's family lived and the tools they used to work surrounding marshes.

Bewilderwood (www.bewilderwood.co.uk; Hornig Rd, Hoveton; adult/child £15.50/13.50; ☺ 10am-5.30pm Easter-Oct) A forest playground for children and adults alike, with zip wires, jungle bridges, tree houses and old-fashioned outdoor adventure involving plenty of mud, mazes and marsh walks.

St Helen's Church (Ranworth; ☺ 9am-5pm) The Broads' most impressive ecclesiastical attraction is this 14th-century church, known locally as the 'Cathedral of the Broads'. It features a magnificent painted medieval rood screen and a 15th-century *antiphoner* – a rare illustrated book of prayers.

Bure Valley Steam Railway (www.bvrw.co.uk; Aylsham; adult/child return £13/6.50; ☺ 2-6 trains daily Apr-Oct; ℙ) Steam buffs will love this train, which puffs along 9 miles of narrow-gauge tracks between Aylsham and Wroxham. You can make the return trip by boat.

Blakeney

POP 801

The pretty village of Blakeney was once a busy fishing and trading port before its harbour silted up. These days it offers an inviting seafront walk lined with yachts, and boat trips out to a 500-strong colony of common and grey seals that live, bask and breed on nearby Blakeney Point.

🌾 Tours

Bishop's Boats   BOATING
(☑ 01263-740753; www.bishopsboats.com; Blakeney Quay; adult/child £12/6; ☺ 1-4 daily Apr-Oct) Hour-long trips to see the seals at Blakeney Point; the best time to come is between June and August when the common seals pup.

Beans Seal Trips   BOATING
(☑ 01263-740505; www.beansboattrips.co.uk; Morston Quay; adult/child £12/6; ☺ 1-4 daily Apr-Oct) Boat journeys out to the hundreds-strong Blakeney Point seal colony. The departure point is Morston Quay, 1½ miles east of Blakeney.

🛏 Sleeping & Eating

Kings Arms   INN ££
(☑ 01263-740341; www.blakeneykingsarms.co.uk; Westgate St; s/d £60/80; ℙ) Sweet, simple, old-style rooms (expect bright colours and pine) in a pub that's so welcoming you might not want to leave. Order some substantial pub grub (their fish and chips are famous; mains from £8 to £15; meals served noon to 9pm) then, for some great theatre gossip, ask landlady Marjorie about her career on the stage.

How Do I Get Around?

Driving around the Broads is missing the point and pretty useless. The key centres of Wroxham, on the A1151 from Norwich, and Potter Heigham, on the A1062 from Wroxham, are reachable by bus from Norwich and Great Yarmouth, respectively. From there, you can either take to the water or to the trails.

Exploring by Boat

Launches range from large cabin cruisers to little craft with outboards; they can be hired for anything from a couple of hours' gentle messing about on the water to week-long trips. Tuition is given. Depending on boat size, facilities and season, an eight-person boat costs from around £18 per hour, from £68 for four hours and from £114 for one day. Week-long rental ranges from around £660 to £1330, including fuel and insurance. **Broadland Day Boats** (☑ 01692-667659; www.dayboathire.com; Ludham) hires boats and canoes. **Barnes Brinkcraft** (☑ 01603-782625; www.barnesbrinkcraft.co.uk; Wroxham) does short- and long-term rental, while **Broads Tours** (☑ 01603-782207; www.broads.co.uk; Wroxham) lets out boats by the day and week, and runs boat trips. **Blakes** (☑ 0345-498 6184; www.blakes.co.uk) arranges all manner of boating holidays.

Exploring by Canoe

Paddlers can find canoes for hire for £27 to £35 per day; **Rowan Craft** (www.rowancraft.com; Geldeston) and **Waveney River Centre** (www.waveneyrivercentre.co.uk; Burgh St Peter) are recommended. **Mark the Canoe Man** (www.thecanoeman.com; half-day trips £25) knows the secrets of the Broads and arranges guided trips to areas the cruisers can't reach (from £25), as well as offering canoe and kayak hire, weekend camping canoe trails (two nights £65) and two-day canoe and bushcraft trips (adult/child £175/125).

Exploring by Foot & Bike

A web of walking trails stretches across the region, including the 61-mile **Weavers' Way**, which stretches from Cromer to Great Yarmouth, taking in some choice landscapes along the way. The Broads' highest point, How Hill, is just 12m above sea level, so superhero levels of fitness are not required. The section between Aylsham and Stalham is open to bicycles.

Broadland Cycle Hire (www.norfolkbroadscycling.co.uk) and **Martha's Cottage** (www.marthascottagecyclehire.co.uk; Barnby) are among the bicycle-rental firms. Expect to pay between £12 and £18 per day; child seats and tandems are also available.

Moorings MODERN BRITISH ££
(☑ 01263-740054; www.blakeney-moorings.co.uk; High St; mains £7-22; ☺ 10.30am-9pm Tue-Sat, to 5pm Sun) Perfectly pitched fish dishes have won this bistro a loyal following – try the roast monkfish with squid and tangy harissa, or keep it simple with avocado-dotted sweet local crab; the classic meat and veg dishes are tempting too. Mustn't-miss puddings include plum crumble with custard, and a gooey treacle sponge.

Wells-next-the-Sea

POP 2165

Charming Wells excels at both land and sea. Rows of attractive Georgian houses and flint cottages snake down to a boat-lined quay; to the north sits a vast golden beach, backed by pine-covered dunes.

◉ Sights

Wells Beach BEACH
(ⓟ) Fringed by dense pine forests and undulating dunes, Wells' sandy shore stretches for miles to the west, with brightly coloured beach huts clustering beside the water and wooden steps leading up into the woods. It's all tucked away at the end of a mile-long road; you can walk, drive or hop on a miniature train. Parking is available.

Wells & Walsingham Railway HERITAGE RAILWAY
(www.wellswalsinghamrailway.co.uk; Stiffkey Rd; adult/child return £9/7; ☺ 4-5 trains daily Apr-Oct; ⓟ) The longest 10.25in narrow-gauge railway in the world puffs for 5 picturesque

miles from Wells to the village of Little Walsingham, the site of religious shrines and the ruined but still impressive Walsingham Abbey.

🛏 Sleeping & Eating

Wells YHA
HOSTEL £

(☑ 0845-371 9544; www.yha.org.uk; Church Plains; dm £20-26, d £49-65; P) Set in the heart of town in an ornately gabled early-20th-century church hall.

★ Old Customs House
B&B ££

(☑ 01328-711463; www.eastquay.co.uk; East Quay; s £80-90, d £100-110; P 🛜) The stately but comfy feel here comes courtesy of worn wood panels, alcoves full of books and gorgeous creek views. Choose from the snug Captain's Quarters or a grand four-poster room. Breakfasts see you discussing what you'd like with the owner – perhaps goats-cheese omelette or smoked haddock.

Wells Beach Cafe
CAFE £

(Wells Beach; mains £4; ⊙10am-5pm Easter-Oct, to 4pm Nov-Easter; 🛜) This locals' favourite rustles up bacon baps, homemade chilli and decadent hot chocolates. Outside sits a corral of picnic tables; inside there's a wood-burning stove for when the wind whips in.

Crown
BRITISH ££

(☑ 01328-710209; www.crownhotelnorfolk.co.uk; The Buttlands; mains £7-20; ⊙noon-2.30pm & 6-9pm) Renowned for robust dishes made from locally sourced ingredients.

ℹ Information

Tourist Office (☑ 01328-710885; www.visitnorthnorfolk.com; Staithe St; ⊙10am-4pm Mon-Sat, to 1pm Sun Apr-Oct)

Holkham

Little Holkham may have only two big assets, but both are highly impressive: a grand country-house estate and a spectacular stretch of sandy shore.

◉ Sights

★ Holkham National Nature Reserve
WILDLIFE RESERVE

(www.holkham.co.uk; parking per 2hr/day £3/6.50) Beach, dunes, salt marsh, grazing marsh, pinewoods and scrub – a high number of habitats pack into 37-sq-km Holkham Reserve. It's easily accessed from the car park at Lady Anne's Dr in Holkham village. From there, ribboning pathways lead through forests, via bird hides and on to an expansive, pristine shore.

Holkham Hall & Estate
HISTORIC BUILDING

(www.holkham.co.uk; Holkham; adult/child £15/7.50, parking £3; ⊙noon-4pm Sun, Mon & Thu Apr-Oct; P) Holkham Hall is the ancestral seat of the original Earl of Leicester and still belongs to his descendants. A severe Palladian mansion, it's largely unadorned on the outside but the interior is sumptuous, with a red velvet–lined saloon, copies of Greek and Roman statues, the luxurious Green State Bedroom, and fluted columns in the Marble Hall. It's set in a vast deer park (open 9.30am to 5pm daily), which was designed by William Kent.

Burnham Deepdale

POP 800

Walkers flock to this lovely coastal spot, with the tiny village of Burnham Deepdale (which merges seamlessly into Brancaster Staithe) strung along a rural road. Edged by the beautiful Norfolk Coast Path, surrounded by beaches and reedy marshes, alive with bird life and criss-crossed by cycling routes, Burnham Deepdale is also the base for a whole host of water sports.

◉ Sights

Titchwell Marsh
NATURE RESERVE

(RSPB; www.rspb.org.uk; Titchwell; parking £5; ⊙dawn-dusk; P) Tiny Titchwell has a big asset: the Titchwell Marsh Nature Reserve, where marshland, sandbars and lagoons attract vast numbers of birds. Summer brings marsh harriers, avocets, terns and nesting bearded tits; in winter you'll see more than 20 species of wading birds and countless ducks and geese.

Titchwell Marsh is some 2 miles west of Burnham Deepdale.

🛏 Sleeping & Eating

Deepdale Farm
HOSTEL £

(☑ 01485-210256; www.deepdalefarm.co.uk; Burnham Deepdale; dm £25-30, d £30-60, camping £10-20; P @ 🛜) For backpackers it really doesn't get much better than Deepdale Farm: spick-and-span en-suite dorms and doubles in converted stables, a homely well-equipped kitchen, a barbecue area, and a cosy lounge warmed by a wood-burning stove. Campers

WORTH A TRIP

THE QUEEN'S SANDRINGHAM ESTATE

Both monarchists and those bemused by the English system will have plenty to mull over at Sandringham (www.sandringhamestate.co.uk; Sandringham; adult/child £14/7; ☉11am-4.45pm Easter-Sep, to 3.45pm Oct; P), the Queen's country estate. It's set in 25 hectares of beautifully landscaped gardens, and wandering around sumptuous reception rooms regularly used by the royals reveals a wealth of objets d'art and glinting gifts from European and Russian royal families.

Sandringham was built in 1870 by the then Prince and Princess of Wales (who later became King Edward VII and Queen Alexandra) and the house's features and furnishings remain much as they were in Edwardian days. The stables, meanwhile, now house a flag-waving museum filled with diverse royal memorabilia. The superb vintage-car collection includes the very first royal motor from 1900, and the buggy in which the Queen Mother would bounce around race tracks.

There are guided tours (£3.50, 11am and 2pm Wednesday and Saturday) of the gardens. The shop stocks organic goodies produced on the vast estate. Sandringham is 6 miles northeast of King's Lynn off the A149. Bus 11 runs from King's Lynn (£4.70, 30 minutes, hourly).

get to go glam in a tepee or yurt, or casual in a good old tent.

★ **Titchwell Manor**   HOTEL £££
(☎ 01485-210221; www.titchwellmanor.com; Titchwell; d £125-235; P @ 🛜) Dreamy Titchwell Manor is a swish, oh-so-contemporary hotel set in a grand Victorian house; expect lovingly upcycled furniture and bold colours in chic rooms ranging from those beside the herb-garden courtyard to ones with corking sea views. The stylish restaurant and terrace set the scene for modern tapas and acclaimed à la carte dishes (mains £12 to £31; food served from noon to 2pm and 6pm to 9pm).

★ **White Horse**   MODERN BRITISH ££
(☎ 01485-210262; www.whitehorsebrancaster. co.uk; Main Rd, Brancaster Staithe; mains £13-22; ☉11am-9pm; P 🛜) The White Horse gastropub's imaginative menu more than sets it apart from its competitors. Choose from seafood and tapas-style dishes including brown crab custard, cod and dill, scorched bass or tempura Brancaster oysters. The bedrooms (doubles £140 to £230) embody the seaside with their subtle colour schemes.

🛈 Information

Tourist Office (☎ 01485-210256; www.deepdalefarm.co.uk; Burnham Deepdale; ☉8am-11am & 2-8pm Mon-Sat, to 7pm Sun)

King's Lynn & Around
POP 12,200

Once one of England's most important ports, King's Lynn was long known as 'the Warehouse on the Wash'. In its heyday, it was said you could cross from one side of the River Great Ouse to the other by simply stepping from boat to boat. Something of the salty port-town tang can still be felt in old King's Lynn, with its cobbled lanes, vibrant weekly markets, and narrow streets flanked by old merchants' houses.

◉ Sights

King's Lynn Minster   CHURCH
(St Margaret's Church; www.stmargaretskingslynn. org.uk; St Margaret's Pl; ☉8am-6pm) The patchwork of styles here includes Flemish brasses and a remarkable 17th-century moon dial, which tells the tide, not the time. You'll find historic flood-level markings by the west door.

Opposite, the 1421 Trinity Guildhall has an attractive stone facade.

Stories of Lynn   MUSEUM
(www.kingslynntownhall.com; Saturday Market Pl; adult/child £5/3.50; ☉10am-4.30pm) A £2-million revamp has seen archive sources converted into multimedia exhibits, so you'll experience the stories of local seafarers, explorers, mayors and ne'er-do-wells. It's all set in the 15th-century Guildhall and parts of the town's Georgian jail, where you get to roam around the cells.

Lynn Museum   MUSEUM
(www.museums.norfolk.gov.uk; Market St; adult/child £4.20/3.20; ☉10am-5pm Tue-Sat, noon-4pm

Sun) High points here include a large hoard of Iceni gold coins and the Seahenge Gallery, which tells the story behind the construction and preservation of the early Bronze Age timber circle, which survived for 4000 years, despite being submerged on the Norfolk shoreline – it was only discovered in 1998. The exhibits include a life-size replica of the monument, which you can stand inside.

True's Yard
MUSEUM

(www.truesyard.co.uk; North St; adult/child £3/1.50; ⊙10am-4pm Tue-Sat) Housed in two restored fishers' cottages – the only remainder of the district's once bustling, fiercely independent fishing community – this museum explores the lives and traditions of the fisherfolk, who were packed like sardines into cottages such as these.

Castle Rising
CASTLE

(www.castlerising.co.uk; Castle Rising; adult/child £4.50/3; ⊙10am-6pm Apr-Oct, to 4pm Wed-Sun Nov-Mar; P) There's something bordering on ecclesiastical about the beautifully embellished keep of this castle, built in 1138 and set in the middle of a massive earthwork – unsurprisingly it shares stonemasons with some of East Anglia's finest cathedrals. Castle Rising was also once the home of Queen Isabella, who (allegedly) arranged the gruesome murder of her husband, Edward II. It's 4 miles northeast of King's Lynn. Bus 11 runs here (£2, 15 minutes, hourly).

Houghton Hall
HISTORIC BUILDING

(www.houghtonhall.com; near King's Lynn; adult/child £15/5; ⊙11am-4.30pm Wed, Thu & Sun May–late Sep; P) Built for Britain's first de-facto prime minister, Sir Robert Walpole, in 1730, the grand Palladian-style Houghton Hall is worth seeing for the ornate staterooms alone, where stunning interiors overflow with gilt, tapestries, velvets and period furniture. The surrounding grounds, home to 600 deer, and the 2-hectare walled garden are dotted with contemporary sculptures, making for grand but pleasant rambling. Houghton Hall is just off the A148, 13 miles east of King's Lynn.

Festivals & Events

King's Lynn Festival
CULTURAL

(www.kingslynnfestival.org.uk; ⊙Jul) East Anglia's most important cultural gathering, with a diverse mix of music, from medieval ballads to opera, as well as literary talks.

Sleeping & Eating

★ Bank House
BOUTIQUE HOTEL ££

(☎01553-660492; www.thebankhouse.co.uk; King's Staithe Sq; s £85-129, d £115-220; P🖥) There's so much to love here: a quayside setting, gently funky decor and luxury bathrooms all make this stylish Georgian town house pretty hard to turn down. The best bedroom (the expansive Captain's Room) is gorgeous; but even cheaper, river-view 'Cosy' is still charming.

Downstairs, the hip purple and pink themed brasserie (dishes £5 to £14; served noon to 8.30pm) serves seriously good modern British food.

Market Bistro
MODERN BRITISH ££

(☎01553-771483; www.marketbistro.co.uk; 11 Saturday Market Pl; mains £14-22; ⊙noon-2pm & 6-8.30pm Tue-Sat) A commitment to Norfolk ingredients has won this friendly, family-run eatery heaps of fans. Seasonal specials might include succulent local asparagus with quail egg or pan-fried haddock with pickled cockles and seaweed sauce. A combo of their small dishes (£3 to £4) is ideal for a light lunch.

ℹ Information

Tourist Office (☎01553-763044; www.visitwestnorfolk.com; Purfleet Quay; ⊙10am-5pm Mon-Sat, noon-5pm Sun Apr-Sep, to 4pm Oct-Mar) Arranges guided heritage walks (adult/child £5/1) at 2pm Tuesdays, Fridays and Saturdays between May and October.

ℹ Getting There & Away

Bus The **Coasthopper** (www.coasthopper.co.uk) bus runs from King's Lynn along the shore all the way to Cromer (£8.60, 2½ hours).

Train There are hourly trains from Cambridge (£8, 50 minutes) via Ely, and also from London King's Cross (£24, 1¾ hours).

Birmingham, the Midlands & the Marches

Includes ➡

Birmingham 392
Warwickshire. 402
Staffordshire. 412
Worcestershire 414
Herefordshire 417
Shropshire. 421
Nottinghamshire . . . 436
Lincolnshire. 443
Northamptonshire. . . 450
Leicestershire 451
Derbyshire. 457
Peak District 463

Best Places to Eat

➡ The Cross (p406)

➡ Hammer & Pincers (p457)

➡ Hercules Revived (p456)

➡ Chatsworth Estate Farm Shop Cafe (p474)

Best Places to Sleep

➡ Warwick Castle Accommodation (p405)

➡ George Hotel (p449)

➡ Brownsover Hall (p411)

➡ Hotel Maiyango (p454)

Why Go?

If you're searching for quintessential English landscapes – green valleys, chocolate-box villages of wonky black-and-white timbered houses, woodlands steeped in legend such as Nottinghamshire's Sherwood Forest, and stately homes that look like the last lord of the manor just clip-clopped out of the stables – you'll find it here in the country's heart.

You'll also find the relics of centuries of industrial history, exemplified by the World Heritage–listed mills of Ironbridge and the Derwent Valley, and by today's dynamic cities, including Britain's second-largest, Birmingham: a canal-woven industrial crucible reinvented as a cultural melting pot and creative hub, with striking 21st-century architecture and red-hot restaurant, bar and nightlife scenes. Beyond them are tumbling hills where the air is so clean you can taste it. Walkers and cyclists flock to these areas, particularly the Peak District National Park and the Shropshire Hills, to vanish into the vastness of the landscape.

When to Go

➡ February or March (depending when Lent falls) sees the wonderful chaos of Shrovetide football in Ashbourne.

➡ Shakespeare takes a back seat to contemporary wordsmiths at Stratford's Literary Festival in April/May.

➡ Foodies will want to head to Ludlow's famous Food and Drink Festival in September.

➡ From May to September, the Long Mynd and Stiperstones Shuttle runs from the Carding Mill Valley near Church Stretton to the villages atop the Long Mynd heath and moorland plateau in the glorious Shropshire Hills.

➡ June to September is the best season for walking and cycling in the Peak District.

Birmingham, the Midlands & the Marches Highlights

1 Library of Birmingham (p392) Surveying the buzzing city of Birmingham from its library's rooftop 'secret garden'.

2 Peak District (p463) Hiking, cycling or driving through England's inaugural national park.

3 Woolsthorpe Manor (p447) Contemplating the apple tree that inspired Isaac Newton's theories on gravity at his former home.

4 Ironbridge Gorge (p424) Museum-hopping in the birthplace of the Industrial Revolution.

5 King Richard III: Dynasty, Death & Discovery (p451) Learning about King Richard III's life, death and the extraordinary discovery of his remains in Leicester.

6 Stratford-upon-Avon (p406) Visiting the Bard's schoolroom and reimagined town house before catching a Royal Shakespeare Company performance in his Tudor home town.

7 Morgan Motor Company (p416) Touring Great Malvern's venerable car factory and taking a car for a spin through the surrounding hills.

8 Burghley House (p448) Wandering the opulent halls and grand gardens of this stately Stamford home.

Activities

Famous walking trails such as the Pennine Way and Limestone Way struggle across the Peak District's hills, while challenging cycling routes include the Pennine Cycleway. The Marches, tracing the English–Welsh border, are also wonderful walking territory.

Watersports abound at Rutland Water; Hereford and Ironbridge Gorge offer canoeing and kayaking.

Getting There & Around

Birmingham Airport (BHX; 0871 222 0072; www.birminghamairport.co.uk) and **East Midlands Airport** (EMA; 0871 271 0711; www. eastmidlandsairport.com), near Derby, are the main air hubs.

There are excellent rail connections to towns across the Midlands. **National Express** (08717 818181; www.nationalexpress.com), at Birmingham Coach Station, and local bus companies connect larger towns and villages, though services are reduced in the low season. For general route information, consult **Traveline** (0871 200 2233; www.travelinemidlands.co.uk). Ask locally about discounted all-day tickets.

BIRMINGHAM

POP 1,073,045

Regeneration, renewal and grand-scale construction continue at a breathless pace in Britain's second-largest city. A state-of-the-art library, gleaming shopping centre atop revitalised New St Station, beautifully restored Victorian buildings and a tram-line extension through the city's heart are just some of the recently completed initiatives of its Big City Plan. These come hot on the heels of the striking Mailbox and Bullring shopping malls and iconic Selfridges building's 'bubblewrapped' facade. Work has started on the first phase of the centrepiece Paradise development's new hotels, public spaces, and glitzy residential and commercial buildings, due to open in 2018.

Alongside Birmingham's picturesque canals, waterside attractions, outstanding museums and galleries is an explosion of gastronomic restaurants, cool and/or secret cocktail bars and craft breweries. Thriving legacies of the city's industrial heritage include its Jewellery Quarter, Cadbury manufacturing plant and former custard factory turned cutting-edge creative hub. 'Brum', as it's dubbed by locals, is buzzing.

History

Birmingham was first mentioned in the Domesday Book of 1086, where it was described as a small village, home to a handful of villagers and two ploughs, with a total value of £1. From these humble beginnings, Brum exploded into an industrial and mercantile hub, building its fortunes first on the wool trade and then on metalworking from the 16th century.

The Lunar Society brought together the leading geologists, chemists, scientists, engineers and theorists of the mid-18th century and Birmingham became the world's first industrialised town, attracting a tide of workers from across the nation.

In the mid-1800s enlightened mayors such as Joseph Chamberlain (1836–1914) cleaned out the slums and filled the centre with grand civic buildings. Later, WWII bombers and overzealous town planners took their toll, and swaths of the centre were demolished in a bid to transform Birmingham into 'Britain's Motor City'.

Recent years have seen an explosion of regeneration projects, with 21st-century landmarks appearing all over the city.

Sights

City Centre

Birmingham's grandest civic buildings are clustered around pedestrianised Victoria Square, at the western end of New St, dominated by the stately facade of Council House (Victoria Sq), built between 1874 and 1879. The square was given a facelift in 1993, with modernist sphinxes and a fountain topped by a naked female figure, nicknamed 'the floozy in the jacuzzi' by locals, overlooked by a disapproving statue of Queen Victoria.

To the west, Centenary Square is bookended by the art-deco Hall of Memory War Memorial, the International Convention Centre (ICC; Broad St) and Symphony Hall. There's a gleaming golden statue of Birmingham's Industrial Revolution leading lights Matthew Boulton, James Watt and William Murdoch. Centenary Sq's showpiece is the spiffing Library of Birmingham.

★ **Library of Birmingham**   LIBRARY
(www.libraryofbirmingham.com; Centenary Sq; ⊙ground fl 9am-9pm Mon & Tue, 11am-9pm Wed-Fri, 11am-5pm Sat, rest of bldg 11am-7pm Mon & Tue, to 5pm Wed-Sat;) Resembling a glittering

BIRMINGHAM IN TWO DAYS

Start off in the centre, dropping into the eclectic **Birmingham Museum & Art Gallery**. Walk west through Centenary Sq, stopping to check out the **Library of Birmingham** (p392) before reaching the Birmingham Canals. From here you can take a **canal cruise** (p397) or while away an afternoon at the **National Sea Life Centre** (p394) or **Ikon Gallery**. Dine that night at one of Birmingham's cutting-edge restaurants such as **adam's** (p399). On day two, indulge your inner shopaholic at the gleaming shopping malls of the **Bullring** (p401) and **Mailbox** (p401), which both have good options for lunch. In the afternoon, catch up on some social history at the museum **Birmingham Back to Backs**. After dark, kick off a pub crawl at the **Lost & Found** (p399).

stack of gift-wrapped presents, the Francine Houben–designed Library of Birmingham is an architectural triumph. Opened in 2013, it features a subterranean amphitheatre, spiralling interior, viewing decks and glass elevator to the 7th-floor 'secret garden' with panoramic views over the city. In addition to its archives, photography and rare-book collections (including Britain's most important Shakespeare collection), there are gallery spaces, 160-plus computers and a cafe. The British Film Institute Mediatheque provides free access to the National Film Archive.

Birmingham Museum & Art Gallery MUSEUM
(📞 0121-348 8038; www.birminghammuseums. org.uk; Chamberlain Sq; ⏰ 10am-5pm Sat-Thu, 10.30am-5pm Fri; 🚼) FREE Major Pre-Raphaelite works by Rossetti, Edward Burne-Jones and others are among the highlights of the delightful Birmingham Museum and Art Gallery's impressive collection of ancient treasures and Victorian art.

Birmingham Back to Backs HISTORIC BUILDING
(NT; 📞 0121-666 7671; www.nationaltrust.org.uk; 55-63 Hurst St; tours adult/child £7.85/4.55; ⏰ 1-5pm Tue-Thu, 10am-5pm Fri-Sun) Quirky tours of this cluster of restored back-to-back terraced houses take you through four working-class homes, telling the stories of those who lived here between the 1840s and the 1970s. Book ahead by phone for the compulsory guided tour.

For an even more vivid impression of what life was like here, you can book to stay in basic three-storey period cottages at 52 and 54 Inge St (doubles with wi-fi from £119). Guests receive a free Back to Backs tour.

Town Hall HISTORIC BUILDING
(📞 0121-780 3333; www.thsh.co.uk; Victoria Sq) Constructed in 1834 and styled after the Temple of Castor and Pollux in Rome, Birmingham's neoclassical Town Hall is now used as a venue for classical concerts and stage performances.

Birmingham Cathedral CATHEDRAL
(📞 0121-262 1840; www.birminghamcathedral. com; Colmore Row; entry by donation; ⏰ 8am-6.30pm Mon-Fri, 9am-5pm Sat & Sun) Dedicated to St Philip, this small but perfectly formed cathedral was constructed in a neoclassical style between 1709 and 1715. Pre-Raphaelite artist Edward Burne-Jones was responsible for the magnificent stained-glass windows.

Thinktank MUSEUM
(📞 0121-348 0000; www.birminghammuseums. org.uk; Millennium Point, Curzon St; adult/child £13/9.50; ⏰ 10am-5pm) A 10-minute walk northeast of the centre, surrounded by the footprints of vanished factories, the Millennium Point development incorporates this entertaining and ambitious attempt to make science accessible to children. Highlights include galleries on the past (Birmingham's industrial breakthroughs), present (how stuff works) and future, as well as an outdoor science garden and digital planetarium (included in the admission price).

◉ Birmingham Canals

During the industrial age, Birmingham was a major hub on the English canal network and today the city has more miles of canals than Venice. Narrow boats still float through the heart of the city, passing a string of glitzy wharfside developments.

Ikon Gallery GALLERY
(📞 0121-248 0708; www.ikon-gallery.org; 1 Oozells Sq; ⏰ 11am-5pm Tue-Sun) FREE Within the glitzy Brindley Pl development of banking offices and designer restaurants, a converted Gothic schoolhouse contains the

Birmingham

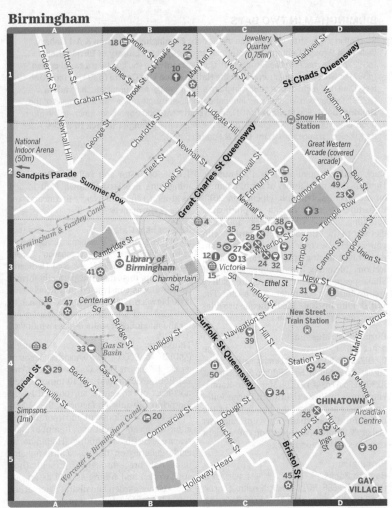

cutting-edge Ikon Gallery. Prepare to be thrilled, bemused or outraged, depending on your take on conceptual art.

National Sea Life Centre AQUARIUM
(☑0121-643 6777; www.visitsealife.com; 3a Brindley Pl; £17.50; ☺10am-5pm Mon-Fri, to 6pm Sat & Sun) The Sir Norman Foster–designed National Sea Life Centre is England's largest inland aquarium. Its tanks teem with exotic marine life including razor-jawed hammerhead sharks, turtles and otters. Prepurchase tickets online for fast-track entry and get discounts of up to 40% off walk-in rates. Book online

too for 15-minute behind-the-scenes tours (£1.50) offering access to otherwise out-of-bounds areas, and for one-hour feeding tours (£65 to £105; minimum age 12), feeding turtles, penguins or (if you're game) sharks.

◉ Jewellery Quarter

Birmingham has been a major jewellery player since Charles II acquired a taste for it in 17th-century France. The gentrifying Jewellery Quarter, three-quarters of a mile northwest of the centre, still produces 40% of UK-manufactured jewellery. Dozens of work-

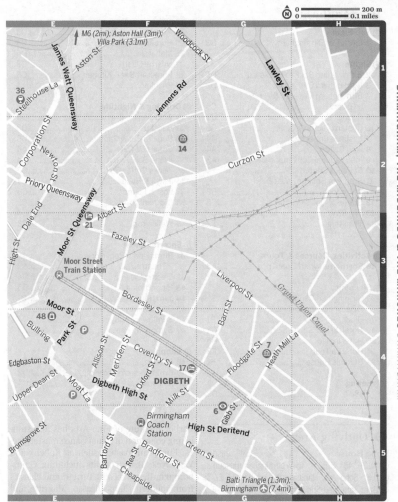

shops open to the public are listed in the free booklet *Jewellery Quarter: the Essential Guide,* available from tourist offices and local businesses, or visit www.jewelleryquarter.net.

Take the metro from Snow Hill or the train from Moor St to Jewellery Quarter station.

**Museum of the
Jewellery Quarter**   MUSEUM
(☑0121-348 8140; www.birminghammuseums.org. uk; 75 Vyse St; adult/child £7/3; ☺10.30am-5pm Tue-Sat) The Smith & Pepper jewellery factory is preserved as it was on its closing day in 1981 after 80 years of operation. Guided tours

lasting around one hour explain the long history of the trade in Birmingham and let you watch master jewellers at work. Entry to the temporary exhibition space and shop is free.

St Paul's Church   CHURCH
(www.stpaulsjq.church; St Paul's Sq; ☺10am-4pm Tue-Sat) St Paul's Sq is dominated by this beautiful 18th-century Georgian church, where 'Birmingham Brains' Matthew Boulton and James Watt came to pray. Free organ recitals take place on the first Thursday of the month from 1.15pm to 1.45pm (no reservations necessary).

Birmingham

◎ **Top Sights**
1 Library of Birmingham B3

◎ **Sights**
2 Birmingham Back to Backs D5
3 Birmingham Cathedral D2
4 Birmingham Museum & Art
 Gallery C3
5 Council House C3
6 Custard Factory G5
7 Eastside Projects G4
8 Ikon Gallery A4
9 International Convention Centre A3
10 St Paul's Church B1
11 Statue of Boulton, Watt &
 Murdoch B3
12 Statue of Queen Victoria C3
13 The River C3
14 Thinktank F2
15 Town Hall C3

⦿ **Activities, Courses & Tours**
16 Sherborne Wharf Boat Trips A3

⊟ **Sleeping**
17 Birmingham Central
 Backpackers F4
18 Bloc B1
19 Hotel du Vin C2
20 Hotel Indigo B5
21 Hotel La Tour E3
22 St Pauls House B1

⊗ **Eating**
23 1847 .... D2

24 Adam's C3
25 Bureau C3
26 Maharaja D5
27 Nosh & Quaff C3
28 Purecraft Bar & Kitchen C3
29 Pushkar A4

◎ **Drinking & Nightlife**
30 Arcadian Centre D5
31 Bacchus D3
32 Bodega Bar & Cantina C3
33 Canalside Cafe A4
34 Island Bar C4
35 Jake's Coffee Box C3
36 Jekyll & Hyde E1
37 Lost & Found C3
38 Old Joint Stock C3
39 Victoria C4
40 Wellington C3

◎ **Entertainment**
41 Birmingham Repertory
 Theatre A3
42 Electric Cinema D4
43 Hippodrome D5
44 Jam House B1
45 O2 Academy C5
46 Sunflower Lounge D4
47 Symphony Hall A3

⊡ **Shopping**
48 Bullring E4
49 Great Western Arcade D2
50 Mailbox C4

◉ Outlying Areas

Soho House   MUSEUM
(☏0121-348 8150; www.birminghammuseums.
org.uk; Soho Ave, Handsworth; adult/child £7/3;
⊙11am-3pm Wed-Sun Easter-Oct) Situated 1.5
miles northwest of Birmingham's Jewellery
Quarter, Soho House is where industrialist
Matthew Boulton lived from 1766 to 1809.
Among the restored 18th-century chambers is the dining room where Boulton and
members of the esteemed Lunar Society met
to discuss their world-changing ideas during the greatest technological leap forward
since the invention of the wheel. From Priory
Queensway, take bus 74 or 75 to the Lozells
stop, from where it's a five-minute walk.

★ Barber Institute of Fine Arts   GALLERY
(☏0121-414 7333; http://barber.org.uk; University
of Birmingham, Edgbaston; ⊙10am-5pm Mon-Fri,
11am-5pm Sat & Sun) FREE At the University of
Birmingham, 3 miles south of the centre, the
Barber Institute of Fine Arts has an astonishing collection of Renaissance masterpieces; European masters such as Rubens and
Van Dyck; British greats including Gainsborough, Reynolds and Turner; and classics
from modern titans Picasso, Magritte and
others. Trains run from New St to University
station, from where it's a 10-minute walk.

Cadbury World   MUSEUM
(☏0844 880 7667; www.cadburyworld.co.uk; Linden
Rd, Bournville; adult/child £16.75/12.30; ⊙11am-
4.30pm, hours vary) The next best thing to Willy
Wonka's chocolate factory is Cadbury World,
4 miles south of Birmingham. It aims to educate visitors about the history of cocoa and
the Cadbury family, but sweetens the deal
with free samples, displays of chocolate-mak-
ing machines, and chocolate-themed rides.
Opening hours vary; bookings are essential
at peak times. Last entry is 90 minutes before closing. Frequent trains run from Bir-

mingham New St Station to Bournville, from where it's a signposted 10-minute walk.

Aston Hall
HISTORIC BUILDING

(☑ 0121-348 8100; www.birminghammuseums. org.uk; Trinity Rd, Aston; house adult/child £8/3, grounds free; ☺ 11am-4pm Tue-Sun Easter-Oct) Set in lush grounds 3 miles north of the centre, this well-preserved hall was built in extravagant Jacobean style between 1618 and 1635. The sumptuous interiors are full of friezes, moulded ceilings and tapestries. Trains run from New St to Aston station, then it's a 10-minute walk.

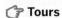 Tours

Big Brum Buz
BUS TOUR

(☑ 0121-427 2555; www.birmingham-tours.co.uk; day ticket adult/child £12/5; ☺ 10.30am, 12.30pm & 2.30pm Sat & Sun May-Sep) Hop-on/hop-off bus tour visiting the Jewellery Quarter, Golden Mile, Edgbaston and Digbeth.

Sherborne Wharf Boat Trips
BOAT TOUR

(☑ 0121-455 6163; http://sherbornewharf.co.uk; Sherborne St; adult/child £8/6; ☺ 11.30am, 1pm, 2.30pm & 4pm Easter-Nov, Sat & Sun Dec-Easter) Nostalgic narrow-boat cruises from the quayside by the International Convention Centre.

Festivals & Events

Frankfurt Christmas Market & Craft Fair
CHRISTMAS MARKET

(www.birmingham.gov.uk/frankfurtmarket; ☺ mid-Nov–mid-Dec) Some 200 food, drink and craft stalls from Birmingham's twin city in Germany and from local purveyors fill the centre during the UK's largest Christmas market from mid-November to mid-December.

Sleeping

Chains dominate Birmingham's hotel scene, which is aimed at business travellers, ensuring high weekday prices. Look out for cheap deals at weekends or for longer stays. Accommodation is often tight but 14 new hotels are now in the pipeline and due for completion over the coming years.

B&Bs are concentrated outside the centre in Acocks Green (to the southeast) or Edgbaston and Selly Oak (to the southwest).

Birmingham Central Backpackers
HOSTEL £

(☑ 0121-643 0033; www.birminghambackpackers. com; 58 Coventry St; dm/d/tr/q incl breakfast from £14/36/57/72; @ ☎) Despite the railway-bridge-right-next-door setting, Birmingham's purple and turquoise backpacker hostel is recommended for its convenience to the bus station and choice of clean, multicoloured dorms or Japanese-capsule-style pods. Excellent facilities include a lounge with DVDs and regular movie nights, a bar (note you can't BYO alcohol) and a self-catering kitchen.

★ Hotel La Tour
HOTEL ££

(☑ 0121-718 8000; http://hotel-latour.co.uk; Albert St; d from £119; ❋ ☎) Sunlight streams through floor-to-ceiling windows into the public areas and spacious rooms of this state-of-the-art independent hotel, purpose-built in 2012. Tech-savvy room features include digitally controlled 'do not disturb' signs and media hubs. There's a 24-hour gym and a swish Modern British restaurant, **Mr White's English Chophouse**, run by star chef Marco Pierre White.

St Pauls House
BOUTIQUE HOTEL ££

(☑ 0121-272 0999; www.saintpaulshouse.com; 15-20 St Paul's Sq; d from £119; P ❋ ☎) Opened in 2016, this independent addition to Birmingham's accommodation scene has 34 fresh, contemporary rooms with welcoming touches such as hot-water bottles in woollen covers. Upcycled decor in its hip bar and restaurant includes industrial-style ropes referencing the building's original use as a rope factory. The park-facing Jewellery Quarter location is a winner.

Hotel du Vin
BOUTIQUE HOTEL ££

(☑ 0121-794 3605; www.hotelduvin.com; 25 Church St; d from £124; ❋ @ ☎) Housed in the handsome Victorian precincts of the former Birmingham Eye Hospital, this red-brick beauty has real class, with wrought-iron balustrades, classical murals and seasoned charms. Art deco-inspired rooms have spectacular bathrooms; there's a spa and gym, a bistro with shabby-chic worn floorboards and a stellar wine list, plus a pub and lounge bar with comfy, duffed-up leather furniture.

Hotel Indigo
BOUTIQUE HOTEL ££

(☑ 0121-643 2010; www.hotelindigobirmingham. co.uk; The Cube, Wharfside St; d from £90; ☎ ❋) A stylish operation on the 23rd and 24th floors of the Mailbox's annex, The Cube, Hotel Indigo marries a handy location with snazzy amenities including a small swimming pool and great views from its 52 rooms (some with balconies). Panoramic vistas continue on the 25th floor from the **Marco Pierre White Steakhouse Bar & Grill** and **Laurent Perrier Champagne Bar**.

Bloc

HOTEL ££

(📞 0121-212 1223; www.blochotels.com; St Paul's, Caroline St; d from £75; ✲ 🛜) Located in the Jewellery Quarter, Bloc excels in sharp, contemporary pod design. Rooms are tiny but space is cleverly stretched: flatscreen TVs are built into walls; there's under-bed storage; and bathrooms are compact but with luxe shower heads. Book carefully: rooms come with window or without. Good online specials.

🍴 Eating

Dining options span cool cafes and cosy pubs to gastronomic extravaganzas, with dozens of innovative new openings every year. Inexpensive restaurants are scattered throughout Chinatown, on the southwestern side of the Bullring shopping mall.

Praza

INDIAN ££

(📞 0121-456 4500; http://praza.co.uk; 94-96 Hagley Rd, Edgbaston; mains £11-12, banquet menus £29-39; ⏰ 5-11.30pm Mon-Sat) The runaway success of Indian restaurant/cocktail bar Pushkar (p398) led the owners to open this sister restaurant in Edgbaston, with its own signature dishes (*nilgiri* – slow-cooked chicken in fragrant herb curry) and cocktails (Red Carpet, with Midori, cucumber, vodka, strawberries and cranberry juice). The monumental Grade II–listed Georgian mansion has *Great Gatsby*–style art-deco styling and two levels of dining.

Bureau

GASTROPUB ££

(📞 0121-236 1110; www.thebureaubar.co.uk; 110 Colmore St; mains £7-19.50, platters £12; ⏰ kitchen 10am-10pm Tue-Sat, to 8pm Sun & Mon, bar 10am-10.30pm Mon, to midnight Tue-Thu, to 1am Fri & Sat, to 8pm Sun) While this gleaming marble ex-office building dating from 1902 serves stupendous cocktails (such as hickory-smoked Bloody Marys), it's above all worth visiting for its food. Winning dishes include a duck Scotch egg (soft-boiled duck egg encased in confit of duck and a deep-fried breadcrumb shell, served in a nest of watercress with red-onion jam). Its roof terrace is a suntrap.

Purecraft Bar & Kitchen

GASTROPUB ££

(📞 0121-237 5666; www.purecraftbars.com; 30 Waterloo St; mains £11-18; ⏰ kitchen noon-10pm Mon-Sat, to 5pm Sun, bar 11am-11pm Mon-Thu, 11am-midnight Fri & Sat, noon-10pm Sun) Fabulous dishes created in the open kitchen of this craft-beer-lover's paradise come with suggested beer pairings. The menu changes monthly but might include Lawless Lager–battered fish and chips (with Veltins Pilsner); Brewer's Grain asparagus and broad-bean risotto (with Odell St Lupulin American Pale Ale); grilled plaice with beer-and-parsley butter and Jersey Royal new potatoes (with Purity Mad Goose).

Nosh & Quaff

AMERICAN ££

(📞 0121-236 4246; http://noshandquaff.co.uk; 130 Colmore Row; mains £10-18, whole lobster £25; ⏰ 11am-11pm) North American fare at this cavernous, uberhip venue spans gourmet burgers, hot dogs and slow-cooked, hickory-glazed ribs, plus sides such as charred corn on the cob and sweet-potato wedges with sour cream, but the star is the whole lobster flown in live from Canada and dressed with garlic and lemon-butter sauce. The rockin' bar serves great craft beers.

Pushkar

INDIAN ££

(📞 0121-643 7978; http://pushkardining.com; 245 Broad St; 2-/3-course lunch menus £11/14, mains £8-19; ⏰ noon-2.30pm & 5-11.30pm Mon-Fri, 5-11.30pm Sat, 5-11pm Sun) Classy north Indian and Punjabi cuisine is served up in this glass-fronted, white tableclothed, gold-trimmed dining room. The elegant presentation extends to boxed menus and serviette-wrapped naan bread as well as stunning cocktails. Lunch menus are an excellent deal. Its swanky spin-off, Praza (p398), in Edgbaston, is also superb.

1847

VEGETARIAN ££

(📞 0121-236 2313; www.by1847.com; 26 Great Western Arcade, Colmore Row; 2-/3-course menus £19.75/25.50; ⏰ noon-3pm & 5-10pm Mon-Fri, noon-10.30pm Sat, noon-8pm Sun; 🖉🖐) 🍃 Occupying two levels in a gorgeous, heritage-listed Victorian shopping arcade, this chic spot proves that vegetarian and vegan food can be cutting-edge, from starters such as mushroom and liquorice pâté, wild-mushroom cappuccino and pear and fennel confit to mains including cider-battered halloumi, and lush desserts such as passionfruit and chia crème brûlée, and spiced clotted cream. Kids' menus available.

Maharaja

INDIAN ££

(📞 0121-622 2641; www.maharajarestaurant.co.uk; 25 Hurst St; mains £6.75-11.25; ⏰ noon-2pm & 5.30-11pm Mon-Sat; 🖉) Impeccable service sets this intimate north Indian restaurant apart from its neighbours, as does the superior food. Creative starters, naan breads and a dish of the day keep the menu fresh; the homemade paneer (pillowy Indian cottage cheese) is exceptional.

★ Simpsons
MODERN BRITISH **£££**

(☑ 0121-454 3434; www.simpsonsrestaurant.co.uk; 20 Highfield Rd; menus lunch £35, dinner £55-85; ⊙ noon-2pm & 7-9pm Mon-Thu, noon-2pm & 7-9.30pm Fri & Sat, noon-4.30pm Sun; 🅿 🖶) It's worth the 2.5-mile journey southwest of the centre to this gorgeous Georgian mansion in leafy Edgbaston for sensational Michelin-starred menus (kids and vegetarians catered for). You can also stay in one of four luxurious bedrooms upstairs (from £110; Monday to Saturday only) or take an all-day cookery class (from £135 including three-course lunch, Saturdays). Reservations recommended.

Adam's
MODERN BRITISH **£££**

(☑ 0121-643 3745; www.adamsrestaurant.co.uk; New Oxford House, 16 Waterloo St; 3-course lunch menu £35, dinner menus £60-85; ⊙ noon-2pm & 7-9.30pm Tue-Sat) Michelin-starred restaurant Adam's has proved such a success story that it recently located to larger, ritzier premises and still wows with intricately prepared and presented flavour combinations such as venison with banana, shallots and red cabbage, purple broccoli with brown shrimp and Béarnaise sauce, or sea trout with morels, broad beans and oregano. Book well ahead.

🍷 Drinking & Nightlife

Like all British cities, Birmingham has plenty of chain pubs, but fantastic independents continue to spring up all over the city.

Nightlife hubs in Birmingham include Broad St (aka the 'golden mile' – some say for the prevalence of fake tan here) and Chinatown's **Arcadian Centre** (www.thearcadian.co.uk; Hurst St). Postindustrial Digbeth has alternative clubs and club events in and around the Custard Factory (p400).

★ Jake's Coffee Box
COFFEE

(off Colmore Row; ⊙ 7am-4pm Mon-Thu, 7am-3pm Fri, 8am-2pm Sat) A classic red British telephone box on a pedestrian laneway has been ingeniously repurposed as a tiny coffee bar, where Jake brews espressos, flat whites, Americanos, cappuccinos and lattes using Birmingham-roasted Quarterhorse beans. He also serves snacks including gourmet sausage rolls (pork, asparagus and black pepper; pork and wild boar), brownies, choc-chip cookies and carrot cake, plus occasional BBQs.

★ Jekyll & Hyde
PUB

(☑ 0121-236 0345; www.thejekyllandhyde.co.uk; 28 Steelhouse Lane; ⊙ noon-11pm Mon-Thu, to midnight Fri, to 1am Sat) Potent cocktails (or rather 'elixirs, concoctions and potions') at this trippy spot are served in sweets jars, watering cans, teapots and miniature bath-tubs – even a washbag (with rum-mint toothpaste and kaffir lime). Downstairs, Mr Hyde's emporium has a cosy drawing room and *Alice in Wonderland*–themed courtyard; upstairs is Dr Jekyll's Gin Parlour with more than 90 different gins.

Lost & Found
BAR

(http://the-lostandfound.co.uk; 8 Bennett's Hill; ⊙ 11am-11pm Mon-Thu, to 1am Fri & Sat, to 10pm Sun) Fictitious Victorian-era explorer/professor Hettie G Watson is the inspiration for the botanical-library theme of this bar in an 1869-built former bank. Inside the domed entrance, elevated seating is surrounded by plants, birdcages, books and maps, while a bookcase conceals the entrance to Hettie's 'secret emporium' bar (try your luck around 7.30pm on a Friday or Saturday).

Wellington
PUB

(www.thewellingtonrealale.co.uk; 37 Bennett's Hill; ⊙ 10am-midnight) The pastel wallpaper, timber bar and polished brass give the impression the Welly is frozen in time, but this specialist real ale pub has been recently spruced up and shelters a timber-decked roof terrace. Its 15 hand-pulled beers (and three ciders) include favourites from Black Country and Wye Valley as well as rare brews.

Bacchus
BAR

(☑ 0121-632 5445; www.nicholsonspubs.co.uk; Burlington Arcade, New St; ⊙ 11am-11pm Sun-Thu, to 1am Fri & Sat) Buried beneath the Burlington Arcade, this darkened drinking den has the ambience of a decadent underworld. Down a faux-marble-encased staircase, crumbling

LOCAL KNOWLEDGE

DIGBETH'S CREATIVE QUARTER

Just over a mile southeast of the centre, Digbeth's creative quarter centres on the **Custard Factory** (☑0121-224 7777; www.custardfactory.co.uk; Gibb St) , a hip art and design enclave set in the converted buildings of the factory that once churned out British favourite Bird's Custard. The open-plan space is now full of small galleries, quirky design boutiques, vintage-clothing outlets, skateboard shops and affordable, offbeat cafes. There's also a mini skate ramp and free ping-pong tables.

Check out the artist-run experimental gallery **Eastside Projects** (www.eastsideprojects.org; 86 Heath Mill Lane; ⊘noon-5pm Wed-Sat) nearby.

pillars and giant Grecian murals give way to soaring medieval-style stone arches, swords, suits of armour and candelabras.

Old Joint Stock PUB
(☑0121-200 1892; www.oldjointstocktheatre.co.uk; 4 Temple Row West; ⊘8am-11pm Mon-Fri, 9am-11pm Sat, 10am-5pm Sun; 🛜) A vast high-ceilinged temple of a pub, housed in a former bank and beloved by a high-spirited after-work crowd. Upstairs, an 80-seat theatre puts on plays and comedy shows.

Canalside Cafe CAFE
(☑0121-643 3170; 35 Worcester Bar, Gas St; ⊘9am-11pm Mon-Sat, to 10.30pm Sun) Narrow boats glide past the terrace of this 18th-century lock-keeper's cottage, where the low-ceilinged interior is strung with nautical paraphernalia and warmed by an open fire. Drop by for a cuppa, real ale or cider (or warming mulled cider in winter).

☆ Entertainment

Tickets for most Birmingham events can be purchased through entertainment megacorp **TicketWeb** (☑0333 321 9990; www.ticketweb.co.uk; ⊘phone lines open 9am-8pm Mon-Fri, 10am-4pm Sat & Sun). Free publications listing gigs and events include the excellent *Brum Notes* (www.brumnotes.com).

Live Music

The **Barclaycard Arena** (☑0121-780 4141; www.barclaycardarena.co.uk; King Edwards Rd), north of Brindley Pl, and the **National Exhi**bition Centre Arena (☑0121-780 4141; www.thenec.co.uk; North Ave; 🛜), near Birmingham Airport, host stadium-fillers from the world of rock and pop.

Sunflower Lounge LIVE MUSIC
(☑0121-632 6756; http://thesunflowerlounge.com; 76 Smallbrook Queensway; ⊘bar noon-1am Mon-Thu, to 2am Fri & Sat, to 11pm Sun) This quirky little indie bar matches a magnificent alternative soundtrack with a regular program of live gigs and DJ nights.

Jam House LIVE MUSIC
(☑0121-200 3030; www.thejamhouse.com; 3-5 St Paul's Sq; ⊘6pm-midnight Tue & Wed, to 1am Thu, to 2am Fri & Sat) Pianist Jools Holland was the brains behind this moody, smart-casual music venue (dress accordingly). Acts range from jazz big bands to famous soul crooners. Over 21s only.

O2 Academy LIVE MUSIC
(☑box office 0844 477 2000; www.academy-musicgroup.com/o2academybirmingham; 16-18 Horsefair, Bristol St; ⊘box office noon-4pm Mon-Sat) Birmingham's leading venue for big-name rockers and tribute bands as well as up-and-coming talent.

Symphony Hall CLASSICAL MUSIC
(☑0121-345 0600; www.thsh.co.uk; Broad St) The City of Birmingham Symphony Orchestra's official home is the ultramodern Symphony Hall. Shows also take place in the handsome auditorium at the Town Hall (p393).

Theatre & Cinema

Electric Cinema CINEMA
(www.theelectric.co.uk; 47-49 Station St; standard/deluxe seats £7.80/13.50) Topped by its art deco sign, this is the UK's oldest working cinema, operating since 1909. It screens mainly art-house films. Be waited upon in plush two-seater sofas or have a drink in the small bar (complete with an absinthe fountain).

Birmingham Repertory Theatre THEATRE
(☑0121-236 4455; www.birmingham-rep.co.uk; Centenary Sq) Founded more than a century ago, today 'the Rep' has three performance spaces: the Main House; the more experimental Door; and a 300-seat studio theatre presenting edgy drama and musicals, with an emphasis on contemporary work.

Hippodrome THEATRE
(☑0844 338 5000; www.birminghamhippodrome.com; Hurst St) Hosts the Birmingham Royal Ballet.

Sport

Birmingham has three football (soccer) clubs within striking distance: Birmingham City Football Club, West Bromwich Albion ('West Brom') and, most famously, Aston Villa Football Club, who play at **Villa Park** (☏ 0333 323 5353; www.avfc.co.uk; Trinity Rd, Witton; tours adult/child £15/10).

Shopping

Bustling markets sell fresh food and cheap imported clothes in the pedestrian precincts surrounding the Bullring.

Great Western Arcade   SHOPPING ARCADE
(www.greatwesternarcade.co.uk; btwn Colmore Row & Temple Row; ⊙ arcade 6.30am-10pm Mon-Sat, 10.50am-5.30pm Sun, shop hours vary) This glass-roofed, tiled-floored Victorian-era arcade is a jewel filled with mostly independent shops.

Mailbox   MALL
(www.mailboxlife.com; 61 Wharfside St; ⊙ mall 10am-7pm Mon-Sat, 11am-5pm Sun, shop hours vary) Birmingham's stylish canalside shopping experience, the redevelopment of the former Royal Mail sorting office, comes complete with designer hotels, a fleet of upmarket restaurants, the luxury department store Harvey Nichols and designer boutiques. Its super-snazzy metallic extension, The Cube, houses Marco Pierre White's **Steakhouse Bar & Grill** on the 25th floor.

Bullring   MALL
(www.bullring.co.uk; St Martin's Circus; ⊙ 10am-8pm Mon-Fri, 9am-8pm Sat, 11am-5pm Sun) Split into two vast retail spaces – the East Mall and West Mall – the Bullring has all the international brands and chain cafes you could ask for, plus the standout architectural wonder of Selfridges, which looks out over the city like the compound eye of a giant robot insect.

Information

As in most large cities, it's wise to avoid walking alone late at night in unlit areas. And as in most British cities, the centre, especially south of the Bullring and on and around Broad St, can be rowdy with revellers on weekend nights.

Digbeth bus station and its surrounds can be quite rough after dark.

Birmingham Children's Hospital (☏ 0121-333 9999; www.bch.nhs.uk; Steelhouse Lane) Has an accident and emergency department.

Heartlands Hospital (☏ 0121-424 2000; www.heartofengland.nhs.uk; Bordesley Green East) Located 4 miles east of the centre; has an accident and emergency department.

Heart of England Tourist Board (☏ 01905-887690; www.visitheartofengland.com)

Police Station (☏ emergency 999, nonemergency 101; www.west-midlands.police.uk; Steelhouse Lane)

Tourist Office (☏ 0844 888 3883; www.visitbirmingham.com; cnr Corporation & New Sts; ⊙ 9am-5pm Mon-Sat, 10am-4pm Sun) Kiosk with racks of info on activities, transport and sights.

Getting There & Away

AIR

Birmingham Airport (p392), 8 miles east of the centre, has direct flights to destinations around the UK and Europe as well as direct long-haul routes to Dubai, India, the USA and Canada.

Fast and convenient trains run regularly between New St and Birmingham International station (£3.60, 20 minutes, every 10 minutes). The station is linked to the terminal by the Air-Rail Link monorail (free; two minutes; frequent), which runs from 5.15am to 2am.

Alternatively, take bus 97 or 900 (£2.30, 30 minutes, up to two hourly) from Moor St Queensway, which run 24 hours.

A taxi from the airport to the centre costs about £30.

BUS

Most intercity buses run from **Birmingham Coach Station** (☏ 0871 781 8181; Mill Lane, Digbeth), but the X20 to Stratford-upon-Avon (£5.20, 1½ hours, up to 14 daily) also leaves from a more convenient stop on Carr's Lane, opposite Moor St Station.

National Express coaches link Birmingham with major cities across the country, including the following.

London Victoria £5 to £12.50, 2¾ hours, every 30 minutes

Manchester £4, three hours, 12 daily

Oxford £5, 2¼ hours, six daily

TRAIN

Most long-distance trains leave from New St Station, but Chiltern Railways runs to London Marylebone (£48, two hours, half-hourly) from Birmingham Snow Hill, and London Midland runs to Stratford-upon-Avon (£7.70, one hour, half-hourly) from Snow Hill and Moor St stations.

Construction on the High Speed Rail (HS2) line – connecting London with Birmingham in just 40 minutes – is set to commence in 2017 and be completed by 2026.

Useful services from New St:

Derby £16.60, 40 minutes, four per hour

Leicester £13.40, one hour, two per hour

London Euston £51.20, 1½ hours, every 15 minutes

Manchester £35.50, 1¾ hours, half-hourly

Nottingham £18.10, 1¼ hours, three per hour

Shrewsbury £14.30, one hour, two per hour

ⓘ Getting Around

CAR

During central Birmingham's ongoing construction, traffic into and around the city is severely disrupted and parking is limited. Check with your accommodation about access (don't rely on your satnav). Most roadworks are expected to be completed by late 2018.

All the big car-hire companies have town and airport offices.

PUBLIC TRANSPORT

Local buses run from a convenient hub on Corporation St, just north of the New St junction. For routes, pick up a free copy of the *Network Birmingham Map and Guide* from the tourist office. Single-trip tickets start from £1.90.

Commuter trains to destinations in the north of Birmingham (including Aston) operate from Moor St train station, close to Selfridges.

Birmingham's single tram line, the **Metro** (http://nxbus.co.uk), links New St Station with Wolverhampton via the Jewellery Quarter, West Bromwich and Dudley. Tickets start from £1. An extension from New St to Birmingham Town Hall and Centenary Sq should be open by the time you read this.

Various saver tickets covering buses and trains are available from **Network West Midlands** (☑ 0121-2147 7550; www.network-westmidlands.com; New St station; ⊘ 8.30am-5.30pm Mon-Sat) at New St Station. **TOA Taxis** (☑ 0121-427 8888; www.toataxis.co.uk) is a reliable black-cab taxi firm.

WARWICKSHIRE

Warwickshire could have been just another picturesque English county of rolling hills and market towns were it not for the birth of a rather well-known wordsmith. William Shakespeare was born and died in Stratford-upon-Avon, and the sights linked to his life are a magnet for tourists around the globe. Famous Warwick Castle attracts similar crowds. Elsewhere visitor numbers dwindle but Kenilworth has atmospheric castle ruins, Rugby celebrates the sport that takes its name at its World Rugby Hall of Fame, and Coventry claims two extraordinary cathedrals and an unmissable motoring museum.

ⓘ Getting There & Around

Coventry is the main transport hub, with frequent rail connections to London Euston and Birmingham New St.

Coventry

POP 337,428

Coventry was once a bustling hub for the production of cloth, clocks, bicycles, automobiles and munitions. It was this last industry that drew the German Luftwaffe in WWII: on the night of 14 November 1940, the city was so badly blitzed that the Nazis coined a new verb, *coventrieren,* meaning 'to flatten'. The city faced a further setback with the collapse of the British motor industry in the 1980s, but is undergoing a resurgence today thanks to its redeveloped and expanded university, and its proximity to London. A handful of medieval streets that escaped the bombers offer a glimpse of old Coventry.

◎ Sights

★ **Coventry Transport Museum** MUSEUM
(☑ 024-7623 4270; www.transport-museum.com; Hales St; ⊘ 10am-5pm) FREE This stupendous museum has hundreds of 'cars', from horseless carriages to jet-powered, land-speed record breakers. There's a brushed-stainless-steel DeLorean DMC-12 (of *Back to the Future* fame) with gull-wing doors, alongside a gorgeous Jaguar E-type, a Daimler armoured car and, for 1970s British-design-oddity enthusiasts, a Triumph TR7 and an Austin Allegro 'Special'. View the Thrust SCC, the current holder of the World Land Speed Record and the Thrust 2, the previous record holder.

Coventry Cathedral CATHEDRAL
(☑ 024-7652 1210; www.coventrycathedral.org.uk; Priory Row; adult/child £6/free; ⊘ cathedral 10am-4pm Mon-Sat, noon-3pm Sun, ruins 9am-5pm daily) The evocative ruins of **St Michael's Cathedral**, built around 1300 but destroyed by Nazi incendiary bombs in the Blitz, stand as a permanent memorial to Coventry's darkest hour and as a symbol of peace and reconciliation. Climb the 180 steps of the **Gothic spire** for panoramic views (adult/child £2.50/free).

Symbolically adjoining St Michael's Cathedral's sandstone walls is the Sir Basil Spence–designed modernist architectural masterpiece **Coventry Cathedral**, with a futuristic organ, stained glass and Jacob Epstein statue of the devil and St Michael.

Herbert Art Gallery & Museum GALLERY

(☑ 024-7623 7521; www.theherbert.org; Jordan Well; ⊘ 10am-4pm Mon-Sat, noon-4pm Sun) FREE Behind Coventry's twin cathedrals, the Herbert has an eclectic collection of paintings and sculptures (including work by TS Lowry and Stanley Spencer), a delightful cafe and lots of activities aimed at kids. The history gallery and thought-provoking gallery on peace and reconciliation are worth a look-in.

St Mary's Guildhall HISTORIC BUILDING

(☑ 024-7683 3328; www.stmarysguildhall.co.uk; Bayley Lane; ⊘ 10am-4pm Sun-Thu mid-Mar–Sep) FREE One of the most evocative insights into pre-WWII Coventry is this half-timbered and brick hall where the town's trades came together in the Middle Ages to discuss town affairs. As one of England's finest guildhalls, it was chosen to be a jail for Mary Queen of Scots. Stained-glass windows glorify the kings of England; further down the hall stands WC Marshall's statue of Lady Godiva. Look out for the medieval tapestry depicting Henry VI.

🛏 Sleeping & Eating

Coventry makes an easy day trip from Birmingham but if you want to stay, the tourist office can help find accommodation.

Blue Bistro BISTRO ££

(☑ 024-7622 9274; www.blue-bistro.com; 21 Spon St; mains £12-17.50; ⊘ 5-9pm Wed-Sat, 1-6pm Sun) A half-timbered building dating from 1450 with exposed beams and wooden furniture is the setting for beautifully cooked and presented bistro fare (braised lamb shanks, BBQ pork ribs, pan-fried sea bass...).

Playwrights CAFE ££

(☑ 024-7623 1441; www.playwrightsrestaurant. co.uk; 4-6 Hay Lane; mains lunch £5-8.50, dinner £10-19.50; ⊘ 10am-9pm Mon-Thu, 9am-10.30pm Fri & Sat, 10am-8pm Sun; 🖉 👪) On the lovely cobbled lane leading from Earl St to the cathedral, this bright, inviting cafe, bar and bistro is as good for breakfast as it is for lunch or an intimate dinner. Vegetarians and vegans are catered for with separate menus, as are kids. Tables are set up on the cobbles in warmer weather.

❶ Information

The **tourist office** (☑ 024-7622 5616; www. visitcoventryandwarwickshire.co.uk; Bayley Lane; ⊘ 9.30am-12.30pm & 1-4.30pm Mon-Fri, from 10am Sat & Sun) is housed in the restored tower of St Michael's Cathedral.

❶ Getting There & Away

National Express buses serve most parts of the country.

Buses X17 and X19 (every 15 minutes) go to Kenilworth (£2.70, 25 minutes) and Warwick (£2.90, 35 minutes).

Regular services include the following:

Birmingham (£4.50, 30 minutes, every 10 minutes)

London Euston (£49, 1¼ hours, every 10 to 20 minutes)

Rugby (£5.70, 10 minutes, up to four per hour)

Warwick

POP 58,679

Regularly name-checked by Shakespeare, Warwick was the ancestral seat of the Earls of Warwick, who played a pivotal role in the Wars of the Roses. Despite a devastating fire in 1694, Warwick remains a treasure-house of medieval architecture with rich veins of history and charming streets, dominated by the soaring turrets of Warwick Castle.

◉ Sights

★ **Warwick Castle** CASTLE

(☑ 0871 265 2000; www.warwick-castle.com; Castle Lane; castle adult/child £25.20/22.20, castle & dungeon £30.20/27.20; ⊘ 10am-6pm Apr-Sep, to 5pm Oct-Mar; P 🤶) Founded in 1068 by William the Conqueror, stunningly preserved Warwick Castle is the biggest show in town. The ancestral home of the earls of Warwick remains impressively intact, and the Tussauds Group has filled the interior with flamboyant, family-friendly attractions that bring the castle's rich history to life. Waxworks populate the private apartments; there are also jousting tournaments, daily trebuchet firings, themed evenings and a dungeon. Discounted online tickets provide fast-track entry. A fabulous range of accommodation options (p405) opened in 2016.

Collegiate Church of St Mary CHURCH

(☑ 01926-403940; www.stmaryswarwick.org.uk; Old Sq; church entry by £2 donation, tower adult/ child £2.50/1; ⊘ 10am-6pm Apr-Sep, to 4.30pm Oct-Mar) This magnificent 1123-founded Norman church was badly damaged in the Great Fire of Warwick in 1694 but is packed with 16th- and 17th-century tombs. Highlights include the Norman crypt with a 14th-century extension; the impressive Beauchamp Chapel, built between 1442 and 1464 to enshrine the mortal remains of the earls of Warwick;

Warwick

Warwick

◎ Top Sights
1 Warwick Castle C4

◎ Sights
2 Collegiate Church of St Mary B3
3 Lord Leycester Hospital A4

⌂ Sleeping
4 Rose & Crown A3
5 Warwick Castle Accommodation B4

✕ Eating
6 Tailors A3

and, up 134 steps, the **tower**, which provides supreme views over town (kids must be aged over eight).

Lord Leycester Hospital HISTORIC BUILDING
(☎ 01926-491422; www.lordleycester.com; 60 High St; adult/child £5.90/4.90, garden only £2; ☺ 10am-

5pm Tue-Sun Apr-Sep, to 4pm Oct-Mar) A survivor of the 1694 fire, the wonderfully wonky Lord Leycester Hospital has been used as a retirement home for soldiers (but never as a hospital) since 1571. Visitors can wander around the chapel, guildhall, regimental museum and restored walled garden, which includes a knot garden and a Norman arch.

🛏 Sleeping & Eating

Park Cottage Guest House B&B ££
(☎ 01926-410319; www.parkcottagewarwick. co.uk; 113 West St; s £59-80, d £80-99, f £92.50-115; ℗ 🛜 👪) Southwest of the centre, this stand-alone 16th-century wattle-and-daub building once served as the dairy for Warwick Castle. There are seven pretty rooms, each with a teddy bear, original floors and a courtyard garden. Two of its rooms can accommodate up to two adults and two children.

Rose & Crown

PUB **££**

(📞 01926-411117; www.roseandcrownwarwick. co.uk; 30 Market Pl; s/d/f incl breakfast from £80/100/105; 🛜🚼) Dating from the 17th century, this inn on the town square has five lovely, spacious and tastefully decorated rooms upstairs from the pub and another eight in the building across the lane, as well as great ales and bottled beers and superior food (mains £12.50 to £27). Four of its rooms are set up for families.

★ Warwick Castle Accommodation

RESORT

(📞 01926-406660; www.warwick-castle.com; Warwick Castle; tower ste/lodge/glamping tent per night from £550/203/149; 🅿🛜🚼) Accommodation offerings at Warwick Castle cater for all budgets, and include two days' castle admission. The castle itself now contains two four-poster-bed Tower Suites (including a private tour, champagne and breakfast). The riverside Knight's Village has woodland and knight-themed lodges (all with terraces and some with kitchenettes) and medieval entertainment. Themed tents (with shared bathrooms) make up the Glamping ground.

Tailors

MODERN BRITISH **£££**

(📞 01926-410590; www.tailorsrestaurant.co.uk; 22 Market Pl; 2-/3-course lunch menus £18/23, 2-/3-/6-course dinner menus £29.50/39.50/62.50; ⏰ noon-1.30pm & 6.30-8.45pm Tue-Sat) Set in a former tailor's shop, this elegant restaurant, owned and run by two young-gun chefs, serves prime ingredients – guinea fowl, pork belly and lamb from named farms – complemented by the likes of beetroot meringue, black truffle and fennel candy, and black-pudding crumble. One to watch.

❶ Information

Warwick's **tourist office** (📞 01926-492212; www.visitwarwick.co.uk; Court House, Jury St; ⏰ 9.30am-4.30pm Mon-Fri, 10am-4.30pm Sat, 10am-4pm Sun) is within the flagstone-floored Court House (1725).

❶ Getting There & Away

BUS

Buses depart from outside **Westgate House** (Market St).

National Express coaches serve London Victoria (£12.50, 3½ hours, up to four daily).

Stagecoach X16, X17 and X18 run to Coventry (£5.20, 1¼ hours, every 15 minutes Monday to Saturday) via Kenilworth (£3.75, 35 minutes).

Stagecoach bus 18A goes to Stratford-upon-Avon (£4.30, 45 minutes, half-hourly Monday to Saturday, hourly Sunday).

TRAIN

The train station is half a mile northeast of the centre on Station Rd.

Trains run to Birmingham (£6.80, 40 minutes, half-hourly), Stratford-upon-Avon (£6.60, 30 minutes, hourly) and London Marylebone (£31.80, 1½ hours, every 20 minutes).

Kenilworth

POP 23,480

An easy deviation off the A46 between Warwick and Coventry, the atmospheric ruin of Kenilworth Castle was the inspiration for Walter Scott's *Kenilworth*, and it still feels pretty inspiring today. The town is essentially split into two by Finham Brook: the historic village-like area, of most interest to visitors, is on the northern side, while the southern side is the commercial centre.

◉ Sights

Kenilworth Castle

CASTLE

(EH; 📞 01926-852078; www.english-heritage.org. uk; Castle Green; adult/child £10.10/6; ⏰ 10am-6pm mid-Mar–Sep, shorter hours Oct–mid-Mar; 🅿) This spine-tingling ruin sprawls among fields and hedges on Kenilworth's outskirts. Built in the 1120s, the castle survived the longest siege in English history in 1266, when the forces of Lord Edward (later Edward I) threw themselves at the moat and battlements for six solid months. The fortress was dramatically extended in Tudor times, but it fell in the English Civil War and its walls were breached and water defences drained. Don't miss the magnificent restored Elizabethan gardens.

Stoneleigh Abbey

HISTORIC BUILDING

(📞 01926-858535; www.stoneleighabbey.org; adult/child £9.50/4.50, garden only £4.50/free; ⏰ tours 11.30am, 1pm & 2.30pm Sun-Thu Easter-Oct, garden 11am-5pm Sun-Thu Easter-Oct; 🅿) The kind of stately home that makes movie directors go weak at the knees, this 850-year-old country house 2 miles east of Kenilworth, off the B4115 by the River Avon, name-drops Charles I and Jane Austen among its roll-call of visitors. Completed in 1726 and only viewable on tours (included in admission), the abbey's splendid Palladian west wing contains richly detailed plasterwork ceilings and wood-panelled rooms. The landscaped grounds are fine picnic territory.

🛏 Sleeping & Eating

The Old Bakery
B&B **££**

(☑ 01926-864111; www.theoldbakery.eu; 12 High St; s/d/tr from £75/95/115; ☺ bar 5.30-11pm Mon-Sat, to 10.30pm Sun; ℗ 🛜) Located down High St east of the castle, this appealing B&B has attractively attired modern rooms and a cosy, welcoming bar serving real ales on the ground floor.

Harringtons on the Hill
MODERN BRITISH **££**

(☑ 01926-852074; www.harringtonsonthehill. com; 42 Castle Hill; mains £10-19; ☺ noon-3pm & 6-11pm Mon-Sat, noon-4pm Sun) In an adorable bow-fronted cottage festooned with flower boxes opposite Kenilworth Castle, chef Ryan New re-creates his success at some of London's top tables. Dishes include pan-fried sea bass in garlic butter, bacon-wrapped pork medallions, and venison with horseradish mash and redcurrant jus – at impressively reasonable prices.

⭐ The Cross
GASTROPUB **£££**

(☑ 01926-853840; www.thecrosskenilworth.co.uk; 16 New St; 2-/3-course lunch menus £25/30, 5-course dinner tasting menu £65, with wines extra £35, mains £25-32; ☺ noon-2pm & 6.30-10pm Mon-Thu, noon-2pm & 6-10pm Fri, noon-2.30pm & 6-10pm Sat, noon-4pm Sun; 🅿🍴) One of England's culinary jewels, this Michelin-starred gastropub occupies a romantic 19th-century inn. Prepare to be dazzled by exquisite creations such as seared scallops with smoked butter and roast cauliflower, squab pigeon with cracked wheat and yoghurt, and a Black Forest sphere with toasted-almond ice cream.

ℹ SHAKESPEARE HISTORIC HOMES

Five of the most important buildings associated with Shakespeare contain museums that form the core of the visitor experience at Stratford. All are run by the Shakespeare Birthplace Trust (www.shakespeare.org.uk).

Tickets for the three houses in town – Shakespeare's Birthplace, Shakespeare's New Place and Hall's Croft – cost adult/child £17.50/11.50. If you also visit Anne Hathaway's Cottage and Mary Arden's Farm, you can buy a combination ticket covering all five properties (£26.25/17).

Vegetarian menus are available; junior gourmands have their own three-course children's menu (£12).

ℹ Getting There & Away

From Monday to Saturday, buses X17 and X19 run every 15 minutes between Coventry (£2.70, 25 minutes) and Kenilworth and on to Warwick (£3.75, 20 minutes). There are no buses on Sunday.

Stratford-upon-Avon

POP 27,455

The author of some of the most quoted lines ever written in the English language, William Shakespeare was born in Stratford in 1564 and died here in 1616. Experiences linked to his life in this unmistakably Tudor town range from the touristy (medieval re-creations and Bard-themed tearooms) to the humbling (Shakespeare's modest grave in Holy Trinity Church) and the sublime (taking in a play by the world-famous Royal Shakespeare Company).

◉ Sights

⭐ Shakespeare's Birthplace
HISTORIC BUILDING

(☑ 01789-204016; www.shakespeare.org.uk; Henley St; incl Shakespeare's New Place & Halls Croft adult/child £17.50/11.50; ☺ 9am-5.30pm Jul & Aug, to 5pm Sep-Jun) Start your Shakespeare quest at the house where the world's most popular playwright supposedly spent his childhood days. In fact, the jury is still out on whether this really was Shakespeare's birthplace, but devotees of the Bard have been dropping in since at least the 19th century, leaving their signatures scratched on to the windows. Set behind a modern facade, the house has restored Tudor rooms, live presentations from famous Shakespearean characters, and an engaging exhibition on Stratford's favourite son.

⭐ Shakespeare's New Place
HISTORIC SITE

(☑ 01789-204016; www.shakespeare.org.uk; cnr Chapel St & Chapel Lane; incl Shakespeare's Birthplace & Hall's Croft adult/child £17.50/11.50; ☺ 9am-5.30pm Jul & Aug, to 5pm mid-Mar-Jun, Sep & Oct, 10am-4pm Nov–mid-Mar) When Shakespeare retired, he swapped the bright lights of London for a comfortable town house at New Place, where he died of unknown causes in April 1616. The house was demolished in 1759, but an attractive Elizabethan knot garden occupies part of the grounds.

A major restoration project has uncovered Shakespeare's kitchen and incorporated new exhibits in a reimagining of the house as it would have been. You can also explore the adjacent Nash's House, where Shakespeare's granddaughter Elizabeth lived.

Hall's Croft   HISTORIC BUILDING

(📞01789-204016; www.shakespeare.org.uk; Old Town; incl Shakespeare's Birthplace & Shakespeare's New Place adult/child £17.50/11.50; ⊘10am-5pm mid-Mar–Oct) The handsome Jacobean town house belonging to Shakespeare's daughter Susanna and her husband, respected doctor John Hall, stands south of the centre. The exhibition offers fascinating insights into medicine in the 16th and 17th centuries, and the lovely walled garden sprouts with aromatic herbs employed in medicinal preparations.

Holy Trinity Church   CHURCH

(📞01789-266316; www.stratford-upon-avon.org; Old Town; Shakespeare's grave adult/child £2/1; ⊘8.30am-6pm Mon-Sat, 12.30-5pm Sun Apr-Sep, shorter hours Oct-Mar) The final resting place of the Bard is said to be the most visited parish church in all of England. Inside are handsome 16th- and 17th-century tombs (particularly in the Clopton Chapel), some fabulous carvings on the choir stalls and, of course, the grave of William Shakespeare, with its ominous epitaph: 'cvrst be he yt moves my bones'.

Anne Hathaway's Cottage   HISTORIC BUILDING

(📞01789-204016; www.shakespeare.org.uk; Cottage Lane, Shottery; adult/child £10.25/6.50; ⊘9am-5pm mid-Mar–Oct, closed Nov–mid-Mar) Before tying the knot with Shakespeare, Anne Hathaway lived in Shottery, 1 mile west of the centre of Stratford, in this delightful thatched farmhouse. As well as period furniture, it has gorgeous gardens and an orchard and arboretum, with examples of all the trees mentioned in Shakespeare's plays. A footpath (no bikes allowed) leads to Shottery from Evesham Pl. The **City Sightseeing** (📞01789-299123; www.city-sightseeing.com; adult/child £13.90/6.95; ⊘every 30min Apr-Sep, less frequently Oct-Mar) bus stops here.

Mary Arden's Farm   HISTORIC SITE, FARM

(📞01789-204016; www.shakespeare.org.uk; Station Rd, Wilmcote; adult/child £13.25/8.50; ⊘10am-5pm mid-Mar–Oct, closed Nov–mid-Mar) Shakespeare genealogists can trace the family tree to the childhood home of the Bard's mother at Wilmcote, 3 miles west of Stratford. Aimed squarely at families, the working farm traces country life over the centuries, with nature trails, falconry displays and a collection of rare-breed farm animals. You can get here on the City Sightseeing bus, or cycle via Anne Hathaway's Cottage, following the Stratford-upon-Avon Canal towpath.

Shakespeare's School Room   HISTORIC SITE

(www.shakespearesschoolroom.org; King Edward VI School, Church St; adult/child £8.90/5.50; ⊘11am-5pm Mon-Fri during school term, 10am-5pm Sat, Sun & school holidays) Shakespeare's alma mater, King Edward VI School (still a prestigious grammar school today), incorporates a vast black-and-white timbered building, dating from 1420, that was once the town's guildhall. Upstairs, in the Bard's former classroom, you can sit in on mock-Tudor lessons, watch a short film and test yourself on Tudor-style homework.

It's adjacent to the 1269-built **Guild Chapel** (cnr Chapel Lane & Church St; ⊘services 10am Wed, noon 1st Sat of month Apr-Sep).

🚩 Tours

Guided Town Walks   WALKING

(📞07855-760377; www.stratfordtownwalk.co.uk; adult/child £6/3; ⊘11am Mon & Fri, 11am & 2pm Sat & Sun) Popular and informative, these two-hour guided town walks depart from Waterside, opposite Sheep St.

Avon Boating   BOATING

(📞01789-267073; www.avon-boating.co.uk; The Boathouse, Swan's Nest Lane; river cruises adult/child £6/4; ⊘9am-dusk Easter-Oct) Avon Boating runs 40-minute river cruises that depart every 20 minutes from either side of the main bridge. It also rents rowboats, canoes and punts (per hour £6) and motorboats (per hour £33).

Stratford Town Ghost Walk   WALKING

(📞07855-760377; www.stratfordtownwalk.co.uk; adult/child £6/4; ⊘7.30pm Fri & Sat) Chill-seekers can take the two-hour Stratford Town Ghost Walk departing from Waterside, opposite Sheep St.

🎊 Festivals & Events

Stratford Literary Festival   LITERATURE

(📞01789-470185; www.stratfordliteraryfestival. co.uk; ⊘Apr or May) A highlight of Stratford's cultural calendar is the week-long annual Stratford Literary Festival, which attracts literary big-hitters of the calibre of John Simpson and Jonathan Miller.

Stratford-upon-Avon

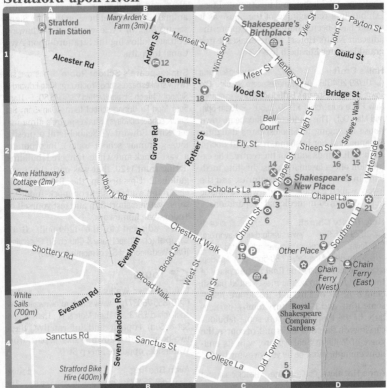

🛏 Sleeping

B&Bs are plentiful, particularly along Grove Rd and Evesham Pl, but vacancies can be hard to find during the high season; check listings on www.shakespeare-country.co.uk. The tourist office can help with bookings for a £5 fee.

Stratford-upon-Avon YHA   HOSTEL £
(☑ 0845 371 9661; www.yha.org.uk; Hemmingford House, Wellesbourne, Alveston; dm/d/camping pod from £19/90/89; P@🛜🛝) Set in a large 200-year-old mansion 1.5 miles east of the town centre, this superior hostel attracts travellers of all ages. Of its 32 rooms and dorms, 16 are en suite, as are four-person camping pods with kitchenettes. There's a canteen, bar and kitchen. Buses X15, X18 and 18A run here from Bridge St. Wi-fi is available in common areas.

Falcon Hotel   HOTEL ££
(☑ 01789-279953; www.sjhotels.co.uk; Chapel St; d/f from £85/145; P🛜🛝) Definitely request a room in the original 15th-century building, not the soulless modern annex or dingy 17th-century garden house of this epicentral hotel. This way you'll get the full Tudor experience – creaky floorboards, wonky timbered walls and all. Open fires blaze in the public areas but the best asset is the bargain-priced-for-Stratford car park (£5). Family rooms sleep three people.

Emsley Guesthouse   B&B ££
(☑ 01789-299557; www.theemsley.co.uk; 4 Arden St; d £65-90, f £105-130; P🛜) This lovely five-bedroom Victorian property has a personable owner, very clean and attractive accommodation, and a large, pretty family room at the top with an exposed-beam ceiling. Weekends require a two-night minimum stay.

Stratford-upon-Avon

◎ Top Sights
1 Shakespeare's Birthplace...................C1
2 Shakespeare's New Place...................C2

◎ Sights
3 Guild Chapel...C2
4 Hall's Croft..C3
5 Holy Trinity Church C4
6 Shakespeare's School Room...............C3

✦ Activities, Courses & Tours
7 Avon Boating.......................................E2
8 City Sightseeing...................................E1
9 Guided Town Walks.............................D2
   Stratford Town Ghost Walk .... (see 9)

🛏 Sleeping
10 Arden Hotel..D3
11 Church Street Townhouse...................C3
12 Emsley Guesthouse............................B1
13 Falcon Hotel.......................................C2

✖ Eating
   Church Street Townhouse......... (see 11)
14 Edward Moon's C2
15 Fourteas D2
16 Lambs...D2

🍷 Drinking & Nightlife
17 Dirty Duck D3
18 Old Thatch Tavern.............................. C1
19 Windmill Inn C3

✪ Entertainment
20 Royal Shakespeare Company E2
21 Swan Theatre.....................................D3

White Sails B&B ££

(☎01789-550469; www.white-sails.co.uk; 85 Evesham Rd; s £75-100, d £105-130; ❄🛜) Plush fabrics, framed prints, brass bedsteads and shabby-chic tables and lamps set the scene at this intimate property on the town's western edge. The four individually furnished rooms come with flatscreen TVs, climate control and glamorous bathrooms.

Church Street Townhouse BOUTIQUE HOTEL £££

(☎01789-262222; www.churchstreet-th.co.uk; 16 Church St; d from £110; 🛜) Some of the dozen rooms at this exquisite hotel have free-standing claw-foot bathtubs, and all have iPod docks, flatscreen TVs and luxurious furnishings. Light sleepers should avoid room 1, nearest the bar. The building itself is a centrally located 400-year-old gem with a first-rate restaurant and bar. There's a minimum two-night stay on weekends.

Arden Hotel HOTEL £££

(☎01789-298682; www.theardenhotelstratford.com; Waterside; d incl breakfast from £129; 🅿@) Facing the Swan Theatre, this elegant property has a sleek brasserie and champagne bar. Its 45 rooms feature designer fabrics and its bathrooms are full of polished stone.

✖ Eating

Fourteas TEAROOM £

(☎01789-293908; www.thefourteas.co.uk; 24 Sheep St; dishes £4-7, afternoon tea with/without Prosecco £18.50/14; ◷9.30am-5pm Mon-Sat, 11am-4pm Sun) ✐ Breaking with Stratford's Shakespearean theme, this tearoom takes the 1940s as its inspiration with beautiful old teapots, framed posters and staff in period costume. As well as premium loose-leaf teas and homemade cakes, there are hearty breakfasts, delicious sandwiches (fresh poached salmon, brie and grape), a hot dish of the day and indulgent afternoon teas (gluten-free options available).

Church Street Townhouse
BISTRO ££

(☎01789-262222; www.churchstreettownhouse.com; 16 Church St; mains £11-24; ⊙kitchen noon-3pm & 5-9.45pm, bar 8am-midnight Mon-Sat, to 10.30pm Sun; ⓢ) This lovely restaurant is a fantastic place for immersing yourself in Stratford's historic charms. The food is delightful and the ambience impeccably congenial and well presented. Music students from Shakespeare's old grammar school across the way tinkle the piano ivories daily at 5.30pm, though it can be hard to hear over the bar noise.

Lambs
MODERN EUROPEAN ££

(☎01789-292554; www.lambsrestaurant.co.uk; 12 Sheep St; mains £13-19; ⊙5-9pm Mon, noon-2pm & 5-9pm Tue-Sat, noon-2pm & 6-9pm Sun) Lambs swaps Shakespeare chintz in favour of Venetian blinds and modern elegance but throws in authentic 16th-century ceiling beams for good measure. The menu embraces Gressingham duck, deep-fried goats cheese and slow-roasted lamb shank, backed up by a strong wine list.

Edward Moon's
MODERN BRITISH ££

(☎01789-267069; www.edwardmoon.com; 9 Chapel St; mains £10-17; ⊙11am-2.30pm & 5-9.30pm Mon-Fri, 11am-3pm & 5-10pm Sat, 11am-3pm & 5-9pm Sun) Named after a famous travelling chef who cooked up the flavours of home for the British colonial service, this snug eatery serves delicious, hearty English dishes, many livened up with herbs and spices from the East. Kids get pared-down versions of adult dishes.

🍷 Drinking & Nightlife

★ Old Thatch Tavern
PUB

(www.oldthatchtavernstratford.co.uk; Greenhill St; ⊙11.30am-11pm Mon-Sat, noon-5pm Sun; ⓢ) To truly appreciate Stratford's olde-worlde atmosphere, join the locals for a pint at the town's oldest pub. Built in 1470, this thatched-roofed, low-ceilinged treasure has great real ales and a gorgeous summertime courtyard.

Dirty Duck
PUB

(Black Swan; Waterside; ⊙11am-11pm Mon-Sat, to 10.30pm Sun) Also called the 'Black Swan', this enchanting riverside alehouse is the only pub in England to be licensed under two names. It's a favourite thespian watering hole, with a roll-call of former regulars (Olivier, Attenborough et al) that reads like a who's who of actors.

Windmill Inn
PUB

(Church St; ⊙10am-11pm Sun-Thu, to midnight Fri & Sat) Ale was flowing here at the same time as rhyming couplets gushed from Shakespeare's quill – which means this pub with low ceilings has been around a while.

☆ Entertainment

★ Royal Shakespeare Company
THEATRE

(RSC; ☑box office 01789-403493; www.rsc.org.uk; Waterside; tours adult £6.50-8.50, child £3-4.50, tower adult/child £2.50/1.25; ⊙tour times vary, tower 10am-6.15pm Sun-Fri, 10am-12.15pm & 2-6.15pm Sat Apr-Sep, 10am-4.30pm Sun-Fri, 10am-12.15pm & 2-4.30pm Sat Oct-Mar) Stratford has two grand stages run by the world-renowned Royal Shakespeare Company – the **Royal Shakespeare Theatre** and the **Swan Theatre** (☎01789-403493; www.rsc.org.uk; Waterside) on Waterside – as well as the smaller **Other Place** (☑box office 01789-403493; www.rsc.org.uk; 22 Southern Lane). The theatres have witnessed performances by such legends as Lawrence Olivier, Richard Burton, Judi Dench, Helen Mirren, Ian McKellan and Patrick Stewart. Various one-hour **guided tours** take you behind the scenes.

ℹ Information

The **tourist office** (☎01789-264293; www.discover-stratford.com; Bridge Foot; ⊙9am-5.30pm Mon-Sat, 10am-4pm Sun) is just west of Clopton Bridge.

ℹ Getting There & Away

BUS

National Express coaches and other bus companies run from Stratford's Riverside bus station (behind the Stratford Leisure Centre on Bridgeway). Services include the following:

Birmingham National Express; £8.50, one hour, two per day

London Victoria National Express; £7, three hours, three per day

Oxford National Express; £10.80, one hour, two per day

CAR

If you're driving, be warned that town car parks charge high fees, 24 hours a day.

TRAIN

From Stratford-upon-Avon train station, London Midland runs to Birmingham (£7.70, 50 minutes, half-hourly), Chiltern Railways serves London Marylebone (£28.90, two hours, up to two per hour) and East Midlands runs to Warwick (£6.60, 30 minutes, hourly).

The nostalgic **Shakespeare Express Steam Train** (☑ 0121-708 4960; www.shakespeare-express.com; adult/child £20/15) chugs twice every Sunday in July and August between Stratford and Birmingham Snow Hill; journey time is one hour.

ℹ Getting Around

From 10am to 6pm April to October, a 1937-built, hand-wound **chain ferry** (1-way 50p) yo-yos across the Avon (one way 50p).

A bicycle is handy for getting out to the outlying Shakespeare properties. **Stratford Bike Hire** (☑ 07711-776340; www.stratford-bikehire.com; The Stratford Greenway, 7 Seven Meadows Rd; bike rental per half-/full day from £10/15; ☉ 9.30am-5pm) will deliver to your accommodation for free within a 6-mile radius of Stratford.

Rugby

POP 101,373

Warwickshire's second-largest hub, Rugby is an attractive market town whose history dates back to the Iron Age. But it's most famous for the sport that was invented here and now takes its name, and is a place of pilgrimage for fans.

The game was invented at prestigious Rugby School in 1823 when William Webb Ellis is said to have caught the ball during a football match and broken the rules by running with it. Situated just across from the **Webb Ellis Rugby Football Museum** (☑ 01788-567777; 5-6 Matthews St; ☉ 9.30am-5pm Mon-Sat) **FREE**, the school itself is closed to the public, but you can peek at the hallowed ground through the gates on Barby Rd. A gleaming golden **statue of William Webb Ellis** (Lawrence Sheriff St) stands outside the main Rugby School gates on Lawrence Sheriff St.

A whizz-bang new interactive World Rugby Hall of Fame has opened in the **Rugby Art Gallery, Museum & Library** (☑ 01788-533201; www.ragm.co.uk; Little Elborow St; ☉ 10am-5pm Tue-Fri, to 4pm Sat; ☎) **FREE**.

🛏 Sleeping & Eating

★ **Brownsover Hall** HISTORIC HOTEL **££**
(☑ 01788-546100; www.brownsoverhall.co.uk; Brownsover Lane, Old Brownsover; d from £82; **P** ☎) Set in 2.8 hectares of woodland and manicured gardens 2.7 miles north of Rugby, this Grade II–listed Gothic Revival manor (where Frank Whittle designed the turbojet engine) has 47 rooms, split between the creaking old house with monumental central timber staircase and the more modern converted stables. Friendly staff are ultraefficient. Ask about dinner, bed and breakfast packages.

Manor Farm Shop & Cafe CAFE, DELI **£**
(☑ 01788-869002; www.manorfarmcatthorpe.co.uk; Main St; Catthorpe; dishes £4-11; ☉ cafe & shop 9am-6pm Mon-Sat, 10am-5pm Sun; ☑ 🖫) 🍴 On this working farm 4.5 miles northeast of Rugby, you can pet rare-breed animals, pick your own fruit (priced by weight) and browse the deli. Blackboard specials at the barn-like cafe might include pies (cottage; steak and ale), liver and bacon casserole, and rabbit stew, along with vegetarian options such as cheesy leek and potato bake, and full English breakfasts.

Café Vin Cinq FRENCH, INTERNATIONAL **££**
(☑ 01788-541304; www.cafevincinq.com; 25 High St; mains £14-20; ☉ 6-10pm Mon-Fri, 11am-2.30pm & 6-10pm Sat) French fare mostly figures on the menu (coq au vin, bouillabaisse, top-tier steak), but successful forays elsewhere span Thailand (fiery red curry) to British home turf (puddings include Eton-mess cheesecake and warm treacle tart with clotted cream). The space is beautiful, both inside (vintage furniture, patterned wallpaper, chandeliers) and out (look for the aqua facade and red-and-white-checked pavement tables).

WORTH A TRIP

ALTON TOWERS

Phenomenally popular **Alton Towers** (☑ 0871 222 3330; www.altontowers.com; Farley Lane, Alton; adult/child £51.60/45.60, water park £17.50/12.75; ☉ amusement park 10am-6pm mid-Jul–Aug, to 5pm Easter–mid-Jul, Sep & Oct, closed Nov-Easter, water park 10am-8pm mid-Jul–Aug, to 4pm Sep–mid-Jul) , 4 miles east of Cheadle off the B5032, offers maximum G-force for your buck. Wild rides include the Th13teen, Nemesis, Oblivion and 2016-opened Galactica coasters. Gentler thrills span carousels and stage shows to a pirate-themed aquarium and splashtastic **water park** (check ahead for seasonal closures). Book online to skip ticket queues and take advantage of discounted entry deals. The on-site **hotel** (doubles from £192) offers themed rooms plus perks such as an hour's early park entry.

☕ Drinking

★ William Webb Ellis   PUB

(22 Warwick St; ⏰11am-11pm Mon-Thu, to 1am Fri & Sat, to 10pm Sun) Rugby's passion for its home-grown sport reaches fever pitch here. Memorabilia covers the walls, staff wear jerseys, cocktails are all rugby-themed (whisky-based 'Half Time'; Kahlúa- and vodka-laced 'Full Time'; Baileys and sambuca 'Scrum Shot'…), as is the food (provenance-inspired 'Six Nations Sausages'), and TVs not only screen live matches but also reruns of vintage fixtures. Unmissable.

ⓘ Information

Rugby's **tourist office** (☎01788-533217; www.enjoyrugby.co.uk; Little Elborow St; ⏰10am-4pm Mon-Sat) is inside the Rugby Art Gallery, Museum and Library.

ⓘ Getting There & Away

Rugby is 13 miles east of Coventry, served by regular trains (£5.70, 10 minutes, up to four hourly). Trains also serve Birmingham (£9.50, 40 minutes, two to four per hour) and Leicester (£14, one hour, hourly).

STAFFORDSHIRE

Despite being wedged between the ever-expanding conurbations of Birmingham and Manchester, Staffordshire is surprisingly green, with the northern half of the county rising to meet the rugged hills of the Peak District.

ⓘ Getting There & Around

Regular trains and National Express buses serve Stafford and other major towns. The main local bus operator is **First Group** (☎08456 020 121; www.firstgroup.com). The public-transport pages at www.staffordshire.gov.uk and Traveline (p392) have details of services.

Lichfield

POP 32,219

Even without its magnificent Gothic cathedral – one of the most spectacular in the country – this charming cobbled market town would be worth a visit to tread in the footsteps of lexicographer and wit Samuel Johnson, and natural philosopher Erasmus Darwin, grandfather of Charles. Johnson once described Lichfield folk as 'the most sober, decent people in England', which was rather generous considering that this was the last place in the country to stop burning people at the stake.

◉ Sights

★ Lichfield Cathedral   CATHEDRAL

(☎01543-306100; www.lichfield-cathedral.org; 19 Cathedral Close; admission by donation; ⏰7am-6.15pm Mon-Fri, 8am-6.15pm Sat, 7.30am-4.30pm Sun) Crowned by three dramatic towers, Lichfield Cathedral is a Gothic fantasy, constructed in stages from 1200 to 1350. The enormous vaulted nave is set slightly off line from the choir, creating a bizarre perspective when viewed from the west door, and carvings inside the cathedral still bear signs of damage caused by Civil War soldiers sharpening their swords.

Erasmus Darwin House   HISTORIC BUILDING

(☎01543-306260; www.erasmusdarwin.org; Beacon St; ⏰11am-5pm Apr-Oct, to 4pm Thu-Sun Nov-Mar) **FREE** After turning down the job of royal physician to King George III – perhaps a lucky escape, considering the monarch's descent into madness – Erasmus Darwin became a leading light in the Lunar Society, debating the origins of life with luminaries including Wedgwood, Boulton and Watt decades before his grandson Charles came up with the theory of evolution. The former house of the 'Grandfather of Evolution' contains some intriguing personal effects. At the back, a fragrant herb garden leads to Cathedral Close.

Samuel Johnson Birthplace Museum   MUSEUM

(☎01543-264972; www.samueljohnsonbirthplace.org.uk; Breadmarket St; ⏰10.30am-4.30pm Apr-Sep, 11am-3.30pm Oct-Mar) **FREE** This absorbing museum charts the life of the pioneering lexicographer, poet and critic Samuel Johnson, who moved to London from his native Lichfield and devoted nine years to producing the first major dictionary of the English language. Johnson's first dictionary helped define the word 'dull' with this example: 'to make dictionaries is dull work'. On the 1st floor, a short dramatised film narrates Johnson's life story. It's a lovely property to explore.

Lichfield Museum   MUSEUM

(☎01543-256611; www.stmaryslichfield.co.uk; Market Sq; museum free, tower adult/child £3/1.50; ⏰9.30am-3.30pm daily late Mar–mid-Sep, Mon-Sat mid-Sep–late Mar) Exhibits cover 1300 years of Lichfield history at this museum inside the old St Mary's Church. Climb the tower's 120 steps for sweeping city views.

Sleeping & Eating

George Hotel
HOTEL ££

(☏ 01543-414822; www.thegeorgelichfield.co.uk; 12-14 Bird St; s/d from £90/105; P ☎) Part of the Best Western group, this old Georgian pub has been upgraded into a comfortable midrange hotel with 44 rooms that scores points for location rather than atmosphere.

Damn Fine Cafe
CAFE £

(www.damnfinecafelichfield.co.uk; 16 Bird St; dishes £4-10; ⊙ 9am-4pm Tue, Thu & Fri, to 3.30pm Wed, to 5pm Sat, 10am-4pm Sun; 🖘) Teeming with locals, this cafe is a handy spot for sandwiches, soup, filling bacon-and-sausage breakfasts (served all day) or vegetarian toad-in-the-hole. Order and pay at the counter.

Chapters Cathedral Coffee Shop
CAFE £

(☏ 01543-306125; 19 Cathedral Close; dishes £3.50-8; ⊙ 9am-5pm Mon-Sat, 10am-4pm Sun Jul & Aug, 9am-4pm Mon-Sat, 10am-4pm Sun Sep-Jun) Ensconced in a fine 18th-century house overlooking its 13th-century walled garden on one side and the cathedral on the other, Chapters serves morning and afternoon tea and Sunday lunches.

★ Trooper
GASTROPUB ££

(☏ 01543-480413; www.thetrooperwall.co.uk; Watling St, Wall; mains £9.50-23; ⊙ kitchen noon-9.15pm Mon-Wed, to 9.45pm Thu-Sat, to 8pm Sun, bar noon-midnight Mon-Sat, to 10pm Sun; 🖘) 🖉 Situated 3 miles southwest of Lichfield in the tiny village of Wall, this idyllic gastropub prides itself on ingredients such as 28-day aged steak (served with hand-cut, beef-dripping-fried chips and sweet tomato chutney) and pork belly (with apple and quince jus) plus vegetarian options using herbs from its gardens. It has fabulous real ales and a sunny beer garden too.

Wine House
MODERN BRITISH ££

(☏ 01543-419999; www.thewinehouselichfield. co.uk; 27 Bird St; mains £10-40; ⊙ noon-10pm Mon-Sat, to 6pm Sun) Astutely selected whites, reds, champagnes and rosés, including many by-the-glass options, complement the seriously good cooking at these smart, red-brick premises. Choices range from pancetta-wrapped, fig-stuffed pork fillet to steamed Scottish mussels with tail-on tiger prawns and squid-ink risotto.

WORTH A TRIP

LORD LICHFIELD'S SHUGBOROUGH

The regal, neoclassical mansion **Shugborough** (☏ 0845 459 8900; www. shugborough.org.uk; Great Haywood; adult/child £15/9, garden only £3.50; ⊙ 11am-5pm Wed-Mon mid-Mar–mid-Oct, garden 11am-5pm daily year-round) is the ancestral home of royal photographer Lord Lichfield. A good proportion of the wall space is devoted to his work; the highlight is the staterooms' collection of exquisite Louis XV and XVI furniture. One-hour guided tours (included in admission) run between 11am and 1pm. Shugborough is 6 miles east of Stafford on the A513; bus 825 linking Stafford and Lichfield stops 1 mile from the manor (£3.10, 20 minutes, half-hourly Monday to Saturday, hourly Sunday).

Drinking & Nightlife

★ Whippet Inn
PUB

(www.whippetinnmicro.co.uk; 21 Tamworth St; ⊙ noon-2.30pm & 4.30-10pm Wed & Thu, noon-10pm Fri & Sat, noon-5pm Sun) 🖉 All of the ales at this adorable little one-room micropub are sourced within a 50-mile radius of Lichfield and there's also a wonderful selection of handcrafted cloudy and clear West Country, Welsh and Scottish ciders, along with British wines, but it resolutely doesn't serve lager, keg beer or spirits. Artisan bar snacks include pork pies, Scotch eggs and sausage rolls.

ℹ Information

The **tourist office** (☏ 01543-256611; www. stmaryslichfield.co.uk; Market Sq; ⊙ 9.30am-4pm Mon-Sat year-round plus 10am-4pm Sun Easter-Sep) is in the Lichfield Museum.

ℹ Getting There & Away

The bus station is opposite the main Lichfield City train station on Birmingham Rd. Bus 825 serves Stafford (£3.60, 1½ hours, half-hourly Monday to Saturday, none on Sunday).

Lichfield has two train stations:

Lichfield City Trains to Birmingham (£5, 35 minutes, every 20 minutes) leave from Lichfield City station in the centre.

Lichfield Trent Valley Trains to London Euston (£37, 1¾ hours, up to two per hour) run from Lichfield Trent Valley station on the eastern side of town 1.5 miles east of the centre.

WORTH A TRIP

THE POTTERIES - STOKE-ON-TRENT

Situated at the heart of the Potteries (the famous pottery-producing region of Staffordshire) Stoke-on-Trent is famed for its ceramics. Don't expect cute little artisanal producers: this was where pottery shifted to mass production during the Industrial Revolution, and Stoke today is a sprawl of industrial townships tied together by flyovers and bypasses. There are dozens of active potteries that you can visit in the greater area, including the famous Wedgwood factory.

The **tourist office** (☏ 01782-236000; www.visitstoke.co.uk; Bethesda St, Hanley; ◷ 10am-5pm Mon-Sat, 11am-4pm Sun) has information on all the potteries that are open to the public.

Potteries Museum & Art Gallery (☏ 01782-236000; www.stokemuseums.org.uk; Bethesda St, Hanley; ◷ 10am-5pm Mon-Sat, 11am-4pm Sun) For a thorough overview of the Potteries area's history, this museum/gallery houses an extensive ceramics display, from Toby jugs and jasperware to outrageous ornamental pieces. Other highlights include treasures from the 2009-discovered Staffordshire Hoard (the largest hoard of Anglo-Saxon gold and silver metalwork ever found, incorporating 5.1kg of gold, 1.4kg of silver and some 3500 pieces of jewellery); displays on the WWII Spitfire, created by the Stoke-born aviator Reginald Mitchell; and artworks by TS Lowry and Sir Henry Moore.

Wedgwood Visitor Centre (☏ 01782-282986; www.worldofwedgwood.com; Wedgwood Dr, Barlaston; factory tour & museum adult/child £15/7.50, factory tour only £10/5, museum only £7.50/3.75; ◷ 10am-5pm Mon-Fri, to 4pm Sat & Sun) Set in attractive parkland 8 miles south of Hanley, the modern production centre for Josiah Wedgwood's porcelain empire displays an extensive collection of historic pieces, including plenty of Wedgwood's delicate, neoclassical blue-and-white jasperware. The fascinating industrial process is revealed, and there's an interesting film on Josiah's life and work, including his involvement in canal-building and opposition to slavery.

WORCESTERSHIRE

Famed for its eponymous condiment, invented by two Worcester chemists in 1837, Worcestershire marks the transition from the industrial heart of the Midlands to the peaceful countryside of the Welsh Marches. The southern and western fringes of the county burst with lush countryside and sleepy market towns, while the capital is a classic English county town, whose magnificent cathedral inspired the composer Elgar to write some of his greatest works.

🏃 Activities

The 210-mile riverside **Severn Way** winds through Worcestershire en route from Plynlimon in Wales to the sea at Bristol. A shorter challenge is the 100-mile **Three Choirs Way**, linking Worcester to Hereford and Gloucester. The Malvern Hills (p417) are also prime country for walking and cycling; information is available at www.malvernhillsaonb.org.uk.

ℹ Getting There & Away

Worcester is a convenient rail hub. Kidderminster is the southern railhead of the quaint Severn Valley Railway (p429).

Buses and trains connect larger towns, but bus services to rural areas can be frustratingly infrequent; search the transport pages at www.worcestershire.gov.uk or Traveline (p392) for bus companies and timetables.

Worcester

POP 99,600

Worcester (pronounced *woos*-ter) has enough historic treasures to forgive the architectural eyesores from the postwar love affair with all things concrete. The home of the famous Worcestershire sauce (an unlikely combination of fermented tamarinds and anchovies), this ancient cathedral city was the site of the last battle of the Civil War, the Battle of Worcester, which took place on 3 September 1651. The defeated Charles II only narrowly escaped the pursuing Roundheads by hiding in an oak tree, an event still celebrated in Worcester every 29 May, when government buildings are decked out with oak sprigs.

◎ Sights

★ **Worcester Cathedral**　　　　CATHEDRAL
(☏ 01905-732900; www.worcestercathedral.co.uk; 8 College Yard; cathedral free, tower adult/child £4/2,

tours £4/free; ⊘7.30am-6pm, tower 11am-5pm Sat Apr-Oct, tours 11am & 2.30pm Mon-Sat Apr-Nov, Sat Dec-Mar) Rising above the River Severn, Worcester's majestic cathedral is best known as the final resting place of Magna Carta signatory King John. The strong-legged can tackle the 249 steps to the top of the **tower**, from where Charles II surveyed his troops during the disastrous Battle of Worcester. Hour-long **tours** run from the gift shop. Several works by local composer Edward Elgar had their first public outings here – to appreciate the acoustics, come for **evensong** (5.30pm Monday to Saturday, 4pm Sunday).

Commandery   MUSEUM
(☑01905-361821; www.worcester.gov.uk; College St; adult/child £5.50/2.50; ⊘10am-5pm Tue-Sat, 1.30-5pm Sun) The town's history museum is housed in a splendid Tudor building that served as King Charles II's headquarters during the Battle of Worcester. Engaging audio guides and interactive exhibits tell the story of Worcester during key periods in its history. A highlight is the 'painted chamber', covered with intriguing 15th-century religious frescos.

Royal Worcester Porcelain Works   MUSEUM
(☑01905-21247; www.museumofroyalworcester. org; Severn St; adult/child £6/free; ⊘10am-5pm Mon-Sat Mar-Oct, to 4pm Nov-Feb) Up there with the country's most famous potteries, the Royal Worcester porcelain factory gained an edge over its rivals by picking up the contract to provide fine crockery to the English monarchy. An entertaining audio tour reveals some quirkier sides to the Royal Worcester story, including its brief foray into porcelain dentures and 'portable fonts' designed for cholera outbreaks. The shop has some splendid pieces, from monk-shaped candle-snuffers to decorated thimbles and pill boxes.

🛏 **Sleeping & Eating**

Diglis House Hotel   HOTEL **££**
(☑01905-353518; www.diglishousehotel.co.uk; Severn St; d £78-153; P🞄) Next to the boathouse in a gorgeous waterside setting, this rambling yet cosy 28-room Georgian house is a short stroll from the cathedral. The best rooms have four-poster beds, luxe bathrooms and river views. Guests can work out at the nearby gym for free.

Lenchford Inn   INN **££**
(☑01905-620229; www.thelenchfordinn.co.uk; Shrawley; d/tr/f from £75/90/95; P🞄) An easy 8-mile drive north of Worcester, this

sprawling inn on the banks of the Severn is a haven of tranquillity. Its nine en suite rooms (including family rooms) are old-fashioned but spacious and squeaky clean, and all open onto a communal balcony or terrace with river views. There's a cavernous restaurant (kids' menu available) and sociable bar.

Mac & Jac's   DELI, CAFE **£**
(www.macandjacs.co.uk; 44 Friar St; dishes £4.50-14; ⊘9am-5pm Mon-Sat) This Friar St outfit has a lovely deli downstairs and a relaxing cafe upstairs for caffeine, sandwiches with fillings such as brie and grape, and a wholesome menu of hot dishes such as crispy pork belly with toasted almonds and coriander. Look out for gourmet supper evenings (two-/three-course menus £27/33). There's a second location in Great Malvern (p417).

★ **Old Rectifying House**   MODERN BRITISH **££**
(☑01905-619622; www.theoldrec.co.uk; North Parade; mains £13-24.50; ⊘kitchen noon-3pm & 6-9pm Tue-Thu, noon-9.30pm Fri & Sat, noon-6pm Sun, bar noon-11pm Tue-Thu, to 12.30am Fri & Sat, to 11pm Sun) Worcester's hippest dining space has a candlelit, painted-brick interior and umbrella-shaded courtyard tables. Its switched-on menu features dishes such as roast pigeon breast with black pudding and watercress or dry-aged rib-eye with duck egg and red-wine jus. DJs often hit the decks in the lounge bar, which mixes mighty cocktails including 'Walnut of Wall St'.

🍷 **Drinking & Entertainment**

★ **Cardinal's Hat**   PUB
(☑01905-724006; www.the-cardinals-hat.co.uk; 31 Friar St; ⊘noon-11pm Mon-Sat, to 10.30pm Sun; 🞄) Dating from the 14th century, and claiming a resident ghost, Worcester's oldest pub has had a grand makeover that highlights its original features including log-burning stoves. English craft beers and ciders dominate the taps; its menu concentrates on locally sourced British classics (Scotch eggs, pies, kippers, artisan cheese platters). Upstairs are four Georgian-style boutique guest rooms (doubles £80 to £125).

Marr's Bar   LIVE MUSIC
(☑01905-613336; www.marrsbar.co.uk; 12 Pierpoint St; ⊘8pm-late) The best live-music venue for miles around, Marr's still has its original sprung dance floors from its days as a dance studio. There's a lively schedule of gigs, acts, comedy shows, acoustic and jamming evenings most nights.

ℹ Information

Located inside the Grade I–listed Guildhall, dating from 1721, the **tourist office** (☏ 01905-726311; www.visitworcestershire.org/worcester; Guildhall, High St; ⊙ 9.30am-5pm Mon-Sat) has details of history-focused town walks.

ℹ Getting There & Away

BUS

The **bus station** is inside the Crowngate Centre on Friary Walk. National Express has services to London Victoria (£19.20, 3½ hours, two daily).

TRAIN

Worcester Foregate is the main rail hub, but services also run from Worcester Shrub Hill. Regular trains:

Birmingham £8.10, one hour, every 20 minutes

Great Malvern £5.20, 15 minutes, up to four per hour

Hereford £9.40, 50 minutes, hourly

Ledbury £6.80, 25 minutes, hourly

London Paddington £18, 2½ hours, hourly

Great Malvern

POP 32,900

Tumbling down the side of a forested ridge about 7 miles southwest of Worcester is the picturesque spa town of Great Malvern, the gateway to the Malverns, a soaring 9-mile-long range of volcanic hills that rise unexpectedly from the surrounding meadows. In Victorian times, the medicinal waters were prescribed as a panacea for everything from gout to 'sore eyes' – you can test the theory by sampling Malvern water at public wells dotted around the town.

WORTH A TRIP

ELGAR BIRTHPLACE MUSEUM

England's most popular classical composer is celebrated with appropriate pomp and circumstance at **Elgar Birthplace Museum** (☏ 01905-333224; www.elgarmuseum.org; Crown East Lane, Lower Broadheath; adult/child £7.50/3.50; ⊙ 11am-5pm Fri-Thu Easter–mid-Sep) , housed in the humble country cottage where Edward Elgar was born in 1857. Admission includes an audio guide with musical interludes so that you can appreciate what all the fuss is about.

The cottage is 4 miles west of Worcester; you'll need your own transport.

◉ Sights

★ Morgan Motor Company   MUSEUM

(☏ 01684-584580; www.morgan-motor.co.uk; Pickersleigh Rd; museum free, tours adult/child £20/10; ⊙ museum 8.30am-5pm Mon-Thu, to 3pm Fri, tours 10am, 12.30pm & 2.30pm Mon-Fri) FREE Morgan has been handcrafting elegant sports cars since 1909, and you can still see the mechanics at work on two-hour guided tours of the unassuming shed-like buildings comprising the factory (prebooking essential), and view a fleet of vintage classics adjacent to the museum. If buying one of these beautiful machines is beyond your budget, you can rent one per day/week from £200/975, including insurance, for a spin through the Malvern Hills.

Great Malvern Priory   MONASTERY

(☏ 01684-561020; www.greatmalvernpriory.org.uk; Church St; ⊙ 9am-5pm) FREE The 11th-century Great Malvern Priory is packed with remarkable features, from original Norman pillars to surreal modernist stained glass. The choir is enclosed by a screen of 15th-century tiles and the monks' stalls are decorated with delightfully irreverent 14th-century misericords, depicting everything from three rats hanging a cat to the mythological reptile, the basilisk. Charles Darwin's daughter Annie is buried here.

Malvern Museum of Local History   MUSEUM

(☏ 01684-567811; www.malvernmuseum.co.uk; Priory Gatehouse, Abbey Rd; adult/child £2/50p; ⊙ 10.30am-5pm Mar-Oct) Straddling Abbey Rd in the grand Priory Gatehouse (c 1470), the town museum offers a thorough exploration of Great Malvern's claims to fame, including spring waters, medieval monasteries, the Malvern Hills and Morgan Motors.

☞ Tours

Great Malvern Walking Tours   WALKING

(adult/child £3/50p; ⊙ tours 10.30am Sat & Sun Apr-Sep) Walking tours departing from the tourist office (p417) explore the town's medieval and Victorian history over 1½ hours (no reservations needed).

🛏 Sleeping & Eating

Como House   B&B ££

(☏ 01684-561486; www.comohouse.co.uk; Como Rd; s/d £45/70; P ❄ 🤝) This handsome stone house benefits from a quiet location away from the central bustle. Rooms are snug, the garden is a delight and the mood is restoratively calm. Vegetarian and gluten-free breakfasts are available on request, and the friendly owners will pick you up from the station and drop you off by the walking trails.

Abbey Hotel HOTEL **£££**
(☑ 01684-892332; www.sarova-abbeyhotel.com; Abbey Rd; d £149-205; P @ ⊞) Tangled in vines like a Brothers Grimm fairy-tale castle, this stately property has 103 elegant rooms in a prime location by the museum and priory.

Mac & Jac's CAFE **£**
(www.macandjacs.co.uk; 23 Abbey Rd; dishes £4.50-14; ⊗ 9am-7pm Tue-Sat, 10am-4pm Sun) Creative salads, flatbreads, sharing plates, spelt risotto and a savoury tart of the day are served up at this fresh addition to the town's dining scene. It's the sister branch of the popular Worcester (p415) cafe, set in a chic white-painted shopfront near the Great Malvern Priory.

St Ann's Well Cafe CAFE, VEGETARIAN **£**
(☑ 01684-560285; www.stannswell.co.uk; St Ann's Rd; dishes £2-4.50; ⊗ 11.30am-3.30pm Tue-Fri, 10am-4pm Sat & Sun Easter-Sep; ☑) A s-t-e-e-p climb above St Ann's Rd (so best to check opening times beforehand), this quaint cafe is set in an early-19th-century villa, with mountain-fresh spring water bubbling into a carved basin by the door. All-vegetarian food (including vegan options) spans soups to pies, filled baguettes, cakes, pastries and puddings.

Fig Tree MODERN BRITISH **££**
(☑ 01684-569909; www.thefigtreemalvern.co.uk; 99b Church St; mains £8-17.50; ⊗ noon-2pm & 5.30-9.30pm Tue-Sat) Tucked down an alleyway off Church St, this 19th-century former stable serves Mediterranean-inspired fare such as marinated pork chops with caramelised apple, red onion and rosemary potatoes, and chargrilled chicken with minted yoghurt and saffron rice.

☆ Entertainment

Theatre of Small Convenience THEATRE
(☑ 01684-568933; www.wctheatre.co.uk; Edith Walk; shows adult/child £2.50/1.50; ⊗ Easter-Sep) Set in a converted Victorian public lavatory decked out with theatrical Italianate flourishes, this quirky place has just 12 seats and a program running from puppet shows to poetry and opera. Shows usually last five to 10 minutes.

Malvern Theatres THEATRE
(☑ 01684-892277; www.malvern-theatres.co.uk; Grange Rd) One of the country's best provin-

> ### WALKING IN THE MALVERN HILLS
>
> The jack-in-the-box Malvern Hills, which dramatically pop up out of the Severn plains on the boundary between Worcestershire and Herefordshire, rise to the lofty peak of the Worcester Beacon (419m), reached by a steep 3-mile climb above Great Malvern. More than 100 miles of trails traipse over the various summits, which are mostly capped by exposed grassland, offering the kind of views that inspire orchestral movements.
>
> The Great Malvern **tourist office** (p417) has racks of pamphlets covering popular hikes, including a map of the mineral-water springs, wells and fountains of the town and surrounding hills. The enthusiast-run website www.malverntrail.co.uk is also a goldmine of useful walking information.
>
> A single £4 parking ticket per day is valid at locations throughout the hills.

cial theatres, this long-established cultural hub packs in a lively program of classical music, dance, comedy, drama and cinema.

ⓘ Information

The **tourist office** (☑ 01684-892289; www.visitthemalverns.org; 21 Church St; ⊗ 10am-5pm Apr-Oct, 10am-5pm Mon-Sat, to 4pm Sun Nov-Mar) is a mine of walking and cycling information.

ⓘ Getting There & Away

Buses are limited, making trains your best bet. The train station is east of the centre, off Ave Rd.
Services include the following:
Hereford £7.90, 35 minutes, hourly
Ledbury £5, 10 minutes, hourly
Worcester £5.20, 15 minutes, up to four hourly

HEREFORDSHIRE

Adjoining the Welsh border, Herefordshire is a patchwork of fields, hills and cute little black-and-white villages, many dating back to the Tudor era and beyond.

🏃 Activities

As well as the famous **Offa's Dyke Path**, walkers can follow the **Herefordshire Trail**

SUPPING CIDER - HEREFORDSHIRE STYLE

The **Herefordshire Cider Route** (www.ciderroute.co.uk) drops in on numerous local cider producers, where you can try before you buy, and then totter off to the next cidery. Mindful of road safety, tourist offices have maps and guide booklets to help you explore by bus or bicycle.

Westons Cider Mills (☎ 01531-660108; www.westons-cider.co.uk; The Bounds, Much Marcle; tours adult/child £10/4; ☺ 9am-5pm Mon-Fri, 10am-5pm Sat & Sun) If you only have time to visit one Herefordshire cider-maker, make it Westons Cider Mills, just under a mile west of the tiny village of Much Marcle, its house brew is even served in the Houses of Parliament. Informative tours (1½ hours) start at 11am, 12.30pm, 2pm and 3.30pm, with free cider and perry tastings for the grown-ups. There's also a fascinating bottle museum.

Walwyn Arms (☎ 01531-660601; www.bucaneer.co.uk; Much Marcle; mains £9.50-17; ☺ kitchen noon-2.30pm & 6-9.30pm Mon-Sat, noon-4pm & 6-9pm Sun, bar 11am-11pm Mon-Sat, to 10pm Sun) Westons ciders are served at this welcoming country pub, just across from Westons Cider Mills. Cider is also used in many dishes, such as the scrumptious twice-baked, mature cheddar and Old Rosie scrumpy soufflé, and cider-battered haddock fillet, with chips and mushy peas. It also has great lunchtime sandwiches (eg prawn and Bloody Mary mayonnaise) on hand-cut bread.

(www.herefordshiretrail.com) on a 150-mile circular loop through Leominster, Ledbury, Ross-on-Wye and Kington. Only slightly less ambitious is the 136-mile **Wye Valley Walk** (www.wyevalleywalk.org), which runs from Chepstow in Wales through Herefordshire and back out again to Plynlimon. Then there's the **Three Choirs Way**, a 100-mile route connecting the cathedrals of Hereford, Worcester and Gloucester.

Cyclists can trace the **Six Castles Cycleway** (NCN Route 44) from Hereford to Leominster and Shrewsbury, or NCN Route 68 to Great Malvern and Worcester.

ⓘ Getting Around

Trains run frequently to destinations including Hereford and Ledbury, with bus connections on to the rest of the county. For bus timetables, contact Traveline (p392).

Hereford

POP 60,000

Surrounded by apple orchards and rolling pastures at the heart of the Marches, straddling the River Wye, Hereford is best known for prime steaks, cider and the Pretenders (three of the original band members – guitarist James Honeyman-Scott, bassist Pete Farndon and drummer Martin Chamers – were locals). Its key draw for visitors is its magnificent cathedral.

⊙ Sights & Activities

★ Hereford Cathedral   CATHEDRAL

(☎ 01432-374202; www.herefordcathedral.org; 5 College Cloisters; cathedral entry by £5 donation, Mappa Mundi £6; ☺ cathedral 9.15am-5.30pm Mon-Sat, to 3.30pm Sun, Mappa Mundi 10am-5pm Mon-Sat mid-Mar–Oct, to 4pm Nov–mid-Mar) After Welsh marauders torched the original Saxon cathedral, the Norman rulers of Hereford erected a larger, grander cathedral on the same site, which was subsequently remodelled in a succession of medieval architectural styles.

The signature highlight is the magnificent **Mappa Mundi**, a single piece of calfskin vellum intricately painted with some rather fantastical assumptions about the layout of the globe in around 1290. The same wing contains the world's largest surviving chained library of rare manuscripts manacled to the shelves.

Cider Museum & King Offa Distillery   BREWERY

(☎ 01432-354207; www.cidermuseum.co.uk; Pomona Pl; adult/child £5.50/3; ☺ 10am-5pm Mon-Sat Apr-Oct, 11am-3pm Mon-Sat Nov-Mar) Displays at this brewery and museum cover cider-making history and you can sample the delicious modern brews. Look for the fine *costrels* (minibarrels) used by agricultural workers to carry their wages, which were partially paid in cider. It's half a mile west of the centre; follow Eign St and turn south along Ryelands St.

Ultimate Left Bank
CANOEING

(☑ 01432-264807; www.leftbankcanoehire.co.uk; 15 Bridge St; canoe hire half-day/day £20/25) Rents open canoes to paddle along the River Wye.

🛏 Sleeping

Charades
B&B £

(☑ 01432-269444; www.charadeshereford.co.uk; 32 Southbank Rd; s/d from £55/61; [P] [@] [?]) Handy for the bus station, this imposing Victorian house has six inviting rooms with high ceilings, big and bright windows, and some with soothing countryside views. The house itself has character in spades – look for old service bells in the hall and the plentiful *Titanic* memorabilia.

Kidwells Guest House
B&B £

(☑ 01432-270315; www.kidwellshouse.com; 9 Newtown Rd; s/d £55/65, without bathroom £35/55; [P] [?]) The 20 comfortable rooms at this welcoming B&B in the north of town come in varying categories, including two with big balconies and one with its own courtyard. A sunlit conservatory opens onto a large garden.

★ Castle House
BOUTIQUE HOTEL £££

(☑ 01432-356321; www.castlehse.co.uk; Castle St; s/d/ste from £130/150/190; [P] [?]) Set in a regal Georgian town house that was once the luxurious digs of the Bishop of Hereford, this tranquil 16-room hotel has a sophisticated restaurant, sunny garden spilling down to the river, and magnificent rooms and suites. Another eight newer rooms (some wheelchair accessible) are a short walk away at 25 Castle St.

🍽 Eating & Drinking

★ A Rule of Tum
BURGERS £

(☑ 01432-351764; www.aruleoftum.com; 32 Aubrey St; burgers £7-9.50; ☺ noon-10pm Mon-Sat, to 8pm Sun) Exposed brick, elongated wooden benches and a courtyard garden are the backdrop for brioche-bun burgers that justify the trip to Hereford alone. Standouts include the Hereford Hop (pulled beef shin, Hereford Hop cheese, dill pickles and mustard mayo), Welsh lamb with celeriac slaw, and portobello mushroom with tangy Shropshire blue cheese (veggie burgers are cooked on a separate grill).

La Madeleine
FRENCH ££

(☑ 01432-265233; www.church-street-cafe-restaurant-hereford.co.uk; 17 Church St; mains £7.50-17, 2-course dinner menu £15; ☺ 9.30am-4pm Mon, Tue & Thu, to 10pm Wed, to 10.30pm Fri, to 4.30pm Sat; [♿]) La Madeleine's pretty, bare-boards interior, outdoor tables in the vine-draped garden and stylish French menu – breakfast croissants, lunchtime tarts and dinner dishes such as fillet steak with horseradish crème fraiche, fries and green-bean salad – are enough to make any Parisian homesick. Shakes in vintage milk bottles are a kid favourite. During evening services, last orders are at 8pm.

★ Beer in Hand
PUB

(www.beerinhand.co.uk; 136 Eign St; ☺ 5-10pm Mon-Thu, 4-11pm Fri & Sat, noon-11pm Sun) Ciders at this independent pub are sublime and most are locally sourced. It's also the tap room for its own Odyssey beers (such as Black Out, a dark-malt, full-bodied American Black Ale brewed with fresh oranges, which it brews on the nearby National Trust Brockhampton Estate). There are board games but no TVs.

Lichfield Vaults
PUB

(www.lichfieldvaultshereford.co.uk; 11 Church St; ☺ 10.30am-midnight Sun-Thu, to 2am Fri & Sat; [?]) On a cobbled lane near the cathedral, sociable 18th-century pub 'The Lich' opens to a decked beer garden out back. Regular live-music events include a monthly blues Sunday lunch. Jovial Greek Cypriot host Andy serves up superior Greek food including meatballs, meze plates and more.

Venue
CLUB

(www.venuehereford.co.uk; Gaol St; ☺ 10pm-3am Fri & Sat) Edgy, underground DJs and alternative sounds are constantly on the billing at Hereford's leading club (formerly known as the Jailhouse). Look out for secret sets by big-name spinners.

ℹ Information

Hereford's **tourist office** (☑ 01432-268430; www.visitherefordshire.co.uk; St Owen St; ☺ 9.30am-4pm Wed-Fri) is inside the town hall.

ℹ Getting There & Away

BUS

The bus station is on Commercial Rd, 500m northeast of the town centre. National Express goes to London Victoria (£21.10, 4½ hours, up to four daily) and Gloucester (£5.60, one hour, four daily).

Local services to destinations including Ross-on-Wye (Bus 44; £3.90, 50 minutes, five daily Monday to Friday, four Saturday) depart from St Owen St in the town centre.

TRAIN

The train station is 950m northeast of the centre.

Regular services:

Birmingham (£16, 1½ hours, hourly)

Ledbury (£6.20, 15 minutes, hourly)

London Paddington (£39.70, three hours, hourly – either direct or with a change in Newport, South Wales)

Ludlow (£9.80, 25 minutes, half-hourly)

Worcester (£9.40, 50 minutes, half-hourly)

Ross-on-Wye

POP 10,582

Set on a red sandstone bluff over a kink in the River Wye, hilly Ross-on-Wye was propelled to fame in the 18th century by Alexander Pope and Samuel Taylor Coleridge, who penned tributes to philanthropist John Kyrle, Man of Ross, who dedicated his life and fortune to the poor of the parish.

◎ Sights

Market House   GALLERY

(☑ 01989-260675; www.madeinross.co.uk; Market Pl; ◎ 10am-4pm) 🎫 FREE The 17th-century Market House sits atop weathered sandstone columns in Market Pl. The salmon-on-pink building is now home to artist collective Made in Ross, whose members live and work in a 20-mile radius, and exhibit and sell their arts and crafts here. Regular markets take place on the square out front.

🛏 Sleeping & Eating

White House Guest House   B&B ££

(☑ 01989-763572; www.whitehouseross.com; 13 Wye St; s/d/tr/f £50/70/90/100; 🅿 🛜 👪 🐾) This 18th-century stone house has a scenic location across the road from the River Wye. Vivid window boxes give it a splash of colour, and the seven quiet and comfortable rooms (some with river views) are decorated in shades of burgundy and crisp white. Family rooms sleep up to four people.

Truffles Delicatessen   DELI £

(www.trufflesdeli.co.uk; 46 High St; dishes £2.50-5.50; ◎ 8am-5pm Mon-Sat, 11am-5pm Sun) Packed to the rafters with local artisan products (cheeses, breads, chutneys et al), Truffles also has stellar sandwiches, soups and salad boxes to takeaway for a riverside picnic.

Pots & Pieces   CAFE £

(www.potsandpieces.com; 40 High St; dishes £3-6; ◎ 9am-4.45pm Mon-Fri, 10am-4.45pm Sat year-round plus 11am-3.45pm Sun Jun-Sep) Browse ceramics and crafts at this tearoom by the market place, and choosing from cakes such as lemon drizzle, coffee, and walnut and carrot. Savoury options includes quiches, sandwiches and a soup of the day.

King's Head   MODERN BRITISH ££

(☑ 01989-763174; www.kingshead.co.uk; 8 High St; mains £12-19; ◎ kitchen noon-2.15pm & 6.30-9pm, bar noon-11pm; 🛜 🐾) Dating from the 14th century, this unassuming inn is a charmer, with a low-lit front dining room and glass conservatory. Menu favourites include beer-battered haddock, pan-seared salmon with basil mash and Welsh lamb loin with red cabbage. Some of its 15 chocolate- or oyster-toned rooms (double £65 to £105) have four-poster beds; there's limited guest parking.

Ledbury

POP 9636

Creaking with history and dotted with antique shops, Ledbury's crooked black-and-white streets zero in on a delightfully leggy medieval **Market House**. The timber-framed structure is precariously balanced atop a series of wooden posts supposedly taken from the wrecked ships of the Spanish Armada.

Almost impossibly cute Church Lane, crowded with tilting timber-framed buildings, runs its cobbled way from High St to the town church.

At the top of the lane lies the 12th-century church of **St Michael & All Angels** (www.ledburyparishchurch.org.uk; Church St; ◎ 9am-5.30pm Easter-Oct, to 4pm Nov-Mar), with a splendid 18th-century spire and tower divided from its medieval nave.

🛏 Sleeping & Eating

Verzon House Hotel   HOTEL £££

(☑ 01531-670381; www.verzonhouse.com; Hereford Rd, Trumpet; s/d/ste from £80/110/180; 🅿 🛜) 🎫 The ultimate country-chic retreat, this lovely Georgian farmhouse 3.8 miles northwest of Ledbury on the A438 has eight luxuriously appointed rooms with tactile fabrics, free-standing baths, goose-down pillows, and deep-pile carpets. Locally sourced produce underpins the menu at its smart brasserie (two-/three-course lunch menus £23/27, dinner mains £14 to £32).

Feathers Hotel   HOTEL £££

(☑ 01531-635266; www.feathers-ledbury.co.uk; 25 High St; d from £110; 🅿 🛜 🐾) A Ledbury landmark, this black-and-white Tudor hotel looms over the main road. Of its 22 rooms, those in the oldest part of the building come with sloping floorboards, painted beams and much more character than rooms in the modern extension. There's an atmospheric wood-panelled restaurant, **Quills** (mains £10-26), and an indoor heated swimming pool.

Chez Pascal   FRENCH ££
(✆ 01531-634443; www.chezpascal.co.uk; Church Lane; mains £14-16; ⊗ 9.30am-5.30pm Mon-Thu, to 11pm Fri & Sat) Set in a delightful courtyard with garden tables, this place is the locals' go-to address for fine dining. French owner/chef/*patissier* Pascal's mains include classics such as pan-fried pheasant in red wine, seafood ragout and fish gratin, but it's his desserts such as ginger and lemon torte and raspberry tarts that are the stars of the show.

🛍 Shopping

★ **Three Counties Cider Shop**   DRINKS
(www.onceuponatree.co.uk; 5a The Homend; ⊗ 10am-5.30pm Tue-Thu, to 6pm Fri & Sat) The aroma of apples pervades this charming little shop filled with artisan cider, perry and juices from producers in three counties (Herefordshire, Worcestershire and Gloucestershire). A dozen ciders and perries are on tap to try; you can also buy locally produced gourmet goods including cider chocolates, chutneys and jams.

ℹ️ Getting There & Away

Buses are limited but regular train services include the following:
Great Malvern £5, 10 minutes, hourly
Hereford £6.20, 15 minutes, hourly
Worcester £6.80, 25 minutes, hourly

SHROPSHIRE

Sleepy Shropshire is a glorious scattering of hills, castles and timber-framed villages tucked against the Welsh border. Highlights include castle-crowned Ludlow, industrial Ironbridge and the beautiful Shropshire Hills, which offer the best walking and cycling in the Marches.

🏃 Activities

Walking
The rolling Shropshire Hills call out to walkers like a siren. Between Shrewsbury and Ludlow, the landscape rucks up into dramatic folds, with spectacular trails climbing the flanks of **Wenlock Edge** and the **Long Mynd** near Church Stretton. The county is also crossed by long-distance trails, including the famous **Offa's Dyke Path** and the popular **Shropshire Way**, which meanders around Ludlow and Church Stretton.

Cycling
Mountain bikers head for the muddy tracks that traverse the **Long Mynd** near Church Stretton, while road riders aim for the **Six Castles Cycleway** (NCN 44), which runs for 58 miles from Shrewsbury to Leominster.

Tourist offices sell copies of *Cycling for Pleasure in the Marches*, a pack of five maps and guides covering the entire county. You can also download free cycling guides from www.travelshropshire.co.uk.

ℹ️ Getting There & Around

Shrewsbury is the local transport hub, with good bus and rail connections. Church Stretton and Ludlow also have handy rail services.

From May to September, Shropshire Hills Shuttles (www.shropshirehillsshuttles.co.uk) runs useful bus services along popular hiking routes on weekends and bank holidays.

Shrewsbury

POP 71,715

A delightful jumble of winding medieval streets and timbered Tudor houses leaning at precarious angles, Shrewsbury was a crucial front in the conflict between the English and the Welsh in medieval days. Even today, the road bridge running east towards London is known as the English Bridge to mark it out from the Welsh Bridge leading northwest towards Holyhead. Shrewsbury is also the birthplace of Charles Darwin (1809-82).

The pronunciation of the town's name has long been a hot topic. In 2015, a charity debate hosted by University Centre Shrewsbury declared '*shroos*-bree' (rhyming with 'grew') the winner over the posher '*shrows*-bree' (rhyming with 'grow'), as did a survey by the *Shropshire Star,* though you'll still hear both pronunciations in the town and across British media.

◉ Sights

St Mary's Church   CHURCH
(www.visitchurches.org.uk; St Mary's St; ⊗ 10am-5pm Mon-Sat May–early Dec, to 4pm Mon-Sat early Dec–Apr) The fabulous interior of this tall-spired medieval church contains an impressive collection of stained glass, including a 1340 window depicting the Tree of Jesse

Shrewsbury

Shrewsbury

◎ Sights
1 Shrewsbury Abbey	D2
2 Shrewsbury Castle	C1
3 St Mary's Church	C2

◉ Activities, Courses & Tours
4 Sabrina	A2
5 Shrewsbury Walking Tours	B3

🛏 Sleeping
6 Lion & Pheasant	C3
7 Old House Suites	C3

✖ Eating
8 Drapers Hall	C2
9 Ginger & Co	B3
10 Golden Cross	B3
11 No 4 Butcher Row	B2

🍷 Drinking & Nightlife
12 Armoury	A2
13 Henry Tudor House	C3

✪ Entertainment
14 Old Market Hall Film & Digital Media	B2
15 Theatre Severn	A1

(a biblical representation of the lineage of Jesus) and a magnificent oak ceiling in the nave, which largely collapsed in a huge gale in 1894 when the top of the spire blew off. Much of the glass in the church is sourced from Europe, including some outstanding Dutch glass from 1500.

Shrewsbury Abbey   CHURCH
(☑ 01743-232723; www.shrewsburyabbey.com; Abbey Foregate; admission by donation; ⏰ 10am-4pm Apr-Oct, 10.30am-3pm Nov-Mar) All that remains of a vast, cruciform Benedictine monastery founded in 1083 is the lovely red-sandstone Shrewsbury Abbey. Twice used for meetings of the English Parliament, the Abbey church lost its spire and two wings when the monastery was dissolved in 1540. It sustained further damage in 1826 when engineer Thomas Telford ran the London–Holyhead road right through the grounds. Nevertheless, you can still see some impressive Norman, Early English and Victorian features, including an exceptional 14th-century west window.

Shrewsbury Castle   CASTLE
(☑ 01743-358516; www.shropshireregimentalmuseum.co.uk; Castle St; adult/child £4/1; ⏰ 10.30am-5pm Mon-Wed, Fri & Sat, to 4pm Sun Jun–mid-Sep, to 4pm Mon-Wed, Fri & Sat mid-Feb–

May & mid-Sep–mid-Dec) Hewn from flaking red Shropshire sandstone, the town castle contains the **Shropshire Regimental Museum**. There are fine views from **Laura's Tower** and the battlements. The lower level of the **Great Hall** dates from 1150.

Tours

Sabrina BOATING
(✆ 01743-369741; www.sabrinaboat.co.uk; Victoria Quay; adult/child £8/4; ⊙ hourly 11am-4pm Mar-Oct) Enjoy Shrewsbury from the water on board the Sabrina, which cruises the River Severn. Ghost cruises run from 7pm to 10.30pm on Monday evenings. There are music nights from 7.30pm to 10.30pm on Tuesdays. All trips last 45 minutes and leave from Victoria Quay near the Welsh Bridge.

Shrewsbury Walking Tours WALKING
(✆ 01743-258888; adult/child £7.50/2.50; ⊙ 2pm Mon-Sat, 11am Sun May-Sep, 2pm Tue-Sat, 11am Sun Oct, 2pm Sat Nov-Mar) Guided 1½-hour circuits of the historic centre depart from the tourist office (p424).

Sleeping

Old House Suites B&B ££
(✆ 07813-610904; www.theoldhousesuites.com; The Old House, 20 Dogpole; ste £85-100; P ☎) Shrewsbury's most historic place to hang your tricorn, the Old House has three lavish suites, all with views of the garden from a gloriously crooked timbered Tudor town house that was once owned by one of Catherine of Aragon's courtiers. The owner conducts hour-long history tours of the property for guests. It's up the steps from the Dogpole bus stop.

Lion & Pheasant BOUTIQUE HOTEL ££
(✆ 01743-770345; www.lionandpheasant.co.uk; 50 Wyle Cop; s/d incl breakfast from £99/119) This former coaching inn is now a stylish town house offering 22 individually styled rooms with comfy goose- and duck-down pillows. Original features throughout the property include magnificent exposed timber beams. Classy modern British fare is served in the white-washed restaurant (mains £14 to £23).

Corbet Arms PUB ££
(✆ 01743-709232; www.thecorbetarms.com; Church Rd, Uffington; d £65-105; P ☎ 🖭) Peacefully situated 4 miles east of Shrewsbury in the pint-sized village of Uffington, this family-friendly pub has nine beautifully appointed en suite rooms reached by a staircase. Try for top-floor room 10, which has exposed beams, a spacious sitting area and panoramic views of the surrounding countryside. High-quality pub food includes outstanding Sunday roasts.

Eating & Drinking

Ginger & Co CAFE £
(30-31 Princess St; dishes £4-9.50; ⊙ 8.30am-5pm Mon-Sat, 10am-4pm Sun; 🖉) 🍴 A successful crowd-funding campaign propelled the opening of this airy, L-shaped cafe filled with upcycled furniture. It's a great option for a light brunch or lunch (smashed avocado on artisan toast with oak-smoked streaky bacon), snacks (lemon and Earl Grey scones with homemade raspberry jam), good coffee and vitamin-packed smoothies. Gluten-free, dairy-free and vegan options abound.

★ **Golden Cross** MODERN BRITISH ££
(✆ 01743-362507; www.goldencrosshotel.co.uk; 14 Princess St; mains £10.50-19.50; ⊙ noon-2.30pm & 5.30-9.30pm Tue-Sat, noon-2.30pm Sun) Overwhelmingly romantic, this candlelit inn dating from 1428 has an impeccably executed menu spanning mains such as roast pumpkin and chestnut gnocchi or garlic- and rosemary-marinated lamb with creamed leek to lush desserts like rose *panna cotta* with poached rhubarb. Upstairs, five exquisite guest rooms (doubles £75 to £150) have luxurious touches including freestanding bathtubs and chaise longues.

No 4 Butcher Row CAFE ££
(✆ 01743-366691; www.number-four.com; 4 Butcher Row; lunch mains £7-12, 2-/3-course dinner menus £18/22; ⊙ 9am-4pm Mon-Wed, to 11pm Thu-Sat; 🖭) Tucked away near St Alkmond's Church, this hip, bare-boards split-level cafe is best known for its fantastic breakfasts, from eggs Benedict to bacon baguettes or a full English with freshly squeezed juices. Light lunches include burgers and gourmet salads (eg black pudding, spinach, mozzarella and potato); dinner is a more upmarket affair (slow-roast pork belly with apple and potato mash).

Drapers Hall FRENCH £££
(✆ 01743-344679; www.drapershallrestaurant. co.uk; 10 St Mary's Pl; mains £18-24; ⊙ noon-2.30pm & 6.30-9pm; P ☎) The sense of history is palpable in this beautifully preserved 16th-century hall, fronted by an elegant Elizabethan facade. Award-winning Anglo-French haute cuisine is served in rooms adorned with wood panelling and artwork, and upstairs there are spectacular heirloom-filled bedrooms (doubles £90 to £155).

WORTH A TRIP

ATTINGHAM PARK

Built in imposing neoclassical style in 1785, **Attingham Park** (NT; ☎ 01743-708123; www.nationaltrust.org.uk; Atcham; house & grounds adult/child £11.25/5.60, grounds only £6.75/3.35; ◷ house 10.30am-5.30pm mid-Mar–early Nov, grounds 8am-7pm May-Sep, 9am-6pm Mar-Apr & Oct, 9am-5pm Nov-Feb) looks like something straight out of a period drama with its grand columned facade, manicured lawns, and stagecoach turning circle in the courtyard. The landscaped grounds swirl around an ornamental lake and are home to some 300 fallow deer. The restored walled garden is a picture.

Attingham Park is 4 miles southeast of Shrewsbury; take bus 81 or 96 (£2.10, 20 minutes, six per day Monday to Saturday).

Henry Tudor House　　　　　　　PUB
(www.henrytudorhouse.com; Barracks Passage; ◷ noon-11pm Mon-Thu, 11am-1am Fri & Sat, noon-10pm Sun) Tucked off Wyle Cop, this seriously overhanging black-and-white beauty was built in the early 15th century and is where Henry VII stayed before the Battle of Bosworth. Today it melds old and new with a zinc bar, light-filled conservatory and bird-cage-encased chandeliers. Live gigs regularly take to the stage. Superb food too.

Armoury　　　　　　　　　　　　PUB
(www.armoury-shrewsbury.co.uk; Victoria Quay; ◷ noon-11pm Mon-Sat, to 10.30pm Sun) Despite being a modern creation, this cavernous brick space with long wooden tables, floor-to-ceiling bookshelves, assorted collectables and the aromas of fine cooking feels like it has been here for generations.

☆ Entertainment

Old Market Hall Film & Digital Media　　　　　CINEMA
(☎ 01743-281281; www.oldmarkethall.co.uk; The Square; tickets adult/child £8/6.50; ◷ 10am-9pm Mon-Sat, noon-6pm Sun; ☎) Catch mainstream and art-house movies in a charming Elizabethan setting.

Theatre Severn　　　　　　　THEATRE
(☎ 01743-281281; www.theatresevern.co.uk; Frankwell Quay) This much-acclaimed riverside theatre and music venue hosts everything from pop gigs and comedy nights to plays and classical concerts.

ⓘ Information

The **tourist office** (☎ 01743-258888; www.visitshrewsbury.com; The Square; ◷ 10am-5pm daily Apr-Oct, Tue-Sun Nov-Mar) shares space with the Shrewsbury Museum and Art Gallery.

ⓘ Getting There & Away

BUS

The **bus station** (Smithfield Rd) is beside the river.

Regular services:

Birmingham National Express; £6.70, 1½ hours, three daily

Church Stretton Bus 435; £3, 45 minutes, hourly Monday to Friday, every two hours Saturday

Ironbridge Bus 96; £3, 50 minutes, every two hours Monday to Saturday

London Victoria National Express; £20.70, 5½ hours, three daily

Ludlow Bus 435; £3.85, 1½ hours, hourly Monday to Friday, every two hours Saturday

TRAIN

The train station is on the northeastern edge of the centre at the bottom of Castle Foregate.

Trains to destinations in England and Wales include the following:

Birmingham £14.60, one hour, every two hours

Holyhead £45.60, 2½ hours, up to two per hour

London Euston £70.40, 2¾ hours, every 20 minutes

Ludlow £12.70, 30 minutes, half-hourly

Swansea £26.50, three hours, hourly

ⓘ Getting Around

Dave Mellor Cycles (☎ 01743-366662; www.davemellorcycles.com; 9a New St, Frankwell; per half/full day £7.50/15; ◷ 9am-6pm Mon-Sat) Rents bikes for adults (no kids' bikes available).

Ironbridge Gorge

POP 2582

Strolling or cycling through the woods, hills and villages of this peaceful river gorge, it's hard to believe such a sleepy enclave could really have been the birthplace of the Industrial Revolution. Nevertheless, it was here that Abraham Darby perfected the art of smelting iron ore with coke in 1709, making it possible to mass-produce cast iron for the first time.

Abraham Darby's son, Abraham Darby II, invented a new forging process for producing single beams of iron, allowing Abraham Darby III to astound the world with the first-ever iron bridge, constructed in 1779. The bridge remains the focal point of this World Heritage Site, and 10 very different museums tell the story of the Industrial Revolution in the buildings where it took place.

⊙ Sights & Activities

★ Iron Bridge
BRIDGE

FREE The flamboyant, arching and gravel-strewn Iron Bridge, which gives the area its name, was built to flaunt the new technology invented by the pioneering Darby family. At the time of its construction in 1779, nobody could believe that anything so large – it weighs 384 tonnes – could be built from cast iron without collapsing under its own weight. There's a small exhibition on the bridge's history at the former **toll house** (www.ironbridge.org.uk; ⊘10am-5pm Sat & Sun Mar–early Nov, to 4pm Sat & Sun early Nov–Feb, daily during school holidays) FREE.

★ Museum of the Gorge
MUSEUM

(☑01952-433424; www.ironbridge.org.uk; The Wharfage; adult/child £4.50/3.15; ⊘10am-5pm) An ideal place to kick off your Ironbridge Gorge visit is the Museum of the Gorge. Occupying a Gothic riverside warehouse, it offers an overview of the World Heritage Site using film, photos and exhibits, including a 12m-long 3D model of the town in 1796.

Blists Hill Victorian Town
MUSEUM

(☑01952-433424; www.ironbridge.org.uk; Legges Way; adult/child £16.25/10.75; ⊘10am-5pm early Mar–early Nov, to 4pm early Nov–early Mar) Set at the top of the Hay Inclined Plane (a cable lift that once transported coal barges uphill from the Shropshire Canal), Blists Hill is a lovingly restored Victorian village repopulated with townsfolk in period costume, busy with day-to-day chores. There's even a bank, where you can exchange your modern pounds for shillings to use at the village shops. In summer, a Victorian fair is an added attraction for young ones.

Museum of Iron
MUSEUM

(www.ironbridge.org.uk; Wellington Rd; adult/child, £8.85/5.65, incl Darby Houses £9.25/6.35; ⊘10am-5pm) Set in the brooding buildings of Abraham Darby's original iron foundry, the Museum of Iron contains some excellent interactive exhibits. As well as producing the girders for the Iron Bridge, the factory became famous for heavy machinery and extravagant ornamental castings, including the gates for London's Hyde Park.

Darby Houses
MUSEUM

(☑01952-433424; www.ironbridge.org.uk; Darby Rd; adult/child £5.30/3.75, incl Museum of Iron Darby Houses £9.25/6.35; ⊘10am-5pm early Mar–early Nov) Just uphill from the Museum of Iron, these beautifully restored 18th-century homes housed generations of the Darby family in gracious but modest Quaker comfort. In the Rosehill house, kids and adults can try on Victorian dress and view china displays. The highlight of the Darby family house is the study where Abraham Darby III designed the Iron Bridge. Admission includes access to the family's Quaker cemetery.

Coalport China Museum & Tar Tunnel
MUSEUM

(www.ironbridge.org.uk; Coalport High St; museum adult/child £8.85/5.65, Tar Tunnel £3.40/2.50; ⊘10am-5pm early Mar–early Nov) As ironmaking fell into decline, Ironbridge diversified into manufacturing china pots, using the fine clay mined around Blists Hill. Dominated by a pair of towering bottle kilns, the atmospheric old china-works now contains an absorbing museum tracing the history of the industry, with demonstrations of traditional pottery techniques.

A short stroll along the canal brings you to the 200-year-old **Tar Tunnel**, an artificial watercourse that was abandoned when natural bitumen started trickling from its walls.

Jackfield Tile Museum
MUSEUM

(☑01952-433424; www.ironbridge.org.uk; adult/child £8.85/5.65; ⊘10am-5pm) Once the largest tile factory in the world, Jackfield was famous for its encaustic tiles, with ornate designs produced using layers of different coloured clay. Tiles are still produced here today for period restorations. Gas-lit galleries re-create ornately tiled rooms from past centuries, including Victorian public conveniences. The museum

> ### ⓘ IRONBRIDGE GORGE PASSPORT
>
> The 10 Ironbridge museums are administered by the Ironbridge Gorge Museum Trust (p428). You'll save considerably by buying a passport ticket (adult/child £25/15) at any of the museums or the tourist office. Valid for 12 months, it allows unlimited entry to all of Ironbridge Gorge's sites.

BIRMINGHAM, THE MIDLANDS & THE MARCHES IRONBRIDGE GORGE

Ironbridge Gorge

N↑

500 m
0.25 miles

Enlargement scale:
100 m
0.05 miles

**Inset labels:**
High St
Waterloo St
16
10
Severn
Ironbridge Rd
17
The Wharfage
Iron Bridge 1
12
Severn Bank
7
14
Ladywood
Ironbridge Rd

**Main map labels:**
Telford Golf Club
Coalport High St 4
3
Legges Way
Ironbridge Rd
Woodside Roundabout
Telford (5mi)
Lees Farm Roundabout
Church Rd
8
The Lloyds
11
Calcutts Rd
Severn
Madeley Rd
Woodside Ave
13
Waterloo St
High St
See Enlargement
Darby Rd
9
6
Wellington Rd
5
Beech Rd
Paradise Rd
Dale End
The Wharfage
Broseley Pipeworks (200m)
15
Buildwas Rd
Dale End Park
Museum of the Gorge
2
1

Ironbridge Gorge

◎ **Top Sights**
1 Iron Bridge F2
2 Museum of the Gorge...........................A3

◎ **Sights**
3 Blists Hill Victorian Town E3
4 Coalport China Museum & Tar
   Tunnel...E4
5 Darby Houses A1
6 Enginuity A1
7 Iron Bridge Tollhouse...............................F2
8 Jackfield Tile Museum...........................D4
9 Museum of Iron.......................................A1

◉ **Activities, Courses & Tours**
10 Ironbridge Leisure..................................G1
   Shropshire Raft Tours ....(see 2)

◻ **Sleeping**
11 Calcutts House...D3
12 Library House F1
13 Ye Olde Robin Hood C3

◉ **Eating**
14 D'arcys at the Station F2
15 Deli-Dale...A2
16 Pondicherry...G1
17 Restaurant Severn F1

is on the south bank of the Severn – cross the footbridge at the bottom of the Hay Inclined Plane. Tile-decorating **workshops** take place on Tuesdays (from 10am; £5).

Enginuity   MUSEUM
(www.ironbridge.org.uk; Wellington Rd; adult/child £8.85/6.95; ⊙10am-5pm) Kids will love this levers-and-pulleys science centre where they can control robots, move a steam locomotive with their bare hands (and a little engineering know-how) and power up a vacuum cleaner with self-generated electricity.

Shropshire Raft Tours   RAFTING
(☑ 01592-426100; www.shropshirerafttours.co.uk; The Wharfage; rafting trips adult/child £14.95/6.95; ⊙by reservation 9am, 11.30am, 2pm & 4.30pm Easter-Oct, plus 7pm Jul & Aug) 🛶 Ironbridge Gorge might not have any rapids but you can take a gentle, highly enjoyable 90-minute trip along a 1.2-mile stretch of the River Severn floating past stunning gorge scenery with this eco-conscious outfit. Life jackets are provided.

Ironbridge Leisure   CANOEING, KAYAKING
(☑ 01952-426111; 31 High St; kayak/canoe rental from £30; ⊙9am-8pm Sat & Sun Easter-Oct) In summer, when the river is at a safe level, you can rent canoes and kayaks to explore the gorge and surrounding areas on 5-mile excursions (around three hours) or multiday camping trips.

🛏 Sleeping

Ye Olde Robin Hood   PUB £
(☑ 01952-433071; www.holdensyeolderobin-hoodinnironbridge.co.uk; 33 Waterloo St; s/d from £50/70; 🅿🛜🐾) The three spotless rooms at this quaint, white-washed, traditional inn on the banks of the River Severn come with king-size mattresses. The bar is a sociable spot where you're treated like a regular from the moment you walk in the door.

★**Library House**   B&B ££
(☑01952-432299; www.libraryhouse.com; 11 Severn Bank; s/d from £75/95; 🅿🛜) Up an alley off the main street, this lovingly restored Georgian library building is hugged by vines, backed by a beautiful garden and decked out with stacks of vintage books, curios, prints and lithographs. There are four charmingly well-preserved, individually decorated rooms, named Milton, Chaucer, Eliot and Hardy. The affable dog whipping around is Millie.

Calcutts House   B&B ££
(☑01952-882631; www.calcuttshouse.co.uk; Calcutts Rd; s/d from £50/65; 🅿🛜) This former ironmaster's pad dates from the 18th century. It's tucked away on the south bank around the corner from the Jackfield Tile Museum (p425), about a mile east of the bridge. Its traditionally decorated rooms have heaps of character, and one is furnished with an outsized 200-year-old four-poster bed.

🍴 Eating

Deli-Dale   DELI £
(☑01952-432508; www.deli-dale.com; Dale End, Coalbrookdale; dishes £3.50-6; ⊙8.30am-4.30pm Mon-Wed & Fri, 9am-4pm Sat, 10-4pm Sun; 🛜🐾) This wonderful deli is far and away the best place in the area for a light meal. Steaming-hot soups, salads, cakes and sandwiches are all freshly made; take them away or else dine in the cosy shop or at umbrella-shaded picnic tables in the courtyard. Call 48 hours ahead to order bountiful picnic baskets (£12 to £21.50).

WORTH A TRIP

COSFORD ROYAL AIR FORCE MUSEUM

The famous **Cosford Royal Air Force Museum** (01902-376200; www.raf-museum.org.uk; Shifnal; 10am-5pm), 13 miles east of Ironbridge, is run by the Royal Air Force, whose pilots steered many of these winged wonders across the skies. Among the 70 aircraft displayed are the Vulcan bomber (which carried Britain's nuclear deterrent) and the tiny helicopter-like FA330 Bachstelze glider that was towed behind German U-boats to warn them of enemy ships. You can also try out a Black Hawk simulator. It's a half-mile walk from Cosford train station, on the Birmingham–Shrewsbury line.

Pondicherry   INDIAN ££
(01952-433055; www.pondicherryrestaurant.co.uk; 52 Waterloo St; mains £11-16; 6-11pm Mon-Thu, to midnight Fri & Sat, to 10.30pm Sun) Original features of this 1862-built former police station and courtroom include four lock-up cells (one's now the takeaway waiting area), the magistrate's bench, and blue-painted bars on the windows. Above-average contemporary Indian cuisine includes crowd-pleasers such as tandoori platters and chicken tikka masala along with chef specialities such as lamb *saag mamyam* (braised Staffordshire lamb with spinach and spices).

D'arcys at the Station   MEDITERRANEAN ££
(01952-884499; www.darcysironbridge.co.uk; Ladywood; mains £11.50-15; 6-9.30pm Tue-Sat) Just over the bridge by the river, the handsome old station building is the backdrop for flavoursome Mediterranean dishes, from Moroccan chicken to Cypriot kebabs and Tuscan bean casserole.

Restaurant Severn   BRITISH, FRENCH £££
(01952-432233; www.restaurantsevern.co.uk; 33 High St; 2-/3-course lunch £18.95/20.95, dinner from £25.95/27.95; 6.30-8.30pm Wed-Sat, noon-1.30pm Sun) The highly praised fare at this small, unadorned riverside restaurant is a winning English–French hybrid. The locally sourced menu changes weekly but incorporates creations such as Shropshire venison medallions with cognac and sundried cranberry sauce. Menu prices rise slightly on Fridays and Saturdays.

Information

The **tourist office** (01952-433424; www.visitironbridge.co.uk; The Wharfage; 10am-5pm) is located at the Museum of the Gorge.
Ironbridge Gorge Museum Trust (01952-433424; www.ironbridge.org.uk)

Getting There & Away

The nearest train station is 6 miles away at Telford, from where you can travel to Ironbridge on bus 96 (£2.10, 15 minutes, six per day Monday to Saturday). The same bus continues from Ironbridge's tourist office to Shrewsbury (£3, 50 minutes). Bus 99 runs from Bridgnorth (£3.20, 45 minutes, nine per day Monday to Saturday) and bus 88 runs to Much Wenlock (£3.60, 25 minutes, every two hours Monday to Saturday).

Getting Around

At weekends and on bank holidays from Easter to mid-September, the Gorge Connect bus (£2.20; Museum Passport holders £1) runs from Telford bus station to all the museums on the north bank of the Severn.

Much Wenlock & Around
POP 3041

With one of those quirky names that abound in the English countryside, Much Wenlock is as charming as it sounds. Surrounding the time-worn ruins of Wenlock Priory, the streets are studded with Tudor, Jacobean and Georgian houses, and locals say hello to everyone.

Sights

Guildhall   HISTORIC BUILDING
(01952-727509; Wilmore St; 11am-4pm Fri-Mon Apr-Oct) **FREE** Built in classic Tudor style in 1540, the wonky Guildhall features some splendidly ornate woodcarving. One of the pillars supporting it was used for public floggings in medieval times.

Wenlock Priory   RUINS
(EH; 01952-727466; www.english-heritage.org.uk; 5 Sheinton St; adult/child incl audio guide £4.70/2.80; 10am-6pm Apr-Sep, to 5pm Oct, to 4pm Sat & Sun Nov-Mar;) The maudlin Cluniac ruins of Wenlock Priory rise up from vivid green lawns, sprinkled with animal-shaped topiary. Raised by Norman monks over the ruins of a Saxon monastery from AD 680, the hallowed remains include a finely decorated chapterhouse and an unusual carved lavabo, where monks came to ceremonially wash before eating.

🛏 Sleeping & Eating

Wilderhope Manor YHA   HOSTEL £

(☑0845 371 9149; www.yha.org.uk; Longville-in-the-Dale; dm/d/f from £16/65/99; P) A gloriously atmospheric gabled greystone Elizabethan manor, with spiral staircases, wood-panelled walls, an impressive stone-floored dining hall and spacious, oak-beamed rooms – this is hostelling for royalty. It's 7.5 miles southwest of Much Wenlock, best reached by your own wheels.

Raven Hotel   HOTEL ££

(☑01952-727251; www.ravenhotel.com; Barrow St; d £120-130, ste £150; P 🐱) Much Wenlock's finest place to stay is this 17th-century coaching inn and converted stables with oodles of historical charm and rich country-chic styling. Overlooking a flower-filled courtyard, the excellent **restaurant** (lunch mains £12.50 to £18, dinner two-/three-/five-/seven-course menus £29/39/45/59) serves classic Mediterranean and British fare.

Fox   PUB FOOD ££

(☑01952-727292; 46 High St; mains £10-23; ⊕5-9pm Mon-Fri, noon-9pm Sat, noon-8pm Sun; 🐱) Warm yourself by the massive fireplace, then settle down in the dining room to savour locally sourced venison, pheasant and beef, swished down with a pint of Shropshire ale. Candlelit dinners here are lovely. It also has five contemporary rooms (single/double/family from £65/85/115).

ℹ Information

The **tourist office** (☑01952-727679; www.shropshire.gov.uk; The Square; ⊕10.30am-1pm & 1.30-5pm Apr-Oct, 10.30am-1pm & 1.30-4pm Fri-Sun Nov-Mar) has a modest museum of local history (admission free).

ℹ Getting There & Away

Bus 436 links Shrewsbury with Much Wenlock (£3.10, 35 minutes, hourly Monday to Saturday) and continues on to Bridgnorth (£3, 20 minutes). Bus 18 runs to Ironbridge (£2.90, 30 minutes, every two hours Monday to Saturday).

Bridgnorth & Around

POP 12,212

Cleaved into two by a dramatic sandstone bluff that tumbles down to the River Severn, Bridgnorth is one of Shropshire's finest-looking historic towns, with a wealth of architectural charm despite much of the High Town succumbing to fire in 1646 during the Civil War.

Around its namesake church, the High Town's adorable **St Leonard's Close** contains some of the most attractive buildings and almshouses in town, including a splendid six-gabled house, once part of the grammar school.

A 19th-century cliff railway – Britain's steepest – and several narrow lanes drop down from the High Town to the Low Town, including the vertiginous pedestrian Cartway, at the bottom of which is **Bishop Percy's House**, dating from 1580.

◉ Sights & Activities

Daniels Mill   MILL

(☑01746-762753; www.danielsmill.co.uk; The Cankhorn, Eardington; adult/child £5/4; ⊕11am-4pm Thu-Sun Easter-Oct) England's largest working water-powered mill still produces flour for local bakers. Visitors get a personal tour of the working machinery from the resident miller. It's located 1 mile south of the centre, reached on foot or with your own wheels.

Severn Valley Railway   RAIL

(☑01299-403816; www.svr.co.uk; Hollybush Rd; adult 1-way/return £13.50/19, child £9.50/13; ⊕daily May-Sep, Sat & Sun Oct-Apr) Bridgnorth is the northern terminus of the Severn Valley Railway; its historic steam or diesel locomotives chug down the valley to Kidderminster (one hour), starting from the station on Hollybush Rd. Check the calendar for additional event dates.

Cyclists can follow a beautiful 20-mile section of the Mercian Way (NCN Route 45) beside the railway line towards the Wyre Forest.

Bridgnorth Cliff Railway   RAIL

(☑01746-762052; www.bridgnorthcliffrailway.co.uk; entrances 6a Castle Tce & Underhill St; return £1.60; ⊕8am-8pm Mon-Sat & noon-8pm Sun May-Sep, to 6.30pm Oct-Apr) Britain's steepest inland railway has trundled 50m up the cliff since 1892. At the top, a pedestrian walkway (affording astonishing night-time panoramas) curves around the bluff to a pretty park dotted with scattered masonry, some leaning at an incredible angle (all that remains of **Bridgnorth Castle**), and passes the grand and imposing Thomas Telford–designed and cupola-topped **St Mary's Church**.

🛌 Sleeping & Eating

Severn Arms Hotel
HOTEL ££

(☑ 01746-764616; www.thesevernarms.co.uk; 3 Underhill St; s with/without en suite from £32/46, d £66, f £75; 🛜) At the bottom of the bluff conveniently positioned right next to the cliff railway, this comfortable riverside Georgian property has fabulous bridge views. The helpful owners can direct you to parking a few minutes' walk away over the bridge. Family rooms can sleep up to two adults and two children.

Cinnamon Cafe
CAFE £

(☑ 01746-762944; Waterloo House, Cartway; dishes £5-8; ⊙ 9am-6pm Mon-Fri, 10am-4pm Sat; 🚸🐾) Sweeping views extend from the dining room and terrace of this licensed cafe near the top of the Cartway. It serves up savoury bakes (many vegetarian and vegan), plus quiches, homemade muesli and cakes.

❶ Information

Bridgnorth's **tourist office** (☑ 01746-763257; www.visitbridgnorth.co.uk; Listley St; ⊙ 9.30am-5pm Mon-Fri, 9am-5pm Sat) is inside the town library.

❶ Getting There & Away

Bus 436 runs from Shrewsbury to Bridgnorth (£3.40, one hour, hourly Monday to Saturday), via Much Wenlock (£3.40, 25 minutes). Bus 99 runs to Ironbridge (£3.40, 30 minutes, every two hours Monday to Saturday).

Church Stretton & Around

POP 2789

Tucked in a deep valley formed by the Long Mynd and the Caradoc Hills, Church Stretton is an ideal base for walks or cycle tours through the Shropshire Hills. Although black-and-white timbers are heavily in evidence, most of the buildings in town are 19th-century fakes, built by the Victorians who flocked here to take the country air.

◉ Sights & Activities

Walking is the big draw here. The tourist office has maps and details of local mountain-biking circuits and horse-riding stables (riding info is also available at www.shropshireriding.co.uk).

Church Stretton clings to the steeply sloping sides of the Long Mynd, Shropshire's most famous hill, which rises to 517m. Dubbed 'Little Switzerland' by the Victorians, this desolate but dramatic bluff is girdled by walking trails that offer soaring views over the surrounding countryside. Most people start walking from the National Trust car park (per day £3.60) at the end of the Carding Mill Valley (www.cardingmill-valley.org.uk), half a mile west of Shrewsbury Rd. A small **tearoom** (Carding Mill Valley; dishes £3.50-7.50; ⊙ 10am-5pm Apr-Oct, to 4pm Nov-Mar) here provides refreshments.

A maze of single-track roads climbs over the Long Mynd to the adjacent ridge of Stiperstones, crowned by a line of spooky-looking crags. You can continue right over the ridge, passing the Bog tourist office and cafe in a Victorian-era school next to the ruins of an abandoned mining village, heading to the village of Snailbeach, with its intriguing mining relics.

Snailbeach
MINE

(☑ 01952-405105; www.shropshiremines.org.uk) The former lead- and silver-mining village of Snailbeach is littered with intriguing, rusting machinery relics. The Bog Centre (☑ 01743-792484; www.bogcentre.co.uk; The Bog, Stiperstones; ⊙ noon-5pm Mon, 10am-5pm Tue-Sun Easter-Sep, noon-4pm Mon, 10am-4pm Tue-Sun Oct–early Nov; 🛜) sells self-guided trail leaflets (50p) to explore the site, or you can join one of two guided tours. The 30-minute Day Level & Surface Tour (every 30 minutes 11am to 4pm Sunday June to September; adult/child £7.50/3) covers the mine's exterior and entrance. The 2½-hour Roberts/Perkins Level Tour (by reservation Sunday June to September; adult/child £5/3) takes you deep into the mine.

Plush Hill Cycles
CYCLING

(☑ 01694-720133; www.plushhillcycles.co.uk; 8 The Square; per half/full day from £17/22; ⊙ 9am-5.30pm Mon, Tue, Thu & Fri, 9am-5pm Sat, 10am-4pm Sun) Plush Hill Cycles rents a range of mountain bikes and electric bikes. Rates include helmets, maps and child seats; a £50 cash deposit is required. Handily, it offers free delivery within a 10-mile radius if you spend £40 or more.

🛌 Sleeping & Eating

Bridges Long Mynd YHA
HOSTEL £

(☑ 01588-650656; www.yha.org.uk; Bridges; dm from £19, camping per person from £8; 🅿) 🌿 On the far side of the Long Mynd, this wonderfully isolated hiker favourite is housed in a former school in the tiny hamlet of Bridges. No wi-fi, no mobile-phone reception, no credit cards, no online bookings. Cross the

Mynd to Ratlinghope, from where it's 1.1 miles southwest, or take the Long Mynd & Stiperstones Shuttle (p431) bus.

Mynd Guest House B&B ££
(☑ 01694-722212; www.myndhouse.co.uk; Ludlow Rd, Little Stretton; s/d from £55/80; P 🛜) Just under 2 miles south of Church Stretton, this inviting guesthouse has splendid views across the valley and backs directly onto the Mynd. The four rooms are named after local hills; there's a small bar and lounge stocked with local books; and a room for drying your boots.

Berry's Coffee House CAFE £
(☑ 01694-724452; www.berryscoffeehouse.co.uk; 17 High St; dishes £3.50-8; ⏰ 9am-5pm; ✍) 🍃 A particularly cosy cafe with loads of rooms in an 18th-century house, Berry's offers an organic, free-range, fair-trade, home-cooked menu, including Shropshire breakfasts and locally produced Shropshire white wines, ales and ciders. No credit cards.

Bridges PUB FOOD ££
(☑ 01588-650260; www.thebridgespub.co.uk; Ratlinghope; mains lunch £5.50-9.50, dinner £10-18; ⏰ kitchen 11.30am-9pm Mon-Sat, 12.30-8.30pm Sun, bar 11am-11pm; 👬🐕) Some 5 miles northeast of Church Stretton, at the base of Long Mynd by the river, this is one of those secret country pubs revered for its live music, riverside terrace, relaxed accommodation (dorm/double from £27/55) and impressive food (lamb shank and mint sauce; beef lasagne...). Mini burgers, battered fish and sausages are among the choices on the kids' menu.

ℹ Information

Adjoining the library, Church Stretton's **tourist office** (☑ 01694-723133; www.churchstretton. co.uk; Church St; ⏰ 9.30am-1pm & 1.30-5pm Mon-Sat Apr-Sep, 9.30am-1pm & 1.30-3pm Mon-Sat Oct-Mar) has abundant walking information and free internet terminals.

ℹ Getting There & Away

BUS

Bus 553 runs from Shrewsbury to Bishop's Castle via Stiperstones and Snailbeach (£3.70, one hour, five daily Monday to Saturday).

From May to September, the **Long Mynd & Stiperstones Shuttle** (www.shropshirehillsaonb. co.uk; Day Rover ticket £7; ⏰ May-Sep) runs from the Carding Mill Valley near Church Stretton to the villages atop the Long Mynd, passing the YHA at Bridges, and Stiperstones near the Snailbeach mine.

TRAIN

Trains between Ludlow (£7.10) and Shrewsbury (£6.20) stop in Church Stretton hourly, taking 15 minutes from either end. Alternatively, take bus 435 from Shrewsbury or Ludlow (£2.95, 40 minutes, hourly Monday to Friday, every two hours Saturday).

Bishop's Castle
POP 1630

Set amid blissfully peaceful Shropshire countryside, Bishop's Castle is a higgledy-piggledy tangle of timbered town houses and Old Mother Hubbard cottages. The High St climbs from the town church to the refurbished Georgian **town hall** (1765) abutting the crooked 16th-century **House on Crutches** (☑ 01588-630556; www. hocmuseum.org.uk; High St; ⏰ 2-5pm Sat & Sun Apr-Sep) FREE, which also houses the small town **museum**.

Local artists' work is exhibited in the gallery upstairs from the **tourist office** (☑ 01588-630023; www.bishopscastletownhall. co.uk; High St; ⏰ 10am-4pm Mon-Sat).

◉ Sights & Activities

Walkers can hike from north Bishop's Castle along the **Shropshire Way** (www.shropshirewalking.co.uk), which joins up with the long-distance **Offa's Dyke Path** and **Kerry Ridgeway** to the west. The northern sections of the Shropshire Way climb to the high country of the Stiperstones and the Long Mynd near Church Stretton. Bishop's Castle also lies on the popular **Six Castles Cycleway** (NCN Route 44) between Shrewsbury and Leominster.

★**Kerry Vale Vineyard** WINERY
(☑ 01588-620627; www.kerryvalevineyard.co.uk; Pentreheyling; tours £10-25; ⏰ tours noon Wed, Sat, Sun & bank holidays Apr-Oct, shop & cafe 10am-4pm Tue-Sun mid-Mar–Dec) More than 6000 vines are now planted over 2.4 hectares of the former Pentreheyling Roman Fort, where pottery and metalwork have been uncovered and are displayed at the winery shop. Tours range from a 90-minute guided walk through the vines, with a talk on the site's Roman history and three tastings, to three-hour guided visits with five tastings, a tutorial and afternoon tea including the vineyard's own sparkling wine. Or pop by the cafe for a tasting flight (from £2).

🛏 Sleeping & Eating

Poppy House   B&B **££**

(☑ 01588-638443; www.poppyhouse.co.uk; 20 Market Sq; s/d from £40/60, cafe dishes £2.50-9.50; ⊙ cafe 10am-4pm Wed-Mon; 🛜🅿) Attached to a friendly **cafe**, this sweet guesthouse has lovely, individual rooms with latch-doors and loads of old beams. Doubles cost £80 on Saturday nights. Children aged five to 16 are charged £20 per night when staying in their parents' rooms; under fives stay free.

Castle Hotel   HOTEL **££**

(☑ 01588-638403; www.thecastlehotelbishops castle.co.uk; Market Sq; s/d/f incl breakfast from £75/95/140; 🅿🛜🅿🐾) This solid-looking 18th-century coaching inn was built with stones from the now-vanished Bishop's Castle, which also contributed the gorgeous wood panelling in the dining room (mains £11 to £22). All 12 en suite rooms are lovely, with modern fabrics meeting old antique furniture; three-bed family rooms and cots are available. Doubles start at £115 on weekends.

New Deli   DELI **£**

(35 High St; dishes £2.50-8.50; ⊙ 9.30am-4.30pm Tue-Sat) 🥗 Locally made English and Welsh cheeses and breads, along with hams, salamis and sausages, premade salads, preserves, chutneys and pickles, cakes and biscuits, and ales, wines and liqueurs at this enticing deli mean you're spoiled for choice for picnic fare while walking in the surrounding hills.

🍷 Drinking

Three Tuns   PUB

(www.thethreetunsinn.co.uk; Salop St; ⊙ noon-11pm Mon-Sat, to 10pm Sun; 🛜) Bishop's Castle's finest watering hole is attached to the tiny Three Tuns Brewery, which has been rolling barrels of nut-brown ale across the courtyard since 1642. It's a lively local, and the ales are delicious. Jazz, blues and brass bands perform regularly in summer.

❶ Getting There & Away

Bus 553 runs to and from Shrewsbury (£3.60, 1¼ hours, four per day Monday to Saturday).

Ludlow

POP 11,003

On the northern bank of the swirling River Teme, this genteel market town fans out from the rambling ruins of its fine Norman castle, with some superb black-and-white Tudor buildings lining its cobbled streets.

◉ Sights & Activities

Ludlow is ringed by wonderful landscapes. Starting just outside Ludlow Castle's entrance, the waymarked **Mortimer Trail** walking route runs for 30 miles through idyllic English countryside to Kington in Herefordshire. The tourist office has leaflets describing the trail, or visit www.explore-mortimercountry.com.

Hire bikes from **Wheely Wonderful** (☑ 01568-770755; www.wheelywonderfulcycling.co.uk; Petchfield Farm, Elton; adult/child bikes per day from £20/15; ⊙ 9am-5pm Mon-Sat, by reservation Sun Apr-Oct), 5 miles west of Ludlow.

Ludlow Castle   CASTLE

(☑ 01584-873355; www.ludlowcastle.com; Castle Sq; adult/child £5/2.50; ⊙ 10am-6pm daily Aug, to 5pm Apr-Jul & Sep, to 4pm Oct, Nov, Feb & Mar, to 4pm Sat & Sun Dec & Jan) Perched in an ideal defensive location atop a cliff above a crook in the river, the town castle was built to ward off the marauding Welsh – or to enforce the English expansion into Wales, perspective depending. Founded after the Norman conquest, the castle was dramatically expanded in the 14th century.

The Norman chapel in the inner bailey is one of the few surviving round chapels in England, and the sturdy keep (built around 1090) offers wonderful views over the hills.

Church of St Laurence   CHURCH

(www.stlaurences.org.uk; 2 College St; admission by £3 donation; ⊙ 10am-5pm) One of Britain's largest parish churches, the church of St Laurence contains grand Elizabethan alabaster tombs and delightfully cheeky medieval misericords carved into its medieval choir stalls, including a beer-swilling chap raiding his barrel. The Lady Chapel contains a marvellous **Jesse Window** originally dating from 1330 (although the glass is mostly Victorian). Four windows in St John's Chapel date from the mid-15th century, including the honey-coloured **Golden Window**. Climb 200 steps up the **tower** (included in donation) for stunning views.

Ludlow Brewing Company   BREWERY

(☑ 01584-873291; www.theludlowbrewingcompany.co.uk; The Railway Shed, Station Dr; tours £6; ⊙ tours 3pm Mon-Fri, 2pm Sat, pub 10am-5pm Mon-Thu, to 6pm Fri, to 4pm Sat) 🥗 Up an inconspicuous laneway, the Ludlow Brewing

Company produces award-winning all-natural brews and sells directly from the brewery and its airy, post-industrial-style bar. Hour-long tours include one pint and six samples.

Ghost Walk WALKING
(www.shropshireghostwalks.co.uk; adult/child £5/4; ⊘8pm Fri Easter-Dec) Search for spooks on this 90-minute ghost walk from outside the Church Inn on the Buttercross.

✯ Festivals & Events

Ludlow Spring Festival CULTURAL
(www.ludlowspringestival.co.uk; ⊘mid-May) The three-day Ludlow Spring Festival uses the castle as its dramatic backdrop for more than 100 beer, cider and food stalls, a vintage car show and live concerts.

Ludlow Food & Drink Festival FOOD & DRINK
(www.foodfestival.co.uk; ⊘Sep) Established in 1995, the Ludlow Food and Drink Festival spans a long weekend in September.

🛏 Sleeping

Feathers Hotel HISTORIC HOTEL ££
(✆01584-875261; www.feathersatludlow.co.uk; 21 Bull Ring; s/d/f from £95/145/180; P🅿🛜👪) Behind the impossibly ornate timbered Jacobean facade, this 1619-built treasure is all tapestries, creaky wood furniture, timber beams and stained glass: you can almost hear the cavaliers toasting the health of King Charles. The best rooms are in the old building; rooms in the newer wing lack the character and romance. The **restaurant** (two-/three-course menus £34.50/42) is highly recommended.

Clive BOUTIQUE HOTEL ££
(✆01584-856565; www.theclive.co.uk; Bromfield Rd, Bromfield; d/f incl breakfast from £89/137.50; P❄🛜👪) For foodies, this is Ludlow's ultimate place to stay. Located 4 miles northwest of town adjoining the Ludlow Food Centre (p436), it has its own top-end restaurant; breakfast is served at the Ludlow Kitchen (p433). Many of its 15 spacious rooms are on ground level; family rooms have two sleeping areas separated by a bathroom, giving parents and kids their own space.

Charlton Arms INN ££
(✆01584-872813; www.charltonarms.co.uk; Ludford Bridge; d £100-160; P🅿🛜👪) The pick of the rooms at this landmark inn overlook the River Teme, and the pick of those have terraces (one with an outdoor hot tub as well as a four-poster bed). A family room sleeps three people. Its restaurant, also opening to a terrace, serves top-quality Modern British cuisine, and there's a large free car park and superb service.

Dinham Hall Hotel HOTEL £££
(✆01584-876464; www.dinhamhall.com; Dinham Rd; s/d/ste from £120/135/235; P🅿🛜👪) A resplendent 18th-century country manor, Dinham Hall has views of the castle and the river from gorgeous rooms full of heirloom furniture. Its superb fine-dining restaurant, **Elliots**, is renowned for its afternoon teas (from 3pm; per person from £18).

🍴 Eating & Drinking

Green Cafe CAFE £
(✆01584-879872; www.thegreencafe.co.uk; Mill on the Green, Linney; dishes £5-11; ⊘10am-4pm Tue-Sun Feb-Dec; 🦺) The Slow Food–accredited Green Cafe takes full advantage of its riverside position overlooking the weir with 25 alfresco seats (plus another 30 inside). Outstanding food spans warm salt brisket-beef baps (soft bread rolls) to ox tongue with hazelnut pesto and lemon polenta cake. Wines, beers and ciders are from small-scale producers. Kids' menus include hot chocolates or smoothies.

Ludlow Kitchen CAFE £
(✆01584-856020; www.ludlowkitchen.co.uk; Bromfield Rd, Bromfield; breakfast £3.50-8.50, lunch mains £7-12.50; ⊘7am-5.30pm Mon-Sat, 8am-4pm Sun; 🚗) 🌱 Produce from the Ludlow Food Centre (p436) artisanal farm shop is served at this sunlit cafe 4 miles northwest of Ludlow off Bromfield Rd (the A49). Fantastic breakfasts (homemade toasted muesli; full English fry-ups with farmhouse eggs, organic bacon and black pudding; eggs royale) are the precursor to lunch dishes such as Ludlow Brewing Company beer-battered cod with zingy tartar.

Fish House SEAFOOD £
(✆01584-879790; www.thefishhouseludlow.co.uk; 50 Bull Ring; taster plates £4-10, shellfish platter £68; ⊘noon-3pm Wed-Sat) Except on Saturdays when it's first-come, first-served, bookings are recommended for the barrel tables at this stylish fish and oyster bar. It sources Britain's best seafood: Whitby dressed crab, Arbroath smokies and Bigbury Bay oysters. Taster plates come with organic bread, lemon and mayo. The house shellfish platter, available Fridays and Saturdays only, is best washed down with champagne.

1. Ploughman's lunch 2. Scones with jam and cream 3. A typical cooked English breakfast 4. Fish and chips

Flavours of England

England has shaken off its reputation for bland food. Today, wherever you go in the country it's possible to find good quality dishes, which focus on locally sourced or seasonally grown ingredients. There's still no English equivalent of 'bon appetit' but at least the term can be used genuinely these days – instead of with a dash of irony.

Breakfast

For many visitors to England, the culinary day begins in a hotel or B&B with the phenomenon known as the 'Full English' – a large plateful of mainly fried food that may be a shock if you usually have just a bowl of cereal. But perseverance is recommended, as there's enough fuel here to see you through hours of sightseeing.

Lunch & Dinner

For lunch or an evening meal, England has a good range of local and international options to suit all budgets, but you should definitely sample two quintessentially English eateries: the cafe and the pub. In cities, cafes are a good cheaper option, while in country areas they're often called teashops – perfect for a traditional afternoon tea with scones, jam and cream. Pubs are the obvious place to sample traditional English beer, as well as being a reliable option for good-value meals. The most food-focused establishments are now called 'gastropubs'.

English Classics

Fish & chips Long-standing favourite, best sampled in coastal towns.

Sandwich Global snack today, but an English 'invention' from the 18th century.

Ploughman's lunch Bread and cheese,a pub menu regular, perfect with a pint.

Roast beef & Yorkshire pudding Traditional English Sunday lunch.

Cumberland sausage Northern speciality, so big it's coiled to fit on your plate.

Cornish pasty Once restricted to the southwest, now available country-wide.

Wheatsheaf Inn   PUB
(www.wheatsheafludlow.co.uk; Lower Broad St; ⊙noon-11pm) Under the medieval Broadgate, the quiet little Wheatsheaf Inn has stone walls, exposed wooden beams, two toasty fireplaces and a good choice of local ales.

Church Inn   PUB
(www.thechurchinncom; Buttercross, King St; ⊙10am-midnight Mon-Thu, to 1am Fri & Sat, to 11pm Sun) The hop-strewn Church Inn is a cosy little escape with a pulpit at the bar. It's tucked away on the narrow lane beside the old butter market.

☆ Entertainment

Ludlow Assembly Rooms   CINEMA
(☑01584-878141; www.ludlowassemblyrooms. co.uk; adult standard/balcony £7/8, child £6.50/7.50) Overlooking the market square, the Ludlow Assembly Rooms double as the town cinema.

🛍 Shopping

★ Ludlow Food Centre   FOOD & DRINKS
(☑01584-856000; www.ludlowfoodcentre.co.uk; Bromfield Rd, Bromfield; ⊙9am-5.30pm Mon-Sat, to 4.30pm Sun) 🌱 More than 80% of the cheeses, meats, breads, fruit and vegetables are sourced from the surrounding region and tantalisingly displayed at this enormous farm shop stocking over 4000 products in all. Watch through viewing windows to see traditional preserves, pies, ice cream and more being made. It's signposted 4 miles northwest of Ludlow off Bromfield Rd (the A49).

Ludlow Market   MARKET
(www.ludlowmarket.co.uk; Castle Sq; ⊙9.30am-2pm Mon, Wed, Fri & Sat) Ludlow Market takes place on the market square on the site of the old Victorian town hall, demolished overnight in 1986. Various spin-off markets (farmers markets, flea markets, book markets and craft markets) take place on Thursdays and Sundays.

ℹ Information

Ludlow's **tourist office** (☑01584-875053; www.visitshropshirehills.co.uk; Castle Sq; ⊙10am-5pm daily Apr-Sep, to 4pm Mon-Sat Oct-Mar) contains a small local-history exhibit (adult/child £1/free).

ℹ Getting There & Away

Bus 435 runs to Shrewsbury (£3.85, 1½ hours, hourly Monday to Friday, every two hours Saturday) via Church Stretton (£2.95, 40 minutes).

Trains run frequently from the station on the north edge of town to Hereford (£9.80, 25 minutes, half-hourly) and Shrewsbury (£12.70, 30 minutes, half-hourly), some via Church Stretton (£7.10, 15 minutes, hourly).

NOTTINGHAMSHIRE

Say Nottinghamshire and people think of one thing – Robin Hood. Whether the hero woodsman existed is hotly debated, but the county plays up its connections to the outlaw. Storytelling seems to be in Nottinghamshire's blood – local wordsmiths include provocative writer DH Lawrence, of *Lady Chatterley's Lover* fame, and hedonistic poet Lord Byron. The city of Nottingham is the bustling hub, but venture into the surrounding countryside and you'll discover historic towns and stately homes surrounding the green bower of Sherwood Forest.

ℹ Getting There & Around

National Express and **Trent Barton** (☑01773-712265; www.trentbarton.co.uk) buses provide the majority of bus services. See **Traveline** (☑0871 200 2233; www.travelineeastmidlands. co.uk) for timetables. Trains run frequently to most large towns, and to many smaller villages in the Peak District.

Nottingham & Around
POP 310,800

Forever associated with men in tights and a sheriff with anger-management issues (aka the Robin Hood legend) Nottingham is a dynamic county capital with big-city aspirations, atmospheric historical sights, and a buzzing music and club scene thanks to its spirited student population.

◎ Sights

★ Nottingham Castle   CASTLE, GALLERY
(☑0115-876 1400; www.nottinghamcastle.org.uk; Lenton Rd; adult/child £6/5, cave tours £5/free; ⊙10am-5pm daily mid-Feb–Oct, to 4pm Wed-Sun Nov–mid-Feb, cave tours hourly noon-3pm) Nottingham's castle crowns a sandstone outcrop worm-holed with caves and tunnels. Founded by William the Conqueror, the original castle was held by a succession of English kings before falling in the English Civil War. Its 17th-century manor-house-like replacement contains a local-history **museum** and **art gallery**. Various cave tours include one through underground passageway **Mortimer's Hole**,

emerging alongside five 17th-century cottages comprising the **Museum of Nottingham Life at Brewhouse Yard** (☑0115-876 1400; www.nottinghamcity.gov.uk; Castle Blvd; adult/child £2.50/free; ☺noon-4pm Sat & Sun year-round). The much-photographed **statue of Robin Hood** (Castle Rd) stands in the former moat.

City of Caves   CAVE
(☑0115-988 1955; www.cityofcaves.com; Drury Walk, Upper Level, Broadmarsh Shopping Centre; adult/child £7.95/5.95, incl Galleries of Justice £15/11.75; ☺10.30am-4pm) Over the centuries, the sandstone underneath Nottingham has been carved into a honeycomb of caverns and passageways. Audio tours (Monday to Friday) and performance tours (weekends and school holidays) lead you from the top level of the Broadmarsh shopping centre through a WWII air-raid shelter, a medieval underground tannery, several pub cellars and a mock-up of a Victorian slum dwelling. Book ahead.

Galleries of Justice   MUSEUM
(☑0115-952 0555; www.galleriesofjustice.org.uk; High Pavement; adult/child £9.95/7.95, incl City of Caves £15/11.75; ☺9am-6pm Mon-Fri, 10am-5.30pm Sat & Sun, tours 10am-4pm Mon-Fri, 10.30am-4pm Sat & Sun) In the grand Georgian Shire Hall, the Galleries of Justice offers a ghoulish stroll through centuries of British justice, including medieval trials by fire and water. Audio tours run on Mondays and Tuesdays; live-action tours with 'gaolers' run from Wednesday to Sunday (daily during school holidays).

Nottingham Contemporary   GALLERY
(☑0115-948 9750; www.nottinghamcontemporary.org; Weekday Cross; ☺10am-6pm Tue-Sat, 11am-5pm Sun) FREE Behind its lace-patterned concrete facade, Nottingham Contemporary holds edgy, design-driven exhibitions of paintings, prints, photography and sculpture.

St Mary's Church   CHURCH
(www.nottinghamchurches.org; High Pavement; ☺8am-6.30pm) The most atmospheric time to visit this historic church dating from Saxon times is during evensong (6.15pm Wednesday, 6.30pm Sunday).

Wollaton Hall   HISTORIC BUILDING
(☑0115-876 3100; www.wollatonhall.co.uk; Wollaton Park, Derby Rd; tours adult/child £5/3, grounds free; ☺tours 11am, 2pm & 3pm, grounds 8am-8pm Mon-Fri, 9am-8pm Sat & Sun mid-Feb–Oct, 9am-7pm Mon-Fri, 10am-7pm Sat & Sun Nov–mid-Feb) Built in 1588 for land owner and coal mogul Sir Francis Willoughby by avant-garde architect Robert Smythson, Wollaton Hall sits within 200 hectares of grounds roamed by fallow and red deer. Along with extravagant rooms from the Tudor, Regency and Victorian periods, there's a natural-history museum and industrial museum.

Wollaton Hall is 2.5 miles west of Nottingham city centre; take bus 30 or 2 from Victoria bus station (£2.20, 15 minutes, every 15 minutes Monday to Saturday, half-hourly Sunday).

Newstead Abbey   HISTORIC BUILDING
(☑01623-455900; www.newsteadabbey.org.uk; adult/child house £7/5, garden only £1; ☺house noon-5pm Sat & Sun, garden 10am-5pm daily) The evocative lakeside ruins of Newstead Abbey are inextricably associated with the original tortured romantic, Lord Byron (1788–1824), who owned the house until 1817. Founded as an Augustinian priory in around 1170, it was converted into a residence in 1539.

Newstead Abbey is 12 miles north of Nottingham, off the A60. Pronto buses (£3.20, 25 minutes, every 10 minutes Monday to Saturday, half-hourly Sunday) from Victoria bus station stop at the gates, a mile from the house and gardens.

🏃 **Activities & Tours**

★**Ezekial Bone Tours**   WALKING
(☑07941 210986; www.ezekialbone.com; Robin Hood Town Tours adult/child £12/7; ☺Robin Hood Town Tours by reservation 2pm Sat Mar-Oct) Hugely entertaining, history-focused **Robin Hood town tours** are led by 'modern-day Robin Hood' Ezekial Bone (aka historian/actor/writer Ade Andrews). Tours last 2½ hours, departing from the Cross Keys pub. Check Bone/Andrews' website for 90-minute **Lace Market tours** and 80-minute **Guts & Gore** ghost tours, plus **Robin Hood Sherwood Forest tours** by request.

National Ice Centre   SKATING
(☑0843 373 3000; www.national-ice-centre.com; Bolero Sq; skating £6.50, skate hire £2) The UK's first ice centre with twin Olympic-sized (60m x 30m) rinks sits on Bolero Sq, named for Nottingham skaters Jayne Torvill and Christopher Dean's historic 1984 gold-medal-winning routine. The complex incorporates the East Midland's premier entertainment venue, the **Motorpoint Arena**, which hosts sporting fixtures, competitions and performances. Daily skating session times (including weekend disco sessions) are posted online.

Nottingham

☆ Festivals & Events

Goose Fair CULTURAL
(www.nottinghamcity.gov.uk; ⊙ early Oct) The five-day Goose Fair has evolved from a medieval travelling market to a modern funfair.

Robin Hood Beer & Cider Festival DRINK
(www.beerfestival.nottinghamcamra.org; ⊙ mid-Oct) In the castle grounds, this four-day tasting festival features more than 1000 beers and 200 ciders.

Robin Hood Pageant CULTURAL
(www.nottinghamcastle.org.uk; ⊙ late Oct) This family-friendly pageant takes place over two days in late October.

🛏 Sleeping

Igloo Hybrid Hostel HOSTEL £
(☏ 0115-948 3822; www.igloohostel.co.uk; 4-6 Eldon Chambers, Wheeler Gate; dm from £19, s/d sleep box from £29/64, s without/with en suite from £34/48, d without/with en suite £72/98; 🛜)

Opened in 2015, the sister property of the much-loved **Igloo Backpackers Hostel** (☏ 0115-947 5250; www.igloohostel.co.uk; 110 Mansfield Rd; dm/d from £19/44; 🛜) has an epicentral location footsteps from the Old Market Sq. Its Japanese capsule-style 'Sleep Boxes' incorporate USB ports and reading lights; there's a well-equipped self-catering kitchen and a sociable courtyard garden.

★ Lace Market Hotel BOUTIQUE HOTEL ££
(☏ 0115-948 4414; www.lacemarkethotel.co.uk; 29-31 High Pavement; s/d incl breakfast from £85/135; 🅿 ✳ 🛜) In the heart of the trendy Lace Market, this elegant Georgian town house's sleek rooms have state-of-the-art furnishings and amenities; some come with air-conditioning. Its fine-dining restaurant, Merchants (p440), and adjoining genteel pub, the **Cock & Hoop** (www.lacemarkethotel.co.uk; 25 High Pavement; ⊙ 11am-11pm Mon-Thu, to midnight Fri, to 1am Sat, to 10.30pm Sun), are both superb.

Nottingham

◎ **Top Sights**
1 Nottingham Castle A4

◎ **Sights**
2 City of Caves C3
3 Galleries of Justice D3
4 Museum of Nottingham Life at
   Brewhouse Yard B4
5 Nottingham Contemporary C3
6 St Mary's Church D3
7 Statue of Robin Hood B3

◉ **Activities, Courses & Tours**
8 Ezekial Bone Tours C2

◎ **Sleeping**
9 Hart's A2
10 Igloo Hybrid Hostel B2
11 Lace Market Hotel D3
12 St James Hotel A3

◎ **Eating**
13 Annie's Burger Shack D2
14 Aubrey's Traditional Crêperie A1

15 Delilah Fine Foods C2
   Hart's Restaurant .... (see 9)
   Merchants .... (see 11)
16 Purecraft Bar & Kitchen C2

◎ **Drinking & Nightlife**
17 Brass Monkey D3
18 Cock & Hoop D3
19 Crafty Crow A3
20 Dragon A1
21 Malt Cross B2
22 NG1 .... D1
23 Tilt C2
24 Ye Olde Trip to Jerusalem B3

◎ **Entertainment**
25 Broadway Cinema D1
26 Nottingham Playhouse A2
27 Theatre Royal & Royal Concert
   Hall B1

◎ **Shopping**
28 Victoria Shopping Centre C1

St James Hotel   BOUTIQUE HOTEL **££**
(☑ 0115-941 1114; www.stjames-hotel.com; St James's Tce; s/d/ste £74.50/89.50/204.50; 🛜) Stunning patterned wallpaper, richly coloured textured fabrics and designer elements such as stag heads made from stainless steel set the striking St James apart. It's in an increasingly vibrant area right by Nottingham Castle and historic pubs plus hip new bars and restaurants. More than 500 books line its library shelves; parking is available next door (per 24 hours £11).

Hart's   BOUTIQUE HOTEL **£££**
(☑ 0115-988 1900; www.hartsnottingham.co.uk; Standard Hill, Park Row; incl breakfast d £93-212, ste £127-302; 🅿🛜) Within the former Nottingham General Hospital compound, the city's swishest hotel has ultracontemporary rooms in a striking modernist building; its renowned **restaurant** (☑ 0115-988 1900; www.hartsnottingham.co.uk; Standard Hill, Park Row; mains £16-30; ☉ noon-2.30pm & 6-10pm; ✐) is housed in a historic red-brick wing. Work out in the small gym or unwind in the private garden.

✕ Eating

★ **Delilah Fine Foods**   DELI, CAFE **£**
(www.delilahfinefoods.co.uk; 12 Victoria St; dishes £4-16, platters £15-35; ☉ 8am-7pm Mon-Fri, 9am-7pm Sat, 11am-5pm Sun; ✐) 🍃 Impeccably selected cheeses (more than 150 varieties), pâtés, meats and more from artisan producers are available to take away or eat on-site at this gourmand's dream, housed in a grand former bank with mezzanine seating.

Annie's Burger Shack   BURGERS, AMERICAN **£**
(www.anniesburgershack.com; 5 Broadway; burgers £8.90-13.20, breakfast £6-10; ☉ 8-10.15am & noon-11.30pm Mon-Thu, 8-10.15am & noon-12.30am Sat, noon-11.30pm Sun; 🛜) More than 30 different burgers (available in vegan, veggie or meat versions) are on the menu at Annie's, a wildly popular joint in the Lace Market that stays true to its owner's US roots (and adds real ales to its offerings). Midweek breakfast menus feature American classics (blueberry pancakes with maple syrup and bacon; Boston franks 'n beans). Book ahead.

Aubrey's Traditional Crêperie   CREPERIE **£**
(www.aubreystraditionalcreperie.com; 14-16 West End Arcade; dishes £2.75-8; ☉ 10am-6pm Wed-Sat; ✐) Traditional down to its savoury galettes made with buckwheat flour, its sweet crêpes including salted caramel and its Breton ciders, this little hole-in-the-wall is a charming spot for an inexpensive lunch. Alongside the classics, there are galettes you'll never see in Brittany, such as black olives, caramelised onions, sun-dried tomatoes and balsamic, or ginger, chilli relish, rucola and chorizo, too.

Purecraft Bar & Kitchen
GASTROPUB ££

(☑ 0115-934 9040; www.purecraftbars.com; 13 St Peter's Gate; mains £9-16, platters £8.50-9.50; ⊗ kitchen noon-10pm Mon-Sat, to 6pm Sun, bar 11am-11pm Mon-Thu, 11am-midnight Fri & Sat, noon-10pm Sun) Purecraft matches artisan beers from around the world with well-crafted fare, including platters (Wyre Forest–reared pig board; British cheese board), light bites (such as a Scotch egg with Purity-beer ketchup, stout-cured ham and Old Winchester cheese rarebit), Wagyu burgers, and traditional pork pies with homemade piccalilli pickle relish.

The original of its two locations is in Birmingham (p398).

Merchants
GASTRONOMY £££

(☑ 0115-948 4414; www.lacemarkethotel.co.uk; 29-31 High Pavement; mains £19-30, 2-/3-course lunch menus £14.50/18.50, 3-course dinner menu £45; ⊗ 7-10am, noon-2pm & 5-10pm Mon-Sat, 7-10.30am & noon-2pm Sun) A stunning, coffered-ceilinged dining room sets the stage for some of Nottingham's finest dining. Knock-out combinations include Texel lamb with pistachio and courgette; Irish sea trout with samphire and radish; and morrels, broad beans and goats curd. Follow up with equally adventurous desserts such as poached-rhubarb panna cotta with black-pepper crumble and basil ice cream.

Restaurant Sat Bains
GASTRONOMY £££

(☑ 0115-986 6566; www.restaurantsatbains.com; Lenton Lane; 7-/10-course tasting menus £85/95; ⊗ 6-9pm Wed & Thu, 6-9.45pm Fri & Sat; 🅿) Chef Sat Bains has been awarded two Michelin stars for his wildly inventive Modern European cooking. Book well in advance and beware of hefty cancellation charges. It also has eight chic **guest rooms** (double £140 to £190, suite £285). It's 2 miles southwest of the centre off the A52.

🍷 Drinking & Nightlife

★ Ye Olde Trip to Jerusalem
PUB

(☑ 0115-947 3171; www.triptojerusalem.com; Brewhouse Yard, Castle Rd; ⊗ 11am-11pm Sun-Thu, to midnight Fri & Sat) Carved into the cliff below the castle, this atmospheric alehouse claims to be England's oldest pub. Founded in 1189, it supposedly slaked the thirst of departing crusaders, and its rooms and cobbled courtyards are still the most ambient place in Nottingham for a pint. Book ahead for informal tours (£2.50) of its cellars and caves.

★ Crafty Crow
PUB

(www.craftycrownotts.co.uk; 102 Friar Lane; ⊗ noon-11pm Sun-Thu, 11am-midnight Fri & Sat; 🎐) 🍺 Rotating brews at this beer specialist include several from its own Nottingham-based Magpie Brewery, made from British hops and malts, plus hand-pulls from local microbreweries and more than a dozen craft beers and ciders on tap. Timber-planked walls line the TV-free split-level space; don't miss the bathrooms with sinks and taps made out of kegs. Gastropub food is locally sourced.

Dragon
PUB

(www.the-dragon.co.uk; 67 Long Row; ⊗ noon-midnight Mon-Thu, noon-2am Fri & Sat, 11am-10pm Sun; 🎐) The Dragon has a fabulous atmosphere at any time, thanks to homemade food, a good beer garden and funky music on weekends. But it peaks from 7.30pm on Tuesdays when it hosts the Racing Room (race entry £5) – an awesome Scalextric slot-car race around a scale model of Nottingham along 180ft of track.

Brass Monkey
BAR

(www.brassmonkeybar.co.uk; 11 High Pavement; ⊗ 5pm-3am Mon-Sat, 8pm-3am Sun) Nottingham's original cocktail bar rocks the Lace Market with DJ sets and quirky takes on favourites such as elderflower mojitos. The roof terrace gets packed on summer evenings.

Tilt
COCKTAIL BAR

(www.tiltbar.co.uk; 9 Pelham St; ⊗ 5pm-midnight Tue-Thu, to 1.30am Fri & Sat) This tiny 1st-floor cocktail bar serves up a brilliant array of live blues offerings as well as cocktails that are giving their competition (in Nottingham, that's a lot!) a run for their money. House specialities include a Blues Blazer (cognac and Drambuie flamed with vanilla sugar and orange peel).

NG1
CLUB

(☑ 0115-958 8440; www.ng1club.co.uk; 76-80 Lower Parliament St; ⊗ 11pm-6am Fri, to 6.30am Sat) A fixture on Notthingham's late-night scene, NG1 is unpretentious, hedonistic fun, with four bars and two dance floors belting out house, electro, pop and more. It's gay-friendly and all-welcoming.

Malt Cross
PUB

(www.maltcross.com; 16 St James's St; ⊗ 11am-11pm Mon-Fri, 10am-midnight Sat, 10am-10pm Sun) A fine place for a pint, the Malt Cross occupies a stately old Victorian music hall,

SHERWOOD FOREST NATIONAL NATURE RESERVE

If Robin Hood wanted to hide out in Sherwood Forest today, he'd have to disguise himself and the Merry Men as day trippers on mountain bikes. Now covering just 182 hectares of old growth forest, it's nevertheless a major destination for Nottingham city dwellers.

Until a proposed new visitor centre opens, the **Sherwood Forest Visitor Centre** (www.nottinghamshire.gov.uk; Swinecote Rd, Edwinstowe; ⊙10am-5.30pm Easter-Oct, to 4.30pm Nov-Mar), on the B6034, is an uninspiring collection of faded late-20th-century buildings housing cafes, gift shops et al. It's the departure point for walking trails passing Sherwood Forest landmarks such as the **Major Oak** (1 mile return), a broad-boughed oak tree (propped up by supporting rods) alleged to have sheltered Robin of Locksley.

For informative guided walks through forest, contact **Ezekial Bone Tours** (p437).

Sherwood Pines Cycles (☑01623-822855; www.sherwoodpinescycles.co.uk; Sherwood Pines Forest Park, Clipstone; bike hire adult/child per hour £9/8, per day £28/20; ⊙9am-5pm Thu-Tue, to 7pm Wed) rents bikes. From Nottingham, take the Sherwood Arrow bus (£5, 55 minutes, four per day Monday to Saturday, two on Sunday).

Robin Hood Festival (www.nottinghamshire.gov.uk; ⊙early Aug) The week-long Robin Hood Festival is a massive medieval reenactment that takes place in the forest in early August.

where past performers included Charlie Chaplin. It's now a community space run by the Christian Charity Trust hosting art exhibitions and live music. Top-notch bar food includes towering burgers.

☆ Entertainment

Nottingham Playhouse THEATRE
(☑0115-941 9419; www.nottinghamplayhouse. co.uk; Wellington Circus) Beside Anish Kapoor's enormous *Sky Mirror* dish, the Playhouse puts on serious theatre, from stage classics to the avant-garde. Nottingham's artistic community congregates at its attached restaurant and bar.

Theatre Royal &
Royal Concert Hall THEATRE, LIVE MUSIC
(☑0115-989 5555; www.trch.co.uk; Theatre Sq; ⊙booking office 9.30am-8.30pm Mon-Sat) Sharing the same building and booking office, the Theatre Royal and Royal Concert Hall host musicals, touring theatre shows and veteran music acts. Backstage tours can be arranged (£6.50, 90 minutes).

Broadway Cinema CINEMA, GALLERY
(www.broadway.org.uk; 14-18 Broad St; cinema tickets adult/child £8.20/4) Along with an independent cinema, this artistic hub has a media-arts gallery and a cafe-bar where you can actually hear yourself talk.

❶ Information

Nottingham's friendly **tourist office** (☑0844 477 5678; www.experiencenottinghamshire. com; The Exchange, 1-4 Smithy Row; ⊙9.30am-5.30pm Mon-Sat year-round, plus 11am-5pm Sun late Jul–Aug & mid–late Dec) has racks of info and Robin Hood merchandise.

❶ Getting There & Away

AIR

East Midlands Airport (p392) is 13.5 miles southwest of central Nottingham; Skylink buses pass the airport (one way/return £5/9.90, one hour, at least hourly, 24 hours).

BUS

Local services run from the Victoria bus station, behind the **Victoria Shopping Centre** (Lower Parliament St) on Milton St. Bus 100 runs to Southwell (£4.15, 55 minutes, every 30 minutes Monday to Saturday, hourly Sunday) and bus 90 to Newark (£5, 50 minutes, every 30 minutes Monday to Friday, hourly Saturday, every two hours Sunday).

Long-distance buses operate from the **Broadmarsh bus station** (Collin St).

Frequent National Express services:

Birmingham £10.90, 2¼ hours, eight daily
Derby £7.80, 40 minutes, six Monday to Saturday, four Sunday
Leicester £5.50, 55 minutes, hourly or better
London Victoria £14, 3½ hours, hourly or better

TRAIN

The train station is on the southern edge of the town centre.

Derby £7.30, 30 minutes, four hourly

Lincoln £11.30, one hour, hourly

London King's Cross/St Pancras £29.50, two hours, at least two per hour Monday to Saturday, at least hourly Sunday

Manchester £23.50, two hours, up to two per hour

ⓘ Getting Around

For information on buses within Nottingham, call **Nottingham City Transport** (☑ 0115-950 6070; www.nctx.co.uk). A Robin Hood Day Ticket gives you unlimited travel on buses and trams within the city for £4.50.

Trams are operated by **Nottingham Express Transit** (www.thetram.net; single/day ticket from £2.20/4). A single-stage bus ticket costs £1.10.

Nottingham City Council's bike-share scheme, **City Card Cycles** (www.citycardcycles.co.uk; per day £1), has rental bikes available from Nottingham's tourist office and Broadmarsh bus station. Register using a credit card, then use the code sent to your phone to unlock the bikes.

Southwell

POP 6900

A graceful scattering of grand, wisteria-draped country houses, pretty little Southwell is straight out of the pages of a novel from the English Romantic period.

◉ Sights

★ Southwell Minster CHURCH

(www.southwellminster.org; Church St; suggested donation £5; ⊙ 8am-7pm Mar-Oct, to 6.30pm Nov-Feb) Rising from the village centre, the awe-inspiring Southwell Minster, built over Saxon and Roman foundations, blends 12th- and 13th-century features including zigzag door frames and curved arches. Its chapterhouse features some unusual stained glass and detailed carvings of faces, animals and leaves of forest trees.

Southwell Workhouse MUSEUM

(NT; www.nationaltrust.org.uk; Upton Rd; adult/child £8/4; ⊙ noon-5pm daily Aug, Wed-Sun mid-Feb–Jul & Sep-Nov) On the road to Newark, 1 mile east of the village centre, the Southwell Workhouse is a sobering reminder of the tough life faced by paupers in the 19th century. You can explore the factory floors and workers' chambers accompanied by an audio guide narrated by 'inmates' and 'officials'.

Free one-hour guided tours of the exteriors take place at 11am.

🍴 Sleeping & Eating

Saracen's Head Hotel HISTORIC HOTEL ££

(☑ 01636-812701; www.saracensheadhotel.com; Market Pl; s/d/f/ste incl breakfast from £90/100/130/150; P🅿🛜♿🐾) Set around a flower-filled courtyard in the village heart, this rambling, black-and-white timbered coaching inn has 27 beautifully refurbished rooms (some with four-poster beds and clawfoot baths) across its old and new wings. Illustrious past guests included Charles I, Lord Byron and Dickens. Its oak-panelled restaurant serves traditional British fare (two-/three-course menus £15.95/19.95).

Mosedales Bakery BAKERY £

(7 King St; dishes £3-8; ⊙ 9am-4pm Mon-Fri, 8.30am-4pm Sat, 9.30am-3pm Sun) Queues at this central village bakery regularly extend out the door.

ⓘ Getting There & Away

Bus 100 runs from Nottingham (£4.15, 55 minutes, half-hourly Monday to Saturday, hourly on Sunday). For Newark-on-Trent, take bus 28 or 29 (£4, 20 minutes, half-hourly).

Newark-on-Trent

POP 37,457

Newark-on-Trent paid the price for backing the wrong side in the English Civil War. After surviving four sieges by Oliver Cromwell's men, the town was ransacked by Roundheads when Charles I surrendered in 1646. Today, the riverside town is a peaceful place worth a stop to wander its castle ruins.

◉ Sights

Newark Castle CASTLE

(www.newark-sherwooddc.gov.uk/newarkcastle; Castle Gate; grounds admission free, tours adult/child £5/2.50; ⊙ grounds 9am-6pm, tours 11am, 1pm & 3pm Wed & Fri-Sun) In a pretty park overlooking the River Trent, the ruins of Newark Castle include an impressive Norman gate and a series of underground passages and chambers. The real King John, portrayed as a villain in the Robin Hood legend, died here in 1216. Book tour tickets online at www.palacenewarktickets.com. Concerts, festivals and various cultural events regularly take place in the grounds.

Newark Air Museum MUSEUM
(☑ 01636-707170; www.newarkairmuseum.org;
Drove Lane, Winthorpe; adult/child £8.50/4.50;
⊙ 10am-5pm Mar-Oct, to 4pm Nov-Feb) Situated
2 miles east of Newark by the Winthorpe
Showground, this air museum has an impressive collection of aircraft, including a
fearsome Vulcan bomber.

✖ Eating & Drinking

Old Bakery Tea Rooms TEAROOM £
(☑ 01636-611501; www.oldbakerytearooms.co.uk;
4 Queens Head Ct; mains £6-12; ⊙ 9.30am-5pm
Mon-Sat; ☑) Everything, including to-die-for
scones, is baked fresh on the premises at the
Old Bakery Tea Rooms, housed in an enchanting *Hansel and Gretel*–like 15th-cen-
tury Tudor building. Lunch specials include
soups, frittata, bruschetta and smoked-salmon brioche. Cash only.

Castle Barge BAR
(www.castlebarge.co.uk; The Wharf; ⊙ 10.30am-
11pm) Moored on the River Trent overlooking Newark Castle, this former grain barge,
which once plied the waters between Hull
and Gainsborough, is an idyllic spot for a
local ale. It serves decent food; there's additional picnic seating on the riverbanks.

ℹ Information

The **tourist office** (☑ 01636-655765; www.
newark-sherwooddc.gov.uk/tourism; 14 Apple-
ton Gate; ⊙ 10am-5pm) is on the northeastern
edge of the historic centre.

ℹ Getting There & Away

Buses 28 and 29 serve Southwell (£4, 25 minutes, up to four per hour).

Newark has two train stations:

Newark North Gate Trains on the East Coast
Main Line serve London King's Cross (£20, 1½
hours, two per hour) and the north.
Newark Castle East Midlands trains serve
Leicester (£12.80, 1¼ hours, hourly), Notting-
ham (£6.10, 30 minutes, two per hour) and
Lincoln (£5.10, 30 minutes, up to two hourly).

LINCOLNSHIRE

Lincolnshire unfolds over low hills and the
sparsely populated, pancake-flat Fens where
the farmland is strewn with windmills and,
more recently, wind turbines. Surrounding
the history-steeped county town of Lincoln
you'll find seaside resorts, scenic waterways,

serene nature reserves and stone-built towns
tailor-made for English period dramas.

Two of the county's most famous 'yellow-
bellies' (as Lincolnshire locals call themselves) were Sir Isaac Newton, whose home,
Woolsthorpe Manor, can be visited, and
the late former prime minister Margaret
Thatcher, the daughter of a humble green-
grocer from the market town of Grantham.

🏃 Activities

Traversing the area occupied by Norse invaders in the 9th century, the 147-mile **Viking
Way** walking trail snakes across the gentle
hills of the Lincolnshire Wolds from the banks
of the River Humber to Oakham in Rutland.

Cyclists can find information on routes
across the county in any of the local tourist
offices. The 33-mile **Water Rail Way** is a flat,
sculpture-lined on-road cycling route that
follows the River Witham through classic
Fens countryside along the former railway
line between Lincoln and Boston.

Detailed information on activities is available at www.visitlincolnshire.com.

ℹ Getting There & Around

East Midlands trains connect Lincoln, Newark
Castle and Nottingham. Newark North Gate and
Grantham lie on the East Coast Main Line be-
tween London King's Cross and Edinburgh.

Local buses link Lincolnshire's towns but services are slow and infrequent. Check the transport pages at www.lincolnshire.gov.uk, which
also has cycling route info.

Comprehensive transport information is available from Traveline (p436).

Lincoln

POP 96,200

Ringed by historic city gates – including the
Newport Arch on Bailgate, a relic from the
original Roman settlement – this beautiful
city's old centre is a tangle of cobbled medieval streets surrounding a colossal 12th-
century cathedral. The lanes that topple
over the edge of Lincoln Cliff are lined with
Tudor town houses, ancient pubs and quirky
independent stores.

Flanking the River Witham at the base of
the hill, the new town is less absorbing, but
the revitalised Brayford Waterfront development by the university is a popular spot to
watch the boats go by.

◉ Sights

★ Lincoln Cathedral   CATHEDRAL
(☑ 01522-561600;   www.lincolncathedral.com;
Minster Yard; adult/child joint ticket with castle
£16/10, cathedral £8/4.80 Mon-Sat, by donation
Sun; ⊙ 7.15am-8pm Mon-Fri, to 6pm Sat & Sun Jul
& Aug, 7.15am-6pm Mon-Sat, to 5pm Sun Sep-Jun,
evensong 5.30pm Mon-Sat, 3.45pm Sun) Towering over the city like a medieval skyscraper,
Lincoln's magnificent cathedral is a breathtaking representation of divine power on
earth. The great tower rising above the
crossing is the third-highest in England at
83m, but in medieval times, a lead-encased
wooden spire added a further 79m, topping
even the great pyramids of Giza. One-hour
guided tours (included in admission) take
place at least twice daily; there are also tours
of the roof and tower (£4, book in advance).

★ Lincoln Castle   CASTLE
(☑ 01522-554559; www.lincolncastle.com; Castle
Hill; adult/child joint ticket with cathedral £16/10, castle, Magna Carta exhibition & walls £12/7.20, walls only
£5/3; ⊙ 10am-5pm Apr-Sep, to 4pm Oct-Mar) One
of the first castles erected by the victorious
William the Conqueror to keep his new kingdom in line, Lincoln Castle offers awesome
views over the city and miles of surrounding
countryside. A major restoration program,
completed in 2015, has opened up the entire
castle walls and given the 1215 Magna Carta
(one of only four copies) a swanky, subterranean new home. One-hour guided tours, included in castle admission, depart from the
eastern gate; check the blackboard for times.

Bishops' Palace   HISTORIC SITE
(EH; ☑ 01522-527468; www.english-heritage.org.uk;
Minster Yard; adult/child £5.70/3.40; ⊙ 10am-6pm
Wed-Sun Easter-Sep, to 5pm Wed-Sun Oct, to 4pm
Sat & Sun Nov-Easter) Beside Lincoln Cathedral
lie the time-ravaged but still imposing ruins
of the 12th-century Bishops' Palace, gutted
by parliamentary forces during the Civil War.
From here, the local bishops once controlled
a diocese stretching from the Humber to the
Thames. Entertaining audio guides are in-
cluded in admission. Free 30-minute guided
tours take place at noon, 2pm and 4pm on
Fridays from Easter to October.

Collection   MUSEUM
(www.thecollectionmuseum.com;   Danes   Tce;
⊙ 10am-4pm, from 10.45am 1st Mon of month)
FREE Archaeology bursts into life with loads
of hands-on displays. Kids can handle artefacts and dress up in period costume. Check

out the crushed skull of a 4000-year-old 'yel-
lowbelly' (the local term for, well, the locals),
pulled from a Neolithic burial site near Sleaford. Free one-hour tours run at 2pm on Saturdays. Look out for various evening events.

Usher Gallery   GALLERY
(www.thecollectionmuseum.com;   Danes   Tce;
⊙ 10am-4pm, from 10.45am 1st Mon of month)
FREE A handsome Edwardian building decorated with carvings of cow skulls houses
an impressive collection of works by greats
such as Turner, Lowry and English watercol-
ourist Peter de Wint (1784–1849).

Museum of Lincolnshire Life   MUSEUM
(www.lincolnshire.gov.uk;   Old   Barracks,   Burton
Rd; ⊙ 10am-4.30pm) FREE Displays at this
charming community museum housed in
an old Victorian barracks span everything
from Victorian farm implements to the tin-
can tank built in Lincoln for WWI. Around
the corner from the museum is the cute little
Ellis Mill (www.lincolnshire.gov.uk; Mill Rd; ⊙ 2-
5pm Sat & Sun Apr-Sep, 2-4pm Sun Oct-Mar) FREE,
which ground the town's flour in the 18th
century and is still in use today.

⟲ Tours

Ghost Walks   WALKING
(☑ 01522-874056; adult/child £5/3; ⊙ 7pm Wed-
Sat year-round) Genuinely spooky 75-minute
ghost walks depart adjacent to the tourist
office in Castle Sq.

Brayford Belle   BOATING
(☑ 01522-881200;   www.lincolnboattrips.co.uk;
Brayford Wharf North; adult/child £7/4; ⊙ tours
11am, 12.15pm, 1.30pm, 2.45pm & 3.45pm Easter–mid-Oct) Boat trips aboard the *Brayford
Belle* travel along the River Witham and
Fossdyke Navigation, a canal system dating
back to Roman times. No credit cards.

Walking Tours   WALKING
(☑ 01522-521256; www.lincolnguidedtours.co.uk;
adult/child £4/free; ⊙ tours 11am daily Jul & Aug,
Sat & Sun Jun, Sep & Oct) History-focused
90-minute guided walking tours run from
outside the tourist office.

🛏 Sleeping

★ Castle Hotel   BOUTIQUE HOTEL ££
(☑ 01522-538801; www.castlehotel.net; Westgate;
incl breakfast s £90-130, d £110-150, coach house
£250-270; [P ☎ ⚇]) Each of the Castle Hotel's
18 rooms have been exquisitely refurbished
in olive, truffle and oyster tones, as has its

Lincoln

Lincoln

◎ Top Sights

1 Lincoln Castle	C2
2 Lincoln Cathedral	D2

◎ Sights

3 Bishops' Palace	D2
4 Collection	C3
5 Ellis Mill	B1
6 Museum of Lincolnshire Life	B1
7 Usher Gallery	D2

✪ Activities, Courses & Tours

8 Brayford Belle	B4
9 Ghost Walks	C2
Walking Tours	(see 9)

🛌 Sleeping

10 Bail House	C1

11 Castle Hotel	C1
12 White Hart Hotel	C2

✪ Eating

13 Bronze Pig	B1
14 Jew's House	C2
15 La Bottega Delitalia	C3
16 Old Bakery	B1
Reform	(see 11)
17 Wig & Mitre	C2

🍷 Drinking & Nightlife

18 Electric Bar & Restaurant	B3
19 Strugglers Inn	B1

✪ Entertainment

20 Home Nightclub	C3
21 Lincoln Drill Hall	C3

four-person coach house. Built on the site of Lincoln's Roman forum in 1852, the red-brick building's incarnations variously included a school and WWII lookout station. Take advantage of great-value dinner, bed and breakfast deals linked to its award-winning restaurant Reform (p446).

Bail House
B&B **££**

(☏01522-541000; www.bailhouse.co.uk; 34 Bailgate; d/f from £69/179; P@🛜🌊🐾) Stone walls, worn flagstones, secluded gardens and one room with an extraordinary timber-vaulted ceiling are just some of the charms of this lovingly restored Georgian town house in central Lincoln. There's limited on-site parking, a garden and children's playground, and even a seasonal heated outdoor swimming pool. Family rooms sleep four.

White Hart Hotel
HOTEL **££**

(☏01522-526222; www.whitehart-lincoln.co.uk; Bailgate; d/tr/ste from £110/150/160; P🛜) You can't get more venerable than this grand dame of Lincoln hotels, sandwiched between the castle and cathedral, with a history dating back 600 years. Its flowing countrified rooms include triples with three single beds.

Eating

La Bottega Delitalia
CAFE, DELI **£**

(☏01522-537775; 9 West Pde; dishes £3-7.50; ⊙8.30am-4pm Mon-Wed, to 9pm Thu & Fri, to 3pm Sat) Authentic Italian fare such as lobster ravioli in creamy tomato and basil sauce is made from scratch at this inexpensive cafe-deli. Cash only.

ℹ MINIMISING LINCOLN'S HILLS

Walking between Lincoln's old and new towns can feel like an Everest expedition, but fortunately there are alternatives.

Lincoln's **Steep Hill Shuttle** (www.visitlincoln.com; single ticket adult/child £1.50/70p, all-day pass £3/1.60; ⊙9.10am-2.45pm & 4.10-5.20pm Mon-Sat) runs every 20 minutes, making 13 stops including the castle, cathedral, Newport Arch, Brayford Waterfront and the train and bus stations.

To tour the city in comfort, hop aboard the open-topped **Tour Lincoln** (www.visitlincoln.com; adult/child £10/4; ⊙10.30am-4.30pm Jun-Sep, 10.30am-4.30pm Sat & Sun Mar-May & Oct) bus, which stops at nine key sights. Tickets are sold at the tourist office and on board. Tours last one hour; tickets are valid all day. One child under 16 travels free per paying adult.

Bronze Pig
MODERN BRITISH **££**

(☏01522-524817; www.thebronzepig.co.uk; 4 Burton Rd; mains £16-27; ⊙by reservation 7-9.30pm Wed-Sat, noon-3pm Sun) BBC *Masterchef* finalist, Irishman Eamonn Hunt, and Sicilian chef Pompeo Siracusa have taken Lincoln's dining scene by storm since opening the Bronze Pig. Their exceptional Modern British cooking has an Italian accent and food is locally sourced. Reserve well ahead and prepare to be wowed.

Reform
MODERN BRITISH **££**

(☏01522-538801; www.castlehotel.net; The Castle Hotel, Westgate; mains £12.50-22; ⊙noon-2.30pm & 7-9pm Mon-Sat, noon-3pm & 7-9pm Sun) Local, seasonal produce at the Castle Hotel's sophisticated restaurant stars in starters such as Parma-ham-wrapped rabbit and liver terrine, and mains including smoked duck breast with orange-pickled carrots. The real show-stoppers here, however, are desserts, from caramelised banana *tarte Tatin* with clotted cream and peanut brittle to lemon drizzle cake with lemon and mint sorbet and lemon panna cotta.

Old Bakery
MODERN BRITISH **££**

(☏01522-576057; www.theold-bakery.co.uk; 26-28 Burton Rd; mains £17.50-26, 2-/3-course lunch menus £14.50/18, 5-course tasting menu £48, with wines £65; ⊙7-8.30pm Tue & Wed, noon-1.30pm & 7-8.30pm Thu-Sat, noon-1.30pm Sun) 🌱 The menu at this long-established spot is built around local produce and – appropriately – freshly baked bread. It also offers regular half-day cookery lessons (from £95) and has three quaint guest rooms upstairs (doubles £75 to £80; two are en suite and the third has a private but separate bathroom).

Wig & Mitre
PUB FOOD **££**

(☏01522-535190; www.wigandmitre.com; 30 Steep Hill; mains £12.50-19.50; ⊙kitchen 8.30am-10.30pm Mon-Sat, to 10pm Sun, bar 8.30am-midnight Mon-Sat, to 11pm Sun; 🍴) Civilised pub-restaurant the Wig & Mitre has an excellent menu yet retains the ambience of a friendly local. Food is served throughout the day, from morning fry-ups to lunchtime sandwiches and filling evening roasts. Look out for wine tastings and gourmet evenings.

Jew's House
MODERN EUROPEAN **££**

(☏01522-524851; www.jewshouserestaurant.co.uk; 15 The Strait (Steep Hill); 2-/3-course lunch menu £16.50/19.95, mains £16-24.50; ⊙7-9.30pm Tue, noon-2pm & 7-9.30pm Wed-Sat) This local favourite serves up gourmet fare in atmos-

AROUND GRANTHAM

Grantham, around 40kms from Lincoln, has few sights itself but there are some fascinating properties in the surrounding countryside.

Woolsthorpe Manor (NT; www.nationaltrust.org.uk; Water Lane; house & grounds adult/child £6.45/3.27, grounds only £3.50/2.27; ◷11am-5pm Wed-Mon Mar-Oct, Fri-Sun Nov-Feb) Sir Isaac Newton fans may feel the gravitational pull of the great man's birthplace, about 8 miles south of Grantham. The humble 17th-century house contains reconstructions of Newton's rooms; the apple that inspired his theory of gravity allegedly fell from the tree in the garden. There's a nifty kids' science room and a cafe. Take Centrebus 28 from Grantham (£2.60, 25 minutes, four per day Monday to Saturday).

Belton House (NT; ☏01476-566116; www.nationaltrust.org.uk; Belton; house & grounds adult/child £13.10/8.40, grounds only £10.30/7; ◷house 12.30-5pm Wed-Sun Mar-Oct, closed Nov-Feb, grounds 9.30am-5.30pm Mar-Oct, to 4pm Nov-Feb) Amid 14.2 hectares of elegant formal gardens, Belton House is a dream location for English period dramas, *Jane Eyre*, *Tom Jones* and the Colin Firth version of *Pride and Prejudice* among them. Built in 1688 in classic Restoration style, the house retains stunning original features including ornate woodcarvings by master Dutch carver Grinling Gibbons. It's off the A607 2.5 miles northeast of Grantham, served by Stagecoach bus 1 (£2.20, 15 minutes, hourly Monday to Saturday, every two hours Sunday).

Belvoir Castle (☏01476-871001; www.belvoircastle.com; Belvoir; castle tours adult/child £15/8, gardens only £8/5; ◷castle tours by reservation, gardens 11am-5pm Mar-Sep, hours can vary) The Duke and Duchess of Rutland's ancestral home, Belvoir (pronounced 'beaver') is a 19th-century baroque and Gothic fantasy built over the ruins of three previous castles. Still inhabited by the Manners family, it overflows with tapestries, priceless furniture and ancient oil paintings. Although the castle is in Leicestershire, Grantham (6 miles east in Lincolnshire) is the nearest town. Bus 9 (£2.60, 20 minutes, four per day Monday to Saturday) stops at Chequers Inn, from where it's a 20-minute walk.

Chequers Inn (☏01476-870701; www.chequersinn.net; Main St, Woolsthorpe by Belvoir; mains £11-20; ◷kitchen noon-2.30pm & 6-9.30pm Mon-Sat, noon-4pm & 6-8.30pm Sun, bar 10am-11pm Mon-Sat, noon-9pm Sun; 🐾) Dine on some of the finest food in the Midlands in the rambling garden bordering a sheep-filled paddock or inside by the open fire of this charming inn, 7 miles southwest of Grantham. There's a fabulous range of ciders and real ales on tap and, across the lane, the former stables house four simple but stylish guest rooms (single/double/loft £50/70/120).

pheric surrounds in one of England's oldest houses; the Romanesque Jew's House was constructed around 1160. For the ultimate indulgence, go for the six-course tasting menu (by reservation, £70).

🍷 Drinking & Nightlife

Strugglers Inn　　　　　　　　PUB
(83 Westgate; ◷noon-midnight Tue & Wed, to 1am Thu-Sat, to 11pm Sun & Mon) A sunny walled-courtyard beer garden out back, a cosy interior and a superb selection of real ales on tap make this the pick of Lincoln's independent pubs.

Electric Bar & Restaurant　　　BAR
(☏01522-565182; www.electricbarandrestaurant.co.uk; 5th fl, DoubleTree by Hilton Lincoln, Brayford Wharf North; ◷11am-11pm Sun-Thu, to midnight Fri & Sat; 🛜) On the top floor of Lincoln's snazzy four-star DoubleTree Hilton Hotel, this swish spot with glittering river views has a great cocktail list with more than 40 choices, including pineapple and black-pepper daiquiris, and 'Lincoln Aphrodisia' with limoncello, passionfruit and Prosecco. Live jazz plays regularly; the restaurant serves sophisticated British dishes with a retro twist.

☆ Entertainment

Home Nightclub　　　　　　LIVE MUSIC
(www.homelincoln.co.uk; Park St; ◷11.30am-11pm Mon & Wed, to 3am Tue & Thu-Sat, 7pm-3am Sun) Spread over six rooms with live music and dance tunes and a total of eight bars, this cavernous venue is a home from home for Lincoln's students.

LINCOLNSHIRE: BOMBER COUNTY

Following WWI the Royal Air Force (RAF) was formed in 1918 and two years later its college was established in Lincolnshire. During WWII, England's 'Bomber County' was home to numerous squadrons and by 1945 had more airfields (49) than any other in the country. US Navy flying boats flew antisubmarine patrols and B-29 bombers were based here.

Lincoln's tourist office (p448) has details of the county's aviation legacies.

Battle of Britain Memorial Flight Visitor Centre (☑01522-552222; www.lincolnshire. gov.uk/bbmf; Dogdyke Rd, Coningsby; hangar tours adult/child £6.50/4.50; ⊙10am-5pm Mon-Fri) See spitfires and the four-engined *Lancaster City of Lincoln* at the Battle of Britain Memorial Flight Visitor Centre on 90-minute hangar tours. Interconnect bus 5 (£4.10, 50 minutes, hourly Monday to Saturday) runs here from Lincoln.

Lincolnshire Aviation Heritage Centre (☑01790-763207; www.lincsaviation.co.uk; East Kirkby, near Spilsby; adult/child £7/3; ⊙9.30am-5pm Mon-Sat Easter-Oct, 10am-4pm Mon-Sat Nov-Easter) An original WWII Bomber Command airfield complete with its original wartime control tower is now home to the Lincolnshire Aviation Heritage Centre. It's 30 miles southeast of Lincoln via the A153; there's no public transport.

Waddington Air Show (www.waddingtonairshow.co.uk; ⊙Jul) The RAF's Waddington Air Show takes place in Waddington, 3 miles south of Lincoln, on the first weekend in July. Book tickets and accommodation well ahead.

Lincoln Drill Hall　　　ARTS CENTRE
(☑01522-873894; www.lincolndrillhall.com; Freeschool Lane) Downhill near the train station, this late 19th-century former drill hall hosts bands, orchestras, stage shows, comedy and daytime festivals.

ℹ Information

Lincoln's friendly **tourist office** (☑01522-545458; www.visitlincoln.com; 9 Castle Hill; ⊙10am-5pm Mon-Sat, 10.30am-4pm Sun, hours can vary) is located in a 16th-century black-and-white building.

ℹ Getting There & Away

BUS

The **bus station** (Melville St) is just northeast of the train station in the new town.

National Express runs direct bus services from Lincoln to London Victoria (£20.20, 5¼ hours, up to two daily) and Birmingham (£17, 3¼ hours, one daily).

Local Stagecoach buses include bus 1 to Grantham (£5, 1¼ hours, hourly Monday to Saturday, five on Sunday).

TRAIN

The train station is 250m east of the Brayford Waterfront development in the new town.

Boston £13.60, 1¼ hours, hourly, change at Sleaford

Newark-on-Trent (Newark Castle) £5.10, 25 minutes, half-hourly Monday to Saturday, fewer on Sunday

Nottingham £11.30, one hour, hourly

Sheffield £14.50, 80 minutes, hourly

York £37.10, two hours, up to two per hour

Stamford

POP 19,704

One of England's prettiest towns, Stamford seems frozen in time, with elegant streets lined with honey-coloured limestone buildings and hidden alleyways dotted with alehouses, interesting eateries and small independent boutiques. A forest of historic church spires rises overhead and the gently gurgling River Welland meanders through the town centre. It's a favourite with filmmakers seeking the postcard vision of England, and appears in everything from *Pride and Prejudice* to the *Da Vinci Code*.

◎ Sights

★**Burghley House**　　　HISTORIC BUILDING
(www.burghley.co.uk; house & garden adult/child £14/7, garden only £8.50/5.50; ⊙house 11am-5pm Sat-Thu mid-Mar–Oct, park & garden 8am-6pm Jun-Sep, to 5pm mid-Mar–May & Oct) Set in more than 810 hectares of grounds, landscaped by Lancelot 'Capability' Brown, opulent Burghley House (pronounced 'bur-lee') was built by Queen Elizabeth's chief adviser William Cecil, whose descendants still live here. It bristles with cupolas, pavilions, belvederes and chimneys; the lavish staterooms are a particular

highlight. In early September, the renowned Burghley Horse Trials take place here. The estate is 1.3 miles southeast of Stamford; follow the marked path for 15 minutes through the park by Stamford train station.

St Mary's Church   CHURCH
(www.stamfordstmary.com; St Mary's St; ⊘ 8am-6pm, hours can vary) A charmingly wonky broach spire tops the 12th-century St Mary's Church. Classical concerts are held here in summer; tickets (from £14) are sold at Stamford's tourist office.

🛏 Sleeping & Eating

Stamford Lodge   B&B ££
(☑ 01780-482932; www.stamfordlodge.co.uk; 66 Scotgate; s/d £75/95; 🛜) Centrally situated, this 18th-century former bakehouse has four fresh, modern rooms and excellent breakfasts made from ingredients sourced from local farmers markets.

★ George Hotel   HISTORIC HOTEL £££
(☑ 01780-750750; www.georgehotelofstamford.com; 71 St Martin's; s/d/4-poster from £120/195/260; 🅿🛜🐾) Stamford's luxurious landmark inn opened its doors in 1597. Today its 45 individually sized and decorated rooms impeccably blend period charm and modern elegance. Superior modern British cuisine is served at its oak-panelled restaurant, while its more informal garden-room restaurant hosts afternoon teas in its courtyard. Its two bars include a champagne bar.

William Cecil at Stamford   HISTORIC HOTEL £££
(☑ 01780-750070; www.hillbrookehotels.co.uk; High St, St Martins; s/d/tr/f from £100/135/185/215; 🅿🛜) Within the Burghley Estate, this stunningly renovated hotel has 27 rooms inspired by Burghley House, with period furnishings and luxuries such as Egyptian cotton linens and complimentary organic vodka. Family rooms sleep two adults and two kids. The smart restaurant creates stylish British classics and opens to a wicker-chair-furnished patio.

No 3 The Yard   MODERN BRITISH ££
(☑ 01780-756080; www.no3theyard.co.uk; 3 Ironmonger St; mains £14.50-21.50; ⊘11.30am-2.30pm & 6-9.30pm Tue-Thu, 11.30am-2.30pm & 6-10pm Fri & Sat, noon-3pm Sun) Tucked away in a courtyard off a narrow laneway, No 3 The Yard serves upmarket fare such as pan-fried sea trout with minted Jersey Royal new potatoes, Norfolk samphire and lemon hollandaise. Try a multicourse menu (two-/three-

course lunch menus £16/19.50, three-course dinner menu £22) for an excellent deal.

Tobie Norris   PUB
(www.kneadpubs.co.uk; 12 St Pauls St; ⊘11am-11pm Mon-Thu, to midnight Fri & Sat, noon-10.30pm Sun) A wonderful stone-walled, flagstone-floored pub, the Tobie Norris has a warren of rooms with open fireplaces, a sunny, flower-filled courtyard and wholesome local ales. Wood-fired pizzas (more than 40 different kinds) are a speciality.

ℹ Information

The **tourist office** (☑ 01780-763203; www.southwestlincs.com; 27 St Mary's St; ⊘ 9.30am-5pm Mon-Sat; 🛜) is inside the Stamford Arts Centre.

ℹ Getting There & Away

Centrebus 4 runs to Grantham (£4.10, one hour, three per day Monday to Friday, two Saturday) and National Express to London Victoria (£15.50, four hours, one daily).

Trains run to Birmingham (£22.80, 1½ hours, hourly), Nottingham (£24.30, 1½ hours, hourly) via Leicester (£13.40, 40 minutes), and Stansted Airport (£32.70, 1¾ hours, hourly) via Cambridge (£23.70, 1¼ hours) and Peterborough (£8, 15 minutes).

Boston

POP 66,500

It's hard to believe that sleepy Boston was the inspiration for its larger and more famous American cousin. Although no Boston citizens sailed on the *Mayflower*, the port became a conduit for persecuted Puritans fleeing Nottinghamshire for religious freedom in the Netherlands and America. In the 1630s, the fiery sermons of Boston vicar John Cotton inspired many locals to follow their lead, among them the ancestors of John Quincy-Adams, the sixth American president. These pioneers founded a namesake town in the new colony of Massachusetts and the rest, as they say, is history.

⊙ Sights

St Botolph's Church   CHURCH
(www.parish-of-boston.org.uk; Church St; tower adult/child £3/1; ⊘ church visiting hours 8.30am-4pm Mon-Sat, 7.30am-4pm Sun, tower 10am-3.30pm Mon-Sat, 1-3.30pm Sun, last climb 3pm) Built in the early 14th century, St Botolph's Church (the name Boston is a corruption of 'St Botolph's Stone') is known locally as the

Stump, in reference to the truncated appearance of its 88m-high tower. Puff your way up the 365 steps on a clear day and you'll see out to Lincoln, 32 miles away.

Guildhall MUSEUM
(☑ 01205-365954; www.bostonguildhall.co.uk; South St; ⏰ 10.30am-3.30pm Wed-Sat) FREE Before escaping to the New World, the Pilgrim Fathers were briefly imprisoned in the 14th-century Guildhall. It's one of Lincolnshire's oldest brick buildings, dating from the 1390s and situated close to the River Witham. Inside are fun interactive exhibits, as well as a restored 16th-century courtroom and a re-created Georgian kitchen. Regular temporary exhibitions are also free.

Maud Foster Windmill MILL
(☑ 01205-352188; www.maudfoster.co.uk; 16 Willoughby Rd; adult/child £4/2; ⏰ 10am-5pm Wed & Sat; 🅿) About 800m northeast of Market Pl, England's tallest working windmill has seven floors that creak and tremble with every turn of the sails; it sells bags of flour milled on-site. Self-caterers can stay in the granary next door (double from £430 for three nights including a windmill tour and parking; children not permitted).

ℹ Information
The **tourist office** (☑ 01205-365954; www. bostonguildhall.co.uk; South St; ⏰ 10.30am-3.30pm Wed-Sat) is inside the Guildhall.

WORTH A TRIP

SULGRAVE MANOR

The impressively preserved Tudor mansion **Sulgrave Manor** (☑ 01295-760205; www.sulgravemanor.org.uk; Manor Rd, Sulgrave; adult/child £7.90/3.60, garden only £3.60/free; ⏰ 10am-5pm Sat-Thu Aug, Sat & Sun late Mar-Jul, Sep & Oct) was built by Lawrence Washington in 1539. The Washington family lived here for almost 120 years before Colonel John Washington, the great-grandfather of America's first president George Washington, sailed to Virginia in 1656.

Sulgrave Manor is 20 miles southwest of Northampton, just off the B4525 near Banbury; you'll need your own wheels to get here.

ℹ Getting There & Away
Trains connect Boston with Leicester (£22.80, 2½ hours, hourly) and Lincoln (£13.60, 1¼ hours, hourly) via a change at Sleaford.

NORTHAMPTONSHIRE

Dotted with villages full of pincushion cottages with thatched roofs and Tudor timbers, Northamptonshire also has a string of stately manors, including the ancestral homes of George Washington and Diana, Princess of Wales.

ℹ Getting Around
Northampton is the county's hub for transport; Traveline (p436) has timetable information for buses and trains. Trains run by London Midland are useful for getting to/from Northampton.

Stoke Bruerne
POP 373

About 8 miles south of Northampton, brightly painted barges frequent this charming little village nestled against the Grand Union Canal, the main drag of England's canal network. From here, you can follow the waterways all the way to Leicester, Birmingham or London.

◉ Sights & Activities

Canal Museum MUSEUM
(www.canalrivertrust.org.uk/the-canal-museum/ stoke-bruerne; 3 Bridge Rd; adult/child £4.75/2.75; ⏰ 10am-5pm Apr-Oct, shorter hours Nov-Mar) A converted corn mill houses the entertaining Canal Museum, which charts the history of the canal network and its bargemen, lock-keepers and pit workers. Scale models abound; outside you can see the historic narrowboat *Sculptor,* listed on the National Historic Boat Register.

Indian Chief CRUISE
(☑ 01604-862428; www.boatinn.co.uk; cruises adult/child £3.50/2.50; ⏰ 11.30am-3pm Sun & bank-holiday weekends) One-hour canal trips aboard the *Indian Chief* narrowboat depart year-round from the Boat Inn (p451).

🛏 Sleeping

Waterways Cottage B&B ££
(☑ 01604-863865; www.waterwayscottage.co.uk; Bridge Rd; d £55-80; 🅿🛜) Right on the canal, Waterways Cottage is an adorable thatched

cottage right off the front of a biscuit box. There's a two-night minimum stay.

Boat Inn
PUB FOOD **££**

(☎ 01604-862428; www.boatinn.co.uk; mains £6.50-24; ⏰ kitchen noon-3pm & 6-9pm Mon-Fri, noon-9pm Sat, noon-8.30pm Sun, bar 9am-11pm Mon-Sat, to 10.30pm Sun) A canalside landmark, this sociable local pub has a relaxed bistro and more formal restaurant and a great range of ales.

❶ Getting There & Away

If you're not travelling by canal boat, then your own wheels are the next-best mode of transport.

Bus 86 runs between Stoke Bruerne and Northampton (£4.50, 45 minutes, four per day Monday to Saturday) as does bus X4 (£4.50, 25 minutes, four per day Sunday).

LEICESTERSHIRE

Leicestershire was a vital creative hub during the Industrial Revolution, but its factories were a major target for German air raids in WWII and most towns in the county still bear the scars of war-time bombing. Nevertheless, there are some impressive remains, from Elizabethan castles to Roman ruins. The busy, multicultural capital Leicester is enjoying new-found fame due to the recent discovery and reburial of King Richard III's remains and its football team's against-all-odds 2016 Premier League win – one of the greatest upsets in British sporting history.

❶ Getting There & Around

Leicester is well served by buses and trains. For bus routes and timetables, visit the 'Roads and Transport' pages at www.leicestershire.gov.uk.

Regular buses connect Rutland to Leicester, Stamford and other surrounding towns.

Leicester

POP 337,653

Built over the buried ruins of two millennia of history, Leicester (*les*-ter) suffered at the hands of the Luftwaffe and postwar planners but an influx of textile workers from India and Pakistan from the 1960s transformed the city into a bustling global melting pot.

The astonishing 2012 discovery and 2013 identification of the remains of King Richard III in a Leicester car park sparked a flurry of developments, including a spiffing visi-

---

WORTH A TRIP

ALTHORP HOUSE

The ancestral home of the Spencer family, **Althorp House** (☎ 01604-770107; www.spencerofalthorp.com; adult/child £18.50/11; ⏰ 11am-3pm early Jul–early Sep, hours vary May–early Jul & early–late Sep, closed late Sep–Apr) is the final resting place of Diana, Princess of Wales, commemorated by a memorial. The outstanding art collection features works by Rubens, Gainsborough and Van Dyck. Tickets are limited; prebook by phone or online.

Althorp – pronounced 'altrup' – is off the A428, 5.5 miles northwest of Northampton; a taxi costs around £20. Stagecoach Northampton–Rugby bus 96 (£2.35, hourly, Monday to Saturday) passes the estate gates, from where it's a 1-mile walk. Profits go to charities supported by the Princess Diana Memorial Fund.

---

tor centre on the site, and the restoration of the cathedral, where the king was reburied in 2015. And sporting history was made in 2016, when Leicester City Football Club won the Premier League against 5000:1 odds at the beginning of the season, having never won a top-division championship in the club's 132-year existence.

◎ Sights & Activities

★ **King Richard III: Dynasty, Death & Discovery**
HERITAGE CENTRE

(www.kriii.com; 4a St Martin's Pl; adult/child £7.95/4.75; ⏰ 10am-4pm Sun-Fri, to 5pm Sat) Built following the incredible 2012 discovery and 2013 DNA testing of King Richard III's remains, Leicester's high-tech King Richard III visitor centre encompasses three fascinating sections. Dynasty explores his rise to become the final Plantagenet king. Death delves into the Battle of Bosworth, when Richard became the last English king to be killed in battle. Discovery details the University of Leicester's archaeological dig and identification, and lets you view the site of the grave in which he was found.

★ **Leicester Cathedral**
CATHEDRAL

(www.leicestercathedral.org; Peacock Lane; ⏰ 10am-5pm Mon-Sat, 12.30-2.30pm Sun) **FREE** Pride of place at this substantial medieval cathedral goes to the contemporary

Leicester

Leicester

◎ Top Sights
1 King Richard III: Dynasty, Death	
& Discovery	B3
2 Leicester Cathedral	B2

◎ Sights
3 Great Hall	A3
4 Guildhall	B2
5 Jewry Wall Museum	A2
Leicester Castle	(see 3)
6 Magazine	B3
7 New Walk Museum & Art Gallery	D4
8 Newarke Houses Museum	A3
9 St Mary de Castro	A3
10 St Nicholas Church	A2

🛏 Sleeping
| 11 Belmont Hotel | D4 |
| 12 Hotel Maiyango | A2 |

⊗ Eating
13 Boot Room	B3
14 Good Earth	C2
15 Walkers	B2
16 White Peacock	C3

🍷 Drinking & Nightlife
17 Bread & Honey	C3
18 Globe	B2
19 XY Club	C3

✪ Entertainment
| 20 Curve Theatre | D2 |
| 21 Phoenix Square | D2 |

🛍 Shopping
| 22 Leicester Market | C2 |

FINDING KING RICHARD III

It's an amazing story. Philippa Langley, a member of the Richard III Society, spent four-and-a-half years researching the whereabouts of King Richard's remains after his demise at Bosworth (p454). The 1924-founded society's aim is to research the king's life and to achieve a more balanced characterisation of him than that of a cruel and calculating figure, as portrayed by Shakespeare and various authors and historians. Langley narrowed it down to a Leicester car park, built over the site of the long-since-demolished Greyfriars church. But it took her another three years to persuade the city council to excavate.

Archaeologists from the University of Leicester carried out the dig in August 2012, unearthing a skeleton just three weeks later. In February 2013, the bones were confirmed by DNA analysis as those of the late king.

The university was also able to undertake a facial reconstruction using the king's skull, giving the modern world its first true image of Richard III. The reconstruction is on permanent display at Leicester's state-of-the-art King Richard III: Dynasty, Death & Discovery (p451) visitor centre along with the site where he'd been buried for more than 500 years.

Richard's remains were reburied in Leicester Cathedral (p451) in 2015 following a procession from Bosworth.

A free Richard III Audio Tour, downloadable from Leicester's tourist office (p456), covers key Richard sites in the city and county.

limestone tomb atop the vault where the remains of King Richard III were reburied in 2015, following the discovery of his skeleton nearby. Look too for the striking carvings on the cathedral's roof supports.

Guildhall
HISTORIC BUILDING
(www.leicester.gov.uk/leisure-and-culture; Guildhall Lane; ⊙11am-4.30pm) FREE Leicester's perfectly preserved 14th-century guildhall, one of England's finest, is reputed to be the most haunted building in Leicester. You can search for spooks in the magnificent Great Hall, the wood-panelled 'Mayor's Parlour' and the old police cells, which contain a reconstruction of a 19th-century gibbet.

New Walk Museum & Art Gallery
MUSEUM, GALLERY
(www.leicester.gov.uk/leisure-and-culture; 53 New Walk; ⊙10am-5pm Mon-Sat, 11am-5pm Sun; 🛜) FREE Highlights of this grand Victorian museum include the dinosaur galleries, the painting collection (with works by Turner and Degas) and the Egyptian gallery, where real mummies rub shoulders with displays about Boris Karloff's *The Mummy* film. Littlies under five can let loose in the interactive Den.

National Space Centre
MUSEUM
(www.spacecentre.co.uk; Exploration Drive; adult/child £14/11; ⊙10am-4pm Mon-Fri, to 5pm Sat & Sun) Although British space missions usually launch from French Guiana or Kazakhstan, Leicester's space museum is a fascinating introduction to the mysteries of the spheres. The ill-fated *Beagle 2* mission to Mars was controlled from here. Fun, kid-friendly displays cover everything from astronomy to the status of current space missions. The centre is off the A6 about 1.5 miles north of the city centre. Take bus 54 (15 minutes, every 20 minutes) from Charles St.

Newarke Houses Museum
MUSEUM
(www.leicester.gov.uk/leisure-and-culture; The Newarke; ⊙10am-5pm Mon-Sat, 11am-5pm Sun) FREE Sprawling over two 16th-century mansions, this entertaining museum details the lifestyle of locals through the centuries. Don't miss the walk-through re-creation of a WWI trench, and the trophies of the Royal Leicestershire Regiment, including an outrageous snuff box made from a tiger's head.

Leicester Castle
RUINS
(Castle View) Scattered around the Newarke Houses Museum are the ruins of Leicester's medieval castle, where Richard III spent his final days before the Battle of Bosworth. The most impressive chunk of masonry is the monumental gateway known as the Magazine (Newarke St), once a storehouse for cannonballs and gunpowder. Clad in Georgian brickwork, the 12th-century Great Hall (Castle Yard) stands behind a 15th-century gate near the church of St Mary de Castro (www.stmarydecastro.org.uk; 15 Castle View; ⊙noon-2pm Mon-Fri, 2-4pm Sat), where Geoffrey Chaucer was married in 1366.

WORTH A TRIP

BOSWORTH BATTLEFIELD

Given a few hundred years, every battlefield ends up simply a field, but the site of the Battle of Bosworth – where Richard III met his maker in 1485 – is enlivened by the entertaining **Bosworth Battlefield Heritage Centre** (☎01455-290429; www.bosworthbattlefield.org.uk; Ambion Lane, Sutton Cheney; adult/child £7.95/4.75; ☻heritage centre 10am-5pm, last admission 4pm, grounds 7am-dusk) full of skeletons and musket balls. Enthusiasts in period costume reenact the battle each August. The battlefield is 16 miles southwest of Leicester at Sutton Cheney, off the A447. A taxi from Leicester costs around £25.

Jewry Wall Museum   MUSEUM
(www.visitleicester.info; St Nicholas Circle; ☻11am-4.30pm Feb-Oct) FREE You can see fine Roman mosaics and frescos in this museum exploring the history of Leicester from Roman times to the modern day. In front of the museum is the **Jewry Wall**, part of Leicester's Roman baths. Tiles and masonry from the baths were incorporated in the walls of neighbouring **St Nicholas Church** (www.stnicholasleicester.com; St Nicholas Circle; admission by donation; ☻2-4pm Sat, 5.30-6.30pm Sun). A free audio tour is downloadable from the tourist office (p456) website.

Great Central Railway   RAIL
(☎01509-632323; www.gcrailway.co.uk; return adult/child £16/9) Steam locomotives chug from Leicester North station on Redhill Circle to Loughborough Central, following the 8-mile route along which Thomas Cook ran the original package tour in 1841. The locos operate most weekends year-round and some summer weekdays; check timetables online.

For Leicester North station, take bus 127 (£4.20, 20 minutes, every 10 minutes) from Haymarket bus station (p456) on Charles St.

✼ Festivals & Events

Leicester Caribbean Carnival   CULTURAL
(www.leicestercarnival.com; ☻Aug) Colourful costumes galore fill Leicester on the first Saturday in August during the biggest Caribbean celebration in the country after London's Notting Hill Carnival. Musicians perform on two stages; there's a fun fair, a supervised play area for kids, and a slew of food and drink stalls.

Leicester Comedy Festival   COMEDY
(www.comedy-festival.co.uk; ☻Feb) England's longest-running comedy festival draws big names as well as fresh talent for eight days in February, when more than 700 shows take place in more than 60 different venues.

🛏 Sleeping

★**Hotel Maiyango**   BOUTIQUE HOTEL ££
(☎0116-251 8898; www.maiyango.com; 13-21 St Nicholas Pl; d from £79; ✳🐾) At the end of the pedestrian High St, this sophisticated pad has 14 spacious rooms, decorated with handmade Asian furniture, contemporary art and massive plasma TVs. In addition to its candlelit **Maiyango Restaurant & Bar**, serving the city's best cocktails, it also has a fabulous **Kitchen Deli** gourmet cafe and store.

Belmont Hotel   HOTEL ££
(☎0116-254 4773; www.belmonthotel.co.uk; 20 De Montfort St; s/d/f from £60/75/89; ᴘ✳@🐾♿) Owned and run by the same family for four generations, the 19th-century Belmont has stylish contemporary, individually designed rooms and a fantastic location overlooking leafy New Walk. Family rooms have a double bed and bunks. Its restaurant is highly regarded; the two bars, Jamie's and Bowie's, open to a terrace and a conservatory respectively.

🍴 Eating

Walkers   BAKERY £
(Walker & Son; www.walkerspies.co.uk; 4-6 Cheapside; dishes 90p-£5; ☻8.30am-5.30pm Mon-Sat) For lunch on the run, you can't beat Walkers' towering pork pies. These are the original premises where Walkers was founded in 1824; it's since sold its famous crisp brand but the pies remain a family business today. Other pie varieties include chicken, bacon and mushroom, farmhouse steak, game and pulled pork. There's a handful of pavement tables out front.

Good Earth   VEGETARIAN £
(☎0116-262 6260; 19 Free Lane; mains £3.50-6.50; ☻10am-3pm Mon-Fri, to 4pm Sat; 🖉) 🍴 This venerable vegetarian cafe is justifiably popular for its daily changing wholesome veggie bakes; huge, fresh salads; and homemade cakes.

Boot Room   BISTRO ££
(☎0116-262 2555; www.thebootroomeaterie.co.uk; 29 Millstone Lane; mains £13-19.50; ☻noon-2pm

& 5.30-9.30pm Tue-Fri, noon-2.30pm & 5.30-10pm Sat;) A former shoe factory now houses this contemporary independent bistro. Premium ingredients are used in dishes from roast Cornish cod with smoked tomato risotto to duck leg with Clonakilty black pudding. Save room for the soufflé of the day for dessert.

White Peacock
MODERN BRITISH £££

(0116-254 7663; www.the-white-peacock.co.uk; 14-16 King St; 2-/3-course lunch menus £15/18, 2-/3-course dinner menus £26.50/28.50; ⊙noon-3pm & 5.30-9.45pm Tue-Fri, noon-3pm & 6-9.45pm Sat) The beautiful Grade II–listed building housing this fine-dining restaurant overlooks pedestrianised New Walk. Chef Phillip Sharpe's ambitious menus might start with goats-cheese panna cotta with balsamic jelly and move on to roast pork belly with black pudding and smoked-celeriac purée, ending with Turkish-delight crème brûlée with dark chocolate and pistachio sorbet.

Drinking & Nightlife

Bread & Honey
COFFEE

(15 King St; ⊙7.30am-2.30pm Mon-Sat;) Beans from single farm estates and co-ops sourced and roasted by London-based Monmouth are brewed up at this little bare-boards hole-in-the-wall; the flat whites here are the best for miles. It also whips up smoothies in summer, steaming soups in winter, and fantastic cakes (chocolate fudge cake with white-chocolate icing; honey-glazed banana loaf) all year.

XY Club
CLUB

(www.xyclub.co.uk; 2 King St; ⊙10.30pm-6am Fri & Sat) Behind a towering mock-Tudor facade, XY's resident and visiting DJs serve up diverse beats. Special weeknight events are listed on the website.

Globe
PUB

(www.everards.co.uk; 43 Silver St; ⊙11am-11pm Sun-Thu, to 1am Fri & Sat) In the atmospheric Lanes – a tangle of alleys south of the High St – this old-fashioned pub has fine draught ales and a crowd that rates its drinks by quality rather than quantity.

Entertainment

Curve Theatre
THEATRE

(0116-242 3595; www.curveonline.co.uk; 60 Rutland St; backstage tours adult/child £3/2) This sleek artistic space hosts big-name shows and some innovative modern theatre, and has good accessibility for theatre-goers who are aurally or visually impaired. Call the ticket office to book backstage tours. The bar is a sophisticated place for a sundowner.

Phoenix Square
CINEMA

(0116-242 2800; www.phoenix.org.uk; 4 Midland St; tickets adult/child from £7.50/5.50) Phoenix is Leicester's premier venue for art-house films and digital media.

De Montfort Hall
LIVE MUSIC

(0116-233 3111; www.demontforthall.co.uk; Granville Rd) Big orchestras, ballets, musicals and other big song-and-dance performances are on the bill at this huge venue.

Shopping

Leicester Market
MARKET

(www.leicestermarket.co.uk; Market Pl; ⊙outdoor market 7am-6pm Mon-Sat, indoor market 9am-5pm Mon-Sat) More than 300 stalls at Leicester's indoor and outdoor markets sell everything from organic vegetables to aromatic spices, fish and shellfish, new and secondhand clothes, and homewares, electronic goods, cosmetics, jewellery, flowers and fabrics.

LOCAL KNOWLEDGE

THE GOLDEN MILE

Lined with sari stores, jewellery emporiums and curry houses, Belgrave Rd – aka the Golden Mile – is an essential stop for authentic Indian vegetarian food.

There are more top-notch eateries than you can shake a chapatti at. Top pick is **Bobby's** (0116-266 0106; www.eatatbobbys.com; 154-156 Belgrave Rd; dishes £3.75-6; ⊙11am-10pm Mon-Fri, 10am-10pm Sat & Sun;), famed for its *namkeen* – lentil-flour snacks that come in myriad shapes and sizes. Shops along the strip sell *mithai* (Indian sweets), which involve sugary combinations of nuts, fruit and milk curds.

Belgrave Rd is about 1 mile northeast of the Leicester's centre – follow Belgrave Gate and cross Burleys Flyover, or take bus 2 or 127 (seven minutes, every five minutes) from **St Margaret's bus station** (p456) or bus 5 from **Haymarket bus station** (p456).

ℹ Information

Leicester's helpful **tourist office** (☎ 0116-299 4444; www.visitleicester.info; 51 Gallowtree Gate; ⏰ 9.30am-5.30pm Mon-Sat, 10am-4pm Sun) has reams of city and countywide info. Ask about guided walking tours (£5; times vary).

ℹ Getting There & Away

BUS

Intercity buses operate from **St Margaret's bus station** (Gravel St), north of the centre. The useful Skylink bus runs to East Midlands Airport (£7, 50 minutes, at least hourly, 24 hours) and continues on to Derby (one hour).

National Express services:

Coventry £6.70, 45 minutes, four daily
London Victoria £14, 2¾ hours, four daily
Nottingham £5, 45 minutes, four daily

TRAIN

East Midlands trains:

Birmingham £13.40, one hour, two per hour
London St Pancras £79.50, 1¼ hours, two to four hourly

ℹ Getting Around

The centre is cut off from the suburbs by a tangle of underpasses and flyovers, but downtown Leicester is easy to get around on foot.

Local buses depart from **Haymarket bus station** (Charles St) and nearby St Margaret's bus station. For unlimited transport on local buses, buy a Flexi Day Ticket (£5).

WORTH A TRIP

GASTROPUB: HERCULES REVIVED

One of the joys of travelling through the Midlands is chancing upon a picture-perfect country pub serving food that could hold its own in the world's gastronomic capitals. And **Hercules Revived** (☎ 01455-699336; www.herculesrevived.co.uk; Sutton Cheney; mains £10.50-21.50; ⏰ noon-2.30pm & 6-9.30pm Mon-Sat, noon-2.30pm & 6-8pm Sun), in a 17th-century coaching inn, is just 1.2 miles east of Bosworth Battlefield (p454). Inspired starters (Stilton brûlée!) precede amazing mains such as seared duck breast in wild-blackberry sauce.

RUTLAND

Tiny Rutland was merged with Leicestershire in 1974, but in 1997 regained its 'independence' as England's smallest county.

Rutland Water

Rutland centres on Rutland Water, a vast artificial reservoir created by the damming of the Gwash Valley in 1976. Covering 4.19 sq miles, the reservoir attracts some 20,000 birds, including ospreys.

◉ Sights & Activities

Rutland Water
Nature Reserve   NATURE RESERVE
(www.rutlandwater.org.uk; Egleton; adult/child incl parking £5.70/3.30; ⏰ 9am-5pm Mar-Oct, to 4pm Nov-Feb) Near Oakham, the Rutland Water Nature Reserve has hides where you can view the abundant birdlife.

Normanton Church   CHURCH
(☎ 01780-686800; www.anglianwater.co.uk; Normanton; ⏰ hours vary Apr-Oct, closed Nov-Mar) **FREE** This quaint church is saved from inundation by a limestone barrier wall. Inside are displays on the history of the Rutland reservoir. Many concerts and private events such as weddings take place here, so check ahead to make sure it's open.

Rutland Belle   CRUISE
(☎ 01572-787630; www.rutlandwatercruises.com; Whitwell; adult/child £8.50/5.50; ⏰ hourly noon-3pm Mon-Sat, 11am-3pm Sun mid-Jul–Aug, shorter hours Apr–mid-Jul, Sep & Oct) Take a 45-minute cruise from Whitwell to Normanton on the southern shore of the Rutland reservoir, returning to Whitwell.

Rutland Watersports   WATER SPORTS
(☎ 01780-460154; www.anglianwater.co.uk/leisure; Whitwell Leisure Park, Bull Brigg Lane, Whitwell; windsurf/kayak/SUP rental per hour from £7; ⏰ 9am-7pm Fri-Tue, to 8pm Wed & Thu Apr-Oct, shorter hours Nov-Mar) Aquatic activities offered by Rutland Watersports include windsurfing, kayaking and SUP (stand-up paddleboarding). You can rent gear or take lessons.

Rutland Sailing School   BOATING
(☎ 01780-721999; www.rutlandsailingschool.co.uk; Gibbet Lane, Edith Weston; sailboat hire per hour from £20, half-day sailing courses adult/child from £125/105; ⏰ 7.30am-dusk Apr-Oct) Rents boats and runs sailing courses.

Rockblok
CLIMBING

(☎01780-460060; www.rockblok.com; Whitwell Leisure Park, Bull Brigg Lane, Whitwell; climbing/ high ropes £4/10, bike hire adult/child £23/10; ⊙9am-7pm mid-Mar–mid-Sep, to 4pm mid-Sep– mid-Mar) Tackle a vertigo-inducing high-ropes course, an outdoor climbing wall or rent bikes for a gentle pedal around the Rutland lake shore.

Giant-Bike
CYCLING

(☎01780-720888; www.giant-rutland.co.uk; Normanton; bike rental per day adult/child £23/10; ⊙9am-6pm) Close to the Normanton boat jetty, Giant-Bike rents road bicycles, along with tandems, electric bikes and trailers.

🛌 Sleeping

Hambleton Hall
HISTORIC HOTEL £££

(☎01572-756991; www.hambletonhall.com; Hambleton; s/d incl breakfast from £220/295; 🅿🐾) One of England's finest country hotels, rambling former hunting lodge Hambleton Hall, built in 1881, sits on a peninsula jutting out into Rutland Water, 3 miles east of Oakham. Its luxurious floral rooms and Michelin-starred restaurant (two-/three-course lunch menus £29/37.50, three-course dinner menus £69) are surrounded by gorgeous gardens.

ⓘ Information

Situated near Empingham, the **Rutland Water Visitor Centre** (☎01780-686800; www. rutlandwater.org.uk; Skyes Lane, Empingham; ⊙9am-5pm mid-Mar–mid-Sep) has a snack kiosk, walking and cycling trails, and information on the area.

ⓘ Getting There & Away

Bus 9 links Oakham with Stamford (£3.10, 45 minutes, hourly Monday to Saturday) via Rutland Water's north shore.

Trains link Oakham with Leicester (£12.20, 30 minutes, hourly or better).

DERBYSHIRE

The Derbyshire countryside is painted in two distinct tones: the lush green of rolling valleys criss-crossed by dry stone walls, and the barren mottled brown hilltops of the high, wild moorlands. The biggest draw here is the Peak District National Park, which preserves some of England's most evocative scenery, attracting legions of hikers, climbers, cyclists and cave enthusiasts.

WORTH A TRIP

GASTROPUB: HAMMER & PINCERS

For a mind-blowing meal, head to the idyllic gastropub **Hammer & Pincers** (☎01509-880735; www.hammerandpincers. co.uk; 5 East Rd, Wymeswold; mains £14.50-24.50, 8-course menu £45, with wine £65; ⊙noon-2pm & 6-9.30pm Tue-Sat, to 4pm Sun; 🐾), set in bucolic gardens at the edge of the cute village of Wymeswold. Everything is homemade, down to the breads and condiments; seasonal specialities might include cider-cured sea trout, gin-marinated pheasant and rosemary rhubarb sorbet. Don't miss its signature twice-baked cheese soufflé. It's 16 miles north of Leicester via the A46.

ⓘ Getting There & Away

East Midlands Airport (p392) is the nearest air hub, and Derby is well served by trains, but connecting services to smaller towns are few. In the Peak District, the Derwent Valley Line runs from Derby to Matlock. Edale and Hope lie on the Hope Valley Line from Sheffield to Manchester.

For a comprehensive list of Derbyshire bus routes, visit the 'Transport and Roads' pages at www.derbyshire.gov.uk.

Derby
POP 252,500

Gloriously sited at the southeastern edge of the Derbyshire hills that roll towards the Peak District, Derby is one of the Midlands' most energetic, creative cities. This was one of the crucibles of the Industrial Revolution: almost overnight, a sleepy market town was transformed into a major manufacturing centre, producing everything from silk to bone china, and later locomotives and Rolls-Royce aircraft engines. The city suffered the ravages of industrial decline in the 1980s, but bounced back with impressive cultural developments and a rejuvenated riverfront.

⊙ Sights

Derby Cathedral
CATHEDRAL

(www.derbycathedral.org; 18 Irongate; ⊙8.30am-5.15pm Mon-Sat, 8am-6pm Sun) Founded in AD 943 and reconstructed in the 18th century. Derby Cathedral's vaulted ceiling towers above a fine collection of medieval tombs, including the opulent grave of the oft-married

CONKERS & THE NATIONAL FOREST

The National Forest (www.nationalforest.org) is an ambitious project to generate new areas of sustainable woodland by planting 30 million trees in Leicestershire, Derbyshire and Staffordshire, covering a total area of 128,000 acres or 200 sq miles. More than eight million saplings have already taken root, and all sorts of visitor attractions are springing up in the forest.

Conkers (☑ 01283-216633; www.visitconkers.com; Rawdon Rd, Moira; adult/child £9.05/7.95; ☺ 10am-6pm Easter–mid-Sep, to 5pm mid-Sep–Easter) A family-oriented nature centre, Conkers has interactive displays, indoor and outdoor playgrounds (the latter includes high and low ropes courses), a viewing tower and boardwalks through the woodlands. It's 20 miles northwest of Leicester off the A444.

Hicks Lodge (☑ 01530-274533; Willesley Wood Side, Moira; bike rental per day adult/child £30/15; ☺ trails 8am-dusk, bike hire & cafe 9am-5pm Fri-Wed, 9am-9pm Thu mid-Feb–Oct, 10am-4pm Mon-Wed & Fri, 9am-9pm Thu, 9am-5pm Sat & Sun Nov–mid-Feb) Bike trails through the National Forest include a flat 2km path around the lake from this cycle centre, which rents wheels and organises guided tours and night rides. The attached cafe serves coffee, cakes and sandwiches.

National Forest YHA (☑ 0845 371 9672; www.yha.org.uk; 48 Bath Lane, Moira; dm/d/f from £15/49/65; 🅿 🛜) Situated 300m west of Conkers along Bath Lane, this hostel has impressive ecofriendly features (such as greywater and solar biomass boiler usage), spotless en suite rooms, and a restaurant serving local produce and organic wines. Family rooms sleep up to five people.

Bess of Hardwick, who at various times held court at Hardwick Hall, Chatsworth House and Bolsover Castle. Peregrine falcons nest in the tower; follow their progress at www.derbyperegrines.blogspot.com.

Derby Museum & Art Gallery MUSEUM
(www.derbymuseums.org; The Strand; ☺ 10am-5pm Tue-Sat, noon-4pm Sun) FREE Local history and industry displays include fine ceramics produced by Royal Crown Derby and an archaeology gallery.

Quad GALLERY, CINEMA
(☑ 01332-290606; www.derbyquad.co.uk; Market Pl; gallery free, cinema tickets £5-17; ☺ gallery 11am-6pm Mon-Sat, noon-6pm Sun, cinema 11am-9pm) A striking modernist cube on Market Pl, Quad contains a futuristic art gallery and an art-house cinema.

Royal Crown Derby Factory MUSEUM
(☑ 01332-712800; www.royalcrownderby.co.uk; Osmaston Rd; museum & factory tour adult/child £5/2.50, museum only £2/1; ☺ museum 10am-4pm Mon-Sat, factory tours 1.30pm Tue-Thu, shop 10am-5pm Mon-Sat, tearoom 10am-4pm Tue-Fri) Derby's historic potteries still turn out some of the finest bone china in England, from edgy Asian-inspired designs to the kind of stuff your grandma collects. Reservations are essential for factory tours lasting 90

minutes, including a visit to the museum. Royal Crown Derby's china (including seconds and discontinued items) is sold at its on-site shop, and is used as tableware at its elegant tearoom.

🛏 Sleeping

Cathedral Quarter Hotel HOTEL ££
(☑ 01332-546080; www.cathedralquarterhotel.com; 16 St Mary's Gate; s/d incl breakfast from £60/80; 🛜) A bell's peal from the cathedral, this grand Georgian edifice houses Derby's finest digs. The service is as polished as the grand marble staircase and there's an on-site spa and fine-dining restaurant.

Farmhouse at Mackworth INN ££
(☑ 01332-824324; www.thefarmhouseatmackworth.com; 60 Ashbourne Rd; d/f incl breakfast from £70/90; 🅿 🛜 🐾) Overhauled by pub conglomerate Marston's, designer inn the Farmhouse at Mackworth is just 2.5 miles northwest of Derby in undulating countryside, with the bonus of plentiful free parking. Its 10 boutique rooms have checked fabrics, rustic timber cladding and chrome fittings, plus amenities including Nespresso machines and fluffy robes. There's a fabulous bar and restaurant with a Josper charcoal oven. Family rooms sleep three.

Eating

Forge BURGERS £
(☑ 01332-987030; www.forgederby.com; 1-6 Blacksmiths Yard, Sadler Gate; burgers £7.50-13; ☻kitchen noon-9pm Mon-Sat, noon-5pm Sun) Creative twists on burgers made from local ingredients (English flour, Derbyshire beef) include the Fire Starter (jalapeños, red chillies and hot-pepper sauce) and the love-it-or-hate-it PJ (with peanut butter and raspberry jam), with more than two dozen choices in all. Its terrace opens onto the paved Blacksmiths Yard, home to more great restaurants and bars.

Wonky Table BISTRO ££
(☑ 01332-295000; www.wonkytable.co.uk; 32 Sadler Gate; mains lunch £5.50-12, dinner £15-18; ☻5-10pm Mon, noon-2pm & 5-10pm Tue-Sat) Inside an inviting retro-vintage dining room with exposed-brick walls, Wonky Table features a slimmed-down daytime menu plus sandwiches such as warm goats cheese with caramelised onion and walnuts. But it really comes into its own at dinner with dishes including honey and balsamic goose breast, rosemary-crusted lamb rump, and beetroot and goats-cheese risotto balls with watercress cream.

Darleys MODERN BRITISH £££
(☑ 01332-364987; www.darleys.com; Waterfront, Darley Abbey Mill; mains £21.50-25, 2-/3-course lunch menus £20/25; ☻noon-2pm & 7-9pm Mon-Sat, noon-2.30pm Sun) Two miles north of the centre, this upmarket restaurant has a gorgeous setting in a bright, converted mill overlooking the river. Classy fare spans semolina-coated lamb belly with mint jelly to guinea-fowl Kiev with wilted spinach, and raspberry and rhubarb soufflé.

Drinking & Nightliife

★Brooklyn Social BAR
(34-35 Sadler Gate; ☻noon-midnight Mon-Thu, noon-1am Fri & Sat, 11am-11pm Sun) Opened by Derby local Tom Warner following stints in East London and the US, this triple-decker Grade II–listed space is styled after a neon-lit American dive bar, with retro, vintage and industrial decor. Cocktails (such as Stewed, Screwed and Tattooed, with Sailor Jerry spiced rum with ginger beer, honey and fiery Tabasco) and craft beers complement its awesome burgers.

★Old Bell Hotel PUB
(www.bellhotelderby.co.uk; 51 Sadler Gate; ☻11.30am-11.30pm Sun-Thu, to 1.30am Fri & Sat) Dating from 1650 and hosting Bonnie Prince Charlie's soldiers in 1745, this history-steeped black-and-white inn languished from late last century until its recent restoration by valiant local entrepreneur Paul Hurst. There's a crackling open fire and a central courtyard (and, allegedly, more than a few ghosts). Top-notch food here includes fine-dining restaurant Zest.

Silk Mill PUB
(www.silkmillderby.co.uk; 19 Full St; ☻noon-11pm Mon-Thu, to midnight Fri & Sat, to 10.30pm Sun; 🛜) Live music plays at this real-ale pub several times a week including Sunday jazz.

Ye Olde Dolphin PUB
(☑ 01332-267711; www.yeoldedolphin.co.uk; 5a Queen St; ☻11.30am-11pm Mon-Thu, 11.30am-midnight Fri, 11am-midnight Sat, noon-11pm Sun) Dating from 1530, Derby's oldest pub has a hearty menu and live music in the beer garden from Thursday to Saturday. Ask about its ghost tours.

Shopping

Bennetts DEPARTMENT STORE
(www.bennettsirongate.co.uk; 8 Irongate; ☻9am-5pm Mon-Sat, 11am-4pm Sun) Founded as an ironmongers in 1734 and still retaining an ironmongery, Derby's historic department store has evolved over the centuries to sell beautiful clothes, homewares, gifts and more. On the 1st-floor interior balcony, the excellent **Lisa Jean at Bennetts Brasserie** (☑ 01332-344621; www.lisajean-bennetts.co.uk; 8 Irongate; mains £8.50-12.50, 5-course champagne breakfast £24; ☻9am-3pm Mon-Sat, 11am-2pm Sun) specialises in five-course champagne breakfasts (served until 2pm).

ℹ Information

Derby's **tourist office** (☑ 01332-643411; www.visitderby.co.uk; Market Pl; ☻9.30am-4.30pm Mon-Sat Apr-Sep, 10am-3.30pm Mon-Sat Oct-Mar) is situated under the Assembly Rooms in the main square.

ℹ Getting There & Around

AIR

East Midlands Airport (p392), 11.5 miles southeast of Derby, is served by regular Skylink buses (£4.30, 30 minutes, at least hourly, 24 hours).

KEDLESTON HALL

Kedleston Hall (NT; Kedleston; house & gardens adult/child £12/6, garden only £5/2.50; ⊙ house noon-5pm Sat-Thu Feb-Oct, garden 10am-6pm Feb-Oct, to 4pm Nov-Jan) Sitting pretty in vast landscaped grounds, this neoclassical mansion is a must for fans of stately homes. Entering the house through a grand portico, you'll reach the breathtaking Marble Hall with massive alabaster columns and statues of Greek deities.

Kedleston Hall is 5 miles northwest of Derby, off the A52. Bus 114 between Derby and Ashbourne (£3.20, 30 minutes, up to six per day Monday to Saturday) passes the Smithy, 1 mile northwest of Kedleston.

BUS

Local and long-distance buses run from Derby's bus station, immediately east of the Westfield shopping mall. Highpeak has hourly buses between Derby and Buxton (£5.90, 1¾ hours), via Matlock (£4.30, 35 minutes) and Bakewell (£4.80, 1¼ hours). Five buses continue to Manchester (£8, 2¼ hours).

Other services:

Leicester Skylink; £7, 1½ hours, one to two per hour

Nottingham Red Arrow; £5, 35 minutes, every 10 minutes Monday to Saturday, three per hour Sunday

TRAIN

The train station is about half a mile southeast of the centre on Railway Tce.

Birmingham £18.40, 40 minutes, four hourly

Leeds £33.60, 1½ hours, two hourly

London St Pancras £72, 1¾ hours, up to four hourly

Ashbourne

POP 7800

Perched at the southern edge of the Peak District National Park, Ashbourne is a pretty patchwork of steeply slanting stone streets lined with cafes, pubs and antique shops.

🛏 Sleeping & Eating

Compton House   B&B **££**

(☎ 01335-343100; www.comptonhouse.co.uk; 27-31 Compton St; d £70; [P][🛜]) Fresh, clean, frilly rooms, a warm welcome and a central location make this the pick of Ashbourne's B&Bs.

Flower Cafe   CAFE **£**

(5 Market Pl; mains £5.50-12.50; ⊙ 8.30am-5pm; [🖋]) Soups such as parsnip, chorizo and chestnut, broccoli and Stilton, and spicy bean and lentil are a year-round speciality at this cute-as-a-button cafe where everything is homemade. In summer it also cooks deli-

cious quiches (cheesy leek and mushroom; bacon, brie and cranberry...). Gluten-free and dairy-free dishes are plentiful.

Bramhalls   DELI, CAFE **£**

(☎ 01335-342631; www.bramhallsdeli.co.uk; 22 Market Pl; dishes £4-8; ⊙ 8am-5pm Mon-Sat, 9am-5pm Sun) A great little deli and cafe, Bramhalls serves stylish light meals and sandwiches, and excellent homemade pastries, breads, cold meats as well as more than 60 varieties of cheese.

Drinking

Smith's Tavern   PUB

(36 St John's St; ⊙ 11am-3pm & 5-11pm Sun-Fri, noon-10.30pm Sat) On the main shopping street, this tiny pub has a big selection of real ales and an old piano at the back.

ℹ Information

The **tourist office** (☎ 01335-343666; www.visit-ashbourne.co.uk; Market Pl; ⊙ 10am-5pm Jun-Aug, shorter hours Mar-May & Sep-Dec, closed Jan & Feb) is inside Ashbourne's town hall.

ℹ Getting There & Around

Bus services include the following:

Buxton Highpeak routes 441 and 442; £4.30, 1¼ hours, eight daily Monday to Saturday, five Sunday.

Derby Trent Barton Swift; £4, 40 minutes, hourly Monday to Saturday, five Sunday.

Cycle Hire Centre (☎ 01335-343156; www.peakdistrict.gov.uk/visiting/cycle; Mapleton Lane; half-day/day from £14/17; ⊙ 9.30am-5.30pm Mar-Nov, shorter hours Dec-Feb)

Matlock Bath

POP 753

Unashamedly tacky, Matlock Bath (not to be confused with the larger, work-a-day town of Matlock 2 miles north) looks like a seaside resort that somehow lost its way and ended up at the foot of the Peak District National Park. Following the River Derwent through a sheer-walled gorge, the main promenade is lined with amusement arcades, tearooms, fish-and-chip shops, pubs and shops catering to the bikers who congregate here on summer weekends. Outside summer, the town is considerably quieter.

◉ Sights & Activities

Steep paths climb the eastern side of the gorge, reached by pedestrian bridges from the A6. The tourist office has details of longer, more challenging walks in the hills.

Beware: many of the lanes up the side of the valley are too narrow for cars, with no space for turning (or parking).

Peak District Lead Mining Museum   MUSEUM
(☑01629-583834; www.peakdistrictleadmining-museum.co.uk; The Grand Pavilion, South Pde; museum adult/child £4/3, mine £4.50/3.50, combined ticket £7/5; ⊙10am-5pm Apr-Oct, 11am-3pm Wed-Fri, to 4pm Sat & Sun Nov-Mar) An educational introduction to the mining history of Matlock is provided by this enthusiast-run museum set in an old Victorian dance hall. Kids can wriggle through its maze of tunnels and shafts while adults browse historical displays. At noon and 2pm daily from April to October (at weekends only from November to March) you can go into the workings of the **Temple Mine** and pan for 'gold' (well, shiny minerals). Reservations for mine tours are recommended.

Heights of Abraham   AMUSEMENT PARK
(☑01629-582365; www.heightsofabraham.com; Dale Rd; adult/child £15/10.50; ⊙10am-4.30pm daily mid-Mar–Oct, Sat & Sun mid-Feb–mid-Mar, closed Nov–mid-Feb) A spectacular **cable-car ride** (accessible with admission ticket only) from the bottom of the gorge brings you to this hilltop leisure park, its cave and mine tours and fossil exhibitions are a winner with kids.

Peak Rail   RAIL
(☑01629-580381; www.peakrail.co.uk; adult/child £8.50/4.50; ⊙Mar-Nov, hours vary) From a tiny platform by Sainsbury's supermarket on the outskirts of the town of Matlock (not Matlock Bath), nostalgic steam trains trundle along a 4-mile length of track to the nearby village of Rowsley, home to Caudwell's Mill (p461). Tickets include unlimited travel on the day of purchase.

🛏 Sleeping

Hodgkinson's Hotel & Restaurant   HOTEL ££
(☑01629-582170; www.hodgkinsons-hotel.co.uk; 150 South Pde; d/f incl breakfast from £95/145; P🕸🖥) The eight rooms at this central Grade II–listed Victorian beauty conjure up Matlock's golden age with antique furnishings, flowery wallpaper and cast-iron fireplaces. Arrive early to nab one of its five parking spaces. The restaurant (two-/three-course menus £26/29) has just 18 seats so bookings are advised. Service is superb.

DERWENT VALLEY MILLS

Unlikely as it may sound, the industrial mills that line the Derwent Valley are ranked up there with the Taj Mahal on the Unesco World Heritage list.

Cromford Mill (☑01629-823256; www.cromfordmills.org.uk; Mill Lane, Cromford; tour adult/child £3/2.50; ⊙9am-5pm, tours 11am, 1pm & 2.30pm Sat-Thu, by reservation 11am Fri) Founded in the 1770s by Richard Arkwright, the Cromford Mill was the first modern factory, producing cotton on automated machines, powered by a series of waterwheels along the River Derwent. This prototype inspired a succession of mills, ushering in the industrial age. The Arkwright Society runs fascinating tours. It's 1 mile south of Matlock Bath (a 20-minute walk), or you can take the train one stop to Cromford (70p, three minutes, hourly).

Caudwell's Mill (☑01629-734374; www.caudwellsmill.co.uk; Rowsley; mill tours adult/child £4.50/2; ⊙mill tours 9.30am-4.30pm, shop 9am-5pm) This chugging, grinding, water-powered mill still produces flour the old-fashioned way – 25 different types are for sale, along with eight different oat products, and yeast and biscuits. The mill has various craft workshops and a tearoom. You can get to Rowsley direct from Matlock Bath by Highpeak bus (£2.80, 15 minutes, hourly) on the route to Bakewell, or take the **Peak Rail** (p461) steam train and follow the riverside path from the station.

Grouse & Claret INN ££

(☑ 01629-733233; www.grouseclaretpub.co.uk; Station Rd, Rowsley; d/f incl breakfast from £75/90; ⓟ ⚆ ⚇) In the village of Rowsley, 6.2 miles northwest of Matlock Bath, this 18th-century stone inn has been revamped by pub operator Marston's and now has eight comfy, country-style wallpapered rooms (some sleeping up to three people), a restaurant and a huge, sunny beer garden with umbrella-shaded tables.

Ashdale Guest House B&B ££

(☑ 01629-57826; www.ashdaleguesthouse.co.uk; 92 North Pde; s/d from £50/70; ⓟ ⚆ ⚇) Just beyond the bling of the amusement-arcade-lined main promenade framed by towering monkey-puzzle trees, this tall 1840s-built stone house has four spacious, tastefully decorated rooms and organic breakfasts.

🛍 Shopping

Scarthin Books BOOKS

(www.scarthinbooks.com; The Promenade, Cromford; ⊙ 9am-6pm Mon-Sat, noon-6pm Sun) More than 100,000 new and secondhand books cram 12 rooms in this biblio-paradise, which hosts regular literary events and has a vegetarian cafe (dishes £3.50 to £6.50) serving organic pizza, wraps, pies and burritos.

ℹ Information

The **tourist office** (☑ 01629-583834; www. visitpeakdistrict.com; The Grand Pavilion, South Pde; ⊙ 10am-5pm Apr-Oct, 11am-3pm Wed-Fri, to 4pm Sat & Sun Nov-Mar) is located at the Peak District Lead Mining Museum.

ℹ Getting There & Away

Matlock is a hub for buses around the Peak District.

Bakewell Highpeak; £3.30, 30 minutes, hourly

Derby Transpeak; £4.30, 35 minutes, hourly

Trains run hourly between Matlock Bath and Derby (£5.60, 30 minutes, hourly).

Chesterfield & Around

POP 104,300

The eastern gateway to the Peaks, Chesterfield is worth a stop to see the astonishing crooked spire rising atop St Mary & All Saints Church and the magnificent Elizabethan mansion Hardwick Hall nearby.

👁 Sights

St Mary & All Saints Church CHURCH

(☑ 01246-206506; www.chesterfieldparishchurch. org.uk; Church Walk; spire tours adult/child £5/3; ⊙ church 9am-5pm Mon-Sat, 8am-6.30pm Sun, spire tours Mon-Sat) **FREE**. Dating from 1360, the 68m-high spire is twisted in a right-handed corkscrew and leans several metres southwest. It's the result of the lead casing on the south-facing side having buckled in the sun. Learn more at the engaging **Chesterfield Museum & Art Gallery** (☑ 01246-345727; www.chesterfield.gov.uk/museum; St Mary's Gate; ⊙ 10am-4pm Mon & Thu-Sat; **FREE**).

Hardwick Hall HISTORIC BUILDING

(NT; www.nationaltrust.org.uk; house & garden adult/child £13.10/6.55, garden only £6.55/3.30, incl Hardwick Old Hall £19.10/10.15; ⊙ house 11am-5pm Wed-Sun late Feb–Oct, to 3pm Wed-Sun Nov–late Feb, garden 9am-6pm daily year-round) One of the most complete Elizabethan mansions in the country, Hardwick Hall was designed by eminent architect Robert Smythson. The hall featured all the latest mod-cons of the time, including fully glazed windows. The atmospheric interiors are decked out with magnificent tapestries and oil paintings of forgotten dignitaries.

The hall was home to the 16th-century's second-most powerful woman, Elizabeth, Countess of Shrewsbury (known to all as Bess of Hardwick) who amassed a staggering fortune by marrying wealthy noblemen with one foot in the grave. Hardwick Hall was constructed using her inheritance from hubby number four, who shuffled off this mortal coil in 1590.

Set aside time to explore the formal gardens or the longer walking trails of Hardwick Park.

Next door to the manor is Bess' first house, **Hardwick Old Hall** (EH; www.english-heritage.org.uk; adult/child £6.60/4, incl Hardwick Hall £19.10/10.15; ⊙ 10am-6pm Wed-Sun Easter-Sep, to 5pm Oct, shorter hours Nov-Easter), now a romantic ruin administered by English Heritage.

Hardwick Hall is 10 miles southeast of Chesterfield, just off the M1; it's best reached by your own wheels.

ℹ Information

The **tourist office** (☑ 012246-345777; www. visitchesterfield.info; Rykneld Sq; ⊙ 9am-6pm Mon-Sat) is directly opposite St Mary and All Saints Church.

ⓘ Getting There & Away

BUS
From Chesterfield coach station on Beetwell St, bus 170 serves Bakewell (£3.30, 50 minutes, hourly).

TRAIN
Chesterfield lies on the main rail line between Nottingham (£12.50, 45 minutes, up to three per hour) and Derby (£11.10, 25 minutes, up to three per hour), which continues to Sheffield (£5.10, 15 minutes, up to three per hour). The station is just east of the centre.

PEAK DISTRICT

Rolling across the Pennines' southernmost hills is the glorious Peak District National Park. Ancient stone villages are folded into creases in the landscape, and the hillsides are littered with stately homes and rocky outcrops. The Dark Peak is dominated by exposed moorland and gritstone 'edges', while to the south, the White Peak is made up of the limestone dales.

No one knows how the Peak District got its name – certainly not from the landscape, which has hills and valleys, gorges and lakes, wild moorland and gritstone escarpments, but no peaks. The most popular theory is that the region was named for the Pecsaetan, the Anglo-Saxon tribe who once populated this part of England.

Founded in 1951, the Peak District was England's first national park and is Europe's busiest. But even at peak times, there are 555 sq miles of open English countryside in which to soak up the scenery.

⚐ Activities

Climbing & Caving
The limestone sections of the Peak District are riddled with caves and caverns, including a series of 'showcaves' in Castleton, Buxton and Matlock Bath. For serious caving (or potholing) trips, the first port of call should be the website www.peakdistrictcaving.info, run by caving store **Hitch n Hike** (01433-651013; www.hitchnhike.co.uk; Hope Rd, Bamford; ☺9am-5.30pm), near Castleton, which has gear and advice for climbing.

England's top mountaineers train in this area, which offers rigorous technical climbing on a series of limestone gorges, exposed tors (crags) and gritstone 'edges' that extend south into the Staffordshire Moorlands.

Gritstone climbing in the Peak District is predominantly on old-school trad routes, requiring a decent rack of friends, nuts and hexes. Bolted sport routes are found on several limestone crags in the Peak District, but many use ancient pieces of gear and most require additional protection. The crags are best reached with your own transport; check seasonal bus services with tourist offices.

Cycling
Plunging dales and soaring scarps provide a perfect testing ground for cyclists, and local tourist offices are piled high with cycling maps and trail guides. For easy traffic-free riding, head for the 17.5-mile **High Peak Trail**, which follows the old railway line from Cromford, near Matlock Bath, to Dowlow near Buxton. The trail winds through beautiful hills and farmland to Parsley Hay, where the **Tissington Trail**, part of NCN Route 68, heads south for 13 miles to Ashbourne. Trails are off-road on dedicated cycle paths, suitable for road bikes.

Mirroring the Pennine Way, the **Pennine Bridleway** is another top spot to put your calves through their paces. Around 120 miles of trails have been created between Middleton Top and the South Pennines, and the route is suitable for horse riders, cyclists and walkers. You could also follow the **Pennine Cycleway** (NCN Route 68) from Derby to Buxton and beyond. Other popular routes include the **Limestone Way**, running south from Castleton to Staffordshire, and the **Monsal Trail & Tunnels** between Bakewell and Wyedale, near Buxton.

ⓘ PEAK DISTRICT TRANSPORT PASSES

Handy bus passes cover travel in the Peak District.

The Peaks Plus ticket (Peaks Plus adult/child £7.50/5, Peaks Plus Xtra £12.50/7) offers all-day travel on Trent Barton buses, including the Transpeak between Ashbourne, Matlock Bath and Buxton. Its Peaks Plus Xtra ticket includes all transport on Transpeak and TM buses between Derby, Sheffield and Buxton.

The Derbyshire Wayfarer ticket (adult/child £12.40/6.20) covers buses and trains throughout the county and as far afield as Sheffield. One child under 16 travels free per paying adult.

Peak District National Park

Peak Tours (☎ 01457-851462; www.peak-tours.com; mountain-bike rental per day £20) delivers rental bikes anywhere in the Peak District, and offers guided cycling tours. The Peak District National Park Authority (p465) operates several cycle-hire centres renting road, mountain, tandem and electric bikes as well as kids' bikes.

Walking

The Peak District is one of the most popular walking areas in England, with awe-inspiring vistas of hills, dales and sky that attract legions of hikers in summer. The White Peak is perfect for leisurely strolls, which can start from pretty much anywhere. Be sure to close gates behind you as you go. When exploring the rugged territory of the Dark Peak, make sure your boots are waterproof and beware of slipping into rivulets and marshes.

The Peak's most famous walking trail is the **Pennine Way**, which runs north from Edale for more than 250 miles, finishing in the Scottish Borders. If you don't have three weeks to spare, you can reach the pretty town of Hebden Bridge in Yorkshire comfortably in three days.

The 46-mile **Limestone Way** winds through the Derbyshire countryside from Castleton to Rocester in Staffordshire, following footpaths, tracks and quiet lanes. Many people walk the 26-mile section between Castleton and Matlock in one long, tiring day, but two days is better. Tourist offices have a detailed leaflet.

Other popular routes include the **High Peak Trail**, **Tissington Trail**, and **Monsal Trail & Tunnels**. Numerous short walks are available.

ℹ️ Information

Tourist offices or national-park visitor centres include Buxton, Bakewell, Castleton and Edale. The **Peak District National Park Authority** (www. peakdistrict.gov.uk) website has reams of information on transport, activities and local events.

ℹ️ Getting There & Away

Buses run from regional centres such as Sheffield and Derby to destinations across the Peak District. Be aware that buses are much more frequent at weekends, and many services close down completely in winter. Bakewell and Matlock (not Matlock Bath) are the two main hubs – from here you can get anywhere in the Peak District. Timetables are available from all tourist offices as well as Traveline (p436). Trains run to Matlock Bath, Buxton, Edale and several other towns and villages.

Buxton

POP 24,001

The 'capital' of the Peak District National Park, albeit just outside the park boundary, Buxton is a confection of Georgian terraces, Victorian amusements and parks in the rolling hills of the Derbyshire dales. The town built its fortunes on its natural warm-water

springs, which attracted health tourists in Buxton's turn-of-the-century heyday.

Today, visitors are drawn here by the flamboyant Regency architecture and the natural wonders of the surrounding countryside. Tuesdays and Saturdays are market days, bringing colour to the grey limestone marketplace.

◎ Sights

Buxton's historic centre overflows with Victorian pavilions, concert halls and glasshouse domes. Its most famous building is the turreted Opera House (p468).

★**Pavilion Gardens**   GARDENS
(www.paviliongardens.co.uk; ⊘9.30am-5pm) FREE
Adjoining Buxton's opulent Opera House (p468) is the equally flamboyant Pavilion Gardens. These 9.3 hectares are dotted with domed pavilions; concerts take place in the bandstand throughout the year. The main building contains a tropical greenhouse, a nostalgic cafe and the tourist office (p468).

Devonshire Dome   HISTORIC BUILDING
(Devonshire Rd) A glorious piece of Victoriana, the Devonshire Dome forms part of the campus of the University of Derby. It is also home to **Devonshire Spa** (☑01298-330334; www.devonshiredome.co.uk; 1 Devonshire Rd; 2hr body spa £20, ocean or frangipani wrap £50, day package from £95; ⊘9am-6pm Tue, Wed, Sat & Sun, to 9pm Thu & Fri), which offers a full range of pampering treatments.

Buxton Baths   HISTORIC BUILDING
(The Crescent) In Victorian times, spa activities centred on the extravagant Buxton Baths complex, built in grand Regency style in 1854. The various bath buildings are fronted by a grand, curving facade, known as the **Crescent**, inspired by the Royal Crescent in Bath. It's expected to reopen in 2019 as a five-star hotel and spa.

Slopes   PARK
(⊘24hr) Opposite the Crescent, aptly named park the Slopes rises steeply in a series of grassy terraces. Climbing them provides the definitive view over Buxton's Victorian rooftops.

Buxton
Museum & Art Gallery   MUSEUM, GALLERY
(www.derbyshire.gov.uk/leisure/buxton_museum; Terrace Rd; ⊘9.30am-5.30pm Tue-Fri, to 5pm Sat year-round, plus 10.30am-5pm Sun Easter-Sep) FREE In a handsome Victorian building,

Buxton

Buxton

⊙ Top Sights
1 Pavilion Gardens................................... A2

⊙ Sights
2 Buxton Baths C2
3 Buxton Museum & Art Gallery............. C3
4 Crescent.. C2
5 Devonshire Dome.................................. B1
6 Slopes... C2

⊕ Activities, Courses & Tours
7 Buxton Tram B2
  Devonshire Spa.............................. (see 5)
8 Roman Buxton Town Walks.................. A2

⊜ Sleeping
9 Grosvenor House................................... B2

10 Old Hall Hotel....................................... B2
11 Roseleigh Hotel A4

⊗ Eating
12 Columbine Restaurant........................... C3
13 Number 13 .... C3

⊙ Drinking & Nightlife
14 Barbarella's C1
15 Old Sun Inn B4

⊕ Entertainment
16 Opera House.. B2

⊕ Shopping
17 Scrivener's Books &
    Bookbinding...................................... B4

the town museum displays local historical bric-a-brac and curiosities from Castleton's Victorian-era 'House of Wonders', including Harry Houdini's handcuffs.

Poole's Cavern　CAVE
(☎01298-26978; www.poolescavern.co.uk; adult/child £9.75/5.25; ⊙9.30am-5pm Mar-Oct, 10am-4pm Sat & Sun Nov-Feb) A pleasant mile-long

stroll southwest from the centre brings you to Poole's Cavern. This magnificent natural limestone cavern is reached by descending 28 steps; the temperature is a cool 7°C. Tours lasting 50 minutes run every 20 minutes from March to October and at 10.30am, 12.30pm and 2.30pm from November to February.

From the cavern's car park, a 20-minute walk leads up through Grin Low Wood to **Solomon's Temple**, a ruined tower with fine views over the town.

🏃 Activities

★ Buxton Tram   BUS
(☑ 01298-79648; adult/child £6/4; ☺ hourly 10am-5pm Easter-Oct, 11am-4pm Nov-Easter) From the Pavilion Gardens (p465), this vintage milk float takes you on a 12mph, hour-or-so circuit of the centre on its entertaining 'Wonder of the Peak' tour. There are only eight seats, so booking ahead is recommended.

The same company also offers hour-long walking tours at 2pm daily (adult/child £6/4) from the same departure point.

Roman Buxton Town Walks   WALKING
(walking tours by donation; ☺ 11am daily Jun-Aug, Sat Sep-May) Hour-long Roman Buxton town walks depart from the tourist office (p468).

Parsley Hay Cycle Hire   CYCLING
(☑ 01298-84493; www.peakdistrict.gov.uk/visiting/cycle; bike hire per half/full day adult from £14/17, child from £9/12; ☺ 9.30am-5pm Mar-Oct, 10am-4pm Nov-Feb) Rent mountain bikes, tandems and electric bikes from the Peak District National Park Authority's Parsley Hay Cycle Hire, 8 miles south of Buxton on the A515 at the junction of the High Peak and Tissington Trails.

🛏 Sleeping

Old Hall Hotel   HISTORIC HOTEL ££
(☑ 01298-22841; www.oldhallhotelbuxton.co.uk; The Square; s/d incl breakfast from £69/79; 🛜🍴) There's a tale to go with every creak of the floorboards at this history-soaked establishment, supposedly the oldest hotel in England. Among other esteemed residents, Mary, Queen of Scots, stayed here from 1576 to 1578, albeit against her will. The rooms are still the grandest in town, and there are several bars, lounges and dining options.

Roseleigh Hotel   B&B ££
(☑ 01298-24904; www.roseleighhotel.co.uk; 19 Broad Walk; s/d from £44/55; P@🛜) This gorgeous family-run B&B in a roomy old Victorian house has lovingly decorated rooms, many with fine views over the Pavilion Gardens. The owners are a welcoming couple, both seasoned travellers, with plenty of interesting stories. There's a minimum two-night stay on summer weekends.

Grosvenor House   B&B ££
(☑ 01298-72439; www.grosvenorbuxton.co.uk; 1 Broad Walk; s/d/f from £55/70/100; P🛜🍴) Overlooking the Pavilion Gardens, the Grosvenor is an old-school Victorian guesthouse with a huge parlour overlooking the park. Its eight rooms (including one family room sleeping three people) have floral upholstery, floral drapes and, well, floral everything else, really. There's a minimum two-night stay at peak times, when singles aren't available.

🍴 Eating & Drinking

Columbine Restaurant   MODERN BRITISH ££
(☑ 01298-78752; www.columbinerestaurant.co.uk; 7 Hall Bank; mains £13.50-20; ☺ 7-10pm Mon & Wed-Sat) 🍴 On the lane leading down beside the town hall, this understated restaurant is the top choice among in-the-know Buxtonites. The chef conjures up imaginative dishes primarily made from local produce. Bookings recommended. Two of its three dining areas are in the atmospheric stone cellar.

Number 13   MODERN BRITISH ££
(☑ 01298-25397; www.number13.co.uk; cnr Market St & South Ave; mains £9-17; ☺ 4.30-10.30pm Mon-Fri, noon-10.30pm Sat & Sun) 🍴 Burgers, pies, steaks and fish dishes are the stock-in-trade of this busy town-centre restaurant. Live jazz swings in the bar on Sunday afternoons. Upstairs, basic double **rooms** cost £50 per night.

Barbarella's   WINE BAR
(www.barbarellaswinebar.co.uk; 7 The Quadrant; ☺ noon-11pm Sun-Thu, to midnight Fri & Sat; 🛜🍴) Black-and-white paisley wallpaper, chandeliers and glossy timber tables make this sleek retro wine bar the hottest drinking den in Buxton. Stellar food too.

Old Sun Inn   PUB
(www.theoldsuninnbuxton.com; 33 High St; ☺ noon-11pm Mon & Wed, to 11.30pm Tue, Thu & Sun, to midnight Fri & Sat) The cosiest of Buxton's pubs, with a warren of rooms full of original features, a dozen ales on tap, and a lively crowd that spans the generations.

WORTH A TRIP

CATHEDRAL OF THE PEAK

Cathedral of the Peak (☏01298-871317; www.tideswellchurch.org; Commercial Rd, Tideswell; ☺9am-6pm) dominates the former lead-mining village of Tideswell, 10km east of Buxton. The massive parish church of St John the Baptist – aka the Cathedral of the Peak – has stood here virtually unchanged since the 14th century. Look out for the wooden panels inscribed with the Ten Commandments and grand 14th-century tomb of local landowner Thurston de Bower, depicted in full medieval armour. It's 8 miles east of Buxton, linked by buses 65 and 68 (£2.40, 30 minutes, hourly Monday to Saturday, every two hours Sunday).

⭐ Entertainment

Opera House   OPERA
(☏0845 127 2190; www.buxtonoperahouse.org.uk; Water St; tours £2.50; ☺tours usually 11am Sat) Buxton's gorgeously restored Opera House hosts a full program of drama, dance, concerts and comedy. It's the focal point for festivities including the **Buxton Festival** (www.buxtonfestival.co.uk; ☺Jul).

🛍 Shopping

Scrivener's Books & Bookbinding   BOOKS
(☏01298-73100; www.scrivenersbooks.co.uk; 42 High St; ☺9.30am-5pm Mon-Sat, noon-4pm Sun) At this delightfully chaotic bookshop, sprawling over five floors, books are filed in piles and the Dewey system has yet to be discovered.

Cavendish Arcade   ARCADE
(www.cavendisharcade.co.uk; Cavendish Circus; ☺9am-6pm Mon-Sat, 10am-5pm Sun, shop hours vary) Retaining its original eggshell-blue tiles, Cavendish Arcade houses boutiques selling upmarket gifts.

ⓘ Information

Buxton's helpful, well-organised **tourist office** (☏01298-25106; www.visitpeakdistrict.com; Pavilion Gardens; ☺9.30am-5pm; 🖥) has useful leaflets on walks in the area.

ⓘ Getting There & Away

Buses stop on both sides of the road at **Market Pl** (Market Pl). The hourly Highpeak runs to Derby (£5.90, 1¾ hours), via Bakewell (£3.80,

30 minutes) and Matlock Bath (£3.30, one hour). Five Highpeak services run to Manchester (£5.30, 1¼ hours).

To reach Sheffield take bus 65 (£5.80, 1¼ hours, every two hours Monday to Saturday, three services Sunday).

Northern Rail has trains to/from Manchester (£10.10, one hour, hourly).

Castleton & Around

POP 706

Guarding the entrance to the forbidding Winnats Pass gorge, charming Castleton is a magnet on summer weekends for Midlands visitors – come midweek if you want to enjoy the sights in relative peace and quiet. The village's streets are lined with leaning stone houses, with walking trails criss-crossing the surrounding hills. A wonderfully atmospheric castle crowns the ridge above, and the bedrock below is riddled with fascinating caves.

◎ Sights & Activities

Situated at the base of 517m-high Mam Tor, Castleton is the northern terminus of the **Limestone Way**, which follows narrow, rocky Cave Dale, far below the east wall of the castle. The tourist office has maps and leaflets, including details of numerous easier walks.

Peveril Castle   CASTLE
(EH; www.english-heritage.org.uk; adult/child £5.10/3; ☺10am-6pm Easter-Sep, to 5pm Oct, to 4pm Sat & Sun Nov-Easter) Topping the ridge to the south of Castleton, a 350m walk from the town centre, this evocative castle has been so ravaged by the centuries that it almost looks like a crag itself. Constructed by William Peveril, son of William the Conqueror, the castle was used as a hunting lodge by Henry II, King John and Henry III, and the crumbling ruins offer swooping views over the Hope Valley.

Castleton Museum   MUSEUM
(☏01629-816572; www.peakdistrict.gov.uk; Buxton Rd; ☺10am-5.30pm late Jul–early Sep, to 5pm Apr–late Jul & early Sep–Oct, shorter hours early Nov–Mar) FREE Attached to the tourist office (p470), the cute town museum has displays on everything from mining and geology to rock climbing, hang-gliding and the curious Garland Festival (☺29 May).

Driving Tour
Peak District

START BAKEWELL
END BUXTON
LENGTH 52 MILES; ONE TO TWO DAYS

Although you can drive this route in just a few hours, there's a lot to see and do, so pack your hiking boots and consider breaking your journey overnight. Fuel your car at the pretty town of ① **Bakewell**, famed for its distinctive Bakewell Pudding. Head south on the A6 for 3.5 miles to Rowsley and turn left on winding Church Lane for 2 miles to visit the atmospheric medieval manor ② **Haddon Hall** (p473).

Return to Rowsley, turn left on the A6 and left on the B6012 – follow it for 2.9 miles before turning right to reach the 'Palace of the Peak', ③ **Chatsworth House** (p473).

Back on the B6012, turn right to join the A619. At Baslow, home to the country hotel and Michelin-starred restaurant Fischer's Baslow Hall, turn left at the roundabout and travel along the A623 for 3.4 miles to the turn-off for ④ **Eyam**. Drive up the hill to reach its quaint museum, where you can

learn about the town's poignant plague history. There's fantastic walking here.

Continue up the hill and turn right on Edge Rd, then right on Sir William Hill Rd and left on the B601 at Grindleford. Continue to Hathersage and turn left on the A6187 to Hope Valley. From here, turn right on the A6013, passing Ladybower Reservoir, to reach the ⑤ **Derwent Dam Museum** (p471). Pop in to learn about the Dambusters squadron's 'bouncing bombs' tests here during WWII.

It's 5.8 miles back to the Hope Valley turn-off. Then turn right onto Hathersage Rd, right again on Edale Rd and follow the valley to stretch your legs at another prime walking destination, ⑥ **Edale**. Scenery peaks when you travel southwest towards Castleton, climbing the steep hill near 517m-high Mam Tor, to Winnats Rd, then following the spectacular former coral-reef canyon Winnats Pass to explore ⑦ **Speedwell Cavern** (p470).

From Speedwell Cavern, head west along Arthurs Way on to Winnats Rd. Turning right on the A623 brings you to the riot of Victoriana in the former spa town of ⑧ **Buxton**.

Peak Cavern
CAVE

(☑ 01433-620285; www.peakcavern.co.uk; Peak Cavern Rd; adult/child £10.25/8.25, incl Speedwell Cavern £17/13.50; ☺ 10am-5pm daily Apr-Oct, Sat & Sun Nov-Mar) Castleton's most convenient cave is easily reached by a pretty streamside 250m walk south of the village centre. It has the largest natural cave entrance in England, known (not so prettily) as the Devil's Arse. Dramatic limestone formations are lit with fibre-optic cables. Buy tickets ahead online in peak season.

Speedwell Cavern
CAVE

(☑ 01433-620512; www.speedwellcavern.co.uk; Winnats Pass; adult/child £11/9, incl Peak Cavern £17/13.50; ☺ 10am-5pm daily Apr-Oct, Sat & Sun Nov-Mar) Just over half a mile west of Castleton at the mouth of Winnats Pass, this claustrophobe's nightmare is reached via an eerie boat ride through flooded tunnels, emerging by a huge subterranean lake called the Bottomless Pit. New chambers are discovered here all the time by potholing expeditions.

Treak Cliff Cavern
CAVE

(☑ 01433-620571; www.bluejohnstone.com; adult/child £9.50/5.20; ☺ 10am-4.15pm Mar-Oct, to 3.15pm Nov-Feb) Captivating Treak Cliff has a forest of stalactites and exposed seams of colourful Blue John Stone, which is still mined to supply the jewellery trade. Tours focus on the history of mining; kids can polish their own Blue John Stone during school holidays. It's just under a mile west of Castleton's village centre.

Blue John Cavern
CAVE

(☑ 01433-620638; www.bluejohn-cavern.co.uk; adult/child £11/6; ☺ 9.30am-5.30pm Apr-Oct, to dusk Nov-Mar) Up the southeastern side of Mam Tor, 2 miles west of Castleton, Blue John is a maze of natural caverns with rich seams of Blue John Stone that are still mined every winter. You can get here on foot up the closed section of the Mam Tor road.

🛏 Sleeping

Rowter Farm
CAMPGROUND £

(☑ 01433-620271; 2-person sites £10; ☺ Easter-Oct; ⓟ 🐾) About 2 miles west of central Castleton, this simple camping field (no lounge area or shop) has a stunning location up in the hills. Showers cost 50p. Drivers should approach via Winnats Pass (take the left fork at the top, and the first left immediately after); on foot, follow the Cave Dale path.

Ye Olde Nag's Head Hotel
PUB ££

(☑ 01433-620248; www.yeoldenagshead.co.uk; Cross St; d £50-95; 🐾🐾) The cosiest of the 'residential' pubs along the main road offers 10 comfortable, well-appointed rooms (some with four-poster beds and spas), ale tasting trays and a popular restaurant, plus regular live music.

Causeway House
B&B ££

(☑ 01433-623921; www.causewayhouse.co.uk; Back St; s/d from £35/75) The floors within this ancient character-soaked stone cottage are worn and warped with age, but the quaint bedrooms are bright and welcoming. Doubles have en suites but the two single rooms (one of which can be used as a twin) share a bathroom.

🍴 Eating

Three Roofs Cafe
CAFE £

(www.threeroofscafe.co.uk; The Island; dishes £6-11; ☺ 9.30am-4.30pm; 🐾) Castleton's most popular purveyor of cream teas, opposite the turn-off to the tourist office, also has filling sandwiches, pies and jacket potatoes.

1530
ITALIAN ££

(☑ 01433-621870; www.1530therestaurant.co.uk; Cross St; mains lunch £5-7.50, dinner £8-17; ☺ noon-2pm & 6-8.30pm Wed & Thu, noon-2pm & 6-9.30pm Fri & Sat, noon-2pm & 6-8pm Sun & Mon; 🐾) Crispy thin-crust pizzas and fresh pastas such as king prawn, crab, crayfish and calamari linguine are the speciality of Castleton's swish Italian flag-bearer.

★ Samuel Fox
MODERN BRITISH £££

(☑ 01433-621562; www.samuelfox.co.uk; Stretfield Rd, Bradwell; mains lunch £12.50-14, dinner £13.50-21; ☺ kitchen 6-9pm Wed & Thu, noon-2pm & 6-9pm Fri & Sat, 1-8pm Sun Feb-Dec; ⓟ🐾) In the Hope Valley village of Bradwell, 2.5 miles southeast of Castleton, this enchanting inn owned by pedigreed chef James Duckett serves exceptional Modern British cuisine: rare roasted venison with pickled red cabbage and roast pheasant with braised sprouts, bacon and parsnips. Rates for the gorgeous pastel-shaded guest rooms upstairs (single/double £95/130) include a sumptuous breakfast plus sherry, grapes and chocolates.

ℹ Information

The tourist office (☑ 01629-816572; www.peakdistrict.gov.uk; Buxton Rd; ☺ 10am-5.30pm late Jul–early Sep, to 5pm Apr–late Jul & early

Sep–Oct, shorter hours early Nov–Mar) is in the Castleton Museum.

ℹ️ Getting There & Away

Bus services include the following:

Bakewell Bus 173; £3.10, 50 minutes, four daily via Hope (five minutes) and Tideswell (20 minutes)

Buxton Bus 68; £3.90, one hour (departs Castleton in the morning and returns in the afternoon Monday to Saturday)

The nearest train station is at Hope, an easy 2-mile walk east of Castleton, on the line between Sheffield (£5.50, 30 minutes, every two hours) and Manchester (£11.10, 55 minutes, hourly).

Derwent Reservoirs

North of the Hope Valley, the upper reaches of the Derwent Valley were flooded between 1916 and 1935 to create three huge reservoirs to supply Sheffield, Leicester, Nottingham and Derby with water. These constructed lakes soon proved their worth – the **Dambusters** squadron carried out practice runs over Derwent Reservoir before unleashing their 'bouncing bombs' on the Ruhr Valley in Germany in WWII. Their exploits are detailed in the **Derwent Dam Museum** (www.dambusters.org.uk; Fairholmes; ⊙10am-4pm Sun) **FREE** in the western tower atop the dam.

These days, the Ladybower, Derwent and Howden Reservoirs are popular destinations for walkers, cyclists and mountain bikers – and lots of ducks, so drive slowly!

Fairholmes is a good base for walking and cycling, with a **cycle-hire centre** (☑01433-651261; www.peakdistrict.gov.uk; Fairholmes; per half/full day adult £14/17, child £10/12; ⊙10am-4.30pm Mon-Fri, to 5.30pm Sat & Sun Apr-Oct, 10am-3.30pm Sat & Sun Nov-Mar).

Fairholmes' **tourist office** (☑01433-650953; www.peakdistrict.gov.uk; Fairholmes; ⊙10am-4.30pm Mon-Fri, to 5.30pm Sat & Sun Apr-Oct, 10am-3.30pm Sat & Sun Nov-Mar) dispenses walking and cycling advice.

Fairholmes is 2 miles north of the A57 linking Sheffield and Manchester. Buses are limited at best, so you really need your own wheels.

Edale

POP 316

Surrounded by majestic Peak District countryside, this cluster of stone houses centred on a pretty parish church is an en-chanting place to pass the time. Edale lies between the White and Dark Peak areas, and is the southern terminus of the Pennine Way. Despite the remote location, the Manchester–Sheffield train line passes through the village, bringing throngs of weekend visitors.

🏃 Activities

Walking is the number-one drawcard here, with plenty of diverting strolls for less committed hill walkers.

As well as trips to Hollins Cross and Mam Tor, on the ridge dividing Edale from Castleton, you can walk north onto the **Kinder Plateau**, dark and brooding in the mist, gloriously high and open when the sun's out. This was the setting for a famous act of civil disobedience by ramblers in 1932 that paved the way for the legal 'right to roam' and the creation of England's national parks.

Weather permitting, a fine circular walk starts by following the **Pennine Way** through fields to **Upper Booth**, then up a path called Jacobs Ladder and along the southern edge of Kinder, before dropping down to Edale via the steep rocky valley of Grindsbrook Clough, or the ridge of Ringing Roger.

🛏️ Sleeping & Eating

Upper Booth Farm CAMPGROUND £
(☑01433-670250; www.upperboothcamping.co.uk; Upper Booth; sites per person/car £6/4, camping barn per person £8; ⊙Easter–early Nov; **P**) 🌱 Located along the Pennine Way 1.8 miles west of Edale, this peaceful campsite is set on a working farm and is surrounded by spectacular scenery. For hikers, there's a camping barn and small shop. Customised hampers (from £20; preorder when booking) can be filled with locally baked cakes, breads, biscuits, flapjacks, eggs, honey, BBQ meats and preserves, and more.

Fieldhead Campsite CAMPGROUND £
(☑01433-670386; www.fieldhead-campsite.co.uk; sites per person/car from £6/3.50; ⊙Apr-Sep; **P 🛜 ♿**) Right next to the Moorland Tourist Office (p472), this pretty and well-equipped campsite spreads over six fields, with some pitches right by the river. Showers cost 20p.

Edale YHA HOSTEL £
(☑0845 371 9514; www.yha.org.uk; Rowland Cote, Nether Booth; dm/d/f from £11.50/65/69; **P @ 🛜**) Spectacular views across to Back Tor unfold from this country-house hostel

1.5 miles east of Edale, signposted from the Hope road. Check availability ahead as it's often busy with school groups.

Stonecroft
B&B ££

(☑ 01433-670262; www.stonecroftguesthouse.co.uk; Grindsbrook; s/d from £55/99; P �) ✎ This handsomely fitted-out stone house, built in the 1900s, has two comfortable bedrooms. Vegetarians and vegans are well catered for – host Julia is an award-winning chef and the organic breakfast (with gluten-free options) is excellent. Packed lunches (£7.50) are available by request when booking. Bike rental costs £30 per day. Free pickup from the train station can be arranged.

Rambler Inn
PUB FOOD ££

(☑ 01433-670268; www.theramblerinn.com; Grindsbrook; mains £9-20; ⊙ kitchen noon-9.30pm Mon-Sat, to 8pm Sun, bar noon-11pm Mon-Fri, to midnight Sat, to 9pm Sun; P ☎ ⓦ ⓗ ⓢ) Edale's heart and soul, this cosy stone pub serves real ales, and filling fare such as steaks, pork pies and local lamb casseroles. There's a kids' menu, B&B **rooms** (double/triple/family from £85/105/125) and occasional live music.

ⓘ Information

Topped by a sedum turf 'living roof' with a waterfall splashing across its glass panels, the eco-conscious **Moorland Tourist Office** (☑ 01433-670207; www.peakdistrict.gov.uk; Fieldhead; ⊙ 9.30am-5pm Apr-Sep) has maps and displays on the moors.

ⓘ Getting There & Away

Trains run from Edale to Manchester (£11, every hour, 45 minutes) and Sheffield (£7.10, every two hours, 40 minutes).

Eyam

POP 926

Quaint little Eyam (ee-em), a former lead-mining village, has a poignant history. In 1665 the town was infected by the dreaded Black Death plague, carried here by fleas on a consignment of cloth from London, and the village rector, William Mompesson, convinced villagers to quarantine themselves. Some 270 of the village's 800 inhabitants succumbed, while surrounding villages remained relatively unscathed. Today, Eyam's sloping streets of old cottages backed by rows of green hills are delightful to wander.

⊙ Sights & Activities

Eyam Parish Church
CHURCH

(www.eyam-church.org; Church St; ⊙ 9am-6pm Easter-Sep, to 4pm Oct-Easter) Many victims of the village's 1665 Black Death plague outbreak were buried at Eyam's church. You can view stained-glass panels and moving displays telling the story of the outbreak. The churchyard contains a Celtic cross carved in the 8th century.

Eyam Museum
MUSEUM

(www.eyam.museum.org.uk; Hawkhill Rd; adult/child £2.50/2; ⊙ 10am-4.30pm Tue-Sun Easter-Oct) Vivid displays on the Eyam plague are the centrepiece of the engaging town museum, alongside exhibits on the village's history of lead-mining and silk-weaving.

⌁ Sleeping

Crown Cottage
B&B ££

(☑ 01433-630858; http://crown-cottage.co.uk; Main Rd; s/d from £50/70; P ☎) Opposite the post office, this walker- and cyclist-friendly stone house full of pottery ornaments is crammed to the rafters most weekends, when there's a minimum two-night stay. There's secure bike storage and a piano for guests to play.

Miner's Arms
PUB ££

(☑ 01433-630853; www.theminersarmseyam.co.uk; Water Lane; s/d £45/70; ☎) Although its age isn't immediately obvious, this traditional village inn was built shortly before the Black Death hit Eyam in 1665. Inside you'll find beamed ceilings, affable staff, a blazing open fireplace, comfy en suite rooms and good-value pub food (mains £8 to £12.50).

ⓘ Getting There & Away

Bus services include the following:

Bakewell Bus 275; £3.60, 20 minutes, three per day Monday to Saturday

Buxton Buses 65 and 66; £3.60, 40 minutes, five per day Monday to Saturday, three Sunday

Sheffield Bus 65; £5.70, 40 minutes, five per day Monday to Saturday, three Sunday

---

Bakewell & Around

POP 3950

The second-largest town in the Peak District, charming Bakewell is a great base for exploring the limestone dales of the White Peak. Filled with storybook stone buildings, the town is ringed by famous walking trails

> WORTH A TRIP
>
> ## CHATSWORTH HOUSE
> ··
> Known as the 'Palace of the Peak', the vast edifice **Chatsworth House** (☑01246-565300; www.chatsworth.org; house & gardens adult/child £20/12, gardens only £12/7, playground £6, park admission free; ⊙10.30am-5pm late May–early Sep, shorter hours mid-Mar–late May & early Sep–early Jan), 3 miles northeast of Bakewell, has been occupied by the earls and dukes of Devonshire for centuries. Inside, the lavish apartments and mural-painted staterooms are packed with priceless paintings and period furniture. The house sits in 25 sq miles of grounds and ornamental gardens, some landscaped by Lancelot 'Capability' Brown. Kids will love the farmyard adventure playground.
>
> From Bakewell, take bus 218 (£2.40, 15 minutes, half-hourly).

and stately homes, but it's probably best known for its famous Bakewell Pudding, a pastry shell filled with jam and frangipane invented here in 1820.

⊙ Sights

All Saints Church CHURCH
(www.bakewellchurch.co.uk; South Church St; £2 donation requested; ⊙9am-5pm Apr-Oct, to 4pm Nov-Mar) Up on the hill above Rutland Sq, All Saints Church is packed with ancient features, including a 14th-century font, a pair of Norman arches, some fine heraldic tombs, and a collection of crude stone gravestones and crosses dating from the 12th century.

Old House Museum MUSEUM
(www.oldhousemuseum.org.uk; Cunningham Pl; adult/child £4/2; ⊙11am-4pm) Set in a time-worn stone house near All Saints Church, the Old House Museum explores local history. Check out the Tudor loo and the displays on wattle and daub, a traditional technique for building walls using woven twigs and cow dung.

Thornbridge Brewery BREWERY
(☑01629-815999; www.thornbridgebrewery.com; Buxton Rd; tours adult/child £7.50/3; ⊙tours 3pm Wed & Fri, shop 9am-4.30pm Mon-Fri, 10am-2pm last Sun of month) Vibrant brews from this riverside brewery include a fruity strawberry-blonde ale, I Love You Will You Marry Me; a Rhubarbe De Saison; Bamberg smoked-bock beer; and Vienna-style lager Kill Your Darlings; as well as collaborations with international independents. Tours lasting 1½ hours take you behind the scenes and include tastings in Thornbridge glasses, which you get to keep afterwards. Under-fives aren't permitted on tours. It's half a mile from the centre on the northwestern edge of town.

Haddon Hall HISTORIC SITE
(www.haddonhall.co.uk; Haddon Rd; adult/child £13.50/7; ⊙10.30am-5pm daily May-Sep, Sat-Mon Apr & Oct, to 4pm early–mid Dec) With stone turrets, time-worn timbers and walled gardens, Haddon Hall, 2 miles south of Bakewell on the A6, looks exactly like a medieval manor house should. Founded in the 12th century, it was expanded and re-modelled throughout medieval times. The 'modernisation' stopped when the house was abandoned in the 18th century. Take the Highpeak bus from Bakewell (£2.30, 10 minutes, hourly) or walk along the footpath through the fields, mostly on the east side of the river.

🏃 Activities

Walking and cycling are, of course, the main activities in the area. The scenic **Monsal Trail** follows the path of a disused railway line from Combs Viaduct on the outskirts of Bakewell to Topley Pike in Wye Dale (about 3 miles east of Buxton) including a number of reopened old railway tunnels, covering 8.5 miles in all.

For a rewarding shorter walk, follow the Monsal Trail for 3 miles to the dramatic viewpoint at **Monsal Head**, where you can pause for refreshment at the **Monsal Head Hotel** (☑01629-640250; www.monsalhead.com; Monsal Trail; mains £11.50-16; ⊙kitchen noon-8pm Sun-Thu, to 9pm Fri & Sat; P🐾), which serves real ales and excellent Modern British cuisine. With more time to kill, continue to **Miller's Dale**, where viaducts give a spectacular vista across the steep-sided valley. The tourist offices at Bakewell and Buxton have full details.

Other walking routes go to the stately homes Haddon Hall and Chatsworth House.

🛏 Sleeping

Melbourne House & Eastthorpe B&B **££**
(📞 01629-815357; www.bakewell-accommodation.
co.uk; Buxton Rd; d from £70; P 🔊) Occupying a
picturesque, creeper-covered building (Melbourne House) dating back more than three
centuries and a new annex (Easthorpe),
with uncluttered, neutral-toned rooms, this
inviting B&B is handily situated on the main
road leading to Buxton.

Rutland Arms Hotel HOTEL **£££**
(📞 01629-812812; www.rutlandarmsbakewell.
co.uk; The Square; s £64-76, d £92-165; P 🔊🐾)
Jane Austen is said to have stayed in room
2 of this aristocratic, recently refurbished
stone coaching inn while working on *Pride
and Prejudice*. The more expensive of its 33
rooms have lots of Victorian flourishes.

🍴 Eating & Drinking

Bakewell's streets are lined with sweet
tearooms and bakeries selling Bakewell
Pudding.

⭐ Chatsworth Estate
Farm Shop Cafe
CAFE, DELI **£**
(www.chatsworth.org; Pilsley; dishes £4.50-10;
⏰ cafe & shop 9am-5pm Mon-Sat, 10am-5pm
Sun; 🅿) One of the finest places to eat
in the Peak District, this bucolic cafe serves
hearty breakfasts (eggs Benedict with Chat-
sworth-cured bacon or salmon; strawber-
ry-and-honey Chatsworth yoghurt with
muesli) until 11.30am before turning out
lunches (steak-and-kidney suet pudding;
traditional roasts) until 3pm, and an afternoon menu. Over half the products at its adjacent farm shop are produced on the estate.

Old Original Bakewell
Pudding Shop
BAKERY, TEAROOM **£**
(www.bakewellpuddingshop.co.uk; The Square;
dishes £7-12; ⏰ 8.30am-6pm Mon-Sat, 9am-6pm
Sun) One of those that claims to have invented the Bakewell Pudding, this place
has a lovely 1st-floor tearoom with exposed
beams. It serves light meals and afternoon
teas on tiered trays.

Piedaniel's
FRENCH **££**
(📞 01629-812687; www.piedaniels-restaurant.com;
Bath St; mains lunch £12, dinner £15-25; ⏰ noon-
2pm & 7-9pm Tue-Sat) Chefs Eric and Christi-
ana Piedaniel's Modern French cuisine is the
toast of the in-town restaurants. A whitewashed dining room is the exquisite setting
for the likes of prawn and fennel bisque with
quenelles (feather-light flour, egg and cream
dumplings) followed by lobster and salmon
thermidor or lemon sole stuffed with scallop
mousse.

⭐ Fischer's Baslow Hall
GASTRONOMY **£££**
(📞 01246-583259; www.fischers-baslowhall.
co.uk; 259 Calver Rd, Baslow; 2-/3-/7-course lunch
menus £20/27/60, 2-/3-/9-course dinner menus
£55/72/80; ⏰ noon-2pm & 7-9pm; 🔊🅿) Some 4
miles northeast of Bakewell, this 1907-built
manor house has a magnificent Michelin-starred dining room showcasing British
produce (Derbyshire lamb, Yorkshire game,
Cornish crab...) along with vegetables from
its kitchen garden.

Six sumptuous floral bedrooms are in the
main house, with another five in the adjacent garden house (doubles from £200);
weekend-night stays (from £344) include a
three-course meal.

Castle Inn
PUB
(📞 01629-812103; www.oldenglishinns.co.uk;
Bridge St; ⏰ 8am-10pm Sun-Thu, to midnight Fri &
Sat; 🔊🐾🅿) The ivy-draped Castle Inn is one
of the better pubs in Bakewell, with four centuries of practice in rejuvenating hamstrung
hikers (and their dogs – pets are warmly
welcomed here). Gourmet burgers are a
menu highlight (mains from £8 to £19). It
also has four comfortable rooms (double/
family from £85/95). Enter via Castle St.

ℹ Information

Bakewell's **tourist office** (📞 01629-816558;
www.visitpeakdistrict.com; Bridge St;
⏰ 9.30am-5pm Apr-Oct, 10.30am-4.30pm Nov-
Mar) is inside the old Market Hall; helpful staff
can book accommodation.

ℹ Getting There & Away

Bakewell lies on the Highpeak bus route. Buses
run hourly to Buxton (£3.30, 30 minutes), Derby
(£4.80, 1¼ hours) and Matlock Bath (£3.30, 30
minutes). Five services a day continue to Manchester (£6, 1¾ hours).

Other services:

Castleton Bus 173; £3.10, 50 minutes, four
per day

Chesterfield Bus 170; £3.30, 50 minutes,
hourly

Yorkshire

Includes ➡

York 480
Harrogate 491
Scarborough 494
Helmsley
& Around 499
Whitby 502
Skipton 506
Hawes 511
Richmond 512
Leeds 514
Haworth 522
Sheffield 523
Hull 525
Beverley 527

Best Places to Eat

➡ Pipe and Glass Inn (p528)

➡ Norse (p493)

➡ Hare Inn (p500)

➡ Crafthouse (p517)

➡ Cochon Aveugle (p488)

Best Places to Sleep

➡ Millgate House (p513)

➡ Windmill (p495)

➡ West Park (p492)

➡ Art Hostel (p516)

Why Go?

With a population as big as Scotland's and an area half the size of Belgium, Yorkshire is almost a country in itself. It has its own flag, its own dialect and its own celebration, Yorkshire Day (1 August). While local folk are proud to be English, they're even prouder to be natives of 'God's Own County'.

What makes Yorkshire so special? First, there's the landscape – with its brooding moors and green dales rolling down to a dramatic coastline, Yorkshire has some of Britain's finest scenery. Second, there's the sheer breadth of history – every facet of the British experience is represented here, from Roman times to the 21st century.

But Yorkshire's greatest appeal lies in its people. Industrious and opinionated, they have a wry wit and shrewd friendliness. Stay here for a while and you'll come away believing, like the locals, that God is indeed a Yorkshirewoman. .

When to Go

➡ The weeklong Jorvik Festival in February sees York taken over by a Viking invasion.

➡ Spring brings drifts of yellow daffodils to brighten the roadsides in the Dales and North York Moors; the Three Peaks Race takes place in Horton-in-Ribblesdale.

➡ Agriculture is celebrated at the Great Yorkshire Show in Harrogate in July. At the same time of year Yorkshire's coastal sea cliffs become a frenzy of nesting seabirds.

➡ September is the ideal time for hiking in the Yorkshire Dales; the Walking Festival in Richmond also takes place in this month. York goes all gourmet with its annual 10-day food festival, while Harrogate gets green-fingered during its Autumn Flower Show.

Yorkshire Highlights

1 **York** (p480)
Exploring the medieval streets of the city and its awe-inspiring cathedral.

2 **Yorkshire Dales National Park** (p506) Getting off the beaten track and exploring the lesser-known corners.

3 **Fountains Abbey** (p498) Wandering among the atmospheric medieval ruins.

4 **Scarborough** (p494) Being beside the seaside, and enjoying this town's traditional bucket-and-spade atmosphere.

5 **North Yorkshire Moors Railway** (p501) Riding on one of England's most scenic train lines.

6 **Whitby** (p502) Sitting on the pier and tucking into the world's best fish and chips.

7 **Castle Howard** (p490) Reliving the story of *Brideshead Revisited* amid the aristocratic splendour.

8 **Malham Cove** (p509) Pulling on your hiking boots and tackling the steep paths around this scenic cove.

9 **National Coal Mining Museum for England** (p521) Discovering mining's dark side.

10 **National Media Museum** (p519) Enjoying the high-tech, hands-on exhibits.

History

As you drive through Yorkshire on the main A1 road, you're following in the footsteps of the Roman legions who conquered northern Britain in the 1st century AD. In fact, many Yorkshire towns – including York, Catterick and Malton – were founded by the Romans, and many modern roads (including the A1, A59, A166 and A1079) follow the alignment of Roman roads.

When the Romans departed in the 5th century, native Britons battled for supremacy with invading Teutonic tribe the Angles and, for a while, Yorkshire was part of the Kingdom of Northumbria. In the 9th century the Vikings arrived and conquered most of northern Britain, an area that became known as the Danelaw. They divided the territory that is now Yorkshire into *thridings* (thirds), which met at Jorvik (York), their thriving commercial capital.

In 1066 Yorkshire was the scene of a pivotal showdown in the struggle for the English crown, when the Anglo-Saxon king, Harold II, rode north to defeat the forces of the Norwegian king, Harold Hardrada, in the Battle of Stamford Bridge, before returning south for his appointment with William the Conqueror – and a fatal arrow – in the Battle of Hastings.

The inhabitants of northern England did not take the subsequent Norman invasion lying down. In order to subdue them, the Norman nobles built a chain of formidable castles throughout Yorkshire, including those at York, Richmond, Scarborough, Pickering and Helmsley. The Norman land grab formed the basis of the great estates that supported England's medieval aristocrats.

By the 15th century, the duchies of York and Lancaster had become so wealthy and powerful that they ended up battling for the English throne in the Wars of the Roses (1455–87). The dissolution of the monasteries by Henry VIII from 1536 to 1540 saw the wealth of the great abbeys of Rievaulx, Fountains and Whitby fall into the hands of noble families, and Yorkshire quietly prospered for 200 years, with fertile farms in the north and the Sheffield cutlery business in the south, until the big bang of the Industrial Revolution transformed the landscape.

South Yorkshire became a centre of coal mining and steel-making while West Yorkshire nurtured a massive textile industry, and the cities of Leeds, Bradford, Sheffield and Rotherham flourished. By the late 20th century another revolution was taking place. The heavy industries had died out, and the cities of Yorkshire were reinventing themselves as shiny, high-tech centres of finance, higher education and tourism.

 ## Activities

Yorkshire's varied landscape of wild hills, tranquil valleys, high moors and spectacular coastline offers plenty of opportunities for outdoor activities. See www.outdooryorkshire.com for more details.

Cycling

Yorkshire's hosting of the start of the 2014 Tour de France saw a huge upsurge in interest in cycling, and resulted in the establishment of the **Tour de Yorkshire** (www.letour.yorkshire.com) annual cycle race from 2015. The county has a vast network of country lanes that are perfect for road cyclists, although the national parks also attract lots of motorists so even minor roads can be busy at weekends.

North York Moors   MOUNTAIN BIKING
(www.mtb-routes.co.uk/northyorkmoors) Off-road bikers can avail themselves of the network of bridleways, former railways and disused mining tracks now converted for two-wheel use. Dalby Forest (www.forestry.gov.uk/dalbyforest), near Pickering, sports purpose-built mountain-biking trails of all grades from green to black, and there are newly waymarked trails at the Sutton Bank visitor centre.

Moor to Sea Cycle Route   CYCLING
(www.moortoseacycle.net) A network of routes between Pickering, Danby and the coast includes a 20-mile traffic-free route that follows a disused railway line between Whitby and Scarborough.

White Rose Cycle Route   CYCLING
(www.sustrans.org.uk; NCN Rte 65) A 131-mile road cruise from Middlesborough to York and on to Hull and Hornsea, via the dramatic western scarp of the North York Moors and the rolling Yorkshire Wolds, with a traffic-free section on the old railway between Selby and York.

Yorkshire Dales Cycleway   CYCLING, MOUNTAIN BIKING
(www.cyclethedales.org.uk) An exhilarating 130-mile loop, taking in the best of the national park; the website also details the route followed by Stage 1 of the 2014 Tour de France. There's lots of scope for off-road riding, with about 500 miles of bridleways and trails – for inspiration, go to www.mtbthedales.org.uk.

Walking

For shorter walks and rambles, the best area is the **Yorkshire Dales**, with a great selection of walks through scenic valleys or over wild hilltops, with a few higher summits thrown in for good measure. The East Riding's **Yorkshire Wolds** hold hidden delights, while the quiet valleys and dramatic coast of the **North York Moors** also offer many opportunities.

Cleveland Way   WALKING

(www.nationaltrail.co.uk/clevelandway) A venerable moor-and-coast classic that circles the North York Moors National Park on its 109-mile, nine-day route from Helmsley to Filey.

Coast to Coast Walk   WALKING

(www.wainwright.org.uk/coasttocoast.html) One of England's most popular walks: 190 miles across northern England from the Lake District through the Yorkshire Dales and North York Moors National Parks. The Yorkshire section takes a week to 10 days and offers some of the finest walking of its kind in England.

Dales Way   WALKING

(www.dalesway.org.uk) A charming and not-too-strenuous 80-mile amble from the Yorkshire Dales to the Lake District, following the River Wharfe through the heart of the Dales and finishing at Bowness-on-Windermere.

Pennine Way   WALKING

(www.nationaltrail.co.uk/pennineway) The Yorkshire section of England's most famous walk runs for more than 100 miles via Hebden Bridge, Malham, Horton-in-Ribblesdale and Hawes, passing near Haworth and Skipton.

White Rose Way   WALKING

(www.whiteroseway.co.uk) A long-distance trail covering the 104 miles from Leeds' city centre to Scarborough, taking in remote and picturesque Yorkshire villages along the way.

Wolds Way   WALKING

(www.nationaltrail.co.uk/yorkshirewoldsway) A beautiful but oft-overlooked walk that winds through the most scenic part of Yorkshire's East Riding district.

ℹ Information

The **Yorkshire Tourist Board** (www.yorkshire.com) has plenty of general leaflets and brochures, for postal and email enquiries only. For more detailed information, contact local tourist offices.

ℹ Getting There & Around

The major north–south road transport routes – the M1 and A1 motorways – run through the middle of Yorkshire, serving the key cities of Sheffield, Leeds and York. If you're arriving by sea from northern Europe, Hull in the East Riding district is the region's main port.

Traveline Yorkshire (☑ 0871 200 2233; www.yorkshiretravel.net) provides public-transport information for all of Yorkshire.

BUS

Long-distance coaches operated by **National Express** (☑ 08717 818181; www.national express.com) serve most cities and large towns in Yorkshire from London, the south of England, the Midlands and Scotland.

Bus transport around Yorkshire is frequent and efficient, especially between major towns. Services are more sporadic in the national parks, but are still adequate for reaching most places, particularly in summer months (June to September).

TRAIN

The main rail line between London and Edinburgh runs through Yorkshire, with at least 10 trains calling each day at York and Doncaster, where you can change trains for other Yorkshire destinations. There are also direct links to northern cities such as Manchester and Newcastle. For timetable information, contact **National Rail Enquiries** (☑ 08457 48 49 50; www.nationalrail.co.uk). There are direct services between the major towns and cities of Yorkshire.

NORTH YORKSHIRE

This, the largest of Yorkshire's four counties – and the largest county in England – is also the most beautiful. Unlike the rest of northern England, it has survived almost unscathed by the Industrial Revolution. Since the Middle Ages, North Yorkshire has been almost exclusively about sheep and the woolly wealth they produce.

Rather than closed-down factories, mills and mines, the human-made monuments dotting the landscape in these parts are of the stately variety – the great houses and wealthy abbeys that sit, ruined or restored, as a reminder that there was plenty of money to be made off the sheep's back.

All the same, North Yorkshire's biggest attraction is an urban one. While the genteel spa town of Harrogate and the bright and breezy seaside resorts of Scarborough and Whitby have many fans, nothing compares to the unparalleled splendour of York, England's most-visited city outside London.

York

POP 198,000

Nowhere in northern England says 'medieval' quite like York, a city of extraordinary cultural and historical wealth that has lost little of its pre-industrial lustre. A magnificent circuit of 13th-century walls encloses a medieval spider's web of narrow streets. At its heart lies the immense, awe-inspiring York Minster, one of the most beautiful Gothic cathedrals in the world. York's long history and rich heritage is woven into virtually every brick and beam, and the modern, tourist-oriented city – with its myriad museums, restaurants, cafes and traditional pubs – is a carefully maintained heir to that heritage.

Try to avoid the inevitable confusion by remembering that around these parts, *gate* means street and *bar* means gate.

History

In AD 71 the Romans built a garrison called Eboracum, which in time became a large fort with a civilian settlement around it. Hadrian used it as the base for his northern campaign, while Constantine the Great was proclaimed emperor here in AD 306. When the Roman Empire collapsed, the town was taken by the Anglo-Saxons, who renamed it Eoforwic and made it the capital of the independent kingdom of Northumbria.

In 625 a Roman priest, Paulinus, arrived and converted King Edwin and his nobles to Christianity; two years later they built the first wooden church here. For most of the next century, the city was a major centre of learning, attracting students from all over Europe. In 866 the next wave of invaders arrived, this time the Vikings, who gave the town a more tongue-friendly name, Jorvik. It was their capital for the next 100 years, and during that time they turned the city into an important trading port.

King Eadred of Wessex drove out the last Viking ruler in 954 and reunited Danelaw with the south, but trouble quickly followed. In 1066 King Harold II fended off a Norwegian invasion at Stamford Bridge, east of York, but was defeated by William the Conqueror a few months later in the Battle of Hastings.

After William's two wooden castles were captured by an Anglo-Scandinavian army, he torched the entire city (and Durham) and the surrounding countryside. The Normans then set about rebuilding it, adding a grand new minster. Over the next 300 years York (a contraction of the Viking name Jorvik) prospered through royal patronage, textiles, trade and the Church.

Throughout the 18th century the city was a fashionable social centre dominated by the aristocracy, who were drawn by its culture and new racecourse. When the railway arrived in 1839, thousands of people were employed in new industries that sprang up around it, such as confectionery (the Terry's and Rowntree's brands were founded here). These industries went into decline in the latter half of the 20th century, but by then a new invader was asking for directions at the city gates, armed only with a guidebook.

◎ Sights

★ **York Minster**   CATHEDRAL
(www.yorkminster.org; Deangate; adult/child £10/free, incl tower £15/5; ⊙9am-5.30pm Mon-Sat, 12.45-5pm Sun, last admission 30min before closing) The remarkable York Minster is the largest medieval cathedral in all of northern Europe, and one of the world's most beautiful Gothic buildings. Seat of the archbishop of York, primate of England, it is second in importance only to Canterbury, seat of the primate of *all* England – the separate titles were created to settle a debate over the true centre of the English church. If this is the only cathedral you visit in England, you'll still walk away satisfied.

The first church on this site was a wooden chapel built for the baptism of King Edwin of Northumbria on Easter Day 627, whose location is marked in the crypt. It was replaced with a stone church built on the site of a Roman basilica, parts of which can be seen in the foundations. The first Norman minster was built in the 11th century and, again, you can see surviving fragments in the foundations and crypt.

The present minster, built mainly between 1220 and 1480, manages to encompass all the major stages of Gothic architectural development. The transepts (1220–55) were built in Early English style; the octagonal chapter house (1260–90) and nave (1291-1340) in the Decorated style; and the west towers, west front and central (or lantern) tower (1470–72) in Perpendicular style.

➡ **Nave**

Entrance to the minster is via the west door, which leads into the unusually tall and wide nave. The aisles (to the sides) are roofed in stone, in contrast to the central roof, which is wood painted to look like stone. On both sides of the nave are painted stone shields of the nobles who met with Edward II at a parliament in York. Also note the dragon's head projecting from the gallery – it's a crane believed to have been used to lift a font cover. There are several fine windows dating from the early 14th century, but the most impressive is the **Great West Window** (1338) above the entrance, with its beautiful heart-shaped stone tracery.

➡ **Transepts & Chapter House**

The south transept was badly damaged by fire in 1984, but has been fully restored. It is dominated by the exquisite **Rose Window** commemorating the union of the royal houses of Lancaster and York, through the marriage of Henry VII and Elizabeth of York, which ended the Wars of the Roses and began the Tudor dynasty

Opposite, in the north transept, is the magnificent **Five Sisters Window**, with five lancets over 15m high. This is the minster's oldest complete window; most of its tangle of coloured glass dates from around 1250. Just beyond it to the right is the 13th-century **chapter house**, a fine example of the Decorated style. Sinuous and intricately carved stonework – there are more than 200 expressive carved heads and figures – surrounds an airy, uninterrupted space.

➡ **Choir Screen & East Window**

Separating the choir from the nave is a superb 15th-century choir screen with 15 statues depicting the kings of England from William I to Henry VI. Beyond the screen and the carved wooden stalls of the choir is the lady chapel and, behind it, the high altar, which is dominated by the huge **Great East Window** (1405). At 23.7m by 9.4m – roughly the size of a tennis court – it is the world's largest medieval stained-glass window and the cathedral's single most important treasure. Needless to say, its epic size matches the epic theme depicted within: the beginning and end of the world as described in Genesis and the Book of Revelations.

➡ **Undercroft**

A set of stairs in the south transept leads down to the undercroft (open 10am to 5pm Monday to Saturday, 1pm to 5pm Sunday), the very bowels of the building. In 1967 the minster foundations were shored up when the central tower threatened to collapse; while engineers worked frantically to save the building, archaeologists uncovered Roman and Norman remains that attest to the site's ancient history – one of the most ex-

traordinary finds was a Roman culvert, still carrying water to the Ouse. An interactive exhibition here, **York Minster Revealed**, leads visitors through 2000 years of history on the site of the cathedral. The nearby **treasury** houses 11th-century artefacts including relics from the graves of medieval archbishops.

➡ **Crypt**

The crypt, entered from the choir close to the altar, contains fragments from the Norman cathedral, including the font showing King Edwin's baptism, which also marks the site of the original wooden chapel. Look out for the **Doomstone**, a 12th-century carved stone showing a scene from the Last Judgement with demons casting doomed souls into Hell.

➡ **Tower**

At the heart of York's cathedral is the massive tower, which is well worth climbing for the unparalleled views of York. You'll have to tackle a fairly claustrophobic climb of 275 steps and, most probably, a queue of people with cameras in hand. Access to the tower is from the south transept.

★ **National Railway Museum**   MUSEUM
(www.nrm.org.uk; Leeman Rd; ⊙10am-6pm; P ♿)
FREE While many railway museums are the sole preserve of lone men in anoraks comparing dog-eared notebooks and getting high on the smell of machine oil, coal smoke and nostalgia, this place is different. York's National Railway Museum – the biggest in the world, with more than 100 locomotives – is so well presented and crammed with fascinating stuff that it's interesting even to folk whose eyes don't mist over at the thought of a 4-6-2 A1 Pacific class thundering into a tunnel.

Highlights for the trainspotters among us include a replica of George Stephenson's **Rocket** (1829), the world's first 'modern' steam locomotive; the sleek and streamlined **Mallard**, which set the world speed record for a steam locomotive in 1938 (126mph); a

ⓘ THE YORK PASS

If you plan on visiting a number of sights, you can save yourself some money by using a YorkPass (www.yorkpass.com). It gives you free access to more than 30 pay-to-visit sights in and around York, including York Minster, Jorvik and Castle Howard. You can buy it at York tourist office or online; prices for one/two/three days are adult £38/50/60, child £20/26/30.

York

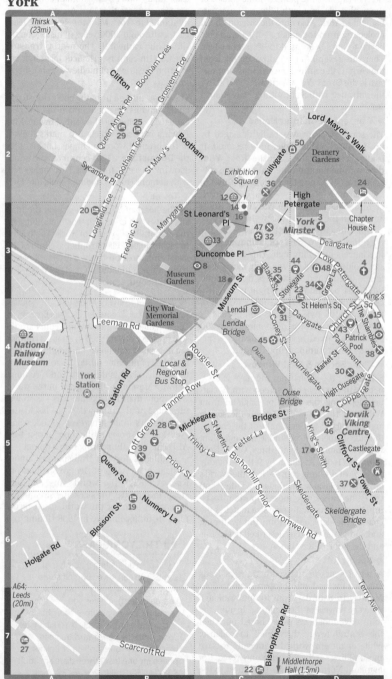

Thirsk
(23mi)

Clifton

Bootham Cres

Grosvenor Tce

21

Queen Anne's Rd

Bootham Tce

25
29

Sycamore Pl

St Mary's

Bootham

Lord Mayor's Walk

Deanery
Gardens

50

Gillygate

24

Exhibition
Square

36

High
Petergate

Chapter
House St

York
Minster

3

12
14
16

St Leonard's
Pl

Marygate

Frederic St

Longfield Tce

20

13

Duncombe Pl

47 32

Deangate

Low Petergate

44
35

48

4

Museum
Gardens

8

18

Museum St

Stonegate

34
23

Grape La

King's
Sq

St Helen's Sq

The Shambles

15
10

City War
Memorial
Gardens

Leeman Rd

Lendal

Coney St

31

Davygate

Church St

43

Patrick
Pool

Parliament St

National
Railway
Museum

2

Lendal
Bridge

45

Market St

38

30

York
Station

Station Rd

Rougier St

Ouse

Spurriergate

High Ousegate

Coppergate

Jorvik
Viking
Centre

1

Local &
Regional
Bus Stop

Tanner Row

Ouse
Bridge

Bridge St

42

46

Castlegate

5

Station Rd

Tott Green

Micklegate

28
41

St Martin's La

Trinity La

Fetter La

King's Staith

17

37

Tower St

Queen St

39

Priory St

Bishophill Senior

Cromwell Rd

Skeldergate

Skeldergate
Bridge

7

Blossom St

19

Nunnery La

Holgate Rd

Terry Ave

A64;
Leeds
(20mi)

27

Scarcroft Rd

Bishopthorpe Rd

22

Middlethorpe
Hall (1.5mi)

1960s Japanese **Shinkansen bullet train**; and the world-famous **Flying Scotsman**, the first steam engine to break the 100mph barrier (now restored to full working order). There's also a massive 4-6-2 loco from 1949 that's been cut in half to demonstrate how it works (daily talk at 4pm).

Even if you're not a rail nerd, you'll enjoy looking through the gleaming, silk-lined carriages of the **royal trains** used by Queens Mary, Adelaide and Victoria and King Edward VII, or having a *Brief Encounter* moment over tea and scones at the museum's station platform cafe. Allow at least two hours to do it all justice.

The museum is about 400m west of the train station and if you don't fancy walking you can ride the roadtrain (adult/child £2/1, April to October) that runs between the minster and museum every 30 minutes from 11am to 4pm.

★ **Jorvik Viking Centre** MUSEUM
(www.jorvik-viking-centre.co.uk; Coppergate; adult/child £10.25/7.25; ◷10am-5pm Apr-Oct, to 4pm Nov-Mar) Interactive multimedia exhibits aimed at bringing history to life often achieve exactly the opposite, but the much-hyped Jorvik manages to pull it off with aplomb. Thoroughly restored and re-imagined following flood damage in 2015, it's a smells-and-all reconstruction of the Viking settlement unearthed here during excavations in the late 1970s, experienced via a 'time-car' monorail that transports you through 9th-century Jorvik (the Viking name for York). You can reduce time waiting in the queue by booking your tickets online.

While some of the 'you will now travel back in time' malarkey is a bit naff, it's all done with a sense of humour tied to historical authenticity that will give you a pretty good idea of what life must have been like in Viking-era York. In the museum exhibition at the end of the monorail, look out for the Lloyds Bank coprolite, a fossilised human stool that measures an eye-watering 9in long and half a pound in weight, and must be the only turd in the world to have its own Wikipedia entry.

Yorkshire Museum MUSEUM
(www.yorkshiremuseum.org.uk; Museum St; adult/child £7.50/free; ◷10am-5pm) Most of York's Roman archaeology is hidden beneath the medieval city, so the superb displays in the Yorkshire Museum are invaluable if you want to get an idea of what Eboracum was

York

◉ Top Sights
1 Jorvik Viking Centre D5
2 National Railway Museum A4
3 York Minster..D3

◉ Sights
4 Church of the Holy Trinity..................D3
5 Clifford's Tower D5
6 Dig...E4
7 Henry VII Experience...........................B5
8 Museum Gardens C3
9 Richard III Experience E2
10 The Shambles.......................................D4
11 York Castle Museum E6
12 York City Art Gallery C2
13 Yorkshire Museum C3

◉ Activities, Courses & Tours
14 Association of Voluntary
      Guides..C3
15 Ghost Hunt of York..............................D4
16 York Citysightseeing C3
17 YorkBoat D5
18 Yorkwalk..C3

◉ Sleeping
19 Bar Convent B6
20 Beech House..A3
21 Brontë House...B1
22 Dairy Guesthouse C7
23 Fort D3
24 Grays Court..D2
25 Hedley House Hotel..............................B2
26 Monkgate Guesthouse.........................F2

27 Mount Royale Hotel & Spa A7
28 Safestay York B5
29 St Raphael B2

◉ Eating
30 Ate O'Clock..D4
31 Bettys...C4
32 Café Concerto C3
33 Cochon Aveugle E5
34 El Piano D3
35 Mannion's C3
36 No 8 Bistro C2
37 Olive Tree...D5
      Parlour at Grays Court................ (see 24)
38 Shambles Kitchen D4
39 Your Bike Shed B5

◉ Drinking & Nightlife
40 Blue Bell E4
41 Brigantes Bar...B5
42 King's Arms..D5
43 Pivní...D4
44 Ye Olde Starre D3

◉ Entertainment
45 City Screen Picturehouse....................C4
46 Grand Opera House D5
47 York Theatre Royal C3

◉ Shopping
48 Antiques Centre D3
49 Fossgate Books.....................................E4
50 Inkwell D2

like. There are maps and models of Roman York, funerary monuments, mosaic floors and wall paintings, and a 4th-century bust of Emperor Constantine. Kids will enjoy the dinosaur exhibit, centred around giant ichthyosaur fossils from Yorkshire's Jurassic coast.

Museum Gardens   GARDENS
(entrances on Museum St & Marygate; ◔ dawn-dusk) FREE In the grounds of the peaceful Museum Gardens, you can see the **Multangular Tower**, a part of the City Walls that was once the western tower of the Roman garrison's defensive ramparts. The Roman stonework at the base has been built over with 13th-century additions. On the other side of the gardens are the ruins of **St Mary's Abbey** dating from 1270 to 1294. The ruined **Gatehall** was its main entrance, providing access from the abbey to the river.

The Shambles   STREET
The Shambles takes its name from the Saxon word *shamel,* meaning 'slaughterhouse' –

in 1862 there were 26 butcher shops on this street. Today the butchers are long gone, but this narrow cobbled lane, lined with 15th-century Tudor buildings that overhang so much they seem to meet above your head, is the most picturesque in Britain, and one of the most visited in Europe, often crammed with visitors intent on buying a tacky souvenir before rushing back to the tour bus.

York Castle Museum   MUSEUM
(www.yorkcastlemuseum.org.uk; Tower St; adult/child £10/free; ◔ 9.30am-5pm) This excellent museum has displays of everyday life through the centuries, with reconstructed domestic interiors, a Victorian street and a prison cell where you can try out a condemned man's bed – in this case, that of highwayman Dick Turpin (imprisoned here before being hanged in 1739). There's a bewildering array of evocative objects from the past 400 years, gathered together by a certain Dr Kirk from the 1920s onwards for fear the items would become obsolete and disappear completely.

Dig   MUSEUM
(www.digyork.com; St Saviour's Church, St Saviourgate; adult/child £6.50/6; ⊘10am-5pm, last admission 4pm; 🚻) Under the same management as Jorvik (p483), Dig cashes in on the popularity of archaeology programs on TV by giving you the chance to be an 'archaeological detective', unearthing the secrets of York's distant past as well as learning something of the archaeologist's world – what they do, how they do it and so on. Aimed mainly at kids, it's much more hands-on than Jorvik and a lot of its merit depends on how good – and entertaining – your guide is.

Clifford's Tower   CASTLE
(EH; www.english-heritage.org.uk; Tower St; adult/child £5.20/3.10; ⊘10am-6pm Apr-Sep, to 5pm Oct) There's precious little left of York Castle except for this evocative stone tower, a highly unusual four-lobed design built into the castle's keep after the original one was destroyed in 1190 during anti-Jewish riots. An angry mob forced 150 Jews to be locked inside the tower and the hapless victims took their own lives rather than be killed. There's not much to see inside, but the views over the city are excellent.

Church of the Holy Trinity   CHURCH
(www.holytrinityyork.org; Goodramgate; ⊘10am-5pm Tue-Sat May-Sep, to 4pm Oct-Apr) **FREE**
Tucked away behind an inconspicuous gate and seemingly cut off from the rest of the town, the Church of the Holy Trinity is a fantastically atmospheric old building, having survived almost unchanged for the past 200 years (it has no electricity or running water). Inside are rare 17th- to 18th-century box pews, 15th-century stained glass and wonky walls that seem to have been built without plumb line or spirit level.

York City Art Gallery   GALLERY
(www.yorkartgallery.org.uk; Exhibition Sq; adult/child £7.50/free; ⊘10am-5pm Mon-Fri, to 6pm Sat, 11am-4pm Sun) After a major restoration, York Art Gallery reopened in 2015 with a new art garden and an exhibition dedicated to British ceramics (www.centreofceramicart.org.uk) – the **Wall of Pots** houses more than 1000 pieces dating from Roman times to the present day. As well as an impressive collection of Old Masters, there are works by LS Lowry, Picasso, Grayson Perry, David Hockney, and the controversial York artist William Etty who, in the 1820s, was the first major British painter to specialise in nudes.

👉 Tours

Ghost Hunt of York   WALKING
(www.ghosthunt.co.uk; adult/child £6/4; ⊘tours 7.30pm) The kids will just love this award-winning and highly entertaining 75-minute tour laced with authentic ghost stories. It begins at the top end of The Shambles, whatever the weather (it's never cancelled) and there's no need to book, just turn up and wait till you hear the handbell ringing...

Yorkwalk   WALKING
(www.yorkwalk.co.uk; adult/child £6/5; ⊘tours 10.30am & 2.15pm Feb-Nov) Offers a series of two-hour walks on a range of themes, from the classics – Roman York, the snickelways (narrow alleys) and City Walls – to walks focused on chocolates and sweets, women in York, and the inevitable graveyard, coffin and plague tour. Walks depart from Museum Gardens Gate on Museum St; there's no need to book.

YorkBoat   BOATING
(www.yorkboat.co.uk; King's Staith; adult/child from £8/4; ⊘tours 10.30am, noon, 1.30pm & 3pm Feb-Nov) Hour-long cruises on the River Ouse, departing from King's Staith and, 10 minutes later, Lendal Bridge. Special lunch, dinner and evening cruises are also offered.

York Citysightseeing   BUS
(www.city-sightseeing.com; day ticket adult/child £13/5; ⊘9am-5.30pm Easter-Nov) Hop-on, hop-off route with 20 stops, calling at all the main sights. Buses leave every 10 to 30 minutes from Exhibition Sq near York Minster.

Association of Voluntary Guides   WALKING
(www.avgyork.co.uk; ⊘tours 10.15am year-round, 2.15pm Apr-Oct, 6.15pm Jun-Aug, 1.15pm Nov-Mar) **FREE** Free two-hour walking tours of the city, setting out from Exhibition Sq in front of York Art Gallery.

🎉 Festivals & Events

Jorvik Viking Festival   CULTURAL
(www.jorvik-viking-festival.co.uk) For a week in mid-February, York is invaded by Vikings as part of this festival, which features battle re-enactments, themed walks, markets and other bits of Viking-related fun.

York Food Festival   FOOD & DRINK
(www.yorkfoodfestival.com) For 10 days in September/October, discover all that's good to eat and drink in Yorkshire, with food stalls, tastings, a beer tent, cookery demonstrations and more.

LOCAL KNOWLEDGE

YORK CITY WALLS

If the weather's good, don't miss the chance to walk York's **City Walls** (www.yorkwalls.org. uk), which follow the line of the original Roman walls and give a whole new perspective on the city. Allow 1½ to two hours for the full circuit of 4.5 miles or, if you're pushed for time, the short stretch from Bootham Bar to Monk Bar is worth doing for the views of the minster.

Start and finish in the Museum Gardens or at **Bootham Bar** (on the site of a Roman gate), where a multimedia exhibit provides some historical context, and travel clockwise. Highlights include **Monk Bar**, which is the best-preserved medieval gate and still has a working portcullis, and **Walmgate Bar**, England's only city gate with an intact barbican.

At Monk Bar you'll find the **Richard III Experience** (www.richardiiiexperience.com; Monk Bar; adult/child incl Henry VII Experience £5/3; ⊙10am-5pm Apr-Oct, to 4pm Nov-Mar), a museum which sets out the case of the murdered 'Princes in the Tower' and invites visitors to judge whether their uncle, Richard III, killed them. The **Henry VII Experience** (www.richardiii experience.com; Micklegate Bar; adult/child incl Richard III Experience £5/3; ⊙10am-4pm) at Micklegate Bar charts the history of the city walls and the reign of England's first Tudor king.

York Christmas CHRISTMAS
(www.visityork.org/christmas) Kicking off with St Nicholas Fayre market in late November, the run-up to Christmas is an extravaganza of street decorations, market stalls, carol singers and mulled wine.

🛏 Sleeping

Beds can be hard to find in midsummer, even with inflated high-season rates. The tourist office's accommodation booking service charges £4, which might be the best four quid you spend if you arrive without a reservation.

Prices get higher the closer you are to the city centre. However, there are plenty of decent B&Bs on the streets north and south of Bootham. Southwest of the centre, B&Bs are clustered around Scarcroft, Southlands and Bishopthorpe Rds.

★ Fort HOSTEL £
(☎01904-620222; www.thefortyork.co.uk; 1 Little Stonegate; dm/d from £18/74; 🖀) This boutique hostel showcases the work of young British designers, creating affordable accommodation with a dash of character and flair. There are six- and eight-bed dorms, along with six doubles, but don't expect a peaceful retreat – the central location is in the middle of York's nightlife, and there's a lively club downstairs (earplugs are provided!).

Safestay York HOSTEL £
(☎01904-627720; www.safestayyork.co.uk; 88-90 Micklegate; dm/tw from £18/75; @🖀🌢) Housed in a Grade I Georgian building that was once home to the High Sheriff of Yorkshire, this is a large and well-equipped boutique hostel with cool decor and good facilities. It's popular with school groups and stag and hen parties – don't come here looking for peace and quiet!

York YHA HOSTEL £
(☎0845 371 9051; www.yha.org.uk; 42 Water End, Clifton; dm/q from £15/79; 🅿@🖀🌢) Originally the Rowntree (Quaker confectioners) mansion, this handsome Victorian house makes a spacious and child-friendly youth hostel, with most of its rooms four-bed dorms. Often busy, so book early. It's about a mile northwest of the city centre; there's a riverside footpath from Lendal Bridge (poorly lit, so avoid after dark). Alternatively, take bus 2 from the train station or Museum St.

★ Hedley House Hotel HOTEL ££
(☎01904-637404; www.hedleyhouse.com; 3 Bootham Tce; d/f from £105/115; 🅿🖀🌢) 🏊 This redbrick terrace-house hotel sports a variety of smartly refurbished, family-friendly accommodation, including rooms that sleep up to five, and some self-catering apartments – plus it has a sauna and spa bath on the outdoor terrace at the back, and is barely five minutes' walk from the city centre through the Museum Gardens.

Bar Convent B&B ££
(☎01904-643238; www.bar-convent.org.uk; 17 Blossom St; s/d £67/96; 🖀) This elegant Georgian redbrick mansion just outside Micklegate Bar, less than 10 minutes' walk from the train station, houses a working convent, a cafe, a conference centre and exhibition, and also offers excellent B&B accommodation. Open to visitors of all faiths and none. Charming bedrooms are modern and well

equipped, breakfasts are superb, and there's a garden and hidden chapel to enjoy.

Beech House B&B **££**
(☑ 01904-634581; www.beechhouse-york.co.uk; 6-7 Longfield Tce; s/d from £50/80; 🐾) Smart, businesslike bedrooms and a warm welcome from the friendly owners promise a comfortable stay at this redbrick terrace house. It enjoys an excellent location, both quiet and central, with the city centre a 10-minute walk away through the Museum Gardens.

Monkgate Guesthouse B&B **££**
(☑ 01904-655947; www.monkgateguesthouse.com; 65 Monkgate; s/d/f from £50/78/117; ᴾ🐾🌀) This attractive guesthouse lies just outside the city walls. It has seven brightly decorated bedrooms including a special family suite that has a separate bedroom for two kids.

St Raphael B&B **££**
(☑ 01904-645028; www.straphaelguesthouse. co.uk; 44 Queen Anne's Rd; d/tr £94/125; ᴾ🐾) Set in a historic house with that distinctively English half-timbered look, this B&B has a great central location, bright and airy bedrooms, and the smell of home-baked bread wafting up from the breakfast room.

Dairy Guesthouse B&B **££**
(☑ 01904-639367; www.dairyguesthouse.co.uk; 3 Scarcroft Rd; d/f from £80/100; 🐾) A lovely Victorian home that has retained many of its original features, including pine doors, stained glass and cast-iron fireplaces. But the real treat here is the flower- and plant-filled courtyard leading to the cottage-style rooms. Minimum two-night stay at all times.

Brontë House B&B **££**
(☑ 01904-621066; www.bronte-guesthouse.com; 22 Grosvenor Tce; s/d/f from £45/85/115; 🐾) The Brontë has five homely en suite rooms, each individually decorated; top of the range is the romantic double bedroom with a carved 19th-century headboard and velvet canopy. Breakfasts are served in a period dining room with magnificent carved oak sideboard, and include Yorkshire black pudding and local farm eggs.

★ **Middlethorpe Hall** HOTEL **£££**
(☑ 01904-641241; www.middlethorpe.com; Bishopthorpe Rd; s/d from £118/126; ᴾ🐾✖🐾) This breathtaking 17th-century country house is set in 8 hectares of parkland, once the home of diarist Lady Mary Wortley Montagu. The rooms are divided between the main house, restored courtyard buildings and three cottage suites. All are beautifully decorated with original antiques and oil paintings that have been carefully selected to reflect the period.

Grays Court HISTORIC HOTEL **£££**
(☑ 01904-612613; www.grayscourtyork.com; Chapter House St; d from £170; ᴾ🐾) Although it's practically in the shadow of York Minster, this medieval mansion feels more like a country-house hotel, set in lovely gardens ringed by the old city walls, with bedrooms that combine antique furniture with modern comfort and design. The oldest part of the building is 11th century, and King James I once dined in the Long Gallery, now an excellent restaurant, **Parlour at Grays Court** (p488).

Mount Royale Hotel & Spa HOTEL **£££**
(☑ 01904-628856; www.mountroyale.co.uk; The Mount; s/d/ste from £95/125/225; ᴾ🐾✖) A grand, early-19th-century heritage-listed building converted into a superb luxury hotel, complete with a solarium, beauty spa and outdoor heated tub and swimming pool. The rooms in the main house are gorgeous, but best of all are the open-plan garden suites, reached via an arcade of tropical fruit trees and bougainvillea.

🍴 Eating

★ **Mannion's** CAFE, BISTRO **£**
(☑ 01904-631030; www.mannionandco.co.uk; 1 Blake St; mains £6-11; ⊙ 9am-5.30pm Mon-Fri, to 6pm Sat, 10am-5pm Sun) Expect to queue for a table at this busy bistro (no reservations), with its maze of rustic, wood-panelled rooms and selection of daily specials. Regulars on the menu include eggs Benedict for breakfast, a chunky Yorkshire rarebit made with home-baked bread, and lunch platters of cheese and charcuterie from the attached deli. Oh, and pavlova for pudding.

Shambles Kitchen FAST FOOD **£**
(☑ 01904-674684; www.shambleskitchen.co.uk; 28 The Shambles; mains £6; ⊙ 9am-4pm Mon-Fri, to 5pm Sat, 10am-4pm Sun; 🖉) 🌱 Fast food doesn't mean unhealthy at this hugely popular little takeaway (there are only three tables inside). The place is best known for its pulled-pork sandwiches on sourdough bread, but there are also yummy vegetarian wraps, daily specials such as Goan curry and Korean chicken, and a choice of freshly made juices and smoothies.

Your Bike Shed CAFE **£**
(☑ 01904-633777; www.yourbikeshed.co.uk; 148-150 Micklegate; mains £4-7; ⊙ 9am-5pm Mon-Sat,

10am-5pm Sun; 🛜🚲♿) 🍴 Reinvigorated by the 2014 Tour de France (which began in Yorkshire) and the annual Tour de Yorkshire (from 2015), York's cycling scene has latched onto this cool cafe and bike workshop. Fitted out with recycled furniture and classic bikes, it serves reviving portions of halloumi burger, pie and peas, and carrot cake to hungry cyclists, washed down with excellent coffee.

★ No 8 Bistro
BISTRO ££

(📞01904-653074; www.no8york.co.uk/bistro; 8 Gillygate; 3-course lunch/dinner £16/25; ⊙noon-10pm Mon-Thu, 9am-10pm Fri-Sun; 🛜♿) 🍴 A cool little place with modern artwork mimicking the Edwardian stained glass at the front, No 8 offers a daylong menu of classic bistro dishes using fresh local produce, including Jerusalem artichoke risotto with fresh herbs, and Yorkshire lamb slow-cooked in hay and lavender. It also does breakfast (mains £6 to £9) and Sunday lunch (two courses £18). Booking recommended.

★ Parlour at Grays Court
CAFE, BRITISH ££

(www.grayscourtyork.com; Chapter House St; mains £9-20; ⊙10am-5pm & 6-9pm; 🛜) An unexpected pleasure in the heart of York, this 16th-century mansion (now a hotel) has more of a country-house atmosphere. Relax with coffee and cake in the sunny garden, enjoy a light lunch of Yorkshire rarebit, or indulge in a dinner of scallops and sea bass in the oak-panelled Jacobean gallery. The daytime menu includes traditional afternoon tea (£18.50).

Café Concerto
CAFE, MEDITERRANEAN ££

(📞01904-610478; www.cafeconcerto.biz; 21 High Petergate; mains lunch £6-9, dinner £13-19; ⊙9am-9pm) Walls papered with sheet music, chilled jazz on the stereo, and battered, mismatched tables and chairs set the bohemian tone in this comforting coffee shop-cum-bistro. Expect breakfasts, bagels and cappuccinos big enough to float a boat in during the day, and a sophisticated Mediterranean-style menu in the evening.

Ate O'Clock
BISTRO ££

(📞01904-644080; www.ateoclock.co.uk; 13a High Ousegate; mains £8-18; ⊙noon-2pm & 6-9.30pm Tue-Fri, noon-2.30pm & 5.30-9.30pm Sat; 🛜) 🍴 A tempting menu of classic bistro dishes (sirloin steak, slow-roasted pork belly, pan-fried duck breast) made with fresh Yorkshire produce has made this place hugely popular with locals – book a table to avoid disappointment. A three-course dinner costs £19.50 from 6pm to 7.55pm Tuesday to Thursday.

Olive Tree
MEDITERRANEAN ££

(📞01904-624433; www.theolivetreeyork.co.uk; 10 Tower St; mains £9-21; ⊙noon-2pm & 5.30-10pm) Local produce gets a Mediterranean makeover at this bright and breezy bistro. Classic pizza and pasta dishes are complemented by more ambitious recipes such as crayfish and chorizo risotto, and Moroccan lamb stew. The set menu (lunch and dinner, pre-6.30pm Friday and Saturday) offers two courses for £15.

Bettys
TEAHOUSE ££

(www.bettys.co.uk; St Helen's Sq; mains £6-14, afternoon tea £18.95; ⊙9am-9pm Sun-Fri, 8.30am-9pm Sat; ♿) Old-school afternoon tea, with white-aproned waiters, linen tablecloths and a teapot collection ranged along the walls. The house speciality is the Yorkshire Fat Rascal, a huge fruit scone smothered in melted butter, but the smoked haddock with poached egg and hollandaise sauce (seasonal) is our favourite lunch dish. No bookings – queue for a table at busy times.

El Piano
VEGAN ££

(📞01904-610676; www.el-piano.com; 15 Grape Lane; lunch £12, 2-course dinner £15; ⊙11am-10pm Mon-Sat, noon-9pm Sun; 🛜🚲♿) 🍴 With a menu that's 100% vegan, nut-free and gluten-free, this colourful, Hispanic-style spot is a vegetarian haven. Downstairs there's a lovely cafe, and upstairs, three themed rooms. The menu offers dishes such as felafel, onion bhaji, corn fritters and mushroom-and-basil salad, either in tapas-size portions or as mixed platters. There's also a takeaway counter.

★ Cochon Aveugle
FRENCH £££

(📞01904-640222; www.lecochonaveugle.uk; 37 Walmgate; 6-/9-course tasting menu £40/60; ⊙6-9pm Tue-Sat) 🍴 Black-pudding macaroon? Strawberry and elderflower sandwich? Blowtorched mackerel with melon gazpacho? Fussy eaters beware – this small restaurant with huge ambition serves an ever-changing tasting menu (no à la carte) of infinite imagination and invention. You never know what will come next, except that it will be delicious. Bookings essential.

🍺 Drinking & Nightlife

★ Blue Bell
PUB

(📞01904-654904; bluebellyork@gmail.com; 53 Fossgate; ⊙11am-11pm Mon-Thu, to midnight Fri & Sat, noon-10.30pm Sun) This is what a proper English pub looks like – a tiny, 200-year-old wood-panelled room with a smouldering fireplace, decor untouched since 1903, a pile of ancient board games in the corner, friendly and efficient bar staff, and Timothy Taylor and Black Sheep ales on tap. Bliss, with froth on top – if you can get in (it's often full).

Ye Olde Starre
PUB

(www.taylor-walker.co.uk; 40 Stonegate; ⊙11am-11pm Sun-Wed, to midnight Thu-Sat; 🛜🐕) Licenced since 1644, this is York's oldest pub – a warren of small rooms and a small beer garden, with a half-dozen real ales on tap. It was used as a morgue by the Roundheads (supporters of parliament) during the Civil War, but the atmosphere has improved considerably since then.

Pivní
CRAFT BEER

(www.pivni.co.uk; 6 Patrick Pool; ⊙noon-11.30pm Sun-Thu, 11am-11.30pm Fri & Sat; 🛜) A slick, modern pub set in an ancient half-timbered house, Pivní provides an atmospheric setting for sampling its range of more than 80 draught and bottled craft beers from all over the world.

Brigantes Bar
CRAFT BEER

(☑01904-675355; www.brigantesyork.co.uk; 114 Micklegate; ⊙noon-11pm) On a street that is notorious for its Saturday-night drunken revelry, Brigantes is a wood-panelled haven of peace and sophistication, with 10 hand-pulled ales (mostly from Yorkshire) on tap and a dining room that serves classic comfort food such as nachos, burgers and fish and chips.

King's Arms
PUB

(☑01904-659435; King's Staith; ⊙11am-11pm Mon-Sat, noon-10.30pm Sun) York's best-known pub enjoys a fabulous riverside location, with tables spilling out onto the quayside. It's the perfect spot on a summer evening, but be prepared to share it with a few hundred other people.

☆ Entertainment

York Theatre Royal
THEATRE

(☑01904-623568; www.yorktheatreroyal.co.uk; St Leonard's Pl) Well-regarded productions of theatre, opera and dance are staged here.

Grand Opera House
LIVE MUSIC, COMEDY

(☑0844 871 3024; www.facebook.com/GrandOperaHouseYork; Clifford St) Despite the name, there are no operas staged here; instead, there's a wide range of entertainment, from live bands and popular musicals to stand-up comics and pantomime.

City Screen Picturehouse
CINEMA

(☑0871 902 5726; www.picturehouses.co.uk; 13-17 Coney St; 🛜🐕) An appealing modern building in a converted printing works, screening both mainstream and art-house films. There's also a nice cafe-bar on the terrace overlooking the river.

🛍 Shopping

Coney St, Davygate and the adjoining streets are the hub of York's city-centre shopping scene, but the real treats are the secondhand bookshops, and antique, bric-a-brac and independent shops to be found along Gillygate, Colliergate, Fossgate and Micklegate.

Fossgate Books
BOOKS

(☑01904-641389; fossgatebooks@hotmail.co.uk; 36 Fossgate; ⊙10am-5.30pm Mon-Sat) A classic, old-school secondhand bookshop, with a maze of floor-to-ceiling shelves crammed with titles covering every subject under the sun, from crime fiction and popular paperbacks to arcane academic tomes and 1st editions.

Inkwell
MUSIC

(☑07846 610777; www.ink-well.co.uk; 10 Gillygate; ⊙10am-5.30pm Mon-Sat, 11am-4pm Sun) Laid out like an old schoolroom, complete with desks and blackboard, this place is a welcoming haven for anyone interested in vinyl records: as well as new and reissued vinyl, there are wooden crates filled with secondhand LPs, and you can even buy record players to play them on. There's also a good selection of secondhand books and comics.

Antiques Centre
ANTIQUES

(www.theantiquescentreyork.co.uk; 41 Stonegate; ⊙9am-5.30pm Mon-Sat, to 4pm Sun) A Georgian townhouse with a veritable maze of rooms and corridors, showcasing the wares of about 120 dealers selling everything from lapel pins and snuffboxes to oil paintings and longcase clocks. And the house is haunted as well…

ℹ Information

Post Office (22 Lendal; ⊙8.30am-5.30pm Mon-Fri, to 4pm Sat)

York Hospital (☑01904-631313; www.yorkhospitals.nhs.uk; Wiggington Rd) Has an emergency department; located a mile north of the centre.

York Tourist Office (☑01904-550099; www.visityork.org; 1 Museum St; ⊙9am-5pm Mon-Sat, 10am-4pm Sun) Visitor and transport info for all of Yorkshire, plus accommodation bookings, ticket sales and internet access.

❶ Getting There & Away

BUS

York does not have a bus station; intercity buses stop outside the train station, while local and regional buses stop here and also on **Rougier St**, about 200m northeast of the train station.

For timetable information, call **Traveline York-shire** (✆ 0871 200 2233; www.yorkshiretravel. net) or check the computerised 24-hour information points at the train station and Rougier St. There's a bus information point in the train station's Travel Centre.

Birmingham £29, 3½ hours, one daily
Edinburgh £40, 6¼ hours, one daily
London from £25, 5½ hours, three daily
Newcastle £15.40, 2¼ hours, two daily

CAR

A car is more hindrance than help in the city centre, so use one of the Park & Ride car parks at the edge of the city. If you want to explore the surrounding area, rental options include **Europcar** (✆ 0844 846 0872; www.europcar. co.uk; Queen St; ⊙8am-6pm Mon-Fri, to 3pm Sat), located next to the long-stay car park at the train station.

TRAIN

York is a major railway hub, with frequent direct services to many British cities.

Birmingham £45, 2¼ hours, two per hour
Cambridge (change at Peterborough) £71, 2¾ hours, hourly
Edinburgh £60, 2½ hours, every 30 minutes
Leeds £13.90, 25 minutes, every 15 minutes
London Kings Cross £80, two hours, every 30 minutes
Manchester £25, 1½ hours, every 15 minutes
Newcastle £25, one hour, every 30 minutes
Scarborough £14, 50 minutes, hourly

❶ Getting Around

Central York is easy to get around on foot – you're never more than 20 minutes' walk from any of the major sights.

BICYCLE

The tourist office has a useful free map showing York's cycle routes, or visit iTravel-York (www. itravelyork.info/cycling). Castle Howard (15 miles northeast of York via Haxby and Strensall) is an interesting destination, and there's also a section of the **Trans-Pennine Trail cycle path** (www.transpenninetrail.org.uk) from Bishopthorpe in York to Selby (15 miles) along the old railway line.

You can rent bikes from **Cycle Heaven** (✆ 01904-622701; www.cycle-heaven.co.uk; York Railway Station, Station Rd; ⊙8.30am-

5.30pm Mon-Fri, 9am-5pm Sat year-round, 11am-4pm Sun May-Aug) at the train station for £20 per day.

BUS

Local bus services are operated by First York (www.firstgroup.com/york). Single fares range from £1 to £3, and a day pass valid for all local buses is £4 (available on the bus or at Park & Ride car parks).

TAXI

Station Taxis (✆ 01904-623332; www.yorkstationtaxis.co.uk; Train Station, Station Rd) has a kiosk outside the train station.

Castle Howard

Stately homes may be two a penny in England, but you'll have to try pretty damn hard to find one as breathtaking as Castle Howard (www.castlehoward.co.uk; adult/child house & grounds £17.50/9, grounds only £9.95/7; ⊙house 10.30am-4pm, last admission 4pm, grounds 10am-5pm; 🅿), a work of theatrical grandeur and audacity set in the rolling Howardian Hills. This is one of the world's most beautiful buildings, instantly recognisable from its starring role in the 1980s TV series *Brideshead Revisited* and in the 2008 film of the same name (both based on Evelyn Waugh's 1945 novel).

When the Earl of Carlisle hired his pal Sir John Vanbrugh to design his new home in 1699, he was hiring a man who had no formal training and was best known as a playwright. Luckily, Vanbrugh hired Nicholas Hawksmoor, who had worked as Christopher Wren's clerk of works – not only would Hawksmoor have a big part to play in the house's design, but he and Vanbrugh would later work wonders with Blenheim Palace. Today the house is still home to the Hon Simon Howard and his family and he can often be seen around the place.

If you can, try to visit on a weekday when it's easier to find the space to appreciate this hedonistic marriage of art, architecture, landscaping and natural beauty. As you wander about the peacock-haunted grounds, views open up over Vanbrugh's playful Temple of the Four Winds, Hawksmoor's stately mausoleum and the distant hills, but the great baroque house with its magnificent central cupola is an irresistible visual magnet. Inside, the house is full of treasures – the breathtaking Great Hall with its soaring Corinthian pilasters, Pre-Raphaelite stained glass in the chapel, and corridors lined with classical antiquities.

The entrance courtyard has a good cafe, a gift shop and a farm shop filled with foodie delights from local producers.

Castle Howard is 15 miles northeast of York, off the A64. There are several organised tours from York; check with the tourist office for up-to-date schedules. Stephenson's of Easingwold (www.stephensonsofeasingwold.co.uk) bus 181 links York with Castle Howard (£10 return, 40 minutes, four times daily Monday to Saturday year-round, three on Sunday May to September).

Harrogate

POP 73,580

The quintessential Victorian spa town, prim and pretty Harrogate has long been associated with a certain kind of old-fashioned Englishness – the kind that seems the preserve of retired army majors and formidable dowagers who take the *Daily Telegraph* and always vote Tory. They come to Harrogate to enjoy the flower shows and gardens that fill the town with magnificent displays of colour, especially in spring and autumn. It is fitting that the town's most famous visitor was Agatha Christie, who fled here incognito in 1926 to escape her broken marriage.

And yet, this picture of Victoriana redux is not quite complete. While it's undoubtedly true that Harrogate remains a firm favourite of visitors in their golden years, the town has plenty of smart hotels and trendy eateries catering to the boom in Harrogate's newest trade – conferences. All those dynamic young sales-and-marketing guns have to eat and sleep somewhere.

◎ Sights & Activities

Royal Pump Room Museum   MUSEUM
(www.harrogate.gov.uk; Crown Pl; adult/child £4/2.35; ⊙ 10.30am-5pm Mon-Sat, 2-5pm Sun Apr-Oct, to 4pm Nov-Mar) You can learn all about Harrogate's history as a spa town in the ornate Royal Pump Room, built in 1842 over the most famous of the town's sulphurous springs. It gives an insight into how the phenomenon of visiting spas to 'take the waters' shaped the town and records the illustrious visitors it attracted. At the end, you get the chance to sample the spa water, if you dare.

The ritual of visiting spa towns as a health cure became fashionable in the 19th century and peaked during the Edwardian era in the

WORTH A TRIP

KIRKHAM PRIORY & STONE TROUGH INN

The picturesque ruins of **Kirkham Priory** (EH; www.english-heritage.org.uk; adult/child £4.50/2.70; ⊙ 10am-6pm Wed-Sun Apr-Sep, daily Aug, 10am-5pm Wed-Sun Oct; P) rise gracefully above the banks of the River Derwent, sporting medieval floor tiles and an impressive 13th-century gatehouse encrusted with heraldic symbols.

The traditional country inn **Stone Trough Inn** (☑ 01653-618713; Kirkham; mains £11-18; ⊙ food served noon-9pm Mon-Sat, to 8pm Sun; P 🛜 👪 🐾) is full of cosy nooks, with exposed stone walls, timber beams and open fires, and serves gourmet-style pub classics (eg fish and chips, steak pie with peas and gravy). An added attraction is the outdoor terrace with great views over the Derwent valley and the ruins of Kirkham Priory. Three-course Sunday lunch is £17.

years before WWI. Charles Dickens visited Harrogate in 1858 and described it as 'the queerest place, with the strangest people in it, leading the oddest lives of dancing, newspaper-reading and dining' – sounds quite pleasant, really.

Montpellier Quarter   AREA
(www.montpellierharrogate.com) The most attractive part of town is the Montpellier Quarter, overlooking Prospect Gardens between Crescent Rd and Montpellier Hill. It's an area of pedestrianised streets lined with restored 19th-century buildings that are now home to art galleries, antique shops, fashion boutiques, cafes and restaurants – an upmarket annex to the main shopping area around Oxford and Cambridge Sts.

Turkish Baths   SPA
(☑ 01423-556746; www.turkishbathsharrogate.co.uk; Parliament St; £15.50-29.50, guided tours per person £3.75; ⊙ guided tours 9-10am Wed) Plunge into Harrogate's past at the town's fabulously tiled Turkish Baths. This mock-Moorish facility is gloriously Victorian and offers a range of watery delights: hot rooms, steam rooms, plunge pools and so on. A visit is likely to last about 1½ hours. There's a complicated schedule of opening hours that are by turns single sex or mixed, so call or check online

for details. If you prefer to remain dry, there are also guided tours of the building.

🎇 Festivals & Events

Spring Flower Show HORTICULTURE
(www.flowershow.org.uk; £16-17.50) The year's main event, held in late April. A colourful three-day extravaganza of blooms and blossoms, flower competitions, gardening demonstrations, market stalls, crafts and gardening shops.

Great Yorkshire Show AGRICULTURE
(www.greatyorkshireshow.co.uk; adult/child £27/13) Staged over three days in mid-July by the Yorkshire Agricultural Society. Expect all manner of primped and prettified farm animals competing for prizes, and entertainment ranging from showjumping and falconry to cookery demonstrations and hot-air-balloon rides.

🛏 Sleeping

★ Bijou B&B **££**
(☑ 01423-567974; www.thebijou.co.uk; 17 Ripon Rd; s/d from £59/94; P 🛜) Bijou by name and bijou by nature, this jewel of a Victorian villa sits firmly at the boutique end of the B&B spectrum – you can tell that a lot of thought and care have gone into its design. The husband-and-wife team who own the place make fantastic hosts, warm and helpful but unobtrusive.

Hotel du Vin BOUTIQUE HOTEL **££**
(☑ 01423-856800; www.hotelduvin.com/locations/harrogate; Prospect Pl; r/ste from £95/255; P 🛜) An extremely stylish boutique hotel – the loft suites with exposed oak beams, hardwood

> ### HARLOW CARR BOTANICAL GARDENS
>
> A huge green thumbs-up to Harrogate's gardeners: the town has some of the most beautiful public gardens in England. Flower fanatics should make for the **Harlow Carr Botanical Gardens** (www.rhs.org.uk/gardens/harlow-carr; Crag Lane, Beckwithshaw; adult/child £11/5.50; ⊙ 9.30am-6pm Mar-Oct, to 4pm Nov-Feb), the northern showpiece of the Royal Horticultural Society, which are 1.5 miles southwest of town; take the B6162 Otley Rd, or walk through the Pine Woods southwest of the Valley Gardens. Last admission is one hour before closing time.

floors and designer bathrooms are among the nicest rooms in town, but even the standard bedrooms are spacious and very comfortable (though they can be noisy), each with a huge bed draped in soft Egyptian cotton.

Acorn Lodge B&B **££**
(☑ 01423-525630; www.acornlodgeharrogate.co.uk; 1 Studley Rd; s/d from £49/89; P 🛜) Attention to detail makes the difference between an average and an excellent B&B, and the details at Acorn Lodge are spot on: stylish decor, crisp cotton sheets, powerful showers and perfect poached eggs for breakfast. The location is good too, just 10 minutes' walk from the town centre.

Arden House B&B **££**
(☑ 01423-509224; www.ardenhousehotel.co.uk; 69-71 Franklin Rd; s/d from £58/80; P 🛜) This grand old Edwardian house has been given a modern makeover with stylish contemporary furniture, Egyptian-cotton bed linen and posh toiletries, but still retains some lovely period details, including tiled cast-iron fireplaces. Attentive service, good breakfasts and a central location are the icing on the cake.

★ West Park BOUTIQUE HOTEL **£££**
(☑ 01423-524471; www.thewestparkhotel.com; 19 West Park; r/ste from £140/200; 🛜) Overlooking the grassy expanse of the Stray just five minutes' walk south of the town centre, this classy hotel combines tastefully designed modern bedrooms with a popular restaurant and cocktail bar. Treat yourself to one of the two penthouse suites and you can watch TV while soaking in the bath-tub, or sip champagne on the private roof terrace.

🍴 Eating

Fat Badger PUB FOOD **££**
(☑ 01423-505681; www.thefatbadgerharrogate.com; Cold Bath Rd; mains £10-16; ⊙ food served noon-9.30pm Mon-Thu, to 10pm Fri & Sat, to 9pm Sun; 🛜🚼) This is a Harrogate (ie posh) interpretation of a typical English pub, all polished wood, gilt-framed mirrors, wing-back armchairs and leather-bench booths, with the occasional stuffed animal for decoration. It's a convivial spot to enjoy a pub lunch of mussels with bacon and cider, or steak and chips, followed by a pint of Yorkshire ale at one of the outdoor tables.

Bettys TEAROOM **££**
(☑ 01423-814070; www.bettys.co.uk; 1 Parliament St; mains £6-14, afternoon tea £18.95; ⊙ 9am-9pm; 🚼) A classic tearoom in a classic location

EAT & DRINK LIKE A LOCAL

Yorkshire pudding The classic local dish, these puffy batter puddings are traditionally served with roast beef, but Yorkshire tearooms often serve them as a dish in themselves, with gravy. Try them at Ye Olde Naked Man (p510) in Settle.

Theakston's ale Theakston's was turning out best bitter long before the term 'craft beer' had been thought of. Try it at pubs all over Britain, or at Theakston's Brewery (p495) in Masham.

Wensleydale cheese Famous as the favourite snack of animated characters Wallace and Gromit, this crumbly white cheese is made in the heart of the Yorkshire Dales. Try it at the source, at Wensleydale Creamery (p511) in Hawes.

Yorkshire rhubarb Traditionally grown in the 'rhubarb triangle' near Wakefield, Yorkshire forced rhubarb (early-season rhubarb grown in darkness) has achieved Protected Designation of Origin status. Try the Michelin-starred rhubarb trifle at the Pipe and Glass (p528) near Beverley.

Curd tart A very old Yorkshire dish, a bit like cheesecake, traditionally baked for the Whitsun holiday. Try it at Bettys (p492) in Harrogate.

Parkin A rich and sticky cake made with oatmeal and flavoured with ginger and treacle. Try it at Thomas of Helmsley (p501).

with views across the park, Bettys is a local institution. It was established in 1919 by a Swiss immigrant confectioner who took the wrong train, ended up in Yorkshire and decided to stay. There are exquisite home-baked breads, scones and cakes, quality tea and coffee, and a gallery hung with art nouveau marquetry.

Le Jardin BISTRO ££
(☎01423-507323; www.lejardin-harrogate.com; 7 Montpellier Pde; mains £9-15; ⊙11.30am-2.30pm & 6-11.30pm Mon-Sat, noon-3pm Sun; 🚌) This cool little bistro has a snug atmosphere, especially in the evening when candlelight adds a romantic glow; the food is basic bistro fare – grilled chicken, gammon steak, sausage and mash. During the day, locals throng to the tables to enjoy great salads, sandwiches and homemade ice cream. The early-bird menu offers two/three courses for £9.95/12.95 from 6pm to 7pm.

★**Norse** SCANDINAVIAN £££
(☎01423-202363; www.norserestaurant.co.uk; 22 Oxford St; 4-/8-course tasting menu £40/60; ⊙6-9pm Tue-Sat) Norse injects some fun into fine dining, with a choice of tasting menus that blends the best of British produce with Scandinavian inspiration to produce unusual flavour combinations such as beetroot, cocoa and horseradish; pork, oyster and peas; and yoghurt, gooseberry and orange blossom. The drinks list includes carefuly chosen craft beers and cocktails plus wine. Bookings essential.

Drinking & Nightlife

★**Bean & Bud** COFFEE
(☎01423-508200; www.beanandbud.co.uk; 14 Commercial St; ⊙8am-5pm Mon-Sat; 🛜) Small and unpretentious, this place has been around since 2010 and serves what might be the finest cup of coffee in town, if not Yorkshire. There's a choice of two freshly ground blends every day, plus a selection of top-quality white, green, oolong and black teas.

Harrogate Tap CRAFT BEER
(☎01423-501644; www.harrogatetap.co.uk; Station Pde; ⊙11am-11pm Sun-Thu, 11am-midnight Fri, 10am-midnight Sat; 🛜) Set in a restored red-brick railway-station building dating from 1862, the Tap does a grand job of conjuring up the ambience of a bustling Victorian pub, but with the added attractions of a dozen hand-pulled cask ales, another dozen keg taps, and a menu of around 130 bottled craft beers from all over the world.

North Bar CRAFT BEER
(☎01423-520772; www.northbar.com/harrogate; Cheltenham Pde; ⊙8am-11pm Mon-Thu, 8am-midnight Fri, 9am-midnight Sat, 10am-11pm Sun; 🛜) Spread over three floors, this new branch of Leeds' famous North Bar not only brings a bit of big-city chic to Harrogate's rather staid pub scene, but also a refreshingly international beer menu and all-day service that kick-starts the morning with quality coffee and croissants.

☆ Entertainment

Royal Hall LIVE MUSIC
(☑ 01423-500500; www.royalhall.co.uk; Ripon Rd)
A gorgeous Edwardian theatre that is now
part of the conference-and-events venue
Harrogate International Centre. The musical program covers orchestral and choral
performances, piano recitals, jazz and more.

Harrogate Theatre THEATRE
(☑ 01423-502116; www.harrogatetheatre.co.uk;
Oxford St) A historic Victorian theatre that
dates from 1900, staging variety, comedy,
musicals and dancing.

ⓘ Information

Harrogate Tourist Office (☑ 01423-537300;
www.visitharrogate.co.uk; Crescent Rd; ☉ 9am-
5.30pm Mon-Sat, 10am-1pm Sun Apr-Oct,
9.30am-5pm Mon-Sat Nov-Mar)
Post Office (11 Cambridge Rd; ☉ 9.30am-
5.30pm Mon-Sat)

ⓘ Getting There & Away

Bus Harrogate & District (www.harrogatebus.
co.uk) bus 36 connects Harrogate with Leeds
(£6.50, 45 minutes, every 10 to 20 minutes)
and Ripon (£6.20, 30 minutes, every 15 minutes).

Train There are trains to Harrogate from Leeds
(£8.20, 35 minutes, every 30 minutes) and
York (£8.50, 40 minutes, hourly).

Scarborough

POP 61,750

Scarborough retains all the trappings of the
classic seaside resort, but is in the process of
reinventing itself as a centre for the creative
arts and digital industries. The Victorian spa
has been redeveloped as a conference and
entertainment centre, a former museum has
been converted into studio space for artists, a vast new water park opened in 2016,
and there's free, open-access wi-fi along the
promenade beside the harbour – an area
being promoted as the town's bar, cafe and
restaurant quarter.

As well as the usual seaside attractions,
Scarborough offers excellent coastal walking, a geology museum, one of Yorkshire's
most impressively sited castles, and a renowned theatre that is the home base for
popular playwright Alan Ayckbourn, whose
plays always premiere here.

◉ Sights

★ Scarborough Castle CASTLE
(EH; www.english-heritage.org.uk; Castle Rd; adult/
child £6.10/3.70; ☉ 10am-6pm Apr-Sep, to 5pm Oct,
to 4pm Sat & Sun Nov-Mar) The massive medieval keep of Scarborough Castle occupies a
commanding position atop its headland. Legend has it that Richard I loved the views from
here so much that his ghost just keeps coming back. Take a walk out to the edge of the
cliffs, where you can see the 2000-year-old
remains of a **Roman signal station**; clearly
the Romans appreciated this viewpoint too.

★ Rotunda Museum MUSEUM
(www.rotundamuseum.co.uk; Vernon Rd; adult/
child £3/free; ☉ 10am-5pm Tue-Sun; ♿) The Rotunda Museum is dedicated to the coastal
geology of northeast Yorkshire, which has
yielded many of Britain's most important
dinosaur fossils. The strata in the local cliffs
were also important in deciphering England's geological history. Founded by William Smith, 'the father of English geology',
who lived in Scarborough in the 1820s, the
museum has original Victorian exhibits as
well as a hands-on gallery for kids.

Sea Life Sanctuary AQUARIUM
(www.sealife.co.uk; Scalby Mills; adult/child 2yr
& under £18/free; ☉ 10am-6pm, last admission
5pm; Ⓟ ♿) At this family-oriented attraction
(tickets are much cheaper if you buy online)
you can see coral reefs, turtles, octopuses,
seahorses, otters and many other fascinating creatures, though the biggest draw is
the **Seal Pool** (feeding times 11.30am and
2.30pm). The centre is at the far north end
of North Beach; the miniature North Bay
Railway (p498) runs the three-quarter-mile
route. A lot of the attractions are outdoors,
so it's not an ideal rainy-day refuge.

Peasholm Park PARK
(www.peasholmpark.com; Columbus Ravine;
☉ 24hr) FREE Set back from North Bay, Scarborough's beautiful Edwardian pleasure gardens are famous for their summer sessions of
Naval Warfare (adult/child £4.10/2.30; ☉ 3pm
Mon, Thu & Sat Jul & Aug), when large model
ships reenact famous naval battles on the
boating lake (check the website for dates).

St Mary's Church CHURCH
(Castle Rd; ☉ 10am-4pm Mon-Fri, 1-4pm Sun May-
Sep) FREE This church dates from the 12th to
the 15th centuries (boards inside explain its
history), but it is most notable for the little

BREWERIES IN MASHAM VILLAGE

Masham is 9 miles northwest of Ripon on the AG108 to Leyburn. Bus 159 from Richmond to Ripon stops at Masham.

Theakston's Brewery (☑01765-680000; www.theakstons.co.uk; The Brewery, Masham; tour adult/child £7.50/4.75; ☉10.30am-5.30pm Jul & Aug, to 4.30pm Sep-Jun) Founded in 1827, and still run by the Theakston family (despite a spell in the ownership of global brewer Scottish & Newcastle), Theakston's has long been one of Yorkshire's most famous breweries. Old Peculier, its best-known ale, takes its name from the Peculier of Masham, a parish court established in medieval times to deal with offences such as drunkenness and brawling. There's a visitor centre which doubles as a bar, and four tours a day (six in August) of the brewery works.

Black Sheep Brewery (☑01765-680101; www.blacksheepbrewery.com; Wellgarth, Masham; tours adult/child £8.50/4.95; ☉10am-5pm Sun-Wed, to 11pm Thu-Sat; [P][♿]) Founded in 1992 by the 'black sheep' of the Theakston family, who refused to work for the multinational company that took over Yorkshire's highly regarded Theakston's brewery in 1987, this place has grown to be just as famous as its near neighbour. There are four tours a day, plus an excellent restaurant where you can wash down your lunch with a pint of the brewery's own ale.

cemetery across the lane that contains the **grave of Anne Brontë**, sister of Charlotte and author of *The Tenant of Wildfell Hall*.

🏃 Activities

There are some decent waves on England's northeast coast, supporting a growing surf scene. A top spot is **Cayton Bay**, 4 miles south of town, where you'll find **Scarborough Surf School** (☑01723-585585; www.scarboroughsurfschool.co.uk; Cayton Bay). The best time for waves is September to May.

Back in town, you can get information and advice from the **Secretspot Surf Shop** (☑01723-500467; www.secretspot.co.uk; 4 Pavilion Tce; ☉9am-5pm Mon-Fri) near the train station.

🛏 Sleeping

YHA Scarborough　　　　　　HOSTEL £
(☑01723-361176; www.yha.org.uk; Burniston Rd; dm/q from £18/70; [P][♿]) An idyllic hostel set in a converted 17th-century water mill, 2 miles north of town along the A166 to Whitby. Take bus 3 or 3A from York Place to the Ivanhoe pub; it's a five-minute walk from there.

★Waves　　　　　　　　　　B&B ££
(☑01723-373658; www.scarboroughwaves.co.uk; 39 Esplanade Rd, South Cliff; s/d from £54/79; [P][🛜])
🍃 Crisp cotton sheets and powerful showers make for comfortable accommodation at this retro-styled B&B, but it's the second B that's the real star – the breakfasts range from vegan-friendly fruit salads and smoothies to fry-ups, kippers and kedgeree. A unique selling point is the jukebox in the lounge, loaded

with 1960s and '70s hits. It's 0.75 miles south of the centre, off the A165 (Ramshill Rd).

★Windmill　　　　　　　　　B&B ££
(☑01723-372735; www.scarborough-windmill.co.uk; Mill St; d from £85; [P][🛜]) Quirky doesn't begin to describe this place, a beautifully converted 18th-century windmill in the middle of town. There are two self-catering cottages and three four-poster doubles around a cobbled courtyard, but try to secure the balcony suite (from £110 a night) in the upper floors of the windmill itself, with great views from the wraparound balcony.

Helaina　　　　　　　　　　B&B ££
(☑01723-375191; www.hotelhelaina.co.uk; 14 Blenheim Tce; r from £90; ☉daily Apr-Nov, Fri & Sat only Feb & Mar; [🛜]) Location, location, location – you'd be hard-pressed to find a place with a better sea view than this elegant guesthouse perched on the clifftop overlooking North Beach. And the view inside is pretty good too, with sharply styled contemporary furniture and cool colours. The cheaper rooms are on the small side; it's worth paying extra for a sea-view room (from £100).

Interludes　　　　　　　　　B&B ££
(☑01723-360513; www.interludeshotel.co.uk; 32 Princess St; s/d £45/70; [🛜]) Established in 1991 by owners with a flair for the theatrical, this lovely, gay-friendly Georgian guesthouse is plastered with old theatre posters, prints and other thespian mementoes. The individually decorated rooms feature flights of fancy that will put a smile on your face. No children.

Scarborough

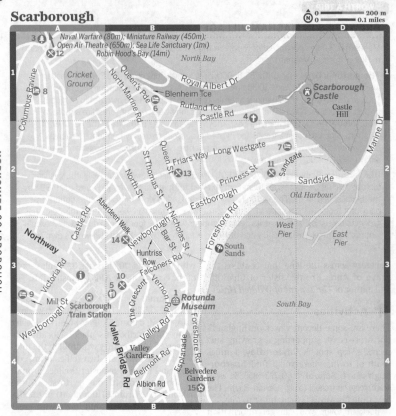

Scarborough

◎ Top Sights
1 Rotunda Museum	B3
2 Scarborough Castle	D1

◎ Sights
3 Peasholm Park	A1
4 St Mary's Church	C1

⊕ Activities, Courses & Tours
5 Secretspot Surf Shop	B3

🛏 Sleeping
6 Helaina	B1
7 Interludes	C2
8 North Bay Guest House	A1
9 Windmill	A3

✖ Eating
10 Cafe Fish	B3
11 Golden Grid	C2
12 Jeremy's	A1
13 Lanterna	B2
14 Roasters	B3

✪ Entertainment
15 Scarborough Spa	B4

North Bay Guest House　　B&B **££**
(☑ 01723-374406; therussells1@btinternet.com; 137 Columbus Ravine; s/d from £34/79; 🛜 ♿ 🐾) Cosy and colourful bedrooms, big breakfasts and wonderfully welcoming owners create exceptional value at this excellent B&B, within easy walking distance of Peasholm Park, North Bay Railway and the beach at North Bay.

✖ Eating

Roasters　　CAFE **£**
(www.roasterscoffee.co.uk; 8 Aberdeen Walk; mains £4-7; ☺ 9am-5pm) A funky coffee shop with chunky pine tables, bentwood chairs and an excellent range of freshly ground coffees. There's a juice and smoothie bar too, and the

lunch menu includes ciabatta sandwiches, salads and jacket potatoes.

⭐**Cafe Fish** SEAFOOD ££
(☎01723-500301; www.cafefish.co.uk; 19 York Pl; mains £11-26; ⊘5.30-10pm) 🍴 This is the place to come for top-quality local seafood without the fuss: freshly landed Scarborough lobster and crab, Scottish oysters, mussels and scallops, and North Sea cod, haddock and hake all simply prepared and reasonably priced. For those who don't want fish, there's a decent choice of meat and vegetarian dishes too.

⭐**Jeremy's** BRITISH, FRENCH ££
(☎01723-363871; www.jeremys.co; 33 Victoria Park Ave; mains £16-25, 3-course lunch Sun £25; ⊘6-9.30pm Thu-Sat, noon-3pm Sun, plus 6-9.30pm Tue & Wed Jul & Aug; 🚼) 🍴 A fantastic neighbourhood bistro run by a chef who won his Michelin credentials with Marco Pierre White, this off-the-beaten-track gem sports an art deco ambience and a menu that blends the best of Yorkshire and British produce with French inventiveness and flair. Best to book at weekends.

Golden Grid FISH & CHIPS ££
(☎01723-360922; www.goldengrid.co.uk; 4 Sandside; mains £9-20; ⊘11.30am-11pm; 🚼) The Golden Grid is a sit-down fish restaurant that has been serving the best cod in Scarborough since 1883. Its starched white tablecloths and starched white aprons are staunchly traditional, as is the menu: as well as cod and chips, oysters, and freshly landed crab and lobster, there's sausage and mash, roast beef and Yorkshire pudding, and steak and chips.

⭐**Lanterna** ITALIAN £££
(☎01723-363616; www.lanterna-ristorante.co.uk; 33 Queen St; mains £15-24; ⊘7-9.30pm Tue-Sat) 🍴 A snug, old-fashioned Italian trattoria that specialises in fresh local seafood (including lobster, from £32) and classic dishes from the old country such as *stufato de ceci* (chickpea stew with oxtail) and white-truffle dishes in season (October to December, £30 to £45). As well as sourcing Yorkshire produce, the chef imports delicacies direct from Italy.

☆ **Entertainment**

Open Air Theatre CONCERT VENUE
(☎01723-818111; www.scarboroughopenairtheatre. com; Burniston Rd) Europe's largest open-air theatre, with its stage on an island in a lake, stages big-name concerts throughout the summer season.

Scarborough Spa MUSIC, DANCE
(☎01723-821888; www.scarboroughspa.co.uk; Foreshore Rd; 🛜🚼) The revitalised spa complex stages a varied program of entertainment, especially in the summer months: orchestral performances, variety shows, popular musicals and old-fashioned afternoon-tea dances.

ℹ️ **Information**

There's free wi-fi internet access along the harbourfront from West Pier to East Pier.

There's a small **information point** (☎01723-383636; www.discoveryorkshirecoast.com; Stephen Joseph Theatre, Westborough; ⊘9am-5pm) in the lobby of the theatre; a second kiosk operates in summer at the Open-Air Theatre box office, opposite the entrance to Peasholm Park.

ℹ️ **Getting There & Away**

BUS

Bus 128 (www.eyms.co.uk) travels along the A170 from Helmsley to Scarborough via Pickering, while Arriva (www.arrivabus.co.uk) buses 93 and X93 come from Middlesborough and Whitby via Robin Hood's Bay. Coastliner (www. coastliner.co.uk) bus 843 runs to Scarborough from Leeds and York.

Helmsley £7.60, 1¾ hours, hourly Monday to Saturday, four times on Sunday

Leeds £12.30, 2¾ hours, hourly

Whitby £5.70, one hour, every 30 minutes

York £11.30, 1¾ hours, hourly

TRAIN

Hull £12, 1½ hours, hourly

Leeds £20, 1¼ hours, hourly

York £14, 50 minutes, hourly

ℹ️ **Getting Around**

Tiny Victorian-era funicular railways rattle up and down Scarborough's steep cliffs between town and beach. The **Central Tramway** (www. centraltramway.co.uk; Marine Pde; per person 90p; ⊘9.30am-5.45pm Feb-Jun, Sep & Oct, to 9.30pm Jul & Aug) connects the Grand Hotel with the promenade, while the **Spa Cliff Lift** (www.scarboroughspa.co.uk/cliff_lift; Esplanade; per person £1; ⊘at least 10am-5pm, hours vary, check website) runs between Scarborough Spa and the Esplanade.

Open-top bus 109 shuttles back and forth along the seafront between Scarborough Spa and the Sands complex on North Bay (£2, every 20 minutes 9.30am to 3pm). The service runs daily from Easter to September, weekends only in October. An all-day, hop on-hop off ticket costs £3.

WORTH A TRIP

FOUNTAINS ABBEY & STUDLEY ROYAL

Fountains Abbey & Studley Royal (NT; www.fountainsabbey.org.uk; adult/child £13/6.50; ⊙10am-6pm Apr-Sep, to 5pm Sat-Thu Oct-Mar; ℗) The alluring and strangely obsessive water gardens of the Studley Royal estate were built in the 18th century to enhance the picturesque ruins of 12th-century Fountains Abbey. Together, they present a breathtaking picture of pastoral elegance and tranquillity that have made them a Unesco World Heritage site and the most visited of all the National Trust's pay-to-enter properties.

After falling out with the Benedictines of York in 1132, a band of rebel monks came here to establish their own monastery. Struggling to make it alone, they were formally adopted by the Cistercians in 1135. By the middle of the 13th century, the new abbey had become the most successful Cistercian venture in the country. After the Dissolution, when Henry III confiscated church property, the abbey's estate was sold into private hands, and between 1598 and 1611 **Fountains Hall** was built using stone from the abbey ruins. The hall and ruins were united with the Studley Royal estate in 1768.

Studley Royal was owned by John Aislabie, once Chancellor of the Exchequer, who dedicated his life to creating the park after a financial scandal saw him expelled from parliament. The main house of Studley Royal burnt down in 1946, but the superb landscaping, with its serene artificial lakes, survives almost unchanged from the 18th century.

The remains of the abbey are impressively grandiose, gathered around the sunny Romanesque **cloister**, with a huge vaulted **cellarium** leading off the west end of the church. Here, the abbey's 200 lay brothers lived, and food and wool from the abbey's farms were stored. At the east end is the soaring **Chapel of Nine Altars** and on the outside of its northeast window is a Green Man carving (a pre-Christian fertility symbol).

A choice of scenic walking trails leads for a mile from the abbey ruins to the famous water gardens, designed to enhance the romantic views of the ruined abbey. Don't miss **St Mary's Church** (⊙noon-4pm Apr-Sep) above the gardens.

Fountains Abbey is 4 miles west of Ripon off the B6265. Bus 139 travels from Ripon to Fountains Abbey visitor centre year-round (£2.60 return, 15 minutes, four times daily Monday to Saturday, seven on Sundays in summer).

The miniature **North Bay Railway** (www. nbr.org.uk; return adult/child £3.50/2.70; ⊙10.30am-3pm daily Apr-Sep, Sat & Sun year-round) also runs to North Beach.

For a taxi, call **Station Taxis** (✆01723-366366; www.taxisinscarborough.co.uk); £5 should get you to most places in town.

NORTH YORK MOORS NATIONAL PARK

Inland from the north Yorkshire coast, the wild and windswept North York Moors rise in desolate splendour. Three-quarters of all the world's heather moorland is found in Britain, and this is the largest expanse in England. Ridge-top roads climb up from lush green valleys to the bleak open moors, where weather-beaten stone crosses mark the lines of ancient roadways. In summer, heather blooms in billowing drifts of purple haze.

This is classic walking country. The moors are criss-crossed with footpaths old and new, and dotted with pretty, flower-bedecked villages. The national park is also home to one of England's most picturesque steam railways.

The park produces the useful *Out & About* visitor guide, available from tourist offices and hotels. See also www.northyorkmoors.org.uk.

ℹ Information

There are two national park visitor centres, providing information on walking, cycling, wildlife and public transport.

Moors National Park Centre (✆01439-772737; www.northyorkmoors.org.uk; Lodge Lane, Danby; ⊙10am-5pm Apr-Oct, 10.30am-4pm Nov-Mar, Sat & Sun only Jan & Feb; ♿)
Sutton Bank National Park Centre (✆01845-597426; www.northyorkmoors.org.uk; Sutton Bank, by Thirsk; ⊙10am-5pm Apr-Oct, 10.30am-4pm Nov-Mar, Sat & Sun only Jan & Feb; ☎)

ℹ Getting Around

On Sundays and bank holiday Mondays from late May to September, a number of minibus services aimed at hikers shuttle around various locations within the national park; all are detailed on the Moorsbus (www.moorsbus.org) website.

For example, the **Moors Explorer** (☑ 01482-592929; www.eyms.co.uk) service runs from Hull to the Moors National Park Centre in Danby, via Beverley, Pickering, Hutton-le-Hole and the Lion Inn at Blakey, with a shuttle between Danby and Pickering. An all-day hop-on, hop-off ticket costs £12.50.

The North Yorkshire Moors Railway (www.nymr.co.uk), running between Pickering and Whitby, is an excellent way of exploring the central moors in summer. If you're planning to drive on the minor roads over the moors, beware of wandering sheep and lambs – hundreds are killed by careless drivers every year.

Helmsley & Around

POP 1515

Helmsley is a classic North Yorkshire market town, a handsome huddle of old stone houses, historic coaching inns and – inevitably – a cobbled market square (market day is Friday), all basking under the watchful gaze of a sturdy Norman castle. Nearby are the romantic ruins of Rievaulx Abbey, several excellent restaurants and a fistful of country walks.

◉ Sights

Helmsley Castle   CASTLE
(EH; www.english-heritage.org.uk; Castlegate; adult/child £6.40/3.80; ☺10am-6pm Apr-Sep, to 5pm Oct, to 4pm Sat & Sun Nov-Mar; P) The impressive ruins of 12th-century Helmsley Castle are defended by a striking series of deep ditches and banks, to which later rulers added the thick stone walls and defensive towers. Only one tooth-shaped tower survives today, following the dismantling of the fortress by Sir Thomas Fairfax after the Civil War. The castle's tumultuous history is well explained in the visitor centre.

Helmsley Walled Garden   GARDENS
(www.helmsleywalledgarden.org.uk; adult/child £7.50/free; ☺10am-5pm Apr-Oct) Helmsley Walled Garden would be just another plant-and-produce centre were it not for its dramatic setting next to Helmsley Castle and its fabulous selection of flowers, fruits and vegetables (some of them rare), not to mention the herbs, which include 40 varieties of mint. If you're into horticulture with a historical twist, this is Eden.

Duncombe Park Gardens   GARDENS
(www.duncombepark.com; adult/child £5/3; ☺10.30am-5pm Sun-Fri Apr-Aug; P🐾) South of Helmsley lies the superb ornamental landscape of Duncombe Park estate, laid out in 1718 for Thomas Duncombe (whose son would later build Rievaulx Terrace) with the stately Georgian mansion of Duncombe Park House at its heart. From the house (not open to the public) and formal gardens, wide grassy walkways and terraces lead through woodland to mock-classical temples, while longer walking trails are set out in the landscaped parkland, now protected as a nature reserve.

★ **Rievaulx Abbey**   RUINS
(www.english-heritage.org.uk; adult/child £8/4.80; ☺10am-6pm Apr-Sep, to 5pm Oct, to 4pm Sat & Sun Nov-Mar; P) In the secluded valley of the River Rye about 3 miles west of Helmsley, amid fields and woods loud with birdsong, stand the magnificent ruins of Rievaulx Abbey (*ree*-voh). The extensive remains give a wonderful sense of the size and complexity of the community that once lived here, and their story is fleshed out in a series of fascinating exhibits in a new museum and visitor centre.

This idyllic spot was chosen by Cistercian monks in 1132 as a base for their missionary activity in northern Britain. St Aelred, the third abbot, famously described the abbey's setting as 'everywhere peace, everywhere serenity, and a marvellous freedom from the tumult of the world'. But the monks of Rievaulx were far from unworldly and soon created a network of commercial interests ranging from sheep farms to lead mines.

There's an excellent 3½-mile **walking trail** from Helmsley to Rievaulx Abbey; Helmsley tourist information point can provide route leaflets and advise on buses if you don't want to walk both ways. This route is also the opening section of the Cleveland Way.

On the hillside above the abbey is **Rievaulx Terrace** (www.nationaltrust.org.uk; adult/child £5.95/3; ☺11am-5pm May-Aug, to 4pm Mar, Apr, Sep & Oct; P🐾), built in the 18th century by Thomas Duncombe II as a place to admire views of the abbey. Note that there's no direct access between the abbey and the terrace, and the two sites have separate admission fees. Their entrance gates are about a mile apart along a narrow road (steeply uphill if you're heading from the abbey to the terrace).

🛏 Sleeping

Canadian Fields   CAMPGROUND ££
(☑ 01439-772409; www.canadianfields.co.uk; Gale Lane; safari tents £60-90; ☺Feb–mid-Nov; P🐾) This luxury campsite 3 miles east of Helmsley offers comfortable and unusual accommodation in 'safari tents': spacious canvas-walled cabins with kitchens, electricity

North York Moors National Park

and wood-burning stoves. There are also sites where you can pitch your own tent (from £15 a night), and a bar-restaurant housed in a giant tepee provides a convivial social hub.

Helmsley YHA
HOSTEL £

(☑ 0845 371 9638; www.yha.org.uk; Carlton Lane; dm/q from £15/49; P ☎ ✚) This hostel's location, just 400m east of the market square at the start of the Cleveland Way, means it's often busy, so book in advance.

Feathers Hotel
INN ££

(☑ 01439-770275; www.feathershotelhelmsley. co.uk; Market Pl; s/d from £90/100; P ☎ ✚ ☀) One of a number of old coaching inns on the market square that offer B&B, decent grub and a pint of hand-pumped real ale. There are four-poster beds in some bedrooms and historical trimmings throughout.

Feversham Arms
HOTEL £££

(☑ 01439-770766; www.fevershamarms.com; High St; r from £200; P ☎ ☀) A rustic hotel given a designer makeover, the Feversham Arms has a snug and sophisticated atmosphere where country charm meets boutique chic. Individually decorated bedrooms are complemented by an excellent restaurant, spa treatments and a heated outdoor pool in the central courtyard.

✖ Eating

★ Hare Inn
MODERN BRITISH £££

(☑ 01845-597769; www.thehare-inn.com; Scawton; per person £30-60; ☻ noon-2.30pm & 6-9pm Wed-Sat, noon-4pm Sun; P) ✐ The phrase 'hidden gem' is overused, but here it is entirely appropriate – drowsing in a secluded hamlet 4 miles west of Helmsley, the Hare is a 21st-century restaurant in a 13th-century inn, where gourmet dining is relaxed, informal and even fun. There's no á la carte, just a choice of three tasting menus that change continually to take advantage of seasonal produce.

★ Star Inn
MODERN BRITISH £££

(☑ 01439-770397; www.thestaratharome.co.uk; Harome; mains £16-29; ☻ 11.30am-2pm Tue-Sat, 6.15-9.30pm Mon-Sat, noon-6pm Sun; P ✚) ✐ This thatch-roofed country pub is home to a Michelin-starred restaurant, with a menu specialising in top-quality produce from the surrounding countryside: Whitby crab with pickled cockles and avocado 'ice', or roast English quail with braised salsify and bergamot preserve. There's also a set three-course menu for £25 (Monday to Saturday). Harome is about 2 miles southeast of Helmsley off the A170.

The Star is the sort of place you won't want to leave, and the good news is you don't have to – the adjacent lodge has nine magnificent bedrooms (£170 to £260), each decorated in classic but luxurious country style.

🔒 Shopping

Hunters of Helmsley   FOOD & DRINKS
(☏ 01439-771307; www.huntersofhelmsley.com; 13 Market Pl; ⊙ 9am-4.30pm Sun-Thu, 8am-5.30pm Fri & Sat) Offers a cornucopia of locally made chutneys, jams, beers, cheeses, bacon, gourmet pies and sausage rolls, jams, sweets and ice cream – a great place to stock up for a posh picnic.

Thomas of Helmsley   FOOD & DRINKS
(☏ 01439-770249; 18 Market Pl; ⊙ 7.30am-5.30pm Mon-Sat, 10am-4pm Sun) A butcher and deli specialising in local produce, including delicious homemade sausages.

ⓘ Information

There's a **tourist office** (www.visitryedale.co.uk; Cut-Price Bookstore, 11 Market Pl; ⊙ 9.30am-5.30pm Mon-Sat, 11am-4.30pm Sun) in a local bookshop, providing leaflets, maps and public-transport advice.

ⓘ Getting There & Away

All buses stop in the main square. Bus 31X runs from York to Helmsley (£7.60, 1¼ hours, four daily Monday to Saturday). From Scarborough, take bus 128 (£7.60, 1¾ hours, hourly Monday to Saturday, four times on Sunday) via Pickering.

Pickering

POP 6590

Pickering is a lively market town with an imposing Norman castle that advertises itself as the 'gateway to the North York Moors'. That gateway is the terminus of the wonderful North Yorkshire Moors Railway, a picturesque survivor from the great days of steam.

Two scenic drives head north across the moors: the A169 to Whitby leads past the **Hole of Horcum** beauty spot and the hiking trails of **Goathland**; and the Blakey Ridge road (beginning 6 miles west of town) passes through the pretty village of **Hutton-le-Hole** and the famous **Lion Inn** on the way to Danby.

◉ Sights

North Yorkshire Moors Railway   HERITAGE RAILWAY
(NYMR; www.nymr.co.uk; Pickering-Whitby day-return ticket adult/child £30/13.50; ⊙ Apr-Oct) This privately owned railway runs for 18 miles through beautiful countryside from Pickering to Whitby. Lovingly restored steam locos pull period carriages resplendent with polished brass and bright paintwork, appealing to railway buffs and day trippers alike. For visitors without wheels, it's excellent for reaching out-of-the-way spots and devising walks between stations.

Pickering Castle   CASTLE
(EH; www.english-heritage.org.uk; Castlegate; adult/child £5.10/3.10; ⊙ 10am-6pm Apr-Sep, to 5pm Oct) Pickering Castle is a lot like the castles we drew as kids: thick stone outer walls circle the keep, and the whole lot is perched atop a high motte (mound) with great views of the surrounding countryside. Founded by William the Conqueror, it was added to and altered by later kings.

🛏️ Sleeping & Eating

★ **Eleven Westgate**   B&B ££
(☏ 01751-475111; www.elevenwestgate.co.uk; 11 Westgate; s/d £65/89; 🕸🚲) Just a few minutes' walk west of the town centre, Eleven Westgate is a pretty house with patio and garden offering top-value accommodation in cosy bedrooms. Cyclists are well catered for, with a bike wash, drying room and secure storage. Breakfast choices include the full Yorkshire fry-up or a vegetarian version.

17 Burgate   B&B ££
(☏ 01751-473463; www.17burgate.co.uk; 17 Burgate; s/d £95/110; P 🕸) ✿ Tea and cake on arrival set the mood at this elegant Georgian town house; its quiet and luxurious bedrooms exude a period atmosphere. Breakfast (cooked on an Aga stove, of course) makes the most of locally sourced produce, along with homemade marmalade and muesli.

★ **White Swan Hotel**   HOTEL £££
(☏ 01751-472288; www.white-swan.co.uk; Market Pl; r from £149; P 🕸🚲) ✿ The top spot in town successfully combines a smart pub, a superb restaurant serving local produce cooked with a Continental twist (mains £14 to £25), and a luxurious boutique hotel. Nine modern rooms in the converted coach house up the ante, with flatscreen TVs and other stylish paraphernalia adding to the luxury found throughout the hotel.

Pickering Station Tearoom   CAFE £
(Park St; mains £4-6; ⏱8.30am-4pm) The tea-room at Pickering station serves excellent home-baked goodies and tasty lunch specials such as Yorkshire pudding with roast beef and gravy.

❶ Information

The **tourist office** (Morlands Newsagent, 7 Market Pl; ⏱5am-5.30pm Mon-Sat, to 12.30pm Sun) has the usual details, as well as plenty of railway-related info.

❶ Getting There & Away

Bus 128 between Helmsley (£4.50, 40 minutes) and Scarborough (£5.50, 50 minutes) runs hourly via Pickering. Bus 840 between Leeds and Whitby links Pickering with York (£8.80, 70 minutes, hourly).

Whitby

POP 13,215

Whitby is a town of two parts, split down the middle by the River Esk. It's also a town with two personalities – on the one hand, a busy commercial and fishing port (once home to 18th-century explorer Captain James Cook) with a bustling quayside fish market; on the other, a traditional seaside resort, complete with sandy beach, amusement arcades and promenading holidaymakers. Keeping a watchful eye over the town is an atmospheric ruined abbey atop the East Cliff, the inspiration and setting for part of Bram Stoker's Gothic horror story *Dracula*.

Whitby is also famous for the jet (fossilised wood) that has been mined from its sea cliffs for centuries. This smooth black substance was popularised in the 19th century when Queen Victoria took to wearing mourning jewellery made from Whitby jet. In recent years these morbid associations have seen the rise of a series of hugely popular Goth festivals.

◉ Sights

★**Whitby Abbey**   RUINS
(EH; www.english-heritage.org.uk; adult/child £7.90/4.70; ⏱10am-6pm Apr-Sep, to 5pm Oct, to 4pm Tue-Sat Nov, to 4pm Sat & Sun Dec-Mar; ℗) There are ruined abbeys; and there are picturesque ruined abbeys. And then there's Whitby Abbey, dominating the skyline above the East Cliff like a great Gothic tombstone silhouetted against the sky. Looking as though it was built as an atmospheric film set rather than a monastic establishment, it is hardly surprising that this medieval hulk inspired the Victorian novelist Bram Stoker (who holidayed in Whitby) to make it the setting for Count Dracula's dramatic landfall.

From the end of Church St, the 199 steps of **Church Stairs** will lead you steeply up to Whitby Abbey. By car, you have to approach from the A171 Scarborough road to the east side of the bridge over the River Esk.

★**Captain Cook**
Memorial Museum   MUSEUM
(www.cookmuseumwhitby.co.uk; Grape Lane; adult/child £5.40/3.50; ⏱9.45am-5pm Apr-Oct, 11am-3pm Mar) This fascinating museum occupies the house of the ship owner with whom Cook began his seafaring career. Highlights include the attic where Cook lodged as a young apprentice, Cook's own maps and letters, etchings from the South Seas, and a wonderful model of the *Endeavour*, with the crew and stores all laid out for inspection.

Whitby Sands   BEACH
Whitby Sands, stretching west from the harbour mouth, offers donkey rides, ice-cream vendors and bucket-and-spade escapades, though the sand is mostly covered at high tide. The beach can be reached on a path from Whitby Pavilion, or from West Cliff via the **cliff lift** (per person 60p; ⏱10am-5.30pm May-Sep), an elevator that has been in service since 1931.

Whitby Museum   MUSEUM
(www.whitbymuseum.org.uk; Pannett Park; adult/child £5/free; ⏱9am-5pm Mon-Sat, 9.30am-4.30pm Sun; ♿) Set in a park to the west of the town centre is the wonderfully eclectic Whitby Museum, with displays of fossil plesiosaurs and dinosaur footprints, Captain Cook memorabilia, ships in bottles, jet jewellery and the gruesome 'Hand of Glory', a preserved human hand reputedly cut from the corpse of an executed criminal.

🏃 Activities

Whitby Whale Watching   WILDLIFE
(🖉07941 450381; www.whitbywhalewatching.net; Brewery Steps; per person £40) Join a four-hour cruise offshore to spot marine wildlife. Sightings of seals, porpoises and dolphins are almost guaranteed year-round, but August and September offer the best chances of seeing whales (usually Minke whales, more rarely humpback, sei and fin).

Trailways CYCLING
(☑01947-820207; www.trailways.info; Old Railway Station, Hawsker; per day from £17; ⊘9.30am-6pm) Bike-rental place in an old railway station on the Whitby to Scarborough cycle path, 2.5 miles southeast of Whitby.

⚑ Festivals & Events

Whitby Goth Weekends CULTURAL
(www.whitbygothweekend.co.uk; tickets 1/2 days £34/65) Goth and steampunk heaven, with live-music gigs, events and the Bizarre Bazaar – dozens of traders selling Goth gear, jewellery, art and music. Held twice yearly in late April or early May and late October or early November.

Whitby Spring Session MUSIC, ART
(www.moorandcoast.co.uk; tickets from £40) Beards, sandals and real ale abound at this traditional festival of folk music, dance and dubious Celtic art on the May Bank Holiday weekend.

⌖ Sleeping

YHA Whitby HOSTEL £
(☑0845 371 9049; www.yha.org.uk; Church Lane; dm/tw £23/59; Ⓟ◉⦿⊕) With an unbeatable setting in an old mansion next to the abbey, this hostel is incredibly popular – you'll have to book well in advance to get your body into one of the bunks here. Hike up the 199 steps from the town, or take bus 97 from the train station to Whitby Abbey (twice hourly Monday to Saturday).

Harbour Grange HOSTEL £
(☑01947-600817; www.whitbybackpackers.co.uk; Spital Bridge; dm from £18; Ⓟ) Less than 10 minutes' walk from the train station, this clean and basic hostel is conveniently located and has great views – it has picnic tables right beside the harbour. There's an 11.30pm curfew – just the ticket for a night when you don't want to paint the town red.

★La Rosa Hotel HOTEL ££
(☑01947-606981; www.larosa.co.uk/hotel; 5 East Tce; d £86-135; ⦿) ⌀ Weird, but wonderful. Lewis Carroll, author of *Alice in Wonderland,* once stayed in this house while holidaying in Whitby. And entering today is like stepping through the looking glass into an antique world of love-it-or-hate-it Victorian bric-a-brac and kitsch. Eight quirky and atmospheric bedrooms (one with a wooden bath!), great sea views, no TVs, and breakfast served in a basket in your room.

Trailways APARTMENT ££
(☑01947-820207; www.trailways.info; Hawsker; per week high season £699; Ⓟ) If travelling on the North Yorkshire Moors Railway has given you a taste for trains, how about sleeping in one? Trailways has a beautifully converted InterCity 125 coach parked at the old Hawsker train station on the Whitby–Scarborough cycle route, offering luxurious self-catering accommodation with all mod cons for two to six people.

Langley Hotel B&B ££
(☑01947-604250; www.langleyhotel.com; 16 Royal Cres; s/d from £70/105; ⦿) With its cream-and-crimson colour scheme, and a gilt four-poster bed in one room, this grand old guesthouse exudes a whiff of Victorian splendour. Go for room 1, 2 or 6, if possible, to make the most of the panoramic views – the same as those enjoyed in 1897 by Bram Stoker, author of *Dracula,* who holidayed a few doors along at No 6.

Shepherd's Purse GUESTHOUSE ££
(☑01947-820228; www.theshepherdspurse.com; Sanders Yard, Church St; d £65-85; ⦿) This place offers a romantic hideaway clustered around a hidden courtyard off busy Church St. The en suite bedrooms are charmingly rustic and, while the four-poster beds can feel a bit as though they've been shoehorned in, the atmosphere is cute rather than cramped. Two-night minimum stay April to October; breakfast is not provided.

YORKSHIRE WHITBY

CAPTAIN COOK – WHITBY'S ADOPTED SON

Although he was born in Marton (now a suburb of Middlesborough), the renowned explorer Captain James Cook has been adopted by Whitby. Ever since the first tourists got off the train in Victorian times, local entrepreneurs have mercilessly cashed in on Cook's memory, as endless Endeavour Cafes and Captain Cook Chip Shops testify.

Still, Whitby played a key role in Cook's eventual success as a world-famous explorer. It was here that he first went to sea, serving his apprenticeship with local ship owners, and the design of the ships used for his voyages of discovery – including the *Endeavour* – were based on the design of Whitby 'cats', flat-bottomed ships that carried coal from Newcastle to London.

Whitby

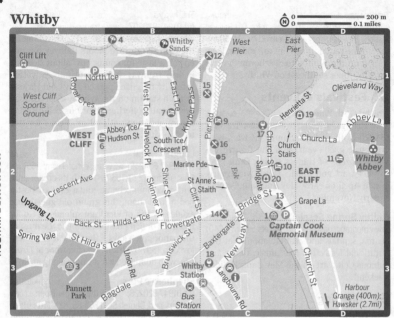

Whitby

◎ Top Sights
1 Captain Cook Memorial Museum.........C2
2 Whitby Abbey.....................................D2

◎ Sights
3 Whitby Museum....................................A3
4 Whitby Sands.......................................B1

◎ Activities, Courses & Tours
5 Whitby Whale Watching.......................C2

◎ Sleeping
6 Argyle House.......................................A2
7 La Rosa Hotel......................................B1
8 Langley Hotel......................................A1
9 Marine Hotel.......................................C1
10 Shepherd's Purse................................C2

11 YHA Whitby..D2

◎ Eating
12 Fisherman's Wife................................C1
13 Humble Pie 'n' Mash C2
14 Java Cafe-Bar.....................................C2
15 Magpie Cafe.......................................C1
16 Moon & Sixpence C2

◎ Drinking & Nightlife
17 Duke of York C2
18 Station Inn C3

◎ Shopping
19 Fortune's Kippers................................D1
20 Hildoceras..C2

Argyle House　　　　　　　　B&B **££**
(☏01947-821877; www.argyle-house.co.uk; 18
Hudson St; per person £37-43; ☜) ✐ Lovely
Victorian guesthouse near the West Sands,
comfortable as old slippers, with kippers for
breakfast. Discount available for multinight
stays.

★ Marine Hotel　　　　　　　INN **£££**
(☏01947-605022; www.the-marine-hotel.co.uk; 13
Marine Pde; r £100-195; ☜) Feeling more like
minisuites than ordinary hotel accommodation, the four bedrooms at the Marine are
quirky, stylish and comfortable; it's the sort
of place that makes you want to stay in rather than go out. Ask for one of the two rooms
with a balcony – they have great views
across the harbour.

✖ Eating

Humble Pie 'n' Mash　　　　　BRITISH **£**
(www.humblepie.tccdev.com; 163 Church St; mains
£6; ☉noon-8pm Mon-Sat, to 4pm Sun) ✐ Superb homemade pies with fillings ranging

from lamb, leek and rosemary to roast veg and goats cheese, served in a cosy timber-framed cottage.

Java Cafe-Bar
CAFE **£**

(✆ 01947-821973; 2 Flowergate; mains £5-8; ⏰ 8am-6pm; 🛜) A cool little diner with stainless-steel counters and retro decor, music videos on the flatscreen and a menu of healthy salads, sandwiches and wraps washed down with excellent coffee.

★ Fisherman's Wife
SEAFOOD **££**

(✆ 01947-603500; thefishermanswife.co.uk; Khyber Pass; mains £8-15; ⏰ noon-8.30pm Mon-Thu, to 8.45pm Fri & Sat, to 8pm Sun; 🖼) 🍴 With a prime location overlooking the beach and harbour entrance and smart staff dressed in navy-blue aprons, this is the place to enjoy local seafood in style. Whitby lobster (half/whole around £20/36 depending on market prices) is served as a salad, grilled with garlic, or thermidor style, while local crab comes with smoked salmon, avocado, apple and fennel.

★ Moon & Sixpence
BRASSERIE **££**

(✆ 01947-604416; www.moon-and-sixpence.co.uk; 5 Marine Pde; mains £9-18; ⏰ 9am-midnight; 🛜) 🍴 This brasserie and cocktail bar has a prime position, with views across the harbour to the abbey ruins. The seafood-dominated menu concentrates on hearty, straightforward dishes such as chunky vegetable soup, seafood chowder, fish pie, homemade burgers, and mussels and chips. Excellent breakfasts too, including local Fortune's kippers with brown bread and butter.

Magpie Cafe
SEAFOOD **££**

(www.magpiecafe.co.uk; 14 Pier Rd; mains £8-23; ⏰ 11.30am-9pm; 🛜 🖼) 🍴 The Magpie flaunts its reputation for serving the 'World's Best Fish and Chips'. Damn fine they are too, but the world and his dog knows about it and summertime queues can stretch along the street. Takeaway fish and chips cost £4.95; the sit-down restaurant is more expensive, but offers a wide range of seafood dishes, from grilled sea bass to paella.

Drinking & Nightlife

Station Inn
PUB

(www.stationinnwhitby.co.uk; New Quay Rd; ⏰ 10am-midnight Mon-Sat, to 11.30pm Sun; 🛜) The best place in town for atmosphere and real ale, with its impressive range of cask-conditioned beers including Timothy Taylor's Golden Best and Ossett Silver King. Live music Wednesday, Friday, Saturday and Sunday.

Duke of York
PUB

(www.dukeofyork.co.uk; Church St; ⏰ 11am-11pm Sun-Thu, to 11.30pm Fri, to midnight Sat; 🛜) A popular watering hole at the bottom of the Church Stairs, serving Timothy Taylor ales, fish and chips, and great views over the harbour.

Shopping

Fortune's Kippers
FOOD

(✆ 01947-601659; www.fortuneskippers.co.uk; 22 Henrietta St; ⏰ 9am-3pm Mon-Sat, 10am-1pm Sun) Fortune's has been making kippers (smoked herring) at this little smokehouse since 1872, and still turns out some of Britain's best; they're on the breakfast menu in many of Whitby's hotels and B&Bs. How to cook them? Either smear with butter and grill until bubbling, or poach in boiling water for five minutes.

Hildoceras
GIFTS & SOUVENIRS

(✆ 01947-604188; 12 Sandgate; ⏰ 10am-6pm) Fascinating gift shop selling all kinds of stuff, including fossils, minerals, crystals, insects preserved in amber, jewellery and leather goods.

ℹ Information

Whitby Tourist Office (✆ 01947-602674; www.visitwhitby.com; Langbourne Rd; ⏰ 9.30am-6pm Apr-Oct, to 4.30pm Nov-Mar)

ℹ Getting There & Away

Bus Two buses, 93 and X93, run south to Scarborough (£5.70, one hour, every 30 minutes), with every second bus going via Robin Hood's Bay (£4, 15 minutes, hourly); and north to Middlesborough (£5.70, one hour, hourly), with fewer services on Sunday.

DRACULA IN WHITBY

The famous story of *Dracula*, inspiration for a thousand lurid horror movies, was written by Bram Stoker while holidaying in Whitby in 1897 (a blue plaque at 6 Royal Cres marks the house where he stayed). Although most Hollywood versions of the tale concentrate on deepest, darkest Transylvania, a large part of the original book was set in Whitby, and many of the sites can still be seen today.

Get hold of a *Dracula Trail* leaflet (£1) from the tourist office, which will lead you around all the places in town linked to Bram Stoker and Dracula.

The Coastliner service 840 runs from Leeds to Whitby (£13.50, 3¼ hours, six times daily Monday to Saturday) via York and Pickering.

Train Coming from the north, you can get to Whitby by train along the Esk Valley Railway from Middlesborough (£6.80, 1½ hours, four per day), with connections from Durham and Newcastle. From the south, it's easier to get a train from York to Scarborough, and then a bus from Scarborough to Whitby.

Robin Hood's Bay

Picturesque Robin Hood's Bay has nothing to do with the hero of Sherwood Forest – the origin of its name is a mystery, and the locals call it Bay Town or just Bay. But there's no denying that this fishing village is one of the prettiest spots on the Yorkshire coast.

Leave your car at the parking area in the upper village (£3.50 for four hours), where 19th-century ships' captains built comfortable Victorian villas, and walk downhill to Old Bay, the oldest part of the village (don't even think about driving down). This maze of narrow lanes and passages is dotted with tearooms, pubs, craft shops and artists' studios (there's even a tiny cinema) and at low tide you can go down onto the beach and fossick around in the rock pools.

◉ Sights

Old Coastguard Station INTERPRETATION CENTRE
(www.nationaltrust.org.uk; The Dock; ⊘10am-5pm Apr-Nov, to 4pm Sat & Sun Dec-Mar) **FREE** National Trust visitor centre housing an exhibition about local geology and natural history.

✕ Eating & Drinking

Swell Cafe CAFE **£**
(www.swell.org.uk; Chapel St; mains £3-8; ⊘9.30am-3.30pm Mon-Fri, to 4pm Sat & Sun; ☎⊞) Great coffee, soup, salads and sandwiches, and a terrace with a view over the beach.

Ye Dolphin PUB
(☎01947-880337; King St; ⊘11.30am-11pm Mon-Sat, noon-11pm Sun; ☎⊞) The Bay's best pub for ambience and real ale; the local folk-music club meets here on Friday evenings.

ⓘ Getting There & Away

Robin Hood's Bay is 6 miles southeast of Whitby. Bus 93 runs hourly between Whitby and Scarborough via Robin Hood's Bay; the bus stop is at the top of the hill, in the new part of town.

YORKSHIRE DALES NATIONAL PARK

The Yorkshire Dales – named from the old Norse word *dalr*, meaning 'valleys', and protected as a national park since the 1950s – is the central jewel in the necklace of three national parks strung across the throat of northern England, with the dramatic fells of the Lake District to the west and the brooding heaths of the North York Moors to the east.

From well-known names such as Wensleydale and Ribblesdale to the obscure and evocative Langstrothdale and Arkengarthdale, the park's glacial valleys are characterised by a distinctive landscape of high heather moorland, stepped skylines and flat-topped hills. Down in the green valleys, patchworked with drystone dykes and little barns, are picture-postcard villages where sheep and cattle still graze on village greens. And in the limestone country of the southern Dales you'll find England's best examples of karst scenery (created by rainwater dissolving the underlying limestone bedrock).

ⓘ Getting There & Around

About 90% of visitors to the park arrive by car, and the narrow roads can become extremely crowded in summer. Parking can also be a serious problem. If you can, try to use public transport as much as possible.

Bus services are limited, and many run in summer only, some on Sundays and bank holidays only; pick up a DalesBus timetable from tourist offices, or consult the Dalesbus (www.dalesbus. org) website. The main routes run from Richmond to Ribblehead via Reeth, Keld and Hawes; from Richmond to Leyburn; and from Skipton to Kettlewell via Grassington.

By train, the best and most interesting access to the Dales is via the famous **Settle–Carlisle Line** (p512). Trains run between Leeds and Carlisle, stopping at Skipton, Settle and numerous small villages, offering unrivalled access to the hills straight from the station platform.

Skipton
POP 14,625

This busy market town on the southern edge of the Dales takes its name from the Anglo-Saxon *sceape ton* (sheep town). There are no prizes for guessing how it made its money. Market days bring crowds from all over and giving the town something of a festive atmosphere.

GOATHLAND

This picture-postcard halt on the North Yorkshire Moors Railway stars as Hogsmeade train station in the Harry Potter films, and the village appears as Aidensfield in the British TV series *Heartbeat*. It's also the starting point for lots of easy and enjoyable walks, often with the chuff-chuff-chuff of passing steam engines in the background.

One of the most popular hikes is to head northwest from the train station (via a gate on the platform on the far side from the village) to the hamlet of Beck Hole, where you can stop for a pork pie and a pint of Black Sheep at the wonderfully atmospheric **Birch Hall Inn** (www.beckhole.info; Beck Hole; ⊙11am-11pm May-Sep, shorter hours & closed Tue Oct-Apr; 🚻🍺), where it's like stepping into the past. Return to Goathland via the waterfall at Mally-an Spout (total 4 miles).

An alternative to the hike is to walk or cycle from Goathland along Beck Hole Rd (just over 1 mile); best not to drive, as the road is narrow and twisty and there's nowhere to park.

◉ Sights & Activities

High St
STREET

Skipton's pride and joy is the broad and bustling High St, one of the most attractive shopping streets in Yorkshire. There's a **general market** on High St four days a week (Monday, Wednesday, Friday and Saturday), and on the first Sunday of the month the nearby canal basin hosts a **farmers market** (9am to 3pm).

Skipton Castle
CASTLE

(www.skiptoncastle.co.uk; High St; adult/child £7.80/4.90; ⊙10am-6pm Mon-Sat, noon-6pm Sun Apr-Sep, to 5pm Oct-Mar) A gate to the side of the church at the north end of High St leads to Skipton Castle, one of the best-preserved medieval castles in England, a fascinating contrast to the ruins you'll see elsewhere.

Pennine Cruisers
BOATING

(www.penninecruisers.com; The Wharf, Coach St; per person £4; ⊙10.30am-dusk Mar-Oct) No trip to Skipton is complete without a cruise along the Leeds–Liverpool Canal, which runs through the middle of town. Pennine Cruisers runs half-hour trips to Skipton Castle and back.

🛏 Sleeping

Park Hill
B&B ££

(☎01756-792772; www.parkhillskipton.co.uk; 17 Grassington Rd; d £85; 🅿@🛜) 🍴 From the complimentary glass of sherry on arrival to the hearty breakfasts based on local produce, farm-fresh eggs and home-grown tomatoes, this B&B provides a real Yorkshire welcome. It enjoys an attractive rural location half a mile north of the town centre, on the B6265 road towards Grassington.

Carlton House
B&B ££

(☎01756-700921; www.carltonhouseskipton.co.uk; 46 Keighley Rd; s/d from £40/60) A handsome house with five pretty and comfortable rooms (there are no frills, but lots of floral prints) this B&B is deservedly popular on account of its friendly welcome, and is just a short walk south of the town centre.

🍴 Eating & Drinking

Bizzie Lizzies
FISH & CHIPS £

(☎01756-701131; www.bizzielizzies.co.uk; 36 Swadford St; mains £6-10; ⊙11am-9pm; 🚻🍺) An award-winning sit-down fish-and-chip restaurant overlooking the canal. There's also a takeaway counter offering fish and chips for £5, open to 11.30pm.

★Le Caveau
BRITISH ££

(☎01756-794274; www.lecaveau.co.uk; 86 High St; mains £17-20; ⊙noon-2.30pm & 7-9.30pm Tue-Fri, 5-9.30pm Sat) 🍴 Set in a stylishly decorated 16th-century cellar with barrel-vaulted ceilings, this friendly bistro offers a seasonal menu built lovingly around fresh local produce. Daily specials include dishes such as home-cured sea trout with mustard aioli, and cider-marinated pork fillet with crispy black pudding. On weekdays you can get a two-course lunch for £12.

Filmore & Union
HEALTH FOOD ££

(☎01756-700738; www.filmoreandunion.com; 66 High St; mains £8-16; ⊙8am-6pm Mon-Wed, to 10pm Thu-Sat, 9am-5pm Sun; 🛜🍴🍺) This San Francisco–inspired, Yorkshire-based chain of restaurants (there are branches in York, Leeds, Beverley and Harrogate) specialises in fresh salads, smoothies and juices. There are lots of vegetarian, vegan, low-sugar and gluten-free options alongside healthy meat dishes including burgers, steaks and chicken *shawarma* (skewers).

Narrow Boat PUB
(www.narrowboatskipton.co.uk; 38 Victoria St; ⊙noon-11pm; 🛜🕿) A traditionally styled pub with a great selection of local ales and foreign beers, friendly service and bar meals.

ℹ Information

The **tourist office** (📞 01756-792809; www.welcometoskipton.com; High St; ⊙ 9.30am-4pm Mon-Sat & 10am-4pm 1st Sun of month) is in the town hall.

ℹ Getting There & Away

Skipton is the last stop on the Metro rail network from Leeds (£9.40, 45 minutes, half-hourly, hourly on Sunday). Three buses a day (weekdays only) link Skipton with Settle (£6.20, 40 minutes)

Grassington

The perfect base for jaunts around the south Dales, Grassington's handsome Georgian centre teems with walkers and visitors throughout the summer months, soaking up an atmosphere that – despite the odd touch of faux rusticity – is as attractive and traditional as you'll find in these parts.

Highlight of the year is June's Grassington Festival, a two-week celebration of the arts.

🛏 Sleeping & Eating

Ashfield House B&B ££
(📞 01756-752584; www.ashfieldhouse.co.uk; Summers Fold; r from £105; 🅿@🛜) A secluded 17th-century country house behind a walled garden, with exposed stone walls, open fireplaces and an all-round cosy feel. It's just off the main square.

Yorkshire Dales National Park

★ **Devonshire Fell** HOTEL £££

(☎01756-718111; www.devonshirefell.co.uk; Burnsall; r from £129; P@❄⚟☎) This former gentleman's club for mill owners has a very contemporary feel, with beautiful modern furnishings crafted by local experts. The conservatory (used as a restaurant and breakfast room) has a stunning view over the valley. It's 3 miles southeast of Grassington on the B6160.

Corner House Cafe CAFE £

(☎01756-752414; www.cornerhousegrassington.co.uk; 1 Garr's Lane; mains £6-9; ⏰10am-4pm; ❄⚟☎) This cute little white cottage, just uphill from the village square, serves good coffee and unusual homemade cakes (citrus and lavender syrup sponge is unexpectedly delicious), as well as tasty lunch specials such as *croque monsieur* (gourmet toasted ham-and-cheese sandwich) or chicken and chorizo gratin. Breakfast, served till 11.30am, ranges from cinnamon toast to the full English fry-up.

✿ Festivals & Events

Grassington Festival ART

(www.grassington-festival.org.uk) Highlight of the cultural year in the Yorkshire Dales is the Grassington Festival, a two-week arts extravaganza held in June that attracts many big names in music, theatre and comedy, and also includes offbeat events like drystone-walling workshops.

ℹ Information

The **tourist office** (☎01756-751690; Hebden Rd; ⏰10am-5pm Apr-Oct, to 4pm Sat & Sun Nov, Dec, Feb & Mar) is beside the big car park on the edge of town.

ℹ Getting There & Away

Grassington is 6 miles north of Skipton; take bus 72 from Skipton bus or train station (£3.90, 30 minutes, hourly Monday to Saturday), or X43 (hourly, Sunday) from the bus station only. For onward travel, bus 72 continues up the valley to the villages of Kettlewell and Buckden.

Malham

POP 120

Stretching west from Grassington to Ingleton is the largest area of limestone country in England, a distinctive landscape pockmarked with potholes, dry valleys, limestone pavements and gorges. Two of the most spectacular features – Malham Cove and Gordale Scar – lie near the pretty village of Malham.

✈ Activities

★ **Malham Cove** AMPITHEATRE

A 0.75-mile walk north from Malham village lies Malham Cove, a huge rock amphitheatre lined with 80m-high vertical cliffs. Peregrine falcons nest here in spring, when the Royal Society for the Protection of Birds (RSPB) sets up a birdwatching lookout. You can hike up the steep steps on the left-hand side of the cove (on the Pennine Way footpath) to see the extensive limestone pavement above the cliffs. Another 1.5 miles further north is **Malham Tarn**, a glacial lake and nature reserve.

A mile east of Malham is spectacular **Gordale Scar**, a deep limestone canyon with scenic cascades and remains of an Iron Age settlement.

🛏 Sleeping

YHA Malham HOSTEL £

(☎0845 371 9529; www.yha.org.uk; dm/tw £25/55; P❄⚟) You will find this recently refurbished, purpose-built hostel across the bridge from the village centre. The facilities are top-notch, including a shop, a bar and a cafe, and young children are well catered for.

★ **Beck Hall** HOTEL ££

(☎01729-830332; www.beckhallmalham.com; d £90-110; P❄⚟☎) Ideally located for walks to Malham Cove, this rambling 17th-century country house has a gurgling beck (stream) flowing through the garden, 18 individually decorated rooms, all chunkily rustic with old-style furnishings and some with antique four-poster beds, and a lovely oak-panelled lounge with an open fire in winter.

ℹ Information

The **national park centre** (☎01969-652380; www.yorkshiredales.org.uk; ⏰10am-5pm Apr-Oct, to 4pm Sat & Sun Nov-Mar) in the car park at the southern edge of the village has the usual information. See also www.malhamdale.com.

ℹ Getting There & Away

There are between two and five buses a day (except Tuesday and Thursday) from Skipton to Malham (£4, 45 minutes), and the Malham Tarn Shuttle bus links Settle and Malham (£3.50, 25 minutes) four times daily on Sundays only, Easter to October. Check the Dalesbus website (www.dalesbus.org) or ask at Skipton tourist office for details. Note that Malham is reached via narrow roads that can get very congested in summer, so leave your car at the national park centre and walk into the village.

Ribblesdale & the Three Peaks

Scenic Ribblesdale cuts through the south-western corner of the Yorkshire Dales National Park, where the skyline is dominated by a trio of distinctive hills known as the Three Peaks: Whernside (735m), Ingleborough (724m) and Pen-y-ghent (694m). Easily accessible via the Settle–Carlisle railway line, this is one of England's most popular areas for outdoor activities, attracting thousands of hikers, cyclists and cavers each weekend.

At the head of the valley, 5 miles north of Horton, is the spectacular 30m-high Ribblehead Viaduct, built in 1874 and, at 400m, the longest on the Settle–Carlisle Line. You can hike there along the Pennine Way and travel back by train from Ribblehead station.

Settle

POP 3660

The busy market town of Settle, dominated by its grand neo-Gothic town hall, is the gateway to Ribblesdale and marks the beginning of the scenic part of the famous Settle–Carlisle railway line. Narrow cobbled streets lined with shops and pubs lead out from the central market square (Tuesday is market day), and the town offers plenty of accommodation options.

OFF THE BEATEN TRACK

EXPLORING THE DALES

Whether on two wheels or four, one of the joys of the Yorkshire Dales is exploring the hidden corners of the lesser-known valleys. From Swaledale, climb up to the moors above Arkengarthdale in search of the **Tan Hill Inn** (☑01833-628246; www.tanhillinn.com; Tan Hill, Reeth; ⊙8am-11.30pm Jul & Aug, noon-9.30pm Sep-Jun; 🐕🏧🍺), Britain's highest pub, or seek out the picture-postcard village green at **West Burton**, at the entrance to Bishopdale. From Grassington, make your way north along lovely Littondale and stop for a pint at the **Falcon Inn** (www.thefalconinn.com; Arncliffe; ⊙noon-3pm & 7-11pm Mon-Thu, noon-11pm Fri & Sat, noon-10.30pm Sun), where beer is still served from a jug on the counter.

Eating

Ye Olde Naked Man CAFE £
(Market Pl; mains £4-8; ⊙9am-5pm Thu-Tue, to 4pm Wed; 🧒) Formerly an undertaker's (look for the 'naked man' on the outside wall, dated 1663), Ye Olde Naked Man serves superb Yorkshire pudding with a choice of fillings.

ℹ Information

The **tourist office** (☑01729-825192; Town Hall, Cheapside; ⊙9.30am-4pm Mon-Sat year-round, to 4pm Sun Apr-Oct, 10am-2pm Sun Nov-Mar) has maps and guidebooks.

ℹ Getting There & Away

Trains from Leeds heading to Carlisle stop at Settle station near the town centre (£12.40, one hour, every two hours).

Horton-in-Ribblesdale

POP 560

A favourite with outdoor enthusiasts, the little village of Horton-in-Ribblesdale and its railway station is 5 miles north of Settle. Everything centres on the Pen-y-Ghent Cafe, which acts as the village tourist office, wet-weather retreat and hikers' information centre.

Horton is the starting point for climbing Pen-y-ghent and doing the Three Peaks Walk; it's also a stop on the Pennine Way.

🛏 Sleeping & Eating

Holme Farm Campsite CAMPGROUND £
(☑01729-860281; tent sites £4 plus per person £3, shower £1) A basic, no-frills campsite next door to the Golden Lion pub, much used by Pennine Way hikers.

Golden Lion INN £
(☑01729-860206; www.goldenlionhotel.co.uk; s/d from £45/70, bunkhouse per person £12; 🅿🧒) The Golden Lion is a lively pub that offers comfortable B&B rooms, a 15-bed bunkhouse, and three public bars where you can tuck into a bit of grub washed down with a pint of hand-pulled ale.

Pen-y-Ghent Cafe CAFE £
(mains £3-6; ⊙9am-5.30pm Mon & Wed-Fri, 8am-5.30pm Sat & Sun; 🅿🏧🧒) A traditional cafe run by the same family since 1965, the Pen-y-Ghent fills walkers' fuel tanks with fried eggs and chips, homemade scones and pint-sized mugs of tea. It also sells maps, guidebooks and walking gear.

Hawes

POP 885

Hawes is the beating heart of Wensleydale, a thriving and picturesque market town (market day is Tuesday) with several antique, art and craft shops that has the added attraction of its own waterfall in the village centre. On busy summer weekends, however, Hawes' narrow arteries can get seriously clogged with traffic. Leave the car in the parking area beside the national park centre at the eastern entrance to the village.

◎ Sights

Dales Countryside Museum MUSEUM
(☑ 01969-666210; www.dalescountrysidemuseum.org.uk; Station Yard; adult/child £4.50/free; ⊙ 10am-5pm, closed Jan; P) Sharing a building with the national park centre, the Dales Countryside Museum is a beautifully presented social history of the area that explains the forces shaping the landscape, from geology to lead mining to land enclosure.

Wensleydale Creamery MUSEUM
(www.wensleydale.co.uk; adult/child £2.50/1.50; ⊙ 10am-4pm; P⊞) Wensleydale Creamery is devoted to the production of a crumbly white cheese that's the favourite of animation characters Wallace and Gromit. You can visit the cheese museum, watch cheesemakers in action in the viewing gallery, and then try-before-you-buy in the shop (which is free to enter). A new interactive exhibit for kids explains the process from grass to cow to cheese.

Hardraw Force WATERFALL
(www.hardrawforce.com; Hardraw; per person £2.50; P) About 1.5 miles north of Hawes is 30m-high Hardraw Force, the highest unbroken waterfall in England, but by international standards not that impressive (except after heavy rain). Access is via a lovely landscaped walk (400m) from the car park behind the Green Dragon Inn (p511), which levies an admission fee.

Sheepdog Demonstrations FARM
(www.sheepdogdemo.co.uk; Hardraw; adult/child £5/1; ⊙ 6.30pm Thu May-Aug, 2.30pm Thu Sep & Oct; P) On Thursdays from May to October, a local farmer gives demonstrations of working sheepdogs, held in a field 800m north of Hawes on the minor road towards Hardraw.

🛏 Sleeping & Eating

Bainbridge Ings Caravan & Camp Site CAMPGROUND £
(☑ 01969-667354; www.bainbridge-ings.co.uk; hikers & cyclists per person £6, site, car & 2 adults £16; 🛜🐾) An attractive site set around a spacious farmhouse in stone-walled fields about half a mile east of Hawes. Fresh-laid eggs are sold on-site.

YHA Hawes HOSTEL £
(☑ 0845 371 9120; www.yha.org.uk; Lancaster Tce; dm/tw £25/55; 🛜🐾) A modern place on the western edge of town, at the junction of the main A684 (Aysgarth Rd) and B6255, this is a family-friendly hostel with great views of Wensleydale. Cheaper rates (dorm bed from £13) on weekdays.

Herriot's Guest House B&B ££
(☑ 01969-667536; www.herriotsinhawes.co.uk; Main St; s/d from £48/80; 🛜) A delightful guesthouse set in an old stone building close to the bridge by the waterfall, Herriot's has seven comfy en suite bedrooms set above an art gallery and coffee shop.

Green Dragon Inn INN ££
(☑ 01969-667392; www.greendragonhardraw.co.uk; Hardraw; B&B per person £35-50; P🛜🐾) A fine old pub with flagstone floors, low timber beams, ancient oak furniture and Theakston's on draught. The Dragon serves up a tasty steak-and-ale pie and offers bunkhouse accommodation (per person £17.50), camping (per person £8) or B&B in plain but adequate rooms, as well as a pair of larger, more comfortable suites. One mile northwest of Hawes.

Cart House TEAROOM £
(☑ 01969-667691; Hardraw; mains £4-7; ⊙ 10am-5pm mid-Mar-Oct) This craft shop and tearoom offers a healthy diet of homemade soup, organic bread and a 'Fellman's Lunch' of Wensleydale cheese, pickle and salad. There's a basic campsite at the back (£8 per person, including tent and car). One mile northwest of Hawes.

❶ Information

Hawes National Park Centre (☑ 01969-666210; Station Yard; ⊙ 10am-5pm Apr-Oct, limited hours Nov, Dec, Feb & Mar, closed Jan)

❶ Getting There & Away

Buses 156 and 157 run from Hawes to Leyburn (£5.50, 50 minutes, four daily), where you can connect with buses to or from Richmond.

YORKSHIRE HAWES

From Garsdale station on the Settle–Carlisle Line, bus 113 runs to Hawes (20 minutes, two to four daily Monday to Friday). On Sundays and bank holidays from April to September, bus 831 goes from Richmond to Hawes (£4, one hour and 20 minutes, twice daily) via Reeth and Keld, and on to Ribblehead station (£3.50, 25 minutes). Confirm bus times with Traveline Yorkshire or a tourist office before using these routes.

Richmond

POP 8415

The handsome market town of Richmond is one of England's best-kept secrets, perched on a rocky outcrop overlooking the River Swale and guarded by the ruins of a massive castle. A maze of cobbled streets radiates from the broad, sloping market square (market day is Saturday), lined with elegant Georgian buildings and photogenic stone cottages, with glimpses of the surrounding hills and dales peeking through the gaps.

👁 Sights & Activities

Richmond Castle CASTLE
(EH; www.english-heritage.org.uk; Tower St; adult/child £5.90/3.50; 🕙10am-6pm Apr-Sep, to 5pm Oct, to 4pm Sat & Sun Nov-Mar) The impressive heap that is Richmond Castle, founded in 1070, was one of the first castles in England since Roman times to be built of stone. It's had many uses through the years, including a stint as a prison for conscientious objectors during WWI (there's a small and sobering exhibition about their part in the castle's history). The best part of a visit is the view from the top of the remarkably well-preserved 30m-high keep, which towers over the town.

Richmondshire Museum MUSEUM
(www.richmondshiremuseum.org.uk; Ryder's Wynd; adult/child £3/free; 🕙10.30am-4.30pm Easter-Oct) The Richmondshire Museum is a delight, with local history exhibits including an early Yorkshire cave-dweller and displays about lead mining, which forever altered the Swaledale landscape a century ago. You can also see the original set that served as James Herriot's surgery in the TV series *All Creatures Great and Small*.

Green Howards Museum MUSEUM
(www.greenhowards.org.uk; Trinity Church Sq; adult/child £4.50/free; 🕙10am-4.30pm Feb-Dec) Military buffs will enjoy the three floors of this museum, which pays tribute to the famous Yorkshire regiment.

Georgian Theatre Royal TOURS
(www.georgiantheatreroyal.co.uk; Victoria Rd; adult/child £5/2; 🕙tours hourly 10am-4pm Mon-Sat mid-Feb–mid-Nov) The Georgian Theatre Royal, built in 1788, is the most complete Georgian playhouse in Britain. Tours include a look at the country's oldest surviving stage scenery, painted between 1818 and 1836.

SETTLE–CARLISLE LINE

The 72-mile **Settle–Carlisle Line** (SCL; www.settle-carlisle.co.uk), built between 1869 and 1875, offers one of England's most scenic railway journeys. The line's construction was one of the great engineering achievements of the Victorian era: 5000 labourers armed with picks and shovels built 325 bridges and 21 viaducts and blasted 14 tunnels in horrific conditions – nearly 200 of them died in the process. Trains run between Leeds and Carlisle via Settle about eight times per day. (The section between Appleby and Armathwaite is closed for repairs until March 2017.)

The first section of the journey from Leeds is along the Aire Valley, stopping at Keighley, where the **Keighley & Worth Valley Railway** (p522) branches off to Haworth, Skipton (gateway to the southern Dales) and Settle. The train then labours up the valley beside the River Ribble, through Horton-in-Ribblesdale, across the spectacular **Ribblehead Viaduct** and then through Blea Moor Tunnel to reach remote **Dent station**, at 350m the highest main-line station in the country.

The line reaches its highest point (356m) at Ais Gill, where it leaves the Dales behind before easing down to Kirkby Stephen. The last halts are Appleby and Langwathby, just northeast of Penrith (a jumping-off point for the Lake District), before the train finally pulls into Carlisle.

The entire journey from Leeds to Carlisle takes two hours and 40 minutes. Various hop-on, hop-off passes are also available for one or three days. You can pick up a free SCL timetable – which includes a colour map of the line and brief details about places of interest – from most Yorkshire stations.

✴️ Festivals & Events

Richmond Walking
& Book Festival LITERATURE
(www.booksandboots.org) In September/October Richmond hosts 10 days of guided walks, talks, films and other events.

🛏️ Sleeping

★ Old Dairy B&B ££
(☑ 01748-886057; www.olddairylowrow.wordpress.com; Low Row, Swaledale; r £65-75; 🅿 🛜 🐾) Near Reeth, 15 miles west of Richmond, the Old Dairy is a lovingly restored 200-year-old house in the very heart of the Dales with two homely guest bedrooms enjoying lovely views across the dale. The owners are a fount of knowledge on local walking, cycling and mountain biking, and can provide stargazing and astrophotography guidance from their 'dark sky' garden.

Frenchgate Hotel HOTEL ££
(☑ 01748-822087; www.thefrenchgate.co.uk; 59-61 Frenchgate; s/d from £88/118; 🅿 🛜) Nine elegant bedrooms occupy the upper floors of this converted Georgian town house, now a boutique hotel decorated with local art. The rooms have cool designer fittings that set off a period fireplace here, a Victorian roll-top bath there. Downstairs there's an excellent restaurant (three-course dinner £39) and a hospitable lounge with oak beams and an open fire.

Frenchgate Guest House B&B ££
(☑ 01748-823421; www.66frenchgate.co.uk; 66 Frenchgate; s/d from £70/100; 🛜 🐾) A gorgeous guesthouse perched at the top of a cobbled lane and decorated in period style. Two of the eight luxurious bedrooms have superb views across the valley of the River Swale, as does the breakfast room.

★ Millgate House B&B £££
(☑ 01748-823571; www.millgatehouse.com; Market Pl; r £125-165; 🅿 @ 🐾) 🐾 Behind an unassuming grey door lies the unexpected pleasure of one of the most attractive guesthouses in England. While the house itself is a Georgian gem crammed with period details, it is overshadowed by the multi-award-winning garden at the back, which offers superb views over the River Swale and the Cleveland Hills. If possible, book the Garden Suite.

MOUNTAIN-BIKING YORKSHIRE'S DALES
....

The epicentre of mountain-biking in the Yorkshire Dales, the **Dales Bike Centre** (☑ 01748-884908; www.dalesbikecentre.co.uk; Fremington; bike hire per day £35; ⊙ 9am-5pm; 🛜), 12 miles west of Richmond, provides bike hire (both mountain and road bikes), a bike shop and repair service, advice and trail maps, guided rides (£199 per day for up to eight people), a brilliant cafe (best coffee in the Dales) and comfortable bunkhouse accommodation for up to 14 people (four-bunk room £116 a night).

🍴 Eating & Drinking

Cross View Tearooms TEAROOM £
(www.crossviewtearooms.co.uk; 38 Market Pl; mains £5-10; ⊙ 9am-5.30pm; 🛜 👶) 🐾 So popular with locals that you might have to queue for a table at lunchtime, the Cross View is the place to go for a hearty breakfast, homemade cakes, a hot lunch, or just a nice cup of tea.

★ George & Dragon PUB FOOD ££
(☑ 01748-518373; www.georgeanddragonhudswell.co.uk; Hudswell; mains £8-10; ⊙ food served noon-2pm & 6-9pm Mon-Sat, noon-4pm Sun; 🛜 👶) A mile and a half west of Richmond, on a minor road south of the river, the George & Dragon is a genuine local pub, owned and managed by the community. It serves a small menu of freshly prepared pub grub, including sausage and mash, rabbit pie, and roast beef and Yorkshire pudding. The terrace at the back offers outdoor drinking and dining with gorgeous views across the dale.

Rustique FRENCH ££
(☑ 01748-821565; www.rustiquerichmond.co.uk; Chantry Wynd, Finkle St; mains £12-22; ⊙ noon-9pm) 🐾 Tucked away in an arcade, this cosy bistro has consistently impressed with its mastery of French country cooking, from *confit de canard* (duck slow roasted in its own fat) to *moules marinière* (mussels with white wine, garlic and cream). Booking is recommended.

Black Lion Hotel PUB
(www.blacklionhotelrichmond.co.uk; Finkle St; ⊙ 11am-11pm; 🛜 👶) Cosy bars, low beams and good beer and food.

ℹ Information

There's a **tourist office** (🖉 01609-532980; www.richmond.org; Richmond Library, Queens Rd; ⊙10am-6pm Mon & Thu, to 5pm Tue & Fri, to noon Wed, to 1pm Sat) in the local library with the usual maps and guides, plus several leaflets showing walks in town and the surrounding countryside.

ℹ Getting There & Away

From Darlington (on the railway between London and Edinburgh) it's easy to reach Richmond on bus X26 or X27 (£4.70, 30 minutes, every half-hour, hourly on Sunday). All buses stop in Market Pl.

On Sundays and bank-holiday Mondays only, from May to September, the Northern Dalesman bus 830 runs from Richmond to Hawes (£4, 1½ hours, one daily) via Reeth, and continues to Ribblehead (£6.50, two hours, one daily).

WEST YORKSHIRE

It was the tough and unforgiving textile industry that drove West Yorkshire's economy from the 18th century onward. The woollen mills, factories and canals built to transport raw materials and finished products defined much of the county's landscape. But that's all in the past, and recent years have seen the transformation of this once hard-bitten area into quite the picture postcard.

Leeds and Bradford, two adjoining cities so big they've virtually become one, are undergoing radical redevelopment and reinvention, prettifying their town centres and tempting more adventurous tourists with new museums, galleries and restaurants. Beyond the cities lies a landscape of wild moorland dissected by deep valleys dotted with old mill towns and villages, scenes that were so vividly described by the Brontë sisters, West Yorkshire's most renowned literary export and biggest tourist draw.

ℹ Getting Around

The Metro is West Yorkshire's highly efficient train and bus network, centred on Leeds and Bradford, which are also the main gateways to the county. For transport information, contact **West Yorkshire Metro** (🖉 0113-245 7676; www. wymetro.com).

Day Rover tickets (£8) are good for one day's unlimited travel on Metro buses and trains after 9.30am on weekdays and all day at weekends. A range of additional Rover tickets covering buses and/or trains, plus heaps of useful Metro maps and timetables, are available from bus and train stations and tourist offices in West Yorkshire.

Leeds

POP 751,500

One of the fastest-growing cities in the UK, Leeds is the glitzy embodiment of rediscovered northern self-confidence. A decade and a half of redevelopment has seen the city centre transform from near-derelict mill town into a vision of 21st-century urban chic, with skyscraping office blocks, glass-and-steel waterfront apartment complexes and renovated Victorian shopping arcades. The financial crisis of 2008–10 saw many flagship development projects grind to a halt, but tower cranes have sprouted on the skyline again.

The openings of the Leeds Arena entertainment venue and Leeds Trinity shopping centre in 2013 have been followed by a new southern entrance to the train station, a new Hilton Hotel near Leeds Arena, and yet another retail mall, Victoria Gate, to the east of Vicar Lane. Now something of a shopping mecca, it's little wonder the city has garnered the nickname 'Knightsbridge of the North'.

◉ Sights

★ Royal Armouries   MUSEUM

(www.royalarmouries.org; Armouries Dr; ⊙10am-5pm; P ♿) FREE Leeds' most interesting museum was originally built in 1996 to house armour and weapons from the Tower of London, but subsequently expanded to cover 3000 years' worth of combat and self-defence. It all sounds a bit macho, but the exhibits are as varied as they are fascinating, covering subjects as varied as jousting, fencing and Indian elephant armour. To get here, walk east along the river from Centenary Footbridge (10 minutes), or take bus 70 from Infirmary St (50p, 10 minutes, four per hour).

Leeds Industrial Museum   MUSEUM

(www.leeds.gov.uk/armleymills; Canal Rd, Armley; adult/child £3.80/1.90; ⊙10am-5pm Tue-Sat, 1-5pm Sun; P ♿) One of the world's largest textile mills has been transformed into a museum telling the story of Leeds' industrial past, both glorious and ignominious. The city grew rich from the textile industry, but at some cost in human terms – working conditions were Dickensian. As well as a selection of mill machinery, there's a particularly informative display about how cloth is made. The museum is 2 miles west of the city centre; take bus 15 from the train station.

Leeds

Leeds

◎ Sights

1 Leeds Art Gallery	A1

🛏 Sleeping

2 42 The Calls	D4
3 Art Hostel	D3
4 Chambers	A3
5 Quebecs	A3
6 Roomzzz Leeds City	C4

✖ Eating

7 Art's Cafe Bar & Restaurant	C3
Belgrave Music Hall & Canteen	(see 19)
8 Crafthouse	B3
9 Friends of Ham	B3
10 Pintura	C3
11 Shears Yard	D3

🍷 Drinking & Nightlife

12 Bar Fibre	C3
13 HiFi Club	C3
14 North Bar	C2
15 Reliance	D1
16 Sandinista	C1
17 Whitelocks	C3
18 Wire	C3

✪ Entertainment

19 Belgrave Music Hall & Canteen	C1
20 City Varieties	C2

🛍 Shopping

21 Corn Exchange	C3
22 Harvey Nichols	C2
23 Victoria Quarter	C2

Leeds Art Gallery   GALLERY
(www.leeds.gov.uk/artgallery; The Headrow;
⊙10am-5pm Mon, Tue & Thu-Sat, noon-5pm Wed,
1-5pm Sun; 🛜) **FREE** The municipal gallery – closed for roof repairs until 2017 – is
packed with 19th- and 20th-century British

heavyweights – Turner, Constable, Stanley Spencer, Wyndham Lewis et al – along with contemporary pieces by more recent arrivals such as Antony Gormley, sculptor of the *Angel of the North*.

Kirkstall Abbey CHURCH
(www.leeds.gov.uk/kirkstallabbey; Abbey Rd, Kirkstall; ⊙10am-4.30pm Tue-Sun Apr-Oct, to 4pm Nov-Mar) FREE Leeds' most impressive medieval structure is the beautiful Kirkstall Abbey, founded in 1152 by Cistercian monks from Fountains Abbey in North Yorkshire, and one of the best-preserved medieval abbeys in Britain. Across the road is the **Abbey House Museum** (www.leeds.gov.uk/museums andgalleries; Abbey Walk, Kirkstall; adult/child £4.20/2.10; ⊙10am-5pm Tue-Sun; P). The abbey and museum are 3 miles northwest of the centre; take bus 33, 33A or 757.

✲ Festivals & Events

Leeds Festival MUSIC
(www.leedsfestival.com) The August Bank Holiday (the weekend preceding the last Monday in August) sees 50,000-plus music fans converge on Bramham Park, 10 miles outside the city centre, for the Leeds Festival. Spread across four stages, it's one of Englands's biggest rock-music extravaganzas.

🛏 Sleeping

★ Art Hostel HOSTEL £
(☑0113-345 3363; www.arthostel.org.uk; 83 Kirkgate; dm/tw £22.50/55;) Set in an appealingly grungy 200-year-old brick building in the middle of Leeds' nightlife zone, this brand-new hostel is a great advert for the revitalisation of the city centre. Each room has been individually designed by a local artist, and the hostel is full of recycled furniture and innovative ideas.

Roomzzz Leeds City APARTMENT ££
(☑0203 504 5555; www.roomzzz.co.uk; 10 Swinegate; 2-person apt from £79; @) This outfit offers bright and modern luxury apartments complete with fitted kitchen, with the added advantage of 24-hour hotel reception, and a great city-centre location; a second branch, Roomzzz Leeds City West, is half a mile west on Burley Rd.

42 The Calls BOUTIQUE HOTEL ££
(☑0113-244 0099; www.42thecalls.co.uk; 42 The Calls; r from £89; @) This pioneer of the boutique-hotel scene (it opened in 1991), set in a 19th-century grain mill overlooking

the river, is looking a little frayed around the edges but its bold colours and designer aesthetic still appeal, although the smaller 'study' rooms are pretty compact. Breakfast is not included in standard rates – it'll cost you £15 for the full English.

★ Chambers APARTMENT £££
(☑0113-386 3300; www.morethanjustabed.com; 30 Park Pl; 2-person apt from £145; P) This grand Edwardian office building in one of the most attractive parts of the city centre has been converted into luxury serviced apartments, ranging from two-person studios to a two-bedroom penthouse (£360 a night) which will sleep up to four adults. Decor and design are in keeping with the beauty of the architecture, and service is spot on.

★ Quebecs BOUTIQUE HOTEL £££
(☑0113-244 8989; www.quebecshotel.co.uk; 9 Quebec St; d/ste from £99/179; @) Victorian grace at its opulent best is the theme of Quebecs, a conversion of the former Leeds & County Liberal Club. The elaborate wood panelling and heraldic stained-glass windows in the public areas are mirrored in the contemporary design of the bedrooms. Booking online can get you a suite for as little as half the rack rate.

🍴 Eating

Belgrave Music Hall & Canteen STREET FOOD £
(www.belgravemusichall.com; 1 Cross Belgrave St; mains £4-8; ⊙food served 11am-10pm) The Belgrave is a bar and music venue that also has a great kitchen – make that two kitchens. One serves artisan pizza (watch out for the napalm chilli sauce), the other probably the best burgers in Yorkshire, all at great-value prices. And every 2nd Saturday of the month the place hosts the **Belgrave Feast** (11am to 8pm), an art market and street food festival.

★ Friends of Ham DELI ££
(☑0113-242 0275; www.friendsofham.co.uk; 4-8 New Station St; mains £7-20; ⊙11am-11pm Mon-Thu, to 1am Fri & Sat, to 10pm Sun;) 🌿 We're not sure how to describe this place, other than that it's a stylish bar that serves the finest charcuterie and cheeses – Spanish, French, British – accompanied by fine wines and craft beers. The food is carefully selected and prepared, and utterly delicious; you can order individual tapas-like portions, or huge sharing platters with olive-oil-drizzled bread. Also, brunch (11am till noon).

Pintura

BASQUE **££**

([📋] 0113-430 0915; www.pinturakitchen.co.uk; Unit 3.26, Trinity Leeds; tapas £4-8; ⊙ noon-10pm Mon-Fri, 10am-10pm Sat & Sun) 🍴 Set beside the northern entrance to the Trinity shopping mall (from Lands Lane), this tapas bar is huge (spread over three floors) but always packed, so it must be doing something right. Seek out the more authentically Basque dishes – *bacalao* (salt cod) and *morcilla* (black pudding) – among the classic Spanish crowd-pleasers like *albondigas* (meatballs) and *gambas a la plancha* (prawns in garlic and chilli).

Shears Yard

MODERN BRITISH **££**

([📋] 0113-244 4144; www.shearsyard.com; 11-15 Wharf St; mains £11-25; ⊙ 5.30-10pm Tue-Sat, 11am-3pm Sat, noon-5pm Sun; [🍴]) 🍴 Acres of exposed brick, concrete floors and a soaring roof provide an industrial-chic setting (it's a former rope-making yard) for painterly presentations of imaginative (and intriguingly described) dishes such as ox-cheek fritter with roast-onion consommé, or squid with puffed potato and coriander emulsion. A two-/three-course dinner menu is available for £16.50/19.50 Tuesday, Wednesday and Thursday evenings, and before 7pm on Friday.

Art's Cafe Bar & Restaurant

INTERNATIONAL **££**

(www.artscafebar.co.uk; 42 Call Lane; mains £7-17; ⊙ noon-11pm; [🛜]) 🍴 Local art on the walls and a bohemian vibe throughout make this a popular place for quiet reflection, a chat and a really good cup of coffee. The dinner menu offers six classic dishes, while the early-bird menu (pre-7pm, except Saturday) offers three courses for £15.

⭐ Crafthouse

MODERN BRITISH **£££**

([📋] 0113-897 0444; www.crafthouse-restaurant. com; Level 5, Trinity Leeds, 70 Boar Lane; mains £22-37; ⊙ noon-2.45pm & 5-10pm Mon-Sat, noon-10pm Sun; [🛜][♿]) 🍴 This rooftop restaurant makes a big impression, with cool grey and black decor and huge picture windows overlooking the neighbouring church tower. The food is similarly striking, with bold flavour combinations such as charcoal salmon with nasturtium leaves, or quail with sour green strawberry. A two-/three-course set menu (£20/25) is available on Sundays.

🍷 Drinking & Nightlife

Reliance

CRAFT BEER

([📋] 0113-295 6060; www.the-reliance.co.uk; 76-78 North St; ⊙ noon-11pm Mon-Thu, to midnight Fri & Sat, to 10.30pm Sun; [🛜]) 🍴 Despite being relatively new, the Reliance is one of those comfortable-as-old-slippers bars where you can happily while away an afternoon reading or chatting, pausing only to order another pint of Roosters pale ale (brewed in Yorkshire, of course) or snack on a platter of homemade charcuterie (yes, they make it themselves).

Bar Fibre

CLUB

(www.barfibre.com; 168 Lower Briggate; ⊙ noon-1am Sun-Thu, to 3am Fri, to 4am Sat) Leeds' most popular gay bar, which spills out onto the cheekily named Queen's Court, is where the beautiful people congregate; dress code is...dressy, so look your best or you won't get in. There's another cluster of gay bars downhill at the junction of Lower Briggate and The Calls.

Sandinista

COCKTAIL BAR

(www.sandinista.co.uk; 5/5a Cross Belgrave St; ⊙ 3pm-3am Mon-Thu, noon-3am Fri-Sun; [🛜]) This laid-back bar has a Latin look and a unifying theme (it's named after the Clash's fourth album), attracting an eclectic clientele with its independent taste in music and unpretentious atmosphere. If you enjoy a well-mixed cocktail, but aren't too fussed about looking glam, this is the spot for you.

Whitelocks

PUB

(www.whitelocksleeds.com; 6-8 Turk's Head Yard; ⊙ 11am-midnight Mon-Thu, to 1am Fri & Sat, to 11pm Sun; [🛜][♿][🐾]) There's lots of polished wood, gleaming brass and colourful stained glass in this popular traditional pub, which dates from 1715. Theakston's, Deuchars IPA and several other real ales are on tap, there's a log fire in winter, and in summer the crowds spill out into the courtyard.

North Bar

CRAFT BEER

(www.northbar.com; 24 New Briggate; ⊙ 11am-1am Mon & Tue, to 2am Wed-Sat, noon-midnight Sun; [🛜]) There's a Continental feel to this long and narrow, minimalist bar, enhanced by the unfamiliar beer labels, from Dortmunder and Duvel to Schneider and Snake Dog. In fact, North is dedicated to the best of world beers, with more than a dozen ales on tap and scores more in bottles. Good selection of malt whisky too.

HiFi Club

CLUB

(www.thehificlub.co.uk; 2 Central Rd; ⊙ 11pm-3am Wed & Fri-Sun) This intimate club makes a good break from the hard-core sound of electronic dance: if it's Tamla Motown or the percussive beats of dance-floor jazz that shake your

HISTORIC SALTAIRE VILLAGE

Salts Mill (www.saltsmill.org.uk; Victoria Rd; ☺10am-5.30pm Mon-Fri, to 6pm Sat & Sun; P) Saltaire, a Victorian-era landmark and Unesco World Heritage Site, was an industrial village purpose-built in 1851 by philanthropic wool baron and teetotaller Titus Salt. The village's huge factory is now Salts Mill, a splendidly bright and airy cathedral-like building where the main draw is a permanent exhibition of works by Bradford-born artist David Hockney.

In a fitting metaphor for the shift in the British economy from making things to selling them, this former engine of industry is now a shrine to retail therapy, with shops selling books, crafts and outdoor equipment, and a cafe and restaurant.

Saltaire's **tourist office** (☎01274-437942; www.saltairevillage.info; Salts Mill, Victoria Rd; ☺10am-5pm Apr-Sep, to 4pm Oct-Mar) has maps of the village and provides information on local walks.

Saltaire is easily reached by train from Leeds (£3.70, 15 minutes, every 30 minutes).

booty, this is the spot for you. Also has stand-up comedy sessions on Saturday evenings.

Wire CLUB
(www.wireclub.co.uk; 2-8 Call Lane; ☺11pm-3am) This small, atmospheric basement club, set in a forest of Victorian cast-iron pillars with brick-vaulted ceilings, throbs to a different beat every night, from rock and roll to drum and bass; the only rule is: no mainstream music. Popular with local students.

☆ Entertainment

★**Belgrave Music Hall & Canteen**
(☎0113-234 6160; www.belgravemusichall.com; 1 Cross Belgrave St; ☺11am-midnight Sun-Wed, to 1am Thu, to 3am Fri & Sat) The Belgrave has it all – as well as being the city's best live-music venue, its three floors encompass a huge bar bristling with craft-beer taps, two kitchens (p516) serving the best street food in town, loads of shared tables and sofa space for socialising, and a fantastic roof terrace with views across the city. Why would you ever leave?

City Varieties LIVE MUSIC, COMEDY
(www.cityvarieties.co.uk; Swan St) Founded in 1865, City Varieties is the world's longest-running music hall, where the likes of Harry Houdini, Charlie Chaplin and Lily Langtry once trod the boards. Reopened after a major revamp in 2011, the program now features stand-up comedy, live music, pantomime and old-fashioned variety shows.

🛍 Shopping

Victoria Quarter MALL
(www.victoria-quarter.co.uk; Vicar Lane) The mosaic-paved, stained-glass-roofed Victorian arcades of Victoria Quarter, between Brig-

gate and Vicar Lane, are well worth visiting for aesthetic reasons alone. Dedicated shoppers can join the footballers' wives browsing boutiques by Louis Vuitton, Vivienne Westwood and Swarovski. The flagship store here, of course, is **Harvey Nichols** (www.harveynichols.com; 107-111 Briggate; ☺10am-7pm Mon-Sat, 11am-5pm Sun).

Corn Exchange SHOPPING CENTRE
(www.leedscornexchange.co.uk; Call Lane; ☺10am-6pm Mon-Sat, 10.30am-4.30pm Sun; 🖥) The dramatic Corn Exchange, built in 1865 to house grain-trade merchants, has a wonderful wrought-iron roof that today shelters a fine collection of independent shops and boutiques selling everything from art and fashion to jewellery and beauty products.

ℹ Information

Leeds Tourist Office (☎0113-242 5242; www.visitleeds.co.uk; Leeds Art Gallery, Headrow; ☺10am-5pm Mon-Sat, 11am-3pm Sun; 🖥) is in the basement of the city art gallery, next to the gallery shop.

Post Office (St John's Centre, 116 Albion St; ☺9am-5.30pm Mon-Sat)

ℹ Getting There & Away

AIR

Leeds Bradford International Airport (www.leedsbradfordairport.co.uk) is 11 miles northwest of the city via the A65, and has flights to a range of domestic and international destinations. The Flying Tiger (www.flyingtigerbus.co.uk) 757 bus runs between Leeds bus station and the airport (£3.60, 40 minutes, every 20 to 30 minutes, hourly on Sunday). A taxi costs about £20.

BUS

National Express (www.nationalexpress.com) serves most major cities, while Yorkshire Coastliner (www.coastliner.co.uk) buses run to York, Scarborough and Whitby. A Day Tripper Plus (£15) gives unlimited travel on all Coastliner buses for a day.

London £10 to £20, five hours, hourly

Manchester £3 to £6, 1¼ hours, every 30 minutes

Scarborough £12.30, three hours

Whitby £13.50, 3¾ hours

York £6.50, 1¼ hours

TRAIN

Leeds City station has good rail connections with the rest of the country, and is also the starting point for trains on the famous Settle–Carlisle railway line (p512).

London King's Cross £85, 2¼ hours, hourly

Manchester £20, one hour, hourly

Sheffield £13, one hour, twice hourly

York £13.90, 25 minutes, every 15 minutes

GETTING AROUND

Leeds City Bus (www.wymetro.com) runs every few minutes from 6.30am to 7.30pm Monday to Saturday, linking the **bus** and train stations with all the main shopping areas in the city centre (£1 flat fare); CityBus 70 South Bank (50p flat fare) links the train station and Infirmary St with Leeds Dock (for the Royal Armouries).

Various WY Metro Day Rover passes covering trains and/or buses are good for reaching Bradford, Haworth and Hebden Bridge.

Bradford

POP 522,452

Their suburbs may have merged into one sprawling urban conurbation, but Bradford remains far removed from its much more glamorous neighbour, Leeds. Thanks to its role as a major player in the wool trade, Bradford attracted large numbers of immigrants from Bangladesh and Pakistan during the 20th century. Despite occasional racial tensions, these new arrivals have helped reinvigorate the city and give it new energy (plus a reputation for superb curry restaurants). A high point of the year is the colourful Bradford Festival, a multicultural celebration of music, dance, arts, crafts and food.

⊙ Sights

★**National Media Museum**   MUSEUM
(www.nationalmediamuseum.org.uk; off Little Horton Lane; ⊙10am-6pm) FREE Bradford's top attraction is the National Media Museum, an impressive glass-fronted building that chronicles the story of photography, film, TV, radio and the web from 19th-century cameras and early animation to digital technology and the psychology of advertising. There's lots of hands-on stuff too – you can film yourself in a bedroom scene, pretend to be a TV newsreader, or play 1970s and 80s video games. There's also an **IMAX cinema** (www.picturehouses.com; National Media Museum; adult/child £12/9.50) here.

The museum looks out over **City Park**, Bradford's award-winning central square, which is home to the Mirror Pool, the country's largest urban water feature.

Festivals & Events

Bradford Festival   CULTURAL
(www.bradfordfestival.org.uk) This colourful Bradford Festival in July is a high point of the year: a multicultural celebration of music, dance, arts, crafts and food, with most events happening around City Park in the town centre.

✕ Eating

Bradford is famous for its curries – it was voted the Curry Capital of Britain for five years running from 2011 to 2015 – so don't miss out on trying one of the city's hundred or so restaurants. A great help is the Bradford Curry Guide (www.visitbradford.com/explore/Bradford_Curry_Guide.aspx), which helps sort the rogan josh from the rubbish nosh.

Kashmir   INDIAN £
(☑01274-726513; 27 Morley St; mains £4-6; ⊙11am-2am Sun-Thu, to 4am Fri & Sat; ✐) Bradford's oldest curry house has top tucker, served with no frills and no booze (although it is BYO). Whatever you do, go for a table upstairs, as the soul-destroying, windowless basement has all the character of a 1950s factory canteen. It's just around the corner from the National Media Museum.

Zouk Tea Bar   INDIAN ££
(☑01274-258025; www.zoukteabar.co.uk; 1312 Leeds Rd; mains £8-12; ⊙noon-midnight; 🛜✐🖶) This modern and stylish cafe-restaurant staffed by chefs from Lahore serves everything from *chana puri* (curried chickpeas) for lunch to legendary lamb Nihari (slow-cooked lamb with a thick and spicy sauce) for dinner.

ℹ️ Getting There & Away

Bradford is on the Metro train line from Leeds (£3.80, 20 minutes, three or four per hour).

Hebden Bridge

POP 4235

Tucked tightly into a fold of a steep-sided valley, Yorkshire's funkiest little village is a former mill town that refused to go gently with the dying of industry's light. Instead, it raged a bit and then morphed into an attractive little tourist trap with a distinctly bohemian atmosphere. The town is home to university academics, artists, diehard hippies and a substantial gay community. All of this explains the abundance of craft shops, organic cafes and secondhand bookstores.

The town centre was badly hit by flooding at Christmas 2015, but most businesses were quickly back on their feet. There are many cultural events on the calendar, culminating in late June/early July with the annual Hebden Bridge Arts Festival (hebdenbridgeartsfestival.co.uk).

◉ Sights & Activities

Heptonstall VILLAGE
(www.heptonstall.org) Above Hebden Bridge lies the much older village of Heptonstall, its narrow cobbled street lined with 500-year-old cottages and the ruins of a beautiful 13th-century church. But it's the churchyard of the newer St Thomas' Church (1854) that draws literary pilgrims, for here is buried the poet Sylvia Plath (1932–63), wife of another famous poet, Ted Hughes (1930–98), who was born in nearby Mytholmroyd.

Gibson Mill HISTORIC BUILDING
(NT; www.nationaltrust.org.uk; adult/child £4.50/2.20; ⏱11am-4pm Sat-Thu Mar-Oct, to 3pm Sat & Sun Nov-Feb; P) 🚶 This renovated 19th-century cotton mill houses a visitor centre with exhibitions covering the industrial and social history of the mill and its former workers. It is set amid the woods and waterfalls of local beauty spot **Hardcastle Crags** (open dawn to dusk, admission free), 1.5 miles north of town, reachable via a 30-minute riverside walk.

Hebden Bridge Cruises CRUISE
(☑07966 808717; http://hebdenbridgecruises.com; Stubbing Wharf, King St; per person £15; ⏱1pm & 2.15pm Sat) Join a colourful canal boat for a guided cruise along the Rochdale Canal, with tea and scones included in the price. Departs from the Stubbing Wharf pub, half a mile west of the town centre.

🛏️ Sleeping & Eating

Hebden Bridge Hostel HOSTEL £
(☑01422-843183; www.hebdenbridgehostel.co.uk; Birchcliffe Centre, Birchcliffe Rd; dm/tw/q £20/55/75; ⏱Easter-early Nov; P@🛜) 🚶 Just 10 minutes' walk uphill from the town centre, this hostel is set in a peaceful stone building, complete with sunny patio, tucked behind a former Baptist chapel (look for the green hostel signs). There's a cosy library, comfy and clean en suite rooms, and a vegetarian-food-only kitchen. The hostel is closed from 10.30am to 5pm daily.

★ Thorncliffe B&B B&B ££
(☑01422-842163; www.thorncliffe.uk.net; Alexandra Rd; s/d £55/75; 🛜) This delightful Victori-

---

YORKSHIRE'S WORLD-CLASS ART

Yorkshire Sculpture Park (www.ysp.co.uk; Bretton Park, near Wakefield; parking 2hr/all day £5/8; ⏱10am-5pm; P♿🐕) One of England's most impressive collections of sculpture is scattered across the formidable 18th-century estate of Bretton Park, 200-odd hectares of lawns, fields and trees. A bit like the art world's equivalent of a safari park, the Yorkshire Sculpture Park showcases the work of dozens of sculptors both national and international. But the main focus of this outdoor gallery is the work of local heroes Barbara Hepworth (1903–75), who was born in nearby Wakefield, and Henry Moore (1898–1986).

Hepworth Wakefield (☑01924-247360; www.hepworthwakefield.org; Gallery Walk, Wakefield; parking £5; ⏱10am-5pm Tue-Sun; P) West Yorkshire's standing in the international arts scene got a boost in 2011 when the Yorkshire Sculpture Park was joined by this award-winning gallery of modern art, housed in a stunningly angular building on the banks of the River Calder. The gallery has been built around the works of Wakefield-born sculptor Barbara Hepworth, perhaps best known for her work Single Form, which graces the UN Headquarters in New York.

HISTORY OF COAL

For close to three centuries, West and South Yorkshire were synonymous with coal production. The collieries shaped and scarred the landscape and entire villages grew up around the pits. The industry came to a shuddering halt in the 1980s, but the imprint of coal is still very much in evidence, even if there's only a handful of collieries left. One of these, the former Caphouse Colliery, **National Coal Mining Museum for England** (www.ncm.org.uk; Overton, near Wakefield; ⊙10am-5pm, last tour 3.15pm; P ♠) FREE is now this fascinating museum, a superb testament to the inner workings of a coal mine.

The highlight of a visit is the underground tour (departing every 10 minutes): equipped with helmet and head-torch, you descend almost 140m in the 'cage', then follow subterranean passages to the coal seam where massive drilling machines now stand idle. Former miners work as guides and explain the detail – sometimes with a suitably authentic and almost impenetrable mix of local dialect (known in Yorkshire as 'Tyke') and technical terminology.

At ground level there are audiovisual displays, some fascinating memorabilia (including sketches by Henry Moore), and exhibits about trade unions, strikes and the wider mining communities – only a bit over-romanticised in parts. You can also stroll round the pit-pony stables (their equine inhabitants also now retired) or the slightly eerie bathhouse, unchanged since the miners scrubbed off the coal dust for the last time and emptied their lockers.

The museum is 10 miles south of Leeds on the A642 between Wakefield and Huddersfield, reached via Junction 40 on the M1. By public transport, take a train from Leeds to Wakefield (£3.50, 15 to 30 minutes, at least hourly), and then bus 232 towards Huddersfield (£3.10, 25 minutes, hourly)

an house is perched on the hill above town, and the guest accommodation is perched at the top of the house – a spacious and peaceful attic double with private bathroom and lovely views across the valley, and a 1st-floor en suite double room, but without the views. A continental, vegetarian breakfast is served in your room.

Mooch CAFE £
(☑01422-846954; 24 Market St; mains £4-9; ⊙9am-8pm Wed-Mon; ⊛🍴♠) This chilled-out little cafe-bar exemplifies Hebden's alternative atmosphere, with a menu that includes a full-vegan breakfast, brie-and-grape ciabatta, and Mediterranean lunch platters of olives, hummus, stuffed vine leaves, tabouli and more. There's also Krombacher beer on draught, excellent espresso, and outdoor tables through the back.

★ **Green's Vegetarian Café** VEGETARIAN ££
(☑01422-843587; www.greensvegetariancafe.co.uk; Old Oxford House, Albert St; mains lunch £5-9, dinner £11; ⊙11am-3pm Wed-Sun, 6.30-10pm Fri & Sat; 🍴) 🌱 One of Yorkshire's best vegetarian restaurants, Green's adopts a gourmet attitude towards veggie and vegan cuisine, serving dishes such as Sicilian *caponata* (aubergines, red pepper, celery, olives and capers) with spaghetti, and Thai green curry with chickpeas, squash and tofu. Breakfast

(11am to noon) includes superb scrambled free-range eggs on toasted focaccia. Book a table to avoid disappointment, especially for dinner.

☆ Entertainment

Trades Club LIVE MUSIC
(☑01422-845265; www.thetradesclub.com; Holme St) Built in 1923 as a social club by the local trades unions, this place was revived in the 1980s and has since gone on to become one of the UK's coolest live-music venues, hosting names as big and diverse as the Buzzcocks, Patti Smith, the Fall and Martha Wainwright in recent years, as well as a host of up-and-coming indie talent.

ⓘ Information

Hebden Bridge Visitor & Canal Centre
(☑01422-843831; www.hebdenbridge.co.uk; Butlers Wharf, New Rd; ⊙10am-5pm mid-Mar–mid-Oct, shorter hours rest of year) has a good stock of maps and leaflets on local walks and bicycle routes, and information on the weekly flea market and farmers market.

ⓘ Getting There & Away

Hebden Bridge is on the train line from Leeds (£5.40, 50 minutes, every 20 minutes Monday to Saturday, hourly on Sunday) to Manchester (£9.50, 30 minutes, three or four per hour).

Haworth

POP 6380

It seems that only Shakespeare himself is held in higher esteem than the beloved Brontë sisters – Emily, Anne and Charlotte – judging by the eight million visitors a year who trudge up the hill from the train station to pay their respects at the handsome parsonage where the literary classics *Jane Eyre* and *Wuthering Heights* were penned.

Not surprisingly, the whole village is given over to Brontë-linked tourism, but even without the literary associations Haworth is still worth a visit, though you'll be hard-pressed not to be overwhelmed by the cottage industry that has grown up around the Brontës and their wonderful creations.

Sights

Haworth Parish Church CHURCH

(Church St; ⏱9am-5.30pm Mon-Sat) Your first stop in Haworth should be the parish church, a lovely old place of worship built in the late 19th century on the site of the older church that the Brontë sisters knew, which was demolished in 1879. The Brontë family vault lies beneath a pillar in the southeast corner, and a polished brass plaque on the floor commemorates Charlotte and Emily; Anne is buried at St Mary's Church in Scarborough.

Brontë Parsonage Museum MUSEUM

(www.bronte.org.uk; Church St; adult/child £7.50/3.75; ⏱10am-5.30pm Apr-Oct, to 5pm Nov-Mar) Set in a pretty garden overlooking Haworth parish church and graveyard, the house where the Brontë family lived from 1820 to 1861 is now a museum. The rooms

> **STEAM ENGINES & RAILWAY CHILDREN**
>
> The **Keighley & Worth Valley Railway** (www.kwvr.co.uk; adult/child return £11/5.50, Day Rover £16/8) runs steam and classic diesel engines between Keighley and Oxenhope via Haworth. It was here, in 1969, that the classic 1970 movie *The Railway Children* was shot: Mr Perks was stationmaster at Oakworth, where the Edwardian look has been meticulously maintained. Trains operate about hourly at weekends all year, and in holiday periods they run hourly every day.

are meticulously furnished and decorated exactly as they were in the Brontë era, including Charlotte's bedroom, her clothes and her writing paraphernalia. There's also an informative exhibition, which includes the fascinating miniature books the Brontës wrote as children.

Activities

Above Haworth stretch the bleak moors of the South Pennines – immediately familiar to Brontë fans. The tourist office has leaflets on local walks to endless Brontë-related places. A 6.5-mile favourite leads to **Top Withins**, a ruined farm thought to have inspired *Wuthering Heights,* even though a plaque clearly states that the farmhouse bore no resemblance to the one Emily wrote about.

Other walks can be taken around the **Brontë Way**, a longer route linking Bradford and Colne via Haworth. Alternatively, you can walk or cycle the 8 miles south to Hebden Bridge via the scenic valley of Hardcastle Crags.

Sleeping

Apothecary Guest House B&B £

(☑01535-643642; www.theapothecaryguesthouse. co.uk; 86 Main St; s/d £40/60; 🛜) A quaint and ancient building at the top end of the main street with oak beams and narrow, slanted passageways that lead to smallish rooms with cheerful decor; excellent value.

YHA Haworth HOSTEL £

(☑0845 371 9520; www.yha.org.uk; Longlands Dr; dm/tw £13/29; 🅿@🛜♿) In keeping with Haworth's Brontë heritage, the YHA hostel is set in a brooding Victorian Gothic mansion complete with games room, lounge, cycle store and laundry. It's on the northeastern edge of town, off Lees Lane.

★ Old Registry B&B ££

(☑01535-646503; www.theoldregistryhaworth. co.uk; 2-4 Main St; r £80-125; 🛜) This place is a bit special. It's an elegantly rustic guesthouse where each of the carefully themed rooms has either a four-poster bed, a whirlpool bath or valley views. The Secret Garden room sports floral textiles and a glorious view across parkland to the lower village with, if you're lucky, a steam train chuffing sedately by.

Ye Sleeping House
B&B ££

(☑ 01535-546992; www.yesleepinghouse.co.uk; 8 Main St; s/d from £58/64; P 🛜 🐾) This welcoming B&B has a cosy, country-cottage atmosphere, with just three small rooms and a friendly resident cat. Try to get the one en-suite room, which can sleep a family of four and has great views over the valley.

✖ Eating

Cookhouse
CAFE, BISTRO £

(☑ 01535-958904; www.thecookhousehaworth. co.uk; Main St; mains £4-9; ⊙10am-5.30pm; 🛜 🐾) A bright and breezy cafe that serves a bracing breakfast menu (till 11.45am) that includes eggs Benedict and bacon, cheese and onion hash, and mouth-watering lunch dishes such as bangers and mash with onion gravy, pulled pork sandwiches with barbecue sauce or toasted crumpets with Wensleydale cheese and chutney.

Cobbles & Clay
CAFE £

(www.cobblesandclay.co.uk; 60 Main St; mains £5-8; ⊙8.45am-5pm; 🖍 🐾) This attractive, child-friendly cafe not only offers fair-trade coffee and healthy salads and snacks – Tuscan bean stew, or hummus with pita bread and raw veggie sticks – but also provides the opportunity to indulge in a bit of pottery painting.

Haworth Old Hall
PUB FOOD ££

(☑ 01535-642709; www.hawortholdhall.co.uk; Sun St; mains £10-15) A 16th-century pub serving real ale and decent food, with a glorious beer garden for alfresco drinking and dining. If you want to linger longer, two comfortable doubles cost from £60 each.

❶ Information

The **Haworth Tourist Office** (☑ 01535-642329; www.visitbradford.com/discover/Haworth.aspx; 2-4 West Lane; ⊙10am-5pm Apr-Sep, to 4pm Oct-Mar) has an excellent supply of information on the village, the surrounding area and, of course, the Brontës.

❶ Getting There & Away

From Leeds, the easiest approach is via Keighley, which is on the Metro rail network. Bus 500 (www.keighleybus.co.uk) runs from Keighley bus station to Haworth (£2.20, 20 minutes, hourly) and continues to Todmorden and Hebden Bridge. However, the most interesting way to get from Keighley to Haworth is via the Keighley & Worth Valley Railway (p522).

SOUTH YORKSHIRE

What wool was to West Yorkshire, so steel was to South Yorkshire. A confluence of natural resources – coal, iron ore and ample water – made this part of the country a crucible of the British iron and steel industries. From the 18th to the 20th centuries, the region was the industrial powerhouse of northern England.

Sheffield's and Rotherham's blast furnaces and the coal pits of Barnsley and Doncaster may have closed long ago, but the hulking reminders of that irrepressible Victorian dynamism remain, not only in the old steelworks and pit heads (some of which have been converted into museums and exhibition spaces), but also in the grand civic buildings that grace Sheffield's city centre, fitting testaments to the untrammelled ambitions of their 19th-century patrons.

Sheffield

POP 551,800

Steel is everywhere in Sheffield. Today, however, it's not the steel of the foundries, mills and forges that made the city's fortune, nor the canteens of cutlery that made 'Sheffield Steel' a household name, but the steel of scaffolding and cranes, of modern sculptures and supertrams, and of new steel-framed buildings rising against the skyline.

The steel industry that made the city famous is long since gone, but after many years of decline Sheffield is on the up again – like many of northern England's cities, it has grabbed the opportunities presented by urban renewal with both hands and is working hard to reinvent itself. The new economy is based on services, shopping and the 'knowledge industry' that flows from the city's universities.

Since 2000 the city centre has been in the throes of a massive redevelopment that will continue into 2020 and beyond, so expect building sites and roadworks for several years to come.

◉ Sights

★ Kelham Island Museum
MUSEUM

(www.simt.co.uk; Alma St; adult/child £6/free; ⊙10am-4pm Mon-Thu, 11am-4.45pm Sun; P 🐾) Sheffield's prodigious industrial heritage is the subject of this excellent museum, set on a human-made island in the city's oldest industrial district. Exhibits cover all

WORTH A TRIP

MAGNA

At its peak, the Templeborough steelworks was the world's most productive steel smelter, with six 3000°C, electric-arc furnaces producing 1.8 million tonnes of metal a year. The mile-long **Magna** (☎ 01709-720002; www.visitmagna.co.uk; Sheffield Rd, Templeborough, Rotherham; adult/child £11.95/9.95; ☻ 10am-5pm, last entry 4pm; P ⊞), which once had a 10,000-strong workforce, is now an unashamed celebration of heavy industry, and a hands-on paradise for kids of all ages, with a huge range of science and technology exhibits. Magna is 4 miles northeast of Sheffield, just off the M1 motorway near Rotherham; phone in advance to check opening times.

A vast, dimly lit building, smelling vaguely of machine oil, hot metal and past glory, houses a series of displays based on the themes of earth, air, water and fire. The latter section is especially impressive, with a towering tornado of flame as a centrepiece and the chance to use a real electric arc to create your own tiny puddle of molten steel (if only for a moment or two). The hourly 'Big Melt' – a massive sound, light and fireworks show – memorably reenacts the firing up of one of the original arc furnaces.

aspects of industry, from steel-making to knife-sharpening – don't miss Little Mesters Lane, where the city's last remaining cutler (knife-maker) continues his trade. The most impressive display is the thundering 12,000-horsepower River Don steam engine (the size of a house) that gets powered up twice a day – don't miss it. The museum is 800m north of the city centre.

Winter Gardens GARDENS
(Surrey St; ☻ 8am-6pm; ☎) Pride of place in Sheffield's city centre goes to this wonderfully ambitious public space with a soaring glass roof supported by graceful arches of laminated timber. The 21st-century architecture contrasts sharply with the nearby Victorian **town hall** and the **Peace Gardens** – complete with fountains, sculptures, and lawns full of lunching office workers whenever there's a bit of sun.

Graves Gallery GALLERY
(www.museums-sheffield.org.uk; Surrey St; ☻ 11am-4pm Tue-Sat) FREE This gallery has a neat and accessible display of British and European art from the 16th century to the present day; the big names represented include Turner, Sisley, Cézanne, Gaugin, Miró, Klee, Picasso and Damien Hirst.

Abbeydale Industrial Hamlet MUSEUM
(www.simt.co.uk; Abbeydale Rd S; adult/child £4/ free; ☻ 10am-4pm Mon-Thu, 11am-4.45pm Sun; P ⊞) In the days before steel mills, metalworking was a cottage industry (just like wool and cotton). For a glimpse of that earlier, more innocent era, you can explore the restored 18th-century forges, workshops and machines at this industrial museum,

4 miles southwest of the centre on the A621 (towards the Peak District).

🛏 Sleeping & Eating

Leopold Hotel BOUTIQUE HOTEL ££
(☎ 0845 078 0067; www.leopoldhotel.co.uk; 2 Leopold St; r from £70; ☎) Housed in a former grammar-school building, Sheffield's first boutique hotel brings some much-needed style and sophistication to the city's accommodation scene (but without a London-sized price tag). Rooms can suffer late-night noise from the bars on Leopold Sq – ask for a quiet room at the back.

Houseboat Hotels HOUSEBOAT ££
(☎ 01909 569393; www.houseboathotels.com; Victoria Quays, Wharfe St; s/d/q from £79/99/159; P ⊞) Here's something a bit different: kick off your shoes and relax on board your very own permanently moored houseboat, complete with self-catering kitchen and patio area. Guests are entitled to discounts on the gym and pool facilities at the Hilton across the road.

Marmaduke's CAFE £
(www.marmadukescafedeli.co.uk; 22a Norfolk Row; mains £6-11; ☻ 9am-5pm Mon-Sat, 10am-4pm Sun; ☎ ⊿) ✔ This appealingly cramped and chaotic cafe, crammed with recycled furniture and fittings and run by a young and enthusiastic crew, serves a breakfast menu (until 11.30am) that highlights local and organic produce, and lunch dishes that range from deli sandwiches and quiche to vegetarian specials such as the halloumi and herb burger.

Street Food Chef
TEX-MEX **£**

(☑ 0114-275 2390; www.streetfoodchef.co.uk; 90 Arundel St; mains £3-6; ⊙10am-10pm Mon-Sat, to 9pm Sun) Local students flock to this down-to-earth Mexican canteen for its freshly prepared, great-value meals, including nachos, burritos, tacos and quesadillas with a choice of chilli-laced meat or veggie fillings, available to sit in or take away.

★ Vero Gusto
ITALIAN **££**

(☑ 0114-276 0004; www.verogusto.com; 12 Norfolk Row; mains £9-27; ⊙11am-11pm Tue-Sat; 🖀) 🍷 Gusto is a *real* Italian restaurant, from the Italian owners serving homemade Italian food to the genuine Italian coffee enjoyed by Italian customers reading Italian newspapers...you get the idea. Coffee and home-baked Italian cakes and pastries are served in the afternoon, plus lunch and dinner menus of exquisite Italian cuisine. It's best to book for dinner.

🍷 Drinking & Entertainment

Fat Cat
CRAFT BEER

(☑ 0114-249 4801; www.thefatcat.co.uk; 23 Alma St; ⊙noon-11pm Sun-Thu, to midnight Fri & Sat) One of Sheffield's finest pubs, the Fat Cat serves a wide range of real ales (some brewed on the premises) in a wonderfully unreconstructed interior. There are three bars (one nonsmoking), good pub grub, and a roaring fire in winter. It's north of the city centre, and handy for Kelham Island Museum.

Showroom
CINEMA

(☑ 0114-275 7727; www.showroomworkstation.org.uk; 15 Paternoster Row) This is the largest independent cinema in England, set in a grand art deco complex and screening a great mix of art-house, offbeat and not-quite-mainstream films.

❶ Information

Post Office (Norfolk St; ⊙8.30am-5.30pm Mon-Fri, to 3pm Sat)

Sheffield Tourist Office (☑ 0114-275 7754; www.welcometosheffield.co.uk; Surrey St; ⊙9.30am-5pm Mon-Fri, to 4pm Sat, closed 1-1.30pm)

❶ Getting There & Away

For all travel-related info for Sheffield and South Yorkshire, contact **Travel South Yorkshire** (☑ 01709-515151; www.travelsouthyorkshire.com).

BUS

The bus station, called the Interchange, is just east of the centre, about 250m north of the train station.

Leeds £4.70, one hour, hourly
Manchester £8.70, 1½ hours, four daily
London £14, four hours, four daily

TRAIN

Leeds £13, one hour, twice hourly
London St Pancras £75, 2½ hours, hourly
Manchester £15, one hour, twice hourly
York £16, 1¼ hours, twice hourly

EAST RIDING OF YORKSHIRE

The rolling farmland of the East Riding of Yorkshire meets the sea at Hull, a no-nonsense port that looks to the broad horizons of the Humber estuary and the North Sea for its livelihood. Just to its north, and in complete contrast to Hull's salt and grit, is Beverley, the East Riding's most attractive town, with lots of Georgian character and one of England's finest churches.

Hull
POP 284,320

Properly known as Kingston-upon-Hull (the ancient harbour on the River Hull was granted a royal charter in 1299 and became King's Town), Hull has long been the principal port of England's east coast, with an economy that grew up around wool and wine trading, whaling and fishing.

Named as UK City of Culture 2017 (www.hull2017.co.uk), the town has set about redeveloping its waterfront and Old Town; a minor cultural renaissance has taken place in the Fruitmarket district around Humber St, where derelict buildings have been reclaimed as artists' studios and performance spaces.

Though it's not going to win any prizes for prettiness, Hull has a gritty appeal for those who appreciate Britain's industrial past and enjoy getting away from the beaten tourist path. Famous as the home of poet Philip Larkin, the city harbours some fine Victorian civic architecture, a clutch of fascinating museums and one of Britain's best aquariums.

◎ Sights & Activities

★ The Deep
AQUARIUM

(☑01482-381000; www.thedeep.co.uk; Tower St; adult/child £12/10; ◷10am-6pm, last entry 5pm; [P][♿]) Hull's biggest tourist attraction is The Deep, Britain's most spectacular aquarium, housed in a colossal angular building that appears to lunge above the muddy waters of the Humber like a giant shark's head. Inside, it's just as dramatic, with echoing commentaries and computer-generated interactive displays that guide you through the formation of the oceans and the evolution of sea life.

The largest aquarium tank is 10m deep, filled with sharks, stingrays and colourful coral fishes, with moray eels draped over rocks like scarves of iridescent slime. A glass elevator plies up and down inside the tank, though you'll get a better view by taking the stairs. Don't miss the cafe on the top floor, which has a great view of the Humber estuary.

Ferens Art Gallery
GALLERY

(☑01482-300300; www.hullcc.gov.uk/ferens; Queen Victoria Sq; ◷10am-5pm Mon-Sat, 1.30-4.30pm Sun) FREE Following extensive renovations, the Ferens Art Gallery reopened in 2017 as part of Hull's City of Culture celebrations, with an exhibition of Spencer Tunick's Sea of Hull (a photographic installation where more than 3000 naked volunteers, covered in blue body paint, filled the city streets). The permanent art collection ranges from old masters like Frans Hals to modern works by Stanley Spencer, Peter Blake, David Hockney and Gillian Wearing.

Arctic Corsair
HISTORIC SITE

(www.hullcc.gov.uk/museums; ◷10am-4.30pm Wed & Sat, 1.30-4.30pm Sun Apr-Oct) FREE Marooned in the mud of the River Hull around the back of the Streetlife Museum, this Atlantic trawler is a veteran of the 1970s so-called 'Cod Wars' when the UK and Iceland clashed over fishing rights. Free guided tours – request at Hull & East Riding Museum (www.hullcc.gov.uk/museums; High St; ◷10am-5pm Mon-Sat, 1.30-4.30pm Sun) FREE reception desk – reveal the hardships of fishing north of the Arctic Circle.

Spurn Lightship
MUSEUM

(www.hullcc.gov.uk/museums; Castle St; ◷1.30-4pm Sun late Jun–mid-Sep) FREE Built in 1927, this lighthouse-ship once served as a navigation mark for ships entering the notorious Humber estuary. Now safely retired in the marina, it houses an engaging exhibition about its own history, and offers an interesting contrast between the former living quarters of captain and crew.

Old Town
AREA

Hull's Old Town, whose grand public buildings retain a sense of the prosperity the town once knew, occupies the thumb of land between the River Hull to the east and Princes Quay to the west. The most impressive legacy is the Guildhall (Low Gate; ◷8.30am-4.30pm Mon-Thu, to 3.30pm Fri) FREE, a huge neoclassical building that dates from 1916.

🛏 Sleeping & Eating

Garden Mews
B&B £

(☑01482-215574; http://the-garden-mews-gb.book.direct; 13-14 John St; s/d/f from £30/45/60; [奈][♿]) Overlooking leafy Kingston Sq, and close to the New Theatre, this is one of the best-value B&B options in the city centre; the rooms are nothing fancy, but are tidy and comfortable, and the owners are friendly and helpful.

Kingston Theatre Hotel
HOTEL ££

(☑01482-225828; www.kingstontheatrehotel.com; 1-2 Kingston Sq; s/d/ste £75/110/190; [奈][♿]) One of Hull's most pleasant places to stay, this hotel has elegant bedrooms, friendly service and an excellent breakfast, and enjoys a quiet location on a park-like square opposite the New Theatre. Good discounts available via website.

Bait
SEAFOOD ££

(☑01482-343088; www.baithull.co.uk; 13-15 Princes Ave; mains £11-18; ◷noon-2.30pm & 5-9pm Tue-Thu, noon-9.30pm Fri-Sun) 🍴 Hull's seafaring tradition is reflected in a menu dominated by the best of British seafood, including Lindisfarne oysters au naturel, lobster bisque, grey mullet with cider and onion chutney, smoked haddock risotto and good old-fashioned fish pie. There are meat and vegetarian dishes too, and the rustic, chunky-timber decor engenders a lively and informal atmosphere.

Fudge AMERICAN **££**
(📞01482-441019; www.fudgefood.com; 93 Princes Ave; mains £8-17; ⊘10.30am-3pm Tue-Thu & Sun, 9am-3pm Fri & Sat, 6-9pm Tue-Sun; 🛜👶) This funky cafe decked out in pink and peppermint colours serves hearty brunches, cakes and coffee all day, but also offers a tempting USA-style menu of dishes that include juicy burgers (beef or veggie), creole chicken, po' boys and deli sandwiches.

★1884 Dock Street Kitchen MODERN BRITISH **£££**
(📞01482-222260; www.1884dockstreetkitchen. co.uk; Humber Dock St; mains £17-33; ⊘noon-2pm Tue-Sat, 6-9.30pm Mon-Sat, noon-3pm Sun; 🛜) ✒ Poster boy for the city's redeveloping waterfront, this big and bold enterprise tries to blend British cuisine with a sepia-tinted, late-19th-century New York-steakhouse look, and just about pulls it off. As well as the steaks, the menu is strong on Scottish seafood, Yorkshire pork and Lancashire lamb, and dishes dotted with wild garlic and duck egg. Three-course lunch menu £21.

🍷 Drinking & Entertainment

Olde Black Boy PUB
(📞01482-215040; 150 High St; ⊘5.30-11.30pm Mon-Tue, 12.30-11.30pm Wed-Sun) A favourite watering hole of poet Philip Larkin, Hull's oldest pub has been serving ale since 1726. Oak floors and roof beams, dark-wood panelling and a snug log fire in winter make for a great atmosphere, and there's live folk music on Wednesdays.

Fuel CLUB
(www.fuel-hull.co.uk; 6 Baker St; ⊘11pm-3am Wed, 8pm-6am Fri & Sat; 🛜) A nondescript facade conceals what is currently Hull's hottest club, proudly but not exclusively gay, with camp comedy and drag shows as well as DJs and dancers.

Fruitspace LIVE MUSIC, COMEDY
(📞01482-221113; www.fruitspace.co.uk; 62-63 Humber St; 🛜) A focus for the cultural revival of Hull's Fruitmarket district, this former in-

dustrial space is now a multipurpose venue incorporating a bar, cinema and stage. There are regular live gigs by local bands (and occasional big names), a monthly comedy club and, on the third Sunday of the month, the Humber Street Market.

ℹ Information

Hull Tourist Office (📞01482-300300; www. visithullandeastyorkshire.com; 1 Paragon St; ⊘10am-5pm Mon-Sat, 11am-3pm Sun)

Beverley

POP 30,590

Handsome, unspoilt Beverley is one of the most attractive towns in Yorkshire, largely on account of its magnificent minster – a rival to any cathedral in England – and the tangle of streets that lie beneath it, each brimming with exquisite Georgian and Victorian buildings.

All the sights are a short walk from either the train or bus station. There's a large market on Saturdays in the square called Saturday Market, and a smaller one on Wednesdays in the square called...Wednesday Market.

◉ Sights

★Beverley Minster CHURCH
(www.beverleyminster.org; St John St; ⊘9am-5pm Mon-Sat, noon-5pm Sun Mar-Oct, to 4pm Nov-Mar; 🛜) **FREE** One of the great glories of English religious architecture, Beverley Minster is the most impressive church in the country that is not a cathedral. The soaring lines of the exterior are imposing, but it is inside that the charm and beauty lie. The 14th-century north aisle is lined with original stone carvings, mostly of musicians; much of our knowledge of early musical instruments comes from these images. You'll also see goblins, devils and grotesque figures. Look out for the bagpipe player.

Construction began in 1220 – the third church to be built on this site, with the first dating from the 7th century – and continued for two centuries, spanning the Early English, Decorated and Perpendicular periods of the Gothic style.

Close to the altar, the elaborate and intricate **Percy Canopy** (1340), a decorative frill above the tomb of local aristocrat Lady Eleanor Percy, is a testament to the skill of the sculptor and the finest example of Gothic stone carving in England. In complete

PIPE & GLASS INN

Set in a picturesque hamlet 4 miles northwest of Beverley, the **Pipe and Glass Inn** (🅙 01430-810246; www.pipe andglass.co.uk; West End, South Dalton; mains £11-30; ⊗ noon-2pm & 6.30-9.30pm Tue-Sat, noon-4pm Sun; 🅿🔊🎐🛉) is a charming country pub which has held a Michelin star since 2010. The setting may be delightfully informal, with weathered timber tables, stone hearths and leather sofas, but a great deal of care is lavished on the food – even seemingly simple dishes such as fish pie are unforgettable.

If you want to stay the night, there are five luxurious bedrooms to choose from (£180 to £225 per night, including breakfast).

contrast, in the nearby chancel is the 10th-century Saxon **frith stool**, a plain and polished stone chair that once gave sanctuary to anyone escaping the law.

In the roof of the tower is a restored treadwheel crane, where workers ground around like hapless hamsters to lift the huge loads necessary to build a medieval church. Access to the roof is by guided tour only (per person £5).

Beverley Westwood PARK
(Walkington Rd) The western edge of Beverley is bounded by this large area of common pasture studded with mature trees, which has been used as grazing for local livestock for centuries. The land, owned 'in common' by the community since 1380, is overseen by the Pasture Masters, a group of men elected from the Freemen of Beverley each March. Contented cows amble across the unfenced road, while walkers stroll and enjoy the gorgeous views of Beverley Minster.

🛏 Sleeping & Eating

⭐ **YHA Beverley Friary** HOSTEL £
(🅙 0845 371 9004; www.yha.org.uk; Friar's Lane; dm/d from £15/49; 🅿🔊🛉) In Beverley, the cheapest accommodation also has the best setting and location. This hostel is housed in a beautifully restored 14th-century Dominican friary mentioned in Chaucer's The

Canterbury Tales, and is only 100m from the minster and a short walk from the train station.

Kings Head INN ££
(🅙 01482-868103; www.kingsheadpubbeverley. co.uk; 38 Saturday Market; r from £90; 🔊) A Georgian coaching inn given a modern makeover, the Kings Head is a lively pub with 10 bright and stylish rooms above the bar. The pub opens late on weekend nights, but earplugs are supplied for those who don't want to join the revelry!

Vanessa Delicafe CAFE ££
(🅙 01482-868190; www.vanessadelicafe.co.uk; 21-22 Saturday Market; mains £7-15; ⊗ 9am-4.30pm Mon-Sat, 10am-3.30pm Sun; 🔊🛉) This popular cafe sits above a delicatessen, with sofas and bookshelves scattered among the tables, and window seats overlooking the market square. Settle down for cappuccino and cake with the Sunday papers, or tuck into hearty lunch specials such as venison burger or a Yorkshire platter of pork pie, roast ham, cheese and chutney.

Grant's Bistro 22 MODERN BRITISH £££
(🅙 01482-887624; www.grantsbistro.co.uk; 22 North Bar Within; mains £14-25; ⊗ noon-2pm Fri & Sat, 6-9.30pm Mon-Sat; 🎐) 🍴 A great place for a romantic dinner à deux, with dark-wood tables, fresh flowers and candlelight. The menu makes the most of fresh local beef, game and especially seafood, with dishes such as pan-fried scallops with black pudding, and a decent choice of vegetarian options. A two-/three-course lunch is £15/20.

ℹ Information

Beverley Tourist Office (🅙 01482-391672; www.visithullandeastyorkshire.com/beverley; 34 Butcher Row; ⊗ 9.30am-5pm Mon-Sat)

ℹ Getting There & Away

There are frequent bus services from Hull, including numbers 121, 122, 246 and X46/X47 (£4.05, 30 minutes, every 20 minutes). Bus X46/X47 links Beverley with York (£6.45, 1¼ hours, hourly).

Trains run regularly to Scarborough (£13.70, 1¼ hours, every two hours) and Hull (£6.80, 15 minutes, twice hourly).

Manchester, Liverpool & Northwest England

Includes ➡

Manchester	532
Chester	543
Liverpool	547
Blackpool	556
Lancaster	557
Douglas	561
Castletown & Around	562
Peel	563

Best Places to Eat

➡ Northcote Hotel (p560)

➡ Manchester House (p540)

➡ Little Fish Cafe (p561)

➡ Simon Radley at the Grosvenor (p546)

➡ Salt House (p554)

Best Places to Sleep

➡ Inn at Whitewell (p560)

➡ 2 Blackburne Terrace (p553)

➡ King Street Townhouse (p538)

➡ Stone Villa (p545)

➡ Richmond Hotel (p552)

Why Go?

Two rival cities with rich traditions, a medieval masterpiece, an island unto itself and some of the finest countryside in England...this is just a flavour of what the northwest has to offer. Dominating the region is Manchester, arguably England's most exciting city and the unofficial capital of the north. Just across the Pennines is Liverpool, fiercely proud of its own heritage and well able to put it up to its bigger neighbour in all matters from food to football. Near to both is Chester, a historic Tudor postcard with a legacy dating back to Roman times. And, just to prove that the northwest isn't all about humankind's concrete footprint, you can get away from it all in some of Britain's most beautiful – and walkable – countryside, in northern Lancashire and on the Isle of Man.

When to Go

➡ The world's most famous steeplechase – the Aintree Grand National – is run just outside Liverpool over the first weekend in April.

➡ May and June are Tourist Trophy (TT) Festival season on the Isle of Man – beloved of motor enthusiasts the world over.

➡ In the arts, the highlight is the Manchester International Festival, a biennial showstopper held in July.

➡ Music buffs should visit Liverpool in the last week of August for madness at Creamfields dance-fest and for the Mathew St Festival, an ode to all things Beatles.

➡ The football (soccer) season runs from late August until May.

CALDERALE

Hebden Bridge

Todmorden

Cross Hill

Skipton

Colne

Burnley

Haslingden

M65

Gargrave

Gisburn

A59

Barley

Pendle Hill ▲

Whalley

Blackburn

Great Whernside (705m) ▲

NORTH YORKSHIRE

Malham

Long Preston

Ribble Way

Newton

Clitheroe

Hurst Green

Goosnargh

Preston

Yorkshire Dales National Park

Hawes

Pen-y-ghent (695m) ▲

Stainforth

Whitewell

Forest of Bowland

Dunsop Bridge

Slaidburn

Chipping

Longridge

LANCASHIRE

M6

Garsdale Head

Dent ⋒

Whernside (735m) ▲

Ribblehead

Ingleborough (723m) ▲

A65

Ingleton

Ribble

Kirkham

Dent

Barbon

Kirkby Lonsdale

Arkholme

Lancaster

Preesall

Cockerham

Glasson

Kirkham

Lytham St Anne's

Killington Reservoir

Forest Hall

Kendal

Heaves

Milnthorpe

Arnside

M6

Halton

Carnforth

Morecambe Bay

Morecambe

Heysham

Fleetwood

Poulton-le-Fylde

6 Blackpool

CUMBRIA

Troutbeck Bridge

Coniston Water

Newby Bridge

Penny Bridge

Ulverston

Broughton-in-Furness

Lake District National Park

Coniston

Bootle

Haverigg

Barrow-in-Furness

Barrow Island

Seascale

Ravenglass

A595

IRISH SEA

To Isle of Man (38mi) (see inset)

Isle of Man

Point of Ayre

Andreas

Ramsey

Maughold

Laxey

Baldrine

5 Isle of Man

Douglas

Jurby

Bellaugh

Snaefell (621m) ▲

Crosby

St Marks

Ronaldsway Airport

Castletown

Peel

St John's

Dalby

Port Erin

Port St Mary

Cregneash

Calf of Man

St Mary

IRISH SEA

0 — 10 km
0 — 5 miles

N

Isle of Man

Manchester, Liverpool & Northwest England Highlights

1 International Slavery Museum

(p550) Learning a history lesson at Liverpool's most emotionally charged museum.

2 Beatles' Childhood Homes

(p551) Visiting the Liverpool houses where John and Paul grew up – and wrote their earliest hits.

3 HOME (p541) Catching a show at Manchester's exciting and provocative arts centre.

4 City Walls

(p543) Tramping Chester's fortifications like the Romans did 2000 years ago.

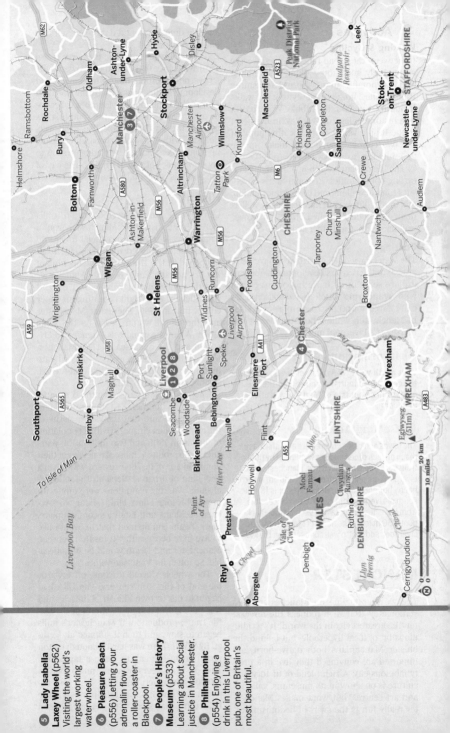

5 Lady Isabella Laxey Wheel (p562)
Visiting the world's largest working waterwheel.

6 Pleasure Beach (p556) Letting your adrenalin flow on a roller-coaster in Blackpool.

7 People's History Museum (p533)
Learning about social justice in Manchester.

8 Philharmonic (p554) Enjoying a drink in this Liverpool pub, one of Britain's most beautiful.

🏃 Activities

Walking & Cycling

In between the urban bits, the northwest is surprisingly good for walking and cycling options, notably in northern Lancashire's Ribble Valley, home to plenty of good walks including the 70-mile Ribble Way (p558). The historic village of Whalley, in the heart of the Ribble Valley, is the meeting point of the two circular routes that make up the 260-mile Lancashire Cycle Way (p558).

The Isle of Man has top-notch walking and cycling opportunities. Regional tourism websites contain walking and cycling information, and tourist offices stock free leaflets as well as maps and guides (usually £1 to £5) that cover walking, cycling and other activities.

Boating

The waterways of the northwest have been crucial to the region's development. You can explore some of its more important canals with **Wandering Duck** (www.wanderingduck. co.uk; 2-night trip per person incl meals from £145) in Manchester, while a boat trip across the Mersey is a Liverpool must-do.

ℹ️ Information

Visit north west (www.visitnorthwest.com) is the centralised tourist authority; for the Isle of Man check out **Isle of Man** (www.visitisleofman.com).

ℹ️ Getting Around

The towns and cities covered are all within easy reach of each other, and are well linked by public transport. The two main cities, Manchester and Liverpool, are only 34 miles apart and are linked by hourly bus and train services. Chester is 18 miles south of Liverpool, but is also easily accessible from Manchester by train or via the M56. Blackpool is 50 miles to the north of Manchester and Liverpool, and is also well connected on the M6.

MANCHESTER

POP 527,240

The weather tagline on Manchester radio station Key 103FM introduces the forecast for 'the greatest city in the world'. It's a ridiculous bit of local hyperbole, but behind the bluster Mancunians both native-born and imported are convinced they live in a pretty fabulous city. A rich blend of history and culture is on show in its museums, galleries and art centres, but what makes Manchester really fun is the swirl of hedonism that lets you dine, drink and dance yourself into happy oblivion.

The uncrowned capital of the north is also the driving force of the Northern Powerhouse, a government programme of investment and development that looks to corral northern England's 15 million people into a collective force to rival London and the southeast. As a result, the city centre looks like a construction site, with a host of new buildings rising up from streets that are being dug up so as to lay down miles of new tram line. The city of the future is being built today.

History

Canals and steam-powered cotton mills were what transformed Manchester from a small, disease-infested provincial town into a big, disease-infested industrial city. It all happened in the 1760s, with the opening of the Bridgewater Canal between Manchester and the coal mines at Worsley in 1763, and with Richard Arkwright patenting his super cotton mill in 1769. Thereafter Manchester and the world would never be the same again. When the canal was extended to Liverpool and the open sea in 1776, Manchester – dubbed 'Cottonopolis' – kicked into high gear and took off on the coal-fuelled, steam-powered gravy train.

There was plenty of gravy to go around, but the good burghers of 19th-century Manchester made sure that the vast majority of the city's swollen citizenry (with a population of 90,000 in 1801, and two million 100 years later) who produced most of it never got their hands on any of it. Their reward was life in a new kind of urban settlement: the industrial slum. Working conditions were dire, with impossibly long hours, child labour, work-related accidents and fatalities commonplace. Mark Twain commented that he would like to live here because the 'transition between Manchester and Death would be unnoticeable'. So much for Victorian values.

The wheels started to come off towards the end of the 19th century. The USA had begun to flex its own industrial muscles and was taking over a sizeable chunk of the textile trade; production in Manchester's mills began to slow, and then it stopped altogether. By WWII there was hardly enough cotton produced in the city to make a tablecloth. The postwar years weren't much better: 150,000 manufacturing jobs were lost between 1961 and 1983, and the port – still the UK's third largest in 1963 – finally closed

MANCHESTER IN ONE DAY

Start your exploration in the light-filled galleries of the **Manchester Art Gallery** (p533), home to one of the most important collections in the north. The **Museum of Science & Industry** (p533) will take up at least a couple of hours – more if you've got kids or you're a science geek. Alternatively, the **People's History Museum** (p533) is a fascinating exploration of social history. Lunch on Chinese food at **Tattu** (p539) or take your pick at **The Kitchens** (p538)

Hop on the tram to Salford Quays, where you can explore the **Imperial War Museum North** (p537) or take a guided tour of the norther headquarters of the **BBC** (p537); fans of Manchester United should take the tour of **Old Trafford** (p539), where they'll get to stand in the tunnel and pretend they're players. Make dinner reservations for **Manchester House** (p540).

After dinner, head to the Northern Quarter and have your choice of ale at the **Port Street Beer House** (p540) or a more musical pint at **The Castle Hotel** (p540); there's often a gig on at the attached venue, or you can head south towards Castlefield and take in a film or a play at the superb **HOME** (p541) arts centre.

in 1982 due to declining traffic. The nadir came on 15 June 1996, when an IRA bomb wrecked a chunk of the city centre, but the subsequent reconstruction proved to be the beginning of the glass-and-chrome revolution so much in evidence today.

⊙ Sights

⊙ City Centre

★ People's History Museum   MUSEUM
(☑ 0161-838 9190; www.phm.org.uk; Left Bank, Bridge St; ⊙ 10am-5pm) FREE The story of Britain's 200-year march to democracy is told in all its pain and pathos at this superb museum, housed in a refurbished Edwardian pumping station. You clock in on the 1st floor (literally: punch your card in an old mill clock, which managers would infamously fiddle with so as to make employees work longer) and plunge into the heart of Britain's struggle for basic democratic rights, labour reform and fair pay.

Amid displays like the (tiny) desk at which Thomas Paine (1737–1809) wrote *Rights of Man* (1791), and an array of beautifully made and colourful union banners, are compelling interactive displays, including a screen where you can trace the effects of all the events covered in the museum on five generations of the same family. The 2nd floor takes up the struggle for equal rights from WWII to the current day, touching on gay rights, antiracism initiatives and the defining British sociopolitical landmarks of the last 50 years, including the founding of the National Health Service (NHS), the Miners' Strike and the widespread protests against the Poll Tax.

★ Museum of Science & Industry   MUSEUM
(MOSI; ☑ 0161-832 2244; www.msimanchester.org.uk; Liverpool Rd; special exhibits £2.50-4; ⊙ 10am-5pm) FREE Manchester's rich industrial legacy is explored in this excellent museum set within the enormous grounds of the old Liverpool St Station, the oldest rail terminus in the world. The large collection of steam engines, locomotives and original factory machinery tell the story of the city from the sewers up, while a host of new technology (flight simulator, 4D cinema) look to the future. Take Metrolink to Deansgate-Castlefield or Metroshuttle No 2.

It's an all-ages kind of museum, but the emphasis is on making sure the young 'uns don't get bored – they could easily spend a whole day poking about, testing an early electric-shock machine here and trying out a printing press there. You can get up close and personal with fighter jets and get to grips with all kinds of space-age technology. In the Revolution Manchester Gallery a unique barcode activates a series of games and challenges that you can follow up on at home. A unifying theme is that Manchester and Mancunians had a key role to play: this is the place to discover that Manchester was home to the world's first stored-program computer (a giant contraption nicknamed 'baby') in 1948 and that the world's first submarine was built to the designs of local curate Reverend George Garrett in 1880.

★ Manchester Art Gallery   ART MUSEUM
(☑ 0161-235 8888; http://manchesterartgallery.org; Mosley St; tours 20min/1hr free/£80; ⊙ 10am-5pm

Manchester

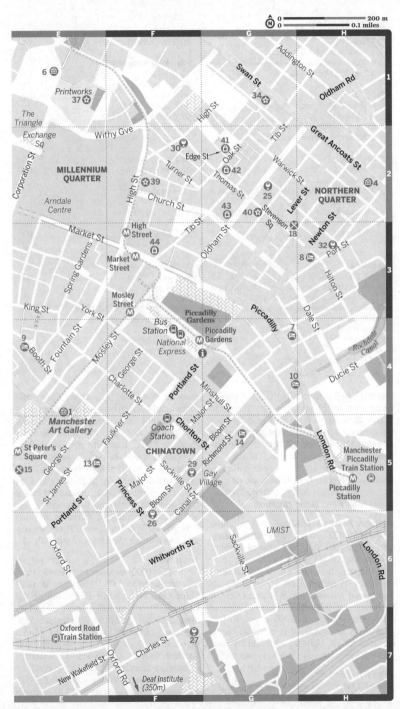

Manchester

◉ **Top Sights**
1 Manchester Art Gallery E4
2 Museum of Science & Industry A5
3 People's History Museum B3

◉ **Sights**
4 Greater Manchester Police
  Museum H2
5 John Rylands Library C4
6 National Football Museum E1

◉ **Sleeping**
7 ABode G4
8 Hatters H3
9 King Street Townhouse E4
10 Malmaison G4
11 Midland Hotel D5
12 Radisson Blu Edwardian C5
13 Roomzzz E5
14 Velvet Hotel G5

◉ **Eating**
15 Fumo E5
16 Manchester House B3
17 Mr Cooper's House & Garden D5
18 Rosylee Tearooms G3
19 San Carlo Cicchetti C3
20 Sculpture Hall Cafe D4
    Smoak Grill ....(see 10)
21 Tattu B4
    The French ....(see 11)

22 The Kitchens A4

◉ **Drinking & Nightlife**
23 Brewdog C5
24 Britons Protection C6
25 Castle Hotel G2
26 Club Alter Ego F6
27 Fac251 ....F7
28 Liar's Club C3
29 Molly House F5
30 Odd F2
31 Peveril of the Peak D6
32 Port Street Beer House H3

◉ **Entertainment**
33 AMC Cinemas C6
34 Band on the Wall G1
35 Bridgewater Hall D6
36 HOME D7
37 Odeon Cinema E1
38 Royal Exchange D2
39 Ruby Lounge F2
40 Soup Kitchen G2

◉ **Shopping**
41 Manchester Craft & Design
   Centre G2
42 Oi Polloi G2
43 Oxfam Originals G2
44 Tib Street Market F3

Mon-Wed & Fri-Sun, to 9pm Thu) **FREE** A superb collection of British art and a hefty number of European masters are on display at the city's top gallery. The older wing has an impressive selection that includes 37 Turner watercolours, as well as the country's best assemblage of Pre-Raphaelite art. The newer gallery is home to 20th-century British art starring Lucien Freud, Francis Bacon, Stanley Spencer, Henry Moore and David Hockney.

National Football Museum   MUSEUM
(☎0161-605 8200; www.nationalfootballmuseum. com; Corporation St, Urbis, Cathedral Gardens; ⊙10am-5pm) **FREE** This blockbuster museum charts the evolution of British football from its earliest days to the multi-billion-pound phenomenon it is today. One of the highlights is **Football Plus**, a series of interactive stations that allow you to test your skills in simulated conditions; buy a credit (2 for £5, eight for £10) and try your luck – it's recommended for kids over seven.

John Rylands Library   LIBRARY
(☎0161-306 0555; www.library.manchester.ac.uk/ rylands; 150 Deansgate; ⊙10am-5pm Tue-Sat,

noon-5pm Mon & Sun) **FREE** Less a library and more a cathedral to books, Basil Champneys' stunning building is a breathtaking example of Victorian Gothic, no more so than the Reading Room, complete with high-vaulted ceilings and stained-glass windows. The collection of early printed books and rare manuscripts is equally impressive, and includes a Gutenberg Bible, the earliest extant New Testament text and the country's second-largest assembly of works by Britain's first printer, William Caxton. There are regular tours; check the website for details.

Town Hall   HISTORIC BUILDING
(☎0161-234 5000; www.manchester.gov.uk; Albert Sq; clock-tower tour £9; ⊙9am-5pm Mon-Sat) Manchester's most impressive building is the Grade I–listed town hall, completed in 1877 after a design by Alfred Waterhouse. Visitors can go into the building, best explored by organised tour with either **Manchester Guided Tours** (☎07505-685 942; www.manchesterguidedtours.com; tours £8; ⊙11am) or **New Manchester Walks** (☎07769-298 068; www.newmanchesterwalks.com; £8-10); climb

the 85m-high tower and grab a bite in the beautiful Sculpture Hall cafe. Unfortunately, the grandest room of all, the Great Hall (decorated with murals by Ford Madox Ford) is open only for official business.

⊙ Salford Quays

Just west of the city centre lies Salford Quays, home to some of Manchester's big-ticket attractions and MediaCityUK, the northern hub of both the BBC and ITV. It is easily reached via Metrolink (£2.80). Check out www.mediacityuk.co.uk for more info.

Imperial War Museum North MUSEUM
(☑ 0161-836 4000; www.iwm.org.uk/north; Trafford Wharf Rd; ⊙10am-5pm) FREE Inside Daniel Libeskind's aluminum-clad architectural stunner is a war museum with a difference, exploring the effects of conflict on society rather than fetishising the instruments of destruction. Six mini exhibitions within the main hall examine war since the beginning of the 20th century from a variety of perspectives, including the role of women and the influence of science and technology. Catch the Metrolink to Harbour City or MediaCityUK.

MediaCityUK MEDIA CENTRE
(☑ 0161-886 5300; www.mediacityuk.co.uk; Salford Quays; adult/child £11/7.25; ⊙tours 10.30am, 12.30pm & 3pm Mon-Wed, Sat & Sun) The BBC's northern home is but one significant element of this vast, 81-hectare site. Besides hosting six departments of the national broadcaster (BBC Breakfast, Children's, Sport, Radio 5 Live, Learning, and Future Media & Technology), it is also home to the set of the world's longest-running soap opera, the perennially popular *Coronation Street* (which broadcasts on ITV). To get here take the Metrolink to MediaCityUK.

There are no plans as yet to offer tours of the Corrie set, but you can visit the BBC's impressive set-up and see the sets of some of TV's most iconic programs on a guided 90-minute tour that also includes a chance for kids to 'make' a program in an interactive studio; see www.bbc.co.uk/showsandtours. For refueling, there are plenty of cafes and restaurants in the area.

Lowry ARTS CENTRE
(☑ 0161-876 2020; www.thelowry.com; Pier 8, Salford Quays; ⊙11am-6pm Sun-Fri, 10am-8pm Sat) With multiple performance spaces, bars, restaurants and shops, this contemporary arts centre attracts more than a million visitors a year to its myriad functions, which include everthing from big-name theatrical productions to comedy, kids' theatre and even weddings. The centre is also home to 300 beautifully humanistic depictions of urban landscapes by LS Lowry (1887–1976), who was born in nearby Stretford, and after whom the complex is named. Get here by Metrolink to Harbour City or MediaCity UK.

🎊 Festivals & Events

Screenings at the Garden Leftbank FILM
(www.spinningfieldsonline.com; The Garden, Irwell Sq, Spinningfields; ⊙5.30pm Thu May-Jul) FREE Summer season of outdoor films, complete with deckchairs, beginning in May. Grab some food from The Kitchens and enjoy the show.

Manchester International Festival ART
(☑ 0161-238 7300; www.mif.co.uk) A three-week-long biennial arts festival of artist-led new work across visual arts, performance and popular culture. The next festival is scheduled for July 2017.

Manchester Food & Drink Festival FOOD & DRINK
(www.foodanddrinkfestival.com; ⊙mid-Oct) Manchester's superb foodie scene shows off its wares over 10 days in mid-October. Farmers markets, pop-up restaurants and gourmet events are just part of the UK's biggest urban food fest.

🛏 Sleeping

★Manchester YHA HOSTEL $
(☑ 0845 371 9647; www.yha.org.uk; Potato Wharf; dm/d from £10/80; ☝@☂) This purpose-built canalside hostel in the Castlefield area is one of the best in the country. It's a top-class option with four- and six-bed dorms, all with bathroom, as well as three doubles and a host of good facilities. Potato Wharf is just left off Liverpool Rd.

Hatters HOSTEL $
(☑ 0161-236 9500; http://hattershostels.com; 50 Newton St; dm/s/d from £16/35/50; ☝@☂) The old-style lift and porcelain sinks are the only leftovers of this former milliner's factory, now one of the best hostels in town. The location is a boon: smack in the heart of the Northern Quarter, you won't have to go far to get the best of alternative Manchester.

ABode HOTEL $$

(📞0161-247 7744; www.abodemanchester.co.uk; 107 Piccadilly St; r from £100; ❄@🛜) The original fittings at this converted textile factory have been combined successfully with 61 bedrooms divided into four categories of ever-increasing luxury: Comfortable, Desirable, Enviable and Fabulous on Fifth, the latter being five seriously swanky top-floor suites.

Midland Hotel HOTEL $$

(📞0161-236 3333; www.qhotels.co.uk; 16 Peter St; r from £100; ❄@🛜) This newly refurbished Grade II–listed Edwardian hotel is back to its elegant best. Its 312 rooms are all elegantly appointed: the junior suites have a separate lounge while the seven Midland suites once entertained royalty. Downstairs, Simon Rogan's The French (p540) and **Mr Cooper's House & Garden** (www.mrcoopershouseandgarden.co.uk; Midland Hotel, 16 Peter St; mains £15-25; ⏰noon-2pm & 5-10pm Mon-Thu, noon-2.30pm & 5-10pm Fri-Sat, 1-8pm Sun) restaurants are among the best in the city.

Roomzzz APARTMENT $$

(📞0161-236 2121; www.roomzzz.co.uk; 36 Princess St; r from £99; ❄@🛜) The inelegant name belies the designer digs inside this beautifully restored Grade II building, which features serviced apartments equipped with a kitchen and the latest connectivity gadgetry, including sleek iMac computers and free wifi throughout. There's a small pantry, with food for sale downstairs. Highly recommended if you're planning a longer stay.

Malmaison HOTEL $$

(📞0161-278 1000; www.malmaison.com; Piccadilly St; r from £105; ❄@🛜) Drop-dead trendy and full of red crushed velvet, deep purples, art deco ironwork and signature black-and-white tiles, Malmaison Manchester follows the chain's quirky design style and passion for cool, although rarely at the expense of comfort: the rooms are terrific. The **Smoak Grill** (📞0161-278 1000; Piccadilly St; mains £14-26, steaks £25-45) downstairs is hugely popular.

Radisson Blu Edwardian HOTEL $$

(📞0161-835 9929; www.radissonblu-edwardian.com/manchester; Peter St; r from £100; P@🛜) Gladstone, Dickens and Fitzgerald...just some of the names associated with the historic Free Trade Hall, now an elegant business hotel with high-end trimmings and decor. It has done its best to preserve the memories of the building's most famous visitors: suites are named after Bob Dylan and Shirley Bas-

sey, while meeting rooms carry the names of Disraeli, Thackeray and Pankhurst.

⭐**King Street Townhouse** BOUTIQUE HOTEL $$$

(📞0161-667 0707; www.eclectichotels.co.uk; 10 Booth St; r/ste from £210/£350; ❄@🛜🏊) Arguably the city centre's finest lodgings is in this beautiful 1872 Italian Renaissance-style former bank, now an exquisite boutique hotel with 40 bedrooms ranging from snug to suite. Furnishings are the perfect combination of period elegance and contemporary style. On the top floor is a small spa with an infinity pool overlooking the town hall; downstairs is a nice bar and restaurant.

Velvet Hotel BOUTIQUE HOTEL $$$

(📞0161-236 9003; www.velvetmanchester.com; 2 Canal St; r from £115; 🛜) Nineteen beautiful bespoke rooms each oozing style: there's the sleigh bed in room 24, the double bath of room 34, the saucy framed photographs of a stripped-down David Beckham (this is Gay Village, after all!). Despite the tantalising decor and location, this is not an exclusive hotel and is as popular with straight visitors as it is with the same-sex crowd.

🍴 Eating

Manchester's choice of restaurants is second only to London. Spinningfields, just off Deansgate, has some of the most interesting spots in the centre while the Northern Quarter is great for offbeat cafes and organic eats.

Sculpture Hall Cafe CAFE $

(Town Hall, Albert Sq; mains £3.95-6.95, afternoon tea £12.50; ⏰8am-4pm Mon-Fri, 10am-4pm Sat & Sun) The lovely cafe in the town hall has sandwiches, salads, traditional Lancashire hotpots (a kind of stew topped with sliced potatoes) as well as afternoon tea, which comes with savoury and sweet treats like potted Yorkshire ham rillette and Manchester sponge cake. The champagne version costs £19.95.

The Kitchens INTERNATIONAL $

(http://thekitchensleftbank.com; Irwell Sq; mains £4-12; ⏰noon-3pm Mon-Wed, to 9pm Thu-Sun, Bangers & Bacon 7am-midnight Mon-Fri, from 9.30am Sat & Sun) Gathered under the one roof are a number of 'street food' producers including Bangers and Bacon (@bangersandbacon), Chaat Cart (Indian street food; @chaatcart), the Hip Hop Chip Shop (@thehiphopchippy), Dim Sum Su (@dimsumsu) and Well Hung (@wellhungkitchen), which serves 28-day aged steaks and sandwiches. They're all terrific: check the Twitter handles for updates.

MANCHESTER'S FOOTBALL SIDES

If modern football is made up of equal parts spectacle, soap opera and sporting drama, then Manchester has the ingredients to offer the greatest show on earth. Home to two of the world's best-known clubs, in 2016 the city welcomed the world's most famous managers: the 'Chosen One', José Mourinho has taken over at United, while Josep 'Pep' Guardiola has lent his stylish and successful brand of football to City. They're both enormously successful, and their very presence will draw some of the best talent in the world, but what will really attract the world's attention is the intensity of their rivalry, which became acrimonious when Mourinho was in charge of Real Madrid and Guardiola of Barcelona. Let the show begin...

Old Trafford (Manchester United Museum & Tour) (☑0161-868 8000; www.manutd. com; Sir Matt Busby Way; tours adult/child £18/12; ☺museum 9.30am-5pm, tours every 10min 9.40am-4.30pm except match days) You don't have to be a fan of the world's most famous football club to enjoy a visit to their impressive 75,000-plus capacity stadium, but it helps. The museum tour includes a walk down the tunnel onto the edge of the playing surface of the 'Theatre of Dreams', where Manchester United's superstar footballers exercised their Premier League supremacy for 20 years, guided by the peerless Sir Alex Ferguson. To reach here take the Metrolink to Old Trafford.

Other highlights of the excellent tour include a seat in the stands, a stop in the changing rooms and a peek at the players' lounge (from which the manager is banned unless invited by the players) – all ecstatic experiences for a Man United devotee. The museum has a comprehensive history of the club and a state-of-the-art call-up system that means you can view your favourite goals.

Etihad Stadium Tour (☑0161-444 1894; www.mcfc.co.uk; Etihad Campus; tours adult/child £17/11; ☺9am-5pm Mon-Sat, 10am-4pm Sun except match days) On this 70-minute tour of Manchester City's home ground you'll visit the players' dressing room, lounge and warm-up room; sit in the manager's seat in the dugout; get a bird's-eye view from the directors' box; and stand in the tunnel with the (recorded) roar of 55,000 fans in your ears. There's also a small museum and the inevitable steer into the kit shop. To reach here catch Metrolink to Etihad Campus.

MANCHESTER, LIVERPOOL & NORTHWEST ENGLAND MANCHESTER

★ **Rosylee Tearooms** CAFE **$$**
(www.rosylee.com; 11 Stevenson Sq; mains £10-12, 2-/3-course menu £11.95/14.95; ☺noon-9pm Mon-Thu, 10am-10pm Fri-Sat, 10am-6pm Sun) A touch of Edwardian and Georgian elegance in the heart of the Northern Quarter, this gorgeous tearooms has expanded its menu to offer a range of British classics like beer-battered haddock and chips and steak suet pudding. The afternoon tea (£18.25 or £25.25 if you want a glass of bubbles) is superb.

San Carlo Cicchetti ITALIAN **$$**
(www.sancarlocicchetti.co.uk; King St W, House of Fraser; small plates £6.95-8.95; ☺8am-11pm Mon-Fri, from 9am Sat, 9am-10pm Sun) Celebrity chef Aldo Zilli has designed the superlative menu at this ornate Italian restaurant on the ground floor of House of Fraser. Instead of big plates of carb overload, though, you get smaller dishes known as *cicchetti*. The truffle and pecorino ravioli are divine. It also serves more standard egg dishes for breakfast.

Tattu CHINESE **$$**
(☑0161-819 2060; www.tattu.co.uk; Gartside St, 3 Hardman Sq, Spinningfields; mains £14-27; ☺noon-3pm & 5-10.45pm Mon-Thu, noon-10.45pm Fri-Sun) One of the most beautiful restaurants in town is this newish and supremely elegant Chinese spot in Spinningfields. From the nautical-themed downstairs bar (dark-wood booths, hanging anchors) to the upstairs deck, where you can dine beneath a cherry tree, the decor is as stylish as the food is tasty; we loved the saffron miso black cod.

Fumo ITALIAN **$$**
(www.sancarlofumo.co.uk; 1 St Peter's Sq; dishes £4.50-7.95; ☺noon-11pm Mon-Sat, to 10pm Sun) This glass-fronted restaurant specialises in Venetian-style tapas known as *cicchetti* – you can take your pick from a broad-ranging menu that includes a variety of carpaccios, pasta, meats and even minipizzas. It's part of the same group that run the equally good San Carlo Cicchetti on the ground floor of House of Fraser.

LOCAL KNOWLEDGE

GREATER MANCHESTER POLICE MUSEUM

One of the city's best-kept secrets is the superb **Greater Manchester Police Museum** (www.gmpmuseum. co.uk; 57a Newton St; ⊙10.30am-3.30pm Tue) housed within a former Victorian police station. The original building has been magnificently – if a little creepily – brought back to life, and you can wander in and out of 19th-century cells where prisoners rested their heads on wooden pillows; visit a restored magistrates' court from 1895 and examine the case histories (complete with mugshots and photos of weapons) of some of the more notorious names to have passed through its doors.

★**Manchester House** MODERN BRITISH $$$
(www.manchesterhouse.uk.com; Tower 12, 18-22 Bridge St; mains £37, 10-/14-course tasting menu £70/95;) This much-praised restaurant atop a nondescript '60s-era tower serves molecular cuisine, but with a Manchester twist. Chef Aiden Byrne offers a simplified version of Blumenthal and Adriá, but without sacrificing any of the taste: the constantly changing menu (including exclusively veggie) is simply exceptional and this is one of the best places to eat in the northwest. Reservations are essential.

The French MODERN BRITISH $$$
(☑0161-932 4198; www.the-french.co.uk; Midland Hotel, 16 Peter St; 6-/10-course menu £65/85; ⊙noon-1.30pm & 6.30-9.30pm) The revamped restaurant of the Midland Hotel (where Rolls met Royce to make motoring history) is now home to Simon Rogan's exquisite Modern British cuisine, which uses exclusively local produce grown on his farm in Cartmel, Cumbria, home to his Michelin-starred L'Enclume restaurant. The 10-course tasting menu (not available lunchtime Wednesday to Friday) is a feast you won't soon forget.

Drinking & Nightlife

★**Port Street Beer House** CRAFT BEER
(39-41 Port St; ⊙4pm-midnight) Fans of real ale love this Northern Quarter boozer with its seven hand pulls, 18 draught lines and more than 100 beers from around the world, including gluten-free ales and some heavy hit-

ters: Brewdog's Tactical Nuclear Penguin is a 32% stout but at £45 a bottle you won't need more than one. It hosts regular tastings and tap takeovers.

★**Sankey's** CLUB
(☑0161-950 4201; www.sankeys.info; Radium St, Ancoats; admission free-£6; ⊙10.30pm-5am Fri & Sat) If you're a fan of techno, electro or any kind of nonmainstream house music, then a pilgrimage to Sankeys – where The Chemical Brothers, Daft Punk and others got their start – should on no account be missed. Its commitment to top-class music is unwavering, with world-renowned DJs mixing it up with residents. One of the best clubs in Britain.

Castle Hotel PUB
(66 Oldham St; ⊙noon-1am Sun-Thu, to 2am Fri-Sat) Old-fashioned boozer founded in 1776 with a strong musical heritage: John Peel interviewed Joy Division's Ian Curtis here in 1979 and some of its fine selection of ales – Build a Rocket Boys, Trooper – are named after songs by local band Elbow. There's a small music venue attached that hosts regular gigs.

Brewdog BAR
(35 Peter St; ⊙noon-1am Mon-Sat, to midnight Sun) The Manchester branch of this bolshie Scottish brewery ('we brew hardcore beer for punks' is their tagline) has all of the beers that have made it such a huge hit across the country – 5am Red Ale, Brixton Porter and Dead Pony Pale Ale – as well as some stronger IPAs from its Amplified range.

Britons Protection PUB
(☑0161-236 5895; 50 Great Bridgewater St; ⊙noon-midnight Mon-Thu, to 1am Fri & Sat, to 11pm Sun) Whisky – over 300 different kinds of it (the Cu Dhub 'black whisky' is a particular treat with its touch of coffee and honey) – is the beverage of choice at this liver-threatening, proper English pub that also does homestyle meals (gammon, pies etc). An old-fashioned boozer with open fires in the back rooms and a cosy atmosphere...perfect on a cold evening.

Liar's Club BAR
(www.theliarsclub.co.uk; 19a Back Bridge St; ⊙5pm-4am Mon-Sat, to 3am Sun; ⊛) A basement bar designed in the style of a speakeasy/tiki lounge, the Liar's Club serves strong cocktails to an assorted clientele of revellers, students and off-duty bar staff. A great atmosphere any night of the week.

Odd BAR

(☑0161-833 0070; www.oddbar.co.uk; 30-32 Thomas St; ☉11am-midnight Sun-Wed, to 1am Thu, to 2am Fri & Sat) This eclectic little bar – with its oddball furnishings, wacky tunes and anti-establishment crew of customers – is the perfect antidote to the increasingly similar look of so many modern bars. A slice of Mancuniana to be treasured.

Fac251 CLUB

(☑0161-272 7251; www.factorymanchester.com; 112-118 Princess St; admission £1-6; ☉11pm-4am Mon-Sat) Located in Tony Wilson's former Factory Records HQ, Fac251 is one of the most popular venues in town. There are three rooms, all with a broad musical appeal, from drum and bass to Motown and indie rock. Something for everybody, from Monday's Quids In (for students) to the Big Weekender on Saturday (commercial R & B).

☆ Entertainment

★HOME ARTS CENTRE

(☑0161-200 1500; http://homemcr.org; 2 Tony Wilson Pl, First St; tickets £5-20; ☉box office noon-8pm; bar 10am-11pm Mon-Thu & Sun, to midnight Fri-Sat) One of Britain's best new arts centres, Home has two theatre spaces that host provocative new work in a variety of contexts, from proscenium sets to promenade pieces. The five cinema screens show the latest indie releases as well as classics. There's also a ground-floor bar and a cafe on the first floor.

Cinemas

AMC Cinemas CINEMA

(www.amccinemas.co.uk; The Great Northern, 235 Deansgate; ☉noon-11pm) A 16-screen multiplex in a retail centre that was formerly a goods warehouse for the Northern Railway Company.

Odeon Cinema CINEMA

(www.odeon.co.uk; The Printworks, Exchange Sq; ☉noon-11pm) A 20-screen complex in the middle of the Printworks centre.

Classical Music

Bridgewater Hall CONCERT VENUE

(☑0161-907 9000; www.bridgewater-hall.co.uk; Lower Mosley St) The world-renowned Hallé Orchestra has its home at this enormous and impressive concert hall, which hosts up to 250 concerts and events a year. It has a widespread program that includes opera, folk music, children's shows, comedy and contemporary music.

Cricket

Lancashire County Cricket Club CRICKET

(☑0161-282 4000; www.lccc.co.uk; Warwick Rd; tickets £15, test matches £40; 🚇Old Trafford) The genteel game of cricket is a big deal here and the biggest game of Lancashire's season is the Roses match against Yorkshire. They – and their limited overs team, the Lancashire Lightning – play their matches at Old Trafford (same name, different but adjacent ground to the football stadium), where international test matches are also played occasionally.

GAY & LESBIAN MANCHESTER

The city's gay scene is unrivalled outside London and caters to every taste. Its healthy heart beats loudest in the Gay Village, centred on handsome Canal St. Here you'll find bars, clubs, restaurants and – crucially – karaoke joints that cater almost exclusively to the pink pound.

Big Weekend (☑0161-831 7700; www.manchesterpride.com; ☉Aug) One of the UK's biggest Pride festivals, attracting in excess of 500,000 people over the August Bank Holiday at the end of the month.

Molly House (www.themollyhouse.com; 26 Richmond St; ☉noon-midnight Mon & Tue, to 1am Wed, Thu & Sun, to 2am Fri & Sat) You won't go far wrong in this bar, which has terrific ales, a fine tapas menu and a door policy that encourages relaxed contemplation over adrenalin-charged debauchery.

Club Alter Ego (105-107 Princess St; ☉11pm-5am Thu-Sat) Look no further for your clubbing needs.

For more information, check with the **Lesbian & Gay Foundation** (☑0161-235 8035; http://lgbt.foundation; 5 Richmond St; ☉4-10pm). Up-to-date information is also available at www.visitmanchester.com under LGBT.

Live Music

Soup Kitchen
LIVE MUSIC

(http://soup-kitchen.co.uk; 31-33 Spear St; £3-5; ☉noon-11pm Mon-Wed & Sun, to 1am Thu, to 4am Fri & Sat) By day a typical Northern Quarter canteen-style cafe, but at night this is one of the city's best places to catch live music, with a full schedule of gigs by all kinds of indie acts passing through town. When the bands are done, the excellent DJs kick in and it often goes until 6am.

Deaf Institute
LIVE MUSIC

(www.thedeafinstitute.co.uk; 135 Grosvenor St; ☉10am-midnight) Excellent midsized venue in a former institute for the deaf; also includes a smaller venue in the basement and a cafe on the ground floor. It's where you'll hear alt rock and pop by dozens of local bands we guarantee you've never heard of (as well as some visiting bands you may have).

Ruby Lounge
LIVE MUSIC

(☑0161-834 1392; www.therubylounge.com; 28-34 High St; tickets around £8; ☉noon-midnight, clubs 11pm-3am) Terrific live-music venue in the Northern Quarter that features mostly rock bands. It gets very loud. After the bands there's usually a club night that runs until late.

Band on the Wall
LIVE MUSIC

(☑0161-834 1786; www.bandonthewall.org; 25 Swan St; ☉5-11pm) A top-notch venue that hosts everything from rock to world music, with splashes of jazz, blues and folk thrown in.

Theatre

Royal Exchange
THEATRE

(☑0161-833 9833; www.royalexchange.co.uk; St Anne's Sq) Interesting contemporary plays are standard at this magnificent, modern theatre-in-the-round.

🛍 Shopping

King St, with its 14 listed buildings, is Manchester's most elegant shopping street, lined with high-end boutiques and independent retailers. The Northern Quarter is all about boho indie styles, while Spinningfields has a handful of swanky shops. Market St and the Arndale Centre are where you'll find the mainstay of the city's high-street shopping.

Manchester Craft
& Design Centre
ARTS & CRAFTS

(www.craftanddesign.com; 17 Oak St; ☉10am-5.30pm Mon-Sat, 11am-5pm Sun) This award-winning centre (in a building dating from 1873) stocks jewellery, ceramics, bags and furnishings all handmade by local designers. There's also a cafe on the premises.

Oi Polloi
CLOTHING

(www.oipolloi.com; 63 Thomas St; ☉10am-6pm Mon-Sat) Besides the impressive range of casual footwear, this hip boutique also stocks a range of designers including A Kind of Guise, LA Panoplie, Nudie Jeans Co and Fjällräven.

Oxfam Originals
VINTAGE

(Unit 8, Smithfield Bldg, Oldham St; ☉10am-6pm Mon-Sat, noon-5pm Sun) If you're into retro, this terrific store has high-quality gear from the 1960s and '70s. Shop in the knowledge that it's for a good cause.

Tib Street Market
MARKET

(☑0161-234 7357; Tib St; ☉10am-5pm Sat) Up-and-coming local designers get a chance to display their wares at this weekly market where you can pick up everything from purses to lingerie and hats to jewellery.

ℹ Information

Cameolord Chemist (St Peter's Sq; ☉8am-midnight)

Manchester Royal Infirmary (Oxford Rd; ☉24hr)

Post Office (Town Hall Annexe, Albert Sq; ☉9am-6pm Mon-Fri)

Visitor Information Centre (www.visitmanchester.com; 1 Piccadilly Gardens; guided tours daily £8; ☉10am-5.15pm Mon-Sat, to 4.30pm Sun)

ℹ Getting There & Away

AIR

Manchester Airport (☑0161-489 3000; www.manchesterairport.co.uk) The airport is 12 miles south of the city.

Bus (30 minutes, £4.10) Every 20 minutes to Manchester **Coach Station** (Chorlton St)

Metrolink (40 minutes, £4.20) Every 12 minutes; change at Cornbrook or Firswood for city centre.**Taxi** (25 to 40 minutes, £20 to £30)

Train (20 minutes, £5) Every 10 minutes to Piccadilly Station.

BUS

National Express (☑08717 81 81 81; www.nationalexpress.com) serves most major cities from the **coach station** (p542), including the following:

Leeds (£4, one hour, hourly)

Liverpool (£6.50, 1½ hours, hourly)

London (£20.70, 4¼ hours, hourly)

TRAIN

Manchester Piccadilly (east of Piccadilly Gardens) is the main station for most mainline train services across Britain; Victoria Station (north of the National Football Museum) serves destinations in the northwest including Blackburn, Halifax and Huddersfield but also Leeds and Liverpool. The two stations are linked by Metrolink. Off-peak fares are considerably cheaper. Destinations include the following:

Blackpool (£16.90, 1¼ hours, half-hourly)

Liverpool Lime St (£9.20, 45 minutes, half-hourly)

London Euston (£110, three hours, seven daily)

Newcastle (£64.90, three hours, six daily)

ℹ Getting Around

The excellent public transport system can be used with a variety of Day Saver tickets. For enquiries about local transport, including night buses, contact**Travelshop** (☑ 0161-228 7811; www.tfgm.com; 1 Piccadilly Gardens; ☉ 7am-6pm Mon-Sat, 10am-6pm Sun).

BUS

The Metroshuttle is a free service with three separate routes around the heart of Manchester every 10 minutes. Pick up a map from the tourist office. Most local buses start from **Piccadilly Gardens**.

METROLINK

The Metrolink (www.metrolink.co.uk) light-rail network is the best way to get between Victoria and Piccadilly train stations (and the G-Mex for Castlefield), as well as further afield to Salford Quays, Didsbury and other suburbs. It also serves the airport, but you need to change at either Cornbrook or Firswood. Trams run every few minutes throughout the day from 6am to 11pm. Buy your tickets from the platform machine.

TRAIN

Castlefield is served by Deansgate station with suburban rail links to Piccadilly, Oxford Rd and Salford stations.

CHESTER

POP 79,645

With a red-sandstone, Roman-era wall wrapped around a tidy collection of Tudor- and Victorian-era buildings, Chester is one of English history's greatest gifts to the contemporary visitor. The walls were built when this was Castra Devana, the largest Roman fortress in Britain.

Beyond the cruciform-shaped historic centre, Chester is an ordinary, residential town; it's hard to believe today, but throughout the Middle Ages Chester made its money as the most important port in the northwest. However, the River Dee silted up over time and Chester fell behind Liverpool in importance.

◉ Sights

★ City Walls   LANDMARK

A good way to get a sense of Chester's unique character is to walk the 2-mile circuit along the walls that surround the historic centre. Originally built by the Romans around AD 70, the walls were altered substantially over the following centuries but have retained their current position since around 1200. The tourist office's *Walk Around Chester Walls* leaflet is an excellent guide and you can also take a 90-minute guided walk.

Of the many features along the walls, the most eye-catching is the prominent **Eastgate**, where you can see the most famous clock in England after London's Big Ben, built for Queen Victoria's Diamond Jubilee in 1897.

At the southeastern corner of the walls are the **wishing steps**, added in 1785. Local legend claims that if you can run up and down these uneven steps while holding your breath your wish will come true.

Just inside Southgate, known here as **Bridgegate** (as it's located at the northern end of the Old Dee Bridge), is the **Bear & Billet** (www.bearandbillet.com; 94 Lower Bridge St; ☉ noon-11.30pm) pub, Chester's oldest timber-framed building, built in 1664, and once a toll gate into the city.

★ Rows   ARCHITECTURE

Besides the City Walls, Chester's other great draw is the Rows, a series of two-level galleried arcades along the four streets that fan out in each direction from the **Central Cross**. The architecture is a handsome mix of Victorian and Tudor (original and mock) buildings that house a fantastic collection of individually owned shops.

Chester Cathedral   CATHEDRAL

(☑ 01244-324756; www.chestercathedral.com; 12 Abbey Sq; ☉ 9am-6pm Mon-Sat, 11am-4pm Sun) **FREE** Originally a Benedictine abbey built on the remains of an earlier Saxon church dedicated to St Werburgh (the city's patron saint), it was shut down in 1540 as part of Henry VIII's dissolution frenzy, but reconsecrated as a cathedral the following year. Despite a substantial Victorian facelift,

Chester

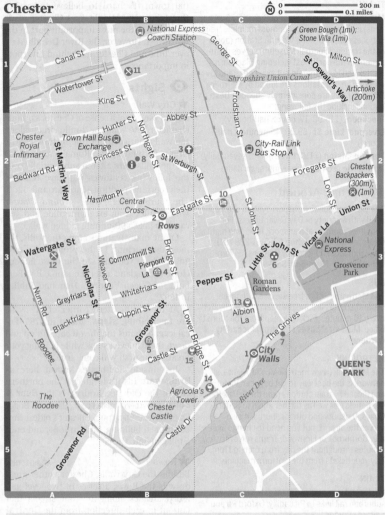

Chester

◎ Top Sights
1 City Walls	C4
2 Rows	B3

◎ Sights
3 Chester Cathedral	B2
4 Dewa Roman Experience	B3
5 Grosvenor Museum	B4
6 Roman Amphitheatre	C3

◎ Activities, Courses & Tours
Cathedral Tours	(see 3)
7 Chester Boat	C4
8 Chester Tour	B2

◎ Sleeping
9 ABode Chester	A4
10 Chester Grosvenor Hotel & Spa	C2

◎ Eating
11 Joseph Benjamin	B1
12 Mockingbird Taproom	A3
Simon Radley at the Grosvenor	(see 10)

◎ Drinking & Nightlife
13 Albion	C3
14 Bear & Billet	C4
15 Brewery Tap	B4

the cathedral retains much of its original 12th-century structure. You can amble about freely, but the **tours** (adult/child 1hr tour £8/6, 30min tour £6; ☺1hr tour 11am & 3pm daily, 30min tour 12.30pm & 1.15pm Mon-Tue, also 2pm & 4pm Wed-Sat) are excellent, as they bring you to to the top of the panoramic bell tower.

Grosvenor Museum MUSEUM
(📞01244-972197; www.grosvenormuseum.co.uk; 27 Grosvenor St; ☺10.30am-5pm Mon-Sat, 1-4pm Sun) **FREE** Excellent museum with the country's most comprehensive collection of Roman tombstones. At the back of the museum is a preserved Georgian house, complete with kitchen, drawing room, bedroom and bathroom.

Dewa Roman Experience MUSEUM
(📞01244-343407; www.dewaromanexperience.co.uk; Pierpoint Lane; adult/child £5.50/3.95; ☺9am-5pm Mon-Sat, 10am-5pm Sun Feb-Nov, 10am-4pm Dec-Jan) What was life like in Roman times? Begin your journey in the hold of a galley ship, where Grapus the Oars Master talks about the dangers of life at the edge of the known world. You then walk down a reconstructed Roman street lined with a granary, barracks, bathhouse and tavern – all built to serve the needs of the 20th Legion.

Roman Amphitheatre ARCHAEOLOGICAL SITE
(Little St John St) **FREE** Just outside the city walls is what was once an arena that seated 7000 spectators (making it the country's largest); some historians have suggested that it may have also been the site of King Arthur's Camelot and that his knights' 'round table' was really just this circular construction. Excavations continue; during summer months there are occasional shows held here.

Blue Planet Aquarium AQUARIUM
(www.blueplanetaquarium.com; adult/child £17/12.25; ☺10am-5pm Mon-Fri, to 6pm Sat & Sun) Things aren't done by halves around Chester, where you'll find the country's largest aquarium, Blue Planet. It's home to 10 different kinds of shark, which can be viewed from a 70m-long moving walkway that lets you eye them up close. The aquarium is 9 miles north of Chester at junction 10 of the M53 to Liverpool. Buses 1 and 4 run there every half-hour from Chester Town Hall Bus Exchange.

Tours

Chester Tour WALKING TOUR
(www.chestertours.org.uk; Northgate St, Town Hall Visitor Information Centre; adult/concession £7/6) Ninety-minute guided walking tours covering various aspects of the city's history, including the Chester Tour (10.30am and 2pm daily), and a handful of seasonal walks that run from Easter to the end of October. Recommended are the Walls Walk (11.30am Wednesday and Saturday) and the Rows Revealed (11.30am Monday and Thursday), which includes finding a 16th-century priest hole hidden behind a fireplace. The tours depart from the town hall.

Chester Boat BOAT TOUR
(📞01244-325394; www.chesterboat.co.uk; Boating Station, Souters La, The Groves; tours £6.50-20) Runs 30-minute and two hour-long cruises up and down the Dee, including a foray into the gorgeous Eaton Estate, home of the duke and duchess of Westminster. All departures are from the riverside along the promenade known as the Groves.

🛏 Sleeping

Chester Backpackers HOSTEL $
(📞01244-400185; www.chesterbackpackers.co.uk; 67 Boughton; dm/s/d from £16/22/34; ☏) Comfortable dorm rooms with nice pine beds in a typically Tudor white-and-black building. It's just a short walk from the city walls and there's also a pleasant garden.

★Stone Villa B&B $$
(📞01244-345014; www.stonevillachester.co.uk; 3 Stone Pl, Hoole Rd; s/d from £60/85; P☏; ☐9) This award-winning, beautiful 1850 villa has everything you need for a memorable stay. Elegant bedrooms, a fabulous breakfast and welcoming, friendly owners all add up to one of the best lodgings in town. The property is about a mile from the city centre.

ABode Chester HOTEL $$
(📞01244-347000; www.abodechester.co.uk; Grosvenor Rd; r from £100; P❀☏) Contemporary hotel with 84 rooms all equipped with handcrafted Vispring beds and handsome bathrooms complete with monsoon showers. Good toiletries, flatscreen TVs and cashmere throws on the bed give it a touch of elegance. The 5th-floor restaurant bore TV chef Michael Caines' name until December 2015, but though he's no longer involved it is still an excellent dining choice.

★ **Chester Grosvenor**
Hotel & Spa   HOTEL $$$
(☑ 01244-324024; www.chestergrosvenor.com; 58 Eastgate St; r from £195; P@☎) The black-and-white timbered Grosvenor is the city's top hotel by location – right next to the Eastgate Clock – and quality, offering a five-star experience throughout. The lobby's main feature is the chandelier, with 28,000 pieces of crystal; move on from there to the huge rooms with exquisite period furniture. There's also a top spa (open to nonguests) and a Michelin-starred restaurant, Simon Radley at the Grosvenor.

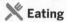 **Eating**

Mockingbird Taproom   CAJUN $$
(www.mockingbirdtaproom.co.uk; 85 Watergate St; mains £10-15; ⊙ noon-10pm Mon-Wed, to 1am Thu-Fri, 10am-1am Sat, to 11pm Sun) If you like your food with a kick, then the menu at this Cajun-inspired place is for you. Burgers, crawfish, oysters, ribs and a selection of burritos, nachos and fajitas all come with a choose-your-own level of spiciness, but we went for a mean-lookin' gumbo, Lucifer Licked: chicken, sweet potato and spicy sausage – finished with the Taproom's own 'Howling at the Moon' sauce. Hot.

Artichoke   MODERN BRITISH $$
(www.artichokechester.co.uk; The Steam Mill, Steam Mill St; mains £13-17; ⊙ 10am-3.30pm & 5-10pm Mon-Sat, 10am-8pm Sun) One of a number of warehouse conversions along the Shropshire Union Canal (now known as the Canal Quarter), this cafe-bar serves sandwiches and smaller bites as well as tasty main courses like sea trout in a sweet pea wasabi velvet cream, and confit of duck legs with Jersey potatoes, pancetta and red cabbage. It's a popular drinking spot too.

Joseph Benjamin   MODERN BRITISH $$
(☑ 01244-344295; www.josephbenjamin.co.uk; 140 Northgate St; ⊙ noon-3pm Tue-Sat, also 6-9.30pm Thu-Sat & noon-4pm Sun) A bright star in Chester's culinary firmament is this combo restaurant, bar and deli that delivers carefully prepared local produce to take out or eat in. Excellent sandwiches and gorgeous salads are the mainstay of the takeaway menu, while the more formal dinner menu features fine examples of modern British cuisine.

★ **Simon Radley**
at the Grosvenor   MODERN BRITISH $$$
(☑ 01244-324024; www.chestergrosvenor.com; 58 Eastgate St, Chester Grosvenor Hotel; tasting menu £99, à la carte menu £75; ⊙ 6.30-9pm Tue-Sat) Simon Radley's formal restaurant (you're instructed to arrive 30 minutes early for drinks and canapés) has served near-perfect Modern British cuisine since 1990, when it was first awarded the Michelin star that it has kept ever since. The food is divine and the wine list extensive. One of Britain's best, but why no second star? Smart attire, no children under 12.

 Drinking & Nightlife

Brewery Tap   PUB
(www.the-tap.co.uk; 52-54 Lower Bridge St; ⊙ noon-11pm, to 10.30pm Sun) If you're looking for the best pint in the city, the aficionados at the Campaign for Real Ale (CAMRA) reckon you'll get it at this boozer in a Grade II–listed Jacobean banqueting hall; its seven taps offer a rotating range of quality brews from all over England.

Albion   PUB
(www.albioninnchester.co.uk; Park St; ⊙ noon-11pm) No children, no music and no machines or big screens (but plenty of Union Jacks). This 'family hostile' Edwardian classic pub is a throwback to a time when ale-drinking still had its own rituals. Still, this is one of the finest pubs in northwest England precisely because it doggedly refuses to modernise.

❶ **Information**

Tourist Office (☑ 01244-402111; www.visitchester.com; Town Hall, Northgate St; ⊙ 9am-5.30pm Mon-Sat, 10am-5pm Sun Mar-Oct, 9.30am-4.30pm Mon-Fri, 9am-4pm Sat, 10am-4pm Sun Nov-Feb)

❶ **Getting There & Around**

BUS
Local buses leave from the **Town Hall Bus Exchange** (Princess St). **National Express** (☑ 08717 81 81 81; www.nationalexpress.com) coaches stop on Vicar's Lane, just opposite the tourist office by the Roman amphitheatre. Destinations include the following:

Birmingham £13.90, two hours, four daily
Liverpool £8, one hour, four daily
London £27.60, 5½ hours, three daily
Manchester £7.60, 1¼ hours, three daily

TRAIN

The train station is about a mile from the city centre via Foregate St and City Rd, or Brook St. City-Rail Link buses are free for people with rail tickets, and operate between the station and **Bus Stop A** (Frodsham St). Destinations include the following:

Liverpool (£6.90, 45 minutes, hourly)
London Euston £69, 2½ hours, hourly
Manchester £12.60, one hour, hourly

LIVERPOOL

POP 467,500

Few English cities are as shackled by reputation as Liverpool, and none has worked so hard to outgrow the clichés that for so long have been used to define it.

A hardscrabble town with a reputation for wit and an obsessive love of football, Liverpool also has an impressive cultural heritage: it has more listed buildings than any other city outside London, its galleries and museums are among the best in the country, and its ongoing program of urban regeneration is slowly transforming the city centre into one of the most pleasant cities in northern England to have a wander in. And then there are the Beatles: Liverpool cherishes them not because they're wedded to the past but because the Beatles are such a central part of the tourist experience that it would be crazy *not* to do so.

The main attractions are Albert Dock (west of the city centre) and the trendy Ropewalks area (south of Hanover St and west of the two cathedrals). Lime St station, the bus station and the Cavern Quarter – a mecca for Beatles fans – lie just to the north.

History

Liverpool grew wealthy on the back of the triangular trading of slaves, raw materials and finished goods. From 1700 ships carried cotton goods and hardware from Liverpool to West Africa, where they were exchanged for slaves, who in turn were carried to the West Indies and Virginia, where they were exchanged for sugar, rum, tobacco and raw cotton.

As a great port, the city drew thousands of Irish and Scottish immigrants, and its Celtic influences are still apparent. Between 1830 and 1930, however, nine million emigrants – mainly English, Scots and Irish, but also Swedes, Norwegians and Russian Jews – sailed from here to the New World.

The start of WWII led to a resurgence of Liverpool's importance. More than one million American GIs disembarked here before D-Day and the port was, once again, hugely important as the western gateway for transatlantic supplies. The GIs brought with them the latest American records, and Liverpool was thus the first European port of call for the new rhythm and blues that would eventually become rock and roll. Within 20 years, the Mersey Beat was *the* sound of British pop, and four mop-topped Scousers had formed a skiffle band...

⊙ Sights

The wonderful Albert Dock is the city's biggest tourist attraction and the key to understanding the city's history, but the city centre is where you'll find most of Liverpool's real day-to-day life.

LIVERPOOL IN ONE DAY

Start your day at the **Beatles Story** on the Albert Dock: it's an excellent intro to the Fab Four but fans should make sure to have booked a morning tour to **Mendips** and **20 Forthlin Road**, the childhood homes of John Lennon and Paul McCartney respectively, which leaves from Albert Dock. If you're not a die-hard Beatles fan, then visit the **Museum of Liverpool** and, just south, the **International Slavery Museum**. Lunch at **Salt House** or **Etsu**.

If you've still got a cultural hunger, you can head to the city centre to explore the **Walker Art Gallery** or the wonderful natural science exhibits of the **World Museum**. Football fans should make the trip to **Anfield** and take the tour of **Liverpool Football Club** (☑0151-263 9199, ticket office 0151-220 2345; www.liverpoolfc.com; Anfield Rd). For dinner you could make a reservation for **London Carriage Works** or **The Art School**.

After dinner, be sure to get a drink at the **Philharmonic**, after which you can take in a gig across the street at the **Philharmonic Hall**. If you're into something a little more adrenalised, the clubs of the Baltic Triangle are worth a punt: our favourite is **Constellations**, which always has something interesting going on.

Liverpool

200 m
0.1 miles

Dauby St
Pembroke Pl
London Rd
Brownlow Hill
Mt Pleasant
Oxford St
Hope St
Myrtle St
Catherine St
Blackburne Tce
Canning St
Blackburne Pl
Falkner St
Rice St
Hope Pl
Hardman St
Rodney St
Leece St
Upper Duke St
Liverpool Cathedral
Great George St
Berry St
Renshaw St
Mt Pleasant
Brownlow Hill
Clarence St
Russell St
Hotham St
Lord Nelson St
National Express Coach Station
Walker Art Gallery
World Museum
William Brown St
Lime St Train Station
Arriva Express Bus 500
Lime St
Lime St
Clayton Sq
Copperas Hill
Ranelagh St
Central
Church St
School La
Hanover St
Wood St
Bold St
Concert St
See St
Campbell Sq
Slater St
Parr St
Duke St
ROPEWALKS
Nelson St
CHINATOWN
Park La
Tabley St
Wapping Dock
Wapping
Liver St
Strand St
Liverpool ONE Bus Station
Salthouse Dock
Strand St
Wapping Basin
Monarch's Quay
King's Pde
ALBERT DOCK
Beatles Story
International Slavery Museum
Canning Half Tide Basin
Canning Dock
PIER HEAD
Museum of Liverpool
Mann Island
James St
Water St
Goree Piazza
New Quay
Brunswick St
Mersey Ferry
Chapel St
Rumford St
Town Hall
Castle St
Cook St
Mathew St
Harrington St
Lord St
Temple La
Paradise St
Williamson Sq
Cavern Quarter
Victoria St
Queen Sq
Hatton Gdn
Dale St
Moorfields
Tithebarn St
Old Hall St
King Edward St
Bath St
William Jessop Way
Princes Dock
Mersey Tunnel
Mersey
District (200m); Constellations (350m)

Queen Sq

Liverpool

⦿ Top Sights
1 Beatles Story C4
2 International Slavery
   Museum C3
3 Liverpool Cathedral F4
4 Museum of Liverpool C3
5 Walker Art Gallery E1
6 World Museum E1

⦿ Sights
7 Beatles Story Pier Head C3
8 Merseyside Maritime
   Museum C3
9 St George's Hall E1
10 Tate Liverpool C3
11 Western Approaches
   Museum C2

⦿ Activities, Courses & Tours
12 Beatles' Childhood Homes
   Tour D4
13 Magical Mystery Tour C4

⦿ Sleeping
14 2 Blackburne Terrace G4
15 Hard Days Night Hotel D2
16 Hope Street Hotel F3

17 Liverpool YHA D4
18 Malmaison B1
19 Radisson Blu B1
20 Richmond Hotel D1
21 Tune Hotel C2

⦿ Eating
22 Etsu C2
23 HOST F3
   London Carriage Works .... (see 16)
24 Monro E3
25 Salt House D3
26 The Art School G3

⦿ Drinking & Nightlife
27 24 Kitchen Street E4
28 Arts Club E3
29 Everyman Bistro D2
30 Philharmonic G3
31 Red Door F3
32 The Merchant E3

⦿ Entertainment
33 Cavern Club D2
34 O2 Academy E1
35 Philharmonic Hall G3

MANCHESTER, LIVERPOOL & NORTHWEST ENGLAND LIVERPOOL

⦿ City Centre

★ **World Museum**   MUSEUM
(☏ 0151-478 4399; www.liverpoolmuseums.org.uk/
wml; William Brown St; ⊗ 10am-5pm) FREE Natural history, science and technology are the
themes of the oldest museum in town, which
opened in 1853. Its exhibits range from live
bugs to human anthropology. This vastly entertaining and educational museum is spread
across five themed floors, from the live fish
aquarium on the 1st floor to the planetarium
on the 5th, where you'll also find exhibits
dedicated to space (moon rocks, telescopes
etc) and time (clocks and timepieces from the
1500s to 1960). Highly recommended.

★ **Liverpool Cathedral**   CHURCH
(☏ 0151-709 6271; www.liverpoolcathedral.org.
uk; Upper Duke St; visitor centre & tower admission £5.50; ⊗ 8am-6pm) Liverpool's Anglican
cathedral is a building of superlatives. Not
only is it Britain's largest church, it's also the
world's largest Anglican cathedral. It is the
work of Sir Gilbert Scott, who also gave us
the red telephone box and the Southwark
Power Station in London, now the Tate Modern. The central bell is the world's third largest (with the world's highest and heaviest

peal), while the organ, with its 9765 pipes, is
likely the world's largest operational model.

The visitor centre features *Great Space;*
this 10-minute, panoramic high-definition
movie about the history of the cathedral is
followed by your own audiovisual tour, courtesy of a headset. Your ticket also gives you
access to the cathedral's 101m tower, from
which there are terrific views of the city and
beyond – on a clear day you can see Blackpool Tower. The cathedral is also home to a
collection of artworks, including a piece over
the West Doors called *For You* by Tracey
Emin: a pink neon sign that says 'I felt you
and I knew you loved me'.

★ **Walker Art Gallery**   GALLERY
(☏ 0151-478 4199; www.liverpoolmuseums.org.uk/
walker; William Brown St; ⊗ 10am-5pm) FREE
The city's foremost art gallery is the national gallery for northern England, housing
an outstanding collection of art from the
14th to the 21st centuries. Its strong suits
are Pre-Raphaelite art, modern British art
and sculpture – not to mention the rotating
exhibits of contemporary expression. It's a
family-friendly place too: the ground-floor
Big Art for Little People gallery is designed
for under-eights and features interactive

LIVERPOOL'S FOOTBALL SIDES

Anfield Stadium Tour (www.liverpoolfc.com; Anfield Stadium; stadium tour adult/child £19.50/13.50) Fans of Liverpool FC will relish the Anfield Stadium Tour as it grants them entry to the home dressing room and down the tunnel past the famous 'This is Anfield' sign into the pitchside dugout. The tour is currently an abridged version, however, while the Main Stand is being redeveloped: from January 2017 a bigger and better tour will be launched.

The ground is 2.5 miles northeast of the city centre. Take bus 26 or 27 from Liverpool ONE bus station or bus 17 from Queen St Bus Station.

Goodison Park Tours (☑ 0151-530 5212; www.evertonfc.com; adult/child £12/6; ☺ 11am & 1pm Mon, Wed & Fri, 10am, noon, 2pm & 4pm Sun) Tours (75 minutes) of Everton FC's Goodison Park stadium, including the ubiquitous visit to the dressing room and the pitchside dugout. Compared to other more modern stadiums, Goodison is almost quaintly antiquated. There are no tours on match day or the afternoon before a home match.

exhibits and games that will (hopefully) result in a lifelong love affair with art.

St George's Hall
CULTURAL CENTRE

(☑ 0151-707 2391; http://liverpoolcityhalls.co.uk; William Brown St; ☺ 10am-5pm) **FREE** Liverpool's most impressive building is the Grade I-listed St George's Hall, a magnificent example of neoclassical architecture that is as imposing today as it was when it was completed in 1854. Curiously, it was built as law courts and a concert hall – presumably a judge could pass sentence and then relax to a string quartet.

Inside, you can visit the recently refurbished courtroom and robing room, stop by the cells below, and get a nice vantage point on the Great Hall, home to Britain's third-largest organ (its 7737 pipes were pipped by the organ in London's Albert Hall, and then both were topped by the gargantuan organ built for Liverpool Cathedral). The building also hosts concerts, corporate gigs and a host of other civic get-togethers; it is also the focal point of any citywide celebration.

Western Approaches Museum
MUSEUM

(www.liverpoolwarmuseum.co.uk; 1-3 Rumford St; adult/child £6/4; ☺ 10.30am-4.30pm Mon-Thu & Sat Mar-Oct, last admission 1hr before closing) The secret command centre for the Battle of the Atlantic, the Western Approaches, was abandoned at the end of the war with virtually everything left intact. You can get a good glimpse of the labyrinthine nerve centre of Allied operations, including the all-important map room, where you can imagine playing a real-life, full-scale version of Risk.

◉ Albert Dock

Liverpool's biggest tourist attraction is Albert Dock, 2.75 hectares of water ringed by enormous cast-iron columns and impressive five-storey warehouses that make up the country's largest collection of protected buildings and are a World Heritage Site. A fabulous development program has really brought the dock to life – here you'll find several outstanding museums and an extension of the Tate Gallery, as well as a couple of top-class restaurants and bars.

★ Beatles Story
MUSEUM

(☑ 0151-709 1963; www.beatlesstory.com; adult/child £14.95/9; ☺ 9am-7pm, last admission 5pm) Liverpool's most popular museum won't illuminate any dark, juicy corners in the turbulent history of the world's most famous foursome – there's ne'er a mention of internal discord, drugs or Yoko Ono – but there's plenty of genuine memorabilia to keep a Beatles fan happy. Your ticket also gets you entry to the exhibit (p551) at the Beatles Story extension on Pier Head.

Particularly impressive is the full-size replica Cavern Club (which was actually tiny) and the Abbey Rd studio where the lads recorded their first singles, while George Harrison's crappy first guitar (now worth half a million quid) should inspire budding, penniless musicians to keep the faith.

★ International Slavery Museum
MUSEUM

(☑ 0151-478 4499; www.liverpoolmuseums.org.uk/ism; ☺ 10am-5pm) **FREE** Museums are, by their very nature, like a still of the past, but the extraordinary International Slavery Museum resonates very much in the present. It reveals slavery's unimaginable horrors – including Liverpool's own role in the triangular slave trade – in a clear and uncompromising manner. It does this through a remarkable series of multimedia and other displays, and it doesn't baulk at confronting racism, slavery's shadowy ideological justification for this inhumane practice.

The history of slavery is made real through a series of personal experiences, including a carefully kept ship's log and captain's diary. These tell the story of one slaver's experience on a typical trip, departing Liverpool for West Africa. The ship then purchased or captured as many slaves as it could carry before embarking on the gruesome 'middle passage' across the Atlantic to the West Indies. The slaves that survived the torturous journey were sold for sugar, rum, tobacco and raw cotton, which were then brought back to England for profit. Exhibits include original shackles, chains and instruments used to punish rebellious slaves – each piece of metal is more horrendous than the next.

It's heady, disturbing stuff, but as well as providing an insightful history lesson, we are reminded of our own obligations to humanity and justice throughout the museum, not least in the Legacies of Slavery exhibit, which explores the continuing fight for freedom and equality.

Merseyside Maritime Museum MUSEUM
(☑0151-478 4499; www.liverpoolmuseums.org.uk/maritime; ⊙10am-5pm) **FREE** The story of one of the world's great ports is the theme of this excellent museum and, believe us, it's a graphic and compelling page-turner. One of the many great exhibits is Emigration to a New World (in the basement), which tells the story of nine million emigrants and their efforts to get to North America and Australia; the walk-through model of a typical ship shows just how tough conditions on board really were.

Tate Liverpool GALLERY
(☑0151-702 7400; www.tate.org.uk/liverpool; special exhibitions adult/child from £5/4; ⊙10am-5.50pm) **FREE** Touted as the home of modern art in the north, this gallery features a substantial checklist of 20th-century artists across its four floors, as well as touring exhibitions from the mother ship on London's Bankside. But it's all a little sparse, with none of the energy we'd expect from the world-famous Tate. The **Clore Learning Centre** lets kids (and adults) take a break from the serious business of viewing art to make their own.

North of Albert Dock

The area to the north of Albert Dock is known as **Pier Head**, after a stone pier built in the 1760s. This is still the departure point for ferries across the River Mersey, and was for millions of migrants their final contact with European soil.

The Museum of Liverpool is an impressive architectural interloper, but pride of place in this part of the dock still goes to the trio of Edwardian buildings known as the 'Three Graces', dating from the days when Liverpool's star was still ascending: the Port of Liverpool Building, the Cunard Building and the Royal Liver Building, which is topped by Liverpool's symbol, the famous 5.5m copper Liver Bird.

★**Museum of Liverpool** MUSEUM
(☑0151-478 4545; www.liverpoolmuseums.org.uk/mol; Pier Head; ⊙10am-5pm) **FREE** Liverpool's storied past is explored through an interactive exploration of the city's cultural and historical milestones: the railroad, poverty, wealth, *Brookside* (a popular '80s TV soap opera set in the city), the Beatles and football (the film on the meaning of the game to the city is worth the 15 minutes). The desire to tell all of the city's rich story means there isn't a huge amount of depth, but the kids will love it.

The museum is constantly introducing new elements and temporary exhibitions, with a view towards ensuring that all visits are connected with a contemporary experience of the city. Recent exhibits include Liverpool and War (the collection of photographs taken during the Blitz in WWII is especially poignant) and Pride and Prejudice, an exploration of the city's LGBT identity.

Beatles Story Pier Head EXHIBITION
(☑0151-709 1963; www.beatlesstory.com; Mersey Ferries Terminal, Pier Head; adult/child £14.95/9; ⊙10am-6pm) If you haven't had enough Beatles at the main Beatles Story museum, your ticket also gains you entry to the annexe on Pier Head, with its rotating Fab Four–related photo exhibitions, a 4D cinema and a shop with a huge collection of Beatles merchandise.

👉 Tours

★**Beatles' Childhood Homes Tour** TOUR
(☑0151-427 7231; www.nationaltrust.org.uk; Jury's Inn, 31 Keel Wharf, Wapping Dock; adult/child £23/7.25; ⊙10am, 11am, 2.15pm & 3.15pm Wed-Sun Mar-Nov) The most intimate portrait of John and Paul comes courtesy of the National Trust–organised tour of their childhood homes. John lived at Mendips with his Aunt Mimi from 1945 to 1963 (which is also the

time period covered by Sam Taylor-Wood's superb 2009 biopic of the young Lennon, *Nowhere Boy*), while Paul lived at a plain terraced home at 20 Forthlin Rd. All tours depart from Jury's Inn on Wapping Dock bar the 3.15pm tour, which goes from Speke Hall (www.nationaltrust.org.uk).

A particular highlight of 20 Forthlin Rd is the lounge room where John and Paul wrote early songs like 'Love Me Do' and 'I Saw Her Standing There'.

Magical Mystery Tour   TOUR
(☑0151-703 9100; www.cavernclub.org; per person £16.95; ⏱tours hourly 11am-4pm) Two-hour tour that takes in all Beatles-related landmarks – their birthplaces, childhood homes, schools and places such as Penny Lane and Strawberry Field – before finishing up in the Cavern Club (which isn't the original). Departs from opposite the tourist office on Albert Dock.

Beatles Fab Four Taxi Tour   DRIVING TOUR
(☑0151-601 2111; www.thebeatlesfabfourtaxitour.co.uk; 2/3hr tour £50/60) Themed tours of the city's mop-top landmarks: there's the three-hour original Lennon tour or the two-hour Epstein express tour. Pick-ups arranged when booking. Up to five people per tour.

★ Festivals & Events

Gin Festival Liverpool   FOOD & DRINK
(www.ginfestival.com; Lutyens Crypt, Metropolitan Cathedral of Christ the King; admission £7.50; ⏱late Jul) One hundred different kinds of gin, including 40 new varieties and bespoke blends, are available for consumption at the

---

THE GRAND NATIONAL
....
The world's most famous steeplechase, and one of England's most cherished events, the Grand National (☑0151-522 2929; www.aintree.co.uk; Aintree Racecourse, Ormskirk Rd; ☒300, 311, 345, 350 & 351 from Liverpool ONE bus station, ☒Aintree from Liverpool Central) takes place on the first Saturday in April across 4.5 miles and over the most difficult fences in world racing. Its protagonists are 40-odd veteran stalwarts of the jumps, ageing bruisers full of the oh-so-English qualities of grit and derring-do. Book tickets well in advance.

Aintree is 6 miles north of the city centre.

UK's largest festival devoted to the drink. The festival takes place in the crypt of the Catholic cathedral – buy your drinks token (£5 per drink) and off you go! Over 18s only.

Liverpool International Music Festival   MUSIC
(☑0151-239 9091; www.limfestival.com; ⏱late Jul) A festival showcasing local bands and international acts across five different venues spread throughout the city during the last weekend of July

International Beatleweek   MUSIC
(www.cavernclub.org; ⏱late Aug) Tribute bands keep the crowds entertained across a week in late August of Beatles-inspired music and talks organised by the Cavern Club.

Creamfields   MUSIC, DANCE
(www.creamfields.com; ⏱Aug Bank Holiday) An alfresco dance-fest that brings together some of the world's best DJs and dance acts during the last weekend in August. It takes place at the Daresbury Estate near Halton, Cheshire.

☐ Sleeping

Tune Hotel   HOTEL $
(☑0151-239 5070; www.tunehotels.com; 3-19 Queen Bldgs, Castle St; r from £40; ❉@令) A slightly upscale version of a pod hotel, Tune offers a comfortable night's sleep (courtesy of a superb mattress and good-quality linen) in a range of en suite rooms. The cheapest of them have no windows and are quite small, but at this price and in this location, it's an easy sacrifice to make. Bathrooms have power showers.

Liverpool YHA   HOSTEL $
(☑0845-371 9527; www.yha.org.uk; 25 Tabley St; dm from £11; ℗令) It may have the look of an Eastern European apartment complex, but this award-winning hostel, adorned with plenty of Beatles memorabilia, is one of the most comfortable you'll find anywhere in the country. The dorms with en suite bathrooms even have heated towel rails.

★ Richmond Hotel   HOTEL $$
(www.richmondliverpool.com; 24 Hatton Garden; d from £80, 2-bedroom apt from £199) Centrally located and fully renovated, the Richmond offers a convenient choice of accommodation, from classic doubles and suites to fully equipped, self-catering one-, two-and three-bedroom apartments. All of the rooms have high-spec decor, including 50in

(NEVER) LET IT BE

They broke up more than 40 years ago and two of their members are dead, but the Beatles are bigger business than ever in Liverpool.

Most of it centres around tiny Mathew St, site of the original Cavern Club, which is now the main thoroughfare of the 'Cavern Quarter'. Here you can shuck oysters in the Rubber Soul Oyster Bar, buy a George pillowcase in the From Me to You shop and put it on the pillows of the Hard Day's Night Hotel. Ringo may have disparaged the city in 2008 by declaring that he missed nothing about it, but the city's tourist authorities continue to exploit Liverpool's ties to the world's most famous group and have done so with enormous success – the original, Beatles-oriented Mathew St Festival was enormously popular, attracting over 350,000 fans; it's now the Liverpool International Music Festival (p552) and explores music beyond the Fab Four.

Wandering around Mathew St is plenty of fun – and the Beatles Shop is best for memorabilia – but if you really want a bit of Beatles lore, you'll have to visit the National Trust–owned **Mendips**, the home where John lived with his aunt from 1945 to 1963, and **20 Forthlin Road**, the plain terraced home where Paul grew up; you can only do so by prebooked Beatle's Childhood Home Tour (p551). The 3.15pm tour leaves from Speke Hall.

If you'd rather do it yourself, the tourist offices stock the *Discover Lennon's Liverpool* guide and map, and Ron Jones' *The Beatles' Liverpool*.

---

flatscreen TVs and fancy toiletries. Guests also have access to the hotel spa.

Hope Street Hotel   BOUTIQUE HOTEL **$$**
(☑ 0151-709 3000; www.hopestreethotel.co.uk; 40 Hope St; r/ste from £90/120; @🖘) One of the classiest digs in town is this handsome boutique hotel on the city's most elegant street. King-sized beds draped in Egyptian cotton, oak floors with underfloor heating, LCD TVs and sleek modern bathrooms are but the most obvious touches of sophistication at this supremely cool address. Breakfast, taken in the marvellous London Carriage Works, is £16.50.

Radisson Blu   HOTEL **$$**
(☑ 0151-966 1500; www.radissonblu.co.uk; 107 Old Hall St; r from £90; @🖘) The rooms at this funky Scandinavian design hotel are divided into 'Ocean', with regal blues and views of the docks and the Mersey, and 'Urban', with luscious reds and purples and city views. Each comes with all the designer gadgetry you'd expect: flatscreen TVs, free high-speed wi-fi and superhip bathrooms. They're not especially huge, but they're very cool, baby.

Malmaison   HOTEL **$$**
(☑ 0151-229 5000; www.malmaison.com; 7 William Jessop Way, Princes Dock; r/ste from £80/125; 🅿@🖘) Malmaison's preferred colour scheme of plum and black is everywhere in this purpose-built hotel, which gives it an air of contemporary sophistication. Everything

about the Liverpool Mal is plush, from the huge beds and the deep baths to the heavy velvet curtains and the excellent buffet breakfast. After a while, you'll ignore the constantly piped music of the Beatles.

Hard Days Night Hotel   HOTEL **$$**
(☑ 0151-236 1964; www.harddaysnighthotel.com; Central Bldgs, North John St; r £70-115, ste from £500; @🖘) You don't have to be a fan to stay here, but it helps: unquestionably luxurious, the 110 ultramodern rooms are decorated with specially commissioned drawings of the Beatles. And if you opt for one of the suites, named after Lennon and McCartney, you'll get a white baby grand in the style of 'Imagine' and a bottle of fancy bubbly.

★ **2 Blackburne Terrace**   B&B **$$$**
(www.2blackburneterrace.com; 2 Blackburne Tce; r £160-180; 🅰@🖘) This exquisite B&B is in a converted Grade II–listed Georgian town house built in 1826. The four rooms are all beautifully appointed with gorgeous period furniture and the attention to detail is superb, from the birdseye maple French secretaire in Room 2 to the free-standing bath in Room 3. All have great views of the cathedral.

✖ Eating

The foodie revolution has completely overhauled the local dining scene, resulting in a host of trendy new spots, the establishment

NIGHTLIFE: THE BALTIC TRIANGLE

Forget Ropewalks – most of Liverpool's best nightlife is in the Baltic Triangle, a once-run-down area of warehouses roughly between the city centre and the docks just north of Toxteth that is now the city's self-styled creative hub. Best spots to check out include **24 Kitchen Street** (www.facebook.com/24kitchenstreet; 24 Kitchen St; tickets £8-12; ⊙9pm-4am Fri & Sat), the-recycling-yard-turned-multipurpose-venue **Constellations** (☑051-345 6302; www.constellations-liv.com; 37-39 Greenland St; ⊙9am-midnight Mon-Thu, to 2am Fri & Sat, 10am-midnight Sun) and **District** (☑07812-141 936; www.facebook.com/District-473098799400626; 61 Jordan St; ⊙7pm-4am Fri-Sat), the first venue to open in the area.

of some exceptional gastropubs and the emergence of a handful of fine-dining restaurants as good as any you'll find anywhere in Britain. You'll find the widest choice in Ropewalks, along Hardman and Hope Sts, and in the streets around Dale St.

★ **Salt House**   SPANISH **$$**
(www.salthousetapas.co.uk; Hanover Sq; tapas £5-8; ⊙noon-10.30pm) Liverpool has grown fond of its Spanish tapas bars, and this gorgeous spot – half deli, half restaurant – is the best of them. The cooking is authentic, varied and delicious, from the choice of charcuterie to the wonderful fish dishes. The takeaway counter at the deli does fab sandwiches too.

The Art School   MODERN BRITISH **$$**
(☑0151-230 8600; www.theartschoolrestaurant.co.uk; 1 Sugnall St; 2-/3-course prix fixe £23.50/29, tasting menu £89; ☑) The old lantern room of a Victorian 'home for destitute children' is now one of the top spots in town for contemporary British cuisine, courtesy of chef Paul Askew (ex–London Carriage Works). Take your pick of expertly presented British classics from a series of menus, including two vegetarian and one vegan. The wine list is superb.

Etsu   JAPANESE **$$**
(☑0151-236 7530; www.etsu-restaurant.co.uk; 25 The Strand, off Brunswick St; mains £12.95-16.95, 15-piece sashimi £14; ⊙noon-2.30pm & 5-9pm Tue, Thu & Fri, 5-9pm Wed & Sat, 4-9pm Sun) The best

Japanese food in town is to be had in this contemporary spot on the ground floor of an office building. The speciality of the house is its fresh sushi and sashimi, but you'll find the usual selection of Japanese classics, from chicken *kara-age* (crispy fried chicken pieces marinated in soy, ginger and garlic) to *unagi don* (grilled eel over rice).

HOST   ASIAN, FUSION **$$**
(www.ho-st.co.uk; 31 Hope St; mains £10-14; ⊙11am-11pm Mon-Sat, noon-10pm Sun; ☑⊞) A bright, airy room with the look of a chic, contemporary New York brasserie serves up excellent pan-Asian dishes like Indonesian braised lamb with fried rice, and red duck coconut curry with lychees. The starter nibbles are pretty delicious too.

Monro   GASTROPUB **$$**
(☑0151-707 9933; www.themonro.com; 92 Duke St; 2-course lunch £12.50, dinner mains £11.50-18; ⊙11am-11pm) ✐ The Monro has fast become one of the city's favourite spots for lunch, dinner and, especially, weekend brunch. The constantly changing menu of classic British dishes made with ingredients sourced as locally as possible has transformed this handsome old pub into a superb dining experience. It's tough to find pub grub this good elsewhere.

London Carriage Works   MODERN BRITISH **$$$**
(☑0151-705 2222; www.thelondoncarriageworks.co.uk; 40 Hope St; 2-/3-course meal £19.50/25.50, mains £15-30; ⊙7-10am, noon-3pm & 5-10pm Mon-Fri, 8-11am & noon-10pm Sat, to 9pm Sun) Head chef Dave Critchley has picked up where Paul Askew left off and continues to set the culinary tone for the city. This award-winning restaurant successfully blends ethnic influences from around the globe with staunch British favourites and serves up the result in a beautiful dining room – actually more of a bright glass box divided only by a series of sculpted glass shards. Reservations are recommended.

🍷 Drinking & Nightlife

★ **Philharmonic**   PUB
(36 Hope St; ⊙10am-midnight) This extraordinary bar, designed by the shipwrights who built the *Lusitania*, is one of the most beautiful bars in all of England. The interior is resplendent with etched and stained glass, wrought iron, mosaics and ceramic tiling – and if you think that's good, just wait until you see inside the marble men's toilets, the only heritage-listed lav in the country.

Red Door
COCKTAIL BAR

(21-23 Berry St; ⊙7pm-2am Mon-Wed, 6pm-4am Thu, 5pm-4am Fri & Sat, 5pm-1am Sun) The cocktail fad is given full expression at this lovely bar, where the bartenders take an almost annoying pride in the theatrical quality of their creations – the 'Rise and Shine' (Southern Comfort, orange juice, grenadine and banana liqueur) comes topped with smoking dry ice for effect. It also has a big selection of gins.

The Merchant
BAR

(40 Slater St; ⊙noon-midnight Mon-Thu & Sun, to 2am Fri, to 3am Sat) This new bar is in a converted merchant's house and has something of a Scandi feel to it – stripped-back walls, wooden bar tables – which made it the 'in' spot at the time of writing. The bar serves 50 different craft beers, gin by the goblet and – wait for it – Prosecco on tap. Good DJs provide the soundtrack.

Everyman Bistro
BAR

(www.everymanplayhouse.com; Williamson Sq; ⊙8.30am-11pm Mon-Thu, to midnight Fri & Sat; 🛜) This Liverpool institution reopened in 2014 in a new location and is better than ever. The downstairs bar and bistro are packed most evenings, making this one of the best places in town for a drink and a bite. The wifi is stronger than in most other bars.

Arts Club
CLUB

(☑0151-707 6171; www.academymusicgroup.com/artsclubliverpool; 90 Seel St; £4-11; ⊙Mon-Sat) This converted theatre is home to one of Liverpool's most beloved clubs, despite going through several name and management changes. It still hosts some fabulous nights, with a mix of live music and DJs keeping everyone entertained with some of the best music in town.

⭐ Entertainment

Philharmonic Hall
CLASSICAL MUSIC

(☑0151-709 3789; www.liverpoolphil.com; Hope St) One of Liverpool's most beautiful buildings, the art deco Phil is home to the city's main classical orchestra, but it also stages the work of avant-garde musicians such as John Cage and Nick Cave.

Cavern Club
LIVE MUSIC

(☑0151-236 1965; www.cavernclub.org; 8-10 Mathew St; admission before/after 2pm free/£4; ⊙10am-midnight Mon-Wed & Sun, to 1.30am Thu, to 2am Fri & Sat) It's a faithful reconstruction of the club where the Beatles played their early gigs, and not even on the same spot (the original club was a few doors away), but the 'world's most famous club' is still a great spot to see local bands, including (invariably) Beatles cover bands.

O2 Academy
LIVE MUSIC

(☑0151-794 6868; www.academymusicgroup.com/o2academyliverpool; Liverpool University, 11-13 Hotham St; ⊙7-11pm) This midsize venue fits about 1200 people and is the place to see those bands that are on the rise (or on the fall).

ℹ Information

Merseyside Police Headquarters (☑0151-709 6010; Canning Pl)
Royal Liverpool University Hospital (☑0151-706 2000; Prescot St)
Post Office (Liverpool ONE; ⊙9am-5.30pm Mon-Sat)
Tourist Office (☑0151-707 0729; www.visitliverpool.com; Anchor Courtyard; ⊙10am-6pm) Small office in Albert Dock.

ℹ Getting There & Away

AIR

Liverpool John Lennon Airport (☑0870-750 8484; www.liverpoolairport.com; Speke Hall Ave) serves a variety of international destinations as well as destinations in the UK (Belfast, London and the Isle of Man). The airport is 8 miles south of the centre.
Arriva Express (www.arriva.co.uk; £4.30; ⊙4.45-12.15am) bus 500 runs every 30 minutes to Liverpool ONE bus station. The journey is about 30 minutes. A taxi to the city centre should cost no more than £20.

BUS

The **National Express Coach Station** (www.nationalexpress.com; Norton St) is 300m north of Lime St train station. There are services to/from most major towns including the following:
Birmingham £13.20, 2½ hours, five daily
London £25.80, five to six hours, six daily

DON'T MISS

BEST PUBS FOR A PINT IN THE NORTHWEST

Philharmonic (p554), Liverpool

Port Street Beer House (p540), Manchester

Albion (p546), Chester

Peveril of the Peak (☑0161-236 6364; 127 Great Bridgewater St; ⊙11am-11pm), Manchester

Manchester £2, one hour, hourly
Newcastle £12, 5½ hours, three daily

TRAIN

Liverpool's main station is Lime St. It has hourly services to almost everywhere, including the following:
Chester £6.90, 45 minutes
London Euston £31, 3¼ hours
Manchester £8.20, 45 minutes

ⓘ Getting Around

BOAT

The famous **Mersey ferry** (www.merseyferries. co.uk; 1 way/return £2.60/3.20) crossing for Woodside and Seacombe departs from Pier Head Ferry Terminal, next to the Royal Liver Building (to the north of Albert Dock).

CAR & MOTORCYCLE

You won't really have much use for a car in Liverpool, but if you have a car the good news is that parking in most sheltered and open car parks is relatively cheap – usually between £2.50 and £3.50 *per day*. The only exception is the huge car park at Liverpool ONE, which costs £2.50 an hour and £16 for a day. Car break-ins are a significant problem, so leave absolutely nothing of value in the car.

PUBLIC TRANSPORT

Liverpool ONE Bus Station (www.merseytravel.gov.uk; Canning Pl) is in the city centre. Local public transport is coordinated by Merseytravel (www.merseytravel.gov.uk). The Saveaway ticket (adult/child £5.20/2.70) allows for one day's off-peak (after 9.30am) travel on all bus, train and ferry services throughout Liverpool and the Wirral (on the far side of the Mersey). Tickets are available at shops throughout the city.

Merseyrail (www.merseyrail.org) is an extensive suburban rail service linking Liverpool with the Greater Merseyside area. There are four stops in the city centre: Lime St, Central (handy for Ropewalks), James St (close to Albert Dock) and Moorfields (for the Liverpool War Museum).

TAXI

ComCab (☑ 0151-298 2222)

LANCASHIRE

As you travel north, past the concrete blanket that covers much of the southern half of the county, Lancashire's undulating landscape begins to reveal itself in all its bucolic glory. East of Blackpool – the faded queen of beachside holidays – the Ribble Valley is a gentle and beautiful appetiser for the Lake District that lies beyond the county's northern border. Lancaster is the county's handsome, Georgian capital.

Blackpool

POP 142,065

Blackpool's enduring appeal – in the face of low-cost airlines transporting its natural constituents to sunnier coasts – is down to its defiant embrace of a more traditional kind of holiday, coupled with the high-tech adrenalin hit of its famed Pleasure Beach amusement park.

The town is also famous for its tower and its three piers. A successful ploy to extend the brief summer holiday season is the Illuminations, when, from early September to early November, 5 miles of the Promenade are illuminated with thousands of electric and neon lights.

◉ Sights

Blackpool Pleasure Beach AMUSEMENT PARK
(☑ box office 0871-222 9090, enquiries 0871-222 1234; www.blackpoolpleasurebeach.com; Ocean Beach; Pleasure Beach Pass £6, 1-day Unlimited Ride wristband adult/child £30/27; ☺ hours vary, usually 10am-8pm in summer) The main reason for Blackpool's immense popularity is the Blackpool Pleasure Beach, a 16-hectare collection of more than 145 rides that attracts some seven million visitors annually. As amusement parks go, it's easily the best in Britain.

Rides are divided into categories, and once you've gained entry to the park with your Pleasure Beach Pass you can buy tickets for individual categories or for a mixture of them all. Alternatively, an Unlimited Ride wristband includes the £6 entrance fee; there are great discounts if you book your tickets online in advance. There's also the option of a Speedy Pass (£15), which saves you the hassle of queuing for rides by allocating you a specific ride time - rent it and add as many people to it as you want. You can go one better with the VIP Speedy Pass (£25), which cuts queuing time by 50%; or with the VIP Plus Speedy Pass (£45), which reduces wait time to almost nothing. There are no set times for closing; it depends how busy it is.

Blackpool Tower ENTERTAINMENT COMPLEX
(☑ 0844-856 1000; www.theblackpooltower. com; Tower Pass door price adult/child £53.45/41;

from 10am, closing hours vary) Built in 1894, this 154m-high tower is Blackpool's most recognisable landmark. Watch a 4D film on the town's history in the **Blackpool Tower Eye** (a 2011 addition), before taking the elevator up to the observation deck, which has splendid views and only a (thick) glass floor between you and the ant-sized people below. Visitors are strongly urged to buy their tickets online as buying them at the door can be up to 50% more expensive.

Down at ground level, the **dungeon** exhibit sits alongside the old Moorish circus and the magnificent rococo ballroom, with its extraordinary sculptured and gilded plasterwork, murals, chandeliers and couples gliding across the beautifully polished wooden floor to the melodramatic tones of a huge Wurlitzer organ. There's also **Jungle Jim's** adventure playground for kids.

Sleeping

Number One   BOUTIQUE HOTEL **$$**
(01253-343901; www.numberoneblackpool.com; 1 St Lukes Rd; s/d from £85/125; P) Far fancier than anything else around, this stunning boutique guesthouse is all luxury and contemporary style. Everything exudes a discreet elegance, from the dark-wood furniture and high-end mod cons to the top-notch breakfast. It's on a quiet road just set back from the South Promenade near the Pleasure Beach amusement park.

Big Blue Hotel   HOTEL **$$**
(01253-400045; www.bigbluehotel.com; Blackpool Pleasure Beach; r from £90; P@) A handsome family hotel with smartly kitted-out rooms. Kids are looked after with DVD players and computer games, while its location at the southern entrance to Blackpool Pleasure Beach should ensure that everyone has something to do.

Information

Tourist office (01253-478222; www.visitblackpool.com; Festival House, Promenade; 9am-6pm Mon-Tue, to 5pm Wed-Sat, 10am-4pm Sun)

Getting There & Away

BUS
The central coach station is on Talbot Rd, near the town centre. Services include the following:
London £38.10, seven hours, four daily
Manchester £8.60, 1¾ hours, four daily

TRAIN
The main train station is Blackpool North, about five blocks east of the North Pier on Talbot Rd. Most arrivals change in Preston, but there's a direct service from the following:
Manchester £16.90, 1¼ hours, half-hourly
Liverpool £18.10, 1½ hours, seven daily
Preston £7.80, 30 minutes, half-hourly

Getting Around

With more than 14,000 car-parking spaces in Blackpool, you'll have no problem parking. A host of travel-card options for trams and buses ranging from one day to a week are available at the tourist office and most newsagents. The tramway (one stop £1.60, up to 16 stops £2.60; from 10.30am Apr-Oct) shuttles funsters for 11 miles, including along the pier as far as the Fylde Coast (also serving the central-corridor carparks), every eight minutes or so throughout the day.

Lancaster
POP 140,000

Lancashire's handsome Georgian county town is a quiet enough burg these days, but all around is evidence of the wealth it accrued in its 18th-century heyday, when it was an important trading port and a key player in the slave trade.

Sights

Lancaster Castle   CASTLE
(01524-64998; www.lancastercastle.com; Castle Park; adult/child £8/6.50; 10am-5pm, guided tours hourly 10am-3pm Mon-Fri, every 30min Sat & Sun) Lancaster's most imposing building is the castle, built in 1150 but added to over the centuries: the **Well Tower** dates from 1325 and is also known as the Witches' Tower because its basement dungeon was used to imprison the accused in the infamous Pendle Witches Trial of 1612. Also dating from the early 14th century is the impressive twin-towered **gatehouse**. Visits are by guided tour only as the castle is used as a Crown Court.

Also imprisoned here was George Fox (1624–91), founder of the Quaker movement. The castle was heavily restored in the 18th and 19th centuries to suit a new function as a prison, and it continued to house Category C prisoners until 2011 – the A wing of the prison is now part of the guided tour.

Priory Church
CHURCH

(Priory Cl; ⊙9.30am-5pm) Immediately next to Lancaster Castle is the equally fine priory church, founded in 1094 but extensively re-modelled in the Middle Ages.

Judges' Lodgings
MUSEUM

(Church St; adult/child £3/2; ⊙11am-4pm Mon-Fri, from noon Sat & Sun Jun & Jul, 1-4pm Mon-Sat Easter-May & Aug-Oct) The former home of witch-hunter Thomas Covell (who 'caught' the poor Pendle women), Lancaster's oldest town house, a Grade I–listed Georgian building, is now home to a **Museum of Furnishings** by master builders Gillows of Lancaster, whose work graces the Houses of Parliament. It also houses a **Museum of Childhood**, which has memorabilia from the turn of the 20th century.

Williamson Park & Tropical Butterfly House
GARDENS

(Tropical Butterfly House adult/child £3.20/2.60; ⊙10am-5pm Apr-Sep, to 4pm Oct-Mar; ☐25 or 25A from train station) Lancaster's highest point is the 22-hectare spread of this elegant park, the highlights of which are (besides the views) the **Tropical Butterfly House**, full of exotic and stunning species, and the **Ashton Memorial**, a 67m-high baroque folly built by Lord Ashton (the son of the park's founder, James Williamson) for his wife. The memorial stands on what was once Lancaster Moor, the spot where until 1800 those sentenced to death at the castle were brought to meet the hangman.

🛏 Sleeping

Borough
BOUTIQUE HOTEL $$

(☑01524-64170; www.theboroughlancaster.co.uk; 3 Dalton Sq; r £100; P@🛜) The Borough has nine beautifully appointed rooms – each with an Italian marble wet-room bathroom for added luxury – spread over two floors of this elegant Georgian building. The downstairs bar has a microbrewery attached, so you don't have to go far to get your fill of locally made cask ales.

Sun Hotel & Bar
HOTEL $$

(☑01524-66006; www.thesunhotelandbar.co.uk; 63-65 Church St; r from £90; P🛜) A fine hotel in a 300-year-old building with a rustic, old-world look that stops at the bedroom doors – beyond them are 16 stylish and contemporary rooms. The pub downstairs is one of the best in town and a top spot for a bit of grub; mains cost between £10 and £12.

Whale Tail Cafe
VEGETARIAN $

(www.whaletailcafe.co.uk; 78a Penny St; mains £6-8; ⊙9am-4.30pm Mon-Sat, 10am-3pm Sun; 🖉) 🍃 This gorgeous 1st-floor veggie restaurant has an elegant dining room and a more informal plant-filled courtyard for lunch on a sunny day. The spicy bean burger is particularly good. Food here is locally produced and, where possible, organic.

RIBBLE VALLEY

Known locally as 'Little Switzerland', Lancashire's most attractive landscapes lie east of the brash tackiness of Blackpool and north of the sprawling urban areas of Preston and Blackburn.

The northern half of the valley is dominated by the sparsely populated moorland of the Forest of Bowland, which is a fantastic place for walks, while the southern half features rolling hills, attractive market towns and ruins, with the River Ribble flowing between them.

Ribble Valley Food Trail (www.ribblevalleyfoodtrail.com) An award-winning food trail highlighting the produce of more than 30 local growers, chefs and restaurateurs, showcasing the rich gourmet bounty available in the region. Download the brochure from the website.

Ribble Way One of the most popular long-distance paths in northern England is the Ribble Way, a 70-mile footpath that follows the River Ribble from its source at Ribblehead (in the Yorkshire Dales), passing through Clitheroe to the estuary at Preston.

Lancashire Cycle Way (www.visitlancashire.com) The Ribble Valley is well covered by the northern loop of the Lancashire Cycle Way; for more information about routes, safety and so on, contact **Blazing Saddles** (☑01442-844435; www.blazingsaddles.co.uk; 35 West End, Hebden Bridge, West Yorkshire), a Yorkshire-based bike shop.

ℹ Information

Tourist Office (☑ 01524-582394; www.
visitlancashire.com; The Storey, Meeting House
Lane; ⊙ 9am-5pm Mon-Sat)

ℹ Getting There & Away

Lancaster Bus Station is the main hub for transport throughout Lancashire, with regular buses to all the main towns and villages.

Lancaster is on the main west-coast railway line and on the Cumbrian coast line. Destinations include the following:

Carlisle £21.80, one hour, hourly

Manchester £17.40, one hour, hourly

Morecambe £3.20, 15 minutes, half-hourly

Clitheroe

POP 14,765

The Ribble Valley's largest market town is best known for its impressive Norman keep, built in the 12th century and now, sadly, standing empty; from it there are great views of the river valley below.

◉ Sights

**Norman Keep
& Castle Museum**   HISTORIC BUILDING
(Castle Hill; museum adult/child £4.20/3.10;
⊙ keep dawn-dusk, museum 11am-4pm Mar-Oct,
noon-4pm Mon, Tue & Fri-Sun Nov-Feb) Dominating the skyline for the last 800 years is this Norman keep, England's smallest and the only remaining castle in the country to have kept a royal garrison during the Civil War. It was built in 1186 and captured by royalist troops in 1644, but managed to avoid destruction afterwards. The extensive grounds are home to a museum that explores 350 million years of local history.

✦ Festivals & Events

Clitheroe Food Festival   FOOD & DRINK
(http://clitheroefoodfestival.com; ⊙ mid-Aug) A food festival showcasing local producers that attracts in excess of 20,000 people during the second Saturday of August. One of the highlights is the Pudding Feast, where locals compete for the best homemade dessert.

⌂ Sleeping & Eating

Old Post House Hotel   HOTEL $$
(☑ 01200-422025; www.posthousehotel.co.uk;
44-48 King St; s/d from £65/95; 🅿 🛜) A former post office is now Clitheroe's most handsome hotel, with 11 superbly decorated rooms.

Emporium   BRITISH
(Moor La; mains £14-19; ⊙ noon-2.30pm & 6.30-9.30pm Mon-Sat, noon-4.30pm Sun) This combination craft shop, bar, cafe and restaurant is one of the most popular spots in town. The excellent menu in the brasserie keeps the focus firmly on local dishes, with a particular emphasis on meat dishes (Goosnargh chicken and duck, locally sourced lamb and beef). On Sundays there's live jazz.

ℹ Information

Tourist Office (☑ 01200-425566; www.
visitribblevalley.co.uk; Church Walk; ⊙ 9am-5pm Mon-Sat)

ℹ Getting There & Away

Clitheroe has direct bus services to all the small towns and villages in northern Lancashire as well as bigger towns like Blackburn (bus 22, 40 minutes, every half-hour).

There are direct trains to Manchester from Clitheroe (£10.80, 1½ hours, 10 daily).

Forest of Bowland

This vast grouse-ridden moorland is somewhat of a misnomer. The use of 'forest' is a throwback to an earlier definition, when it served as a royal hunting ground. Today it is an Area of Outstanding Natural Beauty (AONB), which makes for good walking and cycling. The **Pendle Witch Way**, a 45-mile walk from Pendle Hill to northeast of Lancaster, cuts right through the area, and the Lancashire Cycle Way runs along the eastern border. The forest's main town is **Slaidburn**, about 9 miles north of Clitheroe on the B6478.

Other villages worth exploring are **Newton**, **Whitewell** and **Dunsop Bridge**.

⌂ Sleeping & Eating

Slaidburn YHA   HOSTEL $
(☑ 0845-371 9343; www.yha.org.uk; King's House;
dm £13; ⊙ Apr-Oct) A converted 17th-century village inn that is especially popular with walkers and cyclists.

Hark to Bounty Inn   INN $$
(☑ 01200-446246; www.harktobounty.co.uk;
Slaidburn; s/d from £45/90) This marvellous 13th-century inn has atmospheric rooms with exposed oak beams. An excellent restaurant downstairs specialises in homemade herb breads (mains £10 to £17).

★ **Inn at Whitewell**   INN $$$
(☑ 01200-448222; www.innatwhitewell.com; s/d from £95/132) Once the home of Bowland's forest keeper, this superb guesthouse with antique furniture, peat fires and Victorian claw-foot baths is one of the finest accommodations in northern England. Everything is top-notch, including the views: it's like being in the French countryside. Its restaurant (mains £19-26) is top-notch too.

★ **Northcote Hotel**   MODERN BRITISH $$$
(☑ 01254-240555; www.northcote.com; Northcote Rd, Langho; mains £45-55; ☺ noon-2pm & 7-9.30pm) One of the finest restaurants in northern England, Northcote's Michelin-starred menu is the unpretentious, delicious creation of chef Nigel Haworth and sommelier Craig Bancroft. Duck, lamb, beef and chicken are given the Modern British treatment and the result is fantastic. Upstairs are 26 beautifully styled bedrooms (from £265), making this one of the northwest's top gourmet getaways. Bookings recommended.

ISLE OF MAN

Forget what you may have heard on the mainland: there's nothing odd about the Isle of Man (Ellan Vannin in Manx, the local lingo) and even its famous tail-less cat isn't that strange. No, the island's reputation for oddity is entirely down to its persistent insistence that it do its own thing, rejecting England's warm embrace in favour of a semiautonomous status (it is home to the world's oldest continuous parliament, the Tynwald), which really just lets it continue operating as a popular tax haven.

What you'll find here is beautiful scenery in the lush valleys, barren hills and rugged coastlines. In 2016 Unesco designated the Isle of Man a Biosphere Reserve (one of five in the UK) marking it out as one of the most beautiful spots in Britain to enjoy nature. That bucolic charm is shattered during the world-famous summer season of Tourist Trophy (TT) motorbike racing, which attracts around 50,000 punters and bike freaks every May and June. Needless to say, if you want a slice of silence, be sure to avoid the high-rev bike fest.

🏃 Activities

With plenty of great marked trails, the Isle of Man is a firm favourite with walkers and is regularly voted one of the best walking destinations in Britain. Ordnance Survey (OS) Landranger Map 95 (£8.99) covers the whole island, while the free *Walks on the Isle of Man* is available from the tourist office in Douglas. There are four waymarked long-distance paths on the island:

Bayr Ny Skeddan (14 miles) The 'Herring Road' is a coastal path between Castletown and Peel; the route was the traditional path taken by Manx fishermen.

Heritage Trail (26 miles) A coastal footpath along the old Douglas-to-Peel railway line, waymarked with a blue sign showing a gull in flight.

Millennium Way (26 miles) Runs the length of the island between Sky Hill and Castle Rushen amid spectacular scenery.

Raad ny Foillan (95 miles) The most demanding of all the island's walks is the 'Road of the Gull,' a well-marked path that makes a complete circuit of the island and normally takes about five days to complete.

The island has six designated off-road mountain-biking trails, each with varying ranges of difficulty. See www.visitisleofman.com for details.

🎉 Festivals & Events

Isle of Man
Food & Drink Festival   FOOD & DRINK
(www.gov.im; Villa Marina Gardens, Douglas; £3; ☺ mid-Sep) Over two days in mid-September more than 50 of the island's producers gather to showcase their wares. There's plenty of street food, baked goods, beer and cider, as well as music.

Isle of Man Walking Festival   WALKING
(www.iomevents.com; ☺ mid-May) Takes place over five days in May.

ℹ Information

Most of the island's historic sites are operated by Manx Heritage (www.manxnationalheritage.im). You can also check out www.iomevents.com for listings of what's on in the Isle of Man, along with accommodation and other tourist information.

Tourist Office (☑ 01624-686766; www.visitisleofman.com; Sea Terminal Bldg, Douglas; ☺ 9.15am-7pm May-Sep, closed Sun Oct-Apr)

ℹ Getting There & Away

AIR
Ronaldsway Airport (www.iom-airport.com) is 10 miles south of Douglas near Castletown. The following airlines have services to the island:

Aer Lingus Regional (www.aerlingus.com; from £30)

Citywing (www.citywing.com; from £40)

Easyjet (www.easyjet.com; from £20)

Flybe (www.flybe.com; from £21)

BOAT

Isle of Man Steam Packet (www.steam-packet.com; foot passenger single/return from £18/33, car & 2 passengers return from £150) offers a car ferry and high-speed catamaran service from Liverpool and Heysham to Douglas. From mid-April to mid-September there's also a service to Dublin and Belfast.

🛈 Getting Around

Buses link the airport with Douglas every 30 minutes between 7am and 11pm. Taxis have fixed fares to destinations throughout the island; a cab to Douglas costs £20, to Peel £25.

The island has a comprehensive bus service (www.gov.im); the tourist office in Douglas has timetables and sells tickets. It also sells the Go Explore ticket (one day adult/child £16/8, 3 day £32/16), which gives you unlimited public-transport use, including the tram to Snaefell and Douglas' horse-trams.

Bikes can be hired from **Simpsons Ltd** (☑ 01624-842472; www.cyclehire.im; 15-17 Michael St, Peel; per day/week £15/90; ☺ 9am-5pm Mon-Sat) in Peel.

Petrolheads will love the scenic, sweeping bends that make for some exciting driving – and the fact that outside of Douglas town there's no speed limit. Naturally, the most popular drive is along the Tourist Trophy (TT) route. Car-hire operators have desks at the airport, and charge from around £38 per day.

The 19th-century electric and steam **rail services** (☑ 01624-663366; www.iombusandrail. info; ☺ Mar-Oct) are a thoroughly satisfying way of getting from A to B:

Douglas–Castletown–Port Erin Steam Train
Return £12.40

Douglas–Laxey–Ramsey Electric Tramway
Return £12.40

Laxey–Summit Snaefell Mountain Railway
Return £12

Douglas

POP 27,000

The island's largest town and most important commercial centre is a little faded around the edges and a far cry from its Victorian heyday when it was, like Blackpool across the water, a favourite with British holidaymakers. The bulk of the island's hotels and restaurants are still here – as well

as most of the finance houses that are frequented so regularly by tax-allergic Brits.

👁 Sights

Manx Museum &
National Art Gallery   MUSEUM

(MH; www.manxnationalheritage.im; Kingswood Grove; ☺ 10am-5pm Mon-Sat) **FREE** This modern museum begins with an introductory film to the island's 10,000-year history and then races through it, making various stops including Viking gold and silver, the history of the Tynwald, the island's internment camps during WWII and famous TT races. Also part of the museum is the National Art Gallery, which has works by the island's best-known artists including Archibald Knox and John Miller Nicholson.

🛏 Sleeping

Saba's Glen Yurt   YURT $$

(www.sabasglenyurt.com; Close Ny Howin, Main Rd, Union Mills; 2-person yurt £110) 🍴 In the conservation area of Union Mills you can bed down in a solar-powered eco-yurt that comes equipped with a king-sized bed and a wood burner. Outside are hot tubs filled with steaming water that you can sink in to up to your shoulders. It's 2.5 miles northeast of town on the road to Peel.

Inglewood   BOUTIQUE HOTEL $$

(☑ 01624-674734; www.inglewoodhotel-isleofman. com; 26 Palace Tce, Queens Promenade; s/d incl breakfast from £42.50/85; 🅿@🛜) Sea-view suites in this beautifully refurbished, friendly hotel have big wooden beds and leather sofas. The homemade breakfasts are superb, and the residents' bar specialises in whisky from all over the world.

Claremont Hotel   HOTEL $$$

(☑ 01624-617068; www.claremonthoteldouglas.com; 18-22 Loch Promenade; r from £200; 🅿✳@🛜) The island's fanciest hotel is this newly refurbished classic hotel on the promenade, with huge rooms kitted out with handsome wooden floors and comfortable beds with crisp linen.

🍴 Eating

⭐ **Little Fish Cafe**   SEAFOOD $$

(www.littlefishcafe.com; 31 North Quay; mains £11.50-14.50; ☺ 9am-9pm) Superb seafood presented in a variety of ways, from hake with mustard and lemon butter to a Kerala-style fish curry. For brunch, the Queenie Po'Boy –

battered Manx queenies (queen scallops), paprika mayo and avocado on sourdough brioche – is divine. It also does meat dishes, but the real focus is on the sea.

14North MODERN BRITISH **$$**
(📞 01624-664414; www.14north.im; 14 North Quay; mains £18-22; ☺ noon-2.30pm & 6-9.30pm Mon-Sat) An old timber merchant's house is now home to this smart restaurant specialising in local dishes including pickled herring, lamb rump and, of course, queenies.

Tanroagan SEAFOOD **$$**
(📞 01624-472411; www.tanroagan.co.uk; 9 Ridgeway St; mains £17-20; ☺ noon-2pm & 6-9.30pm Mon-Sat) The place for all things from the sea, this elegant restaurant serves fresh fish straight off the boats, giving them the merest of Continental twists or just a spell on the hot grill. Reservations are recommended.

 Drinking & Nightlife

Bath & Bottle COCKTAIL BAR
(6 Victoria St; ☺ noon-2.30pm & 5-11pm Tue-Wed, to 1am Thu, noon-2am Fri-Sat) A cocktail bar styled like a gin joint from the roaring twenties – it does excellent cocktails and on Wednesdays at 8pm there are classic films in the Speakeasy Cinema.

Bar George BAR
(www.bargeorge.im; St George's Chambers, 3 Hill St; ☺ 11am-midnight) An elegant option for a glass of wine.

Around Douglas

North of the capital, the dominant feature is Snaefell (621m), the island's tallest mountain. You can follow the Tourist Trophy (TT) circuit up and over the mountain towards Ramsey, or take the alternate route along the coast, going through Laxey, where you can also take the electric tram to near the top of Snaefell, from which it's an easy walk to the summit.

◉ Sights

Grove Museum of Victorian Life MUSEUM
(MH; www.manxnationalheritage.im; Andreas Rd, Ramsey; adult/child £5/2.50; ☺ 10am-5pm Jun-Aug, to 4pm Sep) On the edge of Ramsey, on the north of the island, is this imposing house, built in the mid-19th century by Liverpool shipping merchant Duncan Gibb as a summer retreat for himself and his family. The house has been maintained pretty much

as it was in its Victorian heyday, and you can wander through its period rooms – and even learn what it was like to be a scullery maid! The house was occupied by the Gibb family until the 1970s.

Maughold Church & Stone Crosses CHRISTIAN
(MH; www.manxnationalheritage.im; Maughold) The church in the small village of Maughold is on the site of an ancient Celtic monastery founded in AD 600; a small shelter houses quite a good selection of stone crosses and ancient inscriptions dating from the 6th to the 13th centuries.

★ **Great Laxey Wheel** WATER WHEEL
(MH; www.manxnationalheritage.im; Mines Rd, Laxey; adult/child £5/2.50; ☺ 9.30am-5pm Apr-Oct) It's no exaggeration to describe the Lady Isabella Laxey Wheel, built in 1854 to pump water from a mine, as a 'great' wheel: it measures 22m across and can draw 1140L of water per minute from a depth of 550m. The largest wheel of its kind in the world, it's named after the wife of the then lieutenant-governor.

Lonan Old Church CHURCH
The wheel-headed cross at Lonan Old Church, just north of Douglas, is the island's most impressive early Christian cross.

Castletown & Around

At the southern end of the island is Castletown, a quiet harbour town that was originally the capital of the Isle of Man. The town is home to the old parliament and one of the finest castles on the island.

◉ Sights

Castle Rushen CASTLE
(MH; www.manxnationalheritage.im; Castletown Sq, Castletown; adult/child £6/3; ☺ 10am-5pm Apr-Aug, to 4pm Sep-Oct) Castletown is dominated by the impressive 13th-century Castle Rushen. You can visit the gatehouse, medieval kitchens, dungeons and the Great Hall. The flag tower affords fine views of the town and coast.

Nautical Museum MUSEUM
(MH; www.manxnationalheritage.im; Bridge St, Castletown; adult/child £5/2.50; ☺ 10am-4pm Easter-Oct) This small museum displays, among other things, its pride and joy, *Peggy*, a boat built in 1791 and still housed in its original boathouse.

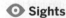
MANCHESTER, LIVERPOOL & NORTHWEST ENGLAND AROUND DOUGLAS

Balladoole
Iron Age Fort
ARCHAEOLOGICAL SITE

 This collection of ancient monuments between Castletown and Cregneash includes a Bronze Age grave dating to 10,000 BC, a Christian chapel from around 900 AD and the remains of a 36ft-long Viking ship used to bury a man and a woman. The buried ship was uncovered in 1945 by a German refugee and a team from the local WWII internment camp.

Cregneash Village Folk Museum
MUSEUM

(MH; www.manxnationalheritage.im; adult/child £5/2.50; ⊙10am-5pm Apr-Aug, to 4pm Sep) On the southern tip of the island, the Cregneash Village Folk Museum recalls traditional Manx rural life.

✗ Eating

Castle Deli @ Radcliffe Butchers
DELI $

(4 Malew St, Castletown; ⊙8am-5pm Mon-Sat) Decent sandwiches with meats from the butcher next door. The selection of cheeses and fish is pretty good too.

Port Erin & Port St Mary

Port Erin is a smallish Victorian seaside resort that plays host to the small **Railway Museum** (Station Rd; adult/child £2/1; ⊙9.30am-4.30pm Apr-Oct, guided tours also 7.30pm & 9.30pm Thu, 11am-1pm Sun mid-Jul–mid-Sep). Port St Mary lies across the headland and is linked to by steam train.

⦿ Sights

Calf of Man
BIRD SANCTUARY

(www.manxnationalheritage.im; ⊙Apr-Sep) This small island just off Cregneash is on one of western Britain's major bird migration routes, and 33 species breed annually here, including Manx shearwaters, kittiwakes, razorbills and shags. Other species normally observed on the island include peregrines, hen harriers, choughs and ravens. It's been an official bird sanctuary since 1939. **Gemini Charter** (☎01624-832761; www.geminicharter.co.uk; trips £25-30 per person) runs birdwatching trips to the island from Port St Mary.

⨇ Sleeping

Aaron House
B&B $$

(☎01624-835702; www.aaronhouse.co.uk; The Promenade, Port St Mary; r from £70) Victori-

an-style Aaron House is a B&B that has fussed over every detail, from the gorgeous brass beds and claw-foot baths to the old-fashioned photographs on the walls. The sea views are also sensational.

Falcon's Nest Hotel
HOTEL

(☎01624-834077; www.falconsnesthotel.co.uk; Station Rd, Port Erin; s/d from £55/90; 🐾) The Victorian Falcon's Nest Hotel, once supremely elegant, is now just handsome in a nostalgic sort of way. The rooms aren't noteworthy, but the views over the water are superb.

Peel
POP 4280

Peel is the west coast's most appealing town, with a fine sandy beach.

⦿ Sights

Peel Castle
CASTLE

(MH; www.manxnationalheritage.im; adult/child £5/2.50; ⊙10am-5pm Jun-Aug, to 4pm Sep-Oct) Peel's big attraction is the ruin of the 11th-century Peel Castle, stunningly positioned atop St Patrick's Island and joined to Peel by a causeway.

House of Manannan
MUSEUM

(MH; www.manxnationalheritage.im; adult/child £6/3; ⊙10am-5pm) The House of Manannan museum uses interactive displays to explain Manx history and its seafaring traditions. It includes reconstructions of a Viking longship and longhouse and a Celtic roundhouse.

⨇ Sleeping & Eating

Fernleigh Hotel
B&B $$

(☎01624-842435; www.isleofman-bedandbreakfast.com; Marine Pde; d from £75; ⊙Feb-Nov; 🅿🐾) Comfortable and family-run B&B with 12 decent bedrooms.

Creek Inn
PUB FOOD $

(☎01624-842216; www.thecreekinn.co.uk; East Quay; mains around £8; ⊙10am-11pm) For a better-than-average bite, head to this seadog kind of pub on the waterfront. It has a decent bar menu, including Manx queenies (scallops served with white cheese sauce).

The Lake District & Cumbria

Includes ➡

Windermere
& Around 568

Ambleside 574

Grasmere. 577

Hawkshead 579

Coniston 581

Elterwater & Great
Langdale 583

Keswick 588

Borrowdale 591

Buttermere 592

Kendal 595

Carlisle. 598

Why Go?

'No part of the country is more distinguished by its sublimity', mused the grand old bard of the lakes, William Wordsworth, and a couple of centuries on his words still ring true. In terms of natural splendour, nowhere in England can compare to the Lake District. For centuries, poets, painters and perambulators alike have been flocking here in search of inspiration and escape, and it's still the nation's favourite place to revel in the majesty of the English landscape.

The main draw here is undoubtedly the Lake District National Park – England's largest, at 885 sq miles. Every bend in the road reveals more eye-popping views: deep valleys, plunging passes, glittering lakes, whitewashed inns, barren hills. But it's worth exploring beyond the national park's boundaries too: the old towns of Carlisle, Kendal and Penrith are full of historical interest and Cumbria's coast has a windswept charm all of its own.

Best Places to Eat

➡ Lake Road Kitchen (p577)

➡ L'Enclume (p597)

➡ Old Stamp House (p577)

➡ Rogan & Company (p597)

➡ Drunken Duck (p580)

When to Go

➡ The Lake District is the UK's most popular national park; visit in early spring and late autumn for the smallest crowds.

➡ The weather is also notoriously fickle – showers can strike at any time of year, so bring wet-weather gear just in case.

➡ Cumbria's largest mountain festival is held in Keswick in mid-May, while the Beer Festival in June welcomes ale aficionados from across the globe.

➡ Ambleside's traditional sports day on the last Saturday in July features events such as hound trailing and Cumbrian wrestling; Grasmere's annual sports day takes place on the August Bank Holiday.

➡ In November the world's greatest liars congregate on Santon Bridge for their annual fibbing contest.

Best Places to Sleep

➡ Forest Side (p578)

➡ Brimstone Hotel (p583)

➡ Daffodil Hotel (p578)

➡ Augill Castle (p600)

➡ Wasdale Head Inn (p587)

History

Neolithic settlers arrived in the Lake District around 5000 BC. The region was subsequently occupied by Celts, Angles, Vikings and Romans. During the Dark Ages it marked the centre of the ancient kingdom of Rheged.

During the Middle Ages, Cumbria marked the start of the 'Debatable Lands', the wild frontier between England and Scotland. Bands of raiders known as Border Reivers regularly plundered the area, prompting the construction of defensive *pele* towers and castles at Carlisle, Penrith and Kendal.

The area became a centre for the Romantic movement during the 19th century, largely thanks to the Cumbrian-born poet William Wordsworth, who also championed the need to protect the Lake District's landscape from overdevelopment – a dream that was achieved in 1951 when the Lake District National Park was formed.

The present-day county of Cumbria was formed from the neighbouring districts of Cumberland and Westmorland in 1974.

🏃 Activities

Cycling

Cycling is a great way to explore the Lake District and Cumbria, as long as you don't mind the hills. For short mountain-bike rides, the trails of Grizedale Forest (p581) and Whinlatter Forest Park (p589) are very popular.

Long-distance touring routes include the 70-mile **Cumbria Way** between Ulverston, Keswick and Carlisle; the 140-mile **Sea to Sea Cycle Route** (C2C, NCN 7; www.c2c-guide.co.uk), which begins in Whitehaven and cuts east across the northern Pennines to Newcastle; and the 173-mile **Reivers Route** (NCN 10; www.reivers-route.co.uk) from the River Tyne to Whitehaven.

Several local buses (including bus 599 from Bowness to Grasmere, bus X33 from Ambleside to Ravenglass and the Cross Lakes Experience) have space for bikes. There's also the new summer-only bus 800 along Windermere's eastern shore, which can carry 12 bikes. It runs several times a day in July and August, plus on weekends in May and June. You pay the standard bus fare plus £1.50 for each bike. For more information see www.golakes.co.uk/travel/by-bus.aspx.

Walking

For many people, hiking is the main reason for a visit to the Lake District. All tourist offices and bookshops sell maps and guidebooks, such as Collins' *Lakeland Fellranger* and Ordnance Survey's *Pathfinder Guides*. Purists prefer Alfred Wainwright's seven-volume *Pictorial Guides to the Lakeland Fells* (1955–66) – part walking guides, part illustrated artworks, part philosophical memoirs – with painstakingly hand-penned maps and text.

Maps are essential: the Ordnance Survey's 1:25,000 *Landranger* maps are used by most official bodies, while some hikers prefer the Harvey *Superwalker* 1:25,000 maps.

Long-distance trails that pass through Cumbria include the 54-mile **Allerdale Ramble** from Seathwaite to the Solway Firth, the 70-mile **Cumbria Way** from Ulverston to Carlisle and the 191-mile **Coast to Coast** from St Bees to Robin Hood's Bay in Yorkshire. Door-to-door baggage services such as **Coast to Coast Packhorse** (☑ 017683-71777; www.c2cpackhorse.co.uk) or **Sherpa Van** (☑ 0871-520 0124; www.sherpavan.com) transport luggage from one destination to the next.

Other Activities

Cumbria is a haven for outdoor activities, including rock climbing, orienteering, horse riding, archery, fell (mountain) running and *ghyll* (waterfall) scrambling. Contact the Outdoor Adventure Company (p595), Rookin House (p574) or Keswick Adventure Centre (p589).

🛈 Getting There & Away

National Express coaches run direct from London Victoria and Glasgow to Windermere, Carlisle and Kendal.

Carlisle is on the main West Coast train line from London Euston to Manchester and Glasgow. To get to the Lake District, you need to change at Oxenholme for Kendal and Windermere. The lines around the Cumbrian Coast and between Settle and Carlisle are particularly scenic.

🛈 Getting Around

Traveline (☑ 0871-200 2233; www.travelinenortheast.info) provides comprehensive travel information.

There are round-the-lake ferry services on Windermere, Coniston Water, Ullswater and Derwentwater. Windermere also has a **ferry service** (p573).

Traffic can be heavy during peak season and holiday weekends. Many Cumbrian towns use timed parking permits for on-street parking, which you can pick up free from local shops and tourist offices.

Cumbria & the Lake District Highlights

1 Scafell Pike (p587) Climbing to the summit of England's highest mountain.

2 Hill Top (p579) Spotting the inspirations for Beatrix Potter's tales.

3 Steam Yacht Gondola (p581) Cruising Coniston Water in stately 19th-century style.

4 Grizedale Forest (p581) Cycling woodland trails surrounded by outdoor art.

5 Honister Pass (p590) Delving into the depths of the Lake District's last slate mine.

6 La'al Ratty (p598) Catching the miniature steam trains into Eskdale.

7 Dove Cottage (p577) Exploring Wordsworth's much-loved Lakeland cottage.

8 Carlisle Castle (p598) Patrolling the battlements of Carlisle's mighty medieval fortress.

9 Sarah Nelson's Shop (p579) Sampling world-famous gingerbread in Grasmere.

10 Helvellyn (p594) Braving the ridge walk via Striding Edge to the summit.

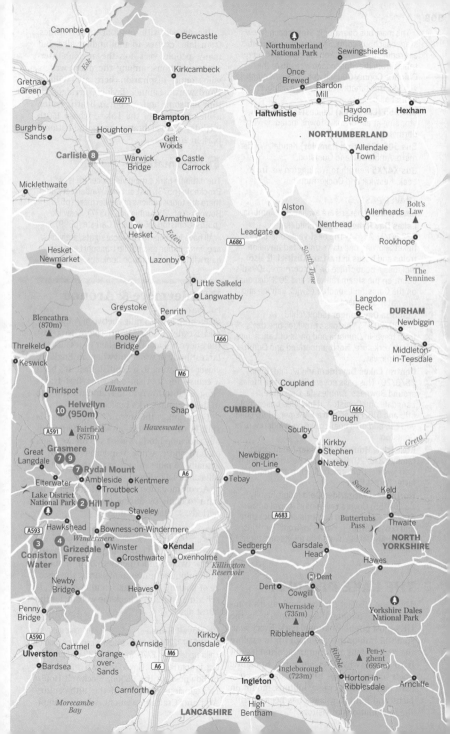

The main bus operator is Stagecoach (www.stagecoachbus.com). Services on most routes are reduced in winter. You can download timetables from the Stagecoach website or the Cumbria County Council website (www.cumbria.gov.uk). Bus timetables are also available from tourist offices.

Bus 555 (Lakeslink) Lancaster to Keswick, stopping at all the main towns including Windermere and Ambleside.

Bus 505 (Coniston Rambler) Kendal, Windermere, Ambleside and Coniston.

Bus X4/X5 Penrith to Workington via Troutbeck, Keswick and Cockermouth.

TRAVEL PASSES

Several travel passes are available in Cumbria.

Lakes Day Ranger (adult/child/family £22.50/11.25/44) The best-value one-day ticket allowing one day's unlimited travel on trains and buses in the Lake District. It also includes a boat cruise on Windermere, 10% discount on the steam railways and 20% discount on the Coniston Launch, Keswick Launch and Ullswater Steamers.

Cumbria Day Ranger (adult/child £41.90/20.95) This pass provides one day's train travel in Cumbria and parts of Lancashire, North Yorkshire, Northumberland and Dumfries and Galloway.

Central Lakes Dayrider (adult/child/family £8/6/20) This pass covers Stagecoach buses around Bowness, Ambleside, Grasmere, Langdale and Coniston; it includes buses 599, 505 and 516. For an extra £4/2 per adult/child you can add on a boat cruise on Windermere or Coniston.

Keswick & Honister Dayrider (adult/child/family £8/6/20) Buses from Keswick through Borrowdale, Buttermere, Lorton and the Whinlatter Forest Park.

North West Megarider Gold (adult/family £27.30/55) Covers seven days' travel on all Stagecoach buses in Cumbria and Lancashire, and cross-border services to/from Dumfries. The family ticket covers two adults and three children.

THE LAKE DISTRICT

The Lake District (or Lakeland, as it's commonly known round these parts) is by far the UK's most popular national park. Every year, some 15 million people pitch up to explore the region's fells and countryside and it's not hard to see why. Ever since the Romantic poets arrived in the 19th century, its postcard panorama of craggy hilltops, mountain tarns and glittering lakes has been stirring the imaginations of visitors.

It's awash with outdoor opportunities, from lake cruises to mountain walks, but many people visit for the region's literary connections: among the many writers who found inspiration here are William Wordsworth, Samuel Taylor Coleridge, Arthur Ransome and, of course, Beatrix Potter, a lifelong lover of the Lakes, whose 150th birthday was celebrated across the national park in 2016.

ⓘ Information

The national park's main visitor centre is at Brockhole (p573), just outside Windermere, and there are tourist offices in Windermere (p573), Bowness (p573), Ambleside (p577), Keswick (p591), Coniston (p582) and Carlisle (p599).

All have information on local sights, activities, accommodation and public transport and can help with accommodation bookings.

Windermere & Around

POP 5423

Stretching for 10.5 miles between Ambleside and Newby Bridge, Windermere isn't just the queen of Lake District lakes – it's also the largest body of water anywhere in England, closer in stature to a Scottish loch. It's been a centre for tourism since the first trains chugged into town in 1847 and it's still one of the national park's busiest spots.

Confusingly, the town of Windermere is split in two: Bowness-on-Windermere (usually shortened to Bowness) sits on the lake's eastern shore, while Windermere Town is actually 1.5 miles inland, at the top of a steep hill called Lake Road.

Accommodation (and parking) can be hard to come by during holidays and busy periods, so plan accordingly.

◎ Sights

The long-awaited reopening of **Windermere Jetty** (www.windermerejetty.org), a multi-million-pound museum exploring the history of boating in the Lakes and elsewhere, is scheduled for 2017; check the website for the latest news.

Blackwell House   HISTORIC BUILDING
(☏ 01539-722464; www.blackwell.org.uk; adult/child under 16yr £7.70/free; ⊙ 10.30am-5pm Apr-Oct, to 4pm Feb, Mar, Nov & Dec) Two miles south of Bowness on the B5360, Blackwell House is a glorious example of the 19th-century Arts and Crafts movement, which champi-

Lake District

oned handmade goods and craftsmanship over the mass-produced mentality of the Industrial Revolution.

Designed by Mackay Hugh Baillie Scott for Sir Edward Holt, a wealthy brewer, the house shimmers with Arts and Crafts details: light, airy rooms, bespoke craftwork, wood panelling, stained glass and Delft tiles. The mock-medieval Great Hall and serene White Drawing Room are particularly fine. The cafe has brilliant views over Windermere.

Fell Foot Park   GARDENS
(NT; www.nationaltrust.org.uk/fell-foot-park; ⊗8am-8pm Apr-Sep, 9am-5pm Oct-Mar, cafe 10am-5pm) **FREE** Located at the southern end of Windermere, 7 miles south of Bowness, this 7-hectare lakeside estate originally belonged to a manor house. It's now owned by the National Trust and its shoreline paths and grassy lawns are ideal for a sunny day picnic. There's a small cafe and rowing boats are available for hire.

Lakes Aquarium   AQUARIUM
(☏015395-30153; www.lakesaquarium.co.uk; Lakeside; adult/child £6.95/4.95; ⊗9am-6pm Apr-Oct) At the southern end of the lake near Newby Bridge, this aquarium explores a range of underwater habitats from tropical Africa through to Morecambe Bay. Windermere Lake Cruises (p570) and the Lakeside & Haverthwaite Railway (p570) stop right beside the aquarium or you could catch bus 6/X6 from Bowness. There's a £1 discount per ticket for online bookings.

**Lakeland
Motor Museum**   MUSEUM
(☏015395-30400; www.lakelandmotormuseum.co.uk; Backbarrow; adult/child £8.50/5; ⊗9.30am-5.30pm Apr-Sep, to 4.30pm Oct-Mar) Two miles south of Newby Bridge on the A590, this car museum houses a wonderful collection of antique cars: classic (Minis, Austin Healeys, MGs), sporty (DeLoreans, Audi Quattros, Aston Martins) and downright odd (Scootacars,

---

ℹ NATIONAL TRUST LAKE DISTRICT CAMPSITE BOOKINGS

National Trust Lake District Campsite Bookings (NT; ☎ 015394-32733; www.nationaltrust.org.uk/features/camping-in-the-lake-district; ⏰ 10am-5pm Mon-Fri) This centralised service handles reservations for all NT campsites in the Lake District. Bookings can be made up to 24 hours before arrival. Online bookings cost £2.50 and must be for a minimum of two nights.

Amphicars). There are also quirky exhibits on the history of caravans and vintage bicycles.

A separate building explores Donald and Malcolm Campbell's record attempts on Coniston Water, with replicas of the 1935 Bluebird car and 1967 *Bluebird K7* boat.

Lakeside & Haverthwaite Railway HERITAGE RAILWAY

(☎ 015395-31594; www.lakesiderailway.co.uk; adult/child/family return £6.70/4.10/19, 1-day rover ticket adult/child £10/5; ⏰ mid-Mar–Oct) Originally built to carry ore and timber to the ports at Ulverston and Barrow, these vintage steam trains puff their way between Haverthwaite, near Ulverston, and Newby Bridge and Lakeside. There are five to seven trains a day, timed to correspond with the Windermere cruise boats; you can also buy combo tickets that include a lake cruise to Bowness or Ambleside.

🏃 Activities

Windermere Lake Cruises BOATING

(☎ 015394-43360; www.windermere-lakecruises.co.uk; tickets from £2.70) Since the launch of the first passenger ferry in 1845, cruising has been an essential part of every Windermere itinerary. Some vessels are modern, but there are some period beauties dating back to the 1930s.

There are various colour-coded cruise options exploring different areas of the lake. All boats allow you to disembark and catch a later ferry back.

The Freedom of the Lake ticket (adult/child/family £19.50/9.75/52.50) allows a day's unlimited travel on all routes.

The most popular route is the **Islands Cruise** (adult/child/family £8/4/21), a 45-minute circular cruise around Windermere's shoreline and islands. The north-lake **Red Cruise** (adult/child/family £10.50/6.30/30) goes from Bowness to Ambleside, while the south-lake **Yellow Cruise** (adult/child/family £11/6.50/31.50) heads down to Lakeside and the Lakes Aquarium.

Running in summer only, the **Green Cruise** (adult/child/family £8/4/21) takes in Waterhead/Ambleside via Wray Castle and Brockhole Visitor Centre. Seasonal twilight cruises also run in summertime and if you're visiting other local attractions, such as the Lakeland Motor Museum and the Lakes Aquarium, ask about the various combination tickets that are available.

From April to October, rowing boats (£15 per hour) and motor boats (from £31 for two adults per hour; children under 16 free) can be hired from the pier at Bowness. Remember there's a 10mph speed limit on the lake.

🛏 Sleeping

Lake District Backpackers Lodge HOSTEL £

(☎ 015394-46374; www.lakedistrictbackpackers.co.uk; High St, Windermere Town; dm/r £16.50/39; @) In a small, old-style house down a little lane near the train station, this basic hostel lacks pizazz, but it's pretty much the only option in town for budgeteers. There are two small four-bed dorms, plus two private rooms with a double bed and a single bed above. The kitchen is tiny but the lounge is cosy.

★ Rum Doodle B&B ££

(☎ 015394-45967; www.rumdoodlewindermere.com; Sunny Bank Rd, Windermere Town; d £85-119; P ☎) Named after a classic travel novel about a fictional mountain in the Himalayas, this B&B zings with imagination. Its rooms are themed after places and characters in the book, with details like book-effect wallpaper, vintage maps and old suitcases. Top of the heap is The Summit, snug under the eaves with a separate sitting room. Two-night minimum in summer.

★ Boundary B&B ££

(☎ 015394-48978; www.boundaryonline.com; Lake Rd, Windermere Town; d £99-210; P ☎) A refined choice, sleek and chic, with neutral-toned rooms all named after great English cricketers: top picks are Hobbs, with bay window and vast bathroom, and Ranji, with cute flamingo wallpaper and a free-standing in-room bathtub. The downstairs lounge has a trendy wood burner and copies of *Wisden's Almanac* to browse.

Windermere Town

1 Park Road
B&B **££**

(☏ 015394-42107; www.1parkroad.com; 1 Park Rd, Windermere Town; d £82-112; 🅿 🛜) It's the little treats that keep this cosy guesthouse a cut above: bath goodies from Pure Lakes and The White Company, iPod docks in every room and homemade baked beans and marmalade for breakfast. Rooms are comfortable and the rates stay reasonable year-round – a rarity in Windermere.

Gilpin Lodge
HOTEL **£££**

(☏ 015394-88818; www.gilpinlodge.co.uk; Crook Rd; r £335-615; 🅿) Windermere's B&Bs might be pushing up their rates to silly levels, but this famously posh country-house retreat shows them how it should be done. The fabulously fancy rooms are named after fells; garden suites even have their own decks and outdoor hot tubs; and the new Lake House comes with its own chauffeur.

A superb restaurant, spa and hectares of grounds complete the package.

Windermere Town

🛏 Sleeping

1 1 Park Road	C3
2 Boundary	B4
3 Lake District Backpackers Lodge	B1
4 Rum Doodle	B4

🍴 Eating

5 Homeground	C2
6 Hooked	B2

Samling
HOTEL **£££**

(☏ 015394-31922; www.thesamlinghotel.co.uk; Ambleside Rd; r £220-670) If money's no object, this deluxe country house is the choice. The chic rooms and cottages are classically styled and feature luxury touches such as split-level mezzanines, rain showers and private lounges. Its restaurant has a Michelin star too. Early bookings score a substantial

LOCAL KNOWLEDGE

WINDERMERE & THE ISLANDS

Like many places in Cumbria, Windermere gets its name from the old Norse, Vinandr mere (Vinandr's lake; so Lake Windermere is actually a tautology). Encompassing 5.7 sq miles between Ambleside and Newby Bridge, the lake is a mile wide at its broadest point, with a maximum depth of about 220m. It's a nice place to hire a boat for the afternoon.

The lake's shoreline is owned by a combination of private landholders, the National Park Authority and the National Trust, but the lakebed itself (and thus the lake itself) officially belongs to the people of Windermere (local philanthropist Henry Leigh Groves purchased it on their behalf in 1938).

There are 18 islands on Windermere: the largest is **Belle Isle**, encompassing 16 hectares and an 18th-century Italianate mansion, while the smallest is **Maiden Holme**, little more than a patch of soil and a solitary tree.

discount. The hotel is 3 miles northwest of Windermere Town, off the A591.

Cranleigh   HOTEL £££

(📞 015394-43293; www.thecranleigh.com; Kendal Rd, Bowness-on-Windermere; d £119-189, ste £305-515; 🅿️🛜) This guesthouse has gone all out on the decor, but strip away the snazziness and it's still just a B&B. It's worth bumping up to the superior for the spacious bathrooms or maybe blowing the budget on one of the two over-the-top suites (check out the Sanctuary, complete with Bose stereo, glass bath and picture-fireplace).

✖️ Eating

Homeground   CAFE £

(📞 015394-44863; www.homegroundcafe.co.uk; 56 Main Rd, Windermere Town; coffees £2-4, mains £7-10; ⏰ 9am-5pm) Windermere gets its own boutique coffee house, serving excellent flat whites, pour overs and ristrettos, accompanied by a fine display of milk art. It's super for brunch too, with bang-on-trend options like a lavish eggs Benedict and maple-bacon waffles. All in all, a thoroughly welcome new addition to town.

⭐ Mason's Arms   PUB FOOD ££

(📞 015395-68486; www.masonsarmsstrawberry bank.co.uk; Winster; mains £12.95-18.95) Three miles east near Bowlands Bridge, the marvellous Mason's Arms is a local secret. The rafters, flagstones and cast-iron range haven't changed in centuries, and the patio has to-die-for views across fields and fells. The food is hearty – Cumbrian stewpot, slow-roasted Cartmel lamb – and there are lovely rooms and cottages for rent too (£175 to £350). In short, a cracker.

Brown Horse Inn   PUB FOOD ££

(📞 015394-43443; www.thebrownhorseinn.co.uk; Winster; mains £11.95-17.95; ⏰ lunch noon-2pm, dinner 6-9pm) Three miles from Windermere in Winster, the Brown Horse is one of Windermere's top dining pubs. Produce is sourced from the Brown Horse Estate, furnishing the chefs with meat and game such as venison, spring lamb and pigeon. Beams and fireplaces conjure rustic atmosphere and there are two home-brewed ales on tap (Old School and Best Bitter). Worth the drive.

Watermill   PUB FOOD ££

(📞 01539-821309; www.watermillinn.co.uk; Ings; mains £12-20; ⏰ 11am-11pm Mon-Sat, to 10.30pm Sun) Two miles from Windermere in Ings, this resolutely traditional inn is exactly what you'd expect from a Cumbrian pub – beamed ceilings, whitewashed walls, log fires, hand pumps and all. Throw in good food and a choice of 16 ales – including home-brewed Collie Wobbles – and it's no wonder it's scooped lots of local awards.

Porto   BISTRO ££

(📞 015394-48242; www.porto-restaurant.co.uk; 3 Ash St, Bowness-on-Windermere; mains £14.95-24.45, set menu £18.95; ⏰ noon-4pm & 6-10pm Wed-Mon) The classiest address in Bowness, tucked away in a whitewashed building on Ash St, and serving adventurous British bistro food (slate plates and sparse presentation present and correct). Head chef David Bewick previously worked with Gordon Ramsay and Nigel Haworth so he knows what's what. The afternoon tea is a cracker too.

Hooked   SEAFOOD ££

(📞 015394-48443; www.hookedwindermere.co. uk; Ellerthwaite Sq, Windermere Town; mains £19.95-21.95; ⏰ 5.30-10.30pm Tue-Sun) Seafood might not be something you immediately think of when deciding what to eat in Windermere, but Paul White's first-class fish restaurant is well worth considering. He likes to keep things classic: hake with Mediterranean veg and pesto, sea trout with peas and pancetta or lemon sole with capers and parsley butter. It's small, so bookings are essential.

Angel Inn PUB FOOD **££**
(☑ 015394-44080; www.the-angelinn.com; Helm Rd, Bowness-on-Windermere; mains £10.95-16.50; ⊙ 11.30am-4pm & 5-9pm) This smart gastropub sits atop a grassy knoll near the Bowness shoreline and offers superior pub grub: think deli boards and Thai chicken supreme. Arrive early if you want to bag a table on the lawn – the lake views are great, so they go fast. A recent refurb has brightened up its rooms (£90 to £150) with natural fabrics and checked accents.

Drinking & Nightlife

Hawkshead Brewery BREWERY
(☑ 01539-822644; www.hawksheadbrewery.co.uk; Mill Yard, Staveley) This craft brewery has its own beer hall in Staveley, 3 miles east of Windermere. Core beers include Hawkshead Bitter, dark Brodie's Prime and fruity Red. Guided tours can be arranged in advance.

Hole in T' Wall PUB
(☑ 015394-43488; Fallbarrow Rd, Bowness-on-Windermere; ⊙ 11am-11pm) Bowness' oldest boozer, dating back to 1612 and offering lashings of rough-beamed, low-ceilinged atmosphere.

ℹ Information

Bowness Tourist Office (☑ 0845 901 0845; bownesstic@lake-district.gov.uk; Glebe Rd, Bowness-on-Windermere; ⊙ 9.30am-5.30pm) Bowness' tourist office is beside the lake jetties.

Brockhole National Park Visitor Centre (☑ 015394-46601; www.lake-district.gov.uk; ⊙ 10am-5pm Easter-Oct, to 4pm Nov-Easter) In a 19th-century mansion 3 miles north of Windermere on the A591, this is the Lake District's flagship visitor centre. It also has a teashop, an adventure playground and gardens.

Windermere Tourist Office (☑ 015394-46499; www.windermereinfo.co.uk; Victoria St, Windermere Town; ⊙ 8.30am-5pm) Windermere's tourist office is now run by the outdoor-activity provider **Mountain Goat** (☑ 015394-45161; www.mountain-goat.com; Victoria St, Windermere).

ℹ Getting There & Away

BOAT
To cross Windermere by car, bike or on foot, head south of Bowness to the **Windermere Ferry** (www.cumbria.gov.uk/roads-transport/highways-pavements/windermereferry.asp; car/bicycle/pedestrian £4.40/1/50p; ⊙ every 20 minutes 6.50am-9.50pm Mon-Fri, 9.10am-9.50pm Sat & Sun Mar-Oct, to 8.50pm Nov-Feb), which shuttles between Ferry Nab on the east bank to Ferry House on the west bank.

BUS
There's one daily National Express coach from London (£31.50, eight hours) via Lancaster and Kendal.

Bus 555/556 Lakeslink (£5.20 to £10.80, at least hourly including Sundays) Starts at the train station, stopping at Troutbeck Bridge (five minutes), Brockhole Visitor Centre (seven minutes), Ambleside (£5.20, 15 minutes), Grasmere (£6.50, 30 minutes) and Keswick (£10.80, one hour). In the opposite direction it continues to Kendal (£6.70, 25 minutes).

Bus 505 Coniston Rambler (£3.50 to £4.50, hourly including Sundays) Travels from Bowness to Coniston (£4.50, 50 minutes) via Troutbeck, Brockhole, Ambleside, Skelwith Fold, Hawkshead and Hawkshead Hill. Two buses a day serve Kendal.

Bus 599 Lakes Rider (£4 to £6.50, three times hourly including weekends) Open-top bus between Bowness, Troutbeck, Brockhole, Rydal Church (for Rydal Mount), Dove Cottage and Grasmere. Some buses stop at Windermere train station.

OFF THE BEATEN TRACK

WRAY CASTLE & CLAIFE HEIGHTS
Windermere's quieter west side is a good place to escape the crowds. North of the ferry landings at Ferry House, a network of woodland paths winds across Claife Heights, while the nearby National Trust–owned estate of Wray Castle (NT; www.nationaltrust.org.uk/wray-castle; adult/child £8.50/4.25; ⊙ 10am-5pm) encompasses 25 hectares of lakeside grounds and a turreted 19th-century mansion, once used as a holiday home by Beatrix Potter's family.

TRAIN

Windermere is the only town inside the national park accessible by train. It's on the branch line to Kendal and Oxenholme.

DESTINATION	ONE-WAY FARE (£)	DURATION
Edinburgh	61.20	2½hr
Glasgow	53.50	2¼-2¾hr
Kendal	4.70	15min
Lancaster	13.90	45min
London Euston	102.50	3½hr
Manchester Piccadilly	36.20	1½hr

Troutbeck

Nestled among the fells to the north of Windermere, on the road towards Kirkstone Pass, this rural hamlet feels a world away from the Bowness bustle, with wonderful views over Windermere.

⊙ Sights & Activities

Townend   HISTORIC BUILDING
(NT; ☑ 01539-432628; www.nationaltrust.org.uk/townend; adult/child £5.90/3.25; ☉1-5pm Wed-Sun Mar-Oct, daily school holidays) Reopened after major renovations, the historic farmhouse at Townend contains a collection of vintage farming tools, possessions and furniture that belonged to the Browne family, who owned the house until 1943. Hourly guided tours run from 11am to 1pm.

Rookin House   OUTDOORS
(☑ 017684-83561; www.rookinhouse.co.uk; Troutbeck) This activities centre between Penrith and Keswick offers a huge range of outdoor fun, from the usual horse riding, clay-pigeon shooting and archery to the weird and wonderful (ever fancied driving a JCB or an Argo cat? Now's your chance).

🍽 Sleeping & Eating

Queen's Head   INN ££
(☑ 015394-32174; www.queensheadhotel.com; d £99-110; ℙ) This 17th-century coaching inn and pub in Troutbeck is a winning blend of old and new. The bedrooms are surprisingly fancy, with bright bedspreads, flatscreen TVs and teddy bears, but it's the solid food and ale that keeps the place busy (mains £12.95 to £16.95). There's a three-course menu (£20) chalked up over the fireplace.

★ Mortal Man   PUB FOOD ££
(☑ 015394-33193; www.themortalman.co.uk; Troutbeck; mains £8.95-15.95; ℙ🐾) Troutbeck's oldest pub, dating from 1689, with a gabled facade, traditional rooms (£89 to £105) and a cracking fell-view beer garden. The food mainly centres on 'pub classics' such as bangers and mash and shepherd's pie. In case you're wondering about the curious name, have a look at the pub sign on your way in – it's taken from an old Lakeland rhyme.

❶ Getting There & Away

Bus 508 from Windermere costs £3.20. It travels every two hours Monday to Friday, with four daily on Saturday and Sunday.

Ambleside

POP 2529

Once a busy mill and textile centre at Windermere's northern tip, Ambleside is an attractive little town, built from the same slate and stern grey stone that's so characteristic of the rest of Lakeland. Ringed by fells, it's a favourite base for hikers, with a cluster of outdoors shops and plenty of cosy pubs and cafes providing fuel for adventures.

⊙ Sights & Activities

Armitt Museum   MUSEUM
(☑ 015394-31212; www.armitt.com; Rydal Rd; adult/child £3.50/free; ☉10am-5pm) Despite some damage incurred during the 2015 floods, Ambleside's excellent little museum is now back up and running. It hosts some intriguing seasonal exhibitions alongside its core collection, populated with artefacts relating to important Lakeland characters such as Beatrix Potter, National Trust founder Canon Hardwicke Rawnsley and pioneering photographers Herbert Bell and the Abraham Brothers. There are also original canvases by the modernist artist Kurt Schwitters, a German refugee who settled in Ambleside after WWII.

★ Rydal Mount   HISTORIC BUILDING
(☑ 015394-33002; www.rydalmount.co.uk; adult/child £7.50/3.50, grounds only £4.50; ☉9.30am-5pm Mar-Oct, 11am-4pm Wed-Mon Nov, Dec & Feb) The poet William Wordsworth's most famous residence in the Lake District is undoubtedly Dove Cottage (p577), but he actually spent a great deal more time at Rydal Mount, 1.5 miles northwest of Ambleside, off the A591. This was the Wordsworth family's home from 1813 until the poet's death in 1850 and the house

contains a treasure trove of Wordsworth memorabilia. Bus 555 (and bus 599 from April to October) stops at the end of the drive.

Downstairs you can wander around the library, dining room and drawing room (look out for William's pen, inkstand and picnic box in the cabinets as well as a famous portrait of the poet by the American painter Henry Inman hanging above the fireplace). Upstairs are the family bedrooms and Wordsworth's attic study, containing his encyclopedia and a sword belonging to his brother John, who was lost in a shipwreck in 1805.

The gardens are lovely too; Wordsworth fancied himself as a landscape gardener and much of the grounds were laid out according to his designs. Below the house is Dora's Field, a peaceful meadow in which Wordsworth planted daffodils in memory of his eldest daughter, who died from tuberculosis in 1847.

Stock Ghyll Force   WALKING

Ambleside's most popular walk is the half-hour stroll up to the 18m waterfall of Stock Ghyll Force; the trail is signposted behind the old Market Hall at the bottom of Stock Ghyll Lane. If you feel energetic, you can follow the trail beyond the falls up **Wansfell Pike** (482m), a reasonably steep walk of about two hours.

Low Wood Watersports   BOATING

(☑015394-39441; www.englishlakes.co.uk/watersports; Low Bay Marina) This watersports centre offers waterskiing, sailing and kayaking and has row boats and motor boats for hire. Kayaks cost from £15 per hour, canoes £18 per hour.

🛏 Sleeping

★ Ambleside YHA   HOSTEL £

(☑0845 371 9620; www.yha.org.uk; Lake Rd; dm £21-30; ▣🛜) One of the YHA's flagship Lake District hostels, this huge lakeside house is a fave for activity holidays (everything from kayaking to ghyll scrambling). Great facilities (kitchen, bike rental, boat jetty and bar) mean it's heavily subscribed, so book well ahead. Families can book out dorms as private rooms. The hostel is halfway between Ambleside and Windermere on Lake Rd (the A591).

Low Wray   CAMPSITE £

(NT; ☑bookings 015394-63862; www.ntlakescampsites.org.uk; campsites £13-35.50, eco pods £45-55; ⊙campsite arrivals 3-7pm Sat-Thu, to 9pm Fri Mar-Oct) One of the most popular of the National Trust's four Lakeland campsites, in a fine spot along Windermere's shores,

3 miles from Ambleside along the B5286. There are 120 tent pitches, nine hard pitches for caravans, plus a handful of camping pods and two safari tents. Choose from lake view, woodland, field or water's edge. Bus 505 stops nearby.

Regent Hotel   HOTEL ££

(☑015394-32254; www.regentlakes.co.uk; Waterhead Bay; d £99-195; ▣🛜♿) This small lakeside hotel is a bit of a bargain. The rooms offer different settings: some have balconies overlooking the garden, others have bunks for the kids or walk-in wet rooms and a few sneak in views over Windermere. The top-floor Sail Loft has romantic skylights and its own private deck terrace.

Gables   B&B ££

(☑015394-33272; www.thegables-ambleside.co.uk; Church Walk; d £102-122; ▣🛜) One of Ambleside's best-value B&Bs in a double-gabled house (hence the name) in a quiet spot overlooking the recreation ground. Spotty cushions and colourful prints keep things cheery, but room sizes are variable (in this instance, bigger is definitely better). Guests receive discounts at the owner's restaurant, **Sheila's Cottage** (☑015394-33079; The Slack; mains £12.50-18; ⊙noon-2.30pm & 6.30-10pm).

Riverside   B&B ££

(☑015394-32395; www.riverside-at-ambleside.co.uk; Under Loughrigg; d £112-122; ▣🛜) Lodged beside the River Rothay half a mile from town, this detached Victorian villa is distinguished by its luxuries: walking guides, ethical bath products and fresh chutneys from the Hawkshead Relish Company. Two rooms have spa baths, one a pine four-poster.

Lakes Lodge   B&B ££

(☑015394-33240; www.lakeslodge.co.uk; Lake Rd; r £106-129; ▣🛜) This modish mini hotel offers a touch more luxury than Ambleside's other guesthouses. The rooms are all about clean lines, stark walls and zero clutter and most have a full-size wall mural featuring

---

LAKE GLAMPING

Wild in Style (yurts 4 nights from £290, vardo wagons 3 nights £285) constructs yurts and gypsy 'vardo' caravans, and is currently located at two campsites in the Lake District: Low Wray (p575) near Ambleside and Hoathwaite near Coniston.

TOP FIVE CLASSIC LAKELAND HIKES

The Lake District's most famous fell-walker, the accountant-turned-author Alfred Wainwright, recorded 214 official fells in his seven-volume *Pictorial Guides* (as if that weren't enough, he usually outlines at least two possible routes to the top or in the case of Scafell Pike, five). If you only have limited time, here are five hikes that offer a flavour of what makes fell walking in the Lake District so special.

Scafell Pike (978m) The daddy of Lakeland hikes, a six- to seven-hour slog to the top of England's highest peak. The classic route is from Wasdale Head.

Helvellyn (950m) Not for the faint hearted; a vertiginous scramble along the knife-edge ridge of Striding Edge. It takes at least six hours starting from Glenridding or Patterdale.

Blencathra (868m) A mountain on its own, Blencathra offers a panoramic outlook on Keswick and the northern fells. Count on four hours from Threlkeld.

Haystacks (597m) Wainwright's favourite mountain and the place where his ashes were scattered. It's a steep, three-hour return hike from Buttermere village.

Catbells (451m) The fell for everyone, accessible to six-year-olds and septuagenarians. It's on the west side of Derwentwater and takes a couple of hours to climb.

a local beauty spot. Some are in the main building while others are in an attached annexe. Breakfast is served in a puce-and-lime-coloured dining room.

Randy Pike   B&B **£££**
(☑ 015394-36088; www.randypike.co.uk; r Mon-Fri £200, Sat & Sun £225) Managed by the owners of Grasmere's Jumble Room restaurant, Andy & Chrissy Hill, this former hunting lodge feels more like a stay in the country with friends than a night in a B&B. The three rooms ooze bohemian style: distressed wood floors, quirky furniture and mix-and-match fabrics, plus iPods loaded up with music. There's even a Tardis in the garden.

The house is about 2.5 miles from Ambleside, off the B5286 to Hawkshead.

Waterhead Hotel   HOTEL **£££**
(☑ 08458-504503; www.englishlakes.co.uk; Lake Rd; r £140-350; [P][⊛][⊛][⊛]) Ambleside's main hotel has a super position beside the lake shore. The exterior is classic Lakeland, all solid stone and bay windows, but inside it's very much a modern hotel with spacious rooms stocked with heritage furniture and designer fabrics, and a sophisticated restaurant, the Mountain View. It's very family friendly and there are good online discounts.

 Eating

Apple Pie   CAFE **£**
(☑ 015394-33679; www.applepieambleside.co.uk; Rydal Rd; lunches £4-10; ⊗ 9am-5.30pm) For a quick lunch stop, you won't go far wrong at this friendly little caff, which serves stuffed sandwiches, hot pies, baked spuds and yummy cakes (the apple pie is a local legend). It also has some great-value rooms (doubles £60 to £80) in the house next door.

Zeffirelli's   ITALIAN **£**
(☑ 015394-33845; www.zeffirellis.com; Compston Rd; pizzas & mains £8-14; ⊗ 11am-10pm) A beloved local landmark, Zeff's is often packed out for its quality pizza and pasta. The £20.75 Double Feature deal includes two courses and a ticket to the cinema (p577) next door.

Fellini's   VEGETARIAN **££**
(☑ 015394-32487; www.fellinisambleside.com; Church St; mains £12.95; ⊗ 5.30-10pm; [⊘]) Fear not, veggies: even in the land of the Cumberland sausage and the tattie hotpot (lamb, vegetable and potato stew), you won't go hungry thanks to Fellini's sophisticated 'vegeterranean' food. The dishes are creative – think brazil nut, hazelnut and almond roast or onion, leek and feta filo pie.

Lucy's on a Plate   CAFE, BISTRO **££**
(☑ 015394-31191; www.lucysofambleside.co.uk; Church St; mains £12.95-20.95; ⊗ 10am-5pm Mon-Fri, to 10pm Sat & Sun) This long-standing boho bistro has been an Ambleside feature for years – and it's still popular. The decor's eclectic – mix-and-match furniture, knick-knacks – and the dishes are similarly quirky (for Rumpy Pumpy, Wild About Bambi and Bobbing Bobotie, read roast lamb, venison and South African stew).

⭐**Lake Road Kitchen** BISTRO £££
(☑015394-22012; www.lakeroadkitchen.co.uk;
Lake Rd; 5-/8-course tasting menu £50/80; ◷6-
9.30pm Wed-Sun) This much-lauded new
bistro has brought some dazzle to Ambleside's dining scene. Its Noma-trained head
chef James Cross explores the 'food of the
north', and his multicourse tasting menus
are chock-full of locally sourced, seasonal
and foraged ingredients, from shore-sourced
seaweed to forest-picked mushrooms. Presentation is impeccable, flavours are experimental and the Scandi-inspired decor is just
so. A meal not to miss.

⭐**Old Stamp House** BISTRO £££
(☑015394-32775; www.oldstamphouse.com; Church
St; dinner mains £19-26; ◷12.30-2pm Wed-Sat,
6.30-10pm Tue-Sat) An Ambleside treat: classy
food with impeccable Cumbrian provenance.
The dishes feel simultaneously familiar and
fresh – Herdwick hogget (lamb) freshened
with peas, beans and barley stew or roast
duck with salsify, chicory and orange. It's in
the cellar of the building where Wordsworth
once worked as Distributor of Stamps: beams,
whitewashed walls, scuffed wood and mono-
chrome photos set a stylish scene.

🍷 Drinking & Entertainment

Ambleside has plenty of pubs: locals favour
the **Golden Rule** (☑015394-32257; www.
robinsonsbrewery.com/goldenrule; Smithy Brow)
for its ale selection, while the **Royal Oak**
(☑015394-33382; www.johnbarras.com/pub/roy
al-oak-ambleside/s6627/; Market Pl) packs in the
post hike punters.

Zeffirelli's Cinema CINEMA
(☑015394-33100; Compston Rd; tickets before/
after 6.45pm £7/8.50) Ambleside's two-screen
Zeffirelli's Cinema is next to Zeffirelli's restaurant, with extra screens in a converted
church down the road.

ℹ Information

Hub (☑015394-32582; tic@thehubofamble-
side.com; Central Bldgs, Market Cross; ◷9am-
5pm) The tourist office and the post office are
both here.

ℹ Getting There & Around

BICYCLE
Biketreks (☑015394-31505; www.biketreks.
net; Rydal Rd; per day £20)
Ghyllside Cycles (☑015394-33592; www.
ghyllside.co.uk; The Slack; per day £18)

BUS
Bus 555 Runs at least hourly (including
Sundays) to Grasmere and Keswick (£8.20),
Bowness and Windermere (£5.20) and Kendal
(£6.70) in the opposite direction.
Bus 599 Open-top service that leaves at least
hourly (including weekends) to Grasmere
(£8.20), Bowness (£5.20), Windermere (£5.20)
and Brockhole Visitor Centre; four buses daily
continue to Kendal (£6.70). Prices similar to
bus 555.
Bus 505 To Hawkshead and Coniston (£4.20,
hourly including Sundays).
Bus 516 To Elterwater and Langdale (£3.70,
seven daily).

Grasmere
POP 1458

Even without its connections to the Romantic poets, gorgeous Grasmere would still be
one of the Lakes' biggest draws. It's one of the
prettiest of the Lakeland hamlets, huddled at
the edge of an island-studded lake surrounded by woods, pastures and slate-coloured
hills, but most of the thousands of trippers
come in search of its famous former resident,
the poet William Wordsworth, who set up
home at nearby Dove Cottage in 1799. With
such a rich literary heritage, Grasmere, unsurprisingly, gets busy.

👁 Sights

⭐**Dove Cottage** HISTORIC BUILDING
(☑015394-35544; www.wordsworth.org.uk; adult/
child £7.50/4.50; ◷9.30am-5.30pm) On the
edge of Grasmere, this tiny, creeper-clad cottage (formerly a pub called the Dove & Olive
Bough) was famously inhabited by William
Wordsworth between 1799 and 1808. The
cottage's cramped rooms are full of artefacts: try to spot the poet's passport, a pair of
his spectacles and a portrait (given to him by
Sir Walter Scott) of his favourite dog Pepper.
Entry is by timed ticket to avoid overcrowd-
ing and includes an informative guided tour.

Wordsworth lived here happily with his
sister Dorothy, wife Mary and three children
John, Dora and Thomas until 1808 when the
family moved to another nearby house at
Allen Bank and the cottage was rented by
Thomas de Quincey (author of *Confessions
of an English Opium Eater*).

Tickets also include admission to the
Wordsworth Museum & Art Gallery next
door, which houses one of the nation's main
collections relating to the Romantic movement, including many original manuscripts

and some creepy death masks of some famous Romantic figures.

St Oswald's Church
CHURCH

(Church Stile) In the churchyard of this tiny chapel in the centre of Grasmere are the Wordsworth's family graves: look out for tombstones belonging to William, Mary, Dorothy and all three children. Samuel Taylor Coleridge's son Hartley is also buried here.

Grasmere Lake & Rydal Water
LAKE

Quiet paths lead along the shorelines of Grasmere's twin-set lakes. Rowing boats can be hired at the northern end of Grasmere Lake from the **Grasmere Tea Gardens** (☑ 015394-35590; Stock Lane; ⊙ 9.30am-5pm), which is a five-minute walk from the village centre.

🛌 Sleeping

Grasmere Hostel
HOSTEL £

(☑ 015394-35055; www.grasmerehostel.co.uk; Broadrayne Farm; dm £20-23; P @) This stylish indie hostel has a vaguely Scandi feel, with unexpected luxuries like a Nordic sauna, skylights, two kitchens and en suite bathrooms for each dorm. Porthole windows provide impressive views over the fells. It's in a converted farmhouse on the A591 about 1.5 miles north of the village, near the Traveller's Rest pub.

Heidi's Grasmere Lodge
B&B ££

(☑ 0774-382 7252; www.heidisgrasmerelodge.co.uk; Red Lion Sq; d £99-130; 🕏) This plush B&B plonked above Heidi's cafe in the centre of the village offers six superfeminine rooms full of frilly cushions and Cath Kidston-style patterns. They're quite small but very comfy: room 6 has its own sun patio, reached via a spiral staircase.

How Foot Lodge
B&B ££

(☑ 015394-35366; www.howfootlodge.co.uk; Town End; d £76-85; P) Just a stroll from Dove Cottage, this stone house has six rooms finished in fawns and beiges; the nicest are the deluxe doubles, one with a sun terrace and the other with a private sitting room. Rates are an absolute bargain considering the location.

★ Forest Side
BOUTIQUE HOTEL £££

(☑ 015394-35250; www.theforestside.com; r incl full board £279-399; P 🕏) For out-and-out luxury, this boutique beauty is the place. Run by renowned hotelier Andrew Wildsmith, it's a design palace: chic interiors decorated with crushed-velvet sofas, bird-of-paradise wallpaper, stag heads and 20 swish rooms classed from 'Cosy' to 'Jolly Good', 'Superb', 'Grand' and 'Master'. Chef Kevin Tickle previously worked at L'Enclume, and now runs the stellar restaurant here using produce from the kitchen garden.

★ Daffodil Hotel
BOUTIQUE HOTEL £££

(☑ 015394-63550; www.daffodilhotel.co.uk; d £99-159, ste £179-259; P 🕏 🛗) Opened in 2012, this upscale hotel occupies a Victorian building but the 78 rooms zing with modern style: swirly carpets, art prints and bold shades of lime, purple and turquoise. There's a choice of lake or valley views and lovely bathrooms with pan-head showers and Molton Brown bath products. A fine restaurant and luxurious spa complete the package. Rather good.

It's just off the A591 heading north towards Grasmere from Ambleside; if you pass Dove Cottage, you've missed it.

🍴 Eating & Drinking

Baldry's Tea Room
CAFE £

(☑ 015394-35301; Red Lion Sq; lunch £5-9; ⊙ 10am-5pm) As traditionally English as a Sunday roast, this old-school tearoom is the spot for a classic cream tea served in a bone-china pot and accompanied by buttery scones, flapjacks or a slice of Victoria sponge. There are rarebits, salads and corned beef sandwiches for lunch too.

★ **Jumble Room** MODERN BRITISH **££**
(☑ 015394-35188; www.thejumbleroom.co.uk; Langdale Rd; dinner mains £14.50-21; ☺ 5.30-9.30pm Wed-Mon) Husband-and-wife team Andy and Crissy Hill have turned this village bistro into a much-loved dining landmark. It's a really fun and friendly place to dine. Spotty crockery, cow murals and primary colours set the boho tone, matched by a magpie menu taking in everything from lentil dhal and Japanese-spiced steak to pinatubo chicken (cooked in Asian spices and coconut milk).

Lewis's BISTRO **££**
(☑ 015394-35266; Broadgate; mains £12.50-18.95; ☺ noon-2pm & 6-9pm) Formerly Sara's Bistro, this small restaurant turns out hearty dishes ranging from roast lamb with red wine jus to Morecambe Bay sea bass with samphire. It's enthusiastically run by its eponymous owner. This is homespun rather than haute cuisine and a little overpriced, but worth a try.

Traveller's Rest PUB
(☑ 015394-35604; www.lakedistrictinns.co.uk/ travellers-rest; A591, near Grasmere; mains £8-16; ☺ 10am-11pm) With its sputtering fires and inglenook bar, this 16th-century coaching inn on the A591 makes a fine place for a pint and a simple pie supper.

🛍 Shopping

★ **Sarah Nelson's Gingerbread Shop** FOOD
(☑ 015394-35428; www.grasmeregingerbread.co. uk; Church Cottage; ☺ 9.15am-5.30pm Mon-Sat, 12.30-5pm Sun) In business since 1854, this famous sweetshop next to the village church makes Grasmere's essential souvenir: traditional gingerbread with a half-biscuit, half-cakey texture (six/12 pieces for £3.50/5.95) cooked using the original top-secret recipe. Friendly service by ladies dressed in frilly pinafores and starched bonnets is an added bonus.

ℹ Getting There & Away

The regular 555 bus runs from Windermere to Grasmere (15 minutes) via Ambleside, Rydal Church and Dove Cottage. The open-top 599 (two or three per hour in summer) runs from Grasmere via Ambleside, Troutbeck Bridge, Windermere and Bowness. Both buses charge the same fares: Grasmere to Ambleside is £5.80, to Windermere it's £6.50.

Hawkshead

POP 1640

Lakeland villages don't come much more perfect than pint-sized Hawkshead, a jumble of whitewashed cottages, cobbled lanes and old pubs lost among bottle-green countryside between Ambleside and Coniston. The village has literary cachet too – Wordsworth went to school here and Beatrix Potter's husband, William Heelis, worked here as a solicitor for many years (his old office is now an art gallery).

Cars are banned in the village centre.

◉ Sights

Beatrix Potter Gallery GALLERY
(NT; www.nationaltrust.org.uk/beatrix-potter-gallery; Red Lion Sq; adult/child £6/3; ☺ 10.30am-5pm Sat-Thu mid-Mar–Oct) As well as being a children's author, Beatrix Potter was also a talented botanical painter and amateur naturalist. This small gallery (housed in what were once the offices of Potter's husband, solicitor William Heelis) contains a collection of her watercolours depicting local flora and fauna. She was particularly fascinated by mushrooms. The gallery celebrated Beatrix Potter's 150th birthday in 2016 with a special exhibition featuring extracts from the author's coded journal.

★ **Tarn Hows** LAKE
(NT; www.nationaltrust.org.uk/coniston-and-tarn-hows) **FREE** Two miles off the B5285 from Hawkshead, a winding country lane wends its way to this famously photogenic artificial lake, now owned by the National Trust. Trails wind their way around the lake shore and surrounding woodland – keep your eyes peeled for red squirrels in the treetops.

There's a small National Trust car park, but it fills quickly. Several buses, including the 505, stop nearby.

★ **Hill Top** HISTORIC BUILDING
(NT; ☑ 015394-36269; www.nationaltrust.org.uk/ hill-top; adult/child £10/5, admission to garden & shop free; ☺ house 10am-5.30pm Mon-Thu, 10am-4.30pm Fri-Sun, garden to 5.45pm Mon-Thu, to 5pm Fri-Sun) Two miles south of Hawkshead in the tiny village of Near Sawrey, this idyllic farmhouse was purchased in 1905 by Beatrix Potter and was used as inspiration for many of her tales: the house features directly in *Samuel Whiskers, Tom Kitten, Pigling Bland* and *Jemima Puddleduck,* among others, and you might recognise the kitchen

THE LAKE DISTRICT & CUMBRIA HAWKSHEAD

❶ THE CROSS LAKES EXPERIENCE

....

If you're not driving, the **Cross Lakes Experience** (www.mountain-goat.co.uk/Cross-Lakes-Experience; adult/child return £12.45/7.15; ☉ Apr-Nov) is a handy way to travel from Bowness to Hawkshead, including travel on the Windermere Ferry (p573) and a minibus on to Hill Top and Hawkshead. It's operated by Mountain Goat (p573).

garden from *Peter Rabbit*. Entry is by timed ticket; it's very, very popular, so try visiting in the late afternoon or on weekdays to avoid the worst crowds.

Clad in climbing ivy and stocked with memorabilia, the house looks like something out of a storybook, but Beatrix only actually lived here until her marriage to William Heelis. In 1913 the newly wed couple moved to a larger farm at Castle Cottage nearby, where the author wrote many more tales and lived until her death in 1943.

She bequeathed Hill Top (along with Castle Cottage and more than 1600 hectares of land) to the National Trust with the proviso that the house should be left with her belongings and decor in situ. The house formed the centrepiece for celebrations to mark the author's 150th birthday in 2016.

🛏 Sleeping & Eating

Hawkshead YHA   HOSTEL £

(☎ 0845-371 9321; www.yha.org.uk; dm £10-21; ▣@🛜) This impressive YHA is lodged in a Grade II–listed Regency house overlooking Esthwaite Water, a mile from Hawkshead along the Newby Bridge road. It's a fancy spot considering the bargain prices: the dorms and kitchen are large and there are camping pods outside as well as bike rentals. The 505 stops at the end of the lane.

Yewfield   B&B ££

(☎ 015394-36765; www.yewfield.co.uk; Hawkshead Hill; s £49, d £106-140; ▣🛜) ✎ This rambling Victorian mansion is one of the best options around Hawkshead, although it's out of the way on the road to Coniston, near Tarn Hows. It's run by the owners of Zeffirelli's in Ambleside and offers a range of comfortable rooms and antique-stocked lounges, plus ecofriendly touches like a wood-mass boiler and all-veggie breakfasts. Discounts available for three nights.

Summer Hill Country House   HOTEL ££

(☎ 015394-36180; www.summerhillcountryhouse. com; Hawkshead Hill; d £102-122; ▣@🛜) On Hawkshead Hill, this 1700s house has a wonderfully out-of-the-way setting, 3 miles from both Coniston and Hawkshead. The five rooms vary in shape and size, but all feature posh bath products and net-connected Mac Minis for getting online or watching DVDs. The garden boasts sculptures and a summer house that belonged to John Ruskin.

Love Shack   COTTAGE £££

(☎ 015394-41242; www.lakedistrictloveshack.com; Cunsey; ☉ 3 days £500-850, r per week £700-1250) ✎ Built on the site of a 1960s love shack (hence the name), this supercool, ecofriendly cabin is the brainchild of artists Karen Guthrie and Adam Sutherland. It's a mix of modern and retro – reclaimed timber, organic paints and oak floors meet funky furnishings and shagadelic love seats, all in a secluded woodland location not far from Near Sawrey.

Queen's Head   PUB FOOD ££

(☎ 015394-36271; www.queensheadhawkshead.co. uk; Main St; mains £12-15; ☉ noon-3pm & 6-10pm) The best choice of several pubs in Hawkshead, with the requisite head-knockingly low ceilings and oak-panelled walls. Decent food plus pleasant four-poster rooms (£98–£158) above and more in a modern annexe.

⭐ **Drunken Duck**   PUB FOOD £££

(☎ 015394-36347; www.drunkenduckinn.co.uk; Barngates; lunch mains £7-12, dinner mains £22; ☉ noon-2pm & 6-10pm; ▣🛜) Long one of the Lakes' premier dining destinations, the Drunken Duck blends historic pub and fine-dining restaurant. On a wooded crossroads on the top of Hawkshead Hill, it's renowned for its luxurious food and home-brewed ales, and the flagstones and sporting prints conjure a convincing country atmosphere. Book well ahead for dinner or take your chances at lunchtime.

If you fancy staying, you'll find the rooms (£105 to £325) are just as fancy as the food. The pub's tricky to find: drive along the B5286 from Hawkshead towards Ambleside and look out for the brown signs.

❶ Getting There & Away

Hawkshead is linked with Windermere, Ambleside and Coniston by bus 505 (£3.50 to £4.50; hourly including Sundays).

Coniston

POP 641

Hunkered beneath the pock-marked peak known as the **Old Man of Coniston** (803m), this lakeside village was originally established to support the local mining industry and the surrounding hilltops are littered with the remains of old copper workings. These days most people visit with two things in mind: to cruise on the lovely old Coniston Launch or to tramp to the top of the Old Man, a steep but rewarding return hike of around 7 miles.

Coniston's other claim to fame is as the location for a string of world-record speed attempts made by Sir Malcolm Campbell and his son, Donald, between the 1930s and 1960s. Tragically, after beating the record several times, Donald was killed during an attempt in 1967 when his futuristic jetboat *Bluebird* flipped at around 320mph. The boat and its pilot were recovered in 2001, and Campbell was buried in the cemetery of St Andrew's church.

👁 Sights

Brantwood   HISTORIC BUILDING
(☑ 015394-41396;   www.brantwood.org.uk;
adult/child £7.50/free, gardens only £4.95/free;
⊙ 10.30am-5pm mid-Mar–mid-Nov, to 4pm Wed-Sun mid-Nov–mid-Mar) John Ruskin (1819–1900) was one of the great thinkers of 19th-century society. A polymath, philosopher, painter and critic, he expounded views on everything from Venetian architecture to lace-making. In 1871 Ruskin purchased this lakeside house and spent the next 20 years modifying it, championing handmade crafts (he even designed the wallpaper). Look out for his vast hoard of shells and several works by JMW Turner.

Boats run regularly from Coniston. Alternatively, look out for signs on the B5285.

Coniston Water   LAKE
Coniston's gleaming 5-mile lake – the third largest in the Lake District after Windermere and Ullswater – is a half-mile walk from town along Lake Rd.

The best way to explore the lake is on one of the two cruise services or, better still, by paddle. Dinghies, rowing boats, canoes, kayaks and motor boats can be hired from the **Coniston Boating Centre** (☑ 015394-41366; www.conistonboatingcentre.co.uk; Coniston Jetty).

🏃 Activities

Coniston Water famously inspired Arthur Ransome's classic children's tale *Swallows and Amazons*. Peel Island, towards the southern end of the lake, doubles in the book as Wild Cat Island, while the *Gondola* steam yacht allegedly gave Ransome the idea for Captain Flint's houseboat.

★ **Steam Yacht Gondola**   BOATING
(NT;   ☑ 015394-63850;   www.nationaltrust.org.uk/steam-yacht-gondola; Coniston Jetty; half lake adult/child return £11/5.50, full lake adult/child/family £21.50/10/51) 🛥 Built in 1859 and restored in the 1980s by the National Trust, this wonderful steam yacht looks like a cross between a Venetian *vaporetto* and an English houseboat, complete with cushioned saloons and polished wood seats. It's a stately way of seeing the lake, especially if you're visiting Brantwood, and it's even ecofriendly: since 2008 it's been powered by waste wood.

THE LAKE DISTRICT & CUMBRIA CONISTON

GRIZEDALE FOREST

Grizedale Forest (www.forestry.gov.uk/grizedale) The forest, stretching for 2428 hectares across the hilltops between Coniston Water and Esthwaite Water, has nine walking trails and seven cycling trails to explore – some are easy and designed for families while others are geared towards hardcore hikers and bikers. Along the way you'll spot more than 40 outdoor sculptures hidden in the undergrowth, created by artists since 1977 (there's a useful online guide at (www.grizedalesculpture.org). Visit the tourist office (☑ 0300 067 4495; grizedale@forestry.gsi.gov.uk; ⊙ 10am-5pm summer, 10am-4pm winter) for more information.

Velo Bikes (☑ 01229-860335; www.velobikes.co.uk; adult/child per half-day from £20/12; ⊙ 9am-5pm) Rents out mountain bikes and supplies trail maps. Last hire at 3pm.

Bowkerstead Farm (☑ 01229-860208; www.grizedale-camping.co.uk; Satterthwaite; adult/child £7/3, camping pods £30; ⊙ Apr-Sep) Pitch beside the trees of Grizedale Forest, either in your own tent, a luxury yurt or a timber eco pod. There's also a bunk-barn for hikers and a farm shop for supplies.

There are several 45-minute half-lake trips per day from mid-March to October. Longer 105-minute full-lake cruises run a few times per week and cover the history of Ransome, the Campbells and Ruskin. There's also a Walkers' Cruise and special picnic and Sunday-afternoon-tea cruises in summer. There's a 10% discount for National Trust members.

Coniston Launch BOATING
(☑ 015394-36216; www.conistonlaunch.co.uk; Coniston Jetty; northern service adult/child return £11/5.50, southern £16.50/8.25) ✐ Coniston's two modern launches have been solar powered since 2005. The regular 45-minute **northern service** calls at the Waterhead Hotel, Torver and Brantwood, while the 105-minute **southern service** sails from Monday to Thursday with a different theme depending on the day; it's Swallows and Amazons on Monday and Wednesday, and the Campbells on Coniston on Tuesday and Thursday.

🛏 Sleeping

Coppermines YHA HOSTEL £
(☑ 0845-371 9630; www.yha.org.uk; dm from £16; ⊙ reception 7-11am & 5-10pm Easter-Oct) Up a steep rock road 1.5km from the village, this rustic hostel once provided accommodation for local copper miners. It's now a walkers' favourite, allowing guests to get an early start on the Old Man; dorms are small but there's a kitchen, showers and even a licensed bar.

Lakeland House B&B ££
(☑ 015394-41303; www.lakelandhouse.co.uk; Tilberthwaite Ave; s £30-60, d £65-99, ste £90-160) You're smack-bang in the centre of Coniston at this good-value, basic B&B above Hollands cafe. The rooms have been recently renovated with fresh colours and updated bathrooms; some have dormer windows, others views of the Old Man. The Lookout Suite has its own sitting room and in-room bathtub.

Bank Ground Farm B&B ££
(☑ 015394-41264; www.bankground.com; East of the Lake; d from £90; 🅿) This lakeside farmhouse has literary cachet: Arthur Ransome used it as the model for Holly Howe Farm in *Swallows and Amazons*. Parts of the house date back to the 15th century, so the rooms are snug. Some have sleigh beds, others exposed beams. The tearoom is a beauty too,

and there are cottages for longer stays. Two-night minimum.

🍴 Eating & Drinking

Steam Bistro BISTRO ££
(☑ 01539-441928; www.steambistro.co.uk; Tilberthwaite Ave; 2-/3-course menu £18.95/22.95; ⊙ 6-11pm Wed-Sun) This swish new bistro has become the go-to address for Coniston dining. Its magpie menu borrows lots of global flavours – you'll find everything from crispy chilli beef with pak choi to Greek-style *kleftiko* (slow-cooked lamb) with minted pesto on the specials board. Even better, they're all *prix fixe* (fixed-price menus).

Sun Hotel PUB
(☑ 015394-41248; www.thesunconiston.com; ⊙ 10am-11pm) Famously used as an HQ by Donald Campbell during his fateful campaign, this trad boozer is a good place for a pint, with a fell-view beer garden and cosy crannies to hunker down in – look out for Campbell memorabilia. Food (mains £12 to £20) is hit-and-miss at busy times. It's up a small hill beside the bridge over Church Beck.

Black Bull PUB
(☑ 015394-41335; www.conistonbrewery.com/black-bull-coniston.htm; Yewdale Rd; ⊙ 10am-11pm) Coniston's main meeting spot, the old Black Bull offers a warren of rooms and a popular outside terrace. The pub grub's good (mains £8 to £18) but it's mainly known for its home-brewed ales: Bluebird Bitter and Old Man Ale are always on tap and there are seasonal ones too.

ℹ Information

Coniston Tourist Office (☑ 015394-41533; www.conistontic.org; Ruskin Ave; ⊙ 9.30am-5.30pm Easter-Oct, to 4pm Nov-Easter) This privately run tourist office has stacks of info on the Coniston area, including a schedule of guided walks.

ℹ Getting There & Away

Bus 505 runs to Windermere (£4.50, hourly including Sundays) via Ambleside, with a couple of daily connections to Kendal (£9.50, 1¼ hours).

The Coniston Bus-and-Boat ticket (adult/child £18/8) includes return bus travel on the 505, plus a trip on the launch and entry to Brantwood.

Elterwater & Great Langdale

Travelling north from Coniston, the road passes into the wild, empty landscape of Great Langdale, one of Lakeland's iconic hiking valleys. As you pass the pretty village of Elterwater, imposing fells stack up like dominoes along the horizon, looming over a pastoral patchwork of tumbledown barns and lime-green fields.

Activities

Langdale's best-known hike is the multipeak route up and over the **Langdale Pikes**: Pike O' Stickle (709m), Loft Crag (682m), Harrison Stickle (736m) and Pavey Ark (700m). Across the valley are the rippled summits of **Bowfell** (902m) and the **Crinkle Crags**, which represent a serious challenge even for experienced walkers.

Sleeping

Great Langdale Campsite   CAMPSITE **£**
(NT; ☎ 015394-63862; www.nationaltrust.org.uk/features/great-langdale-campsite; Great Langdale; sites £13-23, extra adult £6, pods £35-57.50; ⊗ arrivals 3-7pm Sat-Thu, to 9pm Fri; P) Quite possibly the most spectacularly positioned campsite in the Lake District, spread out over grassy meadows overlooked by Langdale's fells. It gets crowded in high season, but 140 sites can be booked in advance; another 30 are on a first-come, first-served basis. Camping pods and yurts are also available.

Langdale YHA   HOSTEL **£**
(☎ 0845-371 9748; www.yha.org.uk; High Close, Loughrigg; dm £13-25; ⊗ reception 7-10am & 5-10.15pm Mar-Oct; P @) If you didn't know this was a hostel, you'd think it was a grand country hotel: vast, Victorian, set in private grounds with its own arboretum. Big dorms with sash windows overlook the fells and there's a cavernous kitchen and lounge (with original ornate fireplace). The cafe serves breakfast, packed lunches and a two-course 'supper club'.

★ Old Dungeon Ghyll   HOTEL **££**
(☎ 015394-37272; www.odg.co.uk; Great Langdale; s £58, d £116-132; P ⊗ 🐾) Affectionately known as the ODG, this inn is awash with Lakeland heritage: many famous walkers have stayed here, including Prince Charles and mountaineer Chris Bonington. It's endearingly olde worlde (well-worn furniture,

four-poster beds) and even if you're not staying, the slate-floored, fire-warmed Hiker's Bar is a must for a posthike pint – it's been the hub of Langdale's social life for decades.

★ Brimstone Hotel   HOTEL **£££**
(☎ 015394-38062; www.brimstonehotel.co.uk; Langdale Estate, Great Langdale; r £220-350; P) This lavish cottage complex on the Langdale Estate takes luxury to another level. The huge suites are more London-chic than Lakeland-cosy; mezzanine floors, sleek tiles, private patios and futuristic log-burners are standard, and then of course there's a reading room, spa, restaurant and private woodland. A new spa is being built, which should be open by the time you read this.

★ Eltermere Inn   HOTEL **£££**
(☎ 015394-37207; www.eltermere.co.uk; Elterwater; r £145-295; P 🐾) This charming inn is one of Lakeland's loveliest backwater boltholes. Rooms are simple and classic, tastefully decorated in fawns and taupes with quirky features such as window seats and free-standing baths. The food's excellent too, served in the inn's snug bar; afternoon tea is served on the lawn on sunny days.

Eating

Stickle Barn   PUB FOOD **£**
(☎ 015394-37356; Great Langdale; mains £6-12) A walkers' fave, this lively pub near the Old Dungeon Ghyll serves filling food such as curries, chillis and hotpots.

Chesters by the River   CAFE **££**
(☎ 015394-32553; www.chestersbytheriver.co.uk; Skelwith Bridge; lunch mains £8-15; ⊗ 9am-5pm) Beside a rattling brook at Skelwith Bridge, halfway between Ambleside and Elterwater, this smart cafe is definitely more gourmet than greasy spoon: delicious salads, specials and cakes make it well worth a stop. There's a chic gift shop too; items include slate souvenirs from the workshop around the corner.

ℹ️ Getting There & Away

Bus 516 (six daily Monday to Friday, seven on weekends) is the only bus, with stops at Ambleside, Skelwith Bridge, Elterwater and the Old Dungeon Ghyll Hotel in Great Langdale. The fare from Ambleside all the way into Great Langdale is £4.80.

1. A cyclist climbs Chapel Fell in the Pennine hills (p604) 2. Surfers at Newquay (p325) 3. Hadrian's Wall (p617) has a range of easy walks

England's Great Outdoors

The English love the great outdoors, and every weekend sees a mass exodus from the towns and cities to the hills, moors and coastline. Hiking and biking are the most popular pursuits but there's a huge range of activities available – and getting wet and muddy can actually be a highlight of your trip!

Walking

England can seem crowded, but away from the cities there are many beautiful areas, perfect for walking. You can go for a short riverside stroll or a major hike over mountain ranges – or anything in between. The best places include the Cotswolds, the Lake District and the Yorkshire Dales.

Cycling

A bike is ideal for getting to know England's countryside. Areas such as Suffolk, Yorkshire and Wiltshire offer a vast network of quiet country roads ideal for cycle touring. For off-road fun, mountain bikers can go further into the wilds in places such as the Peak District, the North Yorkshire Moors and the South Downs.

Horse Riding

If you want to explore the hills and moors at a more leisurely place, seeing the wilder parts of England from horseback is the way to go. In rural areas and national parks such as Dartmoor and Northumberland, there are riding centres catering to all levels of proficiency.

Surfing

England may not be an obvious destination for surfers, but conditions can be surprisingly good at key locations. Top of the list are the west-facing coasts of Cornwall and Devon, while there are smaller scenes on the east coast, notably in Norfolk and Yorkshire.

Eskdale

POP 304

Historically the valley of Eskdale was known for its many mines, which extracted rich reserves of iron, copper and other minerals from the surrounding fells. These days it's hikers' country and a pocket-sized steam railway that formerly served the mines has now been turned into a much-loved tourist attraction.

The village of Eskdale Green holds a traditional country fair over the August Bank Holiday, when local shepherds and breeders show off their prize Herdwicks and there are displays of hound trailing, fell running and local craftwork.

🛏 Sleeping & Eating

Fisherground Farm CAMPSITE £
(☑019467-23349; www.fishergroundcampsite.co.uk; adult/child £6.50/3.50, car £2.50; ☉Mar-Oct; 🌃) Family-friendly camping in idyllic Eskdale, handy for the Ravenglass & Eskdale Railway. It gets very busy in summer so it's better reserved for the shoulder months.

Stanley House B&B ££
(☑019467-23327; www.stanleyghyll-eskdale.co.uk; Eskdale; s £64, d £110-120, f £140-170; 🅿🛜🐕) 🍃 This turn-of-the-century house is halfway down the Eskdale valley, near Beckfoot station. It's a real home away from home: guests are given the run of the place with cosy lounges, rhododendron-filled gardens and an 'open larder' stocked with help-your-self beans, bread and spaghetti hoops. First-floor rooms are dog friendly and the house's hot water and heating comes from an eco-friendly biomass boiler.

Woolpack Inn PUB FOOD ££
(☑019467-23230; www.woolpack.co.uk; Boot; mains £8.50-14.95; 🅿) This old Eskdale inn has a split personality: half contemporary cafe, half trad pub. Each has its own corresponding menu: salads, cakes and light bites in the cafe, filling tatie hotpot and Cumberland bangers in the inn. Rooms are plain but decent value (singles £60, doubles £80 to £110) and most have views of the Eskdale fells.

ℹ Getting There & Away

The trains of the Ravenglass & Eskdale Railway (p598) run up the valley as far as the village of Dalegarth, a short walk from Boot.

Wasdale

Carving its way for 5 miles from the Cumbrian coast, the craggy, wind-lashed valley of Wasdale is where the Lake District scenery takes a turn for the wild. Ground out by a long-extinct glacier, the valley is home to the Lake District's highest and wildest peaks, as well as the steely grey expanse of Wastwater, England's deepest and coldest lake.

Wasdale's fells are an irresistible draw for hikers, especially those looking to conquer England's tallest mountain, **Scafell Pike** (978m).

THE STEEPEST ROAD IN ENGLAND?

Zigzagging over fells between the valleys of **Little Langdale** and **Eskdale** is one of the Lake District's most infamous mountain roads. Used since ancient times and later substantially improved by the Romans, this old packhorse route provided a vital trading link between the central valleys of Lakeland and the ports dotted along the Cumbrian Coast. En route it traverses both of England's highest road passes, **Wrynose** and **Hardknott**, and in places the road reaches forbidding gradients of 1 in 3. At the top of Hardknott Pass, there's a ruined Roman fort where you can still see the remains of the walls, parade ground and commandant's house. The views from here to the coast are stunning.

It's perfectly drivable if you take things slow and steady, but probably best avoided if you're a hesitant reverser or don't like driving next to steep drops (caravans and buses should definitely steer clear). Things to note: it's single-carriage most of the way, and passing places are few and far between, so be prepared for vehicles going the opposite way. Also make sure your brakes are in good order and top up the water in your radiator – you'll do most of the road in first or second gear.

To get to the passes from Ambleside, follow road signs on the A593 to Skelwith Bridge, then turn off to Little Langdale. When you reach the Three Shires Inn, the road gets really steep. Alternatively, you can approach from the west: drive along the A595 coast road and turn off towards Eskdale, then follow the road past Boot to the passes.

⊙ Sights & Activities

Wastwater   LAKE
In his 1810 *Guide to the Lakes,* William Wordsworth described Wastwater as 'long, narrow, stern and desolate', and it's a description that still seems apt. The lake itself is owned by the National Trust and is the deepest body of water in the national park (around 79m at its deepest point). It's also one of the coldest and clearest; very little life can survive in its inhospitable waters, apart from the hardy Arctic char.

★ Scafell Pike   HIKING
The roof of England at 978m, England's highest mountain features on every self-respecting hiker's bucket list. The classic route starts from Wasdale Head; it's hard going but within the reach of most moderately fit walkers, although it's steep and hard to navigate in bad weather. It's a return trip of around six to seven hours and proper gear is essential: raincoat, rucksack (backpack), map, food and water, and decent hiking boots. A favourable weather forecast is preferable to make the most of the views.

🛏 Sleeping

Wasdale Hall YHA   HOSTEL £
(☑ 0845-371 9350; www.yha.org.uk; Wasdale Hall, Nether Wasdale; dm £18-30; ⊙ reception 8-10am & 5-10.30pm; [P]) This lakeside hostel on the shores of Wastwater has the kind of location you'd normally pay through the nose for. It's in a 19th-century mock-Tudor mansion that still boasts most of its period architecture, including original roof trusses and latticed windows. It has the usual self-catering facilities plus a very decent restaurant.

Wasdale Head Campsite   CAMPSITE £
(NT; ☑ bookings 015394-63862; www.ntlakescampsites.org.uk; sites £13-23, extra adult £6, pods £35-57.50; ⊙ reception 8-10.30am Mon-Fri, 8-10.30am & 5-6.30pm Sat & Sun) This National Trust campsite is in a fantastically wild spot, nestled beneath the Scafell range. Facilities are basic (laundry room, showers), but the views are out of this world. Camping pods and tipis provide a bit more shelter in case Wasdale's notorious weather decides to make an appearance.

★ Wasdale Head Inn   B&B ££
(☑ 019467-26229; www.wasdale.com; s £59, d £118-130, tr £177; [P][☎]) Hunkering beneath the brooding bulk of Scafell Pike, this 19th-century hostelry is full of hill-walking heritage. It's wonderfully old-fashioned and covered in vintage photos and climbing memorabilia. The rooms are cosy, with roomier suites in a converted stable. The wood-panelled dining room serves fine food, with humbler grub and ales from the Great Gable Brewing Co available in Ritson's Bar.

❶ Getting There & Away

There are no longer any scheduled bus services to Wasdale Head.
Gosforth Taxis (☑ 01946-734800)

Cockermouth

POP 9146
Set at the confluence of the River Cocker and River Derwent, the Georgian town of Cockermouth is best known as the birthplace of William Wordsworth and the home base of the renowned Jenning's Brewery. Unfortunately, its position beside two major rivers means it has suffered serious flooding – most recently in 2009 and 2015, when much of the town centre was swamped.

⊙ Sights

★ Wordsworth House   HISTORIC BUILDING
(NT; ☑ 01900-824805; Main St; adult/child £7.20/3.60; ⊙ 11am-5pm Sat-Thu Mar-Oct) The Romantic poet William Wordsworth was born on 7 April 1770 at this handsome Georgian house at the end of Main St. Built around 1745, the house has been meticulously restored based on accounts from the Wordsworth archive: the kitchen, drawing room, study and bedrooms all look much as they would have to a young William. Costumed guides help bring things to life. Unfortunately the ground floor and kitchen garden were inundated in the 2015 floods; restoration work is ongoing.

Jennings Brewery   BREWERY
(☑ 01900-821011; www.jenningsbrewery.co.uk; adult/child £9/4.50; ⊙ guided tours 1.30pm Wed-Sat) Real-ale aficionados will be familiar with the Jennings name – it has been brewing beers since 1874 and its pints are pulled at pubs all over the Lake District. Guided tours trace the brewing process, followed by a tasting session of Cocker Hoop and Sneck Lifter in the Old Cooperage Bar. Children must be over 12.

ENNERDALE

If you really want to leave the outside world behind, the remote valley of Ennerdale is definitely the place. Just to the north of Wasdale, this valley and its namesake lake were once home to slate mines and large timber plantations, but these are slowly being removed and the valley is being returned to nature as part of the Wild Ennerdale project (www.wildennerdale.co.uk).

Needless to say, the valley is paradise if you prefer your trails quiet. Several popular routes head over the fells to Wasdale, while walking towards Buttermere takes you past the **Black Sail YHA** (0845-371 9680; www.yha.org.uk; dm £25-30; ⊙ reception 8am-10am & 5-10pm, hostel open mid-Mar–Oct) , a marvellously remote hostel inside a shepherd's bothy. Much loved by mountaineers and hikers, it's become a YHA landmark. Space is very limited, so make sure you book ahead.

🛏 Sleeping & Eating

Six Castlegate   B&B **££**
(01900-826749; www.sixcastlegate.co.uk; 6 Castlegate; s £60-80, d £80-90; P ⊛) Georgian and Grade II–listed, this elegant B&B has a hint of grandeur. All the rooms are named after fells: go for Blencathra, Melbreak or Latrigg if you're after maximum space.

Old Homestead   B&B **££**
(01900-822223; www.byresteads.co.uk; Byresteads Farm; s £40-50, d £60-80; P) Byre is an old English dialect word meaning 'cowshed', but you certainly won't be roughing it with the animals at this lovely farm conversion. The rooms are sweet and traditional, blending classic pine, flagstones and rendered walls with modern luxuries like power showers and underfloor heating. The Cruck Rooms and Master's Loft are the pick of the bunch. It's 2 miles from Cockermouth.

★ Merienda   CAFE **£**
(017687-72024; www.merienda.co.uk; 7a Station St; mains £4-8; ⊙8am-9pm Mon-Thu, 8am-10pm Fri & Sat, 9am-9pm Sun) This Cockermouth fave is now open daily and has recently opened a second branch in Keswick. The interior is light and airy and the Med-tinged food is packed with flavour, with a good balance between meat and veggie-friendly dishes. Carnivores might enjoy a generous slow-cooked BBQ brisket burger, while herbivores should try the excellent baked eggs with feta and aubergine.

ℹ Information

Tourist Office (01900-822634; www.cockermouth.org.uk; 4 Old Kings Arms Lane; ⊙10am-4pm Mon-Fri, to 2pm Sat) In a new location just off the main street, next to Boots Chemists.

ℹ Getting There & Away

Bus X4/X5 (half-hourly Monday to Saturday, hourly Sunday) travels from Cockermouth to Keswick (£5.30) and Penrith (£7.10).

Keswick

POP 4821

The most northerly of the Lake District's major towns, Keswick has perhaps the most beautiful location of all: encircled by cloud-capped fells and nestled alongside the idyllic, island-studded lake of Derwentwater, a silvery curve criss-crossed by puttering cruise boats. It's also brilliantly positioned for further adventures into the nearby valleys of Borrowdale and Buttermere.

Sadly, the town suffered heavy damage during the 2015 floods when the rivers Greta and Derwent burst their banks; the lake level rose by roughly a metre and the A591 between Keswick and Grasmere was partially washed away, effectively cutting off the north and south halves of the national park. Many businesses found themselves under metres of water and two bridges on the popular Keswick to Threlkeld Railway Path vanished. The town is slowly getting back to business, but you can still expect some disruption and ongoing renovations when you visit.

◎ Sights

★ Keswick Museum   MUSEUM
(017687-73263; www.keswickmuseum.org.uk; Station Rd; adult/child £4/2.50; ⊙10am-4pm) Finally reopened after a long program of refurbishment, Keswick's quirky town museum explores the area's history, from ancient archaeology through to the arrival of industry in the Lakes. It's a diverse collection, taking in everything from neolithic axe-heads

mined in the Langdale valley to a huge collection of taxidermied butterflies. Its best-known exhibits are a 700-year-old mummified cat and the Musical Stones of Skiddaw, a weird instrument made from hornsfel rock that was once played for Queen Victoria.

Castlerigg Stone Circle MONUMENT
FREE Set on a hilltop a mile east of town, this jaw-dropping stone circle consists of 48 stones that are between 3000 and 4000 years old, surrounded by a dramatic ring of mountain peaks.

Lakes Distillery DISTILLERY
(☑017687-88850; www.lakesdistillery.com; tours £12.50; ☺11am-6pm) The first and only distillery in the Lake District, this spirit-maker has made a big splash since opening in 2014. It's located on a 'model farm' built during the 1850s and was founded by a team of master distillers; so far its range includes a gin, a vodka and a flagship whisky. Guided tours take you through the process and include a tasting of the three spirits, plus a £5 voucher for use in the shop.

Activities

Hiking opportunities abound around Keswick. The most popular is Catbells (451m), a mini mountain on the west shore of Derwentwater, which is easily reached via the Keswick Launch. More challenging options include the imposing bulk of Skiddaw (931m), which looms north of town, and Blencathra (868m), another classic fell to the northeast.

The 2015 floods damaged parts of the paths on all three fells, but they were navigable at the time of writing – check with the tourist office to make sure.

★**Keswick Launch** BOATING
(☑017687-72263; www.keswick-launch.co.uk; round-the-lake adult/child/family £10.25/5.15/24) Shimmering to the south of Keswick, studded with islands and ringed by craggy fells, Derwentwater is undoubtedly one of the prettiest of the Lakeland lakes.

As always, getting out on the water is the best way to explore. The Keswick Launch runs regular cross-lake excursions, and rowboats and motor boats (£12/27 per hour) can be hired next to the jetties.

Keswick Adventure Centre OUTDOORS
(☑017687-75687; www.keswickadventurecentre.co.uk; Newlands) This activity centre in Keswick organises hikes and has a climbing wall.

Whinlatter Forest Park OUTDOORS
(www.forestry.gov.uk/whinlatter) **FREE** Encompassing 4.6 sq miles of pine, larch and spruce, Whinlatter is England's only true mountain forest, rising sharply to 790m about 5 miles from Keswick. The forest is a designated red squirrel reserve; you can check out live video feeds from squirrel cams at the visitor centre (☑01768-778469; ☺10am-4pm).

It's also home to two exciting mountain-bike trails and the **Go Ape** (www.goape.co.uk/days-out/whinlatter; adult/child £33/25; ☺9am-5pm mid-Mar–Oct) treetop assault course. You can hire bikes from **Cyclewise** (☑017687-78711; www.cyclewise.co.uk; Whinlatter Forest Park; 3hr hire adult/child £19/15; ☺10am-5pm), next to the visitor centre.

Keswick Mountain Bikes CYCLING
(☑017687-75202; www.keswickbikes.co.uk; 133 Main St; adult bikes per day £15-40; ☺9.30am-5.30pm) Mountain bikes can be hired from Keswick Mountain Bikes. The road-specific shop is above the Lakeland Pedlar Cafe.

Festivals & Events

Keswick Mountain Festival OUTDOORS
(www.keswickmountainfestival.co.uk) This May festival celebrates all things mountainous.

Keswick Beer Festival BEER
(www.keswickbeerfestival.co.uk) Lots and lots of beer is drunk during Keswick's real-ale fest in June.

Sleeping

★**Howe Keld** B&B ££
(☑017687-72417; www.howekeld.co.uk; 5-7 The Heads; s £60-85, d £112-130; [P][�]) This gold-standard B&B pulls out all the stops: goose-down duvets, slate-floored bathrooms, chic colours and locally made furniture. The best rooms have views across Crow Park and the golf course, and the breakfast is a pick-and-mix delight. Free parking is available on The Heads if there's space.

★**Lookout** B&B ££
(☑017687-80407; www.thelookoutkeswick.co.uk; Chestnut Hill; d £95-120; [P][�]) The clue's in the name: this fine B&B is all about the views – there's a stunning panorama of fells filling every window. It's in a gabled 1920s house but feels modern with cappuccino-and-cream colour schemes, wooden beds and minimalist glass showers. Take Penrith Rd west and turn right onto Chestnut Hill; the B&B is on the left.

HONISTER PASS & MINE

From Borrowdale, a narrow, perilously steep road snakes up the fellside to Honister Pass, home to the last working slate mine left in the UK.

Honister Slate Mine (☎ 017687-77230; www.honister-slate-mine.co.uk; mine tour adult/child £12.50/7.50; ⊙ tours 10.30am, 12.30pm & 3.30pm Mar-Oct) Underground tours venture deep into the bowels of Honister's old 'Edge' and 'Kimberley' mines (a tour into the 'Cathedral' mine runs on Friday by request, but you'll need eight people and it costs £19.75).

Via Ferrata (classic route adult/child £35/25, Xtreme £39.50/29.50) Part of the Honister Slate Mine, the UK's first 'iron way' is a vertiginous system of clifftop ropes and ladders once used by slate miners. It's exhilarating, but unsurprisingly you'll need a head for heights. There's also an extreme version that involves traversing a single rope 'Infinity Bridge' – not for the faint-hearted. All-day pass including mine tour costs adult/child £56.50/43.50.

Linnett Hill   B&B ££
(☎ 017687-44518; www.linnetthillkeswick.co.uk; 4 Penrith Rd; s £48, d £85-95; 🤖) Much recommended by travellers, this lovingly run B&B has lots going for it: crisp white rooms, a great location near Fitz Park and keen prices that stay the same year-round. Breakfast is good too: there's a blackboard of specials to choose from and the dining room has gingham-check tablecloths and a crackling wood burner.

Powe House   B&B ££
(☎ 017687-73611; www.powehouse.com; Portinscale; s £48-65, d £84-92; P🤖) Pleasantly removed from the Keswick crush about a mile from town in Portinscale, this smart detached house has six great-value bedrooms. Ask for room 3 or room 5 if you're after maximum space or room 2 if you'd like a view of Skiddaw from your bed.

★**Cottage in the Wood**   HOTEL £££
(☎ 017687-78409; www.thecottageinthewood.co.uk; Braithwaite; d Sun-Thu £110-190, Fri & Sat £120-205; ⊙ restaurant 6.30-9pm Tue-Sat; P🤖) For a secluded spoil, head for this out-of-the-way bolthole, on the road to Whinlatter Forest, in a completely modernised coaching inn. Elegant rooms survey woods and countryside: the Mountain View rooms overlook the Skiddaw Range, but we liked the superprivate Attic Suite and the Garden Room, with its wood floors and wet-room. The restaurant's fantastic too (set dinner menu £55).

✕ Eating & Drinking

Pumpkin Cafe   CAFE £
(☎ 017687-75973; 19 Lake Rd; lunches £4-8; ⊙ 8.30am-5pm Mon-Sat) An ever-popular lunch stop, this cafe-bakery-deli is under new owners but the menu remains the same. Order a deli sandwich or a mix-and-match Mediterranean salad and chase it down with a flat white and a slice of heavenly carrot cake. There's seating upstairs or you can order to go.

Morrel's   BRITISH ££
(☎ 017687-72666; www.morrels.co.uk; Lake Rd; 3-course menu £21.95, mains £12-19.50; ⊙ 5.30-9pm Tue-Sun) Probably the best option for dinner in town, Morrel's is a modern bistro serving fusion dishes like Cajun salmon, Asian-style pork belly and summer risotto. Glossy wood, spotlights and pop-art prints of Steve McQueen and Marilyn Monroe give it character.

Pheasant Inn   PUB FOOD ££
(☎ 017687-76234; www.the-pheasant.co.uk; Bassenthwaite Lake; mains £13.50-21; ⊙ restaurant 7-9pm Tue-Sat, noon-2pm Sun, bistro noon-4.30pm & 6-9pm) A short drive along Bassenthwaite Lake is this fine-dining pub. Hunting prints and pewter tankards cover the old bar, stocked with vintage whiskies and Lakeland ales, and the two restaurants (informal bistro and smart restaurant) serve superior country food. The afternoon tea's done in the proper English fashion too, served on a tiered cakestand with scones and cucumber sandwiches.

Square Orange   CAFE, BAR
(☎ 017687-73888; www.thesquareorange.co.uk; 20 St John's St; ⊙ 10am-11pm Sun-Thu, 10am-midnight Fri & Sat) This lively little hang-out has become a real draw for Keswick's hipsters, shakers and drinkers, with regular live music, a tapas and pizza menu, an impressive range of wines and ales and the best coffee in town. There are even board games to keep you entertained.

Dog & Gun
PUB

(☑ 017687-73463; 2 Lake Rd; ⊙ 11am-11pm)
Benches, beams, hearths, rugs: the old Dog
is the picture of a Lakeland pub. Look out
for Thirst Rescue ale, which donates part of
its proceeds to the Keswick Mountain Rescue Team.

🔒 Shopping

★ **George Fisher**
SPORTS & OUTDOORS

(☑ 017687-72178; www.georgefisher.co.uk; 2 Borrowdale Rd; ⊙ 9am-5.30pm Mon-Sat, 10am-4pm
Sun) Quite possibly the most famous outdoors shop in the Lake District, founded
in 1967 and still the place where discerning
hikers go to buy their gear (even if it is a
bit more expensive than the chains). There
are three floors of boots, tents and gear,
and the boot-fitting service is legendarily
thorough.

ℹ️ Information

Tourist Office (☑ 017687-72645; keswicktic@
lake-district.gov.uk; Moot Hall, Market Pl;
⊙ 9.30am-5.30pm Apr-Oct, to 4.30pm Nov-
Mar) The town's tourist office is well run and
the staff are very informed; it also sells discounted tickets for the Keswick Launch.

Post Office (48 Main St; ⊙ 9am-5.30pm Mon-
Fri, to 12.30pm Sat)

ℹ️ Getting There & Away

The **Keswick & Honister Dayrider** (p568) buys
unlimited travel on buses in the Keswick area,
including to Borrowdale and Buttermere. Useful
buses from Keswick:

Bus 555/556 Lakeslink Hourly to Grasmere
(£7.70, 40 minutes), Ambleside (£8.20, 45
minutes), Windermere (£8.90, one hour) and
Kendal (£9.60, 1½ hours).

Bus 77/77A Circular route (five to seven daily)
from Keswick via Portinscale, Catbells, Grange,
Seatoller, Honister Pass, Buttermere, Lorton
and Whinlatter.

Bus 78 (at least hourly Monday to Friday, half-
hourly weekends) The main Borrowdale bus,
with stops at Lodore, Grange, Rosthwaite and
Seatoller.

Borrowdale

POP 417

With their patchwork of craggy hills, broad
fields, tinkling streams and drystone walls,
the side-by-side valleys of Borrowdale and
Buttermere are many people's idea of the
quintessential Lakeland landscape. Once
a centre for mineral mining (especially for

slate, coal and graphite), this is walkers'
country these days and, apart from the odd
rickety barn or puttering tractor, there's precious little to spoil the view.

South of Keswick, the B5289 tracks Derwentwater into the heart of Borrowdale,
winding past the small farming villages
of Grange-in-Borrowdale, Rosthwaite and
Stonethwaite.

👁 Sights & Activities

Lodore Falls
WATERFALL

At the southern end of Derwentwater, this
famous waterfall featured in a poem by Robert Southey, but it's only worth visiting after
a good spell of rain. It's in the grounds of
the Lodore Hotel; there's an honesty box for
donations.

Bowder Stone
OUTDOORS

A mile south from Grange, a turn-off leads
up to the geological curiosity known as the
Bowder Stone, a 1870-ton lump of rock left
behind by a retreating glacier. A small stepladder leads to the top of the rock.

Watendlath Tarn
LAKE

This National Trust–owned tarn is reached
via a turn-off on the B5285 south of Keswick.
On the way the road passes over one of the
Lake District's most photographed packhorse crossings at **Ashness Bridge**. Parking
at the tarn is free for NT members, but the
road is narrow and has few passing places
so it's more pleasant to walk up in summer.

Platty+
BOATING

(☑ 017687-76572; www.plattyplus.co.uk; kayaks
& canoes per hour £8-15) Based at the Lodore
Boat Landings at the southern end of Derwentwater, this company hires out kayaks,
canoes, rowing boats and sailing dinghies. It
also runs instruction courses.

🛏 Sleeping & Eating

Derwentwater
Independent Hostel
HOSTEL £

(☑ 017687-77246; www.derwentwater.org; Barrow
House; dm £20.50-22.50, d £49-54, tr £72-77, q
£93-104; P @) Built as a 19th-century mansion, this grand Grade II–listed house is
one of Britain's most architecturally ostentatious hostels. Previously YHA-owned, now
private, it's a thing of beauty: many rooms
have original features like plasterwork and
fireplaces. The 88 beds are split across 11
bedrooms; smaller dorms can be booked by
groups and families.

★ Langstrath Inn
B&B ££

(☎ 017687-77239; www.thelangstrath.com; Stonethwaite; d £106-136; ☺ restaurant noon-2-30pm & 6-8.30pm Tue-Sun; P 🛜) This simple country inn makes one of the best little bases in Borrowdale, we reckon. Its eight rooms are snug and simple, with crimson throws and the occasional roof beam to add character – but it's the views that really sell the place. Hearty, unpretentious food (dinner mains £13.95) and ales from Hawkshead Brewery are served in the restaurant.

Yew Tree Farm
B&B ££

(☎ 017687-77675; www.borrowdaleherdwick.co.uk; Rosthwaite; d £85; P) There are floral patterns galore at this sturdy Cumbrian farmhouse in rural Rosthwaite, with three rooms snuggled among cob walls and tiny windows (no wi-fi or TV!). It's run by working sheep farmers and you'll be able to spot Herdwicks in the nearby fields. Breakfast is huge and the **Flock In Tea-Room** over the road serves delicious cakes and puddings.

❶ Getting There & Away

Bus 77/77A (£2.30 to £7.70, five to seven daily) makes a circular route from Keswick via all of Borrowdale's villages, over Honister Pass and through Buttermere. Bus 78 (£2.30 to £4, at least hourly) shuttles through Borrowdale as far as Seatoller. If you're planning on making a return journey the same day, it's cheaper to buy the **Keswick & Honister Dayrider** (p568) than a return fare.

Buttermere

POP 121

Up and over Honister Pass, the road drops sharply into the deep bowl of Buttermere, gouged out by a steamroller glacier and backed by a string of impressive peaks and emerald-green hills. The valley's twin lakes, **Buttermere** and **Crummock Water**, were once joined but became separated by glacial silt and rockfall. The little village of Buttermere sits halfway between the two and provides a wonderfully cosy base for exploring the rest of the valley and the many nearby fells, including **Haystacks** (597m), the favourite mountain and the last resting place of the patron saint of Lakeland walkers, the author Alfred Wainwright.

From here the B5289 exits the valley's northern edge and heads back towards Keswick.

🛏 Sleeping & Eating

Buttermere YHA
HOSTEL £

(☎ 0845-371 9508; www.yha.org.uk; dm £10-30; ☺ reception 8.30-10am & 5-10.30pm, hostel mid-Mar–Oct; P 🛜 ♿) Perched in a perfect position on the Honister–Buttermere road, this excellent hostel has rooms looking out across the lake. The decor is smart, colourful and surprisingly modern. There's a great cafe-kitchen and plenty of quads and six-bed dorms – but note that the hostel is open to individual travellers at weekends and during summer holidays.

★ Kirkstile Inn
PUB FOOD ££

(☎ 01900-85219; www.kirkstile.com; mains £11.50-15.95) A finer country pub you could not hope to find. Hidden away near the little lake of Loweswater, a mile or so north of Buttermere, the Kirkstile is a joy: crackling fires, oak beams, worn carpets, wooden bar and all. Rooms (singles £64, doubles £98 to £115) are quaint; some have views across Lorton Vale.

It's particularly known for its award-winning ales (try the Loweswater Gold).

Bridge Hotel
PUB FOOD ££

(☎ 017687-70252; www.bridge-hotel.com; mains £10-16; P 🛜) As the name suggests, it's right beside Buttermere's village bridge. There's standard pub food in the bar or more upmarket fare in the smart-casual restaurant. Frilly rooms (singles £74.50, doubles £159 to £169) and an antique ambience define the old Bridge.

❶ Getting There & Away

Bus 77/77A (£5.60, five to seven daily) serves Buttermere and Honister Pass from Keswick. For return journeys the same day, save a bit of cash by buying the Keswick & Honister Dayrider (p568).

Ullswater & Around

After Windermere, the second-largest lake in the Lake District is **Ullswater**, stretching for 7.5 miles between **Pooley Bridge** and **Glenridding** and **Patterdale** in the south. Carved out by a long-extinct glacier, the deep valley in which the lake sits is flanked by an impressive string of fells, most notably the razor ridge of **Helvellyn**, Cumbria's third-highest mountain at 950m. The area is also famous as the place where William Wordsworth was inspired to write his best-known poem, 'Daffodils'.

Driving Tour
Borrowdale & Buttermere

START KESWICK
END KESWICK
LENGTH 28 MILES; THREE TO FOUR HOURS

This is one of the Lakes' most beautiful road trips, taking in the unspoilt scenery of the Borrowdale, Buttermere and Lorton Valleys. It's a perfect day trip out of Keswick.

Begin with breakfast in **1 Keswick**, then head along the B5289 into Borrowdale. First stop is **2 Lodore Falls** (p591), a pretty cascade at the southern end of Derwentwater. Next, detour to the little hamlet of **3 Grange-in-Borrowdale**, where a trail leads up the slate-strewn sides of Castle Crag, a small fell with great views over Borrowdale. From Grange, carry on to the huge boulder known as the **4 Bowder Stone** (p591), shifted into position by the long-gone glacier that carved out the Borrowdale Valley. Pootle on to **5 Rosthwaite** for cake at the Flock In Tea-Room or to **6 Seatoller** for lunch.

In the afternoon tackle the steep crawl up to **7 Honister Pass** (p590), where you can

pick up some slate souvenirs, take a tour down into the depths of the old slate mine or tackle the hair-raising *via ferrata*.

From here the road drops down into the beautiful valley of **8 Buttermere**. Spot the zigzag peaks of High Stile, Haystacks and Red Pike looming over the lake, stop off for a drink at the Fish Inn and remember to pay your respects to hiker and author Alfred Wainwright inside St James' Church.

Continue along the shore of Crummock Water past **9 Loweswater**, where you could make an optional but very worthwhile detour via the excellent Kirkstile Inn. When you reach **10 Low Lorton**, a right-hand turn carries you over Whinlatter Pass to **11 Whinlatter Forest** (p589). The forest park makes a good spot for a late-afternoon stop; there's a pleasant cafe at the visitor centre, as well as informative displays on the local wildlife.

There are a couple of great options for dinner on your way back to Keswick: Cottage in the Wood (p590) just before **12 Braithwaite** or the traditional Pheasant Inn (p590) on the shores of Bassenthwaite Lake.

Sadly, the Ullswater area was one of the areas worst affected by the terrible storms of 2015. The lake level rose by around a metre and the becks burst their banks, sending cascades of water through Pooley Bridge and Glenridding, swamping shops, destroying bridges and causing massive damage to the lake shore. It's been a long haul back to normality and no doubt you'll still see the storm's effects when you visit.

👁 Sights & Activities

Gowbarrow Park
& Aira Force   PARK, WATERFALL
FREE This rolling park stretches out across the lake shore between Pooley Bridge and Glenridding. Well-marked paths lead up to the impressive 20m waterfall of Aira Force. Another waterfall, High Force, is further up the hillside.

South of Gowbarrow Park is Glencoyne Bay, where the springtime daffodils inspired William Wordsworth to pen the immortal lines: 'I wandered lonely as a cloud/That floats on high o'er vales and hills/When all at once I saw a crowd/A host of golden daffodils.'

★ Helvellyn   HIKING
Along with Scafell Pike, this challenging hike is the one everyone wants to do. The classic ascent takes in the twin ridges of Striding and Swirral Edge, which are spectacular but very exposed and involve some scrambling and dizzyingly steep drops on either side – if you're at all nervous of heights, Helvellyn is probably not the fell for you. The usual routes climb up through Glenridding or Patterdale. Always check the weather forecast and take all the necessary supplies.

Ullswater 'Steamers'   BOATING
(☑ 017684-82229; www.ullswater-steamers.co.uk; round-the-lake adult/child £13.90/6.95) Back in service after 2015's damaging storms, Ullswater's historic steamers are a memorable way to explore the lake. The various vessels include the stately *Lady of the Lake*, launched in 1877, supposedly the world's oldest working passenger boat. The boats run east–west from Pooley Bridge to Glenridding via Howtown; there are nine daily sailings in summer, three in winter.

🛏 Sleeping & Eating

Helvellyn YHA   HOSTEL £
(☑ 0845-371 9742; www.yha.org.uk; Greenside; dm £13-25; ⊙ Easter-Oct) This back-of-beyond hostel is a favourite of hikers looking to get an early start on Helvellyn. It's in an old miner's cottage about a 900m hike up from the valley. Dorms are small and facilities are basic, but meals are provided by hostel staff. There's even a bar.

Old Water View   B&B ££
(☑ 017684-82175; www.oldwaterview.co.uk; Patterdale; d £98; P ⊛ 🐾) Patterdale has several B&Bs, but this one's the pick. It's a simple place focusing on the essentials: friendly service, comfy rooms and good value. The split-level Bothy room is ideal for families, with attic beds for the kids, while Little Gem overlooks a stream and Place Fell is said to have been a favourite of Alfred Wainwright.

Lowthwaite B&B   B&B ££
(☑ 017684-82343; www.lowthwaiteullswater.com; Matterdale; d £96; P ⊛) This lovely farmhouse in Matterdale is all about the good life. The globetrotting owners have filled the place with souvenirs, such as chunky wooden beds made in Tanzania that match the house's hefty wooden beams (the owners previously ran expeditions up Kilimanjaro). It's a couple of miles from the lake, off the A5091 to Dockray. Two-night minimum on weekends.

Fellbites   CAFE ££
(☑ 01768-482781; Glenridding; lunch mains £3.95-9.95, dinner mains £12.50-18; ⊙ 9am-8.30pm Thu-Tue, to 5.30pm Wed) This cafe beside the main car park in Glenridding has something to fill you up at any time of day: generous fry-ups for breakfast; soups, pulled-pork burgers and rarebits for lunch; lamb shanks and duck breast for dinner. It's honest, no-fuss grub.

Traveller's Rest   PUB FOOD ££
(☑ 017684-82298; Glenridding; mains £5.50-15; ⊙ 10am-11pm) Down a pint with a view of the fells at Traveller's Rest, a Glenridding stalwart. The food might be plain (steaks, pies, mixed grills) but the portions are huge.

ℹ Information

Ullswater Tourist Office (☑ 017684-82414; ullswatertic@lake-district.gov.uk; Glenridding; ⊙ 9am-5pm Apr-Oct) has comprehensive advice on hikes and activities around Ullswater.

ℹ Getting There & Away

The Ullswater Bus-and-Boat Combo ticket (adult/child/family £15.50/8.50/33) includes a day's travel on bus 108 with a return trip on an Ullswater Steamer; buy the ticket on the bus.

Bus 108/508 travels from Penrith to Patterdale via Pooley Bridge and Glenridding (£5.20, nine daily Monday to Friday, four on weekends).

Kendal

POP 28,586

Technically Kendal isn't in the Lake District, but it's a major gateway town. Often known as the 'Auld Grey Town' thanks to the sombre grey stone used for many of its buildings, Kendal is a bustling shopping centre with some good restaurants, a funky arts centre and intriguing museums. But it'll forever be synonymous in many people's minds with its famous mint cake, a staple item in the nation's hiking packs ever since Edmund Hillary and Tenzing Norgay munched it during their ascent of Everest in 1953.

◉ Sights & Activities

Abbot Hall Art Gallery GALLERY
(☑ 01539-722464; www.abbothall.org.uk; adult/child £7/free, joint ticket with Museum of Lakeland Life & Industry £8.60; ⊙ 10.30am-5pm Mon-Sat Apr-Oct, to 4pm Nov-Mar) Kendal's fine art gallery houses one of the northwest's best collections of 18th- and 19th-century art. It's especially strong on portraiture and Lakeland landscapes: look out for works by Constable, John Ruskin and local boy George Romney, a key figure in the Kendal School. Look out for signposts as you head south along Kirkland Rd.

Museum of Lakeland Life & Industry MUSEUM
(☑ 01539-722464; www.lakelandmuseum.org.uk; adult/child £5/free, joint ticket with Abbot Hall Art Gallery £8.60; ⊙ 10.30am-5pm Mon-Sat Mar-Oct, to 4pm Nov-Feb) Directly opposite Abbot Hall, this museum re-creates various scenes from Lakeland life during the 18th and 19th centuries, including a farmhouse parlour, a Lakeland kitchen, an apothecary and the study of Arthur Ransome, author of *Swallows and Amazons* – look out for some of his original sketchbooks.

Levens Hall HISTORIC BUILDING
(☑ 015395-60321; www.levenshall.co.uk; house & gardens adult/child £12.80/5, garden only £9.50/4; ⊙ house noon-4.30pm, gardens 10am-5pm Sun-Thu Mar-Oct) This Elizabethan manor is built around a mid-13th-century *pele* tower and fine Jacobean furniture litters the house, although the real draw is the 17th-century topiary garden: a surreal riot of pyramids, swirls, curls, pompoms and peacocks straight out of *Alice in Wonderland*.

A major project to reface the West Elevation with lime mortar should be completed by the time you read this.

Outdoor Adventure Company OUTDOORS
(☑ 01539-722147; www.theoutdooradventurecompany.co.uk; Old Hutton) An experienced outdoors centre near Kendal offering lots of activities from archery to tank-driving.

⚞ Festivals & Events

Kendal Calling MUSIC
(www.kendalcalling.co.uk) The Lake District's largest outdoor music festival is held in July and welcomes around 12,000 people to the Lowther Deer Park near Kendal. Recent headliners include Madness, The Charlatans, Elbow and Kaiser Chiefs.

Kendal Mountain Festival OUTDOORS
(www.mountainfest.co.uk) Annual mountain-themed celebration encompassing films, books and talks in November.

🛏 Sleeping & Eating

Kendal is a bit low on quality sleeping options and it's easily visited from Windermere.

Brew Brothers CAFE £
(☑ 01539-722237; www.brew-brothers.co.uk; 69 Highgate; mains £8.50-10; ⊙ 8.30am-5.30pm Mon-Sat) The hipster cafe comes to Kendal at this new number on Highgate. With its scruffy wood furniture and black-aproned baristas, it's got the aesthetic down, but its owners are Lakeland through and through – they previously ran a cafe in Windermere. Go for smashed avocado and poached eggs for brekkie, then for lunch wolf down a hot smoked-salmon sandwich. Yum.

1657 Chocolate House CAFE £
(☑ 01539-740702; 54 Branthwaite Brow; lunches £3-8) A chocaholic's delight: handmade chocolates and Kendal mint cake in the basement, plus umpteen varieties of hot chocolate in the upstairs cafe.

★ Punch Bowl Inn PUB FOOD ££
(☑ 015395-68237; www.the-punchbowl.co.uk; Crosthwaite; mains £13.95-19.95; ⊙ noon-4pm & 5.30-8.30pm; ℗) If you don't mind a drive, there's no doubt – this renowned gastropub in the village of Crosthwaite is the best place to eat around Kendal. Whitewashed outside,

carefully modernised inside, it's a cosy, inviting space to dine. Chef Scott Fairweather's superb food blends classic dishes with cheffy ingredients (oyster mousse, potato croquettes, pea fricassée, salsify).

The rooms (£105 to £305) are lovely too: they're all different, but the nicest ones have reclaimed beams, sloping eaves, slate-floored bathrooms and his-and-hers clawfoot tubs.

New Moon   BISTRO ££
(✆01539-729254; www.newmoonrestaurant.co.uk; 129 Highgate; mains £12.95-17.50; ⊙11.30am-2.15pm & 5.30-9pm Tue-Sat) For bistro dining in Kendal, this long-standing address is the place, with a varied menu encompassing almond-crusted cod, veggie tarts, Moroccan-style chicken, Cumbrian rump steak and plenty more besides – so you're pretty much guaranteed to find a taste to tickle your fancy. The two-course pre-7pm menu is great value at £13.95.

☆ Entertainment

Brewery Arts Centre   THEATRE, CINEMA
(✆01539-725133; www.breweryarts.co.uk; Highgate) A cracking arts centre with a gallery, cafe, theatre and two cinemas, hosting the latest films as well as music, theatre, dance and much more.

🛍 Shopping

★Low Sizergh Barn   FOOD
(✆015395-60426; www.lowsizerghbarn.co.uk; ⊙9am-5.30pm) A prodigious selection of Lakeland goodies are available at this farm shop, just outside Kendal on the A590. Breads from Grange Bakery, meats from Mansergh Hall, cheeses from Thornby Moor Dairy and beers from the Coniston Brewery Co are just some of the treats in store. There's also a farm trail and woodland walk to follow if the weather's nice.

ℹ Getting There & Away

The train line from Windermere runs to Kendal (£4.70, 15 minutes, hourly) en route to Oxenholme.

Bus 555/556 Regular bus (half-hourly Monday to Saturday, hourly at weekends) to Windermere (£6.70, 30 minutes), Ambleside (£6.90, 40 minutes) and Grasmere (£8.90, 1¼ hours).

Bus 106 To Penrith (£10.80, 80 minutes, one or two daily Monday to Friday).

CUMBRIAN COAST

While the central lakes and fells pull in a never-ending stream of visitors, surprisingly few ever make the trek west to explore Cumbria's coastline. And that's a shame: while it might not compare to the wild grandeur of Northumberland or the rugged splendour of Scotland's shores, Cumbria's coast is well worth exploring – a bleakly beautiful landscape of long sandy bays, grassy headlands, salt marshes and seaside villages stretching all the way from Morecambe Bay to the shores of the Solway Coast. There's an important seabird reserve at St Bees Head and the majestic grounds of Holker Hall are well worth a wander.

Historically, Cumbria's coast served the local mining, quarrying and shipping industries and Barrow-in-Furness remains a major shipbuilding centre. More controversial is the nuclear plant of Sellafield, a major employer but still dividing opinion half-a-century on from its inception.

⊙ Sights

★Holker Hall   HISTORIC BUILDING
(✆015395-58328; www.holker.co.uk; adult/child £12/free; ⊙house 11am-4pm, grounds 10.30am-5pm Wed-Sun Mar-Oct) Three miles east of Cartmel on the B5278, Holker Hall has been the family seat of the Cavendish family for nigh on four centuries. Though parts of the house date from the 16th century, the house was almost entirely rebuilt following a devastating fire in 1871. It's a typically ostentatious Victorian affair, covered with mullioned windows, gables and copper-topped turrets outside and filled with a warren of lavishly over-the-top rooms inside.

Muncaster Castle   CASTLE
(✆01229-717614; www.muncaster.co.uk; adult/child £13.50/6.75; ⊙gardens & owl centre 10.30am-5pm, castle noon-4pm Sun-Fri) This crenellated castle, 1.5 miles east of Ravenglass, was originally built around a 14th-century *pele* tower, constructed to resist Reiver raids. Home to the Pennington family for seven centuries, the castle's architectural highlights are its great hall and octagonal library, and outside you'll find an ornamental maze and splendid grounds. The castle is also home to a hawk and owl centre, which stages several flying displays a day.

Muncaster is also known for its numerous ghosts: keep your eyes peeled for the Mun-

CARTMEL

Tiny Cartmel is known for three things: its 12th-century **Cartmel Priory** (⊙9am-5.30pm May-Oct, to 3.30pm Nov-Apr), one of only a handful to have survived the ravages of the dissolution of the monasteries largely unscathed, its **miniature racecourse** and its world-famous sticky toffee pudding, sold at the **Cartmel Village Shop** (☑015395-36280; www.cartmelvillageshop.co.uk; ⊙9am-5pm Mon-Sat, 10am-4.30pm Sun).

More recently it's become known as the home of chef Simon Rogan (dubbed Cumbria's answer to Heston Blumenthal). His flagship restaurant, **L'Enclume** (☑015395-36362; www.lenclume.co.uk; Cavendish St, Cartmel; set lunch £49, lunch & dinner menu £130; ⊙noon-1.30pm & 6.30-8.30pm Tue-Sun), showcases his boundary-pushing cuisine and madcap presentation as well as his passion for foraged ingredients.

He also runs a less formal bistro, **Rogan & Company** (☑015395-35917; www.roganandcompany.co.uk; The Square, Cartmel; 2-/3-course set lunch £18/24, mains £18.95-26.95; ⊙noon-2pm Tue-Sat, 6.30-9pm Mon-Sat, 12.30-5pm Sun), across the village. This village bistro focuses on classic British dishes like pork belly, butter-poached cod and roasted plaice, perfected and perfectly presented. It's cosy and welcoming, with fires and wooden interiors, and the Sunday roast is an utter feast. Bookings are essential for both.

Also worth a visit is the **Cavendish Arms** (☑015395-36240; www.thecavendisharms.co.uk; Cavendish St, Cartmel; mains £16-21; ⊙11am-11pm), where you'll be treated to seriously upmarket food. Exposed beams, worn wood and a sunflower-yellow facade conjure an olde-worlde vibe, and there's a sunny beer garden too.

caster Boggle and a malevolent jester known as Tom Fool (hence 'tomfoolery').

Laurel & Hardy Museum
MUSEUM

(☑01229-582292; www.laurel-and-hardy.co.uk; Brogden St, Ulverston; adult/child £5/2.50; ⊙10am-5pm Easter-Oct, closed Mon & Wed rest of year) Founded by avid Laurel and Hardy collector Bill Cubin back in 1983, this madcap museum in Ulverston (the birthplace of Stan Laurel) has new premises inside the town's old Roxy cinema. It's crammed floor-to-ceiling with cinematic memorabilia, from original posters to film props, and there's a shoebox-sized cinema showing back-to-back Laurel and Hardy classics. Now run by Bill's grandson, it's a must for movie buffs.

South Lakes Safari Zoo
ZOO

(www.southlakessafarizoo.com; Melton Tce, Lindal-inFurness, Ulverston; adult/child £16.50/9; ⊙10am-5pm) This zoo has recently reinvented itself as the UK's first pedestrian safari, in which visitors can wander up close to the animals, hand-feed giraffes and lemurs and see vultures, macaws and condors flying past (thankfully the keepers still take charge of the big cats). There are regular feeding opportunities throughout the day – £3 buys a pass for one feeding session. Though it's still essentially a zoo, the lack of cages makes for an intriguing and different experience.

St Bees Head
WILDLIFE RESERVE

(RSPB; stbees.head@rspb.org.uk) Five-and-a-half miles south of Whitehaven and 1½ miles north of the tiny town of St Bees, this wind-battered headland is one of Cumbria's most important reserves for nesting seabirds. Depending on the season, species nesting here include fulmars, kittiwakes and razorbills as well as Britain's only population of resident black guillemots. There are over 2 miles of cliff paths to explore.

ℹ️ Getting There & Around

The Furness and Cumbrian Coast railway lines loop 120 miles from Lancaster to Carlisle, stopping at the coastal resorts of Grange, Ulverston, Ravenglass, Whitehaven and Workington. The **Cumbria Coast Day Ranger** (adult/child £19.50/9.75) covers a day's unlimited travel on the line and works out cheaper than a return journey from Carlisle or Lancaster.

Northern & Eastern Cumbria

Many visitors speed through the northern and eastern reaches of Cumbria in a headlong dash for the Lake District, but it's worth taking the time to venture inland from the national park. It might not have the big-name fells and chocolate-box villages, but it's full of interest: traditional towns, crumbling

LOCAL KNOWLEDGE

RAVENGLASS & ESKDALE RAILWAY

Affectionately known as La'al Ratty, the pocket-sized **Ravenglass & Eskdale Railway** (☑ 01229-717171; www.ravenglass-railway.co.uk; adult/child/family return £13.50/6.75/38; 🖼) was originally built to ferry iron ore from the Eskdale mines to the coast. These days it's one of Cumbria's most beloved family attractions, with miniature steam trains that chug for 7 miles along the Eskdale valley between the coastal town of Ravenglass and the village of Dalegarth. There are seven to 14 trains a day depending on the season. A five-day Ratty Rover pass costs £40/20/110 per adult/child/family.

castles, abandoned abbeys and sweeping moors, all set alongside the magnificent Roman engineering project of Hadrian's Wall.

Carlisle

POP 75,306

Carlisle isn't Britain's prettiest city, but it has history and heritage aplenty. Precariously perched on the frontier between England and Scotland, in the area once ominously dubbed the 'Debatable Lands', Cumbria's capital is a city with a notoriously stormy past: sacked by the Vikings, pillaged by the Scots and plundered by the Border Reivers, the city has been on the front line of England's defences for more than 1000 years.

Reminders of the past are evident in its great crimson castle and cathedral, built from the same rosy-red sandstone as most of the city's houses. On English St, you can also see two massive circular **towers** that once flanked the city's gateway.

The closest section of Hadrian's Wall begins at nearby Brampton.

⊙ Sights

★ **Carlisle Castle** CASTLE

(EH; ☑ 01228-591922; www.english-heritage.org.uk/visit/places/carlisle-castle/; Castle Way; adult/child £6.40/3.80, joint ticket with Cumbria's Museum of Military Life £9.20/5.15; ⊙10am-5pm Apr-Sep, to 4pm Oct-Mar) Carlisle's brooding, rust-red castle lurks on the north side of the city. Founded around a Celtic and Roman stronghold, the castle's Norman keep was added in 1092 by William Rufus, and later refortified by Henry II, Edward I and Henry VIII (who added the supposedly cannon-proof towers). From the battlements, the stirring views stretch as far as the Scottish borders.

The castle also houses **Cumbria's Museum of Military Life** (☑ 01228-532774; adult/child £4/2, joint ticket with Carlisle Castle £9.20/5.15; ⊙10am-6pm Apr-Oct, to 5pm Sat-Thu Nov-Mar), which houses collections of military memorabilia associated with the region's regiments.

The castle has witnessed some dramatic events over the centuries: Mary, Queen of Scots, was imprisoned here in 1568, and the castle was the site of a notorious eight-month siege during the English Civil War, when the Royalist garrison survived by eating rats, mice and the castle dogs before finally surrendering in 1645. Look out for some medieval graffiti and the 'licking stones' in the dungeon, which Jacobite prisoners supposedly lapped for moisture.

Carlisle Cathedral CHURCH

(☑ 01228-548151; www.carlislecathedral.org.uk; 7 The Abbey; suggested donation £5, photography £1; ⊙7.30am-6.15pm Mon-Sat, to 5pm Sun) Built from the same red sandstone as Carlisle castle, Carlisle's cathedral began life as a priory church in 1122 and became a cathedral when its first abbot, Athelwold, became the first bishop of Carlisle. Among its notable features are the 15th-century choir stalls, the barrel-vaulted roof and the 14th-century East Window, one of the largest Gothic windows in England. Surrounding the cathedral are other priory relics, including the 16th-century **Fratry** and the **Prior's Tower**.

Tullie House Museum MUSEUM

(☑ 01228-618718; www.tulliehouse.co.uk; Castle St; adult/child £7.70/free; ⊙10am-5pm Mon-Sat, 11am-5pm Sun) Carlisle's flagship museum covers 2000 years of the city's past. The Roman Frontier Gallery explores Carlisle's Roman foundations, while the Border Galleries cover the Bronze Age through to the Industrial Revolution. Two new galleries flesh out the story: the Border Reivers covers the marauding bandits who once terrorised the area, while the Vikings Revealed exhibition displays finds from the Cumwhitton Viking cemetery, including helmets, swords and grave goods. The top-floor Lookout has cracking views of the castle.

Settle to Carlisle Railway   HERITAGE RAILWAY
(www.settle-carlisle.co.uk; day-ranger ticket adult/
child £15/7.50) This historic railway route
travels from Carlisle to Settle in North Yorkshire and is famous for its views across the
Yorkshire Dales.

🛏 Sleeping

★ Willowbeck Lodge   B&B ££
(☏ 01228-513607;   www.willowbeck-lodge.com;
Lambley Bank, Scotby; d £100-130; P ?) If staying in the city centre isn't important, then
this palatial B&B is the top choice in the
city. The four rooms are huge, contemporary and plush, with luxuries like underfloor
heating, Egyptian-cotton bedding and tasteful shades of beige and taupe. Some rooms
have balconies overlooking the gardens and
pond. There's also a restaurant, Fini's Kitch-
en (mains £14 to £22).

Crown & Mitre   HISTORIC HOTEL ££
(☏ 01228-525491;   www.peelhotels.co.uk/hotels/
crown-and-mitre-hotel-carlisle-cumbria-england;
English St; d £72.50-118.50; P ? ≋) You will not
find a grander edifice in Carlisle than this
imposing Edwardian pile, built as the city's
poshest hotel following the arrival of the railway. It still has a hint of its original splendour
in the lobby and staircase, but the rooms feel
pretty corporate these days. It's worth up-
grading to King for more up-to-date decor.

Warwick Hall   B&B £££
(☏ 01228-561546;   www.warwickhall.org; Warwick-
on-Eden; s £88-130, d £128-164) This fine country
house 2 miles from the centre along Warwick
Rd is a real country retreat. With its huge
rooms, high ceilings and old-fashioned decor, it feels a bit like staying on an aristocratic
friend's estate. There are hectares of grounds
and even a stretch of river for fishing.

✕ Eating

Hell Below & Co   FUSION £
(☏ 01228-548481;   www.hellbelowandco.co.uk;   14
Devonshire St; mains £8-9.50; ☉ 11am-midnight
Mon-Sat) A new menu has given this trendy
brick-walled, bare-wood bar-bistro a fresh
lease of life: it spans the gamut from cheese
and charcuterie sharing boards to steaks,
fajitas and flat-iron chicken. If you're not
hungry, inventive cocktails like bubblegum
sours and starburst cosmos are served.

Foxes Cafe Lounge   CAFE £
(☏ 01228-491836;   www.foxescafelounge.co.uk;   18
Abbey St; mains £4-8; ☉ 8am-4.30pm) Swing by

this cool cafe for a pastry and cappuccino or
an apple-and-elderflower smoothie – or better still, settle in for a hearty brunch (available in carnivorous and veggie versions).

David's   BRITISH ££
(☏ 01228-523578; www.davidsrestaurant.co.uk;   62
Warwick Rd; 2-course lunch £16.95, dinner mains
£15.95-25.50; ☉ noon-3.30pm & 6.30-11pm Tue-
Sat) For many years this town-house restaurant has been the address for formal dining
in Carlisle and there's no sign that's going to
change. It majors in rich, traditional dishes
with a strong French flavour: lamb with a
pistachio crust and port gravy, roast chicken
with leek and tarragon mash. The house is
full of period architecture too.

🍷 Drinking & Entertainment

Botchergate is the centre of Carlisle's nightlife. It gets rowdy at closing time.

Fats   PUB
(☏ 01228-511774; 48 Abbey St; ☉ 11am-11pm) A
less hectic alternative to Botchergate's pubs.
DJs and comedy nights are held regularly.

Brickyard   CONCERT VENUE
(☏ 01228-512220; www.thebrickyardonline.com; 14
Fisher St) Carlisle's grungy gig venue, housed
in the former Memorial Hall.

ℹ Information

Tourist Office (☏ 01228-625600; www.histor
ic-carlisle.org.uk; Greenmarket; ☉ 9.30am-5pm
Mon-Sat, 10.30am-4pm Sun)

ℹ Getting There & Away

BUS

National Express coaches depart from the bus
station on Lonsdale St for destinations including
London (£29.60 to £34.50, 7½ hours, two or
three direct daily), Manchester (£27.70, three to
3½ hours, three daily) and Glasgow (£19.70, two
hours, four to six daily).

Keswick bus 554; £12.10, 70 minutes, four
daily Monday to Saturday, three on Sunday

Penrith bus 104; £6.50, 40 minutes, half-
hourly Monday to Saturday, nine on Sunday

TRAIN

Carlisle is on the west-coast line from London
to Glasgow. It's also the terminus for the scenic
Cumbrian Coast and Tyne Valley Lines, as well
as the historic Settle to Carlisle Railway (p599)
across the Yorkshire Dales. The following are the
main destinations:

Glasgow £28, 1¼ hours

SOUTH TYNEDALE RAILWAY

The heritage narrow-gauge **South Tynedale Railway** (☑ 01434-381696, timetable 01434-382828; www.south-tynedale-railway.org.uk; adult/child return to Lintley £10/4; ☉ Apr-Oct), the highest such in England, puffs for 3.5 miles of scenic track between Alston in Cumbria and Lintley in Northumberland. En route you pass over three landmark viaducts at South Tyne, Gilderdale and Whitley.

Lancaster £30, 45 minutes
London Euston £113.50, 3½ hours
Manchester £56, 2 hours, 10 minutes
Newcastle-upon-Tyne £15.90, 1½ hours

🛈 Getting Around

To book a taxi, call **Radio Taxis** (☑ 01228-527575) or **Cumbria Cabs** (☑ 01228-899599).

Penrith

POP 15,181

Just outside the borders of the national park, red-brick Penrith perhaps has more in common with the stout market towns of the Yorkshire Dales. It's a solid, traditional place with plenty of cosy pubs and quaint teashops and a lively market on Tuesdays. It's also the main gateway for exploring the picturesque Eden Valley.

◉ Sights

Rheged   VISITOR CENTRE
(☑ 01768-868000; www.rheged.com; ☉ 10am-6pm) Cunningly disguised as a Lakeland hill 2 miles west of Penrith, this visitor centre houses an Imax cinema and temporary exhibitions. There's also a large retail hall selling Cumbrian foodstuffs and souvenirs. Local chef Peter Sidwell runs cooking classes and is also responsible for the cafe menu.

Penrith Castle   RUIN
(☉ 7.30am-9pm Easter-Oct, to 4.30pm Nov-Easter) The ruins of Penrith Castle loom on the edge of town opposite the train station. Built in the 14th century by William Strickland (later Bishop of Carlisle and Archbishop of Canterbury), it was later expanded by Richard III to resist Scottish raids, one of which razed the town in 1345.

🛏 Sleeping & Eating

Brooklands   B&B **££**
(☑ 01768-863395; www.brooklandsguesthouse. com; 2 Portland Pl; s £40-60, d £85-95; 🛜) The town's top B&B by some considerable margin, lodged in a terrace of red-brick houses on Portland Pl. It's Victorian outside, but inside it has fancy furnishings and posh extras such as White Company toiletries, in-room fridges and chocolates on the tea tray. There's a four-poster room too.

★ **Augill Castle**   HOTEL **£££**
(☑ 01768-341967; www.stayinacastle.com; Kirkby Stephen; r £180-240; 🅿🛜🐾) If you've always dreamt of staying in a bona fide British castle, then this stately pile in Kirkby Stephen is definitely the place. All the trappings are here – crenellated turrets, stained-glass windows, cavernous rooms – and inside the design vibe is rather groovy, with a mix of antique furniture and contemporary furnishings. There's even a minicinema. It's 25 miles southeast of Penrith.

★ **Four & Twenty**   BISTRO **££**
(☑ 01768-210231; www.fourandtwentypenrith.co. uk; 14 King St; lunch mains £10, dinner mains £14-18; ☉ noon-2.30pm & 6.30-9.30pm Tue-Sat) Proper fine dining with a reasonable price tag is the modus operandi at this fine bistro, which blends sleek decor with rustic wood, banquette seats and mix-and-match furniture. Expect sophisticated dishes such as twice-baked Stilton soufflé and braised blade of beef with caramelised onion rösti. If you're going to eat out in Penrith, this is the place to do it.

🛈 Information

The Tourist Office (☑ 01768-867466; pen. tic@eden.gov.uk; Middlegate; ☉ 9.30am-5pm Mon-Sat, 1-4.45pm Sun) also houses Penrith's tiny museum.

🛈 Getting There & Away

There are frequent train connections to Carlisle (£10.50, 15 minutes) and Lancaster (£18.50, one hour).

The bus station is northeast of the centre, off Sandgate.

Carlisle bus 104; £6.50, 40 minutes, half-hourly Monday to Saturday, nine on Sunday
Cumbrian coast (bus X4/X5; £6.50 to £10.20, half-hourly Monday to Saturday, hourly Sunday) Via Rheged, Keswick and Cockermouth.

Newcastle & Northeast England

Includes ➡

Newcastle-
upon-Tyne 605
Tynemouth 613
Durham 614
Barnard Castle 616
Hadrian's Wall 617
Northumberland
National Park 624
Northumberland
Coast 626

Best Places to Eat

➡ Jolly Fisherman (p627)

➡ Cross Lanes Organic Farm Shop (p617)

➡ Bouchon Bistrot (p622)

➡ Broad Chare (p609)

➡ House of Tides (p610)

Best Places to Sleep

➡ Langley Castle Hotel (p622)

➡ Marshall Meadows Country House Hotel (p632)

➡ Otterburn Castle Country House Hotel (p625)

➡ Jesmond Dene House (p609)

Why Go?

The irrepressible city of Newcastle-upon-Tyne anchors England's northeast. Set on the mighty River Tyne, this former industrial powerhouse's steep hills are lined with handsome Victorian buildings, and many of its one-time factories and warehouses have been transformed into galleries, museums, bars and entertainment venues. Newcastle's nightlife is legendary, and revelling in an evening on the tiles here is a quintessential experience.

Newcastle is also an ideal gateway for escaping into the northeast's utterly wild, starkly beautiful countryside – from the rounded Cheviot Hills to brooding Northumberland National Park and the remote North Pennines. Spectacular Hadrian's Wall cuts a lonely path through the landscape, dotted with dramatic fortress ruins that are haunting reminders of the bloody struggle with the Scots to the north, while the region's unspoilt coastline takes in long, desolate beaches, wind-worn castles and tiny, magical islands offshore.

When to Go

➡ Costumed re-enactments and Roman celebrations take place throughout the year at Hadrian's Wall.

➡ The best time to discover the region's miles of wide sandy beaches is during the summer season (June to August), although for surfers, Tynemouth's world-class waves are best (if chilliest) in winter and spring.

➡ September and October are great for losing yourself in the autumnal landscapes of Northumberland National Park.

➡ September is also the month to grab a Newkie Brown ale, or your running shoes, and join the party along the route of Tyneside's Great North Run, one of the world's biggest half-marathons.

Newcastle & Northeast England Highlights

1 **Victoria Tunnel**
(p607) Exploring a
coal-wagon tunnel
and WWII air-raid
shelter beneath
Newcastle's streets.

2 **Kielder
Observatory** (p624)
Stargazing from this
observatory in the
Northumberland
International Dark
Sky Park.

3 **Holy Island
(Lindisfarne)** (p630)
Negotiating the tidal
causeway to reach
this other-worldly
pilgrimage site.

4 **Bowes Museum**
(p617) Viewing
extraordinary objets
d'art in this château-
housed museum at
Barnard Castle.

5 **Berwick
Walls** (p631)
Circumnavigating

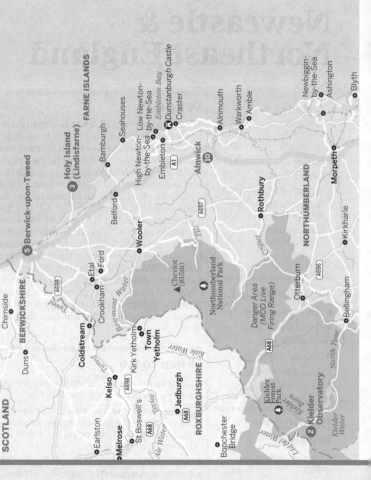

Newcastle &
Northeast England

SCOTLAND

EAST LOTHIAN

Cockburnspath

Grantshouse

Coldingham • St Abbs

Eyemouth

B6355

Duns

Chirnside

Earlston

BERWICKSHIRE

Melrose

St Boswell's

Kelso

A698

Coldstream

Crookham

Etal
Ford

Kirk Yetholm

Town
Yetholm

Jedburgh

A68

ROXBURGHSHIRE

Bonchester
Bridge

Ale Water

Teviot

Tweed

A698

A698

Tweed

Bowmont Water

Kale Water

2 **Kielder
Observatory**

Kielder
Forest
Park

Kielder Water

Kielder
Water

Kielder
Burn

4

Danger Area
(MOD Live
Firing Range)

A68

North Tyne

Bellingham

Otterburn

A696

Kirkharle

Rothbury

NORTHUMBERLAND

Northumberland
National Park

▲Cheviot
(815m)

Wooler

Belford

5 **Berwick-upon-Tweed**

3 **Holy Island
(Lindisfarne)**

FARNE ISLANDS

Bamburgh

Seahouses

High Newton-
by-the-Sea

Embleton

A1

Low Newton-
by-the-Sea

Embleton Bay

6 *Dunstanburgh Castle*

Craster

Alnwick

10

A697

Coquet

Till

Alnmouth

Warkworth

Amble

Newbiggin-
by-the-Sea

Ashington

Morpeth

A696

Blyth

N O R T H

S E A

N

0   20 km
0   10 miles

To Ijmuiden

Whitley Bay
Tynemouth
Wallsend
South Shields
Sunderland
Seaham
Peterlee
8 Hartlepool

Belsay
Ponteland
Newcastle Airport
Newcastle-upon-Tyne 1
Angel of the North
Beamish Open-Air Museum 9
Stanley
Consett
Knitsley
Durham 6
Croxdale
Sedgefield
Billingham
Redcar
Saltburn-by-the-Sea
Loftus
Danby
Castleton
North York Moors National Park 4
Leven
Esk
Seven
Guisborough
Middlesbrough
Stokesley
Eaglescliffe
Stockton-on-Tees
Bishop Auckland
Shildon
Darlington
Northallerton

Corbridge
Hexham
Hedley on the Hill
A68
Derwent Reservoir
Edmundbyers
Blanchland
Wolsingham
Frosterley
Crook
West Auckland
Pierce Bridge
DURHAM
Hamsterley Forest
Raby Castle
Barnard Castle
Bowes
Teesdale 4
Catterick
Bedale
A1
NORTH YORKSHIRE
Richmond
The Pennines
Reeth
Yorkshire Dales National Park
Hawes

Hadrian's Wall 7
Haltwhistle
South Tyne
Carlisle (20mi)
Allendale Town
Alston
Allenheads
Nenthead
Killhope
Wear
Stanhope
Weardale
North Pennines
Langdon Beck
Ireshopeburn
Newbiggin
Middleton-in-Teesdale
Pennine Way
Brough
Tees
Greta
Bowes
B6278
B6277
Appleby
Coupland
Kirkby Stephen
B6270
Newbiggin-on-Line
Tebay
A683
A685
A66
M6
Eden
CUMBRIA
Buttertubs Pass

the Elizabethan walls of England's northernmost city, Berwick-upon-Tweed.

6 **Durham River Cruises** (p615) Cruising on the tranquil River Wear, taking in Durham's city, castle and wondrous cathedral.

7 **Hadrian's Wall** (p617) Hiking along the remains of this Roman wall.

8 **Hartlepool** (p612) Learning about the fascinating maritime and wartime history of this coastal town.

9 **Beamish Open-Air Museum** (p616) Reliving the northeast's industrial age at this working museum.

10 **Alnwick Castle** (p626) Wandering the halls of Harry Potter's Hogwarts, aka Alnwick Castle.

History

Violent history has shaped this region more than any other in England, primarily because of its frontier position. Although Hadrian's Wall didn't serve as a defensive barrier, it marked the northern limit of Roman Britain and was the Empire's most heavily fortified line. Following the Romans' departure, the region became part of the Anglian kingdom of Bernicia, which united with the kingdom of Deira (encompassing much of modern-day Yorkshire) to form Northumbria in 604.

The kingdom changed hands and borders shifted several times over the next 500 years as Anglo-Saxons and Danes struggled to seize it. The land north of the River Tweed was finally ceded to Scotland in 1018, while the nascent kingdom of England kept everything below it.

The arrival of the Normans in 1066 saw William I eager to secure his northern borders against the Scots. He commissioned most of the castles you see along the coast, and cut deals with the prince bishops of Durham to ensure their loyalty. The new lords of Northumberland became very powerful because, as Marcher Lords (from the use of 'march' as a synonym of 'border'), they kept the Scots at bay.

Northumberland's reputation as a hotbed of rebellion intensified during the Tudor years, when the largely Catholic north, led by the seventh duke of Northumberland, Thomas Percy, rose up against Elizabeth I in the defeated Rising of the North in 1569. The Border Reivers, raiders from both sides of the border in the 16th century, kept the region in a perpetual state of lawlessness that only subsided after the Act of Union between England and Scotland in 1707.

Coal mines were the key to the 19th-century industrialisation of the northeast, powering steelworks, shipyards and armament works that grew up along the Tyne and Tees. In 1825 the mines also spawned the world's first steam railway, the Stockton & Darlington, built by local engineer George Stephenson. Social strife emerged in the 20th century, however, with mines, shipbuilding, steel production and the railway industry all winding down during the Great Depression and postwar years. Reinventing the northeast has been a mammoth task but continues apace.

🏃 Activities

Walking and cycling opportunities abound in this region. But be prepared for wind and rain at any time of year and for very harsh conditions in winter. Regional tourism websites contain walking and cycling information, and tourist offices stock maps and guides covering walking, cycling and other activities.

Cycling

The northeast has some of England's most inspiring cycle routes.

Part of the National Cycle Network (NCN), a long-time favourite is the 200-mile Coast & Castles Cycle Route (www.coast-and-castles.co.uk), which runs south–north along the glorious Northumberland coast between Newcastle-upon-Tyne and Berwick-upon-Tweed and Edinburgh, Scotland.

The 140-mile Sea to Sea Cycle Route (www.c2c-guide.co.uk) runs across northern England between the Cumbrian coast (Whitehaven or Workington) and Tynemouth or Sunderland via the northern Lake District and wild North Pennines' hills.

The other coast-to-coast option is the Hadrian's Cycleway (www.hadrian-guide.co.uk), a 175-mile route between South Shields or Tynemouth and Ravenglass in Cumbria along Hadrian's Wall.

Walking

The North Pennines – along with the Cheviots further north – are considered 'England's last wilderness'. Long routes through the hills include the famous Pennine Way National Trail, which keeps mainly to the high ground between the Yorkshire Dales and the Scottish border, but also crosses sections of river valley and some tedious patches of plantation. The whole route is around 270 miles, but the 70-mile section between Bowes and Hadrian's Wall is a fine four-day taster.

Hadrian's Wall has a huge range of easy loop walks taking in forts and other historical highlights.

One of the finest walks along the windswept Northumberland coast, between the villages of Craster and Bamburgh via Dunstanburgh, includes two of the region's most spectacular castles. Another superb coastal trail is the 30-mile Berwickshire Coastal Path (www.walkhighlands.co.uk/borders/berwickshire-coastal-path.shtml) from Berwick-upon-Tweed to the village of Cockburnspath in Scotland.

ℹ️ Getting There & Around

BUS

Bus transport around the region can be difficult, particularly around the more remote reaches of western Northumberland. Contact **Traveline** (☑ 0871-200 2233; www.travelinenortheast. info) for information on connections, timetables and prices.

TRAIN

The East Coast Main Line runs north from London King's Cross to Edinburgh via Durham, Newcastle and Berwick; Northern Rail operates local and interurban services in the north, including west to Carlisle.

There are numerous Rover tickets for single-day travel and longer periods; check www. networkonetickets.co.uk.

Newcastle-upon-Tyne

POP 280,200

Against its dramatic backdrop of Victorian elegance and industrial grit, this fiercely independent city harbours a spirited mix of heritage and urban sophistication, with excellent art galleries and a magnificent concert hall, along with boutique hotels, some exceptional restaurants and, of course, interesting bars: Newcastle is renowned throughout Britain for its thumping nightlife, bolstered by an energetic, 42,000-strong student population. The city retains deep-rooted traditions, embodied by the no-nonsense, likeable locals.

Allow at least a few days to explore the Victorian city centre and quayside areas along the Tyne and across the river in Gateshead, as well as the rejuvenated Ouseburn Valley to the east, shabby-chic Jesmond to the north, and, on the coast, the surf beaches of Tynemouth.

◉ Sights

◉ City Centre

Newcastle's grand Victorian centre, a compact area bordered roughly by Grainger St to the west and Pilgrim St to the east, is one of the most compelling examples of urban rejuvenation in England. Down by the quays are the city's most recognisable attractions – the iconic bridges (p605) that span the Tyne and the striking buildings that flank it.

Newcastle Castle CASTLE
(☑ 0191-230 6300; www.newcastlecastle.co.uk; Castle Garth; adult/child £6.50/3.90; ◎ 10am-5pm) The stronghold that put both the 'new' and 'castle' into Newcastle has been largely swallowed up by the train station, leaving only a few remaining fragments including the square Norman keep and the Black Gate, both fresh from a £1.67-million restoration.

Exhibits inside the two buildings cover the history of the city, its castle and its residents from Roman times onwards. The 360-degree city views from the keep's rooftop are the best in town.

★ **Discovery Museum** MUSEUM
(https://discoverymuseum.org.uk; Blandford Sq; ◎ 10am-4pm) **FREE** Tyneside's rich history is explored at this unmissable museum. Exhibitions spread across three floors of the former Co-operative Wholesale Society building around the mightily impressive 30m-long *Turbinia,* the fastest ship in the world in 1897 and the first to be powered by steam turbine. Other highlights are a section on shipbuilding on the Tyne, with a scale model of the river in 1929, and the 'Story of Newcastle', spanning the city's history from Pons Aelius (Roman Newcastle) to Cheryl Cole.

★ **Great North Museum** MUSEUM
(☑ 0191-208 6765; https://greatnorthmuseum.org. uk; Barras Bridge; general admission free, planetarium adult/child £2.50/1.50; ◎ 10am-5pm Mon-Fri, to 4pm Sat, 11am-4pm Sun) The contents of Newcastle University's museums and the prestigious Hancock Museum's natural-history exhibits come together in the latter's neoclassical building. The result is a fascinating jumble of dinosaurs, Roman altar stones, Egyptian mummies, Samurai warriors and impressive taxidermy. Standout exhibits include a life-size *Tyrannosaurus rex* recreation and an interactive model of Hadrian's Wall showing every milecastle and fortress. There's also lots of hands-on stuff

> **BRIDGING THE TYNE**
>
> The most famous view in Newcastle is the cluster of Tyne bridges, the most famous of these being the **Tyne Bridge** (1925–28). Its resemblance to Australia's Sydney Harbour Bridge (1923–32) is no coincidence, as both were built by the same company, Dorman Long of Middlesbrough. The quaint little **Swing Bridge** (1876) pivots in the middle to let ships through. Nearby, the **High Level Bridge** (1849), designed by Robert Stephenson, was the world's first combined road and railway bridge. The most recent addition is the multiple-award-winning **Millennium Bridge** (aka Blinking Bridge; 2002), which opens like an eyelid to let ships pass.

Newcastle-upon-Tyne

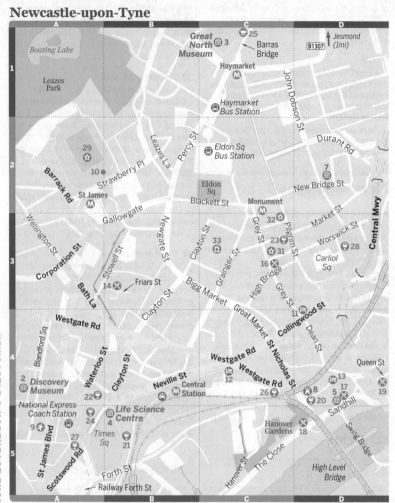

for kids and a planetarium with screenings throughout the day.

Laing Art Gallery
GALLERY

(www.laingartgallery.org.uk; New Bridge St; ⊙10am-5pm Tue-Sat, 2-5pm Sun) FREE The exceptional collection at the Laing includes works by Gainsborough, Gauguin and Henry Moore, and an important collection of paintings by Northumberland-born artist John Martin (1789–1854). Check the 'What's On' section of the website for free events including talks and tours. Temporary exhibitions often incur an extra charge.

★ Life Science Centre
MUSEUM

(☑ 0191-243 8210; www.life.org.uk; Times Sq; adult/child £14/8; ⊙10am-6pm Mon-Sat, 11am-6pm Sun) Part of a sober-minded institute devoted to the study of genetic science, this centre lets you discover the secrets of life through a fascinating series of hands-on exhibits. The highlight is the Motion Ride, a simulator that lets you 'experience' bungee jumping and the like (the 4D film changes every year). There are lots of thought-provoking arcade-style games, and if the information sometimes gets lost on the way, never mind, kids will love it. Book ahead at busy times.

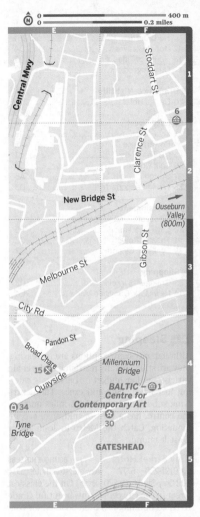

Mornings on school days see it filled with groups; visit after 2pm to avoid the crowds.

⊙ Ouseburn Valley

Now semiregenerated, Newcastle's 19th-century industrial heartland, Ouseburn Valley, 1 mile east of the city centre, has potteries, glass-blowing studios and other creative workspaces, along with pubs, bars and entertainment venues.

★**Victoria Tunnel**   HISTORIC SITE
(☑0191-261 6596; www.ouseburntrust.org.uk; Arch 6, Stepney Bank; tours adult/child £6/4; ⊙ by res-

ervation) Walking Newcastle's streets, you'd never know this extraordinary tunnel runs for 2.5 miles beneath your feet. Built between 1839 and 1842 as a coal-wagon thoroughfare, it was used as an air-raid shelter during WWII. Volunteer-led, two-hour tours take you through an atmospheric 700m-long level section of the tunnel. Book ahead as numbers are limited to 12 participants, and wear good shoes and a washable jacket for the limewashed walls. Tours finish at Ouse St, near the Quayside.

Ouseburn Farm   FARM
(☑0191-232 3698; www.bykerbridge.org.uk/farm; Ouseburn Rd, adjacent Lime St; ⊙9.30am-4.30pm Mon-Fri, 10.30am-4.30pm Sat & Sun) FREE Shetland ponies, sheep, goats, pigs, chickens and agricultural crops are the last thing you'd expect to find in Newcastle, but you can see them all at this community farm. Eggs, dairy products and more are sold at its farm shop and used in dishes served at its tearoom.

**Seven Stories – The Centre for
Children's Books**   MUSEUM
(www.sevenstories.org.uk; 30 Lime St; adult/child £7.70/6.60; ⊙10am-5pm Mon-Sat, to 4pm Sun) A marvellous conversion of a handsome Victorian mill has resulted in Seven Stories, a very hands-on museum dedicated to the wondrous world of children's literature. Across the seven floors you'll find original manuscripts and artwork from the 1930s onwards, and a constantly changing program of kid-oriented exhibitions, activities and events designed to encourage the AA Milnes of the new millennium.

⊙ Gateshead

The area of Newcastle south of the Tyne is the 'town' (neighbourhood, really) of Gateshead. Local authorities are now promoting the whole kit-and-caboodle-on-Tyne as 'NewcastleGateshead'.

★**BALTIC – Centre for
Contemporary Art**   GALLERY
(www.balticmill.com; Gateshead Quays; ⊙10am-6pm) FREE Once a huge mustard-coloured grain store, BALTIC is now a huge mustard-coloured art gallery rivalling London's Tate Modern. There are no permanent exhibitions; instead, rotating shows feature the work and installations of some of contemporary art's biggest show-stoppers. The complex has artists in residence, a performance space, a cinema, a bar, a spectacular

Newcastle-upon-Tyne

◎ Top Sights
1 BALTIC – Centre for
   Contemporary Art F4
2 Discovery Museum...............................A4
3 Great North Museum C1
4 Life Science Centre B5

◎ Sights
5 Bessie Surtees House D4
6 Biscuit Factory....................................F1
7 Laing Art Gallery D2
8 Newcastle Castle D4

⊙ Activities, Courses & Tours
9 Lane 7 ....A5
10 St James Park Tours............................A2

⊕ Sleeping
11 Grey Street Hotel.................................D4
12 Royal Station Hotel..............................C4
13 Vermont Hotel D4

⊗ Eating
14 Blackfriars B3
15 Broad Chare..E4
16 Fat Hippo Underground C3

Herb Garden ....(see 26)
17 Hop & Cleaver.....................................D4
18 House of Tides....................................D5
19 Quay Ingredient..................................D4

◎ Drinking & Nightlife
20 Bridge Hotel..D4
21 Digital..B5
22 Eazy Street A4
23 Lola Jeans C3
24 Powerhouse...A5
25 QB Tea House C1
26 Split Chimp C4
27 Switch A5
28 World Headquarters D3

⊕ Entertainment
29 Newcastle United Football Club............A2
30 Sage Gateshead F5
31 Theatre Royal C3
32 Tyneside Cinema C3

◎ Shopping
33 Grainger Market C3
34 Newcastle Quayside Market E4

rooftop restaurant (bookings essential) and a ground-floor restaurant with riverside tables. A 4th-floor outdoor platform and 5th-floor viewing box offer fabulous panoramas of the Tyne.

🏃 Activities

★Lane 7   BOWLING
(☑0191-261 6161; http://lane7.co.uk; 80-90 St James's Blvd; bowling from £6; ⊘4pm-midnight Mon-Thu, 11am-2am Fri & Sat, 11am-midnight Sun) Not only does this supercool bowling alley have 10 walnut lanes, it also has a slot-car Racing Ring, ping-pong tables, Donkey Kong arcade games, pool tables and a karaoke room, as well as a gastropub menu (pulled-pork buns; gourmet hot dogs) and a craft-beer bar. Kids are welcome until 7pm.

🎉 Festivals & Events

Great North Run   SPORTS
(www.greatrun.org) Newcastle's 13.1-mile half-marathon takes place in mid-September. Entry is by ballot, otherwise join the locals cheering on the entrants along the route, which goes from the city centre across the Tyne Bridge and through Gateshead to South Shields.

🛏 Sleeping

Although city-centre options are increasing, they are still generally restricted to the chain variety – either budget or business – catering to party people and execs. The gentrifying suburb of Jesmond, 1.5 miles north of the centre, has a host of midrange accommodation. Catch the Metro to Jesmond or West Jesmond.

Grey Street Hotel   BOUTIQUE HOTEL **$$**
(☑0191-230 6777; www.greystreethotel.co.uk; 2-12 Grey St; d from £70; ❄️🛜) On the classiest street in the city centre, this beautiful Grade II–listed building has been adapted for contemporary needs, including triple glazing on the sash windows. Individually designed rooms have big beds and handsome modern furnishings.

Newcastle Jesmond Hotel   HOTEL **$$**
(☑0191-239 9943; www.newcastlejesmondhotel. co.uk; 105 Osborne Rd; s/d/f from £55/75/105; 🅿️🛜👪) Rooms aren't huge at this freshly refurbished red-brick property footsteps from the bars and restaurants of Osborne Rd, but they're cosy, comfy and come with the bonus of free parking (though spaces are limited, so get in quick). Family rooms sleep three people. Wi-fi can be patchy.

Royal Station Hotel
HOTEL $$

(📞0191-232 0781; www.royalstationhotel.com; Neville St; s/d from £58/63; P🌐🏊) Newcastle's hotels don't come better located than this Grade I– and II–listed Victorian beauty attached to Central Station. Above the chandeliered lobby, the 144 streamlined, unfussy rooms include cheaper, broom-cupboard-size 'small doubles' (from £60); there's a small indoor pool. Staff couldn't be friendlier or more helpful. Arrive early – the 20 free on-street car spaces are first-come, first-served.

Avenue
B&B $$

(📞0191-281 1396; 2 Manor House Rd; s/d/f from £45/70/85; 🌐📶) In a peaceful residential area, this basic but well-run, family-friendly B&B has good breakfasts and friendly hosts.

★ Jesmond Dene House
HOTEL $$$

(📞0191-212 3000; http://jesmonddene-house.co.uk; Jesmond Dene Rd; s/d/ste from £109/119/169; P✴@🌐) Large, gorgeous bedrooms at this exquisite property are furnished in a modern interpretation of the Arts and Crafts style and have stunning bathrooms complete with underfloor heating, as well as the latest tech. The fine-dining restaurant (p610) is sublime.

Vermont Hotel
HERITAGE HOTEL $$$

(📞0191-233 1010; www.vermont-hotel.com; Castle Garth; d/ste from £119/179; P🌐📶) Early 20th-century elegance reigns at this magnificent stone building (the former County Hall), which has an art deco ballroom, 101 rooms with marble bathrooms and glossy timber (including interconnecting rooms for families and sumptuous suites), two bars and a fine-dining restaurant. Limited on-site parking is first-come, first-served but free. Its 11 luxury self-catering apartments (two-/four-person apartments from £169/229) are located nearby.

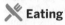 Eating

✕ City Centre

Quay Ingredient
CAFE $

(📞0191-447 2327; http://quayingredient.co.uk; 4 Queen St; dishes £3-17; ⊘8am-5pm; 🌐) Beneath the Tyne Bridge's soaring steel girders, this chic little hole in the wall has a devoted following for its eggs Benedict (and Florentine, and Montreal), but don't discount the rest of the menu: Craster kippers with pickled beetroot, scampi with homemade tartar sauce, pulled beef with bourbon....

WORTH A TRIP

SEGEDUNUM FORT

The last strong post of Hadrian's Wall was the fort of **Segedunum** (📞0191-278 4217; htttp://segedunumromanfort.org.uk; Buddle St, Wallsend; adult/child £5.95/free; ⊘10am-5pm Jun–mid-Sep, to 4pm Easter-May & mid-Sep–early Nov, to 2.30pm Mon-Fri early Nov-Easter) , 5 miles east of Newcastle at the 'wall's end', now the Newcastle suburb of Wallsend. Beneath the 35m-high tower, which you can climb for terrific views, is an absorbing site that includes a reconstructed Roman bathhouse (with steaming pools and frescos) and a museum offering a fascinating insight into life during Roman times.

Segedeunum is a three-minute walk from the Wallsend Metro station (from Newcastle £3.20, 20 minutes).

★ Broad Chare
GASTROPUB $$

(📞0191-211 2144; www.thebroadchare.co.uk; 25 Broad Chare; mains £10-19.50; ⊘kitchen noon-2.30pm & 5.30-10pm Mon-Sat, noon-5pm Sun) Spiffing English classics and splendid cask ales are served in the dark-wood bar and mezzanine of this perfect gastropub. Starters such as crispy pig ears, pork pies and venison terrine are followed by mains including a divine grilled pork chop with black pudding and cider sauce and desserts such as treacle tart with walnut brittle to finish.

Fat Hippo Underground
BURGERS $$

(📞0191-447 1161; www.fathippo.co.uk; 2-6 Shakespeare St; burgers £8-14; ⊘noon-10pm Mon-Thu, 11am-10.30pm Fri & Sat, 11am-10pm Sun) An arched brick basement houses this city-centre offshoot of Jesmond favourite the Fat Hippo (p610). Its namesake Fat Hippo burger comes with double beef patties, bacon, chorizo, cheese, onion rings and secret house sauce; there are some great chicken and veggie burgers as well as triple-cooked fries. Kids' burgers cost £5.

Hop & Cleaver
GASTROPUB $$

(📞0191-261 1037; www.hopandcleaver.com; 44 Sandhill; mains £9-18; ⊘kitchen noon-9pm Sun-Thu, to 10pm Fri & Sat, bar 11am-1am) Inside the magnificent Jacobean **Bessie Surtees House** (http://historicengland.org.uk; 41-44 Sandhill; ⊘10am-4pm Mon-Fri) **FREE**, this hip spot is great for a drink (it brews its own small-batch craft beers) but the food (including house-smoked meats) is equally brilliant:

ANGEL OF THE NORTH

Nicknamed the Gateshead Flasher, this extraordinary 200-tonne, rust-coloured, winged human frame **Angel of the North** (Durham Rd, Low Eighton) has loomed over the A1 (M) some 6 miles south of Newcastle since 1998. Sir Antony Gormley's iconic work (which saw him knighted in 2014) stands 20m high, with a wingspan wider than a Boeing 767. Bus 21 from Newcastle's Eldon Sq (£2.10, 20 minutes) stops here. There's a free car park by the base.

smoky brisket with apple-and-onion fritters; 12-hour cooked pulled pork with homemade slaw and BBQ sauce; charred, Bourbon-marinated ribs; beer-steamed and roasted chicken. Veggie options exist but are limited.

★ **House of Tides**   GASTRONOMY $$$
(☑ 0191-230 3720; http://houseoftides.co.uk; 28-30 The Close; 7-/8-course lunch menus £35/60, with wine £65/110, 8-course dinner menu £68, with wine £118; ☺ noon-2pm & 6-9.30pm Tue-Fri, noon-2pm & 5-10pm Sat) A 16th-century merchant's house is now the home of Newcastle's most celebrated restaurant. Michelin-starred chef Kenny Atkinson (a past two-time winner of the BBC's Great British Menu) works with premium ingredients – Orkney scallops, Norfolk quail, wild blackberries, black truffles and nasturtiums – on regularly changing menus. Vegetarians and other dietary requirements can be catered by prior arrangement.

★ **Blackfriars**   BRITISH $$$
(☑ 0191-261 5945; www.blackfriarsrestaurant. co.uk; Friars St; mains £12-25; ☺ noon-2.30pm & 5.30-11pm Mon-Sat, noon-4pm Sun) 🍷 A 12th-century friary is the atmospheric setting for 'modern medieval' cuisine. Check the table-mat map for the provenance of your cod, woodpigeon or rare-breed pork. Everything else is made from scratch on site, including breads, pastries, ice creams and sausages. Bookings recommended.

✕ Jesmond

Fat Hippo   BURGERS $$
(☑ 0191-340 8949; www.fat-hippo.co.uk; 35a St Georges Tce, West Jesmond; burgers £8-14; ☺ noon-9.30pm Mon-Thu, noon-10pm Fri, 11am-10pm Sat, 11am-9.30pm Sun) Humongous burgers arrive on wooden planks with stainless-steel buckets of triple-fried, hand-cut chips at this local success story. Stinky Pete comes with blue cheese, jalapeño peppers and red-onion jam; 4x4 has a whopping four patties. Veggie options include Mac the Ripper (mac 'n cheese balls with lettuce and white BBQ sauce). Sides span deep-fried gherkins to house-made slaw.

Pizzeria Francesca   PIZZERIA $$
(134 Manor House Rd; pizza & pasta £5-8.40, mains £9-17; ☺ noon-2.30pm & 5-9.30pm Mon-Sat) Excitable waiters and huge portions of pizza and pasta keep locals queuing at the door of this chaotic, cheerful neighbourhood restaurant – get in line and wait because you can't book in advance.

Jesmond Dene House   MODERN BRITISH $$$
(☑ 0191-212 5555; http://jesmonddene-house.co.uk; Jesmond Dene Rd; mains £16-36, 2-/3-course lunch menus £19.50/22; ☺ 7-10am, noon-5pm & 7-9pm Mon-Thu, 7-10am, noon-5pm & 7-9.30pm Fri, 7.30-10.30am, noon-5pm & 7-9.30pm Sat, 7.30-10.30am & noon-9pm Sun) 🍷 Head chef Michael Penaluna is the architect of an exquisite regional menu – venison from County Durham, oysters from Lindisfarne and herbs plucked straight from the garden. The result is a gourmet extravaganza.

🍷 Drinking & Nightlife

Newcastle can get seriously rowdy on Friday and Saturday nights, especially the areas around Bigg Market (just south of Newgate St) and Newcastle Central Station. Less raucous alternatives include Jesmond's bars and the Ouseburn Valley, which attracts a mellower, arty crowd.

🍷 City Centre

★ **Bridge Hotel**   PUB
(http://sjf.co.uk/our-pubs/bridge-hotel; Castle Sq; ☺ 11.30am-11pm Mon-Thu, to midnight Fri & Sat, noon-10.30pm Sun) Dating from 1901, this jewel of a traditional pub retains original features including Victorian snugs, carved woodwork, stained-glass windows and mosaic tiles. At least 11 hand-pulled ales are on tap; mellow live music (folk; singer-songwriters) plays almost every night. Its panoramic beer garden overlooking the High Level and Tyne bridges incorporates part of Newcastle's medieval city walls.

Lola Jeans   COCKTAIL BAR
(www.lolajeans.co.uk; 1-3 Market St; ☺ noon-midnight Mon-Thu, to 1am Fri-Sun) At this Jazz

Age–styled bar, dazzling cocktails – Fog on the Tyne (Bols Genever, Newcastle Brown Ale reduction, rose lemonade and nettle cordial); Garden of Babylon (white rum, passionfruit, lime, sugar snap peas, brown sugar and mango); Hot Buttered Horchata (dark rum, condensed almond milk and chai spices) – come in vintage glassware and are accompanied by a classy BBQ menu.

World Headquarters CLUB
(www.welovewhq.com; Curtis Mayfield House, Carliol Sq; ⊙11pm-4am, days vary) Dedicated to the genius of black music – funk, rare groove, dance-floor jazz, northern soul, genuine R&B, lush disco, proper house, reggae and more – this brilliant club is a world away from commercial blandness.

Split Chimp PUB
(www.splitchimp.pub; Arch 7, Westgate Rd; ⊙4-9pm Tue, 4-10pm Wed, 3-10pm Thu, 1-11pm Fri & Sat) Covered in retro chimp montages but actually named for the wood that's wedged behind ale casks to tip them, this tiny, two-level micropub inside a railway viaduct has a 31ft-long skittle alley and hosts occasional live music. Hand-pulled local ales rotate on the taps; it also has craft beers, ciders and wine.

QB Tea House TEAHOUSE
(☑0191-261 4861; www.quilliambrothers.com; Claremont Buildings, 1 Eldon Pl; ⊙10am-midnight Mon-Fri, 9am-midnight Sat) Set up by a trio of brothers as 'an alternative to Newcastle's boozy scene', this hip Hungarian-style teahouse with postindustrial decor has over 100 types of tea as well as a tiny cinema screening cult films (dates vary), plus various gigs and art events.

Digital CLUB
(http://yourfutureisdigital.com; Times Sq; ⊙11pm-3am Mon & Thu-Sat) A two-floored cathedral to dance music, this megaclub was voted one of the top 20 clubs in the world by *DJ Magazine* thanks to one of the best sound systems you're ever likely to hear. Live acts rock the house too.

⬤ Ouseburn Valley

★ Tyne Bar PUB
(☑0191-265 2550; www.thetyne.com; 1 Maling St; ⊙noon-11pm Mon-Thu, to midnight Fri & Sat, to 10.30pm Sun; ☎) An outdoor stage hosting free gigs, a free jukebox, beer-garden-style seating under one of the brick arches of the Glasshouse Bridge and a sprawling expanse of grass with knockout river views make this tucked-away waterfront pub a magnet for in-the-know locals. Free bar food is laid on between 7pm and 9pm on Tuesdays.

Ship Inn PUB
(☑0191-222 1322; Stepney Bank; ⊙noon-10pm Mon-Thu, to midnight Fri & Sat, to 11pm Sun) Maritime memorabilia and historic photos of the Ouseburn Valley fill this red-brick charmer, which has been pouring pints since the early 1800s. On busy days the elbow-bending spills out onto the small green in front.

☆ Entertainment

The Crack (www.thecrackmagazine.com) has comprehensive theatre, music, cinema and club listings for the entire northeast.

Sage Gateshead LIVE MUSIC
(☑0191-443 4661; www.sagegateshead.com; Gateshead Quays) Norman Foster's magnificent chrome-and-glass horizontal bottle is a stunner in itself but, as the home of the Northern Sinfonia and Folkworks, also presents outstanding live music.

GAY & LESBIAN NEWCASTLE
....

Newcastle's dynamic gay scene centres on the 'Pink Triangle', formed by Waterloo, Neville and Collingwood Sts, though venues stretch south to Scotswood Rd. Check www.gaynewcastle.co.uk for venues, parties and events.

Eazy Street (www.eazy-street.co.uk; 8-10 Westmorland Rd; ⊙noon-3am) Called Camp David in a previous life, this gay and all-welcoming bar draws a crowd for its nightly feast of DJs and cabaret drag shows.

Powerhouse (9-19 Westmorland Rd; ⊙11pm-4am Mon, 10pm-4am Tue-Thu, 10pm-5am Fri & Sat) Mixed but mainly gay, this massive four-floor club has flashing lights, a pumping sound system and lots of suggestive posing.

Switch (10a Scotswood Rd; ⊙9pm-1.30am Mon, 9pm-2am Thu, 6pm-2.30am Fri, 5pm-3am Sat, 5pm-2am Sun) This small late-night bar, formerly known as Loft, remains supremely popular.

WORTH A TRIP

HARTLEPOOL

Steelworks and shipyards made this North Sea coastal town's fortunes in the 19th century, but also made it a WWI target. On 16 December 1914 it was hit by 1150 shells, killing 117 people including 29-year-old Durham Light Infantry Private Theophilus Jones, the war's first soldier killed on British soil. Hartlepool's defence batteries returned fire, damaging three enemy ships and becoming England's only coastal battery to fire its guns in the conflict.

After WWII the collapse of both the steel and ship-building industries saw Hartlepool languish until the revitalisation of its marina around the turn of the millennium, and it makes a fascinating stop to explore its wartime and maritime heritage.

Hartlepool's Maritime Experience (☑ 01429-860077; www.hartlepoolsmaritimeexperience.com; Jackson Dock, Maritime Ave; adult/child £9.25/7; ☉ 10am-5pm Easter-Oct, 11am-4pm Nov-Easter) This superb family attraction incorporates both the Museum of Hartlepool, with exhibits from the Bronze Age to today, and the 1817-built HMS *Trincomalee*, the oldest British warship still afloat, as well as re-created businesses – gunsmith, swordsmith and so on – along its historic quayside. Costumed staff and audio guides do a great job of bringing it to life.

Heugh Gun Battery Museum (☑ 01429-270746; www.heughbattery.com; Moor Tce; adult/child £5/3; ☉ 10am-4pm Thu-Sun) Atop the windswept Hartlepool Headland, about 2 miles west of the centre, you can visit the underground magazines, parade ground, museum and panoramic observation tower at the 19th-century Heugh (pronounced 'yuff') Gun Battery – one of Hartlepool's two defence batteries to return WWI fire.

Bus 22 to/from Durham (£6.10, 1¼ hours, hourly) stops at the train station. Trains link Hartlepool with Newcastle (£9.20, 45 minutes, hourly).

Tyneside Cinema
CINEMA

(☑ 0191-227 5500; www.tynesidecinema.co.uk; 10 Pilgrim St) Opened in 1937 as Newcastle's first newsreel cinema, this art deco picture house with plush red-velvet seats still screens newsreels (11.15am daily) as well as mainstream and offbeat movies, and archive British Pathé films. Free one-hour guided tours of the building run at 11am on Monday, Tuesday, Friday and Saturday.

Theatre Royal
PERFORMING ARTS

(☑ 08448 112121; www.theatreroyal.co.uk; 100 Grey St) The winter home of the Royal Shakespeare Company is full of Victorian splendour and has an excellent program of drama, along with major musicals, pantomimes, opera, ballet, comedy and contemporary dance.

Head of Steam @ The Cluny
LIVE MUSIC

(www.headofsteam.co.uk; 36 Lime St; ☉ noon-11pm Mon-Thu, to midnight Fri & Sat, to 10.30pm Sun) Based at the artist cooperative 36 Lime St, touring acts and local talent – from experimental prog-rock heads to up-and-coming pop goddesses – fill the bill every night of the week. This is the original of several other venues in Newcastle and throughout Britain.

Shopping

Newcastle Quayside Market
MARKET

(under the Tyne Bridge; ☉ 9am-4pm Sun) Stalls displaying jewellery, photographic prints, art, clothing, homewares and more set up along the quays around the Tyne Bridge every Sunday. Buskers and food stalls add to the street-party atmosphere.

Grainger Market
MARKET

(www.graingermarket.org.uk; btwn Grainger & Clayton Sts; ☉ 9am-5.30pm Mon-Sat) Trading since 1835, Newcastle's gorgeous, heritage-listed covered market has over 100 stalls selling everything from fish, farm produce, meat and vegetables to clothes, accessories and homewares. Between alleys 1 and 2, look out for the historic Weigh House, where goods were once weighed. There are some fantastic food stalls to pick up lunch on the run.

ⓘ Information

Newcastle currently doesn't have a physical tourist office, but information is available at www.newcastlegateshead.com.

Newcastle City Centre Police Station (☑ emergency 999, non-emergency 101; www.northumbria.police.uk; Forth Banks; ☉ 24hr)

ⓘ Getting There & Away

AIR

Newcastle International Airport (☎0871 882 1121; www.newcastleairport.com), 7 miles north of the city off the A696, has direct services to many UK and European cities as well as long-haul flights to Dubai. Tour operators fly charters to the USA, Middle East and Africa.

The airport is linked to town by the Metro (£3.30, 25 minutes, every 12 minutes).

BUS

Local and regional buses leave from Haymarket or Eldon Sq bus stations. National Express buses arrive and depart from the **coach station** (St James Blvd) on St James Blvd. For local buses around the northeast, the excellent-value Explorer North East ticket (adult/child £9.70/8.60) is valid on most services.

Buses X15 and X18 run north to Berwick-upon-Tweed (£6.80, two hours, every two hours). National Express offers services to Edinburgh (£13.40, three hours, three daily), London (£22, seven hours, three daily) and Manchester (£22.50, 4½ hours, four daily).

TRAIN

Newcastle is on the main rail line between London and Edinburgh and is the starting point of the scenic Tyne Valley Line west to Carlisle.

Alnmouth (for bus connections to Alnwick) £10.30, 25 minutes, hourly

Berwick-upon-Tweed £7.50, 45 minutes, up to two per hour

Carlisle £15.90, 1½ hours, hourly

Durham £6.80, 10 minutes, every 20 minutes

Edinburgh £49, 1½ hours, every 30 minutes

Hartlepool £9.20, 45 minutes, hourly

London King's Cross £138, three hours, every 30 minutes

York £40, one hour, at least two per hour

ⓘ Getting Around

CAR

Two tollway **vehicle tunnels** (TT2; www.tt2. co.uk; 1 way £1.70, notes & copper coins not accepted) travel beneath the Tyne.

PUBLIC TRANSPORT

There's a large bus network, but the best means of getting around is the excellent Metro (www. nexus.org.uk), with single fares from £1.70. Several saver passes are also available.

The DaySaver (£2.80 to £4.80) gives unlimited Metro travel for one day for travel after 9am, and the DayRover (adult/child £7/3.90) gives unlimited travel on all modes of transport in the Tyne and Wear county for one day for travel any time.

TAXI

On weekend nights taxis can be rare; try **Noda Taxis** (☎0191-222 1888; www.noda-taxis. co.uk), which has a kiosk outside the entrance to Central Station.

Tynemouth

POP 67,520

The mouth of the Tyne, 9 miles east of Newcastle, is one of the best surf spots in England, with great all-year breaks off the immense, crescent-shaped Blue Flag beach, which occasionally hosts the National Surfing Championships.

◉ Sights & Activities

Tynemouth Priory   RUINS
(EH; www.english-heritage.org.uk; Pier Rd; adult/child £5.20/3.10; ⊙10am-6pm Apr-Sep, to 5pm Oct, 10am-4pm Sat & Sun Nov-Mar) Built by Benedictine monks on a strategic bluff above the mouth of the Tyne in the 11th-century ruins, Tynemouth Priory was ransacked during the Dissolution in 1539. The military took over for four centuries, only leaving in 1960, and today the skeletal remains of the priory church sit alongside old military installations, their guns aimed out to sea at an enemy that never came.

Tynemouth Surf Company   SURFING
(☎0191-258 2496; www.tynemouthsurf.co.uk; Grand Pde; ⊙10am-5.30pm) For all your surfing needs, call into this friendly surf company, which also provides two-hour group lessons for £25 per person at 2pm daily (when the surf's up) from March to October. The

---

NEWCASTLE UNITED FOOTBALL CLUB TOUR

Newcastle United Football Club (NUFC; ☎0844 372 1892; www.nufc.co.uk; St James Park, Strawberry Pl) is more than just a football team – it's the collective expression of Geordie hope and pride. The club's hallowed ground, St James Park, is always packed, but you can take a stadium tour (adult/child £15/8, rooftop tours £20/15; ⊙ stadium tours 11.30am, 12.30pm & 2.30pm non-match days, 10.30am match days, rooftop tours noon & 2pm Sat non-match days) that includes the dugout and changing rooms, as well as rooftop tours. Match tickets go on public sale about two weeks before a game.

adjoining chilled surf cafe morphs into a cool bar and live-music venue at night.

🛏 Sleeping & Eating

Grand Hotel   HERITAGE HOTEL $$$
(☑ 0191-293 6666; www.grandhotel-uk.com; Grand Pde; incl breakfast d £96-199, f £156-196) Many of the 46 rooms at this landmark 1872-built hotel (the one-time summer residence of the duke and duchess of Northumberland) and neighbouring town house overlook the beach, and some have four-poster beds and spa baths, though wi-fi's only reliable in public areas. Its Victorian-style bar, drawing room serving high tea, and fine-dining restaurant (mains £12 to £22) are excellent.

Barca Art Cafe   CAFE $$
(☑ 0191-257 7959; www.barcaart.co.uk; 68 Front St; mains £12-17; ⊙ kitchen 5-10pm Mon-Sat, noon-6pm Sun, bar noon-1am daily) This funky hybrid restaurant, bar and art gallery (the works by local artists are all for sale) has an ambitious, contemporary menu, although vegetarian options, aside from some of its tapas dishes, are few. DJs spin on Saturday nights from 10pm.

❶ Getting There & Away

From Newcastle, the easiest way to reach Tynemouth is by Metro (£3.20, 25 min, every 12 min).

Durham

POP 48,069

England's most beautiful Romanesque cathedral, a huge castle, and, surrounding them both, a cobweb of hilly, cobbled streets usually full of upper-crust students attending England's third university of choice (after Oxford and Cambridge) make Durham an ideal day trip from Newcastle or overnight stop.

◉ Sights

★ Durham Cathedral   CATHEDRAL
(www.durhamcathedral.co.uk; Palace Green; cathedral by donation, tower adult/child £5/2.50, cathedral guided tours adult/child £5/4.50; ⊙ cathedral 7.30am-6pm Mon-Sat, to 5.30pm Sun, tower noon-2pm Wed & Sat, cathedral tours 10.30am, 11am & 2pm Jun-Aug, 11am & 2pm Sep-May) This monumental cathedral is the definitive structure of the Anglo-Norman Romanesque style, a resplendent monument to the country's ecclesiastical history and, since 1986, a Unesco World Heritage Site. Beyond the main door – and the famous Sanctuary Knocker, which medieval felons would strike to gain 37 days asylum within the cathedral before standing trial or leaving the country – the interior is spectacular. Climbing the tower's 325 steps rewards you with show-stopping vistas.

Durham was the first European cathedral to be roofed with stone-ribbed vaulting, which upheld the heavy stone roof and made it possible to build pointed transverse arches – the first in England, and a great architectural achievement. The central tower dates from 1262, but was damaged in a fire caused by lightning in 1429 and unsatisfactorily patched up until it was entirely rebuilt in 1470. The western towers were added in 1217-26.

The northern side of the beautiful, 1175-built Galilee Chapel features rare surviving examples of 12th-century wall painting (thought to feature portraits of Sts Cuthbert and Oswald). Galilee Chapel also contains the tomb of the Venerable Bede, the 8th-century Northumbrian monk turned historian: his *Ecclesiastical History of the English People* is still the prime source of information on the development of early Christian Britain. Among other things, Bede introduced the numbering of years from the birth of Jesus. He was first buried at Jarrow, but in 1022 a miscreant monk stole his remains and brought them here.

Other highlights include the 14th-century Bishop's Throne; the beautiful stone Neville Screen (1372-80), which separates the high altar from St Cuthbert's tomb; and the mostly 19th-century Cloisters where you'll find the Monk's Dormitory, now a library of 30,000 books. There are audiovisual displays on the building of the cathedral and St Cuthbert, and a rolling program of exhibitions.

★ Durham Castle   CASTLE
(☑ 0191-334 2932; www.dur.ac.uk/durham.castle; Palace Green; admission by guided tour only, adult/child £5/3.50; ⊙ by reservation) Built as a standard motte-and-bailey fort in 1072, Durham Castle was the prince bishops' home until 1837, when it became the University of Durham's first college. It remains a university hall today. Highlights of the 45-minute tour include the 17th-century Black Staircase and the beautifully preserved Norman chapel (1080).

Each successive prince bishop sought to put his particular imprint on the place, but restoration and reconstruction were necessary in any case as the castle is built of soft stone on soft ground.

Durham

🏃 Activities

Browns Boathouse BOATING
(📞0191-386 3779; Elvet Bridge; per hour adult/child £6/4; ⏰10am-6pm Easter-late Sep) Rent a row boat for a romantic river excursion.

Prince Bishop River Cruiser BOATING
(📞0191-386 9525; www.princebishoprc.co.uk; Browns Boathouse, Elvet Bridge; adult/child £8/5; ⏰cruises 12.30pm, 2pm & 3pm Jun-Sep, call for times Oct-May) Wonderfully scenic one-hour cruises take you out on the Wear.

🛏 Sleeping & Eating

Honest Lawyer INN $$
(📞0191-378 3780; www.strhotels.co.uk; Croxdale Bridge, Croxdale; d £58-83, f £89-110; 🅿🛜🛗🐾) An easy 3-mile drive south of Durham on the A167, this handy spot has mostly motel-style rooms with countrified chequered fabrics and parking outside the door. Family rooms sleep up to four people. The main

Durham

⊙ **Top Sights**
| 1 Durham Castle | B3 |
| 2 Durham Cathedral | B4 |

⊕ **Activities, Courses & Tours**
| Browns Boathouse | (see 3) |
| 3 Prince Bishop River Cruiser | C2 |

⊖ **Sleeping**
| 4 The Townhouse | D3 |

⊗ **Eating**
| 5 Cellar Door Durham | C3 |
| 6 Tealicious | C3 |

⊖ **Drinking & Nightlife**
| 7 Shakespeare Tavern | C3 |

building has a timber bar and restaurant serving good pub grub in generous portions.

WORTH A TRIP

BEAMISH OPEN-AIR MUSEUM

County Durham's living, breathing, working **Beamish Open-Air Museum** (☎0191-370 4000; www.beamish.org. uk; Beamish; adult/child £18.50/10.50; ☻10am-5pm Easter-Oct, closed Nov-Mar) offers an unflinching glimpse into industrial life in the northeast during the 19th and 20th centuries. Spread over 120 hectares, it is instructive and fun for all ages. Allow at least three hours here.

Beamish is 9 miles northwest of Durham. Take bus 28 or 28A from Newcastle (£4.90, one hour, every 30 minutes) or 128 from Durham (£3.40, 30 minutes, hourly).

★ **Townhouse** BOUTIQUE HOTEL $$$
(☎0191-384 1037; www.thetownhousedurham. co.uk; 34 Old Elvet; d £99-200; 🛜) Each of the Townhouse's 11 opulent-and-then-some rooms has a theme, with Le Jardin featuring a shed and garden furniture; Premiere a huge projection screen and popcorn machine; and the Edwardian Express re-creating a night in a yesteryear sleeper compartment. The most 'normal' room is the Garden Lodge, complete with outdoor tub and underfloor heating. The restaurant is superb.

Tealicious CAFE $
(☎0191-340 1393; www.tealicioustearoom.co.uk; 88 Elvet Bridge; dishes £2-5.50, high tea adult/child £12.50/6.95; ☻10am-4pm Tue-Sat, noon-4pm Sun) Inside this quaint pastel-blue and white building, amid vintage decor, treats include homemade cakes (such as white-chocolate cheesecake or ginger and lime), sandwiches, and over a dozen blends of tea served from individual pots on fine bone china. High tea here is a treat. It's tiny so book ahead.

Cellar Door Durham MODERN BRITISH $$
(☎0191-383 1856; www.thecellardoordurham.co.uk; 41 Saddler St; mains £11-22, 2-/3-course lunch menus £14/17; ☻10.30am-10.30pm) Accessed from an inconspicuous door on Saddler St, this 12th-century building has glorious river views, including from the alfresco terrace. The Mediterranean-meets-Britain menu features starters such as twice-baked Camembert soufflé, mains including beef ribs with smoked mash and beer-pickled onions, and desserts such as chocolate and brown butter terrine with pistachio ice cream. Service is spot on.

🍷 Drinking

Shakespeare Tavern PUB
(63 Saddler St; ☻11am-11.30pm) Built in 1190, this authentic-as-it-gets locals' boozer is complete with dartboard, cosy snugs, a terrific selection of beers and spirits, and wise-cracking characters propping up the bar – as well as, allegedly, a resident ghost. Folk-music jam sessions take place on Wednesday evenings.

ℹ️ Information

Durham's **tourist office** (World Heritage Site Visitor Centre; ☎0191-334 3805; www.thisisdurham. com; 7 Owengate; ☻9.30am-6pm mid-Jun–Aug, to 5pm early Apr–mid-Jun, Sep & Oct, to 4.30pm Nov–early Apr) is in the shadow of the castle.

ℹ️ Getting There & Around

BUS

The **bus station** (North Rd) is on the western side of the river.

Destinations include the following:
Hartlepool Bus 57A; £6.10, 1¼ hours, hourly
London National Express; £28, 6½ hours, four daily
Newcastle Bus 21, X12 and X21; £4.10, 1¼ hours, at least four hourly

TAXI

Pratt's (☎0191-386 4040; http://prattstaxis. co.uk) is a reliable taxi company.

TRAIN

The East Coast Main Line provides speedy connections to destinations including the following:
Edinburgh £61, 1½ hours, hourly
London King's Cross £138, three hours, every 30 minutes
Newcastle £6.80, 10 minutes, three hourly
York £33.90, 50 minutes, four hourly

Barnard Castle

POP 5694

The charming market town of Barnard Castle, better known as 'Barney', is a traditionalist's dream, full of antiquarian shops and atmospheric old pubs. It's a wonderful setting for the town's twin draws: a daunting ruined castle and an extraordinary French chateau.

👁 Sights

Barnard Castle CASTLE
(EH; www.english-heritage.org.uk; Scar Top; adult/child £5/3; ☻10am-6pm Easter-Sep, to 5pm Oct, 10am-4pm Sat & Sun Nov-Easter) Built on a cliff

above the River Tees by Guy de Bailleul and rebuilt around 1150, Barnard Castle was partly dismantled some four centuries later, but its ruins still manage to cover two very impressive hectares with wonderful river views. Also here is a sensory garden.

★ **Bowes Museum**   MUSEUM
(www.thebowesmuseum.org.uk; Newgate; adult/child £10.50/free; ⊙10am-5pm) A monumental chateau half a mile east of the centre contains the lavishly furnished Bowes Museum. Funded by 19th-century industrialist John Bowes, and opened in 1892, this brainchild of his Parisian actress wife, Josephine, was built by French architect Jules Pellechet to display a collection the Bowes had travelled the world to assemble. The star attraction is the marvellous 18th-century mechanical swan, which performs every day at 2pm. If you miss it, a film shows it in action.

Look for works by Canaletto, El Greco and Goya as well as 55 paintings by Josephine herself. Among the 15,000 other objets d'art are incredible dresses from the 17th century through to the 1970s as part of an exhibit on textiles through the ages, and clocks, watches and tableware in gold and silver in the precious-metals section. It also houses finds unearthed from the nearby Binchester Roman Fort.

🛏 Sleeping & Eating

Old Well Inn   INN $$
(☑01833-690130; http://theoldwellinn.co.uk; 21 The Bank; s/d incl breakfast from £60/83; 🛜) Built over a huge well (not visible), this old coaching inn has 10 enormous rooms. No 9 is the most impressive with its own private entrance, flagstone floors and a bath. The pub has regional ales on tap that you can sip in the leafy beer garden in fine weather.

Jersey Farm Country Hotel   HOTEL $$
(☑01833-638223; www.jerseyfarmhotel.co.uk; Darlington Rd; s/d from £72/99; 🅿🛜🐾) Another genteel farmhouse conversion, right? Wrong. The 22 rooms here sport cool retro colour schemes and gadgets galore. The restaurant is a clean-cut affair (mains £7.50 to £16). It's 1.3 miles east of the town centre signposted just off Darlington Rd (the A67).

★ **Cross Lanes**
Organic Farm Shop   DELI, CAFE
(☑01833-630619; www.crosslanesorganics.co.uk; Cross Lanes; dishes £4.50-11; ⊙cafe 8.30am-4pm, shop 8.30am-5pm Mon-Sat, 10am-5pm Sun; 🛜♿)

KNITSLEY FARM SHOP & CAFE

It's worth stopping off at **Knitsley Farm Shop & Cafe** (☑01207-592059; www.knitselyfarmshop.co.uk; East Knitsley Grange Farm, Knitsley; dishes £3.50-9.50; ⊙shop 10am-5pm Tue-Sat, to 4pm Sun, cafe 10am-5pm Tue-Fri, 9.30am-5pm Sat, 9.30am-4pm Sun), 12 miles northwest of Durham en route to Northumberland National Park and Hadrian's Wall, to stock up on its incredible cheeses, meats, homemade sweets, cakes and breads. It's even better if you can make time to dine at its wonderful cafe on fresh-as-it-gets soups, farmyard sausages, and pulled-pork and crackling baps.

🍃 Sheep graze on the grass-covered roof of this award-winning farm shop and cafe 1.5 miles south of Barnard Castle. The cavernous interior brims with all-organic produce; breakfasts (home-cured bacon, homemade sausages and eggs from the farm's chickens) segue into lunches including gourmet sandwiches, steak or veggie burgers and wood-fired pizzas, and 'rustic afternoon tea' with organic cream and wild-fruit jams.

ℹ Information

Tourist Office (☑01833-631107; www.thisisdurham.com; 3 Horsemarket; ⊙10am-4pm Mon & Wed-Sat) In the Witham building's arts and community centre.

ℹ Getting There & Away

Barnard Castle is poorly served by public transport so you really need your own wheels.

Hadrian's Wall

Named in honour of the emperor who ordered it built, Hadrian's Wall was one of Rome's greatest engineering projects. This enormous 73-mile-long wall was built between AD 122 and 128 to separate Romans and Scottish Picts. Today, the awe-inspiring sections that remain are testament to Roman ambition and tenacity.

When completed, the mammoth structure ran across the island's narrow neck, from the Solway Firth in the west almost to the mouth of the Tyne in the east. Every Roman mile (0.95 miles) there was a gateway guarded by a small fort (milecastle) and

RABY CASTLE

Sprawling **Raby Castle** (www.rabycastle. com; Staindrop; castle, gardens & park adult/child £10/4.50, gardens & park only £6/2.50; ⊙1-4.30pm Sun-Fri Jul & Aug, 1-4.30pm Sun-Wed May, Jun & Sep) was a stronghold of the Catholic Neville family until it engaged in some ill-judged plotting (the 'Rising of the North') against the oh-so Protestant Queen Elizabeth in 1569. Most of the interior dates from the 18th and 19th centuries, but the exterior remains true to the original design, built around a courtyard and surrounded by a moat. It's 6.8 miles northeast of Barnard Castle; take bus 85A (£3, 15 minutes, every two hours Monday to Saturday).

between each milecastle were two observation turrets. Milecastles are numbered right across the country, starting with Milecastle 0 at Wallsend – where you can visit the wall's last stronghold, Segedunum (p609) – and ending with Milecastle 80 at Bowness-on-Solway.

A series of forts were developed as bases some distance south (and may predate the wall), and 16 lie astride it.

Activities

The **Hadrian's Wall Path** (www.national-trail.co.uk/hadrians-wall-path) is an 84-mile national trail that runs the length of the wall from Wallsend in the east to Bowness-on-Solway in the west. The entire route should take about seven days on foot, giving plenty of time to explore the rich archaeological heritage along the way.

ⓘ Information

There are tourist offices in Hexham, Haltwhistle and Corbridge. The Walltown Visitor Centre (p624), aka the Northumberland National Park Visitor Centre, is located at Greenhead.

Hadrian's Wall Country (http://hadrianswall-country.co.uk) is the official portal for the area.

ⓘ Getting There & Around

BUS

The AD122 Hadrian's Wall bus (five daily, Easter to late September) is a hail-and-ride service that runs between Hexham and Carlisle, with one bus a day starting and ending at Newcastle's Central Station and not all services covering the entire route.

Bikes can be taken aboard AD122 buses, but space is limited. Bus 185 zips between Birdoswald Roman Fort and Carlisle via Haltwhistle the rest of the year (three daily, Monday to Saturday only).

Bus 10 links Newcastle with Hexham (1½ hours, every 30 minutes).

West of Hexham the wall runs parallel to the A69, which connects Carlisle and Newcastle. Buses 85 and 685 run along the A69 hourly, passing 2 miles to 3 miles south of the main sites throughout the year.

All these services can be used with the Hadrian's Wall Rover Ticket (adult/child 1 day £12.50/6.50, 3 days £25/13, 7 days £50/26), available from bus drivers and tourist offices. Show your Rover Ticket to get 10% off admission to all museums and attractions.

CAR & MOTORCYCLE

Your own wheels are the easiest way to get around, with one fort or garrison usually just a short hop from the next. Parking costs £4/15 per day/week; tickets are valid at all sites along the wall.

The B6318 follows the course of the wall from the outskirts of Newcastle to Birdoswald. The main A69 road and the railway line follow 3 or 4 miles to the south.

TRAIN

The railway line between Newcastle and Carlisle (Tyne Valley Line; £15.90, 1½ hours, hourly) has stations at Corbridge, Hexham, Haydon Bridge, Bardon Mill, Haltwhistle and Brampton. Not all services stop at all stations.

Corbridge

POP 3011

Above a green-banked curve in the Tyne, Corbridge's shady, cobbled streets are lined with old-fashioned shops and pubs. Inhabited since Saxon times when there was a substantial monastery, many of its charming buildings feature stones from nearby Corstopitum.

◉ Sights

Corbridge Roman Site & Museum   HISTORIC SITE

(EH; www.english-heritage.org.uk; Corchester Lane; adult/child £6.10/3.70; ⊙10am-6pm Easter-Sep, to 5pm Oct, 10am-4pm Sat & Sun Nov-Easter) What's left of the Roman garrison town of Corstopitum lies about half a mile west of Market Pl on Dere St, once the main road from York to Scotland. It's the oldest fortified site in the area, predating the wall itself by some 40 years. Most of what you see here, though, dates from around AD 200, when the fort had developed into a civilian settlement and was the main base along the wall.

You get a sense of the domestic heart of the town from the visible remains. The Corbridge Museum displays Roman sculpture and carvings, including the amazing 3rd-century **Corbridge Lion**.

🛏️ Sleeping & Eating

2 The Crofts
B&B $$

(☎01434-633046; www.2thecrofts.co.uk; Newcastle Rd; s/d from £55/75; P 🛜) By far the best place in town to drop your pack, this secluded B&B occupies a beautiful period home half a mile east of the town centre. The two high-ceilinged, spacious rooms are en suite and the energetic owner cooks a mean breakfast (packed lunches can also be organised). Guests are welcome to play the piano.

★ Corbridge Larder
DELI, CAFE $

(☎01434-632 948; www.corbridgelarder.co.uk; 18 Hill St; dishes £4-7, dinner mains £10; ☺9am-5pm

Mon-Fri, 9am-5pm & 6.30-10.30pm Sat, 10am-4pm Sun) Gourmet picnic fare at this fabulous deli includes bread, over 100 varieties of cheese, chutneys, cakes, chocolates and wine (you can get hampers made up) as well as made-to-order sandwiches, pies, quiches, tarts, and antipasti and meze delicacies. Upstairs from the wonderland of provisions there's a small sit-down cafe. On Saturday evenings it hosts dinners accompanied by live music.

Black Bull
BRITISH $$

(www.oldenglishinns.co.uk; Middle St; mains £8-17; ☺kitchen noon-9pm, bar noon-midnight; 🛜) A menu of British comfort food, such as beef burgers, fish in beer batter and slow-cooked lamb, and a series of low-ceilinged, atmospheric dining rooms, make this tavern dating from 1755 a cosy spot to hole up. Sundays offer a choice of five different roasts.

Hadrian's Wall & Northumberland National Park

Hadrian's Wall

ROME'S FINAL FRONTIER

Of all Britain's Roman ruins, Emperor Hadrian's 2nd-century wall, cutting across northern England from the Irish Sea to the North Sea, is by far the most spectacular; Unesco awarded it world cultural heritage status in 1987.

We've picked out the highlights, one of which is the prime remaining Roman fort on the wall, Housesteads, which we've reconstructed here.

Housesteads' granaries
Nothing like the clever underground ventilation system, which kept vital supplies of grain dry in Northumberland's damp and drizzly climate, would be seen again in these parts for 1500 years.

Birdoswald Roman Fort
Explore the longest intact stretch of the wall, scramble over the remains of a large fort then head indoors to wonder at a full-scale model of the wall at its zenith. Great fun for the kids.

Housesteads Roman Fort
See Illustration Right

Milecastle

North Gate

Interval Tower

- Birdoswald Roman Fort
- Harrow Scar Milecastle
- Greenhead
- Brampton
- Haltwhistle
- Roman Army Museum
- Once Brewed
- Irthing
- Sewingshields
- Housesteads Roman Fort & Museum
- Hadrian's Wall
- B6318
- Vindolanda Roman Fort & Museum
- A69
- Bardon Mill
- South Tyne
- Haydon Bridge
- Chollerford
- Chesters Roman Fort & Museum
- Low Brunton
- Acomb
- Hexham
- N
- 0 — 10 km
- 0 — 5 miles

Chesters Roman Fort
Built to keep watch over a bridge spanning the River North Tyne, Britain's best-preserved Roman cavalry fort has a terrific bathhouse, essential if you have months of nippy northern winter ahead.

Hexham Abbey
This may be the finest non-Roman sight near Hadrian's Wall, but the 7th-century parts of this magnificent church were built with stone quarried by the Romans for use in their forts.

Housesteads' hospital
Operations performed at the hospital would have been surprisingly effective, even without anaesthetics; religious rituals and prayers to Aesculapius, the Roman god of healing, were possibly less helpful for a hernia or appendicitis.

Housesteads' latrines
Communal toilets were the norm in Roman times and Housesteads' are remarkably well preserved – fortunately no traces remain of the vinegar-soaked sponges that were used instead of toilet paper.

QUICK WALL FACTS & FIGURES

» **Latin name** Vallum Aelium

» **Length** 73.5 miles (80 Roman miles)

» **Construction date** AD 122–128

» **Manpower for construction**
Three legions (around 16,000 men)

» **Features** At least 16 forts, 80 milecastles, 160 turrets

» **Did you know** Hadrian's wasn't the only Roman wall in Britain – the Antonine Wall was built across what is now central Scotland in the AD 140s, but it was abandoned soon after

Commanding Officer's House

Farms

Workshop

Headquarters

Barracks

West Gate

Angle Tower

Housesteads' gatehouses
Unusually at Housesteads neither of the gates faces the enemy, as was the norm at a Roman fort – builders aligned them east-west. Ruts worn by cart wheels are still visible in the stone.

SCALING THE WALL

The main concentration of sights is in the central, wildest part of the wall, roughly between Corbridge in the east and Brampton in the west. All our suggested stops are within this area and follow an east–west route. The easiest way to travel is by car, scooting along the B6318, but special bus AD122 will also get you there. Hiking along the designated Hadrian's Wall Path (84 miles) allows you to appreciate the achievement up close.

FREE GUIDES

At some sites knowledgeable volunteer heritage guides are on hand to answer questions and put meat on the wall's stony bones.

ⓘ Information

Corbridge's **tourist office** (📞 01434-632815; www.visitnorthumberland.com; Hill St; ⏰ 10am-4.30pm Mon-Sat Easter-Oct, closed Nov-Mar) occupies a corner of the library.

ⓘ Getting There & Away

Buses 85, 685 and X85 between Newcastle (£4.80, 45 minutes, hourly) and Carlisle (£7.10, 2¼ hours, hourly) come through Corbridge, as does bus 10 from Newcastle (£5.10, one hour, every 30 minutes) to Hexham (£3, 20 minutes, every 30 minutes), where you can connect with the Hadrian's Wall bus AD122.

Corbridge is also on the railway line between Newcastle (£6.20, 45 minutes, hourly) and Carlisle (£14.10, 1½ hours, hourly).

Hexham

POP 13,100

Bustling Hexham is a handsome if somewhat scuffed market town centred on its grand Augustinian abbey. Its cobbled alleyways have more shops and amenities than any other Hadrian's Wall town between Carlisle and Newcastle.

◉ Sights

Hexham Abbey   CHURCH
(www.hexhamabbey.org.uk; Beaumont St; suggested donation £3; ⏰ 9.30am-5pm, Saxon crypt 11am & 3.30pm) Dominating tiny Market Pl, Hexham's stately abbey is a marvellous example of Early English architecture. It cleverly escaped the Dissolution of 1537 by rebranding as Hexham's parish church, a role it still has today. The highlight is the 7th-century **Saxon crypt**, the only surviving element of St Wilifrid's Church, built with inscribed stones from Corstopitum in 674.

Old Gaol   HISTORIC BUILDING
(www.hexhamoldgaol.org.uk; Hallgate; adult/child £3.95/2.50; ⏰ 11am-4.30pm Mon-Sat Aug, 11am-4.30pm Tue-Sat Apr-Jul & Sep, 11am-4.30pm Tue & Sat Oct, Nov, Feb & Mar, closed Dec) Completed in 1333 as England's first purpose-built prison, today this strapping stone structure's four floors tell the history of the jail in all its gruesome glory. The history of the Border Reivers – a group of clans who fought, kidnapped, blackmailed and killed each other in an effort to exercise control over a lawless tract of land along the Anglo-Scottish border throughout the 16th century – is also retold, along with tales of the punishments handed out in the prison.

🛏 Sleeping & Eating

Hallbank Guest House   B&B $$
(📞 01434-605567; www.hallbankguesthouse.com; Hallgate; d/f from £120/130; 🅿🖧) Behind the Old Gaol, this fine Edwardian house combines period elegance with stylishly furnished rooms with patterned wallpaper, autumnal colours and huge beds. Evening meals can be arranged on request. It's very popular so book ahead.

Deli at Number 4   DELI, CAFE $
(📞 01434-608091; www.deliatnumber4.co.uk; 4 Beaumont St; dishes £2-6; ⏰ 9am-5pm Mon-Sat, 11am-5pm Sun) 🖉 Opposite Hexham's abbey, colourful window displays of artisan breads, local cheeses, olives, jams, homemade cakes and more entice you into this deli, and the aromas from the kitchen lure you upstairs to dine on soups, sandwiches and various specials.

★ Bouchon Bistrot   FRENCH $$
(📞 01434-609943; www.bouchonbistrot.co.uk; 4-6 Gilesgate; mains £12-20, 2-/3-course lunch menus £14/15; ⏰ noon-2pm & 6-9.30pm Mon-Sat) Hexham may be an unlikely setting for some true fine dining, but this Gallic affair has an enviable reputation. Classically inspired dishes range from proper French onion soup with gruyère or garlic snails to pan-fried Coley fillet with watercress velouté. Ingredients are as fresh as nature can provide; the wine list is an elite selection of champagnes, reds and whites.

ⓘ Information

Hexham's **tourist office** (📞 01670-620450; www.visitnorthumberland.com/hexham;

LANGLEY CASTLE HOTEL

Soaring above 12 acres of gardens, the 1350-built **Langley Castle Hotel** (📞 01434-688888; www.langleycastle.com; Langley; s/d lodge from £129.50/159, s/d castle from £199.50/245,; 🅿🖧📶) is a beauty, with creaking hallways filled with suits of armour and an alleged resident ghost. Its nine castle rooms are gorgeously appointed with antique furnishings (most have four-poster beds); there are splendid views of the castle from its adjacent, recently converted lodge. Check for dinner, bed and breakfast packages.

Queen's Hall, Beaumont St; ⏰10am-5pm Mon-Fri, to 4pm Sat) is inside the library.

ℹ Getting There & Away

Buses 85, 685 and X85 between Newcastle (£4.80, 1¼ hours, every 30 minutes) and Carlisle (£6.60, 1½ hours, every 30 minutes) come through Hexham; the AD122 Hadrian's Wall bus connects with other towns along the wall. Bus 10 (£5.50, 1½ hours, every 30 minutes) also links Hexham with Newcastle.

Hexham is on the scenic railway line between Newcastle (£6.90, 40 minutes, hourly) and Carlisle (£13, one hour, hourly).

Haltwhistle & Around

POP 3811

The village of Haltwhistle, little more than two intersecting streets, has more key Hadrian's Wall sights in its surrounds than anywhere else along the wall, but tourist infrastructure here is surprisingly underdeveloped.

Haltwhistle is one of the places that claims to be the geographic centre of the British mainland, although the jury is still out.

◉ Sights

★Housesteads Roman Fort & Museum
HISTORIC SITE

(EH; www.english-heritage.org.uk; Haydon Bridge; adult/child £7/4.10; ⏰10am-6pm Easter-Sep, to 5pm Oct, to 4pm Nov-Easter) The most dramatic site of Hadrian's Wall – and the best-preserved Roman fort in the whole country – is at Housesteads, 4 miles north of Bardon Mill on the B6318, and 6.5 miles northeast of Haltwhistle. From here, high on a ridge and covering 2 hectares, you can survey the moors of Northumberland National Park, and the snaking wall, with a sense of awe at the landscape and the aura of the Roman lookouts.

Up to 800 troops were based at Housesteads at any one time. Its remains include an impressive hospital, granaries with a carefully worked out ventilation system and barrack blocks. Most memorable are the spectacularly situated communal flushable latrines. Information boards show what the individual buildings would have looked like in their heyday. There's a scale model of the entire fort in the small museum at the ticket office.

Vindolanda Roman Fort & Museum
HISTORIC SITE

(www.vindolanda.com; Bardon Mill; adult/child £6.07/3.86, with Roman Army Museum £9.55/5.50; ⏰10am-6pm Apr-Sep, to 5pm Oct, to 4pm Nov-Mar)

The extensive site of Vindolanda offers a fascinating glimpse into the daily life of a Roman garrison town. The time-capsule museum is just one part of this large, extensively excavated site, which includes impressive parts of the fort and town (excavations continue) and reconstructed turrets and temple.

It's 1.5 miles north of Bardon Mill between the A69 and B6318, and 5.8 miles northeast of Haltwhistle.

Roman Army Museum
MUSEUM

(www.vindolanda.com; Greenhead; adult/child £5/2.95, with Vindolanda £9.55/5.50; ⏰10am-6pm Apr-Sep, to 5pm Oct, 10am-4pm Sat & Sun Nov-Mar) On the site of the Carvoran Roman Fort a mile northeast of Greenhead, near Walltown Crags, this revamped museum has three new galleries covering the Roman army and expanding and contracting Empire; the wall (with a 3D film illustrating what the wall was like nearly 2000 years ago and today); and colourful background detail to Hadrian's Wall life (such as how the soldiers spent their R&R time in this lonely outpost of the Empire).

Birdoswald Roman Fort
HISTORIC SITE

(EH; ☎01697-747602; www.english-heritage.org.uk; Gilsland, Greenhead; adult/child £6.10/3.70; ⏰10am-6pm Apr-Sep, to 5pm Oct, 10am-4pm Sat & Sun Nov-Mar) Technically in Cumbria, the remains of this once-formidable fort on an escarpment overlooking the beautiful Irthing Gorge are on a minor road off the B6318, about 3 miles west of Greenhead. The longest intact stretch of wall extends from here to Harrow's Scar Milecastle.

🛏 Sleeping

Greenhead
HOSTEL, B&B $

(☎01697-747411; www.greenheadhotelandhostel.co.uk; Greenhead; dm/d incl breakfast from £15/85; ⏰Apr-Sep; 🅿🛜) A converted 1866-built Methodist chapel by a trickling stream houses this independent hostel 3 miles west of Haltwhistle near the Roman Army Museum. There's a laundry and roomy kitchen, but if you don't feel like cooking, Greenhead's hotel across the road has a restaurant and bar with wi-fi. It's served by the Hadrian's Wall bus AD122.

★Ashcroft
B&B $$

(☎01434-320213; www.ashcroftguesthouse.co.uk; Lanty's Lonnen, Haltwhistle; s/d/apt from £72/94/140; 🅿🛜🚗) British B&Bs don't get better than this elegant Edwardian vicarage surrounded by nearly a hectare of beautiful-

CHESTERS ROMAN FORT & MUSEUM

The superbly preserved Roman cavalry remains at **Chesters Roman Fort & Museum** (EH; ☑ 01434-681379; www.english-heritage.org.uk; Chollerford; adult/child £6.20/3.70; ⊙10am-6pm Easter-Sep, to 5pm Oct, 10am-4pm Sat & Sun Nov-Easter) are set among idyllic green woods and meadows near the village of Chollerford. Originally constructed to house up to 500 troops from Asturias in northern Spain, they include part of a bridge (best appreciated from the eastern bank), four gatehouses, a bathhouse and an underfloor heating system. The museum has a large Roman sculpture collection; there's a simple tearoom on site. It's served by Hadrian's Wall bus AD122.

ly manicured, terraced lawns and gardens. Inside, the nine rooms – some with private balconies and terraces – have soaring ceilings and every 21st-century gadget imaginable. Breakfast is served in a grand dining room; there's also a self-catering apartment on the grounds sleeping up to five people.

Holmhead Guest House　　　　B&B $$
(☑ 01697-747402;　http://bandb-hadrianswall.co.uk; Greenhead; campsites per person £7, dm/s/d from £13.50/55/70; P🐾🛜🏠) Built using recycled bits of the wall on whose foundations it stands, this superb farmhouse half a mile north of Greenhead offers comfy rooms, a basic bunk barn and five unpowered campsites. The Pennine Way and the Hadrian's Wall Path pass through the grounds and Thirlwall Castle's jagged ruins loom above. Ask to see the 3rd-century Roman graffiti.

ℹ Information

On the main street, Haltwhistle's small **tourist office** (☑ 01434-321863; www.visitnorthumberland.com; Mechanics Institute, Westgate; ⊙10am-4.30pm Mon-Fri, to 1pm Sat Apr-Oct, 10am-1pm & 1.30-4.30pm Mon-Fri, 10am-1pm Sat Nov-Mar) has information on the wall's attractions.

The Northumberland National Park's visitor centre, **Walltown Visitor Centre** (☑ 01697-747151; www.northumberlandnationalpark.org.uk; Greenhead; ⊙10am-6pm Apr-Sep, to 5pm Oct, 10am-4pm Sat & Sun Nov-Mar) is located at Greenhead.

ℹ Getting There & Away

Bus 685 runs to Hexham (£3.40, 25 minutes, hourly) and Newcastle (£6.50, 1½ hours, hourly).

Haltwhistle is also linked by train to Hexham (£6.40, 20 minutes, hourly) and Newcastle (£12.60, one hour, hourly).

Northumberland National Park

England's last great wilderness is the 405 sq miles of natural wonderland that make up the country's least populated national park. The finest sections of Hadrian's Wall run along its southern edge and the landscape is dotted with prehistoric remains and fortified houses – the thick-walled *peles* were the only solid buildings built here until the mid-18th century.

Adjacent to the national park, the Kielder Water & Forest Park is home to the vast artificial lake Kielder Water, holding 200,000 million litres. Surrounding its 27-mile-long shoreline is England's largest plantation forest, with 150 million spruce and pine trees.

The lack of population here helped see the area awarded dark-sky status by the International Dark Skies Association in late 2013 (the largest such designation in Europe), with controls to prevent light pollution.

◉ Sights

★ **Kielder Observatory**　　OBSERVATORY
(☑ 0191-265 5510; www.kielderobservatory.org; Black Fell, off Shilling Pot; public observing session adult/child £16.50/15; ⊙by reservation) For the best views of the Northumberland International Dark Sky Park, attend a stargazing session at this state-of-the-art, 2008-built observatory. In addition to public observing there are a host of events, including family astronomy, astrophotography and star camps. Book well ahead for all events, which sell out quickly, and dress as you would for the ski slopes (it's seriously chilly here at night). At the signs towards Kielder Observatory and Skyspace, turn left; it's a 2-mile drive up the track.

Cragside House, Garden & Estate　　HISTORIC BUILDING, GARDENS
(NT;　☑ 01669-620333;　www.nationaltrust.org.uk; adult/child £15.80/7.90, gardens & estate only £10.20/5.10;　⊙house 11am-5pm Tue-Sun mid-Mar–Oct, gardens 10am-6pm Tue-Sun mid-Mar–Oct) Situated 1 mile northeast of Rothbury is the astonishing country retreat of the first

Lord Armstrong. In the 1880s the house had hot and cold running water, a telephone and alarm system, and was the first in the world to be lit by electricity, generated through hydropower. The sprawling Victorian gardens feature lakes, moors and one of Europe's largest rock gardens. Visit late May to mid-June to see Cragside's famous rhododendrons in bloom. It's just off the B6341.

Chillingham Castle CASTLE
(☑ 01668-215359; www.chillingham-castle.com; Chillingham; castle adult/child £9.50/5.50, Chillingham Wild Cattle £8/3, castle & Chillingham Wild Cattle £16/6; ◷ castle noon-5pm Sun-Fri Apr-Oct, Chillingham Wild Cattle tours 10am, 11am, noon, 2pm, 3pm & 4pm Mon-Fri, 10am, 11am & noon Sun Easter to Oct, by reservation Nov-Easter) Steeped in history, warfare, torture and ghosts, 12th-century Chillingham is said to be one of the country's most haunted places, with spectres from a phantom funeral to Lady Mary Berkeley seeking her errant husband. Owner Sir Humphrey Wakefield has passionately restored the castle's extravagant medieval staterooms, stone-flagged banquet halls and grisly torture chambers. Chillingham is 6 miles southeast of Wooler.

Bus 470 (three daily Monday to Saturday) between Alnwick (£3.70, 30 minutes) and Wooler (£3.10, 20 minutes) stops at Chillingham.

🏃 Activities

The most spectacular stretch of the **Hadrian's Wall Path** is between Sewingshields and Greenhead in the south of the park.

There are many fine walks through the Cheviots (including a clamber to the top of the 815m-high Cheviot, the highest peak in the range), frequently passing by prehistoric remnants; local tourist offices can provide maps, guides and route information.

Though at times strenuous, cycling is a pleasure here; roads are good and traffic is light.

Kielder Water is a watersports playground (and midge magnet; bring insect repellent), and also has walking and cycling as well as great birdwatching. Visit www.visitkielder. com for more information.

🛏 Sleeping

Wooler YHA HOSTEL $
(☑ 0845 371 9668; www.yha.org.uk; 30 Cheviot St, Wooler; dm/d/hut from £15.50/35/42; ◷ Mar-Nov; P 🛜) In a low, red-brick building above

Wooler, this handy hostel contains 57 beds in a variety of rooms (including four handcrafted 'shepherds' huts' sleeping two to three people on bunk beds), a modern lounge and a small restaurant, as well as a self-catering kitchen, drying room and bike storage.

★**Otterburn Castle
Country House Hotel** HISTORIC HOTEL $$
(☑ 01830-520620; www.otterburncastle.com; Main St, Otterburn; incl breakfast d £90-140, f £110-170; P 🛜 🛜 🅰) Founded by William the Conqueror's cousin Robert Umfraville in 1086 and set in almost 13 hectares of grounds, this story-book castle has 17 recently refurbished, astonishing-value rooms, some with four-poster beds. Exceptional modern British fare is served in its wood-panelled **Oak Room Restaurant** (two-/three-course menus £29.50/35.50). Cheaper meals are available in the **Stable Bar & Bistro** (mains £8.50 to £16.50).

Katerina's Guest House B&B $$
(☑ 01669-620691; www.katerinasguesthouse. co.uk; High St, Rothbury; d £80; 🛜) Beamed ceilings, stone fireplaces and en-suite rooms with fridges and canopied four-poster beds make Katerina's one of Rothbury's best choices. Bakeries, cafes and pubs abound along the street.

ℹ Information

For information, contact the **National Park** (☑ 01434-605555; www.northumberlandnationalpark.org.uk). As well as tourist offices in towns including **Wooler** (☑ 01668-282123; www. wooler.org.uk; Cheviot Centre, 12 Padgepool Pl, Wooler; ◷ 10am-4.30pm Apr-Oct, 10am-4.30pm Mon-Sat Nov-Mar) and **Rothbury** (☑ 01669-620887; www.visitkielder.com; Coquetdale Centre, Church St, Rothbury; ◷ 10am-4.30pm Mon-Sat, 10.30am-4pm Sun Apr-Oct, closed Nov-Mar), there's a national park office, the **Walltown Visitor Centre** (p624), near Haltwhistle. All offices can help find accommodation.

ℹ Getting There & Around

Public transport options are limited at best – to explore properly you really need your own wheels.

Bus 808 (£3.70, 55 minutes, one daily Monday to Saturday) runs between Otterburn and Newcastle.

Bus 15 serves Alnwick from Rothbury (£4, 25 minutes, four daily Monday to Saturday).

Buses 470 and **473** link Wooler and Alnwick (£3.90, 50 minutes, hourly). Buses 267 and 464 run between Wooler and Berwick-upon-Tweed (£3.90, 50 minutes, hourly)

Northumberland Coast

Northumberland's coast, like its wild and remote interior, is sparsely populated. You won't find any hurdy-gurdy seaside resorts, but instead charming, castle-crowned villages strung along miles of wide, sandy beaches that you might just have to yourself.

Alnwick

POP 8116

Northumberland's historic ducal town, Alnwick (pronounced 'annick') is an elegant maze of narrow cobbled streets beneath its colossal medieval castle. Alnwick is also home to an enchanting bookshop and spectacular Alnwick Garden.

◉ Sights

★ Alnwick Castle   CASTLE
(www.alnwickcastle.com; The Peth; adult/child £14.95/7.75, with Alnwick Garden £25.60/10.90; ⊙10am-5.30pm Easter-Oct) Set in parklands designed by Lancelot 'Capability' Brown, the imposing ancestral home of the duke of Northumberland has changed little since the 14th century. It's a favourite set for film-makers and starred as Hogwarts for the first couple of Harry Potter films. The interior is sumptuous and extravagant; the six rooms open to the public – staterooms, dining room, guard chamber and library – have an incredible display of Italian paintings, including Titian's *Ecce Homo* and many Canalettos.

Various free tours include several focusing on Harry Potter and other productions that have used the castle as a backdrop, including British comedy series *Blackadder*.

For the best views of the castle's exterior, take The Peth to the River Aln's northern bank and follow the woodland trail east.

Alnwick Garden   GARDENS
(www.alnwickgarden.com; Denwick Lane; adult/child £12.10/4.40, with Alnwick Castle £25.60/10.90; ⊙10am-6pm Easter-Oct, to 4pm Nov-Easter) This 4.8-hectare walled garden incorporates a series of magnificent green spaces surrounding the breathtaking Grand Cascade – 120 separate jets spurting some 30,000L of water down 21 weirs. Half a dozen other gardens include a Franco-Italian-influenced Ornamental Garden (with over 15,000 plants), Rose Garden and fascinating Poison Garden, home to some of the deadliest – and most illegal – plants in the world, including cannabis, magic mushrooms, belladonna and tobacco.

⏢ Sleeping

★ Alnwick Lodge   B&B, CAMPGROUND **$$**
(☑ 01665-604363; www.alnwicklodge.com; West Cawledge Park, A1; tent sites from £12, B&B s/d/f from £55/72/100; P 🛜 ♿ 🐾) Situated 2 miles south off the A1, this gorgeous Victorian farmstead has 15 antique-filled rooms with quirky touches like free-standing, lidded baths. Cooked breakfasts are served around a huge circular banqueting table. You can also go 'glamping' in restored gypsy caravans, wagons and shepherds' huts (from £45, linen per bed £15; shared bathrooms), or pitch up on the sheltered meadow.

White Swan Hotel   HOTEL **$$**
(☑ 01665-602109; www.classiclodges.co.uk; Bondgate Within; d/f from £115/135; P 🛜 ♿ 🐾) Alnwick's top address is this 300-year-old coaching inn in the heart of town. Rooms are all superbly appointed (including family rooms that sleep up to four). Its architectural showpiece is the fine-dining **Olympic Restaurant** (☑01665-602109; www.classiclodges.co.uk; Bondgate Within; mains £11-18, 2-/3-course lunch menus £12/15, 3-course dinner menu £31.50; ⊙noon-3pm & 5-9pm).

🍷 Drinking

Bari Tea   CAFE
(www.baritea.co.uk; 28 Narrowgate; ⊙11am-4pm Easter-Sep, 11am-4pm Thu-Mon Oct-Easter; 🛜) Some 30 different varieties of loose-leaf tea are on offer at this tearoom, accompanied by scones, cakes and slices. High tea costs £10 for two people.

🛍 Shopping

★ Barter Books   BOOKS
(☑01665-604888; www.barterbooks.co.uk; Alnwick Station, Wagon Way Rd; ⊙9am-7pm) If you're familiar with the renaissance of the WWII 'Keep Calm and Carry On' slogan, it's thanks to this wonderfully atmospheric secondhand bookshop in Alnwick's Victorian former railway station. While converting the station, the owner came across a set of posters – the framed original is above the till – and turned it into a successful industry.

Coal fires, velvet ottomans, reading rooms and a cafe make this a place you could spend days in, the silence interrupted only by the tiny rumble of the toy train that runs along the track above your head.

Taste of Northumberland FOOD, DRINK
(4-6 Market Pl; ⊙10am-3pm Mon-Sat) 🖉 Alnwick-distilled rum and Lindisfarne-made mead along with a range of boutique English gins and Scottish whiskies are sold at this locavore shop in the town centre. Alnwick rum is also used in seasonal Christmas puddings sold here.

ℹ Information

Alnwick's **tourist office** (📞 01670-622152; www.visitalnwick.org.uk; 2 The Shambles; ⊙9.30am-5pm Mon-Sat, 10am-4pm Sun Easter-Oct, 10am-4pm Mon-Sat Nov-Easter) is by Market Pl.

ℹ Getting There & Away

Buses X15 and X18 run to Berwick-upon-Tweed (£6.10, 50 minutes, every two hours) and Newcastle (£6.30, one hour, every two hours).

Alnwick's nearest train station is at Alnmouth, connected to Alnwick by bus X18 (£2.70, 10 minutes, hourly). Alnmouth's train services include Berwick-upon-Tweed (£13.60, 20 minutes, up to two per hour), Edinburgh (£38.90, one hour, up to two per hour) and Newcastle (£10.30, 30 minutes, up to two per hour).

Craster

POP 305

Sandy, salty Craster is a small, sheltered fishing village about 6 miles northeast of Alnwick, and is famous for its kippers. In the early 20th century, 2500 herring were smoked here daily. The kippers still produced today often grace the Queen's breakfast table.

⊙ Sights

Dunstanburgh Castle CASTLE
(EH; www.english-heritage.org.uk; Dunstanburgh Rd; adult/child £5.20/3.10; ⊙10am-6pm Easter-Sep, to 4pm Oct, 10am-4pm Sat & Sun Nov-Easter) The dramatic 1.5-mile walk along the coast from Craster (not accessible by car) is the most scenic path to this moody, weather-beaten castle. Its construction began in 1314 and it was strengthened during the Wars of the Roses, but left to crumble, becoming ruined by 1550. Parts of the original wall and gatehouse keep are still standing and it's a tribute to its builders that so much remains.

You can also reach the castle on foot from Embleton (1.5 miles), but access can be cut off at high tide.

🍴 Eating

★ Jolly Fisherman GASTROPUB $$
(📞 016650-576461; www.thejollyfishermancraster.co.uk; Haven Hill; mains lunch £7-10, dinner £15-22; ⊙kitchen 11am-3pm & 5-8.30pm Mon-Sat, noon-7pm Sun, bar 11am-11pm Mon-Thu, to midnight Sat, to 9pm Sun; 🚸) Crab (in sensational soup, sandwiches, fish platters and more) is the speciality of this superb gastropub, but Paul Bocuse–trained chef John Blackmore's other amazing creations include roast pheasant with tarragon mustard, and game pie with Northumbrian venison and wood pigeon. Great wine list, wonderful real ales, a roaring fire in the bar and stunning beer garden overlooking Dunstanburgh Castle too.

🛍 Shopping

★ Robson & Sons FOOD
(📞 01665-576223; www.kipper.co.uk; Haven Hill; kippers per kilo from £9; ⊙9am-4.30pm Mon-Sat, 10am-4pm Sun) Four generations have operated this traditional fish smokers; loyal customers include the Royal Family. It's best known for its kippers, but also smokes salmon and other fish.

ℹ Information

Craster's **tourist office** (📞 01665-576007; www.visitnorthumberland.com; Quarry Car Park; ⊙10am-4.30pm Easter-Oct) opens in the warmer months.

ℹ Getting There & Away

Bus X18 runs to Berwick-upon-Tweed (£6.10, 1½ hours, every two hours) and Newcastle (£5.60, 1½ hours, every two hours). Bus 418 links Craster to Alnwick (£5.10, 30 minutes, hourly).

> **LOCAL KNOWLEDGE**
>
> ### AMBLE PUFFIN FESTIVAL
>
> For eight days from late May to early June, the town of Amble celebrates the hatching of puffin chicks on Coquet Island (just offshore) with **Amble Puffin Festival** (http://amblepuffinfest.co.uk). Events include local history talks, guided birdwatching walks, exhibitions, watersports, a craft fair, a food festival and live music. There's also a kayak fishing competition and a daily teddy bear parachute drop.

Embleton Bay

Beautiful Embleton Bay, a pale wide arc of sand, stretches from Dunstanburgh past the endearing, sloping village of Embleton and curves in a broad vanilla-coloured strand around to end at Low Newton-by-the-Sea, a tiny whitewashed, National Trust–preserved village.

Sights & Activities

Behind the bay is a path leading to the **Newton Pool Nature Reserve**, an important spot for breeding and migrating birds such as black-headed gulls and grasshopper warblers. There are a couple of hides where you can peer out at them. You can continue walking along the headland beyond Low Newton, where you'll find **Football Hole**, a delightful hidden beach between headlands.

The easiest access to Dunstanburgh Castle (p627) is from Craster; the walk to the castle from Embleton Bay can be cut off at high tide.

Sleeping & Eating

Joiners Arms   PUB $$$
(☑01665-576112; http://joiners-arms.com; High Newton-by-the-Sea; d £140-155; P ☏ ⊛ ☙) Locals love this gastropub and for good reason: ingredients are sourced nearby, the seafood and steaks are excellent (mains £13 to £20) and families are warmly welcomed. But for visitors, it's also a fantastic place to stay: five contemporary guest rooms are individually and exquisitely decorated with details like exposed brick, free-standing baths and four-poster beds.

Ship Inn   PUB FOOD $$
(☑01665-576262; www.shipinnnewton.co.uk; Low Newton-by-the-Sea; mains £8.50-18; ⊘kitchen noon-2.30pm & 7-8pm Wed-Sat, noon-2.30pm Sun-Tue, bar 11am-11pm Mon-Sat, 11am-10pm Sun Apr-Oct, reduced hours Nov-Mar) ✎ Set around a village green, this wonderful pub brews 26 different beers – blond, wheat, rye, bitter, stout and seasonal – using local River Coquet water. The food is first-rate, too, from local crab to slow-cooked Peelham Farm lamb shanks with lemon and parsley couscous. No credit cards. Live music often plays at weekends.

Getting There & Away

Bus X18 to Newcastle (£5.60, 1¾ hours, every two hours) and Berwick-upon-Tweed (£5.50, 1¼ hours, every two hours) stops outside the Join-

ers Arms. Bus 418 (£5.10, 40 minutes, hourly) links the village of Embleton with Alnwick.

Bamburgh

POP 300

High up on a basalt crag, Bamburgh's mighty castle looms over the quaint village – a clutch of houses around a pleasant green – which continues to commemorate the valiant achievements of local heroine Grace Darling.

Sights

Bamburgh Castle   CASTLE
(www.bamburghcastle.com; Links Rd; adult/child £10.75/5; ⊘10am-5pm mid-Feb–Oct, 11am-4.30pm Sat & Sun Nov–mid-Feb) Northumberland's most dramatic castle was built around a powerful 11th-century Norman keep by Henry II. The castle played a key role in the border wars of the 13th and 14th centuries, and in 1464 was the first English castle to fall during the Wars of the Roses. It was restored in the 19th century by the great industrialist Lord Armstrong, and is still home to the Armstrong family.

Its name is a derivative of Bebbanburgh, after the wife of Anglo-Saxon ruler Aedelfrip, whose fortified home occupied this basalt outcrop 500 years earlier. Antique furniture, suits of armour, priceless ceramics and artworks cram the castle's rooms and chambers, but top billing goes to the neo-Gothic **King's Hall** with wood panelling, leaded windows and hefty beams supporting the roof.

RNLI Grace Darling Museum   MUSEUM
(www.rnli.org; 1 Radcliffe Rd; ⊘10am-5pm Easter-Sep, 10am-4pm Tue-Sun Oct-Easter) FREE
Born in Bamburgh, Grace Darling was the lighthouse keeper's daughter on Outer Farne who rowed out to the grounded, flailing SS *Forfarshire* in 1838 and saved its crew in the middle of a dreadful storm. This refurbished museum even has her actual coble (row boat) as well as a film on the events of that stormy night. Grace was born just three houses down from the museum and is buried in the churchyard opposite.

Her ornate wrought-iron and sandstone tomb was built tall so as to be visible to passing ships.

Eating

★ **Mizen Head**   MODERN BRITISH $$
(☑01668-214254; www.mizen-head.co.uk; Lucker Rd; mains £10-32.50; ⊘6-9pm Mon-Wed, noon-1.45pm & 6-9pm Thu-Sun; P ☏) Bamburgh's

Driving Tour
Northumberland Coast

START NEWBIGGIN-BY-THE-SEA
END BERWICK-UPON-TWEED
LENGTH 78 MILES; ONE DAY

It's possible to shadow the coast to the Scottish border from Tynemouth, but the scenery really picks up at **1 Newbiggin-by-the-Sea**. Newbiggin's beach was restored in 2007, when over 500,000 tonnes of Skegness' sand was relocated here to counteract erosion, and Sean Henry's gigantic bronze sculpture *The Couple* was installed offshore.

Continuing north along the A1068 coast road for 13 miles brings you to the fishing port of **2 Amble**, with a boardwalk along the seafront and puffin cruises. Less than 2 miles north, biscuit-coloured **3 Warkworth** is a cluster of houses around a loop in the River Coquet, dominated by the craggy ruin of 14th-century Warkworth Castle. The castle features in Shakespeare's *Henry IV* Parts I and II, and the 1998 film *Elizabeth* was shot here. A few hundred metres upriver, the tiny 14th-century Warkworth Hermitage is carved into the rock.

Some 5 miles north of Warkworth is **4 Alnmouth**, with brightly painted houses and pretty beaches. It's another 5 miles inland to the bustling town of **5 Alnwick** to see its imposing castle – which starred as Harry Potter's Hogwarts – and glorious Alnwick Garden. Turn back towards the coast and follow the B1339 for 4.7 miles before turning east on Windside Hill to **6 Craster**, famed for its smoked kippers, which you can buy direct from the smokery. Don't miss a meal at the Jolly Fisherman, which has spectacular views of brooding Dunstanburgh Castle. Around 5 miles north at **7 Low Newton-by-the-Sea**, in Embleton Bay, pause for a pint brewed at the Ship Inn.

Past the village of Seahouses (the departure point for the Farne Islands), quaint **8 Bamburgh** is home to the most dramatic castle yet. Another 17 miles on, via a tidal causeway (check tide times!), the sacred priory ruins of isolated, otherworldly **9 Holy Island (Lindisfarne)** still attract spiritual pilgrims. Return to the mainland where, 14 miles north, you can walk almost the entire length of the Elizabethan walls encircling England's northernmost city, beautiful **10 Berwick-upon-Tweed**.

best place to eat and/or stay is this stunning restaurant with rooms. Local seafood – lobster thermidor, roast turbot with asparagus, tarragon and lemon butter – is the kitchen's speciality, along with chargrilled steaks. Its six rooms with chequered fabrics and black-and-white coastal prints are light, bright and spacious (doubles from £100 to £140). Switched-on staff know their stuff.

ℹ Getting There & Away

Take bus X18 north to Berwick-upon-Tweed (£6, 35 minutes, every two hours) or south to Newcastle (£6.10, two hours, every two hours).

Holy Island (Lindisfarne)

POP 160

There's something almost other-worldly about this tiny, 2-sq-mile island. Connected to the mainland by a narrow causeway that only appears at low tide, cutting the island off from the mainland for about five hours each day, it's fiercely desolate and isolated, scarcely different from when St Aidan arrived to found a monastery in 635.

As you cross the empty flats, it's easy to imagine the marauding Vikings who repeatedly sacked the settlement between 793 and 875, when the monks finally took the hint and left. They carried with them the illuminated *Lindisfarne Gospels* (now in the British Library in London) and the miraculously preserved body of St Cuthbert, who lived here for a couple of years but preferred the hermit's life on Inner Farne. A priory was re-established in the 11th century, but didn't survive the Dissolution in 1537.

◎ Sights

Lindisfarne Priory RUINS
(EH; www.english-heritage.org.uk; adult/child £6/3.60; ☉10am-6pm Apr-Sep, to 5pm Oct, 10am-4pm Sat & Sun Nov-Mar) The skeletal, red and grey ruins of the priory are an eerie sight and give a glimpse into the isolated life of the Lindisfarne monks. The later 13th-century St Mary the Virgin Church is built on the site of the first church between the Tees and the Firth of Forth, and the adjacent museum displays the remains of the first monastery and tells the story of the monastic community before and after the Dissolution. Hours can vary according to tides.

Lindisfarne Heritage Centre MUSEUM
(www.lindisfarne-centre.com; Marygate; adult/child £4/2; ☉10am-5pm Apr-Oct, shorter hours Nov-Mar) Flick through 20 pages of the luminescent *Lindisfarne Gospels* on touch screens at this heritage centre. It also has some fascinating exhibits on the Vikings and the sacking of Lindisfarne in 793. Opening times are tide-dependent.

Lindisfarne Castle CASTLE
(NT; www.nationaltrust.org.uk; adult/child £7.30/3.60; ☉10am-3pm Tue-Sun mid-Feb–Oct & some weekends Nov–mid-Feb) Built atop a rocky bluff in 1550, this tiny, storybook castle was extended and converted by Sir Edwin Lutyens from 1902 to 1910 for Mr Hudson, the owner of *Country Life* magazine – you can imagine some of the decadent Gatsby-style parties to have graced its alluring rooms. It's half a mile east of the village. Opening times can vary due to tide times.

🛏 Sleeping & Eating

Crown & Anchor INN $$
(☎01289-389215; http://holyislandcrown.co.uk; Market Pl; s £55-80, d £70-100; 🐾) The only locally run inn on the island is a relaxed, down-to-earth spot with brightly coloured guest rooms and solid pub grub (steak-and-ale pie, rib-eye steak with onion rings; mains £6.50 to £18), but the biggest winner is the beer garden with a postcard panorama of the castle, priory and harbour.

Manor House Hotel HOTEL $$
(☎01289-389207; http://manorhouseholyisland.com; Market Sq; s/d/f incl breakfast from £60/95/180; P🛜) Wake up to views of the harbour, priory and castle from some of the 10 modern rooms at this 1870s manor. Rates fall outside summer; be sure to book ahead. Its Priory Restaurant (mains £9 to £14), on the ground floor, opens to a large beer garden and utilises seasonal, local produce. Bike storage is available.

Lindisfarne Inn INN $$
(☎01289-381223; www.lindisfarneinn.co.uk; Beal; s/d/f from £70/76/125; P🛜🐾) Although on the mainland (on the A1 next to the turn-off to the causeway), this is a handy alternative to island accommodation and/or dining if you're cutting it fine with crossing times. Its 21 spotless, modern rooms are set far back enough that road noise isn't a problem. Well-above-average bar food includes a catch-of-the-day fisherman's pie (mains £10 to £20). There's wi-fi in the bar only.

FARNE ISLANDS

During breeding season (roughly May to July), you can see feeding chicks of 20 seabird species (including puffin, kittiwake, Arctic tern and eider duck), and some 6000 grey seals, on the **Farne Islands** (NT; www.nationaltrust.org.uk; adult/child excl boat transport £5.75/2.90; ☺ by reservation, season & conditions permitting Apr-Oct), a rocky archipelago three miles offshore from the fishing village of Seahouses. Four boat operators, contactable through Seahouses' **tourist office** (☑ 01670-625593; http://visitnorthumberland.com; Seafield car park, Seahouses; ☺ 10am-4.30pm Easter-Oct), depart from Seahouses' dock, including **Billy Shiel** (☑ 01665-720308; www.farne-islands.com; adult/child 2.5hr tour £15/10, 6hr tour £35/20).

Crossings can be rough (impossible in bad weather); wear warm, waterproof clothing and an old hat to guard against the birds!

Bus X18 links Seahouses with Berwick-upon-Tweed (£5.70, 45 minutes, every two hours) and Newcastle (£6.60, two hours, every two hours). Bus 418 runs to Alnwick (£5.30, 55 minutes, hourly).

Pilgrim's Coffee House   COFFEE, CAFE
(www.pilgrimscoffee.com; Marygate; ☺ 9.30am-5pm Sun-Fri, to 9pm Sat Mar-Nov, closed Dec-Feb, hours can vary; 🛜) 🍴 Fairtrade organic beans and compostable packaging are used by this fabulous independent coffee roastery. The living-room-like dining space with Chesterfield armchairs and a blazing open fire is a cosy spot for sandwiches, jacket potatoes, and homemade cakes, slices and shortbread, plus pizzas and cocktails on Saturday nights. On sunny days the courtyard garden is a treat.

🛍 Shopping

St Aidan's Winery   FOOD, DRINK
(Lindisfarne Mead; www.lindisfarne-mead.co.uk; Prior Lane; ☺ 9am-5pm Easter-Oct, 10am-5pm Nov-Easter depending on tides) 🍴 Mead made on Lindisfarne by St Aidan's Winery to a traditional Roman recipe using locally drawn water and honey. Free tastings let you try its three varieties – original, blood orange and spiced – as well as some of its fortified wines (ginger, wild strawberry, elderberry, blackberry, cherry and more). Other products include mead-based chocolate truffles and jams.

ⓘ Getting There & Around

The island can sometimes be reached by bus 477 from Berwick-upon-Tweed (£4.50, 40 minutes, depends on tides); check with Berwick's tourist offices for updated information.

Drivers need to pay close attention to crossing-time information posted at tourist offices and on notice boards throughout the area, and at www.holy-island.info. Every year drivers are caught midway by the incoming tide and have to abandon their cars.

Park in the signposted car park (£4.60 per day). A shuttle bus (£2 return) runs from the car park to the castle every 20 minutes from Easter to September; alternatively it's a level 300m walk to the village centre and 1 mile to the castle.

Berwick-upon-Tweed

POP 11,500

England's northernmost city is a picturesque fortress town, cleaved by the River Tweed, which is spanned by the Grade I–listed Berwick Bridge (aka Old Bridge), built from sandstone between 1611 and 1624, and the Royal Tweed (1925–28).

Berwick is the stubborn holder of two unique honours: it is the most fought-over settlement in European history (between 1174 and 1482 it changed hands 14 times between the Scots and the English); and its football team, Berwick Rangers, are the only English team to play in the Scottish League (albeit in lowly Scottish League Two). Although firmly English since the 15th century, Berwick retains its own identity, with locals south of the border speaking with a noticeable Scottish whirr.

⊙ Sights

★ **Berwick Walls**   HISTORIC SITE
(EH; www.english-heritage.org.uk; ☺ dawn-dusk) **FREE** You can walk almost the entire length of Berwick's hefty Elizabethan walls, begun in 1558 to reinforce an earlier set built during the reign of Edward II. The mile-long walk is a must, with wonderful, wide-open views. Only a small fragment remains of the once mighty **border castle**, most of the building having been replaced by the train station.

Berwick Barracks
MUSEUM, GALLERY

(EH; www.english-heritage.org.uk; The Parade; adult/child £4.60/2.80; ⊘10am-6pm Easter-Sep, to 4pm Oct, closed Nov-Easter) Designed by Nicholas Hawksmoor, Britain's oldest purpose-built barracks (1717) now house an assortment of museums and art galleries, covering a history of the town and British soldiery since the 17th century. The **Gymnasium Gallery** hosts big-name contemporary art exhibitions.

Cell Block Museum
MUSEUM

(Marygate; adult/child £2/50p; ⊘tours 10am & 2pm Mon-Fri Easter-Sep) The original jail cells in the upper floor of the town hall (1750–61) have been preserved as a chilling museum devoted to crime and punishment. Tours take in the public rooms, museum, jail and belfry.

☞ Tours

Time to Explore Guided Tours
WALKING

(☏01289-330218; www.visitberwick.com; 106 Marygate; Town & Walls adult/child £7/free; ⊘by reservation 11am Mon-Fri Easter-Oct) Passionate local Derek Sharman leads 1¼-hour Town & Walls tours taking in Berwick's highlights. Tours depart from the tourist office.

🛏 Sleeping

Berwick YHA
HOSTEL $

(☏0845 371 9676; www.yha.org.uk; Dewars Lane; dm/d from £10/58; ▣@⊛) A 240-year-old granary has been converted into a state-of-the-art hostel with 55 beds in all-en-suite dorms and private rooms. Contemporary facilities include a TV room, a laundry and wi-fi in common areas. Staff are terrifically friendly and helpful.

★Marshall Meadows
Country House Hotel
HERITAGE HOTEL $$

(☏01289-331133; http://marshallmeadowshotel. co.uk; Marshall Meadows; incl breakfast s £70-90, d £89-139, f £99-149; ▣⊛▣) England's most northerly hotel, just 600m from the Scottish border, is a treasure. Set in 6 hectares of woodland and ornamental gardens, the Georgian manor has 19 rooms (including a ground-floor family room) with countrified checked and floral fabrics, two cosy bars with open fireplaces and a conservatory. Breakfast (including kippers) is served in the oak-panelled restaurant (two-/three-course dinner menus £21.95/29.95).

The Berwickshire Coastal Path walking trail runs alongside the property.

Granary Guesthouse
B&B $$

(☏01289-304403; www.granaryguesthouse. co.uk; 11 Bridge St; s/d from £80/96; ▣⊛) ⊘ In a charming town-centre location, Berwick's most romantic B&B has three fresh, elegant and contemporary guest rooms, locally sourced and/or organic breakfasts (gluten-free options available) and an on-site beauty treatment room offering massages.

🍴 Eating & Drinking

Audela
MODERN BRITISH $$

(☏01289-308827; www.audela.co.uk; 41-47 Bridge St; breakfast dishes £5.50-9.50, mains lunch £5.50-11.50, dinner £8-19; ⊘9am-9pm; ☝) ⊘ Named for the last vessel to be built at Berwick Shipyard (in 1979), Audela is the town's top table. Local suppliers provide the ingredients for dishes like twice-backed Northumberland cheese soufflé, halibut with lemon butter sauce and herb-crusted rack of lamb, served in a striking sage-green dining room. Lunchtime gourmet sandwiches include Berwick crab and lime mayo.

Barrels Alehouse
PUB

(59-61 Bridge St; ⊘noon-midnight Sun-Thu, to 1am Fri & Sat; ⊛) Berwick's best watering hole attracts a mixed, laid-back crowd who can be found sipping real ales and micro-distilled gins and whiskies at all hours. On Friday nights, live music plays in the atmospherically dingy basement bar.

ℹ Information

The **tourist office** (☏01670-622155; www. visitberwick.com; 106 Marygate; ⊘10am-5pm Mon-Sat, 11am-4pm Sun Easter-Sep, 10am-4pm Mon-Sat Oct-Easter) is in the centre of town.

ℹ Getting There & Away

BUS

Buses stop on Golden Sq (where it meets Marygate). National Express coaches between Edinburgh (£11.60, 1¼ hours, twice daily) and London (£33, eight hours, twice daily) stop here.

Other options include buses X15 (via Alnwick) and X18 to Newcastle (£6.80, 2½ hours, every two hours) and bus 477 to Holy Island, aka Lindisfarne (£4.50, 40 minutes, depends on tides; check with Berwick's tourist offices for updated information).

TRAIN

On the East Coast Main Line linking London and Edinburgh, Berwick-upon-Tweed is almost exactly halfway between Edinburgh (£25.10, 40 minutes, two per hour) and Newcastle (£26.10, 45 minutes, two per hour).

Understand
England

ENGLAND TODAY **634**

A monumental vote to exit Europe signals a time of great change for England, and it's not come without some tensions and much soul searching.

HISTORY **636**

From Stonehenge to the challenges of the 21st century, England's history is varied – and never, ever dull.

FOOD & DRINK **648**

Fish and chips or chicken tikka masala? Real ale or fine wine? This chapter will totally tickle your taste buds.

ARCHITECTURE **655**

In England the artistry of architecture is never far away. From ancient castles and cathedrals, to modern creations - there's plenty to impress.

LANDSCAPE **660**

A geographical variety pack: from sandy beaches to high mountains, with diverse wildlife and stunning national parks.

ARTS **665**

Shakespeare, Wordsworth, Turner, the *Angel of the North*, the Beatles and James Bond – they're all here.

SPORTING ENGLAND **672**

Where to see the football (aka soccer), rugby, cricket, tennis and more. You might even see England win. Occasionally …

England Today

Events in recent times have been seismic for the English. For decades as Scottish and Welsh nationalism gained ground, the English seemed to become less certain about their own identity. But in 2016 the country had the chance to define itself – facing a referendum vote on either remaining an integral part of Europe or breaking away. The country, technically, made a clear call to leave. But the detail revealed a divided England, and the long-term consequences remain opaque.

Best on Film

Brief Encounter (1945) Classic tale of buttoned-up English love affair.

My Beautiful Laundrette (1985) Touching and comic study of racism and homophobia in Thatcher-era London.

War Horse (2011) Rite-of-passage story of a young man surviving WWI.

Pride (2014) Comic, compassionate depiction of lesbian and gay activists raising money for families hit by the UK Miners' Strike (1984-5).

Suffragette (2015) Compelling account of the pre-WWI fight to secure votes for women.

Best in Print

Notes from a Small Island (Bill Bryson; 1995) It's dated, but this American's fond take on British behaviour is a classic, and still spot on today.

The English (Jeremy Paxman; 1998) A perceptive take on the national character.

The Rotters Club (Jonathan Coe; 2001) Growing up in the 1970s, amid strikes, IRA bombings and punk rock.

Watching the English (Kate Fox; 2004) A fascinating field guide to the nation's peculiar habits.

A Week in December (Sebastian Faulks; 2009) A state-of-the-nation satire on 2007 London life.

English or European?

On 24 June 2016, England awoke to monumental news. By a slim referendum vote the UK had opted to leave the EU, cutting ties stretching back 43 years. Within hours of the 'Brexit' result the prime minister, David Cameron, who'd campaigned to remain within the EU, announced his resignation. The pound fell to its worst level for 31 years; the FTSE 100 share index fell to an eight-year low.

The result mattered so much because since 1973 English and EU laws and procedures had become intertwined, from migration to trade, from fishing to human rights, from weights and measures to the environment. The closeness of that relationship was a comfort to some but an anathema to others. Remain supporters felt protected by Europe-wide civil rights; Leave campaigners felt Britain's right to shape its own destiny was under threat. For some it was about whether they saw themselves as English or European. These divisions were brought sharply into focus by a fierce, often acrimonious, referendum campaign.

The economy and health service were central issues, but – against the backdrop of a Europe-wide refugee crisis – the real flashpoint was immigration, an issue that's bubbled uncomfortably under the surface of English politics for decades. This time the debate revolved around whether Britain should regain the right to fix levels of immigration from within the EU. One camp argued England didn't have enough resources to cope with more migrants, the other pointed to the ranks of EU workers fulfilling crucial roles. There were bitter arguments over whether levels of migration meant 'Englishness' itself was 'under threat'. For some it was a debate about latent racism, for others it was about sovereignty.

The referendum result was close: 52% to 48%, revealing a country polarised by different views. Some argued the country was freed from the shackles of an ailing EU while others saw a country cast dangerously adrift. The result showed the English capital and the rest of the country were out of synch, as London voted overwhelmingly (by 60%) to stay within Europe. There were similar divisions along age lines: 73% of 18- to 24-year-olds wanted to remain; 60% of those aged over 65 wanted to exit – suggesting young English people see themselves as far more European than the generations before. And while turnout was high, at 72%, it still means around one in four potential voters either couldn't decide or couldn't be bothered to cast a ballot. It was a referendum, then, that highlighted division rather than expressing a clear statement of English identity.

The vote to leave the EU also leaves broader uncertainties in England's political, economic and social landscapes. Regulations affecting almost every aspect of English life will have to be renegotiated, from customs and border controls to pan-European mobile-phone charges, driving regulations and health cover. Over the next few years, visitors to England, and English people themselves, will have plenty to keep an eye on. Theresa May, who replaced David Cameron as prime minister in July 2016, will be kept very busy.

Divisions & Unions
Perhaps that lack of clarity has something to do with the differences between England, Britain and the UK. They're confusing but crucial. Great Britain is the collective name for England, Scotland and Wales. The UK is the political union between Great Britain and Northern Ireland (not to be confused with the British Isles – a purely geographical term for islands including Great Britain and Ireland). And if you can find an English person who can nail the finer points of those distinctions, bravo. It tends to mean people in England are often a little unsure how to identify themselves (English, British or from the UK?), something you'll often spot in general conversation.

These distinctions might have bigger consequences because the EU referendum results are divided by country: England and Wales voted to leave the EU, but Scotland and Northern Ireland voted to remain. Within hours of the result, Scotland's First Minister, Nicola Sturgeon, said that to stop Scotland being taken out of the EU against its will, a second Scottish Independence referendum was now 'highly likely'. In 2014 Scotland had voted to remain within the UK. Then, some 45% of Scottish voters wanted independence. In England, only 19% of people wanted Scotland to leave. Meanwhile, there were calls in Northern Ireland for a broader poll on whether it should now unite with the Republic of Ireland. England's place within its closest union, and the shape of this union, has become very uncertain.

Keep Calm & Carry On
One thing the English are sure about, though, is the monarchy. It consistently enjoys popular support; a 2012 poll found only 22% of people thought Britain would be better off as a republic.

POPULATION: **53 MILLION**

AREA: **50,345 SQ MILES (130,395 SQ KM)**

GDP GROWTH (UK): **2.2%**

INFLATION (UK): **2%**

UNEMPLOYMENT (UK): **4.9%**

if England were 100 people
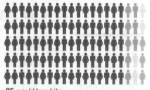
85 would be white
8 would be Asian
4 would be black
3 would be mixed/other

belief systems
(% of population)

60 Christian   32 No religion   5 Muslim

1.5 Hindu   1.5 Other

population per sq km

England   UK   London
† ≈ 260 people

History

Tiny geographically, England is immensely complex historically. And the extent to which its past shapes its present is profound. To really understand England you need to delve into its history, packed with drama and intrigue, with characters including incomers and invaders all leaving their mark. The result? The rich mix of culture, landscape and language that shaped the nation. For many, this vibrant heritage – whether seen in Stonehenge, Hadrian's Wall, Canterbury Cathedral or the Tower of London – is England's big draw.

Stone Age & Iron Age

The country of England is part of the island of Great Britain (along with Wales and Scotland). The words 'England' and 'Britain' are not synonymous, although visitors sometimes miss the distinction. Getting a grip on this basic principle will ease your understanding of English history and culture.

Stone tools discovered on a beach in Norfolk suggest human habitation in England stretches back at least 840,000 years. These early peoples were nomadic hunter-gatherers, but by around 4000 BC, most had settled down, notably in open areas such as Salisbury Plain in southern England. Alongside fields they built burial mounds (today called barrows), but their most enduring legacies are the great stone circles of Avebury and Stonehenge, still clearly visible today.

Move on a millennium or two and it's the Iron Age. Better tools meant trees could be felled and more land turned over to farming. As landscapes altered, this was also a time of cultural change: a new wave of migrants – the Celts – arrived in Britain from the European mainland. It's not clear if the new arrivals absorbed the indigenous people, or vice versa, but the end result was the widespread adoption of Celtic language and culture, and the creation of a Celtic-British population – today often known as the Britons (or Ancient Britons to distinguish them from today's natives).

By around 100 BC, the Ancient Britons had separated into about 20 different tribes, including the Cantiaci (in today's county of Kent), the Iceni (today's Norfolk) and the Brigantes (northern England). Did you notice the Latin-sounding names? That's because the tribal tags were handed out by the next arrivals on England's shores...

TIMELINE	4000 BC	55 BC	AD 43
	Neolithic peoples migrate from continental Europe. Differing significantly from previous arrivals, instead of hunting and moving on, they eventually settle in one place and start farming.	Relatively small groups of Roman invaders under the command of General Julius Caesar make forays into southern England from the northern coast of Gaul (today's France).	Emperor Claudius leads the first proper Roman invasion of Britain. His army wages a ruthless campaign, and the Romans control most of southern England by AD 50.

The Romans

Although there had been some earlier expeditionary campaigns, the main Roman invasion of what is now England began in AD 43. They called their newly won province Britannia, and within a decade most of southern England was under Roman control. It wasn't a walkover though: some locals fought back, most famously the warrior-queen Boudica, who led a rebel army against Londinium, the Roman port on the present site of London.

Opposition was mostly sporadic, however, and no real threat to Roman military might. By around AD 80 Britannia comprised much of today's England and Wales. Though it's tempting to imagine noble natives battling courageously against occupying forces, Roman control and stability was possibly welcomed by the general population, tired of feuding chiefs and insecure tribal territories.

Roman settlement in Britain continued for almost four centuries, and intermarriage was common between locals and incomers (many from other parts of the Empire – including modern-day Belgium, Spain and Syria – rather than Rome itself). A Romano-British population thus evolved, particularly in the towns, while indigenous Celtic-British culture remained in rural areas.

Along with stability and wealth, the Romans paved the way for another cultural facet: a new religion called Christianity, after it was recognised by Emperor Constantine in the 4th century. Recent research also suggests Celtic Christians may have brought the religion to Britain even earlier. But by this time, although Romano-British culture was thriving in Britannia, back in its Mediterranean heartland the Empire was already in decline.

It was an untidy finale. The Romans were not driven out by the Ancient Britons (after more than 300 years, Romano-British culture was so established there was nowhere for many to go 'home' to). In reality,

Probably constructed from around 3000 BC, Stonehenge has stood on Salisbury Plain for more than 5000 years, making it older than the pyramids of Egypt.

LEGACY OF THE LEGIONS

To control their new territory, the Romans built garrisons across England. Many developed into towns, which can be recognised by names ending in 'chester' or 'caster' (from the Latin *castrum*, meaning military camp) – Lancaster, Winchester, Manchester and, of course, Chester, to name but a few. The Romans also built roads, initially so soldiers could march quickly from place to place, and later so that trade could develop. Wherever possible the roads were straight lines (because it was efficient, not – as the old joke goes – to stop Ancient Britons hiding round corners) and included Ermine St between London and York, Watling St between Kent and Wales, and the Fosse Way between Exeter and Lincoln. As you travel around England, you'll notice many modern highways still follow Roman roads. In a country better known for old lanes and turnpike routes winding through the landscape, these ruler-straight highways stand out on the map.

c 60	c 200	c 410	5th century
The Iceni warrior queen Boudica (also known as Boadicea) leads a rebel army against the Romans, destroys the Roman town of Colchester and gets as far as their port at Londinium (now London).	The Romans build a defensive wall around the city of London with four main entrance gates, still reflected today by the districts of Aldgate, Ludgate, Newgate and Bishopsgate.	As the classical world's greatest empire declines after more than three centuries of relative peace and prosperity, Roman rule ends in Britain with more of a whimper than a bang.	Teutonic tribes – known today as the Anglo-Saxons – from the area now called Germany migrate to England, and quickly spread across much of the country.

Britannia was simply dumped by the rulers in Rome, and the colony slowly fizzled out. But some historians are tidy folk, and the end of Roman power in England is often dated at AD 410.

A History of England in 100 Places by John Julius Norwich is a fascinating handbook mixing history with geography, covering a range of locations 'from Stonehenge to the Gherkin' (the latter an ubermodern piece of London architecture).

The Anglo-Saxons

When Roman power faded, the province of Britannia went downhill. Romano-British towns were abandoned and rural areas became no-go zones as local warlords fought over fiefdoms. The vacuum didn't go unnoticed, and once again migrants crossed from the European mainland – this time Germanic tribes called Angles and Saxons.

Historians disagree on what happened next; either the Anglo-Saxons largely overcame or absorbed the Romano-British and Celts, or the indigenous tribes simply adopted Anglo-Saxon language and culture. Either way, by the late 6th century much of England was predominantly Anglo-Saxon, divided into separate kingdoms dominated by Wessex (in southern England), Mercia (today's Midlands) and Northumbria (northern England).

Some areas remained unaffected by the incomers, but the overall impact was immense – the name England means 'land of the Angles', and today the core of the English language is Anglo-Saxon, many place names have Anglo-Saxon roots, and the very term 'Anglo-Saxon' has become a (much abused and factually incorrect) byword for 'pure English'.

The Vikings & Alfred the Great

In the 9th century England was yet again invaded by a bunch of pesky Continentals. This time it was the Vikings, from today's Denmark. They quickly conquered the eastern and northeastern areas of England, then started to expand into central England. Blocking their route were the Anglo-Saxon armies heading north, led by Alfred the Great, the king of Wessex and one of English history's best-known characters.

Thus England was divided in two: north and east was the Viking land, known as 'Danelaw', while south and west was Anglo-Saxon territory. Alfred was hailed as king of the English – the first time the Anglo-Saxons regarded themselves as a truly united people. His capital was Winchester; if you come to visit the famous cathedral, look out for the nearby statue of Alfred in the city centre.

Alfred's son and successor was Edward, known as Edward the Elder. After more battles, he gained control of Danelaw, and thus became the first king to rule the whole country – a major milestone in English history.

But it was hardly cause for celebration. Later in the 10th century, more raids from Scandinavia threatened the fledgling English unity, and as England came to the end of the 1st millennium AD, the future was anything but certain.

8th century	9th century	927	1066
King Offa of Mercia orders the construction of a clear border between his kingdom and Wales – a defensive ditch called Offa's Dyke that is still visible today.	Vikings come from what is today Denmark and conquer east and northeast England. They establish their capital at Jorvik, today's city of York.	Athelstan, grandson of Alfred the Great and son of Edward the Elder, is the first monarch to be crowned king of England, building on his ancestors' success in regaining Viking territory.	Incumbent King Harold II is defeated by an invading Norman army at the Battle of Hastings, and England finds itself with a new monarch: William the Conqueror.

1066 & All That

In 1066 when King Edward the Confessor died, the crown passed to Harold II, his brother-in-law. That should've settled things, but Edward had a cousin in Normandy (in northern France) called William, who thought *he* should have succeeded to the throne of England.

The end result was the Battle of Hastings of 1066, the most memorable of dates for anyone who has studied English history. William sailed from Normandy with an army, the Saxons were defeated, and King Harold II was killed – by an arrow in the eye, according to legend. William became king of England, earning himself the prestigious epithet Conqueror.

In the years after the invasion, the French-speaking Normans and the English-speaking Anglo-Saxons kept pretty much to themselves. At the top of the feudal system came the monarch, and below that came the land-owning nobles: barons and baronesses, dukes and duchesses, plus the bishops. Then came earls, knights and lords – and their ladies. At the bottom were landless peasants or 'serfs', and this strict hierarchy became the basis of a class system that to a certain extent still exists in England today.

Royal & Holy Squabbling

William's successor, William II, was assassinated during a hunting trip and was succeeded by Henry I, then Stephen of Blois, then Henry II; thus establishing the House of Plantagenet. This period also established the long-standing English tradition of competition for the throne, and introduced an equally enduring tendency of bickering between royalty and the Church. Things came to a head in 1170 when Henry II had the 'turbulent priest' Thomas Becket murdered in Canterbury Cathedral.

Perhaps the next king, Richard I, wanted to make amends for his forebears' unholy sentiments by fighting against what were then seen as Muslim 'infidels' in the Holy Land (today's Israel and the Palestinian Territories, plus parts of Syria, Jordan and Lebanon). Unfortunately, Richard was too busy crusading to govern England – although his battles earned him the sobriquet Lionheart – and in his absence the country fell into disarray.

Richard was succeeded by his brother John. According to legend, it was during this time that a nobleman named Robert of Loxley, better known as Robin Hood, hid in Sherwood Forest and engaged in a spot of wealth redistribution.

Plantagenet Progress

By the early 13th century King John's erratic rule was too much for the powerful barons, and they forced him to affirm a document called the Magna Carta (Great Charter), which set limits on the power of the monarch. It was signed at Runnymede, near Windsor; you can still visit the site today.

Despite Anglo-Saxon dominance from around AD 500, the Celtic language was still being spoken in parts of southern England when the Normans invaded in the 11th century.

Medieval Women by Henrietta Leyser looks through a female lens at the period of English history from AD 450 to 1500; a life of work, marriage, sex and children – not necessarily in that order.

1085–86	1096	12th century	1215
The Norman invaders compile the Domesday Book – a thorough census of England's stock and future potential; it's still a vital historical document today.	The official start of the First Crusade – a campaign of Christian European armies against the Muslim occupation of Jerusalem and the 'Holy Land'. A series of crusades continues until 1272.	Oxford University founded. There's evidence of teaching in the area since 1096, but King Henry II's 1167 ban on students attending the University of Paris solidifies Oxford's importance.	King John signs the Magna Carta, limiting the monarch's power for the first time in English history: an early step on the path towards constitutional rule.

The next king was Henry III, followed in 1272 by Edward I – a skilled ruler and ambitious general. During a busy 35-year reign, he was unashamedly expansionist, leading campaigns into Wales and Scotland, where his ruthless activities earned him the title 'Hammer of the Scots'.

Edward I was succeeded by Edward II, who lacked his forebear's military success. He failed in the marriage department too, and came to a grisly end when, it's thought, his wife Isabella and her lover Roger Mortimer had him murdered in Berkeley Castle. Today, fans of ghoulish ends can visit the very spot where it happened.

Houses of Lancaster & York

In 1399 Richard II was ousted by a powerful baron called Henry Bolingbroke, who became Henry IV – the first monarch of the House of Lancaster. He was followed, neatly, by Henry V, who decided it was time to end the Hundred Years' War, a long-standing conflict between England and France. Henry's victory at the Battle of Agincourt and the patriotic speech he was given by Shakespeare in his namesake play ('cry God for Harry, England and St George!') ensured his position among the most famous of English monarchs.

Still keeping things neat, Henry V was followed by Henry VI. His main claims to fame were overseeing the building of great places of worship – King's College Chapel, in Cambridge; Eton Chapel, near Windsor – and suffering from great bouts of insanity.

The Hundred Years' War finally ground to a halt in 1453, but just a few years later, England was plunged into a civil conflict dubbed the Wars of the Roses. Briefly it went like this: Henry VI of the House of Lancaster (emblem: a red rose) was challenged by Richard, Duke of York (emblem: a white rose). Henry was weak and it was almost a walkover for Richard, but Henry's wife, Margaret of Anjou, was made of sterner stuff and her

Today, more than 500 years after the Wars of the Roses, Yorkshire's symbol is still a white rose, while Lancashire's is still a red rose, and rivalry between these two counties is still very strong – especially when it comes to cricket and football.

THE PERILS OF KINGSHIP

The gallop through the story of England's ruling dynasties clearly shows that life is never dull for the person at the top. Despite immense power and privilege, the position of monarch (or, perhaps worse, *potential* monarch) probably ranks as one of history's least safe occupations. English kings to meet an untimely end include Harold II (killed in battle), William II (assassinated), Charles I (beheaded by Republicans), Edward V (allegedly murdered by an uncle), Richard II (probably starved to death), James II (deposed), Edward II (dispatched by his queen and her lover) and William III (died after his horse tripped over a molehill). As you visit the castles and battlefields of England, you may feel a touch of sympathy – but only a touch – for those all-powerful figures continually looking over their shoulders.

1337–1453	1348	1459–71	1485
England battles France in a long conflict known as the Hundred Years' War. It was actually a series of small conflicts. And it lasted for more than a century too...	The arrival of the Black Death. Commonly attributed to bubonic plague, the pandemic kills more than 1.5 million people, over a third of the country's population.	The Wars of the Roses: a conflict between two competing dynasties – the Houses of Lancaster and York. The Yorkists are successful, and King Edward IV gains the throne.	Henry Tudor defeats Richard III at the Battle of Bosworth to become King Henry VII, establishing the Tudor dynasty and ending York-Lancaster rivalry for the throne.

forces defeated the challenger. Then Richard's son Edward entered with an army, turned the tables, drove out Henry and became King Edward IV – the first monarch of the House of York.

Dark Deeds in the Tower

Edward IV hardly had time to catch his breath before facing a challenge from the Earl of Warwick, who teamed up with the energetic Margaret of Anjou to shuttle Edward into exile and bring Henry VI back to the throne. A year later Edward IV came bouncing back, killed Warwick, captured Margaret and had Henry executed in the Tower of London.

Edward IV was succeeded by his 12-year-old son, Edward V. But in 1483 the boy-king was mysteriously murdered, along with his brother, and once again the Tower of London was the scene of the crime.

With the 'little princes' dispatched, the throne was open for their old Uncle Richard. Whether he was the princes' killer remains the subject of debate, but his rule as Richard III was short-lived: in 1485 he was tumbled from the top job by a Welsh nobleman (from the rival Lancastrian line) named Henry Tudor, who became King Henry VII.

Peace & Dissolution

With the Wars of the Roses only recently ended, Henry VII married Elizabeth of York, so uniting the House of Lancaster and the House of York. He adopted the 'Tudor rose' symbol, which features the flower in both colours. Henry also married off his daughter to James IV of Scotland, linking the Tudor and Stuart lines. The result? A much-welcomed period of peace for England.

The next king, Henry VIII, is one of England's best-known monarchs, mainly thanks to his six wives – the result of a desperate quest for a male heir. He also had a profound impact on England's religious history; his rift with the Pope and the Roman Catholic Church led to the separation of the Church of England from papal rule, and to the 'Dissolution' – the infamous closure of many monasteries, the ruins of which can still be seen today at places such as Fountains Abbey and Rievaulx Abbey in Yorkshire.

The Elizabethan Age

Henry VIII was succeeded by his son Edward VI, and his daughter Mary I, but their reigns were short. And so Elizabeth, third in line, unexpectedly came to the throne.

Elizabeth I inherited a nasty mess of religious strife and divided loyalties, but after an uncertain start she gained confidence and turned the country around. Refusing marriage, she borrowed biblical motifs and

The 1955 film version of Shakespeare's *Richard III*, starring Laurence Olivier and John Gielgud, was the award-winning drama of its time, and is well worth watching for a view on this turbulent period in English history.

HISTORY DARK DEEDS IN THE TOWER

Shakespeare's *Henry V* was filmed in 1989 as a superb epic, starring Kenneth Branagh as the eponymous king. Also worth catching is the earlier, wartime movie of the same name starring Laurence Olivier, made in 1944 as a patriotic rallying cry.

1509–47	1558–1603	1605	1644–49
Reign of King Henry VIII. The Pope's disapproval of Henry's serial marriage and divorce partly prompts the English Reformation – the founding of the Church of England.	Reign of Queen Elizabeth I, a period of boundless English optimism. Enter stage right playwright William Shakespeare. Exit due west navigators Walter Raleigh and Francis Drake.	King James' attempts to smooth religious relations are set back by an anti-Catholic outcry following the infamous Gunpowder Plot, a terrorist attempt to blow up Parliament led by Guy Fawkes.	English Civil War. Royalist forces supporting the king are pitted against Oliver Cromwell's army of 'Parliamentarians'. Cromwell is victorious, and England becomes a republic.

became known as the Virgin Queen – perhaps the first English monarch to create a cult image.

The big moments in her 45-year reign included the naval defeat of the Spanish Armada, the far-flung explorations of English seafarers Walter Raleigh and Francis Drake and the expansion of England's trading network, including newly established colonies on the east coast of America – not to mention a cultural flourishing, thanks to writers such as William Shakespeare and Christopher Marlowe.

Meanwhile, Elizabeth's Catholic cousin Mary Stuart (daughter of Scottish King James V) had become queen of Scotland. She'd spent her childhood in France, marrying the French dauphin (crown prince), thereby becoming queen of France as well. After her husband's death (so no longer France's queen), Mary returned to Scotland to rule but was eventually forced to abdicate amid claims of infidelity and murder.

She escaped to England and appealed to Elizabeth for help. But Mary had a strong claim to the English throne. That made her a security risk and she was imprisoned by Elizabeth. Historians dispute whether the former Scottish queen then instigated or was simply the focus of numerous Catholic plots to assassinate Protestant Elizabeth and put Mary on the throne. Either way, Elizabeth held Mary under arrest for nearly 19 years, moving her frequently from house to house. As you travel around England today, you can visit many stately homes (and even a few pubs) that proudly claim, 'Mary Queen of Scots slept here'. Elizabeth eventually ordered Mary's execution in 1587.

> The movie *Elizabeth*, directed by Shekhar Kapur (1998) and starring Cate Blanchett, covers the early years of the Virgin Queen's rule, as she graduates from princess to commanding monarch – a time of forbidden love, unwanted suitors, intrigue and death.

United & Disunited Britain

Elizabeth died in 1603, but despite a bountiful reign, the Virgin Queen had failed to provide an heir. She was succeeded by her closest relative, the Scottish King James, the safely Protestant son of the executed Mary. Thus, he became James I of England and VI of Scotland, the first English monarch of the House of Stuart. James did his best to soothe Catholic-Protestant tensions and united England, Wales and Scotland into one kingdom for the first time – another step towards British unity, at least on paper.

But the divide between king and parliament continued to smoulder, and the power struggle worsened during the reign of Charles I, eventually degenerating into the English Civil War. The antiroyalist (or 'Parliamentarian') forces were led by Oliver Cromwell, a Puritan who preached against the excesses of the monarchy and established Church. His army (known as the Roundheads) was pitched against the king's forces (the Cavaliers) in a conflict that tore England apart. It ended with victory for the Roundheads – the king was executed and England declared a republic, with Cromwell hailed as 'Protector'.

1660 〉	1749 〉	1775–83 〉	1799–1815 〉
After Cromwell's death, conflicting interests beset the republic. The eldest son of Charles I is invited back to take the throne. Charles II is crowned, and the monarchy is restored (the Restoration).	Author and magistrate Henry Fielding founds the Bow Street Runners, London's first professional police force. A 1792 Act of Parliament allowed the Bow Street model to spread across England.	The American War of Independence is the British Empire's first major reversal. William Pitt the Younger becomes the country's youngest-ever prime minister at the age of 24.	The Napoleonic Wars see a weakened Britain threatened with invasion by Napoleon, whose ambitions are curtailed at the famous battles of Trafalgar (1805) and Waterloo (1815).

The Return of the King

By 1653 Cromwell was finding parliament too restricting and assumed dictatorial powers, much to his supporters' dismay. On his death in 1658, he was followed half-heartedly by his son, but in 1660 parliament decided to re-establish the monarchy, as republican alternatives were proving far worse.

Charles II (the exiled son of Charles I) came to the throne, and his rule – known as 'the Restoration' – saw scientific and cultural activity bursting forth after the strait-laced ethics of Cromwell's time. Exploration and expansion were also on the agenda. Backed by the army and navy (which had been modernised by Cromwell), colonies stretched down the American coast, while the East India Company set up headquarters in Bombay, laying foundations for what was to become the British Empire.

The next king, James II, had a harder time. Attempts to ease restrictive laws on Catholics ended with his defeat at the Battle of the Boyne by William III, the Protestant king of Holland, aka William of Orange. William was married to James' daughter Mary. William and Mary had equal rights to the throne, and their joint accession in 1689 was known as the Glorious Revolution.

Empire Building

By 1702, both Mary and William had died. They were succeeded by William's sister-in-law, Anne. During her reign, in 1707, the Act of Union was passed, uniting England, Wales and Scotland under one parliament – based in London – for the first time.

Queen Anne died without an heir in 1714, marking the end of the Stuart line. The throne passed to distant (but still safely Protestant) German relatives – the House of Hanover.

Meanwhile, the British Empire – which, despite its title, was predominantly an English entity – continued to grow in the Americas as well as in Asia, while claims were made to Australia after James Cook's epic voyage of 1769.

The Industrial Era

While the Empire expanded abroad, at home Britain had become the crucible of the Industrial Revolution. Steam power (pioneered by James Watt in the 1760s and 1770s) and steam trains (developed by George Stephenson in the 1820s and 1830s) transformed methods of production and transport, and the towns of the English Midlands became the first industrial cities.

Industrial growth led to Britain's first major period of internal migration, as vast numbers of people from the countryside came to the cities in search of work. At the same time, medical advances improved

A History of England in a Nutshell by John Mathew provides exactly what it says on the cover: a quick overview of the nation's key events in less than 200 pages.

The Isles: A History by Norman Davies provides much-acclaimed and highly readable coverage of the past 10,000 years in England, within the broader history of the British Isles.

HISTORY THE RETURN OF THE KING

1837–1901	1914	1926	1939–45
Reign of Queen Victoria. The British Empire – 'the Empire where the sun never sets' – expands from Canada through Africa and India to Australia and New Zealand.	Archduke Franz Ferdinand of Austria is assassinated in the Balkan city of Sarajevo – the final spark in a decade-long crisis that starts the Great War, now called WWI.	Increasing mistrust of the government, fuelled by soaring unemployment, leads to the General Strike. Millions of workers – train drivers, miners, shipbuilders – down tools and bring the country to a halt.	WWII rages across Europe, and much of Africa and Asia. Britain and Allies, including America, Russia, Australia, India and New Zealand, eventually defeat the armies of Germany, Japan and Italy.

life expectancy, creating a sharp population increase. For many ordinary people the effects of Britain's economic blossoming were dislocation and poverty.

But despite the social turmoil of the early 19th century, by the time Queen Victoria took the throne in 1837 Britain's factories and fleets dominated world trade. The rest of the 19th century was seen as Britain's Golden Age – a period of patriotic confidence not seen since the days of the last great queen, Elizabeth I.

The times were optimistic, but it wasn't all tub-thumping jingoism. Prime Minister Disraeli and his successor, William Gladstone, also introduced social reforms to address the exploitative excesses of the Industrial Revolution. Education became universal, trade unions were legalised and the right to vote was extended in a series of reform acts, finally being granted to all men over the age of 21 in 1918, and to all women in 1928.

One of the finest novels about WWI is *Birdsong* by Sebastian Faulks. Understated, perfectly paced and intensely moving, it tells of passion, fear, waste, incompetent generals and the poor bloody infantry.

World War I

When Queen Victoria died in 1901 the country entered a period of decline. Meanwhile, in continental Europe, the military powers of Russia, Austro-Hungary, Turkey and Germany were sabre-rattling in the Balkan states, a dispute that eventually started the 'Great War' (now known as WWI). By the war's weary end in 1918, millions had died, with hardly a street or village untouched, as the sobering lists of names on war memorials all over England still show.

For the soldiers that did return from WWI, disillusion with the old social order helped make the Labour Party – which represented the working class – a political force, upsetting the balance long enjoyed by the Liberal and Conservative Parties.

The Labour Party came to power for the first time, in coalition with the Liberals, in the 1923 election, but by the mid-1920s the Conservatives were back. The world economy was now in decline and industrial unrest had become widespread.

London is an epic novel by Edward Rutherfurd – or rather around 50 separate mininovels, each set in a key historical era, from the Roman invasion to the Blitz of WWII. Exhaustive and exhausting, but great for a sense of each period.

The situation worsened in the 1930s as the Great Depression meant another decade of misery and political upheaval, and even the Royal Family took a knock when Edward VIII abdicated in 1936 so he could marry Wallis Simpson, a woman who was twice divorced and – horror of horrors – American.

World War II

The next monarch was Edward's less charismatic brother, George VI. Britain dithered through the rest of the decade, with mediocre governments failing to confront the country's deep-set problems.

Meanwhile, Adolf Hitler came to power in Germany and in 1939 invaded Poland. Two days later Britain was once again at war. The German

1945	1946–48	1948	1952
WWII ends, and in the immediate postwar election the Labour Party under Clement Attlee defeats the Conservatives under Winston Churchill, despite the latter's pivotal role in Britain's WWII victory.	The Labour Party nationalises key industries such as shipyards, coalmines and steel foundries. Britain's 'big four' train companies are combined into British Railways.	Aneurin Bevan, the health minister in the Labour government, launches the National Health Service: free medical care for all – the core of Britain as a 'welfare state'.	Princess Elizabeth becomes Queen Elizabeth II when her father, George VI, dies. Her coronation takes place in Westminster Abbey in June 1953.

army swept through Europe and pushed back British forces to the beaches of Dunkirk, in northern France. In June 1940 an extraordinary flotilla of tiny, private vessels (the 'Little Ships') turned total disaster into a brave defeat – and Dunkirk Day is still remembered with pride and sadness in Britain every year.

By mid-1940, most of Europe was controlled by Germany. Russia had negotiated a peace agreement and the USA was neutral, leaving Britain virtually isolated. Into this arena came a new prime minister called Winston Churchill.

Between September 1940 and May 1941, the German air force launched 'the Blitz', a series of (mainly night-time) bombing raids on London and other cities. But morale in Britain remained strong, thanks

WINSTON CHURCHILL

More than a century after becoming part of the British government, Winston Churchill is still one of the country's best-known political figures. He was born in 1874 and, although from an aristocratic family, his early years were not auspicious; he was famously a 'dunce' at school, an image he actively cultivated in later life.

As a young man Churchill joined the British Army and also acted as a newspaper war correspondent, writing several books about his exploits. In 1900 he was elected to parliament as a Conservative MP. In 1904 he defected to the Liberals, the main opposition party. A year later, after a Liberal election victory, he became a government minister. Churchill rejoined the Conservatives in 1924, and held various ministerial positions through the rest of the 1920s. Notable statements during this period included calling Mussolini a 'genius' and Gandhi 'a half-naked fakir'.

Churchill criticised Prime Minister Neville Chamberlain's 1938 'appeasement' of Hitler and called for British rearmament to face a growing German threat, but his political life was generally quiet – so he concentrated on writing. His multivolume *A History of the English-Speaking Peoples* was drafted during this period; although biased and flawed, it remains his best-known work.

In 1939 Britain entered WWII, and by 1940 Churchill was prime minister, taking additional responsibility as Minister of Defence. Hitler might have expected an easy victory in the war, but Churchill's extraordinary dedication (not to mention his radio speeches – most famously saying he had 'nothing to offer but blood, toil, tears and sweat' and promising to 'fight on the beaches...') inspired the British people to resist.

Between July and October 1940 the Royal Air Force withstood Germany's aerial raids to win what became known as the Battle of Britain – a major turning point in the war, and a chance for land forces to rebuild their strength. Britain's refusal to negotiate terms with Germany and the decision to stand alone against Hitler's forces was an audacious strategy, but it paid off and Churchill was lauded as a national hero – praise that continued beyond his death in 1965 and which continues today.

1960–66	1971	1970s	1979
The era of African and Caribbean independence brings the freedom of Nigeria, Tanzania, Jamaica, Trinidad & Tobago, Kenya, Malawi, Gambia and Barbados.	Britain adopts the 'decimal' currency (one pound equals 100 pence) and drops the ancient system of 20 shillings or 240 pennies per pound, the centuries-old bane of school maths lessons.	Much of the decade is characterised by inflation, inept governments (on the left and right), trade-union disputes, strikes, shortages and blackouts, culminating in the 1978–9 'Winter of Discontent'.	A Conservative government led by Margaret Thatcher wins the general election, a major milestone in Britain's 20th-century history, ushering in a decade of dramatic political and social change.

partly to Churchill's regular radio broadcasts. The USA entered the war after the Japanese bombing of Pearl Harbor, and in late 1941 the tide began to turn.

By 1944 Germany was in retreat. Russia pushed back from the east, and Britain, the USA and other Allies were again on the beaches of France. The Normandy landings (D-Day, as it's remembered) marked the start of the liberation of Europe's western side. By 1945 Hitler was dead and the war was over.

Swinging & Sliding

The aftermath of WWII saw an unexpected swing on the political front. An electorate tired of war tumbled Churchill's Conservatives from power in favour of the Labour Party. There was change abroad too, as parts of the British Empire became independent, including India and Pakistan in 1947 and Malaya in 1957, followed by much of Africa and the Caribbean.

But while the Empire's sun may have been setting, Britain's royal family was still going strong. In 1952 George VI was succeeded by his daughter, Elizabeth II.

By the late 1950s, postwar recovery was strong enough for Prime Minister Harold Macmillan to famously remind the British people they had 'never had it so good'. Some saw this as a boast for a confident future, others as a warning about difficult times ahead. But many people didn't care either way, as the 1960s had arrived and grey old England was suddenly more fun and lively than it had been for generations.

The '60s may have been swinging, but by the 1970s decline had set in, thanks to a combination of inflation, an oil crisis and international competition revealing the weaknesses of Britain's economy. Britain joined the European Economic Community in 1973, with the country voting in a referendum to remain two years later; 67% were in favour of remaining.

The rest of the '70s were marked by strikes, disputes and general all-round gloom, but neither the Conservatives (also known as the Tories) under Prime Minister Edward Heath, nor Labour, under Prime Ministers Harold Wilson and Jim Callaghan, proved capable of controlling the strife. The British public had had enough, and the elections of May 1979 saw the arrival of a new prime minister: a previously little-known politician named Margaret Thatcher.

The Thatcher Years

Soon everyone had heard of Margaret Thatcher. Love her or hate her, no one could argue that her methods weren't dramatic, and many policies had a lasting impact, one of the most prominent being the privatisation of state-run industries that had been nationalised in the late 1940s.

1990	1997	2003	2007
Thatcher ousted as leader, and the Conservative Party enters a period of decline, but remains in power, partly due to ineffective Labour opposition.	The general election sees Tony Blair lead 'New' Labour to victory in the polls, with a record-breaking parliamentary majority, ending 18 years of Conservative rule.	Britain joins the USA in the invasion of Iraq, initially with some support from parliament and the public – despite large antiwar demonstrations held in London and other cities.	Tony Blair, Britain's longest-serving Labour prime minister, resigns and Gordon Brown, Chancellor of the Exchequer, takes over as Labour leader and prime minister.

Some commentators argue that in economic terms the Thatcher government's policies were largely successful. Others claim in social terms they were a failure and created a polarised Britain: on one side were the people who gained from the prosperous wave of opportunities in the 'new' industries, while on the other were those who became unemployed and dispossessed as the 'old' industries, such as coal mining and steel production, became an increasingly small part of the country's economy.

Despite policies that were frequently described as uncompromising, by 1988 Margaret Thatcher was the longest-serving British prime minister of the 20th century, although her repeated electoral victories were helped considerably by the Labour Party's ineffective campaigns and destructive internal struggles.

New Labour, New Coalition, New Start

The pendulum started to swing again in the early 1990s. Margaret Thatcher was replaced as leader by John Major, but the voters still regarded Labour with suspicion, allowing the Conservatives to unexpectedly win the 1992 election. It all came to a head in the 1997 election, when 'New' Labour swept to power under a fresh-faced leader called Tony Blair.

Blair and the Labour Party enjoyed an extended honeymoon period, and the next election (in 2001) was another walkover. The Conservative party continued to struggle, allowing Labour to win a historic third term in 2005, and a year later Blair became the longest-serving Labour prime minister in British history.

In May 2010 a record 13 years of Labour rule came to an end, and a coalition government (the first in the UK since WWII) was formed between the Conservatives and the Liberal Democrats.

It was an experiment that ended disastrously for the Lib Dems at the 2015 general election: they lost 49 seats, and were left with just eight MPs. The same vote left the defeated Labour Party searching for a new identity, and the Conservatives back in sole charge.

But just over a year later a referendum saw the people of the UK vote, by 52% to 48%, to leave the EU – in defiance of the main parties, which had wanted the country to stay in.

Handy Historic Websites

www.royal.gov.uk

www.bbc.co.uk/ history

www.victorianweb. org

2010	2014	2015	2016
Labour is narrowly defeated in the general election as the minority Liberal Democrats align with the Conservatives to form the first coalition government in Britain's postwar history.	Scotland votes in a referendum not to become an independent country (by 55% to 45%), so remaining within the UK. It sparks a debate on the possibility of a separate English parliament.	The Conservatives win a surprising 12-seat election majority. Their former coalition partners, the Liberal Democrats, lose 49 seats. Labour is almost wiped out in Scotland. The UK Independence Party secures one seat.	In a referendum on whether to remain within the EU, the UK votes to leave by 52% to 48%. England and Wales vote to leave the EU, but Scotland and Northern Ireland vote to stay in.

Food & Drink

Wherever you travel in England, for every greasy spoon or fast-food joint, there's a local pub or speciality restaurant serving up enticing homemade meals. For decades most towns have boasted Italian, Chinese and Indian restaurants, so spaghetti carbonara, chow mein and vindaloo are no longer considered exotic. London is now regarded as a global gastronomic capital, and it's increasingly easy to find decent food options in other cities, towns and villages across the country.

Meals

For the locals, the English culinary day is punctuated by the three traditional main meals of breakfast, lunch and dinner. And just to keep you on your toes, the last two meals are also called dinner and tea, or lunch and supper – depending on social class and location.

In Yorkshire, the eponymous pudding is traditionally a *starter*, a reminder of days when food was scarce and the pudding was a premeal stomach-filler.

Breakfast

Many people in England make do with toast or a bowl of cereal before dashing to work, but visitors staying in hotels and B&Bs will undoubtedly encounter a phenomenon called the 'Full English Breakfast'. This usually consists of fried bacon, sausages, eggs, tomatoes, mushrooms, baked beans and fried bread. If you don't feel like eating half a farmyard first thing in the morning it's OK to ask for just the eggs and tomatoes, for example. Some B&Bs offer other alternatives such as kippers (smoked fish) or a 'continental breakfast', which completely omits the cooked stuff and may even add something exotic such as croissants.

Lunch

One of the many great inventions that England gave the world is the sandwich, often eaten as a midday meal. Slapping a slice of cheese or ham between two bits of bread may seem a simple concept, but no one apparently thought of it until the 18th century: the Earl of Sandwich (his title comes from a town in southeast England that originally got its name from the Viking word for 'sandy beach') ordered his servants to bring cold meat between bread so he could keep working at his desk or, as some historians claim, keep playing cards late at night.

Another English classic is the ploughman's lunch. Basically it's bread, cheese and pickles, and although hearty yokels probably did carry such food to the fields in the days of yore, the meal was actually invented in the 1960s by the national cheesemakers' organisation to boost consumption, neatly cashing in on public nostalgia and fondness for tradition.

You can still find a basic ploughman's lunch offered in some pubs – and it undeniably goes well with a pint or two of local ale at lunchtime – but these days the meal has usually been smartened up to include butter, salad and dressings. At some pubs you get a selection of cheeses. You'll also find other variations, such as a farmer's lunch (bread and chicken), stockman's lunch (bread and ham), Frenchman's lunch (brie and baguette) and fisherman's lunch (you guessed it, with fish).

Dinner

For generations, a typical English dinner has been 'meat and two veg'. Dressed up as 'evening meal' or dressed down as 'cooked tea', there was little variation: the meat would be pork, beef or lamb, one of the vegetables would be potatoes and the other would inevitably be carrots, cabbage or cauliflower – just as inevitably cooked long and hard. Although tastes and diets are changing, this classic combination still graces the tables of many English families several times a week.

Traditionally, the beef is roast beef (always roast, never 'roasted') and with the beef – especially at Sunday lunches – comes Yorkshire pudding. It's simply roast batter, but crisp and tasty when properly cooked. Another classic English dish brings Yorkshire pudding and sausages together, with the delightful name of 'toad-in-the-hole'.

Yorkshire pudding also turns up in another guise, especially in pubs and cafes in northern England, where a big bowl-shaped pudding is filled with stew, gravy or vegetables. You can even find multicultural crossover Yorkshire puddings filled with curry.

Perhaps the best-known classic English meal is fish and chips, often bought from the 'chippie' as a takeaway wrapped in paper to eat on the spot or enjoy at home. For visitors, English fish and chips can be an acquired taste. Sometimes the chips can be limp and the fish tasteless, especially once you get away from the sea, but in towns with salt in the air this classic deep-fried delight is always worth trying.

> Rick Stein is a TV chef, energetic restaurateur and good-food evangelist. His books *Food Heroes* and *Food Heroes – Another Helping* extol small-scale producers and top-notch local food, from organic veg to wild-boar sausages.

Dessert

After the main course – usually at an evening meal, or if you're enjoying a hearty lunch – comes dessert or 'pudding'. A classic English pudding is rhubarb crumble, the juicy stem of a large-leafed garden plant, stewed and sweetened, then topped with a crunchy mix of flour, butter and more sugar – and served with custard or ice cream. Other favourites include treacle sponge, bread-and-butter pudding and plum pudding, a dome-shaped cake with fruit, nuts and brandy or rum, traditionally eaten at Christmas.

Regional Specialities

With the country's large coastline, it's no surprise that seafood is a speciality in many English regions. Yorkshire's seaside resorts are particularly famous for huge servings of cod – despite it being in danger of overfishing – while restaurants in Devon and Cornwall regularly conjure up prawns, oysters, mussels and scallops. Other local seafood you may encounter elsewhere on your travels include Norfolk crab and Northumberland kippers.

In northern and central England you'll find Cumberland sausage – a tasty mix of minced pork and herbs, so large it has to be spiralled to fit

---

NAME THAT PASTY

A favourite speciality in southwest England is the Cornish pasty. Originally a mix of cooked vegetables wrapped in pastry, it's often available in meat varieties (much to the scorn of the Cornish people) and now sold everywhere in England. Invented long before Tupperware, the pasty was an all-in-one-lunch pack that tin miners carried underground and left on a ledge ready for mealtime. So pasties weren't mixed up, they were marked with their owners' initials – always at one end, so the miner could eat half and safely leave the rest to snack on later without it mistakenly disappearing into the mouth of a workmate. Before going back to the surface, the miners traditionally left the last few crumbs of the pasty as a gift for the spirits of the mine, known as 'knockers', to ensure a safe shift the next day.

on your plate. Look out too for Melton Mowbray pork pies – cooked ham in a casing of pastry, eaten cold. A legal victory in 2005 ensured that only pies from the eponymous Midlands town could carry the Melton Mowbray moniker, in the same way that only fizzy wine from the Champagne region of France can carry that name. Another English speciality that enjoys the same protection is Stilton – a strong white cheese, either plain or in a blue-vein variety. Only five dairies in all of England are allowed to produce cheese with this name.

Perhaps less appealing is black pudding, a large sausage made with pig's blood and oatmeal, and traditionally served for breakfast in northern England.

Eating Out

In England, 'eating out' means simply going to a restaurant or cafe – anywhere away from home. There's a huge choice across the country.

Picnics & Self-Catering

When shopping for food, as well as the more obvious chain stores and corner shops, markets can be a great place for bargains – everything from dented tins of tomatoes to home-baked cakes and organic goats cheese. Farmers markets are always worth a visit; they're a great way for producers to sell good food direct to consumers, with both sides avoiding the grip of the supermarkets.

Cafes & Teashops

The traditional English cafe is nothing like its Continental European namesake. For a start, asking for a brandy with your coffee may cause confusion, as cafes in England rarely serve alcohol. Most are simple places serving simple meals such as meat pie, beans on toast, baked potato or omelette with chips (costing around £3 to £6) and stuff like sandwiches, cakes and other snacks (£2 to £3). Quality varies enormously: some cafes definitely earn their 'greasy spoon' handle, while others are neat and clean.

In London and some other cities, a rearguard of classic cafes – with formica tables, seats in booths and decor unchanged from their 1950s glory days – stand against the onslaught of the international chains. In rural areas, many market towns and villages have cafes catering to tourists, walkers, cyclists and other outdoor types, and in summer they're open every day. Whether you're in town or country, good English cafes are a wonderful institution and always worth a stop during your travels.

Smarter cafes are called teashops (also more often found in country areas) where you might pay a bit more for extras such as neat decor and table service.

NOSE-TO-TAIL CUSINE

One of the many trends enjoyed by Modern British cuisine is the revival of 'nose to tail' cooking – that is, using the whole animal, not just the more obvious cuts such as chops and fillet steaks. This does not mean boiling or grilling a pig or sheep all in one go – although spit-roasts are popular. It means utilising the parts that may at first seem unappetising or, frankly, inedible. So as well as dishes involving liver, heart, chitterlings (intestines) and other offal, traditional delights such as bone marrow on toast, or tripe (stomach) and onions once again grace the menus of fashionable restaurants. The movement is particularly spearheaded by chef Fergus Henderson at his St John restaurant in London and via his influential recipe books *Nose to Tail Eating: A Kind of British Cooking* and *Beyond Nose To Tail*.

NO SMOKING

All restaurants and cafes in England are nonsmoking throughout. Pubs have the same rule, which is why there's often a small crowd of smokers standing on the pavement outside. Some pubs provide specific outdoor smoking areas, ranging from a simple yard to elaborate gazebos with canvas walls and the full complement of lighting, heating, piped music and TV screens – you'd never need to know you were 'outside' at all, apart from the pungent clouds of burning tobacco.

As well as the traditional establishments, in most cities and towns you'll also find coffee shops – independents and international chains – and a growing number of Euro-style cafe-bars, serving decent lattes and espressos and offering bagels or ciabattas rather than beans on toast (you'll probably be able to get that brandy too). Some of these modern places even have outdoor chairs and tables – rather brave considering the narrow pavements and inclement weather much of England enjoys.

Many towns and cities in England hold regular farmers markets – a good chance for food producers large and small to sell direct to the public. For more info and a searchable database, see www.localfoods.org.uk.

Restaurants

London has scores of excellent restaurants that could hold their own in major cities worldwide, while places in Bath, Leeds and Manchester can give the capital a fair run for its money (actually, often for rather less money). We've taken great pleasure in seeking out some of the best and best-value restaurants in England.

Prices vary considerably across the country, with a main course in a straightforward restaurant costing around £10 or less, and anywhere between £10 and £20 at midrange places. Excellent food, service and surroundings can be enjoyed for £20 to £50 – although in London you can, if you want, pay double this.

For vegetarians, England is not too bad. Many restaurants and pubs have at least one token vegetarian dish, while better places offer much more imaginative choices. Vegans will find the going trickier, except of course at dedicated veggie/vegan restaurants.

Pubs & Gastropubs

Not so many years ago, a pub was the place to go for a drink. And that was it. If you felt peckish, your choice might be a ham or cheese sandwich, with pickled onions if you were lucky. Today many pubs serve a wide range of food, and it's usually a good-value option, whether you want a toasted sandwich between museum visits in London, or a three-course meal in the evening after touring castles and stately homes in Yorkshire.

While the food in many pubs is good quality and good value, some places raised the bar to such a degree that a whole new genre of eatery – the gastropub – was born. The finest gastropubs are effectively restaurants (with smart decor, neat menus and uniformed table service; a few have won Michelin stars), while others have gone for a more relaxed atmosphere, with mismatched cutlery, waiters in T-shirts and the day's choices chalked up on a blackboard. The key for all, though, is top-notch no-frills food and drink. For visitors relaxing after a hard day's sightseeing, nothing beats the luxury of a wholesome shepherd's pie washed down with a decent ale without the worry of guessing which fork to use.

Drinking in England

The two beverages most associated with England are probably tea and beer. Both are unlike drinks of the same name found elsewhere in the world, and well worth trying on your travels around the country.

Tea & Coffee

In England, if a local asks 'Would you like a drink?' don't automatically expect a gin and tonic. They may well mean a 'cuppa' (cup of tea), England's best-known beverage. It's usually made with dark tea leaves to produce a strong brown drink, more bitter in taste than tea served in some other Western countries, which is partly why it's usually served with a dash of milk.

Although tea is often billed as the national drink, tea consumption fell by around 20% in the five years to 2015 and coffee is becoming ever more popular. The British coffee-shop market is worth almost £8 billion a year, but with the prices some coffee shops charge, maybe that's not surprising. A final word of warning: when you're ordering a coffee and the server says 'white or black', don't panic. It simply means 'do you want milk in it?'

Beer & Wine

Among alcoholic drinks, England is probably best known for its beer. As you travel around the country you should definitely try some local brews. English beer typically ranges from dark brown to bright amber in colour, and is often served at room temperature. Technically it's ale

FOOD & DRINK GLOSSARY

aubergine – large purple-skinned vegetable; 'eggplant' in the USA and Australia

bangers – sausages (colloquial)

bap – a large, wide, flat, soft bread roll

bevvy – drink (slang; originally from northern England)

bill – the total you need to pay after eating in a restaurant ('check' to Americans)

bitter – ale; a type of beer

black pudding – type of sausage made from dried blood and other ingredients

bun – bread roll, usually sweet, eg currant bun, cream bun

BYO – bring your own (usually in the context of bringing your own drink to a restaurant)

caff – abbreviated form of cafe

candy floss – light sugar-based confectionery; called 'cotton candy' in the USA, 'fairy floss' in Australia

chips – sliced, deep-fried potatoes, eaten hot (what Americans call 'fries')

cider – beer made from apples

clotted cream – cream so heavy or rich that it's become almost solid (but not sour)

corkage – a small charge levied by the restaurant when you BYO (bring your own)

courgette – green vegetable ('zucchini' to Americans)

cream cracker – white unsalted savoury biscuit

cream tea – cup of tea and a scone loaded with jam and cream

crisps – thin slices of fried potato bought in a packet, eaten cold; called 'chips' or 'potato chips' in the USA and Australia

crumpet – circular piece of doughy bread, toasted before eating, usually covered with butter

double cream – heavy or thick cream

dram – whisky measure

but it's often called 'bitter'. This is to distinguish it from lager (the drink that most of the rest of the word calls 'beer') which is generally yellow and served cold.

Beer that's brewed and served traditionally is called 'real ale' to distinguish it from mass-produced brands, and there are many regional varieties. But be ready! If you're used to the 'amber nectar' or 'king of beers', a traditional British brew may come as a shock – a warm, flat and expensive shock. This is partly to do with Britain's climate, and partly to do with the beer being served by hand pump rather than gas pressure. Most important, though, is the integral flavour: traditional British beer doesn't need to be chilled or fizzed to make it palatable.

A new breed of microbreweries has sprung up over the last decade, producing their own varieties of traditional and innovative brews, usually referred to as 'craft beers'. Outside of the microbrewery's own bar, these are usually only available in bottles.

On hot summer days, you could go for shandy – beer and lemonade mixed in equal quantities. You'll usually need to specify 'lager shandy' or 'bitter shandy'. It may seem an astonishing combination for outsiders, but it's very refreshing and of course not very strong.

The Campaign for Real Ale promotes the understanding of traditional British beer. Look for endorsement stickers on pub windows, and for more info see www.camra.org.uk.

FOOD & DRINK DRINKING IN ENGLAND

fish fingers – strips of fish pieces covered in breadcrumbs, usually bought frozen and cooked by frying or grilling

greasy spoon – cheap cafe (colloquial)

ice lolly – flavoured ice on a stick; called 'popsicle' in the USA, 'icy pole' in Australia

icing – thick, sweet and solid covering on a cake

jam – fruit conserve often spread on bread

jelly – sweet dessert of flavoured gelatine; called 'jello' in the US

joint – cut of meat used for roasting

kippers – salted and smoked fish, traditionally herring

pickle – food, usually vegetables (eg onions or beetroot), preserved in vinegar

Pimm's – popular English spirit mixed with lemonade, mint and fresh fruit

pint – beer (as in 'let me buy you a pint')

pop – fizzy drink

salad cream – creamy vinegary salad dressing, much sharper than mayonnaise

scrumpy – a type of strong dry cider

shandy – beer and lemonade mixed together in equal quantities

shepherd's pie – two-layered dish with a ground beef and onion mixture on the bottom and mashed potato on the top, cooked in an oven

shout – to buy a group of people drinks, usually reciprocated (colloquial)

single cream – light cream (to distinguish from *double cream* and *clotted cream*)

snug – a small room in a pub, usually just inside the door

squash – fruit-drink concentrate mixed with water

stout – dark, full-bodied beer made from malt; Guinness is the most famous variety

swede – large root vegetable; sometimes called 'yellow turnip' or 'rutabaga' in the USA

sweets – what Americans call 'candy' and Australians call 'lollies'

treacle – dark treacle is molasses, but in England treacle often means golden syrup

THE OLDEST PUB IN ENGLAND?

Many drinkers are often surprised to learn that the word 'pub' (short for 'public house'), although apparently steeped in history, dates only from the 19th century. But places selling beer have been around for much longer, and 'the oldest pub in England' is a hotly contested title.

One of the country's oldest pubs, with the paperwork to prove it, is Ye Olde Trip to Jerusalem (p440) in Nottingham, which was serving ale to departing crusaders in the 12th century.

Other contenders dismiss Ye Olde Trip as a mere newcomer. A fine old inn called the Royalist Hotel in Stow-on-the-Wold, Gloucestershire, claims to have been selling beer since AD 947, while another pub called Ye Olde Fighting Cocks in St Albans (Hertfordshire) apparently dates back to the 8th century – although the 13th is more likely.

But then back comes Ye Olde Trip with a counterclaim: one of its bars is a cave hollowed out of living rock, and that's more than a million years old.

Another option is cider, available in sweet and dry varieties and, increasingly, as 'craft cider', often with various fruit or herbal flavours added. In western and southwestern counties, you could try 'scrumpy', a very strong dry cider traditionally made from local apples.

Many visitors are surprised to learn that wine is produced in England, and has been since the time of the Romans. Today, more than 400 vineyards and wineries produce around two million bottles a year, many winning major awards. English white sparkling wines have been a particular success story, especially those produced in the southeast, where the growing conditions are similar to those of the Champagne region in France.

Bars & Pubs

In England, the difference between a bar and a pub is sometimes vague, but generally bars are smarter and louder than pubs, possibly with a younger crowd. Drinks are more expensive too, unless there's a gallon-of-vodka-and-Red-Bull-for-a-fiver promotion – which there often is.

As well as beer and wine, pubs and bars offer the usual choice of spirits, often served with a 'mixer', producing English favourites such as gin and tonic, rum and coke or vodka and lime. These drinks are served in measures called 'singles' and 'doubles'. A single is usually 35ml – just over one US fluid ounce. Only more upmarket city bars have a large array of cocktail options.

And finally, two tips: first, if you see a pub called a 'free house', it means it doesn't belong to a brewery or pub company, and thus is 'free' to sell any brand of beer. It doesn't mean the booze is free of charge. Second, remember that drinks in English pubs are ordered and paid for at the bar. You can always spot the freshly arrived tourists – they're the ones sitting forlornly at an empty table hoping to spot a server.

When it comes to gratuities, it's not usual to tip pub and bar staff. However, if you're ordering a large round, or the service has been good all evening, you can say to the person behind the bar '...and one for yourself'. They may not have a drink, but they'll add the monetary equivalent to the total you pay and keep it as a tip.

Architecture

England's architecture spans some five millenniums, ranging from the mysterious stone circle of Stonehenge to London's glittering skyscrapers. If you know what to look for, a veritable design timeline can be traced through any of England's villages, towns and cities, and getting to grips with styles from different eras will greatly enhance your stay. Prepare for Roman baths, parish churches, mighty castles, magnificent cathedrals, humble cottages and grand stately homes.

Early Foundations

The oldest surviving structures in England are the grass-covered mounds of earth, called 'tumuli' or 'barrows', used as burial sites by England's prehistoric residents. These mounds – measuring anything from a rough semisphere just 2m high to much larger, elongated semiovoids 5m high and 10m long – are dotted across the countryside from Cornwall to Cumbria, and are especially common in chalk areas such as Salisbury Plain and the Wiltshire Downs in southern England.

Perhaps the most famous chalk mound – and certainly the largest and most mysterious – is Silbury Hill, near Marlborough. Archaeologists are not sure exactly why this 40m-high conical mound was built – there's no evidence of it actually being used for burial. Theories suggest it was used in cultural ceremonies or as part of the worship of deities in the style of South American pyramids. Whatever its original purpose, it still remains impressive, more than four centuries after it was built.

Even more impressive than giant tumuli are another legacy of the Neolithic era: menhirs (standing stones) especially when they're set out in rings. These include the iconic stone circle of Stonehenge and the even larger Avebury Stone Circle, both in Wiltshire. Again, their original purpose is a mystery, providing fertile ground for hypothesis and speculation. The most recent theories suggest Stonehenge may have been a place of pilgrimage for the sick, like modern-day Lourdes, though it was also used as a burial ground and a place of ancestor worship.

The construction of Stonehenge pushed the limits of technology in the Neolithic era. Some giant menhirs were transported a great distance, and many were shaped slightly wider at the top to take account of perspective – a trick used by the Greeks many centuries later.

Bronze Age & Iron Age

Compared with the large stone circles of the Neolithic era, the surviving architecture of the Bronze Age is on a more domestic scale. Hut circles from this period can still be seen in several parts of England, most notably on Dartmoor.

By the time we reach the Iron Age, the early peoples of England were organising themselves into clans or tribes. Their legacy includes the remains of the forts they built to defend territory and protect themselves from rival tribes or other invaders. Most forts consisted of a large circular or oval ditch, with a steep mound of earth behind. A famous example is Maiden Castle in Dorset.

There are more than a thousand Iron Age hill forts in England. Impressive examples include Danebury Ring, Hampshire; Barbury Castle, Wiltshire; Uffington Castle, Oxfordshire; Carl Wark, Derbyshire; Cadbury Castle, Somerset and the immense Maiden Castle, Dorset.

The Roman Era

Roman remains are found in many English towns and cities, including Chester, Exeter and St Albans – as well as the lavish Roman spa and

England's Top Castles

....

Berkeley Castle
(Gloucestershire)

....

Carlisle Castle
(Cumbria)

....

Corfe Castle
(Dorset)

....

Leeds Castle
(Kent)

....

Skipton Castle
(Yorkshire)

....

Tintagel Castle
(Cornwall)

....

Tower of London
(London)

....

Windsor Castle
(Berkshire)

bathing complex in Bath. But England's largest and most impressive Roman relic is the 73-mile sweep of Hadrian's Wall, built in the 2nd century AD as a defensive line stretching coast to coast across the neck of northern England, in a line from modern-day Newcastle to Carlisle. Originally built to separate marauding Pictish warriors to the north of the wall (in modern Scotland) from the Empire's territories to the south, it later became as much a symbol of Roman power as a necessary defence mechanism.

Medieval Masterpieces

In the centuries following the Norman Conquest of 1066, the perfection of the mason's art saw an explosion of architecture in stone, inspired by the two most pressing concerns of the day: religion and defence. Early structures of timber and rubble were replaced with churches, abbeys and monasteries built in dressed stone. The round arches, squat towers and chevron decoration of the Norman or Romanesque style (11th to 12th centuries) slowly evolved into the tall pointed arches, ribbed vaults and soaring spires of the Gothic (13th to 16th centuries), a history that can often be seen all in the one church – construction often took a couple of hundred years to complete. Many cathedrals remain significant landmarks, such as Salisbury, Winchester, Canterbury and York.

Stone was also put to good use in the building of elaborate defensive structures. Castles range from the atmospheric ruins of Tintagel and Dunstanburgh, and the feudal keeps of Lancaster and Bamburgh, to the sturdy fortresses of Warwick and Windsor. And then there's the most impressive of them all: the Tower of London, guarding the capital for more than 900 years.

Stately Homes of England

The medieval period was tumultuous, but by around 1600 life became more settled, and the nobility started to have less need for their castles. While they were excellent for keeping out rivals or the common riff-raff, they were often too dark, cold and draughty to be comfortable. So many castles saw the home improvements of the day – the installation of larger windows, wider staircases and better drainage. Others were simply abandoned for a brand-new dwelling next door; an example of this is Hardwick Hall in Derbyshire.

Following the Civil War, the trend away from castles gathered pace, as through the 17th century the landed gentry developed a taste for fine 'country houses' designed by the most famous architects of the day. Many became the 'stately homes' that are a major feature of the English landscape, celebrated by Noël Coward's famous song 'The Stately Homes of England', and a major attraction for visitors. Among the most extravagant are Holkham Hall in Norfolk, Chatsworth House in Derbyshire, and Blenheim Palace in Oxfordshire.

THE STIRLING PRIZE FOR ARCHITECTURE

The highlight of the year for aficionados of modern architecture is the announcement of the shortlist for the Stirling Prize for the best new building, an annual award for excellence in architecture organised by the Royal Institute of British Architects (RIBA). Established in 1996, this prestigious award is for 'the building that has made the greatest contribution to the evolution of architecture in the past year'. Famous winners include the Millennium Bridge in Gateshead (2002), 30 St Mary Axe (better known as the Gherkin) in London (2004), the Scottish Parliament Building in Edinburgh (2005), the Everyman Theatre in Liverpool (2014) and Burntwood School in London (2015).

> **HOUSE & HOME**
>
> It's not all about big houses. Alongside the stately homes, ordinary domestic architecture from the 16th century onwards can also still be seen in rural areas: black-and-white 'half-timbered' houses still characterise counties such as Worcestershire, while brick-and-flint cottages pepper Norfolk and Suffolk, and hardy centuries-old farms built with slate or local gritstone are a feature of areas such as Derbyshire and the Lake District.

The great stately homes all display the proportion, symmetry and architectural harmony so in vogue during the 17th and 18th centuries, styles later reflected in the fashionable town houses of the Georgian era – most notably in the city of Bath, where the stunning Royal Crescent is the epitome of the genre.

Victoriana

The Victorian era was a time of great building. A style called Victorian-Gothic developed, echoing the towers and spires that were such a feature of the original Gothic cathedrals. The most famous example of this style is the Palace of Westminster (better known as the Houses of Parliament) and Elizabeth Tower (home to Big Ben), in London. Other highlights include London's Natural History Museum and St Pancras train station.

Through the early 20th century, as England's cities grew in size and stature, the newly moneyed middle classes built streets and squares of smart town houses. Meanwhile, in other suburbs the first town planners oversaw the construction of endless terraces of red-brick two-up-two-down houses to accommodate the massive influx of workers required to fuel the country's factories – the terraces are not especially scenic but are one of the most enduring marks on the English architectural landscape today.

The Postwar Rebuild

During WWII many of England's cities were damaged by bombing, and the rebuilding that followed showed scant regard for the overall aesthetic of the cities, or for the lives of the people who lived in them. The rows of terraces were swept away in favour of high-rise tower blocks, while the 'brutalist' architects of the 1950s and '60s employed the modern and efficient materials of steel and concrete, leaving legacies such as London's South Bank Centre.

Perhaps this is why, on the whole, the English are conservative in their architectural tastes, and often resent ambitious or experimental designs, especially when they're applied to public buildings, or when form appears more important than function. But a familiar pattern often unfolds: after a few years of resentment, first comes a nickname, then grudging acceptance, and finally – once the locals have got used to it – comes pride and affection for the new building. The English just don't like to be rushed, that's all.

With this attitude in mind, over the last few decades, English architecture has started to redeem itself, and many big cities now have contemporary buildings their residents can be proud of and enjoy. Highlights in London's financial district include the bulging cone with the official address of 30 St Mary Axe (but widely known by its nickname, the Gherkin), and the former Millennium Dome (now rebranded as simply the O2), which has been transformed from a source of national embarrassment into one of the capital's leading live-music venues.

England's Finest Stately Homes

Audley End House
(Essex)

Blenheim Palace
(Oxfordshire)

Blickling Hall
(Norfolk)

Burghley House
(Lincolnshire)

Castle Howard
(Yorkshire)

Chatsworth House
(Derbyshire)

Cotehele
(Cornwall)

Kingston Lacy
(Dorset)

CBCK / SHUTTERSTOCK ©

Turner Contemporary gallery (p150), designed by David Chipperfield

Twenty-First Century

Through the first decade of the 21st century, many areas of England placed a new importance on progressive, popular architecture as a part of wider regeneration. Top examples include Manchester's Imperial War Museum North, The Deep aquarium in Hull, Cornwall's futuristic Eden Project, and the Sage concert hall in Gateshead, near Newcastle.

From around 2010, development slowed and some plans were shelved, thanks to the global slowdown, but several significant projects continued, including the Turner Contemporary gallery in Margate (opened 2011) and the futuristic Library of Birmingham (2013).

But England's largest and most high-profile architectural project of recent times was of course the Olympic Park, the centrepiece of the 2012 Games, in the London suburb of Stratford. As well as the main Olympic Stadium, other arenas include the Velodrome and Aquatics Centre – all dramatic structures in their own right, using cutting-edge construction techniques. The velodrome also won the construction industry's 2011 Better Public Buildings Award.

Meanwhile, in the centre of the capital, the tall, jagged Shard was officially opened in July 2012; at 306m, it's one of Europe's tallest buildings. On the other side of the River Thames, two more giant skyscrapers were completed in 2014: 20 Fenchurch St (nickname: the Walkie-Talkie) and the Leadenhall Building (the Cheesegrater). While in 2015 the Tate Modern unveiled a dramatic new, 200ft pyramid-like extension.

So London continues to grow upwards, and English architecture continues to push new boundaries of style and technology. The buildings may look a little different, but it's great to see the spirit of Stonehenge alive and well after all these years.

GLOSSARY OF ENGLISH ARCHITECTURE

BAILEY	OUTERMOST WALL OF A CASTLE
bar	fortified gate (York, and some other northern cities)
barrel vault	semicircular arched roof
brass	memorial consisting of a brass plate set into the side or lid of a tomb, or into the floor of a church to indicate a burial place below
buttress	vertical support for a wall; see also *flying buttress*
campanile	free-standing belfry or bell tower
chancel	eastern end of the church, usually reserved for choir and clergy
choir	area in the church where the choir is seated
cloister	covered walkway linking the church with adjacent monastic buildings
close	buildings grouped around a cathedral
cob	mixture of mud and straw for building
corbel	stone or wooden projection from a wall supporting a beam or arch
flying buttress	supporting *buttress* in the form of one side of an open arch
lancet	pointed window in Early English style
lierne vault	*vault* containing many tertiary ribs
Martello tower	small, circular tower used for coastal defence
minster	traditionally a church connected to a monastery; now a title signalling a church's importance
nave	main body of the church at the western end, where the congregation gather
oast house	building containing a kiln for drying hops
pargeting	decorative stucco plasterwork
pele	fortified house
precincts	see *close*
priory	religious house governed by a prior
quire	medieval term for *choir*
rood	archaic word for cross (in churches)
transepts	north–south projections from a church's *nave*, giving church a cruciform (cross-shaped plan)
undercroft	vaulted underground room or cellar
vault	roof with arched ribs, usually in a decorative pattern

The English Landscape

When it comes to landscapes, England is not a place of extremes; there are no Alps or Himalaya here, no Amazon or Sahara. But there are still very diverse environments, and understanding those differences can keep you enthralled. The country may be small, but even a relatively short journey takes you through a surprising mix of scenery. Seeing the change – subtle in some areas, dramatic in others – as you travel is one of this country's great joys.

Landscape Online

www.nationalparks.
gov.uk

www.landscapes
forlife.org.uk

www.rspb.org.uk

www.countryfile.
com

www.environ-
ment-agency.
gov.uk

Beaches

England has an embarrassment of beaches, from tiny hidden coves in Cornwall to vast neon-lined strands such as Brighton or Blackpool. Other great beaches can be found in Devon, Somerset and along the south coast, in Suffolk, Norfolk, Lancashire, Yorkshire and Northumberland – each with their own distinct character. The best resort beaches earn the coveted international Blue Flag (www.blueflag.org) award, meaning sand and water are clean and unpolluted. Other criteria include the presence of lifeguards, litter bins and recycling facilities, meaning some wild beaches may not earn the award, but are stunning nonetheless.

National Parks

Back in 1810, English poet and outdoor fan William Wordsworth suggested that the wild landscape of the Lake District in Cumbria should be 'a sort of national property, in which every man has a right'. More than a century later, the Lake District had indeed become a national park, along with the Peak District, Dartmoor, Exmoor, the North York Moors, the Yorkshire Dales and Northumberland. Other national parks (or equivalent status) followed, including the Norfolk and Suffolk Broads, the New Forest and the South Downs.

But the term 'national park' can cause confusion. First, in England the parks are not state-owned: nearly all land is private, belonging to farmers, private estates and conservation organisations. Second, they are *not* areas of wilderness as in many other countries.

In England's national parks you'll see crop fields in lower areas and grazing sheep on the uplands, as well as roads, railways and villages, and even towns, quarries and factories in some parks. It's a reminder of the balance that is struck in this crowded country between protecting the natural environment and catering for the people who live in it.

Despite these apparent anomalies, England's national parks still contain mountains, hills, downs, moors, lakes, woods, river valleys and other areas of quiet countryside, all ideal for enjoying nature however you like to experience it.

Protected Areas

As well as national parks, other parts of the English countryside are designated as Areas of Outstanding Natural Beauty (AONBs), the second tier of protected landscape after national parks. Some of the finest AONBs in England include the Chilterns, Cornwall, the Cotswolds, the Isles of Scilly, the North Pennines, the Northumberland Coast, the Suffolk Coast and the Wye Valley.

There are also Conservation Areas, Sites of Special Scientific Interest (SSSIs) and many other types of protected landscape that you can enjoy as you travel around.

Wildlife

For a small country, England has a diverse range of plants and animals. Many native species are hidden away, but there are some undoubted gems, from lowland woods carpeted in shimmering bluebells to stately herds of deer on the high moors. Having a closer look will enhance your trip enormously.

ENGLAND'S NATIONAL PARKS

NATIONAL PARK	FEATURES	ACTIVITIES	BEST TIME TO VISIT
Dartmoor	rolling hills, rocky outcrops, serene valleys; Bronze Age relics; wild ponies, deer, peregrine falcons	walking, mountain biking, horse riding, climbing, winter kayaking	May-Jun (wildflowers bloom)
Exmoor	sweeping moors, craggy sea cliffs; red deer, wild ponies, horned sheep	horse riding, walking, mountain biking	Aug-Sep (heather flowering)
Lake District	majestic fells, rugged mountains, shimmering lakes; literary heritage; red squirrels, ospreys	watersports, walking, mountaineering, rock climbing	Sep-Oct (summer crowds departed, autumn colours abound)
New Forest	woodlands, heath; wild ponies, otters, Dartford warblers, southern damselflies	walking, cycling, horse riding	Apr-Sep (lush vegetation)
Norfolk & Suffolk Broads	expansive shallow lakes, rivers, marshlands; windmills; water lilies, wildfowl, otters	walking, cycling, boating	Apr-May (birds most active)
North York Moors	heather-clad hills, deep-green valleys, isolated villages; merlins, curlews, golden plovers	walking, mountain biking	Aug-Sep (heather flowering)
Northumberland	wild rolling moors, heather, gorse; Hadrian's Wall; black grouse, red squirrels	walking, cycling, mountain biking, climbing	Apr-May (lambs) & Sep (heather flowering)
Peak District	high moors, tranquil dales, limestone caves; kestrels, badgers, grouse	walking, cycling, mountain biking, hang-gliding, climbing	Apr-May (even more lambs)
South Downs	rolling grassy chalky hills, chalky sea-cliffs, gorse, heather; Adonis blue butterflies	walking, mountain biking	Aug (heather flowering)
Yorkshire Dales	rugged hills, lush valleys, limestone pavements; red squirrels, hares, curlews, lapwings, buzzards	walking, cycling, mountain biking, climbing	Apr-May (visitors outnumbered by, you guessed it, lambs)

Animals

Farmland

Perhaps surprisingly, England's most wooded county is Surrey, despite its proximity to London. The soil is too poor for agriculture, so while woodland areas elsewhere in England were cleared, Surrey's trees got a stay of execution.

In rural areas, rabbits are everywhere, but if you're hiking through the countryside be on the lookout for the much larger brown hares, an increasingly rare species. Males who battle for territory by boxing on their hind legs in early spring are, of course, as 'mad as a March hare'.

Common birds of farmland areas (and urban gardens) include the robin, with its instantly recognisable red breast and cheerful whistle; the wren, whose loud trilling song belies its tiny size; and the yellowhammer, with a song that sounds like (if you use your imagination) 'a-little-bit-of-bread-and-no-cheese'. In open fields, the warbling cry of a skylark is another classic, but now threatened, sound of the English outdoors. You're more likely to see a pheasant, a large bird originally introduced from Russia to the nobility's shooting estates, but now considered naturalised.

Alongside rivers the once-rare otter is making a comeback. Elsewhere, in some areas the black-and-white striped badger has been the subject of trial culls – some believe it transmits bovine tuberculosis to cattle, others argue the case is far from proven. Also at the centre of controversy is the fox – amid much national debate, hunting foxes with dogs was banned in 2005. The animal is widespread in the countryside and well adapted to a scavenging life in rural towns, and even city suburbs.

Woodland

In woodland areas, mammals include the small white-spotted fallow deer and the even smaller roe deer. Woodland is full of birds too, but you'll hear them more than see them. Listen out for willow warblers (which have a warbling song with a descending cadence), chiffchaffs (which make a repetitive 'chiff chaff' noise) and the rat-a-tat-tat of woodpeckers.

If you hear rustling among the fallen leaves it might be a hedgehog – a spiny-backed insect-eating mammal – but it's an increasingly rare sound these days; conservationists say they'll be extinct in Britain by 2025, thanks to farming insecticides, decreased habitat and their inability to safely cross roads.

Grey squirrels (introduced from North America) have proved very adaptable, to the extent that England's native red squirrels are severely endangered because the greys eat all the food.

Perhaps unexpectedly, England is home to herds of 'wild' ponies, notably in the New Forest, Exmoor and Dartmoor, but although these ani-

---

WILDLIFE IN YOUR POCKET

Is it a rabbit or a hare? A gull or a tern? Buttercup or cowslip? If you need to know a bit more about England's plant and animal kingdoms, the following field guides are ideal for entry-level naturalists:

➡ *Collins Complete Guide to British Wildlife* by Paul Sterry is portable and highly recommended, covering mammals, birds, fish, plants, snakes, insects and even fungi, with brief descriptions and excellent photos.

➡ If feathered friends are enough, the *Collins Complete Guide to British Birds* by Paul Sterry has clear photos and descriptions, plus when and where each species may be seen.

➡ *Wildlife of the North Atlantic* by world-famous film-maker Tony Soper beautifully covers the animals seen from beach, boat and cliff top in the British Isles and beyond.

➡ The Collins GEM series includes handy little books on wildlife topics such as *Birds, Trees, Fish* and *Wild Flowers*.

mals roam free they are privately owned and regularly managed. There's even a pocket of wild goats near Lynmouth in Devon, where they've apparently gambolled merrily for almost 1000 years.

Mountains & High Moors

On some mountains and high moors the most visible mammal is the red deer. Males of the species grow their famous large antlers between April and July, and shed them again in February. Also on the high ground, well-known and easily recognised birds include the red grouse, which often hides in the heather until almost stepped on, then flies away with a loud warning call; and the curlew, with its stately long legs and elegant curved bill. Look hard, and you may see beautifully camouflaged golden plovers, while the spectacular aerial displays of lapwings are impossible to miss.

Coastal Areas

By the sea, two seal species frequent English coasts: the larger grey seal, which is more often seen, and the misnamed common seal. In areas such as Norfolk and Northumberland, boat trips to see seal colonies are a popular attraction. Dolphins, porpoises, minke whales and basking sharks can sometimes be seen off the western coasts, especially from about May to September when viewing conditions are better – although you may need to go with someone who knows where to look. Boat trips are available from many coastal resorts.

England's estuaries and mudflats are feeding grounds for numerous migrant wading birds; easily spotted are black-and-white oystercatchers with their long red bills, while flocks of ringed plovers skitter along the sand. On the coastal cliffs in early summer, particularly in Cornwall and Yorkshire, countless thousands of guillemots, razorbills, kittiwakes and other breeding seabirds fight for space on crowded rock ledges, and the air is thick with their sound. Even if you're not into birdwatching, this is one of England's finest wildlife spectacles.

Plants

In the rolling hills of southern England and the limestone areas further north (such as the Peak District and Yorkshire Dales), the best places to see wildflowers are the areas that evade large-scale farming – many erupt with great profusions of cowslips and primroses in April and May.

For woodland flowers, the best time is also April and May, before the leaf canopy is fully developed so sunlight can reach plants such as bluebells – a beautiful and internationally rare species. Another classic English plant is gorse: you can't miss this spiky bush in heath areas like Dartmoor, Exmoor and the New Forest. Its vivid yellow flowers show year-round and have a distinctive, coconut-like scent.

In contrast, the blooming season for heather is quite short, but no less dramatic; through August and September areas such as the North York Moors and Dartmoor are covered in a riot of purple.

Environmental Issues

With England's long history of human occupation, it's not surprising that the country's appearance is heavily the result of human interaction with the environment. Since the earliest times, trees have been chopped down and fields created for crops or animals, but the really significant changes to rural areas came after WWII in the late 1940s, continuing into the '50s and '60s, when a drive to be self-reliant in food meant new – intensive and large-scale – farming methods. The result was dramatic: in some areas ancient patchworks of small meadows became landscapes of vast

Wildlife of Britain by George McGavin et al is subtitled 'The Definitive Visual Guide'. Although too heavy to carry around during your travels, this beautiful photographic book is great for pretrip inspiration or posttrip memories.

FOX HUNTING

The red fox, a doglike animal with a characteristic bushy tail and an anthropomorphic reputation for cunning, is a divisive creature in England. The controversy focuses on hunting, and specifically fox hunting with hounds (a type of dog). Supporters say it's been a traditional English rural activity for centuries, and helps control the fox population; opponents say it's a savage blood sport that has little impact on overall numbers. Distaste for this type of hunting is not a new phenomenon; the activity was famously described as 'the unspeakable in pursuit of the inedible' by Oscar Wilde more than a century ago. Fox hunting has been immortalised in thousands of paintings depicting English country life, and in countless rural pub names. Today, some observers believe the hunting debate has come to represent much bigger issues: town versus country, or the relative limits of privilege, state control and individual freedom. Either way, fox hunting with dogs was banned in 2005 by law. And opinion is still very strongly divided.

Although hedgerows around fields have been reduced, new 'hedgerows' have appeared: the long strips of grass and bushes alongside motorways and major roads. These areas support thousands of insect species plus mice, shrews and other small mammals, so kestrels are often seen hovering nearby, unconcerned by traffic.

prairie-like fields, as walls were demolished, woodlands felled, ponds filled, wetlands drained and, most notably, hedgerows ripped out.

In most cases the hedgerows were lines of dense bushes, shrubs and trees forming a network that stretched across the countryside, protecting fields from erosion, supporting a varied range of flowers, and providing shelter for numerous insects, birds and small mammals. But in the rush to improve farm yields, thousands of miles of hedgerows were destroyed in the postwar decades, and between the mid-1980s and the early 2000s another 25% disappeared.

Hedgerows have come to symbolise many other environmental issues in rural areas, and in recent years the destruction has abated, partly because farmers recognise their anti-erosion qualities, and partly because they've been encouraged – with financial incentives from UK or European agencies – to 'set aside' such areas as wildlife havens.

In addition to hedgerow clearance, other farming techniques remain hot environmental issues. Studies suggest the use of pesticides and intensive irrigation results in rivers being contaminated or simply running dry. Meanwhile, monocropping means the fields have one type of grass and not another plant to be seen. These 'green deserts' support no insects, so in turn wild bird populations have plummeted. This picture is not a case of wizened old peasants recalling the idyllic days of their forbears; you only have to be aged about 40 in England to remember a countryside where birds such as skylarks or lapwings were visibly much more numerous.

But all is not lost. In the face of apparently overwhelming odds, England still boasts great biodiversity, and some of the best wildlife habitats are protected (to a greater or lesser extent) by the creation of national parks and similar areas, or private reserves owned by conservation campaign groups such as the Wildlife Trusts (www.wildlifetrusts.org), National Trust (www.nationaltrust.org.uk), Woodland Trust (www.woodlandtrust.org.uk) and the Royal Society for the Protection of Birds (www.rspb.org.uk). Many of these areas are open to the public – ideal spots for walking, birdwatching or simply enjoying the peace and beauty of the countryside – and are well worth a visit as you travel around.

Arts

England's contributions to literature, drama, cinema and pop are celebrated around the world. As you travel around England today you'll encounter landscapes made famous as movie sets and literary locations, and places mentioned in songs. Here we've picked some major creative milestones and focused on works with connections to real locations – so your physical journey through England will be one that connects culture with place.

English Literature

The roots of England's poetic and story-telling heritage stretch back to Nordic sagas and Early English epics such as *Beowulf,* but modern English literature starts around 1387 (yes, that is 'modern' in history-soaked England) when Geoffrey Chaucer produced *The Canterbury Tales.* This mammoth poem is a collection of fables, stories and morality tales using travelling pilgrims – the Knight, the Wife of Bath and so on – as a narrative hook.

William Shakespeare

The next big name in English literature came in the 16th century, when William Shakespeare entered the scene. Best known for his plays, he was also a remarkably prolific and influential poet. 'Shall I compare thee to a summer's day?' is just one of his famous lines still widely quoted today. His birthplace, Stratford-upon-Avon, is stacked with Shakespearean sights.

The Romantic Era

During the late 18th and early 19th centuries, a new generation of writers drew inspiration from human imagination and the natural world (in some cases helped along by a healthy dose of laudanum). Leading lights of the movement were William Blake, John Keats, Percy Bysshe Shelley, Lord Byron and Samuel Taylor Coleridge, and perhaps the best-known English poet of all, William Wordsworth. His famous line from 'Daffodils' –

For extra insight, the *Oxford Guide to Literary Britain and Ireland,* edited by Daniel Hahn and Nicholas Robins, gives details of towns, villages and countryside immortalised by writers, from Geoffrey Chaucer's Canterbury to Jane Austen's Bath.

JANE AUSTEN & THE BRONTËS

The beginning of the 19th century saw the emergence of some of English literature's best-known and beloved writers: Jane Austen and the Brontë sisters.

Austen's fame stems from her exquisite observations of love, friendship, intrigues and passions boiling beneath the strait-laced surface of middle-class social convention, and from the endless stream of movies and TV costume dramas based on her works, such as *Pride and Prejudice* and *Sense and Sensibility.* For visitors today, the location most associated with Jane Austen is the city of Bath – a beautiful place even without the literary link. As one of her heroines said, 'who can ever be tired of Bath?'.

Of the Brontë sisters' prodigious output, Emily Brontë's *Wuthering Heights* is the best known – an epic tale of obsession and revenge, where the dark and moody landscape plays a role as great as any human character. Charlotte Brontë's *Jane Eyre* and Anne Brontë's *The Tenant of Wildfell Hall* are classics of passion and mystery. Fans still flock to their former home in the Yorkshire town of Haworth, perched on the edge of the wild Pennine moors that inspired so many of their books.

'I wandered lonely as a cloud' – was inspired by a waterside walk in the Lake District in northern England.

Victoriana

As industrialisation expanded during the reign of Queen Victoria, so key novels of the time explored social themes. Charles Dickens tackled many prevailing issues of his day: in *Oliver Twist,* he captures the lives of young pickpockets in the London slums; *Bleak House* is a critique of the English legal system; and *Hard Times* criticises the excesses of capitalism. At around the same time, but choosing a rural setting, George Eliot (the pen name of Mary Ann Evans) wrote *The Mill on the Floss,* where the central character struggles against society's expectations.

Thomas Hardy's classic *Tess of the D'Urbervilles* deals with the peasantry's decline, and *The Trumpet Major* paints a picture of idyllic English country life interrupted by war and encroaching modernity. Many of Hardy's works are based in the fictionalised county of Wessex, largely based on today's Dorset and surrounding counties, where towns such as Dorchester are dotted with literary links.

The 20th Century

The end of WWI and the ensuing social disruption fed into the modernist movement, with DH Lawrence perhaps its finest exponent; *Sons and Lovers* follows the lives and loves of generations in the English Midlands as the country changes from rural idyll to an increasingly industrial landscape, while his controversial exploration of sexuality in *Lady Chatterley's Lover* was originally banned as 'obscene'. Other highlights of this period included Daphne du Maurier's romantic suspense novel *Rebecca,* set on the Cornish coast, and Evelyn Waugh's *Brideshead Revisited,* an exploration of moral and social disintegration among the English aristocracy, set partly in Oxford.

The 1970s saw the arrival of two novelists who became prolific for the remainder of the century and beyond. Martin Amis published *The Rachel Papers* then went on to produce a string of novels where common themes included the absurdity and unappealing nature of modern life, such as *London Fields* (1989) and *Lionel Asbo: State of England* (2012). Meanwhile, Ian McEwan debuted with *The Cement Garden,* and earned critical acclaim for finely observed studies of the English character such as *The Child in Time* (1987), *Atonement* (2001) and *On Chesil Beach* (2007), which is set on the eponymous, 18-mile stretch of Dorset shore.

New Millennium

As the 20th century came to a close, the nation's multicultural landscape proved a rich inspiration for contemporary novelists: Hanif Kureishi sowed the seeds with his ground-breaking *The Buddha of Suburbia,* about a group of British-Asians in suburban London; Zadie Smith published her acclaimed debut *White Teeth* in 2000, followed by a string of bestsellers including *The Autograph Man* and 2012's *NW;* Andrea Levy published *Small Island,* about a Jamaican couple settled in postwar London; and Monica Ali's *Brick Lane* was shortlisted for the high-profile Man Booker Prize in 2003.

Other contemporary writers include Will Self, known for his surreal, satirical novels including *The Book of Dave,* and Nick Hornby, best known for novels like *Fever Pitch,* a study of the insecurities of English blokishness. There's also Julian Barnes, whose books include *England, England,* a darkly ironic study of nationalism and tourism among other themes, and *The Sense of An Ending,* winner of the 2011 Man Booker Prize. Not to mention Hilary Mantel, author of many novels on an astoundingly wide range of subjects, and winner of the Man Booker Prize

Helen Fielding's book *Bridget Jones's Diary,* originally a series of newspaper articles, is a fond look at the heartache of a modern single woman's blundering search for love, and the epitome of the late-1990s 'chick-lit' genre. It's also (very loosely) based on *Pride and Prejudice* by Jane Austen.

twice, first in 2009 for historical blockbuster *Wolf Hall* (about Henry VIII and his ruthless advisor Thomas Cromwell), and then in 2012 for its sequel *Bring Up the Bodies*. At the time of writing, the third and final instalment, *The Mirror and the Light*, was still a work in progress.

England's greatest literary phenomenon of the 21st century is JK Rowling's Harry Potter books, a series of other-worldly adventures that have entertained millions of children (and many grown-ups too) since the first book was published in 1996. The magical tales are the latest in a long line of British children's classics enjoyed by adults, stretching back to the works of Lewis Carroll *(Alice's Adventures in Wonderland)*, E Nesbit *(The Railway Children)*, AA Milne *(Winnie-the-Pooh)* and CS Lewis (The Chronicles of Narnia).

For other worlds and other-worldly humour, try two of England's funniest – and most successful – writers: Douglas Adams (*The Hitchhiker's Guide to the Galaxy* and several sequels) and Terry Pratchett (the Discworld series).

ARTS CINEMA

Cinema

English cinema has a long history, with many early directors cutting their teeth in the silent-film industry. Perhaps the best-known of these was Alfred Hitchcock, who directed *Blackmail,* one of the first English 'talkies' in 1929, and who went on to direct a string of films during the 1930s before emigrating to Hollywood in the early 1940s.

War & Postwar

During WWII, films such as *In Which We Serve* (1942) and *We Dive at Dawn* (1943) were designed to raise public morale, while a young director called David Lean produced *Brief Encounter* (1945), the classic tale of buttoned-up English passion, before graduating to Hollywood epics including *Lawrence of Arabia* and *Doctor Zhivago*.

Following the hardships of war, British audiences were in the mood for escape and entertainment. During the late 1940s and early '50s, the domestic film industry specialised in eccentric British comedies epitomised by the output of Ealing Studios: notable titles include *Passport to Pimlico* (1949), *Kind Hearts and Coronets* (1949) and *The Titfield Thunderbolt* (1953).

Swinging '60s

'British New Wave' and 'Free Cinema' explored the gritty realities of British life in semidocumentary style, with directors Lindsay Anderson and Tony Richardson crystallising the movement in films such as *This Sporting Life* (1961) and *A Taste of Honey* (1961). At the other end of the spectrum were the *Carry On* films, the cinematic equivalent of the smutty seaside postcard, packed with bawdy gags and double entendres. The 1960s also saw the birth of another classic English genre: the James Bond films, starring Sean Connery (who is actually Scottish).

The Ladykillers (1955) is a classic Ealing comedy about a band of hapless bank robbers holed up in a London guesthouse, and features Alec Guinness sporting the most outrageous set of false teeth ever committed to celluloid.

Brit Flicks

The 1970s was a tough decade for the British film industry, but the 1980s saw a recovery, thanks partly to David Puttnam's Oscar success with

---

WALLACE & GROMIT

One of the great success stories of English TV and cinema has been Bristol-based animator Nick Park and the production company Aardman Animations, best known for the award-winning man-and-dog duo Wallace and Gromit. This lovable pair first appeared in Park's graduation film *A Grand Day Out* (1989) and went on to star in *The Wrong Trousers* (1993), *A Close Shave* (1995) and the full-length feature *The Curse of the Were-Rabbit* (2005). Known for their intricate plots, film homages and amazingly realistic animation, the Wallace and Gromit films scooped Nick Park four Oscars. Other Aardman works include *Chicken Run* (2000), *Flushed Away* (2006) and *The Pirates!* (2012).

Chariots of Fire (1981), and the newly established Channel Four investing in edgy films such as *My Beautiful Laundrette* (1985).

Another minor renaissance occurred in the 1990s, ushered in by the massively successful *Four Weddings and a Funeral* (1994), featuring Hugh Grant in his trademark role as a floppy-haired, self-deprecating Englishman, a character type he reprised in subsequent hits, including *Notting Hill, About a Boy* and *Love Actually*.

The 'Brit Flick' genre – characterised by themes such as irony, social realism and humour in the face of adversity – went on to include *Brassed Off* (1996), about a struggling colliery band; *The Full Monty* (1997), following a troupe of laid-off steelworkers turned male strippers; and *Billy Elliott* (2000), the story of an aspiring young ballet dancer striving to escape the slagheaps and boarded-up factories of the industrial north.

Meanwhile, films such as *East Is East* (1999) and *Bend it like Beckham* (2002) explored the tensions of modern multicultural Britain, while veteran director Mike Leigh, known for his heavily improvised style, found success with *Life Is Sweet* (1991), *Naked* (1993) and the Palme d'Or–winning *Secrets and Lies* (1996).

Twenty-First Century Box

In the early part of the 21st century, literary adaptations have continued to provide the richest seam of success in the English film industry, including 2012's *Anna Karenina,* directed by Joe Wright and staring Keira Knightley, and of course the blockbuster *Harry Potter* franchise. Biopics are also a perennial favourite: recent big-screen subjects include Elizabeth I (*Elizabeth: The Golden Age,* 2007), Margaret Thatcher (*The Iron Lady,* 2011) and the 19th-century artist JMW Turner (*Mr Turner,* 2014).

Meanwhile, the oldest of English film franchises trundles on: a tough, toned, 21st-century James Bond appeared in 2006 courtesy of Daniel Craig and the blockbuster *Casino Royale* (2006), followed by *Quantum of Solace* (2008), *Skyfall* (2012) and *Spectre* (2015). There has been much debate about who will play the legendary spy next.

Pop & Rock Music

England has been putting the world through its musical paces ever since some mop-haired lads from Liverpool created The Beatles. And while Elvis may have invented rock and roll, it was the Fab Four that transformed it into a global phenomenon, backed by the other bands of the 1960s 'British Invasion': The Rolling Stones, The Who, Cream and The Kinks. And the big names have kept coming ever since.

Glam to Punk

Glam rock arrived in the 1970s, fronted by artists such as the anthemic Queen and the chameleonlike David Bowie (whose passing in 2016 triggered a palpable sense of loss worldwide). Also in the '70s Led Zeppelin laid down the blueprint for heavy metal, and the psychedelia of the previous decade morphed into the prog rock of Pink Floyd and Yes.

At the end of the decade, it was all swept aside as punk exploded onto the scene, most famously with the Sex Pistols, ably assisted by The Clash, The Damned, the Buzzcocks and The Stranglers. Then punk begat New Wave, with acts including The Jam and Elvis Costello blending spiky tunes and sharp lyrics into a more radio-friendly sound.

The '80s

The conspicuous consumption of the early 1980s influenced the era's pop scene. Big hair and shoulder pads became the uniform of the day, with big names including Wham! (a boyish duo headed by an up-and-coming popster called George Michael) and New Romantic bands such

The British Film Institute (BFI; www.bfi.org.uk) is dedicated to promoting film and cinema in Britain, and publishes the monthly academic journal *Sight & Sound*.

The UK's biggest film magazine is *Empire* (www.empireonline.com). For less mainstream opinion check out *Little White Lies* (lwlies.com).

as Spandau Ballet and Duran Duran. Away from the glitz, fans enjoyed the doom-laden lyrics of The Cure, the heavy metal of Iron Maiden and the 'miserabilism' of The Smiths.

Dance & Britpop

The late 1980s and early 1990s saw the rise of ecstasy-fuelled rave culture, centred on famous clubs like Manchester's Haçienda and London's Ministry of Sound. Manchester was also a focus for the burgeoning British 'indie' scene, driven by guitar-based bands such The Stone Roses, James, Happy Mondays and Oasis. Then indie morphed into Britpop, with Oasis, Pulp, Supergrass and Blur, whose distinctively British music chimed with the country's reborn sense of optimism after the landslide election of New Labour in 1997.

New Millennium Sound

The new millennium saw no let-up in the music scene's continual shifting and reinventing. R&B, hip hop and drum and bass fused into grime and dubstep, producing acts like Dizzee Rascal, Tinie Tempah and Stormzy. Initially centred on London, both scenes wield an increasing global influence. Dance acts like Calvin Harris and Disclosure also enjoyed massive international success.

Boy-band One Direction clocked up the sales: their first three albums debuted at number one on the US charts; in 2013 they released the year's biggest-selling British album and were named the top global act. But the spirit of British indie also stays alive thanks to the likes of Arctic Monkeys, Florence & the Machine, Coldplay, Muse, Kasabian, Radiohead and The Horrors.

Meanwhile singer-songwriters have made a comeback, as evidence by performers such as Katie Melua, Ed Sheeran and the all-conquering Adele. Her long-awaited 2015 album, 25, won critical acclaim and proved another international blockbuster, becoming the fastest million-seller in UK history.

Painting & Sculpture

For many centuries, continental Europe – especially the Netherlands, Spain, France and Italy – set the artistic agenda. The first artist with a truly British style and sensibility was arguably William Hogarth, whose riotous canvases exposed the vice and corruption of 18th-century London. His most celebrated work is *A Rake's Progress,* which kick-started a long tradition of British caricatures that can be traced right through to

ARTS PAINTING & SCULPTURE

Movies on the English music scene include: *Backbeat* (1994), about The Beatles' early days; *Sid & Nancy* (1986), Sex Pistols' bassist and his girlfriend; *Quadrophenia* (1979), mods and rockers; *Velvet Goldmine* (1998), glam rock; *24 Hour Party People* (2002), Manchester scene; and *Nowhere Boy* (2009), John Lennon pre-Beatles.

ROCK AND ROLL LOCATIONS...

Fans buy the single, then the T-shirt. But true fans visit the location featured on the album cover. The following are a few favourites:

➤ Abbey Rd, St John's Wood, London – *Abbey Road,* The Beatles

➤ Battersea Power Station, London – *Animals,* Pink Floyd (the inflatable pig has gone)

➤ Berwick St, Soho, London – *(What's the Story) Morning Glory,* Oasis

➤ Big Ben plus a corner of plinth under Boudica's statue, London – *My Generation* (US version), The Who

➤ Durdle Door, Dorset – *North Atlantic Drift,* Ocean Colour Scene

➤ Salford Boys Club, Manchester – *The Queen is Dead,* The Smiths

➤ Thor's Cave, Manifold Valley, near Ashbourne, Peak District National Park – *A Storm In Heaven,* The Verve

➤ Yes Tor, Dartmoor, Devon – *Tomato,* Yes

the work of modern-day cartoonists such as Gerald Scarfe and Steve Bell. You can see it at Sir John Soane's Museum in London.

Some of Henry Moore's work can be seen at the Yorkshire Sculpture Park. Barbara Hepworth is celebrated at the eponymous gallery in Wakefield; her home and garden are also open to visitors in St Ives, Cornwall.

Portraits

While Hogarth was busy satirising society, other artists were hard at work showing it in its best light. The leading figures of 18th-century English portraiture were Sir Joshua Reynolds, Thomas Gainsborough (you can visit his house in Sudbury, Suffolk) and George Romney, while George Stubbs is best known for his intricate studies of animals (particularly horses). Most of these artists are represented at Tate Britain or the National Gallery in London.

Landscape & Fables

In the 19th century leading painters favoured the English landscape. John Constable's best-known works include *Salisbury Cathedral* and *The Hay Wain*. The latter is in the National Gallery; you can also visit the setting, a mill at Flatford in Suffolk. JMW Turner, meanwhile, was fascinated by the effects of light and colour on English scenes, with his works becoming almost entirely abstract by the 1840s.

In contrast, the Pre-Raphaelite painters of the late 19th century preferred a figurative style reflecting the Victorian taste for English fables and fairy tales. Key members of the movement included Dante Gabriel Rossetti, John Everett Millais and William Holman Hunt, all represented at London's Tate Britain or Victoria & Albert Museum.

Stones & Sticks

In the tumultuous 20th century, English art became increasingly experimental. Francis Bacon placed Freudian psychoanalysis on the canvas in his portraits, while pioneering sculptors such as Henry Moore and Barbara Hepworth experimented with natural forms in stone and new materials. At about the same time, the painter LS Lowry was setting his 'matchstick men' among the smokestacks of northern England, and is today remembered by the major art centre that bears his name in Manchester.

Pop Art

The mid-1950s and early '60s saw an explosion of English 'pop art', as artists plundered popular culture for inspiration. Leaders of this new movement included David Hockney. His bold colours and simple lines were ground-breaking at the time, and are still used to great effect half a century later. A contemporary, Peter Blake, codesigned the cut-up collage cover for The Beatles' landmark album *Sgt. Pepper's Lonely Hearts Club Band*. The '60s also saw the rise of sculptor Anthony Caro; creating large abstract works in steel and bronze, he was one of England's most influential sculptors.

Britart & Beyond

Thanks partly to the support (and money) of advertising tycoon Charles Saatchi, a new wave of British artists came to the fore in the 1990s. The movement was dubbed, inevitably, 'Britart'; its leading members in-

ANISH KAPOOR

The sculptor Anish Kapoor has been working in London since the 1970s. He is best known for his large outdoor installations, which often feature curved shapes and reflective materials, such as highly polished steel. His recent works include a major new installation, called *ArcelorMittal Orbit*, in London's 2012 Queen Elizabeth Olympic Park. At over 110m high it is the largest piece of public art in Britain, and one you can actually side down, in a hair-raising 40-second glide.

cluded Damien Hirst, famous (or infamous) for works involving pickled sharks, a cow and calf cut into sections *(Mother and Child Divided)* and a diamond-encrusted skull entitled *For the Love of God*. His pregnant, naked and half-flayed *Verity* towers 20m high beside the harbour mouth at Ilfracombe in north Devon.

A contemporary is Tracey Emin. Once considered an enfant terrible, she incurred the wrath of the tabloids for works such as *My Bed* (a messed-up bedroom scene which sold for £2.5 million in 2014), but is now a respected figure and patron of the new Turner Gallery in Margate, named for the famous English artist JMW Turner.

You can enjoy Shakespeare plays at the rebuilt Globe Theatre in London or at the Royal Shakespeare Company's own theatre in Stratford-upon-Avon.

ARTS THEATRE

Theatre

English theatre can trace its roots back to medieval morality plays, court jesters and travelling storytellers, and possibly even to dramas during Roman times in amphitheatres – a few of which still remain, such as at Chester and Cirencester. But most scholars agree that the key milestone in the story is the opening of England's first theatre – called simply The Theatre – in London in 1576. Within 25 years, the Rose and the Globe theatres appeared, and the stage was set for the entrance of England's best-known playwright.

William Shakespeare

For most visitors to England (and for most locals) English drama means just one name: William Shakespeare. Born in 1564, in the Midlands town of Stratford-upon-Avon (still rich in Shakespearean sights), Shakespeare made his mark in London between around 1590 and 1610, where most of his plays were performed at the Globe Theatre. His brilliant plots and spectacular use of language, plus the sheer size of his canon of work (including classics such as *Hamlet, Romeo and Juliet, Henry V* and *A Midsummer Night's Dream*), have turned him into a national – and international – icon, so that today, almost 400 years after shuffling off his mortal coil, the Bard's plays still pull in big crowds.

English Theatre Today

However you budget your time and money during your visit to England, be sure to see some English theatre. It easily lives up to its reputation as the finest in the world, especially in London, while other big cities also boast their own top-class venues, such as the Birmingham Repertory Theatre, the Bristol Old Vic, Chichester Festival Theatre and the Nottingham Playhouse.

Many accomplished British actors, including Judi Dench, Ralph Fiennes, Brenda Blethyn, Toby Stephens and Simon Callow, juggle high-paying Hollywood roles with appearances on the British stage, while over the last decade or so several American stars have taken hefty pay cuts to tread the London boards, including Glenn Close, Kevin Spacey, Gwyneth Paltrow, Gillian Anderson, Christian Slater and Danny DeVito.

Venues in London include the Donmar Warehouse and Royal Court Theatre, best known for new and experimental works. For big names, most people head for the West End, where famous spots include the Shaftesbury, Adelphi and Theatre Royal at Drury Lane. And then there's *The Mousetrap* – Agatha Christie's legendary whodunit is the world's longest-running play, showing continuously since 1952.

West End Musicals

As well as drama, London's West End means big musicals, with a long history of crowd-pullers such as *Cats, The Wizard of Oz, Les Misérables, Sweeney Todd, The Phantom of the Opera* and *The Lion King*, with many of today's shows raiding the pop world for material, such as *We Will Rock You*, inspired by the music of Queen, and Abba-based *Mamma Mia!*

Sporting England

If you want a short cut to the heart of English culture, watch its people at play. In this sports-mad nation thousands turn out each weekend to cheer their favourite football team. Events such as Wimbledon (tennis), the Six Nations (rugby) and test matches (cricket) keep millions enthralled. And then there are the efforts of enthusiastic amateurs – be it in pub football leagues or village cricket matches, the English reveal a penchant for rules, hierarchies and playing the game.

Football (Soccer)

For the dates and details of major football and cricket matches, horse racing and other sporting fixtures across the country, a great place to start is the sports pages of www.britevents.com.

The English Premier League (www.premierleague.com) has some of the finest teams in the world, dominated in recent years by four top teams (Arsenal, Liverpool, Chelsea and Manchester United), joined in 2012 by a fifth big player in the shape of Manchester City. Their big pockets weren't enough in 2016, however, when unfancied Leicester City stunned the pundits and delighted neutrals by winning the title.

Down in quality from the Premiership, 72 other teams play in the English divisions called the Championship, League One and League Two.

The football season is the same for all divisions (August to May), so seeing a match can easily be tied into most visitors' itineraries, but tickets for the biggest games are like gold dust – your chances of bagging one are low unless you're a club member, or know someone who is. You're better off buying a ticket to see the less fashionable teams – they're cheaper and more easily available. You can often buy tickets on the spot, or at online agencies like www.ticketmaster.co.uk and www.myticketmarket.com.

Cricket

Along with Big Ben, The Beatles and a nice cup of tea, cricket is quintessentially English. Dating from the 18th century (although its roots are much older), the sport spread throughout the Commonwealth during Britain's colonial era. Australia, the Caribbean and the Indian subconti-

---

THE SWEET FA CUP

The Football Association held its first interclub knockout tournament in 1871/72: 15 clubs took part, playing for a nice piece of silverware called the FA Cup – then worth about £20.

Nowadays, around 600 clubs compete for this legendary and priceless trophy. It differs from many other competitions in that every team – from the lowest-ranking part-timers to the stars of the Premier League – is in with a chance. The preliminary rounds begin in August, and the world-famous Cup Final is held in May at the iconic Wembley Stadium in London.

Manchester United and Arsenal have the most FA Cups, but public attention – and affection – is invariably focused on the 'giant-killers': minor clubs that claw their way up through the rounds, unexpectedly beating higher-ranking competitors. One of the best-known giant-killing events occurred in 1992, when Wrexham, then ranked 24th in Division 3, famously came from a goal down to beat league champions Arsenal in the third round.

THE ASHES

The historic test-cricket series between England and Australia known as the Ashes has been played every other year since 1882 (bar a few interruptions during the world wars). It is played alternately in England and Australia, with each of the five matches in the series held at a different cricket ground, always in the summer in the host location.

The contest's name dates back to the landmark test match of 1882, won (for the very first time) by the Australians. Defeat of the mother country by the colonial upstarts was a source of profound national shock: a mock obituary in the *Sporting Times* lamented the death of English cricket and referred to the sport's ashes being taken to Australia.

Later the name was given to a terracotta urn presented the following year to the English captain Ivo Bligh (later Lord Darnley), purportedly containing the cremated ashes of a stump or bail used in this landmark match. Since 1953 this hallowed relic has resided at the Marylebone Cricket Club (MCC) Museum at Lord's. Despite the vast importance given to winning the series, the urn itself is a diminutive 6in (150mm) high.

The recent history of the Ashes is not without drama. In the 2010–11 series England thrashed Australia, winning on Australian turf for the first time since the 1986–87 series. Then in 2013 Australia thrashed England 5-0, repeating the humiliating clean sweep they had inflicted in 2006–07. But the 2015 Ashes saw England – to national delight – defeat Australia 3-2.

nent took to the game with gusto, and today the former colonies delight in giving the old country a good spanking on the cricket pitch.

While many English people follow cricket like a religion, to the uninitiated it can be an impenetrable enigma. Spread over one-day games or five-day 'test matches', progress seems so *slow,* and dominated by arcane terminology like 'innings', 'cover drives', 'googlies', 'outswingers', 'leg-byes' and 'silly mid-off'. Nonetheless, at least one cricket match should be a feature of your travels around England. If you're patient and learn the intricacies, you could find cricket as absorbing as it is for all the Brits who remain glued to their radio or computer all summer long, 'just to see how England's getting on'.

Causing ructions is Twenty20 cricket, a relatively new format which limits the number of balls each team has to score off, putting the emphasis on fast, big-batting scores. Traditionalists see it as changing the character of the game, though there's no doubting its popularity – most Twenty20 matches sell out.

Grounds include Lord's in London, Edgbaston in Birmingham and Headingley in Leeds. Tickets cost from £30 to well over £200. The County Championship pits the best teams from around the country against each other; tickets cost £5 to £25, and only the most crucial games tend to sell out. Details are on the website of the English Cricket Board (www.ecb.co.uk).

The easiest way to watch cricket – and often the most enjoyable – is stumbling across a local game on a village green as you travel around the country. There's no charge for spectators, and no one will mind if you nip into the pub during a quiet spell.

Queen Elizabeth II is a great horse-racing fan, and the royal stables have produced many winners. The 2005 Grand National famously clashed with the marriage of Prince Charles; rumours abound that the start was delayed so the Queen could attend the nuptials *and* see the race.

Horse Racing

The tradition of horse racing in Britain stretches back centuries, and there's a 'meeting' somewhere pretty much every day. For all but the major events you should be able to get a ticket on the day, or buy in advance from the sport's marketing body Great British Racing (www.greatbritishracing.com).

The top event in the calendar is Royal Ascot (www.ascot.co.uk) at Ascot Racecourse in mid-June, where the rich and famous come to see and

England's intriguing sports have equally fascinating histories. No one can say when football was invented, but the word 'soccer' (the favoured term in countries where 'football' means another game) is reputedly derived from 'sock'. In medieval times this was a tough leather foot-cover worn by peasants – ideal for kicking around a pig's bladder in the park on a Saturday afternoon.

In contrast, rugby can trace its roots to a football match in 1823 at Rugby School, in Warwickshire. A player called William Webb Ellis, frustrated at the limitations of mere kicking, reputedly picked up the ball and ran with it towards the goal. True to the sense of English fair play, rather than Ellis being dismissed from the game, a whole new sport was developed around his tactic, and the Rugby Football Union was formally inaugurated in 1871. The Rugby World Cup is named the Webb Ellis Trophy after this enterprising young tearaway.

be seen, and the fashion is almost as important as the nags. Even the Queen turns up to put a fiver each way on Lucky Boy in the 3.15.

Other big events include the Grand National steeplechase at Aintree (www.aintree.co.uk) in early April; and the Derby at Epsom (www.epsomdowns.co.uk) on the first Saturday in June. The latter is especially popular with the masses so, unlike at Ascot, you won't see so many morning suits or outrageous hats.

Rugby

A wit once said that football was a gentlemen's game played by hooligans, while rugby was a hooligans' game played by gentlemen. That may be true, but rugby is very popular, especially since England became world champions in 2003, and then hosted the Rugby Union World Cup in 2015. It's worth catching a game for the display of skill (OK, and brawn), and the fun atmosphere in the grounds. Tickets for games cost around £15 to £50 depending on the club's status and fortunes.

There are two versions of the game: Rugby Union (www.rfu.com) is played more in southern England, Wales and Scotland, and is traditionally thought of as the game of the middle and upper classes. Rugby League (www.therfl.co.uk) is played predominantly in northern England, stereotypically by the 'working classes'. Today, leading rugby union clubs include Leicester, Bath, Exeter and Gloucester, while London has a host of good-quality teams (including Wasps and Saracens). In rugby league, teams to watch include the Wigan Warriors, Bradford Bulls and Leeds Rhinos.

Tennis

Tennis is widely played at club and regional level, but the best-known tournament is the All England Championships – known to all as Wimbledon (www.wimbledon.com) – when tennis fever sweeps through the country in the last week of June and first week of July. There's something quintessentially English about the combination of grass courts, polite applause and spectators in straw hats, with strawberries and cream devoured by the truckload.

Demand for seats at Wimbledon always outstrips supply, but to give everyone an equal chance tickets are sold through a public ballot. You can also take your chance on the spot; about 5000 tickets are sold at the gate each day, including those – at the earlier stages of the championships – for the show courts. But you'll need to be an early riser: dedicated fans start queuing (how English) the night before. See the website for more information.

Around 140,000 punnets of strawberries and 10,000l of cream are consumed each year at Wimbledon during the two-week tennis championships.

A highlight of the international rugby calendar is the annual Six Nations Championship (www.rbs6nations.com), held in February and March, in which England battles against teams from Wales, Scotland, Ireland, France and Italy.

Survival
Guide

DIRECTORY A–Z....676

Accommodation........ 676

Climate............... 678

Customs
Regulations............ 678

Electricity 678

Emergency &
Important Numbers..... 679

GLBTI Travellers 679

Health................. 679

Insurance.............. 679

Internet Access........ 679

Legal Matters 680

Money................. 680

Opening Hours 680

Post................... 681

Public Holidays......... 681

Safe Travel............. 681

Telephone 681

Time.................. 682

Toilets................. 682

Tourist
Information 682

Travellers with
Disabilities............. 682

Visas.................. 683

TRANSPORT 684

GETTING THERE
& AWAY 684

Air 684

Land 684

Sea 685

GETTING AROUND.......685

Air 685

Bicycle 686

Bus & Coach........... 686

Car & Motorcycle....... 686

Local Transport........ 687

Train 687

Directory A–Z

Accommodation

B&Bs

The (bed and breakfast) B&B is a great English institution. At smaller places it's pretty much a room in somebody's house; larger places may be called a 'guesthouse' (halfway between a B&B and a full hotel). Prices start from around £30 per person for a simple bedroom and shared bathroom; for around £35 to £45 per person you get a private bathroom, either down the hall or en suite.

In cities, some B&Bs are for long-term residents or people on welfare; they don't take passing tourists. In country areas, most B&Bs cater for walkers and cyclists, but some don't, so let them know if you'll be turning up with dirty boots or wheels.

When booking, check where your B&B actually is. In country areas, postal addresses include the nearest town, which may be 20 miles away – important if you're walking! Some B&B owners will pick you up by car for a small charge.

Prices Usually quoted per person, based on two people sharing a room. Single rooms for solo travellers are harder to find, and attract a 20% to 50% premium. Some B&Bs simply won't take single people (unless you pay the full double-room price), especially in summer.

Booking Advance reservations are preferred at B&Bs and are essential during popular periods. You can book many B&Bs via online agencies but rates may be cheaper if you book directly. If you haven't booked in advance, most towns have a main drag of B&Bs; those with spare rooms hang up a 'Vacancies' sign. Many B&Bs require a minimum two-night stay on weekends. Some places reduce rates for longer stays (two or three nights) midweek. If a B&B is full, owners may recommend another place nearby (possibly a private house taking occasional guests, not in tourist listings).

Food Most B&Bs serve enormous breakfasts; some offer packed lunches (around £6) and evening meals (around £15 to £20).

Bunkhouses & Camping Barns

A bunkhouse in England is a simple place, usually in country areas, with a communal sleeping area and bathroom, plus stoves for self-catering. You provide a sleeping bag and possibly cooking gear. Most charge around £12 to £15 per person per night.

Camping barns are even more basic: usually converted farm buildings. Take everything you'd need to camp except the tent. Charges are from around £6 to £10 per person.

Camping

Campsites range from farmers' fields with a tap and basic toilet, costing from £5 per person per night, to smarter affairs with hot showers and many other facilities, charging up to £15. You usually need all your own kit.

A few campsites also offer self-catering accommodation in chalets, caravans, tepees, yurts and stylish wooden camping 'pods', often dubbed 'glamping'.

If you're touring Britain with a tent or campervan (motorhome), consider joining the Camping & Caravanning Club (www.campingandcaravanningclub.co.uk), which provides up to 30% discount on its sites for an annual membership fee of £37. The club owns almost 100 campsites and lists thousands more in the invaluable

---

BOOK YOUR STAY ONLINE

For more accommodation reviews by Lonely Planet authors, check out http://lonelyplanet.com/hotels. You'll find independent reviews, as well as recommendations on the best places to stay. Best of all, you can book online.

Big Sites Book (free to members).

Hostels

There are two types of hostel in England: those run by the Youth Hostel Association (YHA; www.yha.org.uk), and independent hostels. Most are listed in the Independent Hostel Guide (www.independent hostelguide.co.uk).

Hostels can be found in rural areas, towns and cities, and are aimed at all types of traveller, young and old. Some hostels are converted cottages, country houses and even castles – often in wonderful locations. Sleeping is usually in dormitories; some hostels also have twin or four-bed rooms.

YHA HOSTELS

The simplest YHA hostels cost around £13 to £17 per person per night. Larger hostels with more facilities are £18 to £30. London's YHA hostels cost from £32. Advance bookings and payments with credit card are usually possible.

You don't have to be a member of the YHA (or another Hostelling International organisation) to stay, but most hostels charge extra if you're not a member (£3 at YHA hostels), so it's usually worth joining. Annual YHA membership costs £20; people aged under 26 and families get discounts.

Most hostel prices vary according to demand and season. Book early for a Tuesday night in May and you'll get the best rate. Book late for a weekend in August and you'll pay top price – if there's space at all. We have generally quoted the cheaper rates (in line with those listed on the YHA's website); you may find yourself paying more.

YHA hostels tend to have complicated opening times and days, especially in remote locations or out of tourist season, so check before turning up.

INDEPENDENT HOSTELS

In rural areas some independent hostels are little more than simple bunkhouses (charging around £13), or almost up to B&B standard (£20 or more). In cities, independent backpacker hostels are usually aimed at young budget travellers. Most are open 24 hours, with a lively atmosphere, a range of rooms (doubles or dorms), a bar, a cafe, wi-fi and laundry. Prices go from around £20 for a dorm bed to £40 for a bed in a private room.

Hotels

There's a massive choice of hotels in England, from small town houses to grand country mansions, from no-frills locations to boutique hideaways. At the bargain end, single/double rooms cost from £45/60. Move up the scale and you'll pay £100/150 or beyond.

If all you want is a place to put your head down, budget chain hotels can be a good option. Most are lacking in ambience, but who cares? You'll only be there for 12 hours, and for eight of them you'll be asleep. Prices vary on demand: at quiet times twin-bed rooms start from £30; at the height of the tourist season you'll pay £60 or more. Options include Ibis Hotels, Premier Inn and Travelodge.

Houseboats

A popular English holiday option is renting a houseboat on one of England's picturesque waterways, combining accommodation and transport for a few days or a week.

Pubs & Inns

As well as selling drinks, many pubs and inns offer lodging, particularly in country areas. For bed and breakfast, you'll pay from £30 per person for a basic room, around £45 for something better. An advantage for solo tourists: pubs often have single rooms.

Rental Accommodation

If you want to stay in one place, renting for a week can be ideal. Choose from neat apartments in cities or quaint old houses (always called 'cottages', whatever the size) in country areas. Cottages for four people cost between £275 and £700 in high season. Rates fall at quieter times and you may be able to rent for a long weekend.

University Accommodation

During holidays, many universities offer accommodation to visitors. You usually get a functional single bedroom, and self-catering flats are also available. Prices range from £25 to £60 per person.

Customs Regulations

Entering or leaving the UK is usually straightforward and hassle-free, save for the occasional inconvenience of long queues at passport control and security.

A referendum result in the UK in June 2016 that favoured withdrawal from the EU renders information in this section highly liable to change; it's important to check the current regulations before travel.

Customs Charges

Britain has a two-tier customs system: one for goods bought duty-free outside the EU; the other for goods bought in another EU country where tax and duty is paid. The UK's 2016 decision to leave the EU (widely known as 'Brexit') may eventually lead to a change in these arrangements, but it will be some time before the details are known.

Following is a summary of the current rules; for more details go to www.gov.uk and search for 'Bringing goods into the UK'.

Duty-free The duty-free limit for goods from outside the EU includes 200 cigarettes or equivalent in cigars, 4L of wine, 1L of spirits, 60cc of perfume and other goods worth up to £390.

Tax and duty paid There is no limit on goods from within the EU (if taxes have been paid), but customs officials use the following guidelines to distinguish personal use from commercial imports: 800 cigarettes, 200 cigars, 10L of spirits, 90L of wine and 110L of beer. Still enough to have one hell of a party.

Climate

London

°C/°F **Temp**
30/86 —
20/68 —
10/50 —
0/32 —

Rainfall Inches/mm
4.9/125
3.9/100
2.9/75
2/50
1/25
0

J F M A M J J A S O N D

Bath

°C/°F **Temp**
30/86 —
20/68 —
10/50 —
0/32 —

Rainfall Inches/mm
4.9/125
3.9/100
2.9/75
2/50
1/25
0

J F M A M J J A S O N D

York

°C/°F **Temp**
30/86 —
20/68 —
10/50 —
0/32 —

Rainfall Inches/mm
4.9/125
3.9/100
2.9/75
2/50
1/25
0

J F M A M J J A S O N D

Electricity

230V/50Hz

Emergency & Important Numbers

England (and UK) country code	☏44
International access code	☏00
Emergency (police, fire, ambulance, mountain rescue or coastguard)	☏112 or ☏999

GLBTI Travellers

England is generally a tolerant place for gay and lesbian people. London, Manchester and Brighton have flourishing gay scenes, and in other sizeable cities you'll find communities not entirely in the closet. That said, you'll still find pockets of homophobic hostility in some areas. Resources include the following:

Diva (www.divamag.co.uk)

Gay Times (www.gaytimes. co.uk)

Switchboard LGBT+ Helpline (www.switchboard.lgbt; 0300 330 0630)

Health

No vaccinations are required to travel to Britain. For more information, check with your medical provider in your own country before you travel.

Health Insurance

➡ If you're an EU citizen, a European Health Insurance Card (EHIC) – available from health centres or, in the UK, post offices – covers you for urgent medical treatment, including pre-existing medical conditions and routine maternity care. However, it will not cover costs such as being flown back home in an emergency, so private travel insurance will also be needed.

➡ Citizens from non-EU countries should find out if there is a reciprocal arrangement for free medical care between their country and the UK.

➡ If you do need health insurance, make sure you get a policy that covers you for the worst possible scenarios, including emergency flights home.

Healthcare Provision

➡ Quality medical treatment is widely available at National Health Service (NHS) hospitals throughout the country, and (much more expensively) through private medical practices.

➡ Chemists (pharmacies) can advise on minor ailments such as sore throats and earaches. In large cities, there's always at least one 24-hour chemist.

➡ For medical advice that is not an emergency you can call the NHS 111 service (phone ☏111).

Insurance

Although everyone in England receives free emergency medical treatment, regardless of nationality, travel insurance is still highly recommended. It will usually cover medical and dental consultation and treatment at private clinics, which can be quicker than NHS places – as well as the cost of any emergency flights – plus the usual stuff like loss of baggage.

Worldwide travel insurance is available at www. lonelyplanet.com/travel-insurance. You can buy, extend and claim online anytime – even if you're already on the road.

Internet Access

➡ 3G and 4G mobile broadband coverage is good in large population centres, but limited or nonexistent in rural areas. However, beware high charges for data

---

PRACTICALITIES

➡ **Newspapers** Tabloids include the *Sun*, *Daily Mail* and *Mirror*; quality 'broadsheets' include (from right to left, politically) the *Telegraph*, *Times*, *Independent* and *Guardian*.

➡ **TV** All TV in England is digital. Leading broadcasters include BBC, ITV and Channel 4. Satellite and cable-TV providers include Sky and Virgin Media.

➡ **Radio** Main BBC stations and wavelengths are Radio 1 (98–99.6 FM), Radio 2 (88–92 FM), Radio 3 (90–92.2 FM), Radio 4 (92–94.4 FM) and Radio 5 Live (909AM or 693AM). National commercial stations include non-highbrow classical specialist Classic FM (100–102 FM) and Virgin Radio UK (digital only). All are available on digital.

➡ **DVD** PAL format (incompatible with NTSC and Secam).

➡ **Smoking** Forbidden in all enclosed public places in England. Most pubs have a smoking area outside.

➡ **Weights & Measures** England uses a mix of metric and imperial measures (eg petrol is sold by the litre but beer by the pint; mountain heights are in metres but road distances in miles).

roaming – check with your mobile/cell-phone provider before travelling.

→ Most hotels, B&Bs, hostels, stations and coffee shops (even some trains and buses) have wi-fi access, charging anything from nothing to £6 per hour.

→ Internet cafes are surprisingly rare in England, especially away from big cities and tourist spots. Most charge from £1 per hour, but out in the sticks you can pay £5 per hour.

→ Public libraries often have computers with free internet access, but only for 30-minute slots, and demand is high. All the usual warnings apply about keystroke-capturing software and other security risks.

Legal Matters

→ Police have the power to detain, for up to six hours, anyone suspected of having committed an offence punishable by imprisonment (including drugs offences). Police have the right to search anyone they suspect of possessing drugs.

→ Illegal drugs are widely available, especially in clubs. Cannabis possession is a criminal offence; punishment for carrying a small amount may be a warning, a fine or imprisonment. Dealers face stiffer penalties, as do people caught with other drugs.

→ On buses and trains (including the London Underground), people without a valid ticket are fined on the spot (£80,

reduced to £40 if you pay within 21 days).

Money

The currency of Britain is the pound sterling (£). Paper money (notes) comes in £5, £10, £20 and £50 denominations. Some shops don't accept £50 notes because fakes circulate.

Other currencies are very rarely accepted, except at some gift shops in London, which may take euros, US dollars, yen and other major currencies.

ATMs

ATMs (usually called 'cash machines' in England) are common in cities and even small towns. Cash withdrawals from some ATMs may be subject to a small charge, but most are free. If you're not from the UK, your home bank will likely charge you for withdrawing money overseas. Watch out for tampered ATMs; one ruse by scammers is to attach a card-reader or minicamera.

Credit & Debit Cards

Visa and MasterCard are widely accepted in England, except at some smaller B&Bs, which take cash or cheque only. Other credit cards, including Amex, are not so widely accepted. Most businesses will assume your card is 'Chip and PIN' enabled (using a PIN instead of signing). If it isn't, you should be able to sign instead, but some places may not accept your card.

Money Changers

Cities and larger towns have banks and exchange bureaux

for changing your money into pounds. Check rates first; some bureaux offer poor rates or levy outrageous commissions. You can also change money at some post offices – very handy in country areas, and exchange rates are fair.

Tipping

Restaurants Around 10% in restaurants and tearooms with table service, 15% at smarter restaurants. Tips may be added to your bill as a 'service charge'. Not compulsory.

Pubs & Bars Not expected if you order drinks (or food) and pay at the bar; usually 10% if you order at the table and your meal is brought to you.

Taxis Usually 10%, or rounded up to the nearest pound, especially in London.

Opening Hours

Banks

→ 9.30am to 4pm or 5pm Monday to Friday; some open 9.30am to 1pm Saturday.

Cafes & Restaurants

Most restaurants and cafes are open for lunch or dinner or both.

→ Standard hours for cafes are 9am to 5pm. Most cafes open daily.

→ In cities, some cafes open at 7am for breakfast, and shut at 6pm or later.

→ In country areas, some cafes open until 7pm or later in the summer. In winter months hours are reduced; some cafes close completely from October to Easter.

→ Standard hours for restaurants: lunch is noon to 3pm, dinner 6pm to 9pm or 10pm (to midnight or later in cities). Most restaurants open daily; some close Sunday evening or all day Monday.

EATING PRICE RANGES

The following price ranges refer to a main dish.

£ less than £10 (London £12)

££ £10 to £20 (London £12 to £25)

£££ more than £20 (London £25)

⇒ A few restaurants open for breakfast (usually 9am), but mainly cafes do this.

Museums & Sights

⇒ Large museums and sights usually open daily.

⇒ Some smaller places open Saturday and Sunday but close Monday and/or Tuesday.

⇒ Smaller places open daily in high season but operate weekends only or completely close in low season.

Post Offices

⇒ 9am to 5pm (5.30pm or 6pm in cities) Monday to Friday.

⇒ 9am to 12.30pm Saturday; main branches to 5pm.

Pubs & Bars

⇒ 11am to 11pm Monday to Thursday, 11am to 1am Friday and Saturday, 12.30pm to 11pm Sunday.

Shops

⇒ 9am to 5.30pm (or 6pm in cities) Monday to Saturday, and often 11am to 5pm Sunday. London and other cities have convenience stores open 24/7.

⇒ In smaller towns and country areas shops often shut for lunch (normally 1pm to 2pm) and on Wednesday or Thursday afternoon.

Post

The British postal service is generally efficient and reliable. Information on post-office locations and postage rates can be found at www.postoffice.co.uk.

Public Holidays

Holidays for the whole of Britain:

New Year's Day 1 January

Easter March/April (Good Friday to Easter Monday inclusive)

May Day First Monday in May

Spring Bank Holiday Last Monday in May

SCHOOL HOLIDAYS

Roads get busy and hotel prices go up during school holidays. Exact dates vary from year to year and region to region, but are roughly as follows:

Easter Holiday Week before and week after Easter.

Summer Holiday Third week of July to first week of September.

Christmas Holiday Mid-December to first week of January.

There are also three, week-long 'half-term' school holidays – usually late February (or early March), late May and late October. These are staggered, so the whole country is not on holiday during the same week.

Summer Bank Holiday Last Monday in August

Christmas Day 25 December

Boxing Day 26 December

If a public holiday falls on a weekend, the nearest Monday is usually taken instead. Most businesses and banks close on official public holidays (hence the quaint term 'bank holiday').

On public holidays, some small museums and places of interest close, but larger attractions have their busiest times. If a place closes on Sunday, it'll probably be shut on bank holidays as well.

Virtually everything – attractions, shops, banks, offices – closes on Christmas Day, although pubs are open at lunchtime. There's usually no public transport on Christmas Day, and a very minimal service on Boxing Day.

Safe Travel

England is a remarkably safe country, but crime is not unknown in London and other cities.

⇒ Watch out for pickpockets and hustlers in crowded areas popular with tourists, such as around Westminster Bridge in London.

⇒ When travelling by tube, tram or urban train services at night, choose a carriage containing other people.

⇒ Many town centres can be rowdy on Friday and Saturday nights when the pubs and clubs are emptying.

⇒ Unlicensed minicabs – a bloke with a car earning money on the side – operate in large cities, and are worth avoiding unless you know what you're doing.

Telephone

Mobile Phones

The UK uses the GSM 900/1800 network, which covers the rest of Europe, Australia and New Zealand, but isn't compatible with the North American GSM 1900. Most modern mobiles can function on both networks, but check before you leave home.

ROAMING CHARGES

The UK's decision to leave the EU (aka 'Brexit') means that British networks will eventually be able to charge whatever they want for roaming on the Continent, and EU network subscribers will have to pay to roaming fees when visiting the UK. However, the UK will remain subject to EU laws for two years after the triggering of Article 50, which may not happen until 2017, so the EU roaming agreement should remain in force until at least 2019.

Other international roaming charges can be high, and you'll probably find it cheaper to get a UK number. This is easily done by buying a SIM card (from £5 including calling credit) and sticking it in your phone. Your phone may be locked to your home network, however, so you'll have to either get it unlocked, or buy a cheap pay-as-you-go phone along with your SIM card (from £10 including calling credit).

Pay-as-you-go phones can be recharged by buying vouchers from shops.

Phone Codes

Dialling to the UK Dial your country's international access code then ☑44 (the UK country code), then the area code (dropping the first 0) followed by the telephone number.

Dialling from the UK The international access code is ☑00; dial this, then add the code of the country you wish to dial.

Reverse-charge (Collect) International Call Dial ☑155 for the operator. It's an expensive option, but not for the caller.

Area Codes in the UK No standard format or length, eg Edinburgh ☑0131, London ☑020, Ambleside ☑015394.

Directory Assistance A host of agencies offer this service – numbers include ☑118 118, ☑118 500 and ☑118 811 – but fees are extortionate (around £6 for a 45-second call); search online for free at www.thephonebook.bt.com.

Mobile Phones Codes usually begin with ☑07.

Free Calls Numbers starting with ☑0800 or ☑0808 are free.

Call Charges Details here: www.gov.uk/call-charges

National Operator ☑100

International Operator ☑155

Time

Britain is on GMT/UTC. The clocks go forward one hour for 'summer time' at the end of March, and go back at the end of October. The 24-hour clock is used for transport timetables.

CITY	TIME DIFFERENCE
Los Angeles	8hr behind
Mumbai	5½hr ahead Nov-Feb, 4½hr Mar-Oct
New York	5hr behind
Paris, Berlin, Rome	1hr ahead
Sydney	9hr ahead Apr-Sep, 10hr Oct, 11hr Nov-Mar
Tokyo	9hr ahead Nov-Feb, 8hr Mar-Oct

Toilets

Public toilets in England are generally clean and modern, but cutbacks in public spending mean that many facilities have been closed down. Your best bet is to use the toilets in free-to-enter museums; those in railway and bus stations often charge a fee (from 20p to 50p), and most pubs and restaurants stipulate that their toilets are for customers only.

Tourist Information

Most English cities and towns have a tourist information centre or visitor information centre – for ease we've called all these places 'tourist offices'.

Tourist offices have helpful staff, books and maps for sale, leaflets to give away, and advice on things to see or do. Some can also assist with booking accommodation. Some are run by national parks and often have small exhibits about the area.

Most tourist offices keep regular business hours; in quiet areas they close from October to March, while in popular areas they open daily year-round. In recent years cost-cutting has seen many smaller tourist offices close down; some have been replaced with 'tourist information points' – racks of leaflets and maps in locations such as public libraries and town halls.

Before leaving home, check the comprehensive website of England's official tourist board, Visit England (www.visitengland.com), covering all the angles of national tourism, with links to numerous other sites.

Travellers with Disabilities

All new buildings have wheelchair access, and even hotels in grand old country houses

---

often have lifts, ramps and other facilities. Hotels and B&Bs in historic buildings are often harder to adapt, so you'll have less choice here.

Modern city buses and trams have low floors for easy access, but few have conductors who can lend a hand when you're getting on or off. Many taxis take wheelchairs, or just have more room in the back.

For long-distance travel, coaches may present problems if you can't walk, but the main operator, National Express (www.nationalexpress.com), has wheelchair-friendly coaches on many routes. For details, ring its dedicated Disabled **Passenger Travel Helpline** (☎0371 781 8181).

On intercity trains there's more room and better facilities, and usually station staff around; just have a word and they'll be happy to help out. A Disabled Person's Railcard (www.disabledpersons-railcard.co.uk) costs £20 and gets you 33% off most train fares.

Download Lonely Planet's free Accessible Travel guide from http://lptravel.to/Ac cessibleTravel.

Useful organisations:

Disability Rights UK (www.disabilityrightsuk.org) Published titles include a *Holiday Guide*. Other services include a key for 7000 public disabled toilets across the UK.

Good Access Guide (www.goodaccessguide.co.uk)

Tourism For All (www.tourism forall.org.uk)

Visas

➡ If you're a citizen of the European Economic Area (EEA) nations or Switzerland,

---

HERITAGE ORGANISATIONS

A highlight of a journey through England is visiting the numerous castles and historic sites that pepper the country. Membership of a heritage organisation gets you free admission (usually a good saving) as well as information handbooks and so on.

National Trust (NT; www.nationaltrust.org.uk) A charity protecting historic buildings and land with scenic importance across England and Wales. Annual membership is £58 (discounts for under-26s and families). A Touring Pass allows free entry to NT properties for one/two weeks (£25/30 per person); families and couples get cheaper rates.

English Heritage (EH; www.english-heritage.org.uk) State-funded organisation responsible for numerous historic sites. Annual membership is £49 (couples and seniors get discounts). An Overseas Visitors Pass allows free entry to most sites for nine/16 days for £25/30 (cheaper rates for couples and families).

---

you don't need a visa to enter or work in the UK – you can enter using your national identity card.

➡ Visa regulations are always subject to change, and immigration restriction is currently big news in the UK, so it's essential to check with your local British embassy, high commission or consulate before leaving home.

➡ At the time of research, if you're a citizen of Australia, Canada, New Zealand, Japan, Israel, the USA and several other countries, you can stay for up to six months (no visa required), but are not allowed to work.

➡ Nationals of many countries, including South Africa, will need to obtain a visa: for more info, see www.gov.uk/check-uk-visa.

➡ The Youth Mobility Scheme (www.gov.uk/tier-5-youth-mobility),

for Australian, Canadian, Japanese, Hong Kong, Monégasque, New Zealand, South Korean and Taiwanese citizens aged 18 to 30, allows working visits of up to two years, but must be applied for in advance.

➡ Commonwealth citizens with a UK-born parent may be eligible for a Certificate of Entitlement to the Right of Abode, which entitles them to live and work in the UK.

➡ Commonwealth citizens with a UK-born grandparent could qualify for a UK Ancestry Employment Certificate, allowing them to work full time for up to five years in the UK.

➡ British immigration authorities have always been tough; dress neatly and carry proof that you have sufficient funds with which to support yourself. A credit card and/or an onward ticket will help.

Transport

GETTING THERE & AWAY

Most overseas visitors reach England by air. As London is a global transport hub, it's easy to fly to England from just about anywhere. The massive growth of budget ('no-frills') airlines has increased the number of routes – and reduced the fares – between England and other countries in Europe.

The other main option for travel between England and mainland Europe is ferry, either port-to-port or combined with a long-distance bus trip, although journeys can be long and financial savings not huge compared with budget airfares.

International trains are much more comfortable and a 'green' option; the Channel Tunnel allows direct rail services between England, France and Belgium, with onward connections to many other European destinations.

Flights, cars and rail tickets can be booked online at lonelyplanet.com/bookings.

Air

The national carrier is British Airways (www.britishairways.com).

London Airports

Heathrow (www.heathrow.com) The UK's main airport for international flights; often chaotic and crowded. About 15 miles west of central London.

Gatwick (www.gatwickairport.com) Britain's number-two airport, mainly for international flights, 30 miles south of central London.

Stansted (www.stanstedairport.com) About 35 miles north-east of central London, mainly handling charter and budget European flights.

Luton (www.london-luton.co.uk) Some 35 miles north of central London, well-known as a holiday-flight airport.

London City (www.londoncityairport.com) A few miles east of central London, specialising in flights to/from European and other UK airports.

Regional Airports

Some planes on European and long-haul routes avoid London and use major regional airports including Manchester and Newcastle. Smaller regional airports such as Southampton and Birmingham are served by flights to and from Continental Europe and Ireland.

Land

Bus & Coach

You can easily get between England and other European countries via long-distance bus (called 'coach' in England). The international network Eurolines (www.eurolines.com) connects a huge number of destinations; you

---

CLIMATE CHANGE & TRAVEL

Every form of transport that relies on carbon-based fuel generates CO_2, the main cause of human-induced climate change. Modern travel is dependent on aeroplanes, which might use less fuel per kilometre per person than most cars but travel much greater distances. The altitude at which aircraft emit gases (including CO_2) and particles also contributes to their climate change impact. Many websites offer 'carbon calculators' that allow people to estimate the carbon emissions generated by their journey and, for those who wish to do so, to offset the impact of the greenhouse gases emitted with contributions to portfolios of climate-friendly initiatives throughout the world. Lonely Planet offsets the carbon footprint of all staff and author travel.

can buy tickets online via one of the national operators.

Services to/from England are also operated by National Express (www.nationalexpress.com). Sample journey times to/from London include Amsterdam (12 hours), Barcelona (24 hours), Dublin (12 hours) and Paris (eight hours).

If you book early, and can be flexible with timings (ie travel when few other people want to), you can get some very good deals. For example, between London and Paris or Amsterdam from about £25 one way (although paying £35 to £45 is more usual).

Train
CHANNEL TUNNEL PASSENGER SERVICE

High-speed Eurostar (www.eurostar.com) passenger services shuttle at least 10 times daily between London and Paris (2½ hours) or Brussels (two hours). Buy tickets from travel agencies, major train stations or the Eurostar website.

The normal one-way fare between London and Paris/Brussels costs around £145; advance booking and off-peak travel gets cheaper fares as low as £29 one way.

CHANNEL TUNNEL CAR SERVICE

Drivers use Eurotunnel (www.eurotunnel.com). At Folkestone in England or Calais in France, you drive onto a train, get carried through the tunnel and drive off at the other end.

Trains run about four times an hour from 6am to 10pm, then hourly through the night. Loading and unloading takes an hour; the journey lasts 35 minutes.

Book in advance online or pay on the spot. The standard one-way fare for a car and up to nine passengers is between £75 and £100 depending on time of day; promotional fares often bring it down to £59 or less.

TRAIN & FERRY CONNECTIONS

As well as Eurostar, many 'normal' trains run between England and mainland Europe. You buy one ticket, but get off the train at the port, walk onto a ferry, then get another train on the other side.

Routes include Amsterdam–London (via Hook of Holland and Harwich). Travelling between Ireland and England, the main train-ferry-train route is Dublin to London, via Dun Laoghaire and Holyhead (Wales). Ferries also run between Rosslare and Fishguard or Pembroke (Wales), with train connections on either side.

Sea
Ferry Routes

The main ferry routes between England and other European countries include the following:

➡ Dover to Boulogne (France)

➡ Dover to Calais (France)

➡ Harwich to Hook of Holland (Netherlands)

➡ Hull to Rotterdam (Netherlands)

➡ Hull to Zeebrugge (Belgium)

➡ Liverpool to Dublin (Ireland)

➡ Newcastle to Amsterdam (Netherlands)

➡ Newhaven to Dieppe (France)

➡ Portsmouth to Santander (Spain)

➡ Portsmouth to Bilbao (Spain)

Ferry Fares

Most ferry operators offer flexible fares, meaning great bargains at quiet times of day or year. For example, short cross-channel routes such as Dover to Calais or Boulogne can be as low as £45 for a car plus two passengers, although around £75 to £105 is more likely. If you're a foot passenger, or cycling, there's less need to book ahead; fares on short crossings cost about £30 to £50 each way.

Ferry Booking

You can book directly with one of the ferry operators listed here, or use the very handy www.directferries.co.uk, a single site covering all sea-ferry routes, plus Eurotunnel.

Brittany Ferries (www.brittanyferries.com)

DFDS Seaways (www.dfdsseaways.co.uk)

P&O Ferries (www.poferries.com)

Stena Line (www.stenaline.com)

GETTING AROUND

Air

England's domestic airline companies include British Airways, FlyBe/Loganair, EasyJet and Ryanair. If you're really pushed for time, flights on longer routes across England (eg Exeter or Southampton to Newcastle) are handy, although you miss the glorious scenery in between. On some shorter routes (eg London to Newcastle, or Manchester to Newquay) trains compare favourably with planes on time, once airport downtime is factored in. On costs, you might get a bargain airfare, but trains can be cheaper if you buy tickets in advance.

Bicycle

London

London is famous for its **Santander Cycles** (☏0343 222 6666; www.tfl.gov.uk/modes/cycling/santander-cycles). Bikes can be hired on the spot from automatic docking stations. For more information visit the website. Other rental options in the capital are listed at www.lcc.org.uk (under Advice/Bike Shops).

Around the Country

The nextbike (www.nextbike.co.uk) bike-sharing scheme currently has stations in Bath, Exeter, Oxford and Coventry, while York and Cambridge also have plentiful bike-rental options. Bikes can also be hired in national parks or forestry sites now primarily used for leisure activities, such as Kielder Water in Northumberland and Grizedale Forest in the Lake District. In some areas, disused railway lines are now bike routes, notably the Peak District in Derbyshire. Rental rates start at about £12 per day, or £20 and up for a quality machine.

Bikes on Trains

Bicycles can be taken free of charge on most local urban trains (although they may not be allowed at peak times when the trains are crowded with commuters), and on shorter trips in rural areas on a first-come, first-served basis – there may be space limits.

Bikes can be carried on long-distance train journeys free of charge, but advance booking is required for most conventional bikes. (Folding bikes can be carried on pretty much any train at any time.) In theory, this shouldn't be too much trouble as most long-distance rail trips are best bought in advance anyway, but you have to go a long way down the path of booking your seat before you start booking your bike – only to find space isn't available. A better course of action is to buy in advance at a major rail station, where the booking clerk can help you through the options.

A final warning: when railways are undergoing repair work, cancelled trains are replaced by buses – and they won't take bikes.

The PlusBike scheme provides all the information you need for travelling by train with a bike. Leaflets are available at major stations, or downloadable from www.nationalrail.co.uk/118390.aspx.

Bus & Coach

If you're on a tight budget, long-distance buses (coaches) are nearly always the cheapest way to get around, although they're also the slowest – sometimes by a considerable margin. Many towns have separate stations for local buses and long-distance coaches; make sure you go to the right one!

National Express (www.nationalexpress.com) The main coach operator, with a wide network and frequent services between main centres. Fares vary: they're cheaper if you book in advance and travel at quieter times, and more expensive if you buy your ticket on the spot and it's Friday afternoon. As a guide, a 200-mile trip (eg London to York) will cost £15 to £25 if you book a few days in advance.

Megabus (www.megabus.com) Operates a budget coach service serving more than 100 destinations around the country. Go at a quiet time, book early and your ticket will be very cheap. Book later, for a busy time and... You get the picture.

Passes & Discounts

National Express offers discount passes to full-time students and under-26s, called Young Persons Coachcards. They cost £10 and give you 30% off standard adult fares. Also available are coachcards for people over 60, families and disabled travellers.

For touring the country, National Express offers Brit Xplorer passes, allowing unlimited travel for seven/14/28 days (£79/139/219). You don't need to book journeys in advance: if the coach has a spare seat, you can take it.

Car & Motorcycle

Travelling by car or motorbike around England means you can be independent and flexible, and reach remote places. Downsides for drivers include traffic jams, the high price of fuel and high parking costs in cities.

Car Rental

Compared with many countries (especially the USA), hire rates are expensive in Britain; the smallest cars start from about £130 per week, and it's around £190 and upwards per week for a medium car. All rates include insurance and unlimited mileage, and can rise at busy times (or drop at quiet times).

Some main players:

Avis (www.avis.co.uk)

Budget (www.budget.co.uk)

Europcar (www.europcar.co.uk)

Sixt (www.sixt.co.uk)

Thrifty (www.thrifty.co.uk)

Another option is to look online for small, local car-hire companies in Britain that can undercut the international franchises. Generally those in cities are cheaper than in rural areas. Using a rental-broker or comparison site such as UK Car Hire (www.ukcarhire.net) or Kayak (www.kayak.com) can also help find bargains.

Motorhome Rental

Hiring a motorhome or campervan (£650 to £1100 a week) is more expensive than hiring a car, but saves on accommodation costs and gives almost unlimited freedom. Sites to check include the following:

Just Go (www.justgo.com)

Wild Horizon (www.wildhorizon.co.uk)

Insurance

It's illegal to drive a car or ride a motorbike in England without (at least) third-party insurance. This will be included with all rental cars. If you're bringing your own car, you will need to arrange this.

Parking

Many cities have short-stay and long-stay car parks; the latter are cheaper though may be less convenient. 'Park & Ride' systems allow you to park on the edge of the city then ride to the centre on frequent nonstop buses for an all-in-one price.

Yellow lines (single or double) along the edge of the road indicate restrictions. Nearby signs spell out when you can and can't park. In London and other big cities, traffic wardens operate with efficiency; if you park on the yellow lines at the wrong time, your car will be clamped or towed away, and it'll cost you £130 or more to get driving again. In some cities there are also red lines, which mean no stopping at all. Ever.

Roads

Motorways and main A-roads deliver you quickly from one end of the country to another. Lesser A-roads, B-roads and minor roads are much more scenic – ideal for car or motorcycle touring. You can't travel fast, but you won't care.

Speed limits are usually 30mph (48km/h) in built-up areas, 60mph (96km/h) on main roads and 70mph (112km/h) on motorways and most (but not all) dual carriageways.

Road Rules

A foreign driving licence is valid in Britain for up to 12 months after entering the country.

Drink-driving is taken very seriously; you're allowed a maximum blood-alcohol level of 80mg/100mL (0.08%) – campaigners want it reduced to 50mg/100mL (0.05%), in line with most European countries (including Scotland).

Some other important rules:

➡ Drive on the left (!).

➡ Wear seatbelts in cars.

➡ Wear helmets on motorcycles.

➡ Give way to your right at junctions and roundabouts.

➡ Always use the left lane on motorways and dual carriageways unless overtaking (although so many people ignore this rule, you'd think it didn't exist).

➡ Don't use a mobile phone while driving unless it's fully hands-free (another rule frequently flouted).

Local Transport

English cities usually have good public-transport systems – a combination of bus, train and tram – often run by a confusing number of separate companies. Tourist offices can provide maps and information.

Local Bus

There are good local bus networks year-round in cities and towns. Buses also run in some rural areas year-round, although timetables are designed to serve schools and businesses, so there aren't many noon and weekend services (and they may stop running during school holidays), or buses may link local villages to a market town on only one day each week.

In tourist areas (especially national parks) there are frequent services from Easter to September. However, it's always worth double-checking at a tourist office before planning your day's activities around a bus that may not actually be running.

LOCAL BUS PASSES

If you're taking a few local bus rides in one area, day passes (with names like Day Rover, Wayfarer or Explorer) are cheaper than buying several single tickets. Often they can be bought on your first bus, and may include local rail services. It's always worth asking ticket clerks or bus drivers about your options.

Taxi

There are two sorts of taxi in England: those with meters that can be hailed in the street; and minicabs, which are cheaper but can only be called by phone. Unlicensed minicabs operate in some cities.

In London, most taxis are the famous 'black cabs' (some with advertising livery in other colours), which charge by distance and time. Depending on the time of day, a 1-mile journey takes five to 10 minutes and costs £6 to £9. Longer journeys are proportionally cheaper.

Apps such as Uber (www.uber.com) or Kabbee (www.kabbee.com) allow you to book a minicab in double-quick time.

In rural areas, taxis need to be called by phone; the best place to find the local taxi's phone number is the local pub. Fares are £3 to £5 per mile.

Traintaxi (www.traintaxi.co.uk) is a portal site that helps 'bridge the final gap' between the train station and your hotel or other final destination.

Train

For long-distance travel around England, trains are generally faster and more comfortable than coaches but can be more expensive, although with discount tickets they're competitive – and often take you through beautiful countryside. The English like to moan about their trains, but around 85%

run on time. The other 15% that get delayed or cancelled mostly impact commuter services rather than long-distance journeys.

Train Operators

About 20 different companies operate train services in England, while Network Rail operates tracks and stations. For some passengers this system can be confusing at first, but information and ticket-buying services are mostly centralised. If you have to change trains, or use two or more train operators, you still buy one ticket – valid for the whole journey. The main railcards and passes are also accepted by all train operators.

Where more than one train operator services the same route, eg York to Newcastle, a ticket purchased from one company may not be valid on trains run by another. So if you miss the train you originally booked, it's worth checking which later services your ticket will be valid for.

Information

Your first stop should be National Rail Enquiries (www.nationalrail.co.uk), the nationwide timetable and fare information service. Its website advertises special offers and has real-time links to station departure boards and downloadable maps of the rail network.

Tickets & Reservations
BUYING TICKETS

Once you've found the journey you need on the National Rail Enquiries website, links take you to the relevant train operator to buy the ticket. This can be mailed to you (UK addresses only) or collected at the station on the day of travel from automatic machines. There's usually no booking fee on top of the ticket price.

You can also use a centralised ticketing service to buy your train ticket. These cover all train services in a single site, and add a small booking fee on top of every ticket price. The main players include the following:

QJump (www.qjump.co.uk)

Rail Easy (www.raileasy.co.uk)

Train Line (www.thetrainline.com)

To use operator or centralised ticketing websites, you always have to state a preferred time and day of travel, even if you don't mind when you go, but you can change it as you go through the process, and with a little delving around you can find some real bargains.

You can also buy train tickets on the spot at stations, which is fine for short journeys (under about 50 miles), but discount tickets for longer trips are usually not available and these must be bought in advance by phone or online.

COSTS

For longer journeys, on-the-spot fares are usually available, but tickets are much cheaper if bought in advance. The earlier you book, the cheaper it gets. You can also save if you travel off-peak. Advance purchase usually gets a reserved seat, too.

Whichever operator you travel with and wherever you buy tickets, these are the three main fare types:

Anytime Buy any time, travel any time – usually the most expensive option.

Off-peak Buy ticket any time, travel off-peak (what is off-peak depends on the journey).

Advance Buy ticket in advance, travel only on specific trains – usually the cheapest option.

For an idea of the price difference, an Anytime single ticket from London to York will cost £112 or more, an Off-peak around £56, with an Advance around £36 to £46, and possibly less if you book

early enough or don't mind arriving at midnight.

The cheapest fares are nonrefundable, so if you miss your train you'll have to buy a new ticket.

Train Passes
DISCOUNT PASSES

If you're staying in England for a while, passes known as Railcards (www.railcard.co.uk) are available:

16-25 Railcard For those aged 16 to 25, or a full-time UK student.

Family & Friends Railcard Covers up to four adults and four children travelling together.

Senior Railcard For anyone over 60.

Railcards cost £30 (valid for one year, available from major stations or online) and get a 33% discount on most train fares, except those already heavily discounted. With the Family card, adults get 33% and children get 60% discounts, so the fee is easily repaid in a couple of journeys.

LOCAL & REGIONAL PASSES

Local train passes usually cover rail networks around a city (many include bus travel too).

If you're concentrating your travels on southeast England (eg London to Dover, Weymouth, Cambridge or Oxford), a Network Railcard (www.network-railcard.co.uk) covers up to four adults and up to four children travelling together outside peak times (£30 per year).

NATIONAL PASSES

For countrywide travel, BritRail (www.britrail.net) passes are available for visitors from overseas. They must be bought in your country of origin (not in England) from a specialist travel agency. Available in different versions (eg England only; all Britain; UK and the Republic of Ireland) for periods from four to 30 days.

Behind the Scenes

SEND US YOUR FEEDBACK

We love to hear from travellers – your comments keep us on our toes and help make our books better. Our well-travelled team reads every word on what you loved or loathed about this book. Although we cannot reply individually to your submissions, we always guarantee that your feedback goes straight to the appropriate authors, in time for the next edition. Each person who sends us information is thanked in the next edition – the most useful submissions are rewarded with a selection of digital PDF chapters.

Visit **lonelyplanet.com/contact** to submit your updates and suggestions or to ask for help. Our award-winning website also features inspirational travel stories, news and discussions.

Note: We may edit, reproduce and incorporate your comments in Lonely Planet products such as guidebooks, websites and digital products, so let us know if you don't want your comments reproduced or your name acknowledged. For a copy of our privacy policy visit lonelyplanet.com/privacy.

OUR READERS

Many thanks to the travellers who used the last edition and wrote to us with helpful hints, useful advice and interesting anecdotes:

Edward Jayamaha, Elaine Snider, Hugh Rooney, Jenn Nelson, John Pattison, Julie Woods, Marcus Gomm, Vivien Palcic, Yvonne Hefford

WRITER THANKS
Belinda Dixon

Researching a place is a real joint effort. It's the result of B&B, bar and hotel staff who share their recommendations; tourist office workers who share their knowledge; random strangers who share their time and countless kindnesses. Huge thanks to all. And, again to James Smart for the gig, LP's behind the scenes teams, and fellow authors for humour, wisdom and travellers' tales.

Oliver Berry

Thanks to James Smart for giving me the gig and for guidance and support along the way; to Kate Ardron, Justin Foulkes, Dave Jones, Kate Whinney, Grace Hickock and Sarah Fox for their tips and suggestions; to the team at Wild Card PR and Watergate Bay for north coast adventures; and to Susie and Gracie Berry as always for keeping the home fires burning. Special thanks to Rosie Hillier for accompanying me on my southwest adventures and for never failing to make me smile.

Fionn Davenport

A big thanks to all my new friends in Manchester for their sterling efforts in getting up to speed with an ever-changing city. Thanks to Laura for accompanying me on my research trips and to the editors at Lonely Planet who helped give shape to my scratchings.

Marc Di Duca

Big thanks to all who helped me throughout the Southeast, especially staff at the tourist offices in Sandwich, Eastbourne and Rye. Thanks also to my wife Tanya and sons Taras and Kirill for accompanying on some long days of research.

Damian Harper

Gratitude to all those people who offered assistance along the way and came up with tips and ideas: Fiona Jenkins, James Munroe, Jon Tyler, Daisy Harper, Amy Williams, Arlene Fraser, Sarah Andrews, Timothy Benjamin and Emma Rosalind. Thanks (and apologies) to anyone I may have overlooked.

Catherine Le Nevez

Cheers first and foremost to Julian, and to all of the locals, fellow travellers and tourism professionals who provided insights, inspiration and good times, especially to Ade Andrews. Huge thanks too, to Destination Editor James Smart,

Senior Cartographer Mark Griffiths and everyone at LP. As ever, *merci encore* to my parents, brother, *belle-sœur* and *neveu*.

Isabella Noble

Cheers to everyone who helped out on the road. Big thanks to my talented co-authors, especially fellow Oxbridger Belinda Dixon for the 'healthy' competition. Thanks also to Ellie, Cathy, Rose and David in the Cotswolds; Becky, Doug, Ali and Christine in Oxford; and Elly for perfect Michelin-starred dining company. Extra special thanks to my favourite research assistants Sarah, Jack, Dan, Andrew and Paps.

ACKNOWLEDGEMENTS

Climate map data adapted from Peel MC, Finlayson BL & McMahon TA (2007) 'Updated World Map of the Köppen-Geiger Climate Classification', Hydrology and Earth System Sciences, 11, 163344.

Cover photograph: St Ives, Cornwall, Pietro Canali/4Corners.

Illustrations: pp76-7 & pp620-1 by Javier Zarracina; pp98-9 by Javier Zarracina and Michael Weldon.

THIS BOOK

This 9th edition of Lonely Planet's *England* guidebook was researched and written by Belinda Dixon, Oliver Berry, Fionn Davenport, Marc Di Duca, Damian Harper, Catherine Le Nevez, Isabella Noble and Neil Wilson. The previous edition was also written by Neil, Belinda, Oliver, Fionn, Marc, Damian and Catherine, along with Peter Dragicevich.

This guidebook was produced by the following:

Destination Editor James Smart

Product Editors Kate Kiely, Kate Chapman

Senior Cartographer Mark Griffiths

Book Designer Wendy Wright

Assisting Editors Imogen Bannister, Melanie Dankel, Andrea Dobbin, Gabby Innes, Helen Koehne, Kellie Langdon, Kristin Odijk, Charlotte Orr, Vicki Smith, Fionnuala Twomey

Assisting Cartographer Valentina Kremenchutskaya

Assisting Book Designer Virginia Moreno

Cover Researcher Naomi Parker

Thanks to Cheree Broughton, Dan Corbett, Joel Cotterell, Sasha Drew, Martin Heng, Liz Heynes, Bella Li, Jenna Myers, Claire Naylor, Karyn Noble, Martine Power, Kirsten Rawlings, Kat Rowan, Ross Taylor, Tony Wheeler

Index

A

abbeys, priories & monasteries, *see also* churches & cathedrals
Abbey Gardens 373
Bath Abbey 305-6
Battle Abbey 510
Cartmel Priory 597
Fountains Abbey & Studley Royal 498
Glastonbury Abbey 316-17
Great Malvern Priory 416
Hailes Abbey 202
Kirkham Priory 491
Lacock Abbey 259
Lindisfarne Priory 630
Priory Church 558
Rievaulx Abbey 499
St Nicholas Priory 271
Tynemouth Priory 613
Wenlock Priory 428-9
Westminster Abbey 58-9
Whitby Abbey 502
accommodation 22, 676-8, *see also individual locations*
activities 29-33, 39-45, 585, **584-5**, *see also* bird-watching, boating, coasteering, diving, horseriding, kayaking & canoeing, pony trekking, rock climbing, sailing, SUPing, surfing, swimming, walking, windsurfing
air travel 684
airports 684
Albert Dock 550-1
Aldeburgh 376-7
Alfred the Great 638
Alnwick 626-7
Ambleside 574-7

amusement parks
Alton Towers 411
Blackgang Chine 236-7
Blackpool Pleasure Beach 556
Dreamland 150
Heights of Abraham 461
aquariums
Blue Planet Aquarium 545
Blue Reef Aquarium 325
Bristol Aquarium 297
Deep, the 526
Ilfracombe Aquarium 292
Lakes Aquarium 569
London Sea Life Aquarium 81
National Marine Aquarium 281-2
National Sea Life Centre 394
Sea Life 247
Sea Life Sanctuary 494
ArcelorMittal Orbit 96
archaeological sites
Avebury Stone Circle 260
Belas Knap Long Barrow 202
Maiden Castle 244
Old Sarum 255
Silbury Hill 260
Stonehenge 11, 256-8, **257**, **10**
Sutton Hoo 374
Uley Bury 204
West Kennet Long Barrow 260-1
architecture 24, 655-9
Museum of Bath Architecture 306
Royal Crescent 306
area codes 21, 682
Arlington Row 192
art galleries & museums 27
Abbot Hall Art Gallery 595
Arnolfini 297
BALTIC - Centre for Contemporary Art 607-8

Barbara Hepworth Museum 328
Barber Institute of Fine Arts 396
Beatrix Potter Gallery 579
Birmingham Museum & Art Gallery 393
Brighton Museum & Art Gallery 165-7
Bristol Museum & Art Gallery 297
Christ Church Picture Gallery 183
Ferens Art Gallery 526
Graves Gallery 524
Hastings Museum & Art Gallery 161
Hayward Gallery 81
Hepworth Wakefield 520
Herbert Art Gallery & Museum 403
Holburne Museum 307
Ikon Gallery 393-4
Jerwood Gallery 161
Laing Art Gallery 606
Laurel & Hardy Museum 597
Leeds Art Gallery 515-16
Manchester Art Gallery 533-4
Manx Museum & National Art Gallery 561-2
Market House 420
National Gallery 68-9
National Portrait Gallery 69
New Walk Museum & Art Gallery 453
Nottingham Contemporary 437
Pallant House Gallery 172-3
Penlee House Gallery & Museum 334
Potteries Museum & Art Gallery 414
Royal Academy of Arts 69
Saatchi Gallery 83

Sainsbury Centre for Visual Arts 380
Tate Britain 79
Tate Liverpool 551
Tate Modern 78, **26**
Tate St Ives 328
Towner Art Gallery 162
Turner Contemporary 150
Usher Gallery 444
Walker Art Gallery 549-50
Wedgwood Visitor Centre 414
White Cube Bermondsey 81
Wordsworth Museum & Art Gallery 577-8
York City Art Gallery 24, 485
Yorkshire Sculpture Park 520
arts 634, 665-71
arts festivals
Cambridge Shakespeare Festival 361
Grassington Festival 509
King's Lynn Festival 388
Latitude Festival 377
Manchester International Festival 537
Royal Academy Summer Exhibition 103
Arundel 171-2
Ashbourne 460
Ashes, the 673
ATMs 680
Austen, Jane 306, 665
Avebury 260-3, **261**

B

Bakewell 472-4
Baltic Triangle 554
Bamburgh 628
Banksy 298
bargaining 23
Barnard Castle 616-17

Map Pages **000**
Photo Pages **000**

Bath 13, 303-12, **304**, **13**
accommodation 218, 308
activities 307
climate 218
drinking & nightlife 311
entertainment 311
festivals & events 307-8
food 218, 310-11
shopping 311-12
sights 303-7
tourist information 312
tours 307
travel seasons 218
travel to/from 312
travel within 312
walking tours 309, **309**
bathrooms 682
Battle 160
Battle of Bosworth 454
Battle of Hastings 160
beaches 27-8
Bournemouth Beach 239
Bude 319
Fowey 342
Kynance Cove 336
Newquay 325
Perranporth Beach 327
Sandbanks 241
Wells Beach 385
Weymouth Beach 247
Whitby 502
Beachy Head 163
Beatles, the 551-2, 553
Becket, Thomas 146
Bedfordshire 210-12
Bedruthan Steps 325
Berwick-upon-Tweed 631-2
Beverley 527-8
Bibury 191-3
bicycle travel, see cycling & mountain biking
bird parks & aviaries, see also wildlife reserves
Abbotsbury Swannery 249-50
Calf of Man 563
Cotswold Falconry Centre 199
International Centre for Birds of Prey 208
birdwatching
Cley Marshes 383
Malham Cove 509
Slimbridge Wetland Centre 204

Map Pages **000**
Photo Pages **000**

Somerset Levels 318
Symonds Yat Rock 209
Titchwell Marsh 386
Birmingham 392-402, **394-5**
accommodation 389, 397-8
climate 389
drinking & nightlife 399-400
entertainment 400-1
festivals & events 397
food 389, 398-9
gay & lesbian travellers 399
itineraries 393
shopping 401
sights 392-7
tours 397
travel seasons 389
travel to/from 401-2
travel within 402
Bishop's Castle 431-2
Blackpool 556-7
Blackpool Tower 556
Blair, Tony 647
Blakeney 384-5
Blenheim Palace 189, **26**
Bletchley Park 213
boating 45
Ambleside 575
Bath 307
Birmingham 397
Blakeney 384
Borrowdale 591
Bristol 298
Cambridge 360-1
Canterbury 146
Chester 545
Coniston 581-2
Dover 157
Durham 615
Eastbourne 163
Hebden Bridge 520
Keswick 589
Lincoln 444
Lymington 232
Norfolk Broads 385
northwest England 532
Oxford 183-4
Padstow 323-4
Plymouth 282
Portsmouth 228
Rutland Water 456
Shrewsbury 423
Skipton 507
southwest England 219
Southwold 377
St Ives 328

St Mary's 346
Stoke Bruerne 450
Stratford-upon-Avon 407
Thames 100
Truro 341
Ullswater 594
West Wight 238
Weymouth 247
Windermere 570
Windsor 216
York 485
Bodleian Library 179
Bodmin Moor 344
Borrowdale 591-2
Boscastle 321
Boston 449-50
Bournemouth 238-40
Bowder Stone 591
Bradford 519-20
Braunton 291-2
Bray 217
breweries 587
Adnams 377
Black Sheep Brewery 495
Foundry Brewpub 148
Greene King Brewery 374
Harveys Brewery 155, 164
Ludlow Brewing Company 432-3
Shepherd Neame Brewery 155
Theakston's Brewery 495
Thornbridge Brewery 473
Brexit 634-5
Bridge of Sighs 179
Bridgnorth 429-30
Brighton 165-71, **166**
Bristol 293-303, **294-5**
accommodation 299
activities 298-9
drinking & nightlife 301
entertainment 301
festivals & events 299
food 299-301
shopping 301-2
sights 295-8
travel to/from 302
travel within 302-3
British Library 90-1
British Museum 90, **92-3**
Brixham 276
Broadstairs 151-2
Broadway 201-2, **14**
Brockenhurst 230-1
Brontës, the 665

Bronze Age 655
Brownsea Island 240
Brunel's SS *Great Britain* 295
Bryher 347
Buckingham Palace 61, 64, 63, **63**
Buckinghamshire 210-12
Buckler's Hard 231-2
Bude 319-21
budgeting 21
Burford 193-4
Burnham Deepdale 386-7
Bury St Edmunds 373-5
bus travel 684-5, 686
business hours 680-1
Buttermere 592
Buxton 465-8, **466**

C
cable cars 97
Cambridge 15, 349, 353-65, **354**, **15**
accommodation 349, 361-2
activities 360-1
climate 349
drinking & nightlife 364
entertainment 364
festivals & events 361
food 349, 362-4
sights 353-60
tours 361
travel seasons 349
travel to/from 365
travel within 365
walking tours 359, **359**
Cambridgeshire 352-67
canoeing 45, see kayaking & canoeing
Canterbury 141-9, **145**
car travel 686-7
Carlisle 598-600
Cartmel 597
Castle Howard 490-1
Castlerigg Stone Circle 589
castles & palaces 25
Alnwick Castle 626
Arundel Castle 171
Bamburgh Castle 628
Banqueting House 65
Belvoir Castle 447
Berkeley Castle 205
Bishop's Palace 313
Blenheim Palace 189, **26**
Buckingham Palace 61, 64, 63, **63**
Carisbrooke Castle 235

Carlisle Castle 598
Castle Rising 388
Castle Rushen 562
Chillingham Castle 625
Clifford's Tower 485, **7**
Colchester Castle 367
Corfe Castle 242
Dartmouth Castle 277
Dover Castle 155
Dunstanburgh Castle 627
Dunster Castle 265
Durham Castle 614
Farnham Castle 174
Fulham Palace 88
Hampton Court Palace 101-2, 62, **62**, **104-5**
Hastings Castle 161
Helmsley Castle 499
Kenilworth Castle 405
Kensington Palace 83
Lancaster Castle 557
Leeds Castle 148
Leicester Castle 453
Lewes Castle 164
Lincoln Castle 444
Lindisfarne Castle 630
Ludlow Castle 432
Lulworth Castle 243
Muncaster Castle 596-7
Newark Castle 442
Norwich Castle 380
Nottingham Castle 436-7
Okehampton Castle 290
Orford Castle 376
Peel Castle 563
Pendennis Castle 338
Penrith Castle 600
Pevensey Castle 163-4
Peveril Castle 468
Pickering Castle 501
Portland Castle 249
Powderham Castle 271
Raby Castle 618
Richmond Castle 512
Royal Pavilion 165
Scarborough Castle 494
Sherborne New Castle 252
Sherborne Old Castle 252
Shrewsbury Castle 422-3
Skipton Castle 507
Sudeley Castle 202
Tintagel Castle 322
Totnes Castle 278
Tower of London 16, 63, 71-2, 641, **16**, **62**, **76-7**
Warwick Castle 403

Windsor Castle 63, 213-15, **62-3**
Wolvesey Castle 224
Wray Castle 573
Castleton 468-71
Castletown 562-3
cathedrals, *see* churches & cathedrals
caves
    Blue John Cavern 470
    Carnglaze Caverns 344
    Cheddar Gorge 314
    City of Caves 437
    Clearwell Caves 208
    Peak Cavern 470
    Peak District 463
    Poole's Cavern 466-7
    Shell Grotto 150
    Speedwell Cavern 470
    Treak Cliff Cavern 470
    Wookey Hole 313
cell phones 20, 681-2
Cerne Abbas 246-7
Cerne Giant 246
Chagford 288-90
Chapel Porth 327
Cheddar Gorge 314
Cheltenham 205-7, **206**
Chesil Beach 249
Chester 543-7, **544**
Chesterfield 462-3
Chichester 172-4
children, travel with 46-8
Chipping Campden 200-1
Chipping Norton 198-9
Christie, Agatha 275, 277
Church Stretton 430-1
churches & cathedrals 25
    Arundel Cathedral 171-2
    Beverley Minster 527-8
    Birmingham Cathedral 393
    Canterbury Cathedral 17, 144, **17**
    Carlisle Cathedral 598
    Cathedral of the Peak 468
    Chester Cathedral 543-4
    Chichester Cathedral 172
    Church of St Laurence 432
    Church of St Mary the Virgin (Bilbury) 192
    Church of St Mary the Virgin (Rye) 160
    Church of St Peter & St Paul 197
    Church of St Senara 332
    Church of the Holy Trinity 485

Collegiate Church of St Mary 403-4
Coventry Cathedral 402
Derby Cathedral 457-8
Durham Cathedral 614
Ely Cathedral 366
Exeter Cathedral 270
Eyam Parish Church 472
Gloucester Cathedral 208
Great St Mary's Church 355
Greyfriars Chapel 146
Haworth Parish Church 522
Hereford Cathedral 418
Holy Trinity (Long Melford) 371
Holy Trinity Church (Stratford-upon-Avon) 407
King's College Chapel 353-5
King's Lynn Minster 387
Kirkstall Abbey 516
Leicester Cathedral 451-3
Lichfield Cathedral 412
Lincoln Cathedral 444
Liverpool Cathedral 549
Norwich Cathedral 378-80
Round Church 356
Salisbury Cathedral 253
Sherborne Abbey 251
Shrewsbury Abbey 422
Southwark Cathedral 79
Southwell Minster 442
St Albans Cathedral 212
St Bartholomew-the-Great 75
St Edmundsbury Cathedral 374
St Helen's Church 384
St James' Church 200
St John the Baptist's Church (Burford) 193
St John the Baptist's Church (Cirencester) 190-1
St Martin's Church 144
St Mary & All Saints Church 462
St Mary's Church (Bury St Edmonds) 374
St Mary's Church (Chipping Norton) 198
St Mary's Church (Painswick) 203-4
St Mary's Church (Shrewsbury) 421-2

St Mary the Virgin (Saffron Walden) 369
St Pancras Church 288
St Paul's Cathedral 73-4
St Paul's Church (Birmingham) 395-6
St Peter's (Sandwich) 154
St Peter & St Paul 372
Truro Cathedral 340
Wells Cathedral 313
Westminster Cathedral 64-5
Winchester Cathedral 222-3
Worcester Cathedral 414-15
York Minster 480-1
Churchill, Winston 645
cider 418
cinema 667-8
Cirencester 190-1
Cley-next-the-Sea 383
Clifton Suspension Bridge 297
climate 29-33, 678, *see also individual regions*
Clitheroe 559
Clovelly 293
coal 521
coasteering 262, 326
Cockermouth 587-8
Colchester 367-8
Coniston 581-2
Cook, Captain James 503
Corbridge 618-19
Corfe Castle 242
Cornwall 19, 318-44, **329**
Cotswolds 14, 175, 190-205, **176**, **192-3**, **14**
    accommodation 175
    activities 177
    climate 175
    food 175
    highlights 176
    travel seasons 175
    travel to/from 177
    travel within 177
Covell, Thomas 558
Coventry 402-3
Cowes 235
Craster 627
credit & debit cards 680
cricket 541, 672-3
Cromer 382-3
Cromwell, Oliver 642-3
Croyde 291-2
culture 634-5
Cumbria 564-600, **566-7**

accommodation 564
activities 565
climate 564
driving tours 593, **593**
food 564
highlights 566-7
history 565
travel seasons 564
travel to/from 565
travel within 565
Cumbrian Coast 596-600
currency 20
customs regulations 678
cycling & mountain biking
43, 585, 686, **585**
Bristol 298
Camel Trail 323
Cotswolds 177
Dartmoor National
Park 285
East Anglia 352
Exmoor National Park
262
Grizedale Forest 581
Isle of Man 560
Isle of Wight 233
Keswick 589
Lincolnshire 443
London 103
New Forest 229-30
Norfolk Broads 385
northeast England 604
northwest England 532
Peak District 463-4
Sherwood Forest
National Nature
Reserve 441
Shropshire 421
southeast England 141
southwest England 219
Yorkshire 478, 513

D

dangers 681
Dartmoor National Park
284-91, **285**
Dartmouth 276-8
Debatable Lands 565
Dedham Vale 368-9
Derby 457-60
Derbyshire 457-63
Derwent Reservoirs 471
Derwent Valley 461
Devon 268-93

Map Pages **000**
Photo Pages **000**

Dickens, Charles 152
disabilities, travellers with
682-3
distilleries
Cotswolds Distillery 199
Lakes Distillery 589
Plymouth Gin Distillery
280
diving 248, 347
Dorchester 244-6
Dorset 238-62
Douglas 561-2
Dover 18, 155-7, **156**, **18**
Dragon Hill 190
drinking 651-4
driving 686-7
driving tours
Borrowdale & Butter-
mere 593, **593**
Cotswolds 194-5, **195**
Dartmoor 289, **289**
Dover to Rye 158-9, **159**
Northumberland Coast
629, **629**
Peak District 469, **469**
Dulverton 263-4
Dunsop Bridge 559
Dunster 265-6
Durdle Door 243
Durham 614-16, **615**

E

East Anglia 349-88, **350-1**
accommodation 349
activities 352
climate 349
food 349
highlights 350
travel seasons 349
travel to/from 352
travel within 352
East Riding of Yorkshire
525-8
East Sussex 158-71
Eastbourne 162-3
Eastgate (clock) 543
Edale 471-2
Eden Project 19, 338, **19**
electricity 678
Elterwater 583
Ely 365-7
Embleton Bay 628
emergencies 21, 679
Ennerdale 588
environmental issues
665-6
Eskdale 586
Essex 367-71

etiquette 23, 682
Eton 213-17, **214**
EU referendum 634-5
events, see festivals &
events
exchange rates 21
Exeter 268-74, **269**
Exford 265
Exmoor National Park
262-8, **263**
Eyam 472

F

falconry 199
Falmouth 337-40
Farne Islands 631
Farnham 174
ferry travel 685
festivals & events 27,
29-33, see also arts
festivals, food & drink
festivals, literary
festivals, music festi-
vals, sporting events
Amble Puffin Festival
627
Bradford Festival 519
Brighton Festival 167
Bristol Shakespeare
Festival 299
Canterbury Festival 146
Chelsea Flower Show
103
Great Yorkshire Show
492
Guy Fawkes Night 33
Isle of Man Walking
Festival 560
Isle of Wight Festival 30
Jorvik Viking Festival
29, 485
Kendal Mountain Festival
595
Keswick Mountain
Festival 589
Lewes Bonfire Celebra-
tions 164
Notting Hill Carnival 32,
106, **31**
Pride (London) 31
Screenings at the Gar-
den Leftbank 537
Spring Flower Show 492
Trooping the Colour 103
Whitby Goth Weekends
503
films 634, 667-8
food 23, 435, 648-54, **434-
5**, see also individual
locations
afternoon tea 17, **17**
charcuterie 24

food & drink festivals
Aldeburgh Food & Drink
Festival 376
Beer Festival 361
Clitheroe Food Festival
559
Cotswold Food &
Farming Festival 30
Falmouth Oyster Festival
340
Gin Festival Liverpool
552
Isle of Man Food & Drink
Festival 560
Keswick Beer Festival
589
Ludlow Food & Drink
Festival 433
Ludlow Spring Festival
433
Manchester Food &
Drink Festival 537
Robin Hood Beer & Cider
Festival 438
Whitstable Oyster
Festival 149
York Food Festival 485
football 18, 129, 262, **18**
Forest of Bowland 559-60
Forest of Dean 207-10
forts
Needles Old & New
Battery 238
Nothe Fort 247
Segedunum 609
fossils 250
Fowey 342-3
fox hunting 664

G

Gainsborough, Thomas 372
gardens, see parks &
gardens
gay travellers 679
Birmingham 399
Brighton 168
London 124
Newcastle-upon-Tyne 611
Glastonbury 315-19, **316**
Gloucestershire 205-9
Golden Hind 276
Grantchester 365
Grantham 447
Grasmere 577-9
Grassington 508-9
Great Langdale 583
Great Malvern 416-18
Greenway 277
Grizedale Forest 581

H

Hadrian's Wall 14, 617-24, **619**, 14, **585**, **620-1**
Haltwhistle 623-4
Hampshire 222-33
Hampstead Heath 100
Hampton Court Palace 63, 101-2, **62**, **104-5**
Hardy, Thomas 244, 245
Harrogate 491-4
Harry Potter 211
Hartlepool 612
Hastings 161-2
Hawes 511-12
Hawkshead 579-80
Haworth 522-3
health 679
Hebden Bridge 520-1
Helmsley 499-501
Helvellyn 592
Henley-on-Thames 217
Heptonstall 520
Hereford 418-20
Herefordshire 417-21
heritage organisations 683
heritage railways
 Babbacombe Cliff Railway 274
 Bodmin & Wenford Railway 344
 Bridgnorth Cliff Railway 429
 Bure Valley Steam Railway 384
 Cliff Railway 267
 Dartmouth Steam Railway 277
 Great Central Railway 454
 Isle of Wight Steam Railway 236
 Keighley & Worth Valley Railway 522
 North Yorkshire Moors Railway 501
 Peak Rail 461
 Ravenglass & Eskdale Railway 598
 Settle-Carlisle Line 512, 599
 Severn Valley Railway 429
 South Tynedale Railway 600
 Swanage Steam Railway 242
 Wells & Walsingham Railway 385-6
Hertfordshire 210-12
Hexham 622-3

hiking, *see* walking
historic buildings, *see* stately homes, manors & historic buildings
history 636-47
 Anglo-Saxons 638
 Battle of Hastings 639
 Churchill, Winston 645
 Elizabethan Age 641-2
 Houses of Lancaster & York 640-1
 Industrial Era 643-4
 Iron Age 636-7
 Romans 637-8
 Stone Age 636-7
 Thatcher, Margaret 646-7
 Tower of London 641
 World War I 644
 World War II 644-5
HMS *Alliance* 228
HMS *Belfast* 79, 81
HMS *Victory* 226
HMS *Warrior* 226
Holkham 386
Holnicote Estate 266
Holy Island (Lindisfarne) 630-1
Honister Pass 590
horse racing 673-4
horse riding 45, 585
 Dartmoor National Park 286
 Exmoor National Park 262
 New Forest 230
Horton-in-Ribblesdale 510
hot springs 301, 307
Hove 165-71, **166**
Hull 525-7
Hyde Park 83

I

i360 Tower 24
ice skating 437
Ilfracombe 292-3
insurance 679
internet access 679-80
internet resources 21
Iron Age 655
Ironbridge Gorge 424-8, **426**
Isle of Man 560-3
Isle of Portland 248-9
Isle of Thanet 151
Isle of Wight 233-8, **234**
Isles of Scilly 345-8
itineraries 34-8, 393, **34**, **35**, **36**, **37**, **38**

J

Jorvik Viking Festival 29, 485
Jurassic Coast 246
Just 332-3

K

Kapoor, Anish 670
kayaking & canoeing 45
 Dartmoor National Park 286
 Exmoor National Park 262
 Forest of Dean 209
 Fowey 342
 Hereford 419
 Ironbridge Gorge 427
 Lizard, the 336
 Lulworth Cove 243
 New Forest 229
 Norfolk Broads 385
 Symonds Yat 209
 Totnes 279
Kendal 595-6
Kenilworth 405-6
Kensington Palace 83
Kent 141-58
Keswick 24, 588-91, **12**
Kew Gardens 101
King's Lynn 387-8
Kynance Cove 336

L

Lacock 259-60
Lake District 13, 568-96, **566-7**, **569**, **12**
 accommodation 570, 575, 578
 driving tour 593, **593**
 highlights 566-7
Lancashire 556-60
Lancaster 557-9
Land's End 333
language 20
Lavenham 372-3
Lawrence, TE 243
Ledbury 420-1
Leeds 514-19, **515**
Leeds Castle 148
legal matters 680
Leicester 451-6, **452**
Leicestershire 451-6
lesbian travellers 679
 Birmingham 399
 Brighton 168
 London 124
 Newcastle-upon-Tyne 611
Lewes 164-5

libraries
 Birmingham 392-3
 Bodleian Library 179
 British Library 90-1
 Lichfield 412-14
Lincoln 443-8, **445**
Lincolnshire 443-50
literary festivals
 Bath Literature Festival 307
 Cheltenham Literature Festival 207
 Dickens Festival 152
 Kendal Mountain Festival 595
 Richmond Walking & Book Festival 513
 Stratford Literary Festival 407
 Ways with Words 377
literary museums
 Beatrix Potter Gallery 579
 Brontë Parsonage Museum 522
 Charles Dickens Museum 91
 Dickens House Museum 152
 Dorset County Museum 244
 Samuel Johnson Birthplace Museum 412
literature 634, 665-7
Liverpool 14, 547-56, **548**, **14**
 accommodation 552-3
 drinking & nightlife 554-5
 entertainment 555
 festivals & events 552
 food 553-4
 history 547
 information 555
 itineraries 547
 sights 547, 549-51
 tours 551-2
 travel to/from 555-6
 travel within 556
Lizard, the 336-7
London 54-139, **56-7**, **94-5**, **23**
 accommodation 54, 106-12
 activities 103
 Bayswater 109-11, 125, **110**
 Belgravia 108-9, 116
 Bloomsbury 90-1, 111-12, 117, 124-5

London continued
Camden Hill 125-6
Camden Town 118, **119**
Chelsea 82-8, 109, 116, 124, 133-5, **86-7**
City 71-5, 107-8, 115, 123, **72-3**
Clerkenwell 112, 119-21, 126
climate 54
Docklands 95-7, 112, 135
drinking & nightlife 122-8
East End 95-7, 112, 122, 127, 135
emergencies 135-6
entertainment 128-32
Farringdon 112, 119-21, 126
festivals & events 103-6
Fitzrovia 117-18
food 54, 112-22
gay & lesbian travellers 124
Greenwich 97-100, 127
Hammersmith 116-17
Hampstead 100-1, 127
Highgate 100-1, 127
highlights 56-7
history 55
Hoxton 91-5, 121-2, 135, **120**
internet access 136
Islington 118-19
Kensington 82-8, 109, 116, 124, 133-5, **86-7**
Knightsbridge 109, 116, 133-5, **86-7**
Marylebone 88-90, 117, 125, **89**
medical services 136
Notting Hill 109-11, 116-17, 125, **110**
Paddington 109-11, 125
Pimlico 108-9
Shepherd's Bush 116-17
shopping 132-9
Shoreditch 91-5, 121-2, 135, **120**
sights 58-102
South Bank 75-82, 108, 115-16, 123-4, **80**
Spitalfields 91-5, 121-2, 135, **120**
St James's 58-65, **60**

St Pancras 90-1, 111-12, 117, 124-5
tourist information 136
tours 102-3
travel seasons 54
travel to/from 136
travel within 136-9
walking tours 70, **70**
West End 65-71, 106-7, 112-15, 122-3, 132-3, **66-7**
Westminster 58-65, **60**
London Eye 78
Long Melford 371-2
Looe 343-4
Looe Island 343
Ludlow 432-6
Lulworth Cove 243-4
Lydford 290-1
Lyme Regis 250-1
Lymington 232-3
Lyndhurst 230-1
Lynmouth 267-8
Lynton 267-8

M

Magna Carta 24
Malham 509
Manchester 532-43, **534-5**
accommodation 537-8
entertainment 541-2
festivals & events 537
food 538-40
football 539
gay & lesbian travellers 541
history 532-3
information 542
shopping 542
sights 533, 536-7
travel to/from 542-3
travel within 543
manors, see stately homes, manors & historic buildings
Margate 150-1
maritime museums
Brixham Heritage Museum 276
Buckler's Hard Story 231
Captain Cook Memorial Museum 502
Cutty Sark 100
Discovery Museum 605
HMS Alliance at the Submarine Museum 228
Lizard Lighthouse Heritage Centre 336

Moot Hall 376
National Maritime Museum (Falmouth) 338
National Maritime Museum (Greenwich) 97
National Museum of the Royal Navy 228
Nautical Museum 562
Ramsgate Maritime Museum 153
RNLI Grace Darling Museum 628
Spurn Lightship 526
St Barbe Museum 232
True's Yard 388
Waterfront Museum 240
markets
Brixham 276
Cotswolds 196
Leicester 455
London 75, 81-2, 118, 134
Ludlow 436
Plymouth 280-1
Matlock Bath 460-2
Matthew 297
measures 679
MediaCityUK 537
Midlands 389-474, **390-1**
accommodation 389
activities 392
climate 389
food 389
highlights 390
travel seasons 389
military & war museums
Battle of Britain Memorial Flight Visitor Centre 448
Berwick Barracks 632
Bosworth Battlefield Heritage Centre 454
Churchill War Rooms 65
Cosford Royal Air Force Museum 428
Green Howards Museum 512
Imperial War Museum (Duxford) 364
Imperial War Museum (London) 78
Imperial War Museum North 537
Lincolnshire Aviation Heritage Centre 448
Royal Armouries 514
Royal Green Jackets Museum 224
Spitfire Memorial Museum 152-3

Western Approaches Museum 550
mining 521
Minster Lovell 196
mobile phones 20, 681-2
monarchy 25, 635
monasteries, see abbeys, priories & monasteries
money 20, 21, 23, 680
money changers 680
Moretonhampstead 288-90
Moreton-in-Marsh 199-200
motorcycle travel 686-7
mountain biking see cycling & mountain biking
Mousehole 333
Much Wenlock 428-9
museums 14, 25-6, see also art galleries & museums, literary museums, maritime museums, military & war museums, Roman sites & museums, science museums, transport museums
Abbeydale Industrial Hamlet 524
Action Stations! 227-8
American Museum in Britain 307
Armitt Museum 574
Ashmolean Museum 183
Ashmolean Museum Broadway 201
Beamish Open-Air Museum 616
Beaney House of Art & Knowledge 146
Beatles Story 550
Beatles Story Pier Head 551
Bill Douglas Cinema Museum 271
Blists Hill Victorian Town 425
Bowes Museum 617
Brighton Museum 165-7
British Museum 90, **92-3**, 92-3
Bude Castle 319-20
Buxton Museum 465-6
Cadbury World 396-7
Canal Museum 450
Canterbury Heritage Museum 144
Castleton Museum 468
Cell Block Museum 632
City Museum (Winchester) 224
Coalport China Museum 425

Collection (Lincoln) 444
Commandery 415
Cregneash Village Folk Museum 563
Dales Countryside Museum 511
Darby Houses 425
Dartmoor Prison Museum 287
Dennis Severs' House 94
Derby Museum & Art Gallery 458
Design Museum 79
Dig 485
Dinosaurland 250
Discovery Museum 605
Ely Museum 366
Eyam Museum 472
Fashion Museum 306
Fitzwilliam Museum 358
Fox Talbot Museum 259
Galleries of Justice 437
Geffrye Museum 94-5
Great North Museum 605-6
Greater Manchester Police Museum 540
Grosvenor Museum 545
Grove Museum of Victorian Life 562
Guildhall (Boston) 450
Guildhall Museum (Sandwich) 154
Hastings Museum 161
Henry Blogg Museum 382
Herschel Museum of Astronomy 306
Hollytrees Museum 367
House of Manannan 563
International Slavery Museum 550-1
Isles of Scilly Museum 345
Jackfield Tile Museum 425-74
Jewry Wall Museum 454
Jorvik Viking Centre 483
Judges' Lodgings 558
Kelham Island Museum 523-4
Keswick Museum 588-9
King Richard III: Dynasty, Death & Discovery 451
Lake Village Museum 317
Lakeland Motor Museum 569-70
Leeds Industrial Museum 514
Lichfield Museum 412-13
Lyme Regis Museum 250

Lynn Museum 388
M Shed 296-7
Madame Tussauds 90
Malvern Museum of Local History 416
Mary Rose Museum 226
Merseyside Maritime Museum 551
Morgan Motor Company 416
Moyse's Hall 374
Museum of Bath Architecture 306
Museum of British Surfing 291
Museum of Farnham 174
Museum of Iron 425
Museum of Lakeland Life & Industry 595
Museum of Lincolnshire Life 444
Museum of Liverpool 551
Museum of London 74
Museum of London Docklands 96
Museum of Norwich at the Bridewell 380
Museum of the Broads 384
Museum of the Gorge 425
Museum of the Jewellery Quarter 395
Museum of Witchcraft 321
National Coal Mining Museum for England 521
National Media Museum 519
Natural History Museum 82
New Forest Museum 230
New Walk Museum & Art Gallery 453
Newarke Houses Museum 453
Norwich Castle 380
Novium Museum 173
Old House Museum 473
Old Operating Theatre Museum 79
Oliver Cromwell's House 366
Peak District Lead Mining Museum 461
People's History Museum 533
Pier Museum 370
Pitt Rivers Museum 178
Polar Museum 360
RAMM 270

Richmondshire Museum 512
River & Rowing Museum 217
Rotunda Museum 494
Royal Cornwall Museum 341
Royal Crown Derby Factory 458
Royal Pump Room Museum 491
Royal Worcester Porcelain Works 415
Russell-Cotes 239
Saffron Walden Museum 369
Salisbury Museum 254-5
Seven Stories - The Centre for Children's Books 607
Sir John Soane's Museum 69, 71
Soho House 396
Southwell Workhouse 442
Stories of Lynn 387
Tullie House Museum 598
Verulamium Museum 212
Victoria & Albert Museum 82, **84-5**
Viktor Wynd Museum of Curiosities, Fine Art & Natural History 97
Wellcome Collection 91
Wellington Arch 65
Wensleydale Creamery 511
West Gate Towers 146
Whitby Museum 502
Whitstable Museum & Gallery 149
Wilson, the 205
Wimbledon Lawn Tennis Museum 102
World Museum 549
World Rugby Museum 132
York Castle Museum 484
Ypres Tower 160
music 668-9
music festivals
Aldeburgh Festival 376
Bath International Music Festival 307
Bestival 32, 237
Creamfields 552
Field Day 103
Folk Festival 361
Glastonbury Festival 30, 315, **31**

International Beatleweek 552
Isle of Wight Festival 237
Kendal Calling 595
Leeds Festival 516
Liverpool International Music Festival 552
Lovebox 106
Meltdown Festival 106
Reading Festival 32, 216
Whitby Spring Session 503
Wireless 106

N
national parks & forests 24, 27, 660, see also nature reserves
Dartmoor National Park 284, **285**
Exmoor National Park 262-8
National Forest 458
North York Moors National Park 498-506, **500**
South Downs National Park 163-4
Yorkshire Dales National Park 506-14, **508**
nature reserves, see also national parks & forests
Cley Marshes 383
Newton Pool Nature Reserve 628
Orford Ness 376
Rutland Water Nature Reserve 456
Sherwood Forest National Nature Reserve 441
St Helens Duver 236
Titchwell Marsh 386
New Forest 229-35
Newark-on-Trent 442-3
Newcastle-upon-Tyne 605-13, **606-7**
Newquay 325-7, **585**
newspapers 679
Newton, Isaac 447
Norfolk 378-88
Norfolk Broads 384-5
North York Moors National Park 498-506, **500**
North Yorkshire 479-98
Northamptonshire 450-1
northeast England 601-32, **602-3**
accommodation 601
activities 604

northeast England
  continued
  climate 601
  driving tours 629, **629**
  food 601
  highlights 602-3
  travel seasons 601
  travel to/from 604-5
Northleach 196-7
Northumberland Coast
  626-32, **629**
Northumberland National
  Park 624-5, **619**
northwest England 529-63,
  530-1
  accommodation 529
  activities 532
  climate 529
  food 529
  highlights 530-1
  travel seasons 529
Norwich 378-82, **379**
Nottingham 436-42, **438**
Nottinghamshire 436-43

O
Okehampton 290-1
Old Trafford (Manchester
  United Museum &
  Tour) 539
opening hours 680-1
Orford 375-6
outdoor activities 39-45,
  585, **584-5**
Oxford 11, 175, 177-88,
  180-1, 11
  accommodation 175,
    184-5
  activities 183-4
  climate 175
  drinking & nightlife 186-7
  entertainment 187
  food 175
  shopping 187
  sights 178-83
  tours 184
  travel seasons 175
  travel to/from 188
  travel within 188
Oyster Card 138

P
Padstow 323-5
Painswick 203-4

painting 669-71
palaces, *see* castles &
  palaces
parks & gardens
  Alnwick Garden 626
  Alum Chine 239
  Batsford Arboretum 199
  Beverley Westwood 528
  Botanic Garden (Oxford)
    180-1
  Bridge End Gardens
    369-70
  Cambridge University
    Botanic Garden 360
  Chalice Well & Gardens
    316
  Chelsea Physic
    Garden 88
  Cornwell 338
  Downs, the 297
  Duncombe Park Gardens
    499
  Eden Project 19, 338, 19
  Fell Foot Park 569
  Fountains Abbey &
    Studley Royal 498
  Glendurgan Garden 338
  Green Park 64
  Hampstead Heath 100
  Harlow Carr Botanical
    Gardens 492
  Helmsley Walled Garden
    499
  Hidcote 200
  Hyde Park 83
  Kensington Gardens 83
  Kew Gardens 101
  Lost Gardens of Heligan
    338
  Museum Gardens 484
  Painswick Rococo
    Garden 203
  Pavilion Gardens 465
  Peasholm Park 494
  Portager Garden 338
  Prior Park Estate 306
  Queen Elizabeth Olympic
    Park 96
  Regent's Park 88
  Richmond Park 102
  Salutation Gardens 154
  Slopes 465
  St James's Park 64
  Stowe Gardens 210
  Trebah Garden 338
  Tremenheere Sculpture
    Garden 334
  Tresco Abbey Garden 347
  Williamson Park &
    Tropical Butterfly
    House 558

Windsor Great Park 215
Winter Gardens 524
Peak District 16, 18, 463-74,
  464, 16, 18
Peel 563
Pendle Witch Way 559
Penrith 600
Penzance 334-6, **335**
Perranporth 327-8
Pickering 501-2
planning, *see also*
  individual regions
  activities 39-45
  budgeting 21
  calendar of events 29-33
  children, travel with 46-8
  England basics 20-1
  first-time visitors 22-3
  itineraries 34-8, **34**, **35**,
    36, **37**, **38**
  repeat visitors 24
  travel seasons 20
plants 663
Plymouth 280-4, **281**
politics 634-5
Polperro 342
pony trekking 45, 262
Poole 240-2
pop music 668-9
Porlock 266
Port Erin 563
Port Isaac 322-3
Port St Mary 563
Porthtowan 327-8
Portsmouth 226-9, **227**
post 681
Postbridge 287-8
Potter, Beatrix 579-80
Pride festivals 106, 167
Princetown 286-7
priories, *see* abbeys,
  priories & monasteries
public holidays 681
pubs 19, 19
punting 360

R
radio 679
rafting 427
railways, *see* heritage
  railways
Ramsgate 152-3
Ransome, Arthur 581, 595
red deer 264
Regent's Park 88
Ribble Valley 558
Ribblesdale 510
Richard III 451, 453

Richmond 512-14
River Thames 100, **98-9**
Robin Hood's Bay 506
Rock 323-5
rock climbing 45
  Cheddar Gorge 314
  Dartmoor National
    Park 286
  Exmoor National Park
    262
  Peak District 463
  Rutland Water 457
rock music 668-9
Rogan, Simon 597
Roman sites & museums
  Birdoswald Roman
    Fort 623
  Brading Roman Villa 235
  Chedworth Roman Villa
    196-7
  Chesters Roman Fort &
    Museum 624
  Corinium Museum 190
  Dewa Roman Experience
    545
  Fishbourne Palace 173
  Hadrian's Wall 14, 617-24,
    619, 14, **585**, **620-1**
  Housesteads Roman Fort
    & Museum 623
  Roman Amphitheatre
    545
  Roman Army Museum
    623
  Roman Baths 13, 303-
    5, **13**
  Roman Museum 144-6
  Roman Painted House
    155-6
  Roman Town House 244
  Vindolanda Roman Fort
    & Museum 623
  Yorkshire Museum 483-4
Ross-on-Wye 420
Royal Family 25, 635
Royal Observatory 97
rugby 674
Rugby 411-12
Runnymede 215-16
Rutland 456-7
Rutland Water 456-7
Ryde 235-6
Rye 158-61

S
safety 681
Saffron Walden 369-70
sailing 45, 282 456
Salisbury 253-6, **254**
Saltaire 518

Sandringham 387
Sandwich 153-4
Scafell Pike 587
Scarborough 494-8, **496**
school holidays 681
science museums
  At-Bristol 297
  Enginuity 427
  Life Science Centre
    606-7
  Magna 524
  Museum of Science &
    Industry 533
  National Space Centre
    453
  Science Museum 82-3
  Thinktank 393
  Wellcome Collection 91
  World Museum 549
sculpture 669-71
Sennen 333
Settle 510
Seven Sisters 18, **18**
Shakespeare, William 15,
  24, 78, 406-7, 665, 671
Sheffield 523-5
Sherborne 251-2
Sherwood Forest 441
shopping 27
Shrewsbury 421-4, **422**
Shropshire 421-36
Silbury Hill 260
Skipton 506-8
Slaughters, the 197
smoking 679
soccer 18, 129, 262, **18**
Somerset 312-18
Somerset Levels 318
South Downs National Park
  163-4
South Yorkshire 523-5
southeast England 140-74,
  142-3
  accommodation 140
  activities 141
  climate 140
  food 140
  highlights 142-3
  travel seasons 140
  travel to/from 141
  travel within 141
Southend-on-Sea 370-1
Southwell 442
southwest England 218-
  348, **220-1**
  accommodation 218
  activities 219
  climate 218
  food 218

highlights 220-1
travel seasons 218
travel within 219-22
Southwold 377-8
sport 672-4
sporting events
  Bumps 361
  Cowes Week 32, 235
  Grand National 29, 552
  Great North Run 608
  Henley Royal Regatta 217
  London Marathon 30
  Royal Ascot 30, 212
  University Boat Race 103
  Virgin Money London
    Marathon 103
  Wimbledon Lawn Tennis
    Championships 30,
    106
St Agnes 348
St Albans 212
St Bartholomew-the-
  Great 75
St Ives 328-32, **330**
St Margaret's Bay 157
St Martin's 347-8
St Mary's 345-6
St Michael's Mount 337
St Paul's Cathedral 73-4
Staffordshire 412-13
Stair Hole Bay 243
Stamford 448-9
stately homes, manors &
  historic buildings 26
  30 St Mary Axe 75
  Althorp House 451
  Apsley House 65
  Aston Hall 397
  Attingham Park 424
  Audley End House 369
  Avebury Manor 260
  Bath Assembly Rooms
    306
  Beaulieu 230-1
  Belton House 447
  Blackwell House 568-9
  Blickling Hall 381
  Brantwood 581
  Burghley House 448-9
  Burlington Arcade 71
  Castle Drogo 288-90
  Castle Howard 490-1
  Chatsworth House 16,
    473, **16**
  Coleton Fishacre 277
  Cotehele House 344
  Cragside House, Garden
    & Estate 624-5
  Dove Cottage 577-8

Eastbridge Hospital 144
Erasmus Darwin House
  412
Felbrigg Hall 382
Forde Abbey 251
Guildhall 74-5
Haddon Hall 473
Hardwick Hall 462
Highgrove 203
Hill Top 579-80
Holker Hall 596
Holkham Hall & Estate
  386
Hospital of St Cross 224
Houghton Hall 388
House Mill 96
Houses of Parliament
  59-60
Inns of Court 75
John Rylands Library
  536
Kedleston Hall 460
Kelmscott Manor 189
Kentwell Hall 371
Kenwood 100
Kielder Observatory 624
Kingston Lacy 242
Lavenham Guildhall 372
Levens Hall 595
Little Hall 372
Lloyd's of London 75
London Dungeon 81
Longleat 259
Lord Leycester Hospital
  404
Manchester Town Hall
  536-7
Melford Hall 371
Minster Lovell Hall 196
Mompesson House 255
Montacute House 319
Newstead Abbey 437
No 10 Downing Street 65
Norman Keep & Castle
  Museum 559
Old Royal Naval College
  97
Osborne House 235
Prideaux Place 323
Queen's House 97-100
Royal Exchange 75
Royal Hospital Chelsea
  83-8
Royal Observatory 97
Rydal Mount 574-5
Shakespeare's Globe 78
Shugborough 413
Snowshill Manor &
  Garden 201
Somerset House 71

Spencer House 65
St George's Hall 550
St John's Gate 95
St Mary's Guildhall 403
Stoneleigh Abbey 405-6
Stourhead 258
Strawberry Hill 102
Sulgrave Manor 450
Supreme Court 64
Townend 574
Tyntesfield House 300
Waddesdon Manor 211
Wilton House 255
Winchester College
  223-4
Woburn Abbey 210
Wollaton Hall 437
Woodchester Mansion
  204-5
Woolsthorpe Manor 447
Wordsworth House 587
Steephill Cove 237-8
Stoke Bruerne 450-1
Stoke-on-Trent 414
Stonehenge 11, 256-8,
  257, **10**
Stourhead 258
Stow-on-the-Wold 197-8
Stratford-upon-Avon 15,
  406-11, **408-9**, **15**
Suffolk 371-8
SUPing
  Newquay 326
  Plymouth 282
  Portland Harbour 248
  Rutland Water 456
surfing 45, 585, **584**
  Bournemouth 239
  Bude 320
  Croyde 291
  Isle of Wight 233
  Newquay 325-6
  Scarborough 495
  southwest England 219
Surrey 174
Sutton Hoo 374
swimming
  Cambridge 360
  London 103
  Penzance 334
  Plymouth 282
  Tunnelsbeaches 292
Symonds Yat 209

T
Tarr Steps 263-4
Tate Britain 79
Tate Modern 78

taxis 687
tea 17
telephone services 20, 681-2
tennis 674
Thames 100, **98-9**
Thames Valley 213-17
Thatcher, Margaret 646-7
theatre 17, 671
Three Peaks 510
time 682
Tintagel 321-2
tipping 23
toilets 682
Tolkien, JRR 184
Torquay 274-6
Totnes 278-9
tourist information 682
Tower Bridge 72-3
Tower of London 16, 63, 71-2, 641, **16**, **62**, **76-7**
train travel 685, 687-8, *see also heritage railways*
transport 684-8
transport museums
    Coventry Transport Museum 402
    London Transport Museum 69
    National Railway Museum 481-3
travel seasons 20
travel to/from England 684-5
travel within England 685-8
trekking, *see walking*
Tresco 346-7
Troutbeck 574
Truro 340-1
tunnels 270
TV 679
Tyne bridges 605
Tynemouth 613-14

U

Uffington White Horse 190
Uley 204-5
Ullswater 592-3
universities
    Cambridge 353-60
    Oxford 178-83

V

Vale of the White Horse 189-90

Ventnor 236-7
Victoria & Albert Museum 82, **84-5**
Victoria Tunnel 607
Vikings 638
visas 683

W

Waddesdon 210-12
walking 18, 40-3, 585
    Ambleside 575
    Bakewell 473
    Cotswolds 177
    Dartmoor National Park 284-5
    East Anglia 352
    Edale 471
    Exmoor National Park 262-3
    Fowey 342
    Haworth 522
    Helvellyn 594
    Herefordshire 417-18
    Isle of Wight 233
    Lake District 576
    Langdale 583
    Lincolnshire 443
    Lyme Regis 250
    Malham Cove 509
    Malvern Hills 417
    New Forest 229
    Norfolk Broads 385
    northeast England 532, 604
    Peak District 464-5
    Shropshire 421
    southeast England 141
    southwest England 219
    Ullswater 594
    Valley of the Rocks 267
    Wasdale 587
    Yorkshire 479
walking tours
    Bath 309, **309**
    Cambridge 359, **359**
    London 70, **70**
Wallace & Gromit 667
war museums, *see military & war museums*
Warwick 403-5, **404**
Warwickshire 402-12
Wasdale 586-7

waterfalls
    Golitha Falls 344
    Gowbarrow Park & Aira Force 594
    Hardraw Force 511
    Lodore Falls 591
    Lydford Gorge 290
weather 29-33, 678, *see also individual regions*
weights 679
Wells 313-15
Wells-next-the-Sea 385-6
West Sussex 171-4
West Wight 238
West Yorkshire 514-23
Weymouth 247-8
whale-watching 502
Whitby 502-6, **504**
White Cliffs of Dover 157-8
Whitewell 559
Whitstable 149-50
Widecombe-in-the-Moor 288
wildlife 661-3
wildlife reserves, *see also bird parks & aviaries*
    Braunton Burrows 291
    Cornish Seal Sanctuary 336
    Holkham National Nature Reserve 386
    St Bees Head 597
    Wild Futures Monkey Sanctuary 343
wildlife-watching 264
Wiltshire 252-3
Winchcombe 202-3
Winchester 222-6, **223**
Windermere 568-74, **571**
Windsor 213-17, **214**
Windsor Castle 63, 213-15, **62-3**
windsurfing 45
    Isle of Wight 233
    Poole Harbour 241
    Portland Harbour 248
    Rutland Water 456
wine 652-4
wineries
    Biddenden Vineyards 155
    Camel Valley Vineyard 320
    Chapel Down Vinery 155
    Kerry Vale Vineyard 431

Sharpham Wine & Cheese 278
St Martin's Vineyard 347
Woburn 210
Woodstock 188-9
Worcester 414-16
Worcestershire 414-17
Wordsworth, William 565, 574-5, 587
World Heritage sites
    Blenheim Palace 189
    Fountains Abbey & Studley Royal 498
    Ironbridge Gorge 424-8
    Jurassic Coast 246
    Saltaire 518
World War I 644
World War II 644-5

Y

York 13, 480-90, **482-3**, **12**
Yorkshire 475-528, **476-7**, **28**
    accommodation 475
    climate 475
    food 475
    highlights 476
    travel seasons 475
    travel to/from 479
    travel within 479
Yorkshire Dales National Park 506-14, **508**

Z

Zennor 332-3
zoos, *see also bird parks & aviaries, wildlife reserves*
    Bristol Zoo Gardens 297-8
    Cotswold Farm Park 198
    Cotswold Wildlife Park 193
    Living Coasts 274
    Longleat 259
    Newquay Zoo 325
    Ouseburn Farm 607
    Paignton Zoo 274
    South Lakes Safari Zoo 597
    Woburn Safari Park 210
    ZSL London Zoo 88-9

Map Legend

Sights

- Beach
- Bird Sanctuary
- Buddhist
- Castle/Palace
- Christian
- Confucian
- Hindu
- Islamic
- Jain
- Jewish
- Monument
- Museum/Gallery/Historic Building
- Ruin
- Shinto
- Sikh
- Taoist
- Winery/Vineyard
- Zoo/Wildlife Sanctuary
- Other Sight

Activities, Courses & Tours

- Bodysurfing
- Diving
- Canoeing/Kayaking
- Course/Tour
- Sento Hot Baths/Onsen
- Skiing
- Snorkelling
- Surfing
- Swimming/Pool
- Walking
- Windsurfing
- Other Activity

Sleeping

- Sleeping
- Camping

Eating

- Eating

Drinking & Nightlife

- Drinking & Nightlife
- Cafe

Entertainment

- Entertainment

Shopping

- Shopping

Information

- Bank
- Embassy/Consulate
- Hospital/Medical
- Internet
- Police
- Post Office
- Telephone
- Toilet
- Tourist Information
- Other Information

Geographic

- Beach
- Gate
- Hut/Shelter
- Lighthouse
- Lookout
- Mountain/Volcano
- Oasis
- Park
- Pass
- Picnic Area
- Waterfall

Population

- Capital (National)
- Capital (State/Province)
- City/Large Town
- Town/Village

Transport

- Airport
- Border crossing
- Bus
- Cable car/Funicular
- Cycling
- Ferry
- Metro station
- Monorail
- Parking
- Petrol station
- S-Bahn/Subway station
- Taxi
- T-bane/Tunnelbana station
- Train station/Railway
- Tram
- Tube station
- U-Bahn/Underground station
- Other Transport

Routes

- Tollway
- Freeway
- Primary
- Secondary
- Tertiary
- Lane
- Unsealed road
- Road under construction
- Plaza/Mall
- Steps
- Tunnel
- Pedestrian overpass
- Walking Tour
- Walking Tour detour
- Path/Walking Trail

Boundaries

- International
- State/Province
- Disputed
- Regional/Suburb
- Marine Park
- Cliff
- Wall

Hydrography

- River, Creek
- Intermittent River
- Canal
- Water
- Dry/Salt/Intermittent Lake
- Reef

Areas

- Airport/Runway
- Beach/Desert
- Cemetery (Christian)
- Cemetery (Other)
- Glacier
- Mudflat
- Park/Forest
- Sight (Building)
- Sportsground
- Swamp/Mangrove

Note: Not all symbols displayed above appear on the maps in this book

Damian Harper

London Damian has been working largely full time as a travel writer (and translator) since 1997 and has also written for *National Geographic Traveler*, the *Guardian*, the *Daily Telegraph*, Abbeville Press (*Celestial Realm: The Yellow Mountains of China*), Lexean, Frequent Traveller, China Ethos and various other magazines and newspapers.

Catherine Le Nevez

Birmingham, the Midlands & the Marches; Newcastle & Northeast England Catherine's wanderlust kicked in when she roadtripped across Europe from her Parisian base aged four, and she's been hitting the road at every opportunity since, travelling to around 60 countries and completing her Doctorate of Creative Arts in Writing, Masters in Professional Writing, and postgrad qualifications in Editing and Publishing along the way. Over the past dozen-plus years she's written scores of Lonely Planet guides and articles covering Paris, France, Europe and far beyond. Her work has also appeared in numerous online and print publications. Topping Catherine's list of travel tips is to travel without any expectations.

Isabella Noble

Oxford, Cotswolds & Around Isabella's travels have taken her across India, Southeast Asia, Australia, North America and Europe. She has lived in southern Spain and Melbourne, though she's now (loosely) based in London. Her work has also been published by lonelyplanet.com, the Hotelegraph, Hg2 | A Hedonist's Guide To, Virgin Atlantic, Emirates' Open Skies and Red Carnation hotels, among others.

Neil Wilson

Yorkshire Neil was born in Scotland and has lived there most of his life. Based in Perthshire, he has been a full-time writer since 1988, working on more than 80 guidebooks for various publishers, including the Lonely Planet guides to Scotland, England, Ireland and Prague. An outdoors enthusiast since childhood, Neil is an active hill-walker, mountain-biker, sailor, snowboarder, fly-fisher and rock-climber, and has climbed and tramped in four continents, including ascents of Jebel Toubkal in Morocco, Mount Kinabalu in Borneo, the Old Man of Hoy in Scotland's Orkney Islands and the Northwest Face of Half Dome in California's Yosemite Valley. Neil also wrote the planning chapters of this book.

OUR STORY

A beat-up old car, a few dollars in the pocket and a sense of adventure. In 1972 that's all Tony and Maureen Wheeler needed for the trip of a lifetime – across Europe and Asia overland to Australia. It took several months, and at the end – broke but inspired – they sat at their kitchen table writing and stapling together their first travel guide, *Across Asia on the Cheap*. Within a week they'd sold 1500 copies. Lonely Planet was born.

Today, Lonely Planet has offices in Franklin, London, Melbourne, Oakland, Dublin, Beijing and Delhi, with more than 600 staff and writers. We share Tony's belief that 'a great guidebook should do three things: inform, educate and amuse'.

OUR WRITERS

Belinda Dixon

Cambridge & East Anglia, Bath & Southwest England Only happy when her feet are suitably sandy, Belinda has been (gleefully) travelling, researching and writing for Lonely Planet since 2006. Belinda also wrote the Understand and Survival Guide chapters. See her VideoBlog posts at https://belindadixon.com

Oliver Berry

Bath & Southwest England, the Lake District & Cumbria Oliver is a writer and photographer based in Cornwall. His first trip abroad was to the south of France, aged two. Since then he's travelled to Corsica, New Zealand, the South Pacific and the midwestern USA. Oliver first started writing for Lonely Planet in 2002, and has written for many titles including *France*, *Great Britain*, *England*, *Western Europe*, *Rarotonga & the Cook Islands* and *South Pacific & Micronesia*.

Fionn Davenport

Manchester, Liverpool & Northwest England Irish by birth and conviction, Fionn has been writing about his native country for more than two decades. He's come and gone over the years, pushed to travel in order to escape Dublin's comfortable stasis and by the promise of adventure, but it has cemented his belief that Ireland remains his favourite place to visit, if not always live in. These days, he has a weekly commute home to Dublin from Manchester, where he lives with his partner Laura and their car Trevor. In Dublin he presents *Inside Culture* on RTE Radio 1 and writes travel features for a host of publications, including the *Irish Times*.

Marc Di Duca

Canterbury & Southeast England A travel author for the past decade, Marc has worked for Lonely Planet in Siberia, Slovakia, Bavaria, England, Ukraine, Austria, Poland, Croatia, Portugal, Madeira and on the Trans-Siberian Railway,

OVER PAGE | MORE WRITERS

Published by Lonely Planet Global Limited
CRN 554153
9th edition – Apr 2017
ISBN 978 1 78657 339 1
© Lonely Planet 2017 Photographs © as indicated 2017
10 9 8 7 6 5 4 3 2 1
Printed in Singapore

Although the authors and Lonely Planet have taken all reasonable care in preparing this book, we make no warranty about the accuracy or completeness of its content and, to the maximum extent permitted, disclaim all liability arising from its use.